Index of American Periodical Verse: 1984

Rafael Catalá

and

James D. Anderson

assisted by

Sarah Park Anderson

and

Martha Park Sollberger

The Scarecrow Press, Inc.
Metuchen, N.J., & London
1986

Library of Congress Catalog Card No. 73-3060
ISBN 0-8108-1918-X
Copyright © 1986 by Rafael Catalá and James D. Anderson
Manufactured in the United States of America

CONTENTS

Ref
016.8115
In38
1984

PREFACE

This, the fourteenth annual volume of the _Index of American Periodical Verse_, covers more English and Spanish language periodicals from Canada, the United States, and Puerto Rico than ever before. More than two hundred publications have been indexed this year, contributing more than 16,000 entries to the _Index_.

The importance of the _Index_ grows as its necessity becomes more apparent in circles of contemporary poetry research. The increasing demand for inclusion corroborates this fact. The _Index_ constitutes an objective measure of poetry in North America, recording not only the publication of our own poets in Canada, the U.S. and Puerto Rico, but also those from other lands and cultures and from other times. Of course, the _Index_'s primary purpose is to show what poems have been published by particular poets, what poems have been translated by particular translators, and who wrote poems with particular titles or first lines. But taken together, the _Index_ reveals trends and influences: the ebb and flow of particular poets, as well as the influence of cultures of other lands and times as represented by their poets published in North American journals.

James D. Anderson has made a major contribution to the _Index_ by designing and refining computer programs which have greatly facilitated the indexing process. This year, he has added programs for automatically adding cross-references and for formatting pages, operations which had been done manually in previous years. Also, I want to express my sincere appreciation to Sarah Park Anderson and Martha Park Sollberger for their valuable assistance.

Rafael Catalá
Co-Editor

v

INTRODUCTION

MICRO-COMPUTER COMPILATION

The 1984 _Index_ was compiled using the Osborne 4 Vixen micro-computer and the Wordstar word-processing program. Once all indexing was complete, the entries were sorted and formatted using a suite of programs written especially for the _Index_ in BASIC. The Osborne Vixen is data-compatible with the IBM Personal Computer, so that after initial sorting of entries on the Osborne, files could be moved to a much larger IBM personal computer for final sorting. After author and translator entries were sorted, entry numbers were automatically generated and title entries were extracted and sorted. New programs this year added cross-references automatically and formatted pages with running heads. Finally, the _Index_ was printed in camera-ready form on a NEC Spinwriter printer.

The principal advantage in computer-based compilation is eliminating the repetitive entry of the same data. Within a single issue of a journal, for example, the journal citation will be the same for every poem, yet in the old card-based method, the citation had to be rewritten on every card. With the computer, it is simply copied, without rekeying, to each entry. Similarly, translations no longer call for a completely new entry for the translator. Instead, the original entry is simply modified, moving the name of the translator to the lead position, and the author to the note.

Persons interested in the precise details of compilation, including the computer programs used, should write to the editors at P.O. Box 38, New Brunswick, NJ 08903-0038. The 1982, 1983 and 1984 _Indexes_ are available from the editors on 5-1/4" floppy disks.

NAMES AND CROSS REFERENCES

With the addition of many more poets with compound surnames and surnames containing various prefixes, we have recognized the need for systematic cross references from alternative forms of surname to the form chosen for entry in the _Index_. We have included these references whenever the form used for entry did not fall under the last element. In addition, many poets publish under different forms of the same name, for example, with or without a middle initial. Often these forms will file next to each other in the index. In such cases, both forms are used, since it is often difficult, if not impossible, to determine with complete assurance whether it is the same poet or different poets with similar names. In other cases, cross references may be used to connect two forms of names possibly referring to the same poet. When the poets are known to use different forms of the same name, alternative forms may be indicated by using the format authorized by the Anglo-American Cataloguing Rules, Second Edition. For example:

KNIGHT, Arthur W. (Arthur Winfield)

This heading indicates that this poet has poems published under two forms of name: Arthur W. Knight and Arthur Winfield Knight.

FORMAT AND ARRANGEMENT OF ENTRIES

The basic format and style of the Index remain unchanged. Poets are arranged alphabetically by surname and forenames. In creating this alphabetical sequence, we have adopted principles of the filing rules issued in 1980 by the American Library Association and the Library of Congress. Names are arranged on the basis of their spelling, rather than their pronunciation, so that, for example, names beginning with 'Mac' and 'Mc' are no longer interfiled. Similarly, the space consistently counts as a filing element, so that similar compound and prefixed surnames are often separated by some distance, as illustrated in the following examples. Note that "De BOLT" precedes "DeBEVOISE" by a considerable number of entries.

De ANGELIS	Van BRUNT
De BOLT	Van DUYN
De GRAVELLES	Van HALTEREN
De LOACH	Van TOORN
De PALCHI	Van TROYER
De RONSARD	Van WERT
De VAUL	Van WINCKEL
DEAL	VANCE
DeBEVOISE	Vander DOES
DeFOE	VANDERBEEK
DEGUY	VanDEVENTER
Del VECCHIO	
DeLISLE	
DeMOTT	
DENNISON	
Der HOVANESSIAN	
DESY	
DeYOUNG	

Abbreviations are also arranged on the basis of spelling, rather than pronunciation, so that "ST. JOHN" is not filed as "SAINT JOHN", but as "S+T+space+JOHN". Punctuation is not considered; a hyphen is filed as if it were a space and apostrophes and accents are ignored for purposes of filing. Finally, numerals are arranged in numerical order preceding alphabetical letters rather than as if they were spelled out.

Under each poet's name, poems are arranged alphabetically by title or, if there is no title, by first line. Initial articles in the major languages are ignored in the arrangement. Poem titles and first lines are placed within quotation marks. All significant words of titles are capitalized, but in first lines, only the first word and proper nouns are capitalized. Incomplete excerpts from larger works are followed by the note "Excerpt" or, if they consist of complete sections, by "Selection". The title, first line or number of the excerpt, if given, follows this note. For example:

WALCOTT, Derek
    "Midsummer" (Selections: XXXIV-XXXVI). Agni (18) 83, p. 5-7.

WEBB, Phyllis
    "The Vision Tree" (Selection: "I Daniel"). PoetryCR (5:2) Wint 83-84, p. 11.

WAINWRIGHT, Jeffrey
    "Heart's Desire" (Excerpt: "Some Propositions and Part of a Narrative"). Agni (18) 83, p. 37.

WATTEN, Barret
    "One Half" (Excerpts). ParisR (24:86) Wint 82, p. 112-113.

If an excerpt is a complete "sub-work", it receives an independent entry, with reference to the larger work in a note. For example:

ANDERSON, Jack
    "Magnets" (from The Clouds of That Country). PoNow (7:2, #38) 83, p. 23.

Notes about dedications, joint authors, translators, and sources follow the title, enclosed in parentheses. A poem with more than one author is entered under each author. Likewise, a translated poem is entered under each translator, as well as its author(s). Each entry includes the names of all authors and all translators. Multiple authors or translators are indicated by the abbreviation "w.", standing for "with". Translators are indicated by the abbreviation "tr. by", standing for "translated by", and original authors are indicated by the abbreviation "tr. of", standing for "translation of". For example:

AGGESTAM, Rolf
    "Old Basho" (tr. by Erland Anderson and Lars Nordström). NewRena (16) Spr 83, p. 25.

ANDERSON, Erland
    "Old Basho" (tr. of Rolf Aggestam, w. Lars Nordström). NewRena (16) Spr 83, p. 25.

NORDSTROM, Lars
    "Old Basho" (tr. of Rolf Aggestam, w. Erland Anderson). NewRena (16) Spr 83, p. 25.

The journal citation includes an abbreviation standing
for the journal title, followed by volume and issue numbers,
date, and pages. The journal abbreviation is underlined.
An alphabetical list of these journal abbreviations is in-
cluded at the front of the volume, along with the full
journal title, name of editor(s), address, the numbers of
the issues indexed in this volume of the Index, and sub-
scription information. A separate list of indexed periodi-
cals is arranged by full journal title, with a reference to
the abbreviated title. Volume and issue numbers are in-
cluded within parentheses, e.g., (16:5) stands for volume
16, number 5; (21) refers to issue 21 for a journal which
does not use volume numbers. Dates are given using abbrevia-
tions for months and seasons. Year of publication is indi-
cated by the last two digits of the year, e.g. 84. Please
see the separate list of abbreviations.

Compiling this year's Index has been an adventure into
the wealth and variety of poetry published in U. S., Puerto
Rican and Canadian periodicals as well as the intricacies of
bringing this wealth together and organizing it into a
consistent index. The world of poetry publication is a
dynamic one, with new journals appearing, older journals
declining, dying, reviving and thriving. This year saw the
loss of ten journals and the addition of twenty-five new
ones. These are listed at the front of the volume. Keeping
up with these changes is a big order, and we solicit our
reader's suggestions as to journals which should be included
in future volumes of the Index, and also, journals which
could be dropped. Editors who would like their journals
considered for inclusion in future volumes should send sam-
ple issues to:

Rafael Català, Editor
Index of American Periodical Verse
P.O. Box 38
New Brunswick, NJ 08903-0038

Although indexing is indispensable for the organization
of any literature so that particular works can be found when
needed and scholarship and research facilitated, it is a
tedious business. I know that we have made mistakes. We
solicit your corrections and suggestions, which you may send
to me at the above address.

James D. Anderson
Co-Editor

ABBREVIATIONS

dir., dirs.	director, directors
ed., eds.	editor, editors
(for.)	price for foreign countries
(ind.)	price for individuals
(inst.)	price for institutions
(lib.)	price for libraries
NS	new series
p.	page, pages
po. ed.	poetry editor
pub.	publisher
mss.	manuscripts
(stud.)	price for students
tr. by	translated by
tr. of	translation of
U.	University
w.	with

Months

Ja	January	Jl	July
F	February	Ag	August
Mr	March	S	September
Ap	April	O	October
My	May	N	November
Je	June	D	December

Seasons

Aut	Autumn, Fall	Spr	Spring
Wint	Winter	Sum	Summer

Years

81	1981	83	1983
82	1982	84	1984

PERIODICALS ADDED

Periodical acronyms are followed by the titles.

Amelia: AMELIA
BilingR: BILINGUAL REVIEW
BlueBldgs: BLUE BUILDINGS
Callaloo:CALLALOO
EverG: EVERGREEN REVIEW
GrahamHR: GRAHAM HOUSE REVIEW
GrandS: GRAND STREET
GreenfR: GREENFIELD REVIEW
KenR: KENYON REVIEW
LindLM: LINDEN LANE MAGAZINE
MidAR: MID-AMERICAN REVIEW
NoDaQ: NORTH DAKOTA QUARTERLY
Open24: OPEN 24 HOURS
Origin: ORIGIN
PaintedB: PAINTED BRIDE QUARTERLY
Paunch: PAUNCH
PoeticJ: POETIC JUSTICE
PraF: PRAIRIE FIRE
SnapD: SNAPDRAGON
Stepp: STEPPINGSTONE
TarRP: TAR RIVER POETRY
TexasR: TEXAS REVIEW
Veloc: VELOCITIES
WoosterR: WOOSTER REVIEW
Writ: WRIT
YellowS: YELLOW SILK

PERIODICALS DELETED

The following periodicals have been deleted from the Index
because (1) we have been notified that publication has
ceased or that it no longer publishes poetry, or (2) no 1983
or 1984 issues have been received after repeated requests.

Caribe: CARIBE
Catalyst: CATALYST
CEAFor: THE CEA FORUM -- No longer publishes poetry
EnPas: EN PASSANT
Focus: FOCUS/MIDWEST -- no longer published
MendoR: MENDOCINO REVIEW
Notarte: NOTICIAS DE ARTE
RevIn: REVISTA/REVIEW INTERAMERICANA
Shout: A SHOUT IN THE STREET--No longer published
Sky: SKYWRITING

PERIODICALS INDEXED

Arranged by acronym, with names of editors, ad-
dresses, issues indexed, and subscription informa-
tion. New titles added to the Index in 1984 are
marked with an asterisk (*).

13thM: 13TH MOON, Marilyn Hacker, ed., P.O. Box 309, Cathed-
ral Station, New York, NY 10025. Issues indexed: (8:1/2).
Subscriptions: $19.50/3 volumes, $13.00/2 volumes; Single
issues: $6.50.

Abatis: ABATIS, Duane Locke, ed., U. of Tampa, Tampa, FL
33606. Issues indexed: No 1984 issues received. Subscrip-
tions: $9.50/2 issues; Single issues: $5.

Abraxas: ABRAXAS, Ingrid Swanberg, ed., 2518 Gregory St.,
Madison, WI 53711. Issues indexed: (29/30-31/32). Sub-
scriptions: $8/4 issues.

Academe: ACADEME, Bulletin of the American Association of
University Professors, David S. Green, Paul Strohm, Sarah
G. Womack, eds., Suite 500, 1012 14th St., N.W., Washing-
ton, DC 20005. Issues indexed: (70:1-5). Subscriptions:
$30/yr., $32/yr. (for.).

Agni: THE AGNI REVIEW, Sharon Dunn, ed., P.O. Box 660,
Amherst, MA 01004. Issues indexed: (20-21). Subscrip-
tions: $15/2 yrs., $8/yr.; Single issues: $3.50.

*Amelia: AMELIA, Frederick A. Raborg, Jr., ed., 329 "E" St.,
Bakersfield, CA 93304. Issues indexed: (1:1-2) [1:1 Ap
84 not numbered]. Subscriptions: US, Canada, Mexico,
$28/2 yrs., $15/yr.; $27/yr., $52/2 yrs. (for.); Single
issues: $4.75.

AmerPoR: THE AMERICAN POETRY REVIEW, David Bonanno, Stephen
Berg, Arthur Vogelsang, et al., eds., World Poetry, Inc.,
Temple U Center City, 1616 Walnut St., Room 405, Phila-
delphia, PA 19103. Issues indexed: (13:1-6). Subscrip-
tions: $25/3 yrs., $30/3 yrs. (for.), $17/2 yrs., $21/2
yrs. (for.), $9.50/yr., $11.50/yr. (for.); classroom rate
$6/yr per student; Single issues: $1.95.

AmerS: THE AMERICAN SCHOLAR, Joseph Epstein, ed., United
Chapters of Phi Beta Kappa, 1811 Q St. NW, Washington, DC
20009. Issues indexed: (53:1-4). Subscriptions: $39/3
yrs., $16/yr. plus $3/yr. (for.); Single issues: $4.75.

Annex: ANNEX 21, Patrick Worth Gray, ed., UNO-Community
Writer's Workshop, University of Nebraska at Omaha, Oma-
ha, NE 68182. Issues indexed: No 1984 issues received.

"Temporarily discontinued"; Single issues: $4.95.

Antaeus: ANTAEUS, Megan Ratner, Managing ed., The Ecco Press, 18 W. 30th St., New York, NY 10001. Issues indexed: (52-53). Subscriptions: $16/yr.; Single issues: $5.

AntigR: THE ANTIGONISH REVIEW, George Sanderson, ed., St. Francis Xavier U., Antigonish, Nova Scotia B2G 1C0 Canada. Issues indexed: (56-59). Subscriptions: $14/4 issues; Single issues: $4.

AntR: THE ANTIOCH REVIEW, Robert S. Fogarty, ed., David St. John, Po. ed., Antioch College, P.O. Box 148, Yellow Springs, OH 45387. Issues indexed: (42:1-4). Subscriptions: $25/yr. (inst.), $18/yr. (ind.), $30/yr. (for.); Single issues: $4.75; P.O. Box 1308-R, Ft. Lee, NJ 07024.

Areito: AREITO, Max Azicri, Emilio Bejel, et al., eds., GPO Box 2174, New York, NY 10116. Issues indexed: (9:36, 10:37-38). Subscriptions: $18/yr. (inst.), $12/yr. (ind)., $20/yr. (for.); Single issues: $3; Back issues: $3.50.

Argo: ARGO, Incorporating DELTA, Hilary Davies & David Constantine, eds, Old Fire Station, 40 George St., Oxford OX1 2AQ England; Ray Fleming, U.S. ed., Dept. of Comparative Literature, Miami U., Oxford OH. Issues indexed: (5:2-3, 6:1). Subscriptions: $10/yr.; Single issues $3.

ArizQ: ARIZONA QUARTERLY, Albert Frank Gegenheimer, ed., U. of Arizona, Tucson, AZ 85721. Issues indexed: (40:1-4). Subscriptions: $10/3 yrs., $5/yr.; Single issues: $1.50.

Ascent: ASCENT, Daniel Curley, et al., eds., English Dept., U. of Illinois, 608 South Wright St., Urbana, IL 61801. Issues indexed: (9:2-3, 10:1). Subscriptions: $3/yr., $4.50/yr. (for.); Single issues: $1 (bookstore), $1.50 (mail).

Atlantic: THE ATLANTIC, William Whitworth, ed., Peter Davison, Po. ed., 8 Arlington St., Boston, MA 02116. Issues indexed: (253:1-6, 254:1-6). Subscriptions: $29.95/3 yrs., $15.95/2 yrs., $9.95/yr., plus $5/yr. (for.); Single issues: $2.

BallSUF: BALL STATE UNIVERSITY FORUM, Frances M. Rippy, Dick Renner, eds., Ball State U., Muncie, IN 47306. Issues indexed: (24:3). Subscriptions: (vol. 24) $8/yr., Single issues: $2.50; (vol. 25) $10/yr., Single issues: $3.

BelPoJ: THE BELOIT POETRY JOURNAL, David M. Stocking, Marion M. Stocking, eds., RFD 2, Box 154, Ellsworth, ME 04605. Issues indexed: (34:3-4, 35:1-2). Subscriptions: $17/3 yrs., $6/yr.; Single issues: $1.50.

BerksR: BERKSHIRE REVIEW, Stephen Fix, et al., eds., Williams College, Box 633, Williamstown, MA 01267. Issues indexed: (19).

*BilingR: BILINGUAL REVIEW, Gary D. Keller, ed., Box M, Campus Post Office, SUNY Binghampton, Binghampton, NY 13901. Issues indexed: (10:1, 11:1).

BlackALF: BLACK AMERICAN LITERATURE FORUM, Joe Weixlmann, ed., PH 237, Indiana State U., Terre Haute, IN 47809. Issues indexed: (18:1-4). Subscriptions: $8/yr. (ind.), $10/yr. (inst.), $12/yr. (for.); Statesman Towers West 1005, Indiana State U., Terre Haute, IN 47809.

BlackWR: BLACK WARRIOR REVIEW, Gabby Hyman, ed., Lynn Domina, po. ed., U. of Alabama, P.O. Box 2936, University, AL 35486-2936. Issues indexed: (10:2, 11:1). Subscriptions: $5.50/yr. (ind.), $7.50/yr. (inst.); Single issues: $3.

*BlueBldgs: BLUE BUILDINGS: An International Magazine of Poetry and Translations, Tom Urban, Ruth Doty et al., eds., Dept. of English, Drake U., Des Moines, IA 50311. Issues indexed: (7-8). Subscriptions: $4/2 issues; Single issues: $2.

BlueBuf: BLUE BUFFALO, Roberts Hilles, David Maulsby, et al., eds., c/o Dandelion, 922 - 9 Avenue, S.E., Calgary, Alberta, Canada, T2G 0S4. Issues indexed: (2:2). Single issues: $1.

Blueline: BLUELINE, Alice Gilborn, ed. & publisher; Jane Z. Carroll, po. ed. Blue Mountain Lake, NY 12812. Issues indexed: (5:2, 6:1). Subscriptions: $5/yr., $6/yr. (for.); Back issues: $2.50.

Bogg: BOGG, John Elsberg, ed., 422 N. Cleveland St., Arlington, VA 22201; George Cairncross, ed., 31 Belle Vue St., Filey, N. Yorks YO14 9HU, UK. Issues indexed: (52). Subscriptions: $7.50/3 issues; Single issues: $3.

Bound: BOUNDARY 2, William V. Spanos, ed., Dept. of English, State U. of New York, Binghamton, NY 13901. Issues indexed: (12:1-2). Subscriptions: $25/yr. (inst.), $15/yr. (ind.), $13/yr (stud.); Single issues: $8 (double), $5 (single).

*Callaloo: CALLALOO: A Black South Journal of Arts and Letters, Charles H. Rowell, ed., Dept. of English, U. of Kentucky, Lexington, KY 40506-0027. Issues indexed: (7:1-3, issues 20-22). Subscriptions: $10/yr.; $18/2 yrs; $12/yr. (for.); Single issues: $5.

CalQ: CALIFORNIA QUARTERLY, Elliot L. Gilbert, ed., Robert Swanson, Po. ed., 100 Sproul Hall, U. of California, Davis, CA 95616. Issues indexed: (23/24, 25). Subscriptions: $7/yr.; Single issues: $2.

Calyx: CALYX, Margarita Donnelly, Managing ed., P.O. Box B, Corvallis, OR 97339. Issues indexed: (8:2-3). Subscriptions: $10/yr., $18/2 yrs., $24/3 yrs., plus $4/yr. (for.), $9/yr. (for. airmail); Single issue: $5.

CanLit: CANADIAN LITERATURE, W. H. New, ed., U. of British
Columbia, 2029 West Mall, Vancouver, B.C. V6T 1W5 Canada.
Issues indexed: (100-103). Subscriptions: $20/yr. (ind.),
$25/yr. (inst.) plus $5/yr. outside Canada; Single is-
sues: $7.50.

CapeR: THE CAPE ROCK, Harvey Hecht, et al., eds., Southeast
Missouri State U., Cape Girardeau, MO 63701. Issues
indexed: (19:2-3). Subscriptions: $3/yr.; Single issues:
$2.

CapilR: THE CAPILANO REVIEW, Ann Rosenberg, ed., Capilano
College, 2055 Purcell Way, North Vancouver, B.C. V7J 3H5
Canada. Issues indexed: (28-33). Subscriptions: $17.50/8
issues (ind.), $9/4 issues (ind.), $10/4 issues (lib.),
plus $1/4 issues (for.); Single issues: $3.

CarolQ: CAROLINA QUARTERLY, Mary Titus, ed., Ellen Caldwell,
po. ed., Greenlaw Hall 066-A, U. of North Carolina,
Chapel Hill, NC 27514. Issues indexed: (36:2-3, 37:1).
Subscriptions: $12/yr. (inst.), $10/yr. (ind.), $11/yr.
(for.); Single issues: $4; Back issues: $4.

CEACritic: THE CEA CRITIC, College English Association,
Michael Payne, ed., Dept. of English, Bucknell Univ.,
Lewisburg, PA 17837. Issues indexed: (45:3/4; 46:1/2-3/4;
47: 1/2). Subscriptions: $24/yr. (lib., inst.), $20/yr.
(ind.).

CentR: THE CENTENNIAL REVIEW, Linda Wagner, ed., 110 Morrill
Hall, Michigan State U., East Lansing, MI 48824-1036.
Issues indexed: (28:1-3, 28:4/29:1). Subscriptions: $8/2
yrs., $5/yr., plus $2/yr. (for.); Single issues: $1.50.

CharR: THE CHARITON REVIEW, Jim Barnes, ed., Division of
Language and Literature, Northeast Missouri State U.,
Kirksville, MO 63501. Issues indexed: (10:1-2). Sub-
scriptions: $7/4 issues; Single issues: $2.

Chelsea: CHELSEA, Sonia Raiziss, ed., P.O. Box 5880, Grand
Central Station, New York, NY 10163. Issues indexed:
(42/43). Subscriptions: $9/2 issues or double issue, $9
(for.); Single issues: $5, $5.50 (for.).

ChiR: CHICAGO REVIEW, Steve Heminger & Steve Schroer, eds.,
Michael Alper & Michael Donaghy, po. eds., U. of Chicago,
Faculty Exchange, Box C, Chicago, IL 60637. Issues in-
dexed: (34:2-3). Subscriptions: $35/3 yrs., $24/2 yrs.,
$13/yr., $10/yr. (ind.), plus $2/yr. (for.); Single is-
sues: $3.75.

ChrC: THE CHRISTIAN CENTURY, James M. Wall, ed., 407 S.
Dearborn St., Chicago, IL 60605. Issues indexed: (101:1-
40). Subscriptions: $24/yr.; Single issues: $1.25.

CimR: CIMARRON REVIEW, Neil J. Hackett, ed., Terry Hummer,
Po. ed., 208 Life Sciences East, Oklahoma State U.,
Stillwater, OK 74078. Issues indexed: (66-69). Subscrip-
tions: $10/yr.; Single issues: $2.50.

ClockR: CLOCKWATCH REVIEW, James Plath, ed., 737 Penbrook Way, Hartland, WI 53029. Issues indexed: No 1984 issues published. Subscriptions: $6/yr.; Single issues: $3.

ColEng: COLLEGE ENGLISH, National Council of Teachers of English, Donald Gray, ed., Brian O'Neill, Po. cons., Dept. of English, Indiana U., Bloomington, IN 47405. Issues indexed: (46:1-8). Subscriptions: $35/yr. (inst.), $30/yr. (ind.), plus $4/yr. (for.); Single issues: $4; NCTE, 1111 Kenyon Rd., Urbana, IL 61801.

Comm: COMMONWEAL, Peter Steinfels, ed., Rosemary Deen, Marie Ponsot, Po. eds., 232 Madison Ave., New York, NY 10016. Issues indexed: (111:1-22). Subscriptions: $43/2 yrs., $47/2 yrs. (Canada), $53/2 yrs. (for.), $24/yr., $26/yr. (Canada), $29/yr. (for.); Single issues: $1.25.

ConcPo: CONCERNING POETRY, Ellwood Johnson, ed., Robert Huff, Po. ed., Dept. of English, Western Washington U., Bellingham, WA 98225. Issues indexed: (17:1-2). Subscriptions: $6/yr. (USA, Canada), $7/yr. (for.); Single issues: $3.80.

Cond: CONDITIONS, Elly Bulkin, Jan Clausen, Rima Shore, eds., P.O. Box 56, Van Brunt Station, Brooklyn, NY 11215. Issues indexed: (3:4, issue 10). Subscriptions: $25/3 issues (inst.), $15/3 issues (ind), $9/3 issues "hardship" rate, free to women in prisons and mental institutions; Single issues: $6 (ind.), $9 (inst.).

Confr: CONFRONTATION, Martin Tucker, ed., English Dept., C. W. Post College, Long Island U., Greenvale, NY 11548. Issues indexed: (27/28). Subscriptions: $20/3 yrs., $15/2 yrs., $8/yr.; Single issues: $5.

CrabCR: CRAB CREEK REVIEW, Linda Clifton, ed., 806 N. 42nd, Seattle WA 98103. Issues indexed: (1:3, 2:1). Subscriptions: $15/2 yrs., $8/yr.; Single issues: $3.

CreamCR: CREAM CITY REVIEW, Jesse Glass, Jr., ed., Eamonn Wall, po. ed., English Dept., P.O. Box 413, U. of Wisconsin-Milwaukee, Milwaukee, WI 53201. Issues indexed: (9:1/2) [Note: the 1983 index should have read (8:1-2), not (18:1-2)]. Subscriptions: $6/yr; Back issues: $3; Single issues: $3.50.

CropD: CROP DUST, Edward C. Lynskey ed., Route 2, Box 358, Warrenton, VA 22186. Issues indexed: No 1984 issues published. Subscriptions: $5/2 issues (ind.), $8/2 issues (lib.); Single issues: $2.50.

CrossC: CROSS-CANADA WRITERS' QUARTERLY, Ted Plantos, ed., Bruce Hunter, Po. ed., Box 277, Station F, Toronto, Ontario M4Y 2L7 Canada. Issues indexed: (6:1-4). Subscriptions: $12/yr. (ind.), $14/yr. (inst.), $16/yr (for.); Single issues: $3.95.

CutB: CUTBANK, Suzanne Hackett, Jon Davis, eds., Dept. of English, U. of Montana, Missoula, MT 59812. Issues in-

dexed: (22). Subscriptions: $14/2 yrs., $7.50/yr.; Single
issues: $4.

Dandel: DANDELION, Robert Hilles, Beverly Harris, eds., John
McDermid, Claire Harris, Po. eds., Alexandra Centre, 922
- 9th Ave., S.E., Calgary, Alberta T2G 0S4 Canada. Issues
indexed: (11:1-2). Subscriptions: $15/2 yrs., $8/yr.,
$12/yr. (inst.); Single issues: $4.

DekalbLAJ: THE DEKALB LITERARY ARTS JOURNAL, William S.
Newman, ed., DeKalb Community College, 555 N. Indian
Creek Dr., Clarkston, GA 30021. Issues indexed: (17:1/2,
20th anniversary issue). Single issues: $10.

DenQ: DENVER QUARTERLY, Eric Gould, ed., U. of Denver,
Denver, CO 80208. Issues indexed: (18:4, 19:1). Sub-
scriptions: $18/2 yrs., $10/yr., plus $1/yr. (for.);
Single issues: $2.50

Descant: DESCANT, Karen Mulhallen, ed., P.O. Box 314, Sta-
tion P, Toronto M5S 2S8, Ontario, Canada. Issues in-
dexed: (44/45-47). Subscriptions: $18/yr (ind.), $26/yr.
(inst.); Single issues: $6.50-$8.

EngJ: ENGLISH JOURNAL, National Council of Teachers of Eng-
lish, Ken Donelson, Alleen Pace Nilsen, eds., College of
Education, Arizona State U., Tempe, AZ 85287. Issues
indexed: (73:1-8). Subscriptions: $35/yr. (inst.),
$30/yr. (ind.), plus $4/yr. (for.); Single issues: $4;
NCTE, 1111 Kenyon Rd., Urbana, IL 61801.

Epoch: EPOCH, C. S. Giscombe, ed., 251 Goldwin Smith Hall,
Cornell U., Ithaca, NY 14853. Issues indexed: (33:2-3,
34:1). Subscriptions: $8/yr., $10/yr. (for.); Single
issues: $3.

*EvergR: EVERGREEN REVIEW, Barney Rosset & Fred Jordan,
eds., c/o Grove Press, 196 W. Houston St., New York, NY
10014; Issues indexed: (98); Single issues: $5.95.

Field: FIELD, Stuart Friebert, David Young, eds., Rice Hall,
Oberlin College, Oberlin, OH 44074. Issues indexed: (30-
31). Subscriptions: $12/2 yrs., $7/yr.; Single issues:
$3.50; Back issues: $10.

FourQt: FOUR QUARTERS, John Christopher Kleis, ed., Richard
Lautz, Po. ed., La Salle U., 20th & Olney Aves., Phila-
delphia, PA 19141. Issues indexed: (33:2-4, 34:1). Sub-
scriptions: $13/2 yrs., $8/yr.; Single issues: $2.

Gargoyle: GARGOYLE MAGAZINE, Richard Peabody, Jr., ed./pub.,
Gretchen Johnsen, po. ed., Paycock Press, P.O. Box 3567,
Washington, DC 20007. Issues indexed: (24, 25/26); 20/21
was "all fiction issue." Subscriptions: $8/yr. (ind.),
$10/yr. (inst.); Single issues: $5.95-7.95.

GeoR: GEORGIA REVIEW, Stanley W. Lindberg, ed., U. of Geor-
gia, Athens, GA 30602. Issues indexed: (38:1-4). Sub-
scriptions: $15/2 yrs., $9/yr., plus $3/yr. (for.); Sin-

gle issues: $4.

<u>Germ</u>: GERMINATION, Allan Cooper, ed. & pub., Leigh Faulkner,
Assoc. ed., 428 Yale Ave., Riverview, New Brunswick E1B
2B5, Canada. Issues indexed: (8:1-2). Subscriptions:
$6/2 issues (ind.), $8/2 issues (inst.); Single issues:
$3.50.

*<u>GrahamHR</u>: GRAHAM HOUSE REVIEW, Peter Balakian & Bruce
Smith, eds., Colgate U. Press, Box 5000, Colgate U.,
Hamilton, NY 13346; Issues indexed: (7); Subscriptions:
$17/2 yrs; Single issues: $4.50.

<u>Grain</u>: GRAIN, Saskatchewan Writers Guild, Brenda Riches,
ed., Box 1154, Regina, Saskatchewan S4P 3B4 Canada. Is-
sues indexed: (12:1-4). Subscriptions: $15/2 yrs.,
$9/yr.; Single issues: $3.

*<u>GrandS</u>: GRAND STREET, Ben Sonnenberg, ed., 50 Riverside
Dr., New York, NY 10024. Issues indexed: (3:1-4, 4:1).
Subscriptions: $20/yr. (ind.), $24/yr. (for.); $24/yr.
(inst.), $28/yr. (for.); Single issues: $5.

*<u>GreenfR</u>: GREENFIELD REVIEW, Joseph Bruchac III, ed., R.D.
1, Box 80, Greenfield Center, NY 12833. Issues indexed:
(11:3/4, 12:1/2). Subscriptions: $8/2 double issues; $10
(lib.); Single issues: $4.

<u>HangL</u>: HANGING LOOSE, Robert Hershon, <u>et al</u>., eds., 231
Wyckoff St., Brooklyn, NY 11217. Issues indexed: (45-
46). Subscriptions: $18/9 issues, $12/6 issues, $6.50/3
issues; Single issues: $2.50.

<u>Harp</u>: HARPER'S MAGAZINE, Lewis H. Lapham, ed., Two Park
Ave., New York, NY 10016. Issues indexed: (268:1604-
1609, 269:1610-1615). Subscriptions: $18/yr., plus $2/yr.
(USA possessions, Canada), plus $3/yr. (for.); Single
issues: $2; P.O. Box 1937, Marion, OH 43305.

<u>HarvardA</u>: THE HARVARD ADVOCATE, Rachel Leheny, Managing
ed., Sophie Volpp, po. ed., Advocate House, 21 South St.,
Cambridge, MA 02138. Issues indexed: (117:4/118:1,
118:2). Subscriptions: $8.50/yr. (ind.), $10/yr. (inst.),
$15/yr. (for.).

<u>HiramPoR</u>: HIRAM POETRY REVIEW, English Department, Hiram
College, David Fratus & Carol Donley, eds., Box 162, Hi-
ram, OH 44234. Issues indexed: (36-37). Subscriptions:
$2/yr.; Single issues: $1.

<u>HolCrit</u>: THE HOLLINS CRITIC, John Rees Moore, ed., Hollins
College, VA 24020. Issues indexed: (21:1-5). Subscrip-
tions: $5/yr., $6.50/yr. (for.).

<u>Hudson</u>: THE HUDSON REVIEW, Paula Deitz, Frederick Morgan,
eds., 684 Park Ave., New York, NY 10021. Issues indexed:
(37:1-4). Subscriptions: $16/yr., $26/2 yrs., $38/3 yrs.,
$17/yr. (for.); Single issues: $4.50.

Humanist: THE HUMANIST, Lloyd L. Morain, ed., P.O. Box 146, 7 Harwood Dr., Amherst, NY 14226-0146. Issues indexed: (44:1-6). Subscriptions: $35/3 yrs., $25/2 yrs., $15/yr., plus $3/yr. (for.); Single issues: $2.50; Back issues: $3.

Images: IMAGES, Gary Pacernick, ed., Dept. of English, Wright State U., Dayton, OH 45435. Issues indexed: No 1984 issues received. Subscriptions: $3/yr.; Single issues: $1.

IndR: INDIANA REVIEW, Jane Hilberry, ed., Monica Barron, Jim Brock, et al., po. eds., 316 N. Jordan Ave., Bloomington, IN 47405. Issues indexed: (7:1-3). Subscriptions: $10/yr., $12/yr. (inst.) ; Supporting subscriptions $25; Single issues: $4.

Inti: INTI, Revista de Literatura Hispanica, Roger B. Carmo-sino, ed., Dept. of Modern Languages, Providence College, Providence, RI 02918. Issues indexed: No 1984 issues received. Subscriptions: $20/yr. (inst.), $16/yr. (ind.).

Iowa: IOWA REVIEW, David Hamilton, ed., 308 EPB, U. of Iowa, Iowa City, IA 52242. Issues indexed: (14:1-3). Sub-scriptions: $20/yr. (lib., inst.), $12/yr. (ind.), plus $3/yr. (for.); Single issues: $5.

KanQ: KANSAS QUARTERLY, Harold Schneider, et al., eds., Dept. of English, Denison Hall, Kansas State U., Manhat-tan, KS 66506. Issues indexed: (16:1/2-4). Subscrip-tions: $20/2 yrs., $12/yr. (USA, Canada, Latin America), $22/2 yrs., $13/yr. (other countries); Single issues: $4.

Kayak: KAYAK, George Hitchcock, Marjorie Simon, Gary Fisher, eds., 325 Ocean View Ave., Santa Cruz, CA 95062. Issues indexed: (64) "Final issue". Single issues: $2.

*KenR: KENYON REVIEW, Philip D. Church, Galbraith M. Crump, eds., Kenyon College, Gambier, OH 43022. Issues indexed: (NS 6:1-4). Subscriptions: Kenyon Review, P.O. Box 1308L, Fort Lee, NJ 07024; $15/yr., $28/2 yrs., $39/3 yrs. (ind.); $18/yr. (inst.); +$5 (for.); Single issues: $6.50; Back issues: $3.

LetFem: LETRAS FEMENINAS, Asociacion de Literatura Femenina Hispanica, Dr. Adelaida Martinez, ed., Texas A & M U., Asociacion de Literatura Femenina Hispanica, Modern Lan-guages Dept., College Station, TX 77843-4238. Issues indexed: No 1984 issues received. Subscriptions: $15/yr.

*LindLM: LINDEN LANE MAGAZINE, Herberto Padilla, pub., Bel-kis Cuza Malé, ed., P.O. Box 2384, Princeton, NJ 08540-0384. Issues indexed: (3:1-2/3/4). Subscriptions: $10/yr. (ind.), $16/yr. (inst.), $20/yr. (for.); Single issues: $2.

LitR: THE LITERARY REVIEW, Walter Cummins, ed., Fairleigh Dickinson U., 285 Madison Ave., Madison, NJ 07940. Is-

sues indexed: (27:2-4, 28:1). Subscriptions: $12/yr.,
$15/yr. (for.), $22/2 yrs., (ind.), $28/2 yrs. (for.);
Single issues: $4.50, $5.50/yr (for.).

LittleBR: THE LITTLE BALKANS REVIEW, Gene DeGruson, po. ed.,
The Little Balkans Press, Inc., 601 Grandview Heights
Terr., Pittsburg, KS 66762. Issues indexed: (4:3-4).
Subscriptions: $10/yr.; Single issues: $3.50.

LittleM: THE LITTLE MAGAZINE, Dennis Cooney, Robin de Cres-
pigny, et al., eds, Dragon Press, P.O. Box 78, Pleasant-
ville, NY 10570. Issues Indexed: (14:3). Subscriptions:
$13/4 issues (inst.), $12/4 issues (ind.), $14/4 issues
(for.); Single issues: $3.

LittleR: THE LITTLE REVIEW, John McKernan, ed., Little Re-
view Press, Box 205, Marshall U., Huntington, WV 25701.
Issues indexed: No 1984 issues received; next issue anti-
cipated in 1986. Subscriptions: $2.50/yr.; Single issues:
$1.25.

Mairena: MAIRENA, Manuel de la Puebla, ed., Himalaya 257,
Urbanizacion Monterrey, Rio Piedras, PR 00926. Issues
indexed: (5:13-14, 6:16-18). Subscriptions: $10/yr.
(inst.), $15/yr. (for. inst.), $6/yr. (ind.), $10/yr.
(for. ind.).

MalR: THE MALAHAT REVIEW, Constance Rooke, ed., P.O. Box
1700, Victoria, British Columbia, Canada V8W 2Y2. Issues
indexed: (67-69). Subscriptions: $40/3 yrs., $15/yr.
(USA, Canada), $50/3 yrs., $20/yr. (other countries),
$10/yr. (stud.); Single issues: $7 (USA, Canada), $8
(other countries).

ManhatR: THE MANHATTAN REVIEW, Philip Fried, ed., 304 Third
Ave., Apt. 4A, New York, NY 10010. Issues indexed:
(3:2). Subscriptions: $8/2 issues (ind.), $12/2 issues
(inst.), plus $2.50/2 issues (outside USA & Canada); Back
issues: $4.

MassR: THE MASSACHUSETTS REVIEW, John Hicks, ed., Memorial
Hall, U. of Massachusetts, Amherst, MA 01003. Issues
indexed: (25:1-4). Subscriptions: $12/yr., $14/yr.
(for.); Single issues: $4.

Meadows: THE MEADOWS, Bev Tucker, ed., Art Dept., Truckee
Meadows Community College, 7000 Dandini Blvd., Reno, NV
89512. Issues indexed: No 1984 issues received.

MemphisSR: MEMPHIS STATE REVIEW, William Page, ed., Dept. of
English, Memphis State U., Memphis, TN 38152. Issues
indexed: (4:2, 5:2). Subscriptions: $3/yr.; Single is-
sues: $2.

Mester: MESTER, Librada Hernandez-Lagoa, ed., Dept. of Spa-
nish and Portuguese, U. of California, Los Angeles, CA
90024. Issues indexed: (13:1-2). Subscriptions: $14/yr.
(inst.), $8/yr. (ind.), $5/yr. (stud.); Single issues: $7
(inst.), $4 (ind.)

Metam: METAMORFOSIS, Lauro Flores, Director, Centro de Estu-
dios Chicanos, GN-09, U. of Washington, Seattle, WA
98195. Issues indexed: (5:2/6:1). Single issues: $5.

MichQR: MICHIGAN QUARTERLY REVIEW, Laurence Goldstein, ed.,
3032 Rackham Bldg., U. of Michigan, Ann Arbor, MI 48109.
Issues indexed: (23:1-4). Subscriptions: $24/2 yr.,
$13/yr. (ind.), $15/yr. (inst.); Single issues: $3.50;
Back issues: $2.

*MidAR: MID-AMERICAN REVIEW, Robert Early, ed., George Loon-
ey, po. ed., 106 Hanna Hall, Dept. of English, Bowling
Green State U., Bowling Green, OH 43403. Issues indexed:
(4:1-2). Subscriptions: $6/yr., $10/2 yrs., $14/3 yrs.

MidwQ: THE MIDWEST QUARTERLY, James B. Schick, ed., Michael
Heffernan, po. ed., Pittsburg State U., Pittsburg, KS
66762. Issues indexed: (25:2-4, 26:1). Subscriptions:
$6/yr. plus $2 (for.); Single issues: $2.

MinnR: THE MINNESOTA REVIEW, Fred Pfeil, Laura Rice-Sayre,
Michael Sprinker, eds, Anne E. Krosby, Henry Sayre, Rich-
ard Daniels, po. eds., Dept. of English, Oregon State U.,
Corvallis, OR 97331. Issues Indexed: (NS 22-23). Sub-
scriptions: $20/2 yrs. (inst. & for.), $12/2 yrs. (ind.),
$12/yr. (inst. & for.), $7/yr. (ind.); Single issues: $4.

MissouriR: THE MISSOURI REVIEW, Speer Morgan, ed., Sherod
Santos & Garrett Hongo, po. eds., Dept. of English, 231
Arts and Science, U. of Missouri, Columbia, MO 65211.
Issues indexed: (7:2-3, 8:1). Subscriptions: $18/2 yrs.,
$10/yr.

MissR: MISSISSIPPI REVIEW, Frederick Barthelme, ed., The
Center for Writers, Southern Station, Box 5144, Hatties-
burg, MS 39406-5144. Issues indexed: (12:3, 13:1/2, nos.
36-37/38). Subscriptions: $26/3 yrs., $18/2 yrs.,
$10/yr., plus $2/yr. (for.); Single issues: $5.

ModernPS: MODERN POETRY STUDIES, Jerry McGuire, ed., 207
Delaware Ave., Buffalo, NY 14202. Issues indexed: No
1984 issues received. Subscriptions: $9/3 issues
(inst.), $7.50/3 issues (ind.).

MoodySI: MOODY STREET IRREGULARS, Joy Walsh, ed., P.O. Box
157, Clarence Center, NY 14032. Issues indexed: (14).
Subscriptions: $5/3 issues (ind.), $6/3 issues (lib.);
Single issues: $3.

MSS: MSS, M. L. Rosenberg, J. Higgins, eds., State U. of NY
at Binghamton, Binghamton, NY 13901. Issues indexed:
(3:2/3, 4:1/2). Subscriptions: $18/2 yrs. (ind.), $25/2
yrs. (lib.); $10/yr. (ind.), $15/yr. (lib.); Single is-
sues: $4., Double issues: $6.

Mund: MUNDUS ARTIUM, Rainer Schulte, ed., U. of Texas at
Dallas, Box 830688, Richardson, TX 75080-0688. Issues
indexed: (14:2). Subscriptions: $10/2 issues (inst.),
$8/2 issues (ind.). Single issues: $4.50.

<u>Nat</u>: THE NATION, Victor Navasky, ed., Grace Schulman, po.
   ed., 72 Fifth Ave., New York, NY 10011. Issues indexed:
   (238:1-25, 239:1-22). Subscriptions: $72/2 yrs., $40/yr.,
   $20/half yr. plus $7/yr. (Mexico, Canada), plus $13/yr.
   (other for.); Single issues: $1.25; Nation Subscription
   Service, P.O. Box 1953, Marion, OH 43305.

<u>NegC</u>: NEGATIVE CAPABILITY, Sue Brannam Walker, ed., 6116
   Timberly Road North, Mobile, AL 36609. Issues indexed:
   (4:1-4). Subscriptions: $12/yr. (ind.), $14/yr. (inst.),
   $13/yr. (for.); Single issues: $3.50.

<u>NewEngR</u>: NEW ENGLAND REVIEW AND BREAD LOAF QUARTERLY, Sydney
   Lea, Jim Schley, eds., Box 170, Hanover, NH 03755. Is-
   sues indexed: (6:3-4, 7:1-2). Subscriptions: $12/yr.;
   Single issues: $4-7.

<u>NewL</u>: NEW LETTERS, David Ray, ed., U. of Missouri-Kansas
   City, 5310 Harrison, Kansas City, MO 64110. Issues in-
   dexed: (50:2/3-4, 51:1-2). Subscriptions: $50/5 yrs.,
   $25/2 yrs., $15/yr. (ind.); $60/5 yrs., $30/2 yrs.,
   $18/yr. (lib.); Single issues: $4.

<u>NewOR</u>: NEW ORLEANS REVIEW, John Mosier, <u>et al.</u>, eds., Box
   195, Loyola U., New Orleans, LA 70118. Issues indexed:
   (11:1-3/4). Subscriptions: $25/yr. (inst.), $20/yr.
   (ind.), $30/yr. (for.); Single issues: $7-11.

<u>NewRena</u>: THE NEW RENAISSANCE, Louise T. Reynolds, ed., Stan-
   wood Bolton, po. ed., 9 Heath Road, Arlington, MA 02174.
   Issues indexed: (18). Subscriptions: $19/6 issues, $10/3
   issues; $23/6 issues, $12/3 issues (Canada, Mexico, Eur-
   ope); $25/6 issues, $13/3 issues (elsewhere); Single
   issues: $4.75.

<u>NewRep</u>: THE NEW REPUBLIC. Issues indexed: (189:5-26, 190:1-
   26, 191:1-25); The <u>New</u> <u>Republic</u> is the only journal which
   refuses to supply a complementary subscription for index-
   ing; indexing was done by Martha Sollberger, Indiana, PA.

<u>NewWR</u>: NEW WORLD REVIEW, Marilyn Bechtel, ed., 162 Madison
   Ave., 3rd Floor, New York, NY 10016. Issues indexed:
   (52:1-6). Subscriptions: $5/yr. $6/yr. (for.); Single
   issues: $1.

<u>NewYorker</u>: THE NEW YORKER, Howard Moss, po. ed., 25 W. 43rd
   St., New York, NY 10036. Issues indexed: (59:46-52,
   60:1-45). Subscriptions: $52/2 yrs., $32/yr.; $44/yr.
   (Canada); $52/yr. (for.); Single issues: $1.50.

<u>NewYRB</u>: THE NEW YORK REVIEW OF BOOKS, Robert B. Silvers,
   Barbara Epstein, eds., 250 W. 57th St., New York, NY
   10107. Issues indexed: (30:21/22, 31:1-20). Subscrip-
   tions: $30/yr.; Single issues: $2; Subscription Service
   Dept., P.O. Box 940, Farmingdale, NY 11737.

<u>Nimrod</u>: NIMROD, Francine Ringold, ed., Joan Flint, <u>et al.</u>,
   po. eds., Arts and Humanities Council of Tulsa, 2210 S.
   Main St., Tulsa, OK 74114. Issues indexed: (27:2, 28:1).

Subscriptions: $10/yr., $13/yr. (for.); Single issues: $5.50, $7 (for.).

NoAmR: THE NORTH AMERICAN REVIEW, Robley Wilson, Jr., ed., Peter Cooley, po. ed., U. of Northern Iowa, 1222 West 27th St., Cedar Falls, IA 50614. Issues indexed: (269:1-4). Subscriptions: $9/yr., $10/yr. (Canada, Latin America), $11/yr. (elsewhere); Single issues: 2.50.

*NoDaQ: NORTH DAKOTA QUARTERLY, Robert W. Lewis, ed., Don Eades, po. ed., Box 8237, U. of North Dakota, Grand Forks, ND 58202. Issues indexed: (52:1/2-4). Subscriptions: $10/yr.; Single issues: $4.

Northeast: NORTHEAST, John Judson, ed., Juniper Press, 1310 Shorewood Dr., La Crosse, WI 54601. Issues indexed: (Ser. 3:17-18). Subscriptions: $25/yr.; Single issues: $2.50-$3.

NowestR: NORTHWEST REVIEW, John Witte, ed., Maxine Scates, po. ed., 369 PLC, U. of Oregon, Eugene, OR 97403. Issues indexed: (22:1/2-3). Subscriptions: $30/3 yrs., $21/2 yrs., $11/yr.; $13/2 yrs., $10/yr. (stud.); plus $2/yr. (for.); Single issues: $4.

Obs: OBSIDIAN, Alvin Aubert, ed./pub., Wayne State U., Detroit, MI 48202. Issues indexed: (8). Subscriptions: $8.50/yr., $9.50/yr. (Canada), $11.50/yr. (for.); Single issues: $3; Double issues: $6.

OhioR: THE OHIO REIVEW, Wayne Dodd, ed., Ellis Hall, Ohio U., Athens, OH 45701. Issues indexed: (32-33). Subscriptions: $30/3 yrs., $12/yr.; Single issues: $4.25.

OntR: ONTARIO REVIEW, Raymond J. Smith, ed., 9 Honey Brook Dr., Princeton, NJ 08540. Issues indexed: (20-21). Subscriptions: $21/3 yrs., $15/2 yrs., $8/yr., plus $1/yr. (for.); Single issues: $3.95.

*Open24: OPEN 24 HOURS, Kate Pipkin and Chris Toll, eds, 702 Homestead St., Baltimore, MD 21218. Issues indexed: (3) Single issues: $3.

OP: OPEN PLACES, Eleanor M. Bender, ed., Box 2085, Stephens College, Columbia, MO 65215. Issues indexed: (37). Subscriptions: $15/2 yrs., $8/yr. (USA, Canada), plus $6/yr. (elsewhere); Single issue: $4.

*Origin: ORIGIN. Cid Corman, ed., Michael Heller, USA ed., P.O. Box 981, Stuyvesant Sta., New York, NY 10009. Issues indexed: (5:1-4). Subscriptions: $12/yr. (US, Canada), $15/yr. (for.), $18/yr. (inst.), $21/yr. (for. inst.); The National Poetry Foundation, 305 Neville Hall, U. of Maine, Orono, ME 04469-0122.

OroM: ORO MADRE, Loss and Jan Glazier, eds., 4429 Gibraltar Dr., Fremont, CA 94536. Issues indexed: (2:2-3/4). Subscriptions: $12/4 issues; Single issues: $3.95.

Os: OSIRIS, Andrea Moorhead, ed., Box 297, Deerfield, MA
   01342. Issues indexed: (18-19). Subscriptions: $6/2
   issues (USA, Canada, Mexico), $7/2 issues (elsewhere);
   Single issues: $3.

Outbr: OUTERBRIDGE, Charlotte Alexander, ed., English Dept.
   (A323), College of Staten Island, 715 Ocean Terrace,
   Staten Island, NY 10301. Issues indexed: No 1984 issues
   received. Sub-scriptions: $4/yr.; Single issues: $4.

Paint: PAINTBRUSH, Ben Bennani, ed., English & Foreign Lan-
   guages, Georgia Southwestern College, Americus, GA 31709.
   Issues indexed: No 1984 issues received. Subscriptions:
   $20/3 yrs., $15/2 yrs., $8/yr.; Single issues: $5; Back
   issues: $5.

*PaintedB: PAINTED BRIDE QUARTERLY, Carole Bernstein, et
   al., eds., 230 Vine St., Philadelphia, PA 19106. Issues
   indexed: (21-24). Subscriptions: $9/yr., $17/2 yrs.,
   $15/yr. (lib, inst.); Single issues: $3.

ParisR: THE PARIS REVIEW, George A. Plimpton, et al., eds.,
   Jonathan Galassi, po. ed., 541 East 72nd St., New York,
   NY 10021. Issues indexed: (26:91-94). Subscriptions:
   $1000/life, $48/12 issues, $32/8 issues, $16/4 issues,
   plus $4/4 issues (for.); Single issues: $5; 45-39 171
   Place, Flushing, NY 11358.

PartR: PARTISAN REVIEW, William Phillips, ed., Boston U.,
   141 Bay State Rd., Boston, MA 02215. Issues indexed:
   (51:1-3, 51:4/52:1). Subscriptions: $39/3 yrs., $29/2
   yrs., $16/yr.; $33/2 yrs., $18/yr. (for.); $22/yr.
   (inst.); Single issues: $4.50; Anniversary issue: $8.

*Paunch: PAUNCH, Arthur Efron, ed., Mili Clark, po. ed., 123
   Woodward Ave., Buffalo, NY 14214. Issues indexed:
   (57/58). Subscriptions: $7 (ind.), $10 (lib.), $4
   (stud.)

Peb: PEBBLE, Greg Kuzma, ed., The Best Cellar Press, Dept.
   of English, U. of Nebraska, Lincoln, NE 68588. Issues
   indexed: (23) Poems for the Dead (Special issue). Sub-
   scriptions: $15/4 issues (lib.), $12/4 issues (ind.);
   single issue: $4.

Pequod: PEQUOD, Mark Rudman, ed., Dept. of English, Room
   200, New York U., 19 University Place, New York, NY
   10003. Issues indexed: (16/17). Subscriptions: $17/2
   yrs., $9/yr.; Single issues: $8. The National Poetry
   Foundation, 305 Neville Hall, U. of Maine, Orono, ME
   04469-0122.

Pig: PIG IRON, Jim Villani, Rose Sayre, eds., Pig Iron
   Press, P.O. Box 237, Youngstown, OH 44501. Issues in-
   dexed: (12). Single issues: $7.95.

PikeF: THE PIKESTAFF FORUM, James R. Scrimgeour, Robert D.
   Sutherland, eds./pubs., P.O. Box 127, Normal, IL 61761.
   Issues indexed: (6). Subscriptions: $10/6 issues; Single

issues: $2; Back issues: $2.

Playb: PLAYBOY, Hugh M. Hefner, ed./pub., 919 N. Michigan
Ave., Chicago, IL 60611. Issues indexed: (31:1-12).
Subscriptions: $27/yr., $35 (for.); Single issues: varies.

Ploughs: PLOUGHSHARES, DeWitt Henry, Peter O'Malley, Direc-
tors, Box 529, Cambridge, MA 02139-0529; Editorial of-
fices: Div. of Creative Writing and Literature, Emerson
College, 100 Beacon St., Boston, MA 02116; 214A Waverly
Ave., Watertown, MA 02172. Issues indexed: (10:1-4).
Subscriptions: $14/yr., $16/yr. (for.); Single issues:
$5.

Poem: POEM, Huntsville Literary Association, Robert L. Wel-
ker, ed., U. of Alabama at Huntsville, English Dept.,
Huntsville, AL 35899. Issues indexed: (50-52). Subscrip-
tions: $7.50/yr.; P.O. Box 919, Huntsville, AL 35804.

PoetC: POET AND CRITIC, Michael Martone, ed., 203 Ross Hall,
Iowa State U., Ames, IA 50011. Issues indexed: (15:2-3,
16:1). Subscriptions: 9/yr., plus $1/yr. (for.); Single
issues: $3; Iowa State U. Press, South State St., Ames,
IA 50010.

*PoeticJ: POETIC JUSTICE: Contemporary American Poetry, Alan
Engebretsen, ed., 8220 Rayford Dr., Los Angeles, CA
90045. Issues indexed: (1-8). Subscriptions: $10/yr.;
Single issues: $3.

PoetL: POET LORE, Philip K. Jason, Kevin Madden, Barbara
Lefcowitz, Executive eds., Heldref Publications, 4000
Albemarle St., N.W., Washington, DC 20016. Issues in-
dexed: (79:1-3). Subscriptions: $12/yr., $20/yr. (inst.),
plus $5/yr. (for.); Single issues: $4.50.

Poetry: POETRY, Joseph Parisi, acting ed., 601 S. Morgan
St., P.O. Box 4348, Chicago, IL 60680. Issues indexed:
(143:4-6, 144:1-6, 145:1-3). Subscriptions: $20/yr.,
$24/yr. (for.); Single issues: $2 plus $.60 postage; Back
issues: $2.25 plus $.60 postage.

PoetryCR: POETRY CANADA REVIEW, Robert Billings, ed., 307
Coxwell Ave., Toronto, Ontario M4L 3B5 Canada. Issues
indexed: (5:3-4, 6:1-2). Subscriptions: $10/yr., $22/yr.
(inst.); Single issues: $3.50.

PoetryE: POETRY EAST, Richard Jones, Kate Daniels, eds.,
Star Route 1, Box 50, Earlysville, VA 22936. Issues
indexed: (13/14-15). Subscriptions: $10/yr.; Single is-
sues: $3.50-$6.

PoetryNW: POETRY NORTHWEST, David Wagoner, ed., U. of Wash-
ington, 4045 Brooklyn Ave., NE, Seattle, WA 98105. Is-
sues indexed: (25:1-4). Subscriptions: $8/yr., $9/yr.
(for.); Single issues: $2, $2.25 (for.).

PoNow: POETRY NOW, E. V. Griffith, ed./pub., 3118 K Street,
Eureka, CA 95501. Issues indexed: No 1984 issues re-

ceived. Subscriptions: $19/12 issues, $13/8 issues;
$7.50/4 issues; Single issues: $2.

PortR: PORTLAND REVIEW, Thomas A. Rhodes, ed., Portland
State U., Box 751, Portland, OR 97207. Issues indexed:
(30:1). Single issues: $4.

PottPort: THE POTTERSFIELD PORTFOLIO, Lesley Choyce, ed.,
Pottersfield Press, RR #2, Porters Lake, Nova Scotia B0J
2S0 Canada. Issues indexed: (6). Subscriptions: $10/3
yrs.

*PraF: PRAIRIE FIRE, Andris Taskans, ed., 374 Donald St.,
3rd Floor, Winnipeg, Manitoba R3B 2J2 Canada. Issues
indexed: (5:2/3-4). Subscriptions: $15/yr. (ind.),
$20/yr. (inst.), plus $4 (for.); Single issues: $4.

PraS: PRAIRIE SCHOONER, Hugh Luke, ed., Hilda Raz, po. ed.,
201 Andrews Hall, U. of Nebraska, Lincoln, NE 68588.
Issues indexed: (58:1-4). Subscriptions: $29/3 yrs.,
$20/2 yrs., $11/yr. (ind.); $15/yr. (lib.); Single is-
sues: $3.25.

Prima: PRIMAVERA, Ann Grearen, Rebecca Hecht-Lewis, Jeanne
Krinsley et al., eds., 1212 East 59th, Chicago, IL 60637.
Issues indexed: No 1984 issues published. Single issues:
$5.

Prismal: PRISMAL/CABRAL, Emma Buenaventura, et al., eds.,
Dept. of Spanish and Portuguese, U. of Maryland, College
Park, MD 20742. Issues indexed: (12/13). Subscriptions:
$10/yr. (ind.), $20/yr. (inst.).

Quarry: QUARRY, David Schleich, ed., Box 1061, Kingston,
Ontario K7L 4Y5 Canada. Issues indexed: (33:1-4). Sub-
scriptions: $14/yr., plus $3/yr. (for.); Single issues:
$4.

QRL: QUARTERLY REVIEW OF LITERATURE, T. & R. Weiss, 26
Haslet Ave., Princeton, NJ 08540. Issues indexed: (Poet-
ry series 6, vol. 25). Subscriptions: $15/2 volumes (pa-
per), $20/volume (cloth, inst.) ; Single issues: $10
(paper).

QW: QUARTERLY WEST, Wyn Cooper, ed.; David Rothman & Ann
Snodgrass, po. eds. 317 Olpin Union, U. of Utah, Salt
Lake City, UT 84112. Issues indexed: (18-19). Subscrip-
tions: $12/2 yrs., $6.50/yr.; Single issues: $3.50.

Rácata: JUNTE DEL TALLER RACATA, Programa de Arte y Cultura,
Colegio Comunal Eugenio María de Hostos de la Universidad
de la Ciudad de Nueva York, c/o Prisma Books, 2501 Irving
Ave., S., Minneapolis, MN 55405. Issues indexed: No 1984
issues published.

RagMag: RAG MAG, Beverly Voldseth, ed., Box 12, Goodhue, MN
55027. Issues indexed: (3:1-2). Subscriptions: $5/yr.;
Single issues: $3.

<u>Raritan</u>: RARITAN, Richard Poirier, ed., Rutgers U., 165
College Ave., New Brunswick, NJ 08903. Issues indexed:
(3:3-4, 4:1-2). Subscriptions: $12/yr., $21/2 yrs.;
Single issues: $4; Back issues: $4.50.

<u>RevChic</u>: REVISTA CHICANO-RIQUENA, Nicholas Kanellos, ed., U.
of Houston, University Park, Houston, TX 77004. Issues
indexed: No 1984 issues received. Subscriptions:
$10/yr., $15/yr. (inst.); Single issues: $5.

<u>Salm</u>: SALMAGUNDI, Robert Boyers, ed., Peggy Boyers, Exec.
ed., Skidmore College, Saratoga Springs, NY 12866. Is-
sues indexed: (62, 63/64, 65). Subscriptions: $25/2 yrs.,
$16/yr. (inst.); $15/2 yrs., $9/yr. (ind.); plus
$1.50/yr. (for.); Single issues: $5.

<u>Sam</u>: SAMISDAT, Merritt Clifton, Robin Michelle Clifton,
eds., Box 129, Richford, VT 05476. Issues indexed:
(37:2-4, 38:2-4, 39:1-4, 40:1-2, 41:1-2, releases 146-
148, 150-158, 161-162); Releases 148, 158 & 162 were
indexed from lists supplied by the editor. Subscriptions:
$150/all future issues, $25/1000 pages, $15/500 pages;
Single issues: varies.

<u>SanFPJ</u>: SAN FERNANDO POETRY JOURNAL, Richard Cloke, ed.,
18301 Halsted St., Northridge, CA 91324. Issues indexed:
(6:1-4, 7:1). Subscriptions: $10/yr., $18/2 yrs., $25/3
yrs.; Single issues: $3.

<u>SecC</u>: SECOND COMING, A. D. Winans, ed./pub., Box 31249, San
Francisco, CA 94131. Issues indexed: None, but issue
11:1/2, <u>Second Coming Anthology: Ten Years in Retrospect</u>,
c1984, was indexed in the 1983 volume with a 1983 date.
Subscriptions: $7.50/yr. (lib.), $5.50/yr. (ind.), $9.50
(for.).

<u>SenR</u>: SENECA REVIEW, Deborah Tall, ed., Hobart & William
Smith Colleges, Geneva, NY 14456. Issues indexed: (14:1-
2). Single issues: $3.50.

<u>SewanR</u>: THE SEWANEE REVIEW, George Core, ed., U. of the
South, Sewanee, TN 37375. Issues indexed: (92:1-4).
Subscriptions: $37/3 yrs., $26/2 yrs., $15/yr. (inst.);
$28/3 yrs., $20/2 yrs., $12/yr. (ind.); plus $3/yr.
(for.); Single issues: $4; Back issues: $5-10, plus
$.75/copy postage & handling.

<u>Shen</u>: SHENANDOAH, James Boatwright, ed., Richard Howard, po.
ed., Washington and Lee U., Box 722, Lexington, VA 24450.
Issues indexed: (35:1, 2/3, 4). Subscriptions: $18/3 yrs.,
$13/2 yrs., $8/yr. plus $2/volume (for.); Single issues:
$2.50; Back issues: $4.

<u>SinN</u>: SIN NOMBRE, Nilita Vientos Gaston, Dir., Box 4391, San
Juan, PR 00905-4391. Issues indexed: (14:2-3). Subscrip-
tions: $20/yr. (inst.), $15/yr. (ind.), $10/yr. (stud.,
Puerto Rico); Single issues: $4.25.

SmPd: THE SMALL POND MAGAZINE OF LITERATURE, Napoleon St.
Cyr, ed./pub., Box 664, Stratford, CT 06497. Issues
indexed: (21:1-3, issues 60-62). Subscriptions:
$5.50/yr.; Single issues: $2.50.

*SnapD: SNAPDRAGON, Gail Eckwright, Tina Foriyes, Ron McFar-
land, Co-eds., Dept. of English, U. of Idaho, Moscow, ID
83843. Issues indexed: (6:2, 7:1-2, 8:1). Subscrip-
tions: $3.50 (ind.), $4.50 (inst.).

SoCaR: SOUTH CAROLINA REVIEW, Richard J. Calhoun, Robert W.
Hill, eds., Dept. of English, Clemson U., Clemson, SC
29631. Issues indexed: (16:2, 17:1). Subscriptions: $9/2
yrs., $5/yr. (USA, Canada, Mexico); $10/2 yrs., $5.50/yr.
(elsewhere); Back issues: $3.

SoDakR: SOUTH DAKOTA REVIEW, John R. Milton, ed., Dept. of
English, U. of South Dakota, Box 111, U. Exchange, Ver-
million, SD 57069. Issues indexed: (22:1-4). Subscrip-
tions: $17/2 yrs., $10/yr. (USA, Canada); $20/2 yrs.,
$12/yr. (elsewhere); Single issues: $3.

SouthernHR: SOUTHERN HUMANITIES REVIEW, Patrick D. Morrow,
James P. Hammersmith, eds., 9088 Haley Center, Auburn U.,
Auburn, AL 36849. Issues indexed: (18:1-4). Subscrip-
tions: $8/yr.; Single issues: $2.50.

SouthernPR: SOUTHERN POETRY REVIEW, Robert Grey, ed., Eng-
lish Dept., U. of North Carolina, Charlotte, NC 28223.
Issues indexed: (24:1-2). Subscriptions: $5/yr.; Single
issues: $3.

SouthernR: SOUTHERN REVIEW, James Olney, Lewis P. Simpson,
eds., Louisiana State U., 43 Allen Hall, Baton Rouge, LA
70893. Issues indexed: (20:1-4). Subscriptions: $21/3
yrs., $16/2 yrs., $9/yr.; Single issues: $2.50.

SouthwR: SOUTHWEST REVIEW, Willard Spiegelman, ed., Southern
Methodist U., Dallas, TX 75275. Issues indexed: (69:1-
4). Subscriptions: $20/3 yrs., $14/2 yrs., $8/yr.; Single
issues: $2.50.

Sparrow: SPARROW PRESS POVERTY PAMPHLETS, Felix Stefanile,
ed./Pub., Sparrow Press, 103 Waldron St., West Lafayette,
IN 47906. Issues indexed: (46-47). Subscriptions:
$7.50/3 issues; Single issues: $2.

Spirit: THE SPIRIT THAT MOVES US, Morty Sklar, ed., P.O. Box
1585, Iowa City, IA 52244. Issues indexed: (7:1-2, 8:1).
Single issues: $9.60-$13.60.

SpiritSH: SPIRIT, David Rogers, ed., Seton Hall U., South
Orange, NJ 07079. Issues indexed: (50). Subscriptions:
$4/yr.; Single issues: $2; Back issues: $3.

SpoonRQ: THE SPOON RIVER QUARTERLY, David R. Pichaske, ed.,
P.O. Box 1443, Peoria, IL 61655. Issues indexed: (9:1-4).
Subscriptions: $10/yr.; Single issues: $3.

Stand: STAND, Jon Silkin, et al., eds., 179 Wingrove Road,
Newcastle upon Tyne NE4 9DA, England; Howard Fink, Canad-
ian ed., 4054 Melrose Ave., Montreal, Quebec H4A 2S4
Canada; Lawrence Joseph, USA ed., Apt. 8, 275 Water St.,
New York, NY 10038. Issues indexed: (25:1-4). Subscrip-
tions: $12/yr.; Single issues: $3.

*Stepp: STEPPINGSTONE, James B. Gwyne, ed., Box 1856, Harlem,
NY 10027. Issues indexed: (Sum 82, Wint 83, Wint 84,
Anniversary issue 84). Single issues: $5.

StoneC: STONE COUNTRY, Judith Neeld, ed., The Nathan Mayhew
Seminars of Martha's Vineyard, P.O. Box 132, Menemsha, MA
02552. Issues indexed: (11:3/4, 12:1/2). Subscriptions:
$14/2 yrs., $7.50/yr.; Single issues: $4.50.

Sulfur: SULFUR, Clayton Eshleman, ed., 852 South Bedford
St., Los Angeles, CA 90035. Issues indexed: (3:3, 4:1-2,
issues 9-11). Subscriptions: $22/yr. (inst.), $15/yr.
(ind.), plus $3/yr. (for.); Single issues: $6.

SunM: SUN & MOON, Douglass Messerli, Literary ed., 4330
Hartwick Rd. #418, College Park, MD 20740. Issues in-
dexed: No 1984 issues received. Single issues: $5.95.

Swallow: SWALLOW'S TALE, Joe Taylor, ed., P.O. Box 4328,
Tallahassee, FL 32315. Issues indexed: (3). Subscrip-
tions: $15/3 issues plus 2 books, $9.50/2 issues plus 1
book, $8/yr. - magazine only (inst.).

*TarRP: TAR RIVER POETRY, Peter Makuck, ed., Dept. of Eng-
lish, Austin Bldg., East Carolina U., Greenville, NC
27834. Issues indexed: (23:2, 24:1). Subscriptions:
$5/yr., $8/2 yrs.; Single issues: $2.50.

Tele: TELEPHONE, Maureen Owen, ed., 109 Dunk Rock Rd.,
Guilford, CT 06437. Issues indexed: (19) c1983. Sub-
scriptions: $7/2 issues; Single issues: $4.

Telescope: TELESCOPE, Julia Wendell, Jack Stephens, eds.,
The Galileo Press, 15201 Wheeler Lane, Sparks, MD 21152.
Issues indexed: (3:1-3). Subscriptions: $14/yr. (inst.),
$11/yr. (ind.), $17.50/yr. (for., excluding Canada);
Single issues: $4.50; Sample copies: $2; The Johns Hop-
kins U. Press, Journals Division, Baltimore, MD 21218.

Tendril: TENDRIL, George E. Murphy, Jr., ed., Box 512, Green
Harbor, MA 02041. Issues indexed: (17-18); No. 18: Poet-
ics: Essays on the Art of Poetry: An Anthology from
Tendril Magazine. Subscriptions: $25/9 issues, $17/6
issues, $10/3 issues (ind.); $12/yr. (inst.); Single
issues: $5.95-$10.95.

*TexasR: TEXAS REVIEW, Paul Ruffin, ed., Division of Eng-
lish, Foreign Language, and Journalism, Sam Houston State
U., Huntsville, TX 77341. Issues indexed: (5:1/2-3/4).
Subscriptions: $4/yr., $4.50/yr. (Canada & for.); Single
issues: $2.

ThirdW: THE THIRD WIND, Thomas Paladino, ed., P.O. Box 8277, Boston, MA 02114. Issues indexed: (2). Single issues: $3.50.

13thM: 13TH MOON. See entry at beginning of list, prior to the 'A' entries.

ThRiPo: THREE RIVERS POETRY JOURNAL, Gerald Costanzo, ed., Three Rivers Press, P.O. Box 21, Carnegie-Mellon U., Pittsburgh, PA 15213. Issues indexed: (23/24). Subscriptions: $10/4 issues; Single issues: $2.50.

Thrpny: THE THREEPENNY REVIEW, Wendy Lesser, ed./pub., P.O. Box 9131, Berkeley, CA 94709. Issues indexed: (16-19). Subscriptions: $13/2 yrs., $8/yr., $16/yr. (surface for.), $24/yr. (airmail for.); Single issues: $2.

TriQ: TRIQUARTERLY, Reginald Gibbons, ed., Northwestern U., 1735 Benson Ave., Evanston, IL 60201. Issues indexed: (59-61). Subscriptions: $100/life (ind.), $200/life (inst.), $28/2 yrs. (ind.), $40/2 yrs. (inst.), $16/yr. (ind.), $22/yr. (inst.), plus $4/yr. (for.); Single issues: usually $6.95; Sample copies: $3.

UnderRM: UNDERGROUND RAG MAG. See: RagMag: RAG MAG.

US1: US 1 WORKSHEETS, US 1 Poets Cooperative, 21 Lake Dr., Roosevelt, NJ 08555. Issues indexed: No 1984 issues received. Subscriptions: $5/4 issues; Single issues: $2.50; Back issues: Prices on request.

UTR: UT REVIEW. No longer published; replaced by ABATIS.

*Veloc: VELOCITIES, Andrew Joron, ed., 1509 Le Roy Ave., Berkeley, CA 94708. Issues indexed: (1-4). Single issues: $3.50.

VirQR: THE VIRGINIA QUARTERLY REVIEW, Staige D. Blackford, ed., Gregory Orr, po. consultant., One West Range, Charlottsville, VA 22903. Issues indexed: (60:1-4). Subscriptions: $24/3 yrs., $18/2 yrs., $10/yr., plus $.50/yr. (Canada), $1/yr. (elsewhere); Single issues: $3.

Vis: VISIONS, Bradley R. Strahan, po. ed./pub., Black Buzzard Press, 4705 South 8th Rd., Arlington, VA 22204. Issues indexed: (14-16). Subscriptions: $8/yr., $15.50/2 yrs.; Single issues: $3.

Waves: WAVES, Bernice Lever, ed., Gay Allison, po. ed., 79 Denham Drive, Richmond Hill, Ontario L4C 6H9 Canada. Issues indexed: (12:1, 2/3, 4; 13:1). Subscriptions: $8/yr. (ind.), $12/yr. (lib.); Single issues: $3; Back issues: $2.

WebR: WEBSTER REVIEW, Nancy Schapiro, ed., Pamela Hadas & Jerred Metz, po. eds., Webster U., Webster Groves, MO 63119. Issues indexed: (9:1-2). Subscriptions: $5/yr.; Single issues: $2.50.

WestB: WEST BRANCH, Karl Patten & Robert Taylor, eds., Dept. of English, Bucknell U., Lewisburg, PA 17837. Issues indexed: (14-15). Subscriptions: $8/2 yrs., $5/yr.; Single issues: $3.

WestCR: WEST COAST REVIEW, Fred Candelaria, ed., English Dept., Simon Fraser U., Burnaby, B.C. V5A 1S6 Canada. Issues indexed: (18:3-4, 19:1-2). Subscriptions: $12/yr. (Canada), $15/yr. (USA, for.), $16/yr. (inst.); Single issues: $3.50 (Canada), $4 (USA, for.).

WestHR: WESTERN HUMANITIES REVIEW, Jack Garlington, ed., U. of Utah, Salt Lake City, UT 84112. Issues indexed: (38:1-4). Subscriptions: $20/yr. (inst.), $15/yr. (ind.); Single issues: $4.

Wind: WIND, Quentin R. Howard, ed., RFD Route 1, Box 809K, Pikeville, KY 41501. Issues indexed: (14:50-52). Subscriptions: $6/3 issues (inst.), $5/3 issues (ind.), $7/3 issues (for.); Single issues: $1.50.

WindO: THE WINDLESS ORCHARD, Robert Novak, ed., English Dept., Indiana U.-Purdue U., Fort Wayne, IN 46805. Issues indexed: (44). Subscriptions: $20/3 yrs., $7/yr., $4/yr. (stud.); Single issues: $2.

*WoosterR: WOOSTER REVIEW, Katherine Harper & Warren Hedges, eds., The College of Wooster, Wooster, OH 44691. Issues indexed: (1:1-2). Subscriptions: $5/yr., $8/2 yrs.; Single issues: $2.50.

WorldO: WORLD ORDER, Firuz Kazemzadeh, Betty J. Fisher & Howard Garey, eds., National Spiritual Assembly of the Baha'is of the United States, 415 Linden Ave., Wilmette, IL 60091. Issues indexed: (18:2-4). Subscriptions: $18/2 yrs., $10/yr.; $34/2 yrs., $18/yr. (for.); Single issues: $3.

WormR: THE WORMWOOD REVIEW, Marvin Malone, ed., P.O. Box 8840, Stockton, CA 95208-0840. Issues indexed: (24:1-4, issues 93-96). Subscriptions: $20/4 issues (patrons), $7/4 issues (inst.), $6/4 issues (ind.); Back issues: $3; Single issues: $2.50.

*Writ: WRIT, Roger Greenwald, ed., Innis College, U. of Toronto, 2 Sussex Ave., Toronto, Canada M5S 1JS. Issues indexed: (16). Subscriptions: $12/2 issues (US funds outside Canada); Back issues: $5-10.

WritersL: WRITER'S LIFELINE, Stephen Gill, ed., Box 1641, Cornwall, Ontario K6H 5V6 Canada. Issues indexed: (1984, no. 1-2). Subscriptions: $18/yr; Single issues: $2.

YaleR: THE YALE REVIEW, Kai Erikson, ed., William Meredith, po. ed., 1902A Yale Station, New Haven, CT 06520. Issues indexed: (73:2-4, 74:1). Subscriptions: $22/yr. (inst.), $14/yr. (ind.), plus $3/yr. (for.); Single issues: $5; Back issues: Prices on request.

*<u>YellowS</u>: YELLOW SILK: Journal of Erotic Arts, Lily Pond, ed., P.O. Box 6374, Albany, CA 94706. Issues indexed: (10-13). Subscriptions: $10-$40/yr. (ind., sliding scale), $15/yr. (inst.), plus $4/yr. (for. surface), plus $8/yr. (for. air). Single issues: $3.

<u>YetASM</u>: YET ANOTHER SMALL MAGAZINE, Candace Catlin Hall, ed., Box 14353, Hartford, CT 06114. Issues indexed: (3). Single issues: $1.98.

ALPHABETICAL LIST OF JOURNALS INDEXED, WITH ACRONYMS

13TH MOON: <u>13thM</u>

ABATIS: <u>Abatis</u>
ABRAXAS: <u>Abraxas</u>
ACADEME: <u>Academe</u>
THE AGNI REVIEW: <u>Agni</u>
AMELIA: <u>Amelia</u>:
THE AMERICAN POETRY REVIEW: <u>*merPoR</u>
THE AMERICAN SCHOLAR: <u>AmerS</u>
ANNEX 21: <u>Annex</u>
ANTAEUS: <u>Antaeus</u>
THE ANTIGONISH REVIEW: <u>AntigR</u>
THE ANTIOCH REVIEW: <u>ANTR</u>
AREITO: <u>Areito</u>
ARGO, Incorporating DELTA: <u>Argo</u>
ARIZONA QUARTERLY: <u>ArizQ</u>
ASCENT: <u>Ascent</u>
THE ATLANTIC: <u>Atlantic</u>

BALL STATE UNIVERSITY FORMUM: <u>BallSUF</u>
THE BELOIT POETRY JOURNAL: <u>BelPoJ</u>
BERKSHIRE REVIEW: <u>BerksR</u>
BILINGUAL REVIEW: <u>BilingR</u>:
BLACK AMERICAN LITERATURE FORUM: <u>BlackALF</u>
BLACK WARRIOR REVIEW: <u>BlackWR</u>
BLUE BUFFALO: <u>BlueBuf</u>
BLUE BUILDINGS: <u>BlueBldgs</u>
BLUELINE: <u>Blueline</u>
BOGG: <u>Bogg</u>
BOUNDARY 2: <u>Bound</u>

CALIFORNIA QUARTERLY: <u>CalQ</u>
CALLALOO: <u>Callaloo</u>
CALYX: <u>Calyx</u>
CANADIAN LITERATURE: <u>CanLit</u>
THE CAPE ROCK: <u>CapeR</u>
THE CAPILANO REVIEW: <u>CapilR</u>
CAROLINA QUARTERLY: <u>CarolQ</u>
THE CEA CRITIC: <u>CEACritic</u>
THE CENTENNIAL REVIEW: <u>CentR</u>
THE CHARITON REVIEW: <u>CharR</u>
CHELSEA: <u>Chelsea</u>
CHICAGO REVIEW: <u>ChiR</u>
THE CHRISTIAN CENTURY: <u>ChrC</u>
CIMARRON RIVIEW: <u>CimR</u>
CLOCKWATCH REVIEW: <u>ClockR</u>
COLLEGE ENGLISH: <u>ColEng</u>
COMMONWEAL: <u>Comm</u>
CONCERNING POETRY: <u>ConcPo</u>
CONDITIONS: <u>Cond</u>
CONFRONTATION: <u>Confr</u>
CRAB CREEK REVIEW: <u>CrabCR</u>
CREAM CITY REVIEW: <u>CreamCR</u>
CROP DUST: <u>CropD</u>
CROSS-CANADA WRITERS' QUARTERLY: <u>CrossC</u>
CUTBANK: <u>CutB</u>

DANDELION: <u>Dandel</u>
THE DEKALB LITERARY ARTS JOURNAL: <u>DekalbLAJ</u>
DENVER QUARTERLY: <u>DenQ</u>
DESCANT: <u>Descant</u>

ENGLISH JOURNAL: <u>EngJ</u>
EPOCH: <u>Epoch</u>
EVERGREEN REVIEW: <u>EverG</u>

FIELD: <u>Field</u>
FOUR QUARTERS: <u>FourQt</u>

GARGOYLE MAGAZINE: <u>Gargoyle</u>
GEORGIA REVIEW: <u>GeoR</u>
GERMINATION: <u>Germ</u>
GRAHAM HOUSE REVIEW: <u>GrahamHR</u>
GRAIN: <u>Grain</u>
GRAND STREET: <u>GrandS</u>:
GREENFIELD REVIEW: <u>GreenfR</u>:

HANGING LOOSE: <u>HangL</u>
HARPER'S MAGAZINE: <u>Harp</u>
THE HARVARD ADVOCATE: <u>HarvardA</u>
HIRAM POETRY REVIEW: <u>HiramPoR</u>
THE HOLLINS CRITIC: <u>Hol Crit</u>
THE HUDSON REVIEW: <u>Hudson</u>
THE HUMANIST: <u>Humanist</u>

IMAGES: <u>Images</u>
INDIANA REVIEW: <u>IndR</u>
INTI, REVISTA DE LITERATURA HISPANICA: <u>Inti</u>
IOWA REVIEW: <u>Iowa</u>

JUNTE DEL TALLER RACATA: Rácata

KANSAS QUARTERLY: KanQ
KAYAK: Kayak
KENYON REVIEW: KenR:

LETRAS FEMENINAS: LetFem
LINDEN LANE MAGAZINE: LindLM:
THE LITERARY REVIEW: LitR
THE LITTLE BALKANS REVIEW: LittleBR
THE LITTLE MAGAZINE: LittleM
THE LITTLE REVIEW: LittleR

MAIRENA: Mairena
THE MALAHAT REVIEW: MalR
THE MANHATTAN REVIEW: ManhatR
THE MASSACHUSETTS REVIEW: MassR
THE MEADOWS: Meadows
MEMPHIS STATE REVIEW: MemphisSR
MESTER: Mester
METAMORFOSIS: Metam
MICHIGAN QUARTERLY REVIEW: MichQR
MID-AMERICAN REVIEW: MidAR:
THE MIDWEST QUARTERLY: MidwQ
THE MINNESOTA REVIEW: MinnR
MISSISSIPPI REVIEW: MissR
THE MISSOURI REVIEW: MissouriR
MODERN POETRY STUDIES: ModernPS
MOODY STREET IRREGULARS: MoodySI
MSS: MSS
MUNDUS ARTIUM: Mund

THE NATION: Nat
NEGATIVE CAPABILITY: NegC
NEW ENGLAND REVIEW AND BREAD LOAF QUARTERLY: NewEngR
NEW LETTERS: NewL
NEW ORLEANS REVIEW: NewOR
THE NEW RENAISSANCE: NewRena
THE NEW REPUBLIC: NewRep
NEW WORLD REVIEW: NewWR
THE NEW YORK REVIEW OF BOOKS: NewYRB
THE NEW YORKER: NewYorker
NIMROD: Nimrod
THE NORTH AMERICAN REVIEW: NoAmR
NORTH DAKOTA QUARTERLY: NoDaQ:
NORTHEAST: Northeast
NORTHWEST REVIEW: NowestR

OBSIDIAN: Obs
THE OHIO REIVEW: OhioR
ONTARIO REVIEW: OntR
OPEN 24 HOURS: Open24:
OPEN PLACES: OP
ORIGIN: Origin:
ORO MADRE: OroM
OSIRIS: Os
OUTERBRIDGE: Outbr

PAINTBRUSH: Paint
PAINTED BRIDE QUARTERLY: PaintedB
THE PARIS REVIEW: ParisR
PARTISAN REVIEW: PartR
PAUNCH: Paunch:
PEBBLE: Peb
PEQUOD: Pequod
PIG IRON: Pig
THE PIKESTAFF FORUM: PikeF
PLAYBOY: Playb
PLOUGHSHARES: Ploughs
POEM: Poem
POET AND CRITIC: PoetC
POET LORE: PoetL
POETIC JUSTICE: PoeticJ:
POETRY: Poetry
POETRY CANADA REVIEW: PoetryCR
POETRY EAST: PoetryE
POETRY NORTHWEST: PoetryNW
POETRY NOW: PoNow
PORTLAND REVIEW: PortR
THE POTTERSFIELD PORTFOLIO: PottPort
PRAIRIE FIRE: PraF:
PRAIRIE SCHOONER: PraS
PRIMAVERA: Prima
PRISMAL/CABRAL: Prismal

QUARRY: Quarry
QUARTERLY REVIEW OF LITERATURE: QRL
QUARTERLY WEST: QW

RACATA: Rácata
RAG MAG: RagMag
RARITAN: Raritan
REVISTA CHICANO-RIQUENA: RevChic

SALMAGUNDI: Salm
SAMISDAT: Sam
SAN FERNANDO POETRY JOURNAL: SanFPJ
SECOND COMING: SecC
SENECA REVIEW: SenR
THE SEWANEE REVIEW: SewanR
SHENANDOAH: Shen
SIN NOMBRE: SinN
THE SMALL POND MAGAZINE OF LITERATURE: SmPd
SNAPDRAGON: SnapD:
SOUTH CAROLINA REVIEW: SoCaR
SOUTH DAKOTA REVIEW: SoDakR
SOUTHERN HUMANITIES REVIEW: SouthernHR
SOUTHERN POETRY REVIEW: SouthernPR
SOUTHERN REVIEW: SouthernR
SOUTHWEST REVIEW: SouthwR
SPARROW: Sparrow
SPIRIT: SpiritSH
THE SPIRIT THAT MOVES US: Spirit
THE SPOON RIVER QUARTERLY: SpoonRQ
STAND: Stand
STEPPINGSTONE: Stepp
STONE COUNTRY: StoneC

SULFUR: <u>Sulfur</u>
SUN & MOON: <u>Sun M</u>
SWALLOW'S TALE: <u>Swallow</u>

TAR RIVER POETRY: <u>TarRP</u>:
TELEPHONE: <u>Tele</u>
TELESCOPE: <u>Telescope</u>
TENDRIL: <u>Tendril</u>
TEXAS REVIEW: <u>TexasR</u>:
THE THIRD WIND: <u>ThirdW</u>
13TH MOON: <u>13thM</u>
THREE RIVERS POETRY JOURNAL: <u>ThRiPo</u>
THE THREEPENNY REVIEW: <u>Thrpny</u>
TRIQUARTERLY: <u>TriQ</u>

US 1 WORKSHEETS: <u>US1</u>

VELOCITIES: <u>Veloc</u>:
VIRGINIA QUARTERLY REVIEW: <u>VirQR</u>
VISIONS: <u>Vis</u>

WAVES: <u>Waves</u>
WEBSTER REVIEW: <u>WebR</u>
WEST BRANCH: <u>WestB</u>
WEST COAST REVIEW: <u>WestCR</u>
WESTERN HUMANITIES REVIEW: <u>WestHR</u>
WIND: <u>Wind</u>
THE WINDLESS ORCHARD: <u>WindO</u>
WOOSTER REVIEW: <u>WoosterR</u>
WORLD ORDER: <u>WorldO</u>
THE WORMWOOD REVIEW: <u>WormR</u>
WRIT: <u>Writ</u>:
WRITER'S LIFELINE: <u>WritersL</u>

THE YALE REVIEW: <u>YaleR</u>
YELLOW SILK: <u>YellowS</u>:
YET ANOTHER SMALL MAGAZINE: <u>YetASM</u>

THE AUTHOR INDEX

1. AAL, Katharyn Machan
   "The Ballad of Black Rose." <u>NegC</u> (4:4) Aut 84, p. 12-
      13.
   "Ink on Paper: Kahō, 1899." <u>Amelia</u> (1:2) O 84,
      p. 6.
   "Lithia Emerald." <u>ThirdW</u> (2) Spr 84, p. 38.
   "Poem for My Grandmother." <u>NegC</u> (4:4) Aut 84, p. 14.

2. AARNES, William
   "Forecast of Snow in Minnesota." <u>SouthernR</u> (20:2)
      Spr 84, p. 334-336.
   "Need." <u>Ploughs</u> (10:1) 84, p. 13.

3. ABBOTT, Anthony
   "And must I see him, the father of lies" (tr. of Jean-
      Baptiste Chassignet). <u>WebR</u> (9:2) Wint 85, p. 13.
   "Mortal, imagine here beneath the face" (tr. of Jean-
      Baptiste Chassignet). <u>WebR</u> (9:2) Wint 85, p. 12-13.
   "So many divers torments thrive in us" (tr. of Jean-
      Baptiste Chassignet). <u>WebR</u> (9:2) Wint 85, p. 12.

4. ABBOTT, Mason
   "Girl Talk." <u>Bogg</u> (52) 84, p. 57-58.

5. ABELL, Doug
   "Annie Sadler." <u>Grain</u> (12:1) F 84, p. 20-21.

6. ABERCROMBIE, Virginia
   "Duck Hunt." <u>CrabCR</u> (1:3) Wint 84, p. 8.

7. ABERNATHY, Hugh
   "Two Unpainted Boards." <u>MidAR</u> (4:2) Aut 84, p. 56.

8. ABLON, Steven L.
   "Tornado Weather." <u>SoDakR</u> (22:3) Aut 84, p. 70-71.

9. ABRAHAMOWICZ, Marianna
   "Ballad for a Solonaut" (to the memory of Przemek
      Golba, tr. of Joanna Salamon). <u>Iowa</u> (14:2) Spr-
      Sum 84, p. 195.
   "The Creation of the World" (tr. of Eva Toth). <u>Iowa</u>
      (14:2) Spr-Sum 84, p. 210-211.

10. ABRE-VOLMAR, César
    "Tres Soles." <u>Mairena</u> (5:13) Spr 83, p. 86.

11. ABSE, Dannie
    "A Scream." <u>AmerPoR</u> (13:6) N-D 84, p. 9.
    "Somewhere." <u>Argo</u> (5:3) 84, p. 14.
    "The Vow." <u>Argo</u> (5:3) 84, p. 13.

12. ABSHER, Tom
      "Fish." Poetry (144:6) S 84, p. 331.

13. ABU SAEED
      "For My Daughter, Ruma" (in Bengali). Amelia (1:2)
         O 84, p. 48.
      "For My Daughter, Ruma" (tr. by Rabiul Hasan).
         Amelia (1:2) O 84, p. 49.

14. ABUT, José María
      "Como Todos los Dias." Mairena (6:17) Aut 84, p. 83.
      "Declaracion de Amor a la Vida." Mairena (5:14) Aut
         83, p. 82-83.

15. ACEVEDO RODRIGUEZ, Rafael A.
      "Poesialogia." Mairena (5:13) Spr 83, p. 86-87.

16. ACHUGAR, Hugo
      "Boliche." Metam (5:2/6:1) 84-85, p. 20.
      "Una Falda" (a Idea Vilariño). Metam (5:2/6:1) 84-
         85, p. 20.
      "Tambor." Metam (5:2/6:1) 84-85, p. 21.
      "Toast." Metam (5:2/6:1) 84-85, p. 21.
      "Verbo." Metam (5:2/6:1) 84-85, p. 20.

ACHUGAR FERRARI, Hugo: See ACHUGAR, Hugo

17. ACKER, Peter
      "Barren-Ground Caribou." Waves (12:2/3) Wint 84, p.
         84.

18. ACKERMAN, Diane
      "A. R. Ammons amid the Fungi." Chelsea (42/43) 84,
         p. 282-283.
      "The Archbishop of Puebla Weighs Sister Juana Inès
         de la Cruz' Passion for Study" (Mexico, 1692).
         DenQ (18:4) Wint 84, p. 74-76.
      "Climbing Out." VirQR (60:4) Aut 84, p. 616-618.
      "Lindbergh" (for Martin). VirQR (60:4) Aut 84, p.
         618-619.
      "Lines Written in a Pittsburgh Skyscraper." KenR
         (NS 6:3) Sum 84, p. 42-44.
      "Night on the Nile." KenR (NS 6:3) Sum 84, p. 41.
      "Silhouette." KenR (NS 6:3) Sum 84, p. 41-42.
      "Walking the Planck." Veloc (4) Sum 84, p. 60.

19. ACKERSON, Duane
      "The Matrix." Veloc (2) Spr 83, p. 24.
      "The Pain." Veloc (2) Spr 83, p. 26.

20. ACUFF, Gale, Jr.
      "Death Awaits Its New Clothes." CarolQ (37:1) Aut
         84, p. 38.

21. ADAM, Helen
      "Grain of Hope Rime at the End of the World."
         CreamCR (9:1/2) 84, p. 1-2.

22. ADAMS, B. B.
      "In the Waiting Room." WoosterR (1:1) Mr 84, p. 7-8.

23. ADAMS, Betsy
    "Deletions" (I-III and Epilogue). <u>Veloc</u> (4) Sum 84,
        p. 41-48.

24. ADAMS, David
    "Sunrise Service: Easter 1981." <u>HiramPoR</u> (37) Aut-
        Wint 84, p. 12.

25. ADAMS, Jeanette
    "Langston Hughes Attends the Festival" (For all Past,
        Present and Future Participants in the Langston
        Hughes Choral Speaking Festival at The City
        College of the City University of New York).
        <u>Stepping</u> Wint 84, p. 18-19.

26. ADAMSON, Arthur
    "Lines Written in Early Spring." <u>PoetryCR</u> (5:3) Spr
        84, p. 14.

27. ADAMSON, Jill
    "Guatemalan Morning" (WQ Editors' First Prize Winner:
        Poetry). <u>CrossC</u> (6:1) 84, p. 5.

28. ADAMSON, Robert
    "The Dress." <u>Stand</u> (25:3) Sum 84, p. 21.
    "The Lake." <u>Stand</u> (25:3) Sum 84, p. 20.
    "Window Frame." <u>Stand</u> (25:3) Sum 84, p. 21.

29. ADAN CASTELAR, José
    "Hospital" (tr. by Hardie St. Martin). <u>Nat</u> (238:3)
        28 Ja 84, p. 100.

30. ADDIEGO, John
    "Ash." <u>OhioR</u> (32) 84, p. 75.
    "The Blind, Falling from Trees." <u>OhioR</u> (32) 84, p. 74.
    "Dreaming at 12, 000 Feet." <u>OhioR</u> (32) 84, p. 73.
    "Eggs." <u>OhioR</u> (32) 84, p. 78.
    "The Man You Say You Love" (Chapbook of Poems, In
        memory of Vito Addiego). <u>OhioR</u> (32) 84, p. 65-78.
    "The Man You Say You Love." <u>OhioR</u> (32) 84, p. 71.
    "Natalie." <u>OhioR</u> (32) 84, p. 69.
    "Night." <u>OhioR</u> (32) 84, p. 77.
    "Night School." <u>OhioR</u> (32) 84, p. 76.
    "When the Death of Marilyn Monroe Reached Eastern
        Nevada." <u>OhioR</u> (32) 84, p. 70.
    "A Window." <u>OhioR</u> (32) 84, p. 72.

31. ADILMAN, Mona Elaine
    "Graduate Student." <u>PoetryCR</u> (6:2) Wint 84-85, p. 23.

32. ADLER, Corinne
    "Constructing an Arctic." <u>Calyx</u> (8:3) Aut-Wint 84,
        p. 22.
    "Massage." <u>Calyx</u> (8:3) Aut-Wint 84, p. 23.

ADORNO, Pedro López: <u>See</u> LOPEZ-ADORNO, Pedro

33. ADUNIS
    "I Said to You" (tr. by Ben Bennani). <u>GreenfR</u>
        (11:1/2) Sum-Aut 83, p. 216.

34. AGER, Stephen
    "Beginnings." <u>AntigR</u> (56) Wint 84, p. 9.
    "Broken Mirror." <u>AntigR</u> (56) Wint 84, p. 10.

AGHA SHAHID ALI: <u>See</u> ALI, Agha Shahid

35. AGOOS, Julie
    "In a New Climate." <u>Ploughs</u> (10:4) 84, p. 190-191.
    "Porto Venere." <u>Antaeus</u> (52) Apr 84, p. 76-78.

36. AGOSTINI, Juan Antonio
    "Palabra." <u>Mairena</u> (6:17) Aut 84, p. 74.

37. AGRICOLA, Sandra
    "On a Wide Bed." <u>OhioR</u> (33) 84, p. 52.
    "State of Grace." <u>OhioR</u> (33) 84, p. 53.

38. AGTE, Bruce
    "Flowers." <u>OhioR</u> (33) 84, p. 7.
    "Riverside." <u>OhioR</u> (33) 84, p. 8.
    "Sunlight." <u>OhioR</u> (33) 84, p. 6.

39. AGUERO, Kathleen
    "Body Surfing." <u>HangL</u> (45) Spr 84, p. 3.
    "Charm Bracelet." <u>HangL</u> (45) Spr 84, p. 4-5.
    "Legacy of Hands." <u>WestB</u> (14) 84, p. 82-83.

40. AGUILAR, Pancho
    "Dreadlocks." <u>OroM</u> (2:3/4, issue 7/8) 84, p. 36-37.

41. AGUIRRE, Raul Gustavo
    "Antes y Ahora." <u>Mairena</u> (6:18) 84, p. 111.

42. AHARONI, Ada
    "Anna Frank and I" (three versions, tr. of Amnon
        Shamosh). <u>Descant</u> (47, 15:4) Wint 84, p. 202-204.

43. AHRENS, Robert
    "Our Fair City." <u>SanFPJ</u> (6:2) 84, p. 38-39.

44. AI, Qing
    "Burning the Wasteland Grass" (tr. by George Venn and
        Lu Pei Wu). <u>NowestR</u> (22:3) 84, p. 104.
    "Fish Fossil" (tr. by George Venn and Lu Pei Wu).
        <u>NowestR</u> (22:3) 84, p. 101.
    "Hail" (tr. by George Venn and Lu Pei Wu). <u>NowestR</u>
        (22:3) 84, p. 102.
    "Like an orphan" (tr. by Marilyn Chin). <u>Iowa</u> (14:2)
        Spr-Sum 84, p. 7.
    "Persian Chrysanthemums" (tr. by George Venn and Lu
        Pei Wu). <u>NowestR</u> (22:3) 84, p. 103.
    "Snowy Morning" (tr. by Marilyn Chin). <u>Iowa</u> (14:2)
        Spr-Sum 84, p. 41.

45. AICHINGER, Ilse
    "A Lack of Maids" (tr. by Stuart Friebert). <u>Field</u>
        (31) Aut 84, p. 55.
    "New Alliance" (tr. by Allen H. Chappel). <u>Field</u>
        (30) Spr 84, p. 73.
    "Part of the Question" (tr. by Allen H. Chappel).

<u>Field</u> (30) Spr 84, p. 73-74.
"Plea" (tr. by Stuart Friebert). <u>Field</u> (31) Aut 84,
    p. 53.
"Reading" (tr. by Stuart Friebert). <u>Field</u> (31) Aut
    84, p. 54.
"Temporal Advice." <u>NowestR</u> (22:3) 84, p. 129.
"To My Grandmother" (tr. by Allen H. Chappel).
    <u>Field</u> (30) Spr 84, p. 71-72.

46. AISENBERG, Nadya
    "The Lark Ascending." <u>ThirdW</u> (2) Spr 84, p. 36.
    "Now the Merest Suspicion." <u>LitR</u> (28:1) Aut 84, p.
        128.

47. AJAY, Stephen
    "After Ten Years." <u>YellowS</u> (12) Aut 84, p. 9.
    "Identification." <u>Ploughs</u> (10:1) 84, p. 14.
    "Space." <u>YellowS</u> (12) Aut 84, p. 9.
    "The Twins." <u>Ploughs</u> (10:1) 84, p. 15.
    "Without Compromise." <u>HolCrit</u> (21:2) Ap 84, p. 12.

48. AKEL, Abdul-Latif
    "Self-Portrait" (tr. by the author). <u>Iowa</u> (14:2)
        Spr-Sum 84, p. 118.

49. AKHMADULINA, Bella
    "How do I differ from a woman with a flower" (tr. by
        Mary Maddock). <u>AmerPoR</u> (13:4) Jl-Ag 84, p. 12.
    "Lunatics" (tr. by Mary Maddock). <u>AmerPoR</u> (13:4) Jl-
        Ag 84, p. 12.
    "Muteness" (tr. by Mary Maddock). <u>AmerPoR</u> (13:4) Jl-
        Ag 84, p. 12.

50. AKHMATOVA, Anna
    "After Poems (1913, 1916, 1911, 1959)" (tr. by
        Stephen Berg). <u>Chelsea</u> (42/43) 84, p. 268.
    "Almost in the Album" (from <u>Moscow Triptych</u>, tr. by
        Marianne Andrea). <u>SenR</u> (14:1) 84, p. 55.
    "Creativity" (from <u>Mysteries of Craft</u>, tr. by
        Marianne Andrea). <u>SenR</u> (14:1) 84, p. 54.
    "Dante" (tr. by Marianne Andrea). <u>SenR</u> (14:1) 84,
        p. 53.
    "Dream" (August 14, 1956, tr. by Marianne Andrea).
        <u>Nimrod</u> (28:1) Aut-Wint 84, p. 36.
    "Echo" (tr. by Marianne Andrea). <u>SenR</u> (14:1) 84, p.
        55.
    "I hear the always-sad voice of the oriole" (tr. by
        Jane Kenyon w. Vera Sandomirsky Dunham). <u>OhioR</u>
        (33) 84, p. 30.
    "In Books" (November 25th, 1943, Tashkent, tr. by
        Marianne Andrea). <u>Nimrod</u> (28:1) Aut-Wint 84, p. 35.
    "More about That Summer" (Autumn 1962, tr. by
        Marianne Andrea). <u>Nimrod</u> (28:1) Aut-Wint 84, p. 36.
    "The Muse" (tr. by Marianne Andrea). <u>SenR</u> (14:1)
        84, p. 52.
    "The mysterious spring still lay under a spell" (tr.
        by Jane Kenyon w. Vera Sandomirsky Dunham).
        <u>OhioR</u> (33) 84, p. 30.
    "To Alexander Blok" (tr. by Marianne Andrea).
        <u>Nimrod</u> (28:1) Aut-Wint 84, p. 34.

"While Reading Hamlet" (tr. by Lyn Coffin). <u>NewYRB</u>
(30:21/22) 19 Ja 84, p. 23.
"Yes I loved them, those gatherings late at night"
(tr. by Jane Kenyon w. Vera Sandomirsky Dunham).
<u>OhioR</u> (33) 84, p. 31.

51. AKIMOCHI
"The dread imperial command" (tanka No. 764). <u>NewL</u>
(50:2/3) Wint-Spr 84, p. 230.

52. AKTAN, Feriha
"The Letter" (tr. by Talat Sait Halman). <u>NewRena</u>
(6:1, #18) Spr 84, p. 59.
"Mektup." <u>NewRena</u> (6:1, #18) Spr 84, p. 58.

53. AL-KHANSA
"On the Death of Her Brother" (tr. by Barbara
Feyerabend). <u>SenR</u> (14:1) 84, p. 36.

54. AL-MA'ARRI
"Epigram" (tr. by Andrew Harvey). <u>SenR</u> (14:1) 84,
p. 29.
"If You Have O Soul" (tr. by Andrew Harvey). <u>SenR</u>
(14:1) 84, p. 30.
"Some Thoughts on Dying" (tr. by Barbara Feyerabend).
<u>SenR</u> (14:1) 84, p. 31-33.

55. AL-MAGUT, Mohamed
"Autumn of the Masks" (tr. by Saheb Meshtet and Beth
Tornes). <u>SenR</u> (14:1) 84, p. 41-42.
"Fear" (tr. by Saheb Meshtet and Beth Tornes). <u>SenR</u>
(14:1) 84, p. 39-40.
"In the Night" (tr. by Saheb Meshtet and Beth
Tornes). <u>SenR</u> (14:1) 84, p. 37-38.

56. ALBAN, Laureano
"Solar Creed" (tr. by Frederick H. Fornoff). <u>Vis</u>
(15) 84, p. 14.

57. ALBERTI, Rafael
"Aligi Sassu, Painter" (tr. by Linda Scheer). <u>QRL</u>
(Poetry series 6, v. 25) 84, p. 66.
"Arthrocious (I)" (Sonnet IV, tr. by Linda Scheer).
<u>QRL</u> (Poetry series 6, v. 25) 84, p. 56.
"Arthrocious (II)" (Sonnet V, tr. by Linda Scheer).
<u>QRL</u> (Poetry series 6, v. 25) 84, p. 56-57.
"Autumn in Rome" (tr. by Linda Scheer). <u>QRL</u> (Poetry
series 6, v. 25) 84, p. 33.
"Boredom" (Scenic poem, tr. by Linda Scheer). <u>QRL</u>
(Poetry series 6, v. 25) 84, p. 36-37.
"The Bridge of Breasts" (Remembered from Rome, tr. by
Brian Swann). <u>QRL</u> (Poetry series 6, v. 25) 84,
p. 48.
"Bruno Caruso, Etcher" (tr. by Linda Scheer). <u>QRL</u>
(Poetry series 6, v. 25) 84, p. 65-66.
"Campo de'Fiori" (Sonnet IV, tr. by Linda Scheer).
<u>QRL</u> (Poetry series 6, v. 25) 84, p. 13.
"Carlo Quattrucci Paints the Botanic Gardens" (tr. by
Linda Scheer). <u>QRL</u> (Poetry series 6, v. 25) 84,
p. 68-69.

"Castigos." TriQ (59) Wint 84, p. 196.
"Cats, Cats, and Cats" (Sonnet II, tr. by Brian
  Swann). QRL (Poetry series 6, v. 25) 84, p. 54-55.
"Comet" (tr. by Brian Swann). QRL (Poetry series 6,
  v. 25) 84, p. 34.
"Corrado Cagli, Painter" (tr. by Linda Scheer). QRL
  (Poetry series 6, v. 25) 84, p. 71-72.
"Danger" (tr. by Brian Swann). QRL (Poetry series
  6, v. 25) 84, p. 44.
"Even the Monks Deal in Contraband" (tr. by Brian
  Swann). QRL (Poetry series 6, v. 25) 84, p. 43.
"Finally" (Sonnet VIII, tr. by Linda Sheer). QRL
  (Poetry series 6, v. 25) 84, p. 16.
"Free Verses, Scenes and Songs" (tr. by Linda
  Scheer). QRL (Poetry series 6, v. 25) 84, p. 18.
"Giuseppe Mazzullo, Sculptor" (tr. by Linda Scheer).
  QRL (Poetry series 6, v. 25) 84, p. 70.
"Guido Strazza, Painter" (In Search of Atlantis, tr.
  by Linda Scheer). QRL (Poetry series 6, v. 25)
  84, p. 67.
"Hoy las nubes me trajeron." TriQ (59) Wint 84, p.
  199.
"I Enter Your Churches, Lord" (Sonnet III, tr. by
  Linda Scheer). QRL (Poetry series 6, v. 25) 84,
  p. 55.
"In Rome You Hear" (Sonnet X, tr. by Brian Swann).
  QRL (Poetry series 6, v. 25) 84, p. 60-61.
"Infernal Congratulations" (tr. by Brian Swann).
  QRL (Poetry series 6, v. 25) 84, p. 30.
"Instead of worshippers" (tr. by Brian Swann). QRL
  (Poetry series 6, v. 25) 84, p. 50.
"Intermediate Nocturne 2: Today dark things pass by"
  (Sonnet VII, tr. by Brian Swann). QRL (Poetry
  series 6, v. 25) 84, p. 58-59.
"Invitation in August" (To Vittorio Bodini, tr. by
  Brian Swann). QRL (Poetry series 6, v. 25) 84,
  p. 25.
"Is It a Crime?" (tr. by Linda Scheer). QRL (Poetry
  series 6, v. 25) 84, p. 32.
"It Would Be So Lovely" (tr. by Linda Scheer). QRL
  (Poetry series 6, v. 25) 84, p. 46.
"Lizard" (tr. by Brian Swann). QRL (Poetry series
  6, v. 25) 84, p. 39.
"Love" (tr. by Linda Scheer). QRL (Poetry series 6,
  v. 25) 84, p. 25.
"El mar. La mar." TriQ (59) Wint 84, p. 192.
"Il Mascherone" (tr. by Linda Scheer). QRL (Poetry
  series 6, v. 25) 84, p. 19.
"Me veréis un cometa enloquecido." TriQ (59) Wint
  84, p. 200.
"Monserrato, 20" (tr. by Brian Swann). QRL (Poetry
  series 6, v. 25) 84, p. 9-10.
"Nocturne 1: For a long time I hear your whiskers
  rain" (Sonnet VI, tr. by Brian Swann). QRL
  (Poetry series 6, v. 25) 84, p. 58.
"Nocturne 2: I speak to you today from Rome" (Sonnet
  VIII, tr. by Brian Swann). QRL (Poetry series 6,
  v. 25) 84, p. 59.
"Nocturne: Nights of pain" (tr. by Brian Swann).
  QRL (Poetry series 6, v. 25) 84, p. 30.

"Nocturne: Rome is empty, suddenly" (tr. by Linda
  Scheer). QRL (Poetry series 6, v. 25) 84, p. 44.
"Nocturne: Suddenly, there's no one in Rome" (tr. by
  Brian Swann). QRL (Poetry series 6, v. 25) 84,
  p. 35.
"Nocturne: Take hold of the key to Rome" (tr. by
  Brian Swann). QRL (Poetry series 6, v. 25) 84,
  p. 47.
"Nocturne: The other night I saw" (tr. by Linda
  Scheer). QRL (Poetry series 6, v. 25) 84, p. 24.
"Now Only" (Sonnet I, tr. by Linda Scheer). QRL
  (Poetry series 6, v. 25) 84, p. 54.
"A nymph on the patio of my house" (tr. by Brian
  Swann). QRL (Poetry series 6, v. 25) 84, p. 23.
"Una Pasionaria para Dolores." TriQ (59) Wint 84,
  p. 198.
"Pasquinade" (Sonnet IX, tr. by Linda Scheer). QRL
  (Poetry series 6, v. 25) 84, p. 16-17.
"A Passionflower for Dolores" (tr. by Gabriel Berns).
  TriQ (59) Wint 84, p. 198.
"Poems with Names" (Written in Rome, tr. by Linda
  Scheer). QRL (Poetry series 6, v. 25) 84, p. 64-75.
"The Poet Begs in the Streets" (tr. by Linda Scheer).
  QRL (Poetry series 6, v. 25) 84, p. 62-63.
"Poetic Life" (Sonnet V, tr. by Linda Scheer). QRL
  (Poetry series 6, v. 25) 84, p. 14.
"Prediction" (tr. by Linda Scheer). QRL (Poetry
  series 6, v. 25) 84, p. 39.
"Punishments" (tr. by Gabriel Berns). TriQ (59)
  Wint 84, p. 197.
"La Puttana Andaluza" (Scenic poem, tr. by Linda
  Scheer). QRL (Poetry series 6, v. 25) 84, p. 21-22.
"Roman gatomaquia" (tr. by Brian Swann). QRL
  (Poetry series 6, v. 25) 84, p. 40.
"Roman Religious Art" (Question and plea of J.B.,
  Sonnet VI, tr. by Linda Scheer). QRL (Poetry
  series 6, v. 25) 84, p. 14-15.
"Rome: Danger to Pedestrians" (tr. by Brian Swann and
  Linda Scheer). QRL (Poetry series 6, v. 25) 84,
  p. 1-75.
"Rome, Danger to Pedestrians" (Sonnet II, tr. by
  Brian Swann). QRL (Poetry series 6, v. 25) 84,
  p. 12.
"The sea. My sea" (tr. by Gabriel Berns). TriQ (59)
  Wint 84, p. 192.
"The Seine's chestnut trees" (tr. by Brian Swann).
  QRL (Poetry series 6, v. 25) 84, p. 38.
"Sets of Threes" (tr. by Brian Swann). QRL (Poetry
  series 6, v. 25) 84, p. 20.
"Si Proibisce di Buttare Immondezze" (Sonnet VII, tr.
  by Brian Swann). QRL (Poetry series 6, v. 25)
  84, p. 15.
"Silent Dialogue with a Neighbor" (Scenic poem, tr.
  by Linda Scheer). QRL (Poetry series 6, v. 25)
  84, p. 26-27.
"The Son" (Scenic poem, tr. by Linda Scheer). QRL
  (Poetry series 6, v. 25) 84, p. 31-32.
"St. Peter's Basilica" (to José Miguel Velloso, tr.
  by Linda Scheer). QRL (Poetry series 6, v. 25)
  84, p. 29.

"Still on the subject of piss" (tr. by Linda
    Scheer). QRL (Poetry series 6, v. 25) 84, p. 28-29.
"Strophe for a Monument to the Heroes of the
    Resistance" (for Federico Brook, sculptor, tr. by
    Linda Scheer). QRL (Poetry series 6, v. 25) 84,
    p. 49.
"Summer" (tr. by Gabriel Berns). TriQ (59) Wint 84,
    p. 194-195.
"Take Pity, Lord!" (tr. by Linda Scheer). QRL
    (Poetry series 6, v. 25) 84, p. 34.
"Ten Sonnets" (To Giuseppe Gioachino Belli, homage
    from a Spanish poet in Rome, tr. by Brian Swann
    and Linda Scheer). QRL (Poetry series 6, v. 25)
    84, p. 11-17.
"Three Roman Nocturnes with Don Ramón del Valle-
    Inclán" (tr. by Brian Swann). QRL (Poetry
    series 6, v. 25) 84, p. 58-59.
"Time's Answer" (Sonnet IX, To Bertolt Brecht, tr. by
    Brian Swann). QRL (Poetry series 6, v. 25) 84,
    p. 60.
"To Marco, Dog of Santa Maria in Trastevere" (tr. by
    Brian Swann). QRL (Poetry series 6, v. 25) 84,
    p. 51.
"Today the clouds brought to me" (tr. by Gabriel
    Berns). TriQ (59) Wint 84, p. 199.
"The Two Friends" (Scenic poem, tr. by Linda Scheer).
    QRL (Poetry series 6, v. 25) 84, p. 42-43.
"Ugo Attardi, Painter" (Spain today, tr. by Linda
    Scheer). QRL (Poetry series 6, v. 25) 84, p. 64-65.
"Umberto Mastroianni, Sculptor" (tr. by Linda
    Scheer). QRL (Poetry series 6, v. 25) 84, p. 73-75.
"Urinating Prohibited" (Sonnet III, tr. by Brian
    Swann). QRL (Poetry series 6, v. 25) 84, p. 12-13.
"Verano." TriQ (59) Wint 84, p. 194.
"Vietnam" (Sonnet XI, tr. by Brian Swann). QRL
    (Poetry series 6, v. 25) 84, p. 61.
"Water of innumerable fountains" (tr. by Brian
    Swann). QRL (Poetry series 6, v. 25) 84, p. 45.
"What I've Given Up for You" (Sonnet I, tr. by Brian
    Swann). QRL (Poetry series 6, v. 25) 84, p. 11.
"What to Do?" (Sonnet X, tr. by Linda Scheer). QRL
    (Poetry series 6, v. 25) 84, p. 17.
"When I Leave Rome" (for Ignazio Delogu, tr. by Linda
    Scheer). QRL (Poetry series 6, v. 25) 84, p. 53.
"When Rome Is" (tr. by Linda Scheer). QRL (Poetry
    series 6, v. 25) 84, p. 41.
"While I Sleep" (tr. by Linda Scheer). QRL (Poetry
    series 6, v. 25) 84, p. 37.
"You Haven't Come to Rome to Dream" (tr. by Linda
    Scheer). QRL (Poetry series 6, v. 25) 84, p. 52.
"You may think me a comet gone mad" (tr. by Gabriel
    Berns). TriQ (59) Wint 84, p. 200-201.

58. ALBERTUS, Alexander
    "Upon an Eunuch: A Poet" (After Marvell's Latin).
        Ploughs (10:1) 84, p. 16.

59. ALBIACH, Anne-Marie
    "Enigma VI-VIII." CreamCR (9:1/2) 84, p. 100-102.

60. ALCOSSER, Sandra
    "The Disposition of Hands." NoAmR (269:3) S 84, p.
        36-37.
    "In the Country." NoAmR (269:2) Je 84, p. 13.
    "The Journey." NoAmR (269:3) S 84, p. 33-34.
    "Learning the Gleaner's Song." Poetry (144:1) Ap
        84, p. 13-15.
    "On the Veranda We Drink Gin-and-Tonic." NewYorker
        (60:33) 1 O 84, p. 42.
    "The Photographer Discovers America." NoAmR (269:3)
        S 84, p. 38.

61. ALDAN, Daisy
    "Afterthoughts" (tr. of Malcolm de Chazal). Chelsea
        (42/43) 84, p. 118.
    "Again This Stone." AmerPoR (13:2) Mr-Ap 84, p. 5.

62. ALDRIDGE, Richard
    "Driving North." StoneC (11:3/4) Spr-Sum 84, p. 10.

63. ALEGRE, Carlos
    "El Licor de Tu Cuerpo." Mairena (6:18) 84, p. 96.

64. ALEGRE CUDOS, J. L.
    "La Mano del Frac." LindLM (3:1) Ja-Mr 84, p. 17.

65. ALEGRIA, Claribel
    "Esteli" (tr. by Electra Arenal and Marsha Gabriela
        Dreyer). MinnR (N.S. 22) Spr 84, p. 77-78.
    "I Am Mirror" (tr. by Electa Arenal and Marsha
        Gabriela Dreyer). Confr (27/28) 84, p. 42.

66. ALESHIRE, Joan
    "Migrating Hawks." Tendril (17) Wint 84, p. 15.
    "Perpetual Motion." Poetry (145:3) D 84, p. 151.
    "Persephone." Poetry (145:3) D 84, p. 152.
    "Where Beauty Was Forbidden." AmerPoR (13:6) N-D
        84, p. 37.

67. ALEXANDER, Bonnie L.
    "Hollow." KanQ (16:1/2) Wint-Spr 84, p. 109.

68. ALEXANDER, Francis W.
    "Ignorance Is Unbounded." SanFPJ (6:3) 84, p. 9.
    "Passing the Blame upon the Computer's 'Knowledge'."
        SanFPJ (6:3) 84, p. 12.

69. ALEXANDER, Meena
    "Kabir Was a Weaver." GreenfR (11:3/4) Wint-Spr 84,
        p. 136.

70. ALEXANDER, Will
    "Apocalyptic Sundown Shadows" (To René Guénon).
        Veloc (3) Aut-Wint 83, p. 48-49.

71. ALEXIS, Austin
    "Window-Tree." KanQ (16:1/2) Wint-Spr 84, p. 214.

72. ALEXOPOULOS, Marion
    "John." LittleM (14:3) 84, p. 57-58.

"A Meeting with a Lavatory Cleaner." <u>LittleM</u> (14:3)
     84, p. 55.
"Road Death of a Turtle." <u>LittleM</u> (14:3) 84, p. 56.

73. ALFARO, Rafael
     "En Propio Territorio." <u>Mairena</u> (5:13) Spr 83, p. 58.

74. ALFONSO, Carlos L.
     "La Noche." <u>LindLM</u> (3:1) Ja-Mr 84, p. 30.

75. ALI, Agha Shahid
     "A Dream of Drowning." <u>WebR</u> (9:2) Wint 85, p. 76.
     "The Poverty of Greens." <u>WebR</u> (9:2) Wint 85, p. 75.
     "The Season of the Plains." <u>Agni</u> (21) 84, p. 30-31.

76. ALKALAY-GUT, Karen
     "His Neck." <u>WebR</u> (9:2) Wint 85, p. 93.
     "Night Rider." <u>WebR</u> (9:2) Wint 85, p. 93.

77. ALLBERY, Deb
     "Dormant." <u>WoosterR</u> (1:1) Mr 84, p. 92-93.
     "Extended Family." <u>WoosterR</u> (1:1) Mr 84, p. 94.

78. ALLBERY, Debra
     "Carnies." <u>Ploughs</u> (10:4) 84, p. 194.

79. ALLEN, Blair H.
     "After the Fire Comes the Ice, or, Where the
       Dinosaurs Have Gone." <u>SanFPJ</u> (6:2) 84, p. 9-11.
     "The Day After 'The Day After'." <u>SanFPJ</u> (6:2) 84,
       p. 82-84.
     "The Greenhouse Blues." <u>SanFPJ</u> (6:1) 84, p. 58-60.

80. ALLEN, Carlton C.
     "To Russia--Who Are You." <u>Bogg</u> (52) 84, p. 40.

81. ALLEN, Deborah
     "Fishing for Bass." <u>SoDakR</u> (22:4) Wint 84, p. 85.
     "Gas Station." <u>SoDakR</u> (22:4) Wint 84, p. 90.

82. ALLEN, Deborah L.
     "To Mama Lizzie." <u>PaintedB</u> (21) Wint 84, p. 20.

83. ALLEN, Dick
     "Autobiography Concluding in Seance." <u>AmerPoR</u>
       (13:4) Jl-Ag 84, p. 28.
     "The Clergyman's Wife Composes a Spring Letter."
       <u>Agni</u> (21) 84, p. 19-20.
     "The Poet at Eighteen." <u>Poetry</u> (145:3) D 84, p. 147-
       148.
     "William Rimmer: 'Flight and Pursuit'." <u>Agni</u> (21)
       84, p. 21.

84. ALLEN, Gilbert
     "The Sitter." <u>Amelia</u> (1:2) O 84, p. 54.
     "Snow in Carolina." <u>Wind</u> (14:50) 84, p. 1.

85. ALLEN, Heather
     "The Cartographers." <u>GeoR</u> (38:3) Aut 84, p. 562-563.

86. ALLEN, John
   "Late Leaves of Autumn" (tr. of Irma Klainguti, w.
      Elly Crol). Os (18) 84, p. 13.
   "Survilsan Village" (tr. of Silvio Camenisch, w. Elly
      Crol). Os (18) 84, p. 15.
   "Who Knows" (tr. of Irma Klainguti, w. Elly Crol).
      Os (18) 84, p. 13.

87. ALLEN, Kimalida
   "Inspired by Two Kings and a Queen." BlackALF
      (18:1) Spr 84, p. 36.

88. ALLEN, Michael
   "Fantasy." ColEng (46:2) F 84, p. 127.
   "From 'Remembered Dances for My Brother'." StoneC
      (12:1/2) Aut-Wint 84, p. 20.
   "I am always beginning." Bogg (52) 84, p. 18.
   "The Land Where Rooflines Parallel the Ground."
      IndR (7:3) Sum 84, p. 62-63.

89. ALLEN, Paula Gunn
   "Anatomy Lesson" (for Audre Lorde). GreenfR
      (11:3/4) Wint-Spr 84, p. 38.
   "Dear World." Calyx (8:2) Spr 84, p. 73.
   "Iroquois Sunday, New York, 1982." GreenfR (11:3/4)
      Wint-Spr 84, p. 37-38.
   "Weed." Calyx (8:2) Spr 84, p. 74.

90. ALLEN, Samuel
   "The Apple Trees in Sussex." Callaloo (21, 7:2) Spr-
      Sum 84, p. 18.

91. ALLEN, W. S.
   "Rainbowman." Veloc (2) Spr 83, p. 42.
   "Das Wernher von Braun Lied." WindO (44) Sum-Aut
      84, p. 38.

92. ALLMAN, John
   "The Birth of Time." Agni (21) 84, p. 120.
   "Bullfight." MassR (25:3) Aut 84, p. 475.
   "Camels Led by an Angel." MassR (25:3) Aut 84, p. 474.
   "Croton Dam." Poetry (145:1) O 84, p. 14-15.
   "Darius and the Herdsmen." MassR (25:3) Aut 84, p.
      476.
   "Physics." Agni (21) 84, p. 111-119.
   "The Rising." MemphisSR (4:2) Spr 84, p. 4.
   "Ruffled Grouse in the Forest." MassR (25:3) Aut
      84, p. 473.
   "The Token." Poetry (145:1) O 84, p. 14.
   "William Morris Boating up the Thames to Kelmscott
      Manor 1880." MemphisSR (4:2) Spr 84, p. 12-15.

93. ALMON, Bert
   "Calling Texas." MalR (69) O 84, p. 85.
   "A Lecture in Economics." Quarry (33:3) Sum 84, p. 58.
   "A Sense of Decency." Quarry (33:3) Sum 84, p. 58.
   "Water Music and the Seven Gram Soul." Dandel
      (11:2) Aut-Wint 84-85, p. 70.

94. ALONSO, Dámaso
"A Pizca." MidAR (4:1) Spr 84, p. 92, 94.
"El Alma Era lo Mismo Que una Ranita Verde." MidAR
   (4:1) Spr 84, p. 96, 98.
"En la Sombra." MidAR (4:1) Spr 84, p. 82.
"Hombre." MidAR (4:1) Spr 84, p. 80.
"In the Shadow" (tr. by Robert Early, George Looney
   and Mairi Meredith). MidAR (4:1) Spr 84, p. 83.
"The Life of Man" (tr. by Robert Early, George Looney
   and Mairi Meredith). MidAR (4:1) Spr 84, p. 85, 87.
"Man" (tr. by Robert Early, George Looney and Mairi
   Meredith). MidAR (4:1) Spr 84, p. 81.
"A Man in the Company of Himself" (from Hijos de la
   Ira, tr. by Robert Early, George Looney and Mairi
   Meredith. Translation Chapbook Series, Number
   One). MidAR (4:1) Spr 84, p. 79-102.
"Monsters" (tr. by Robert Early, George Looney and
   Mairi Meredith). MidAR (4:1) Spr 84, p. 89, 91.
"Monstruos." MidAR (4:1) Spr 84, p. 88, 90.
"Myself" (tr. by Robert Early, George Looney and
   Mairi Meredith). MidAR (4:1) Spr 84, p. 101.
"The Soul Is a Little Green Frog" (tr. by Robert
   Early, George Looney and Mairi Meredith). MidAR
   (4:1) Spr 84, p. 97, 99.
"To the Mite" (tr. by Robert Early, George Looney and
   Mairi Meredith). MidAR (4:1) Spr 84, p. 93, 95.
"Vida del Hombre." MidAR (4:1) Spr 84, p. 84, 86.
"Yo." MidAR (4:1) Spr 84, p. 100.

95. ALONSO, Ricardo
"Amanecer en el Escambray." Areíto (9:36) 84, p.
   102.
"Canto Popular." Areíto (9:36) 84, p. 102.

96. ALONSO, Rodolfo
"Deja Vu" (Nueva versión). Mairena (6:18) 84, p.
   116.

97. ALTIZER, Nell
"The Widow's Suite." 13thM (8:1/2) 84, p. 61-63.

98. ALTMANN, Ruth
"Pearl Harbor Day." Tele (19) 83, p. 91.
"Scene." Tele (19) 83, p. 90.

99. ALVAREZ, Ernesto
"Artesana de Sueños" (fragmento). Mairena (6:17)
   Aut 84, p. 73.
"Canto a Cesar Vallejo." Mairena (6:16) Spr 84, p.
   47-60.
"Canto a Cesar Vallejo" (Selections: 2. "Tu Palabra,"
   11. "Destino"). Mairena (5:14) Aut 83, p. 74-75.

100. ALVAREZ, Julia
"Orchids." 13thM (8:1/2) 84, p. 122-125.

101. ALVAREZ CALLE, Manuel
"Los cien adolescentes." Mairena (5:13) Spr 83, p.
   66.
"Tu piel está hecha." Mairena (6:17) Aut 84, p. 81.

102. ALVARO, Alexander
     "The Execution of an Anarchist." PoetryCR (6:2)
        Wint 84-85, p. 27.

103. AMABILE, George
     "The Artist As Historian" (for George Morrissette).
        CanLit (101) Sum 84, p. 56-57.
     "Blithe Spirits." PoetryCR (6:2) Wint 84-85, p. 10.
     "Cat Nap in Two Movements." Dandel (11:2) Aut-Wint
        84-85, p. 62.
     "Evening Out" (for Charli). PoetryCR (6:1) Aut 84,
        p. 3.
     "Misericordia General" (For Robert Emmet Finnegan).
        CanLit (100) Spr 84, p. 11-18.

104. AMADOR, Victoria
     "Night Fantasies." BallSUF (24:3) Sum 83, p. 74.

105. AMALI, Emmanuel
     "Our Neighbours." Stepping (Anniversary Issue I)
        84, p. 12.

106. AMATO, Joseph
     "Buddha in the Limelight." SpoonRQ (9:2) Spr 84,
        p. 42.
     "Our Zen Masters." SpoonRQ (9:2) Spr 84, p. 43.

107. AMEEN, Amy Braverman
     "A Week on the Drawhorse." Blueline (6:1) Sum-Aut
        84, p. 35.

108. AMES, Bernice
     "Hold the Candle, Please." CapeR (19:3) 20th
        Anniverary Issue 84, p. 1.

109. AMICHAI, Yehuda
     "A Modern Girl" (tr. by Edna Amir Coffin). Pequod
        (16/17) 84, p. 124.
     "The Rustle of History's Wings As They Said Then."
        NewRep (189:19) 7 N 83, p. 36.

110. AMMONS, A. R.
     "Burn Out in the Overshoot." Epoch (33:3) Sum-Aut
        84, p. 284.
     "Certainty." NewL (50:2/3) Wint-Spr 84, p. 163.
     "Downing Lines." Raritan (4:1) Sum 84, p. 26.
     "The Gathering." Epoch (33:3) Sum-Aut 84, p. 285-287.
     "Nelly Myers." Peb (23) 84, p. 83-87.
     "Pots and Pans." Raritan (4:1) Sum 84, p. 23-24.
     "Recoveries." Raritan (4:1) Sum 84, p. 25.
     "Sight Seed." Raritan (4:1) Sum 84, p. 22.
     "Spring Tornado." NewL (50:2/3) Wint-Spr 84, p. 163.
     "Two Motions." Chelsea (42/43) 84, p. 124-125.
     "The Yucca Moth." Shen (35:2/3) 84, p. 19.

111. AMPRIMOZ, Alexandre
     "Impression of a Moment." Quarry (33:1) Wint 84,
        p. 41.
     "A Matter of Trust." Quarry (33:1) Wint 84, p. 41-42.
     "Stars." Quarry (33:1) Wint 84, p. 41.

112. AMPRIMOZ, Alexandre L.
     "Algiers." PoetryCR (6:2) Wint 84-85, p. 7.
     "At the Old Dancing School." Descant (47, 15:4)
          Wint 84, p. 56-57.
     "Blurred Impression." PoetryCR (5:4) Sum 84, p. 5.
     "Lesson in Indifference." PoetryCR (6:2) Wint 84-
          85, p. 7.
     "A Liberal at Large" (Overheard on the Riviera).
          PraF (5:2/3) Spr 84, p. 86-87.

113. AMRAM, David
     "This Song's for You Jack." MoodySI (14) Spr 84,
          p. 13.

114. ANAPORTE, J.
     "Benediction." GreenfR (11:1/2) Sum-Aut 83, p. 143.
     "Monsters." GreenfR (11:1/2) Sum-Aut 83, p. 143-144.

115. ANAPORTE, Jean Easton
     "Inexorable Progressions: An Old Theme." PaintedB
          (24) Aut 84, p. 12.
     "Pitfalls of the Lady Poet." PaintedB (21) Wint
          84, p. 6.

116. ANCROM, Nancy
     "Matisse." Tele (19) 83, p. 33.
     "Poverty." Tele (19) 83, p. 33.
     "Vacation Spot." Tele (19) 83, p. 33.

117. ANDERS, Shirley B.
     "Hommage à Gertrude." MichQR (23:2) Spr 84, p. 207.
     "Tobacco Barn." PoetC (16:1) Aut 84, p. 9.

118. ANDERSEN, Marguerite
     "He." PoetryCR (6:1) Aut 84, p. 16.

119. ANDERSEN, Vita
     "Costa del Sol, at Night" (tr. by Jannick Storm and
          Linda Lappin). Iowa (14:2) Spr-Sum 84, p. 183-186.

120. ANDERSON, Barbara
     "Counting on One Hand." Telescope (3:3) Aut 84, p.
          96-97.
     "Significant Others." Telescope (3:3) Aut 84, p.
          94-95.

121. ANDERSON, Beth
     "Living Inside-Out." SanFPJ (6:4) 84, p. 70-71.

122. ANDERSON, Erland
     "Emergency Broadcast" (for Dr. Helen Caldicott).
          GreenfR (12:1/2) Sum-Aut 84, p. 133.

123. ANDERSON, Gerald
     "Consider This." Poetry (144:2) My 84, p. 78.

124. ANDERSON, Jack
     "Artists." HangL (45) Spr 84, p. 8-9.
     "European Lions: A Dozen Views." HangL (45) Spr
          84, p. 10-14.

"The Invention of New Jersey" (for David Antin).
    Chelsea (42/43) 84, p. 168-169.
"Late Music." VirQR (60:2) Spr 84, p. 240-241.
"Murders." HangL (45) Spr 84, p. 6-7.
"A Partial Index to Myself." HangL (45) Spr 84, p.
    15-19.
"The Particulars." VirQR (60:2) Spr 84, p. 239-240.
"The Window in Love." Confr (27/28) 84, p. 192.

125. ANDERSON, Jim
    "Homework." Poetry (144:2) My 84, p. 92-93.
    "Making the Strange Familiar." Poetry (144:2) My
        84, p. 91-92.

126. ANDERSON, Kath M.
    "Coming Back from Venice." CarolQ (36:2) Wint 84,
        p. 88.

127. ANDERSON, Mark
    "Autumn Maneuver" (tr. of Ingeborg Bachmann).
        ParisR (26:92) Sum 84, p. 130.
    "Exile" (tr. of Ingeborg Bachmann). ParisR (26:92)
        Sum 84, p. 129.
    "Go, My Thought" (tr. of Ingeborg Bachmann).
        ParisR (26:92) Sum 84, p. 128.
    "The Heavy Freight" (tr. of Ingeborg Bachmann).
        ParisR (26:92) Sum 84, p. 125.
    "In the Storm of Roses" (tr. of Ingeborg Bachmann).
        ParisR (26:92) Sum 84, p. 131.
    "My Bird" (tr. of Ingeborg Bachmann). ParisR
        (26:92) Sum 84, p. 124-125.
    "Night Portrait of Rome" (tr. of Ingeborg Bachmann).
        ParisR (26:92) Sum 84, p. 131.
    "Shadow Roses Shadow" (tr. of Ingeborg Bachmann).
        ParisR (26:92) Sum 84, p. 126.
    "To the Sun" (tr. of Ingeborg Bachmann). ParisR
        (26:92) Sum 84, p. 127-128.
    "We Have Risen and the Cloisters Are Empty" (tr. of
        Ingeborg Bachmann). ParisR (26:92) Sum 84, p. 126.

128. ANDERSON, Martin
    "Early Traders in Southern China." Waves (12:1)
        Aut 83, p. 58.

129. ANDERSON, Michael
    "Evolution of the Bard, Revised." WormR (24:1,
        issue 93) 84, p. 3-4.
    "Fort Rock." WormR (24:1, issue 93) 84, p. 4-5.
    "The Sky and Sea Darken by Degrees." Grain (12:2)
        My 84, p. 18.
    "Wingwalker, Too High." AntigR (59) Aut 84, p. 136.

130. ANDERSON, Murray (Murray Arden)
    "Horse Stalls." SnapD (8:1) Aut 84, p. 48-49.
    "Prideful Hands." SnapD (6:2) Spr 83, p. 56.
    "Social Security." SnapD (6:2) Spr 83, p. 54-55.
    "Spider Eggs." SnapD (7:1) Aut 83, p. 20-22.

131. ANDERSON, P. F.
    "Milk, Seed, Sun" (from The Wolf Diary). Calyx

(8:3) Aut—Wint 84, p. 28-29.
"Veiled Waters" (from The Wolf Diary). Calyx
(8:3) Aut—Wint 84, p. 26-27.

132. ANDERSON, Sallie
"Walter, 1960." PoetC (15:3) 84, p. 7.

133. ANDERSON, T. J., III
"Emilio's Rain." SanFPJ (6:2) 84, p. 90-91.

134. ANDERSON, Terry
"Gilgamesh." KanQ (16:3) Sum 84, p. 21.
"No One Wants to be Horatio." KanQ (16:3) Sum 84,
p. 22.

135. ANDERSON, Wendell B.
"The Cordillera There Forever." OroM (2:3/4, issue
7/8) 84, p. 43-44.
"The Early Moon." OroM (2:3/4, issue 7/8) 84, p. 44.

136. ANDRADE, Eugenio de
"Coracão Habitado." Mund (14:2) 84, p. 44.
"Corpo Habitado." Mund (14:2) 84, p. 38.
"Cristalizacoes." Mund (14:2) 84, p. 40.
"Crystallizations" (tr. by Alexis Levitin). Mund
(14:2) 84, p. 41.
"Desde a Aurora." Mund (14:2) 84, p. 42, 44.
"Homage to Rimbaud" (tr. by Alexis Levitin).
GreenfR (12:1/2) Sum-Aut 84, p. 87-88.
"Inhabited Body" (tr. by Alexis Levitin). Mund
(14:2) 84, p. 39.
"Inhabited Heart" (tr. by Alexis Levitin). Mund
(14:2) 84, p. 45.
"Names" (tr. by Alexis Levitin). NewOR (11:3/4)
Aut-Wint 84, p. 118.
"Of the Other Side" (tr. by Alexis Levitin).
GreenfR (12:1/2) Sum-Aut 84, p. 88.
"Poetics" (tr. by Alexis Levitin). GreenfR
(12:1/2) Sum-Aut 84, p. 84-85.
"Silence" (tr. by Alexis Levitin). Mund (14:2) 84,
p. 43.
"O Silencio." Mund (14:2) 84, p. 42.
"Since Dawn" (tr. by Alexis Levitin). Mund (14:2)
84, p. 43, 45.
"Solar Matter" (Selections: 45-46, 49, in
Portuguese). CutB (22) Spr-Sum 84, p. 10.
"Solar Matter" (Selections: 45-46, 49, tr. by Alexis
Levitin). CutB (22) Spr-Sum 84, p. 11.
"A Story of the South" (tr. by Alexis Levitin).
GreenfR (12:1/2) Sum-Aut 84, p. 85-86.
"While Asleep" (tr. by Alexis Levitin). GreenfR
(12:1/2) Sum-Aut 84, p. 87.
"Writing on the Wall" (tr. by Alexis Levitin).
GreenfR (12:1/2) Sum-Aut 84, p. 86-87.

137. ANDRADE, Mario de
"The Khaki Lozenge" (tr. by Manoel Cardozo). Vis
(15) 84, p. 7.

138. ANDRADE, Oswald de
     "Frontier" (tr. by Manoel Cardozo). <u>Vis</u> (15) 84,
        p. 8.

139. ANDRE, Michael
     "By Means of Things." <u>Abraxas</u> (31/32) 84, p. 40.

140. ANDREA, Marianne
     "#51. I have not died yet, nor am I yet alone" (tr.
        of Osip Mandelshtam). <u>Confr</u> (27/28) 84, p. 54.
     "Almost in the Album" (from <u>Moscow</u> <u>Triptych</u>, tr.
        of Anna Akhmatova). <u>SenR</u> (14:1) 84, p. 55.
     "At Peredelkino with Pasternak, 1936." <u>Nimrod</u>
        (28:1) Aut-Wint 84, p. 38.
     "Creativity" (from <u>Mysteries</u> <u>of</u> <u>Craft</u>, tr. of Anna
        Akhmatova). <u>SenR</u> (14:1) 84, p. 54.
     "Cruelty Is Rarely Conscious." <u>Wind</u> (14:52) 84, p. 1.
     "Dante" (tr. of Anna Akhmatova). <u>SenR</u> (14:1) 84,
        p. 53.
     "Death and Transfiguration" (Tone Poem by Richard
        Strauss). <u>Wind</u> (14:52) 84, p. 1-2.
     "Dream" (August 14, 1956, tr. of Anna Akhmatova).
        <u>Nimrod</u> (28:1) Aut-Wint 84, p. 36.
     "Echo" (tr. of Anna Akhmatova). <u>SenR</u> (14:1) 84, p.
        55.
     "Elegy for Leningrad, 1944." <u>Nimrod</u> (28:1) Aut-
        Wint 84, p. 39.
     "In Books" (November 25th, 1943, Tashkent, tr. of
        Anna Akhmatova). <u>Nimrod</u> (28:1) Aut-Wint 84, p. 35.
     "The Man with the Prince-Nez." <u>Nimrod</u> (28:1) Aut-
        Wint 84, p. 40.
     "More about That Summer" (Autumn 1962, tr. of Anna
        Akhmatova). <u>Nimrod</u> (28:1) Aut-Wint 84, p. 36.
     "The Muse" (tr. of Anna Akhmatova). <u>SenR</u> (14:1)
        84, p. 52.
     "Plath Reads." <u>WoosterR</u> (1:2) N 84, p. 21.
     "To Alexander Blok" (tr. of Anna Akhmatova).
        <u>Nimrod</u> (28:1) Aut-Wint 84, p. 34.

141. ANDREJCAK, Dawna Maydak
     "Lady Cynthia" (For Ken and his lady). <u>PoeticJ</u> (2)
        83, p. 33.

142. ANDRESEN, Sophia de Mello Breyner (<u>See</u> <u>also</u> BREYNER,
        Sophia de Mello)
     "Assassination of Simonetta Vespucci" (tr. by Lisa
        Sapinkopf). <u>NewOR</u> (11:2) Sum 84, p. 73.
     "Dai-me o Sol das águas azuis e das esferas."
        <u>Mund</u> (14:2) 84, p. 92.
     "E só então saí das minhas trevas." <u>Mund</u>
        (14:2) 84, p. 94.
     "Give me the sun of the blue waters, of the spheres"
        (tr. by Lisa Sapinkopf). <u>Mund</u> (14:2) 84, p. 93.
     "I sent the boat out after the wind" (tr. by Lisa
        Sapinkopf). <u>Mund</u> (14:2) 84, p. 95.
     "Luminosos os dias abolidos." <u>Mund</u> (14:2) 84, p. 92.
     "Luminous the abolished days" (tr. by Lisa
        Sapinkopf). <u>Mund</u> (14:2) 84, p. 93.
     "Mandei para o largo o barco atrás do vento."
        <u>Mund</u> (14:2) 84, p. 94.

"Nas praias que são o rosto branco das amadas
    mortas." <u>Mund</u> (14:2) 84, p. 92.
"Os nossos dedos abriram mãos fechadas." <u>Mund</u>
    (14:2) 84, p. 94.
"On the beaches, which are the white faces of dead
    fleets" (tr. by Lisa Sapinkopf). <u>Mund</u> (14:2)
    84, p. 93.
"Only then did I leave my darkness" (tr. by Lisa
    Sapinkopf). <u>Mund</u> (14:2) 84, p. 95.
"Our fingers opened closed hands" (tr. by Lisa
    Sapinkopf). <u>Mund</u> (14:2) 84, p. 95.
"Poem of geometry and silence" (tr. by Lisa
    Sapinkopf). <u>Mund</u> (14:2) 84, p. 93.
"Poema de geometria e de silêncio." <u>Mund</u> (14:2)
    84, p. 92.
"Women by the Seashore" (Excerpted from <u>Coral</u>, tr.
    by Lisa Sapinkopf). <u>MissR</u> (37/38, 13:1/2) Aut
    84, p. 76.

143. ANDREU, Blanca
    "Me queda la mar media en el triunfo del agua."
        <u>Mairena</u> (6:18) 84, p. 69.

144. ANDREWS, Tom
    "Apologia pro Vita Sua." <u>Wind</u> (14:51) 84, p. 1-2.
    "Walking the Ice." <u>Wind</u> (14:51) 84, p. 1.

145. ANDROLA, Ron
    "Against My Word." <u>Bogg</u> (52) 84, p. 33.
    "Critic Study." <u>Bogg</u> (52) 84, p. 33.
    "Genius Child." <u>Bogg</u> (52) 84, p. 33.
    "A Harrison Fisher Poem." <u>Bogg</u> (52) 84, p. 33.
    "Johnny Cash." <u>Bogg</u> (52) 84, p. 11.
    "June 18, 1983." <u>Bogg</u> (52) 84, p. 9.
    "Micheline." <u>Open24</u> (3) 84, p. 45.
    "Seagulls." <u>Bogg</u> (52) 84, p. 33.

146. ANDRYCHUK, Kristin
    "Candy Cane in July." <u>Quarry</u> (33:3) Sum 84, p. 15.
    "Grey Green Mist." <u>Descant</u> (47, 15:4) Wint 84, p.
        117.
    "The Machine Age." <u>Descant</u> (47, 15:4) Wint 84, p.
        116.
    "My Grandfather." <u>Quarry</u> (33:3) Sum 84, p. 14.

147. ANESTIS, Connie
    "Un Just Spring (with Apologies to E.E. Cummings)."
        <u>EngJ</u> (73:4) Ap 84, p. 32.

148. ANGEL, Ralph
    "Arm and Arm." <u>AmerPoR</u> (13:4) Jl-Ag 84, p. 40.
    "Back Down." <u>PoetryE</u> (15) Aut 84, p. 15-16.
    "Breaking the Rock Down." <u>AmerPoR</u> (13:4) Jl-Ag 84,
        p. 41.
    "History." <u>AmerPoR</u> (13:4) Jl-Ag 84, p. 40.

149. ANGELICA, Clara
    "Beauty and the Beast" (tr. of Paulo Veras). <u>Tele</u>

(19) 83, p. 20.
"Family Album" (tr. of Paulo Veras). <u>Tele</u> (19) 83,
    p. 21.
"Of What Is Not Human" (tr. of Paulo Veras). <u>Tele</u>
    (19) 83, p. 18-19.
"With Marginal Fury" (tr. of Paulo Veras). <u>Tele</u>
    (19) 83, p. 20.

150. ANGELL, Roger
    "Greetings, Friends." <u>NewYorker</u> (60:45) 24 D 84,
        p. 31.

151. ANGLESEY, Zoe
    "The Elect of Violence" (tr. of Roberto Sosa).
        <u>OroM</u> (2:3/4, issue 7/8) 84, p. 7.
    "Undoing a Fable." <u>Vis</u> (16) 84, p. 37.

ANIBAL TRISTE, Juan: <u>See</u> TRISTE, Juan Anibal

152. ANONYMOUS
    "America, I have come and landed" (in Chinese and
        English, tr. by Marlon K. Hom from <u>Songs</u> <u>of</u> <u>Gold</u>
        <u>Mountain</u> I, 14a). <u>GreenfR</u> (11:1/2) Sum-Aut 83,
        p. 157.
    "American laws, more fierce than tigers" (in Chinese
        and English, tr. by Marlon K. Hom from <u>Songs</u> <u>of</u>
        <u>Gold</u> <u>Mountain</u> I, 13b). <u>GreenfR</u> (11:1/2) Sum-
        Aut 83, p. 160.
    "Anonymous Poems on Immigration under the Chinese
        Exclusion Act" (in Chinese and English, tr. by
        Marlon K. Hom from <u>Songs</u> <u>of</u> <u>Gold</u> <u>Mountain</u>
        anthologies, San Francisco, 1911, 1915). <u>GreenfR</u>
        (11:1/2) Sum-Aut 83, p. 149-160.
    "The Close of School." <u>LittleBR</u> (4:3) Spr 84, p. 31.
    "Detention is called 'to await a review'" (in
        Chinese and English, tr. by Marlon K. Hom from
        <u>Songs</u> <u>of</u> <u>Gold</u> <u>Mountain</u> I, 14a). <u>GreenfR</u>
        (11:1/2) Sum-Aut 83, p. 155.
    "Galway Kinnel" (Handed to Galway Kinnell after a
        poetry reading in Tacoma, Washington). <u>Tendril</u>
        (18, special issue) 84, p. 77-78.
    "Home in poverty" (in Chinese and English, tr. by
        Marlon K. Hom from <u>Songs</u> <u>of</u> <u>Gold</u> <u>Mountain</u> I,
        14a). <u>GreenfR</u> (11:1/2) Sum-Aut 83, p. 149.
    "Hundred Names" (Perhaps the oldest Chinese poem
        extant). <u>NewL</u> (50:2/3) Wint-Spr 84, p. 222.
    "I sojourn in America without proper documents" (in
        Chinese and English, tr. by Marlon K. Hom from
        <u>Songs</u> <u>of</u> <u>Gold</u> <u>Mountain</u> I, 13b). <u>GreenfR</u>
        (11:1/2) Sum-Aut 83, p. 152.
    "In Hiroshima Salvias are in bloom" (by Hiroshima A-
        bomb victim, tr. by Takahashi Horioka). <u>NewL</u>
        (50:2/3) Wint-Spr 84, p. 231.
    "In search of a petty gain" (in Chinese and English,
        tr. by Marlon K. Hom from <u>Songs</u> <u>of</u> <u>Gold</u>
        <u>Mountain</u> I, 5a). <u>GreenfR</u> (11:1/2) Sum-Aut 83,
        p. 150.
    "Ishtar and the Shepherd-Man" (in Babylonian).
        <u>YellowS</u> (13) Wint 84, p. 39-40.
    "Ishtar and the Shepherd-Man" (tr. of the Babylonian

by Joe Malone). <u>YellowS</u> (13) Wint 84, p. 39-40.
"The moment I heard we've entered port" (in Chinese
and English, tr. by Marlon K. Hom from <u>Songs of
Gold Mountain</u> I, 13b). <u>GreenfR</u> (11:1/2) Sum-
Aut 83, p. 151.
"My Once upon a Time Husband." <u>LitR</u> (27:3) Spr 84,
p. 293-294.
"Mystic Meditations." <u>PoeticJ</u> (3) 83, p. 22-23.
"Nahuatl Icnocuicatl Song" (From the region of
Chalco. Cantares Mexicanos, Folio 35, recto and
verso). <u>SouthwR</u> (69:2) Spr 84, p. 208-209.
"O my beloved" (Poem inscribed on an Egyptian
statue, 1500 B.C.). <u>PoetryE</u> (13/14) Spr-Sum 84,
p. 192-193.
"So, liberty is the national principle" (in Chinese
and English, tr. by Marlon K. Hom from <u>Songs of
Gold Mountain</u> I, 13b). <u>GreenfR</u> (11:1/2) Sum-
Aut 83, p. 159.
"A south wind stirs" (in transliterated Sanskrit).
<u>YellowS</u> (13) Wint 84, p. 28.
"A south wind stirs" (tr. of the Sanskrit by Andrew
Schelling). <u>YellowS</u> (13) Wint 84, p. 28.
"The spot where the bomb fell" (by Hiroshima A-bomb
victim, tr. by Takahashi Horioka). <u>NewL</u>
(50:2/3) Wint-Spr 84, p. 231.
"Stay at home: many opportunities lost" (in Chinese
and English, tr. by Marlon K. Hom from <u>Songs of
Gold Mountain</u> II, 11a). <u>GreenfR</u> (11:1/2) Sum-
Aut 83, p. 153.
"Three Anglo-Saxon Riddles from <u>The Exeter Book</u>"
(7, 34, 85, in Anglo-Saxon). <u>CimR</u> (69) O 84, p.
57.
"Three Anglo-Saxon Riddles from <u>The Exeter Book</u>"
(7, 34, 85, tr. by Nan Fry). <u>CimR</u> (69) O 84, p.
56.
"Tse'gihi" (Navajo night-chant). <u>Tendril</u> (18,
special issue) 84, p. 83-84.
"Undressing to the waist" (by Hiroshima A-bomb
victim, tr. by Takahashi Horioka). <u>NewL</u>
(50:2/3) Wint-Spr 84, p. 231.
"A weak country, a deprived voice" (in Chinese and
English, tr. by Marlon K. Hom from <u>Songs of Gold
Mountain</u> I, 14a). <u>GreenfR</u> (11:1/2) Sum-Aut 83,
p. 158.
"Western Wind." <u>Tele</u> (19) 83, p. 1.
"Western Wind." <u>Tendril</u> (18, special issue) 84, p.
212.
"Winter taketh embassy in every tree" (8th century).
<u>Abraxas</u> (31/32) 84, p. 20.
"The wooden barracks, all specially built" (in
Chinese and English, tr. by Marlon K. Hom from
<u>Songs of Gold Mountain</u> I, 13b). <u>GreenfR</u>
(11:1/2) Sum-Aut 83, p. 154.
"The wooden cell: a steel barrel" (in Chinese and
English, tr. by Marlon K. Hom from <u>Songs of Gold
Mountain</u> I, 14a). <u>GreenfR</u> (11:1/2) Sum-Aut 83,
p. 156.

153. ANSELMO, Kristine J.
"Loss." <u>SnapD</u> (7:1) Aut 83, p. 27.

154. ANSON, John
    "Discordia Concors." Thrpny (17) Spr 84, p. 12.
    "Frisbee" (for my daughter). Thrpny (18) Sum 84,
        p. 6.

155. ANSON, John S.
    "E. A. Robinson." ArizQ (40:1) Spr 84, p. 84.

156. 'ANTARA
    "On His Own Prowess" (tr. by Barbara Feyerabend).
        SenR (14:1) 84, p. 34-35.
    "She Plays in My Heart" (tr. by Andrew Harvey).
        SenR (14:1) 84, p. 28.

157. ANTIN, David
    "Constructions and Discoveries." Chelsea (42/43)
        84, p. 136-137.

158. ANTONYCH, Bohdan
    "Bitter Night" (tr. by Mark Rudman). Pequod
        (16/17) 84, p. 186.
    "Song on the Indestructability of Matter" (tr. by
        Mark Rudman). Pequod (16/17) 84, p. 185.

159. APOLLINAIRE, Guillaume
    "Rhenane: Les Cloches" (from Alcools, tr. by
        Frederick Lowe). YellowS (13) Wint 84, p. 41.

160. APPEL, Dori
    "Fibroid Tumors." Calyx (8:3) Aut-Wint 84, p. 34.
    "The Oracle." ThirdW (2) Spr 84, p. 74-75.
    "Rehearsal." Calyx (8:3) Aut-Wint 84, p. 33.

161. APPLEMAN, Philip
    "Darwin's Ark" (Selections: "Prologue," "The Worm,"
        "The Gossamer," "The Rabbit"). NoAmR (269:2) Je
        84, p. 14.

162. APPLEWHITE, James
    "The Falling Asleep." SouthernR (20:2) Spr 84, p.
        341.
    "Fictional Family History." Antaeus (53) Aut 84,
        p. 251-252.
    "For W. H. Applewhite." Peb (23) 84, p. 88-94.
    "Graves and Vines." SouthernR (20:2) Spr 84, p. 342.
    "The Story of the Drawer." SouthernR (20:2) Spr
        84, p. 343.

163. AQUILIUS
    "Hellfire to him who discovered hours!" (tr. by
        Janet N. Lembke). Sparrow (46) 84, p. 9.
    "Ut illum di perdant, primus qui horas repperit."
        Sparrow (46) 84, p. 9.

AQUINO, Mario Rosado: See ROSADO AQUINO, Mario

164. ARAD, Miriam
    "When I Said I Shall Wait" (tr. of Amir Gilboa).
        Pequod (16/17) 84, p. 114.

165. ARANA SOTO, Salvador
     "Paralelos." <u>Mairena</u> (5:13) Spr 83, p. 87.

166. ARAUJO, Virginia de
     "Irma." <u>BelPoJ</u> (35:2) Wint 84-85, p. 26-27.
     "Newscast." <u>BelPoJ</u> (35:2) Wint 84-85, p. 28-29.

ARAUZ, Nicomedes Suárez: <u>See</u> SUAREZ ARAUZ, Nicomedes

167. ARB, Siv
     "Living" (tr. by Ingrid Claréus). <u>Abraxas</u>
        (31/32) 84, p. 61.
     "Nowhere to Go" (tr. by Ingrid Claréus). <u>Abraxas</u>
        (31/32) 84, p. 60.
     "Perfect Pitch" (tr. by Ingrid Claréus). <u>Abraxas</u>
        (31/32) 84, p. 61.

168. ARBELECHE, Jorge
     "The Mirror's Place" (tr. by Carolyn Harris and the
        author). <u>Iowa</u> (14:2) Spr-Sum 84, p. 158.

ARCE, Armando Uribe: <u>See</u> URIBE ARCE, Armando

169. ARCE, Manuel José
     "Creditos." <u>Mairena</u> (6:18) 84, p. 215.
     "El Tema del Amor (10)." <u>Mairena</u> (6:18) 84, p. 216.

170. ARCHER, Nuala
     "The Pear Three & Prophecy." <u>Pequod</u> (16/17) 84, p.
        53-54.

ARCY, Michael James d': <u>See</u> D'ARCY, Michael James

171. ARDERY, Julia
     "Scorpia." <u>PraS</u> (58:2) Sum 84, p. 14.
     "Teaching the Seniors." <u>PraS</u> (58:2) Sum 84, p. 13.

ARELLANO, Diana Ramírez de: <u>See</u> RAMIREZ de ARELLANO, Diana

ARELLANO, Olga Ramírez de: <u>See</u> RAMIREZ de ARELLANO, Olga

172. ARENAL, Electa
     "I Am Mirror" (tr. of Claribel Alegria, w. Marsha
        Gabriela Dreyer). <u>Confr</u> (27/28) 84, p. 42.
     "Orchid of Steel" (tr. of Gioconda Belli, w.
        Gabriela Dreye). <u>Nat</u> (238:3) 28 Ja 84, p. 100.

173. ARENAL, Electra
     "Esteli" (tr. of Claribel Alegria, w. Marsha
        Gabriela Dreyer). <u>MinnR</u> (N.S. 22) Spr 84, p. 77-
        78.

174. ARENAS, Bibi
     "Una Casa Nueva." <u>Mairena</u> (5:13) Spr 83, p. 77.

175. ARENAS, Marion
     "Oranges." <u>StoneC</u> (11:3/4) Spr-Sum 84, p. 59.

176. ARENDT, Erich
     "Jewish Cemetery in Prague" (tr. by Suzanne Shipley

Toliver). <u>Sulfur</u> (4:2, issue 11) 84, p. 89-90.

177. AREVALO, Marta de
"Con-Jugar el Verbo." <u>Mairena</u> (6:17) Aut 84, p. 71.

178. ARGUELLES, Ivan
"1929." <u>OroM</u> (2:3/4, issue 7/8) 84, p. 15-16.
"1984." <u>SanFPJ</u> (6:2) 84, p. 35.
"Aqua Pluvia." <u>RagMag</u> (3:2) Aut 84, p. 33.
"Berkeley Where Anything Can Happen." <u>Abraxas</u>
    (31/32) 84, p. 6.
"Between the Lover and the Beloved How Many
    Distances and Legends Spell the Circle to Be
    Unbroken." <u>YellowS</u> (11) Sum 84, p. 29.
"Chance Passing." <u>Abraxas</u> (29/30) 84, p. 35.
"Cordoba." <u>RagMag</u> (3:2) Aut 84, p. 33.
"Daguerrotype." <u>Veloc</u> (2) Spr 83, p. 44.
"The Dark Woman the Lethal Woman Astarte." <u>YellowS</u>
    (11) Sum 84, p. 31.
"Death Mask." <u>Veloc</u> (3) Aut-Wint 83, p. 52.
"Encounter among the Wounds." <u>OroM</u> (2:3/4, issue
    7/8) 84, p. 42.
"Eve." <u>YellowS</u> (10) Spr 84, p. 20.
"Fata Morgana." <u>YellowS</u> (11) Sum 84, p. 31.
"Guernica." <u>SanFPJ</u> (6:2) 84, p. 33-34.
"Hades." <u>Veloc</u> (2) Spr 83, p. 43.
"I Submit My Resignation." <u>Abraxas</u> (31/32) 84, p. 5.
"Lucretius." <u>Os</u> (19) 84, p. 22.
"Orlando." <u>Veloc</u> (1) Sum 82, p. 24.
"A Photograph of Her Breath, an Echo of Her Hair."
    <u>YellowS</u> (11) Sum 84, p. 29.
"The Ruin of Time." <u>Veloc</u> (1) Sum 82, p. 26.
"Tourist." <u>ManhatR</u> (3:2) Wint 84-85, p. 62.
"Vampire." <u>Veloc</u> (3) Aut-Wint 83, p. 51.
"Waiting Room." <u>Abraxas</u> (31/32) 84, p. 7.
"Woman inside the Woman." <u>YellowS</u> (11) Sum 84, p. 30.

179. ARGYROS, Alex
"Before the Beginning." <u>NewOR</u> (11:3/4) Aut-Wint
    84, p. 149.
"The Past." <u>NewOR</u> (11:3/4) Aut-Wint 84, p. 160.

180. ARIBAN
"Mother's Glowing Embers." <u>Calyx</u> (8:2) Spr 84, p. 19.

181. ARIKHA, Anne Atik
"Against Rembrandt." <u>Nat</u> (239:13) 27 O 84, p. 422.

182. ARMANINI, Mark
"The Lamb" (with music). <u>WestCR</u> (19:2) O 84, p. 13-
    19.

183. ARMITAGE, Barri
"Square Dance." <u>GeoR</u> (38:4) Wint 84, p. 729.

184. ARMSTRONG, Bruce
"Wild Berries." <u>Germ</u> (8:1) Spr-Sum 84, p. 23.

185. ARMSTRONG, Thomas
"Anette." <u>Sam</u> (37:3, 147th release) 83, p. 15.

186. ARNEY, Helen Troisi
"On I-74." SpoonRQ (9:2) Spr 84, p. 47.

187. ARNOLD, A. James
"Civil Status" (from Suppots et Supplications:
Interjections, tr. of Antonin Artaud, w. Clayton
Eshleman). Sulfur (3:3, issue 9) 84, p. 43-59.
"Pounding and Gism" (from Suppots et
Supplications: Interjections, tr. of Antonin
Artaud, w. Clayton Eshleman and David Maclagan).
Sulfur (3:3, issue 9) 84, p. 38-42.
"Suppots et Supplications" (Selections, tr. of
Antonin Artaud, w. Clayton Eshleman, David
Rattray, and David Maclagan). Sulfur (3:3,
issue 9) 84, p. 15-59.

188. ARNOLD, Bob
"At the Country Wedding." Northeast (Series 3:18)
84, p. 4.
"Scout." Northeast (Series 3:18) 84, p. 3.

189. ARNOLD, Les
"Blizzard." Grain (12:1) F 84, p. 28.
"Hands." Grain (12:3) Ag 84, p. 29.
"Landscape with the Fall of Icarus." Grain (12:1)
F 84, p. 25.
"Loversmeet." Grain (12:1) F 84, p. 24.
"My Heart the Dancer." Grain (12:3) Ag 84, p. 26.
"Odysseus at the Kitchen Sink." Grain (12:1) F 84,
p. 27.
"A Party at the Doctor's House." Grain (12:1) F
84, p. 26.
"Quiet." Grain (12:3) Ag 84, p. 23.
"Sacred Spring." Grain (12:1) F 84, p. 29.
"The Second Coming." Grain (12:3) Ag 84, p. 23-24.
"Visiting the Sick." Grain (12:3) Ag 84, p. 25.

190. ARONSON, Kristin Janina
"Northern Lights." AntigR (58) Sum 84, p. 103.
"A Wisp of Tinsel." AntigR (58) Sum 84, p. 104.

191. ARP, Jean
"He who tries to bring down a cloud." PoetryE
(13/14) Spr-Sum 84, p. 211.
"Kaspar Is Dead." PoetryE (13/14) Spr-Sum 84, p.
213-214.

192. ARRABAL, Fernando
"The Stone of Madness" (Untitled Prose Poems,
Selections: 1-4, tr. by Laurence Lewis).
Chelsea (42/43) 84, p. 290-291.

193. ARROWSMITH, William
"Another Moon Effect" (tr. of Eugenio Montale).
GrandS (3:1) Aut 83, p. 113.
"Low Tide" (tr. of Eugenio Montale). GrandS (3:1)
Aut 83, p. 114.
"The Return" (Bocca di Magra, tr. of Eugenio
Montale). GrandS (3:1) Aut 83, p. 112.
"Toward Vienna" (tr. of Eugenio Montale). GrandS

(3:1) Aut 83, p. 113.

194. ARRUFAT, Anton
"Recuento (1)." _Mairena_ (6:18) 84, p. 173.

195. ARTAUD, Antonin
"Black Poet" (tr. by Paul Zweig). _Chelsea_ (42/43)
84, p. 117.
"Civil Status" (from _Suppots et Supplications_:
Interjections, tr. by A. James Arnold and Clayton
Eshleman). _Sulfur_ (3:3, issue 9) 84, p. 43-59.
"Codex Artaud" (Excerpts, w. Nancy Spero). _Sulfur_
(3:3, issue 9) 84, p. 60-66.
"Mothers to the Stable" (from _Suppots et
Supplications_: Fragmentations, tr. by David
Rattray). _Sulfur_ (3:3, issue 9) 84, p. 17-19.
"Pounding and Gism" (from _Suppots et
Supplications_: Interjections, tr. by A. James
Arnold, Clayton Eshleman and David Maclagan).
Sulfur (3:3, issue 9) 84, p. 38-42.
"Suppots et Supplications" (Selections, tr. by A.
James Arnold, Clayton Eshleman, David Rattray,
and David Maclagan). _Sulfur_ (3:3, issue 9) 84,
p. 15-59.

196. ARTHUR, Robert P.
"The Eagle Flies." _Poem_ (50) Mr 84, p. 6-7.
"The Haunting." _Poem_ (50) Mr 84, p. 8-9.

197. ARTOPOEUS, Otto F.
"Francis." _ChrC_ (101:19) 30 My 84, p. 565.

198. ARVELO, Mariela
"Hunting" (tr. by the author and Marilyn Chin).
Iowa (14:2) Spr-Sum 84, p. 151.

199. ARVIO, Sarah
"Old Wall" (tr. of Pablo Neruda). _AmerPoR_ (13:5) S-
O 84, p. 13.

200. ASBRIDGE, N. S.
"Reflexion in the Xinese Mode of Heo-Zpouf." _Bogg_
(52) 84, p. 24.
"Two Positions." _Bogg_ (52) 84, p. 13.

201. ASCRIZZI, Lynn Ann
"The Distance Most Disturbing." _WorldO_ (18:4) Sum
84, p. 45.

202. ASEKOFF, L. S.
"Dreams of a Work." _NewYorker_ (60:31) 17 S 84, p.
113.

203. ASHBERY, John
"And can see the many hidden ways merit drains out"
(Haibun 2). _Sulfur_ (3:3, issue 9) 84, p. 114.
"At North Farm." _GeoR_ (38:3) Aut 84, p. 636-637.
"At North Farm." _NewYorker_ (60:8) 9 Ap 84, p. 48.
"Bring them all back to life" (Haibun 5). _Sulfur_
(3:3, issue 9) 84, p. 116.

"But What Is the Reader to Make of This?" <u>GrandS</u>
(3:2) Wint 84, p. 25.
"Dark at four again" (Haibun 4). <u>Sulfur</u> (3:3,
issue 9) 84, p. 115.
"Darlene's Hospital." <u>GrandS</u> (3:2) Wint 84, p. 26-28.
"Ditto, Kiddo." <u>NewYRB</u> (31:10) 14 Je 84, p. 34.
"Down by the Station, Early in the Morning."
<u>NewYorker</u> (60:1) 20 F 84, p. 50.
"I was swimming with the water at my back" (Haibun
3). <u>Sulfur</u> (3:3, issue 9) 84, p. 115.
"Nothing to Steal." <u>PartR</u> (51:4/52:1 Anniversary
issue) 84-85, p. 516-517.
"Purists Will Object." <u>GrandS</u> (3:2) Wint 84, p. 29.
"Six Haibun." <u>Sulfur</u> (3:3, issue 9) 84, p. 113-117.
"To be involved in every phase of directing" (Haibun
6). <u>Sulfur</u> (3:3, issue 9) 84, p. 117.
"Wanting to write something I could think only of my
own ideas" (Haibun 1). <u>Sulfur</u> (3:3, issue 9)
84, p. 113-114.
"Wet Are the Boards." <u>NewYorker</u> (60:37) 29 O 84,
p. 44-45.

ASIS FERNANDEZ, Francisco de: <u>See</u> FERNANDEZ, Francisco de
Asís

204. ASPINWALL, Dorothy
"The Art of Dying" (tr. of Pierre Emmanuel). <u>WebR</u>
(9:1) Spr 84, p. 15.
"Dust" (tr. of Tristan Klingsor). <u>WebR</u> (9:2) Wint
85, p. 18.
"It is perhaps the snow that sets you on fire"
("Untitled", tr. of Ilarie Voronca). <u>WebR</u> (9:2)
Wint 85, p. 18.
"Taedium Vitae" (tr. of Rosaire Dion-Levesque).
<u>WebR</u> (9:1) Spr 84, p. 16.

205. ASTRACHAN, John Mann
"Gifts from Old Lovers." <u>NegC</u> (4:3) Sum 84, p. 35.

206. ATHEARN, Hope
"To the Planetoids and You." <u>Veloc</u> (4) Sum 84, p. 50.

207. ATKINS, Kathleen
"Mr. Rhizor's Geese." <u>BelPoJ</u> (35:2) Wint 84-85, p.
6-7.

208. ATKINSON, Charles
"Back Steps." <u>VirQR</u> (60:4) Aut 84, p. 623-625.
"Bill." <u>PraS</u> (58:2) Sum 84, p. 25-28.
"Break-in on Old Bill." <u>PraS</u> (58:2) Sum 84, p. 24-25.
"More Blessed to Receive." <u>VirQR</u> (60:4) Aut 84, p.
625-626.
"The Patience of Dry Plants." <u>Poetry</u> (144:4) Jl
84, p. 216.
"Plum." <u>Poetry</u> (144:4) Jl 84, p. 216-217.
"Pruning Out of Season." <u>PraS</u> (58:2) Sum 84, p. 28-
29.
"To Split a Round of Oak." <u>Poetry</u> (144:4) Jl 84,
p. 215-216.

209. ATKINSON, Jennifer
     "Fortune-Telling." Poetry (145:2) N 84, p. 78-80.
     "Hail on Stone Mountain." Poetry (145:2) N 84, p.
        74-75.
     "The Magic Words." Poetry (145:2) N 84, p. 75-78.

210. ATLEE, Tom
     "Freedom and Demo." SanFPJ (6:1) 84, p. 38-39.
     "In G(od) We Trust." SanFPJ (6:1) 84, p. 40.
     "Terra Firma Zero." SanFPJ (6:3) 84, p. 55-56.
     "What Win?" SanFPJ (6:3) 84, p. 54.

211. ATWOOD, Margaret
     "Heart Test with an Echo Chamber." CanLit (100)
        Spr 84, p. 19-20.

212. AUBERT, Jimmy
     "North Plains." StoneC (11:3/4) Spr-Sum 84, p. 19.

213. AUDEN, W. H.
     "The Garrison." Shen (35:2/3) 84, p. 20.
     "Musée des Beaux Arts." PoetryE (13/14) Spr-Sum
        84, back cover.

214. AUSLANDER, Rose
     "In Memoriam Paul Celan" (tr. by Carl Clifton
        Toliver). Sulfur (4:2, issue 11) 84, p. 91.

215. AUSTER, Paul
     "A Tomb for Anatole" (Selections: 8, 133, 160, tr.
        of Stéphane Mallarmé). Pequod (16/17) 84,
        p. 227-228.

216. AUSTIN, Annemarie
     "The Fisherman." Argo (5:3) 84, p. 40.
     "Journey." Argo (5:3) 84, p. 41.

217. AUSTIN, Bob
     "Ballad of the Jimco Truckstop." Wind (14:51) 84,
        p. 3-4.
     "Mountain Jack Blues." Abraxas (29/30) 84, p. 51-53.

218. AUSTIN, David
     "Merlin Was an Adjective: He Modified Things."
        EngJ (73:5) S 84, p. 90.

219. AUSTIN, Penelope
     "Photographic Memory" (for Jan Engholm). Telescope
        (3:3) Aut 84, p. 106-107.

AVE, Jeanne: See JEANNE, Ave

220. AWAD, Joseph
     "Now and Then." Comm (111:7) 6 Ap 84, p. 220.

221. AWOONOR, Kofi
     "Grains and Tears." GreenfR (12:1/2) Sum-Aut 84,
        p. 90.
     "Had Death Not Had Me in Tears." GreenfR (12:1/2)
        Sum-Aut 84, p. 90-91.

"I Rejoice." GreenfR (12:1/2) Sum-Aut 84, p. 91.
"So the World Changes." GreenfR (12:1/2) Sum-Aut
    84, p. 92.

222. AXELROD, David Alan
     "Elegy for Jim Baim." HiramPoR (36) Spr-Sum 84, p.
        5-6.
     "Tracing You to a Rented Room." HiramPoR (36) Spr-
        Sum 84, p. 7-8.

223. AXELROD, David B.
     "Plastics." GreenfR (11:1/2) Sum-Aut 83, p. 123-124.
     "See the Specialist." GreenfR (11:1/2) Sum-Aut 83,
        p. 123.

224. AYALA, Carlos
     "Eternidad con el Recuerdo" (fragmento II).
        Mairena (6:18) 84, p. 217.

225. AZRAEL, Mary
     "In My Brother's Garden." PraS (58:2) Sum 84, p. 32.
     "Lament." PraS (58:2) Sum 84, p. 33.
     "Sampler" (for Susanna). PraS (58:2) Sum 84, p. 33-
        34.

AZUCENA TORRES, Alba: See TORRES, Alba Azucena

226. BAAR, Charles
     "Picasso Used to Gaze at the Sun." ThirdW (2) Spr
        84, p. 76.

BAASTAD, Erling Friis: See FRIIS-BAASTAD, Erling

227. BAATZ, Ronald
     "About Death." SmPd (21:2) Spr 84, p. 37.
     "Bad Weather." SmPd (21:2) Spr 84, p. 39.
     "Green Stew." WormR (24:1, issue 93) 84, p. 31-32.
     "Searching Breezes through Me." WormR (24:1, issue
        93) 84, p. 34-35.
     "Solitaire." WormR (24:1, issue 93) 84, p. 33-34.
     "The Stuff My Dreams Are Made Of." WormR (24:1,
        issue 93) 84, p. 32-33.
     "Wild Bears." SmPd (21:2) Spr 84, p. 38.

228. BABER, Terry
     "Ol' Silky Sly." PoeticJ (4) 83, p. 33.

229. BABIN, María Teresa
     "Nuevos Surcos" (Canto X, from La Barca Varada).
        Mairena (5:13) Spr 83, p. 88.

230. BACA, Jimmy Santiago
     "A Beautiful Day." Spirit (7:1) 84, p. 150-151.

BACA, Marc de: See De BACA, Marc

231. BACHAM, Paul
     "Away from the Game." SanFPJ (6:4) 84, p. 33.
     "Heading for an Epilogue." SanFPJ (6:4) 84, p. 38.
     "Politico." SanFPJ (6:4) 84, p. 39.

232. BACHLER, Wolfgang
    "Behind the Shutters" (by Rainer Schulte). <u>Mund</u>
        (14:2) 84, p. 59.
    "The Dead" (tr. by Rainer Schulte). <u>Mund</u> (14:2)
        84, p. 57, 59.
    "Hinter den Fensterläden." <u>Mund</u> (14:2) 84, p. 58.
    "Im Zug." <u>Mund</u> (14:2) 84, p. 58.
    "Meine Grenzen." <u>Mund</u> (14:2) 84, p. 56.
    "My Boundaries" (tr. by Rainer Schulte). <u>Mund</u>
        (14:2) 84, p. 57.
    "On the Train" (tr. by Rainer Schulte). <u>Mund</u>
        (14:2) 84, p. 59.
    "Roads" (tr. by Rainer Schulte). <u>Mund</u> (14:2) 84,
        p. 57.
    "Die Toten." <u>Mund</u> (14:2) 84, p. 56, 58.
    "Wege." <u>Mund</u> (14:2) 84, p. 56.

233. BACHMANN, Ingeborg
    "Autumn Maneuver" (tr. by Mark Anderson). <u>ParisR</u>
        (26:92) Sum 84, p. 130.
    "Exile" (tr. by Mark Anderson). <u>ParisR</u> (26:92) Sum
        84, p. 129.
    "Go, My Thought" (tr. by Mark Anderson). <u>ParisR</u>
        (26:92) Sum 84, p. 128.
    "The Heavy Freight" (tr. by Mark Anderson). <u>ParisR</u>
        (26:92) Sum 84, p. 125.
    "In the Storm of Roses" (tr. by Mark Anderson).
        <u>ParisR</u> (26:92) Sum 84, p. 131.
    "My Bird" (tr. by Mark Anderson). <u>ParisR</u> (26:92)
        Sum 84, p. 124-125.
    "Night Portrait of Rome" (tr. by Mark Anderson).
        <u>ParisR</u> (26:92) Sum 84, p. 131.
    "Shadow Roses Shadow" (tr. by Mark Anderson).
        <u>ParisR</u> (26:92) Sum 84, p. 126.
    "To the Sun" (tr. by Mark Anderson). <u>ParisR</u>
        (26:92) Sum 84, p. 127-128.
    "We Have Risen and the Cloisters Are Empty" (tr. by
        Mark Anderson). <u>ParisR</u> (26:92) Sum 84, p. 126.

234. BACON, Theresa
    "Cob Daughter." <u>PraS</u> (58:2) Sum 84, p. 16-17.
    "The Gramma Poems: Wheelchair." <u>Calyx</u> (8:3) Aut-
        Wint 84, p. 37-38.
    "Minotaur." <u>PraS</u> (58:2) Sum 84, p. 15-16.

235. BADOR, Bernard
    "Cadaver Cracks in the Lotus Pond" (from Sea Urchin
        Harakiri, tr. by Clayton Eshleman). <u>Sulfur</u>
        (4:1, issue 10) 84, p. 64-66.
    "A Cape of Wild Flies" (from Sea Urchin Harakiri,
        edited by Clayton Eshleman). <u>Sulfur</u> (4:1, issue
        10) 84, p. 66-67.
    "Progress" (from Sea Urchin Harakiri, tr. by Clayton
        Eshleman). <u>Sulfur</u> (4:1, issue 10) 84, p. 63-64.
    "Sea Urchin Harakiri" (Selections, tr. by Clayton
        Eshleman). <u>Sulfur</u> (4:1, issue 10) 84, p. 63-67.

236. BAEHR, Anne-Ruth Ediger
    "Doodle of a Hermit." <u>FourQt</u> (33:4) Sum 84, p. 2-3.

57 BALABAN

237. BAEZA FLORES, Alberto
"Palabras de un Viejo Escriba en la Era
Cibernetica." LindLM (3:1) Ja-Mr 84, p. 26.

238. BAHAN, Lee Harlin
"The Catalpa." IndR (7:3) Sum 84, p. 54-55.
"The Cayenne Lilies." Poem (50) Mr 84, p. 1.

239. BAILEY, Alice Morrey
"Fleeting Hour" (First Prize, 13th Annual Kansas
Poetry Contest). LittleBR (4:3) Spr 84, p. 62.

240. BAILEY, Don
"Easter 1983." CrossC (6:2) 84, p. 15.

241. BAILEY, Donald
"While Breath Remains." SanFPJ (6:3) 84, p. 69.

242. BAILEY, Judy
"Economics." SmPd (21:1) Wint 84, p. 17.
"Houses of Parliament." SmPd (21:1) Wint 84, p. 11.

243. BAILIE, Anne
"Roomette on the Night Express" (Christmas Return to
the Midwest). GreenfR (12:1/2) Sum-Aut 84, p.
102-103.

244. BAKER, David
"8-Ball at the Twilite Lounge" (for Ed Byrne).
MemphisSR (5:1) Aut 84, p. 23.
"The Anniversary of Silence" (May 1972, May 1982).
KenR (NS 6:4) Aut 84, p. 80-81.
"Haunts" (a poem for my birthday." SouthernR
(20:2) Spr 84, p. 437-351.
"Mosquitoes." NowestR (22:1/2) 84, p. 121.
"Running the River Lines" (for Tim Gaines). KenR
(NS 6:4) Aut 84, p. 79.
"The Wrecker Driver Foresees Your Death." AmerS
(53:3) Sum 84, p. 351-352.

245. BAKER, Donald W.
"The Brook That Flowed from the Mountain." PoetC
(16:1) Aut 84, p. 14.
"Burnt Oriole." PoetC (16:1) Aut 84, p. 14.
"Death of a Flower." PoetC (16:1) Aut 84, p. 14.
"Survivals." PoetC (16:1) Aut 84, p. 14.

246. BAKER, Lois
"Wild Columbine." PoetryNW (25:1) Spr 84, p. 9.

247. BAKER, Winona
"Summer's cold." Amelia (1:2) O 84, p. 12.

248. BALABAN, John
"After Our War" (Holiday Inn, Oklahoma City, August,
1973). NewL (50:2/3) Wint-Spr 84, p. 220.
"Hitch-Hiking West, the Poet Invokes the Tibetan
Saint, Milarepa (1052-1135)." NewL (50:4) Sum
84, p. 93.
"Landscape with Three Mountains" (tr. of Ho Xuan

Huong). Hudson (37:3) Aut 84, p. 430.
"Let Him Be" (tr. of Georgi Borisov). NewOR (11:1)
    Spr 84, p. 82.
"Mau Than" (A Poem at Tet for To Lai Chanh,
    Selections: 1, 4). Chelsea (42/43) 84, p. 198-199.

249. BALAKIAN, Peter
    "A Country House." Poetry (145:2) N 84, p. 90-91.
    "Fish Mouth" (For my father, in memory). Poetry
        (145:2) N 84, p. 93-94.
    "The Stuffing, East Orange, 1942." Confr (27/28)
        84, p. 197.
    "That Is Why This Day Passes Like a Thousand
        Lilies." Poetry (144:2) My 84, p. 112.
    "Wild Cherry." Poetry (145:2) N 84, p. 91-92.

250. BALAZS, Mary
    "Age Builds by Fissures." KanQ (16:1/2) Wint-Spr
        84, p. 35.
    "Battered Girl." RagMag (3:2) Aut 84, p. 38.
    "I Move about My Life." RagMag (3:2) Aut 84, p. 39.
    "Poetry-in-the-Schools: Marion." CapeR (19:2) Sum
        84, p. 34.
    "The Seventh Grade in Bustleburg." WebR (9:2) Wint
        85, p. 45.
    "What You Live With." CapeR (19:2) Sum 84, p. 35.

251. BALBO, Ned Clark
    "Boating Incident." SnapD (8:1) Aut 84, p. 35.
    "Today, the Rain Walks." HiramPoR (36) Spr-Sum 84,
        p. 9.

252. BALDERSTON, Jean
    "Battlegrounds." LittleM (14:3) 84, p. 26.

253. BALDWIN, Joseph
    "Lavinia." PraS (58:3) Aut 84, p. 86.
    "Novice in the Hunt." PraS (58:3) Aut 84, p. 87.

254. BALDWIN, Sy Margaret
    "After the War." Cond (3:4, issue 10) 84, p. 64.
    "I work Underground" (For the woman miner killed by
        a falling slab of slate. Coalport, Pennsylvania,
        October 1979). Cond (3:4, issue 10) 84, p. 65-66.

255. BALDY, Gary Daniel
    "The Celibate's Son." PoeticJ (3) 83, p. 26.
    "Drought." PoeticJ (8) 84, p. 13.
    "Phone Book Isolation." PoeticJ (4) 83, p. 44.
    "Reassessment." PoeticJ (8) 84, p. 38.
    "Supplication on a Wet Afternoon." PoeticJ (3) 83,
        p. 12.

256. BALL, Angela
    "Fugue." GrandS (4:1) Aut 84, p. 175.
    "A Short Train Ride." PoetC (16:1) Aut 84, p. 43.
    "Tower." Mund (14:2) 84, p. 65.
    "What." Mund (14:2) 84, p. 64-65.

257. BALL, Joseph H.
    "Christ Spoke to Me." HiramPoR (36) Spr-Sum 84, p.
      10.
    "Mary." SmPd (21:1) Wint 84, p. 32.

258. BALLENTINE, Lee
    "American Town." Veloc (2) Spr 83, p. 15.
    "Cascade" (w. Andrew Joron). Veloc (1) Sum 82, p.
      9-10.
    "Eleg." Veloc (1) Sum 82, p. 23.
    "Lock Step." Veloc (3) Aut-Wint 83, p. 50.
    "My Lady Potato." Veloc (1) Sum 82, p. 21.

259. BALLINGER, Susan M.
    "Lunch." Open24 (3) 84, p. 21.

260. BALTENSPERGER, Peter
    "Ankunft." PoetryCR (6:2) Wint 84-85, p. 13.
    "Arrival." PoetryCR (6:2) Wint 84-85, p. 13.
    "The Cross." Germ (8:1) Spr-Sum 84, p. 9.
    "Dark Figures, Dark Ground." Germ (8:1) Spr-Sum
      84, p. 12.
    "Dursten." PoetryCR (6:2) Wint 84-85, p. 13.
    "Fires in the Sky." Germ (8:1) Spr-Sum 84, p. 13.
    "Full Moon." PoetryCR (6:2) Wint 84-85, p. 13.
    "Judgment." PoetryCR (6:2) Wint 84-85, p. 13.
    "October." Germ (8:1) Spr-Sum 84, p. 8.
    "Recognition." Germ (8:1) Spr-Sum 84, p. 10.
    "Strangers." Germ (8:1) Spr-Sum 84, p. 11.
    "Thirsting." PoetryCR (6:2) Wint 84-85, p. 13.
    "The Trap." WestCR (19:2) O 84, p. 29.
    "Urteil " PoetryCR (6:2) Wint 84-85, p. 13.
    "Vollmond." PoetryCR (6:2) Wint 84-85, p. 13.

261. BAMFORTH, Iain
    "An Arrowhead from the Ancient Battlefield of Ch'ang-
      P'ing" (from the Chinese of Li Ho). KenR (NS
      6:2) Spr 84, p. 72-73.
    "Walking Back to China." KenR (NS 6:2) Spr 84, p.
      69-72.

262. BANBERGER, Ellen
    "1978" (tr. of Sergio Vizcaya and Condega Poetry
      Workshop, w. Marc Zimmerman). MinnR (N.S. 22)
      Spr 84, p. 70.
    "Ballad of Monimbo" (tr. of Cajina Vega, w. Marc
      Zimmerman). MinnR (N.S. 22) Spr 84, p. 77, 81.
    "Commander Two" (tr. of Daisy Zamora, w. Marc
      Zimmerman). MinnR (N.S. 22) Spr 84, p. 73.
    "Communique Number 1,000 for My Love" (tr. of Alba
      Azucena Torres, w. Marc Zimmerman). MinnR (N.S.
      22) Spr 84, p. 79.
    "Demonstration" (tr. of Fernando Antonio Silva, w.
      Marc Zimmerman). MinnR (N.S. 22) Spr 84, p. 71-72.
    "The Gourd" (tr. of Pablo Antonio Cuadra, w. Marc
      Zimmerman). MinnR (N.S. 22) Spr 84, p. 67.
    "In la Bartolina" (tr. of Ivan Guevara, w. Marc
      Zimmerman). MinnR (N.S. 22) Spr 84, p. 69.
    "In My Country" (tr. of Pedro Xavier Solis, w.
      Marc Zimmerman). MinnR (N.S. 22) Spr 84, p. 67.

"In the Prison" (tr. of Daniel Ortega, w. Marc
   Zimmerman). MinnR (N.S. 22) Spr 84, p. 70-72.
"In This Country" (tr. of Ernesto Castillo, w. Marc
   Zimmerman). MinnR (N.S. 22) Spr 84, p. 79-80.
"Let's Go, Comrades" (tr. of Francisco de Asís
   Fernández, w. Marc Zimmerman). MinnR (N.S.
   22) Spr 84, p. 81.
"Letter" (tr. of Alejandro Bravo, w. Marc
   Zimmerman). MinnR (N.S. 22) Spr 84, p. 80.
"Manifesto" (tr. of Alejandro Bravo, w. Marc
   Zimmerman). MinnR (N.S. 22) Spr 84, p. 74-76.
"Monimbo" (tr. of Alejandro Bravo, w. Marc
   Zimmerman). MinnR (N.S. 22) Spr 84, p. 68.
"Point Number 1 on the Agenda" (tr. of Rosario
   Murillo, w. Marc Zimmerman). MinnR (N.S. 22)
   Spr 84, p. 69.
"Proverbs and Songs" (tr. of Michele Najlis, w. Marc
   Zimmerman). MinnR (N.S. 22) Spr 84, p. 68.
"The Rigoberto Lopez Perez Unit" (tr. of Daisy
   Zamora, w. Marc Zimmerman). MinnR (N.S. 22) Spr
   84, p. 73-74.
"There Are Discourses Like These" (tr. of Ivan
   Guevara, w. Marc Zimmerman). MinnR (N.S. 22)
   Spr 84, p. 74-77.
"A Time Will Come" (tr. of Daisy Zamora, w. Marc
   Zimmerman). MinnR (N.S. 22) Spr 84, p. 80.
"We Live in a Rush" (tr. of Dora María Tellez, w.
   Marc Zimmerman). MinnR (N.S. 22) Spr 84, p. 72-73.

263. BANDEIRA, Manuel
   "The Morning Star" (tr. by Manoel Cardozo). Vis
   (15) 84, p. 9.

264. BANKS, Kenneth
   "Helen." AntigR (56) Wint 84, p. 67.
   "Magdalene." AntigR (56) Wint 84, p. 68.
   "The Poet." AntigR (56) Wint 84, p. 66.
   "The Tyrian Veil." AntigR (57) Spr 84, p. 115.

265. BANUS, Maria
   "At the End" (tr. by Diana Der Hovanessian). Kayak
   (64) My 84, p. 21.
   "Daimon" (tr. by Diana Der Hovanessian). Kayak
   (64) My 84, p. 19.
   "Patio" (tr. by Diana Der Hovanessian). Kayak (64)
   My 84, p. 19.
   "Prejudice" (tr. by Diana Der Hovanessian). Kayak
   (64) My 84, p. 20.
   "Separation" (tr. by Diana Der Hovanessian). Kayak
   (64) My 84, p. 20.
   "Stripped" (tr. by Diana Der Hovanessian). Kayak
   (64) My 84, p. 21.
   "Time" (tr. by Diana Der Hovanessian). Kayak (64)
   My 84, p. 21.

266. BAQUERO, Gastón
   "Brandeburgo 1526" (Del libro inédito
   Treintaidós magias e invenciones). LindLM
   (3:1) Ja-Mr 84, p. 17.

267. BARADELLE, Marianne
    "Note to a Friend." Quarry (33:1) Wint 84, p. 72.

268. BARAKA, Amina
    "Afroamerican Child" (A Documentation). Stepping
    (Anniversary Issue I) 84, p. 13-15.

269. BARAKA, Amiri
    "Bad News" (for Charlie Richardson). Stepping
    (Premier Issue) Sum 82, p. 8-9.
    "The Fascist." Stepping (Premier Issue) Sum 82, p.
    10.
    "In World War 3 Even Your Muse Will Get Killed!"
    Stepping (Premier Issue) Sum 82, p. 6.
    "Kinda Black." Stepping (Premier Issue) Sum 82, p.
    11-12.
    "Linguistics." Stepping (Premier Issue) Sum 82, p. 5.
    "Terry & the Pirates' Replacement." Stepping
    (Premier Issue) Sum 82, p. 7.

270. BARALE, Michele
    "The Young Make Love Like." Calyx (8:3) Aut-Wint
    84, p. 30.

271. BARANCZAK, Stanislaw
    "December 15, 1979: Dizzy with Success" (tr. by
    Magnus J. Krynski and Robert A. Maguire). Confr
    (27/28) 84, p. 19.
    "December 19, 1979: Clean Hands" (tr. by Magnus J.
    Krynski and Robert A. Maguire). Confr (27/28)
    84, p. 20.

272. BARANOW, Joan
    "Boys." MSS (4:1/2) Aut 84, p. 99.
    "Daniel." LittleM (14:3) 84, p. 59.
    "Dedicated to My Creative Writing Students."
    LittleM (14:3) 84, p. 60-63.

273. BARBA, Rose
    "Paper Hat" (reading Basho, The Narrow Road to the
    Deep North). NewL (50:4) Sum 84, p. 65.

274. BARBAN, Elsa
    "Mirame hacia Adentro." Mairena (5:13) Spr 83, p.
    88-89.

275. BARBARESE, J. T.
    "Joseph." CarolQ (37:1) Aut 84, p. 11.

276. BARBARITO, Carlos
    "En vano me han sido prodigados el océano."
    Mairena (6:17) Aut 84, p. 70.

277. BARBER, Ellen J.
    "Extra Inning" (Ohio High School Creative Writing
    Contest Winner). WoosterR (1:1) Mr 84, p. 86-87.

278. BARBOUR, Doug
    "17.06.79." BlueBuf (2:2) Spr 84, p. 15.
    "The Letter." BlueBuf (2:2) Spr 84, p. 16.

279. BARBOUR, Douglas
     "Alice" (homolinguistic (acrostic) translation of
     Gertrude Stein's "Carafe that is a blind glass").
     <u>Veloc</u> (2) Spr 83, p. 51-52.
     "An Alphabet" (for Barbara Caruso). <u>MalR</u> (69) O
     84, p. 11-18.
     "In the Midnight Hours." <u>CanLit</u> (100) Spr 84, p.
     21-23.
     "These for Those from Whom: #8: AP & AEVV." <u>Veloc</u>
     (2) Spr 83, p. 48-49.

280. BARCIA, Hugo
     "Responso." <u>Mairena</u> (6:17) Aut 84, p. 78.

281. BARCLAY, Heather
     "Darker Than Memory." <u>CrabCR</u> (1:3) Wint 84, p. 19-21.

282. BARDENS, Ann
     "Awakening." <u>KanQ</u> (16:1/2) Wint-Spr 84, p. 58.
     "Salmacis." <u>KanQ</u> (16:1/2) Wint-Spr 84, p. 59.

283. BAREIRO SAGUIER, Ruben
     "Historia Trivial." <u>Mairena</u> (6:18) 84, p. 189.

284. BARG, Lois
     "Independence." <u>PoeticJ</u> (4) 83, p. 31.
     "Mya." <u>PoeticJ</u> (4) 83, p. 6.
     "The Runaway." <u>PoeticJ</u> (7) 84, p. 38.
     "Sunrise." <u>PoeticJ</u> (4) 83, p. 20.

285. BARGAD, W.
     "November '73" (tr. of Dan Pagis). <u>Pequod</u> (16/17)
     84, p. 110.

286. BARGEN, Walter
     "Adam Gives Thanks." <u>WebR</u> (9:2) Wint 85, p. 57.
     "Adam Laments." <u>WebR</u> (9:2) Wint 85, p. 59.
     "Adam's Stroke of Genius." <u>WebR</u> (9:2) Wint 85, p. 58.
     "A Dog's Life." <u>SpoonRQ</u> (9:2) Spr 84, p. 54.
     "Expert Victims." <u>Vis</u> (16) 84, p. 22.
     "Hay Lake, Minnesota." <u>WebR</u> (9:1) Spr 84, p. 66.
     "How Good It Is." <u>WebR</u> (9:1) Spr 84, p. 64.
     "Kinnickinnic River." <u>WebR</u> (9:1) Spr 84, p. 65.
     "Little Creek Baptist Church." <u>Vis</u> (14) 84, p. 17.
     "The Sign." <u>SpoonRQ</u> (9:4) Aut 84, p. 44-45.
     "Walking Down Wind" (Selections: b, e, f). <u>Wind</u>
     (14:50) 84, p. 2-3.

287. BARGER, Rita
     "Forgetting." <u>PoeticJ</u> (3) 83, p. 37.
     "Friends." <u>PoeticJ</u> (4) 83, p. 12.
     "Goodbye." <u>PoeticJ</u> (7) 84, p. 3.
     "It's Your Hands I'm Afraid Of." <u>PoeticJ</u> (8) 84,
     p. 9.
     "Quicksand." <u>PoeticJ</u> (4) 83, p. 12.
     "Your Anger." <u>PoeticJ</u> (2) 83, p. 13.

288. BARI, Karoly
     "Gypsy Wanderers" (tr. by Timothy Kachinske). <u>LitR</u>
     (27:3) Spr 84, p. 304-305.

289. BARILE, Tamara D.
"Becoming" (tr. of Neusa Cardoso). <u>Waves</u> (12:2/3)
Wint 84, p. 70.
"Daily News" (tr. of Neusa Cardoso). <u>Waves</u>
(12:2/3) Wint 84, p. 68.
"Dieu" (tr. of Neusa Cardoso). <u>Waves</u> (12:2/3) Wint
84, p. 66.
"God" (tr. of Neusa Cardoso). <u>Waves</u> (12:2/3) Wint
84, p. 66.
"Megalopole" (tr. of Neusa Cardoso). <u>Waves</u>
(12:2/3) Wint 84, p. 67.
"Megalopolis" (tr. of Neusa Cardoso). <u>Waves</u>
(12:2/3) Wint 84, p. 67.
"Nouvelles Populaires" (tr. of Neusa Cardoso).
<u>Waves</u> (12:2/3) Wint 84, p. 69.
"The Scorpion and the Minuet" (selections, tr. of
Neusa Cardoso). <u>Waves</u> (12:2/3) Wint 84, p. 66-70.
"Le Scorpion et le Menuet" (selections, tr. of Neusa
Cardoso). <u>Waves</u> (12:2/3) Wint 84, p. 66-70.
"Tournant" (tr. of Neusa Cardoso). <u>Waves</u> (12:2/3)
Wint 84, p. 70.

290. BARKER, Christine
"Sometimes." <u>BlueBuf</u> (2:2) Spr 84, p. 28.

291. BARKER, David
"10,000 Volts, Seven Black Widows, All Adults and My
Wife's New Red Pants." <u>WormR</u> (24:2, issue 94)
84, p. 60.
"A Bat Out of Hell." <u>WormR</u> (24:2, issue 94) 84, p.
63-64.
"Cats." <u>WormR</u> (24:2, issue 94) 84, p. 65-66.
"Like a Mad House Light." <u>WormR</u> (24:2, issue 94)
84, p. 56-57.
"Lunch Time." <u>WormR</u> (24:2, issue 94) 84, p. 62.
"Maybe It's the Rinse Cycle." <u>WormR</u> (24:2, issue
94) 84, p. 59.
"No One Calls Me Any More" (Special Section).
<u>WormR</u> (24:2, issue 94) 84, p. 55-66.
"No One Calls Me Any More." <u>WormR</u> (24:2, issue 94)
84, p. 63.
"The Plant Ladies." <u>WormR</u> (24:2, issue 94) 84, p. 56.
"A Poem for the Boss." <u>WormR</u> (24:2, issue 94) 84,
p. 61.
"Pool Party." <u>WormR</u> (24:2, issue 94) 84, p. 64-65.
"Poor." <u>WormR</u> (24:2, issue 94) 84, p. 61-62.
"Something Spanish." <u>WormR</u> (24:2, issue 94) 84, p.
57-58.
"La Strada." <u>WormR</u> (24:2, issue 94) 84, p. 58-59.

292. BARKER, Lucile Angela
"Affirmative Action." <u>Sam</u> (39:1, release 153) 84,
p. 19.

293. BARKER, Lucile Angela Morreale
"For My Unwanted Shadow." <u>ArizQ</u> (40:1) Spr 84, p. 74.

294. BARKETT, Diane DeMichele
"Leveler." <u>SanFPJ</u> (6:2) 84, p. 13.
"Pendulum." <u>SanFPJ</u> (6:1) 84, p. 57.

"Red Badge of Whatever." <u>SanFPJ</u> (6:2) 84, p. 14.
"Tree of Knowledge." <u>SanFPJ</u> (6:2) 84, p. 15.
"Wait, You." <u>SanFPJ</u> (6:1) 84, p. 7.

295. BARKS, Coleman
     "Higdon Cove." <u>PoetryE</u> (15) Aut 84, p. 65.

296. BARLOW, Lolete Falck
     "Old Mobile." <u>NegC</u> (4:3) Sum 84, p. 121.

297. BARNES, Jim
     "Black Mesa Sundown." <u>SouthwR</u> (69:2) Spr 84, p. 181.
     "Consolation." <u>NewL</u> (50:2/3) Wint-Spr 84, p. 245.
     "Dirge." <u>PoetryE</u> (15) Aut 84, p. 47-48.
     "La Plata, Missouri: Clear November Night" (for
        Dagmar Nick). <u>NewL</u> (51:1) Aut 84, p. 96-97.
     "Toy Soldiers." <u>Agni</u> (21) 84, p. 101-102.
     "You Know Who You Are: This Is For You, My Friend."
        <u>NewL</u> (51:1) Aut 84, p. 96.

298. BARNES, Kim
     "Between Nehalem and Manzanita -- Oregon Coast,
        1983." <u>SnapD</u> (8:1) Aut 84, p. 4-5.
     "Infestation." <u>SnapD</u> (8:1) Aut 84, p. 3.

299. BARNES, Mike
     "Calm Jazz Sea." <u>Waves</u> (12:2/3) Wint 84, p. 89.

300. BARNES, Richard
     "Concentrics." <u>Poetry</u> (144:4) Jl 84, p. 220.
     "Poem at Thirty." <u>BlueBldgs</u> (7) 84, p. 45.
     "Watering the Lawn." <u>Poetry</u> (144:4) Jl 84, p. 220-
        221.

301. BARNET, Miguel
     "Patria." <u>Mairena</u> (6:18) 84, p. 175.

302. BARNIE, John
     "Churches." <u>LitR</u> (28:1) Aut 84, p. 44.
     "Patient Griselda." <u>LitR</u> (28:1) Aut 84, p. 45.

303. BARNSTONE, Willis
     "The Angel." <u>NewL</u> (50:2/3) Wint-Spr 84, p. 133.
     "God." <u>NewL</u> (50:2/3) Wint-Spr 84, p. 132-133.
     "It Is Raining" (tr. of Bronislava Volek, w. the
        author). <u>Nimrod</u> (27:2) Spr-Sum 84, p. 75.
     "Looking for You." <u>LitR</u> (28:1) Aut 84, p. 129.
     "Nightingale." <u>MassR</u> (25:2) Sum 84, p. 222.
     "Oil Lamp." <u>SewanR</u> (92:1) Ja-Mr 84, p. 58.
     "Old Song." <u>SouthernPR</u> (24:1) Spr 84, p. 28.
     "Rain" (tr. of Jorge Luis Borges). <u>NewL</u> (50:2/3)
        Wint-Spr 84, p. 134.
     "Reading Li Ch'ing-Chao." <u>MassR</u> (25:2) Sum 84, p.
        222.
     "Supper" (tr. of Bronislava Volek, w. the author).
        <u>Nimrod</u> (27:2) Spr-Sum 84, p. 75.
     "Twilights." <u>Nimrod</u> (27:2) Spr-Sum 84, p. 15.
     "Ubiarco in July." <u>Nimrod</u> (27:2) Spr-Sum 84, p. 14.
     "Wandering Loose in Shaoshan." <u>Chelsea</u> (42/43) 84,
        p. 298.

304. BARONE, Patricia
     "Reduction Block." BlueBldgs (8) 84?, p. 39.

305. BARQUERO, Efrain
     "Yo Te Beso al Irme." Mairena (6:18) 84, p. 136.

306. BARQUET, Jesús J.
     "Imperiosidad de Angel." LindLM (3:1) Ja-Mr 84, p.
     28.

307. BARR, Allan
     "Seeing Nothing at Close Range." AntigR (59) Aut
     84, p. 112.

308. BARR, Bob
     "Upon a Child Who Was Ill in Winter." SoDakR
     (22:2) Sum 84, p. 24.

309. BARR, Tina
     "Household." PraS (58:2) Sum 84, p. 18.
     "Night before Moving." PaintedB (21) Wint 84, p. 9.
     "The Swim." PraS (58:2) Sum 84, p. 19.

310. BARRESI, Dorothy
     "Calvin Coolidge Asleep." MinnR (N.S. 23) Aut 84,
     p. 123-124.
     "The Judas Clock." BlueBldgs (8) 84?, p. 34.
     "Large Families." Tendril (17) Wint 84, p. 16.
     "Last Names" (for my sister). PoetryNW (25:1) Spr
     84, p. 13-15.
     "Renoir's The Luncheon of the Boating Party."
     PoetryNW (25:1) Spr 84, p. 16-17.
     "Small Claims." PoetryNW (25:1) Spr 84, p. 15-16.
     "Song for One More Departure." PoetryNW (25:4)
     Wint 84-85, p. 40-41.

311. BARRETO-RIVERA, Rafael (See also FOUR HORSEMEN)
     "Scrabble Babble." CapilR (31) 84, p. 35.

312. BARRETT, Carol
     "Picture Window." Sam (39:1, release 153) 84, p. 16.
     "Road to Shadow Mountain, Colorado." TarRP (23:2)
     Spr 84, p. 14.
     "Trail Blazing." Nimrod (27:2) Spr-Sum 84, p. 16-17.

BARRETT, Donalee Moulton: See MOULTON-BARRETT, Donalee

313. BARRETT, Lou
     "Piggyback Ride." PoeticJ (8) 84, p. 27.

314. BARRIER, Don
     "Gut Shot." Vis (16) 84, p. 39.
     "Such Feet Little Horse." Vis (16) 84, p. 38.

315. BARRON, Monica
     "Pentwater." Telescope (3:3) Aut 84, p. 52.

316. BARROS, Daniel
     "Carlitos Gardel." _Mairena_ (6:18) 84, p. 114.

317. BARRY, Jan
     "A Childhood Tale." _Sam_ (39:2, release 154) 84, p.
        4-5.
     "A Childhood Tale II." _Sam_ (39:2, release 154) 84,
        p. 10.
     "Gifts." _Sam_ (39:2, release 154) 84, p. 2.
     "Lessons." _Sam_ (39:2, release 154) 84, p. 11-12.
     "A Nun in Ninh Hoa." _Sam_ (39:2, release 154) 84,
        p. 8.
     "Sparrow." _Sam_ (39:2, release 154) 84, p. 6-7.
     "War Baby" (issue title). _Sam_ (39:2, release 154)
        84, p. 1-12.
     "War Baby." _Sam_ (39:2, release 154) 84, p. 3.
     "Young Soldiers, Old War." _Sam_ (39:2, release 154)
        84, p. 9.

318. BARRY, Sebastian
     "A Consolation" (tr. of Steinunn Sigurdardottir, w.
        the author). _NewOR_ (11:2) Sum 84, p. 22.

319. BARTH, R. L.
     "Confiteor." _TriQ_ (59) Wint 84, p. 130.
     "Definition." _TriQ_ (59) Wint 84, p. 130.
     "The Disappearance." _TriQ_ (59) Wint 84, p. 131.
     "For Any Memorial Day." _TriQ_ (59) Wint 84, p. 130.
     "Last Letter" (J.H., who threw himself on a grenade
        to save the lives of six men with him). _Pig_
        (12) 84, p. 36.
     "Marilyn Monroe, a Note to Mail Her and Others."
        TriQ (59) Wint 84, p. 131.
     "A Meditation after Battle." _Pig_ (12) 84, p. 17.
     "To the Lady Who Refused to Purchase My Book of War
        Poems." _TriQ_ (59) Wint 84, p. 130.

BARTHE, Penelope la: _See_ LaBARTHE, Penelope

320. BARTKOWECH, R.
     "Midnight Marching Band." _GreenfR_ (12:1/2) Sum-Aut
        84, p. 155-156.
     "Skyscraper." _WoosterR_ (1:2) N 84, p. 91.

321. BARTKOWECH, Ray
     "The Refusal." _PoeticJ_ (5) 84, p. 31.

322. BARTLETT, Elizabeth
     "Trees." _StoneC_ (11:3/4) Spr-Sum 84, p. 24-25.
     "Undeniable." _AntigR_ (57) Spr 84, p. 33.

323. BARTLETT, Lee
     "And All the Lambs Go Down to Their Final Resting
        Place." _CalQ_ (23/24) Spr-Sum 84, p. 51.
     "In Dreams Begin." _CalQ_ (23/24) Spr-Sum 84, p. 50.
     "Lady in a Green Jacket." _YetASM_ (3) 84, p. 3.
     "Waiting for the Bus." _CalQ_ (23/24) Spr-Sum 84, p.
        49.

324. BARTLETT, Stephen
"Unemployment Line." SanFPJ (6:3) 84, p. 29-30.

325. BARTOLE, Genevieve
"Montmartre." PoetryCR (5:4) Sum 84, p. 8.

326. BARTON, David
"A Death in Hollywood." Telescope (3:3) Aut 84, p.
53-55.

327. BARTON, John
"In My Twenty-fifth Year." WestCR (19:1) Je 84, p.
28-29.
"Laughing Forest." Descant (47, 15:4) Wint 84, p.
7-8.
"Mother Was Gentle." Grain (12:1) F 84, p. 11-13.
"A Skidegate Pole." Descant (47, 15:4) Wint 84, p.
9-10.
"Suddenly Glancing Up from My Book" (after Robin
Skelton). Waves (12:1) Aut 83, p. 20.
"A Summer's Tale." Quarry (33:3) Sum 84, p. 4-6.
"Tapestry." WestCR (19:1) Je 84, p. 29-30.

328. BARTOW, Stuart
"After the People Have Gone." PoeticJ (6) 84, p. 8.

329. BASHŌ
"Ah! summer grasses!" NewL (50:2/3) Wint-Spr 84,
p. 230.
"Fish shop" (Haiku from the Japanese Masters, tr. by
Lucien Stryk and Takashi Ikemoto, calligraphy by
Lloyd J. Reynolds). NewL (50:2/3) Wint-Spr 84,
p. 140.
"Moor" (Haiku from the Japanese Masters, tr. by
Lucien Stryk and Takashi Ikemoto, calligraphy by
Lloyd J. Reynolds). NewL (50:2/3) Wint-Spr 84,
p. 140.

330. BASMAJIAN, Shaunt
"The Jilted Poet." WritersL (1) 84, p. 9.

331. BASSINSKI, Bob
"The Second Nuclear Attack, or the Completion."
PortR (30:1) 84, p. 151.

332. BASTIAN, Richard
"For Ginya." Poem (51) Mr [i.e. Jl] 84, p. 62.
"For My First Love, Roses and Streams" (For Judy).
Poem (51) Mr [i.e. Jl] 84, p. 61.
"Quiet Heroes." Poem (51) Mr [i.e. Jl] 84, p. 63.

BASTOS, Augusto Roa: See ROA BASTOS, Augusto

333. BATAILLE, Gabriel
"Qui Veut Chasser une Migraine." NegC (4:1) Wint
84, p. 53-55.
"Who Wants to Cure a Migraine" (tr. by W. D.
Snodgrass). NegC (4:1) Wint 84, p. 53-55.

334. BATHANTI, Joseph
    "The Holy Men of Loveladies." <u>BelPoJ</u> (35:2) Wint
    84-85, p. 30-31.

335. BATTLO, Jean
    "Irv's Requium." <u>WindO</u> (44) Sum-Aut 84, p. 17.
    "Me, Contemplating 'Astrological Facts and
    Cosmological Theories' in Kung's <u>Does God Exist</u>
    One Morning in June." <u>WindO</u> (44) Sum-Aut 84, p.
    15.

336. BAUCH, Michael
    "Crip." <u>PikeF</u> (6) Aut 84, p. 8.

337. BAUDELAIRE, Charles
    "The Lighthouses" (tr. by James Hatley). <u>WebR</u>
    (9:2) Wint 85, p. 14-15.

338. BAUMEL, Judith
    "Details." <u>Agni</u> (21) 84, p. 81-82.
    "Our Differences." <u>Agni</u> (21) 84, p. 79-80.

339. BAWER, Bruce
    "The Man Given Ten Minutes at the End." <u>PoetryNW</u>
    (25:1) Spr 84, p. 22-23.

340. BAXTER, Charles
    "Falling Asleep in Michigan." <u>BelPoJ</u> (34:3) Spr
    84, p. 1.
    "Imaginary Painting: Beggar in the Snow." <u>MinnR</u>
    (N.S. 22) Spr 84, p. 28.

341. BAYO, Gérard
    "3.885 Hectares." <u>Bound</u> (12:1) Aut 83, p. 224.
    "9,600 Acres" (tr. by Ellen Kocher). <u>Bound</u> (12:1)
    Aut 83, p. 225.
    "Au Sommet de la Nuit" (Selections in French and
    English, tr. by Ellen Kocher). <u>Bound</u> (12:1) Aut
    83, p. 219-225.
    "The Black Woods" (tr. by Ellen Kocher). <u>Bound</u>
    (12:1) Aut 83, p. 223.
    "Le Bois Noir." <u>Bound</u> (12:1) Aut 83, p. 222.
    "Comme une Horloge." <u>Bound</u> (12:1) Aut 83, p. 220.
    "Les Forces de l'Ordre." <u>Bound</u> (12:1) Aut 83, p. 222.
    "Law and Order" (tr. by Ellen Kocher). <u>Bound</u>
    (12:1) Aut 83, p. 223.
    "Like a Clock" (tr. by Ellen Kocher). <u>Bound</u> (12:1)
    Aut 83, p. 221.
    "Soir d'Eté." <u>Bound</u> (12:1) Aut 83, p. 220.
    "Summer Evening" (tr. by Ellen Kocher). <u>Bound</u>
    (12:1) Aut 83, p. 221.

342. BEAKE, Fred
    "Mrs James." <u>Stand</u> (25:3) Sum 84, p. 64-65.

343. BEALE, Judith C.
    "The Children." <u>SouthernR</u> (20:2) Spr 84, p. 371-373.

344. BEALL, Sandra Maness
    "In Einstein's House, in the Closet." <u>BlueBldgs</u>

        (7) 84, p. 49.
    "The Obsession." BlueBldgs (7) 84, p. 49.
    "Walking in the Woods, a genius." BlueBldgs (7)
        84, p. 49.

345. BEAM, Mary Ernestine
    "Still Life." Wind (14:52) 84, p. 2.

BEAR, Ray A. Young: See YOUNG BEAR, Ray A.

346. BEASLEY, Bruce
    "Ascension Day." PoetL (79:1) Spr 84, p. 27.
    "At Easter." SenR (14:1) 84, p. 19-20.
    "Going Back." MissouriR (7:3) 84, p. 30.
    "Pietà." MemphisSR (4:2) Spr 84, p. 28.

347. BECK, Gary
    "Dawn in Cities, XVII." Poem (51) Mr [i.e. Jl] 84,
        p. 58.
    "Holocaust Road." PortR (30:1) 84, p. 139.
    "Idolatry." Poem (51) Mr [i.e. Jl] 84, p. 57.
    "Moon over Vermont." Veloc (4) Sum 84, p. 30.
    "Peace." PortR (30:1) 84, p. 156.
    "Renaissance." Veloc (4) Sum 84, p. 31.

348. BECKER, Therese
    "A Colorless Tale." ThirdW (2) Spr 84, p. 10.

349. BECOUSSE, Raoul
    "Descent under the Sea" (from Le Temps Provisoire,
        tr. by Louis A. Olivier). PikeF (6) Aut 84, p. 14.

350. BEDDOES, Thomas Lovell
    "Hymn: And many voices marshalled in one hymn."
        GrandS (3:4) Sum 84, p. 102.

351. BEDWELL, Carol
    "The Crow" (tr. of Christoph Meckel). PoetL (79:1)
        Spr 84, p. 42-43.
    "Jonas Speakes" (tr. of Christoph Meckel). PoetL
        (79:1) Spr 84, p. 44.
    "Rembrandt, Self-Portraits" (tr. of Christoph
        Meckel). PoetL (79:1) Spr 84, p. 44.

BEEK, Edith van: See Van BEEK, Edith

352. BEEK, F. Ten Harmsen V. D.
    "Good morning? Heavenly Mrs. Ping" (To my despondent
        cat, to console her on the death of her
        offspring, tr. by Pleuke Boyce). MalR (68) Je
        84, p. 26-27.
    "Obscure Correspondence and Its Unhappy
        Consequences, in Two Verses" (tr. by Pleuke
        Boyce). MalR (68) Je 84, p. 28-30.

353. BEGIN, Tom C.
    "Miscount." PottPort (6) 84, p. 31.

354. BEGUIRISTAIN, Mario E.
    "Diciendo lo Indecible." Areíto (9:36) 84, p. 6.

355. BEHAN, Marie
    "Horror Movie." <u>Amelia</u> (1:2) O 84, p. 30-31.

356. BEHAR, Ruth
    "Do Not Drag Me Down." <u>LindLM</u> (3:2/4) Ap-D 84, p. 22.

357. BEHM, Richard
    "After Prospero's Epilogue." <u>NegC</u> (4:3) Sum 84, p. 96-97.
    "The Apple Tree." <u>NegC</u> (4:3) Sum 84, p. 97.
    "Beetle Picking." <u>Poem</u> (50) Mr 84, p. 35.
    "In a Small Town, Hope." <u>SpoonRQ</u> (9:2) Spr 84, p. 53.
    "Meditation at the Edge of Lake Superior." <u>NegC</u> (4:3) Sum 84, p. 98.
    "The Origin and Purpose of Baseball." <u>QW</u> (18) Spr-Sum 84, p. 98-99.
    "A Poem That Could Be about a Giraffe." <u>SnapD</u> (6:2) Spr 83, p. 5.
    "Railroad St. the Doppler Effect." <u>Poem</u> (50) Mr 84, p. 36.
    "What the Woman Who Said She Was Not Crazy Told Me." <u>CalQ</u> (23/24) Spr-Sum 84, p. 123.

358. BEHN, Robin
    "Geographies" (Tom McAfee 1927-1982). <u>AmerPoR</u> (13:4) Jl-Ag 84, p. 21.
    "Living with Sister." <u>AmerPoR</u> (13:4) Jl-Ag 84, p. 21.
    "Night Sail off Raber." <u>AntR</u> (42:3) Sum 84, p. 329.
    "To Rise, So Suddenly" (for Phil Mark). <u>GeoR</u> (38:4) Wint 84, p. 824.

359. BEINING, Guy R.
    "Rebirth #20." <u>Abraxas</u> (29/30) 84, p. 38.

360. BEISCH, June
    "A Fatherless Woman." <u>Tendril</u> (17) Wint 84, p. 18.
    "Two Objects Cannot Occupy the Same Space at the Same Time." <u>Tendril</u> (17) Wint 84, p. 17.

361. BEJEL, Emilio
    "Cuerpos Resucitados." <u>Areíto</u> (9:36) 84, p. 104.
    "Quo Vadis?" <u>Areíto</u> (9:36) 84, p. 15.

BEKY, Iván de: <u>See</u> De BEKY, Iván

362. BELASIK, Paul
    "Owl." <u>SmPd</u> (21:1) Wint 84, p. 13.
    "Shedding." <u>SmPd</u> (21:1) Wint 84, p. 14.

363. BELEVAN, Enriqueta
    "Breve Carta de Amor y Despedida." <u>Mairena</u> (6:18) 84, p. 98.
    "Más allá de la delgadísima voz que no cesa." <u>Mairena</u> (6:16) Spr 84, p. 77.
    "La noche es esta tarde hiriente de sol traspasando." <u>Mairena</u> (6:16) Spr 84, p. 78.
    "Pier Paolo." <u>Mairena</u> (6:16) Spr 84, p. 78.
    "Tocar un cascabel de porcelana en el aire." <u>Mairena</u> (6:16) Spr 84, p. 77.

364. BELFIELD, Judy
     "Basics." <u>Sam</u> (41:2, release 162) 84 or 85, p. 51.
     "Catastrophe for Breakfast, December, 1980."
       <u>SanFPJ</u> (6:2) 84, p. 17.
     "Misanthrope." <u>SanFPJ</u> (6:2) 84, p. 16.

365. BELITT, Ben
     "Possessions" (For Nick Mayer). <u>Salm</u> (63/64) Spr-
       Sum 84, p. 200-203.

366. BELL, Bill
     "Working in America." <u>SanFPJ</u> (6:1) 84, p. 73.

367. BELL, Carolyn Light
     "The Grafting of Hybrids." <u>BlueBldgs</u> (7) 84, p. 43.

368. BELL, Charles G.
     "Sursum Corda." <u>NewL</u> (50:2/3) Wint-Spr 84, p. 107.
     "To Galway." <u>NewL</u> (50:2/3) Wint-Spr 84, p. 106.
     "Weed Farm." <u>NewL</u> (50:2/3) Wint-Spr 84, p. 106.

369. BELL, Marvin
     "Chicago, 1959." <u>TriQ</u> (60) Spr-Sum 84, p. 128-129.
     "Days of Time." <u>AmerPoR</u> (13:2) Mr-Ap 84, p. 4.
     "Drawn by Stones, by Earth, by Things That Have Been
       in the Fire." <u>NewYorker</u> (59:46) 2 Ja 84, p. 34.
     "The Facts of Life." <u>AmerPoR</u> (13:2) Mr-Ap 84, p. 3.
     "He Said To." <u>AmerPoR</u> (13:6) N-D 84, p. 41.
     "In." <u>AmerPoR</u> (13:2) Mr-Ap 84, p. 3.
     "In Those Days." <u>AmerPoR</u> (13:2) Mr-Ap 84, p. 4.
     "Leaving a Resort Town." <u>AmerPoR</u> (13:2) Mr-Ap 84,
       p. 3.
     "One of the Animals." <u>VirQR</u> (60:2) Spr 84, p. 232-
       233.
     "Overcast." <u>Sparrow</u> (46) 84, p. 8.
     "Starfish." <u>NewEngR</u> (6:3) Spr 84, p. 474.
     "They." <u>Antaeus</u> (52) Apr 84, p. 50.
     "Three Letters." <u>VirQR</u> (60:2) Spr 84, p. 230-232.
     "To an Adolescent Weeping Willow." <u>Tendril</u> (18,
       special issue) 84, p. 294-295.
     "To Be." <u>AmerPoR</u> (13:2) Mr-Ap 84, p. 4.
     "Trees As Standing for Something." <u>VirQR</u> (60:2)
       Spr 84, p. 229.
     "Unless It Was Courage." <u>NewYorker</u> (59:50) 30 Ja
       84, p. 40.
     "Who & Where." <u>VirQR</u> (60:2) Spr 84, p. 233-234.
     "A Young Woman Sunning in the Nude." <u>AmerPoR</u>
       (13:2) Mr-Ap 84, p. 4.
     "Youth." <u>Antaeus</u> (52) Apr 84, p. 49.

370. BELL, Sandy
     "What?" <u>PoetryCR</u> (6:1) Aut 84, p. 14.

371. BELLA, István
     "Variations" (tr. by Jascha Kessler). <u>GrahamHR</u>
       (7) Wint 84, p. 57.

BELLA DONNA: <u>See</u> DONNA, Bella

372. BELLADONNA
"Xmas Cock." YellowS (13) Wint 84, p. 24.

373. BELLG, Albert
"Lloyd Reynolds, Calligrapher" (in memoriam). NewL
(50:2/3) Wint-Spr 84, p. 138.

374. BELLI, Gioconda
"Canto al Nuevo Tiempo" (fragmento). Mairena
(6:18) 84, p. 161.
"Orchid of Steel" (tr. by Electa Arenal and Gabriela
Dreye). Nat (238:3) 28 Ja 84, p. 100.
"Other People's Blood" (tr. by David Volpendesta).
Vis (15) 84, p. 27.

375. BELLUCCI, Lucille
"Obi." YellowS (12) Aut 84, p. 30.

376. BELTRAMETTI, Franco
"October October." Origin (5:3) Spr 84, p. 38-43.

377. BEN-TOV, S.
"Earhart Flies through the Monsoon" (Correction to
second stanza as printed in fall 1983 issue).
PraS (58:1) Spr 84, p. 81.

378. BEN-TOV, Sharona
"Carillon for Cambridge Women." ParisR (26:93) Aut
84, p. 192-196.

379. BENAVIE, Barbara
"Fabius Lind's Days" (tr. of A. Leyeles, w. Benjamin
Hrushovski). PartR (51:1) 84, p. 101-102.
"Letter to Sigmund Freud" (tr. of J. L. Teller, w.
Benjamin Hrushovski). PartR (51:1) 84, p. 102-103.

380. BENDER, M. J.
"Palisadian Disturbance." Origin (5:3) Spr 84, p.
5-36.

381. BENDIT, Devy
"Bachelor Party." StoneC (11:3/4) Spr-Sum 84, p.
66-67.
"True Confessions." Open24 (3) 84, p. 18.

382. BENDON, Chris
"Welsh Encounters." PoetryCR (5:4) Sum 84, p. 14.

383. BENEDIKT, Michael
"Big Eyes." MemphisSR (4:2) Spr 84, p. 20.
"Definitive Things." Chelsea (42/43) 84, p. 240.
"Right in the Middle of Everything." ParisR
(26:91) Spr 84, p. 120-121.
"To an Overly Literary Lady" (for C.A.). MemphisSR
(4:2) Spr 84, p. 20.
"The Tornado" (tr. of Aimé Césaire). Chelsea
(42/43) 84, p. 261.

384. BENEY, Zsuzsa
"A Broken Glass" (tr. by Jascha Kessler).

GrahamHR (7) Wint 84, p. 55-56.

385. BENFEY, Christopher
"Flamingos." Ploughs (10:1) 84, p. 18.
"Reading Jane Austen at 3 A.M." Ploughs (10:1) 84,
p. 17.

386. BENGTSDOTTER, Karen
"Growing Up and Anxious." SanFPJ (7:1) 84, p. 85.

387. BENNANI, Ben
"I Said to You" (tr. of Adunis). GreenfR (11:1/2)
Sum-Aut 83, p. 216.

388. BENNETT, Maria
"DC 7B" (tr. of Ernesto Cardenal). CrabCR (2:1)
Sum 84, p. 19.
"Epigrams" (tr. of Ernesto Cardenal). CrabCR (2:1)
Sum 84, p. 16-17.
"Imitation of Propertius" (tr. of Ernesto Cardenal).
CrabCR (2:1) Sum 84, p. 18.
"Murder, Inc." (tr. of Ernesto Cardenal). CrabCR
(2:1) Sum 84, p. 19.

389. BENNETT, Maura Angelus
"Alone on the Airways." PoeticJ (6) 84, p. 9.
"Confrontation." PoeticJ (4) 83, p. 43.

390. BENSEN, Robert
"Driving the County Blacktop." Agni (21) 84, p. 96.
"For One on Whom Murder Was Attempted." Amelia
(1:2) O 84, p. 20.
"The Waves at Matsushima." Agni (21) 84, p. 94-95.

391. BENSKO, John
"Imagery without Purpose." Poetry (144:5) Ag 84,
p. 267-268.
"My Wife's Desire." Poetry (144:5) Ag 84, p. 270.
"Raising Cane." Poetry (144:5) Ag 84, p. 268-269.
"The Right Subject" (Near Yauco, Puerto Rico).
MissR (36, 12:3) Spr 84, p. 78-79.
"Why the Uncurious Travel." MissR (36, 12:3) Spr
84, p. 77.

392. BENTLEY, Beth
"The Clearest Expression of Mixed Emotions."
PoetryNW (25:1) Spr 84, p. 27-28.
"A Sentimental Education." Poetry (143:5) F 84, p.
278-279.

393. BENTLEY, Nelson
"Alice Pigeonfriend: A Mini-Epic." CrabCR (1:3)
Wint 84, p. 12-13.

394. BENTLEY, Roy
"Certain Flowers Persist." FourQt (33:3) Spr 84,
p. 26-27.
"On the Diamond behind Garfield Elementary, Melvin
White Proves There Is But One Boog Powell."
OhioR (33) 84, p. 89.

"On the Failure of All Political Poems." <u>CharR</u>
(10:2) Aut 84, p. 77.

395. BENTTINEN, Ted
"967 A.D." (Reykjavic, Iceland). <u>BelPoJ</u> (35:2)
Wint 84-85, p. 14.
"Agnus Dei." <u>BelPoJ</u> (35:2) Wint 84-85, p. 12-13.
"Antarctic Carnival." <u>YellowS</u> (10) Spr 84, p. 30.
"The Failure of Resuscitation by Silence." <u>StoneC</u>
(12:1/2) Aut-Wint 84, p. 13.
"I Am This Wooden Humming." <u>CharR</u> (10:2) Aut 84,
p. 86.
"Joukahainen" (Harbor market, Helsinki). <u>BelPoJ</u>
(35:2) Wint 84-85, p. 8-9.
"Skålholt." <u>BelPoJ</u> (35:2) Wint 84-85, p. 10-11.

396. BENTZMAN, Bruce Harris
"Tom's Tavern Revisited: a Tale of Ambition."
<u>WindO</u> (44) Sum-Aut 84, p. 52.

397. BENZ, Maudy
"Petals." <u>SouthernPR</u> (24:1) Spr 84, p. 32.

398. BERC, Shelley
"Translations" (I-II). <u>Tele</u> (19) 83, p. 41-43.

399. BERG, Nancy
"Pour the Milky Way in a Glass and Sip It."
<u>PoeticJ</u> (5) 84, p. 19.
"The Travelling Salesman and the Farmer's Daughter."
<u>CrabCR</u> (1:3) Wint 84, p. 12.
"Wobbly Legs." <u>PoeticJ</u> (4) 83, p. 17.

400. BERG, Sharon
"Quarter Moon." <u>PoetryCR</u> (5:4) Sum 84, p. 6.

401. BERG, Stephen
"After Poems (1913, 1916, 1911, 1959)" (tr. of Anna
Akhmatova). <u>Chelsea</u> (42/43) 84, p. 268.

402. BERGAMINI, L. J.
"Climbing Hurricane." <u>Blueline</u> (6:1) Sum-Aut 84,
p. 42.
"Departure." <u>Blueline</u> (5:2) Wint-Spr 84, p. 9.

403. BERGIN, Thomas G.
"Dog Walk." <u>SouthwR</u> (69:4) Aut 84, p. 387.
"No Names, No Pack Drill." <u>SouthwR</u> (69:4) Aut 84,
p. 386.

404. BERGMAN, Denny
"North" (imprisonment of Haitian refugees). <u>SanFPJ</u>
(6:2) 84, p. 25.

405. BERK, Ilhan
"Ben Uyandim Bir Ask Demekti Bu Dunyada." <u>NewRena</u>
(6:1, #18) Spr 84, p. 60.
"I Woke, This Meant a Love in the World" (tr. by
Talat Sait Halman). <u>NewRena</u> (6:1, #18) Spr 84,
p. 61.

406. BERKE, Judith
    "The Red Room." GeoR (38:1) Spr 84, p. 34-35.
    "Tapestry." GeoR (38:1) Spr 84, p. 35.

407. BERKLEY, June
    "Certain Knowledge." EngJ (73:2) F 84, p. 62.

408. BERLIND, Bruce
    "25" (tr. of Lajos Kassák). GrahamHR (7) Wint
        84, p. 54.
    "And There Isn't" (tr. of Dezso Tandori). GrahamHR
        (7) Wint 84, p. 53.
    "Four Squares" (tr. of Agnes Nemes Nagy). Iowa
        (14:2) Spr-Sum 84, p. 196-197.
    "The Ghost" (tr. of Agnes Nemes Nagy). Iowa (14:2)
        Spr-Sum 84, p. 200.
    "Storm" (tr. of Agnes Nemes Nagy). Iowa (14:2) Spr-
        Sum 84, p. 199-200.
    "Streetcar" (to the memory of Sidney Keyes, tr. of
        Agnes Nemes Nagy). Iowa (14:2) Spr-Sum 84, p.
        197-199.
    "To My Craft" (tr. of Agnes Nemes Nagy). Iowa
        (14:2) Spr-Sum 84, p. 201.
    "Underwords." GrahamHR (7) Wint 84, p. 41.

409. BERMAN, Linda
    "Interview" (Excerpts). Mund (14:2) 84, p. 46-47.

410. BERMAN, Ruth
    "Placement Committee." KanQ (16:1/2) Wint-Spr 84,
        p. 63.
    "Tree Ornaments." WindO (44) Sum-Aut 84, p. 35.

BERMUDEZ, Ariel Santiago: See SANTIAGO BERMUDEZ, Ariel

411. BERNARD, April
    "Third Station of the Cross." NewYRB (31:18) 22 N
        84, p. 40.

412. BERNARD, Artis
    "Watching You Swim." PoetL (79:3) Aut 84, p. 136-137.
    "The Young Violinist and the Golden Carp." PoetL
        (79:3) Aut 84, p. 135-136.

413. BERNARD, Judy Clark
    "Mother Nature." Wind (14:51) 84, p. 5.
    "Old Woman." Wind (14:51) 84, p. 5-6.

414. BERNARD, Kenneth
    "Dream." GrandS (3:4) Sum 84, p. 178.

415. BERNAUER, Carol
    "Modern Day." Sam (39:3, release 155) 84, p. 2.
    "Modern Day Companions #2." Sam (39:3, release
        155) 84, p. 6.
    "Modern Day Companions #3." Sam (39:3, release
        155) 84, p. 7.
    "Modern Day Diversions #1." Sam (39:3, release
        155) 84, p. 3.
    "Modern Day Diversions #7." Sam (39:3, release

155) 84, p. 10.
"Modern Day Entertainment #1." _Sam_ (39:3, release
    155) 84, p. 4.
"Modern Day Flukes #37." _Sam_ (39:3, release 155)
    84, p. 11.
"Modern Day Professions #2." _Sam_ (39:3, release
    155) 84, p. 5.
"Modern Day Professions #3." _Sam_ (39:3, release
    155) 84, p. 6.
"Modern Day Professions #9." _Sam_ (39:3, release
    155) 84, p. 7.
"Modern Day Professions #13." _Sam_ (39:3, release
    155) 84, p. 11.
"Modern Days 2!" _Sam_ (39:3, release 155) 84, p. 1-12.
"Modern Flukes." _Sam_ (39:3, release 155) 84, p. 8.

416. BERNHARDT, Suzanne
    "Piecework." _PoeticJ_ (5) 84, p. 32.
    "To Ronnie, Like Your Father." _YetASM_ (3) 84, p. 8.

417. BERNIER, Jack
    "Color Blind Experts." _SanFPJ_ (7:1) 84, p. 26.
    "It's Not Raining Pennies." _SanFPJ_ (6:3) 84, p. 7.
    "News of the Day." _SanFPJ_ (6:2) 84, p. 62.
    "Sorry, Our Lines Are Busy." _SanFPJ_ (6:2) 84, p. 66.
    "Tax Deductible." _SanFPJ_ (6:2) 84, p. 56.
    "Three Thousand Jobs Open." _SanFPJ_ (6:3) 84, p. 8.
    "We Interrupt This Broadcast." _SanFPJ_ (7:1) 84, p.
        27.
    "What? You Lost Your Card?" _SanFPJ_ (6:2) 84, p. 67.
    "Winter and Ashes." _SanFPJ_ (7:1) 84, p. 27.

418. BERNOFSKY, Susan
    "The Goats of São Paulo." _NewOR_ (11:1) Spr 84,
        p. 100.

419. BERNS, Gabriel
    "A Passionflower for Dolores" (tr. of Rafael
        Alberti). _TriQ_ (59) Wint 84, p. 198.
    "Punishments" (tr. of Rafael Alberti). _TriQ_ (59)
        Wint 84, p. 197.
    "The sea. My sea" (tr. of Rafael Alberti). _TriQ_
        (59) Wint 84, p. 192.
    "Summer" (tr. of Rafael Alberti). _TriQ_ (59) Wint
        84, p. 1194-95.
    "Today the clouds brought to me" (tr. of Rafael
        Alberti). _TriQ_ (59) Wint 84, p. 199.
    "You may think me a comet gone mad" (tr. of Rafael
        Alberti). _TriQ_ (59) Wint 84, p. 200-201.

420. BERNSTEIN, Carole
    "Assholes." _PaintedB_ (23) Sum 84, p. 20.
    "Labor Day." _PaintedB_ (23) Sum 84, p. 18.
    "Retrospective." _PaintedB_ (23) Sum 84, p. 19.

421. BERNSTEIN, Sylvia
    "Assassinated on the Street" (tr. of Roque Dalton,
        w. Harold Black and Walter Burrell). _Vis_ (15)
        84, p. 18.
    "For the Eye in the Keyhole" (Partial translation of

Roque Dalton, w. Harold Black and Walter
Burrell). <u>Vis</u> (15) 84, p. 18.
"Insomnia" (tr. of Roque Dalton, w. Harold Black and
Walter Burrell). <u>Vis</u> (15) 84, p. 19.

422. BERRIGAN, Daniel
"Biography." <u>Spirit</u> (7:1) 84, p. 180-181.
"Man Is More." <u>Chelsea</u> (42/43) 84, p. 27.
"One Thinks of Friends in Trouble Elsewhere, or:
Change the Regime But Keep the Prisoners by All
Means." <u>Stepping</u> (Anniversary Issue I) 84, p. 16.

423. BERRIOS PAGAN, Angel A.
"A Mi Hermano el Obrero." <u>Mairena</u> (5:13) Spr 83,
p. 89.

424. BERROCAL, Beatriz
"En las Calles." <u>Mairena</u> (6:16) Spr 84, p. 28.
"Fina Espiga." <u>Mairena</u> (6:16) Spr 84, p. 27-28.
"Humana Trascendencia." <u>Mairena</u> (6:16) Spr 84, p.
29-30.
"Llegas a Mi." <u>Mairena</u> (6:16) Spr 84, p. 27.
"Tu Nombre Tiene." <u>Mairena</u> (5:13) Spr 83, p. 57.
"Y Entonces." <u>Mairena</u> (6:16) Spr 84, p. 28-29.

425. BERRY, D. C.
"Cow Bones." <u>Poetry</u> (144:4) Jl 84, p. 202.
"The Creek Book" (Selection: "A Week on the Chunky
and Chickasawhay"). <u>SouthernR</u> (20:4) Aut 84, p.
874-878.
"Davy Brokenleg." <u>Poetry</u> (144:4) Jl 84, p. 202.
"Geography." <u>Poetry</u> (144:4) Jl 84, p. 201.
"Pier, P. M." <u>Poetry</u> (144:4) Jl 84, p. 201.
"When Insanity Comes a Knocking Throw Away the Door,
The Log of the Pequod 2" (Excerpts, dedicated to
Daryl Dryden and Giovanni Fumagalli). <u>TexasR</u>
(5:1/2) Spr-Sum 84, p. 97-107.

426. BERRY, Donald L.
"As I Walk I Turn over Leaves." <u>StoneC</u> (11:3/4)
Spr-Sum 84, p. 71.

427. BERRY, Wendell
"A Music." <u>Chelsea</u> (42/43) 84, p. 135.

428. BERRYMAN, John
"The Ball Poem." <u>Shen</u> (35:2/3) 84, p. 36.
"Drunks." <u>Shen</u> (35:2/3) 84, p. 44-45.
"Friendless." <u>Shen</u> (35:2/3) 84, p. 44.
"Monkhood." <u>Shen</u> (35:2/3) 84, p. 42-43.
"Revival." <u>Shen</u> (35:2/3) 84, p. 41-42.
"Winter Landscape." <u>Shen</u> (35:2/3) 84, p. 34.

429. BERSIANIK, Louky
"Corps de Noce, Corps de Divorce" (Chanson pour
Aphèlie au bleu regard). <u>CanLit</u> (100) Spr 84,
p. 24-29.

430. BERSSENBRUGGE, Mei-Mei
"Ricochet off Water." <u>Tele</u> (19) 83, p. 14-17.

431. BERTAGNOLLI, Olivia
     "The Right Location." Nimrod (28:1) Aut-Wint 84,
        p. 93.

432. BERTOLINO, James
     "The American." NowestR (22:1/2) 84, p. 120.
     "The Ants." IndR (7:2) Spr 84, p. 16.
     "Chowder." PoetL (79:3) Aut 84, p. 166.
     "The Descent." PoetL (79:3) Aut 84, p. 164.
     "Elephants." PoetL (79:3) Aut 84, p. 167.
     "Gertrude of the Stars." PoetL (79:3) Aut 84, p.
        162-163.
     "The Pothole Sonnet." PoetL (79:3) Aut 84, p. 160-
        161.
     "Precinct Kali." PoetL (79:3) Aut 84, p. 161-162.
     "Saying Atom." PoetL (79:3) Aut 84, p. 170.
     "The Slide." PoetL (79:3) Aut 84, p. 165.
     "Thirteen Ways to Look at Life after Reagan."
        Spirit (7:1) 84, p. 178.
     "This Is." PoetL (79:3) Aut 84, p. 168-169.
     "The Tools." PoetL (79:3) Aut 84, p. 169.
     "The Trace." PoetL (79:3) Aut 84, p. 167.

433. BETT, Stephen
     "Three Characters" (for Ho Hon). Bound (12:1) Aut
        83, p. 171-175.

434. BETTS, Greg
     "Edvard Munch." Waves (12:2/3) Wint 84, p. 71.
     "Rum-headed, footloose and rainfall fluent"
        (Untitled). PottPort (6) 84, p. 34.
     "Stream Song." PottPort (6) 84, p. 34.

435. BEYER, William
     "Journey in Darkness." Wind (14:52) 84, p. 3.

436. BHATT, Sujata P.
     "The Peacock." PaintedB (21) Wint 84, p. 22.
     "The Woodcut." PaintedB (21) Wint 84, p. 21.
     "The Writer." PaintedB (21) Wint 84, p. 23.

437. BIAŁOSZDWSKI, Miron
     "Instinctive Self-Portrait" (tr. by Danuta Lopozyko
        and Peter Harris). LitR (28:1) Aut 84, p. 130.

438. BICKNELL, John
     "Cobblestones." SanFPJ (6:3) 84, p. 51.
     "Losses." SanFPJ (6:2) 84, p. 44.
     "Nicaragua." SanFPJ (6:3) 84, p. 52.

439. BIDART, Frank
     "In the Western Night." NewRep (189:18) 31 O 83,
        p. 28.
     "To the Dead." NewYRB (31:17) 8 N 84, p. 38.

BIEDMA, Jaime Gil de: See GIL de BIEDMA, Jaime

440. BIENVENU, Roberta
     "Elegy: Daffodils on the breakfast table." IndR
        (7:3) Sum 84, p. 53.

441. BIERDS, Linda
     "From the Ghost, the Animal." NewEngR (6:3) Spr
        84, p. 419.
     "Lifting." Swallow (3) 84, p. 105.
     "Off the Aleutian Chain." NewEngR (6:3) Spr 84, p.
        420-421.
     "Pearl." NewYorker (60:39) 12 N 84, p. 54-55.

442. BIGGER, Duff
     "The Comedian Said It." NewL (50:2/3) Wint-Spr 84,
        p. 258.
     "It Is When the Tribe Is Gone." NewL (50:2/3) Wint-
        Spr 84, p. 258.

443. BIGGS, Margaret Key
     "Second Fantasia on the Eve of Saint Agnes." NegC
        (4:1) Wint 84, p. 44-48.

444. BIGNOZZI, Juana
     "Mitologia Familiar." Mairena (6:18) 84, p. 114-115.

445. BILBY, Patricia A.
     "The Writing Group." EngJ (73:5) S 84, p. 51.

446. BILGERE, George
     "The Plum Tree in Spring." ArizQ (40:4) Wint 84,
        p. 304.

447. BILICKE, Tom
     "Senryu." Bogg (52) 84, p. 3.

448. BILL, Jim
     "Zen in the Art of Shooting Rubber Bands." CrabCR
        (2:1) Sum 84, p. 10.

449. BILLINGS, Robert
     "Aisling." PoetryCR (6:2) Wint 84-85, p. 28.
     "At Billings' Bridge Graveyard." PoetryCR (6:2)
        Wint 84-85, p. 28.
     "Caledonia Hill." PoetryCR (6:2) Wint 84-85, p. 28.
     "Cardinal and Lilies." Dandel (11:1) Spr-Sum 84,
        p. 26-27.
     "Greenwood Hill in Winter: 1848." PoetryCR (6:1)
        Aut 84, p. 15.
     "Late Invocation." PoetryCR (6:2) Wint 84-85, p. 28.
     "Naming Flowers" (after moving, for Roo Borson).
        Dandel (11:2) Aut-Wint 84-85, p. 66-67.
     "Reading 'Skunk Hour' at the Briars" (Bicentennial
        Contest Winners, Poetry: Tie for Second). Waves
        (12:4) Spr 84, p. 84-85.
     "Sunday Noon" (for Ruth). Dandel (11:1) Spr-Sum
        84, p. 28.
     "Transparency." Dandel (11:1) Spr-Sum 84, p. 29.

450. BILLY, Allen T.
     "Poetry Reading '2075'." SanFPJ (6:3) 84, p. 40.
     "A Thought." PoeticJ (3) 83, p. 17.
     "Women's Tempo." SanFPJ (6:3) 84, p. 37.

BILOTTA   80

451. BILOTTA, John George
     "Agnr." YellowS (10) Spr 84, p. 39.

452. BINGHAM, Ginger
     "Mail Stop" (after an illustration in a children's
        book). Tendril (17) Wint 84, p. 19.

453. BIRCHARD, Guy
     "Coup de Lance." Origin (5:3) Spr 84, p. 84.
     "Coup de Raccroc." Origin (5:3) Spr 84, p. 83.
     "Coup d'Oeil." Origin (5:3) Spr 84, p. 85.
     "Coup monté." Origin (5:3) Spr 84, p. 86.
     "Triptych." Origin (5:3) Spr 84, p. 87.

454. BIRDSALL, Jane
     "Father and Daughter." BelPoJ (34:4) Sum 84, p. 2.
     "Undertaker's Granddaughter." BelPoJ (34:4) Sum
        84, p. 3.

455. BIRNBAUM, Saul
     "Einstein the Nohilist [sic]." SanFPJ (7:1) 84, p.
        81.
     "Fire and Storm." SanFPJ (7:1) 84, p. 89.
     "Latin-American Tyrant." SanFPJ (7:1) 84, p. 84.

456. BIRNEY, Earle
     "Cry over Aswan." Descant (44/45, 15:1/2) Spr-Sum
        84, p. 130.
     "Ellesmereland 1983." CanLit (100) Spr 84, p. 31.
     "Still Life near Bangalore." CanLit (100) Spr 84,
        p. 30-31.

457. BIRNIE, Christine
     "Even Love Dresses for the Weather." AntigR (56)
        Wint 84, p. 97.
     "Winter as a Second Language." AntigR (56) Wint
        84, p. 98-99.

458. BISHAI, Nadia
     "Poem: The moon is shining" (Beirut, the civil war,
        1975). Iowa (14:2) Spr-Sum 84, p. 87.

459. BISHOP, Elizabeth
     "The Armadillo" (for Robert Lowell). Field (31)
        Aut 84, p. 8-9.
     "At the Fishhouses." Field (31) Aut 84, p. 17-19.
     "The End of March" (For John Malcolm Brinnin and
        Bill Read: Duxbury). Field (31) Aut 84, p. 24-25.
     "Filling Station." Field (31) Aut 84, p. 12-13.
     "First Death in Nova Scotia." Field (31) Aut 84,
        p. 40-41.
     "In the Waiting Room." NewEngR (6:4) Sum 84, p. 528.
     "Objects and Apparitions" (for Joseph Cornell, tr.
        of Octavio Paz). PoetryE (13/14) Spr-Sum 84, p.
        228-229.
     "One Art." Field (31) Aut 84, p. 33.
     "Sonnet: Caught -- the bubble." Field (31) Aut 84,
        p. 44.

460. BISHOP, Michael
     "The Mirroring of Man through Beasts" (In tribute to
     Jèrôme Bosch, tr. of André Frênaud).
     AntiqR (56) Wint 84, p. 120-124.

461. BISLEY, Charles
     "Engines hammer out at night." Quarry (33:3) Sum
     84, p. 35.

462. BISSETT, Bill
     "Baybees Breth." CanLit (100) Spr 84, p. 32.
     "Earlee Wintr Song in th Forest." PoetryCR (6:1)
     Aut 84, p. 3.
     "Me n Arleen Usd to Drive Evree Wher." CanLit
     (100) Spr 84, p. 33.
     "Seeattuuuuuuuuuuuuuuull11ll." CapilR (31) 84, p. 70.
     "Th Elvs Ozone Factorees." PoetryCR (6:2) Wint 84-
     85, p. 18.
     "Timelessness timelessness timelessness
     timelessness." CapilR (31) 84, p. 71.
     "Transplantid." PoetryCR (6:2) Wint 84-85, p. 18.
     "Vowl Man." CapilR (31) 84, p. 74.
     "We Want to Bless Yu All th Stars undr Holee Hevns
     Wing." CapilR (31) 84, p. 72-73.
     "Whn Diefenbaker Went." CanLit (100) Spr 84, p. 34.

463. BITNEY, Kate
     "Sakharov in Exile." Dandel (11:1) Spr-Sum 84, p. 31.

464. BIXBY, R. J.
     "Rand-McNally Black." WoosterR (1:2) N 84, p. 7.

465. BIXLER, Berniece
     "I Leave My Body." Nimrod (27:2) Spr-Sum 84, p. 20.
     "I Send My Love Away." Nimrod (27:2) Spr-Sum 84,
     p. 20.
     "Preview of a Concrete Flower." Nimrod (27:2) Spr-
     Sum 84, p. 18.

466. BJORKLUND, Beth
     "Chalk-Crocus, at dawn" (tr. of Paul Celan).
     Sulfur (4:2, issue 11) 84, p. 8.
     "Pale-Voiced, flayed from the depths" (tr. of Paul
     Celan). Sulfur (4:2, issue 11) 84, p. 8.
     "Stone-Blow behind the beetles" (tr. of Paul Celan).
     Sulfur (4:2, issue 11) 84, p. 9.

467. BLACK, Candace
     "Laundry." GrahamHR (7) Wint 84, p. 28.

468. BLACK, Harold
     "Assassinated on the Street" (tr. of Roque Dalton,
     w. Walter Burrell and Sylvia Bernstein). Vis
     (15) 84, p. 18.
     "For the Eye in the Keyhole" (Partial translation of
     Roque Dalton, w. Walter Burrell and Sylvia
     Bernstein). Vis (15) 84, p. 18.
     "Insomnia" (tr. of Roque Dalton, w. Walter Burrell
     and Sylvia Bernstein). Vis (15) 84, p. 19.
     "Monuments on the Mall." Vis (14) 84, p. 20-21.

469. BLACKBURN, Michael
    "Chalet." Stand (25:1) Wint 83-84, p. 54.
    "E.C.T." Stand (25:4) Aut 84, p. 52.
    "The North Sea at Tynemouth." Stand (25:4) Aut 84,
        p. 52.

470. BLACKBURN, Paul
    "Newsclips 2. (Dec/6-7)." Chelsea (42/43) 84, p.
        161-163.

471. BLACKSHEAR, Helen
    "Migrants." NegC (4:1) Wint 84, p. 98.

472. BLACKWOMON, Julie
    "Johanna Barns" (police report July 3 9:35 a.m.
        female derelict loitering in center city
        restaurant, picked up, taken to Byberry State
        Hospital). PaintedB (23) Sum 84, p. 21-23.

473. BLADES, Joe
    "Doing It en Francais." BlueBuf (2:2) Spr 84, p. 28.
    "Left." CrossC (6:4) 84, p. 8.

474. BLAGA, Lucian
    "Don Quijote" (in Romanian). ConcPo (17:2) Aut 84,
        p. 63.
    "Don Quijote" (tr. by Michael Taub and William
        Harmon). ConcPo (17:2) Aut 84, p. 64.
    "Eve" (tr. by Michael Taub and William Harmon).
        ConcPo (17:2) Aut 84, p. 65.

475. BLAIR, Jeanette
    "Homecoming." SoCaR (16:2) Spr 84, p. 17.
    "Reply to a Poet." SoCaR (16:2) Spr 84, p. 16.
    "Somewhere." SoCaR (16:2) Spr 84, p. 16-17.

476. BLAIR, John M.
    "Joe Prichard." MinnR (N.S. 23) Aut 84, p. 36.

477. BLAKE, George
    "Morning Song." KanQ (16:4) Aut 84, p. 13.
    "Poor Visibility." KanQ (16:1/2) Wint-Spr 84, p. 32.
    "Surprise." KanQ (16:1/2) Wint-Spr 84, p. 33.

478. BLAKE, Rosemary
    "Elegy" (for my father). Waves (12:2/3) Wint 84,
        p. 94-96.

479. BLAKE, William
    "Never Seek to Tell They Love." Tendril (18,
        special issue) 84, p. 260.
    "The Poison Tree." Hudson (37:1) Spr 84, p. 65.

480. BLANCHARD, Lucile
    "Watering the Garden." LitR (28:1) Aut 84, p. 71.

BLAS, Israel Roldan: See ROLDAN BLAS, Israel

481. BLASER, Randall
    "The Dead." PikeF (6) Aut 84, p. 3.

482. BLAUNER, Laurie
     "Lullaby: 1940, Louisiana." GrahamHR (7) Wint 84,
        p. 37.

483. BLAZEK, Douglas
     "At the Iron Works." CreamCR (9:1/2) 84, p. 9.
     "Each Morning, and Each Morning Again." GreenfR
        (11:1/2) Sum-Aut 83, p. 88-89.
     "In Full Agreement." CalQ (25) Aut 84, p. 37.
     "Meditations for Leapers Who Walk Back and Forth
        across the Bridge" (for T. L. Kryss). Abraxas
        (31/32) 84, p. 8-9.
     "Why I Am Inept at Growing a Decent Mustache."
        GreenfR (11:1/2) Sum-Aut 83, p. 89.

484. BLEAKLEY, Alan
     "Seafarers." ManhatR (3:2) Wint 84-85, p. 68-69.

485. BLEHERT, Dean
     "Being Young." Vis (14) 84, p. 30.
     "Mirror Up to Nature." Bogg (52) 84, p. 24.

486. BLENGIO, José Rafael
     "Apuntes para una Declaracion de Fe." Mairena
        (6:17) Aut 84, p. 68.

487. BLESSING, Tom
     "In the Tavern: A Sailor from the Pinta." PoeticJ
        (1) 83, p. 25.
     "Poetry." PoeticJ (3) 83, p. 25.
     "While You Were Gone I Fell Asleep." PoeticJ (3)
        83, p. 27.

488. BLITCH, Lynn Banks
     "Attics of Useful Artifacts." NegC (4:3) Sum 84,
        p. 94-95.

489. BLITT, Rita
     "Statement from the Artist: Dancing on Paper."
        NewL (51:1) Aut 84, p. 18.

490. BLIUMIS, Sarah
     "Everything Is Relative." SpoonRQ (9:2) Spr 84, p.
        31.

491. BLOCH, Chana
     "Pride" (tr. of Dahlia Ravikovitch). Pequod
        (16/17) 84, p. 113.

492. BLODGETT, E. D.
     "Colours of War." PoetryCR (6:2) Wint 84-85, p. 23.
     "Logistics." PoetryCR (6:2) Wint 84-85, p. 23.

493. BLOMAIN, Karen
     "Vineyard Night Soundings." StoneC (11:3/4) Spr-
        Sum 84, p. 76.

494. BLOOMFIELD, Maureen
     "The Wood of Error." Shen (35:1) 83-84, p. 37.

495. BLOSSOM, Laurel
     "Checkpoint." CarolQ (36:2) Wint 84, p. 33.

496. BLOSSOM, Lavina
     "After the Harlequin." ParisR (26:91) Spr 84, p.
     116-117.

497. BLUE, Jane
     "At 5th & Howard." Abraxas (31/32) 84, p. 10-11.
     "Mother Taught Her Daughers to Fish." Abraxas
     (31/32) 84, p. 12-13.

498. BLUE, Janet Buickerood
     "Paper Soldier." Wind (14:51) 84, p. 51.

499. BLUE, Keith
     "The Three Friends" (Excerpt). Open24 (3) 84, p. 26.

500. BLUE CLOUD, Peter
     "A Gentle Earthquake" (for Mt. St. Helens).
     GreenfR (11:3/4) Wint-Spr 84, p. 67-72.
     "Short Coyote Story." GreenfR (11:3/4) Wint-Spr
     84, p. 74.

501. BLUM, Beth
     "Other Footsteps." PoeticJ (6) 84, p. 12-13.

502. BLUM, Jillian
     "Eating the Fruit." LitR (28:1) Aut 84, p. 62.

503. BLUMENTHAL, Michael
     "Back from the Word Processing Course, I Say to My
     Old Typewriter." Poetry (144:1) Ap 84, p. 24-25.
     "The Disappointments of Childhood." Poetry (144:1)
     Ap 84, p. 23-24.
     "Dusk: Mallards on the Charles River." Antaeus
     (53) Aut 84, p. 257.
     "The Earth Was Tepid and the Moon Was Dark." PraS
     (58:1) Spr 84, p. 19.
     "Grace" (The MacDowell Colony, Peterborough, New
     Hampshire). PraS (58:1) Spr 84, p. 22-23.
     "In Assisi." Nat (238:7) 25 F 84, p. 232.
     "The Mountains of Evening" (Sperryville, Virginia).
     PraS (58:1) Spr 84, p. 25-26.
     "Mushroom Hunting in Late August: Peterborough,
     N.H." Nat (238:7) 25 F 84, p. 233.
     "The Old Painter at the Violin" (in memory of Theo
     Fried, 1902-1980). PraS (58:1) Spr 84, p. 24-25.
     "This Year" (for Cynthia, Christmas 1982). PraS
     (58:1) Spr 84, p. 20-21.
     "What a Time!" Poetry (144:1) Ap 84, p. 22-23.
     "Winter Light." PraS (58:1) Spr 84, p. 21-22.

504. BLY, Robert
     "After a Death" (tr. of Tomas Tranströmer).
     Tendril (18, special issue) 84, p. 291.
     "Autumn's End" (tr. of Rainer Maria Rilke). NewL
     (51:2) Wint 84-85, p. 35.
     "Black Tree Trunks." KenR (NS 6:1) Wint 84, p. 22.
     "The Busy Man Speaks." Tendril (18, special issue)

84, p. 70.
"Dark Eyebrows Swim Like Turtles" (from Poems for
    Max Ernst). Chelsea (42/43) 84, p. 181.
"Ferns." KenR (NS 6:1) Wint 84, p. 22.
"The Flounder." Germ (8:2) Aut-Wint 84, p. 30.
"The Fog Horns at Port Townsend." Germ (8:2) Aut-
    Wint 84, p. 31.
"Hearing Fourth of July Drums." NewL (51:2) Wint
    84-85, p. 34.
"The Hermit." Tendril (18, special issue) 84, p.
    30-31.
"The House." KenR (NS 6:1) Wint 84, p. 21.
"How Beautiful the Shiny Turtle" (from Poems for
    Max Ernst). Chelsea (42/43) 84, p. 181.
"In Rainy September." NewRep (190:1/2) 9-16 Ja 84,
    p. 36.
"Merchants Have Multiplied." Chelsea (42/43) 84,
    p. 69.
"Monologue with Its Wife" (tr. of Gunnar Ekelöf).
    Chelsea (42/43) 84, p. 65.
"The Morning Glory." Tendril (18, special issue)
    84, p. 75.
"Night Winds." Atlantic (253:6) Je 84, p. 98.
"Out of the Rolling Ocean, the Crowd." Germ (8:2)
    Aut-Wint 84, p. 32.
"The Pillow." KenR (NS 6:1) Wint 84, p. 21.
"The Poem." NewL (51:2) Wint 84-85, p. 34-35.
"Secrets." Germ (8:2) Aut-Wint 84, p. 33.
"Serious Moment" (tr. of Rainer Maria Rilke). NewL
    (51:2) Wint 84-85, p. 36.
"Turning Inward at Last." Tendril (18, special
    issue) 84, p. 39-40.
"The Way He Turns." KenR (NS 6:1) Wint 84, p. 21.

505. BOATRIGHT, Philip
"For Ariadne." LittleBR (4:4) Sum 84, p. 88.
"Inscription for the Ring She Gave Me." LittleBR
    (4:4) Sum 84, p. 88.
"Inscription from a Persian Tomb." LittleBR (4:4)
    Sum 84, p. 89.
"Lovesong." LittleBR (4:4) Sum 84, p. 88.
"Of the Lotus." LittleBR (4:4) Sum 84, p. 88.
"Om Mani Padme Hum." LittleBR (4:4) Sum 84, p. 89.
"Poem in 7 Lines Pinned to My Mirror by the White
    Goddess." LittleBR (4:4) Sum 84, p. 88.

506. BODLAK, Karen
"February." Waves (12:2/3) Wint 84, p. 75.
"Homecoming for WCW." AntigR (59) Aut 84, p. 81.
"Landscape." PoetryCR (5:3) Spr 84, p. 18.

507. BOE, Deborah
"An Apology to My Lover." Kayak (64) My 84, p. 10.
"Closing the Doors." HangL (45) Spr 84, p. 20.
"Defense to One's Mother for Loving a Bad Man."
    HangL (45) Spr 84, p. 21.
"Enchiladas." HangL (45) Spr 84, p. 25.
"From My Half-Sleep." HangL (45) Spr 84, p. 26.
"Lesson." HangL (45) Spr 84, p. 23.
"Mojave." HangL (45) Spr 84, p. 22-26.

"The Reason I Stay." Kayak (64) My 84, p. 12.
"Sister." HangL (45) Spr 84, p. 24.
"Something I Forgot to Tell You." Kayak (64) My
    84, p. 11.

508. BOEHM, Susan
"Dreaming These Evils into Being." WindO (44) Sum-
    Aut 84, p. 31-32.

509. BOERSMA, Ann
"My Son." PoeticJ (8) 84, p. 32.
"New Colt." PoeticJ (8) 84, p. 26.

510. BOES, Don
"The Bats." PraS (58:2) Sum 84, p. 34-35.
"Guarding the Door." PraS (58:2) Sum 84, p. 35.
"January." PaintedB (24) Aut 84, p. 10.

511. BOGAN, James
"Missouri Litany." NewL (51:2) Wint 84-85, p. 63-67.
"Mrs. Clara Franz: Mother Earth's Daughter." NewL
    (51:2) Wint 84-85, p. 67-70.
"Principles." NewL (51:2) Wint 84-85, p. 71-74.

512. BOGAN, Louise
"To Wystan Auden on His Birthday" (w. Edmund Wilson:
    Alternate lines by E. W. and L. B. -- first line
    by E. W. Composed in 1956). Shen (35:2/3) 84,
    p. 24.

513. BOGEN, Don
"Pasadena." AmerPoR (13:3) My-Je 84, p. 14.
"Pedlar" (Igor Fedorovich Stravinsky 1882-1971).
    AmerPoR (13:3) My-Je 84, p. 14.
"Policies" (for my father). IndR (7:2) Spr 84, p. 22.
"A Priest of Aphrodisias." Stand (25:3) Sum 84, p.
    42.
"A Scholar Gazing at a Flight of Birds." Ploughs
    (10:1) 84, p. 21-22.
"Swan Song." Ploughs (10:1) 84, p. 19-20.
"Winter House." Stand (25:3) Sum 84, p. 43.

514. BOGGILD, Anna
"They Sold the Cove." PottPort (6) 84, p. 16.

515. BOGIN, George
"Family of This World" (tr. of Jules Supervielle).
    PoetryE (15) Aut 84, p. 85-86.
"Finale" (tr. of Jules Supervielle). PoetryE (15)
    Aut 84, p. 82.
"I have always had two skulls" (tr. of Alain
    Bosquet). Mund (14:2) 84, p. 85.
"I was running away from reality" (tr. of Alain
    Bosquet). Mund (14:2) 84, p. 81.
"In New Guinea" (tr. of Alain Bosquet). Mund
    (14:2) 84, p. 81, 83.
"My dearest friend" (tr. of Alain Bosquet). Mund
    (14:2) 84, p. 83.
"Night" (tr. of Jules Supervielle). PoetryE (15)
    Aut 84, p. 84.

"The Snows." NewL (50:4) Sum 84, p. 22.
"A Summer Night on Long Island." MissouriR (7:3)
    84, p. 38.
"The Sun Speaks Softly" (tr. of Jules Supervielle).
    PoetryE (15) Aut 84, p. 83.
"A Sunday at the Beach, 1938." MissouriR (7:3) 84,
    p. 37.
"To Be Human" (after Chekhov, via Harold Clurman).
    Ploughs (10:1) 84, p. 23-24.
"A Twilight." NewL (50:4) Sum 84, p. 22.

516. BOGIN, Magda
     "Despair" (tr. of Roque Dalton). Vis (15) 84, p. 17.

517. BOGIN, Nina
     "Bologna, November 1978." AmerPoR (13:4) Jl-Ag 84,
         p. 44.

518. BOISSEAU, Michelle
     "Equations." OhioR (33) 84, p. 70-71.
     "Mrs. Whitfield." SouthernHR (18:3) Sum 84, p. 255.
     "The Visible Man" (for Bartolomeo Martello). SenR
         (14:1) 84, p. 49-50.

519. BOLES, Rachael
     "Flatiron Poem." Descant (47, 15:4) Wint 84, p.
         126-128.

520. BOLLING, John
     "The Face of Harlem." Stepping (Premier Issue) Sum
         82, p. 13.

521. BOLLS, Imogene
     "Old Indian Pot." SoDakR (22:4) Wint 84, p. 39.

522. BOLLS, Imogene L.
     "Poem for My Father." CapeR (19:3) 20th Anniverary
         Issue 84, p. 2.

523. BOLTON, Barbara Bailey
     "Education." Wind (14:51) 84, p. 46.

524. BOLTON, Joe
     "Another Rainy Night." BlueBldgs (7) 84, p. 42.

525. BOLTZ, Fred
     "Crane in the Marshlands." AntigR (56) Wint 84, p.
         84.

526. BOMBA, Bernard
     "The Crosses of Gdansk, August, 1981." TarRP
         (23:2) Spr 84, p. 27.
     "The Hard Spirit." WestB (14) 84, p. 32-33.
     "The Last Year." WebR (9:2) Wint 85, p. 77.
     "Monday." WoosterR (1:1) Mr 84, p. 10.
     "Pasturing." PoetC (15:3) 84, p. 30.

527. BOND, Anita
     "Letter to Jonathan." KanQ (16:1/2) Wint-Spr 84,
         p. 18.

528. BONGIE, Chris
     "Cain of the Sad Countenance." <u>MalR</u> (69) O 84, p.
     82-84.

529. BONNEFOY, Yves
     "The Clouds" (tr. by Richard Pevear). <u>ParisR</u>
     (26:92) Sum 84, p. 132-144.
     "The Summer of Night" (Excerpted from <u>Words in
     Stone</u>, tr. by Lisa Sapinkopf). <u>MissR</u> (37/38,
     13:1/2) Aut 84, p. 83-87.

530. BONNELL, Paula
     "Dictionary Flowers." <u>NegC</u> (4:1) Wint 84, p. 35-36.
     "In the Rye." <u>SnapD</u> (6:2) Spr 83, p. 58.
     "Montana Rusa." <u>YetASM</u> (3) 84, p. 3.
     "Spring Mourner" (Homage to Sylvia Plath, 1932-
     1963). <u>BlueBldgs</u> (8) 84?, p. 36.

531. BONNER, Carrington
     "Nicaragua Woman." <u>BlackALF</u> (18:1) Spr 84, p. 27.

532. BONOMO, J.
     "By the Sea." <u>PraS</u> (58:2) Sum 84, p. 37.
     "The Cold, the Dark." <u>PraS</u> (58:2) Sum 84, p. 36.
     "Why There Is No Enmity between the Woman and the
     Snake." <u>PraS</u> (58:2) Sum 84, p. 37-38.

533. BOOKER, Betty
     "In Your Sixteenth Year." <u>Wind</u> (14:52) 84, p. 4.
     "October in the Nation of the Black Wall." <u>StoneC</u>
     (12:1/2) Aut-Wint 84, p. 22.
     "The Story Grandfather Would Tell in December."
     <u>Wind</u> (14:52) 84, p. 4.

534. BOOKER, Fred
     "Blue Notes of a White Girl" (Selections, for
     Monique). <u>WestCR</u> (19:1) Je 84, p. 41-44.

535. BOOKER, Julie
     "Tuesday Afternoon." <u>Quarry</u> (33:1) Wint 84, p. 20.
     "White Anger." <u>Quarry</u> (33:1) Wint 84, p. 20-21.

536. BOONE, Bruce
     "A Mutilation (Future Appealed To)" (tr. of La
     Fontaine, w. Robert Glück). <u>Tele</u> (19) 83, p. 53.
     "Mystical Aspirations" (tr. of La Fontaine, w.
     Robert Glück). <u>Tele</u> (19) 83, p. 51-52.

537. BOONE, Gene
     "Living Poetry." <u>WritersL</u> (1) 84, p. 5.
     "My Writing." <u>WritersL</u> (1) 84, p. 5.

538. BOOSE, Maryetta Kelsick
     "Proud Lady." <u>SanFPJ</u> (6:4) 84, p. 21.
     "They Dared to Disobey." <u>SanFPJ</u> (6:4) 84, p. 22.

539. BOOTH, Philip
     "Alba." <u>PoetryNW</u> (25:4) Wint 84-85, p. 39.
     "Argument." <u>Antaeus</u> (52) Apr 84, p. 130.
     "Counting the Ways." <u>NewRep</u> (190:19) 14 My 84, p. 34.

"Creatures." <u>Poetry</u> (144:5) Ag 84, p. 264-266.
"Growing Up in Kankakee." <u>TriQ</u> (60) Spr-Sum 84, p.
    322.
"Liv." <u>NewL</u> (50:2/3) Wint-Spr 84, p. 131.
"Nebraska, U.S.A." <u>Chelsea</u> (42/43) 84, p. 66.
"Parting." <u>PoetryNW</u> (25:4) Wint 84-85, p. 38-39.
"Stove." <u>Tendril</u> (18, special issue) 84, p. 65-66.
"Table." <u>GeoR</u> (38:2) Sum 84, p. 240-241.
"There, Here." <u>NewEngR</u> (7:2) Wint 84, p. 216-217.
"Town Dump." <u>Ploughs</u> (10:1) 84, p. 25-26.
"Watching Out." <u>Blueline</u> (5:2) Wint-Spr 84, p. 46-47.
"The World's Maybe Champion." <u>OntR</u> (20) Spr-Sum
    84, p. 92.

540. BORAS, Helen
    "Suttee." <u>Sam</u> (41:2, release 162) 84 or 85, p. 6.

541. BORCZON, Matthew
    "Constructing a Horizon." <u>HangL</u> (46) Aut 84, p. 73.
    "Fossils." <u>HangL</u> (46) Aut 84, p. 72.
    "P.o.w." <u>HangL</u> (46) Aut 84, p. 74.

542. BORDAO, Rafael
    "Ira de Angeles." <u>LindLM</u> (3:2/4) Ap-D 84, p. 6.

543. BORDEN, Robert
    "Meat Dreams." <u>Pig</u> (12) 84, p. 64-66.

544. BORDERS, Andrew
    "I dream the school will not hold us" (in the story
    "Ritual"). <u>SouthernHR</u> (18:3) Sum 84, p. 242-243.

545. BORGES, Jorge Luis
    "Cyclical Night" (tr. by Robert Lima). <u>Chelsea</u>
    (42/43) 84, p. 170-171.
    "Rain" (tr. by Willis Barnstone). <u>NewL</u> (50:2/3)
    Wint-Spr 84, p. 134.

546. BORISOV, Georgi
    "Let Him Be" (tr. by John Balaban). <u>NewOR</u> (11:1)
    Spr 84, p. 82.

547. BORN, Anne
    "Thanatos" (tr. of Preben Major Sørenson). <u>Stand</u>
    (25:3) Sum 84, p. 55.
    "This Picture" (tr. of Preben Major Sørenson).
    <u>Stand</u> (25:3) Sum 84, p. 55.

548. BORN, Heidi von
    "Change of Earth" (Three poems from the section
    "Bellevue Hospital, New York, tr. by Janice
    Soderling). <u>MalR</u> (67) F 84, p. 104-105.

549. BORSON, Roo
    "All in the Family." <u>MalR</u> (69) O 84, p. 67.
    "Anniversaries." <u>MalR</u> (69) O 84, p. 62.
    "By Flashlight." <u>CanLit</u> (100) Spr 84, p. 42-43.
    "Closed Universe." <u>MalR</u> (69) O 84, p. 66.
    "Definitions of Love, One." <u>PoetryCR</u> (5:4) Sum 84,
    p. 8.

"Fast Forward." PoetryCR (6:1) Aut 84, p. 15.
"The Garden." MalR (69) O 84, p. 63.
"Intertwined Portraits." MalR (69) O 84, p. 64.
"The Long Way Round." MalR (69) O 84, p. 68-69.
"Mostly It Is the Future Which Haunts This House."
    MalR (69) O 84, p. 69.
"A Sense of Proportion." MalR (69) O 84, p. 66.
"Tree-drifting." MalR (69) O 84, p. 65.
"The Whole Night Coming Home" (Prose Poems:
    Selections). MalR (69) O 84, p. 62-69.

550. BORUCH, Marianne
    "The Blue Chair." Ploughs (10:1) 84, p. 28.
    "The Fortune Teller." Ploughs (10:1) 84, p. 27.
    "Grief." IndR (7:3) Sum 84, p. 9.

551. BOSCH, Daniel
    "Three Forms of Possession." StoneC (11:3/4) Spr-
    Sum 84, p. 44-45.

552. BOSCO, Louis J.
    "The Radiant Stone." NowestR (22:1/2) 84, p. 126-128.

553. BOSLEY, Deborah
    "Winter Leavings." SpoonRQ (9:4) Aut 84, p. 47.

554. BOSLEY, Keith
    "Writing in a Notebook" (tr. of Moshe Dor). Pequod
    (16/17) 84, p. 116.

555. BOSQUET, Alain
    "En Nouvelle Guinée." Mund (14:2) 84, p. 80, 82.
    "I have always had two skulls" (tr. by George
    Bogin). Mund (14:2) 84, p. 85.
    "I was running away from reality" (tr. by George
    Bogin). Mund (14:2) 84, p. 81.
    "In New Guinea" (tr. by George Bogin). Mund (14:2)
    84, p. 81, 83.
    "J'ai toujours eu deux crânes." Mund (14:2) 84,
    p. 84.
    "Je fuyais le réel." Mund (14:2) 84, p. 80.
    "Mon ami le plus cher." Mund (14:2) 84, p. 82.
    "My dearest friend" (tr. by George Bogin). Mund
    (14:2) 84, p. 83.

556. BOSS, Laura
    "Last Chance: Atlantic City 3:45 AM" (to G.C.).
    Abraxas (31/32) 84, p. 41.

557. BOSTON, Bruce
    "The Alchemist in Place." Veloc (4) Sum 84, p. 39.
    "The Alchemist Takes a Lover in the Infinite Variety
    of Fire." Veloc (4) Sum 84, p. 38.
    "A Feast for the Vanquished." Veloc (1) Sum 82, p.
    14-15.
    "From the Mouths of Lizards." Veloc (1) Sum 82, p.
    11.
    "The FTL Addict Fixes." Veloc (2) Spr 83, p. 7.
    "In Days of Cataclysm" (after J. G. Ballard).
    Veloc (3) Aut-Wint 83, p. 43.

"The Nativity of Thought" (Refrain with variations
1, 2, ...n). Veloc (2) Spr 83, p. 5-6.
"View from the Abscissa." Veloc (1) Sum 82, p. 12.

558. BOTELHO, Eugene G. E.
"Earth Song LIX." PoeticJ (5) 84, p. 25.

559. BOTTOMS, David
"The Anniversary." Poetry (145:1) O 84, p. 23-24.
"The Desk." Poetry (145:1) O 84, p. 20-22.
"Ice" (For Dave Smith). Poetry (145:3) D 84, p.
132-133.
"Naval Photograph: 25 October 1942: What the Hand
May be Saying." Poetry (145:1) O 84, p. 22-23.
"A Tent beside a River." Poetry (145:1) O 84, p.
19-20.

560. BOTTRALL, Ronald
"Dying." Stand (25:1) Wint 83-84, p. 26.
"Embryo Musician." Stand (25:1) Wint 83-84, p. 26.

561. BOTZWEILER, William
"Dolly Parton's Eggplant Jello Cookbook." PottPort
(6) 84, p. 51.

562. BOU, Antonio
"Cuestion y Silenciario de la Gitana." Mairena
(5:13) Spr 83, p. 90-91.

BOU, Iris M. Landron: See LANDRON BOU, Iris M.

563. BOUCHER, Alan
"The Roads of My Country" (Excerpt, tr. of Sigfus
Dadason). Vis (14) 84, p. 8.
"Time and Water" (Selections, tr. of Steinn
Steinarr). Vis (16) 84, p. 6.
"Water That Runs" (tr. of Steinn Steinarr). Vis
(16) 84, p. 6.
"Wave That Breaks" (tr. of Steinn Steinarr). Vis
(16) 84, p. 6.

564. BOURAOUI, Hédi
"Abandonment." PoetryCR (6:1) Aut 84, p. 16.

565. BOURNE, Daniel
"Afghanistan" (tr. of Tomasz Jastrun). WebR (9:2)
Wint 85, p. 16.
"Did You Know" (after W.C.W.). SpoonRQ (9:4) Aut
84, p. 50.
"Hat" (tr. of Tomasz Jastrun). GreenfR (11:3/4)
Wint-Spr 84, p. 131-132.
"Interrogation and Map" (tr. of Tomasz Jastrun).
GreenfR (11:3/4) Wint-Spr 84, p. 130.
"Intruding." Northeast (Series 3:17) Sum 84, p. 14.
"Polish Dogs" (tr. of Tomasz Jastrun). WebR (9:2)
Wint 85, p. 17.
"Prose" (tr. of Tomasz Jastrun). GreenfR (11:3/4)
Wint-Spr 84, p. 133.
"Reunion" (tr. of Tomasz Jastrun). GreenfR
(11:3/4) Wint-Spr 84, p. 132.

"Rings" (tr. of Tomasz Jastrun). GreenfR (11:3/4)
    Wint-Spr 84, p. 131.
"Tread" (tr. of Tomasz Jastrun). GreenfR (11:3/4)
    Wint-Spr 84, p. 131.
"Visiting Day" (tr. of Tomasz Jastrun). GreenfR
    (11:3/4) Wint-Spr 84, p. 132.
"Walk-ons" (tr. of Tomasz Jastrun). GreenfR
    (11:3/4) Wint-Spr 84, p. 133.

566. BOURNE, Louis
    "Junk" (tr. of Angel Gonzàlez). Stand (25:4) Aut
        84, p. 21.
    "The Kiss" (tr. of Alfonso Carreño). Stand
        (25:4) Aut 84, p. 20.

567. BOURNE, Stephen R.
    "To Have Known a Prophet Isn't Everything" (From
        Land of the Cypress Trees). Waves (12:2/3)
        Wint 84, p. 72-73.

568. BOUVARD, Marguerite Guzman
    "The Crab Apple Tree." SouthwR (69:2) Spr 84, p. 182.
    "Herta." Ploughs (10:1) 84, p. 29-30.
    "In the Desert Botanical Garden." Ploughs (10:4)
        84, p. 52-53.
    "Karel." GreenfR (11:3/4) Wint-Spr 84, p. 149.
    "The Peaks of Otter." LitR (27:2) Wint 84, p. 227.
    "The Sum, Not the Fragments of Many Years."
        GreenfR (11:3/4) Wint-Spr 84, p. 149-150.
    "The Vineyard." LitR (27:2) Wint 84, p. 228.

569. BOWDEN, J. M.
    "Verse." NegC (4:2) Spr 84, p. 56.

570. BOWERING, Marilyn
    "Form and Variation." CanLit (100) Spr 84, p. 44-45.
    "Grandfather Was a Soldier" (Excerpts). MalR (67)
        F 84, p. 26-41.

BOWERS, Cathy Smith: See SMITH-BOWERS, Cathy

571. BOWERS, Neal
    "The Answer Man." NewL (51:1) Aut 84, p. 15.
    "Hedging." SouthernPR (24:1) Spr 84, p. 31.
    "Sitting Up with the Dead." SouthernPR (24:1) Spr
        84, p. 30.
    "Sleeping Late." MichQR (23:1) Wint 84, p. 30.

572. BOWIE, Robert
    "Patience " PoetL (79:1) Spr 84, p. 38.
    "Where Rails Also Sing." WebR (9:2) Wint 85, p. 38.

573. BOWIE, Robert B.
    "Wintermost." SouthwR (69:1) Wint 84, p. 59.

574. BOWLER, Clara Ann
    "Evolution." SanFPJ (6:2) 84, p. 24.
    "Unified Field Theories I" (after James Trefil).
        SanFPJ (6:2) 84, p. 21.
    "Yet Another Coming" (after Yeats). SanFPJ (6:2)

84, p. 37.

575. BOWMAN, P. C.
"The Wrong People." <u>KanQ</u> (16:1/2) Wint-Spr 84, p. 22.

576. BOYCE, Pleuke
"G" (tr. of Rutger Kopland). <u>MalR</u> (68) Je 84, p.
31-35.
"Good morning? Heavenly Mrs. Ping" (To my despondent
cat, to console her on the death of her
offspring, tr. of F. Ten Harmsen V. D. Beek).
<u>MalR</u> (68) Je 84, p. 26-27.
"Obscure Correspondence and Its Unhappy
Consequences, in Two Verses" (tr. of F. Ten
Harmsen V. D. Beek). <u>MalR</u> (68) Je 84, p. 28-30.

577. BOYCE, Robert C.
"Crisis of Identity." <u>Bogg</u> (52) 84, p. 64.

578. BOYCHUK, Bohdan
"Aquarium" (To M.A., tr. of Oleh Olzhych, w. David
Ignatow). <u>Pequod</u> (16/17) 84, p. 188.
"Castle" (tr. of Ihor Kalynec). <u>Pequod</u> (16/17) 84,
p. 198.
"Dutch Painting" (tr. of Oleh Olzhych, w. David
Ignatow). <u>Pequod</u> (16/17) 84, p. 187.
"The Evening" (tr. by Mark Rudman and the author).
<u>Confr</u> (27/28) 84, p. 53.
"Five Poems on One Theme" (tr. by the author and
David Ignatow). <u>Pequod</u> (16/17) 84, p. 191-192.
"In This Immense Aquarium" (tr. of Ihor Kalynec).
<u>Pequod</u> (16/17) 84, p. 199.
"Katerina" (fugue, tr. of Vasyl Holoborodko).
<u>Pequod</u> (16/17) 84, p. 201-204.
"Our Whole Little Province" (tr. of Ihor Kalynec).
<u>Pequod</u> (16/17) 84, p. 200.
"Women" (tr. by David Ignatow and the author).
<u>Confr</u> (27/28) 84, p. 53.

579. BOYD, Greg
"Somebody." <u>WormR</u> (24:4, issue 96) 84, p. 134.
"The Vortex " <u>WormR</u> (24:4, issue 96) 84, p. 134.

580. BOYER, Charles M.
"A Kind of Quiet." <u>SpoonRQ</u> (9:2) Spr 84, p. 17.
"Tambourine Treehouse." <u>SpoonRQ</u> (9:2) Spr 84, p. 18.

581. BOYER, Patsy
"Comprehension" (tr. of Victor Gavirio, w. Mary
Crow). <u>BlackWR</u> (10:2) Spr 84, p. 37.
"Saturday Night" (tr. of Idea Vilariño, w. Mary
Crow). <u>BlackWR</u> (10:2) Spr 84, p. 39.

582. BOZANIC, Nick
"December." <u>MidAR</u> (4:1) Spr 84, p. 56.
"Homecoming." <u>NewOR</u> (11:2) Sum 84, p. 89.

583. BRACKENBURY, Alison
"In the Fifth Week." <u>Stand</u> (25:4) Aut 84, p. 7.

584. BRACKER, Jon
"Teenagers." <u>CrabCR</u> (1:3) Wint 84, p. 15.

585. BRADLEY, George
"Expecting an Angel." <u>Shen</u> (35:2/3) 84, p. 45.

586. BRADLEY, John
"Of the Silence at the Back of Vanity." <u>BlueBldgs</u>
    (8) 84?, p. 27.
"Vanity of Hunger." <u>BlueBldgs</u> (8) 84?, p. 28.
"Vanity of the Plow" (for Joanie). <u>BlueBldgs</u> (8)
    84?, p. 28.
"Window in a Field." <u>BlueBldgs</u> (8) 84?, p. 29.

587. BRADLEY, Robert
"The House Between." <u>PaintedB</u> (24) Aut 84, p. 37.
"The Move West." <u>PaintedB</u> (24) Aut 84, p. 36.
"Reflection Seen in a Shop Window." <u>PaintedB</u> (24)
    Aut 84, p. 38.

588. BRADLEY, Sam
"Declaring the Male." <u>Chelsea</u> (42/43) 84, p. 294.

589. BRAHAM, Jeanne
"Crofter" (Songs from Skye). <u>ThRiPo</u> (23/24) 84, p.
    31.
"False Season." <u>ThRiPo</u> (23/24) 84, p. 32.
"Gillie" (Songs from Skye). <u>ThRiPo</u> (23/24) 84, p. 31.
"Kelpie" (Songs from Skye). <u>ThRiPo</u> (23/24) 84, p. 31.
"Songs fromn Skye." <u>ThRiPo</u> (23/24) 84, p. 31.

590. BRAMBACH, Rainer
"Abschied von der Eifel." <u>MidAR</u> (4:2) Aut 84, p. 72.
"Alleinstehende Männer." <u>MidAR</u> (4:2) Aut 84, p. 64.
"Böses Spiel." <u>MidAR</u> (4:2) Aut 84, p. 74.
"Glückszeichen." <u>MidAR</u> (4:2) Aut 84, p. 68.
"Lucky Signs" (tr. by Stuart Friebert). <u>MidAR</u>
    (4:2) Aut 84, p. 69.
"März in Basel." <u>MidAR</u> (4:2) Aut 84, p. 60.
"March in Basel" (tr. by Stuart Friebert). <u>MidAR</u>
    (4:2) Aut 84, p. 61.
"Men, Isolated, Unmarried" (tr. by Stuart Friebert).
    <u>MidAR</u> (4:2) Aut 84, p. 65.
"One Day among Many" (tr. by Stuart Friebert).
    <u>IndR</u> (7:3) Sum 84, p. 13.
"Poesie." <u>MidAR</u> (4:2) Aut 84, p. 70.
"Poesy" (tr. by Stuart Friebert). <u>MidAR</u> (4:2) Aut
    84, p. 71.
"Salt" (Translation Chapbook Series, Number Two, tr.
    by Stuart Friebert). <u>MidAR</u> (4:2) Aut 84, p. 59-76.
"Salt" (tr. by Stuart Friebert). <u>MidAR</u> (4:2) Aut
    84, p. 67.
"Salz." <u>MidAR</u> (4:2) Aut 84, p. 66.
"So Long to the Eifel" (tr. by Stuart Friebert).
    <u>MidAR</u> (4:2) Aut 84, p. 73.
"Under Appletrees" (tr. by Stuart Friebert). <u>MidAR</u>
    (4:2) Aut 84, p. 63.
"Unter Apfelbäumen." <u>MidAR</u> (4:2) Aut 84, p. 62.
"Wicked Game" (tr. by Stuart Friebert). <u>MidAR</u>
    (4:2) Aut 84, p. 75.

591. BRAND, Dionne
"Calibishie April 1983" (from Chronicles of the
Hostile Sun). PoetryCR (5:4) Sum 84, p. 20.
"Eurocentric" (from Chronicles of the Hostile
Sun). PoetryCR (5:4) Sum 84, p. 20.
"Four hours on a bus across Saskatchewan."
PoetryCR (6:1) Aut 84, p. 15.

592. BRAND, Helena, Sister
"Variation Up-Date: I." EngJ (73:5) S 84, p. 40.
"Variation Up-Date: II." EngJ (73:5) S 84, p. 40.

593. BRAND, Helena S.
"An Unofficial Address by a Losing Candidate."
EngJ (73:3) Mr 84, p. 90.

594. BRAND, Millen
"Local Lives" (Selection: The Honeymoon). Chelsea
(42/43) 84, p. 238-239.

595. BRANDI, John
"Angel Peak: A 2nd Road Song." Spirit (7:1) 84, p.
162-163.
"A Poem for My Mother." GreenfR (11:1/2) Sum-Aut
83, p. 181.
"A Summer Prayer." GreenfR (11:1/2) Sum-Aut 83, p.
182-183.

596. BRASCH, Thomas
"Prewar" (tr. by Reinhold Grimm). NowestR (22:1/2)
84, p. 73.
"Vorkrieg." NowestR (22:1/2) 84, p. 72.

597. BRATHWAITE, Eddard Kamau
"Dread." Stepping (Anniversary Issue I) 84, p. 17-18.

598. BRATTMAN, Steven Ronald
"The Last Scene." Sam (37:3, 147th release) 83, p. 5.

599. BRAUN, Henry
"The Professor." ThRiPo (23/24) 84, p. 53.
"St. Galileo." AmerPoR (13:2) Mr-Ap 84, p. 37.

600. BRAVO, Alejandro
"Letter" (tr. by Marc Zimmerman and Ellen
Banberger). MinnR (N.S. 22) Spr 84, p. 80.
"Manifesto" (tr. by Marc Zimmerman and Ellen
Banberger). MinnR (N.S. 22) Spr 84, p. 74-76.
"Monimbo" (tr. by Marc Zimmerman and Ellen
Banberger). MinnR (N.S. 22) Spr 84, p. 68.
"Todo Continuara en su Puesto." Mairena (6:18) 84,
p. 161-162.

BRAVO, Jorge de: See DEBRAVO, Jorge

601. BREBAN, Nicolae
"Indian Summer" (For Hualing and Paul, tr. by
Malinda Cox). Iowa (14:2) Spr-Sum 84, p. 222-223.

602. BREBNER, Diana
     "The Birds in Paradise." PoetryCR (5:3) Spr 84, p.
     18.

603. BRECHT, Bertolt
     "And What Did the Soldier's Wife Receive?" (tr. by
     Frederick C. Ellert). MassR (25:4) Wint 84, p.
     573, 575.
     "German War Primer (1937)" (Excerpts, tr. by Ed
     Ochester). MinnR (N.S. 23) Aut 84, p. 125.
     "My Poorer Classmates from the Edge of the City"
     (tr. by Ed Ochester). MinnR (N.S. 23) Aut 84,
     p. 126.
     "Und Was Bekam des Soldaten Weib?" MassR (25:4)
     Wint 84, p. 572, 574.
     "Why Should My Name Be Remembered?" (tr. by Bert
     Cardullo). WebR (9:1) Spr 84, p. 98.

604. BREEDEN, David
     "Greetings from Tranquility Lake." Vis (16) 84, p.
     13.

605. BREEDEN, James
     "Before Names of Things." Wind (14:52) 84, p. 13.

606. BREHM, John
     "Autumn." Poetry (145:1) O 84, p. 31-32.
     "Insomnia: For My Grandfather." Poetry (145:1) O
     84, p. 31.

607. BREIL, Ruth
     "A Short Story" (For Alfred and Peter). Stepping
     (Anniversary Issue I) 84, p. 19-20.

608. BREITT, Luke
     "Last of the Coffee" (For Ben Hiatt). OroM (2:3/4,
     issue 7/8) 84, p. 4.
     "Watching Evening Coming On" (For Gary Snyder).
     OroM (2:3/4, issue 7/8) 84, p. 38-39.

609. BREMER, C. R.
     "Bible Sonnet I." DekalbLAJ (20th Anniversary
     Issue) 84, p. 77.
     "In Dogwood Years." DekalbLAJ (20th Anniversary
     Issue) 84, p. 77.

610. BRENNAN, Joan
     "Meal." DekalbLAJ (17:1/2) 84, p. 110.

611. BRENNAN, Lucy
     "A Poet." PoetryCR (6:2) Wint 84-85, p. 27.

612. BRENNAN, Matthew
     "Stone Mountain" (to the memory of Doug Johnson, who
     fell off Stone Mountain, January, 1981). KanQ
     (16:1/2) Wint-Spr 84, p. 109.
     "Waters Have Held Us" (in memory of Deane
     Postlethwaite). WebR (9:1) Spr 84, p. 34.

613. BRESLIN, Paul
     "Orpheus." Poetry (143:5) F 84, p. 285-286.

614. BRETON, André
     "Dukduk." AmerPoR (13:4) Jl-Ag 84, p. 33.
     "No Paradise Is Lost" (for Man Ray). Telescope
     (3:1) Wint 84, p. 7.

615. BRETT, Brian
     "The Shadowy Herd" (A return for Gary Ford).
     PoetryCR (5:4) Sum 84, p. 7.

616. BRETT, Peter
     "Children of Nogales Story." SnapD (8:1) Aut 84,
     p. 6.
     "Fire." SnapD (8:1) Aut 84, p. 7.
     "El Rosario." MidAR (4:2) Aut 84, p. 20.

617. BREWSTER, Elizabeth
     "In October." CanLit (100) Spr 84, p. 46-47.

618. BREWTON, Catherine
     "Grandpa's Hands." CapeR (19:2) Sum 84, p. 16.

619. BREYFOGLE, Valorie
     "To Christopher" (age 7 months). PoeticJ (3) 83,
     p. 13.
     "Uneasy Exit." SpoonRQ (9:4) Aut 84, p. 51.

620. BREYNER, Sophia de Mello (See also ANDRESEN, Sophia
     de Mello Breyner)
     "Biography" (tr. by Alexis Levitin). WebR (9:2)
     Wint 85, p. 9.
     "Blank Page" (tr. by Alexis Levitin). WebR (9:2)
     Wint 85, p. 10.
     "The Dead Soldier" (tr. by Alexis Levitin). WebR
     (9:2) Wint 85, p. 11.
     "Eurydice" (tr. by Alexis Levitin). WebR (9:2)
     Wint 85, p. 9.
     "His Beauty" (tr. by Alexis Levitin). WebR (9:2)
     Wint 85, p. 10.
     "The Minotaur" (tr. by Alexis Levitin). WebR (9:2)
     Wint 85, p. 9.
     "Of Transparency" (tr. by Alexis Levitin). WebR
     (9:2) Wint 85, p. 9.

621. BRIDGES, Pat
     "I Sat Down to Write." YetASM (3) 84, p. 2.

622. BRIDGFORD, Kim
     "A Drop of Summer." KanQ (16:1/2) Wint-Spr 84, p. 92.
     "The Fan." Ascent (9:3) 84, p. 41.
     "That Sudden Clearing Away." TarRP (23:2) Spr 84,
     p. 20-21.
     "Waiting." DekalbLAJ (20th Anniversary Issue) 84,
     p. 78.

623. BRIEFS, E. Castendyk
     "Clockstroke" (tr. of H. L. Pointek). <u>Vis</u> (14) 84,
     p. 16.
     "Consolation" (tr. of H. L. Pointek). <u>Vis</u> (14) 84,
     p. 16.
     "In My Town" (tr. of Sarah Kirsch). <u>Vis</u> (14) 84,
     p. 24.
     "Names" (tr. of H. L. Pointek). <u>Vis</u> (14) 84, p. 16.

624. BRINDEL, June
     "The Appointment." <u>KanQ</u> (16:1/2) Wint-Spr 84, p. 215.

625. BRINGHURST, Robert
     "Two Variations" (I: The Reader, for Celia Duthie.
     II: Larix Lyallii, for Dennis Lee). <u>CanLit</u>
     (100) Spr 84, p. 48-49.

626. BRISBY, Stewart
     "Love Song of the Drunken Moth" (For Yvette).
     <u>PoeticJ</u> (2) 83, p. 24.
     "The Poet." <u>PoeticJ</u> (2) 83, p. 14-15.

627. BRITT, Alan
     "My Car." <u>Open24</u> (3) 84, p. 44.

628. BROCK, Frances R.
     "The Absurd, Off Broadway." <u>KanQ</u> (16:3) Sum 84, p.
     100.

629. BROCK, James
     "Mr Potato Kills Time." <u>CarolQ</u> (37:1) Aut 84, p. 40.
     "Sunday Cleaning" (for Annette and Jane).
     <u>SouthernPR</u> (24:1) Spr 84, p. 46.

630. BROCK, Randall
     "Cold Hard." <u>Wind</u> (14:52) 84, p. 11.
     "Golden Hands." <u>Wind</u> (14:52) 84, p. 16.
     "Stark." <u>Wind</u> (14:52) 84, p. 10.

631. BROCK-BROIDO, Lucie
     "The Bald Angels" (after Rafael Alberti). <u>Epoch</u>
     (33:2) Spr-Sum 84, p. 145-147.
     "The Beginning of the Beginning." <u>AntR</u> (42:4) Aut
     84, p. 454.

632. BROCKLEBANK, Ian
     "The Artist." <u>Bogg</u> (52) 84, p. 46.

633. BROCKLEY, Michael
     "The Shoplifter." <u>WindO</u> (44) Sum-Aut 84, p. 36.

634. BROCKMAN, Fred
     "Driving through Montana after Leaving a Lover."
     <u>SnapD</u> (7:2) Spr 84, p. 37.

635. BROCKMANN, Stephen
     "Revolution in Albania." <u>WindO</u> (44) Sum-Aut 84, p.
     39-40.
     "Vietnam Memorial." <u>SanFPJ</u> (6:3) 84, p. 42-44.

636. BROCKWAY, James
     "Our Gasworks" (tr. of Rutger Kopland). Stand
     (25:1) Wint 83-84, p. 55.
     "A Psalm" (tr. of Rutger Kopland). Stand (25:1)
     Wint 83-84, p. 55.

637. BROCKWELL, Stephen
     "3464 Hutchison: 3 for Easter." AntigR (59) Aut
     84, p. 79-80.

638. BRODERICK, Richard
     "Notes to Myself While Shaving." StoneC (12:1/2)
     Aut-Wint 84, p. 39.

639. BRODINE, Karen
     "Driving through the Mountains at Night." GreenfR
     (11:1/2) Sum-Aut 83, p. 118.
     "Fireweed, a Looseleaf Poem" (Four Selections).
     GreenfR (11:1/2) Sum-Aut 83, p. 115-118.
     "A Pair of Hands." GreenfR (11:1/2) Sum-Aut 83, p.
     116.
     "Wild Blackberries." GreenfR (11:1/2) Sum-Aut 83,
     p. 117.
     "The Year I Was Harriet I Could Do Math and Was
     Bossy." GreenfR (11:1/2) Sum-Aut 83, p. 115.

640. BRODKEY, Harold
     "Rocks." Pequod (16/17) 84, p. 213-214.
     "To Frank O'Hara." ParisR (26:93) Aut 84, p. 207-208.

641. BRODSKY, Joseph
     "Cafe 'Trieste', San Francisco." Confr (27/28) 84,
     p. 17.
     "Gorbunov and Gorchakov" (tr. by Harry Thomas).
     ParisR (26:93) Aut 84, p. 102-145.
     "Sextet." NewYorker (60:46) 31 D 84, p. 24.
     "Tristia" (tr. of Osip Mandelshtam). Confr (27/28)
     84, p. 18.

642. BRODSKY, Louis Daniel
     "Between Seasons." SouthernR (20:4) Aut 84, p. 891-
     893.
     "Street Cleaner." CapeR (19:2) Sum 84, p. 30-31.
     "Willy's Southern Route." SouthernR (20:4) Aut 84,
     p. 890-891.

643. BRODY, Harold
     "Washing." Wind (14:50) 84, p. 21.

644. BRODY, Harry
     "A Country's Music." CharR (10:2) Aut 84, p. 82-84.
     "Watching Stella Die." YetASM (3) 84, p. 8.

645. BROF, Janet
     "My Love Is Hard Right On" (For the compañeros of
     Gradas, tr. of Rosario Murillo). NewEngR (6:4)
     Sum 84, p. 583-584.
     "Requiem in Vita Pro Nobis" (tr. of Rosario
     Murillo). Vis (15) 84, p. 27.

BROIDO, Lucie Brock: See BROCK-BROIDO, Lucie

646. BROMBERG, David
     "Red, White and Black." SanFPJ (6:3) 84, p. 21.

647. BRONK, William
     "To Praise the Music." AntigR (59) Aut 84, p. 103.
     "Where It Ends." AntigR (59) Aut 84, p. 104.

648. BROOKS, David
     "Diary, 14th Entry." Sam (41:1, release 161) 84,
        p. 14.
     "Narcissism on Rye." Sam (39:4, release 156) 84,
        p. 1-12.

649. BROOKS, Gwendolyn
     "Langston Hughes Is Merry Glory." Stepping Wint
        84, p. 11.
     "Malcolm X" (For Dudley Randall). Stepping Wint
        83, p. 13.

650. BROOKS, Jack
     "Blue Chopin." CrossC (6:1) 84, p. 11.

651. BROSMAN, Catharine Savage
     "Birds at Night." SewanR (92:4) O-D 84, p. 531.
     "Homecoming." SewanR (92:4) O-D 84, p. 530.
     "Sayings for Seven Dreams." SewanR (92:4) O-D 84,
        p. 528-529.

652. BROSSARD, Iris
     "Independence Day." Abraxas (31/32) 84, p. 15.

653. BROUGHTON, T. Alan
     "Heart Transplant." Sparrow (46) 84, p. 16.
     "Summer Killer." NewEngR (7:2) Wint 84, p. 192-196.

654. BROWN, Beth
     "Woman without Shadow." GreenfR (11:1/2) Sum-Aut
        83, p. 119.

655. BROWN, Beverly
     "Fireeater." PoetC (15:3) 84, p. 17.

656. BROWN, Bill
     "Talking to You Asleep." NegC (4:2) Spr 84, p. 35.

657. BROWN, Crystal
     "Gilding the Rain." SnapD (7:1) Aut 83, p. 62.

658. BROWN, Emerson
     "The Grenada Invasion 1983." SanFPJ (6:3) 84, p.
        58-59.
     "Our Free Press." SanFPJ (6:3) 84, p. 60.
     "YUPPIE -- The Young Urban Professional of 1984."
        SanFPJ (7:1) 84, p. 40.

659. BROWN, Greg
     "Currents." WorldO (18:3) Spr 84, p. 33.

660. BROWN, Harriet
     "Heat Rising." Telescope (3:2) Spr 84, p. 27.
     "In Our Last World." Telescope (3:1) Wint 84, p. 37.
     "There Is Nothing Quite Like the Heat of It."
        Telescope (3:1) Wint 84, p. 35-36.
     "True North." IndR (7:2) Spr 84, p. 15.
     "Walking Home from the Subway, Carroll Street."
        IndR (7:2) Spr 84, p. 14.

661. BROWN, Harry
     "For Rosie B_____." Wind (14:52) 84, p. 5.
     "Poetry." WindO (44) Sum-Aut 84, p. 52.

662. BROWN, Juanita
     "You Stepped Out of Sepia." CrossC (6:1) 84, p. 15.

663. BROWN, Kurt
     "Cetology." SouthernPR (24:2) Aut 84, p. 13-17.
     "Rita Memorizes the Sound of Leaving." QW (18) Spr-
        Sum 84, p. 69.

664. BROWN, Mae Hill
     "Madrona." Quarry (33:4) Aut 84, p. 75.
     "No Lack of Space." Quarry (33:4) Aut 84, p. 75.
     "Words inside Words." Quarry (33:4) Aut 84, p. 75.

665. BROWN, Marilyn
     "Parallaxis." PaintedB (23) Sum 84, p. 7.

666. BROWN, Melanie Beth
     "If We Had Foreseen All This." CapeR (19:3) 20th
        Anniverary Issue 84, p. 3.

BROWN, Nicole Marchewka: See MARCHEWKA-BROWN, Nicole

667. BROWN, Paul Cameron
     "Upturn the Rock." Amelia (1:2) O 84, p. 71-72.

668. BROWN, Rebecca
     "The Cars." SoCaR (16:2) Spr 84, p. 18-19.

669. BROWN, Ronnie R.
     "Carpool." CrossC (6:1) 84, p. 14.

670. BROWN, Rosellen
     "The Crossroads of the South." Chelsea (42/43) 84,
        p. 236.
     "The Eyes Are Not Alike." OP (37) Spr-Sum 84, p. 14.
     "Some Times." OP (37) Spr-Sum 84, p. 16.
     "Unposted Land." OP (37) Spr-Sum 84, p. 15.
     "A Visit to St. Paul, 1979" (for Trish). OP (37)
        Spr-Sum 84, p. 12-13.

671. BROWN, Russell
     "Dust Bowl #2." Wind (14:51) 84, p. 7.

672. BROWN, Simon
     "Manticore." Bogg (52) 84, p. 42.

673. BROWN, Steven Ford
     "Rome: August 1981." <u>PoetC</u> (16:1) Aut 84, p. 15.
     "The Rooms of Sleep." <u>PoetC</u> (16:1) Aut 84, p. 16.
     "Sickness." <u>PoetC</u> (16:1) Aut 84, p. 17.

674. BROWN, Wayde
     "Chiefs of Africa." <u>PottPort</u> (6) 84, p. 16.

675. BROWN, William J.
     "Danka, Tara, Angel." <u>PaintedB</u> (23) Sum 84, p. 24.

676. BROWNE, Jackson
     "James Dean" (w. Glenn Frey, Don Henley, and J. D.
     Souther, 1974, Benchmark Music, ASCAP). <u>NewOR</u>
     (11:3/4) Aut-Wint 84, p. 95.

677. BROWNE, Michael Dennis
     "Cutting Up a Fallen Tree." <u>GreenfR</u> (12:1/2) Sum-
     Aut 84, p. 115.
     "Leaves Are My Flowers Now." <u>GreenfR</u> (12:1/2) Sum-
     Aut 84, p. 114.
     "To My Wife in Time of War." <u>NowestR</u> (22:1/2) 84,
     p. 28-31.

678. BRUCE, Debra
     "Lula Mae Joins the Procession." <u>MissR</u> (36, 12:3)
     Spr 84, p. 90-91.

679. BRUCHAC, Joseph
     "City Wind" (a bear song). <u>NewL</u> (50:2/3) Wint-Spr
     84, p. 34.
     "The Dancing Boys" (from the Seneca Story).
     <u>Abraxas</u> (31/32) 84, p. 57.
     "Inside the Dream." <u>OroM</u> (2:3/4, issue 7/8) 84, p.
     26.
     "Rembrandt: Two Self Portraits." <u>NewL</u> (50:2/3)
     Wint-Spr 84, p. 34-35.
     "Tahadondeh and the Game Warden." <u>Abraxas</u> (31/32)
     84, p. 56.
     "Tourette's Syndrome." <u>NewL</u> (50:4) Sum 84, p. 20-21.
     "Wahsah Zeh (War Dance) -- As Long As the Grass."
     <u>Spirit</u> (7:1) 84, p. 61-69.
     "Writing by Moonlight." <u>Blueline</u> (6:1) Sum-Aut 84,
     p. 11.

680. BRUEY, Alfred J.
     "Letter from Pennsylvania or Somewhere Else."
     <u>Amelia</u> (1:2) O 84, p. 63.

681. BRUGALETTA, John J.
     "A Working Marriage." <u>Poem</u> (52) N 84, p. 41-44.

682. BRUMMELS, J. V.
     "Billy in the Street: His Wife Considers Her
     Plight." <u>MidwQ</u> (25:4) Sum 84, p. 401-402.
     "Bridge" (for Dan). <u>QW</u> (18) Spr-Sum 84, p. 96-97.
     "A Bystander." <u>MidwQ</u> (25:4) Sum 84, p. 399-400.
     "Death Day." <u>HolCrit</u> (21:4) O 84, p. 17-18.
     "Loretta." <u>Iowa</u> (14:3) Aut 84, p. 58-59.
     "Make Me an Angel." <u>MidwQ</u> (25:4) Sum 84, p. 397-398.

683. BRUMMET, John
     "The Branch." NegC (4:3) Sum 84, p. 48.

684. BRUNN, Don
     "The Little Wedding Honeymoon" (Mr & Mrs Tom Thumb).
     BlueBldgs (7) 84, p. 31.

BRUNT, Lloyd van: See Van BRUNT, Lloyd

685. BRUSH, Thomas
     "Again." PoetryNW (25:3) Aut 84, p. 18-19.
     "Aksarben." IndR (7:2) Spr 84, p. 20.
     "The Children Paint Their Faces." PoetryNW (25:3)
     Aut 84, p. 17-18.

686. BRUSTEHALTER, Earnst
     "Human life is nothing more than the sum of its
     appetites." Open24 (3) 84, p. 41.

687. BRUTUS, Dennis
     "Sedako's cranes are flying." Spirit (7:1) 84, p. 5.
     "You May Not See the Nazis." Stepping (Anniversary
     Issue I) 84, p. 22.

688. BRYAN, Louis E.
     "Made-in-the-U.S.A." PoeticJ (2) 83, p. 9.

689. BRYAN, Sharon
     "The Back of Antelope Island." AmerPoR (13:3) My-
     Je 84, p. 13.
     "Emerson Elementary." Atlantic (254:6) D 84, p. 80.
     "Staunch." Nat (239:7) 15 S 84, p. 216.
     "Volunteer Work." GeoR (38:1) Spr 84, p. 101.

690. BRYANT, Drew
     "History Is for Strangers" (Bicentennial Contest
     Winners: Honourable Mention). Waves (12:4) Spr
     84, p. 88-89.

BRYDYDD, Sion ap: See SION ap BRYDYDD

691. BRYSMAN, Anita
     "The Potter." MalR (67) F 84, p. 95.

692. BRYSON, Debra
     "The Birds Know." AntigR (58) Sum 84, p. 77.

693. BUCCIERO, Patricia
     "M.P.H." PoetryCR (5:4) Sum 84, p. 19.

694. BUCKAWAY, C. M.
     "Lily with Seven Petals." PoetryCR (6:2) Wint 84-
     85, p. 22.
     "Myrrh in Autumn." PoetryCR (6:2) Wint 84-85, p. 22.

695. BUCKLAND, Karen
     "Goodbye." Bogg (52) 84, p. 53.

696. BUCKLEY, B. J.
     "The Stock Pond." Vis (16) 84, p. 12.

697. BUCKLEY, Christopher
     "In the Rain Easing" (for my grandfather, for Phil).
        NewEngR (6:4) Sum 84, p. 579-582.
     "Intransitive." MissouriR (7:3) 84, p. 9.
     "On Being Whole." Chelsea (42/43) 84, p. 373.
     "Some Things" (Fresno 1980, for Cheryl). Telescope
        (3:2) Spr 84, p. 18-22.
     "Spring and the Half Life." SenR (14:2) 84, p. 29-31.
     "La Strada" (for Cheryl). SenR (14:2) 84, p. 27-28.
     "Why I'm in Favor of a Nuclear Freeze." Telescope
        (3:1) Wint 84, p. 78-79.
     "Work & Days" (At Bonny Doon, Santa Cruz, California
        -- for Gary Young). MissouriR (7:3) 84, p. 10.
     "Zurbaran's 'Still Life: Lemons, Oranges and a Rose'
        1633." Hudson (37:1) Spr 84, p. 82.

698. BUCKLEY, M. T.
     "Why the Eskimos Never Answer Their Letters." NewL
        (50:2/3) Wint-Spr 84, p. 184.

699. BUCKLEY, Vincent
     "An Easy Death." Ploughs (10:1) 84, p. 31-34.

700. BUCKNER, Sally
     "More Songs from Holcomb County." CrabCR (2:1) Sum
        84, p. 12-15.
     "Songs from Holcomb County." CrabCR (1:3) Wint 84,
        p. 9-11.

701. BUDBILL, David
     "On Being Native." NewL (50:2/3) Wint-Spr 84, p. 185.

702. BUDDENDECK, David P.
     "Autumn Leaves." PoeticJ (6) 84, p. 39.
     "Escape." PoeticJ (6) 84, p. 32.
     "Love's Life Moment." PoeticJ (6) 84, p. 36.

703. BUDY, Andrea Hollander
     "Pigs." GeoR (38:1) Spr 84, p. 21.

704. BUEHRER, David J.
     "Waking from Dreams." Waves (12:2/3) Wint 84, p. 88.

705. BUELL, Frederick
     "Concerning Starlight." Hudson (37:2) Sum 84, p.
        271-273.

706. BUELL, Thomas
     "The Continent." PortR (30:1) 84, p. 27-28.
     "Tick Ripe for Bursting." PortR (30:1) 84, p. 161.

707. BUETTNER, Shirley
     "Scotch and Water." SpoonRQ (9:4) Aut 84, p. 39.

708. BUGEJA, Michael
     "The Visit." MidAR (4:2) Aut 84, p. 29-30.

709. BUGEJA, Michael J.
     "How to Look at Mirrors, a Love Poem." WestB (15)
        84, p. 70.

"Missing" (The 1983 American Academy of Poets prize-
winning poem). CimR (67) Ap 84, p. 10.
"Pantoum for My Side of the Family." Swallow (3)
84, p. 67.
"Volleyball Becomes Soccer at the International
Picnic." IndR (7:3) Sum 84, p. 60.
"Witness." Amelia (1:2) O 84, p. 67.

710. BUKER, Russell
"Thoughts on the BJ Highway." AntigR (56) Wint 84,
p. 105-107.
"Timothy." PottPort (6) 84, p. 34.

711. BUKOWSKI, Charles
"American Literature II." WormR (24:3, issue 95)
84, p. 87.
"And Then We Got the Green." WormR (24:1, issue
93) 84, p. 38.
"Boor." WormR (24:3, issue 95) 84, p. 113-115.
"The Cats' Behinds." WormR (24:3, issue 95) 84, p.
110-112.
"Confession." WormR (24:4, issue 96) 84, p. 159.
"Counter." WormR (24:3, issue 95) 84, p. 82.
"Dead Dog." WormR (24:3, issue 95) 84, p. 103-106.
"Do You Use a Notebook." WormR (24:3, issue 95)
84, p. 120-121.
"Dog Fight." WormR (24:3, issue 95) 84, p. 81.
"Fight." WormR (24:3, issue 95) 84, p. 92-93.
"Gift." WormR (24:3, issue 95) 84, p. 112-113.
"The Girls." WormR (24:3, issue 95) 84, p. 117-118.
"Guest." WormR (24:3, issue 95) 84, p. 100-101.
"Here I am." OroM (2:3/4, issue 7/8) 84, p. 20-21.
"Horse." WormR (24:3, issue 95) 84, p. 89-90.
"Horses Don't Bet on People & Neither Do I" (A
Wormwood Chapbook). WormR (24:3, issue 95) 84,
p. 81-124.
"Horses Don't Bet on People and Neither Do I."
WormR (24:3, issue 95) 84, p. 119.
"In My Day We Used to Call it Pussy-Whipped."
WormR (24:3, issue 95) 84, p. 122-124.
"Independence Day." WormR (24:3, issue 95) 84, p.
93-96.
"Kenyon Review, After the Sandstorm." WormR (24:3,
issue 95) 84, p. 121.
"Let It Go." WormR (24:3, issue 95) 84, p. 115-116.
"Locks." WormR (24:3, issue 95) 84, p. 82-87.
"The Loser." Sparrow (46) 84, p. 14.
"The Mutilation of the Species." WormR (24:4,
issue 96) 84, p. 159-161.
"My Soul Is Gone." WormR (24:3, issue 95) 84, p.
90-91.
"Of Course." WormR (24:2, issue 94) 84, p. 76.
"The Other Room." WormR (24:3, issue 95) 84, p. 97.
"The Payoff." WormR (24:3, issue 95) 84, p. 110.
"Promenade." WormR (24:2, issue 94) 84, p. 77-78.
"Some of My Readers." WormR (24:1, issue 93) 84,
p. 39.
"Swinging from the Dumb Hook." WormR (24:2, issue
94) 84, p. 76-77.
"Talking to the Barkeep." WormR (24:3, issue 95)

84, p. 106-107.
"There Are So Many Houses and Dark Streets without
    Help." WormR (24:3, issue 95) 84, p. 108-109.
"They Can Ruin Your Day." WormR (24:3, issue 95)
    84, p. 118-119.
"Token Drunk." WormR (24:3, issue 95) 84, p. 97-99.
"The Vampires." WormR (24:3, issue 95) 84, p. 87-89.
"War." WormR (24:3, issue 95) 84, p. 99-100.
"The Wavering Line." WormR (24:3, issue 95) 84, p.
    101-103.

712. BULL, Ruth
"Boom Town." SnapD (7:1) Aut 83, p. 4-5.
"Games in the Back Hills." SnapD (7:1) Aut 83, p. 3.
"Growing Up Maine." SnapD (7:1) Aut 83, p. 6.

713. BULLIS, Jerald
"The Place." NewEngR (6:4) Sum 84, p. 517.

714. BULLOCK, Michael
"Birds in the Garden." Waves (13:1) Aut 84, p. 70.
"Mountains." CanLit (100) Spr 84, p. 56.
"The Plain." Waves (13:1) Aut 84, p. 68.
"Voice." Waves (13:1) Aut 84, p. 68.
"White Vase." Waves (13:1) Aut 84, p. 70.

715. BURCH, Charles
"Jabben." Sparrow (46) 84, p. 30.

716. BURDEN, Jean
"Connection" (for Hildegarde Flanner). Hudson
    (37:4) Wint 84-85, p. 568.

717. BURGESS, A. R.
"Am Not a Jew." NoDaQ (52:3) Sum 84, p. 195.

718. BURGOS, Iris
"Poema: Se va el pasado." Mairena (5:13) Spr 83,
    p. 89-90.

719. BURI, S. G.
"3 To Directorates Almond Water." PraF (5:2/3) Spr
    84, p. 75.
"The Collective Works, A Nother." PraF (5:2/3) Spr
    84, p. 74.
"An Equal Air." PraF (5:2/3) Spr 84, p. 74.
"Morganitas." PraF (5:2/3) Spr 84, p. 72.

720. BURK, Ronnie
"Collage Poem." Open24 (3) 84, p. 24.

721. BURKARD, Michael
"As the Apparition Walked." AmerPoR (13:6) N-D 84,
    p. 6.
"The Clothing of the Heart." AmerPoR (13:6) N-D
    84, p. 3.
"The Dogs on the Cliffs." AmerPoR (13:6) N-D 84,
    p. 7.
"Eerie." AmerPoR (13:6) N-D 84, p. 4.
"The Eternal Husband." AmerPoR (13:6) N-D 84, p. 5.

"Fictions from the Self." <u>AmerPoR</u> (13:6) N-D 84,
    p. 7.
"The Gogol Title." <u>AmerPoR</u> (13:6) N-D 84, p. 3.
"Islands of Feeling." <u>AmerPoR</u> (13:4) Jl-Ag 84, p. 10.
"Islands of Feeling." <u>Tendril</u> (18, special issue)
    84, p.94-95.
"Love's Tongue." <u>AmerPoR</u> (13:6) N-D 84, p. 5.
"The Man I Heard Of." <u>AmerPoR</u> (13:6) N-D 84, p. 6.
"My Aunt and the Sun." <u>AmerPoR</u> (13:6) N-D 84, p. 4.
"Nearing." <u>AmerPoR</u> (13:6) N-D 84, p. 4.
"Series of Photographs (The Genus)." <u>AmerPoR</u>
    (13:6) N-D 84, p. 6.
"The Shadows Are Ripe." <u>AmerPoR</u> (13:6) N-D 84, p. 8.
"Talk to Anyone But Yourself." <u>AmerPoR</u> (13:6) N-D
    84, p. 8.
"White Envelope on Black Sweater." <u>Pequod</u> (16/17)
    84, p. 217.
"Your Voice." <u>Pequod</u> (16/17) 84, p. 218.

722. BURKE, Anne
    "Magic Mongers" (for Ehrich Weiss (Harry Houdini)
        1874-1926, previously published in <u>Blue</u>
        <u>Buffalo</u>). <u>PoetryCR</u> (6:1) Aut 84, p. 14.

723. BURKE, Herbert
    "His Name John Thompson." <u>Germ</u> (8:1) Spr-Sum 84,
        p. 39-43.
    "Shift." <u>Germ</u> (8:2) Aut-Wint 84, p. 42-47.

724. BURKE, Lenny
    "The Sphinx's Daughters." <u>Bogg</u> (52) 84, p. 18.

725. BURNHAM, Deborah
    "The Beached Whale: Wellfleet, Massachusetts, 1840."
        <u>WestB</u> (14) 84, p. 34-35.
    "The Blind Children Learn to Fall." <u>WoosterR</u> (1:1)
        Mr 84, p. 95.
    "The Blind Girl, Thinking." <u>WoosterR</u> (1:1) Mr 84,
        p. 95.
    "Waking Up in Indiana, 1930." <u>GrahamHR</u> (7) Wint
        84, p. 36.
    "Watching Us Sleep." <u>WoosterR</u> (1:1) Mr 84, p. 96.
    "White Monkeys in the Learning Laboratory." <u>WestB</u>
        (14) 84, p. 35.

726. BURNS, Coney
    "The Juke-Box as Messiah." <u>CrossC</u> (6:3) 84, p. 24.
    "Pockets Full of Leaves." <u>CrossC</u> (6:3) 84, p. 24.

727. BURNS, Diane
    "This Ain't No Stoic Look, It's My Face." <u>Abraxas</u>
        (29/30) 84, p. 50.

728. BURNS, Gerald
    "A Book of Spells" (Excerpt). <u>Sulfur</u> (4:1, issue
        10) 84, p. 36-38.

729. BURNS, Michael
    "Summer Solstice, Country Night." <u>KanQ</u> (16:1/2)
        Wint-Spr 84, p. 60.

730. BURNS, Moira
    "Lento for the Late Summer and Anne Sexton" (for Rod
      Jellema). PoetL (79:1) Spr 84, p. 41.
    "The Women of Aran." PoetL (79:1) Spr 84, p. 40.

731. BURNS, Ralph
    "The Big Money." MidwQ (26:1) Aut 84, p. 67.
    "December Twentieth." MidwQ (26:1) Aut 84, p. 70.
    "The Gift" (for W. O. and Michael). MidwQ (26:1)
      Aut 84, p. 69.
    "The House for Sale across the Street." MidwQ
      (26:1) Aut 84, p. 66.
    "The Jay." KenR (NS 6:3) Sum 84, p. 58.
    "Joy." OhioR (33) 84, p. 54.
    "Lacking Sympathy." KenR (NS 6:3) Sum 84, p. 57.
    "March 14-20, 1982, Year of the Eagle" (quoting a
      postage stamp). MidwQ (26:1) Aut 84, p. 64-65.
    "Remembering My Father." MidwQ (26:1) Aut 84, p. 71.
    "The Shetland Islands." MidwQ (26:1) Aut 84, p. 68.
    "Shock Treatment." MidwQ (26:1) Aut 84, p. 63.

732. BURNS, Richard
    "Confidential Memo" (Extract from "The Manager").
      Bound (12:1) Aut 83, p. 16-17.
    "Lullaby" (Extract from "The Manager"). Bound
      (12:1) Aut 83, p. 18.
    "The Manager" (20 Extracts). Bound (12:1) Aut 83,
      p. 15-31.
    "Thursday" (Extract from "The Manager"). Bound
      (12:1) Aut 83, p. 18.
    "To Whom It May Concern" (Extract from "The
      Manager"). Bound (12:1) Aut 83, p. 15-16.

733. BURNS, William
    "All at Once His Leprosy Passed" (Luke: 5). KenR
      (NS 6:3) Sum 84, p. 49.

734. BURR, Gray
    "Cowboy." MassR (25:4) Wint 84, p. 636.

735. BURRELL, Walter
    "Assassinated on the Street" (tr. of Roque Dalton,
      w. Harold Black and Sylvia Bernstein). Vis (15)
      84, p. 18.
    "For the Eye in the Keyhole" (Partial translation of
      Roque Dalton, w. Harold Black and Sylvia
      Bernstein). Vis (15) 84, p. 18.
    "Insomnia" (tr. of Roque Dalton, w. Harold Black and
      Sylvia Bernstein). Vis (15) 84, p. 19.

736. BURRIS, Dorothy
    "Have You Watered the Elephant Today?" NegC (4:1)
      Wint 84, p. 41-42.

737. BURROWS, E. G.
    "Future Talk." BlueBldgs (7) 84, p. 22.

738. BURRUS, Hari
    "No Lo Contendere." NegC (4:4) Aut 84, p. 36-37.

739. BURSK, Christopher
"The Doctors of Tharakien." WoosterR (1:1) Mr 84,
    p. 25-26.
"Foot Soldier." WoosterR (1:1) Mr 84, p. 27.
"Ill at Fifteen." Sparrow (46) 84, p. 7.
"In His Father's House." WoosterR (1:1) Mr 84, p. 29.
"The Injunction" (for Gloria). NowestR (22:1/2)
    84, p. 33.
"Marooned." WoosterR (1:1) Mr 84, p. 28.
"Night Flights." Argo (6:1) 84, p. 5-6.
"Outside the Gates of Norristown Prison." NowestR
    (22:1/2) 84, p. 32.
"Practice." WoosterR (1:1) Mr 84, p. 22-23.
"The Queen Mother." Argo (6:1) 84, p. 4.
"The Thrazien." WoosterR (1:1) Mr 84, p. 24-25.
"Vision." Argo (6:1) 84, p. 8.
"The Way Home from School." WoosterR (1:1) Mr 84,
    p. 21-22.

740. BURT, John
"Her Friends." WebR (9:1) Spr 84, p. 76.
"The Penny and the U-Haul." WebR (9:1) Spr 84, p. 77.
"The Personal Memoirs of U.S. Grant." KanQ (16:3)
    Sum 84, p. 124.
"Plains of Peace." YaleR (73:2) Wint 84, p. 254-258.
"Teratocarcinoma." YaleR (73:3) Spr 84, p. 431.
"Winter: Hunters in Snow" (from the Breughel
    painting). WebR (9:1) Spr 84, p. 75.

741. BURT, Kathryn J.
"Before Nightfall." NewYorker (60:25) 6 Ag 84, p. 36.

742. BURTON, Jonathan
"The Accusation." SanFPJ (6:1) 84, p. 34-36.
"Marching Song." SanFPJ (6:1) 84, p. 36.

743. BUSAILAH, Reja-e
"The Law." HiramPoR (36) Spr-Sum 84, p. 11.
"The Law." Sam (41:2, release 162) 84 or 85, p. 31.

744. BUSCH, Trent
"Aletha." Poetry (144:2) My 84, p. 94.
"Howard Nemerov." SouthernR (20:2) Spr 84, p. 352-
    353.
"Mr. Stevens." Nimrod (27:2) Spr-Sum 84, p. 21-22.
"Staying." Poetry (144:2) My 84, p. 96.
"Woman in a Swing." Poetry (144:2) My 84, p. 95.

745. BUSCHEK, John
"Shifts." AntigR (56) Wint 84, p. 112.

746. BUSH, Barney
"The Last Dream." Vis (14) 84, p. 23.

747. BUSHKOWSKY, Aaron
"The Lush Earth." Waves (12:2/3) Wint 84, p. 92-93.

748. BUSHYEAGER, Peter
"New Jersey Turnpike Night." PaintedB (21) Wint
    84, p. 10-11.

"Things I Can't Remember." <u>PaintedB</u> (21) Wint 84,
    p. 12-13.

749. BUSON
    "Plum-viewing" (Haiku from the Japanese Masters, tr.
    by Lucien Stryk and Takashi Ikemoto, calligraphy
    by Lloyd J. Reynolds). <u>NewL</u> (50:2/3) Wint-Spr
    84, p. 140.

750. BUTCHER, Grace
    "Journey." <u>CapeR</u> (19:3) 20th Anniverary Issue 84,
    p. 4.

751. BUTLER, Jack
    "The Attack of the Zombie Poets." <u>Atlantic</u> (254:3)
        S 84, p. 76.
    "Deuterium Sonnet for a Cassette-Recorder." <u>BelPoJ</u>
        (35:1) Aut 84, p. 7.
    "Keep the Faith." <u>NewOR</u> (11:3/4) Aut-Wint 84, p. 128.
    "Out of the Ghetto of Angels." <u>NewOR</u> (11:3/4) Aut-
        Wint 84, p. 88.
    "A Song for Easter." <u>NewOR</u> (11:3/4) Aut-Wint 84,
        p. 102-103.
    "Withdrawal." <u>PoetryNW</u> (25:2) Sum 84, p. 41-42.

752. BUTLIN, Ron
    "At the Piano." <u>AntigR</u> (57) Spr 84, p. 9.
    "Descriptions of the Falling Snow." <u>AntigR</u> (57)
        Spr 84, p. 10-11.
    "Descriptions of the Falling Snow." <u>Descant</u> (47,
        15:4) Wint 84, p. 173-174.
    "The Embroidress." <u>Descant</u> (47, 15:4) Wint 84, p.
        175.
    "The Gods That I Know Best." <u>Descant</u> (47, 15:4)
        Wint 84, p. 171.
    "Indian Summer." <u>AntigR</u> (57) Spr 84, p. 9.
    "Orpheus' Love Song." <u>AntigR</u> (57) Spr 84, p. 8.
    "These Days." <u>Descant</u> (47, 15:4) Wint 84, p. 172.
    "Two Women." <u>AntigR</u> (57) Spr 84, p. 8.

753. BUTTERS, Christopher
    "The Democrats." <u>SanFPJ</u> (6:4) 84, p. 63.
    "The Main Enemy Is at Home." <u>SanFPJ</u> (6:4) 84, p. 64.
    "War Machine." <u>SanFPJ</u> (6:4) 84, p. 62.

754. BUTTS, W. E.
    "The Visit." <u>MidAR</u> (4:1) Spr 84, p. 173.

755. BYER, Kathryn Stripling
    "All Hallows Eve." <u>GeoR</u> (38:3) Aut 84, p. 550-551.
    "Angels." <u>WestHR</u> (38:2) Sum 84, p. 118.

756. BYLES, Joan Montgomery
    "Hands" (For Peter). <u>Wind</u> (14:52) 84, p. 46.

757. BYRNE, Vera
    "Hakka Woman." <u>PoetryCR</u> (6:1) Aut 84, p. 27.

C., R.: <u>See</u> R. C.

758. CABALLERO BONALD, J. M.
"Inherited Glories" (tr. by Reginald Gibbons).
TriQ (59) Wint 84, p. 205.
"Services Lent" (tr. by Reginald Gibbons). TriQ
(59) Wint 84, p. 207.
"Supplantings" (tr. by Reginald Gibbons). TriQ
(59) Wint 84, p. 206.
"The Uselessness of Antidotes" (tr. by Reginald
Gibbons). TriQ (59) Wint 84, p. 208.

759. CABALQUINTO, Luis
"The Dog-Eater." AmerPoR (13:6) N-D 84, p. 37.

CABAN, David Cortés: See CORTES-CABAN, David

760. CABAÑAS, Esteban
"Poema: Deshabitado el viento, yo busqué la
paloma." Mairena (6:18) 84, p. 192.

761. CABEL, Jesús
"Celebracion de Machu Picchu" (fragmento). Mairena
(6:18) 84, p. 100.

762. CABRAL, Manuel del
"Negro sin Nada en su Casa." Areíto (10:38) 84,
inside back cover.

763. CABRERA, José Antonio
"Sientome Carcomido." Mairena (5:13) Spr 83, p. 91.
"Te Pregunto." Mairena (5:13) Spr 83, p. 92.

CACERES, Fedora Montañez: See MONTAÑEZ CACERES, Fedora

CACHO, Manuel Joglar: See JOGLAR CACHO, Manuel

764. CADER, Teresa
"Parts Do Not Make a Whole." Agni (21) 84, p. 84-86.
"What the Right Hand Gives, the Left Takes Away."
Agni (21) 84, p. 87.

765. CADNUM, Michael
"A Dislike for Flowers." GeoR (38:2) Sum 84, p. 242.
"Tomorrow in the Desert." GeoR (38:1) Spr 84, p. 24.

766. CADSBY, Heather
"Scordatura." PoetryCR (6:1) Aut 84, p. 27.

767. CAGE, John
"Mirage Verbal: Writings through Marcel Duchamp,
Notes" (text derived from Marcel Duchamp,
Notes). PoetryCR (6:1) Aut 84, p. 9.
"Three Mesostics." Chelsea (42/43) 84, p. 381.

768. CAHN, Cynthia
"Ebb Tide" (Route 92). BlueBldgs (7) 84, p. 37.
"In My Darker Moments" (for Francine Hughes,
acquitted of first degree murder in 1977, and
others). BlueBldgs (7) 84, p. 37.
"Report from the State Capitol." KanQ (16:1/2)
Wint-Spr 84, p. 98.

769. CAIN, John
"Upon the Bible Belt." NewL (50:2/3) Wint-Spr 84,
p. 89.

770. CAIN, Kathleen
"On the Death of One of Our Fathers" (for Chief).
Peb (23) 84, p. 44.

771. CAKS, Aleksandrs
"May" (tr. by Inara Cedrins). Thrpny (18) Sum 84,
p. 26.

772. CALANDRO, Ann
"The Cutting Board " WebR (9:1) Spr 84, p. 60.
"Prelude" (For A.L.A.). WebR (9:1) Spr 84, p. 60-61.

773. CALDERWOOD, James L.
"Daddies." AmerS (53:1) Wint 83/84, p. 26.

774. CALDWELL, S. F.
"Election year." SanFPJ (6:4) 84, p. 42.
"Der Fuhrer." SanFPJ (6:4) 84, p. 43.
"Tomorrow the World." SanFPJ (6:4) 84, p. 9.

775. CALLAHAN, Jeff
"November 22, 1963." Wind (14:52) 84, p. 6.
"The Road to the Highway." Wind (14:52) 84, p. 6-7.

CALLE, Manuel Alvarez: See ALVAREZ CALLE, Manuel

776. CALMAN, Nancy Harris
"Night Flying." Vis (16) 84, p. 18.

777. CALVERT, John
"Letters from Stalingrad." WoosterR (1:2) N 84, p.
62-65.

778. CALVERT, Laura
"The New Moon." SouthernR (20:2) Spr 84, p. 368.

779. CAMENISCH, Silvio
"Survilsan Village" (tr. by John Allen and Elly
Crol). Os (18) 84, p. 15.
"Vitget Sursilvan." Os (18) 84, p. 14.

780. CAMERON, Anne
"Iris." CanLit (100) Spr 84, p. 58-59.
"Neuchatlitz." CanLit (100) Spr 84, p. 57-58.

781. CAMERON, Esther
"Argumentum e Silentio" (for René Char, tr. of
Paul Celan). Sulfur (4:2, issue 11) 84, p. 9-10.
"Frankfurt, September" (tr. of Paul Celan). Sulfur
(4:2, issue 11) 84, p. 13.
"Les Globes" (tr. of Paul Celan). Sulfur (4:2,
issue 11) 84, p. 11.
"The Industrious natural resources" (tr. of Paul
Celan). Sulfur (4:2, issue 11) 84, p. 14-15.
"No hand holds me either" (tr. of Paul Celan).
Sulfur (4:2, issue 11) 84, p. 12.

"The Scooped-Out Heart" (tr. of Paul Celan).
    Sulfur (4:2, issue 11) 84, p. 14.
"White, white, white" (tr. of Paul Celan). Sulfur
    (4:2, issue 11) 84, p. 12.

782. CAMERON, Michael
     "Bees and Their Problems." Waves (12:4) Spr 84, p.
         52.
     "Seven Uses for Loneliness." Waves (12:4) Spr 84,
         p. 53.

783. CAMILLO, Victor
     "The Bluesman." NewL (50:4) Sum 84, p. 88.

784. CAMP, James
     "Singing in the Rain: A Success Story." NegC (4:4)
         Aut 84, p. 50.

785. CAMPANA, Dino
     "Autumn Garden" (Florence, tr. by Charles Wright).
         MissouriR (7:3) 84, p. 45.
     "Autumn Garden" (Florence, tr. by Charles Wright).
         Thrpny (19) Aut 84, p. 11.
     "Genoa Woman" (from "Donna Genovese," tr. by Charles
         Wright). Thrpny (17) Spr 84, p. 20.
     "In the Mountains" (From the Falterona to Corniolo --
         deserted valleys, tr. by Charles Wright).
         MissouriR (7:3) 84, p. 46.
     "Orphic Songs" (tr. by Charles Wright). MissouriR
         (7:3) 84, p. 43-47.
     "Song of Darkness" (tr. by Charles Wright).
         MissouriR (7:3) 84, p. 47.
     "Toscanita" (For Bino Binazzi, tr. by Charles
         Wright). Thrpny (19) Aut 84, p. 11.
     "Voyage to Montevideo" (tr. by Charles Wright).
         MissouriR (7:3) 84, p. 43-44.

786. CAMPBELL, Anneke
     "Cranes." Telescope (3:1) Wint 84, p. 80-82.

787. CAMPBELL, Brian
     "A Brief Exercise in Megalomania." PoetryCR (5:4)
         Sum 84, p. 19.

788. CAMPBELL, John
     "7/28." NowestR (22:1/2) 84, p. 129.
     "8/1." NowestR (22:1/2) 84, p. 130.
     "8/2." NowestR (22:1/2) 84, p. 131.
     "8/19." NowestR (22:1/2) 84, p. 132.
     "8/24 (The Farmhouse Finally Speaks)." NowestR
         (22:1/2) 84, p. 133.
     "The Ranch." PoetL (79:1) Spr 84, p. 34-35.

789. CAMPBELL, Mary Belle
     "Attending a Young Man Resting beside a Stream:
         Twilight Image of a Japanese Scroll." StoneC
         (11:3/4) Spr-Sum 84, p. 58-59.

790. CAMPBELL, Mary
     "Justice." Agni (21) 84, p. 34.

791. CAMPBELL, Rick
    "Legend." <u>GeoR</u> (38:3) Aut 84, p. 544.

792. CAMPION, Dan
    "Crows." <u>NegC</u> (4:2) Spr 84, p. 65.
    "The Two Elm Trees." <u>ThirdW</u> (2) Spr 84, p. 69.

793. CANAN, Janine B.
    "Seaside." <u>Vis</u> (16) 84, p. 5.

794. CANDIOTI, Miguel Angel
    "Semen Testimonial." <u>Mairena</u> (5:14) Aut 83, p. 86.

795. CANTONI, Louis J.
    "In a Northern Forest." <u>CapeR</u> (19:3) 20th
    Anniverary Issue 84, p. 5.

796. CANTRELL, Charles
    "Setting the Fires" (after Michael Lesy's <u>Wisconsin
    Death Trip</u>). <u>SouthernPR</u> (24:2) Aut 84, p. 66.

797. CANTWELL, Billie Lou
    "Metamorphosis." <u>PoeticJ</u> (3) 83, p. 37.

798. CANTWELL, Kevin T.
    "North." <u>Poem</u> (51) Mr [i.e. Jl] 84, p. 28.
    "Returning Home from the Field." <u>Poem</u> (51) Mr
    [i.e. Jl] 84, p. 24-25.
    "The Singing Cabbie." <u>Poem</u> (51) Mr [i.e. Jl] 84,
    p. 26-27.

799. CAPELLAN, Angel
    "Lullaby for the Nuclear Age" (For my one-year-old
    daughter). <u>Stepping</u> (Anniversary Issue I) 84,
    p. 23-24.

800. CAPPELLO, Rosemary
    "Leaving." <u>PaintedB</u> (21) Wint 84, p. 7.

801. CARADEC, Odile
    "On Claudine Goux." <u>MichQR</u> (23:4) Aut 84, p. 488.

802. CARB, Alison B.
    "My Father's Whistle." <u>Amelia</u> [1:1] Ap 84, p. 12.

CARBEAU, Mitchell les: <u>See</u> LesCARBEAU, Mitchell

803. CARDENAL, Ernesto
    "DC 7B" (tr. by Maria Bennett). <u>CrabCR</u> (2:1) Sum
    84, p. 19.
    "Epigrams" (tr. by Maria Bennett). <u>CrabCR</u> (2:1)
    Sum 84, p. 16-17.
    "Imitation of Propertius" (tr. by Maria Bennett).
    <u>CrabCR</u> (2:1) Sum 84, p. 18.
    "León" (tr. by Jonathan Cohen). <u>Nat</u> (238:3) 28
    Ja 84, p. 100.
    "Murder, Inc." (tr. by Maria Bennett). <u>CrabCR</u>
    (2:1) Sum 84, p. 19.
    "Oración por Marilyn Monroe" (fragmento).
    <u>Areíto</u> (10:37) 84, inside back cover.

804. CARDILLO, Joe
"Fleetingly Thin." RagMag (3:2) Aut 84, p. 23.

805. CARDONA PEÑA, Alfredo
"Iguanas" (tr. by Nicomedes Suárez Araúz). Nat
(238:3) 28 Ja 84, p. 100.

806. CARDOSO, Neusa
"Absence." PoetryCR (5:3) Spr 84, p. 13.
"Ausência." PoetryCR (5:3) Spr 84, p. 13.
"Becoming" (tr. by Tamara D. Barile). Waves
(12:2/3) Wint 84, p. 70.
"Daily News" (tr. by Tamara D. Barile). Waves
(12:2/3) Wint 84, p. 68.
"Deus." Waves (12:2/3) Wint 84, p. 66.
"Dieu" (tr. by Tamara D. Barile). Waves (12:2/3)
Wint 84, p. 66.
"O Escorpião ea Valsinha" (Selections). Waves
(12:2/3) Wint 84, p. 66-70.
"God" (tr. by Tamara D. Barile). Waves (12:2/3)
Wint 84, p. 66.
"Magalópole." Waves (12:2/3) Wint 84, p. 67.
"Megalopole" (tr. by Tamara D. Barile). Waves
(12:2/3) Wint 84, p. 67.
"Megalopolis" (tr. by Tamara D. Barile). Waves
(12:2/3) Wint 84, p. 67.
"Notícia Popular." Waves (12:2/3) Wint 84, p. 68.
"Nouvelles Populaires" (tr. by Tamara D. Barile).
Waves (12:2/3) Wint 84, p. 69.
"Painting." PoetryCR (5:3) Spr 84, p. 13.
"Pedestre." PoetryCR (5:3) Spr 84, p. 13.
"Pedestrian." PoetryCR (5:3) Spr 84, p. 13.
"Quadro." PoetryCR (5:3) Spr 84, p. 13.
"Reconstrucao." PoetryCR (5:3) Spr 84, p. 13.
"Reconstruction." PoetryCR (5:3) Spr 84, p. 13.
"The Scorpion and the Minuet" (selections, tr. by
Tamara D. Barile). Waves (12:2/3) Wint 84, p.
66-70.
"Le Scorpion et le Menuet" (selections, tr. by
Tamara D. Barile). Waves (12:2/3) Wint 84, p.
66-70.
"Tournant" (tr. by Tamara D. Barile). Waves
(12:2/3) Wint 84, p. 70.
"Viração." Waves (12:2/3) Wint 84, p. 70.

807. CARDOZO, Manoel
"Frontier" (tr. of Oswald de Andrade). Vis (15)
84, p. 8.
"The Khaki Lozenge" (tr. of Mario de Andrade). Vis
(15) 84, p. 7.
"The Morning Star" (tr. of Manuel Bandeira). Vis
(15) 84, p. 9.

808. CARDULLO, Bert
"Why Should My Name Be Remembered?" (tr. of Bertolt
Brecht). WebR (9:1) Spr 84, p. 98.

809. CAREW, Jan
"Catechism of Hope" (for Sheila, Anne, Sekou,
Beverly)." BlackALF (18:1) Spr 84, p. 32.

"For Dennis Brutus." <u>BlackALF</u> (18:1) Spr 84, p. 32.
"Gems & Dust." <u>BlackALF</u> (18:1) Spr 84, p. 33.
"The High Road to Harar." <u>BlackALF</u> (18:1) Spr 84,
    p. 31-32.

810. CAREY, Barbara
    "Everything in Its Place." <u>PoetryCR</u> (6:2) Wint 84-
        85, p. 27.

811. CAREY, Michael A.
    "Gaeilge." <u>Telescope</u> (3:2) Spr 84, p. 14.
    "The Piper of Farragut." <u>MidwQ</u> (25:4) Sum 84, p.
        403-404.

812. CAREY, Michael
    "Summer in Sidney, Iowa." <u>Nimrod</u> (27:2) Spr-Sum
        84, p. 23.

813. CARGYLLE, Dario
    "Ex Cathedra." <u>ChiR</u> (34:2) Spr 84, p. 48.

814. CARLILE, Henry
    "The Cloud and the Plow and the Meaning of Rhyme."
        <u>AmerPoR</u> (13:5) S-O 84, p. 47.
    "Fort Ord, California, 1953." <u>TarRP</u> (24:1) Aut 84,
        p. 6-7.
    "Instruments." <u>TarRP</u> (24:1) Aut 84, p. 7-9.

815. CARLISLE, Thomas John
    "The Annunciation" (Center Panel from the Mérode
        Altarpiece, by Robert Campin, Flemish, about
        1425). <u>ChrC</u> (101:39) 12 D 84, p. 1164.

816. CARLSON, Burton L.
    "Boston 1.12.70." <u>CapeR</u> (19:3) 20th Anniverary
        Issue 84, p. 6.

817. CARLSON, Michael
    "Baybrook." <u>Origin</u> (5:3) Spr 84, p. 63.
    "Images II." <u>Origin</u> (5:3) Spr 84, p. 67.
    "Private Walk / No Trespassing." <u>Origin</u> (5:3) Spr
        84, p. 60-62.
    "Savin Rock 1956." <u>Origin</u> (5:3) Spr 84, p. 59.
    "Self-portrait of Someone Else." <u>Origin</u> (5:3) Spr
        84, p. 65-66.
    "Signal Rock." <u>Origin</u> (5:3) Spr 84, p. 60.
    "Wednesday, 8 February." <u>Origin</u> (5:3) Spr 84, p. 64.
    "Woodmont Beach, after Hurricane Belle." <u>Origin</u>
        (5:3) Spr 84, p. 58.

818. CARLSON, R. S.
    "All the Comforts of the VA." <u>CapeR</u> (19:2) Sum 84,
        p. 39.

819. CARMAGNOLA de MEDINA, Gladys
    "Pre-Requiem." <u>Mairena</u> (6:18) 84, p. 190.

820. CARMELL, Pamela
    "Fossils." <u>LindLM</u> (3:2/4) Ap-D 84, p. 19.

821. CARMI, T.
    "The Gate" (tr. by Grace Schulman). <u>Pequod</u> (16/17)
       84, p. 111.
    "His Shutters Close" (tr. by Grace Schulman).
       <u>Pequod</u> (16/17) 84, p. 112.

822. CARMONA, Julio
    "XXXVIII. Esta es la casa." <u>Mairena</u> (6:18) 84, p. 98.

823. CARNERO, Guillermo
    "Melancolia de Paul Scarron Poeta Burlesco."
       <u>Mairena</u> (6:18) 84, p. 66.

824. CARNEVALE, Robert
    "Exemplary." <u>ParisR</u> (26:94) Wint 84, p. 162.

825. CAROL, Luiza
    "Only One Plain Road." <u>Amelia</u> [1:1] Ap 84, p. 6.

826. CARPATHIOS, Neil
    "After the Rain." <u>WoosterR</u> (1:2) N 84, p. 82-83.
    "Dusk." <u>ThirdW</u> (2) Spr 84, p. 54-55.
    "Ohio Winter." <u>ThirdW</u> (2) Spr 84, p. 53-54.
    "The Road." <u>ThirdW</u> (2) Spr 84, p. 56-57.
    "Upon Walking by the River, in Hope of an
       Inspiration." <u>PoeticJ</u> (1) 83, p. 27.

827. CARPENTER, Bogdana
    "Anabasis" (tr. of Zbigniew Herbert, w. John
       Carpenter). <u>ManhatR</u> (3:2) Wint 84-85, p. 25.
    "Babylon" (tr. of Zbigniew Herbert, w. John
       Carpenter). <u>ManhatR</u> (3:2) Wint 84-85, p. 31.
    "Cradle Song" (tr. of Zbigniew Herbert, w. John
       Carpenter). <u>ManhatR</u> (3:2) Wint 84-85, p. 30.
    "From the Top of the Stairs" (tr. of Zbigniew
       Herbert, w. John Carpenter). <u>MichQR</u> (23:3) Sum
       84, p. 352-354.
    "In Memoriam Nagy Laszlo" (tr. of Zbigniew Herbert,
       w. John Carpenter). <u>ManhatR</u> (3:2) Wint 84-85,
       p. 31-32.
    "Lament" (To the memory of my mother, tr. of
       Zbigniew Herbert, w. John Carpenter). <u>ManhatR</u>
       (3:2) Wint 84-85, p. 27.
    "The Monster of Mr. Cogito" (tr. of Zbigniew
       Herbert, w. John Carpenter). <u>ManhatR</u> (3:2) Wint
       84-85, p. 21-23.
    "Mr. Cogito Looks at His Face in the Mirror" (tr. of
       Zbigniew Herbert, w. John Carpenter). <u>ManhatR</u>
       (3:2) Wint 84-85, p. 19-20.
    "Mr. Cogito--Notes from the House of the Dead" (tr.
       of Zbigniew Herbert, w. John Carpenter).
       <u>ManhatR</u> (3:2) Wint 84-85, p. 34-37.
    "Mr. Cogito on Virtue" (tr. of Zbigniew Herbert, w.
       John Carpenter). <u>ManhatR</u> (3:2) Wint 84-85, p.
       24-25.
    "Mr. Cogito Thinks about Blood" (tr. of Zbigniew
       Herbert, w. John Carpenter). <u>ManhatR</u> (3:2) Wint
       84-85, p. 38-40.
    "The Murderers of Kings" (tr. of Zbigniew Herbert,
       w. John Carpenter). <u>ManhatR</u> (3:2) Wint 84-85,

p. 29.
"The Old Masters" (tr. of Zbigniew Herbert, w. John
    Carpenter). ManhatR (3:2) Wint 84-85, p. 26-27.
"Old Prometheus" (tr. of Zbigniew Herbert, w. John
    Carpenter). ManhatR (3:2) Wint 84-85, p. 20.
"On the Margin of the Trial" (tr. of Zbigniew
    Herbert, w. John Carpenter). ManhatR (3:2) Wint
    84-85, p. 19.
"Photograph" (tr. of Zbigniew Herbert, w. John
    Carpenter). ManhatR (3:2) Wint 84-85, p. 28.
"Prayer of Mr. Cogito--Traveler" (tr. of Zbigniew
    Herbert, w. John Carpenter). ManhatR (3:2) Wint
    84-85, p. 32-34.
"Report from the Besieged City" (tr. of Zbigniew
    Herbert, w. John Carpenter). ManhatR (3:2) Wint
    84-85, p. 42-43.
"Shameful Dreams" (tr. of Zbigniew Herbert, w. John
    Carpenter). ManhatR (3:2) Wint 84-85, p. 27-28.
"To Ryszard Krynicki--A Letter" (tr. of Zbigniew
    Herbert, w. John Carpenter). ManhatR (3:2) Wint
    84-85, p. 40-41.
"We fall asleep on words" (tr. of Zbigniew Herbert,
    w. John Carpenter). ManhatR (3:2) Wint 84-85,
    p. 18.

828. CARPENTER, David
    "Garden Spider." CrossC (6:3) 84, p. 15.

829. CARPENTER, J. D.
    "Barn Dance." CanLit (102) Aut 84, p. 33.
    "Midnight in the City" CanLit (102) Aut 84, p. 34.

830. CARPENTER, John
    "Anabasis" (tr. of Zbigniew Herbert, w. Bogdana
        Carpenter). ManhatR (3:2) Wint 84-85, p. 25.
    "Babylon" (tr. of Zbigniew Herbert, w. Bogdana
        Carpenter). ManhatR (3:2) Wint 84-85, p. 31.
    "Cradle Song" (tr. of Zbigniew Herbert, w. Bogdana
        Carpenter). ManhatR (3:2) Wint 84-85, p. 30.
    "From the Top of the Stairs" (tr. of Zbigniew
        Herbert, w. Bogdana Carpenter). MichQR (23:3)
        Sum 84, p. 352-354.
    "In Memoriam Nagy Laszlo" (tr. of Zbigniew Herbert,
        w. Bogdana Carpenter). ManhatR (3:2) Wint 84-
        85, p. 31-32.
    "Lament" (To the memory of my mother, tr. of
        Zbigniew Herbert, w. Bogdana Carpenter).
        ManhatR (3:2) Wint 84-85, p. 27.
    "The Monster of Mr. Cogito" (tr. of Zbigniew
        Herbert, w. Bogdana Carpenter). ManhatR (3:2)
        Wint 84-85, p. 21-23.
    "Mr. Cogito Looks at His Face in the Mirror" (tr. of
        Zbigniew Herbert, w. Bogdana Carpenter).
        ManhatR (3:2) Wint 84-85, p. 19-20.
    "Mr. Cogito--Notes from the House of the Dead" (tr.
        of Zbigniew Herbert, w. Bogdana Carpenter).
        ManhatR (3:2) Wint 84-85, p. 34-37.
    "Mr. Cogito on Virtue" (tr. of Zbigniew Herbert, w.
        Bogdana Carpenter). ManhatR (3:2) Wint 84-85,
        p. 24-25.

"Mr. Cogito Thinks about Blood" (tr. of Zbigniew
    Herbert, w. Bogdana Carpenter). ManhatR (3:2)
    Wint 84-85, p. 38-40.
"The Murderers of Kings" (tr. of Zbigniew Herbert,
    w. Bogdana Carpenter). ManhatR (3:2) Wint 84-
    85, p. 29.
"The Old Masters" (tr. of Zbigniew Herbert, w.
    Bogdana Carpenter). ManhatR (3:2) Wint 84-85,
    p. 26-27.
"Old Prometheus" (tr. of Zbigniew Herbert, w.
    Bogdana Carpenter). ManhatR (3:2) Wint 84-85,
    p. 20.
"On the Margin of the Trial" (tr. of Zbigniew
    Herbert, w. Bogdana Carpenter). ManhatR (3:2)
    Wint 84-85, p. 19.
"Photograph" (tr. of Zbigniew Herbert, w. Bogdana
    Carpenter). ManhatR (3:2) Wint 84-85, p. 28.
"Prayer of Mr. Cogito--Traveler" (tr. of Zbigniew
    Herbert, w. Bogdana Carpenter). ManhatR (3:2)
    Wint 84-85, p. 32-34.
"Report from the Besieged City" (tr. of Zbigniew
    Herbert, w. Bogdana Carpenter). ManhatR (3:2)
    Wint 84-85, p. 42-43.
"Shameful Dreams" (tr. of Zbigniew Herbert, w.
    Bogdana Carpenter). ManhatR (3:2) Wint 84-85,
    p. 27-28.
"To Ryszard Krynicki--A Letter" (tr. of Zbigniew
    Herbert, w. Bogdana Carpenter). ManhatR (3:2)
    Wint 84-85, p. 40-41.
"We fall asleep on words" (tr. of Zbigniew Herbert,
    w. Bogdana Carpenter). ManhatR (3:2) Wint 84-
    85, p. 18.

831. CARPENTER, William
    "Gaspè." AmerPoR (13:4) Jl-Ag 84, p. 4.
    "Man Climbing Katahdin." AmerPoR (13:4) Jl-Ag 84,
        p. 3.
    "Rain." AmerPoR (13:4) Jl-Ag 84, p. 4.
    "The Red Devil." AmerPoR (13:4) Jl-Ag 84, p. 3.
    "Something Is Adrift in the Water." QW (19) Aut-
        Wint 84-85, p. 86-87.
    "Stairway." Pequod (16/17) 84, p. 76.
    "Woman without a Fan." AmerPoR (13:4) Jl-Ag 84, p. 5.

832. CARPER, Thomas
    "An Aerial Photograph." AmerS (53:4) Aut 84, p. 540.
    "The Monster in the Park." Poetry (144:6) S 84, p.
        342.

833. CARREÑO, Alfonso
    "The Kiss" (tr. by Louis Bourne). Stand (25:4) Aut
        84, p. 20.

834. CARRERA, Margarita
    "Dadme la palabra sola." Mairena (6:18) 84, p. 213.

835. CARRIE, Leann Jackson
    "Susan's Sarah at the Beach." Calyx (8:3) Aut-Wint
        84, p. 31.
    "That Girl." Calyx (8:3) Aut-Wint 84, p. 32.

CARRILLO   120

836. CARRILLO, Jo
     "Sonora's Two Pass at Dawn." Calyx (8:2) Spr 84,
        p. 96.
     "Wind and Seed Abstraction." Calyx (8:2) Spr 84,
        p. 95.

837. CARROLL, Paul
     "Football Weather" (to Jack Kerouac). TriQ (60)
        Spr-Sum 84, p. 291-292.

838. CARROTHERS, Pat
     "Water Music." IndR (7:3) Sum 84, p. 56-57.

839. CARRUTH, Hayden
     "Chicory" (in mem. Paul Goodman). NewEngR (6:3)
        Spr 84, p. 394.
     "Cindy Working, I." PoetryE (15) Aut 84, p. 31-32.
     "Cindy Working, II." PoetryE (15) Aut 84, p. 33-34.
     "The Complete Poems of Septic Tank." NewL (50:4)
        Sum 84, p. 31.
     "Eternity Blues." NewEngR (6:3) Spr 84, p. 395.
     "The Ethics of Altruism in Altoona." WestB (14)
        84, p. 6-7.
     "For Peg: A Remnant of Song Still Distantly
        Sounding." Hudson (37:3) Aut 84, p. 396-397.
     "Fragment." Hudson (37:3) Aut 84, p. 396.
     "Lost." Kayak (64) My 84, p. 22-23.
     "Names." MassR (25:1) Spr 84, p. 125-141.
     "New Hartford." WestHR (38:1) Spr 84, p. 55-57.
     "Not Transhistorical Death, or at Least Not Quite."
        TriQ (61) Aut 84, p. 73-74.
     "Of Distress Being Humiliated by the Classical
        Chinese Poets." TriQ (61) Aut 84, p. 71.
     "The Oldest Killed Lake in North America." Hudson
        (37:3) Aut 84, p. 398.
     "Pa McCabe." NewL (51:2) Wint 84-85, p. 42-43.
     "Poem Catching Up with an Idea." Ploughs (10:1)
        84, p. 35.
     "Reflections." Kayak (64) My 84, p. 23-24.
     "Saturday Morning." GrandS (3:2) Wint 84, p. 158.
     "Septic Tank." NewL (50:4) Sum 84, p. 30-31.
     "Something for Richard Eberhart." Chelsea (42/43)
        84, p. 97.
     "Sometimes When Lovers Lie Quietly Together,
        Unexpectedly One of Them Will Become Aware of the
        Other's Pulse." TriQ (61) Aut 84, p. 72.
     "Song for My Sixtieth Year." Shen (35:1) 83-84, p.
        36.
     "The World As Will and Representation." ParisR
        (26:91) Spr 84, p. 83.

840. CARSON, Anne
     "Canicula di Anna: What Do We Have Here?" QRL
        (Poetry series 6, v. 25) 84, p. 1-39.

841. CARTAÑA, Luis
     "Tres Estudios." Mairena (6:18) 84, p. 176.

842. CARTER, Ellin
     "The Poet Flees from the British Novel." Wind

(14:52) 84, p. 22.

843. CARTER, Jared
   "Dear Friend." ChiR (34:3) Sum 84, p. 22.
   "The Fire's Dream" (from Pincushion's Strawberry).
      AmerPoR (13:3) My-Je 84, p. 47.
   "Lightning." ChiR (34:3) Sum 84, p. 23.

844. CARTER, John
   "How We Survived the Cretaceous Age Together."
      Open24 (3) 84, p. 35.

845. CARTWRIGHT, Keith
   "Between the Rivers" (2 Flood). Wind (14:50) 84,
      p. 4.

846. CARVER, Raymond
   "Afghanistan." ParisR (26:93) Aut 84, p. 47.
   "After Rainy Days." NewL (51:2) Wint 84-85, p. 18.
   "The Ashtray." ParisR (26:93) Aut 84, p. 45-46.
   "The Catch." NewL (51:2) Wint 84-85, p. 18.
   "Fear." ParisR (26:93) Aut 84, p. 41.
   "Hominy and Rain." ParisR (26:93) Aut 84, p. 49-50.
   "Iowa Summer." Chelsea (42/43) 84, p. 185.
   "Listening" (nine poems). NewL (51:2) Wint 84-85,
      p. 11-18.
   "Listening." NewL (51:2) Wint 84-85, p. 17.
   "Medicine." NewL (51:2) Wint 84-85, p. 14.
   "Memory." NewL (51:2) Wint 84-85, p. 15.
   "Movement." ParisR (26:93) Aut 84, p. 40.
   "A Poem Not Against Songbirds." NewL (51:2) Wint
      84-85, p. 16.
   "Radio Waves" (for Antonio Machado). ParisR
      (26:93) Aut 84, p. 37-38.
   "The Road." ParisR (26:93) Aut 84, p. 39.
   "Romanticism" (For my friend Linda Gregg, after
      reading "Classicism"). ParisR (26:93) Aut 84,
      p. 51.
   "A Squall." NewL (51:2) Wint 84-85, p. 14-15.
   "Still Looking Out for Number One." ParisR (26:93)
      Aut 84, p. 48.
   "Trying to Sleep Late on a Saturday Morning in
      November." Chelsea (42/43) 84, p. 185.
   "The Windows of the Summer Vacation Houses." NewL
      (51:2) Wint 84-85, p. 12-13.
   "Woolworth's, 1954." ParisR (26:93) Aut 84, p. 42-44.
   "Work" (For John Gardner, d. Sept. 14, 1982). NewL
      (51:2) Wint 84-85, p. 16.

847. CASACCIA, Gladys
   "Cuando Me Sucede." Mairena (6:18) 84, p. 193.

848. CASAL, Lourdes
   "Areíto por Carlos Muñiz." Areíto (9:36) 84,
      p. 77.

849. CASE, Robert
   "The Spanish Skull." CentR (28:3) Sum 84, p. 224.

850. CASE, Sandra
"Morning Fragments." YetASM (3) 84, p. 5.

851. CASEY, Deb
"Evelyn." PraS (58:2) Sum 84, p. 38.
"A Map for You." PraS (58:2) Sum 84, p. 39.
"Netsuke." MassR (25:4) Wint 84, p. 538.
"Patience at the Window, Waiting." 13thM (8:1/2)
    84, p. 158-159.
"Relations." PraS (58:2) Sum 84, p. 40.

852. CASEY, Michael
"OPC." LittleM (14:3) 84, p. 42-43.

853. CASEY, Philip
"Beneath the Veneer." CreamCR (9:1/2) 84, p. 66-67.

854. CASH, Edna Floyd
"Tohopekaliga." PoeticJ (7) 84, p. 22.

855. CASKEY, Noelle
"Seedbed." YellowS (12) Aut 84, p. 31.
"Siren." YellowS (13) Wint 84, p. 37.
"You Are My Primavera." YellowS (12) Aut 84, p. 31.

856. CASSIDY, John
"The Wasp Trap." Stand (25:1) Wint 83-84, p. 27.

857. CASSITY, Turner
"For the Scrapbook of Mrs. Charles Black." YaleR
    (73:2) Wint 84, p. 301-302.
"Soldiers of Orange." ChiR (34:2) Spr 84, p. 44-47.

858. CASTAÑO, Wilfredo Q.
"Ethnic Diagnosis." OroM (2:3/4, issue 7/8) 84, p.
    48.
"First Time." OroM (2:3/4, issue 7/8) 84, p. 22-23.
"Poem to My Brother Man." OroM (2:3/4, issue 7/8)
    84, p. 3.
"To People Who Pick Food." OroM (2:3/4, issue 7/8)
    84, p. 49-50.

CASTELAR, José Adán: See ADAN CASTELAR, José

859. CASTELNOVO, Columba
"Soledad es una vieja casona." Mairena (6:17) Aut
    84, p. 97.

860. CASTELPOGGI, Atilio Jorge
"Tarjeta de Identificacion." Mairena (6:18) 84, p.
    116.

861. CASTERTON, Julia
"A Terrible Gift I Have Made to Myself." MinnR
    (N.S. 22) Spr 84, p. 31.

862. CASTILLO, Ernesto
"In This Country" (tr. by Marc Zimmerman and Ellen
    Banberger). MinnR (N.S. 22) Spr 84, p. 79-80.

863. CASTILLO, Julia
     "Sueño del Caballero." Mairena (6:18) 84, p. 71.

864. CASTILLO, Otto René
     "Encuentro." Mairena (6:18) 84, p. 212.
     "Invencibles." Mairena (6:18) 84, p. 212.
     "Mourning Flavor" (tr. by David Volpendesta). Vis
          (15) 84, p. 20-21.
     "Vámonos Patria a Caminar." Areíto (10:37) 84,
          p. 35.
     "The Wind Passes through Streets" (tr. by Barbara
          Paschke). Vis (15) 84, p. 22.

865. CASTLE, Sandie
     "Ocean City: A Nice Place to Visit But." Open24
          (3) 84, p. 46-48.
     "Soap Opera in Five Easy Pieces" (for Jay Fisher).
          Open24 (3) 84, p. 48-49.

866. CASTRO, Jan Garden
     "Dark Interiors." Tele (19) 83, p. 129.
     "Reflecting Light." Tele (19) 83, p. 130.

867. CASTRO, Shandra
     "Acontece." Mairena (6:17) Aut 84, p. 84.

868. CASTRO de LEON, José
     "Todo Concluido" (fragmentos). Mairena (5:14) Aut
          83, p. 79.

869. CASULLO, Joanne
     "Bus Ride." KanQ (16:1/2) Wint-Spr 84, p. 155.
     "Language." KanQ (16:1/2) Wint-Spr 84, p. 156.

870. CATALA, Rafael
     "Envejecer." Mairena (5:14) Aut 83, p. 87.
     "Klemente Soto Beles." Areíto (9:36) 84, p. 103.
     "El Proceso Creador" (para Angel Rama). Prismal
          (12/13) Aut 84, p. 53-54.

871. CATINA, Ray
     "Fireworks." PikeF (6) Aut 84, p. 8.

872. CATLIN, Alan
     "Los Adultéros." WoosterR (1:1) Mr 84, p. 41.
     "After Marat, the Charlotte Corday Vacation in the
          White Hotel." CrabCR (2:1) Sum 84, p. 22-23.
     "August 1953." PoeticJ (5) 84, p. 11.
     "The Delta at Sunset." Veloc (2) Spr 83, p. 16.
     "First Hand Viewing the Ground Zero Nevada Desert
          Atomic Bomb Tests 1957." SanFPJ (6:2) 84, p. 22-
          23.
     "Illegal Immigrants Entering the City." WoosterR
          (1:1) Mr 84, p. 41.
     "The Miracle Worker." YetASM (3) 84, p. 2.
     "The Resurrection." Veloc (3) Aut-Wint 83, p. 29.
     "The Rising Gorge." PoeticJ (2) 83, p. 36.
     "Sleepwalking." PoeticJ (2) 83, p. 15.
     "Stuffed Animals." PoeticJ (2) 83, p. 17.
     "The Texas Tower Wallace Stevens." WoosterR (1:2)

N 84, p. 36.
"Wallace Stevens As the Emperor of Ice Cream."
    WoosterR (1:2) N 84, p. 35.
"Wallace Stevens in Florida." WoosterR (1:2) N 84,
    p. 34.
"War Games." PoeticJ (3) 83, p. 6.

873. CATTAFI, Bartolo
     "Archipelagoes" (tr. by Robert White). Chelsea
         (42/43) 84, p. 152.
     "Measurements" (tr. by Robert White). Chelsea
         (42/43) 84, p. 152.

874. CATULLUS
     "VIII. Miser Catulle, desinas ineptire." CimR (67)
         Ap 84, p. 43.
     "8. Miserable Catullus, stop all this foolishness"
         (tr. by Corrinne Hales). CimR (67) Ap 84, p. 42.
     "XI. Furi et Aureli, comites Catulli." CimR (67)
         Ap 84, p. 41.
     "11. Furius and Aurelius, such eager followers" (tr.
         by Corrinne Hales). CimR (67) Ap 84, p. 40.
     "70. My woman says she wishes to marry no one" (tr.
         by Corrinne Hales). CimR (67) Ap 84, p. 44.
     "LXX. Nulli se dicit mulier mea nubere malle."
         CimR (67) Ap 84, p. 44.
     "Catullus 8" (in Latin). Argo (5:3) 84, p. 16.
     "Catullus 8" (tr. by Michael Kelly). Argo (5:3)
         84, p. 17.
     "Catullus 83" (in Latin). Argo (5:3) 84, p. 15.
     "Catullus 83" (tr. by Michael Kelly). Argo (5:3)
         84, p. 15.

875. CAULFIELD, Carlota
     "Fanaim (Yo Espero)." Mairena (6:18) 84, p. 178.
     "Oscuridad Divina." Mairena (6:16) Spr 84, p. 13-14.

876. CAVELL, Kathleen
     "The Season of Devastation" (Excerpt, tr. of Claude
         Esteban, w. Stanley L. Cavell). Pequod (16/17)
         84, p. 240-241.

877. CAVELL, Stanley L.
     "The Season of Devastation" (Excerpt, tr. of Claude
         Esteban, w. Kathleen Cavell). Pequod (16/17)
         84, p. 240-241.

878. CAWLEY, Kevin
     "Dragons." PoetL (79:1) Spr 84, p. 28-29.

879. CAWS, Ian
     "All Souls." Argo (5:3) 84, p. 14.

880. CECIL, Richard
     "Betrayal." Telescope (3:3) Aut 84, p. 80-81.
     "Elegy in a Pet Cemetery." Poetry (144:6) S 84, p.
         343-344.
     "Exile." PoetryE (15) Aut 84, p. 53.
     "Genre Painting." Ploughs (10:4) 84, p. 199-201.
     "Night School." Ploughs (10:4) 84, p. 197-198.

"Ulysses' Second Voyage." <u>AntR</u> (42:1) Wint 84, p. 89.

881. CEDERING, Siv
"The Blue Dress." <u>VirQR</u> (60:3) Sum 84, p. 429-430.
"Shunga." <u>VirQR</u> (60:3) Sum 84, p. 429.

882. CEDRINS, Inara
"May" (tr. of Aleksandrs Caks). <u>Thrpny</u> (18) Sum
84, p. 26.
"Tide" (tr. of Astrid Ivask). <u>Nimrod</u> (27:2) Spr-
Sum 84, p. 55.

883. CELAN, Paul
"Argumentum e Silentio" (for René Char, tr. by
Esther Cameron). <u>Sulfur</u> (4:2, issue 11) 84, p.
9-10.
"Blue of the Lodes in your mouth" (tr. by Katharine
Washburn). <u>Sulfur</u> (4:2, issue 11) 84, p. 16.
"Chalk-Crocus, at dawn" (tr. by Beth Bjorklund).
<u>Sulfur</u> (4:2, issue 11) 84, p. 8.
"Coagula your wound, too" (tr. by Joachim
Neugroschel). <u>Chelsea</u> (42/43) 84, p. 278.
"Death fugue" (Written 1944-45, tr. by John
Felstiner). <u>NewRep</u> (190:13) 2 Ap 84, p. 28.
"Frankfurt, September" (tr. by Esther Cameron).
<u>Sulfur</u> (4:2, issue 11) 84, p. 13.
"Les Globes" (tr. by Esther Cameron). <u>Sulfur</u> (4:2,
issue 11) 84, p. 11.
"Gone into the night, complicit" (tr. by Katharine
Washburn). <u>Sulfur</u> (4:2, issue 11) 84, p. 16.
"The Industrious natural resources" (tr. by Esther
Cameron). <u>Sulfur</u> (4:2, issue 11) 84, p. 14-15.
"Narrow-Wood day under a retinerved sky-leaf" (tr.
by Joachim Neugroschel). <u>Chelsea</u> (42/43) 84, p.
278.
"No hand holds me either" (tr. by Esther Cameron).
<u>Sulfur</u> (4:2, issue 11) 84, p. 12.
"Once, when death was mobbed" (tr. by Katharine
Washburn). <u>Sulfur</u> (4:2, issue 11) 84, p. 16.
"Pale-Voiced, flayed from the depths" (tr. by Beth
Bjorklund). <u>Sulfur</u> (4:2, issue 11) 84, p. 8.
"The Scooped-Out Heart" (tr. by Esther Cameron).
<u>Sulfur</u> (4:2, issue 11) 84, p. 14.
"The Second Cycle of Zeitgehöft" (tr. by Pierre
Joris). <u>Sulfur</u> (4:2, issue 11) 84, p. 17-26.
"Skull-thoughts, mute, on the arrow-path" (tr. by
Joachim Neugroschel). <u>Chelsea</u> (42/43) 84, p. 279.
"Snow-Bed." <u>AmerPoR</u> (13:4) Jl-Ag 84, p. 34.
"Stone-Blow behind the beetles" (tr. by Beth
Bjorklund). <u>Sulfur</u> (4:2, issue 11) 84, p. 9.
"White, white, white" (tr. by Esther Cameron).
<u>Sulfur</u> (4:2, issue 11) 84, p. 12.

884. CELLUCCI, Carol
"Dead or Alive." <u>LittleM</u> (14:3) 84, p. 49.
"Hotel Room, 1931" (after Edward Hopper). <u>LittleM</u>
(14:3) 84, p. 48.
"One Last Song." <u>LittleM</u> (14:3) 84, p. 50.
"What We Do When the Men Are Away." <u>LittleM</u> (14:3)
84, p. 47.

885. CERVIN, Tina
     "Salvadoran Woman Born into America." <u>Vis</u> (15) 84,
     p. 32-34.

886. CESAIRE, Aimé
     "The Tornado" (tr. by Michael Benedikt). <u>Chelsea</u>
     (42/43) 84, p. 261.

887. CHACE, Joel
     "A Feud." <u>Wind</u> (14:51) 84, p. 8.

888. CHAFFIN, Lillie D.
     "Choices." <u>Poem</u> (52) N 84, p. 12-13.
     "Family Reunion." <u>Wind</u> (14:50) 84, p. 5-6.
     "The House That I built." <u>NegC</u> (4:2) Spr 84, p. 39.
     "The Marriage" (for TW). <u>Wind</u> (14:50) 84, p. 6.
     "Submission." <u>Wind</u> (14:50) 84, p. 7.
     "Wilderness." <u>DekalbLAJ</u> (17:1/2) 84, p. 111.
     "Zero Zones." <u>ChrC</u> (101:14) 25 Ap 84, p. 423.

889. CHAFIN, Shirley R.
     "One Last Chance." <u>Wind</u> (14:52) 84, p. 7.
     "Performer." <u>Wind</u> (14:52) 84, p. 43.
     "A Teacher's Immortality." <u>EngJ</u> (73:1) Ja 84, p. 37.
     "A Teacher's Immortality." <u>EngJ</u> (73:3) Mr 84, p. 107.

890. CHALMERS, Emily
     "The Gloves." <u>Iowa</u> (14:3) Aut 84, p. 107-108.

891. CHALPIN, Lila
     "My Collection." <u>NegC</u> (4:4) Aut 84, p. 11.

892. CHAMBERLAIN, Elaine
     "It's Summer at My Sister's House: Mahone Bay 1982."
     <u>AntigR</u> (56) Wint 84, p. 43-46.

893. CHAMBERLAND, Paul
     "Enigme." <u>CanLit</u> (100) Spr 84, p. 60-61.
     "Un Livre de Morale" (trois extraits). <u>CanLit</u>
     (100) Spr 84, p. 61-62.

894. CHAMBERS, Jack
     "And in a Moment." <u>CapilR</u> (33) 84, p. 8.
     "Inmate #2." <u>CapilR</u> (33) 84, p. 11.
     "It Was Difficult." <u>CapilR</u> (33) 84, p. 9.
     "Pasternak's Images." <u>CapilR</u> (33) 84, p. 10.
     "Toronto-London One Way Gray Coach Lines." <u>CapilR</u>
     (33) 84, p. 26-28.

895. CHANDLER, Janet Carncross
     "An Intimate Glimpse into Married Life." <u>Bogg</u> (52)
     84, p. 23.

896. CHANDLER, Michael
     "Autumn." <u>RagMag</u> (3:2) Aut 84, p. 16.
     "Feeling the Area of a Circle." <u>RagMag</u> (3:1) Spr
     84, p. 2.
     "Going to Work." <u>RagMag</u> (3:2) Aut 84, p. 16.
     "Middle Age." <u>RagMag</u> (3:1) Spr 84, p. 3.

897. CHANDLER, Richard
    "A Lily in Ice." NeqC (4:3) Sum 84, p. 10.

898. CHANDLER, Robert
    "Charnel-Houses" (tr. of Eugène Guillevic).
    Stand (25:3) Sum 84, p. 34-35.

899. CHANDLER, Tom
    "The Dancer's Practice" (Piedmont Park, May 1982).
    DekalbLAJ (20th Anniversary Issue) 84, p. 79.
    "November Rain." DekalbLAJ (20th Anniversary
    Issue) 84, p. 79-80.
    "Tonight, Old Bones." DekalbLAJ (20th Anniversary
    Issue) 84, p. 80.

900. CHANDRA, G. S. Sharat
    "Batu Caves, Kuala Lumpur." Stand (25:1) Wint 83-
    84, p. 29.
    "Fable of a Three Year Old." NewL (51:2) Wint 84-
    85, p. 106-107.
    "Lovers." GreenfR (11:1/2) Sum-Aut 83, p. 148.

901. CHANG, Diana
    "Home." StoneC (12:1/2) Aut-Wint 84, p. 35.
    "Present Self." GreenfR (11:3/4) Wint-Spr 84, p.
    113-116.

902. CHANNELL, Carolyn
    "Dance, You Monster, to My Soft Song." SouthwR
    (69:1) Wint 84, p. 48.

CHAO, Hsu: See HSU, Chao

903. CHAPMAN, Jane Autenrieth
    "Down on Sunnyside." Wind (14:50) 84, p. 61.

904. CHAPMAN, R. S.
    "Fillmore West." Abraxas (29/30) 84, p. 72.
    "My Father, the Sailor." Northeast (Series 3:17)
    Sum 84, p. 18.

905. CHAPPEL, Allen H.
    "New Alliance" (tr. of Ilse Aichinger). Field (30)
    Spr 84, p. 73.
    "Part of the Question" (tr. of Ilse Aichinger).
    Field (30) Spr 84, p. 73-74.
    "To My Grandmother" (tr. of Ilse Aichinger). Field
    (30) Spr 84, p. 71-72.

906. CHAPPELL, Fred
    "Latencies." SouthernHR (18:4) Aut 84, p. 326.
    "My Hand Placed on a Rubens Drawing." TarRP (24:1)
    Aut 84, p. 25-27.
    "Perspective." CarolQ (36:2) Wint 84, p. 20.
    "Silver." ChiR (34:3) Sum 84, p. 25.
    "Webern's Mountain." CarolQ (36:2) Wint 84, p. 19.

907. CHAR, René
    "A Bird" (tr. by Michael O'Brien). NewL (51:2)
    Wint 84-85, p. 10.

"End of Solemnities" (tr. by Charles Guenther).
    MissouriR (7:3) 84, p. 27.
"The Library Is on Fire" (to Georges Braque, tr. by
    Charles Guenther). Chelsea (42/43) 84, p. 112-115.
"Lyre." AmerPoR (13:4) Jl-Ag 84, p. 33.
"Le Nu Perdu." AmerPoR (13:4) Jl-Ag 84, p. 31.
"Predecessor" (tr. by Charles Guenther). MissouriR
    (7:3) 84, p. 28.
"Sentry of the Silent" (tr. by Charles Guenther).
    MissouriR (7:3) 84, p. 26.

908. CHARACH, Ron
    "Lena at the Zero-Line." Dandel (11:2) Aut-Wint 84-
        85, p. 76-77.

909. CHARD, John V.
    "Moonlight Nuptials." LitR (28:1) Aut 84, p. 76.

910. CHARIARSE, Leopoldo
    "Al Final del Ontoño." Mund (14:2) 84, p. 8.
    "En el fondo de un sueño estamos solos." Mund
        (14:2) 84, p. 10.
    "End of Autumn" (tr. by Miriam and Gerd Joel).
        Mund (14:2) 84, p. 9.
    "Eternal Walls" (tr. by Miriam and Gerd Joel).
        Mund (14:2) 84, p. 11.

911. CHARLTON, Lindsey D.
    "Seascapes." Waves (12:2/3) Wint 84, p. 80.

912. CHASSIGNET, Jean-Baptiste
    "And must I see him, the father of lies" (tr. by
        Anthony Abbott). WebR (9:2) Wint 85, p. 13.
    "Mortal, imagine here beneath the face" (tr. by
        Anthony Abbott). WebR (9:2) Wint 85, p. 12-13.
    "So many divers torments thrive in us" (tr. by
        Anthony Abbott). WebR (9:2) Wint 85, p. 12.

913. CHATFIELD, Hale
    "Catalyst I" (Selection: A Sportscar to the Road-
        River). HiramPoR (37) Aut-Wint 84, p. 10.
    "Catalyst III" (Excerpt). HiramPoR (37) Aut-Wint
        84, p. 11.
    "Haikuku" (Excerpt, with computer generated lines).
        HiramPoR (37) Aut-Wint 84, p. 8.
    "Lifesongs" (compatible sonnets: 1-4). HiramPoR
        (37) Aut-Wint 84, p. 5-6.
    "A Random Lifesong" (two random collations).
        HiramPoR (37) Aut-Wint 84, p. 7.
    "Some Examples of 'Computer Poems'" (From the
        Programs Described on p. 3-4). HiramPoR (37)
        Aut-Wint 84, p. 5-11.
    "Statewide Artists' Meeting." HiramPoR (37) Aut-
        Wint 84, p. 8-10.

914. CHAVES, Jonathan
    "The Cave of Ghosts." GreenfR (11:1/2) Sum-Aut 83,
        p. 146.
    "Hua-Lien." GreenfR (11:1/2) Sum-Aut 83, p. 145.

915. CHAZAL, Malcolm de
"Afterthoughts" (tr. by Daisy Aldan). Chelsea
(42/43) 84, p. 118.

916. CHECK, Hovan
"The Patriot's Bible." SanFPJ (6:4) 84, p. 69.
"Plundered." SanFPJ (6:4) 84, p. 72.
"A World for the Mushrooms." SanFPJ (6:4) 84, p. 72.

917. CHEN, Eunice
"The Morning Reading" (tr. of Wu Cheng, w. Marilyn
Chin). Iowa (14:2) Spr-Sum 84, p. 58-59.

918. CHENEY-ROSE, Lynne
"Our Lost Selves Singing." CrabCR (1:3) Wint 84,
p. 6.

CHENG, Wu: See WU, Cheng

919. CHERNOFF, Maxine
"The Sheik of Araby." CreamCR (9:1/2) 84, p. 20.
"Tragedy on Ice" (for Paul). CreamCR (9:1/2) 84,
p. 24-25.

920. CHERRY, Kelly
"Day in Blue Shells." NewL (51:1) Aut 84, p. 17.
"The Other Side of Time." PraS (58:2) Sum 84, p.
55-56.

921. CHEW, George T.
"Outside Immigration, I see him waiting." GreenfR
(11:1/2) Sum-Aut 83, p. 161.

922. CHICHETTO, James
"Captain Norman Knight." SanFPJ (6:3) 84, p. 89.
"A History." SanFPJ (6:3) 84, p. 15.
"Pelicans and Rats in Peru, December." SanFPJ
(6:3) 84, p. 92.

923. CHILDERS, David C.
"Amos." SouthernPR (24:1) Spr 84, p. 47.

924. CHIN, Marilyn
"For the Desert Island" (tr. of Tae-ch'ul Shin, w.
the author). Iowa (14:2) Spr-Sum 84, p. 64.
"Hunting" (tr. of Mariela Arvelo, w. the author).
Iowa (14:2) Spr-Sum 84, p. 151.
"I'm Lying on the Bed at a Motel and" (tr. of Tetsuo
Nakagami, w. the author). Iowa (14:2) Spr-Sum
84, p. 63.
"Like an orphan" (tr. of Ai Qing). Iowa (14:2) Spr-
Sum 84, p. 7.
"The Morning Reading" (tr. of Wu Cheng, w. Eunice
Chen). Iowa (14:2) Spr-Sum 84, p. 58-59.
"My Hometown's Base Creatures" (tr. of Wu Cheng, w.
Jesse Wang). Iowa (14:2) Spr-Sum 84, p. 57-58.
"Snowy Morning" (tr. of Ai Qing). Iowa (14:2) Spr-
Sum 84, p. 41.
"Unrequited Love." NewL (50:4) Sum 84, p. 97.
"Wandering Was Always an Important Theme in My

Lyric" (tr. of Tetsuo Nakagami, w. the author).
Iowa (14:2) Spr-Sum 84, p. 62.

925. CHINMOY, Sri
"The Defeat of My Life." ArizQ (40:2) Sum 84, p. 146.

926. CHIOLES, John
"Immigrant" (tr. of Dino Siotis). Os (19) 84, p. 21.
"The Spring" (tr. of Dino Siotis). Os (19) 84, p. 19.

927. CHIROM, Daniel Enrique
"Tres A.M." Mairena (6:18) 84, p. 118.

928. CHITWOOD, Michael
"Driving into the Valley When Painful Duty Called."
GreenfR (12:1/2) Sum-Aut 84, p. 182-183.

929. CHO, Wen-Chun, Lady
"Lament" (tr. by Sam Hamill). CrabCR (1:3) Wint
84, p. 24.

930. CHOCANO, Magdalena
"A Vermeer de Delft." Mairena (6:16) Spr 84, p. 74-
75.
"Dicen que estuvieron contigo y te ayudaban a ir"
(Por Martín Adán). Mairena (6:16) Spr 84,
p. 74.
"Dormiré blandiéndome en un sueño
imprescindible." Mairena (6:16) Spr 84, p. 76.

CHONG-BO, Yi: See YI, Chong-Bo

931. CHOPRA, Shiv
"When I Met You." WritersL (1) 84, p. 12.

932. CHORLTON, David
"Babushka." TarRP (23:2) Spr 84, p. 26.
"Dahlia Petrovna." Abraxas (31/32) 84, p. 38-39.
"The Diary." NegC (4:2) Spr 84, p. 46-47.
"The Edge of My Speech." Abraxas (31/32) 84, p. 37.
"German Blues." WebR (9:2) Wint 85, p. 85.
"Hopper's Woman." WebR (9:2) Wint 85, p. 86.
"Monochromes." WebR (9:2) Wint 85, p. 87.

933. CHOYCE, Lesley
"The Best Watermelon Since the First World War."
PottPort (6) 84, p. 39.
"Love-Feast Prayer." PottPort (6) 84, p. 4.
"The Melting." PottPort (6) 84, p. 52.

934. CHRISTENSEN, Alan
"Checklist for Morning." Amelia (1:2) O 84, p. 76.

935. CHRISTENSEN, Erleen J.
"Heat Wave." KanQ (16:1/2) Wint-Spr 84, p. 59.

936. CHRISTENSEN, Paul
"Losing." ManhatR (3:2) Wint 84-85, p. 69-72.
"The Nap." Sulfur (4:1, issue 10) 84, p. 88-101.
"The Slide." Peb (23) 84, p. 56-57.

937. CHRISTIANSON, Kevin
"Tin Can." NewL (51:1) Aut 84, p. 69.

938. CHRISTINA-MARIE
"Tinsel" (A French Ballade). NeqC (4:4) Aut 84, p. 86-87.

939. CHRISTOPHER, Nicholas
"Cardiac Arrest." NewYorker (60:44) 17 D 84, p. 54.
"Evening." NewYorker (60:34) 8 O 84, p. 48.
"Orange Light." Shen (35:1) 83-84, p. 86.
"Quatrains for Sunlight." Shen (35:1) 83-84, p. 87-89.

940. CHRYSTOS
"Elegy for Jane." Cond (3:4, issue 10) 84, p. 82.
"It Was Your Idea." Cond (3:4, issue 10) 84, p. 81.

941. CHUANG, Tzu
"The Woodcarver" (tr. by Thomas Merton). Germ (8:1) Spr-Sum 84, p. 27-28.

942. CHUBBS, Boyd
"She Grieves for Exits." PottPort (6) 84, p. 52.

943. CHUTE, Robert M.
"Natural Selection." Spirit (7:1) 84, p. 71.

944. CIARDI, John
"The Aging Lover." NewL (51:1) Aut 84, p. 11.
"A Damnation of Doves." NewL (51:1) Aut 84, p. 12.
"For Muhammad Ali." TriQ (59) Wint 84, p. 131.
"From the Second Canto" (from The Divine Comedy, Book 3, tr. of Dante Alighieri). NewYRB (31:20) 20 D 84, p. 9.
"January 1, 1973." NewL (51:1) Aut 84, p. 14.
"Poetry." NewL (51:1) Aut 84, p. 12-13.
"A View." NewL (51:1) Aut 84, p. 13.

CICCO, Pier Giorgio di: See Di CICCO, Pier Giorgio

945. CIGNARELLA, Maria
"Calculation of Probabilities" (To Julio Morejon, tr. of Miguel Sales, w. Robert M. Glickstein). Confr (27/28) 84, p. 37.
"Profile of Winter" (tr. of Miguel Sales, w. Robert M. Glickstein). Confr (27/28) 84, p. 38.

946. CILLONIZ, Antonio
"Gusano de la Conciencia." Mairena (6:18) 84, p. 95.

947. CIMON, Anne
"On Yonge Street, Toronto." CrossC (6:2) 84, p. 11.

948. CINELLI, Joan Eheart
"Second Winter." ChrC (101:4) 1-8 F 84, p. 111.

949. CIORDIA, Javier
"Pathos." Mairena (5:14) Aut 83, p. 88.

950. CIROCCO, William
     "Death Words." <u>Paunch</u> (57/58) Ja 84, p. 90-91.
     "A Name." <u>Paunch</u> (57/58) Ja 84, p. 89.

951. CISNEROS, Antonio
     "The Salt Flats" (tr. by David Tipton). <u>Stand</u>
        (25:3) Sum 84, p. 66-67.

952. CITINO, David
     "Altar Boy." <u>WoosterR</u> (1:1) Mr 84, p. 65.
     "The Appassionata Lectures" (1984 <u>Texas</u> <u>Review</u>
        Poetry Award Chapbook). <u>TexasR</u> (5:3/4) Aut-Wint
        84, p. 33-48.
     "Birds That Come from Trees." <u>WestB</u> (14) 84, p. 41.
     "Cedar Point Amusement Park: Demon Drop." <u>HiramPoR</u>
        (36) Spr-Sum 84, p. 12.
     "Changing the World." <u>SoDakR</u> (22:4) Wint 84, p. 8.
     "Damp Hands, Bad Wire, Typewriter." <u>PoetryNW</u>
        (25:2) Sum 84, p. 38.
     "The Date." <u>MichQR</u> (23:2) Spr 84, p. 208-209.
     "A Defense of Poetry." <u>HolCrit</u> (21:2) Ap 84, p. 17.
     "Distances." <u>Nimrod</u> (28:1) Aut-Wint 84, p. 93.
     "Doctrines of the Pineal." <u>BelPoJ</u> (35:1) Aut 84,
        p. 30-31.
     "Einstein, Placenta, the Caves of Lascaux."
        <u>PoetryNW</u> (25:2) Sum 84, p. 37-38.
     "For the Frost Belt: Three Prayers and One Curse."
        <u>WestB</u> (14) 84, p. 40.
     "From Exile, Sister Mary Appassionata Writes to the
        Creative Writing Class." <u>Tendril</u> (17) Wint 84,
        p. 27.
     "The History of Stone." <u>LitR</u> (28:1) Aut 84, p. 64.
     "The History of Wood." <u>PraS</u> (58:2) Sum 84, p. 58.
     "Homage to the Emptiness." <u>PoetryNW</u> (25:2) Sum 84,
        p. 39.
     "Lecture to the Bioscience Class: Pine and
        Lightning, Cataclysms and Stone." <u>OhioR</u> (32)
        84, p. 102-103.
     "Looking for the Dead." <u>HiramPoR</u> (36) Spr-Sum 84,
        p. 13.
     "The Observer Alters the Observed by the Act of
        Observation" (Heisenberg's Uncertainty
        Principle). <u>Telescope</u> (3:3) Aut 84, p. 113-114.
     "On a Day When I Can't Get Out of Myself." <u>PraS</u>
        (58:2) Sum 84, p. 57.
     "Opening Byron's Tomb, 1938." <u>SouthernHR</u> (18:1)
        Wint 84, p. 9.
     "Painting the Stars." <u>SoDakR</u> (22:1) Spr 84, p. 44.
     "The Pool." <u>GreenfR</u> (12:1/2) Sum-Aut 84, p. 179.
     "September 18: Joseph of Cupertino, Who Had the Gift
        of Flight." <u>LitR</u> (27:2) Wint 84, p. 222-223.
     "The Signature." <u>GreenfR</u> (12:1/2) Sum-Aut 84, p.
        179-180.
     "The Singer." <u>BelPoJ</u> (35:1) Aut 84, p. 31-33.
     "Sister Mary Appassionata Blesses the Kindergarten
        Class." <u>Tendril</u> (17) Wint 84, p. 28.
     "Sister Mary Appassionata Explains to the Classics
        Class Why So Many of the Greatest Lovers, Heroes
        and Saints Were Shepherds." <u>Tendril</u> (17) Wint
        84, p. 25.

"Sister Mary Appassionata Lectures the Anatomy
Class: Doctrines of the Nose." TexasR (5:3/4)
Aut-Wint 84, p. 34.
"Sister Mary Appassionata Lectures the Biorhythm
Class: Doctrines of Time." SouthwR (69:4) Aut
84, p. 388-389.
"Sister Mary Appassionata Lectures the Biorhythm
Class: Doctrines of Time." TexasR (5:3/4) Aut-
Wint 84, p. 40-41.
"Sister Mary Appassionata Lectures the Eighth Grade
Boys and Girls on the Nature of Symmetry."
TexasR (5:3/4) Aut-Wint 84, p. 39.
"Sister Mary Appassionata Lectures the Eighth Grade
Boys and Girls: To Punish the Cities." TexasR
(5:3/4) Aut-Wint 84, p. 46.
"Sister Mary Appassionata Lectures the Eighth Grade
Boys: You're Born with Two Heads, Don't Let the
Little One Rule the Big One." Tendril (17) Wint
84, p. 20.
"Sister Mary Appassionata Lectures the Journalism
Class: Doctrines of Belief." Tendril (17) Wint
84, p. 23.
"Sister Mary Appassionata Lectures the Journalism
Class: Doctrines of Belief." TexasR (5:3/4) Aut-
Wint 84, p. 44.
"Sister Mary Appassionata Lectures the Natural
History Class: Love and Curse, the Wind, the
Words." Tendril (17) Wint 84, p. 26.
"Sister Mary Appassionata Lectures the Parents of
the Eighth Grade Boys and Girls." CimR (69) O
84, p. 19.
"Sister Mary Appassionata Lectures the Parents of
the Eighth Grade Boys and Girls." TexasR
(5:3/4) Aut-Wint 84, p. 45.
"Sister Mary Appassionata Lectures the Pre-Med
Class: Doctrines of Sweat." TexasR (5:3/4) Aut-
Wint 84, p. 37.
"Sister Mary Appassionata Lectures the Science
Class: Doctrines of the Elements." CimR (69) O
84, p. 20-21.
"Sister Mary Appassionata Lectures the Science
Class: Doctrines of the Elements." TexasR
(5:3/4) Aut-Wint 84, p. 43.
"Sister Mary Appassionata Lectures the Social
Behavior Class: Friends, Those Who Love."
Tendril (17) Wint 84, p. 22.
"Sister Mary Appassionata Lectures the Theology
Class." Tendril (17) Wint 84, p. 24.
"Sister Mary Appassionata Lectures the Urban Studies
Class: Gunfire, Bedroom, Passion's Trash."
Tendril (17) Wint 84, p. 21.
"Sister Mary Appassionata Lectures the Zoology
Class: Doctrines of the Beast." TexasR (5:3/4)
Aut-Wint 84, p. 47.
"Sister Mary Appassionata to the Eighth Grade Boys
and Girls: Doctrines of Divination." TexasR
(5:3/4) Aut-Wint 84, p. 42.
"Sister Mary Appassionata to the Introductory
Astronomy Class: Heartbeat and Mass, Every Last
Breath." TexasR (5:3/4) Aut-Wint 84, p. 38.

"Sister Mary Appassionata to the Optometry Class:
Doctrines of the Eye." TexasR (5:3/4) Aut-Wint
84, p. 35-36.
"Sister Mary Appassionata to the Pre-Med Class:
Thinking Ourselves to Death." SouthernPR (24:1)
Spr 84, p. 55.
"Timing." Nimrod (28:1) Aut-Wint 84, p. 92.

953. CLAESON, Eva
"Meeting" (tr. of Barbro Dahlin). LitR (28:1) Aut
84, p. 134.
"Snowed In" (tr. of Barbro Dahlin). LitR (28:1)
Aut 84, p. 134.

954. CLAMPITT, Amy
"A Baroque." NewYorker (60:25) 6 Ag 84, p. 30.
"Cloudberry Summer." NewYorker (60:25) 6 Ag 84, p.
30-31.
"Continental Drift." CreamCR (9:1/2) 84, p. 8.
"The Cooling Tower." NewYorker (60:35) 15 O 84, p.
44.
"A Curfew" (December 13, 1981). GrandS (3:2) Wint
84, p. 97-98.
"Dodona: Asked of the Oracle." Poetry (143:6) Mr
84, p. 332-333.
"Four Poems from Maine." NewYorker (60:25) 6 Ag
84, p. 30-31.
"From the Corridor of a Train." PartR (51:3) 84,
p. 383-384.
"George Eliot Country." NewYorker (60:43) 10 D 84,
p. 52.
"Grasmere." ParisR (26:91) Spr 84, p. 84-87.
"Homer, A. D. 1982" (For Irving Kizner and his class
at Hunter College). Poetry (143:6) Mr 84, p.
331-332.
"Homesick in Woodside, California." NewRep (191:9)
27 Ag 84, p. 32.
"Imago." Sulfur (4:1, issue 10) 84, p. 169-171.
"John Keats: He Dreams of Being Warm." GrandS
(3:1) Aut 83, p. 57-59.
"June Twenty-First, 1983." CreamCR (9:1/2) 84, p.
6-7.
"Keats at Winchester: The Autumn Equinox." GrandS
(3:1) Aut 83, p. 62-63.
"Keats on the Isle of Wight." GrandS (3:1) Aut 83,
p. 60-61.
"Leaving Yánnina." Poetry (143:6) Mr 84, p. 333.
"The Lives of Penguins." AmerS (53:3) Sum 84, p.
326-327.
"The Lives of Penguins." Harp (269:1612) S 84, p.
22-23.
"Losing Track of Language." GrandS (3:2) Wint 84,
p. 100-101.
"Low Tide at Schoodic." NewYorker (60:25) 6 Ag 84,
p. 30.
"A Manhattan Elegy." Shen (35:1) 83-84, p. 15-19.
"The Olive Groves of Thasos." NewYorker (60:20) 2
Jl 84, p. 36.
"Portola Valley." NewRep (191:21) 19 N 84, p. 38.
"Saloniki." GrandS (4:1) Aut 84, p. 129.

"The Spruce Has No Taproot." NewYorker (60:25) 6
   Ag 84, p. 30.
"Tempe in the Rain." SouthwR (69:4) Aut 84, p. 384-
   385.
"Thermopylae." Poetry (143:6) Mr 84, p. 331.
"Vacant Lot with Tumbleweed and Pigeons."
   NewYorker (59:50) 30 Ja 84, p. 32.
"Venice Revisited." NewYorker (60:29) 3 S 84, p. 36.
"Voyages." NewYorker (59:47) 9 Ja 84, p. 36-37.
"Written in Water." GrandS (3:2) Wint 84, p. 99.

955. CLARE, John
   "Written in Northhampton County Asylum." CapilR
   (31) 84, p. 37.

956. CLAREUS, Ingrid
   "Living" (tr. of Siv Arb). Abraxas (31/32) 84, p. 61.
   "Nowhere to Go" (tr. of Siv Arb). Abraxas (31/32)
   84, p. 60.
   "Perfect Pitch" (tr. of Siv Arb). Abraxas (31/32)
   84, p. 61.

957. CLARK, Arthur W.
   "Agenda." Open24 (3) 84, p. 32.
   "Kinetic Poem." Open24 (3) 84, p. 33.

958. CLARK, Brian C.
   "American Eyes." SanFPJ (7:1) 84, p. 73.
   "The Bomb under Big Boy's Butt" (dedicated to Ronnie
   Raygun). SanFPJ (7:1) 84, p. 72.

959. CLARK, J. Wesley
   "The Connoisseur." Bogg (52) 84, p. 17.

960. CLARK, Kevin
   "Granting the Wolf" (For Ken Goldberg). CalQ
   (23/24) Spr-Sum 84, p. 35-40.
   "Small Fires." CalQ (23/24) Spr-Sum 84, p. 41-42.

961. CLARK, Mili
   "The Mower in Therapy." Paunch (57/58) Ja 84, p. 93.

962. CLARK, Patricia
   "Nightfall." Tendril (17) Wint 84, p. 30.
   "A Passage." Tendril (17) Wint 84, p. 29.

CLARK, Ruth Wallace: See WALLACE-CLARK, Ruth

963. CLARK, Tom
   "Poem for Jack Kerouac in California." MoodySI
   (14) Spr 84, p. 11.

964. CLARKE, George Elliott
   "Coming into Intelligence." PottPort (6) 84, p. 6.
   "In Hants County." Germ (8:2) Aut-Wint 84, p. 25.
   "November 22nd, 1963." Germ (8:2) Aut-Wint 84, p. 22.
   "Scratch Danial's." CrossC (6:2) 84, p. 15.
   "Scratch Daniel's." Germ (8:2) Aut-Wint 84, p. 21.
   "Song of the Railway." Germ (8:2) Aut-Wint 84, p. 23.
   "To the Government of Nova Scotia." Germ (8:2) Aut-

Wint 84, p. 24.

965. CLARY, Killarney
"When my heart asked for a way free." Telescope
(3:1) Wint 84, p. 159.

966. CLAYTON, Richard
"Sunday Morning." Bogg (52) 84, p. 34.

967. CLEARY, Brendan
"Abbatoir." Stand (25:2) Spr 84, p. 40.

968. CLEARY, Michael
"Catholic Girls." CapeR (19:3) 20th Anniverary
Issue 84, p. 7.
"Colossus, Wobbling." CapeR (19:2) Sum 84, p. 5.
"Fort Lauderdale Beach Surf Etiquette." Wind
(14:52) 84, p. 8-9.
"Hometown Seasons" (For My Sunbelt Children).
CapeR (19:2) Sum 84, p. 4.
"Sundown, Key West" (For John). TexasR (5:1/2) Spr-
Sum 84, p. 33.

969. CLEARY, Suzanne
"Travels." MSS (4:1/2) Aut 84, p. 59.

970. CLEMENT, Jennifer Sibley
"Wishbone Children." LittleM (14:3) 84, p. 54.

CLEMENTS, Judith Keating: See KEATING-CLEMENTS, Judith

971. CLEMENTS, Susan Hauptfleisch
"Bowl with Splatter-Painted Hand." ArizQ (40:2)
Sum 84, p. 100.

972. CLENMAN, Donia
"The Ballad of Taddle Creek." Descant (47, 15:4)
Wint 84, p. 85.
"Reading the Signs of the Times." Descant (47,
15:4) Wint 84, p. 87-88.
"St. Michael's Cemetery." Descant (47, 15:4) Wint
84, p. 86.

973. CLEWETT, Rick
"The Monroe Doctrine Applied Domestically." Sam
(41:1, release 161) 84, p. 21.
"What's Right?" Sam (39:1, release 153) 84, p. 59.

974. CLIFTON, Harry
"Military Presence, Cobh 1899." Pequod (16/17) 84,
p. 39.

975. CLIFTON, Merritt
"Bonsai Growers." Sam (41:1, release 161) 84, p. 15.
"The Captain Learns Doubt." Sam (37:3, 147th
release) 83, p. 7.
"Our First Woman Priest." Sam (37:3, 147th
release) 83, p. 39.
"To the Tyrant." Sam (41:1, release 161) 84, p. 11.

976. CLIMENHAGA, Joel
"Relics of Religion, Quarantines, Vegetable Blood."
Wind (14:51) 84, p. 13.

977. CLINTON, Robert
"Pilgrim's Progress." Atlantic (254:5) N 84, p. 126.

978. CLOKE, Richard (See also R. C.)
"Boomerang." SanFPJ (7:1) 84, p. 20.
"Democracy Freedom." SanFPJ (6:2) 84, p. 8.
"Don't tell me." SanFPJ (6:4) 84, p. 45.
"Doom." SanFPJ (6:4) 84, p. 59.
"Even if we don't know." SanFPJ (6:4) 84, p. 48.
"If you ever worry." SanFPJ (6:4) 84, p. 63.
"Limbic Chill." SanFPJ (6:1) 84, p. 72.
"Message: Phase A126." SanFPJ (6:1) 84, p. 82.
"Message: Phase A127." SanFPJ (6:1) 84, p. 83.
"Message: Phase A128." SanFPJ (6:2) 84, p. 54.
"Message: Phase A129." SanFPJ (6:2) 84, p. 55.
"Message: Phase A130." SanFPJ (6:4) 84, p. 85.
"Message: Phase A131." SanFPJ (7:1) 84, p. 30-31.
"Message: Phase A132." SanFPJ (7:1) 84, p. 66.
"Message: Phase A133." SanFPJ (7:1) 84, p. 67.
"Nuclear Tech Goes Mini." SanFPJ (6:4) 84, p. 25.
"Pullulation of Pollution." SanFPJ (6:4) 84, p. 18.
"They call it sensory deprivation." SanFPJ (6:4)
84, p. 36.
"This earth." SanFPJ (6:4) 84, p. 44.
"The Unthinkable is being thought!" SanFPJ (6:4)
84, p. 71.
"V.A.L.B." SanFPJ (6:3) 84, p. 38-39.
"We don't have castes in the good old U S of A."
SanFPJ (6:4) 84, p. 42.
"We're all dancing." SanFPJ (6:4) 84, p. 47.

CLOUD, Peter Blue: See BLUE CLOUD, Peter

979. CLOUTIER, Cécile
"Assumer l'ogive de ma main." CanLit (100) Spr 84,
p. 63.
"De grandes plumées de verbes." CanLit (100) Spr
84, p. 63.
"Des cris soyeux." CanLit (100) Spr 84, p. 63.
"Et s'illuminèrent les grands pas bleus." CanLit
(100) Spr 84, p. 64.
"Une goutte de bois." CanLit (100) Spr 84, p. 64.
"Il aurait fallu t'aimer." CanLit (100) Spr 84, p.
64.
"J'aime tant ma maison." CanLit (100) Spr 84, p. 63.
"Mes mains interrogent." CanLit (100) Spr 84, p. 63.
"Mon dernier mot." CanLit (100) Spr 84, p. 64.
"Tout le bleu du monde." CanLit (100) Spr 84, p. 63.

980. CLUCAS, Garth
"An Englishman Goes to a Halloween Party As
Himself." GreenfR (11:3/4) Wint-Spr 84, p. 91-92.

981. COADY, Michael
    "Making a Garden." _Pequod_ (16/17) 84, p. 50-52.
    "The Vendetta of Staggers McGowan." _Pequod_ (16/17)
        84, p. 48-49.

982. COATES, Margaret I.
    "Peace, Where Are You?" _WritersL_ (2) 84, p. 12.
    "Values." _WritersL_ (2) 84, p. 7.

983. COBB, Pamela
    "Evolution." _Amelia_ (1:2) O 84, p. 13.
    "Footsteps." _Amelia_ (1:2) O 84, p. 13.

984. COBIAN, Ricardo
    "Caminante Adjunto." _Areíto_ (9:36) 84, p. 105.

985. COCCIMIGLIO, Vic
    "After a Photograph by David Hawk." _Abraxas_
        (31/32) 84, p. 60.
    "Already." _AmerPoR_ (13:5) S-O 84, p. 32.
    "Medals" (for Donald Hall). _Abraxas_ (29/30) 84, p.
        68.

986. COCHRAN, Jo
    "Cedar Song." _Calyx_ (8:2) Spr 84, p. 97-98.

987. CODRESCU, Andrei
    "Death at the K Mart." _Abraxas_ (31/32) 84, p. 23.
    "Death at the K Mart." _Open24_ (3) 84, p. 23.
    "December 1979." _Abraxas_ (31/32) 84, p. 24.
    "From My New Book Poems about Nothing." _Abraxas_
        (31/32) 84, p. 25.

988. COFER, Judith Ortiz
    "La Tristeza." _SouthernPR_ (24:2) Aut 84, p. 40.

989. COFFEL, Scott
    "Delivery Boy." _MSS_ (4:1/2) Aut 84, p. 60.

990. COFFIN, Edna Amir
    "A Modern Girl" (tr. of Yehuda Amichai). _Pequod_
        (16/17) 84, p. 124.

991. COFFIN, Lyn
    "Abacus" (tr. of Jaroslav Seifert). _ConcPo_ (17:2)
        Aut 84, p. 188.
    "The Blackbird Looks Back." _Paunch_ (57/58) Ja 84,
        p. 75.
    "The Blank Baby" (for Eunice). _MichQR_ (23:1) Wint
        84, p. 65-66.
    "The Dance Studio." _Paunch_ (57/58) Ja 84, p. 76.
    "Mad Poem." _Paunch_ (57/58) Ja 84, p. 77.
    "Paradise Lost" (tr. of Jaroslav Seifert). _ConcPo_
        (17:2) Aut 84, p. 186-188.
    "A Poem at the End" (tr. of Jaroslav Seifert).
        ConcPo (17:2) Aut 84, p. 185.
    "To the King from the Candle." _Paunch_ (57/58) Ja
        84, p. 74.
    "While Reading Hamlet" (tr. of Anna Akhmatova).
        NewYRB (30:21/22) 19 Ja 84, p. 23.

992. COGEOS, Stephanie
"The sun keeps light" ("untitled"). Wind (14:52)
84, p. 5.

993. COGGESHALL, Rosanne
"For George Archibald" (the man who courted Tex, the
whooping crane). SouthernR (20:3) Sum 84, p.
591-593.
"GMH." SouthernR (20:3) Sum 84, p. 593.

994. COHEN, Bruce
"One Solution for Insomnia." GreenfR (12:1/2) Sum-
Aut 84, p. 131.

995. COHEN, Carole
"Revelations." Ascent (10:1) 84, p. 39-40.

996. COHEN, Helen Degen
"I Remember Coming into Warsaw, a Child." SpoonRQ
(9:4) Aut 84, p. 32.
"To the Poet Jimenez, Man of Andalucia." KanQ
(16:1/2) Wint-Spr 84, p. 73.

997. COHEN, Jonathan
"León" (tr. of Ernesto Cardenal). Nat (238:3) 28
Ja 84, p. 100.

998. COHEN, Leonard
"Book of Mercy" (Excerpts). PoetryCR (6:1) Aut 84,
p. 9.

999. COHEN, Marc
"Blithe Cabbage." Shen (35:1) 83-84, p. 79.

1000. COHEN, Marvin
"Past Either and Through Both." Chelsea (42/43)
84, p. 232-235.

1001. COHEN, Miriam A.
"9 a.m. Compression." PoeticJ (2) 83, p. 31.
"Always Chasing the Sun" (To the bank, PLAY).
PoeticJ (4) 83, p. 11.
"As Myself, Dulled." PoeticJ (7) 84, p. 34.
"Cherry Tomato" (for Colette Inez). PoeticJ (3)
83, p. 27.
"Ending Two Cycles." PoeticJ (5) 84, p. 33.
"Identifying w/ Slime-Dazzle." Bogg (52) 84, p. 9.
"Judy at Her Craft." PoeticJ (1) 83, p. 24.
"Losing Blood." PoeticJ (2) 83, p. 37.
"Telephone Giggle Poet." YetASM (3) 84, p. 4.
"What Is Known." Sam (37:3, 147th release) 83, p.
51.

COHN, Mareé Zukor: See ZUKOR-COHN, Mareé

1002. COLANDER, Valerie Nieman
"The Drowning." Wind (14:50) 84, p. 8.
"First Generation." TarRP (24:1) Aut 84, p. 16-17.

1003. COLBY, Joan
      "1943." Poetry (143:6) Mr 84, p. 317-318.
      "Dancing with the Crane." Ascent (9:2) 84, p. 29.
      "For Kay." SnapD (6:2) Spr 83, p. 12-13.
      "Hemlocks." PoeticJ (5) 84, p. 29.
      "Litter." CapeR (19:3) 20th Anniverary Issue 84,
           p. 8.
      "Owls." MidAR (4:1) Spr 84, p. 125-126.
      "Symbiosis." StoneC (12:1/2) Aut-Wint 84, p. 10.
      "The Tornado Chaser." WebR (9:1) Spr 84, p. 37-38.
      "Vegas Hotel Fire, Nov. 22, 1980" (Carbon monoxide
           is major culprit in deaths due to smoke
           inhalation). StoneC (12:1/2) Aut-Wint 84, p.
           11-12.

1004. COLE, April
      "Hunters and Wives." Wind (14:51) 84, p. 6.
      "Ice-God." PoeticJ (2) 83, p. 39.

1005. COLE, Barbara S.
      "Even God must tire." YellowS (13) Wint 84, p. 16.

1006. COLE, Henri
      "Letter to Francis from the Blue Ridge" (after
           Stevens). SouthernR (20:2) Spr 84, p. 374-376.
      "The Marble Queen." Nat (239:17) 24 N 84, p. 560.
      "The Mare." Nat (238:24) 23 Je 84, p. 772.
      "The Prince Enters the Forest." Antaeus (52) Apr
           84, p. 87.
      "V-Winged and Hoary." Antaeus (53) Aut 84, p. 255-
           256.

1007. COLE, Kevin
      "Father's Answer." Thrpny (16) Wint 84, p. 15.

1008. COLE, Michael
      "225. After midnight the heart steals" (tr. of Osip
           Mandelstam, w. Karen Kimball). CharR (10:2)
           Aut 84, p. 94.
      "395. I don't know the woman who searches" (tr. of
           Osip Mandelstam, w. Karen Kimball). CharR
           (10:2) Aut 84, p. 94.
      "Instructions for Self-Exile" (to the memory of
           George Chesnes -- Jurgis Cesnavicius -- who fled
           Lithuania in 1908). Wind (14:52) 84, p. 10.

1009. COLE, Richard
      "The Last Days of Heaven." NewYorker (60:28) 27
           Ag 84, p. 36.

1010. COLE FALTO, Evelyn
      "Estudios Innecesarios." Mairena (5:14) Aut 83,
           p. 23.
      "La Palabra y el Histuario" (Selections). Mairena
           (5:14) Aut 83, p. 23-24.
      "Trabajo Final." Mairena (5:14) Aut 83, p. 23-24.

1011. COLEMAN, Elliott
      "Holy Communion." NewL (50:2/3) Wint-Spr 84, p. 219.
      "Late Words." NewL (50:2/3) Wint-Spr 84, p. 219.

1012. COLEMAN, Horace
      "Poem for a 'Divorced' Daughter." NewL (50:2/3)
      Wint-Spr 84, p. 248.

1013. COLEMAN, Wanda
      "Flight of the California Candor (3)." Epoch
      (34:1) 84-85, p. 43.
      "Propaganda." Epoch (34:1) 84-85, p. 44-46.

1014. COLES, Katharine
      "Distances." GeoR (38:2) Sum 84, p. 288-289.
      "A Room with a View." GeoR (38:4) Wint 84, p. 747-
      748.

1015. COLINAS, Antonio
      "Fria Belleza Virgen." Mairena (6:18) 84, p. 68.

1016. COLLIER, Michael
      "Bruges." AntR (42:1) Wint 84, p. 87.
      "Consider the Garden." Poetry (145:1) O 84, p. 9.
      "Flyer." Poetry (145:1) O 84, p. 8-9.
      "Hamburg." AntR (42:1) Wint 84, p. 86.

1017. COLLINGS, Michael R.
      "Naked to the Sun." Veloc (3) Aut-Wint 83, p. 45.

1018. COLLINS, Denise A.
      "Pink Flamingoes." YetASM (3) 84, p. 7.

1019. COLLINS, Jeffrey
      "Perfect Fit." CapeR (19:3) 20th Anniverary Issue
      84, p. 9.

1020. COLLINS, Martha
      "Alone, One Must Be Careful." WestB (15) 84, p. 97.
      "Chain Letter." PraS (58:2) Sum 84, p. 60.
      "Day." AntR (42:4) Aut 84, p. 461.
      "Dickinson." VirQR (60:4) Aut 84, p. 613-614.
      "Equinox." WestB (15) 84, p. 96.
      "The Green House." Agni (21) 84, p. 54-56.
      "Her Rage." WestB (15) 84, p. 94-95.
      "Light." VirQR (60:4) Aut 84, p. 613.
      "Running." PraS (58:2) Sum 84, p. 59.

1021. COLLINS, Robert
      "Polio." SouthernHR (18:4) Aut 84, p. 323.
      "Running It All Back." Ascent (10:1) 84, p. 20.

1022. COLON, Francisco A.
      "Caerán como guijarros." Mairena (6:17) Aut 84,
      p. 95.

1023. COLON, Salvador
      "Rio Piedras." Areito (9:36) 84, p. 105.

1024. COLON RIVERA, Carmelo
      "A Veces No Quisiera Ser Poeta." Mairena (5:13)
      Spr 83, p. 92-93.

1025. COLON RIVERA, Cecilia
      "Ah Si Esta Lejos." Mairena (6:17) Aut 84, p. 97.

1026. COLON RUIZ, José O.
      "El Campesino." Mairena (5:13) Spr 83, p. 93.
      "Qué extraña canción de agua cansada."
      Mairena (6:17) Aut 84, p. 83.

1027. COLQUITT, Betsy Feagan
      "Afternoon Coming" (from the November 2, 1960
      issue). ChrC (101:22) 4-11 Jl 84, p. 681.

1028. COLQUITT, Clare
      "Runner's Morgen." NegC (4:4) Aut 84, p. 82-83.

1029. COMBS, Bruce
      "Routine Volcanic Activity." PoeticJ (1) 83, p. 5.

1030. COMFORD, Adam
      "Experiments." Veloc (3) Aut-Wint 83, p. 60.
      "July lifts a yellow skull over the palm trees"
      (Acrostic for Jay Kinney). Veloc (3) Aut-Wint
      83, p. 59.
      "Killer whales dance in elliptical orbits"
      (Acrostic for Katerina Valaoritis on her name-
      day). Veloc (3) Aut-Wint 83, p. 59.
      "Two Acrostics." Veloc (3) Aut-Wint 83, p. 59.

1031. COMPTON, S. R.
      "Green Darkness" (Page missing from issue --
      indexed from table of contents). Veloc (2) Spr
      83, p. 45.
      "His watch adlibbed." Veloc (1) Sum 82, p. 7.
      "The Orbit of the Moon." Veloc (2) Spr 83, p. 46.
      "The Wave." Veloc (3) Aut-Wint 83, p. 54-55.

1032. CONCUERA, Arturo
      "Fabula y Metafora del Gallo." Mairena (6:18) 84,
      p. 95.

1033. CONDEE, Nancy
      "Petty Dreads: 6 Poems in Five Lines" (for
      Fénéon). SouthernPR (24:1) Spr 84, p. 45.

1034. CONDEGA POETRY WORKSHOP
      "1978" (w. Sergio Vizcaya, tr. by Marc Zimmerman
      and Ellen Banberger). MinnR (N.S. 22) Spr 84,
      p. 70.

1035. CONDINI, Nereo E.
      "After Neruda." LindLM (3:1) Ja-Mr 84, p. 31.

1036. CONGDON, Kirby
      "Apple Poem." Confr (27/28) 84, p. 212.

1037. CONKLING, Helen
      "At the Winter Solstice." GrandS (4:1) Aut 84, p.
      149.
      "Poem with Tinted Glasses and a Mustache." GrandS
      (4:1) Aut 84, p. 150.

1038. CONN, Jan E.
"Blue Bulls." <u>Germ</u> (8:1) Spr-Sum 84, p. 30.
"Poem for Five Grapefruits." <u>Germ</u> (8:1) Spr-Sum
84, p. 37.
"The Season for Dancing." <u>PoetryCR</u> (5:4) Sum 84,
p. 17.
"South" (for Susan Glickman). <u>Germ</u> (8:1) Spr-Sum
84, p. 38.

CONNA, Thomas de: <u>See</u> DeCONNA, Thomas

1039. CONNELL, Evan S.
"Notes from a Bottle Found on the Beach at Carmel"
(Excerpts). <u>AmerPoR</u> (13:3) My-Je 84, p. 23-28.

1040. CONNELLAN, Leo
"Oil on Wild Birds." <u>GreenfR</u> (11:1/2) Sum-Aut 83,
p. 92.
"Waking Up in Deerfield, Massachusetts" (Written in
The Little Brown House at Deerfield Academy for
Robert William McGlynn). <u>GreenfR</u> (11:1/2) Sum-
Aut 83, p. 93.
"Wawenock." <u>GreenfR</u> (11:1/2) Sum-Aut 83, p. 92.

1041. CONNELLY, Karin Stevens
"Representative Women." <u>LittleM</u> (14:3) 84, p. 36.

1042. CONNELLY, Mark
"After." <u>Telescope</u> (3:1) Wint 84, p. 86.

1043. CONNER, Don
"A Witness." <u>PoeticJ</u> (1) 83, p. 12.

1044. CONNER, Shirley
"Appointments." <u>KanQ</u> (16:1/2) Wint-Spr 84, p. 136-
137.
"Loneliness." <u>KanQ</u> (16:1/2) Wint-Spr 84, p. 137.

1045. CONNIFF, Brian
"A Lake in Indiana." <u>SouthernR</u> (20:2) Spr 84, p.
364-365.

1046. CONNOLLY, J. F.
"The Director." <u>BlueBldgs</u> (7) 84, p. 5.

1047. CONNOR, Jean L.
"Lost." <u>Blueline</u> (5:2) Wint-Spr 84, p. 17.

1048. CONOLEY, Gillian
"The Mexico Divorce Hotel." <u>Tendril</u> (17) Wint 84,
p. 32.
"The Sound I Make Leaving." <u>Tendril</u> (17) Wint 84,
p. 31.
"Tonight I Feel Mortal." <u>Tendril</u> (17) Wint 84, p.
34.
"The Tooth Fairy." <u>Tendril</u> (17) Wint 84, p. 33.

1049. CONRAD, Cherry
"Dear." <u>Ploughs</u> (10:1) 84, p. 36-37.

1050. CONRAD, Nick
"Voyageur Trail" (Grand Portage, Minnesota). KanQ
(16:1/2) Wint-Spr 84, p. 128.

1051. CONTOSKI, Victor
"Incriminating Evidence." HangL (45) Spr 84, p. 27.
"My Wrongs." HangL (46) Aut 84, p. 11.
"Rain after Drought" (for Dzidka). HangL (46) Aut
84, p. 10.

1052. CONTRAIRE, A. U.
"Agape: I Corinthians: 13" (Three Anti-Leo
Buscaglia Poems: III). WindO (44) Sum-Aut 84,
p. 50.
"Little Buscaglia Bears" (Three Anti-Leo Buscaglia
Poems: II). WindO (44) Sum-Aut 84, p. 49-50.
"Pears and Garlic" (Three Anti-Leo Buscaglia Poems:
I). WindO (44) Sum-Aut 84, p. 49.
"Three Anti-Leo Buscaglia Poems." WindO (44) Sum-
Aut 84, p. 49-50.

1053. CONWAY, Jack
"The Brickmen." Amelia (1:2) O 84, p. 14-16.

1054. CONWAY, Rosalind Eve
"Fortune Cookie Future." PoetryCR (6:1) Aut 84,
p. 16.
"King & Bay: 8:00 a.m." CrossC (6:2) 84, p. 11.

1055. COOK, Gregory M.
"We Walk" (from a work in progress: Love in Flight,
1984). PoetryCR (5:4) Sum 84, p. 7.

1056. COOK, Ines
"Arte Poetica." Mairena (6:16) Spr 84, p. 79.
"Qué me dirás ahora." Mairena (6:16) Spr 84,
p. 80.

1057. COOK, Janet Simpson
"Belly Stove." CrossC (6:2) 84, p. 15.

1058. COOK, Lisa
"4 1/2 Hours after He Leaves." SmPd (21:2) Spr
84, p. 23.

1059. COOK-LYNN, Elizabeth
"Within Walking Distance" (A poem for my widowed
mother). Calyx (8:2) Spr 84, p. 90.

1060. COOKSHAW, Marlene
"After the Swim." Descant (47, 15:4) Wint 84, p.
19-20.
"Woodwards, Saturday." Descant (47, 15:4) Wint
84, p. 18.
"You Are Lucky." Quarry (33:4) Aut 84, p. 59-60.

1061. COOLEY, Peter
"Aubade." NewL (50:4) Sum 84, p. 90.
"The Elect." OhioR (32) 84, p. 27.
"Family Portrait in the Park." NewL (50:4) Sum

84, p. 90.
"A Fragment from a Former Life." <u>Abraxas</u> (29/30)
    84, p. 71.
"The Man on the Beach." <u>WestB</u> (14) 84, p. 30-31.
"Passages." <u>WestB</u> (14) 84, p. 31.
"Vanishing Point" (Excerpt). <u>Tendril</u> (18, special
    issue) 84, p. 59.

1062. COON, Betty
    "Cutting a Dress" (For Norma & Silas Wesley).
        <u>WoosterR</u> (1:2) N 84, p. 85.

1063. COOPER, Allan
    "The Axe." <u>AntiqR</u> (56) Wint 84, p. 76.
    "Woodshed." <u>AntiqR</u> (56) Wint 84, p. 75.

1064. COOPER, Michael
    "Cups Shoes Alive Wet and Waterlilies." <u>Tele</u> (19)
        83, p. 9.
    "Ducking." <u>Tele</u> (19) 83, p. 9.
    "Eating Your Lasagna." <u>Tele</u> (19) 83, p. 10-11.
    "House in Connecticut." <u>Tele</u> (19) 83, p. 11.
    "Umbrella." <u>Tele</u> (19) 83, p. 12.

1065. COOPER, Richard
    "April Seventeen." <u>MalR</u> (68) Je 84, p. 93.
    "Metro Dodo Foucault." <u>MalR</u> (68) Je 84, p. 91.
    "Saturday Morning." <u>MalR</u> (68) Je 84, p. 92.

1066. COOPER, Wyn
    "A Circle of Jacks." <u>TexasR</u> (5:3/4) Aut-Wint 84,
        p. 84-85.

1067. COOPERMAN, Robert
    "The Bakers of Unleavened Bread." <u>SmPd</u> (21:1)
        Wint 84, p. 19.
    "Linen Folding." <u>TarRP</u> (23:2) Spr 84, p. 6.
    "The Listening." <u>Nimrod</u> (27:2) Spr-Sum 84, p. 47.
    "Mysteries." <u>SoDakR</u> (22:4) Wint 84, p. 74-75.
    "Odysseus Remembers Nausicaa." <u>SoDakR</u> (22:4) Wint
        84, p. 65-66.
    "On the Disappearance of the Mummy Bound for the
        World's Fiar." <u>HolCrit</u> (21:2) Ap 84, p. 13.
    "Telemachos in Middle Age." <u>HiramPoR</u> (36) Spr-Sum
        84, p. 14.
    "Van Gogh at the Asylum at Saint-Remy." <u>MidAR</u>
        (4:2) Aut 84, p. 116.

1068. CORAZZINI, Sergio
    "For the Hurdy-Gurdy" (tr. by Felix Stefanile).
        <u>Sparrow</u> (46) 84, p. 23.

1069. CORBEN, Beverly
    "Anniversary of Dismay." <u>PoeticJ</u> (8) 84, p. 22.
    "Barn Summer." <u>PoeticJ</u> (4) 83, p. 20.
    "Bathtowel." <u>PoeticJ</u> (6) 84, p. 22.
    "Child's Painting." <u>PoeticJ</u> (4) 83, p. 22.
    "Costa del Sol." <u>PoeticJ</u> (3) 83, p. 25.
    "Frosties." <u>PoeticJ</u> (8) 84, p. 23.
    "Message." <u>PoeticJ</u> (3) 83, p. 24.

"Old Woman." <u>PoeticJ</u> (5) 84, p. 21.
"The Right Place." <u>PoeticJ</u> (5) 84, p. 22.
"Which Shore?" <u>PoeticJ</u> (4) 83, p. 21.

1070. CORBETT, William
      "Judy Watkins' Dream" (from <u>St. Patrick's Day</u>).
      <u>HarvardA</u> (118:2) Spr 84, p. 10.

1071. CORDING, Robert
      "A Boy Adds Black Vultures to His Life-List."
      <u>Poetry</u> (144:2) My 84, p. 97-98.
      "Chardin, Whippoorwill, Towhee." <u>NewYorker</u>
      (60:18) 18 Je 84, p. 42.
      "John Burroughs Thanks Henry Ford for a New Car,
      1914." <u>NewEngR</u> (6:4) Sum 84, p. 628-629.
      "Paired Islands: Assateague and Chincoteague."
      <u>PraS</u> (58:2) Sum 84, p. 61-63.
      "Steiglitz and O'Keeffe: Appropriations." <u>NewEngR</u>
      (6:4) Sum 84, p. 626-627.

1072. CORDONNIER, Max
      "Death of Felix." <u>CapeR</u> (19:3) 20th Anniverary
      Issue 84, p. 10.

CORDOVA, Antonio Ramírez: <u>See</u> RAMIREZ CORDOVA, Antonio

1073. COREY, Stephen
      "Animation." <u>Poetry</u> (144:6) S 84, p. 320.
      "Domestic Life: Nurse and Poet." <u>TarRP</u> (23:2) Spr
      84, p. 17.
      "Freshman Lit & Comp" (For Janet Burroway).
      <u>Poetry</u> (144:6) S 84, p. 319.
      "Gladys." <u>ColEng</u> (46:4) Ap 84, p. 366.
      "Learning to Live in America." <u>SouthernHR</u> (18:3)
      Sum 84, p. 233.
      "Music for My Daughter." <u>SouthernHR</u> (18:3) Sum
      84, p. 244.
      "Preparing to Live among the Old." <u>Poetry</u> (144:6)
      S 84, p. 320-321.
      "Religions." <u>TarRP</u> (23:2) Spr 84, p. 17.
      "Revision." <u>NewRep</u> (190:4) 30 Ja 84, p. 30.
      "Whatever Light." <u>ColEng</u> (46:4) Ap 84, p. 367.

1074. CORLISS, Frank
      "Forecast 1978" (tr. of Jerzy Ficowski). <u>Os</u> (18)
      84, p. 25.
      "Soweto" (tr. of Jerzy Ficowski). <u>Os</u> (18) 84, p. 23.

1075. CORMAN, Cid
      "Next to Nothing" (25 poems for Terry). <u>Origin</u>
      (Series 5:2) Wint 83, p. 29-35.
      "An Orthodoxy." <u>Sparrow</u> (46) 84, p. 22.
      "Realizing westwards." <u>Origin</u> (Series 5:1) Aut
      83, p. 61.

CORMIER-SHEKERJIAN, Regina de: <u>See</u> DeCORMIER-SHEKERJIAN, Regina

1076. CORN, Alfred
      "April." <u>Shen</u> (35:2/3) 84, p. 102-104.
      "The Band." <u>NewRep</u> (191:14) 1 O 84, p. 37.

"Notes from a Child of Paradise" (Excerpts).
ParisR (26:91) Spr 84, p. 179-185.
"Notes from a Child of Paradise" (Selections: VI-
XIV, XVI-XVII, XX-XXI). Poetry (143:5) F 84,
p. 251-265.
"Notes from a Child of Paradise" (Selections: VIII,
XII, XXIX). Nat (238:10) 17 Mr 84, p. 330-331.

1077. CORNELL, Brian R.
"After 20 Years." PottPort (6) 84, p. 24.
"In a Letter from Home #4." PottPort (6) 84, p. 25.
"Last Night's Sleep." Germ (8:1) Spr-Sum 84, p. 20.
"The Root Cellar." Germ (8:1) Spr-Sum 84, p. 19.
"When Your Candle Glows." PottPort (6) 84, p. 24.

1078. CORNFORD, Adam
"The Outer Limits." Veloc (2) Spr 83, p. 11-12.
"Your Time and You" (A Neoprole's Dating Guide).
Veloc (1) Sum 82, p. 5-6.

1079. CORNICK, Jean G.
"By Definition." PoeticJ (7) 84, p. 20.

1080. CORNISH, Sam
"Nat Turner." GreenfR (11:1/2) Sum-Aut 83, p. 96.
"Preacher Nat." GreenfR (11:1/2) Sum-Aut 83, p.
95-96.
"Tice David, Founder of The Underground Railroad,
Reminiscences." GreenfR (11:1/2) Sum-Aut 83,
p. 95.

1081. CORONEL URTECHO, José
"La Paloma." Mairena (6:18) 84, p. 159.

1082. CORRETJER, Juan Antonio
"Cancion de Siempre." Mairena (6:18) 84, p. 24.

1083. CORRIGAN, Paul
"Return to the Lake." BelPoJ (34:3) Spr 84, p. 5-6.
"Two in an Old Canoe" (for Jan). Blueline (5:2)
Wint-Spr 84, p. 16.

1084. CORSO, Gregory
"America Politica Historia, in Spontaneity."
Chelsea (42/43) 84, p. 62-64.

1085. CORTES-CABAN, David
"Hay Frente al Tiempo." Mairena (6:17) Aut 84, p.
79-80.

1086. CORTEZ, Jayne
"Firespritters" (Festac 77). GreenfR (11:1/2) Sum-
Aut 83, p. 15-16.
"There It Is." GreenfR (11:1/2) Sum-Aut 83, p. 13-
14.

1087. CORY, James
"So Little Time" (for Tim Pennypacker). PaintedB
(22) Spr 84, p. 12-13.

1088. CORY, James M.
      "Every Day" (for Kip Jones). FourQt (33:3) Spr
      84, p. 4-5.

1089. COSIER, Tony
      "For Sir John Davies." AntigR (56) Wint 84, p. 126.
      "In Half-Sleep." AntigR (56) Wint 84, p. 126.
      "It Snows Today a Thin Snow." NegC (4:4) Aut 84,
      p. 45.
      "The Newcomer." AntigR (56) Wint 84, p. 125.

1090. COSNER, John
      "In the Wake of Rimbaud." MalR (69) O 84, p. 76-78.

1091. COSTA, Marithelma
      "Te busco desde siempre." Mairena (6:17) Aut 84,
      p. 72.

1092. COTTERILL, Sarah
      "Easter Traffic Jam, San Salvador." PoetryNW
      (25:3) Aut 84, p. 40.
      "Gretel." MinnR (N.S. 22) Spr 84, p. 42.
      "Harp Seals." WebR (9:1) Spr 84, p. 62-63.
      "Jane Todd Crawford, Kentucky, 1830" (Honorable
      Mention). PoetL (79:1) Spr 84, p. 11-14.
      "Leaving Wisconsin for New York in the Sixth
      Month." MinnR (N.S. 22) Spr 84, p. 43-44.
      "Meditations from the Fire Watch: Three Poems."
      PoetryNW (25:3) Aut 84, p. 41-43.

1093. COUCH, Deborah
      "Last Rites." EngJ (73:5) S 84, p. 60.

1094. COUCH, Larry
      "The Poetry Reading." Vis (16) 84, p. 15.

1095. COULOMBE, Michael
      "Jump Shot" (for Matt, 1963-1981). Northeast
      (Series 3:17) Sum 84, p. 17.
      "Jump Shot" (for Matt, 1963-1981). SpoonRQ (9:2)
      Spr 84, p. 2.
      "The Rose in the Snow." SpoonRQ (9:2) Spr 84, p. 3.

1096. COULTER, Page
      "Sugaring-Off in Maine." MinnR (N.S. 23) Aut 84,
      p. 122.

COUNT, Le: See LeCOUNT

1097. COURSEN, H. R.
      "All Hallow's Eve: 1983." SmPd (21:2) Spr 84, p. 24.
      "Doug Kotar (1951-1983), New York Giants (1974-
      1981)." SmPd (21:2) Spr 84, p. 24.
      "Elizabeth: 1967." SmPd (21:2) Spr 84, p. 23.

1098. COURT, Wesli
      "Womansongs" (From the anonymous Middle English).
      HolCrit (21:1) F 84, p. 18.

1099. COURTOT, Martha
       "Letter to My Father." <u>Calyx</u> (8:3) Aut-Wint 84,
          p. 20.

1100. COUTO, Irmelind-Elisabeth
       "Wearing the White Night Gown." <u>Waves</u> (12:4) Spr
          84, p. 46.

1101. COUTO, Nancy Lee
       "The Cradle-Bread." <u>BlueBldgs</u> (7) 84, p. 24.

1102. COUZYN, Jeni
       "Cartography of the Subtle Heart." <u>Descant</u> (47,
          15:4) Wint 84, p. 194.
       "Ceremony of the Afterbirth." <u>CanLit</u> (100) Spr
          84, p. 80-81.
       "Earth-Body, Light-Body." <u>Descant</u> (47, 15:4) Wint
          84, p. 193.
       "Healer of the Light-Body." <u>Descant</u> (47, 15:4)
          Wint 84, p. 191-192.
       "Transformation of the Spirits." <u>CanLit</u> (100) Spr
          84, p. 81-83.
       "Wind." <u>CanLit</u> (100) Spr 84, p. 79-80.

1103. COVAIA, Vince
       "Morbid Fascinations." <u>SouthernPR</u> (24:2) Aut 84,
          p. 50-51.

1104. COVEL, Robert C.
       "Hymn to Allison on Her Natal Day." <u>DekalbLAJ</u>
          (20th Anniversary Issue) 84, p. 81.

1105. COWING, Sheila
       "Backpacker's Wife." <u>StoneC</u> (11:3/4) Spr-Sum 84,
          p. 64.
       "Leaving the Road I Want Only to Be Lost." <u>StoneC</u>
          (11:3/4) Spr-Sum 84, p. 64.

1106. COWNE, Ellen G.
       "The Vocabulary Test." <u>EngJ</u> (73:5) S 84, p. 81.

1107. COWSER, Robert G.
       "The Summer of 1936." <u>CapeR</u> (19:2) Sum 84, p. 38.

1108. COX, Carol
       "Bathers." <u>HangL</u> (46) Aut 84, p. 12-13.
       "Perhaps." <u>HangL</u> (46) Aut 84, p. 14.
       "Runaway." <u>HangL</u> (46) Aut 84, p. 15.

1109. COX, Celeste
       "A Voice Alone." <u>PoeticJ</u> (5) 84, p. 15.

1110. COX, Celeste O.
       "To Alberta" (in honor of Alberta Hunter, the
          legendary blues singer and song writer, and of
          her song "Downhearted Blues"). <u>PoeticJ</u> (6) 84,
          p. 7.

1111. COX, Malinda
       "Indian Summer" (For Hualing and Paul, tr. of

Nicolae Breban). <u>Iowa</u> (14:2) Spr-Sum 84, p.
222-223.

1112. COX, Rosemary D.
"I, Too, Have Felt the Stinging Pain." <u>DekalbLAJ</u>
(17:1/2) 84, p. 112.
"The Love Song of T. Alfred Cranmer." <u>DekalbLAJ</u>
(17:1/2) 84, p. 112-116.
"Paris, Gare du Nord." <u>DekalbLAJ</u> (20th
Anniversary Issue) 84, p. 85.

1113. COZY, David
"For Diablo Canyon." <u>SanFPJ</u> (7:1) 84, p. 77.
"Racism / Enrage." <u>SanFPJ</u> (7:1) 84, p. 78-79.
"Revolution." <u>Sam</u> (39:1, release 153) 84, p. 58.
"Sublimation." <u>SanFPJ</u> (6:4) 84, p. 80.

1114. CRAIG, David
"The Blue Pavilion (1958)." <u>Amelia</u> [1:1] Ap 84,
p. 23.

1115. CRANE, Hart
"Las Cartas de Amor de Mi Abuela" (tr. by Luis
Zalamea). <u>LindLM</u> (3:2/4) Ap-D 84, p. 25.

1116. CRANE, Stephen
"In the desert." <u>Tendril</u> (18, special issue) 84,
p. 67.

1117. CRAPPS, George
"The Main Man." <u>LitR</u> (28:1) Aut 84, p. 74-75.
"One Day a Week." <u>LitR</u> (28:1) Aut 84, p. 75.

1118. CRAWFORD, Robert
"Immaculate Conception." <u>NegC</u> (4:4) Aut 84, p. 70-
71.

1119. CRAWFORD, Tom
"Farmer Creek." <u>PoetryE</u> (15) Aut 84, p. 35.
"Nestucca River Poem" (for Sarah, Quinton and
Marty). <u>PoetryE</u> (15) Aut 84, p. 38-39.
"Pacific City." <u>PoetryE</u> (15) Aut 84, p. 36-37.

1120. CREAGH, Patrick
"Almost a Child's Prayer." <u>Nat</u> (238:14) 14 Ap 84,
p. 456.
"Elegy: As from a sickroom, voices." <u>Nat</u> (238:14)
14 Ap 84, p. 456.
"Monday Morning." <u>Nat</u> (238:14) 14 Ap 84, p. 456.

1121. CREEL, Liz
"Exchange." <u>Poem</u> (51) Mr [i.e. Jl] 84, p. 32-33.
"The Matala Cafe." <u>Poem</u> (51) Mr [i.e. Jl] 84, p. 36.
"The Red Rocks of Hollywood." <u>Poem</u> (51) Mr [i.e.
Jl] 84, p. 34.
"To Johnny Who Could Not See." <u>Poem</u> (51) Mr [i.e.
Jl] 84, p. 35.

1122. CREELEY, Robert
"Bookcase." <u>Epoch</u> (33:2) Spr-Sum 84, p. 148.

"For Jim Dine." Epoch (33:2) Spr-Sum 84, p. 149.
"Help Heaven." Field (30) Spr 84, p. 81.
"Memory, 1930." Poetry (144:6) S 84, p. 346.
"On Saul Bellow's Thesis, That We Think Our Era's
    Awful Because We'll Die in It." Spirit (7:1)
    84, p. 104.
"The Question." NewL (50:4) Sum 84, p. 105.
"She Is." Field (30) Spr 84, p. 81.
"Tell Story." Field (30) Spr 84, p. 82.

1123. CRESPO, José
    "A la Sombra de Leon Felipe." Mairena (6:17) Aut
        84, p. 86.

1124. CRESPO NIEVES, Raúl
    "Haiti." Mairena (6:17) Aut 84, p. 77.

1125. CREW, Louie
    "The Naked Truth." Tele (19) 83, p. 103.

1126. CREWS, Judson
    "Dolores." Abraxas (29/30) 84, p. 47.
    "God and the Devil. Why." WormR (24:2, issue 94)
        84, p. 72.
    "I Have Not Named Anything Its Name." WormR
        (24:1, issue 93) 84, p. 10.
    "If." WormR (24:1, issue 93) 84, p. 10.
    "If Those Memories Have Left Me, How." WormR
        (24:1, issue 93) 84, p. 10.
    "I'll Not Cop Out on Rhododendrons This Ti."
        WormR (24:1, issue 93) 84, p. 9.
    "I'll Not Cop Out on Rhododendrons This Time"
        (corrected reprint). WormR (24:2, issue 94)
        84, p. 72.
    "It Is Almost As If There Were Never." WormR
        (24:1, issue 93) 84, p. 9.
    "I've Ex-." WormR (24:1, issue 93) 84, p. 10.
    "A Stubble of Charred Forest, Several." WormR
        (24:1, issue 93) 84, p. 9.
    "The Telegram." WormR (24:2, issue 94) 84, p. 73.
    "You Took My Clothes Off of Me." OroM (2:3/4,
        issue 7/8) 84, p. 16.

CRIADO, Yolanda Gracia de: See GRACIA de CRIADO, Yolanda

1127. CRIST, Vonnie
    "Ash." SanFPJ (7:1) 84, p. 59.
    "Fanatics." SanFPJ (7:1) 84, p. 59.
    "The Herb Garden." SanFPJ (6:2) 84, p. 89.
    "Parent-Star." SanFPJ (7:1) 84, p. 58.
    "Passenger Pigeon." SanFPJ (6:2) 84, p. 92.

1128. CRIX, John
    "Other Ideas about the A57." Bogg (52) 84, p. 39.

1129. CROCKETT-SMITH, D. L.
    "Bombed." OP (37) Spr-Sum 84, p. 36.
    "Cowboy Eating His Chicken." OP (37) Spr-Sum 84,
        p. 28-29.
    "A Few Fine Lines in Mt. Meigs, Alabama, As Yet

Another Year Passes On." <u>OP</u> (37) Spr-Sum 84,
   p. 30-33.
"Spring Song." <u>OP</u> (37) Spr-Sum 84, p. 34-35.

1130. CROL, Elly
"Late Leaves of Autumn" (tr. of Irma Klainguti, w.
   John Allen). <u>Os</u> (18) 84, p. 13.
"Survilsan Village" (tr. of Silvio Camenisch, w.
   John Allen). <u>Os</u> (18) 84, p. 15.
"Who Knows" (tr. of Irma Klainguti, w. John Allen).
   <u>Os</u> (18) 84, p. 13.

1131. CRONYN, Hume
"Blue Begonias." <u>Kayak</u> (64) My 84, p. 36-37.

1132. CROOKER, Barbara
"Field Guide to North American Birds." <u>BelPoJ</u>
   (35:2) Wint 84-85, p. 19.
"Recipe for Grief." <u>WestB</u> (15) 84, p. 107.

1133. CROOKES, Joyce F.
"The Armchair Philosopher." <u>Sam</u> (41:2, release
   162) 84 or 85, p. 13.

1134. CROSBY, Brooke
"Mud Holes." <u>SnapD</u> (7:2) Spr 84, p. 14-15.

1135. CROSS, Elsa
"Images on the Beach" (tr. by Abby Wolf and Eric
   Walker). <u>Iowa</u> (14:2) Spr-Sum 84, p. 145-146.

1136. CROSSLEY-HOLLAND, Kevin
"Beachcomber" (from "East Coast Portraits"). <u>OntR</u>
   (21) Aut-Wint 84, p. 21.
"Greening." <u>OntR</u> (21) Aut-Wint 84, p. 22.

1137. CROSTON, Julie
"A Story from Cage's Living Room Music (1940)."
   <u>HangL</u> (46) Aut 84, p. 16.

1138. CROW, Mary
"Comprehension" (tr. of Victor Gavirio, w. Patsy
   Boyer). <u>BlackWR</u> (10:2) Spr 84, p. 37.
"Curfew Time." <u>WoosterR</u> (1:2) N 84, p. 48-49.
"From a Bus Window." <u>WoosterR</u> (1:2) N 84, p. 45-46.
"Girl Floating on Air." <u>NewL</u> (50:2/3) Wint-Spr
   84, p. 263.
"Graveyard." <u>WoosterR</u> (1:2) N 84, p. 43-45.
"Happiness" (tr. of Jorge Teillier). <u>WoosterR</u>
   (1:2) N 84, p. 52.
"Innocence of Eye." <u>WoosterR</u> (1:2) N 84, p. 50.
"The Last Island" (tr. of Jorge Teillier).
   <u>WoosterR</u> (1:2) N 84, p. 54.
"Plaza de Mayo" (Waiting for the mothers of the
   missing, Buenos Aires, 1984). <u>WoosterR</u> (1:2) N
   84, p. 49.
"Saturday Night" (tr. of Idea Vilariño, w. Patsy
   Boyer). <u>BlackWR</u> (10:2) Spr 84, p. 39.
"Uses of the Border." <u>LitR</u> (27:2) Wint 84, p. 186-
   187.

"A View of the Sea." <u>WoosterR</u> (1:2) N 84, p. 42-43.
"The Weight of the Day." <u>WoosterR</u> (1:2) N 84, p. 47.

1139. CROWE, Ronald
"Grabbing." <u>DekalbLAJ</u> (17:1/2) 84, p. 111.

1140. CROZIER, L.
"There Are Limits." (for George Morrissette).
<u>CanLit</u> (101) Sum 84, p. 68.

1141. CROZIER, Lorna
"Cat in the Garden." <u>PoetryCR</u> (6:1) Aut 84, p. 19.
"Early Arrival." <u>CrossC</u> (6:4) 84, p. 10.
"Fishing in Air." <u>PoetryCR</u> (6:2) Wint 84-85, p. 11.
"Hours of Insomnia." <u>PoetryCR</u> (6:2) Wint 84-85,
p. 11.
"Loon Song." <u>CrossC</u> (6:4) 84, p. 10.
"No Matter." <u>CrossC</u> (6:4) 84, p. 10.
"The Photograph I Keep of Them." <u>CrossC</u> (6:4) 84,
p. 10.

1142. CRUISE, Stephen
"Blood Red Run." <u>Descant</u> (47, 15:4) Wint 84, p. 1.

1143. CRUM, Robert
"A Child Explains Dying." <u>Ploughs</u> (10:1) 84, p.
38-39.
"Jack, the Following Summer." <u>Ploughs</u> (10:1) 84,
p. 40-41.

1144. CRUMMETT, Vance
"The Poets of Russia." <u>Abraxas</u> (31/32) 84, p. 9.

1145. CRUSZ, Rienzi
"Immigrant" (for Cleta Nora Marcellina Serpanchy).
<u>Quarry</u> (33:4) Aut 84, p. 61.
"Mayaro Sea Sculpture." <u>AntigR</u> (58) Sum 84, p. 85.
"A New Equilibrium" (for Michael). <u>PoetryCR</u> (6:2)
Wint 84-85, p. 11.
"On the Beach." <u>AntigR</u> (58) Sum 84, p. 86.
"The Trouble with Growing Old." <u>PoetryCR</u> (6:2)
Wint 84-85, p. 11.

1146. CRUZ, Juana Inès de la, Sor
"A Modest Gift by Affection Made a Treat" (tr. by
Margaret Sayers Peden). <u>NewL</u> (50:4) Sum 84, p.
64.
"She Assures That She Will Hold a Secret in
Confidence" (tr. by Margaret Sayers Peden).
<u>NewL</u> (50:4) Sum 84, p. 64.

1147. CRUZKATZ, Ida
"Selma: In Memoriam." <u>Sam</u> (37:3, 147th release)
83, p. 34-35.

1148. CSIKSZENTMIHALYI, Mark
"Tango." <u>HarvardA</u> (117:4/118:1) D 84, p. 26.

1149. CSOORI, Sàndor
"By the Time the Day Ends" (tr. by Ivàn de Beky).

<u>Descant</u> (47, 15:4) Wint 84, p. 196.
"Echoes of Great Cavities" (tr. by Iván de Beky).
    <u>Descant</u> (47, 15:4) Wint 84, p. 197.
"Head Bowed" (tr. by Nicholas Kolumban). <u>CharR</u>
    (10:1) Spr 84, p. 76-77.
"Hermit Summer" (tr. by Nicholas Kolumban). <u>CharR</u>
    (10:1) Spr 84, p. 74-75.
"Midnight" (tr. by Nicholas Kolumban). <u>NowestR</u>
    (22:3) 84, p. 91.
"The Poppy Rattles at Night" (tr. by Iván de
    Beky). <u>Descant</u> (47, 15:4) Wint 84, p. 195.
"Winter's Voice Softens" (tr. by Nicholas
    Kolumban). <u>NowestR</u> (22:3) 84, p. 92.
"You Make a Poor Sky Dweller" (tr. by Nicholas
    Kolumban). <u>CharR</u> (10:1) Spr 84, p. 75-76.

1150. CUADRA, Angel
    "Un Plano Ausente." <u>Mairena</u> (6:18) 84, p. 177.

1151. CUADRA, Pablo Antonio
    "The Ceiba" (tr. by Grace Schulman). <u>Nat</u> (238:3)
        28 Ja 84, p. 101.
    "The Gourd" (tr. by Marc Zimmerman and Ellen
        Banberger). <u>MinnR</u> (N.S. 22) Spr 84, p. 67.
    "Las muchachas que juegan construyen una
        astronomía." <u>Mairena</u> (6:18) 84, p. 155.
    "La Pulga" (para lectura de los críticos).
        <u>Mairena</u> (6:18) 84, p. 155.

1152. CUDDY, Dan
    "Lost." <u>Open24</u> (3) 84, p. 41.

CUDOS, J. L. Alegre: <u>See</u> ALEGRE CUDOS, J. L.

1153. CUELHO, Art
    "In Grapevine Sand." <u>Amelia</u> (1:2) O 84, p. 65-66.
    "Priest and River Man." <u>Amelia</u> (1:2) O 84, p. 65.

1154. CUENCA, Luis Alberto de
    "El Regreso." <u>Mairena</u> (6:18) 84, p. 68.

CUESTA, Francisco Ruiz de la: <u>See</u> RUIZ de la CUESTA, Francisco

1155. CULHANE, Brian
    "Estrangement in Athens." <u>Shen</u> (35:1) 83-84, p. 93.

1156. CULLEN, E. J.
    "To William Blake." <u>Swallow</u> (3) 84, p. 88.

1157. CULLEN, John
    "The Beginning." <u>Northeast</u> (Series 3:17) Sum 84,
        p. 6.

1158. CULLUM, J. W.
    "And There Are, Also, Other Awakenings." <u>MidwQ</u>
        (25:2) Wint 84, p. 160.
    "Neoplatonism Comes to an End in the French
        Quarter." <u>MidwQ</u> (25:2) Wint 84, p. 158-159.
    "Rabearivelo, Drunk, Talks to Himself in
        Tananarive." <u>MidwQ</u> (25:2) Wint 84, p. 161.

"Winter Arrives on Upper Moreland Avenue." MidwQ
(25:2) Wint 84, p. 157.

1159. CULP, Mary-Alice
"The Railrodders." BlueBuf (2:2) Spr 84, p. 9.
"White Ribbons." BlueBuf (2:2) Spr 84, p. 10.

1160. CULVER, Marjorie
"The Inhabited House." DekalbLAJ (20th
Anniversary Issue) 84, p. 81-84.

1161. CUMMINGS, Darcy
"In the Vestibule." CarolQ (36:2) Wint 84, p. 37.

1162. CUMMINGS, E. E.
"Poem: ev erythingex Cept." Shen (35:2/3) 84, p.
112.
"Poem: What time is it? it is by every star."
Shen (35:2/3) 84, p. 111.

1163. CUMMINS, James (Jim)
"A Biography." Shen (35:4) 84, p. 97-98.
"The Imaginary Friendship of Li Ho and Tu Mu."
Shen (35:4) 84, p. 99.
"The Perry Mason Sestinas" (Excerpts). Iowa
(14:3) Aut 84, p. 54-55.
"The Perry Mason Sestinas" (Excerpts). MidAR
(4:1) Spr 84, p. 155-156.
"The Perry Mason Sestinas" (Selection: #21). Shen
(35:4) 84, p. 96-97.

1164. CUMPIANO, Ina
"Brujería." BilingR (11:1) Ja-Ap 84, p. 63.
"My Father's Aguacate." BilingR (11:1) Ja-Ap 84,
p. 63-64.
"Naming the Dead." BilingR (11:1) Ja-Ap 84, p. 62.
"Sin Volver." BilingR (11:1) Ja-Ap 84, p. 61.

1165. CUNLIFFE, Dave
"Snafued." Bogg (52) 84, p. 52.
"Two Middle Aged Men Exercise." Vis (14) 84, p. 7.

1166. CUNNINGHAM, J. V.
"Cocktails at six, suburban revelry." Shen
(35:2/3) 84, p. 116.
"Epigrams." Shen (35:2/3) 84, p. 116.
"A periphrastic insult, not a banal." Shen
(35:2/3) 84, p. 116.
"Some twenty years of marital agreement." Shen
(35:2/3) 84, p. 116.

1167. CUNNINGHAM, James
"Fantasy Man" (or, When Dexter Gordon Takes a
Break). BlackALF (18:1) Spr 84, p. 27.
"A Requiem for a Lover of Bigger Thomas."
BlackALF (18:1) Spr 84, p. 27.

1168. CURRY, J. W.
"Stigation." CapilR (31) 84, p. 31.
"Untitled" (for Steven Smith). CapilR (31) 84, p.

56.
"WH." <u>CapilR</u> (31) 84, p. 29.

1169. CURRY, Peggy Simson
"Pioneer Ranching." <u>SoDakR</u> (22:2) Sum 84, p. 48.

1170. CURTIS, Jack
"Crepúsculo." <u>BelPoJ</u> (35:2) Wint 84-85, p. 18.

1171. CURTIS, Redmond
"Impressions in View." <u>AntigR</u> (58) Sum 84, p. 122.

1172. CURTIS, Tony
"Taken to the Sea." <u>PoetryCR</u> (5:4) Sum 84, p. 14.

1173. CUSACK, Margaret
"R.S.V.P." <u>EngJ</u> (73:5) S 84, p. 105.

1174. CUSHMAN, Kim
"Acre of Love." <u>CapeR</u> (19:2) Sum 84, p. 28.
"Everett Morgan's Horses." <u>CapeR</u> (19:2) Sum 84,
p. 26.
"The Welder." <u>CapeR</u> (19:2) Sum 84, p. 27.

1175. CUSHMAN, Stephen
"Descent." <u>WebR</u> (9:2) Wint 85, p. 44.

1176. CUTCHINS, Gerald A.
"Caring." <u>DekalbLAJ</u> (17:1/2) 84, p. 117.
"Sustenance." <u>DekalbLAJ</u> (20th Anniversary Issue)
84, p. 84.

1177. CUTLER, Bruce
"Building." <u>Peb</u> (23) 84, p. 27.

CUTTER, Lionel von: <u>See</u> Von CUTTER, Lionel

1178. CUZA MALE, Belkis
"Adan, Adan." <u>LindLM</u> (3:2/4) Ap-D 84, p. 20.
"Rilke en Toledo." <u>LindLM</u> (3:2/4) Ap-D 84, p. 20.
"Summertime in Princeton." <u>LindLM</u> (3:2/4) Ap-D
84, p. 20.

1179. CYNDIAN, Charles London
"Katherine's Nightmare." <u>BlueBldgs</u> (8) 84?, p. 37.

1180. CZAPLA, Cathy Young
"Connecticut River, July 1976." <u>Spirit</u> (7:1) 84,
p. 185.
"Creek Road." <u>Sam</u> (41:2, release 162) 84 or 85,
p. 26.
"Flying Mountain." <u>Sam</u> (41:1, release 161) 84, p.
27.
"For the Dead." <u>PoeticJ</u> (2) 83, p. 8.
"Lullaby." <u>Pig</u> (12) 84, p. 79.
"Next Mistake." <u>Spirit</u> (7:1) 84, p. 186.
"Skeins." <u>PoeticJ</u> (2) 83, p. 28.

1181. CZECHOWSKI, Heinz
"Oradea" (In memory of Paul Celan, tr. by Suzanne
Shipley Toliver). <u>Sulfur</u> (4:2, issue 11) 84,

p. 92-93.

1182. CZURY, Craig
"Anthracite History." Kayak (64) My 84, p. 26.
"August 2, 1981." Kayak (64) My 84, p. 28.
"Coal Mining Poems." Kayak (64) My 84, p. 26-28.
"Coalscape" (to Blaise Cendrars). Kayak (64) My
    84, p. 27.
"Uncovering the Mine Shaft." Kayak (64) My 84, p.
    27.

D., H. (Doolittle, Hilda): See H. D.

1183. DABNEY, Janice
"The Visitor." CrabCR (1:3) Wint 84, p. 7.
"Zinfandel in 309." CrabCR (2:1) Sum 84, p. 21-22.

1184. DABYDEEN, Cyril
"Backyard & Tenement." Dandel (11:2) Aut-Wint 84-
    85, p. 69.
"Drowning Cats." Dandel (11:2) Aut-Wint 84-85, p.
    68.
"Hemingway" (Cuba, July 1982). CrossC (6:4) 84,
    p. 15.

1185. DACEY, Florence
"After the Attack" (For Rufina Amaya of Mozote, El
    Salvador). Vis (15) 84, p. 36.
"While She Was Being Interrogated, She Witnessed
    the Dismemberment of a Young Boy" (Carolyn
    Forche, about El Salvador). Vis (15) 84, p. 35.

1186. DACEY, Philip
"Anniversary Poem." PoetryNW (25:3) Aut 84, p. 32.
"Dogs." MidAR (4:1) Spr 84, p. 77-78.
"The New Love Poem." PaintedB (21) Wint 84, p. 5.

1187. DADASON, Sigfus
"The Roads of My Country" (Excerpt, tr. by Alan
    Boucher). Vis (14) 84, p. 8.

1188. DAGLARCA, Fazil Hüsnü
"Dead" (tr. by Talat Sait Halman). NewRena (6:1,
    #18) Spr 84, p. 115.
"Ferman." NewRena (6:1, #18) Spr 84, p. 110, 116.
"Imperial Command" (tr. by Talat Sait Halman).
    NewRena (6:1, #18) Spr 84, p. 117.
"Old." NewRena (6:1, #18) Spr 84, p. 110, 114.

1189. DAHL, Chris
"Synopsis of the Fire-Safety Film." PoetryNW
    (25:2) Sum 84, p. 17-18.
"Turning to Pegasus." PoetryNW (25:2) Sum 84, p. 19.

1190. DAHLIN, Barbro
"Meeting" (tr. by Eva Claeson). LitR (28:1) Aut
    84, p. 134.
"Snowed In" (tr. by Eva Claeson). LitR (28:1) Aut
    84, p. 134.

1191. DAILEY, Joel
      "Confessional." <u>Poem</u> (50) Mr 84, p. 13.
      "Head Examined." <u>BlueBldgs</u> (7) 84, p. 8.
      "Meeting Place." <u>Poem</u> (50) Mr 84, p. 15.
      "Night Journal." <u>Poem</u> (50) Mr 84, p. 14.
      "Photograph" (for my father). <u>MidAR</u> (4:1) Spr 84,
         p. 117-118.

1192. DALE, Kathleen
      "The Pottery Keeper." <u>ThirdW</u> (2) Spr 84, p. 18.

1193. D'ALFONSO, Antonio
      "The Family." <u>PoetryCR</u> (6:1) Aut 84, p. 15.

1194. DALIBARD, Jill
      "Clearance." <u>AntigR</u> (58) Sum 84, p. 61.
      "Search." <u>AntigR</u> (58) Sum 84, p. 60.

1195. DALTON, Dorothy
      "Eye Balled." <u>Abraxas</u> (29/30) 84, p. 61.
      "Questions Then: Never Asked of My Father."
         <u>Amelia</u> (1:2) O 84, p. 53.

1196. DALTON, Roque
      "Assassinated on the Street" (tr. by Harold Black,
         w. Walter Burrell and Sylvia Bernstein). <u>Vis</u>
         (15) 84, p. 18.
      "Despair" (tr. by Magda Bogin). <u>Vis</u> (15) 84, p. 17.
      "For the Eye in the Keyhole" (Partial translation
         by Harold Black, w. Walter Burrell and Sylvia
         Bernstein). <u>Vis</u> (15) 84, p. 18.
      "Insomnia" (tr. by Harold Black, w. Walter Burrell
         and Sylvia Bernstein). <u>Vis</u> (15) 84, p. 19.
      "Small Hours of the Night" (tr. by Hardie St.
         Martin). <u>Nat</u> (238:3) 28 Ja 84, p. 100.

1197. DALY, Chris
      "Secret Clearance Sale." <u>PikeF</u> (6) Aut 84, p. 36.

1198. DALY, Desmond
      "Fair Warning." <u>Descant</u> (47, 15:4) Wint 84, p. 130.
      "Premature Withdrawal." <u>Descant</u> (47, 15:4) Wint
         84, p. 129.

1199. DALY, Kevin
      "In the Blessed Seconds." <u>Wind</u> (14:51) 84, p. 9.

1200. DAMACION, Kenneth Zamora
      "Assimilation." <u>Tendril</u> (17) Wint 84, p. 36.
      "Convulsions." <u>CarolQ</u> (37:1) Aut 84, p. 67-68.
      "For Those I've Saved Names For." <u>Tendril</u> (17)
         Wint 84, p. 37.
      "Loneliness." <u>MSS</u> (3:2/3) Spr 84, p. 61.
      "Sleep" (for Karin Ash). <u>Tendril</u> (17) Wint 84, p.
         35.

1201. DAME, Enid
      "Ethel Rosenberg: A Sestina." <u>Cond</u> (3:4, issue
         10) 84, p. 103-104.

159   DANON

1202. DANA, Robert
       "Blue Run." <u>Stand</u> (25:4) Aut 84, p. 5.
       "Watching the Nighthawk's Dive." <u>GeoR</u> (38:2) Sum
          84, p. 398-399.

1203. DANIEL, Hal J., III
       "Just to the Right of the Toilet Paper." <u>Bogg</u>
          (52) 84, p. 26.
       "My One and Only Evening with Blanche." <u>YetASM</u>
          (3) 84, p. 3.
       "No Middle Leg to Stand On." <u>Sam</u> (41:1, release
          161) 84, p. 19.
       "Speed Boats." <u>Sam</u> (39:1, release 153) 84, p. 14.
       "You Can't Whip It at Huey's." <u>Vis</u> (16) 84, p. 35.

1204. DANIEL, John
       "The Sound of Mountain Water." <u>SnapD</u> (7:2) Spr
          84, p. 9.

1205. DANIEL, Lorne
       "Leaving Lodgepole (1976)." <u>BlueBuf</u> (2:2) Spr 84,
          p. 14.
       "The Memory of This House." <u>CrossC</u> (6:4) 84, p. 15.
       "Nightsky." <u>BlueBuf</u> (2:2) Spr 84, p. 13.

1206. DANIEL, Shoshana T.
       "Thrice Gaugin" (for my mother). <u>CrabCR</u> (1:3)
          Wint 84, p. 17-18.

1207. DANIELS, Celia
       "Clans of Stones." <u>KanQ</u> (16:1/2) Wint-Spr 84, p.
          156.

1208. DANIELS, Gabrielle
       "In my country." <u>YellowS</u> (10) Spr 84, p. 6.
       "In my country." <u>YellowS</u> (11) Sum 84, p. 45.

1209. DANIELS, Jim
       "Digger Gets a Dog." <u>PoetryE</u> (15) Aut 84, p. 55-56.
       "Digger Thinks about Numbers." <u>PoetryE</u> (15) Aut
          84, p. 57-58.
       "Digger's Daughter's First Date." <u>PoetryE</u> (15)
          Aut 84, p. 54.
       "Digger's Thanksgiving." <u>MinnR</u> (N.S. 23) Aut 84,
          p. 113.
       "Miles Away." <u>TarRP</u> (24:1) Aut 84, p. 21.
       "Names." <u>OhioR</u> (33) 84, p. 72.

1210. DANIELS, Kate
       "What Will Happen." <u>Pequod</u> (16/17) 84, p. 215-216.

DANIELSON, Anita Endrezze: <u>See</u> ENDREZZE-DANIELSON, Anita

1211. DANN, Jack
       "Night Meetings" (In memory of Loren Eiseley).
          <u>Veloc</u> (4) Sum 84, p. 21-22.

1212. DANON, Ruth
       "Projecting." <u>Tendril</u> (17) Wint 84, p. 41-42.
       "Sensible Shoe Takes a Walk." <u>Tendril</u> (17) Wint

84, p. 39.
"Sensible Shoe Thinks about Nuclear Disaster."
Tendril (17) Wint 84, p. 38.
"Sensible Shoe Thinks about the Discovery of
Kafka's Library." Tendril (17) Wint 84, p. 40.

1213. DANTE ALIGHIERI
"From the Second Canto" (from The Divine Comedy,
Book 3, tr. by John Ciardi). NewYRB (31:20) 20
D 84, p. 9.
"The Inferno" (Selections: "Canto 4: Limbus, Canto
31: Giants, tr. by Wallace Fowlie). SouthernR
(20:1) Wint 84, p. 151-152.
"Purgatorio: Canto I" (tr. by Robert Foster).
Quarry (33:3) Sum 84, p. 43-47.

1214. DANYS, Milda
"Spadina Avenue: Request to Join the Celebration"
(Bicentennial Contest Winners, Poetry: First).
Waves (12:4) Spr 84, p. 81-83.
"Watching the City: An Elegy" (For Marie Uguay,
Montreal poet, died Oct. 1981). Descant (47,
15:4) Wint 84, p. 159-161.

1215. D'ARCY, Michael James
"Holiday Walk." StoneC (12:1/2) Aut-Wint 84, p. 28.

1216. DARGIS, Daniel
"Natale Embrasure." Os (19) 84, p. 28-31.

1217. DARLING, Charles W.
"For Richard." YetASM (3) 84, p. insert.
"In My Father's Study." Sam (39:1, release 153)
84, p. 4-5.
"The Mail." StoneC (12:1/2) Aut-Wint 84, p. 18.
"Waiting." Tendril (17) Wint 84, p. 43-44.

1218. DARLING, Marian
"Meeting at the Village Inn" (for Sheila). StoneC
(11:3/4) Spr-Sum 84, p. 74.

1219. DARLINGTON, Andrew
"The One Was Texas Medicine, the Other Was Just
Railroad Gin." Veloc (3) Aut-Wint 83, p. 40.
"Pace the End to Time/ Breakthru: World #9."
Veloc (3) Aut-Wint 83, p. 39.
"The Secret Life of Mr. Yves Tanguy." Veloc (3)
Aut-Wint 83, p. 42.

1220. DARNELL, Gerald
"Peril."ThirdW (2) Spr 84, p. 26-27.

1221. DASS, Nirmal
"Seeding." Waves (12:4) Spr 84, p. 56.

1222. DAUGHTERS, Marie K.
"Certain Government Officials." SanFPJ (6:2) 84,
p. 88.
"The Street People." SanFPJ (6:2) 84, p. 41.

1223. DAUNT, Jon
      "God Plays Chess with Joan of Arc." <u>MalR</u> (68) Je
      84, p. 88.

1224. DAVENPORT, Doris
      "Teaching Composition in California/With My
      Grandfather near Death in Georgia." <u>BlackALF</u>
      (18:1) Spr 84, p. 10.

1225. DAVEY, Frank
      "Riel." <u>CanLit</u> (100) Spr 84, p. 84-89.

1226. DAVID, Gary
      "Hymn to the Buffalo." <u>GreenfR</u> (12:1/2) Sum-Aut
      84, p. 81.
      "Passing On through Faith." <u>MidAR</u> (4:2) Aut 84,
      p. 124.

1227. DAVIDSON, Anne
      "Event." <u>Poem</u> (51) Mr [i.e. Jl] 84, p. 7.
      "The Illusion Still Unbroken." <u>Poem</u> (51) Mr [i.e.
      Jl] 84, p. 6.
      "Neither Man Nor Mouse." <u>Poem</u> (51) Mr [i.e. Jl]
      84, p. 4-5.
      "The Winds of Katoomba" (Australia). <u>Wind</u> (14:51)
      84, p. 10.

1228. DAVIDSON, Scott
      "Inertia and What Emerges." <u>CutB</u> (22) Spr-Sum 84,
      p. 38-39.

1229. DAVIDSON, Scott L.
      "Driving Late to Work." <u>SnapD</u> (7:1) Aut 83, p. 16-
      17.

1230. DAVIE, Donald
      "Chrysanthemums." <u>Shen</u> (35:2/3) 84, p. 118.
      "Fable of First Person" (tr. of György Somlyó).
      <u>Iowa</u> (14:2) Spr-Sum 84, p. 202-203.
      "The Fountain." <u>Shen</u> (35:2/3) 84, p. 117.
      "Going to Italy." <u>Shen</u> (35:2/3) 84, p. 117-118.

1231. DAVIES, M.
      "The Shepherd's Watch." <u>SpoonRQ</u> (9:2) Spr 84, p.
      51-52.

1232. DAVILA, Angela María
      "No digas más." <u>Mairena</u> (6:18) 84, p. 26.

DAVILA, Marcos Reyes: <u>See</u> REYES DAVILA, Marcos

1233. DAVILA LOPEZ, Antonio
      "Apuntador de Mirajes." <u>Mairena</u> (6:16) Spr 84, p.
      11-12.

1234. DAVIS, Alan
      "Funnels." <u>Sam</u> (39:1, release 153) 84, p. 41.
      "Incident, Chu Lai." <u>Pig</u> (12) 84, p. 17.
      "Omaha, 1982." <u>Pig</u> (12) 84, p. 82.
      "The Red Carpet." <u>Wind</u> (14:52) 84, p. 11.

1235. DAVIS, Albert
        "Mapmaking in the Marsh 1899." SewanR (92:3) J1-S
        84, p. 370-371.

1236. DAVIS, Barbara Nector
        "The Harvest" (Haiku). SanFPJ (6:1) 84, p. 27.
        "Taps." SanFPJ (6:1) 84, p. 28.

1237. DAVIS, Clarence M.
        "Travels with Kathy Collum." Peb (23) 84, p. 54.

1238. DAVIS, Dick
        "Semele." Hudson (37:1) Spr 84, p. 19.

1239. DAVIS, Glover
        "From the First Book of the Ocean to Sandra."
        MissouriR (7:3) 84, p. 23.

1240. DAVIS, Jackson
        "Come Back." Nimrod (28:1) Aut-Wint 84, p. 112-113.

1241. DAVIS, Jon
        "Birthday: The Water Pump." Stand (25:4) Aut 84,
        p. 43.
        "The Curator of the Basement Collection Reveals His
        Secret Fear." GreenfR (12:1/2) Sum-Aut 84, p.
        138.
        "Mr. Celentano Remembers the Night Johnny Paris
        Sang 'Heartbreak Hotel'." PikeF (6) Aut 84, p.
        4-5.
        "That Modern Malice" (for Charlie Parker). GeoR
        (38:3) Aut 84, p. 542-543.
        "The Weed Pullers." GreenfR (12:1/2) Sum-Aut 84,
        p. 137.

1242. DAVIS, Lloyd
        "Bob Hosey Is Dead." Peb (23) 84, p. 65.

1243. DAVIS, Lydia
        "How W. H. Auden Spends the Night in a Friend's
        House." Pequod (16/17) 84, p. 206.
        "Mr. Burdoff's Visit to Germany." Pequod (16/17)
        84, p. 207-212.

1244. DAVIS, Marilyn
        "After the Poetry Reading" (for Grace Butcher).
        HiramPoR (36) Spr-Sum 84, p. 16.
        "Tina's Mother's Morning Meditation" (with lines
        from "An Old-World Thicket," by Christina
        Rossetti). HiramPoR (36) Spr-Sum 84, p. 15.

1245. DAVIS, Mary S.
        "I wrote two letters, both to you, last night"
        (DeKalb County High Schools Literary Award
        Winners: Second Place--Poetry). DekalbLAJ
        (17:1/2) 84, p. 153.

1246. DAVIS, Melody
        "The Camellia Grill." BelPoJ (35:1) Aut 84, p. 16-
        17.

"Potatoes." BelPoJ (35:1) Aut 84, p. 15-16.
"The Tombkeeper, St. Louis Cemetery #1." WestB
   (15) 84, p. 26.

1247. DAVIS, Walter
   "The Second Decade of Illustrations or Captions for
      Chinese Artifacts" (XI-XX). Bound (12:1) Aut
      83, p. 181-185.

1248. DAVIS, William V.
   "Night Thoughts for My Brother." MidAR (4:2) Aut
      84, p. 141.

1249. DAVIS, William Virgil
   "Along the Wall." Hudson (37:1) Spr 84, p. 71.
   "At the End of the Hunt." KanQ (16:1/2) Wint-Spr
      84, p. 19.
   "At the Place of the Skull." ArizQ (40:1) Spr 84,
      p. 65-66.
   "Car Pool." KanQ (16:1/2) Wint-Spr 84, p. 19.
   "Fragments." Hudson (37:1) Spr 84, p. 74.
   "Losses." AntigR (57) Spr 84, p. 75.
   "Man and His Hat." Hudson (37:1) Spr 84, p. 73.
   "Margin of Error." MemphisSR (4:2) Spr 84, p. 29.
   "Mine Disaster." Chelsea (42/43) 84, p. 300.
   "October: With Rain" (for my son). Hudson (37:1)
      Spr 84, p. 74.
   "On the Road." MissR (37/38, 13:1/2) Aut 84, p. 77.
   "The River: A Vision" (for my son). Hudson (37:1)
      Spr 84, p. 72.
   "The Room." Hudson (37:1) Spr 84, p. 73.
   "The Shadow." ArizQ (40:3) Aut 84, p. 241.
   "Winter Roses." Hudson (37:1) Spr 84, p. 72.
   "Winter Solstice." Hudson (37:1) Spr 84, p. 71.

1250. DAVISON, Peter
   "Crossing the Void" (for Stanley Kunitz).
      Atlantic (254:1) Jl 84, p. 84.
   "Last Infirmity." Atlantic (254:3) S 84, p. 77.
   "Moving into Memory." Poetry (144:3) Je 84, p.
      142-143.
   "Questions of Swimming, 1935" (For Robert Penn
      Warren). NewEngR (7:1) Aut 84, p. 112-113.
   "Remembering Eurydice." Poetry (144:3) Je 84, p.
      141-142.
   "The Revenant." Poetry (144:3) Je 84, p. 141.
   "The Vanishing Point" (New Year's Day 1984).
      AmerS (53:4) Aut 84, p. 479-480.

1251. DAWBER, Diane
   "Great Grand Story" (Bicentennial Contest Winners:
      Honourable Mention). Waves (12:4) Spr 84, p. 87.

1252. DAWE, Gerald
   "Darkness" (after the Irish of Sean O'Riordain).
      Pequod (16/17) 84, p. 43.
   "Where I Came In" (for Frank Ormsby). Pequod
      (16/17) 84, p. 42.

1253. DAWSON, Hester Jewell
"Brief Encounter." StoneC (12:1/2) Aut-Wint 84,
p. 27.

De . . .: See also names beginning with "De" without the
following space, filed below in their alphabetic
positions, e.g., DeFOE.

De ANDRADE, Eugenio: See ANDRADE, Eugenio de

De ANDRADE, Mario: See ANDRADE, Mario de

De ANDRADE, Oswald: See ANDRADE, Oswald de

De ARAUJO, Virginia: See ARAUJO, Virginia de

De ARELLANO, Diana Ramírez: See RAMIREZ de ARELLANO, Diana

De ARELLANO, Olga Ramírez: See RAMIREZ de ARELLANO, Olga

De AREVALO, Marta: See AREVALO, Marta de

De ASIS FERNANDEZ, Francisco: See FERNANDEZ, Francisco de
Asis

1254. De BACA, Marc
"Elliptical Wheels." SoCaR (16:2) Spr 84, p. 104.

1255. De BEKY, Iván
"By the Time the Day Ends" (tr. of Sándor
Csoóri). Descant (47, 15:4) Wint 84, p. 196.
"Conflagration" (tr. of György Rónay).
Descant (47, 15:4) Wint 84, p. 201.
"Echoes of Great Cavities" (tr. of Sándor
Csoóri). Descant (47, 15:4) Wint 84, p. 197.
"He Who Has Arrived" (tr. of György Rónay).
Descant (47, 15:4) Wint 84, p. 200.
"On the Skeleton of a Primary Reptile" (tr. of
György Rónay). Descant (47, 15:4) Wint 84,
p. 199.
"The Poppy Rattles at Night" (tr. of Sándor
Csoóri). Descant (47, 15:4) Wint 84, p. 195.
"Report" (tr. of György Rónay). Descant (47,
15:4) Wint 84, p. 198.

De BIEDMA, Jaime Gil: See GIL de BIEDMA, Jaime

De CHAZAL, Malcolm: See CHAZAL, Malcolm de

De CRIADO, Yolanda Gracia: See GRACIA de CRIADO, Yolanda

De CUENCA, Luis Alberto: See CUENCA, Luis Alberto de

De HOYOS, Ramón Ruiz: See RUIZ de HOYOS, Ramón

De JESUS, Teresa: See JESUS, Teresa de

De JOLLY, Paulo: See JOLLY, Paulo de

De la CRUZ, Juana Inés, Sor: See CRUZ, Juana Inés de la, Sor

De la CUESTA, Francisco Ruiz: See RUIZ de la CUESTA,
    Francisco

De la PUEBLA, Manuel: See PUEBLA, Manuel de la

De LEON, Cesar: See LEON, Cesar de

De LEON, Daisy Mora: See MORA de LEON, Daisy

De LEON, José Castro: See CASTRO de LEON, José

1256. De LEON, Kathie
    "Summer." NegC (4:3) Sum 84, p. 91.

De LERGIER, Clara: See LERGIER, Clara de

1257. De LONGCHAMPS, Joanne
    "Letters to Dare." Peb (23) 84, p. 21-25.

1258. De MARIS, Ron
    "Something Domestic." LitR (28:1) Aut 84, p. 114.
    "Summer Houses, Warwick." KanQ (16:1/2) Wint-Spr
        84, p. 33.

De MEDINA, Gladys Carmagnola: See CARMAGNOLA de MEDINA,
    Gladys

De NAPOUT, Lillian Stratta: See STRATTA de NAPOUT, Lillian

De OSBORNE, Elba Díaz: See DIAZ de OSBORNE, Elba

De SENA, Jorge: See SENA, Jorge de

De TORRES, Juan Ruiz: See RUIS de TORRES, Juan

De TORRES, Rosario Esther Ríos: See RIOS de TORRES, Rosario
    Esther

De VILLEGAS, Nestor Díaz: See DIAZ de VILLEGAS, Nestor

De VILLENA, Luis Antonio: See VILLENA, Luis Antonio de

1259. De Vito, E. B.
    "Life-Sized Memory." Comm (111:14) 10 Ag 84, p. 443.

1260. De VRIES, Carrow
    "I'm sick and tired." WindO (44) Sum-Aut 84, p. 14.
    "Oliver, hunchback." WindO (44) Sum-Aut 84, p. 14.
    "Smallness of the town." WindO (44) Sum-Aut 84,
        p. 14.

1261. De VRIES, Daniel
    "Lyrical Sonnet." PoeticJ (3) 83, p. 33.

1262. De VRIES, N.
    "The Expatriate's Lament." Bogg (52) 84, p. 26.

1263. DEAGON, Ann
    "La Giudecca." MemphisSR (5:1) Aut 84, p. 5.
    "The Tiring-Room." SouthernPR (24:1) Spr 84, p.
        18-20.

1264. DEAHL, James
"The Great Falls." PoetryCR (6:2) Wint 84-85, p. 26.

1265. DEAN, Robert
"Sonnet to the SST." NewL (50:4) Sum 84, p. 85.

1266. DEANE, Seamus
"Russian History Lesson" (Derry City, N. Ireland,
1981). Pequod (16/17) 84, p. 40-41.

1267. DEANS, G. N.
"Exhibition (As Seen Through Cold Eyes)." Bogg
(52) 84, p. 42.

1268. DEAVEL, Christine
"On Top of a Small Porch." Iowa (14:3) Aut 84, p. 6.

1269. DEBRAVO, Jorge
"Death Is Naked" (tr. by Michael L. Johnson).
BlueBldgs (8) 84?, p. 24.
"Un Himno Para el Ojo." Mund (14:2) 84, p. 60.
"Hymn for the Eye" (tr. by Michael Johnson). Mund
(14:2) 84, p. 61.
"Psalm to the Animal Earth of Your Abdomen" (tr. by
Michael Johnson). Mund (14:2) 84, p. 61, 63.
"Salmo a la Tierra Animal de tu vientre." Mund
(14:2) 84, p. 60, 62.
"There Are Moments" (tr. by Michael L. Johnson).
BlueBldgs (8) 84?, p. 24.
"Widows of Darkness" (tr. by Michael L. Johnson).
BlueBldgs (8) 84?, p. 24.

1270. DECEMBER, John
"Journal of the Magi." MidAR (4:2) Aut 84, p. 143.
"The Woman on the Plains." MidAR (4:2) Aut 84, p.
142.

1271. DECKER, Michael
"Trees Are Like Waterfalls" (for D.). Shen (35:1)
83-84, p. 64-65.

1272. DECLUE, Charlotte
"Morning Song." Calyx (8:2) Spr 84, p. 80.

1273. DeCONNA, Thomas
"Visit." PoeticJ (7) 84, p. 16.

1274. DeCORMIER-SHEKERJIAN, Regina
"Avilov Writes to Chekhov" (Pablo Neruda Prize for
Poetry: First Prize). Nimrod (28:1) Aut-Wint
84, p. 29-33.
"Coming into the Nearness." BlueBldgs (7) 84, p. 48.
"It Is Then We Will Know." ThirdW (2) Spr 84, p.
42-43.
"Myths." ThirdW (2) Spr 84, p. 41-42.
"Wild Ducks on the River" (The Yellow Room,
Chagall, 1911, for B.W.). BlueBldgs (7) 84, p.
46.

1275. DeFOE, Mark
"The Field." KenR (NS 6:1) Wint 84, p. 23-24.

"Improvisation on the Word 'Shod'." MalR (67) F
84, p. 94.
"Martial Arts." Tendril (17) Wint 84, p. 46-47.

1276. DeFREES, Madeline
"Atlas of Oregon." NowestR (22:1/2) 84, p. 146.
"The Convent at Mystras." GrahamHR (7) Wint 84,
p. 11-12.
"Gallery of the Sarcophagi: Heraklion Museum."
GrahamHR (7) Wint 84, p. 14-15.
"Hagios Panaghiotes: The Church in Tolon."
GrahamHR (7) Wint 84, p. 10.
"Knitting the Sleeve of Care." CutB (22) Spr-Sum
84, p. 5.
"Shadegrown Tobacco: A Presentiment" (for Richard
Hugo). GrahamHR (7) Wint 84, p. 7-9.
"The Widows of Mykonos." GrahamHR (7) Wint 84, p.
13.

1277. DeGENNARO, Lorraine S.
"Winter Son." PoeticJ (4) 83, p. 2.

1278. DeLAURENTIS, Louise Budde
"From a Beginning in Crete." KanQ (16:1/2) Wint-
Spr 84, p. 77.

1279. DELIGIORGIS, Stavros
"Metamorphoses" (Selections: XXI, XXIV, tr. of
Argyris Hionis). Iowa (14:2) Spr-Sum 84, p.
233-234.

1280. DEMING, Alison
"The Stone Breakers" (after Courbet). BlackWR
(11:1) Aut 84, p. 47-48.

1281. DEMING, Alison H.
"Bells" (for my father). Tendril (17) Wint 84, p.
45.

1282. DEMPSTER, Barry
"Answers." Dandel (11:2) Aut-Wint 84-85, p. 58-59.
"Blue Fly." Dandel (11:2) Aut-Wint 84-85, p. 60-61.
"Dreams of Desertion." CanLit (100) Spr 84, p. 90-
91.
"Picasso's Eyes." PoetryCR (6:1) Aut 84, p. 16.
"The Saint." Quarry (33:3) Sum 84, p. 48-50.

1283. DENBERG, Ken
"1923, Albert Einstein Invents Birds." Shen
(35:1) 83-84, p. 61.
"Dear Smillie" (#13). GreenfR (11:3/4) Wint-Spr
84, p. 128.
"Labor." GreenfR (11:1/2) Sum-Aut 83, p. 144-145.

1284. DENIS, Phillipe
"In the Thickness" (tr. by Susanna Lang). Iowa
(14:2) Spr-Sum 84, p. 177-179.

1285. DENNEY, Reuel
"The Portfolio of Benjamin Latrobe: A Celebration."
QRL (Poetry series 6, v. 25) 84, p. 1-56.

1286. DENNIS, Carl
        "The Concert." AmerPoR (13:4) Jl-Ag 84, p. 20.
        "The Dream of Fair Women." Poetry (143:4) Ja 84,
            p. 200.
        "Fear of the Dark." Poetry (143:4) Ja 84, p. 199.
        "Hector's Return." NewRep (189:24) 12 D 83, p. 30.
        "The List." GeoR (38:3) Aut 84, p. 507-508.
        "Mary and Martha." AmerPoR (13:4) Jl-Ag 84, p. 20.
        "More Music." NewYorker (60:30) 10 S 84, p. 48.
        "New Tribes." AmerPoR (13:4) Jl-Ag 84, p. 21.
        "On the Soul." NewYorker (60:23) 23 Jl 84, p. 38.
        "On the Way to School." Poetry (143:4) Ja 84, p.
            197-198.

1287. DENNIS, Michael
        "Daedalus." AntigR (58) Sum 84, p. 133.
        "Fade to Blue." Descant (47, 15:4) Wint 84, p.
            149-150.
        "I Remember the Morning My Grandfather Died."
            AntigR (58) Sum 84, p. 134.
        "Splintered Door and a Frightened Cat." Dandel
            (11:1) Spr-Sum 84, p. 73.
        "You and Your Dog Toto Too." Dandel (11:1) Spr-
            Sum 84, p. 74-75.

1288. DeNORD, Chard
        "Watching on the Railroad." BlackWR (10:2) Spr
            84, p. 46.

1289. DeNOYELLES, Bill
        "I sat with so much space around me." Tele (19)
            83, p. 121.
        "I walk through the barroom." Tele (19) 83, p. 122.
        "Smog levels and denim." Tele (19) 83, p. 121.

1290. DENSMORE, Donald
        "Speaking of Rivers." Stepping Wint 84, p. 25.

1291. DePOY, Phillip
        "The Alphabet of Luciferin." SouthernPR (24:2)
            Aut 84, p. 68.

1292. DEPPE, Theodore
        "Trillium." YetASM (3) 84, p. 6.
        "Vigil, with Sunflowers and Lace." BelPoJ (34:4)
            Sum 84, p. 8-12.

1293. Der HOVANESSIAN, Diana
        "At the End" (tr. of Maria Banus). Kayak (64) My
            84, p. 21.
        "Clever Lamb" (tr. of Gevorg Emin). Mund (14:2)
            84, p. 12.
        "Daimon" (tr. of Maria Banus). Kayak (64) My 84,
            p. 19.
        "Drowning." LitR (28:1) Aut 84, p. 105-106.
        "Forgetting." LitR (28:1) Aut 84, p. 106-107.
        "Patio" (tr. of Maria Banus). Kayak (64) My 84,
            p. 19.
        "Prejudice" (tr. of Maria Banus). Kayak (64) My
            84, p. 20.

"Separation" (tr. of Maria Banus). Kayak (64) My
    84, p. 20.
"Stripped" (tr. of Maria Banus). Kayak (64) My
    84, p. 21.
"Time" (tr. of Maria Banus). Kayak (64) My 84, p.
    21.
"Translating." Agni (20) 84, p. 101-102.
"Why Has This Ache" (tr. of Gevorg Emin). Mund
    (14:2) 84, p. 12.

DerMOLEN, Robert van: See VanderMOLEN, Robert

1294. DERR, Mark
    "Meteor." KanQ (16:1/2) Wint-Spr 84, p. 123.

1295. DERRICOTTE, Toi
    "The Distrust of Logic." NowestR (22:1/2) 84, p. 34.
    "Justice." Cond (3:4, issue 10) 84, p. 12.
    "Morning Coffee: 1945." Cond (3:4, issue 10) 84,
        p. 11.

1296. DERRY, Alice
    "Alice Ropes Kellogg: 1883-1963." PraS (58:2) Sum
        84, p. 65-66.
    "The House" (For Bruce). Poetry (144:2) My 84, p.
        68-70.
    "Learning the Stars." BlueBldgs (8) 84?, p. 33.

1297. DeRUGERIS, C. K.
    "Understudy." Abraxas (31/32) 84, p. 36.

1298. DESNOS, Robert
    "At World's End" (tr. by X. J. Kennedy). Chelsea
        (42/43) 84, p. 116.
    "Comrades" (tr. by William Kulik). AmerPoR (13:5)
        S-O 84, p. 48.

1299. DESY, Peter
    "Boy." SmPd (21:1) Wint 84, p. 24.
    "Depression." SanFPJ (6:1) 84, p. 64.
    "The Girl." Confr (27/28) 84, p. 193.
    "Nude in Candlelight." WebR (9:2) Wint 85, p. 100.
    "Parents." MidAR (4:1) Spr 84, p. 116.
    "Parents." Sam (37:3, 147th release) 83, p. 48.
    "Parents." Waves (12:4) Spr 84, p. 51.
    "Teaching Fellow." EngJ (73:3) Mr 84, p. 70.

1300. DEUTSCH, Laynie Tzena
    "Meeting Frankie at the Moose Lodge." MichQR
        (23:4) Aut 84, p. 559-560.
    "Street." MichQR (23:4) Aut 84, p. 560.

1301. DEUTSCH, R. H.
    "The Conjugation of the Islands." Antaeus (53)
        Aut 84, p. 258.

1302. D'EVELYN, Tom
    "Motel 6." Thrpny (19) Aut 84, p. 12.

1303. DEVLIN, Colleen
       "The Toast." <u>Poetry</u> (143:4) Ja 84, p. 213.

1304. DeVOE, Bill
       "Cassandra's Crying." <u>PoeticJ</u> (7) 84, p. 30.

1305. DEWDNEY, Christopher
       "Points in Time." <u>Sulfur</u> (3:3, issue 9) 84, p. 118.
       "This My Emissary." <u>Sulfur</u> (3:3, issue 9) 84, p.
       119.

1306. DEWEY, Arthur J.
       "Birth of the Baptist." <u>ChrC</u> (101:17) 16 My 84,
       p. 508.

1307. DHARWADKER, Aparna
       "The Half-Hour Argument" (tr. of Shrikant Varma, w.
       Vinay Dharwadker). <u>NewEngR</u> (7:2) Wint 84, p.
       265-268.

1308. DHARWADKER, Vinay
       "At a Quarter to Eight in the Morning" (tr. of
       Mangesh Padgaonkar). <u>MinnR</u> (N.S. 22) Spr 84,
       p. 60.
       "The Half-Hour Argument" (tr. of Shrikant Varma, w.
       Aparna Dharwadker). <u>NewEngR</u> (7:2) Wint 84, p.
       265-268.
       "Salaam" (tr. of Mangesh Padgaonkar). <u>NewEngR</u>
       (6:4) Sum 84, p. 511-514.
       "You" (tr. of Mangesh Padgaonkar). <u>NewEngR</u> (6:4)
       Sum 84, p. 515-516.

Di . . .: <u>See</u> <u>also</u> names beginning with "Di" without the
       following space, filed below in their alphabetic
       positions, e.g., DiPALMA

1309. Di CICCO, Pier Giorgio
       "Language: Post-Feminist." <u>Descant</u> (47, 15:4)
       Wint 84, p. 67-68.
       "Penetration Poem." <u>Descant</u> (47, 15:4) Wint 84,
       p. 64-66.
       "Send Me a Postcard." <u>CanLit</u> (100) Spr 84, p. 92.

1310. Di GIOVANNI, Norman Thomas
       "Instinct" (tr. of Cesare Pavese). <u>Chelsea</u>
       (42/43) 84, p. 123.

1311. Di MICHELE, Mary
       "The Gift of Ourselves." <u>Dandel</u> (11:2) Aut-Wint
       84-85, p. 16.
       "Green Violence." <u>CanLit</u> (101) Sum 84, p. 41-42.
       "Moon Sharks." <u>CanLit</u> (100) Spr 84, p. 93-94.
       "Natural Beauty" (for Roo Borson). <u>Descant</u> (47,
       15:4) Wint 84, p. 74-79.
       "Regrets from the Future Left Behind." <u>Dandel</u>
       (11:2) Aut-Wint 84-85, p. 11-13.
       "Rome Wasted in the Rain." <u>Dandel</u> (11:2) Aut-Wint
       84-85, p. 14-15.

1312. Di PIERO, W. S.
      "The Butterfly." SewanR (92:2) Ap-Je 84, p. 194-195.
      "December 24." AmerS (53:1) Wint 83/84, p. 108.
      "The Iceman." TriQ (60) Spr-Sum 84, p. 378-379.
      "The Incineration." Telescope (3:1) Wint 84, p. 113.
      "Lake Michigan." TriQ (60) Spr-Sum 84, p. 375-376.
      "Likeness." Pequod (16/17) 84, p. 205.
      "Lines for My Daughter." SewanR (92:2) Ap-Je 84,
         p. 196.
      "The Murphy Bed." SewanR (92:4) O-D 84, p. 532-533.
      "Woman Ironing." NewYorker (60:39) 12 N 84, p. 176.

1313. DIAZ, Carlos A.
      "Adivinanza al Final." Mairena (5:14) Aut 83, p. 26.
      "El Dia de la Ira." Mairena (5:14) Aut 83, p. 25-26.
      "Elegias para el Hombre" (Selections). Mairena
         (5:14) Aut 83, p. 25-26.

1314. DIAZ, Jesús
      "Son de Enero." Areíto (9:36) 84, p. 103.

1315. DIAZ de OSBORNE, Elba
      "A Juan Carlos." Mairena (6:16) Spr 84, p. 37-38.
      "Cuenta Corriente." Mairena (6:16) Spr 84, p. 35.
      "Dos Mundos." Mairena (6:16) Spr 84, p. 36-37.
      "Genesis." Mairena (6:16) Spr 84, p. 36.
      "Lepidosirem." Mairena (6:16) Spr 84, p. 37.
      "Profecia." Mairena (6:16) Spr 84, p. 35.
      "Sesiles." Mairena (5:13) Spr 83, p. 76.

1316. DIAZ de VILLEGAS, Nestor
      "Babilonia está cerca." LindLM (3:2/4) Ap-D 84,
         p. 28.
      "En los espejos borrosos ha llovido." LindLM
         (3:2/4) Ap-D 84, p. 28.
      "Orden." LindLM (3:2/4) Ap-D 84, p. 28.
      "Versailles." LindLM (3:2/4) Ap-D 84, p. 28.

1317. DIAZ-DIOCARETZ, Delia
      "Por confundir latitudes." Mairena (6:18) 84, p.
         139.

1318. DIAZ-DIOCARETZ, Myriam
      "Los Mitos del Hombre." Mairena (6:17) Aut 84, p.
         23-24.
      "Mujer de la Tierra." Mairena (6:17) Aut 84, p. 24.

DIAZ OSBORNE, Elba: See DIAZ de OSBORNE, Elba

1319. DIBBEN, Dennis
      "Some Modern Good Turns" (poem found in the 1936
         Boy Scout Manual). NewL (50:2/3) Wint-Spr 84,
         p. 185.
1320. DICKEY, James
      "Drinking from a Helmet." Peb (23) 84, p. 47-53.
      "Immortals" (homage, Vicente Aleixandre, and
         acknowledging translations by Willis Barnstone
         and David Garrison). MemphisSR (5:1) Aut 84,
         p. 28-29.
      "Paestum." Shen (35:2/3) 84, p. 119-122.

1321. DICKEY, Martha
       "Studies from Life." NewL (50:2/3) Wint-Spr 84,
          p. 35.

1322. DICKEY, William
       "Chickens in San Francisco." NewL (50:2/3) Wint-
          Spr 84, p. 88.
       "Coyote's Song." GeoR (38:1) Spr 84, p. 22-23.
       "Decision." CarolQ (36:3) Spr 84, p. 65.
       "Easter Week." NewEngR (6:4) Sum 84, p. 622-624.
       "The Italian Opera." NewEngR (6:4) Sum 84, p. 621.
       "Novgorod." Poetry (143:5) F 84, p. 283-284.
       "Rather Than Musick." Poetry (143:5) F 84, p. 282-
          283.
       "You Cunning White Devils!" NewEngR (6:4) Sum 84,
          p. 625.

1323. DICKSON, John
       "The Aragon Ballroom." TriQ (60) Spr-Sum 84, p.
          295-297.
       "Auld Acquaintance." SpoonRQ (9:4) Aut 84, p. 26-27.
       "Criticism of the Poem." SpoonRQ (9:4) Aut 84, p.
          22-23.
       "Damocles." Poetry (143:6) Mr 84, p. 344.
       "Erasing the Taste of Love Turned Sour by Unliving
          It Back to a Point Preceding Its Inception."
          SpoonRQ (9:4) Aut 84, p. 28.
       "Fugue." Poetry (143:6) Mr 84, p. 345-346.
       "The Legend." SpoonRQ (9:2) Spr 84, p. 11.
       "The Party." SpoonRQ (9:4) Aut 84, p. 24-25.
       "Serenade." SpoonRQ (9:2) Spr 84, p. 12-13.
       "Success." SpoonRQ (9:2) Spr 84, p. 14-15.
       "Wheat." TriQ (60) Spr-Sum 84, p. 293-294.

1324. DIEFENDORF, David
       "Appearances." Pequod (16/17) 84, p. 27-30.

1325. DIFALCO, Salvatore
       "Virtue." Poem (52) N 84, p. 60.
       "You and Me." Poem (52) N 84, p. 61.

1326. DIGBY, John
       "Safe from the Bitter Taste of Exile." Confr
          (27/28) 84, p. 131.

1327. DIGGES, Deborah
       "Darwin's Finches." Field (31) Aut 84, p. 84-85.
       "Gulls Inland." AmerPoR (13:5) S-O 84, p. 5.
       "Laws of Falling Bodies." AmerPoR (13:5) S-O 84,
          p. 5.
       "Letter West." AntR (42:3) Sum 84, p. 326-327.
       "Vesper Sparrows." Antaeus (53) Aut 84, p. 253-254.

1328. DILLON, Andrew
       "Yes, Louis Simpson." ArizQ (40:4) Wint 84, p. 292.

1329. DILLON, Enoch
       "And You Too, Merry Andropov." SanFPJ (6:2) 84,
          p. 28.

1330. DILSAVER, Paul
    "Armageddon." Paunch (57/58) Ja 84, p. 123.
    "At Your Father's Funeral." Paunch (57/58) Ja 84,
        p. 121.
    "The Bethlehem Birth." Paunch (57/58) Ja 84, p. 122.
    "Encounters with the Antichrist" (prose poems
        translated from the void). Paunch (57/58) Ja
        84, p. 110-123.
    "Hereditary Divinity." Paunch (57/58) Ja 84, p. 112.
    "In the Valley of the Shadow." Paunch (57/58) Ja
        84, p. 113.
    "The Inferiority of God." Paunch (57/58) Ja 84,
        p. 117.
    "Our Father." Paunch (57/58) Ja 84, p. 114.
    "The Rise and Fall." Paunch (57/58) Ja 84, p. 118.
    "Seeking the Backdoor to Heaven." Paunch (57/58)
        Ja 84, p. 119.
    "South of the Border." Paunch (57/58) Ja 84, p. 120.
    "Speaking in Tongues." Paunch (57/58) Ja 84, p. 116.
    "Summum Bonum." Paunch (57/58) Ja 84, p. 115.

1331. DING, Zuxin
    "In Spring: Looking into the Distance, on the Wall"
        (tr. of Du Fu, w. Burton Raffel). LitR (27:3)
        Spr 84, p. 296.
    "Moonlit Night" (tr. of Du Fu, w. Burton Raffel).
        LitR (27:3) Spr 84, p. 297.
    "Spring Rain" (tr. of Du Fu, w. Burton Raffel).
        LitR (27:3) Spr 84, p. 297.
    "Tien-mu Mountain, Ascended in a Dream: a Farewell
        Song" (tr. of Li Bai, w. Burton Raffel). LitR
        (27:3) Spr 84, p. 295-296.

DIOCARETZ, Myriam Diaz: See DIAZ-DIOCARETZ, Myriam

1332. DIOMEDE, Matthew
    "Morning Conversation." CentR (28:1) Wint 84, p. 47.

1333. DION, Marc
    "For the Girl Most Likely to Exceed." KanQ (16:3)
        Sum 84, p. 52.

1334. DION-LEVESQUE, Rosaire
    "Taedium Vitae" (tr. by Dorothy Aspinwall). WebR
        (9:1) Spr 84, p. 16.

1335. DIORIO, Margaret T.
    "Lost Cat, Black and White." WindO (44) Sum-Aut
        84, p. 29.

1336. DIORIO, Margaret Toarello
    "End of Summer." ChrC (101:27) 12-19 S 84, p. 830.
    "Friend's Departure." KanQ (16:1/2) Wint-Spr 84,
        p. 113.

1337. DISCH, Tom
    "Entropic Villanelle." Poetry (144:4) Jl 84, p. 205.
    "The Flower Painter" (for June Hildebrand). ChiR
        (34:3) Sum 84, p. 44.
    "Orientating Mr. Blank." ParisR (26:91) Spr 84,

p. 118-119.
"The Prospect behind Us" (for John Berger).
  Chelsea (42/43) 84, p. 422-423.
"Rocks on a Winter Evening." Veloc (4) Sum 84, p.
  10.
"The Thought That Counts." GrandS (3:4) Sum 84,
  p. 140-141.
"To Life." Veloc (3) Aut-Wint 83, p. 5.
"Working on a Tan." Poetry (144:4) Jl 84, p. 205-
  208.

1338. DISCHELL, Stuart
  "The Liquid Face." Agni (20) 84, p. 15.
  "The Original Face." Agni (20) 84, p. 14.
  "The Vagrant Face." Agni (20) 84, p. 13.

1339. DISKIN, Lahna
  "In the Greenhouse." ThirdW (2) Spr 84, p. 35.
  "Onions." ThirdW (2) Spr 84, p. 34.

1340. DISTELHEIM, Rochelle
  "Meeting My Lover." Confr (27/28) 84, p. 240.

1341. DITSKY, John
  "Acapulco." MalR (68) Je 84, p. 89.
  "The Bride Wore Grey" (for Nadeline, on hearing
    that the Javanese were required to pay for
    marriages and divorces with the bodies of rats).
    PraF (5:4) Sum 84, p. 60.
  "Charm." MalR (68) Je 84, p. 90.
  "Compulsion." AntigR (57) Spr 84, p. 134.
  "Disco Bowl." PraF (5:4) Sum 84, p. 59.
  "Erie." AntigR (57) Spr 84, p. 134.
  "The Greek Anthology." NoDaQ (52:3) Sum 84, p. 154.
  "The Hour of the Wolf." NoDaQ (52:3) Sum 84, p. 154.
  "The Lake" (In Memory of Yasunari Kawabata).
    PoetryCR (6:2) Wint 84-85, p. 5.
  "Massacres." Poem (50) Mr 84, p. 17.
  "October Light." Poem (50) Mr 84, p. 19.
  "Ophelia." NoDaQ (52:3) Sum 84, p. 153.
  "Prayer." NewL (50:4) Sum 84, p. 86.
  "Scalpels." Poem (50) Mr 84, p. 20.
  "Survivals." MalR (68) Je 84, p. 90.
  "There, There." Poem (50) Mr 84, p. 18.

1342. DITTA, Joseph M.
  "75 Forebell St., Brooklyn, N.Y." KanQ (16:4) Aut
    84, p. 26.
  "In a Time of Vanishing Graces." KanQ (16:4) Aut
    84, p. 27.

1343. DiVENTI, T. (Tom)
  "Lazy Log Rhythms." Open24 (3) 84, p. 8-9.
  "Paper Chase." Open24 (3) 84, p. 7.

1344. DIXON, Melvin
  "Angels of Ascent." Obs (8:1) Spr 82, p. 203.
  "Silent Reaper" (for Charles H. Rowell). BlackALF
    (18:1) Spr 84, p. 10.

175   DOERR

1345. DJAGAROV, Georgi
    "Bulgaria" (tr. by Spass Nikolov). ConcPo (17:2)
    Aut 84, p. 100-101.

1346. DJANIKIAN, Gregory
    "The Boy in the Mirror." ThRiPo (23/24) 84, p. 38-
    39.
    "You Can't Tell One Assassin from Another" (a
    random comment). ThRiPo (23/24) 84, p. 40.

1347. DOBAL, Carlos
    "The Crime" (tr. by William T. Lawlor). NegC
    (4:4) Aut 84, p. 62.
    "El Crimen." NegC (4:4) Aut 84, p. 63-64.

1348. DOBLER, Patricia
    "Brother Plans to Move, 1983." Kayak (64) My 84,
    p. 30.
    "False Teech, 1947." Kayak (64) My 84, p. 29.
    "How to Winter Out." CapeR (19:3) 20th Anniverary
    Issue 84, p. 11.
    "I Get Jealous of an Old Home Movie." Kayak (64)
    My 84, p. 31.
    "Paper Dolls." OhioR (32) 84, p. 26.
    "Spell for a Jilted Friend." Kayak (64) My 84, p.
    31.
    "Steelmark Day Parade, 1961." Kayak (64) My 84,
    p. 30.
    "Uncles' Advice, 1957." Kayak (64) My 84, p. 29.

1349. DOBLES, Julieta
    "Shadow?" (tr. by Frederick H. Fornoff). Vis (15)
    84, p. 13-14.

1350. DOBYNS, Stephen
    "All That Lies Buried." Antaeus (53) Aut 84, p.
    244-245.
    "Bleeder." Kayak (64) My 84, p. 34-35.

DOC, Keith Lewis: See LEWIS-DOC, Keith

1351. DODD, Wayne
    "Before Divorce." GeoR (38:2) Sum 84, p. 376-377.
    "Of His Life." Peb (23) 84, p. 64.

1352. DODSON, Margaret
    "Child of the People's Republic." PoetL (79:2)
    Sum 84, p. 78-80.
    "Mother Myself." PoetL (79:2) Sum 84, p. 81-83.
    "Night Watch." PoetL (79:2) Sum 84, p. 85.

1353. DODSON, Owen
    "For Billie Holiday: Finally, Lady, You Were Done
    from Us." BlackALF (18:1) Spr 84, p. 5.
    "King Lear and the Fool" (For Frank Silvera).
    BlackALF (18:1) Spr 84, p. 5.
    "The Star." BlackALF (18:1) Spr 84, p. 5.

1354. DOERR, Ken
    "Backbend, Handspring, Full Twist" (For Tom Lyons).

KanQ (16:1/2) Wint-Spr 84, p. 141.

1355. DOLA, Ken
"Poem Dressed in Courting Clothes." PoetryE (15)
Aut 84, p. 19.

1356. DOLCINI, Jerry
"Grange." CutB (22) Spr-Sum 84, p. 9.

1357. DOMENECH, Sylvia
"Este Tiempo Que Me Lleva." Mairena (5:14) Aut
83, p. 93.
"Tarde Perseguida." Mairena (6:17) Aut 84, p. 97.

1358. DOMINGUEZ, Delia
"Conciencia." Mairena (6:17) Aut 84, p. 18.
"Maitines." Mairena (6:17) Aut 84, p. 18.
"Tango." Mairena (6:17) Aut 84, p. 17.

1359. DOMINGUEZ, Ramiro
"Salmos a Deshora: XIII." Mairena (6:18) 84, p.
188-189.

1360. DONAGHY, Michael
"Cloves and cedar smoke in the air" (29 englynion:
II, tr. of Sion ap Brydydd). SenR (14:2) 84,
p. 40.
"Dull the journey. Feeble and muttering the old
men" (29 englynion: XXVIII, tr. of Sion ap
Brydydd). SenR (14:2) 84, p. 41.
"Dull the journey. Long the road reeled in toward
the lantern" (29 englynion: XXVII, tr. of Sion
ap Brydydd). SenR (14:2) 84, p. 41.
"The moment you touch the whorl of my ear" (29
englynion: IV, tr. of Sion ap Brydydd). SenR
(14:2) 84, p. 41.
"Morfydd, daughter of Gwyn" (29 englynion: I, tr.
of Sion ap Brydydd). SenR (14:2) 84, p. 40.
"The Natural and Social Sciences." MassR (25:2)
Sum 84, p. 322.
"Say this rhyme, reader, aloud to yourself" (29
englynion: XXIX, tr. of Sion ap Brydydd). SenR
(14:2) 84, p. 41.
"Smooth the skin on a bowl of milk" (29 englynion:
III, tr. of Sion ap Brydydd). SenR (14:2) 84,
p. 40.

1361. DONAHUE, Neal R.
"Egyptian Chorus." Amelia [1:1] Ap 84, p. 20-22.
"Frontiers." SanFPJ (6:4) 84, p. 89-90.
"Silence." SanFPJ (6:4) 84, p. 92.

1362. DONALDSON, Jeffery
"Toward Penelope." Shen (35:1) 83-84, p. 65-66.
"With Heidegger in a Clearing." GrandS (4:1) Aut
84, p. 64-66.

1363. DONALSON, Mel
"Letter to Frank Wills" (9/82). BlackALF (18:1)
Spr 84, p. 9.

"On the Line" (with eleven million unemployed:
    9/3/82). BlackALF (18:1) Spr 84, p. 9.
"Words of the King" (for Martin Luther King, Jr.).
    BlackALF (18:1) Spr 84, p. 9.

1364. DONLAN, John
    "Something My Father Left Me." Quarry (33:4) Aut
        84, p. 55.

1365. DONNA, Bella
    ". . . New York: They interrogate you about your
        'other' self" (First part of title missing).
        PoeticJ (4) 83, p. 30-31.
    "Hail to the Cockroach!" SanFPJ (7:1) 84, p. 23.
    "Orwell Was an Optimist." SanFPJ (7:1) 84, p. 21-22.

1366. DONNELL, David
    "Abattoir." PoetryCR (6:2) Wint 84-85, p. 15.
    "Cities." PoetryCR (6:2) Wint 84-85, p. 14.
    "Clarities." PoetryCR (6:2) Wint 84-85, p. 14.
    "Graves." PoetryCR (6:2) Wint 84-85, p. 14.
    "How the Medieval Serfs Flew." PoetryCR (6:1) Aut
        84, p. 15.
    "Night Walks." PoetryCR (6:2) Wint 84-85, p. 15.

1367. DONNELLY, Dorothy
    "Metaphor's Lamp." ChrC (101:36) 21 N 84, p. 1093.

1368. DONNELLY, Paul
    "Don't Look Now." Open24 (3) 84, p. 22.
    "Monologue." Open24 (3) 84, p. 22.

1369. DONNELLY, Susan
    "The House of My Birth." Ploughs (10:1) 84, p. 43-
        44.
    "Little Cloud." Ploughs (10:1) 84, p. 47-49.
    "Painting of a Woman with Vines." Ploughs (10:1)
        84, p. 42.
    "That Time, That Country." Ploughs (10:1) 84, p.
        45-46.

1370. DONOVAN, Diane C.
    "Jack-O-Lantern." Amelia (1:2) O 84, p. 47.

1371. DONOVAN, Laurence
    "Sprinkling." KanQ (16:1/2) Wint-Spr 84, p. 114.

1372. DONOVAN, Rhoda
    "Marion, in Winter." Blueline (5:2) Wint-Spr 84,
        p. 18.

1373. DONOVAN, Stewart
    "Awake." AntigR (59) Aut 84, p. 84.
    "Ingonish Inshore" (for Margaret Hawley). AntigR
        (59) Aut 84, p. 82.
    "On Discovering Canada's First Observatory" (for
        Ken Donovan). AntigR (59) Aut 84, p. 83.

1374. DONOVAN, Susan
    "The Landlocked Bride." MassR (25:3) Aut 84, p.

437-438.
"Leonardo's Dream." GeoR (38:3) Aut 84, p. 464.

1375. DOOLEY, Maura
"Even That Routine." Argo (6:1) 84, p. 24.
"Hyacinth." Argo (6:1) 84, p. 23.

DOOLITTLE, Hilda: See H. D.

1376. DOR, Moshe
"Writing in a Notebook" (tr. by Keith Bosley).
Pequod (16/17) 84, p. 116.

1377. DORBIN, Sanford
"Joplin's Joplin." Stepping Wint 84, p. 17.

1378. DORESKI, William
"Green Volvos." BlueBldgs (7) 84, p. 27.
"Poem for Sarah Orne Jewett." PoetryNW (25:4)
Wint 84-85, p. 41-42.

1379. DORIS, Stacy
"Sleeping Beauty." TriQ (61) Aut 84, p. 99.

1380. DORMAN, Sonya
"Blessing the Feet." LittleM (14:3) 84, p. 27.
"Blessing the Hands." LittleM (14:3) 84, p. 27.
"Essay on Elements." Veloc (4) Sum 84, p. 11.
"Island Sunday." BelPoJ (35:2) Wint 84-85, p. 1.
"The Sisters." GrandS (3:4) Sum 84, p. 152-156.
"Study Project for a Natural Scientist." Veloc
(4) Sum 84, p. 12.
"What Is Mine." PoetryNW (25:2) Sum 84, p. 40.

1381. DORMISH, P. J.
"Christmas Eve, Bell Road: A Remembrance." Poem
(51) Mr [i.e. Jl] 84, p. 39.
"Elegy for a Season." Poem (51) Mr [i.e. Jl] 84,
p. 37.
"Indian Summer." Poem (51) Mr [i.e. Jl] 84, p. 38.

1382. DORN, Edward
"Los Mineros." Chelsea (42/43) 84, p. 73-75.

1383. DORSET, Gerald
"Fighting the Odds." Bogg (52) 84, p. 8.
"Traveling through the Land." LittleBR (4:4) Sum
84, p. 40.

1384. DORSETT, Robert
"Blue, As an Abstraction of Carmel." WebR (9:1)
Spr 84, p. 58.
"The Twelve Months of Birds and Flowers of Soken"
(Twelve panels, based on poems by Teika). WebR
(9:1) Spr 84, p. 59.

1385. DORSETT, Thomas
"The few pounds I have on." GreenfR (12:1/2) Sum-
Aut 84, p. 157.
"Four Poems from India." GreenfR (12:1/2) Sum-Aut

84, p. 157-158.
"Most worldmen murder for gold." GreenfR (12:1/2)
    Sum-Aut 84, p. 157-158.
"An old woman dying of cancer." GreenfR (12:1/2)
    Sum-Aut 84, p. 158.
"Praising God without a gong." GreenfR (12:1/2)
    Sum-Aut 84, p. 157.

1386. DOTY, Mark
"Gardenias." Iowa (14:3) Aut 84, p. 103-104.
"Letter from the State Fair." IndR (7:1) Wint 84,
    p. 30-31.
"Paragon Park." MissR (36, 12:3) Spr 84, p. 82-84.
"Replica of the Parthenon." Ploughs (10:4) 84, p.
    118-120.
"Sister." IndR (7:1) Wint 84, p. 24-25.
"Snow." IndR (7:1) Wint 84, p. 26.
"Talking in Your Sleep." IndR (7:1) Wint 84, p.
    27-29.

1387. DOTY, Ruth
"Johnathan Moon." Nimrod (28:1) Aut-Wint 84, p.
    94-98.

1388. DOUBIAGO, Sharon
"Seagull" (A Contemporary Fairy Tale). NoDaQ
    (52:2) Spr 84, p. 6-14.

1389. DOUGHERTY, Fred
"Home from Nam." SanFPJ (6:2) 84, p. 15.
"Soldier's Dream." SanFPJ (6:2) 84, p. 23.

1390. DOUGHERTY, William F.
"Correlative of Ice." DekalbLAJ (17:1/2) 84, p. 117.

1391. DOUGLASS, John D.
"With Our Hands Locked." NegC (4:2) Spr 84, p. 34.

1392. DOUSKEY, Franz
"Facing the Lost." MinnR (N.S. 23) Aut 84, p. 153.

1393. DOVE, Rita
"The Afghani Nomad Coat (Part V)." NowestR
    (22:1/2) 84, p. 134-135.
"Courtship, Diligence." NewEngR (7:1) Aut 84, p. 61.
"Gospel." GeoR (38:3) Aut 84, p. 618-619.
"The Oriental Ballerina" (Georgianna Magdalena
    Hord, 1896-1979). NewEngR (7:1) Aut 84, p. 62-63.
"Pomade." Poetry (144:6) S 84, p. 324-325.
"Primer for the Nuclear Age." Poetry (145:1) O
    84, p. 49.
"Quaker Oats." Ploughs (10:1) 84, p. 50.
"The Wake." Poetry (144:6) S 84, p. 325-326.
"Watching Last Year at Marienbad at Roger
    Haggerty's House in Auburn, Alabama."
    Telescope (3:3) Aut 84, p. 44-45.

1394. DOW, Daniel
"The Songbird's Bid." SanFPJ (6:4) 84, p. 8.

1395. DOWNES, Gwladys
"The Return." CanLit (100) Spr 84, p. 97.
"Scripts." CanLit (100) Spr 84, p. 95-96.

1396. DOWNIE, Glen
"I Am the Light of the World." Mund (14:2) 84, p.
66.
"Primitive Cosmology." CanLit (102) Aut 84, p. 19.
"Should've Seen the One That Got Away" (East Gate
Market, Seoul). Descant (47, 15:4) Wint 84, p.
24.
"Snow in the Heartland." Descant (47, 15:4) Wint
84, p. 25.
"Worker Classification: Material Handler." CanLit
(102) Aut 84, p. 35.

1397. DOWNSBROUGH, Julie
"Sudden Storm." WritersL (2) 84, p. 23.

1398. DOXEY, W. S.
"Crapshoot." Poem (52) N 84, p. 58.
"September." Poem (52) N 84, p. 59.

1399. DOYLE, Donna
"Put an X on the One That Is Different" (For
Andrea). AntigR (59) Aut 84, p. 31-32.

1400. DOYLE, James
"The Procession." HiramPoR (37) Aut-Wint 84, p. 14.
"Salt Fishing." SnapD (8:1) Aut 84, p. 57.
"Study in Brown and White." HiramPoR (37) Aut-
Wint 84, p. 13.

1401. DOYLE, Lynn
"Negotiated Settlements and Immediate Withdrawals."
PoetryNW (25:2) Sum 84, p. 16-17.

1402. DRACH, Ivan
"Synthesis" (tr. by Paul Nemser and Mark Rudman).
Pequod (16/17) 84, p. 197.

DRATLER, Lynne Menzel: See MENZEL-DRATLER, Lynne

1403. DREW, George
"The Drowning of Christopher French." BelPoJ
(35:1) Aut 84, p. 33-35.
"Paying Back Cousin Pete." HolCrit (21:4) O 84,
p. 10.
"Pinnacle Farm." Blueline (5:2) Wint-Spr 84, p.
22-23.

1404. DREYE, Gabriela
"Orchid of Steel" (tr. of Gioconda Belli, w. Electa
Arenal). Nat (238:3) 28 Ja 84, p. 100.

1405. DREYER, Marsha Gabriela
"Esteli" (tr. of Claribel Alegria, w. Electra
Arenal). MinnR (N.S. 22) Spr 84, p. 77-78.
"I Am Mirror" (tr. of Claribel Alegria, w. Electa
Arenal). Confr (27/28) 84, p. 42.

1406. DRISCOLL, Frances
"The Frontier." MassR (25:2) Sum 84, p. 247-248.
"Home Birth." MassR (25:2) Sum 84, p. 249.
"Saturday Night." MassR (25:2) Sum 84, p. 250.

1407. DRISCOLL, Jack
"Arm Wrestling with My Father." Tendril (17) Wint
84, p. 48.
"Finding a Doll in My Father's Workroom." StoneC
(11:3/4) Spr-Sum 84, p. 23.
"Growing Up with Guns." MidAR (4:2) Aut 84, p. 58.
"The Hemophiliac." MemphisSR (5:1) Aut 84, p. 15.
"Omens." CutB (22) Spr-Sum 84, p. 36.
"Palm Reading My Mother's Death." CapeR (19:2)
Sum 84, p. 9.
"Reruns, For All My Sons." CapeR (19:2) Sum 84,
p. 8.
"The Sleepwalker." MidAR (4:1) Spr 84, p. 159-162.
"Sleepwalking beyond the Harvest." MidAR (4:1)
Spr 84, p. 158.
"Strategy." IndR (7:2) Spr 84, p. 23.

1408. DRISKELL, Leon V.
"Knowledge Complete." NegC (4:1) Wint 84, p. 23-24.

1409. DROZ, Vanessa
"Hay un Cuerpo Que Anda." Mairena (5:13) Spr 83,
p. 94.

1410. DRUKER, Phil
"Worms." SnapD (8:1) Aut 84, p. 36-37.

1411. DRURY, John
"Detasseling Corn." Ploughs (10:1) 84, p. 51.
"The Dry Goods Store" (for my mother). Hudson
(37:1) Spr 84, p. 83-84.
"Election Year in Portugal." Shen (35:1) 83-84,
p. 58-59.
"Great South Bay." Hudson (37:1) Spr 84, p. 84.
"Li Po in Chinatown." Shen (35:1) 83-84, p. 58.
"Shrine." SouthernPR (24:1) Spr 84, p. 26-27.

1412. DU, Fu
"In Spring: Looking into the Distance, on the Wall"
(tr. by Burton Raffel and Zuxin Ding). LitR
(27:3) Spr 84, p. 296.
"Look at Spring!" NewL (50:2/3) Wint-Spr 84, p. 225.
"Moonlit Night" (tr. by Burton Raffel and Zuxin
Ding). LitR (27:3) Spr 84, p. 297.
"Night Traveling" (tr. by Sam Hamill). CrabCR
(2:1) Sum 84, p. 24.
"Spring Rain" (tr. by Burton Raffel and Zuxin
Ding). LitR (27:3) Spr 84, p. 297.

1413. DUBIE, Norman
"An Annual of the Dark Physics." AmerPoR (13:5) S-
O 84, p. 25.
"Archangelsk." Telescope (3:3) Aut 84, p. 110.
"The Czar's Last Christmas Letter: A Barn in the
Urals." AmerPoR (13:5) S-O 84, p. 18.

"Danse Macabre." <u>AmerPoR</u> (13:5) S-O 84, p. 23.
"The Diamond Persona." <u>AmerPoR</u> (13:5) S-O 84, p. 25.
"The Elegy for Integral Domains." <u>Antaeus</u> (53)
    Aut 84, p. 246-247.
"February: The Boy Breughel." <u>AmerPoR</u> (13:5) S-O
    84, p. 17-18.
"For Randall Jarrell, 1914-1965." <u>AmerPoR</u> (13:5)
    S-O 84, p. 17.
"The Funeral." <u>AmerPoR</u> (13:5) S-O 84, p. 26.
"Hummingbirds." <u>AmerPoR</u> (13:5) S-O 84, p. 26.
"Leda & the Swan." <u>AmerPoR</u> (13:5) S-O 84, p. 25.
"Letter to Rue Robert de Flers." <u>AmerPoR</u> (13:5) S-
    O 84, p. 24.
"Meister Eckhart." <u>AmerPoR</u> (13:5) S-O 84, p. 26.
"New England Autumn." <u>NewYorker</u> (60:38) 5 N 84,
    p. 54.
"Parish." <u>AmerPoR</u> (13:5) S-O 84, p. 20.
"Through a Glass Darkly" (after Ingmar Bergman).
    <u>AmerPoR</u> (13:5) S-O 84, p. 24.
"To a Young Woman Dying at Weir." <u>AmerPoR</u> (13:5)
    S-O 84, p. 19.
"The Widow of the Beast of Ingolstadt." <u>AmerPoR</u>
    (13:5) S-O 84, p. 26.
"Wintry Night, Its Reticule." <u>Field</u> (31) Aut 84,
    p. 52.

1414. DUBNOV, Eugene
    "The Green Leaf Attached to the Stem" (tr. by C.
    Newman). <u>NowestR</u> (22:3) 84, p. 93.
    "King David" (tr. by the author and John Heath-
    Stubbs). <u>NowestR</u> (22:3) 84, p. 96-98.
    "These Brief and Endless Nights." <u>ArizQ</u> (40:3)
    Aut 84, p. 196.
    "These Squat Towns" (tr. by the author and
    Christopher Newman). <u>PraS</u> (58:2) Sum 84, p. 64.
    "Warming Your Hands" (tr. by the author and C.
    Newman). <u>NowestR</u> (22:3) 84, p. 94-95.

1415. DuBOIS, Rochelle
    "Call It Hope." <u>Calyx</u> (8:2) Spr 84, p. 92.

1416. DUCEY, Jean
    "The Mothers of the Plaza de Mayo." <u>Comm</u> (111:12)
    15 Je 84, p. 367.

1417. DUCHAMP, Marcel
    "Mirage Verbal: Writings through Marcel Duchamp,
    Notes" (by John Cage, text derived from <u>Marcel
    Duchamp, Notes</u>). <u>PoetryCR</u> (6:1) Aut 84, p. 9.

1418. DUDIS, Ellen Kirvin
    "Tree(s)." <u>CarolQ</u> (36:3) Spr 84, p. 33-34.

1419. DUEMER, Joseph
    "Kingdoms." <u>WestHR</u> (38:4) Wint 84, p. 352-354.
    "Old Men Sitting in a Bar." <u>WestHR</u> (38:4) Wint
    84, p. 362.
    "Waves." <u>TarRP</u> (23:2) Spr 84, p. 7.

1420. DUER, David
       "After Harvest." <u>PoetC</u> (16:1) Aut 84, p. 18.
       "Ursa Major: Northwest Sky." <u>PoeticJ</u> (5) 84, p. 4.

1421. DUFFIN, K. E.
       "Arai: Ferry Boats" (Hiroshige). <u>Ploughs</u> (10:1)
       84, p. 53.

1422. DUFFY, Maureen
       "Burning Off." <u>Argo</u> (6:1) 84, p. 36-37.

1423. DUGAN, Alan
       "From a Story in the New York Sunday Times Travel
       Section of Oct. 30, 1983, by Maurice Carroll."
       <u>NowestR</u> (22:1/2) 84, p. 36.
       "I'm waiting for you" ("Untitled poem"). <u>WestHR</u>
       (38:3) Aut 84, p. 269.
       "Pro-Nuke Blues." <u>NowestR</u> (22:1/2) 84, p. 35.
       "Space Is Not Merely a Background for Events, But
       Possesses an Autonomous Structure" (--A.
       Einstein). <u>YaleR</u> (73:3) Spr 84, p. xvii.
       "To a Kid Who Believes in Astrology." <u>GeoR</u> (38:2)
       Sum 84, p. 405.
       "Untitled Poem: Speciously individual." <u>GeoR</u>
       (38:2) Sum 84, p. 405.

1424. DUGGIN, Lorraine
       "To My Brother, Who Wasn't Wearing a Helmet."
       <u>PraS</u> (58:2) Sum 84, p. 68-69.

1425. DUHAIME, A.
       "Après la panne" (Haiku). <u>PoetryCR</u> (6:2) Wint
       84-85, p. 9.
       "Il neige sur le toit" (Haiku). <u>PoetryCR</u> (6:2)
       Wint 84-85, p. 9.
       "Vacances de Noël" (Haiku). <u>PoetryCR</u> (6:2) Wint
       84-85, p. 9.

1426. DUHAMEL, Denise
       "Grammy." <u>WoosterR</u> (1:2) N 84, p. 23.
       "It's Really Easy." <u>WoosterR</u> (1:2) N 84, p. 25.
       "Mrs. Shaw's Cadillac." <u>WoosterR</u> (1:2) N 84, p.
       24-25.

1427. DULTZ, Ron
       "Bright-Eyed Shining Star." <u>PortR</u> (30:1) 84, p. 9-
       10.
       "Dead City." <u>PortR</u> (30:1) 84, p. 177.
       "Oh Wind." <u>PortR</u> (30:1) 84, p. 64-65.
       "The Stoic." <u>PortR</u> (30:1) 84, p. 60.
       "To Our Lady of the Battle." <u>PortR</u> (30:1) 84, p.
       93-94.

1428. DUMBRAVEANU, Anghel
       "At Night on the Shore" (tr. by Adam Sorkin and
       Irina Grigorescu). <u>Mund</u> (14:2) 84, p. 31.
       "Caii de Timp." <u>Mund</u> (14:2) 84, p. 26.
       "Heralds" (tr. by Adam Sorkin and Irina
       Grigorescu). <u>Mund</u> (14:2) 84, p. 27.
       "Hidden Portrait" (tr. by Adam J. Sorkin and Irina

Grigorescu). ConcPo (17:2) Aut 84, p. 70.
"Horses of Time" (tr. by Adam Sorkin and Irina
    Grigorescu). Mund (14:2) 84, p. 27.
"Interior" (tr. by Adam J. Sorkin and Irina
    Grigorescu). ConcPo (17:2) Aut 84, p. 70.
"The Masks" (tr. by Adam Sorkin and Irina
    Grigorescu). Mund (14:2) 84, p. 29.
"Mastile." Mund (14:2) 84, p. 28.
"Noaptea Pe Tarm." Mund (14:2) 84, p. 30.
"Vestitoarele." Mund (14:2) 84, p. 26.

1429. DUNHAM, Vera Sandomirsky
"I hear the always-sad voice of the oriole" (tr. of
    Anna Akhmatova, w. Jane Kenyon). OhioR (33)
    84, p. 30.
"The mysterious spring still lay under a spell"
    (tr. of Anna Akhmatova, w. Jane Kenyon). OhioR
    (33) 84, p. 30.
"Yes I loved them, those gatherings late at night"
    (tr. of Anna Akhmatova, w. Jane Kenyon). OhioR
    (33) 84, p. 31.

1430. DUNLEAVY, Hannah
"I or Eve or Any." PottPort (6) 84, p. 40.
"Short Lesson in Movement." PottPort (6) 84, p. 50.
"Tasha." PottPort (6) 84, p. 50.

1431. DUNLOP, Lane
"The Butterfly" (from Le Parti Pris des Choses,
    tr. of Francis Ponge). Chelsea (42/43) 84, p.
    191.
"The Mollusc" (from Le Parti Pris des Choses, tr.
    of Francis Ponge). Chelsea (42/43) 84, p. 191.

1432. DUNN, Millard
"Stoker." TarRP (24:1) Aut 84, p. 18.

1433. DUNN, Sharon
"Air Hunger." Writ (16) Aut 84, p. 31.
"Family Business." Writ (16) Aut 84, p. 28-29.
"Intensive Care." Writ (16) Aut 84, p. 33.
"Member of the Family." Writ (16) Aut 84, p. 30.
"Mother Dying." Writ (16) Aut 84, p. 32.

1434. DUNN, Stephen
"Birthday Gift." ThRiPo (23/24) 84, p. 24.
"Choosing to Think of It." Antaeus (52) Apr 84,
    p. 51.
"Confession of a Young English Professor." ColEnq
    (46:8) D 84, p. 795-796.
"The Drift." ThRiPo (23/24) 84, p. 22-23.
"Essay on the Personal." Ploughs (10:1) 84, p. 54-
    55.
"From Underneath." SenR (14:2) 84, p. 12-13.
"Halves." PoetryNW (25:4) Wint 84-85, p. 8-9.
"In the Yard." PoetryNW (25:1) Spr 84, p. 6-7.
"Letter Home" (For L.). SenR (14:2) 84, p. 9-10.
"Loss." PoetryNW (25:1) Spr 84, p. 7-8.
"Men Talk." SenR (14:2) 84, p. 11.
"The Obscene." PoetryNW (25:4) Wint 84-85, p. 7-8.

"The Return." PoetryNW (25:1) Spr 84, p. 6.
"The Routine Things around the House." OhioR (32)
    84, p. 12-13.
"Somewhere." QW (18) Spr-Sum 84, p. 46.
"The Substitute." SenR (14:2) 84, p. 7-8.
"Two Women." SenR (14:2) 84, p. 14-15.
"Whiteness." OhioR (32) 84, p. 11.

1435. DUNNE, Carol
    "In the Clare Glens." Poem (52) N 84, p. 54.
    "The Little Vendor of North Main Street." Poem
        (52) N 84, p. 52.
    "My Sister, Her Husband, My Womb." CapeR (19:3)
        20th Anniverary Issue 84, p. 12.
    "On the Stone of a Bully Muscle." WestB (14) 84,
        p. 89.
    "The Real Power." GreenfR (11:3/4) Wint-Spr 84,
        p. 140.
    "Sometimes Making Poems." Tendril (17) Wint 84,
        p. 50.
    "Tooling the Vesper." MissR (36, 12:3) Spr 84, p.
        71-72.
    "Tooling the Vesper." Tendril (17) Wint 84, p. 49.
    "What Salina Sees." Poem (52) N 84, p. 53.

1436. DUNNING, P. L.
    "Puddle at the End of the Slide." Wind (14:51)
        84, p. 38.

1437. DUNNING, Stephen
    "Hardy Street." NewL (50:2/3) Wint-Spr 84, p. 36.
    "Hoo-doo." PoetC (15:2) Wint 84, p. 16.
    "Singing." NewL (51:1) Aut 84, p. 72.
    "Swerve." SouthernPR (24:1) Spr 84, p. 9.
    "Trailer Park." HiramPoR (37) Aut-Wint 84, p. 15.

1438. DUPREE, Edison
    "Another Old Photograph." PoetryNW (25:2) Sum 84,
        p. 31.
    "The Empirical Method." PoetryNW (25:3) Aut 84,
        p. 29.
    "The Funnies." PoetryNW (25:3) Aut 84, p. 28-29.
    "Song of the Man Who Has Hit Bottom." SouthernPR
        (24:1) Spr 84, p. 6.

1439. DURAK, Carol
    "Monologue to His Own Reflection." SnapD (7:1)
        Aut 83, p. 39.

1440. DUREN, Francis
    "Shrew." KanQ (16:4) Aut 84, p. 136.

1441. DUTTON, Paul (See also FOUR HORSEMEN)
    "Lazy Alphabet." CapilR (31) 84, p. 58.
    "Sound Blues for Muddy Waters." CapilR (31) 84,
        p. 59.
    "Time." CapilR (31) 84, p. 60.
    "Unnamed Text." CapilR (31) 84, p. 36.
    "Wah hwah wah wah ters." CapilR (31) 84, p. 57.

1442. DUVAL, Quinton
    "Absent Star" (for my brother John). <u>NewL</u>
    (50:2/3) Wint-Spr 84, p. 242.
    "The Best Days." <u>CharR</u> (10:2) Aut 84, p. 88.
    "Black Horse." <u>CharR</u> (10:2) Aut 84, p. 87.

1443. DUVALL, Johnny, Jr.
    "Photo Circa 1969." <u>MissR</u> (36, 12:3) Spr 84, p. 87.

DUYN, Mona van: <u>See</u> Van DUYN, Mona

1444. DWYER, Cynthia Brown
    "Identification." <u>NewL</u> (50:4) Sum 84, p. 92.
    "September." <u>NewL</u> (50:4) Sum 84, p. 91.

1445. DWYER, David
    "Love and Poetry at Ground Zero." <u>PraS</u> (58:4)
    Wint 84, p. 64-68.
    "Natural Theology in the Garden" (a vision in
    doggerel). <u>Swallow</u> (3) 84, p. 1-2.
    "Old Lovers Drinking Together." <u>Agni</u> (20) 84, p.
    9-12.

1446. DWYER, Deirdre
    "For Georgia O'Keefe and Silk." <u>AntigR</u> (56) Wint
    84, p. 26.

1447. DWYER, Frank
    "Looking Back." <u>AmerPoR</u> (13:4) Jl-Ag 84, p. 45.

1448. DYAK, Miriam
    "If God wants to give you wings." <u>YellowS</u> (13)
    Wint 84, p. 6.

1449. DYBEK, Stuart
    "Corks" (from <u>Outtakes</u>). <u>TriQ</u> (60) Spr-Sum 84,
    p. 365.
    "Entry" (from <u>Outtakes</u>). <u>TriQ</u> (60) Spr-Sum 84,
    p. 362.
    "Flu" (from <u>Outtakes</u>). <u>TriQ</u> (60) Spr-Sum 84, p.
    364.
    "Homage to Giacometti." <u>Chelsea</u> (42/43) 84, p. 295.
    "Lights" (from <u>Outtakes</u>). <u>TriQ</u> (60) Spr-Sum 84,
    p. 363.
    "Lost" (from <u>Outtakes</u>). <u>TriQ</u> (60) Spr-Sum 84,
    p. 367.
    "Mulberry Tree." <u>PraS</u> (58:2) Sum 84, p. 86.
    "The Night Your Dress Lifted." <u>VirQR</u> (60:2) Spr
    84, p. 238.
    "Outtakes" (Selections). <u>TriQ</u> (60) Spr-Sum 84, p.
    362-367.
    "Sleepers." <u>VirQR</u> (60:2) Spr 84, p. 238-239.
    "Strays" (from <u>Outtakes</u>). <u>TriQ</u> (60) Spr-Sum 84,
    p. 366.

1450. E. W.
    "To Market, to Market: Hawthorne's Shopping List."
    <u>NegC</u> (4:3) Sum 84, p. 131.
    "To Market, To Market: Shakespeare's Shopping
    List." <u>NegC</u> (4:2) Spr 84, p. 129.

1451. EADY, Cornelius
"Aerial Ballet." <u>GreenfR</u> (12:1/2) Sum-Aut 84, p.
111-112.
"The Dance." <u>NewL</u> (50:4) Sum 84, p. 87.
"January." <u>Callaloo</u> (20, 7:1) Wint 84, p. 82.
"Miss Johnson Dances for the First Time." <u>PoetL</u>
(79:1) Spr 84, p. 32-33.
"My Mother, If She Had Won Free Dance Lessons."
<u>GreenfR</u> (12:1/2) Sum-Aut 84, p. 110-111.
"November." <u>GreenfR</u> (12:1/2) Sum-Aut 84, p. 109.

1452. EARLE, Jean
"The Garden Girls." <u>Stand</u> (25:2) Spr 84, p. 39.

1453. EARLY, Gerald
"Ghost Writer's Song in Remembrance of Romance"
(for Billie Holiday). <u>AmerPoR</u> (13:5) S-O 84,
p. 3-4.

1454. EARLY, Robert
"A Man in the Company of Himself" (from <u>Hijos de
la Ira</u>, tr. of Dámaso Alonso, w. George
Looney and Mairi Meredith. Translation Chapbook
Series, Number One). <u>MidAR</u> (4:1) Spr 84, p. 79-
102.
"In the Shadow" (tr. of Dámaso Alonso, w. George
Looney and Mairi Meredith). <u>MidAR</u> (4:1) Spr
84, p. 83.
"The Life of Man" (tr. of Dámaso Alonso, w.
George Looney and Mairi Meredith). <u>MidAR</u> (4:1)
Spr 84, p. 85, 87.
"Man" (tr. of Dámaso Alonso, w. George Looney and
Mairi Meredith). <u>MidAR</u> (4:1) Spr 84, p. 81.
"Monsters" (tr. of Dámaso Alonso, w. George
Looney and Mairi Meredith). <u>MidAR</u> (4:1) Spr
84, p. 89, 91.
"Myself" (tr. of Dámaso Alonso, w. George Looney
and Mairi Meredith). <u>MidAR</u> (4:1) Spr 84, p. 101.
"The Soul Is a Little Green Frog" (tr. of Dámaso
Alonso, w. George Looney and Mairi Meredith).
<u>MidAR</u> (4:1) Spr 84, p. 97, 99.
"To the Mite" (tr. of Dámaso Alonso, w. George
Looney and Mairi Meredith). <u>MidAR</u> (4:1) Spr
84, p. 93, 95.

1455. EATON, Charles Edward
"After Degas." <u>SewanR</u> (92:4) O-D 84, p. 535.
"Blue Streak." <u>HolCrit</u> (21:4) O 84, p. 18.
"Clingstone." <u>SouthernPR</u> (24:2) Aut 84, p. 24-25.
"Cloud Pictures." <u>SewanR</u> (92:4) O-D 84, p. 534.
"The Existentialist." <u>MidwQ</u> (25:2) Wint 84, p. 162.
"The Great Chain of Being." <u>ColEng</u> (46:3) Mr 84,
p. 254-255.
"The Niche." <u>CreamCR</u> (9:1/2) 84, p. 89.
"The Oarsman." <u>Chelsea</u> (42/43) 84, p. 275.
"The Plane." <u>Agni</u> (21) 84, p. 32-33.
"Sand Hog." <u>GeoR</u> (38:1) Spr 84, p. 80.
"Slip of the Tongue." <u>GrandS</u> (3:2) Wint 84, p.
156-157.
"The Uprising." <u>Tendril</u> (17) Wint 84, p. 51-52.

1456. EBERHART, Richard
        "Divorce." Shen (35:2/3) 84, p. 122.
        "Ives." Chelsea (42/43) 84, p. 56.
        "The Killer." SouthernR (20:1) Wint 84, p. 116-123.
        "Lilac Feeling." NewL (50:2/3) Wint-Spr 84, p. 247.
        "Listing." Atlantic (253:3) Mr 84, p. 82.
        "Testimony." NowestR (22:1/2) 84, p. 136-138.
        "Throwing Yourself Away." Stand (25:4) Aut 84, p. 4.
        "Trying to Read through My Writing." Chelsea
        (42/43) 84, p. 184.

1457. ECHERRI, Vicente
        "Vision de la Ciudad" (A Gabriel Laguna). LindLM
        (3:1) Ja-Mr 84, p. 15.

1458. ECKMAN, Frederick
        "Alba: Whose Muse?" Sparrow (46) 84, p. 19.

1459. ECONOMOU, George
        "Ameriki 'Amepikh" (Excerpt from Book Two). Bound
        (12:1) Aut 83, p. 167-169.
        "Voluntaries" ("5 Wellfleet, 12:15 p.m. 8/21/79,
        from the deck," "11 Wellfleet, 2:15 p.m.
        7/26/80, from the deck," for James Lechay).
        Nimrod (27:2) Spr-Sum 84, p. 32-33.

1460. EDDINGS, Ann
        "Thinner Shade of Gray." DekalbLAJ (17:1/2) 84,
        p. 118.

1461. EDDY, Gary
        "Desire." GeoR (38:1) Spr 84, p. 36.

1462. EDELMAN, Lee
        "Elegy: You were waiting even then" (For Stuart).
        Nat (238:25) 30 Je 84, p. 808.
        "Grove Street Cemetery, New Haven." Ploughs
        (10:4) 84, p. 211-212.

1463. EDMOND, Murray
        "Hicksville" (for Janet Elepans). PoetryCR (6:1)
        Aut 84, p. 13.

1464. EDMUNDS, Martin
        "Sentence." Agni (21) 84, p. 41.

1465. EDSON, Russell
        "The Rat's Legs." Field (30) Spr 84, p. 50.
        "The Sweet Twilight." Field (30) Spr 84, p. 49.
        "You." Field (30) Spr 84, p. 51.

1466. EDWARDS, Nancy
        "Across the River." Amelia [1:1] Ap 84, p. 13.

1467. EELLS, John S., Jr.
        "Argus, Dreaming." KenR (NS 6:3) Sum 84, p. 51-52.
        "The Forty-Acre Lot." KenR (NS 6:3) Sum 84, p. 50-
        51.
        "Here, in the Desolate City." KenR (NS 6:3) Sum
        84, p. 50.

1468. EGAN, Michael
     "The Cottage Cat." KanQ (16:1/2) Wint-Spr 84, p.
     139.
     "The Gift of Sons."140-141.

1469. EGUZKITZA, Andolin
     "Amodiozko Istorioa." Mester (13:1) My 84, p. 22,
     24.
     "Canción de Placer" (tr. by the author). Mester
     (13:1) My 84, p. 27, 29.
     "Historia de Amor" (tr. by the author). Mester
     (13:1) My 84, p. 23, 25.
     "Plazerezko Kantua." Mester (13:1) My 84, p. 26, 28.

1470. EHERHART, W. D.
     "Child of the Sixties Turns Thirty-five."
     Northeast (Series 3:17) Sum 84, p. 4.

1471. EHRHART, W. D.
     "Climbing to Heaven" (for Brady Shea). NegC (4:3)
     Sum 84, p. 106.
     "Farmer Nguyen." Pig (12) 84, p. 17.
     "The Invasion of Grenada." Sam (41:1, release
     161) 84, p. 12.
     "Letter" (to a North Vietnamese soldier whose life
     crossed paths with mine in Hue, February 5th,
     1968). Pig (12) 84, p. 20.
     "Letter from an Old Lover." Sam (41:2, release
     162) 84 or 85, p. 46.
     "Letter to the Survivors." Sam (41:1, release
     161) 84, p. 13.
     "Sunset" (Dresden Nuclear Power Station, Morris,
     Illinois). Spirit (7:1) 84, p. 93-94.
     "Warning to My Students" (George School, Nov. '81).
     Sam (39:1, release 153) 84, p. 60.

1472. EHRICH, Judith
     "Ridván at Bahjí. WorldO (18:3) Spr 84, p. 32.

1473. EHRINAN, Sally
     "Twins." NegC (4:2) Spr 84, p. 66.

1474. EHRLICH, Helen
     "Assumptions." Veloc (4) Sum 84, p. 59.
     "Space Talk." Veloc (4) Sum 84, p. 58.

1475. EHRLICH, Shelley
     "August and a Pond." PraS (58:2) Sum 84, p. 69.
     "Dreaming My Dead Father Back." Northeast (Series
     3:17) Sum 84, p. 11.
     "Silence." Northeast (Series 3:17) Sum 84, p. 10.
     "Summer Is Tumbling Down." PraS (58:2) Sum 84, p.
     70.

1476. EICH, Günter
     "Jonah" (tr. by Katherine Anne Powell). Field
     (30) Spr 84, p. 47.
     "Keys" (tr. by Katherine Anne Powell). Field (30)
     Spr 84, p. 48.

1477. EICHWALD, Richard
      "The Seasons: A Primer." <u>SewanR</u> (92:2) Ap-Je 84,
      p. 197-198.

1478. EIGNER, Larry
      "The Cripples." <u>Sparrow</u> (46) 84, p. 25.

1479. EINZIG, Barbara
      "George, the Name of a Fish." <u>Ploughs</u> (10:4) 84,
      p. 106-107.

1480. EISENBERG, Ruth F.
      "Deflections." <u>NegC</u> (4:3) Sum 84, p. 117.

1481. EISENBERG, Ruth R.
      "Some Things You Can't Forget" (for Saul N.).
      <u>GreenfR</u> (11:1/2) Sum-Aut 83, p. 177-178.

1482. EKELOF, Gunnar
      "Monologue with Its Wife" (tr. by Robert Bly).
      <u>Chelsea</u> (42/43) 84, p. 65.

1483. ELDER, Karl
      "Anemophobia." <u>PoetC</u> (16:1) Aut 84, p. 6.
      "Cardiophobia." <u>PoetC</u> (16:1) Aut 84, p. 5.
      "Ergasiophobia." <u>PoetC</u> (16:1) Aut 84, p. 7.
      "Pyrophobia." <u>PoetC</u> (16:1) Aut 84, p. 8.
      "Xenophobia." <u>PoetC</u> (16:1) Aut 84, p. 4.

1484. ELDRED, Charlotte
      "In America They Pave the Roads with Gold." <u>WebR</u>
      (9:2) Wint 85, p. 83.
      "My Son." <u>WebR</u> (9:2) Wint 85, p. 84.

1485. ELENKOV, Luchezar
      "Concerned with Something Else While Turnovo's
      Dying" (tr. by Jascha Kessler and Alexander
      Shurbanov). <u>GrahamHR</u> (7) Wint 84, p. 59-60.
      "Poet" (tr. by Jascha Kessler and Alexander
      Shurbanov). <u>GrahamHR</u> (7) Wint 84, p. 58.

1486. ELGIN, Suzette Haden
      "La Jeune Parque" (lines 34-101, tr. of Paul
      Valéry). <u>Veloc</u> (2) Spr 83, p. 35-38.

1487. ELIASON, Ginny
      "Old Lovers." <u>Tendril</u> (17) Wint 84, p. 53.

1488. ELIOT, Eileen
      "Behavior Modification." <u>Vis</u> (16) 84, p. 29-30.
      "Marathon." <u>Vis</u> (14) 84, p. 10-11.
      "Rosary: One Decade." <u>Vis</u> (14) 84, p. 12-14.
      "Second Skin." <u>Vis</u> (16) 84, p. 27-28.

1489. ELIOT, T. S.
      "Dear Madam." <u>KenR</u> (NS 6:3) Sum 84, p. 30.

1490. ELKIN, Roger
      "Pure and Applied." <u>Argo</u> (5:2) 84, p. 20.

1491. ELLEDGE, Jim
       "For Paul Blackburn." CreamCR (9:1/2) 84, p. 80.

1492. ELLEN
       "The Skeletons Will Become Useful Building
          Material." PortR (30:1) 84, p. 164-165.

1493. ELLERT, Frederick C.
       "And What Did the Soldier's Wife Receive?" (tr. of
          Bertolt Brecht). MassR (25:4) Wint 84, p. 573,
          575.
       "Christ Forlorn" (tr. of Christian Morgenstern).
          MassR (25:4) Wint 84, p. 569.
       "The Old Nag" (tr. of Christian Morgenstern).
          MassR (25:4) Wint 84, p. 567.
       "Whereto Now?" (tr. of Heinrich Heine). MassR
          (25:4) Wint 84, p. 571, 573.

1494. ELLIOTT, Harley
       "Short Reality." HangL (46) Aut 84, p. 18.
       "The Skunk." HangL (46) Aut 84, p. 17.

1495. ELLIOTT, Jorge
       "Vices of the Modern World" (tr. of Nicanor Parra).
          Chelsea (42/43) 84, p. 58-60.

1496. ELLIOTT, Mark
       "Dance." Wind (14:50) 84, p. 9-10.

1497. ELLIS, Havelock
       "Her Dream, Half Remembered" (A translation by
          Charles Olson). Sulfur (4:2, issue 11) 84, p.
          151-152.

1498. ELLIS, Ralph J.
       "Ignominy." DekalbLAJ (20th Anniversary Issue)
          84, p. 85.
       "Methuselah (Dart-Man)." DekalbLAJ (20th
          Anniversary Issue) 84, p. 86.

1499. ELLIS, Ron
       "Car Radio." Veloc (4) Sum 84, p. 57.
       "The Pratyeka Cantos" (Canto Five). CreamCR
          (9:1/2) 84, p. 85.
       "Venus Sings to Pioneer." Veloc (4) Sum 84, p. 55-
          56.

1500. ELLIS, Russ
       "The Houses." YellowS (10) Spr 84, p. 8.

1501. ELON, Florence
       "Her Final Portrait" (Berlin). Thrpny (16) Wint
          84, p. 17.

1502. ELOVIC, Barbara
       "Intentions." Poetry (144:1) Ap 84, p. 31.
       "On Soap Operas." GreenfR (11:1/2) Sum-Aut 83, p.
          94.
       "Schooling" (For Connie). Poetry (144:1) Ap 84,
          p. 30.

"Subway Story." Thrpny (18) Sum 84, p. 7.

1503. ELSBERG, John
      "Home-Style Cooking on Third Avenue" (Or, Poem with
        a Sanskrit Image). Bogg (52) 84, p. 8.
      "Trees of a shadow wand." Bogg (52) 84, p. 34.

1504. ELSEY, David
      "Rain." PoeticJ (6) 84, p. 21.

1505. ELSON, Virginia
      "Dugout." Amelia (1:2) O 84, p. 29.

1506. ELTON, Thomas
      "An Apology." CrossC (6:3) 84, p. 20.
      "Crossings." CrossC (6:3) 84, p. 20.
      "Months Later, Your Image." CrossC (6:3) 84, p. 21.
      "Waiting." CrossC (6:3) 84, p. 21.

1507. ELUARD, Paul
      "Les Malheurs des Immortels" (Selections: Between
        the Two Poles of Politeness. The Modesty Well in
        View. Tr. by Ira Sadoff). Chelsea (42/43) 84,
        p. 292.

1508. ELYTIS, Odysseus
      "One Swallow Flying" (Psalm #4 of "The Passion",
        from The Axion Esti, tr. by Edward Morin and
        Lefteris Pavlides). Confr (27/28) 84, p. 57.

1509. EMANS, Elaine V.
      "Autumn Villanelle." KanQ (16:1/2) Wint-Spr 84,
        p. 113.
      "The Cat Who Never Stays Out." TexasR (5:3/4) Aut-
        Wint 84, p. 30.
      "Mouse." KanQ (16:1/2) Wint-Spr 84, p. 112.
      "Song after a Special Breakfast." TexasR (5:3/4)
        Aut-Wint 84, p. 31.

1510. EMANUEL, Lynn
      "The Dig." GeoR (38:2) Sum 84, p. 368.
      "Discovering the Photograph of Lloyd, Earl and
        Priscilla." ThRiPo (23/24) 84, p. 14.
      "Elegy Written in the Vowels of Her Name." ThRiPo
        (23/24) 84, p. 13.
      "Patient." ThRiPo (23/24) 84, p. 15.

1511. EMBLEN, D. L.
      "The State of the Art." EngJ (73:5) S 84, p. 32.

1512. EMERY, Michael J.
      "Blind Faith." WindO (44) Sum-Aut 84, p. 30.
      "Cartographer's Nightmare." WindO (44) Sum-Aut
        84, p. 30.

1513. EMIN, Gevorg
      "Clever Lamb" (tr. by Diana Der Hovanessian).
        Mund (14:2) 84, p. 12.
      "Why Has This Ache" (tr. by Diana Der Hovanessian).
        Mund (14:2) 84, p. 12.

1514. EMMANUEL, Pierre
"The Art of Dying" (tr. by Dorothy Aspinwall).
WebR (9:1) Spr 84, p. 15.
"Quais du Rhône à Lyon." Argo (6:1) 84, p. 20.
"Quays by the Rhone, at Lyons" (tr. by Brian
Merrikin Hill). Argo (6:1) 84, p. 21.
"Simon de Cyrène" (in French). Argo (6:1) 84,
p. 20.
"Simon of Cyrene" (tr. by Brian Merrikin Hill).
Argo (6:1) 84, p. 21.

1515. ENCARNACION, Alfred
"The Plait." CapeR (19:3) 20th Anniverary Issue
84, p. 13.
"Stone for Grandfather" (dead at eighty-five of
hardening of the arteries). CapeR (19:3) 20th
Anniverary Issue 84, p. 14.

1516. ENCARNACION, Angel Manuel
"Ludico Verso." Mairena (6:18) 84, p. 30.

1517. ENDO, Russell Susumu
"To Issei, the First Generation." PaintedB (21)
Wint 84, p. 24.

1518. ENDREZZE-DANIELSON, Anita
"In the Kitchen." SnapD (7:1) Aut 83, p. 18-19.

1519. ENGEBRETSEN, Alan C.
"On the Ever-Blooming Road." Amelia (1:2) O 84,
p. 61.

1520. ENGEL, Mary
"Last Rites." SanFPJ (6:4) 84, p. 78.
"No Body Counts on Holidays." SanFPJ (6:1) 84, p. 9.
"Nursing Home." SanFPJ (6:4) 84, p. 79.

1521. ENGELS, John
"Avocado." SouthernHR (18:3) Sum 84, p. 215.
"Cobra." KenR (NS 6:4) Aut 84, p. 20-21.
"For the Lately Dead." KenR (NS 6:4) Aut 84, p.
19-20.
"Nothing Relents." Peb (23) 84, p. 18-20.
"The Photograph." SouthernHR (18:3) Sum 84, p.
213-215.
"The Pool at Sunrise." KenR (NS 6:4) Aut 84, p.
18-19.
"The Raft." KenR (NS 6:4) Aut 84, p. 21-24.

1522. ENGLE, Ed, Jr.
"The Angelus." Abraxas (29/30) 84, p. 44.

1523. ENGLEBERT, Michel J.
"To a Greased Pole Climber." DekalbLAJ (17:1/2)
84, p. 119.

1524. ENGLER, Robert Klein
"Dim Conjunctions." WebR (9:2) Wint 85, p. 92.
"Jerry." WindO (44) Sum-Aut 84, p. 10.

1525. ENGLISH, Maurice
"The Apple Tree." <u>AmerPoR</u> (13:1) Ja-F 84, p. 47.

1526. ENGMAN, John
"Mushroom Clouds." <u>Telescope</u> (3:1) Wint 84, p. 64-
65.
"Transparent Highway Curves." <u>Telescope</u> (3:1)
Wint 84, p. 66-67.

1527. ENLOE, Glen
"The Essentials of Poetry." <u>Wind</u> (14:51) 84, p. 11.
"Identifying the Body." <u>Wind</u> (14:51) 84, p. 11.

1528. ENSLIN, Theodore
"After the event we know." <u>Origin</u> (5:4) Aut 84,
p. 95.
"If I trace silence." <u>Origin</u> (5:4) Aut 84, p. 96.
"Some Responses to <u>Aegis</u>." <u>Origin</u> (5:4) Aut 84,
p. 95-96.
"What is it you want?" <u>Origin</u> (5:4) Aut 84, p. 96.
"Whatever it is." <u>Origin</u> (5:4) Aut 84, p. 96.
"You tell me that I ask too much." <u>Origin</u> (5:4)
Aut 84, p. 96.

1529. ENZENSBERGER, Hans Magnus
"Canto Sexto" (tr. by Heberto Padilla). <u>LindLM</u>
(3:1) Ja-Mr 84, p. 2.
"Countdown" (in German). <u>NowestR</u> (22:1/2) 84, p. 70.
"Countdown" (tr. by Felix Pollak and Reinhold
Grimm). <u>NowestR</u> (22:1/2) 84, p. 71.
"Course in Poetics" (tr. by Felix Pollak and
Reinhold Grimm). <u>TriQ</u> (61) Aut 84, p. 100.
"Delete Whatever Inapplicable" (tr. by Felix Pollak
and Reinhold Grimm). <u>AmerPoR</u> (13:5) S-O 84, p. 7.
"The Divorce" (tr. by Herbert Graf). <u>Sulfur</u> (3:3,
issue 9) 84, p. 128.
"The Doctrine of Categories" (tr. by Felix Pollak
and Reinhold Grimm). <u>NowestR</u> (22:1/2) 84, p. 65.
"Doomsday" (in German). <u>NowestR</u> (22:1/2) 84, p. 66.
"Doomsday" (tr. by Felix Pollak and Reinhold
Grimm). <u>NowestR</u> (22:1/2) 84, p. 67.
"The Dresses" (tr. by Felix Pollak and Reinhold
Grimm). <u>AmerPoR</u> (13:5) S-O 84, p. 6.
"The Empty House" (tr. by Felix Pollak and Reinhold
Grimm). <u>NowestR</u> (22:1/2) 84, p. 69.
"For the Primer of Senior High" (tr. by Felix
Pollak and Reinhold Grimm). <u>AmerPoR</u> (13:5) S-O
84, p. 7.
"Friedenskongress." <u>NowestR</u> (22:1/2) 84, p. 62.
"Die Furie des Verschwindens" (Selections, tr. by
Herbert Graf). <u>Sulfur</u> (3:3, issue 9) 84, p.
124-129.
"Historical Process" (tr. by Felix Pollak and
Reinhold Grimm). <u>AmerPoR</u> (13:5) S-O 84, p. 7.
"Das Leere Haus." <u>NowestR</u> (22:1/2) 84, p. 68.
"Die Lehre von den Kategorien." <u>NowestR</u> (22:1/2)
84, p. 64.
"Memorial" (tr. by Herbert Graf). <u>Sulfur</u> (3:3,
issue 9) 84, p. 125.
"Obsession" (tr. by Felix Pollak and Reinhold

Grimm). TriQ (61) Aut 84, p. 102.
"Peace Conference" (tr. by Felix Pollak and
Reinhold Grimm). NowestR (22:1/2) 84, p. 63.
"Regardless of" (tr. by Felix Pollak and Reinhold
Grimm). AmerPoR (13:5) S-O 84, p. 6.
"Report from Bonn" (tr. by Herbert Graf). Sulfur
(3:3, issue 9) 84, p. 124-125.
"Residual Light" (tr. by Felix Pollak and Reinhold
Grimm). TriQ (61) Aut 84, p. 101.
"She's Thirty-Three" (tr. by Herbert Graf).
Sulfur (3:3, issue 9) 84, p. 125-126.
"Shit" (tr. by Felix Pollak and Reinhold Grimm).
AmerPoR (13:5) S-O 84, p. 6.
"Short History of the Bourgeoisie" (tr. by Herbert
Graf). Sulfur (3:3, issue 9) 84, p. 129.
"The White Collar Worker" (tr. by Herbert Graf).
Sulfur (3:3, issue 9) 84, p. 126-127.

1530. EPES, W. Perry
"Mother Merrill." NegC (4:3) Sum 84, p. 112-113.

1531. EPLING, Kathy
"There Is a Garden." YellowS (12) Aut 84, p. 20.

1532. EPPLE, Juan Armando
"Estación de Buses." Metam (5:2/6:1) 84-85, p. 23.
"The Oregon Trail." Metam (5:2/6:1) 84-85, p. 22.
"La Pulga Lesa" (a Omar Lara, co-autor del tema, y
a la Burgalesa, of course). Metam (5:2/6:1) 84-
85, p. 24.
"Te Ocultas de Mí." Metam (5:2/6:1) 84-85, p. 23.

1533. EPSTEIN, Elaine
"Catharsis of War" (tr. of Wadym Lesytch). Pequod
(16/17) 84, p. 189-190.

1534. EPSTEIN, Judith
"The First Lady." SanFPJ (6:1) 84, p. 68.
"The First Lady." SanFPJ (6:3) 84, p. 71.
"On the Dole in 1984." SanFPJ (6:1) 84, p. 66.
"USA." SanFPJ (6:1) 84, p. 67.

1535. ERHAN, Ahmet
"Tabutunun Basinda Bir Arkadasin." NewRena (6:1,
#18) Spr 84, p. 72.
"Waiting beside a Friend's Coffin" (tr. by Talat
Sait Halman). NewRena (6:1, #18) Spr 84, p. 73.

1536. ERIAN, Soraya
"His and Her Binoculars." PoetryCR (5:4) Sum 84,
p. 16.

1537. ERICKSON, Catherine
"Perforation." CimR (66) Ja 84, p. 61.

1538. ERWIN, Paul Campbell
"Handful of Dust." DekalbLAJ (17:1/2) 84, p. 120.

1539. ESCH, Jeanne
"In hot desert wind" (Haiku, Third Prize, 13th

Annual Kansas Poetry Contest). LittleBR (4:3)
Spr 84, p. 69.

1540. ESHE, Aisha
"He Can Go Home, I Guess We Pulled the Wrong Nigga
This Time" (would you like a cup of coffee and
some candy for the little girl). BlackALF
(18:1) Spr 84, p. 28.
"Mother." Amelia (1:2) O 84, p. 62.

1541. ESHLEMAN, Clayton
"The Aurignacian Summation." CreamCR (9:1/2) 84,
p. 103-104.
"Cadaver Cracks in the Lotus Pond" (from Sea Urchin
Harakiri, tr. of Bernard Bador). Sulfur (4:1,
issue 10) 84, p. 64-66.
"Cape of Wild Flies" (from Sea Urchin Harakiri,
edited poem of Bernard Bador). Sulfur (4:1,
issue 10) 84, p. 66-67.
"Civil Status" (from Suppots et Supplications:
Interjections, tr. of Antonin Artaud, w. A.
James Arnold). Sulfur (3:3, issue 9) 84, p. 43-
59.
"The peak of the obsidian mountain swarms"
("Untitled"). Sulfur (4:2, issue 11) 84, p.
110-112.
"Pounding and Gism" (from Suppots et
Supplications: Interjections, tr. of Antonin
Artaud, w. A. James Arnold and David Maclagan).
Sulfur (3:3, issue 9) 84, p. 38-42.
"Progress" (from Sea Urchin Harakiri, tr. of
Bernard Bador). Sulfur (4:1, issue 10) 84, p.
63-64.
"Sea Urchin Harakiri" (Selections, tr. of Bernard
Bador). Sulfur (4:1, issue 10) 84, p. 63-67.
"Suppots et Supplications" (Selections, tr. of
Antonin Artaud, w. A. James Arnold, David
Rattray, and David Maclagan). Sulfur (3:3,
issue 9) 84, p. 15-59.

1542. ESPADA, Martin
"Leo Blue's and the Tiger Rose." GreenfR (12:1/2)
Sum-Aut 84, p. 185-186.

1543. ESPOSITO, Nancy
"Ancestor." QRL (Poetry series 6, v. 25) 84, p.
65-67.
"Birding in Mt. Auburn Cemetery." QRL (Poetry
series 6, v. 25) 84, p. 24-25.
"Bluffing Your Way through an Exam" (for Gayle
Zoffer). QRL (Poetry series 6, v. 25) 84, p. 10.
"Borders." QRL (Poetry series 6, v. 25) 84, p. 73.
"Breakfast Piece." QRL (Poetry series 6, v. 25)
84, p. 12-13.
"The Caretaker's Daughter." QRL (Poetry series 6,
v. 25) 84, p. 76-77.
"Changing Hands." QRL (Poetry series 6, v. 25)
84, p. 1-88.
"Dark Horse." QRL (Poetry series 6, v. 25) 84, p.
48.

"The Decorator Views an Interior." QRL (Poetry
    series 6, v. 25) 84, p. 50.
"Dining Out" (for Karen Ebbitt). QRL (Poetry
    series 6, v. 25) 84, p. 41-43.
"Dorothy, Destination: Oz." QRL (Poetry series 6,
    v. 25) 84, p. 70.
"Ex Periculo." QRL (Poetry series 6, v. 25) 84,
    p. 68.
"The Good Shepherd in Industrialist's Clothing"
    (for Larry Indik). QRL (Poetry series 6, v.
    25) 84, p. 19-20.
"Goodwill." QRL (Poetry series 6, v. 25) 84, p.
    28-29.
"Gotham Sometime Later." QRL (Poetry series 6, v.
    25) 84, p. 81-82.
"Ice Storm in the Sun Belt." QRL (Poetry series
    6, v. 25) 84, p. 60.
"In My Ascendancy." QRL (Poetry series 6, v. 25)
    84, p. 83-85.
"Looking into Glass." QRL (Poetry series 6, v.
    25) 84, p. 21-22.
"Migrations" (for Katherine Kadish). QRL (Poetry
    series 6, v. 25) 84, p. 14-15.
"Modalities." QRL (Poetry series 6, v. 25) 84, p.
    55-56.
"Music Room 9" (for Lowry Pei). QRL (Poetry
    series 6, v. 25) 84, p. 78.
"My Sister, Harmonizing" (for Susan). QRL (Poetry
    series 6, v. 25) 84, p. 80.
"Nevada, in Season." QRL (Poetry series 6, v. 25)
    84, p. 74.
"News Item." QRL (Poetry series 6, v. 25) 84, p.
    61-62.
"The Next Instar" (for Aaron Turkewitz). QRL
    (Poetry series 6, v. 25) 84, p. 23.
"Of the Lady of the Streets." QRL (Poetry series
    6, v. 25) 84, p. 75.
"Old Song" (for my father). QRL (Poetry series 6,
    v. 25) 84, p. 79.
"On Cognition" (for Ellen Strenski). QRL (Poetry
    series 6, v. 25) 84, p. 8.
"The Pedagogue's Problem." QRL (Poetry series 6,
    v. 25) 84, p. 47.
"Perhaps Malachi Maynard of Conway Mass." QRL
    (Poetry series 6, v. 25) 84, p. 38-39.
"Plum Island." QRL (Poetry series 6, v. 25) 84,
    p. 17.
"Questions a Son Might Ask" (for Judith Austen).
    QRL (Poetry series 6, v. 25) 84, p. 46.
"Rare Wine of Good Vintage." QRL (Poetry series
    6, v. 25) 84, p. 40.
"The Reading" (Muriel Rukeyser at Harvard,
    4/26/79). QRL (Poetry series 6, v. 25) 84, p. 59.
"Reading for Pleasure." QRL (Poetry series 6, v.
    25) 84, p. 44.
"Rudiment." QRL (Poetry series 6, v. 25) 84, p. 27.
"The Shape the Tongue Takes." AmerPoR (13:5) S-O
    84, p. 7.
"The Shape the Tongue Takes." QRL (Poetry series
    6, v. 25) 84, p. 72.

"Shapeshifting." <u>QRL</u> (Poetry series 6, v. 25) 84,
     p. 45.
"Skilled Labor." <u>QRL</u> (Poetry series 6, v. 25) 84,
     p. 9.
"The Storyteller Tells His Story." <u>QRL</u> (Poetry
     series 6, v. 25) 84, p. 36-37.
"Subject for Art." <u>QRL</u> (Poetry series 6, v. 25)
     84, p. 58.
"The Summer before Apocalypse." <u>QRL</u> (Poetry
     series 6, v. 25) 84, p. 53-54.
"Sunday: Corner of Orchard and Milton." <u>QRL</u>
     (Poetry series 6, v. 25) 84, p. 30-34.
"Survivor." <u>QRL</u> (Poetry series 6, v. 25) 84, p. 63.
"That Soundless Reunion" (Luke Musache, 1882-1964).
     <u>QRL</u> (Poetry series 6, v. 25) 84, p. 64.
"Three Figures Walking through Grass." <u>QRL</u>
     (Poetry series 6, v. 25) 84, p. 11.
"To My Green Lady, with Regret." <u>QRL</u> (Poetry
     series 6, v. 25) 84, p. 51-52.
"Urban Jungle." <u>AmerPoR</u> (13:5) S-O 84, p. 7.
"Urban Jungle." <u>QRL</u> (Poetry series 6, v. 25) 84,
     p. 16.
"Watching off Provincetown." <u>QRL</u> (Poetry series
     6, v. 25) 84, p. 18.
"The Wedding of That Year." <u>QRL</u> (Poetry series 6,
     v. 25) 84, p. 49.
"The Woman in Translation." <u>QRL</u> (Poetry series 6,
     v. 25) 84, p. 71.

1544. ESSARY, Loris
     "As a Fragment, Fourteen Years." <u>GreenfR</u> (11:1/2)
          Sum-Aut 83, p. 105.
     "Un Soir de Carnaval" (A painting by Rousseau, a
          poem ending with an academic quotation).
          <u>MemphisSR</u> (5:1) Aut 84, p. 22.

1545. ESTEBAN, Claude
     "The Season of Devastation" (Excerpt, tr. by
          Stanley L. Cavell and Kathleen Cavell). <u>Pequod</u>
          (16/17) 84, p. 240-241.

1546. ESTEVE, Patricio
     "Funeral Song" (tr. by Linda Lappin, w. the
          author). <u>Iowa</u> (14:2) Spr-Sum 84, p. 159.

1547. ETTER, Dave
     "Cairo." <u>Northeast</u> (Series 3:17) Sum 84, p. 13.
     "Courthouse Square." <u>MidwQ</u> (25:4) Sum 84, p. 405.
     "Fourteen and a Half." <u>MidwQ</u> (25:4) Sum 84, p. 406.
     "Home State" (Selections: 10 pieces). <u>SpoonRQ</u>
          (9:4) Aut 84, p. 5-14.
     "Hotel Nauvoo." <u>SpoonRQ</u> (9:4) Aut 84, p. 6.
     "Ignorance." <u>SpoonRQ</u> (9:4) Aut 84, p. 10.
     "Live at the Silver Dollar" (Another Late-Night
          Fantasy). <u>SpoonRQ</u> (9:2) Spr 84, p. 1.
     "Local Yokel." <u>MidwQ</u> (25:4) Sum 84, p. 407.
     "Lust." <u>SpoonRQ</u> (9:4) Aut 84, p. 9.
     "Mail." <u>SpoonRQ</u> (9:4) Aut 84, p. 7.
     "The Otis Trap." <u>SpoonRQ</u> (9:4) Aut 84, p. 14.
     "Pike County." <u>SpoonRQ</u> (9:4) Aut 84, p. 8.

"Pipe Smoking." SpoonRQ (9:4) Aut 84, p. 13.
"Tallgrass Prairie Plot." SpoonRQ (9:4) Aut 84,
    p. 5.
"Troubles at the Poem Factory." SpoonRQ (9:4) Aut
    84, p. 11.
"The Upper Crust." SpoonRQ (9:4) Aut 84, p. 12.

1548. EULBERG, Mary Thomas, Sister, OSF
    "Shutter closed" (Haiku, First Honorable Mention,
    13th Annual Kansas Poetry Contest). LittleBR
    (4:3) Spr 84, p. 69.

1549. EVANS, Bill
    "Tenth Elegy" (w. Andrew Gent). HangL (46) Aut
    84, p. 19-23.

1550. EVANS, George
    "A.M." Origin (Series 5:1) Aut 83, p. 26-32.
    "American Dream." Origin (Series 5:1) Aut 83, p. 18.
    "The Anchor." Origin (5:4) Aut 84, p. 63.
    "And if I read pomes." Origin (Series 5:1) Aut
    83, p. 34.
    "At that from which the tide pool fills." Origin
    (Series 5:1) Aut 83, p. 36.
    "At the Sound." Origin (Series 5:1) Aut 83, p. 20.
    "Beached Whale." Origin (Series 5:1) Aut 83, p. 19.
    "The Bird's Day." Origin (5:4) Aut 84, p. 58.
    "Don't deny that love." Origin (Series 5:1) Aut
    83, p. 22.
    "The Dresser." Sulfur (4:1, issue 10) 84, p. 85.
    "The Harvestman." Origin (5:4) Aut 84, p. 57.
    "He was smoking a joint." Origin (Series 5:1) Aut
    83, p. 9.
    "How long's it been." Origin (Series 5:1) Aut 83,
    p. 10.
    "How singular." Origin (Series 5:1) Aut 83, p. 35.
    "In Mokelumne Wilderness." Origin (Series 5:1)
    Aut 83, p. 21.
    "In Pieces." Origin (Series 5:1) Aut 83, p. 15.
    "In the Mission Summer, 1983." Origin (5:4) Aut
    84, p. 62.
    "Islands." Sulfur (4:1, issue 10) 84, p. 87.
    "Land's End." Origin (Series 5:1) Aut 83, p. 33.
    "The Loss." Origin (5:4) Aut 84, p. 55.
    "Love's Progressions & Sudden Dreams." Origin
    (Series 5:1) Aut 83, p. 5-7.
    "Morning." Origin (5:4) Aut 84, p. 65.
    "Mushrooms." Origin (Series 5:1) Aut 83, p. 17.
    "On blank space." Origin (Series 5:1) Aut 83, p. 11.
    "Out there the shadow." Origin (Series 5:1) Aut
    83, p. 37.
    "The Prisoner." Origin (5:4) Aut 84, p. 61.
    "Renaissance Drunk." Sulfur (4:1, issue 10) 84,
    p. 84.
    "Running." Origin (5:4) Aut 84, p. 64.
    "Saturday." Origin (Series 5:1) Aut 83, p. 23-24.
    "The Scene." Origin (Series 5:1) Aut 83, p. 16.
    "She was a cloth dyer." Origin (Series 5:1) Aut
    83, p. 8.
    "Summer." Origin (Series 5:1) Aut 83, p. 14.

"Sunday Drive." Origin (5:4) Aut 84, p. 59-60.
"Termagant." Origin (Series 5:1) Aut 83, p. 13.
"TV flickers." Origin (Series 5:1) Aut 83, p. 25.
"The Well-cropped attracts danger." Origin
    (Series 5:1) Aut 83, p. 12.
"Working for the Iceman." Sulfur (4:1, issue 10)
    84, p. 86.
"Wrecking." Origin (5:4) Aut 84, p. 56.
"Xenakis' Psappho" (a percussion). Origin (5:4)
    Aut 84, p. 66.

1551. EVANS, James M.
    "Woodsmoke." WindO (44) Sum-Aut 84, p. 22.

1552. EVANS, Jeptha
    "Commentary." VirQR (60:4) Aut 84, p. 623.
    "Kafka's Derby." VirQR (60:4) Aut 84, p. 621-623.

1553. EVANS, Kathy
    "Note to My Sister." CalQ (25) Aut 84, p. 65.

1554. EVARTS, Prescott, Jr.
    "91 in Vermont." TexasR (5:3/4) Aut-Wint 84, p. 29.
    "The Eye." CimR (69) O 84, p. 28.

1555. EVASON, Greg
    "The Truth." Quarry (33:4) Aut 84, p. 19.

EVELYN, Tom d': See D'EVELYN, Tom

1556. EVERETT, Joann Marie
    "Windless Evening." PoeticJ (8) 84, p. 39.

1557. EVERWINE, Peter
    "Short Novel." NewL (50:2/3) Wint-Spr 84, p. 182.

1558. EWART, Gavin
    "The Body Casts Aside Its Vest and Sings" (a line
        from a book of verse published in 1981).
        PoetryCR (6:2) Wint 84-85, p. 24.
    "The Eclectic Chair." PoetryCR (5:3) Spr 84, p. 12.
    "The Young Pobble's Guide to His Toes." PoetryCR
        (5:3) Spr 84, p. 12.

1559. EXLER, Samuel
    "The Hand." PoetryE (15) Aut 84, p. 20.

1560. FABIAN, R. Gerry
    "New Moon." SanFPJ (6:2) 84, p. 40.
    "Patterns of Personal Poaching." SanFPJ (6:2) 84,
        p. 40.
    "Strangers." SanFPJ (6:2) 84, p. 40.
    "The Takers." BlueBldgs (8) 84?, p. 1.

1561. FAGAN, Cary
    "Zeyde's Last Look." PoetryCR (6:1) Aut 84, p. 11.

1562. FAGAN, Kathy
    "Breath." Ploughs (10:1) 84, p. 56.
    "Brooklyn, 2 A.M." QW (19) Aut-Wint 84-85, p. 88.

"Evangelist & Peregrine." <u>MissouriR</u> (7:3) 84, p. 55.
"Five Poems of Farewell" (New York, 1982: "Winter
    Scene," "The Lit Stations," "Chambers Street,"
    "Morningside Heights," "Street Fires").
    <u>MissouriR</u> (7:3) 84, p. 56-58.
"Migration." <u>Antaeus</u> (52) Apr 84, p. 85-86.
"The Raft." <u>MissouriR</u> (7:3) 84, p. 54.
"Summer Song Cycle." <u>MissouriR</u> (7:3) 84, p. 51-53.

1563. FAGLES, Robert
    "The Exiles" (After Cavafy). <u>Antaeus</u> (52) Apr 84,
        p. 52-63.

1564. FAHEY, W. A.
    "Dawn Song: Her." <u>YellowS</u> (13) Wint 84, p. 5.

1565. FAHRBACH, Helen
    "Windows." <u>SpoonRQ</u> (9:4) Aut 84, p. 38.

1566. FAIERS, Chris
    "Cavern pool." <u>Bogg</u> (52) 84, p. 32.
    "Five Minutes Ago They Dropped the Bomb." <u>Waves</u>
        (13:1) Aut 84, p. 76-77.
    "Light breeze." <u>Bogg</u> (52) 84, p. 32.

1567. FAIR, Kristi
    "Weaverbird's Vacuum Behavior in the Laboratory."
        <u>HiramPoR</u> (37) Aut-Wint 84, p. 16.

1568. FAIR, Susan
    "Bowhead" (For the Ungotts). <u>ThirdW</u> (2) Spr 84,
        p. 14.

1569. FAIRCHILD, B. H.
    "The Arrival of the Future." <u>SouthernPR</u> (24:1)
        Spr 84, p. 35-37.
    "An Attaché Case." <u>MissR</u> (37/38, 13:1/2) Aut
        84, p. 55.
    "Flight." <u>Poetry</u> (145:1) O 84, p. 29-30.
    "The Girl in the Booth." <u>NegC</u> (4:4) Aut 84, p. 42-
        43.
    "Hair." <u>Swallow</u> (3) 84, p. 40.
    "The Impostors." <u>MissR</u> (37/38, 13:1/2) Aut 84, p.
        53.
    "The Limits of My Language." <u>MinnR</u> (N.S. 22) Spr
        84, p. 61-62.
    "Miss Denby." <u>MissR</u> (37/38, 13:1/2) Aut 84, p. 54.
    "The Pleasure Drive." <u>Swallow</u> (3) 84, p. 38-39.
    "Waiting for Sleep." <u>KanQ</u> (16:1/2) Wint-Spr 84,
        p. 95.

1570. FAIRCHOK, Sherry
    "The Last of the Herrigs." <u>Blueline</u> (5:2) Wint-
        Spr 84, p. 6.

1571. FAIRFIELD, C. J.
    "The Sleeping Earth." <u>LittleBR</u> (4:4) Sum 84, p. 39.

1572. FALCO, Edward
    "Jumping the Fence." <u>Telescope</u> (3:3) Aut 84, p.

102-103.

1573. FALK, Marcia
"Clouds." PoetC (16:1) Aut 84, p. 38.
"The Cutting Garden." PoetC (16:1) Aut 84, p. 35.
"Recovery." PoetC (16:1) Aut 84, p. 36.
"Smoke." YetASM (3) 84, p. 7.
"What Calls You Home." PoetC (16:1) Aut 84, p. 37.

1574. FALLEDER, Arnold
"William's Fantasy." DekalbLAJ (17:1/2) 84, p. 121.

1575. FALLON, Peter
"Home." Pequod (16/17) 84, p. 32.
"Nativity." Pequod (16/17) 84, p. 31.

FALTO, Evelyn Cole: See COLE FALTO, Evelyn

1576. FANDEL, John
"The medium white onion." Sparrow (46) 84, p. 10.
"When everything is new and works." Sparrow (46)
84, p. 10.

1577. FARBER, Norma
"Melchior's Monkey." ChrC (101:1) 4-11 Ja 84, p. 5.
"Prosody." CentR (28:1) Wint 84, p. 45.
"Some Poems." CentR (28:1) Wint 84, p. 45-46.

1578. FAREWELL, Patricia
"Learning from Trees." WestB (14) 84, p. 92.

1579. FARGAS, Laura
"Einstein at Princeton." Veloc (4) Sum 84, p. 23-24.
"Endings." Veloc (4) Sum 84, p. 25.

1580. FARMER, Paul
"Drought in Haiti." BelPoJ (34:3) Spr 84, p. 38-39.
"The Mango Lady" (for her children). BelPoJ
(34:3) Spr 84, p. 37-38.

1581. FARNSWORTH, Robert
"Rooms by the Sea." Ploughs (10:1) 84, p. 57-60.

1582. FARRELL, Katy
"The Limits Our Faces Feel." AntigR (57) Spr 84,
p. 18.

1583. FASEL, Ida
"An Invitation." Vis (16) 84, p. 31.

1584. FATISHA
"Elaborations." Stepping (Premier Issue) Sum 82,
p. 17-18.
"What's Left to Be Said?" Stepping (Premier
Issue) Sum 82, p. 14-16.

1585. FAUCHER, Real
"Land Grab in Bolivian Boom Town" (from an ad in
TIME, 12/7/81). Sam (39:1, release 153) 84, p.
35.

"The Velvet Blond." _Wind_ (14:50) 84, p. 11.

1586. FAULKNER, Leigh
"Kejimkujik." _AntigR_ (59) Aut 84, p. 48.
"Near Peggy's Cove." _AntigR_ (59) Aut 84, p. 47.

1587. FAUST, Clive
"The Faces in Cold." _Origin_ (5:3) Spr 84, p. 46.
"The Failures." _Origin_ (5:3) Spr 84, p. 44-45.
"Frost Breath." _Origin_ (5:3) Spr 84, p. 48.
"Keeping It Together." _Origin_ (5:3) Spr 84, p. 47-
48.
"Loosed from Music." _Origin_ (5:3) Spr 84, p. 47.
"Non-Options." _Origin_ (5:3) Spr 84, p. 46-47.
"Solo Concert." _Origin_ (5:3) Spr 84, p. 49-50.
"Thinking and Unsuccess." _Origin_ (5:3) Spr 84, p.
48-49.
"To Stop Thinking With." _Origin_ (5:3) Spr 84, p. 50.
"Worth Living." _Origin_ (5:3) Spr 84, p. 50-51.

1588. FAWCETT, Susan C.
"The Anorexic." _GreenfR_ (11:3/4) Wint-Spr 84, p.
147.
"Looking On" (For my brother David whose retina
tore on his 21st birthday). _GreenfR_ (11:3/4)
Wint-Spr 84, p. 146.

1589. FAY, Julie
"Delaying." _TarRP_ (24:1) Aut 84, p. 29-30.
"Provencal Laundry." _Poetry_ (144:2) My 84, p. 72-73.
"Self Portrait from Venice." _TarRP_ (24:1) Aut 84,
p. 28-29.
"The Stone Woman of Vence." _13thM_ (8:1/2) 84, p.
36-37.

1590. FEARING, Bruce
"Letter to Kenneth/Epistle to Pop." _Bound_ (12:1)
Aut 83, p. 69-80.

1591. FEDULLO, Mick
"Visiting Thomas at the State Hospital."
Telescope (3:2) Spr 84, p. 1-4.

1592. FEELA, David J.
"Father." _PoeticJ_ (6) 84, p. 2.

1593. FEENY, Thomas
"Northbound." _Wind_ (14:52) 84, p. 12-13.
"Springtime." _Wind_ (14:52) 84, p. 12.

1594. FEHLER, Gene L.
"Be Specific, Young Man." _Wind_ (14:52) 84, p. 14.

1595. FEIGERT, Don
"Indian in Tennis Shoes." _HiramPoR_ (36) Spr-Sum
84, p. 17.

1596. FEIJOO, Samuel
"Lake in Bucharest" (tr. by Kathleen Weaver).
MinnR (N.S. 22) Spr 84, p. 57.

1597. FEIN, Cheri
    "Crescent Line." Pequod (16/17) 84, p. 101-102.
    "Direction." Ploughs (10:1) 84, p. 61-62.
    "Venus Beats All." Ploughs (10:1) 84, p. 63-64.

1598. FEINSTEIN, Robert N.
    "La Cucaracha." PortR (30:1) 84, p. 137.

1599. FEIRSTEIN, Frederick
    "Blackout Holiday" (For Jeffrey Atlas). Ploughs
        (10:1) 84, p. 65-66.
    "Mustering Light: a Sequence." KenR (NS 6:3) Sum
        84, p. 67-75.

1600. FELD, Ross
    "On the Heights with You." Pequod (16/17) 84, p.
        135.

1601. FELDMAN, Al
    "I Quench My Thirst at the Gates of Havoc."
        GreenfR (12:1/2) Sum-Aut 84, p. 154.

1602. FELDMAN, Alan
    "Along the Banks of the Don." NewYorker (60:42) 3
        D 84, p. 48.
    "Dissolving the Boundaries." KenR (NS 6:4) Aut
        84, p. 82.
    "Inscrutable." KenR (NS 6:4) Aut 84, p. 82.
    "Self-Portrait." NoAmR (269:1) Mr 84, p. 40.

1603. FELDMAN, Irving
    "An Atlantiad." Shen (35:1) 83-84, p. 25-28.
    "The Judgment of Diana." GrandS (3:2) Wint 84, p.
        79-84.
    "Our Father." NewRep (189:23) 5 D 83, p. 24.
    "Read to the Animals, or Orpheus at the SPCA."
        Shen (35:2/3) 84, p. 124-127.
    "The Return of the Repressed." AmerS (53:3) Sum
        84, p. 350.
    "River." Shen (35:1) 83-84, p. 24-25.

1604. FELDMAN, Ruth
    "Seasons: A Round." SewanR (92:2) Ap-Je 84, p.
        199-200.
    "Shore Line: Boston-New York." CentR (28:4/29:1)
        Aut 84-Wint 85, p. 77.
    "Signorelli Frescoes: Orvieto." SewanR (92:2) Ap-
        Je 84, p. 201.

1605. FELICIANO MENDOZA, Ester
    "Mensaje por el Niño de el Salvador." Mairena
        (6:17) Aut 84, p. 31-32.
    "Nana del Limonero." Mairena (5:13) Spr 83, p. 96.

1606. FELICIANO SANCHEZ, Francisco
    "Arqueologia Divina." Mairena (5:13) Spr 83, p. 96.

1607. FELICIANO SANCHEZ, Jesús Francisco
    "Plenitud en Mi Dios." Mairena (5:13) Spr 83, p. 97.

1608. FELIPE, León
      "Cara o Cruz? Aguila o Sol?" Mairena (6:17) Aut
          84, p. 49-50.
      "El Poeta y el Filosofo." Mairena (6:17) Aut 84,
          p. 48-49.

1609. FELL, Mary
      "Driving in Fog." SouthernPR (24:1) Spr 84, p. 65.
      "How Blue Is It." SouthernPR (24:1) Spr 84, p. 65.
      "Indiana Suite." SouthernPR (24:1) Spr 84, p. 64-66.
      "Only Connect." SouthernPR (24:1) Spr 84, p. 64.
      "Still Life with Highway." SouthernPR (24:1) Spr
          84, p. 65-66.
      "Union Road." SouthernPR (24:1) Spr 84, p. 54.

1610. FELLOWES, Peter
      "Backyard Sabbath." TriQ (60) Spr-Sum 84, p. 323-
          324.

1611. FELSEN, Karl E.
      "I've Never Been to War." Pig (12) 84, p. 61.

1612. FELSTINER, John
      "Death fugue" (Written 1944-45, tr. of Paul Celan).
          NewRep (190:13) 2 Ap 84, p. 28.

1613. FENTON, James
      "Cambodia." GeoR (38:1) Spr 84, p. 168.
      "Lines for Translation into Any Language" (from
          Children in Exile: Poems 1968-1984). Harp
          (268:1608) My 84, p. 31.
      "Wind." NewYRB (31:16) 25 O 84, p. 40.

1614. FERBER, Al
      "Fabled and Mythed Apart." MoodySI (14) Spr 84,
          p. 9.
      "In the Murky Waters." BlueBldgs (8) 84?, p. 38.

1615. FERENCI, George
      "Jew Learning German." AntigR (56) Wint 84, p. 69.

1616. FERGUSON, Joseph
      "Light Will Be Always." CapeR (19:3) 20th
          Anniverary Issue 84, p. 15.

1617. FERLINGHETTI, Lawrence
      "History of the World: A TV Docu-Drama." EvergR
          (98) 84, p. 6-11.
      "Political Poem." Chelsea (42/43) 84, p. 61.

FERNANDEZ, Alvaro Lopez: See LOPEZ FERNANDEZ, Alvaro

1618. FERNANDEZ, Francisco de Asís
      "Let's Go, Comrades" (tr. by Marc Zimmerman and
          Ellen Banberger). MinnR (N.S. 22) Spr 84, p. 81.

FERNANDEZ, Jenri Suárez: See SUAREZ FERNANDEZ, Jenri

1619. FERNANDEZ, Raymond Ringo
      "Treasure Hunt: A Recurrent Dream." Stepping

(Anniversary Issue I) 84, p. 25.

1620. FERNANDEZ GILL, Alicia
"Veleidades de Dios." Mairena (5:13) Spr 83, p. 56.

1621. FERNANDEZ MORENO, César
"Contra el Viento." Mairena (6:18) 84, p. 113.

1622. FERNANDEZ RETAMAR, Roberto
"Quien Pueda Interesar (7)." Mairena (6:18) 84,
p. 171.

1623. FERRARELLI, Rina
"Shy." Wind (14:50) 84, p. 7.
"Steel City." Wind (14:50) 84, p. 7.

1624. FERRE, Rosario
"Pretalamio." Mairena (5:13) Spr 83, p. 97-98.

1625. FERREE, Joel
"Thanking Greater Powers." ChrC (101:28) 26 S 84,
p. 860.

1626. FERRY, David
"Young Woman." NewRep (191:12/13) 17-24 S 84, p. 34.

1627. FERTIG, Mona
"Call It Imagination." Waves (12:4) Spr 84, p. 47.
"Tree History." PoetryCR (6:1) Aut 84, p. 14.

1628. FETTMAN, Edward
"Breakfast" (tr. of Jacques Prevert). GreenfR
(11:1/2) Sum-Aut 83, p. 90.
"The Dunce" (tr. of Jacques Prevert). GreenfR
(11:1/2) Sum-Aut 83, p. 90-91.
"Home Life" (tr. of Jacques Prevert). GreenfR
(11:1/2) Sum-Aut 83, p. 91.

1629. FEYDER, Vera
"Identifying Marks" (from Ferrer le Sombre, tr.
by Louis A. Olivier and Lucia Cordell Getsi).
PikeF (6) Aut 84, p. 14.

1630. FEYERABEND, Barbara
"On His Own Prowess" (tr. of 'Antara). SenR
(14:1) 84, p. 34-35.
"On the Death of Her Brother" (tr. of al-Khansā
). SenR (14:1) 84, p. 36.
"Some Thoughts on Dying" (tr. of al-Ma'arrī).
SenR (14:1) 84, p. 31-33.
"Sonnets to Orpheus" (Selections: I.4, I.11, I.13,
I.14, I.17, I.20, II.5, II.20, II.25, tr. of
Rainer Maria Rilke). SenR (14:1) 84, p. 67-75.

1631. FIAMENGO, Marya
"Yes." CanLit (100) Spr 84, p. 103.

1632. FICKERT, Kurt J.
"Waiting for Apocalypse." PoeticJ (1) 83, p. 10.

1633. FICOWSKI, Jerzy
    "Forecast 1978" (tr. by Frank Corliss). Os (18)
        84, p. 25.
    "Prognoza 1978." Os (18) 84, p. 24.
    "Soveto." Os (18) 84, p. 23.
    "Soweto" (tr. by Frank Corliss). Os (18) 84, p. 23.

1634. FIELD, Crystal MacLean
    "Duchamp's Nude." NewL (50:2/3) Wint-Spr 84, p. 129.

1635. FIELD, Edward
    "Afghanistan." Shen (35:1) 83-84, p. 34-35.
    "Confessions of a Hypochondriac" (Excerpt).
        GrandS (3:4) Sum 84, p. 67.
    "Mae West." Telescope (3:3) Aut 84, p. 119-120.
    "The Return of Frankenstein." Telescope (3:3) Aut
        84, p. 117-118.
    "Stars in My Eyes." Chelsea (42/43) 84, p. 188-190.
    "To Poetry" (To the tune of An Die Musik by
        Schubert). KenR (NS 6:3) Sum 84, p. 48.

1636. FIELD, Greg
    "Home Cooking Cafe." NewL (50:2/3) Wint-Spr 84,
        p. 241.
    "Midnight in Anchorage." NewL (50:2/3) Wint-Spr
        84, p. 241.

1637. FIELD, James M.
    "Mad Magdalens and North American Holy Men"
        (Selections: 24, 18a). BlueBuf (2:2) Spr 84,
        p. 27.

1638. FIELD, S. F.
    "Weathering." SpoonRQ (9:4) Aut 84, p. 56.

1639. FIELDER, William
    "Elegy" (tr. of Kemal Ozer, w. Dionis Coffin Riggs
        and Ozcan Yalim). StoneC (11:3/4) Spr-Sum 84,
        p. 39.
    "Hegira" (tr. of Orhan Veli, w. Dionis Coffin Riggs
        and Ozcan Yalim). StoneC (11:3/4) Spr-Sum 84,
        p. 41.

1640. FIFER, Ken
    "After Fire." NewL (50:2/3) Wint-Spr 84, p. 245.
    "Somewhere Else You Are Getting Dressed." WebR
        (9:1) Spr 84, p. 83.

1641. FILIP, Raymond
    "Belladonna" (In memory of béla egyedi, 1913-
        1982). AntigR (58) Sum 84, p. 68.
    "Emile Nelligan's Navel." PoetryCR (5:4) Sum 84,
        p. 5.
    "Grand Prix Prayer Wheels." AntigR (59) Aut 84,
        p. 64.
    "Social Unrealism." CrossC (6:2) 84, p. 10.
    "Softening to Heaven." CrossC (6:2) 84, p. 10.

1642. FINALE, Frank
    "South River Girls." NegC (4:3) Sum 84, p. 9.

"Summer Recess." <u>Wind</u> (14:52) 84, p. 15.

1643. FINCH, Casey
"England." <u>Iowa</u> (14:3) Aut 84, p. 8-9.

1644. FINCH, Peter
"Difficult Words" (found poem). <u>Kayak</u> (64) My 84, p. 58.
"Hum, quietly" (found poem). <u>Kayak</u> (64) My 84, p. 58.

1645. FINCH, Roger
"The Affinity of Ghosts for Children." <u>Comm</u> (111:22) 14 D 84, p. 687.
"Alice Applies for a Job." <u>Comm</u> (111:22) 14 D 84, p. 687.
"B Is for Beast." <u>SoDakR</u> (22:2) Sum 84, p. 23.
"The Child in the Mirror." <u>CreamCR</u> (9:1/2) 84, p. 81.
"The Conquest of Peru." <u>Poem</u> (51) Mr [i.e. Jl] 84, p. 30-31.
"The Fight between the Jaguar and the Anteater." <u>LitR</u> (28:1) Aut 84, p. 65.
"The Flittermouse." <u>HiramPoR</u> (36) Spr-Sum 84, p. 18.
"Matthiola." <u>Waves</u> (12:1) Aut 83, p. 60.
"More Beautiful Than Beauty Itself." <u>KanQ</u> (16:1/2) Wint-Spr 84, p. 76-77.
"The Night-Scented Stock Opens in Bartok's <u>Music for Strings, Percussion and Celesta</u>." <u>Waves</u> (12:1) Aut 83, p. 61.
"On Looking into Chinggaltai's <u>Grammar of the Mongol Language</u>." <u>WormR</u> (24:4, issue 96) 84, p. 137.
"On Sunset Boulevard." <u>AntigR</u> (59) Aut 84, p. 19-20.
"On the Verandah." <u>WormR</u> (24:4, issue 96) 84, p. 136.
"Peacock on Top of the House" (Detail of an illustration from the manuscript of Amaru Sataka, Rajasthani School, Circa 1680 A.D.). <u>LitR</u> (27:2) Wint 84, p. 178-179.
"Piece of Shadow Work." <u>WebR</u> (9:2) Wint 85, p. 28-31.
"Private Performance" (by the Poulet Quartet at 102 Boulevard Haussmann, Paris, November, 1916). <u>AntigR</u> (59) Aut 84, p. 18-19.
"The Tree That Grew in Brooklyn." <u>FourQt</u> (33:4) Sum 84, p. 4.
"Voiced/Voiceless." <u>SoDakR</u> (22:2) Sum 84, p. 22.
"Vowel Harmony." <u>PoetL</u> (79:2) Sum 84, p. 102.
"Wealth Affords an Opulent Grief." <u>AntigR</u> (57) Spr 84, p. 88.
"What Is Written in Clouds." <u>AntigR</u> (59) Aut 84, p. 17.
"What Is Written in Clouds." <u>Sparrow</u> (47) 84, p. 4.
"What Is Written in Dust." <u>Sparrow</u> (47) 84, p. 6.
"What Is Written in Fields." <u>MichQR</u> (23:2) Spr 84, p. 268.
"What Is Written in Fields." <u>Sparrow</u> (47) 84, p. 3.
"What Is Written in Furniture." <u>Confr</u> (27/28) 84, p. 321.

"What Is Written in Furniture." _Sparrow_ (47) 84,
  p. 20.
"What Is Written in Gardens." _Sparrow_ (47) 84, p.
  18.
"What Is Written in Glass." _Sparrow_ (47) 84, p. 13.
"What Is Written in Leaves." _Sparrow_ (47) 84, p. 7.
"What Is Written in Mist." _Sparrow_ (47) 84, p. 5.
"What Is Written in Moonlight." _Sparrow_ (47) 84,
  p. 12.
"What Is Written in Pine Branches." _Sparrow_ (47)
  84, p. 14.
"What Is Written in Porcelain." _Sparrow_ (47) 84,
  p. 17.
"What Is Written in Rain." _Sparrow_ (47) 84, p. 11.
"What Is Written in Rooms." _Poem_ (51) Mr [i.e.
  Jl] 84, p. 29.
"What Is Written in Rooms." _Sparrow_ (47) 84, p. 19.
"What Is Written in Sand." _Sparrow_ (47) 84, p. 8.
"What Is Written in Stars." _Sparrow_ (47) 84, p. 16.
"What Is Written in Stone." _Sparrow_ (47) 84, p. 9.
"What Is Written in the Sky." _Sparrow_ (47) 84, p.
  10.
"What Is Written in the Wind" (Issue title,
  dedicated with sincere admiration and deepest
  admiration to May Sarton). _Sparrow_ (47) 84, p.
  1-23.
"What Is Written in the Wind." _Sparrow_ (47) 84,
  p. 1.
"What Is Written on the Ceiling." _Sparrow_ (47)
  84, p. 23.
"What Is Written on the Floor." _Sparrow_ (47) 84,
  p. 21-22.
"What Is Written on the Shore." _Sparrow_ (47) 84,
  p. 15.
"What Is Written on the Window." _Sparrow_ (47) 84,
  p. 2.

1646. FINCKE, Gary
  "Arson." _MemphisSR_ (5:1) Aut 84, p. 27.
  "Centralia." _BelPoJ_ (34:4) Sum 84, p. 34-39.
  "The End of Daylight Savings Time." _Amelia_ (1:2)
    O 84, p. 79.
  "Eyewitnesses." _SouthwR_ (69:3) Sum 84, p. 335.
  "The Famous in Selinsgrove." _PoetL_ (79:3) Aut 84,
    p. 140.
  "Fifteen." _Vis_ (14) 84, p. 33.
  "First Halley's Comet Poem" (October 16, 1982).
    CharR (10:1) Spr 84, p. 49.
  "Height." _LitR_ (28:1) Aut 84, p. 110-111.
  "The Last Day to Write Poems." _GreenfR_ (12:1/2)
    Sum-Aut 84, p. 106.
  "Late Friday." _Wind_ (14:51) 84, p. 12-13.
  "Life in One Place." _GreenfR_ (12:1/2) Sum-Aut 84,
    p. 107.
  "Love's Source." _MidAR_ (4:1) Spr 84, p. 45.
  "Night Work." _GrahamHR_ (7) Wint 84, p. 16-17.
  "The Record for Lost Sleep." _PoetL_ (79:3) Aut 84,
    p. 138.
  "Stalling." _GreenfR_ (12:1/2) Sum-Aut 84, p. 105.
  "Street Cleaning." _MemphisSR_ (5:1) Aut 84, p. 26.

"Suicide in Public." WestB (15) 84, p. 72-75.
"These Mornings." PoetL (79:3) Aut 84, p. 139.
"Walking on Every Street in Etna." Wind (14:51)
    84, p. 12.

1647. FINE, Beverly K.
"Autumn Lament." Amelia [1:1] Ap 84, p. 27.

1648. FINK, Robert A.
"The Story of Houses." SouthwR (69:1) Wint 84, p.
    60-61.

1649. FINK, Stan
"The Window." PoeticJ (3) 83, p. 34-35.

1650. FINKE, Gary
"The Coat in the Heart." BlueBldgs (7) 84, p. 6-7.

1651. FINKEL, Donald
"All We Need." ChiR (34:3) Sum 84, p. 21.
"Asiatic Day-Flower." Shen (35:2/3) 84, p. 127.
"The Detachable Man" (2 Selections). OntR (20)
    Spr-Sum 84, p. 35-36.
"Every Day Is the 4th of July." Kayak (64) My 84,
    p. 51.
"The Kindly Ones." GrandS (3:3) Spr 84, p. 15.
"The Lefthanded Juggler." Kayak (64) My 84, p. 50.
"The Lotus Eaters." Chelsea (42/43) 84, p. 102.
"Passing Go Again." OntR (20) Spr-Sum 84, p. 36.
"Salisbury Cathedral from the Bishop's Ground"
    (Constable, 1823). GrandS (3:3) Spr 84, p. 18.
"Savoring the Salt." OntR (20) Spr-Sum 84, p. 35.
"The Tenth Mu." Kayak (64) My 84, p. 51.

1652. FINKELSTEIN, Caroline
"Out of This Melancholy." SenR (14:2) 84, p. 33.

1653. FINLAY, Ian Hamilton
"Meditation." CreamCR (9:1/2) 84, p. 82.

1654. FINLEY, Michael
"At the Koin-o-Kleen." Paunch (57/58) Ja 84, p. 109.
"The Business of Bees." CarolQ (36:3) Spr 84, p. 56.
"The Business of Bees." Paunch (57/58) Ja 84, p.
    107.
"The Iliad." Abraxas (31/32) 84, p. 19.
"Trompe l'Oeil." Paunch (57/58) Ja 84, p. 108.

1655. FINN, Sherrill Morgan
"Birthmarks " YetASM (3) 84, p. 7.

1656. FINNEGAN, James
"Election Day." WebR (9:2) Wint 85, p. 51.
"Faulty Syntax of a Parade." WebR (9:2) Wint 85,
    p. 49-50.

1657. FINNELL, Dennis
"The Deposition." PraS (58:2) Sum 84, p. 73-74.
"Europe." NewEngR (6:4) Sum 84, p. 534.
"The Great Bear over Grand Junction, Colorado."

NewEngR (6:4) Sum 84, p. 535.
"Taking Leave of St. Louis." CharR (10:1) Spr 84,
    p. 65-69.
"Trespassing on McKenzie Creek." CharR (10:1) Spr
    84, p. 64.

1658. FIORENTINO, Hugo A.
    "La Herida de Tu Voz." Mairena (5:14) Aut 83, p. 78.

1659. FIRER, Susan
    "The Wildlife of Death" (for Andrew Firer). HangL
    (46) Aut 84, p. 24.

1660. FIRKINS, Terry
    "After Fall Fashions." Wind (14:50) 84, p. 12.

FIRMAT, Gustavo Pérez: See PEREZ FIRMAT, Gustavo

1661. FIRSCHING, Ellen P.
    "Change (five pennies)." AntigR (57) Spr 84, p.
    72-73.

1662. FIRST DRAFT
    "Scrapbook (Trio)." CapilR (31) 84, p. 32-33.

1663. FISCHER, Raymond P.
    "An Aged Man Remembers April." Poetry (144:1) Ap
    84, p. 39.
    "Time." Poetry (144:1) Ap 84, p. 39.

1664. FISET, Joan
    "Benediction." Ploughs (10:4) 84, p. 114-115.
    "Tomato Vines." BlueBldgs (8) 84?, p. 23.
    "Winter Horses." BlueBldgs (8) 84?, p. 23.

1665. FISH, Karen
    "The Bet: Horse in Motion." Telescope (3:3) Aut
    84, p. 60.
    "My Father Is the Frowning Boy." PoetC (16:1) Aut
    84, p. 19.
    "Venice, Widow in a Gondola 1891" (from a
    photograph by Count Primoli). AntR (42:1) Wint
    84, p. 92.
    "Wishbone" (for Beth & David). YaleR (73:2) Wint
    84, p. 262.

1666. FISHBURN, Katherine
    "Northern Lights." CentR (28:2) Spr 84, p. 108-109.

1667. FISHER, Harrison
    "The Eye at the Center of All Things." NegC (4:1)
    Wint 84, p. 25.

1668. FISHER, Lanette
    "Eviction Notice." San FPJ (6:3) 84, p. 81.

1669. FISHER, Nancy M.
    "Upon Reading Doctorow's Analysis of 1984 in
    Playboy, February 1983." Bogg (52) 84, p. 14.

1670. FISHER, Roy
"The Only Image." Gargoyle (24) 84, p. 98.
"Poem Not a Picture." Gargoyle (24) 84, p. 97.
"Talks for Words" (Excerpt). Gargoyle (24) 84, p.
99.

1671. FISHER, Sally
"Ash Wednesday Again." Spirit (7:1) 84, p. 156-158.
"The New Fish Store." PoetryE (15) Aut 84, p. 66.

1672. FISHER, Will
"Blueberry Juice." RagMag (3:1) Spr 84, p. 5.
"Without His Hat or Bandoleer." RagMag (3:1) Spr
84, p. 4.

1673. FISHMAN, Charles
"The Exit Past." GreenfR (11:1/2) Sum-Aut 83, p.
131.
"Song for the Relief Copters." Pig (12) 84, p. 36.

1674. FISHMAN, Nadell
"The Covenant." Tendril (17) Wint 84, p. 54.

1675. FITCH, Keith
"Blessed Be the Lunatic." PoetryCR (5:3) Spr 84,
p. 18.
"Byron." PoetryCR (5:3) Spr 84, p. 18.
"The Little Prince of Peace." PoetryCR (5:3) Spr
84, p. 18.

1676. FITTERMAN, Rob
"Again." Pequod (16/17) 84, p. 131-132.

1677. FITTERMAN, Robert
"Celia (1887-1971)." Abraxas (29/30) 84, p. 5-7.
"Celia (1887-1971)." Origin (5:3) Spr 84, p. 89-91.
"Cynic." Origin (5:3) Spr 84, p. 94.
"The Garden Cafeteria." Sulfur (4:1, issue 10)
84, p. 112-113.
"The Home." Sulfur (4:1, issue 10) 84, p. 111-112.
"The Lease." Origin (5:3) Spr 84, p. 88.
"Parked in a Hot Car." Origin (5:3) Spr 84, p. 93.
"Pictorial: Upper Volta." Origin (5:3) Spr 84, p.
92.
"The Shelter." Sulfur (4:1, issue 10) 84, p. 113-
114.
"Stalled Bus to Venice." Sulfur (4:1, issue 10)
84, p. 110.

1678. FITZGERALD, Frank S.
"Sunday morning love up." YellowS (13) Wint 84,
p. 12.

1679. FITZGERALD, Jim
"The Awakening" (tr. of Alejandra Pizarnik, w.
Frank Graziano). CharR (10:1) Spr 84, p. 72-73.
"Roads from the Mirror" (tr. of Alejandra Pizarnik,
w. Frank Graziano). CharR (10:1) Spr 84, p. 69-
71.

213 FLINTOFF

1680. FITZGERALD, Judith
"The Body Poetic." Waves (12:4) Spr 84, p. 35.
"Heart Act to Follow." Waves (12:4) Spr 84, p. 33.
"I read you, a novel" ("untitled"). Waves (12:4)
Spr 84, p. 32.
"Speech after Long Silence." Waves (12:4) Spr 84,
p. 36-37.
"Transformation of the Risen." Waves (12:4) Spr
84, p. 34.

1681. FITZGERALD, Robert
"Dedecora Temporum" (Written in 1968). PartR
(51:4/52:1 Anniversary issue) 84-85, p. 529.

1682. FITZMAURICE, Gabriel
"Playtime in the Village." CreamCR (9:1/2) 84, p.
63.

1683. FITZPATRICK, Vincent
"Rimbaud Walks on Foot." NegC (4:2) Spr 84, p. 59.

1684. FLANAGAN, Joanne
"The womb." Sam (41:1, release 161) 84, p. 2.

1685. FLANDERS, Jane
"Cloud Painter" (Suggested by the life and art of
John Constable). Poetry (144:5) Ag 84, p. 249-
250.
"The Fabulous Feats of Madame Houdini." LitR
(28:1) Aut 84, p. 47.
"The Geography of Children." LitR (28:1) Aut 84,
p. 48.
"Headgear from the American Collection" (Mid 20th
Century). WestB (14) 84, p. 38-39.
"The House That Fear Built: Warsaw, 1943."
Chelsea (42/43) 84, p. 435.
"Song of the Jaguar's Wife." LitR (28:1) Aut 84,
p. 49.
"Twirling." WestB (14) 84, p. 37.
"Wild Asters." Poetry (143:4) Ja 84, p. 233.

1686. FLANNER, Hildegarde
"The Feast." PoetryNW (25:2) Sum 84, p. 33-34.
"Few Four-Letter Words." PoetryNW (25:2) Sum 84,
p. 33.
"Homage at Twilight." Salm (65) Aut 84, p. 115.

1687. FLEESON, Tyler
"Dusk" (for Jayne Muirhead). IndR (7:3) Sum 84,
p. 12.

1688. FLEMING, Harold
"At 3 A.M." Wind (14:51) 84, p. 14.
"Now, Especially, No Stump." KanQ (16:1/2) Wint-
Spr 84, p. 75.

1689. FLINTOFF, Eddie
"In Memory of EW, 1st World Soldier, Socialist."
Bogg (52) 84, p. 57.

1690. FLOCK, Miriam
        "From the Dark Lady." GeoR (38:3) Aut 84, p. 484-
           486.

1691. FLOOK, Maria
        "Affidavit." Poetry (144:1) Ap 84, p. 32-33.

FLORES, Alberto Baeza: See BAEZA FLORES, Alberto

1692. FLORES, Angel
        "Untitled Poem (The Caseta Text)" (tr. of Pablo
           Picasso). PoetryE (13/14) Spr-Sum 84, p. 115-117.

1693. FLORES, Margarita Lopez
        "Sandra Cisneros: Leaving Town." SpoonRQ (9:2)
           Spr 84, p. 39.

1694. FLOSDORF, Jim
        "Taurus." Blueline (6:1) Sum-Aut 84, p. 41.

1695. FLYNN, David
        "Tom McAfee." Peb (23) 84, p. 11-12.

FOE, Mark de: See DeFOE, Mark

1696. FOERSTER, Richard
        "Body Surfing." Amelia (1:2) O 84, p. 50.
        "Crossing Over." TarRP (23:2) Spr 84, p. 35.
        "Fear of Earthquakes." SouthernHR (18:2) Spr 84,
           p. 164.
        "Sleep" (For Dana Gioia). Poetry (144:2) My 84,
           p. 79.

1697. FOLLAIN, Jean
        "Age" (tr. by W. S. Merwin). Chelsea (42/43) 84,
           p. 230.
        "Asia" (tr. by W. S. Merwin). Chelsea (42/43) 84,
           p. 231.
        "The Egg" (tr. by W. S. Merwin). Chelsea (42/43)
           84, p. 231.
        "Signs" (tr. by W. S. Merwin). Tendril (18,
           special issue) 84, p. 208.

1698. FOLLIN-JONES, Elizabeth
        "In the Singular." StoneC (12:1/2) Aut-Wint 84,
           p. 67-68.

1699. FONTAINE, Jean de la
        "Mutilation (Future Appealed To)" (tr. by Bruce
           Boone and Robert Glück). Tele (19) 83, p. 53.
        "Mystical Aspirations" (tr. by Bruce Boone and
           Robert Glück). Tele (19) 83, p. 51-52.

1700. FONTANA, Michael
        "Marathon in Rain." Vis (14) 84, p. 9.

1701. FONTENOT, Ken
        "The Conductors of the World." GreenfR (11:1/2)
           Sum-Aut 83, p. 99-100.
        "Family on My Mother's Side." GreenfR (11:1/2)

Sum—Aut 83, p. 101.
"School Days." NewL (51:1) Aut 84, p. 86.
"Thinking about Taniece Buried 1968 in St.
Augustine Churchyard." NewL (50:4) Sum 84, p. 56.

1702. FONVILLE, Dee
"Amnesia" (for Melanie). MemphisSR (4:2) Spr 84,
p. 26.
"The Gift." PoetryNW (25:4) Wint 84-85, p. 36-37.
"Psyche." PoetryNW (25:4) Wint 84-85, p. 35-36.

1703. FORD, Cathy
"Saffron, Rose & Flame" (from "the joan of arc
poems", a suite of one hundred poems based on
the life and works of Joan of Arc). Waves
(12:2/3) Wint 84, p. 64-65.
"Saffron, Rose & Flame" (The Joan of Arc poems: 3
excerpts). Dandel (11:2) Aut-Wint 84-85, p. 63-
65.

1704. FORD, William
"The Graveyard at Rochester, Iowa." KanQ (16:1/2)
Wint-Spr 84, p. 20.
"On Putting the Grandchild to Bed." Poetry
(143:6) Mr 84, p. 319.
"The Pimple." KanQ (16:1/2) Wint-Spr 84, p. 20-21.

FORGE, Christopher Lyle la: See LaFORGE, Christopher Lyle

1705. FORNOFF, Frederick H.
"Shadow?" (tr. of Julieta Dobles). Vis (15) 84,
p. 13-14.
"Solar Creed" (tr. of Laureano Alban). Vis (15)
84, p. 14.

1706. FORREST, Leon
"Richard Hunt's Jacob's Ladder." BlackALF (18:1)
Spr 84, p. 14-15.

1707. FORSTER, Louis
"Accepting Death." Swallow (3) 84, p. 89.
"Visiting Belleville for the Weekend." KanQ
(16:1/2) Wint-Spr 84, p. 191.

1708. FORTIN, Célyne
"Etait-ce une neige de fleurs." Os (18) 84, p. 3-4.

1709. FORTINI, Franco
"April 1961" (tr. by Lawrence R. Smith). PoetryE
(15) Aut 84, p. 74.
"One September Evening" (tr. by Lawrence R. Smith).
PoetryE (15) Aut 84, p. 73.

1710. FOSS, Phillip
"The Goat's Head." CharR (10:1) Spr 84, p. 36-38.

1711. FOSS, Phillip, Jr.
"Burning the Palms." GreenfR (11:1/2) Sum-Aut 83,
p. 138.
"The Shadow Emerging from the Night." GreenfR

(11:1/2) Sum-Aut 83, p. 139.

1712. FOSTER, Barbara
"Controlled Data." WritersL (2) 84, p. 7.

1713. FOSTER, Jeanne Robert
"The Game Protector." Blueline (6:1) Sum-Aut 84,
p. 6-7.

1714. FOSTER, Michael
"Tantrick." YellowS (13) Wint 84, p. 24.

1715. FOSTER, Robert
"Allisan's Desert." PoetryCR (5:4) Sum 84, p. 8.
"Bear Spell." Dandel (11:1) Spr-Sum 84, p. 32.
"Behind Mount Temple." Dandel (11:1) Spr-Sum 84,
p. 32.
"My Bears." Dandel (11:1) Spr-Sum 84, p. 33.
"Purgatorio: Canto I" (tr. of Dante). Quarry
(33:3) Sum 84, p. 43-47.
"Trapped in the Story." MalR (67) F 84, p. 112-113.

1716. FOSTER, Sesshu
"Easy Desktop Human Rights Policy for Bureaucrats
of the U.S. State Dept." SanFPJ (7:1) 84, p. 90.
"Photo." SanFPJ (7:1) 84, p. 91.

1717. FOUR HORSEMEN
"The Prose Tattoo: Selected Performance Scores"
(Selections). PoetryCR (5:3) Spr 84, p. 11.

1718. FOURNIER, Merci
"All the Reasons." Descant (47, 15:4) Wint 84, p.
131.
"When Summer Comes." Descant (47, 15:4) Wint 84,
p. 132.

1719. FOUSHEE, Sandra
"The Light That Stops Us." Ploughs (10:4) 84, p.
182-184.

1720. FOWLER, Adrian
"Fantasy on the Bridge at Upper Ferry." PoetryCR
(6:1) Aut 84, p. 16.

1721. FOWLER, Anne Carroll
"Missing Person." CalQ (25) Aut 84, p. 54.

1722. FOWLIE, Wallace
"The Inferno" (Selections: "Canto 4: Limbus, Canto
31: Giants, tr. of Dante). SouthernR (20:1)
Wint 84, p. 151-152.

1723. FOX, Connie
"Herzog II." Tele (19) 83, p. 22.
"Style." Tele (19) 83, p. 22.
"Wind across Walden." Tele (19) 83, p. 23.

1724. FOX, Dan
"Prayer Machine." Bogg (52) 84, p. 23.

1725. FOX, Gail
      "The Lady" (for Margaret Johnson Seeley).
      PoetryCR (6:2) Wint 84-85, p. 19.
      "The Poem Lives in My Head." PoetryCR (6:1) Aut
      84, p. 6.

1726. FOX, Heather
      "Napalm, Minh, and the Holy Ghost." SanFPJ (6:4)
      84, p. 36.

1727. FOX, Hugh
      "Ghost City and Los Viveres" (from La Cueva
      Sagrada). Abraxas (29/30) 84, p. 56-57.
      "I wanna reinvent my grandmother." GreenfR
      (11:1/2) Sum-Aut 83, p. 87-88.
      "Moon-Fever." NewL (51:1) Aut 84, p. 65.
      "Voices" (Excerpt). Spirit (7:1) 84, p. 112-113.

1728. FOX, Lucia
      "Ellos y Ellas: Poetas." ConcPo (17:2) Aut 84, p.
      180.
      "Male and Female Poets" (tr. by Michael Smith).
      ConcPo (17:2) Aut 84, p. 181.

1729. FOX, Nancy
      "Saturday Nights." FourQt (33:4) Sum 84, p. 27.

1730. FOY, John
      "Nice, Dec. 1983." PoetryCR (6:1) Aut 84, p. 3.
      "Telemachus." PoetryCR (5:3) Spr 84, p. 7.

1731. FRALEY, Michael
      "Beginnings." PoeticJ (5) 84, p. 2.
      "Emissary from Above." PoeticJ (6) 84, p. 36.

1732. FRANCIS, Robert
      "Gray Squirrel." MassR (25:1) Spr 84, p. 20.
      "Light and Shadow." MassR (25:1) Spr 84, p. 19.
      "The Nuthatch." MassR (25:1) Spr 84, p. 20-21.
      "Old Poet." MassR (25:1) Spr 84, p. 21.
      "The Pumpkin Man." MassR (25:1) Spr 84, p. 19.

1733. FRANCISCO, Edward
      "Requiescat" (For Emma Kate Gann -- 1908-1981).
      NeqC (4:1) Wint 84, p. 28-33.

1734. FRANK, Bernhard
      "The True Disciple" (tr. of Paul Verlaine).
      AntiqR (57) Spr 84, p. 25.
      "You Believe in Tea-Leaves" (tr. of Paul Verlaine).
      AntiqR (57) Spr 84, p. 27.

1735. FRANK, Ellen Eve
      "My Dog Is a Spiral Coming toward Me." Pequod
      (16/17) 84, p. 233-237.

1736. FRANKLIN, Walt
      "The Continual Farewell." PoeticJ (1) 83, p. 13-14.
      "Drunk Man Looks at Several Moons and Decides Which
      One Is Real." Vis (16) 84, p. 32.

"Hidden Farm Road." <u>Blueline</u> (6:1) Sum-Aut 84, p. 43.
"Meditation." <u>Blueline</u> (5:2) Wint-Spr 84, p. 19.
"Pastoral." <u>PoeticJ</u> (1) 83, p. 2.
"Romance." <u>PoeticJ</u> (5) 84, p. 13.
"Self-Directions to Christman Hollow" (In appreciation: W. W. Christman, 1865-1937). <u>Wind</u> (14:52) 84, p. 16.
"Wild Food." <u>Sam</u> (37:3, 147th release) 83, p. 18.

1737. FRANZEN, Cola
"The Door" (tr. of Saúl Yurkievich). <u>Mund</u> (14:2) 84, p. 87, 89.
"Rounds" (tr. of Saúl Yurkievich). <u>Mund</u> (14:2) 84, p. 89, 91.
"Why Bother to Read It" (tr. of Saúl Yurkievich). <u>Mund</u> (14:2) 84, p. 87.

1738. FRATE, Frank
"_ _ _ _ _ C.G." <u>Sam</u> (37:2, 146th release) 83, p. 6-7.
"_ _ _ _ _ _ g." <u>Sam</u> (37:2, 146th release) 83, p. 9.
"Bigfoot." <u>Sam</u> (37:2, 146th release) 83, p. 8.
"D.A.W.G." <u>Sam</u> (37:2, 146th release) 83, p. 4.
"Dog Days." <u>Sam</u> (37:2, 146th release) 83, p. 11.
"Junker." <u>Sam</u> (37:2, 146th release) 83, p. 2.
"Lucille." <u>Sam</u> (39:1, release 153) 84, p. 44.
"Millers." <u>Sam</u> (41:2, release 162) 84 or 85, p. 48.
"Obscurity." <u>Sam</u> (37:2, 146th release) 83, p. 12.
"Playing Catch." <u>Sam</u> (37:2, 146th release) 83, p. 3.
"Run - - R." <u>Sam</u> (37:2, 146th release) 83, p. 5.
"Watchers: Investigations IV." <u>Sam</u> (37:2, 146th release) 83, p. 1-12.
"Watchers." <u>Sam</u> (37:2, 146th release) 83, p. 10.

1739. FRATE, Frank C.
"Katy-Did." <u>CapeR</u> (19:2) Sum 84, p. 45.

1740. FRATICELLI, Marco
"Wind rattles the window." <u>CrossC</u> (6:1) 84, p. 21.

1741. FRATRIK, Julie
"Action." <u>Tendril</u> (17) Wint 84, p. 55.
"Advaita." <u>StoneC</u> (12:1/2) Aut-Wint 84, p. 23.

1742. FRAZEE, James
"Dead Man's Float." <u>Iowa</u> (14:3) Aut 84, p. 56.
"The Empty Swimming Pool." <u>Iowa</u> (14:3) Aut 84, p. 57.
"My Father's Lesson." <u>SouthernPR</u> (24:1) Spr 84, p. 8-9.

1743. FRAZIER, Robert
"Biochips." <u>Veloc</u> (2) Spr 83, p. 47.
"Co-Orbital Moons." <u>Veloc</u> (4) Sum 84, p. 20.

1744. FRECHETTE, Jean-Marc
"A Mère Meera." <u>Os</u> (18) 84, p. 18.

1745. FREDERICK, Steve
"Behind the Stone." SanFPJ (6:4) 84, p. 32.
"I See America." SanFPJ (6:4) 84, p. 29-30.

1746. FREEDMAN, Diane P.
"The Clink of Change on Trolleys." Ascent (9:2)
84, p. 17-18.
"Goose Watching in America." Ascent (9:2) 84, p.
16-17.

1747. FREEMAN, James A.
"On Picking Blueberries with My Grandmother for the
Last Time." Wind (14:52) 84, p. 17-18.

FREES, Madeline de: See DeFREES, Madeline

1748. FREISINGER, Randall R.
"Missouri Voices." CharR (10:1) Spr 84, p. 50.
"News Brief." KanQ (16:4) Aut 84, p. 4.
"Only Child." StoneC (12:1/2) Aut-Wint 84, p. 41.
"Plane Geomentry." BlueBldgs (8) 84?, p. 38.
"Running Patterns" (for Bruce). KanQ (16:4) Aut
84, p. 13.

1749. FRENAUD, André
"The Mirroring of Man through Beasts" (In tribute
to Jérôme Bosch, tr. by Michael Bishop).
AntigR (56) Wint 84, p. 120-124.

1750. FRENCH, Bryan
"My Favorite Place." RagMag (3:2) Aut 84, p. 44.

1751. FRENCH, Dayv James (See also JAMES-FRENCH, Dayv)
"The Aviary." MidAR (4:1) Spr 84, p. 127.

1752. FRETWELL, Kathy
"Georgian White Pine." PottPort (6) 84, p. 17.

1753. FREY, Cecelia
"The Man on the Winnipeg Couch." Quarry (33:4)
Aut 84, p. 22.
"To Speak Or." AntigR (59) Aut 84, p. 100.

1754. FREY, Charles
"Guanzhou." PraS (58:4) Wint 84, p. 69-70.
"My Father Enters the Presence of Silence." PraS
(58:4) Wint 84, p. 71.
"Noon that fat man." PraS (58:4) Wint 84, p. 69.

1755. FREY, Glenn
"James Dean" (w. Jackson Browne, Don Henley, and J.
D. Souther, 1974, Benchmark Music, ASCAP).
NewOR (11:3/4) Aut-Wint 84, p. 95.

1756. FRIAR, Kimon
"The Conjunction 'Or'" (tr. of Yánnis Rítsos).
AmerPoR (13:6) N-D 84, p. 25.
"Counterfeit" (tr. of Yánnis Rítsos). AmerPoR

(13:6) N-D 84, p. 26.
"Countryside" (tr. of Yánnis Rítsos). AmerPoR
(13:6) N-D 84, p. 24.
"Deterioration" (tr. of Yánnis Rítsos).
AmerPoR (13:6) N-D 84, p. 26.
"Encounter" (tr. of Yánnis Rítsos). AmerPoR
(13:6) N-D 84, p. 23.
"The Final Obel" (tr. of Yánnis Rítsos).
AmerPoR (13:6) N-D 84, p. 25.
"Forged Passport" (tr. of Yánnis Rítsos).
AmerPoR (13:6) N-D 84, p. 26.
"The Great Hypocrite" (tr. of Yánnis Rítsos).
AmerPoR (13:6) N-D 84, p. 27.
"Helen's House" (tr. of Yánnis Rítsos).
AmerPoR (13:6) N-D 84, p. 27.
"Known Consequences" (tr. of Yánnis Rítsos).
AmerPoR (13:6) N-D 84, p. 27.
"The Meaning of Simplicity" (tr. of Yánnis
Rítsos). AmerPoR (13:6) N-D 84, p. 23.
"The Models" (tr. of Yánnis Rítsos). AmerPoR
(13:6) N-D 84, p. 25.
"The Mountain's Daughter" (tr. of Yánnis
Rítsos). AmerPoR (13:6) N-D 84, p. 26.
"Nocturnal Episode" (tr. of Yánnis Rítsos).
AmerPoR (13:6) N-D 84, p. 26.
"Nocturne" (tr. of Yánnis Rítsos). AmerPoR
(13:6) N-D 84, p. 24.
"The Other Precision" (tr. of Yánnis Rítsos).
AmerPoR (13:6) N-D 84, p. 24.
"Partial Resignation" (tr. of Yánnis Rítsos).
AmerPoR (13:6) N-D 84, p. 26.
"The Relation of the Unrelated" (tr. of Yánnis
Rítsos). AmerPoR (13:6) N-D 84, p. 24.
"Reverential Comparison" (tr. of Yánnis
Rítsos). AmerPoR (13:6) N-D 84, p. 24.
"Silence" (tr. of Yánnis Rítsos). AmerPoR
(13:6) N-D 84, p. 24.
"Strange Times" (tr. of Yánnis Rítsos).
AmerPoR (13:6) N-D 84, p. 25.
"Stripped Naked" (tr. of Yánnis Rítsos).
AmerPoR (13:6) N-D 84, p. 27.
"Summer at Dhiminio" (tr. of Yánnis Rítsos).
AmerPoR (13:6) N-D 84, p. 24.
"Summer Noon at Karlóvasi" (tr. of Yánnis
Rítsos). AmerPoR (13:6) N-D 84, p. 24.
"Summer Sorrow" (tr. of Yánnis Rítsos).
AmerPoR (13:6) N-D 84, p. 27.
"The Unacceptable Man" (tr. of Yánnis Rítsos).
AmerPoR (13:6) N-D 84, p. 25.
"The Uncompromising" (tr. of Yánnis Rítsos).
AmerPoR (13:6) N-D 84, p. 25.
"Wells and People" (tr. of Yánnis Rítsos).
AmerPoR (13:6) N-D 84, p. 26.

1757. FRIEBERT, Stuart
"After the Accident " Sparrow (46) 84, p. 28.
"Daybreak, Summer 1962, American Cemetery,
Luxembourg." CapeR (19:3) 20th Anniverary
Issue 84, p. 16.
"Jane Goodall's Chimps Revert to Cannibalism."

MSS (4:1/2) Aut 84, p. 143-144.
"Lack of Maids" (tr. of Ilse Aichinger). Field
(31) Aut 84, p. 55.
"Lucky Signs" (tr. of Rainer Brambach). MidAR
(4:2) Aut 84, p. 69.
"March in Basel" (tr. of Rainer Brambach). MidAR
(4:2) Aut 84, p. 61.
"Men, Isolated, Unmarried" (tr. of Rainer
Brambach). MidAR (4:2) Aut 84, p. 65.
"Metamorphosis" (tr. of Georg Trakl). Field (30)
Spr 84, p. 66.
"One Day among Many" (tr. of Rainer Brambach).
IndR (7:3) Sum 84, p. 13.
"Plea" (tr. of Ilse Aichinger). Field (31) Aut
84, p. 53.
"Poesy" (tr. of Rainer Brambach). MidAR (4:2) Aut
84, p. 71.
"Reading" (tr. of Ilse Aichinger). Field (31) Aut
84, p. 54.
"Salt" (Translation Chapbook Series, Number Two,
tr. of Rainer Brambach). MidAR (4:2) Aut 84,
p. 59-76.
"Salt" (tr. of Rainer Brambach). MidAR (4:2) Aut
84, p. 67.
"So Long to the Eifel" (tr. of Rainer Brambach).
MidAR (4:2) Aut 84, p. 73.
"The Sudden Feeling Something's Wrong." WestB
(15) 84, p. 93.
"The Tornado Month." CapeR (19:3) 20th Anniverary
Issue 84, p. 17.
"Under Appletrees" (tr. of Rainer Brambach).
MidAR (4:2) Aut 84, p. 63.
"Wicked Game" (tr. of Rainer Brambach). MidAR
(4:2) Aut 84, p. 75.

1758. FRIED, Philip
"At This Instant All Over America." PoetL (79:2)
Sum 84, p. 99.
"Everyone's Humorous Uncle." PoetL (79:2) Sum 84,
p. 98.
"Scroll of Sky Unrolled." CreamCR (9:1/2) 84, p. 3.
"Waking Up I Raise." SouthernPR (24:2) Aut 84, p.
32.

1759. FRIEDMAN, Jeff
"Conch Shell." MSS (3:2/3) Spr 84, p. 126.
"Dogwood Petals." MSS (3:2/3) Spr 84, p. 124.
"For Karl Kline (1935-1971)." MSS (3:2/3) Spr 84,
p. 127-129.
"Jimmy Fendel's Elegy for the Laundromat Owner."
MSS (3:2/3) Spr 84, p. 130-131.
"New Territory." MSS (3:2/3) Spr 84, p. 123.
"Power of Attorney." MSS (3:2/3) Spr 84, p. 125.

1760. FRIEDMAN, Norman
"The Keepsake." Sam (41:1, release 161) 84, p. 6.

1761. FRIEDRICH, Paul
"All the Lost Sons." SpoonRQ (9:2) Spr 84, p. 58.
"I Thought I Saw Some Eskimos." Poem (52) N 84,

p. 5.
"Industrial Accident: Mexico." <u>Poem</u> (52) N 84, p. 6.
"The Tourist." <u>Poem</u> (52) N 84, p. 4.

1762. FRIEND, Robert
"Opening to the Light" (tr. of Gabriel Preil).
<u>Pequod</u> (16/17) 84, p. 118.

1763. FRIESEN, R. J.
"The Traveller." <u>WestCR</u> (19:2) O 84, p. 28.

1764. FRIGGIERI, Oliver
"To a Chilean Woman" (tr. of Lillian Sciberras).
<u>Vis</u> (15) 84, p. 38-39.

1765. FRIIS-BAASTAD, Erling
"Kari & Kerouac." <u>MoodySI</u> (14) Spr 84, p. 9.

1766. FRIMAN, Alice
"Orpheus and Eurydice in Spain, 1981." <u>PaintedB</u>
(21) Wint 84, p. 27-29.
"Plexus to Paul." <u>Confr</u> (27/28) 84, p. 195.

1767. FRITSCH, Janice
"Sleep" (tr. of Louise Herlin, w. Elton Glaser).
<u>WebR</u> (9:1) Spr 84, p. 94-95.

1768. FROSCH, Thomas
"Joshua." <u>DekalbLAJ</u> (17:1/2) 84, p. 121.
"Secrets." <u>DekalbLAJ</u> (17:1/2) 84, p. 122-123.

1769. FROST, Beth
"Child Gathering Stones at Dachau Memorial."
<u>Stepping</u> (Anniversary Issue I) 84, p. 26.

1770. FROST, Carol
"Album." <u>MissouriR</u> (7:3) 84, p. 13.
"The Day of the Body." <u>PraS</u> (58:1) Spr 84, p. 79-81.
"Deerhorns." <u>SenR</u> (14:1) 84, p. 24.
"Girl on a Scaffold." <u>Iowa</u> (14:3) Aut 84, p. 109-
110.
"How I Took Porcupine Quills Out of My Dog."
<u>StoneC</u> (11:3/4) Spr-Sum 84, p. 28.
"Mallard." <u>Tendril</u> (17) Wint 84, p. 57.
"The Migration of Butterflies." <u>MissouriR</u> (7:3)
84, p. 15.
"Punks." <u>Tendril</u> (17) Wint 84, p. 56.
"Roebuck, Jaeger & Farmer's Wife." <u>SenR</u> (14:1)
84, p. 23.
"To Kill a Deer." <u>MissouriR</u> (7:3) 84, p. 14.

1771. FROST, Celestine
"God's Law." <u>LittleM</u> (14:3) 84, p. 31.
"Night Fishing." <u>CrabCR</u> (2:1) Sum 84, p. 6-7.
"The Song." <u>LittleM</u> (14:3) 84, p. 32-33.

1772. FROST, Richard
"What I Did in the War." <u>CimR</u> (68) Jl 84, p. 43-44.

1773. FROST, Robert
    "Birches." <u>Shen</u> (35:2/3) 84, p. 468-469.
    "Hyla Brook." <u>Shen</u> (35:2/3) 84, p. 463.
    "Hyla Brook." <u>Tendril</u> (18, special issue) 84, p.
        256.
    "Out! Out!" <u>Hudson</u> (37:1) Spr 84, p. 62.
    "The Road Not Taken." <u>Tendril</u> (18, special issue)
        84, p. 262.

1774. FRUMKIN, Gene
    "Crises." <u>Chelsea</u> (42/43) 84, p. 437.
    "Disquiet of Reason." <u>Chelsea</u> (42/43) 84, p. 437.
    "The Explanation." <u>Chelsea</u> (42/43) 84, p. 436.
    "Faith." <u>Chelsea</u> (42/43) 84, p. 436.
    "Following." <u>Chelsea</u> (42/43) 84, p. 436.
    "Trick of Memory." <u>Chelsea</u> (42/43) 84, p. 437.

1775. FRY, Nan
    "Three Anglo-Saxon Riddles from <u>The Exeter Book</u>"
        (7, 34, 85, tr. of Anonymous). <u>CimR</u> (69) O 84,
        p. 56.

FU, Du: <u>See</u> DU ,Fu

FU, Tu: <u>See</u> DU ,Fu

1776. FUERTES, Gloria
    "Cabra Sola." <u>Mairena</u> (6:18) 84, p. 52.
    "Cuando Te Nombran." <u>Mairena</u> (6:18) 84, p. 61-62.

1777. FULLER, John
    "In a Railway Compartment." <u>Argo</u> (5:2) 84, p. 47.
    "Sorrel." <u>Argo</u> (5:2) 84, p. 49-50.

1778. FULLER, William
    "Cornea Borealis." <u>CreamCR</u> (9:1/2) 84, p. 32-33.

1779. FULTON, Alice
    "Aviation." <u>Poetry</u> (143:4) Ja 84, p. 207-209.
    "Babies." <u>Poetry</u> (143:4) Ja 84, p. 206-207.
    "My Second Marriage to My First Husband." <u>Poetry</u>
        (143:4) Ja 84, p. 205-206.
    "News of the Occluded Cyclone." <u>NewYorker</u> (60:7)
        2 Ap 84, p. 48.
    "Night Gold." <u>AntR</u> (42:4) Aut 84, p. 464.
    "Scumbling." <u>NewYorker</u> (60:19) 25 Je 84, p. 38.
    "Traveling Light." <u>Poetry</u> (143:4) Ja 84, p. 209-211.
    "Trouble." <u>PaintedB</u> (22) Spr 84, p. 15.

1780. FUNGE, Robert
    "John / Henry" (Excerpts). <u>CharR</u> (10:2) Aut 84,
        p. 73-76.
    "The Tale of a Dog" (from John / Henry). <u>SpoonRQ</u>
        (9:2) Spr 84, p. 55.

1781. FUNKHOUSER, Erica
    "Cryogenics." <u>Poetry</u> (145:3) D 84, p. 139-142.

1782. FUTORANSKY, Luisa
    "Mester de Hechiceria." <u>Mairena</u> (6:18) 84, p. 112.

1783. GABBARD, G. N.
      "R.S.V.P." <u>NewL</u> (50:2/3) Wint-Spr 84, p. 87.

1784. GADOL, Peter
      "Rondeau: Why Phillip Lascelle's Father Set Sail
      for France on August 24, 1922." <u>HarvardA</u>
      (117:4/118:1) D 84, p. 16.

1785. GAERTNER, Ken
      "Ink and Paint on Paper." <u>Comm</u> (111:14) 10 Ag 84,
      p. 443.

1786. GAFFNEY, Elizabeth
      "Reply to Iowa." <u>ColEng</u> (46:8) D 84, p. 796.

1787. GAGNON, Madeleine
      "Un Jour, la Ville." <u>Os</u> (19) 84, p. 9-13.

1788. GAISER, Carolyn
      "Il Mal'occhio." <u>Nat</u> (239:18) 1 D 84, p. 595.
      "Inflation." <u>Nat</u> (239:11) 13 O 84, p. 359.

1789. GALAN, Joaquin
      "Cenizal." <u>Mairena</u> (5:14) Aut 83, p. 90.

1790. GALASSI, Jonathan
      "After Ingres." <u>Pequod</u> (16/17) 84, p. 238-239.
      "At Montale's Grave." <u>Shen</u> (35:4) 84, p. 37.
      "Beloved of the Gods" (tr. of Eugenio Montale).
      <u>Thrpny</u> (19) Aut 84, p. 12.
      "Brooding" (tr. of Eugenio Montale). <u>ParisR</u>
      (26:92) Sum 84, p. 145.
      "Chords: Feelings and Fantasies of an Adolescent
      Girl" (tr. of Eugenio Montale). <u>Antaeus</u> (53)
      Aut 84, p. 84-88.
      "Clizia in '34" (tr. of Eugenio Montale). <u>ParisR</u>
      (26:92) Sum 84, p. 146.
      "Clizia Poems" (tr. of Eugenio Montale). <u>ParisR</u>
      (26:92) Sum 84, p. 145-151.
      "Credo" (tr. of Eugenio Montale). <u>ParisR</u> (26:92)
      Sum 84, p. 151.
      "Floating" (tr. of Eugenio Montale). <u>Antaeus</u> (53)
      Aut 84, p. 82-83.
      "Foursome" (tr. of Eugenio Montale). <u>ParisR</u>
      (26:92) Sum 84, p. 149.
      "The Hiding Places II" (tr. of Eugenio Montale).
      <u>PartR</u> (51:3) 84, p. 382-383.
      "I have such faith in you" (to C., tr. of Eugenio
      Montale). <u>NewYRB</u> (31:10) 14 Je 84, p. 4.
      "In '38" (tr. of Eugenio Montale). <u>ParisR</u> (26:92)
      Sum 84, p. 148.
      "Inside/Outside" (tr. of Eugenio Montale). <u>ParisR</u>
      (26:92) Sum 84, p. 147.
      "Let's go down the road that slopes among tangles
      of brambles" (tr. of Eugenio Montale). <u>Antaeus</u>
      (53) Aut 84, p. 89.
      "Levantine Letter" (tr. of Eugenio Montale).
      <u>Antaeus</u> (53) Aut 84, p. 78-81.
      "Predictions" (tr. of Eugenio Montale). <u>ParisR</u>
      (26:92) Sum 84, p. 146.

"Prose for A.M." (tr. of Eugenio Montale). Stand
    (25:3) Sum 84, p. 13.
"Since Life Is Fleeing" (tr. of Eugenio Montale).
    ParisR (26:92) Sum 84, p. 150.
"Southhampton." Shen (35:4) 84, p. 36.
"Still Life." Atlantic (254:4) O 84, p. 90.
"Winter Lingers On" (tr. of Eugenio Montale).
    Stand (25:3) Sum 84, p. 12.
"Zephyr." NewRep (191:10) 3 S 84, p. 34.

1791. GALEAS, Tulio
    "I See My Country" (tr. by William T. Lawlor).
        Vis (15) 84, p. 23.

GALINDO, José María Rius: See RIUS GALINDO, José María

1792. GALIOTO, Salvatore
    "Hear the Sky." SanFPJ (7:1) 84, p. 71.
    "Ms. Bag Lady." SanFPJ (6:3) 84, p. 76.
    "Musrooms." SanFPJ (6:1) 84, p. 18.
    "Negotiations." SanFPJ (6:3) 84, p. 74-75.
    "Post History." SanFPJ (6:1) 84, p. 19.
    "That Cube." SanFPJ (6:1) 84, p. 20.
    "What Hunter? II." SanFPJ (7:1) 84, p. 69.
    "Wine - Reflections and Perceptions." SanFPJ
        (7:1) 84, p. 70.

1793. GALLAGHER, Brian
    "Airplane Haiku." PaintedB (21) Wint 84, p. 14.

1794. GALLAGHER, Tess
    "Accomplishment." AmerPoR (13:2) Mr-Ap 84, p. 31.
    "Black Ships." AmerPoR (13:2) Mr-Ap 84, p. 31.
    "Black Silk." NewYorker (60:3) 5 Mr 84, p. 48.
    "Boat Ride." BlackWR (10:2) Spr 84, p. 40-45.
    "Boat Ride." Hudson (37:4) Wint 84-85, p. 657.
    "Conversation with a Fireman from Brooklyn." GeoR
        (38:3) Aut 84, p. 630.
    "Each Bird Walking." Nimrod (27:2) Spr-Sum 84, p.
        38-39.
    "Instructions to the Double." Nimrod (27:2) Spr-
        Sum 84, p. 35-36.
    "The Kneeling One." AmerPoR (13:2) Mr-Ap 84, p. 32.
    "Linoleum." AmerPoR (13:2) Mr-Ap 84, p. 32.
    "Not There." Nimrod (27:2) Spr-Sum 84, p. 44.
    "Skylights." Nimrod (27:2) Spr-Sum 84, p. 42.
    "Unsteady Yellow." Nimrod (27:2) Spr-Sum 84, p. 43.

1795. GALLER, David
    "Miss Kelly." Confr (27/28) 84, p. 177.

1796. GALLO, Philip
    "The Cougar." CapeR (19:3) 20th Anniversary Issue
        84, p. 18.

1797. GALVIN, Brendan
    "Beachplums." Ploughs (10:1) 84, p. 68-69.
    "Block Island Cowhorn." TriQ (61) Aut 84, p. 121.
    "Fall Squashes." Poetry (145:2) N 84, p. 65.
    "Finbacks." Ascent (9:3) 84, p. 33-34.

"The Last Man in the Quabbin" (1983 Narrative
    Poetry Prize). PoetL (79:1) Spr 84, p. 6-10.
"Light from Fundy." TriQ (61) Aut 84, p. 124.
"Mosquito Fleet." SouthernHR (18:4) Aut 84, p. 338.
"Night Ways." GeoR (38:1) Spr 84, p. 125-127.
"Old Woods Road." NewYorker (60:4) 12 Mr 84, p. 119.
"Rural Mailboxes." Ploughs (10:1) 84, p. 67.
"Those Times." PoetryNW (25:4) Wint 84-85, p. 12.
"Warmth." NewYorker (59:52) 13 F 84, p. 63.
"Weather Breeder." NewYorker (59:47) 9 Ja 84, p. 98.
"The Winter of Troubled Vision." PoetryNW (25:4)
    Wint 84-85, p. 9-11.
"Wreckers." TriQ (61) Aut 84, p. 122-123.

1798. GALVIN, James
    "Dark Angel." AmerPoR (13:1) Ja-F 84, p. 15.
    "For Our Better Graces." AmerPoR (13:1) Ja-F 84,
        p. 14.
    "The Importance of Green." AmerPoR (13:1) Ja-F
        84, p. 14.
    "Sentences for a Friend Snowed In." Atlantic
        (254:5) N 84, p. 100.
    "They Haven't Heard the West Is Over." AmerPoR
        (13:1) Ja-F 84, p. 14.
    "What Holds Them Apart." Antaeus (52) Apr 84, p.
        37-39.

1799. GALVIN, Martin
    "Legacy." CapeR (19:3) 20th Anniverary Issue 84,
        p. 19.
    "Making Beds." TexasR (5:1/2) Spr-Sum 84, p. 32.

1800. GANDER, Forrest
    "Ono No Komachi." HolCrit (21:2, i.e. 21:3) Je
        84, p. 19.

1801. GANDY, Maurice
    "The Philistine Woman." NeqC (4:1) Wint 84, p. 103.

1802. GANT, Shaun
    "Our Questions about Time Cleared." CutB (22) Spr-
        Sum 84, p. 42.

1803. GARBER, Darrell H.
    "Reaction to the Action Plan in Reaction to the
        Push for Excellence." EnqJ (73:6) O 84, p. 78.

1804. GARCIA, Luis Francisco
    "Mi Mas Preciado Lector." Mairena (6:17) Aut 84,
        p. 93.

GARCIA LORCA, Federico: See LORCA, Federico Garcia

1805. GARCIA ORTEGA, Adolfo
    "Vuelve el Extraño Olor de la Albahaca."
        Mairena (5:14) Aut 83, p. 84.

1806. GARCIA-SIMMS, Michael
    "The Answer." Telescope (3:1) Wint 84, p. 56.
    "Evening in the Adirondacks." Telescope (3:1)

Wint 84, p. 57.

1807. GARDNER, Geoffrey
"Dead Woman's Eyes" (tr. of Jules Supervielle).
NewL (50:2/3) Wint-Spr 84, p. 91.

1808. GARDNER, Isabella
"Card Island or Cod Island?" NewL (50:2/3) Wint-
Spr 84, p. 130-131.
"Nursery Rhymes for Vietnam." Chelsea (42/43) 84,
p. 200.

1809. GARDNER, John
"The Crocus." MSS (4:1/2) Aut 84, p. 331.
"The Fern." MSS (4:1/2) Aut 84, p. 332.
"The Gentian." MSS (4:1/2) Aut 84, p. 333.
"The Holly." MSS (4:1/2) Aut 84, p. 334.
"The Indian Pipe." MSS (4:1/2) Aut 84, p. 335.
"Lilacs." MSS (4:1/2) Aut 84, p. 336.
"My Brother." MSS (4:1/2) Aut 84, p. 232-233.
"The People Who Thought All Men Were Created Equal"
(circa 1949, age 16). MSS (4:1/2) Aut 84, p.
251-252.
"The Potato." MSS (4:1/2) Aut 84, p. 338.
"Queen Anne's Lace." MSS (4:1/2) Aut 84, p. 340.
"The Red Rose." MSS (4:1/2) Aut 84, p. 339.
"Snapdragons." MSS (4:1/2) Aut 84, p. 342.
"Thank you God" (circa 1943). MSS (4:1/2) Aut 84,
p. 250.
"The Thistle." MSS (4:1/2) Aut 84, p. 344.
"The Violet." MSS (4:1/2) Aut 84, p. 346.
"Xanthosma" (for Liz). MSS (4:1/2) Aut 84, p. 343.
"The Yucca." MSS (4:1/2) Aut 84, p. 347.

1810. GARDNER, Stephen
"Notebooks for a New World." Wind (14:50) 84, p.
13-14.

1811. GAREY, Terry A.
"Journey Galactic Voyager." Veloc (1) Sum 82, p. 29.

GARI, Enrique Sacerio: See SACERIO GARI, Enrique

1812. GARIBAY K., A. M.
"Song in Praise of the Chiefs" (Aztec, tr. of
Garibay K.'s Spanish version by Jerome
Rothenberg). Chelsea (42/43) 84, p. 246-247.
"Song of an Initiate" (Huichol, Mexico, tr. of
Garibay K.'s Spanish version by Jerome
Rothenberg). Chelsea (42/43) 84, p. 245.

1813. GARIN, Marita
"Shell." SouthernHR (18:3) Sum 84, p. 244.
"Stone Rubbing" ("Together in death"). IndR (7:2)
Spr 84, p. 47.

1814. GARMANIAN, Steven
"The Sapsucker." KanQ (16:1/2) Wint-Spr 84, p. 152.
"Wind-Chime." KanQ (16:1/2) Wint-Spr 84, p. 153.

1815. GARMON, John
        "Premonitions." <u>Wind</u> (14:52) 84, p. 19.
        "Silences Made of Single Words." <u>KanQ</u> (16:1/2)
            Wint-Spr 84, p. 160-161.
        "What Is Most Needed." <u>Wind</u> (14:52) 84, p. 19-20.

1816. GARNETT, Ruth M.
        "Trump." <u>Stepping</u> (Premier Issue) Sum 82, p. 19-21.

1817. GARRETT, Edward Cortez
        "The Wake." <u>ThirdW</u> (2) Spr 84, p. 15.

1818. GARRETT, George
        "Dialoge." <u>TexasR</u> (5:3/4) Aut-Wint 84, p. 115.

1819. GARRIGUE, Jean
        "Fourth Declamation (Police of the Dead Day)."
            <u>Chelsea</u> (42/43) 84, p. 72.

1820. GARTON, Victoria
        "Roofer on the Courthouse Spire." <u>CapeR</u> (19:3)
            20th Anniverary Issue 84, p. 20.
        "Small Mystery." <u>RagMag</u> (3:2) Aut 84, p. 14.
        "So Many Selves." <u>RagMag</u> (3:2) Aut 84, p. 14.

1821. GARVER, Dan
        "At the University of Melancholy." <u>IndR</u> (7:2) Spr
            84, p. 46.

GASCON, Antonio Ramos: <u>See</u> RAMOS GASCON, Antonio

1822. GASKELL, Ronald
        "Caesar." <u>Poetry</u> (143:6) Mr 84, p. 334-336.

1823. GASPAR, Frank
        "Waking." <u>MassR</u> (25:3) Aut 84, p. 455-456.

1824. GASPAR-HADADI, Litha
        "Sweet, Oh my Savila." <u>YellowS</u> (10) Spr 84, p. 34.

1825. GASPARINI, Len
        "Still Life." <u>CanLit</u> (100) Spr 84, p. 118.

1826. GASTIGER, Joseph
        "Belladonna." <u>TriQ</u> (61) Aut 84, p. 96.
        "It's a Gift." <u>SpoonRQ</u> (9:2) Spr 84, p. 32.
        "Undated Snapshot, Tucked in a Secondhand Book."
            <u>TriQ</u> (61) Aut 84, p. 94-95.

1827. GASTON, Bill
        "Sex Is Red #3." <u>AntigR</u> (56) Wint 84, p. 14.
        "Silver Pennies." <u>AntigR</u> (56) Wint 84, p. 14.

1828. GATENBY, Greg
        "Opus Sectile" (for N.H.). <u>Descant</u> (47, 15:4)
            Wint 84, p. 72.
        "Storm at Varna." <u>Descant</u> (47, 15:4) Wint 84, p. 73.

GATTUTA, Margo la: <u>See</u> LaGATTUTA, Margo

1829. GAUER, Jim
"There Go the Sheep." Pequod (16/17) 84, p. 226.

1830. GAUGER, Jan
"Nothing to Remember You By." NewL (50:2/3) Wint-
Spr 84, p. 137.

1831. GAUTIER, Théophile
"To a Rose Dress: A Translation from Théophile
Gautier" (by Michael L. Johnson). KanQ (16:3)
Sum 84, p. 89.

1832. GAVIRIO, Victor
"Comprehension" (in Spanish). BlackWR (10:2) Spr
84, p. 36.
"Comprehension" (tr. by Patsy Boyer and Mary Crow).
BlackWR (10:2) Spr 84, p. 37.

1833. GAVRONSKY, Serge
"To New York" (for jazz orchestra: trumpet solo,
tr. of Léopold Sédar Senghor). Chelsea
(42/43) 84, p. 242-244.

1834. GAZZOLO, Ana María
"De los trenes aprendo a no quedarme." Mairena
(6:16) Spr 84, p. 81.
"Poema: Aroma amargo." Mairena (6:18) 84, p. 99.
"Tierra roja donde madura la lluvia." Mairena
(6:16) Spr 84, p. 82.
"Traspasaste el domingo." Mairena (6:16) Spr 84,
p. 81.
"Volver como la lluvia." Mairena (6:16) Spr 84,
p. 82.

1835. GEARY, Annette
"Missouri at Flood-Time." CapeR (19:3) 20th
Anniverary Issue 84, p. 21.
"Playground in March." CapeR (19:3) 20th
Anniverary Issue 84, p. 22.

1836. GEIER, Joan Austin
"Great-Grandparents Wedding Portrait." PoeticJ
(4) 83, p. 26.

1837. GEIGER, Geoff
"Appearance & Reality." Sam (37:4, 148th release)
83 or 84, p. 13.
"Death of Burns." Sam (37:4, 148th release) 83 or
84, p. 5.
"Decade" (prose & poetry). Sam (37:4, 148th
release) 83 or 84, p. 1-14.
"Just Another Disaster." Sam (37:4, 148th
release) 83 or 84, p. 14.
"Nostalgia." Sam (37:4, 148th release) 83 or 84,
p. 13.
"The Promise." Sam (37:4, 148th release) 83 or
84, p. 8.
"Rose Garden." Sam (37:4, 148th release) 83 or
84, back cover.

1838. GEISER, Patricia
      "In These." EngJ (73:3) Mr 84, p. 107.

1839. GELBURD, Sue Russell
      "I Sang on National Television with Wayne Newton on
      December 24, 1970." YetASM (3) 84, p. 3.

1840. GELETA, Greg
      "Old Lady Cutler." Wind (14:51) 84, p. 15.

1841. GELLIS, Barrie
      "Ode on Sex and Religion." YellowS (13) Wint 84,
      p. 10.

1842. GELMAN, Juan
      "Arte Poetica." Mairena (6:18) 84, p. 111.

1843. GENCO, Irene Haupel
      "Calling." ChrC (101:35) 14 N 84, p. 1052.

1844. GENDERNALIK, Alfred L.
      "I Seen It." EngJ (73:8) D 84, p. 42.

1845. GENEGA, Paul
      "Change of Scenery." LitR (27:2) Wint 84, p. 182.
      "The Crayfish." LitR (27:2) Wint 84, p. 183.
      "Indoor / Outdoor." WebR (9:2) Wint 85, p. 101-102.

GENNARO, Lorraine S. de: See DeGENNARO, Lorraine S.

1846. GENT, Andrew
      "Orphan." BlueBldgs (7) 84, p. 17.
      "Tenth Elegy" (w. Bill Evans). HangL (46) Aut 84,
      p. 19-23.

1847. GENTLEMAN, Dorothy Corbett
      "The Call." Quarry (33:4) Aut 84, p. 37-38.
      "I Remember." Quarry (33:4) Aut 84, p. 37.

1848. GENYE, Luo
      "I Am Discontented." Harp (268:1609) Je 84, p. 28.

1849. GEORGE, Ann
      "Summer Painting." SouthernPR (24:1) Spr 84, p. 14.

1850. GEORGE, Christopher T.
      "Lawrence of Arabia." Open24 (3) 84, p. 21.

1851. GERBER, Dan
      "Journal Entry." Peb (23) 84, p. 15.
      "No Tongue, No Body, No Mind." Pequod (16/17) 84,
      p. 98.
      "Waiting for the Turtle to Die." Pequod (16/17)
      84, p. 99.

1852. GERGELY, Agnes
      "Joan of Arc: A Sonnet Sequence" (tr. by the author
      and Larry Levis). 13thM (8:1/2) 84, p. 102-109.

1853. GERMAN, Norman
"The Ancient of Days." <u>SanFPJ</u> (6:4) 84, p. 56.
"I'm Not Into Nothingness" (allegro). <u>SanFPJ</u>
(6:4) 84, p. 53.
"Last Honeymoon." <u>CEACritic</u> (46:1/2) Aut-Wint 83-
84, p. 33.
"Negative Capability." <u>CEACritic</u> (46:1/2) Aut-
Wint 83-84, p. 32-33.
"The Wheat Field behind Dolby Elementary."
<u>CEACritic</u> (46:1/2) Aut-Wint 83-84, p. 32.

1854. GERMANAKOS, N. C.
"Romiosini" (Selection: II, tr. of Yannis Ritsos).
<u>Chelsea</u> (42/43) 84, p. 249-251.

1855. GERSHGOREN, Sid
"Little Wind: 27 New Proverbs." <u>CalQ</u> (25) Aut 84,
p. 56-57.

1856. GERSTEIN, Martin
"Razor to the throat." <u>YetASM</u> (3) 84, p. 3.

1857. GERSTEIN, Marvin
"April/Watch/Greece." <u>NegC</u> (4:2) Spr 84, p. 27.

1858. GERSTLE, Val
"I Miss the Yearly Pumpkin." <u>Wind</u> (14:51) 84, p. 16.
"Playing Pin the Tail on the Donkey at Tommy
Yager's Birthday Party." <u>Wind</u> (14:51) 84, p.
16-17.

1859. GERY, John
"The Arbitrary Edge." <u>SoDakR</u> (22:4) Wint 84, p.
86-87.
"Day in the Country." <u>Swallow</u> (3) 84, p. 75.
"The Enemies of Leisure." <u>SoDakR</u> (22:4) Wint 84,
p. 88-89.
"The Fat Lady at the Liquor Store." <u>Swallow</u> (3)
84, p. 76-77.

1860. GETSI, Lucia
"Bottleships." <u>HiramPoR</u> (37) Aut-Wint 84, p. 20-21.
"Class of 1925, Illinois Normal College." <u>SpoonRQ</u>
(9:4) Aut 84, p. 20-21.
"Why I Have to Sell Our Mare." <u>HiramPoR</u> (37) Aut-
Wint 84, p. 17-19.

1861. GETSI, Lucia Cordell
"Identifying Marks" (from <u>Ferrer</u> <u>le</u> <u>Sombre</u>, tr.
of Vera Feyder, w. Louis A. Olivier). <u>PikeF</u>
(6) Aut 84, p. 14.

1862. GETTY, Sarah
"Sit. Anx. Reg. Fert." <u>Shen</u> (35:4) 84, p. 58-61.

1863. GHAI, Gail
"Poem for Patrick" (A mentally retarded child).
<u>PoeticJ</u> (8) 84, p. 12.

1864. GHIGNA, Charles
       "The Bass Fisherman." NegC (4:1) Wint 84, p. 99.

1865. GHIMOSOULIS, Kostís
       "The Survivors. What Became of Them? Who Was the
          Drowned Man?" (in Greek). Argo (5:3) 84, p. 6.
       "The Survivors. What Became of Them? Who Was the
          Drowned Man?" (tr. by Yannis Goumas). Argo
          (5:3) 84, p. 6.
       "To That Dark Handsome Youth Named Death" (in
          Greek). Argo (5:3) 84, p. 6.
       "To That Dark Handsome Youth Named Death" (tr. by
          Yannis Goumas). Argo (5:3) 84, p. 6.

1866. GHITELMAN, David
       "Silver Lake." Agni (21) 84, p. 99-100.

1867. GIACOMELLI, Eloah T.
       "The Horse in the Garden" (tr. of Cassiano
          Ricardo). AntigR (59) Aut 84, p. 120.

1868. GIAMMARINO, Jaye
       "Pops." PoeticJ (2) 83, p. 3.

1869. GIBB, Robert
       "Annulus." WindO (44) Sum-Aut 84, p. 19.
       "Blues for December 21st." Poetry (145:3) D 84,
          p. 127-128.
       "Coming into the Body." Poetry (145:3) D 84, p.
          128-129.
       "Entering Time in a House Photographed by Walker
          Evans." NewL (50:2/3) Wint-Spr 84, p. 76-77.
       "Homestead Park." HiramPoR (37) Aut-Wint 84, p. 24.
       "January." BlueBldgs (7) 84, p. 13.
       "Late Harvest." WindO (44) Sum-Aut 84, p. 20.
       "Lines in a Slow Thaw." Poetry (145:3) D 84, p.
          129-131.
       "March." GrahamHR (7) Wint 84, p. 26-27.
       "Memory: A Poem for a Möbius Strip." HiramPoR
          (37) Aut-Wint 84, p. 22-23.
       "The Return." Wind (14:50) 84, p. 17-18.
       "Song for My Father." NewL (51:1) Aut 84, p. 92-93.
       "Stems." Wind (14:50) 84, p. 15-16.
       "Vespers." SnapD (7:1) Aut 83, p. 60.
       "Weeds." SnapD (7:1) Aut 83, p. 58-59.
       "What the Heart Can Bear." Wind (14:50) 84, p. 16-
          17.

1870. GIBBONS, Reginald
       "Conversation" (tr. of Jaime Gil de Biedma). TriQ
          (59) Wint 84, p. 202.
       "The Eager Interpreter" (for Gloria.). YaleR
          (74:1) Aut 84, p. 27-29.
       "Eating." NewRep (189:27) 31 D 83, p. 34.
       "Family Chronicle" (tr. of Lázaro Santana).
          TriQ (59) Wint 84, p. 215.
       "Industrial Venus" (tr. of Fernando Quiñones).
          TriQ (59) Wint 84, p. 217-218.
       "Inherited Glories" (tr. of J. M. Caballero
          Bonald). TriQ (59) Wint 84, p. 205.

"Out of the World" (tr. of Jorge Guillén). TriQ
    (59) Wint 84, p. 223-226.
"P.S." (tr. of Lázaro Santana). TriQ (59) Wint
    84, p. 216.
"Services Lent" (tr. of J. M. Caballero Bonald).
    TriQ (59) Wint 84, p. 207.
"Supplantings" (tr. of J. M. Caballero Bonald).
    TriQ (59) Wint 84, p. 206.
"The Uselessness of Antidotes" (tr. of J. M.
    Caballero Bonald). TriQ (59) Wint 84, p. 208.

1871. GIBBONS, Robert
    "Sestina of the Singing Wind." NegC (4:3) Sum 84,
        p. 92-93.

1872. GIBBS, Robert
    "Who Asked Me to Be a Reader of Entrails?" CanLit
        (100) Spr 84, p. 119.

1873. GIBBS, Tom
    "The Rose." PoeticJ (8) 84, p. 37.

1874. GIBSON, Becky Gould
    "Her House" (for Bill). Wind (14:50) 84, p. 20-21.
    "Wife's Message." Wind (14:50) 84, p. 19-20.

1875. GIBSON, Margaret
    "From a Single Center." NewEngR (7:1) Aut 84, p.
        117-119.

1876. GIBSON, Stephen L.
    "Ahab in a VW Rabbit." ThirdW (2) Spr 84, p. 77.

1877. GIL de BIEDMA, Jaime
    "Body Is Man's Best Friend" (tr. by Richard
        Sanger). TriQ (59) Wint 84, p. 203.
    "Conversation" (tr. by Reginald Gibbons). TriQ
        (59) Wint 84, p. 202.
    "Le Prince d'Aquitaine a la Tour Abolie" (tr. by
        Richard Sanger). TriQ (59) Wint 84, p. 204.

1878. GILBERT, Virginia
    "Caught in a Bad Time." MSS (4:1/2) Aut 84, p. 64-
        65.

1879. GILBOA, Amir
    "When I Said I Shall Wait" (tr. by Miriam Arad).
        Pequod (16/17) 84, p. 114.

1880. GILDNER, Gary
    "Clackamas." NewEngR (7:1) Aut 84, p. 86-89.
    "First Practice." Tendril (18, special issue) 84,
        p. 20-21.
    "Go Ahead, She Said." Shen (35:1) 83-84, p. 99.

GILL, Alicia Fernández: See FERNANDEZ GILL, Alicia

1881. GILL, Barbara
    "Atomic Sunset" (for our children). SanFPJ (6:4)
        84, p. 7.

"Cultured City." <u>SanFPJ</u> (6:4) 84, p. 26.
"Dream Breakers." <u>SanFPJ</u> (6:4) 84, p. 26.
"Listening to Rose Gallagher." <u>PoeticJ</u> (7) 84, p.
    20.

1882. GILL, Michael J.
    "The Lover's Calendar." <u>HiramPoR</u> (36) Spr-Sum 84,
        p. 19-21.

1883. GILL, Stephen
    "Do Not Depart." <u>WritersL</u> (1) 84, p. 27.
    "Gorious Dawn." <u>WritersL</u> (2) 84, p. 27.

1884. GILLAN, Maria
    "To My Sister." <u>Vis</u> (16) 84, p. 20.

1885. GILLETT, J. T.
    "Fear of Nuclei." <u>YetASM</u> (3) 84, p. 8.

1886. GILLUM, Richard F.
    "Radio Evangelists." <u>ChrC</u> (101:27) 12-19 S 84, p.
        840.

1887. GILPIN, Laura
    "The Bath." <u>Poetry</u> (144:2) My 84, p. 71.

1888. GIMFERRER, Pedro
    "Canto." <u>Mairena</u> (6:18) 84, p. 67.

1889. GINSBERG, Allen
    "Some Writing from a Journal (1959, NY)." <u>Chelsea</u>
        (42/43) 84, p. 70-71.

1890. GINSBERG, David
    "Remnant Mother." <u>DekalbLAJ</u> (17:1/2) 84, p. 123-124.

1891. GINTER, Laurel
    "Quilled on Baxter Mountain." <u>HolCrit</u> (21:2) Ap
        84, p. 16.

1892. GIOIA, Dana
    "Eastern Standard Time." <u>Hudson</u> (37:3) Aut 84, p.
        421-423.
    "His Three Women." <u>Hudson</u> (37:3) Aut 84, p. 423-424.
    "Parts of Summer Weather." <u>Hudson</u> (37:3) Aut 84,
        p. 425.
    "Song from an Open Window" (Rome, 1977, for Harry
        Craig, 1921-1978). <u>NewEngR</u> (7:1) Aut 84, p. 99-
        100.
    "Speech from a Novella." <u>NewYorker</u> (60:23) 23 Jl
        84, p. 32.

GIOVANNI, Norman Thomas di: <u>See</u> Di GIOVANNI, Norman Thomas

1893. GIRARD, Linda Walvoord
    "Back Country" (for Thomas Hardy). <u>SpoonRQ</u> (9:2)
        Spr 84, p. 8.
    "Meeting the 5:27." <u>SpoonRQ</u> (9:2) Spr 84, p. 10.
    "Red Riding Hood." <u>Nimrod</u> (27:2) Spr-Sum 84, p. 45.
    "You, Coming Home." <u>SpoonRQ</u> (9:2) Spr 84, p. 9.

1894. GITLIN, Todd
"The Visitor" (After Anna Akhmatova). CalQ (25)
Aut 84, p. 31.

1895. GITZEN, Julian
"White-Tailed Deer." TexasR (5:1/2) Spr-Sum 84,
p. 66-67.

1896. GIUDICI, Giovanni
"Advice from a Depressed Area" (tr. by Lawrence R.
Smith). PoetryE (15) Aut 84, p. 75.
"Woman" (tr. by Lawrence R. Smith). PoetryE (15)
Aut 84, p. 76.

1897. GIULIANI, Alfredo
"Childish Canzonetta" (tr. by Lawrence R. Smith).
PoetryE (15) Aut 84, p. 77.
"Convalescence" (tr. by Lawrence R. Smith).
PoetryE (15) Aut 84, p. 78.

1898. GLANCY, Diane
"Anny Tarpley." WebR (9:2) Wint 85, p. 52.
"Astoria Boulevard." HiramPoR (36) Spr-Sum 84, p.
22.
"Legend." Spirit (7:1) 84, p. 134.

1899. GLASER, Elton
"Ah the Lovely Holidays" (tr. of Raymond Queneau).
CharR (10:2) Aut 84, p. 93.
"Doctor Snow." LittleM (14:3) 84, p. 25.
"Holograms of the Holy." PoetryNW (25:1) Spr 84,
p. 45-46.
"Prophecy for Yesterday" (tr. of Raymond Queneau).
CharR (10:2) Aut 84, p. 93-94.
"Sleep" (tr. of Louise Herlin, w. Janice Fritsch).
WebR (9:1) Spr 84, p. 94-95.
"Storm Damage." ChiR (34:3) Sum 84, p. 48.

1900. GLASER, Michael
"Husbands." Sam (37:3, 147th release) 83, p. 40.

1901. GLASER, Michael S.
"Images." ChrC (101:18) 23 My 84, p. 548.
"Prayer." Poem (50) Mr 84, p. 25.
"Rearranging the Kitchen." Poem (50) Mr 84, p. 26.
"Secrets." Poem (50) Mr 84, p. 27.
"Sense of Freedom." WoosterR (1:2) N 84, p. 22.

1902. GLASS, Jesse
"The Cannon." NewL (51:1) Aut 84, p. 44-45.
"Madonna." NewL (51:1) Aut 84, p. 43.

1903. GLASS, Jesse, Jr.
"Fireman's Carnival." PoetC (15:3) 84, p. 33.
"Frost." SpoonRQ (9:2) Spr 84, p. 24.
"Going." SpoonRQ (9:2) Spr 84, p. 24.
"In the City." SpoonRQ (9:2) Spr 84, p. 25.
"Mayakovsky Is Dead." Gargoyle (24) 84, p. 132-135.

1904. GLASS, Malcolm
"Box Love." <u>PoetC</u> (15:2) Wint 84, p. 18-19.
"Gliders." <u>TarRP</u> (24:1) Aut 84, p. 9.
"Letting Go." <u>PikeF</u> (6) Aut 84, p. 11.
"Miss Juergensen." <u>YetASM</u> (3) 84, p. 5.
"Roads." <u>NewL</u> (51:1) Aut 84, p. 83.
"The Snake" (for Dave Snyder). <u>PoeticJ</u> (1) 83, p.
16-17.
"Winter, Flags and Children." <u>KanQ</u> (16:1/2) Wint-
Spr 84, p. 21.

1905. GLATSHTEYN, Jacob
"Small Night-Music" (Selections: 1, 12, tr. by
Benjamin Hrushovski and Kathryn Hellerstein).
<u>PartR</u> (51:1) 84, p. 99-100.

1906. GLAZIER, Jan
"Christmas Eve in Wales." <u>OroM</u> (2:3/4, issue 7/8)
84, p. 32-33.

1907. GLAZIER, Loss
"Raga: A Man Is Looking Tired and Wants to Cross
the Road." <u>Pig</u> (12) 84, p. 54-55.
"Shrunken Starlet." <u>Veloc</u> (3) Aut-Wint 83, p. 28.

1908. GLAZIER, Loss Pequeño
"First Birthday Party." <u>OroM</u> (2:3/4, issue 7/8)
84, p. 46-48.

1909. GLAZIER, Lyle
"Azubah Nye." <u>Origin</u> (5:4) Aut 84, p. 5-31.

1910. GLAZNER, Greg
"Meditation in Late August Drought." <u>PortR</u> (30:1)
84, p. 132.
"New Stars." <u>Poetry</u> (144:2) My 84, p. 63-65.
"The Valley" (In memory of Richard Hugo). <u>Poetry</u>
(144:2) My 84, p. 65-67.

1911. GLEASON, Kathi
"Anorexia." <u>ThirdW</u> (2) Spr 84, p. 24.
"Cuttings." <u>ThirdW</u> (2) Spr 84, p. 25.
"Sleepy Hollow Revisited." <u>Blueline</u> (6:1) Sum-Aut
84, p. 22.
"Window on a Northbound Bus." <u>Blueline</u> (6:1) Sum-
Aut 84, p. 23.

1912. GLEN, Emilie
"After Hours." <u>DekalbLAJ</u> (17:1/2) 84, p. 125.
"Aunt Jenny Quotes." <u>SmPd</u> (21:2) Spr 84, p. 28.
"One Light." <u>DekalbLAJ</u> (20th Anniversary Issue)
84, p. 86.
"Snow Up." <u>SmPd</u> (21:2) Spr 84, p. 27.

1913. GLICKMAN, Susan
"The Cold Days." <u>Descant</u> (47, 15:4) Wint 84, p.
70-71.
"Living Alone." <u>Descant</u> (47, 15:4) Wint 84, p. 69.
"Metafiction." <u>PoetryCR</u> (6:2) Wint 84-85, p. 12.

1914. GLICKSTEIN, Robert M.
      "Calculation of Probabilities" (To Julio Morejon,
         tr. of Miguel Sales, w. Maria Cignarella).
         Confr (27/28) 84, p. 37.
      "Profile of Winter" (tr. of Miguel Sales, w. Maria
         Cignarella). Confr (27/28) 84, p. 38.

1915. GLOEGGLER, Edward A.
      "Beings of the Womb." SanFPJ (6:1) 84, p. 22.
      "Economic Alchemy." SanFPJ (6:1) 84, p. 23.
      "The First Laugh." SanFPJ (6:1) 84, p. 24.
      "Hope Rejected." SanFPJ (6:1) 84, p. 22.
      "New Sacrament." SanFPJ (6:1) 84, p. 22.

1916. GLOMBECKI, Gerry
      "Early Morning." CrabCR (2:1) Sum 84, p. 4.

1917. GLOTZER, Marguerite
      "Alison Shaw's Squibnocket Stone Photograph."
         StoneC (11:3/4) Spr-Sum 84, p. 67.

1918. GLOVER, Jon
      "The Last Sermon." Stand (25:2) Spr 84, p. 38.

1919. GLOWNEY, John
      "The Railroad Crossing." PoetryNW (25:4) Wint 84-
         85, p. 33-34.

1920. GLUCK, Louise
      "Psychiatrist's Sestina." Thrpny (19) Aut 84, p. 15.

1921. GLUCK, Robert
      "Mutilation (Future Appealed To)" (tr. of La
         Fontaine, w. Bruce Boone). Tele (19) 83, p. 53.
      "Mystical Aspirations" (tr. of La Fontaine, w.
         Bruce Boone). Tele (19) 83, p. 51-52.

1922. GOBLE, Jo-Anne
      "Indecent Acts." WestCR (19:1) Je 84, p. 45.

1923. GOCKER, Paula
      "An Argument in Support of Letters." KanQ
         (16:1/2) Wint-Spr 84, p. 122.

1924. GODLIN, Deborah
      "Déjà Vu." BlueBuf (2:2) Spr 84, p. 23.
      "Falling/Asleep." BlueBuf (2:2) Spr 84, p. 21.
      "Flight of Birds." BlueBuf (2:2) Spr 84, p. 24.
      "Unbearable, the Cold Rain Coming." BlueBuf (2:2)
         Spr 84, p. 22.

1925. GOEBEL, Ulf
      "The God Within." Paunch (57/58) Ja 84, p. 95.

1926. GOEDICKE, Patricia
      "Big Top." Ploughs (10:4) 84, p. 207-210.
      "The Dance Hall." ThRiPo (23/24) 84, p. 49-50.
      "Double Helix." SnapD (8:1) Aut 84, p. 56.
      "Full Circle." Hudson (37:1) Spr 84, p. 43-48.
      "Jocelyn's House: Wellfleet." MemphisSR (5:1) Aut

84, p. 8-9.
"The King of Childhood." MemphisSR (5:1) Aut 84,
    p. 12.
"Mea Culpa." NewYorker (60:16) 4 Je 84, p. 52-53.
"Not One Leaf." MemphisSR (5:1) Aut 84, p. 10-11.
"Paul Bunyan's Bearskin." Hudson (37:1) Spr 84,
    p. 41-43.
"The Point of Emptiness." NowestR (22:1/2) 84, p.
    139.

1927. GOFF, Charles Rice, III
    "Not Never Here." SanFPJ (6:4) 84, p. 55.
    "Perpetuation." SanFPJ (6:4) 84, p. 54-55.
    "United States: a Peace of Ships." SanFPJ (6:4)
        84, p. 23.

1928. GOLD, Edward
    "Choose Poclain and Be Well-armed" (found in The
        Middle East). MinnR (N.S. 22) Spr 84, p. 59.
    "Isaac." PoetL (79:3) Aut 84, p. 178.
    "Revisions." KanQ (16:1/2) Wint-Spr 84, p. 96.
    "Some Soap" (for Amy). KanQ (16:1/2) Wint-Spr 84,
        p. 96.

1929. GOLDBARTH, Albert
    "19th Century Portraits." NoAmR (269:2) Je 84, p.
        43.
    "20 for Us." Kayak (64) My 84, p. 57.
    "After Semen." MichQR (23:4) Aut 84, p. 500-501.
    "Albert." PraS (58:2) Sum 84, p. 78-79.
    "Arts & Sciences" (Selections). OntR (21) Aut-
        Wint 84, p. 55-64.
    "Blanket." TriQ (60) Spr-Sum 84, p. 148-149.
    "The Body Theory." PoetryNW (25:1) Spr 84, p. 21-22.
    "Book about Rembrandt." OntR (21) Aut-Wint 84, p.
        56.
    "Book Fair/The Topic." PoetL (79:1) Spr 84, p. 21.
    "Cathay." CarolQ (36:2) Wint 84, p. 45-60.
    "Clear Alien." PoetryNW (25:1) Spr 84, p. 20-21.
    "Delivery." MemphisSR (5:1) Aut 84, p. 58.
    "Durer." ThRiPo (23/24) 84, p. 30.
    "Early." Ascent (9:3) 84, p. 14.
    "Gardening" (for Morgan). ParisR (26:94) Wint 84,
        p. 174-175.
    "Ground & Figure." Telescope (3:1) Wint 84, p. 87-
        88.
    "The Hill Land." PoetL (79:1) Spr 84, p. 19.
    "Homage." Ploughs (10:4) 84, p. 138-139.
    "Hunt." BelPoJ (34:3) Spr 84, p. 11-23.
    "In Delicate Times." Gargoyle (24) 84, p. 203.
    "Knees / Dura-Europos." BelPoJ (34:3) Spr 84, p.
        23-31.
    "Lift Mechanics." VirQR (60:3) Sum 84, p. 424.
    "Matchbox." OntR (21) Aut-Wint 84, p. 59-61.
    "My Pajamas." MemphisSR (5:1) Aut 84, p. 51-52.
    "Neologisms." Shen (35:1) 83-84, p. 76-77.
    "Nuevo Mundo." TarRP (24:1) Aut 84, p. 37-38.
    "Of Dazzle." PoetryNW (25:3) Aut 84, p. 16-17.
    "People of the Moon." Tendril (17) Wint 84, p. 79-
        80.

"Poem about the Contract, with Some Language of the
   Contract." PraS (58:2) Sum 84, p. 77-78.
"The Properties of Light." Ascent (10:1) 84, p. 42.
"Reading In." Tendril (17) Wint 84, p. 81-84.
"Rug" (for Sobin & Todd). TarRP (24:1) Aut 84, p.
   35.
"Scar / Beer / Glasses." Poetry (144:5) Ag 84, p.
   295-296.
"Second Level." OntR (21) Aut-Wint 84, p. 62-64.
"Shooting Around." Telescope (3:3) Aut 84, p. 108-
   109.
"Some Vegetables." Ascent (9:3) 84, p. 13-14.
"The Source of Cuttlebone." PoetryNW (25:3) Aut
   84, p. 14-15.
"Spaces." Ascent (9:3) 84, p. 15.
"Speracedes." TarRP (24:1) Aut 84, p. 35-36.
"Symmetrysong." Ascent (9:3) 84, p. 12.
"Tarpan and Aurochs." AmerPoR (13:4) Jl-Ag 84, p.
   19.
"The Threshold for the Definition of 'Numinous' Is
   a Variable." Agni (21) 84, p. 35-36.
"The Triumph of the Digital Watch." MichQR (23:4)
   Aut 84, p. 502.
"U." OntR (21) Aut-Wint 84, p. 57-58.
"Vampire by Noon." ThRiPo (23/24) 84, p. 29.
"Vestigial." Poetry (144:5) Ag 84, p. 293-295.
"The Ways." PoetL (79:1) Spr 84, p. 20.
"Where There Is No Life." PoetryNW (25:3) Aut 84,
   p. 15-16.
"Window Seat." Shen (35:1) 83-84, p. 74-76.
"You're Invited: 1984 Is Donald Duck's 50th
   Birthday Year!" Ascent (10:1) 84, p. 41.

1930. GOLDBERG, Barbara
   "Honeymoon." NewEngR (6:3) Spr 84, p. 450.

1931. GOLDBERG, Beckian
   "Cutting Worms." Nimrod (27:2) Spr-Sum 84, p. 80-81.
   "Emerson's Walk to a Shaker Village." Nimrod
      (27:2) Spr-Sum 84, p. 79.
   "Letter to a Martian Woman." Nimrod (28:1) Aut-
      Wint 84, p. 99-103.

1932. GOLDBERG, Nancy Maxwell
   "Bill of Divorcement" (for Hirsch S. Goldberg).
      DekalbLAJ (17:1/2) 84, p. 126.
   "Sometimes Things Get Out of Hand" (for Hirsch S.
      Goldberg). DekalbLAJ (17:1/2) 84, p. 126.
   "Song for Lorenzo." DekalbLAJ (20th Anniversary
      Issue) 84, p. 87-88.

1933. GOLDBERG, Natalie
   "One More Word." Gargoyle (24) 84, p. 208.

1934. GOLDEN, Renny
   "For the Women Cotton-Pickers of Chinandega."
      Calyx (8:3) Aut-Wint 84, p. 13.
   "Guatemalan Exodus: Los Naturales." Calyx (8:3)
      Aut-Wint 84, p. 14-16.
   "Los Refugiados: A Salvadoran Love Story." Calyx

(8:3) Aut-Wint 84, p. 17.

1935. GOLDENSOHN, Barry
"American Innocents, Oberlin, Ohio, 1954." Salm
(65) Aut 84, p. 108-110.
"The Drawing of Thomas Wyatt by Holbein." Poetry
(144:5) Ag 84, p. 259.
"Home." Poetry (144:5) Ag 84, p. 258-259.
"Librarian of Alexandria." Salm (65) Aut 84, p.
110-111.
"Lulu" (after Alban Berg). MassR (25:1) Spr 84,
p. 79-80.
"The Prisoners." Salm (65) Aut 84, p. 112.
"To All the Gods at Once: A Prayer for Mercy."
Ploughs (10:4) 84, p. 202-204.
"To the Colonised Body." NewRep (191:7/8) 13-20
Ag 84, p. 36.
"Uprooted." Salm (65) Aut 84, p. 111-112.
"US Signal Corps Footage" (for John Peck).
Ploughs (10:1) 84, p. 70.
"War and Peace." Poetry (143:6) Mr 84, p. 313-314.

1936. GOLDENSOHN, Lorrie
"Like a small and perfect animal" (Evening poems).
ThRiPo (23/24) 84, p. 73.
"Open Casket." Ploughs (10:4) 84, p. 76-77.

1937. GOLDERMAN, Cynthia R.
"It Would Be Easy to Say Goodbye to All Good
Things." SanFPJ (6:1) 84, p. 74-75.
"Missiles and Picnics." SanFPJ (6:3) 84, p. 90-91.
"The Prophets of Stonehenge Speak." SanFPJ (6:1)
84, p. 70-71.
"World War 3: Evergreens That Will Never Freeze."
SanFPJ (6:3) 84, p. 25-28.

1938. GOLDIAMOND, Joe
"News of the Tropics." SmPd (21:3) Aut 84, p. 17.

1939. GOLDIN, Judah
"From the Diary of a Royal Psalmist." AmerS
(53:1) Wint 83/84, p. 82.

1940. GOLDMAN, Edward M.
"Nothing Personal" (See N.Y. Times, Dec. 8, 1983).
SanFPJ (6:2) 84, p. 57.

1941. GOLDMAN, Elizabeth
"Season Ticket." HangL (45) Spr 84, p. 28.

1942. GOLDSTEIN, Fran Avnet
"Summer." Wind (14:52) 84, p. 25.

1943. GOLDSTEIN, Jonas L.
"Alley Lights." SanFPJ (7:1) 84, p. 82-83.
"The Challenge." SanFPJ (6:1) 84, p. 12.
"Deliverance." SanFPJ (7:1) 84, p. 86-87.
"Haunting Eyes." SanFPJ (6:3) 84, p. 49.
"The Lip." SanFPJ (6:3) 84, p. 49.

1944. GOLDSTEIN, Laurence
"Personal History." Ploughs (10:1) 84, p. 71-72.

1945. GOLL, Yvan
"In the Fields of Camphor" (tr. by Paul Morris).
WebR (9:1) Spr 84, p. 18.
"The Lake of Salt" (tr. by Paul Morris). WebR
(9:1) Spr 84, p. 17.
"River of Lead" (tr. by Galway Kinnell). Chelsea
(42/43) 84, p. 160.
"To Claire" (Written December 1949 to January 1950
in the hospital where he died. Tr. by Paul
Morris). WebR (9:1) Spr 84, p. 19.

1946. GOM, Leona
"Farmhouse." PoetryCR (5:3) Spr 84, p. 14.
"Sister." Quarry (33:4) Aut 84, p. 6.

1947. GOMEZ, Eduardo
"On Golden Land." LindLM (3:1) Ja-Mr 84, p. 26.

GOMEZ, Florentino Jiménez: See JIMENEZ GOMEZ, Florentino

1948. GOMEZ ROSA, Alexis
"Next: Arlington Station." Areito (10:38) 84,
p. 33.

1949. GOMEZ SANJURJO, José María
"Tiempo: quiero verte de cara." Mairena (6:18)
84, p. 188.

1950. GONZALES, Laurence
"Maneuvers." Shen (35:1) 83-84, p. 11.
"On Clark Lake." Shen (35:1) 83-84, p. 10-11.

1951. GONZALEZ, Angel
"Junk" (tr. by Louis Bourne). Stand (25:4) Aut
84, p. 21.

1952. GOOD, Ruth
"Never Done." PraS (58:2) Sum 84, p. 22-23.
"News Blackout." PraS (58:2) Sum 84, p. 21-22.
"The Venus of Puerta Vallarta" (for Sharon). PraS
(58:2) Sum 84, p. 20-21.

1953. GOODELL, Larry
"Serious Art" (for John Milton on his birthday
December 9th, 1981). Tele (19) 83, p. 5.

1954. GOODENOUGH, J. B.
"Carrying Pain." SnapD (7:1) Aut 83, p. 66.
"End of the Hill Farm." LitR (28:1) Aut 84, p. 117.
"Feast." Poem (50) Mr 84, p. 53.
"Going Back." NeqC (4:2) Spr 84, p. 33.
"In My Dream You Are." Poem (50) Mr 84, p. 54.
"In the Forest." PortR (30:1) 84, p. 59.
"The Innocent." Nimrod (27:2) Spr-Sum 84, p. 46.
"The Last Night at Home." SpoonRQ (9:2) Spr 84,
p. 7.
"The Magician." Nimrod (27:2) Spr-Sum 84, p. 46.

"Market-Day." CapeR (19:2) Sum 84, p. 21.
"Old Man Fishing Cat Swamp." Hudson (37:2) Sum
    84, p. 277-278.
"Places at Table." StoneC (12:1/2) Aut-Wint 84,
    p. 19.
"Revaluations." Hudson (37:2) Sum 84, p. 277.
"Said This Child." SpoonRQ (9:2) Spr 84, p. 5.
"Spring Sowing." SpoonRQ (9:2) Spr 84, p. 6.
"Sunday Songs." FourQt (33:3) Spr 84, p. 3.
"Walking with the Pig." Ploughs (10:1) 84, p. 73.
"What Wrong Is" (Errata from Vol. 10, No. 1).
    Ploughs (10:4) 84, p. 244.
"Widow." CapeR (19:2) Sum 84, p. 22.

1955. GOODIN, Gayle
    "Belinda Fuller." DekalbLAJ (20th Anniversary
        Issue) 84, p. 89.

1956. GOODMAN, Dottie
    "Escort." PoeticJ (7) 84, p. 36.

1957. GOODMAN, Frances
    "Message to Earth." SanFPJ (7:1) 84, p. 25.

1958. GOODMAN, Ryah Tumarkin
    "Against Each Other." Confr (27/28) 84, p. 194.
    "Cherry Music." PoeticJ (6) 84, p. 38.
    "Sometimes." Amelia (1:2) O 84, back cover.
    "Turn to Page Sky." PoeticJ (6) 84, p. 13.

1959. GOODWIN, Amy W.
    "The Margin." ThRiPo (23/24) 84, p. 41.
    "Nor Help for Pain." ThRiPo (23/24) 84, p. 42.

1960. GORBATY, Dorathy
    "Learning to Say We." YellowS (10) Spr 84, p. 35.

1961. GORCZYNSKI, Renata
    "The Gates of the Arsenal" (tr. of Czeslaw Milosz,
        w. Robert Hass). GrandS (3:2) Wint 84, p. 94-96.
    "Going to Lvov" (tr. of Adam Zagajewski). NewRep
        (190:5) 6 F 84, p. 40.

1962. GORDON, Gerry
    "Song." ThirdW (2) Spr 84, p. 19.

1963. GORDON, Guanetta
    "Midas Dream." Amelia [1:1] Ap 84, p. 36.

1964. GORDON, Kirpal
    "The Wall." Wind (14:52) 84, p. 21-22.

1965. GORDON, Mark
    "Winter Landscape." PoetryCR (6:2) Wint 84-85, p.
        25.

1966. GORDON, Roxy
    "Song for a Girl I Used to Know" (Written on Lomas
        Street, Albuquerque, New Mexico, Winter 1972).
        GreenfR (11:3/4) Wint-Spr 84, p. 64.

"When He Dances, a Contrary is Called a Fool
    Dancer" (from a Photo of an Assiniboine Fool
    Dancer taken in 1906 at the Fort Belknap,
    Montana reservation by Sumner W. Matteson).
    GreenfR (11:3/4) Wint-Spr 84, p. 66.

1967. GORE, Robert
    "Dream of the Hunted." AntigR (58) Sum 84, p. 67.
    "Printing Lesson -- Summer." AntigR (58) Sum 84,
    p. 66.

1968. GORHAM, Sarah
    "Bundled Roses." PraS (58:2) Sum 84, p. 72.
    "Laps." PraS (58:2) Sum 84, p. 71.
    "Walkingstick." MichQR (23:3) Sum 84, p. 411.

1969. GORLIN, Debra
    "Second Nature." PraS (58:2) Sum 84, p. 87-88.

1970. GORMAN, LeRoy
    "A diver brings up the body" (haiku). PoetryCR
    (5:3) Spr 84, p. 9.

1971. GORZANSKI, Jerzy
    "Young Faustus Visits the Institute of Oncology and
    Does Research on Experience" (tr. by Danuta
    Lopozyko and Peter Harris). LitR (28:1) Aut
    84, p. 131.

1972. GOSNELL, William
    "Fleeting Lifetime." PortR (30:1) 84, p. 141.

1973. GOSSLING, Susan
    "Poem without End." Open24 (3) 84, p. 27-28.
    "Robot Love." Open24 (3) 84, p. 28.

1974. GOTRO, Paul Edmund
    "Heron." Quarry (33:4) Aut 84, p. 76.

1975. GOUDEY, Andrew
    "Figures in the Light." BlueBuf (2:2) Spr 84, p. 29.

1976. GOULD, Janice
    "Going Home." Calyx (8:2) Spr 84, p. 75.
    "Tanana Valley." Calyx (8:2) Spr 84, p. 83.

1977. GOULD, Roberta
    "Return." Confr (27/28) 84, p. 336.

1978. GOUMAS, Yannis
    "For Young Kerem." Waves (12:2/3) Wint 84, p. 87.
    "The Survivors. What Became of Them? Who Was the
    Drowned Man?" (tr. of Kostis Ghimosoúlis).
    Argo (5:3) 84, p. 6.
    "To That Dark Handsome Youth Named Death" (tr. of
    Kostis Ghimosoúlis). Argo (5:3) 84, p. 6.

1979. GOURLAY, Elizabeth
    "Poem: To Myself." PoetryCR (6:2) Wint 84-85, p. 10.
    "The Postcard." CrossC (6:3) 84, p. 15.

"Survival." <u>CanLit</u> (101) Sum 84, p. 6.

1980. GOVE, Jim
"Some." <u>Sam</u> (37:3, 147th release) 83, p. 27.

1981. GRABILL, James
"Beetle." <u>WoosterR</u> (1:1) Mr 84, p. 101.
"Fall Sayings." <u>GreenfR</u> (12:1/2) Sum-Aut 84, p. 160.
"In Michigan" (for Miriam and Tom). <u>GreenfR</u>
(12:1/2) Sum-Aut 84, p. 160-161.
"Mule Deer." <u>WoosterR</u> (1:1) Mr 84, p. 100.
"The Night Energy Moves in Waves." <u>Spirit</u> (7:1)
84, p. 139-140.

1982. GRACIA de CRIADO, Yolanda
"En Ti." <u>Mairena</u> (6:16) Spr 84, p. 33.
"Nosotros Mismos." <u>Mairena</u> (6:16) Spr 84, p. 31-32.
"La Palabra en Mi." <u>Mairena</u> (6:16) Spr 84, p. 34.
"Regresion." <u>Mairena</u> (6:16) Spr 84, p. 32-33.

1983. GRAD, Judith
"Ice Cream." <u>Vis</u> (14) 84, p. 29.

1984. GRAF, Herbert
"The Divorce" (tr. of Hans Magnus Enzensberger).
<u>Sulfur</u> (3:3, issue 9) 84, p. 128.
"Die Furie des Verschwindens" (Selections, tr. of
Hans Magnus Enzensberger). <u>Sulfur</u> (3:3, issue
9) 84, p. 124-129.
"Memorial" (tr. of Hans Magnus Enzensberger).
<u>Sulfur</u> (3:3, issue 9) 84, p. 125.
"Report from Bonn" (tr. of Hans Magnus
Enzensberger). <u>Sulfur</u> (3:3, issue 9) 84, p.
124-125.
"She's Thirty-Three" (tr. of Hans Magnus
Enzensberger). <u>Sulfur</u> (3:3, issue 9) 84, p.
125-126.
"Short History of the Bourgeoisie" (tr. of Hans
Magnus Enzensberger). <u>Sulfur</u> (3:3, issue 9)
84, p. 129.
"The White Collar Worker" (tr. of Hans Magnus
Enzensberger). <u>Sulfur</u> (3:3, issue 9) 84, p.
126-127.

1985. GRAHAM, Archie
"Island & the Sea." <u>CrossC</u> (6:2) 84, p. 15.

1986. GRAHAM, Chael
"The Dunce" (tr. of Jacques Prevert). <u>Spirit</u>
(7:1) 84, p. 105.

1987. GRAHAM, David
"Here Was Buried Thomas Jefferson." <u>SouthernPR</u>
(24:1) Spr 84, p. 56-58.
"How Straight Up is Curved: Homage to Emily
Dickinson" (For Joe Donahue). <u>NewEngR</u> (6:4)
Sum 84, p. 556-560.
"Testament of Arnaud du Tilh." <u>Nimrod</u> (28:1) Aut-
Wint 84, p. 79-82.

245   GRAZIANO

1988. GRAHAM, Gwendolyn G.
      "For Brandon." HiramPoR (36) Spr-Sum 84, p. 23.

1989. GRAHN, Judy
      "In the Tower of the Crone." GreenfR (11:3/4)
         Wint-Spr 84, p. 85-86.
      "Spider Webster's Declaration: He Is Singing the
         End of the World Again." GreenfR (11:3/4) Wint-
         Spr 84, p. 83-85.

1990. GRANATO, Carol
      "Each Thing in Time Finds." Poem (51) Mr [i.e.
         Jl] 84, p. 51.
      "Ruin." Poem (51) Mr [i.e. Jl] 84, p. 53.
      "The Shocking Hour." Poem (51) Mr [i.e. Jl] 84,
         p. 52.

GRANIELA RODRIGUEZ, Magda: See RODRIGUEZ, Magda Graniela

1991. GRANT, Jamie
      "Adultery on an Ocean-Facing Farm." LittleM
         (14:3) 84, p. 46.
      "Perth's Last Total Eclipse of the Sun Happened
         over 400 Years Ago." LittleM (14:3) 84, p. 45.

1992. GRAVES, Michael
      "The Passionate Grad Stu to His Love." HolCrit
         (21:2, i.e. 21:3) Je 84, p. 20.

1993. GRAVES, Robert
      "Anagrammagic." GrandS (3:1) Aut 83, p. 165-166.

1994. GRAVETT, M.
      "Damp Iron." NegC (4:3) Sum 84, p. 116-117.

1995. GRAY, Alice Wirth
      "The Land of Nod." AmerS (53:1) Wint 83/84, p. 25.

1996. GRAY, Janet
      "Of the Political Correctness of Garp." Abraxas
         (31/32) 84, p. 28.

1997. GRAY, Patrick Worth
      "After a Painting by Paul Kircher." WebR (9:2)
         Wint 85, p. 61.
      "He." WebR (9:2) Wint 85, p. 60.
      "Necessity Is the Mother of the 'Bullet'." Pig
         (12) 84, p. 36.

1998. GRAY, Robert
      "Learning to Walk." HolCrit (21:1) F 84, p. 17.

1999. GRAZIANO, Frank
      "The Awakening" (tr. of Alejandra Pizarnik, w. Jim
         Fitzgerald). CharR (10:1) Spr 84, p. 72-73.
      "Breath." Tendril (17) Wint 84, p. 85.
      "Roads from the Mirror" (tr. of Alejandra Pizarnik,
         w. Jim Fitzgerald). CharR (10:1) Spr 84, p. 69-
         71.

2000. GRAZIDE, Richard
"The Retreat." Wind (14:50) 84, p. 22.

2001. GREEN, Jim
"Blooded" (for Joe Carter). PoetryCR (5:4) Sum
84, p. 5.

2002. GREEN, Linda
"Tent City." SanFPJ (6:3) 84, p. 41.

2003. GREEN, Tim
"Counsels to His Children." SouthwR (69:3) Sum
84, p. 259.

2004. GREENBERG, Uri Zvi
"Naming Souls" (tr. by Jon Silkin and Ezra
Spicehandler). Stand (25:4) Aut 84, p. 65.

2005. GREENE, Jonathan
"Morning Excuse for Not Mowing." Wind (14:50) 84,
p. 23-24.
"Our Stay Was Momentary." Wind (14:50) 84, p. 24.
"Six Days of Thunderstorms." Wind (14:50) 84, p. 23.

2006. GREENWALD, Roger
"Briefing" (tr. of Rolf Jacobsen). Spirit (7:1)
84, p. 141.
"The Catacombs in San Callisto" (tr. of Rolf
Jacobsen). Stand (25:1) Wint 83-84, p. 48.
"Green Light" (tr. of Rolf Jacobsen). Spirit
(7:1) 84, p. 95.
"Thoughts upon Listening in on a Radio Telescope"
(tr. of Rolf Jacobsen). Stand (25:1) Wint 83-
84, p. 49.
"The Time in Malmö on the Earth" (Excerpts, tr.
of Jacques Werup). PoetryE (15) Aut 84, p. 88-93.

2007. GREENWAY, William
"The Book of Days." MissR (37/38, 13:1/2) Aut 84,
p. 81.
"Custer." MissR (37/38, 13:1/2) Aut 84, p. 80.
"New Orleans, 1983." MissR (37/38, 13:1/2) Aut
84, p. 82.
"Wedding." NewL (51:1) Aut 84, p. 87.

2008. GREENWOOD, G. P.
"Reasons." PoetryCR (6:2) Wint 84-85, p. 5.
"Rites of Madness." PoetryCR (6:2) Wint 84-85, p. 7.
"To a Rapist." PoetryCR (5:3) Spr 84, p. 14.

2009. GREGER, Debora
"Dream Lecture, June." Poetry (144:5) Ag 84, p.
251-252.
"The English Tongue." YaleR (73:4) Sum 84, p. 521.
"The Garden of Acclimatization" (for my father).
Agni (21) 84, p. 25-27.
"Habit, Those Yards." NewRep (189:22) 28 N 83, p.
36.
"Passage Overland." Poetry (144:5) Ag 84, p. 252-
253.

"Piranesi in L.A." <u>YaleR</u> (73:4) Sum 84, p. 521-522.
"The Rome of Keats." <u>Poetry</u> (145:1) O 84, p. 28.
"Second Movement: Adagio." <u>SewanR</u> (92:4) O-D 84,
    p. 601-602.
"This Underwater Room Where You Swim, Scaled."
    <u>SewanR</u> (92:4) O-D 84, p. 603.
"Two Rodin Torsos" ("The Prayer," bronze, 49-1/4"
    high, "Grand Torso of a Man," bronze, 40" high).
    <u>Poetry</u> (144:5) Ag 84, p. 253-254.

2010. GREGERSON, Linda
    "Aubade." <u>Salm</u> (65) Aut 84, p. 71.
    "Bachelor's Wives." <u>Ploughs</u> (10:4) 84, p. 74-75.
    "Blason." <u>SenR</u> (14:2) 84, p. 35-36.
    "I See a Voice." <u>SenR</u> (14:2) 84, p. 37-38.
    "Mother Ruin." <u>Atlantic</u> (253:2) F 84, p. 56.
    "Saints' Logic." <u>GrandS</u> (3:3) Spr 84, p. 114-115.

2011. GREGG, Linda
    "Days." <u>ParisR</u> (26:93) Aut 84, p. 170.
    "Saying Goodbye to the Dead." <u>NewYorker</u> (60:2) 27
        F 84, p. 52.
    "Still, Clenched, Attentive." <u>ParisR</u> (26:93) Aut
        84, p. 171.
    "Summer." <u>ParisR</u> (26:93) Aut 84, p. 169.
    "Taken by Each Thing." <u>ParisR</u> (26:93) Aut 84, p.
        170.
    "Twelve Years after the Marriage She Tries to
        Explain How She Loves Him Now." <u>ParisR</u> (26:93)
        Aut 84, p. 171.
    "With a Blessing Rather Than Love Said Nietzsche."
        <u>ParisR</u> (26:93) Aut 84, p. 169.

2012. GREGORY, Mike
    "Parachute." <u>Nimrod</u> (27:2) Spr-Sum 84, p. 74.

2013. GREGORY, Robert
    "Only This Window." <u>Mund</u> (14:2) 84, p. 52.
    "Sheet & Sleeping Woman." <u>Mund</u> (14:2) 84, p. 52.

2014. GREGORY, Sinda
    "My Star Rising Will Give Me Room." <u>IndR</u> (7:1)
        Wint 84, p. 36-44.

2015. GREIG, Geraldine
    "Night Shift." <u>Wind</u> (14:50) 84, p. 25.

2016. GREINER, John
    "Familiar Door." <u>SpoonRQ</u> (9:4) Aut 84, p. 42.
    "Piece of a Thing." <u>SpoonRQ</u> (9:4) Aut 84, p. 41.

2017. GRENIER, R.
    "The Rats" (tr. of Georg Trakl). <u>Field</u> (30) Spr
        84, p. 66.

2018. GRENNAN, Eamon
    "Daughter Lying Awake." <u>OntR</u> (21) Aut-Wint 84, p.
        74-75.
    "From Your Window." <u>OntR</u> (21) Aut-Wint 84, p. 79.
    "Learning Conditions" (Selections). <u>OntR</u> (21) Aut-

Wint 84, p. 73-80.
"Lunch-Break on the Edge of Town." Ploughs (10:1)
    84, p. 74-75.
"Patience in Renvyle." OntR (21) Aut-Wint 84, p. 75.
"Sadness of Birds." OntR (21) Aut-Wint 84, p. 76.
"Search Party" (for Phoebe Palmer). OntR (21) Aut-
    Wint 84, p. 77-79.
"Vespers." OntR (21) Aut-Wint 84, p. 76.
"Winn's Blackbird" (for Winn and Larry Smith).
    OntR (21) Aut-Wint 84, p. 80.

GRESTY, David Ian Price: See PRICE-GRESTY, David Ian

2019. GREVSTAD, Anne
    "The Beach." PikeF (6) Aut 84, p. 21.

2020. GREY, Lucinda
    "Planting Bulbs under the Moon in January." KanQ
        (16:1/2) Wint-Spr 84, p. 174.

2021. GREY, Robert
    "Shoebox Skull." DekalbLAJ (17:1/2) 84, p. 127.

GRIEVE, Christopher Murray: See MacDIARMID, Hugh (pen name
    of Christopher Murray Grieve)

2022. GRIFFIN, Janet R.
    "I Am the Silent Warrior" (Dedicated to the Vietnam
        Veterans). SanFPJ (6:3) 84, p. 62-63.

2023. GRIFFIN, Walter
    "Maze." CapeR (19:3) 20th Anniverary Issue 84, p.
        23.

2024. GRIFFITH, Jonathan
    "In the Beginning." NewL (50:2/3) Wint-Spr 84, p.
        64.

2025. GRIFFITHS, Steve
    "Small Substantial Shadow." Argo (5:2) 84, p. 12.

2026. GRIGORESCU, Irina
    "At Night on the Shore" (tr. of Anghel Dumbraveanu,
        w. Adam Sorkin). Mund (14:2) 84, p. 31.
    "Heralds" (tr. of Anghel Dumbraveanu, w. Adam
        Sorkin). Mund (14:2) 84, p. 27.
    "Hidden Portrait" (tr. of Anghel Dumbraveanu, w.
        Adam J. Sorkin). ConcPo (17:2) Aut 84, p. 70.
    "Horses of Time" (tr. of Anghel Dumbraveanu, w.
        Adam Sorkin). Mund (14:2) 84, p. 27.
    "Interior" (tr. of Anghel Dumbraveanu, w. Adam J.
        Sorkin). ConcPo (17:2) Aut 84, p. 70.
    "The Masks" (tr. of Anghel Dumbraveanu, w. Adam
        Sorkin). Mund (14:2) 84, p. 29.

2027. GRIGSBY, Gordon
    "Interstellar Medium." Vis (14) 84, p. 25.

2028. GRILIKHES, Alexandra
    "Pittsburgh." PaintedB (24) Aut 84, p. 8-9.

2029. GRILL, Neil
      "We Have Looked Everywhere." YetASM (3) 84, p. 4.

2030. GRILLO, Janet
      "Fall" (To My Mother). NegC (4:1) Wint 84, p. 39-40.

2031. GRIMM, Reinhold
      "Countdown" (tr. of Hans Magnus Enzensberger, w.
         Felix Pollak). NowestR (22:1/2) 84, p. 71.
      "Course in Poetics" (tr. of Hans Magnus
         Enzensberger, w. Felix Pollak). TriQ (61) Aut
         84, p. 100.
      "Delete Whatever Inapplicable" (tr. of Hans Magnus
         Enzensberger, w. Felix Pollak). AmerPoR (13:5)
         S-O 84, p. 7.
      "The Doctrine of Categories" (tr. of Hans Magnus
         Enzensberger, w. Felix Pollak). NowestR
         (22:1/2) 84, p. 65.
      "Doomsday" (tr. of Hans Magnus Enzensberger, w.
         Felix Pollak). NowestR (22:1/2) 84, p. 67.
      "The Dresses" (tr. of Hans Magnus Enzensberger, w.
         Felix Pollak). AmerPoR (13:5) S-O 84, p. 6.
      "The Empty House" (tr. of Hans Magnus Enzensberger,
         w. Felix Pollak). NowestR (22:1/2) 84, p. 69.
      "For the Primer of Senior High" (tr. of Hans Magnus
         Enzensberger, w. Felix Pollak). AmerPoR (13:5)
         S-O 84, p. 7.
      "Historical Process" (tr. of Hans Magnus
         Enzensberger, w. Felix Pollak). AmerPoR (13:5)
         S-O 84, p. 7.
      "Obsession" (tr. of Hans Magnus Enzensberger, w.
         Felix Pollak). TriQ (61) Aut 84, p. 102.
      "Peace Conference" (tr. of Hans Magnus
         Enzensberger, w. Felix Pollak). NowestR
         (22:1/2) 84, p. 63.
      "Prewar" (tr. of Thomas Brasch). NowestR (22:1/2)
         84, p. 73.
      "Regardless of" (tr. of Hans Magnus Enzensberger,
         w. Felix Pollak). AmerPoR (13:5) S-O 84, p. 6.
      "Residual Light" (tr. of Hans Magnus Enzensberger,
         w. Felix Pollak). TriQ (61) Aut 84, p. 101.
      "Shit" (tr. of Hans Magnus Enzensberger, w. Felix
         Pollak). AmerPoR (13:5) S-O 84, p. 6.

2032. GRINDE, Olav
      "Your Thoughts, Your Deeds" (tr. of Rolf Jacobsen).
         Stand (25:4) Aut 84, p. 64.

2033. GROLLMES, Eugene
      "Pair of Horses." SpoonRQ (9:2) Spr 84, p. 19.
      "To a Girl in Orange at the Veiled Prophet Fair,
         St. Louis." SpoonRQ (9:2) Spr 84, p. 21.
      "To Patricia at Massanutten Mountain, Virginia:
         Watching for Stars." SpoonRQ (9:2) Spr 84, p. 20.

2034. GRONBACK, Karen
      "In the Wake" (Anthony Kelsey, 1952-1982). YetASM
         (3) 84, p. 7.

2035. GROSHOLZ, Emily
"Egon Schiele's Self Portraits." Salm (63/64) Spr-
Sum 84, p. 251-252.
"Ode to the Senses." Salm (63/64) Spr-Sum 84, p.
253-254.
"The Old Fisherman" (Francois Dejanna, d. 1980,
L'Anse d'Orso, Corsica). Poetry (144:4) Jl 84,
p. 194.
"On a Line from Kavafis." Salm (63/64) Spr-Sum
84, p. 251.
"Siesta." Poetry (144:4) Jl 84, p. 195-196.

2036. GROSS, Harvey
"Andromeda." Nat (239:10) 6 O 84, p. 321.

2037. GROSS, Pamela
"The Desk." StoneC (12:1/2) Aut-Wint 84, p. 16.

2038. GROSS, Philip
"Allies." GrandS (3:2) Wint 84, p. 123-124.
"The Mermaid's Honeymoon." Argo (5:2) 84, p. 4.
"Nursery Rhymes." Argo (5:2) 84, p. 3.
"Passages from Africa." Stand (25:2) Spr 84, p. 4-5.

2039. GROSSMAN, Allen
"The Department" (Siste, viator). Peb (23) 84, p.
7-10.
"The Guardian." GrandS (3:4) Sum 84, p. 13.
"Poland of Death." GrandS (3:4) Sum 84, p. 12.
"Short Walk." GrandS (3:4) Sum 84, p. 15-16.
"The Stare." GrandS (3:4) Sum 84, p. 14.

2040. GROSSMAN, Andrew J.
"Bed of Stones." SnapD (7:2) Spr 84, p. 11.
"The Typist." SnapD (7:2) Spr 84, p. 10.
"The White Marches." Sam (37:3, 147th release)
83, p. 56.

2041. GROSSMAN, Florence
"Tanta." Abraxas (29/30) 84, p. 41.

2042. GROSSMAN, Richard
"Rembrandt Self-portrait, 1659." SouthernR (20:1)
Wint 84, p. 146.

2043. GROVER-ROGOFF, Jay
"In the Lake" (for Bill and Janet Shaw). PoetryNW
(25:1) Spr 84, p. 32-34.
"Monet's Last Self-Portrait." PoetryNW (25:4)
Wint 84-85, p. 37.
"Snow As a Way of Light." SouthernPR (24:1) Spr
84, p. 50.
"Teaching My Students Prosody." GeoR (38:2) Sum
84, p. 262-263.

2044. GROVES, Paul
"Remembering." Argo (6:1) 84, p. 14.

2045. GROW, Eric
"Imaginary Friend." WormR (24:4, issue 96) 84, p.

156.
"Mourning." <u>WormR</u> (24:4, issue 96) 84, p. 157.
"Real Thing." <u>WormR</u> (24:4, issue 96) 84, p. 157.
"Sex." <u>WormR</u> (24:4, issue 96) 84, p. 157-158.
"To a Young Selectric Dying." <u>WormR</u> (24:4, issue
    96) 84, p. 158.
"Why I Don't Like Rock Stars." <u>WormR</u> (24:4, issue
    96) 84, p. 158.

2046. GRUE, Lee Meitzen
"For Celeste: Fifteen and Doubting." <u>NegC</u> (4:1)
    Wint 84, p. 100.

2047. GRUNST, Robert
"The Pine Cone." <u>PraS</u> (58:4) Wint 84, p. 72.
"Smelt." <u>PraS</u> (58:4) Wint 84, p. 73-74.

2048. GRUPP, Art
"Cold Blast." <u>SanFPJ</u> (7:1) 84, p. 33.
"Nightly Vigil." <u>SanFPJ</u> (7:1) 84, p. 38.

2049. GUBMAN, G. D.
"Gemini." <u>Wind</u> (14:51) 84, p. 18.

2050. GUE, Sandra
"An old woman with spindly arthritic legs."
    <u>Northeast</u> (Series 3:17) Sum 84, p. 12.

2051. GUENTHER, Charles
"End of Solemnities" (tr. of René Char).
    <u>MissouriR</u> (7:3) 84, p. 27.
"The Library Is on Fire" (to Georges Braque, tr. of
    René Char). <u>Chelsea</u> (42/43) 84, p. 112-115.
"Predecessor" (tr. of René Char). <u>MissouriR</u>
    (7:3) 84, p. 28.
"Sentry of the Silent" (tr. of René Char).
    <u>MissouriR</u> (7:3) 84, p. 26.

2052. GUERNSEY, Bruce
"The Ironic Dog." <u>Swallow</u> (3) 84, p. 98.

2053. GUESS, Michael L.
"Demise of the Thunderstorms on the Eighth."
    <u>SanFPJ</u> (6:4) 84, p. 46-47.
"Grandson's Elegy of the Cherokee." <u>SanFPJ</u> (6:3)
    84, p. 47.
"Sorrows on the Road to Cali." <u>SanFPJ</u> (6:3) 84,
    p. 45-46.

2054. GUEST, Barbara
"Lunch at Helen Frankenthaler's." <u>Chelsea</u> (42/43)
    84, p. 286.

2055. GUEST, Jerry
"Center." <u>MemphisSR</u> (4:2) Spr 84, p. 48-49.

2056. GUEVARA, Ivan
"In la Bartolina" (tr. by Marc Zimmerman and Ellen
    Banberger). <u>MinnR</u> (N.S. 22) Spr 84, p. 69.
"There Are Discourses Like These" (tr. by Marc

Zimmerman and Ellen Banberger). <u>MinnR</u> (N.S.
22) Spr 84, p. 74-77.

2057. GUGLIELMETTI, Edgardo
"Verdugo del Sol y de la Carne." <u>Mairena</u> (5:14)
Aut 83, p. 94.

2058. GUILLEN, Jorge
"Out of the World" (tr. by Reginald Gibbons).
<u>TriQ</u> (59) Wint 84, p. 223-226.

2059. GUILLEN, Nicolas
"The New Muse" (tr. by Robert Marquez). <u>Vis</u> (15)
84, p. 16.
"The Rivers" (tr. by Robert Marquez). <u>Vis</u> (15)
84, p. 16.
"The Winds" (tr. by Robert Marquez). <u>Vis</u> (15) 84,
p. 15.

2060. GUILLEN, Rafael
"The Front Room" (tr. by Sandy McKinney). <u>TriQ</u>
(59) Wint 84, p. 211-212.
"Mold" (tr. by Sandy McKinney). <u>TriQ</u> (59) Wint
84, p. 213-214.
"Task-Work" (tr. by Sandy McKinney). <u>TriQ</u> (59)
Wint 84, p. 209-210.

2061. GUILLEVIC, Eugène
"Charnel-Houses" (tr. by Robert Chandler). <u>Stand</u>
(25:3) Sum 84, p. 34-35.

GUISCAFRE, Marilyn R. Ramírez: <u>See</u> RAMIREZ GUISCAFRE,
Marilyn R.

2062. GUITART, Jorge
"Anecdota del Abuelito." <u>LindLM</u> (3:2/4) Ap-D 84,
p. 15.
"Edipo y la Esfinge." <u>LindLM</u> (3:2/4) Ap-D 84, p. 15.
"Las Posibilidades." <u>LindLM</u> (3:2/4) Ap-D 84, p. 15.
"Viaje Imaginario al Vedado." <u>LindLM</u> (3:2/4) Ap-D
84, p. 15.

2063. GUITART, Jorge M.
"The Rats." <u>BilingR</u> (11:1) Ja-Ap 84, p. 65.

2064. GUNDY, Jeff
"C. W. Discovers a Tabloid Pome." <u>PikeF</u> (6) Aut
84, p. 10.
"Illinois at Christmas." <u>PikeF</u> (6) Aut 84, p. 11.
"Poems Are Even Now Winging Their Way Back to
Hesston America." <u>PikeF</u> (6) Aut 84, p. 10.
"Water Moving through Concrete" (for Bly). <u>IndR</u>
(7:2) Spr 84, p. 51.

2065. GUNN, Genni
"Blood of Woman" (tr. of Dacia Maraini). <u>Waves</u>
(13:1) Aut 84, p. 63.
"Go Ahead Devour Me Too" (tr. of Dacia Maraini).
<u>Quarry</u> (33:4) Aut 84, p. 50-51.
"His Hair, His Eyes." <u>Quarry</u> (33:4) Aut 84, p. 49.

2066. GUNN, Thom
    "Bow Down." Stand (25:2) Spr 84, p. 9-11.

2067. GUNNARS, Kristjana
    "Albatross." Paunch (57/58) Ja 84, p. 15.
    "Assassin." Paunch (57/58) Ja 84, p. 12.
    "Black Butte." Paunch (57/58) Ja 84, p. 19.
    "Blueprint of St. Francis." Dandel (11:2) Aut-
        Wint 84-85, p. 8-9.
    "Creation." Paunch (57/58) Ja 84, p. 13.
    "Dive." Paunch (57/58) Ja 84, p. 28.
    "Dragonfly." Paunch (57/58) Ja 84, p. 26.
    "Flamingo." Paunch (57/58) Ja 84, p. 14.
    "From Gleneden." Paunch (57/58) Ja 84, p. 22.
    "Greylag." Paunch (57/58) Ja 84, p. 25.
    "Hermaphrodite." Paunch (57/58) Ja 84, p. 11.
    "Hyaena." Paunch (57/58) Ja 84, p. 16.
    "Iguana." Paunch (57/58) Ja 84, p. 23.
    "Kittiwake." Paunch (57/58) Ja 84, p. 20.
    "Lómur." Paunch (57/58) Ja 84, p. 21.
    "Mangrove." Paunch (57/58) Ja 84, p. 17.
    "Mystery." Paunch (57/58) Ja 84, p. 9.
    "North Country Wake" (Selections: 17, 20-21).
        PoetryCR (6:1) Aut 84, p. 26.
    "Poverty Lines." CanLit (100) Spr 84, p. 120-121.
    "Reef" (both a collection of short poems and one
        longpoem). Paunch (57/58) Ja 84, p. 5-29.
    "Reef." Paunch (57/58) Ja 84, p. 27.
    "Sandpiper." Paunch (57/58) Ja 84, p. 10.
    "Seal Rock." Paunch (57/58) Ja 84, p. 24.
    "Self-Asteroids." Dandel (11:2) Aut-Wint 84-85,
        p. 10.
    "Tarantula." Paunch (57/58) Ja 84, p. 29.
    "Victim." Paunch (57/58) Ja 84, p. 8.
    "Wild Waters." PraF (5:2/3) Spr 84, p. 38-40.
    "Winter Ptarmigan." Paunch (57/58) Ja 84, p. 18.
    "Wolf." Paunch (57/58) Ja 84, p. 7.
    "Wordsketch on Indian Summer" (w. Andrew Suknaski).
        PraF (5:2/3) Spr 84, p. 30-31.

2068. GURLEY, George H., Jr.
    "Bird Songs." Poetry (144:1) Ap 84, p. 20.
    "Burning of the Books." Poetry (144:1) Ap 84, p. 21.
    "Native Tongue." KanQ (16:1/2) Wint-Spr 84, p. 38.

2069. GURLEY, James
    "Biddulph's Grove." AntigR (58) Sum 84, p. 10.
    "Coming Up Clean." AntigR (58) Sum 84, p. 9.
    "Prairie Sunset." GreenfR (12:1/2) Sum-Aut 84, p.
        108.

2070. GURNEY, Ivor
    "The Silent One." Stand (25:4) Aut 84, p. 28.
    "Soft Rain." Stand (25:4) Aut 84, p. 32.
    "The Songs I Had." PoetryCR (6:2) Wint 84-85, p. 23.

2071. GUSS, David
    "Cumana in August." Ploughs (10:4) 84, p. 188.
    "Menasha." Ploughs (10:4) 84, p. 187.

2072. GUSTAFSON, Ralph
        "At the Zoo." <u>CanLit</u> (100) Spr 84, p. 123.
        "The Broken Pianola"(for Heitor Villa-Lobos).
            <u>CrossC</u> (6:4) 84, p. 11.
        "Crusted Ochre." <u>PoetryCR</u> (6:1) Aut 84, p. 26.
        "Elms in Storm." <u>PoetryCR</u> (6:2) Wint 84-85, p. 21.
        "The Fall of Snow." <u>CrossC</u> (6:4) 84, p. 11.
        "The Geography of Grass." <u>PoetryCR</u> (6:1) Aut 84,
            p. 26.
        "Impromptu." <u>PoetryCR</u> (6:2) Wint 84-85, p. 21.
        "The Road by the Lake." <u>CanLit</u> (100) Spr 84, p. 122.
        "Stained Glass." <u>CrossC</u> (6:4) 84, p. 11.
        "That Summer." <u>PoetryCR</u> (6:2) Wint 84-85, p. 21.
        "Without Definition." <u>PoetryCR</u> (6:2) Wint 84-85,
            p. 21.

2073. GUSTAVSON, Cynthia M.
        "Dialysis." <u>ChrC</u> (101:39) 12 D 84, p. 1172.

2074. GUSTAVSON, Jeffrey
        "Pond Subjects" (Selections: 3. "Fjord," 4. "High
            School" (for Charles Condrat), 5. "Edmunds!--,"
            6. "Ishmael," 8. "Narcissus" (for G. F.), 13.
            "Letter to My Brother," 16. "Before Lauds").
            <u>Agni</u> (21) 84, p. 42-48.
        "The Scarecrow." <u>Agni</u> (20) 84, p. 16-20.

GUT, Karen Alkalay: <u>See</u> ALKALAY-GUT, Karen

GUZMAN BOUVARD, Marguerite: <u>See</u> BOUVARD, Marguerite Guzman

2075. GWYNN, R. S.
        "Laird of the Maze." <u>SewanR</u> (92:1) Ja-Mr 84, p.
            59-60.

2076. GYURE, James
        "Apparition." <u>TarRP</u> (23:2) Spr 84, p. 4-5.

2077. H. D.
        "Heat." <u>NewYRB</u> (31:5) 29 Mr 84, p. 15.

2078. HABERMAN, Daniel
        "Clumbering in the umbered night" ("Untitled").
            <u>SouthernR</u> (20:2) Spr 84, p. 356.
        "In the purple of an Autumn" ("Untitled").
            <u>SouthernR</u> (20:2) Spr 84, p. 355-356.
        "Morning on the Orient Express." <u>SouthernR</u> (20:2)
            Spr 84, p. 354.
        "One drop upon a rusted leaf" ("Untitled").
            <u>SouthernR</u> (20:2) Spr 84, p. 356.
        "The Sky in an Auburn Haze" (A Ballad). <u>SouthernR</u>
            (20:2) Spr 84, p. 355.

2079. HABIBA
        "Photographs: 1979." <u>Pig</u> (12) 84, p. 61.

2080. HABOVA, Dana
        "Children at Christmas in 1945" (tr. of Vladimir
            Holan, w. C. G. Hanzlicek). <u>AmerPoR</u> (13:2) Mr-
            Ap 84, p. 48.
        "The Vltava in 1946" (tr. of Vladimir Holan, w. C.

G. Hanzlicek). AmerPoR (13:2) Mr-Ap 84, p. 48.

2081. HACKER, Marilyn
"1974." Cond (3:4, issue 10) 84, p. 109.
"April Interval I." Poetry (144:1) Ap 84, p. 1-2.
"April Interval III." Poetry (144:1) Ap 84, p. 2.
"April Interval IV." Poetry (144:1) Ap 84, p. 3.
"Arching in heat, tabbies from the Mairie" (for
    Nadja Tesich, from "Open Windows"). PraS
    (58:4) Wint 84, p. 25.
"Are You Aware of Gender When You Write?" SnapD
    (6:2) Spr 83, p. 3.
"Autumn 1980" (for Judith McDaniel). Cond (3:4,
    issue 10) 84, p. 106-108.
"Cultural Exchanges" (for Catherine Tinker).
    Ploughs (10:4) 84, p. 134-135.
"Fifteen to Eighteen." Cond (3:4, issue 10) 84,
    p. 105.
"Graffiti from the Gare Saint-Manqué" (for Zed
    Bee). Shen (35:2/3) 84, p. 169-173.
"How come, here, you see so many Black people"
    (from "Open Windows"). PraS (58:4) Wint 84, p.
    21.
"How come, she says, if you were what she is" (for
    Nélida Piñon, from "Open Windows"). PraS
    (58:4) Wint 84, p. 22.
"Inheritances." Ploughs (10:4) 84, p. 136-137.
"Late August." Ploughs (10:1) 84, p. 76-77.
"Now that she reads in bed till two A.M." (from
    "Open Windows"). PraS (58:4) Wint 84, p. 23.
"On the back of a letter in French" (for Sára
    Karig, from "Open Windows"). PraS (58:4) Wint
    84, p. 20.
"Open Windows" (Excerpts). PraS (58:4) Wint 84,
    p. 20-25.
"Pastiche Post-Pasta." Shen (35:1) 83-84, p. 78.
"She marched away, tagged 'Unaccompanied Minor'"
    (from "Open Windows"). PraS (58:4) Wint 84, p.
    24.
"Two Young Women." SnapD (6:2) Spr 83, p. 4.

HADADI, Litha Gaspar: See GASPAR-HADADI, Litha

2082. HADAS, Pamela White
"Ballad about a Wall" (tr. of Irina Ratushinskaya,
    w. Ilya Nykin). GrandS (3:3) Spr 84, p. 83.
"Leningrad Triptych" (tr. of Irina Ratushinskaya,
    w. Ilya Nykin). Agni (21) 84, p. 37-38.
"My Lord" (tr. of Irina Ratushinskaya. w. Ilya
    Nykin). Agni (21) 84, p. 39.

2083. HADAS, Rachel
"Amniocentesis" (for Joel, Eleanor, and Katherine).
    PraS (58:2) Sum 84, p. 75.
"Back to School." PraS (58:2) Sum 84, p. 76.
"Little by Little." NewRep (189:7/8) 15-22 Ag 83,
    p. 28.
"Night Piece with Cats (1)." MichQR (23:4) Aut
    84, p. 497.
"Night Piece with Cats (2)." MichQR (23:4) Aut

84, p. 498-499.
"Pantoum on Pumpkin Hill." <u>NewRep</u> (189:14) 3 O
    83, p. 34.
"Rhapsody on Old Clothes." <u>SouthwR</u> (69:4) Aut 84,
    p. 367-369.
"Song for Jonathan." <u>NewEngR</u> (7:1) Aut 84, p. 9-10.
"Tarpon Springs." <u>SouthwR</u> (69:4) Aut 84, p. 370.
"Tent Rocks." <u>SouthwR</u> (69:4) Aut 84, p. 365-366.
"That Walk Away As One: A Marriage Brood." <u>OntR</u>
    (20) Spr-Sum 84, p. 93-97.
"Whether." <u>ParisR</u> (26:94) Wint 84, p. 172-173.

2084. HAECK, Philippe
"Ou Sont les Manteaux." <u>CanLit</u> (100) Spr 84, p.
    130-131.

2085. HAHN, Susan
"Agoraphobia." <u>Poetry</u> (144:3) Je 84, p. 136.
"Waiting at the Gate." <u>Poetry</u> (144:3) Je 84, p.
    137-138.

2086. HAIL, Raven
"Wind Song" (An American Indian song to be sung by
    those waiting at home for a loved one who is
    away at war). <u>LittleBR</u> (4:4) Sum 84, p. 28.

2087. HAINES, John
"Book of the Jungle." <u>Sparrow</u> (46) 84, p. 21.
"The Gardener." <u>Germ</u> (8:1) Spr-Sum 84, p. 31.
"Horns." <u>Germ</u> (8:1) Spr-Sum 84, p. 30-31.
"Paul Klee." <u>Chelsea</u> (42/43) 84, p. 180.
"Rain Country." <u>NewEngR</u> (7:1) Aut 84, p. 1-5.
"The Stone Harp." <u>Chelsea</u> (42/43) 84, p. 180.

2088. HALDEMAN, Joe
"Curves in Space." <u>Veloc</u> (4) Sum 84, p. 51-52.

2089. HALES, Corrinne
"8. Miserable Catullus, stop all this foolishness"
    (tr. of Catullus). <u>CimR</u> (67) Ap 84, p. 42.
"11. Furius and Aurelius, such eager followers"
    (tr. of Catullus). <u>CimR</u> (67) Ap 84, p. 40.
"70. My woman says she wishes to marry no one" (tr.
    of Catullus). <u>CimR</u> (67) Ap 84, p. 44.
"A Fact of Life." <u>MemphisSR</u> (4:2) Spr 84, p. 25.
"In My Mother's Dresser Drawer." <u>MSS</u> (3:2/3) Spr
    84, p. 7.
"Place and Time" (for Alexis Khoury). <u>PraS</u> (58:2)
    Sum 84, p. 30-31.
"Roadside Marker." <u>MidAR</u> (4:2) Aut 84, p. 32.

2090. HALEY, Vanessa
"Luciferin: 1959." <u>MidAR</u> (4:1) Spr 84, p. 121.

2091. HALL, David
"Manhattan Song." <u>NegC</u> (4:2) Spr 84, p. 68-69.

2092. HALL, Donald
"The Baseball Players." <u>Atlantic</u> (254:1) Jl 84,
    p. 94.

"Couplet." <u>NewRep</u> (190:24) 18 Je 84, p. 34.
"Dave Hume." <u>Shen</u> (35:2/3) 84, p. 174.
"A Sister on the Tracks." <u>NewYorker</u> (60:24) 30 Jl
    84, p. 34.
"The Twelve Seasons." <u>SewanR</u> (92:4) O-D 84, p.
    507-511.

2093. HALL, Frances
    "Maledictions: Western Style." <u>SouthwR</u> (69:3) Sum
        84, p. 285.

2094. HALL, James Baker
    "The Maps." <u>Ploughs</u> (10:4) 84, p. 42-43.
    "The Rider." <u>QW</u> (19) Aut-Wint 84-85, p. 85.

2095. HALL, Jim
    "Departing from 28th Street." <u>ThRiPo</u> (23/24) 84,
        p. 64.
    "Last Words." <u>ThRiPo</u> (23/24) 84, p. 62-63.
    "The Mating Reflex." <u>Swallow</u> (3) 84, p. 110-111.
    "Maybe Dats Your Pwoblem Too." <u>Swallow</u> (3) 84, p.
        112-113.

2096. HALL, Joan Joffe
    "Envelope." <u>BelPoJ</u> (34:4) Sum 84, p. 28-32.
    "Four Questions about Surviving." <u>MassR</u> (25:3)
        Aut 84, p. 404.
    "No Hanukah Bush." <u>MassR</u> (25:3) Aut 84, p. 402.
    "Putting Down Roots." <u>MassR</u> (25:3) Aut 84, p. 403.

2097. HALL, Judith
    "The Habit of Surfaces." <u>13thM</u> (8:1/2) 84, p. 144.
    "Malignancies in Winter." <u>13thM</u> (8:1/2) 84, p.
        142-143.
    "Superstitious Elegy." <u>AntR</u> (42:4) Aut 84, p. 459.

2098. HALL, Phil
    "Circling Trout Lake." <u>Dandel</u> (11:2) Aut-Wint 84-
        85, p. 56-57.
    "For the Older Writers." <u>CrossC</u> (6:3) 84, p. 15.
    "Pelvis by Georgia O'Keefe." <u>Quarry</u> (33:3) Sum
        84, p. 53.
    "Portions." <u>PoetryCR</u> (6:2) Wint 84-85, p. 21.
    "Red Skelton." <u>LittleM</u> (14:3) 84, p. 44.
    "Unchosen." <u>CanLit</u> (101) Sum 84, p. 55.

2099. HALL, Theresa M.
    "Lizard Lope to Pea Ridge." <u>DekalbLAJ</u> (20th
        Anniversary Issue) 84, p. 91.

2100. HALL, Walter
    "Black Dog." <u>Gargoyle</u> (24) 84, p. 236.
    "The Last Poem." <u>Gargoyle</u> (24) 84, p. 237-238.

2101. HALLERMAN, Victoria
    "Grandmother in White, Courting." <u>StoneC</u> (11:3/4)
        Spr-Sum 84, p. 73.
    "Seeing, Being Seen." <u>Poetry</u> (144:2) My 84, p. 89-
        90.
    "We Grew Up Playing Bomb Shelter." <u>Poetry</u> (144:2)

My 84, p. 89.

2102. HALLETT, Joseph
      "Conflagration." Poem (52) N 84, p. 38.

2103. HALLEY, Anne
      "My Mother's 1934 Driver's License Considered As
         Evidence." SouthernPR (24:1) Spr 84, p. 38-43.

2104. HALLIDAY, Mark
      "Misery in the World." Ploughs (10:1) 84, p. 78-79.
      "Work." NewRep (191:20) 12 N 84, p. 44-45.

2105. HALMAN, Talat Sait
      "As the Night of Suffering Ends" (tr. of of Aziz
         Nesin). NewRena (6:1, #18) Spr 84, p. 29, 31.
      "Bleeding" (tr. of Izzet Yasar). NewRena (6:1,
         #18) Spr 84, p. 111, 113.
      "Dead" (tr. of Fazil Hüsnü Daglarca). NewRena
         (6:1, #18) Spr 84, p. 115.
      "Gercek Olüm." NewRena (6:1, #18) Spr 84, p. 42.
      "The Girl Grows Smaller" (tr. of Teoman Sarikahya).
         NewRena (6:1, #18) Spr 84, p. 71.
      "Guilt" (tr. of Nurer Ugurlu). NewRena (6:1, #18)
         Spr 84, p. 69.
      "I Woke, This Meant a Love in the World" (tr. of
         Ilhan Berk). NewRena (6:1, #18) Spr 84, p. 61.
      "Imperial Command" (tr. of Fazil Hüsnü
         Daglarca). NewRena (6:1, #18) Spr 84, p. 117.
      "Istanbul" (in Turkish). NewRena (6:1, #18) Spr
         84, p. 44, 46.
      "Istanbul" (tr. by the author). NewRena (6:1,
         #18) Spr 84, p. 45, 47.
      "Just at These Hours" (tr. of Cemal Süreya).
         NewRena (6:1, #18) Spr 84, p. 25, 27.
      "The Letter" (tr. of Feriha Aktan). NewRena (6:1,
         #18) Spr 84, p. 59.
      "Pendulum" (tr. of Yunus Koray). NewRena (6:1,
         #18) Spr 84, p. 67.
      "Ultimate Death" (tr. by the author). NewRena
         (6:1, #18) Spr 84, p. 43.
      "Waiting beside a Friend's Coffin" (tr. of Ahmet
         Erhan). NewRena (6:1, #18) Spr 84, p. 73.

2106. HALPERIN, Joan
      "Basket of Fish Milton Avery 1938." YetASM (3)
         84, p. 6.
      "Saturdays at Fourteen." Confr (27/28) 84, p. 323.

2107. HALPERIN, Mark
      "April." DenQ (19:1) Spr 84, p. 108.
      "The Garden at Twickenham." DenQ (19:1) Spr 84,
         p. 106.
      "In Fall." DenQ (19:1) Spr 84, p. 107.
      "Sold." CrabCR (2:1) Sum 84, p. 28.

2108. HALPERN, Daniel
      "3 A.M. the Rain." BlackWR (10:2) Spr 84, p. 92-93.
      "At Damariscotta Mills" (ending on lines by Lowell
         and Berryman). MemphisSR (5:1) Aut 84, p. 21.

"Autumnal." MissouriR (7:3) 84, p. 11.
"Below Keats' Room, Early Morning" (after Wilbur).
    MissouriR (7:3) 84, p. 12.
"Loose." ParisR (26:94) Wint 84, p. 171.
"Pastiche." TarRP (23:2) Spr 84, p. 2-4.
"Red Setter." TarRP (23:2) Spr 84, p. 1-2.

2109. HALPERN, M. L.
    "Why Not" (tr. by Benjamin Hrushovski and Kathryn
        Hellerstein). PartR (51:1) 84, p. 100-101.

2110. HALSALL, Jalaine
    "Moving On." NeqC (4:4) Aut 84, p. 34-35.

2111. HALSTEAD, Carol
    "Ultra Sound Scan." WestCR (19:2) O 84, p. 23.

2112. HALSTEAD, Peter
    "Flame." KanQ (16:1/2) Wint-Spr 84, p. 110.
    "In the House." KanQ (16:1/2) Wint-Spr 84, p. 110.

2113. HAMBLIN, Robert W.
    "My Daughter at Her Guitar" (Christmas 1981).
        CapeR (19:3) 20th Anniverary Issue 84, p. 26.
    "On the Death of the Evansville University
        Basketball Team in a Plane Crash, December 13,
        1977." CapeR (19:3) 20th Anniverary Issue 84,
        p. 24.
    "View from Room 170." CapeR (19:3) 20th
        Anniverary Issue 84, p. 25.

2114. HAMBURGER, Michael
    "Cat, Dying." GrandS (3:1) Aut 83, p. 82-83.
    "Poisons" (tr. of Marin Sorescu). NowestR (22:3)
        84, p. 124.

2115. HAMEL, Joseph
    "Dreams." PortR (30:1) 84, p. 62.
    "I Welcome the Dark." PortR (30:1) 84, p. 106-107.

2116. HAMERMESH, Cecile
    "Sale on Barbed Wire." ThirdW (2) Spr 84, p. 32.

2117. HAMILL, Janet
    "Bete Noire." Tele (19) 83, p. 44.
    "Insomnia." Tele (19) 83, p. 45.

2118. HAMILL, Paul
    "Member of the House." MidwQ (26:1) Aut 84, p. 72.

2119. HAMILL, Sam
    "Alone" (tr. of Li Po). CrabCR (1:3) Wint 84, p. 24.
    "At Changmen Palace" (tr. of Li Po). CrabCR (2:1)
        Sum 84, p. 24.
    "Eyes cast down, we must walk softly" (tr. of Jaan
        Kaplinski, w. the author). CharR (10:1) Spr
        84, p. 79.
    "George Seferis in Sonora." MidwQ (25:4) Sum 84,
        p. 408-410.
    "Homage to Trakl." MemphisSR (5:1) Aut 84, p. 40-41.

"I Understood" (tr. of Jaan Kaplinski, w. the
    author). MidwQ (25:4) Sum 84, p. 413-414.
"Lament" (tr. of Lady Cho Wen-Chun). CrabCR (1:3)
    Wint 84, p. 24.
"Night Traveling" (tr. of Tu Fu). CrabCR (2:1)
    Sum 84, p. 24.
"Nihil Obstat." MemphisSR (5:1) Aut 84, p. 42.
"Only to go along" (tr. of Jaan Kaplinski, w. the
    author). CharR (10:1) Spr 84, p. 78.
"Poetry Is Standing" (tr. of Jaan Kaplinski, w. the
    author). MidwQ (25:4) Sum 84, p. 412.
"Some roosters wake before dawn some islands grow
    higher in a single day" (tr. of Jaan Kaplinski,
    w. the author). CharR (10:1) Spr 84, p. 77.
"Spring Dreams" (tr. of Meng Hao-jan). CrabCR
    (2:1) Sum 84, p. 24.
"Summer You Poor Summer" (tr. of Jaan Kaplinski, w.
    the author). MidwQ (25:4) Sum 84, p. 411.

2120. HAMILTON, Alfred Starr
    "Awesome." NewL (50:2/3) Wint-Spr 84, p. 246.
    "Rain." NewL (50:2/3) Wint-Spr 84, p. 246.

2121. HAMILTON, Bruce
    "275." SanFPJ (6:1) 84, p. 17.

2122. HAMILTON, Carol
    "Chrysalis." SanFPJ (6:2) 84, p. 71.
    "Killing Cliché." SanFPJ (6:2) 84, p. 72.
    "Survivor." Amelia (1:2) O 84, p. 31.
    "War Is Endemic." SanFPJ (6:2) 84, p. 70.

2123. HAMILTON, Fritz
    "All Roads Leading To" (for Phoebe). SmPd (21:1)
        Wint 84, p. 10.
    "Diaphragm" (Lumber Camp Disaster). Paunch
        (57/58) Ja 84, p. 96.
    "Making It Turkey." WormR (24:2, issue 94) 84, p.
        50-51.
    "Murder for Peace." SanFPJ (7:1) 84, p. 43-44.
    "Nice to End" (for John and Steve). Wind (14:51)
        84, p. 19.
    "To Make It Like Ray!" WormR (24:2, issue 94) 84,
        p. 51.

2124. HAMILTON, Helena
    "For Earle Birney." Waves (12:2/3) Wint 84, p. 60.
    "For Gwendolyn MacEwen." Waves (12:2/3) Wint 84,
        p. 58.
    "For Harold Town." Waves (12:2/3) Wint 84, p. 62.

2125. HAMILTON, Horace
    "Museo Arqueológico Rafael Larco." SouthernR
        (20:1) Wint 84, p. 141-142.

2126. HAMILTON, Neil
    "The House of Mirrors." Quarry (33:1) Wint 84, p.
        46.
    "The man is sick" ("Untitled"). Quarry (33:1)
        Wint 84, p. 45.

2127. HAMILTON, T. G.
"Sam Spencer Owl Child." BlueBuf (2:2) Spr 84, p.
26.

2128. HAMM, Mark
"Just Like God." MalR (67) F 84, p. 116.
"Love Song Number Three" (for Patti Hammond).
MalR (67) F 84, p. 114-115.

2129. HAMMOND, Karla M.
"O Muse." RagMag (3:2) Aut 84, p. 19.
"Sighted." RagMag (3:2) Aut 84, p. 19.

2130. HAMPL, Patricia
"Love." PoetryE (15) Aut 84, p. 18.
"A Place in Florida." PoetryE (15) Aut 84, p. 17.

2131. HAMPSON, Robert
"A Broken Shutter in the Wind." Origin (Series
5:2) Wint 83, p. 62-63.
"Family Circle" (for Barbara, Carole and Cindy).
Origin (Series 5:2) Wint 83, p. 66-67.
"Fieldwork." Origin (Series 5:2) Wint 83, p. 68-69.
"How I found Dr. Livingstone." Origin (Series
5:2) Wint 83, p. 64-65.

2132. HAMPSON, Woesha
"I Am the Washerwoman." Calyx (8:2) Spr 84, p. 93.
"Raft Trip on the Green River." Calyx (8:2) Spr
84, p. 94.

2133. HAN, Yong-Woon (See also MANHAE)
"The Distance" (tr. by Bruce Taylor). LitR (27:3)
Spr 84, p. 310.
"My Sorrow" (tr. by Bruce Taylor). LitR (27:3)
Spr 84, p. 312.
"My Way" (tr. by Bruce Taylor). LitR (27:3) Spr
84, p. 311.
"Waiting" (tr. by Bruce Taylor). LitR (27:3) Spr
84, p. 311.

2134. HANCOCK, Craig
"Teaching at Coxsackie Prison." GreenfR (12:1/2)
Sum-Aut 84, p. 139-140.

2135. HAND, J. C.
"The Facts of Life" (for my daughter). GreenfR
(11:1/2) Sum-Aut 83, p. 124-126.

2136. HANEBURY, Derek
"Coming of Age." Grain (12:1) F 84, p. 15.
"From the Garden of a Quiet House." Grain (12:1)
F 84, p. 14.

2137. HANFT-MARTONE, Marjorie
"That Winter Monday" (for Robert Hayden). Obs
(8:1) Spr 82, p. 204.

2138. HANH, Thich Nhat (See also THICH, Nhat Hanh)
      "Condemnation." NewL (50:2/3) Wint-Spr 84, p. 221-
      222.

2139. HANKLA, Cathryn
      "Of Death, Fire, and the Moon." WebR (9:1) Spr
      84, p. 53.
      "Witch Woman." WebR (9:1) Spr 84, p. 52.

2140. HANNA, Tom
      "Businessmen's Lunch." NewL (50:2/3) Wint-Spr 84,
      p. 137.
      "Sues Seas." NewL (50:2/3) Wint-Spr 84, p. 136-137.

2141. HANNAH, Charles
      "A Quest, I Guess." EngJ (73:5) S 84, p. 90.

2142. HANSEN, Tom
      "Back Room Window -- Dawn to Noon." DekalbLAJ
      (17:1/2) 84, p. 128.
      "Bad Poem." Confr (27/28) 84, p. 310.
      "Complaint" (found poem). Spirit (7:1) 84, p. 135.
      "Crying Uncle." PoetryNW (25:4) Wint 84-85, p. 21-
      22.
      "The Man in the Moon's Loony Brother" (with crayon
      drawing by Paul, age 7). KanQ (16:1/2) Wint-
      Spr 84, p. 61.
      "Places I Never Lived: Faces I Never Loved."
      DekalbLAJ (20th Anniversary Issue) 84, p. 92-93.
      "Rain Song." PoetryNW (25:4) Wint 84-85, p. 23.

2143. HANSON, Charles
      "Christmas 1981." CrabCR (1:3) Wint 84, p. 5.
      "Feeling Winter." StoneC (11:3/4) Spr-Sum 84, p. 31.

2144. HANSON, Howard G.
      "Masking to Meet Ourselves." ArizQ (40:1) Spr 84,
      p. 96.

2145. HANZLICEK, C. G.
      "The Bell Is Struck." ThRiPo (23/24) 84, p. 36.
      "Children at Christmas in 1945" (tr. of Vladimir
      Holan, w. Dana Habova). AmerPoR (13:2) Mr-Ap
      84, p. 48.
      "Flycasting at Sunset." ThRiPo (23/24) 84, p. 37.
      "The Vltava in 1946" (tr. of Vladimir Holan, w.
      Dana Habova). AmerPoR (13:2) Mr-Ap 84, p. 48.

HAO-JAN, Meng: See MENG, Hao-jan

HAQUE, Abu Saeed Zahurul: See ABU SAEED

2146. HARA, Ed
      "Playing with Words." EngJ (73:8) D 84, p. 21.

2147. HARDER, Richard
      "For My Son." CrossC (6:3) 84, p. 25.
      "I've Been Up All Night." CrossC (6:3) 84, p. 25.
      "Some Laws Are." CrossC (6:3) 84, p. 25.
      "What Is a Poet." CrossC (6:3) 84, p. 25.

2148. HARDESTY, Harley C.
    "Noah and the Mushroom." SanFPJ (6:3) 84, p. 50.
    "Silos." SanFPJ (6:4) 84, p. 91.

2149. HARDING, May
    "Of What Substance." GreenfR (12:1/2) Sum-Aut 84,
    p. 104.

2150. HARDING, R. F. G.
    "A Crack in the Ceiling." CanLit (101) Sum 84, p.
    34.

2151. HARDING, Robert
    "Preliminary reports indicate that." Waves
    (12:2/3) Wint 84, p. 74.

2152. HARDY, Thomas
    "The Oxen." TriQ (61) Aut 84, p. 64.

2153. HARJATI, Suwita
    "A Teeny-Tiny Diamond." DekalbLAJ (20th
    Anniversary Issue) 84, p. 93.

2154. HARKINS, Patricia
    "The Taste of Metal." NeqC (4:4) Aut 84, p. 79.

2155. HARLOW, Michael
    "Vlaminck's Tie / The Persistent Imaginal."
    PoetryCR (6:1) Aut 84, p. 13.
    "The War of Course Is Elsewhere." PoetryCR (6:1)
    Aut 84, p. 13.

2156. HARMER, David
    "The Spinner's Final Over." Argo (5:3) 84, p. 39.

2157. HARMON, William
    "Ask me no questions I'll still tell you lies."
    Poetry (144:1) Ap 84, p. 2.
    "A Cloud No Bigger Than a Woman's Hand." CarolQ
    (36:2) Wint 84, p. 76-77.
    "A Cloud No Bigger Than a Woman's Hand"
    (Selections: III.iv-v, IV. "Holy Writ," for
    Krakatoa Ellenbogen). Agni (20) 84, p. 103-104.
    "Crepuscular autumnal moribund." Poetry (144:1)
    Ap 84, p. 27.
    "Don Quijote" (tr. of Lucian Blaga, w. Michael
    Taub). ConcPo (17:2) Aut 84, p. 64.
    "Eve" (tr. of Lucian Blaga, w. Michael Taub).
    ConcPo (17:2) Aut 84, p. 65.
    "Five Poems." Poetry (144:1) Ap 84, p. 26-29.
    "Memoir." CarolQ (37:1) Aut 84, p. 63.
    "Metabolism." CarolQ (37:1) Aut 84, p. 62.
    "O how I O endlessly think endlessly innocent the
    world was." Poetry (144:1) Ap 84, p. 27-28.
    "O. Wow. O." Poetry (144:1) Ap 84, p. 26-27.
    "Way back in my hand-wrestling days." Poetry
    (144:1) Ap 84, p. 28-29.

HARMSEN von der BEEK, F. Ten: See BEEK, F. Ten Harmsen V. D.

2158. HARN, John
"A Sequence of Events." BlueBldgs (7) 84, p. 20.

2159. HARNACK, Curtis
"My Oldest Brother the Moment He Became My
Youngest." GreenfR (12:1/2) Sum-Aut 84, p. 116.
"Summer Lesson." GreenfR (12:1/2) Sum-Aut 84, p.
117.

2160. HARNEY, Stephen
"Poem for My Friends." HarvardA (118:2) Spr 84,
p. 37-38.

2161. HARNEY, Steve
"Anatomy of a Spider Monkey" (for Uncle Tim).
HarvardA (117:4/118:1) D 84, p. 25.
"Wright, James: 'Conversations' Make One Cassette
for His Wife +All Readings (5 Tapes)."
HarvardA (117:4/118:1) D 84, p. 25.

2162. HARPER, Michael
"Alice Braxton Johnson" (for KJH). NewL (50:2/3)
Wint-Spr 84, p. 104-105.

2163. HARPER, Michael S.
"Inauguration Blues." Field (31) Aut 84, p. 61-62.
"The Loon." Field (31) Aut 84, p. 59-60.

2164. HARRELL, William
"Critick draws back from everything that lives."
TriQ (59) Wint 84, p. 133.
"The first decade, the babe is mom's and dad's."
TriQ (59) Wint 84, p. 132.

2165. HARRIS, Carolyn
"The Mirror's Place" (tr. of Jorge Arbeleche, w.
the author). Iowa (14:2) Spr-Sum 84, p. 158.

2166. HARRIS, Claire
"Nude of a Pale Staircase." Waves (13:1) Aut 84,
p. 42-47.

2167. HARRIS, Claire K.
"Where the Sky Is a Pitiful Tent." Descant (47,
15:4) Wint 84, p. 38-45.

2168. HARRIS, Devorah B.
"Body Language." RagMag (3:2) Aut 84, p. 36.
"On the Wire." RagMag (3:2) Aut 84, p. 37.
"To My 8th Grade Class." EngJ (73:3) Mr 84, p. 82.

2169. HARRIS, Jay D.
"The Steel Bronco." PoeticJ (8) 84, p. 6.

2170. HARRIS, Joseph
"Gewgaw in a Taxi." TexasR (5:1/2) Spr-Sum 84, p.
96.
"On Straightening Utrillo." Vis (14) 84, p. 5.
"Return." PortR (30:1) 84, p. 80.

2171. HARRIS, Judith
       "Babysitter." Nimrod (28:1) Aut-Wint 84, p. 69.
       "Her Husband Was a Boxer." Nimrod (28:1) Aut-Wint
       84, p. 70.
       "Story." Nimrod (28:1) Aut-Wint 84, p. 70-72.
       "Sunset over the Houses Will Border This Field."
       Nimrod (28:1) Aut-Wint 84, p. 73-74.
       "Threads" (Selections). Nimrod (28:1) Aut-Wint
       84, p. 69-74.
       "What I Know." Nimrod (28:1) Aut-Wint 84, p. 72-73.

2172. HARRIS, Latif
       "Chile" (for Jack). OroM (2:3/4, issue 7/8) 84,
       p. 40-42.

2173. HARRIS, Mark
       "Conversation between the Borders." Argo (5:3)
       84, p. 25.

2174. HARRIS, Peter
       "Instinctive Self-Portrait" (tr. of Miron
       Białoszdwski, w. Danuta Lopozyko). LitR
       (28:1) Aut 84, p. 130.
       "No Smoking" (tr. Wiesław Kazanecki, w. Danuta
       Lopozyko). LitR (28:1) Aut 84, p. 132.
       "The Pain" (tr. of Marek Wawrzykiewicz, w. Danuta
       Lopozyko). LitR (28:1) Aut 84, p. 133.
       "Young Faustus Visits the Institute of Oncology and
       Does Research on Experience" (tr. of Jerzy
       Gorzanski, w. Danuta Lopozyko). LitR (28:1)
       Aut 84, p. 131.

2175. HARRIS, Rennick W.
       "Ballet Dancer." Amelia (1:2) O 84, p. 34.

2176. HARRIS, Robert
       "Manners." DekalbLAJ (17:1/2) 84, p. 129.

2177. HARRISON, David
       "Food for Thought." PoeticJ (3) 83, p. 8.

2178. HARRISON, James
       "Darwin and the Galapagos." CanLit (103) Wint 84,
       p. 6-9.

2179. HARRISON, Jeffrey
       "The Hummingbird Feeder." Poetry (144:6) S 84, p.
       336.

2180. HARRISON, Keith
       "Last Evening." PoetryNW (25:1) Spr 84, p. 36-37.

2181. HARRISON, Richard
       "The Glove" (Malaya, January 15, 1945). GreenfR
       (11:3/4) Wint-Spr 84, p. 97.
       "Ham, the Father of Canaan." Grain (12:2) My 84,
       p. 20.
       "Jennifer and the Maple Keys." Quarry (33:3) Sum
       84, p. 11.
       "The Mourning of Lot's Wife." CrossC (6:2) 84, p.

11.
"They burned the mannequins." <u>GreenfR</u> (11:3/4)
      Wint-Spr 84, p. 98.
"The War Artist." <u>Grain</u> (12:2) My 84, p. 19.

2182. HARRISON, Sam
      "The Bats." <u>Poem</u> (52) N 84, p. 47.
      "A Morning Spent Waiting for Rain." <u>Poem</u> (52) N
            84, p. 46.
      "Walking Stick." <u>Poem</u> (52) N 84, p. 45.

2183. HARRISON, Tony
      "Marked with D." <u>Hudson</u> (37:1) Spr 84, p. 15.

2184. HARROLD, William
      "Cartography." <u>Open24</u> (3) 84, p. 33.
      "The Night-Wanderers" (after Edward Hopper).
            <u>CreamCR</u> (9:1/2) 84, p. 35.

2185. HARSHMAN, Marc
      "Fishing in June." <u>SpoonRQ</u> (9:2) Spr 84, p. 22.

2186. HART, Jonathan
      "When the night is vacant." <u>Quarry</u> (33:3) Sum 84,
            p. 61.
      "The wind slams the coast." <u>Grain</u> (12:4) N 84, p.
            24.

2187. HART, Max
      "Stranger." <u>Confr</u> (27/28) 84, p. 41.

2188. HARTMAN, Charles O.
      "The Burden of the Desert of the Sea." <u>Agni</u> (20)
            84, p. 70-71.
      "Incentive." <u>Ploughs</u> (10:4) 84, p. 205-206.
      "On My Mother's Birthday." <u>Agni</u> (20) 84, p. 68-69.

2189. HARTSFIELD, Carla
      "The Old House." <u>Descant</u> (47, 15:4) Wint 84, p.
            118-122.
      "A Word about Separation." <u>Descant</u> (47, 15:4)
            Wint 84, p. 123.

2190. HARTWIG, Julia
      "Vigil on a Bay." <u>Iowa</u> (14:2) Spr-Sum 84, p. 194.

2191. HARVEY, Andrew
      "Epigram" (tr. of al-Ma'arrī). <u>SenR</u> (14:1)
            84, p. 29.
      "If You Have O Soul" (tr. of al-Ma'arrī).
            <u>SenR</u> (14:1) 84, p. 30.
      "She Plays in My Heart" (tr. of 'Antara). <u>SenR</u>
            (14:1) 84, p. 28.

2192. HARVEY, Gayle Elen
      "Annunciation." <u>StoneC</u> (11:3/4) Spr-Sum 84, p. 62.
      "Keep It Quiet, Cinderella" (after a drawing by an
            Irish child, age 6 or 7). <u>StoneC</u> (11:3/4) Spr-
            Sum 84, p. 63.
      "One Small House." <u>SnapD</u> (7:1) Aut 83, p. 64.

"Today, the Only Certainty Is Winter." SnapD
    (8:1) Aut 84, p. 51.

2193. HARVEY, Jack
    "The Death of Diamond Bessie." SouthwR (69:3) Sum
        84, p. 242-244.

2194. HARVEY, Joan
    "Floridian Meridian." Os (19) 84, p. 3-5.

2195. HARVEY, Ken J.
    "Another Link." PottPort (6) 84, p. 17.
    "That Ditch." PottPort (6) 84, p. 21.

2196. HARVEY, L. G.
    "Philosopher's Stone." NewL (50:4) Sum 84, p. 43.

2197. HARVEY, Richard F.
    "Papal Visit." SanFPJ (7:1) 84, p. 80.
    "Sonnet for a Soldier" (Chu Lai, Vietnam). Pig
        (12) 84, p. 79.

2198. HARVEY, Sally
    "The Last Time." Tendril (17) Wint 84, p. 86.

2199. HARWOOD, Edmund
    "Death of Badger." Stand (25:2) Spr 84, p. 51.

2200. HASAN, Rabiul
    "For My Daughter, Ruma" (tr. of Abu Saeed).
        Amelia (1:2) O 84, p. 49.

2201. HASKINS, Lola
    "Alexandria, 1982." BelPoJ (35:1) Aut 84, p. 19.
    "Fame." PraS (58:2) Sum 84, p. 88.
    "Invocation." SouthernPR (24:1) Spr 84, p. 5.
    "Kitchen." SouthernPR (24:1) Spr 84, p. 5.
    "Secrets of the Fur Trade: Everywoman's
        Encyclopedia, 1895." SouthwR (69:2) Spr 84, p.
        154.
    "Wings." BelPoJ (35:1) Aut 84, p. 20-27.

2202. HASS, Robert
    "City without a Name" (tr. of Czeslaw Milosz, w.
        the author and Robert Pinsky). Thrpny (16)
        Wint 84, p. 12-13.
    "The Gates of the Arsenal" (tr. of Czeslaw Milosz,
        w. Renata Gorczynski). GrandS (3:2) Wint 84,
        p. 94-96.
    "Meditation at Lagunitas." Tendril (18, special
        issue) 84, p. 186-187.
    "Old Dominion." SoCaR (17:1) Aut 84, p. 87.
    "Slow River" (tr. of Czeslaw Milosz, w. the author
        and Robert Pinsky). NewRep (189:20) 14 N 83,
        p. 31.
    "Songs of Adrian Zielinsky" (tr. of Czeslaw Milosz,
        w. the author). NewRep (189:20) 14 N 83, p. 33.
    "A Story about the Body." NewRep (189:9) 29 Ag
        83, p. 30.

2203. HASSE, Margaret
      "A Notch in the Spiral" (on a theme of Seferis).
      Tendril (17) Wint 84, p. 87.

2204. HATFIELD, Steve
      "Evenly Spaced Out around the Court, the
      Cheerleaders Are Jumping High, Kicking Their
      Legs in the Air." Wind (14:52) 84, p. 23.

2205. HATHAWAY, Baxter
      "Hell's Purgatory" (Selections: 14-17, tr. of
      Edoardo Sanguineti). Chelsea (42/43) 84, p.
      153-155.

2206. HATHAWAY, James
      "1983, San Antonio." NewL (51:2) Wint 84-85, p. 33.
      "Fishing." PoetryE (15) Aut 84, p. 63-64.

2207. HATHAWAY, Jeanine
      "Counsel." KanQ (16:4) Aut 84, p. 28.
      "Magnificat." KanQ (16:4) Aut 84, p. 27.

2208. HATHAWAY, Richard
      "A Winter's Passage." AntigR (59) Aut 84, p. 111.

2209. HATHAWAY, William
      "Greyhound/Science Fiction." CharR (10:2) Aut 84,
      p. 70-72.
      "Letter to a Cousin on This Twentieth Deathday."
      KenR (NS 6:1) Wint 84, p. 25-27.
      "Speaking of Sounds" (For Holley Haymaker). KenR
      (NS 6:1) Wint 84, p. 28.
      "Still Life." Poetry (144:4) Jl 84, p. 218.
      "What Springs to Life." Telescope (3:3) Aut 84,
      p. 46-48.

2210. HATLEN, Burton
      "Take Out the Garbage, etc." MinnR (N.S. 23) Aut
      84, p. 14-16.

2211. HATLEY, James
      "The Lighthouses" (tr. of Charles Baudelaire).
      WebR (9:2) Wint 85, p. 14-15.

2212. HAUG, James
      "Love Canal." MidAR (4:2) Aut 84, p. 57.

2213. HAUSER, Gwen
      "Ode to the Crysanthemums" (poem on the exoticism
      of the white crysanthemums). Waves (12:2/3)
      Wint 84, p. 54-56.
      "Women of the Whole World*" (poem on a painting by
      a Soviet Woman, Andrei Kozka. *The name of a
      women's peace-magazine). PoetryCR (6:2) Wint
      84-85, p. 12.

2214. HAUSMAN, Gerald
      "Desert Water." GreenfR (12:1/2) Sum-Aut 84, p. 82.

2215. HAWKES, John
       "The Bestowal" (individual poems not indexed).
       Sparrow (45) 83.

2216. HAWKINS, Hunt
       "Eduardo Mondlane." _MinnR_ (N.S. 23) Aut 84, p. 68-
         69.
       "Lytton's Corners." _MinnR_ (N.S. 23) Aut 84, p. 69.
       "The Prejohn." _GeoR_ (38:2) Sum 84, p. 366-367.
       "T. S. Eliot's Dinners." _GeoR_ (38:2) Sum 84, p.
         365-366.

2217. HAWKINS, John
       "Dorchester Street: November 22, 1962." _Wind_
         (14:50) 84, p. 57.
       "Easter 1964." _HangL_ (45) Spr 84, p. 29.

2218. HAWLEY, James
       "Ptarmigan Pass." _KanQ_ (16:1/2) Wint-Spr 84, p. 112.

2219. HAXTON, Brooks
       "Bones." _Poetry_ (143:5) F 84, p. 291.
       "The Clarinet." _ChiR_ (34:3) Sum 84, p. 20.
       "Economics." _BelPoJ_ (34:3) Spr 84, p. 8.
       "Glee." _BelPoJ_ (34:3) Spr 84, p. 9-10.
       "Los Angeles." _SouthernR_ (20:1) Wint 84, p. 138-140.
       "Not Wild or Mongolian Now, Nor Ever Truly an Ass."
         ChiR (34:3) Sum 84, p. 19.
       "Odd Man Out." _BelPoJ_ (34:3) Spr 84, p. 9.
       "Peaceable Kingdom." _ChiR_ (34:3) Sum 84, p. 18.
       "Tongue." _Poetry_ (143:5) F 84, p. 292.
       "What Would Make a Boy Think to Kill Bats."
         BelPoJ (34:3) Spr 84, p. 7-8.

2220. HAYDEN, Robert
       "The Whipping." _Obs_ (8:1) Spr 82, p. 62.

HAYDEN, Steve (Editor's error): _See_ NOYES, Steve

2221. HAYES, Ann
       "For Giselbertus the Stone-Carver." _Hudson_ (37:4)
         Wint 84-85, p. 555-556.
       "Of Other Wars." _Hudson_ (37:4) Wint 84-85, p. 554-
         555.

2222. HAYES, Glenn
       "Deathbed." _PoetryCR_ (6:1) Aut 84, p. 27.

2223. HAYES, John E.
       "Taken by the Lake." _GrahamHR_ (7) Wint 84, p. 24-25.

2224. HAYMAN, Lee Ricard
       "Math." _Comm_ (111:7) 6 Ap 84, p. 220.

2225. HAYNES, Pam
       "Always Leave a Way Out for the Spirit."
         MemphisSR (4:2) Spr 84, p. 15.
       "Here, We Are the Hawk." _MemphisSR_ (4:2) Spr 84,
         p. 50.

2226. HAYNES, Pamela
      "Lighting the Lamps." <u>MemphisSR</u> (5:1) Aut 84, p. 25.

2227. HAYS, Jay Bob
      "The Doctor of Children" (for Luvern Hays, M.D.
         dead of cancer January 1, 1966). <u>CapeR</u> (19:3)
         20th Anniverary Issue 84, p. 28.
      "In Greenland Graves." <u>CapeR</u> (19:3) 20th
         Anniversary Issue 84, p. 27.

2228. HAZARD, John
      "Scene." <u>WebR</u> (9:1) Spr 84, p. 54.
      "Writing Your Name" (for my daughter). <u>WebR</u> (9:1)
         Spr 84, p. 55.

2229. HEAD, Gwen
      "Darwin's Moth." <u>Ploughs</u> (10:4) 84, p. 54-55.
      "Hydrangea Blue." <u>Ploughs</u> (10:4) 84, p. 56-57.
      "Kings of England" (after a collage print of
         handmade, hand-dyed paper by Akiko Shimamura,
         one of a series). <u>AntR</u> (42:3) Sum 84, p. 323.

2230. HEAD, Robert Grady
      "Aetiology." <u>Sam</u> (40:1, release 157) 84, p. 16.
      "Alcohol and Atombombs Remove the Veneer of
         Civilization." <u>Sam</u> (40:1, release 157) 84, p. 4.
      "The Atom Bomb Will Cure My Impotence." <u>Sam</u>
         (40:1, release 157) 84, p. 5.
      "Benzedrine Music." <u>Sam</u> (40:1, release 157) 84,
         p. 12.
      "Flow with the Material." <u>Sam</u> (40:1, release 157)
         84, p. 8.
      "Good Colors." <u>Sam</u> (40:1, release 157) 84, p. 14.
      "Here Cums the Bride All Dresst in Fire." <u>Sam</u>
         (40:1, release 157) 84, p. 5.
      "I Bild Myself a Littl House." <u>Sam</u> (40:1, release
         157) 84, p. 10.
      "I Know a Woman Hoo's Warm & Wonderful, Make You
         Weep Like the Morning Star." <u>Sam</u> (40:1,
         release 157) 84, p. 6.
      "If We Could Just Be Certain." <u>Sam</u> (40:1, release
         157) 84, p. 15.
      "In Japan There Were Still Medical Services." <u>Sam</u>
         (40:1, release 157) 84, p. 4.
      "In Praise of Caveman." <u>Sam</u> (40:1, release 157)
         84, p. 2.
      "In Praise of Caveman: The Atom Bomb Poems" (Issue
         title). <u>Sam</u> (40:1, release 157) 84, p. 1-16.
      "In the Rain and on the Grass." <u>Sam</u> (40:1,
         release 157) 84, p. 10.
      "Life." <u>Sam</u> (40:1, release 157) 84, p. 7.
      "Man Cheated of Sex and Honor Wants to Blow It All
         Up." <u>Sam</u> (40:1, release 157) 84, p. 5.
      "Men Again." <u>Sam</u> (40:1, release 157) 84, p. 7.
      "The Most Beautiful Bird in the World." <u>Sam</u>
         (40:1, release 157) 84, p. 8.
      "Plum Brandy." <u>Sam</u> (40:1, release 157) 84, p. 11.
      "The Portly Pompous Man." <u>Sam</u> (40:1, release 157)
         84, p. 6.
      "Say Mass over the Uranium." <u>Sam</u> (40:1, release

157) 84, p. 9.
"Self-Destructive As the Sunshine." <u>Sam</u> (40:1,
      release 157) 84, p. 9.
"Time Is an Aspect of Thermodynamics." <u>Sam</u> (40:1,
      release 157) 84, p. 14.
"Tired of It." <u>Sam</u> (40:1, release 157) 84, p. 12.
"To Relocate." <u>Sam</u> (40:1, release 157) 84, p. 15.
"Wassail." <u>Sam</u> (40:1, release 157) 84, p. 13.
"The Word I Wanted to Say." <u>Sam</u> (40:1, release
      157) 84, p. 13.
"Would Darwin Praise This Struggle?" <u>Sam</u> (40:1,
      release 157) 84, p. 3.
"You'll Both Be Free." <u>Sam</u> (40:1, release 157)
      84, p. 11.

2231. HEADLEY, Doris M.
      "Uncertainties." <u>NegC</u> (4:2) Spr 84, p. 58.

2232. HEANEY, Seamus
      "Alphabets." <u>Harp</u> (269:1615) D 84, p. 31.
      "Changes." <u>Antaeus</u> (53) Aut 84, p. 90-91.
      "Changes." <u>Pequod</u> (16/17) 84, p. 36.
      "Davin on the Broagh Road." <u>Pequod</u> (16/17) 84, p.
            38.
      "The Easter House." <u>Pequod</u> (16/17) 84, p. 37.
      "The Guttural Muse." <u>MidAR</u> (4:2) Aut 84, p. 105.
      "The Loaning." <u>Antaeus</u> (53) Aut 84, p. 93-94.
      "The Railway Children." <u>Antaeus</u> (53) Aut 84, p. 92.
      "Sandstone Keepsake." <u>NewYorker</u> (60:21) 9 Jl 84,
            p. 36.
      "Vowels ploughed into other: opened ground

2233. HEARLE, Kevin
      "The First Demonstration of Muybridge's
            Zoepraxiscope: Palo Alto Stock Farm 1879."
            <u>Telescope</u> (3:3) Aut 84, p. 61.
      "Program Notes for <u>The Art of Cryptic Postcards</u>."
            <u>Telescope</u> (3:3) Aut 84, p. 74-79.

2234. HEARST, James
      "Away with Boards." <u>KanQ</u> (16:1/2) Wint-Spr 84, p.
            97.
      "Never Too Late." <u>NoAmR</u> (269:3) S 84, p. 62.
      "The Trimmed Bush." <u>NoAmR</u> (269:4) D 84, p. 43.
      "Truth." <u>Sparrow</u> (46) 84, p. 15.
      "What Matters." <u>NoAmR</u> (269:4) D 84, p. 43.

2235. HEATH-STUBBS, John
      "King David" (tr. of Eugene Dubnov, w. the author).
            <u>NowestR</u> (22:3) 84, p. 96-98.

2236. HEBERLEIN, Larry
      "Thoreau at a Party." <u>SoDakR</u> (22:4) Wint 84, p.
            61-62.

2237. HEBERT, Anne
      "Love" (tr. by A. Poulin, Jr.). <u>NewEngR</u> (6:4) Sum
            84, p. 561.

2238. HECHT, Anthony
        "The Vow." <u>Peb</u> (23) 84, p. 62-63.

2239. HEDEEN, Paul M.
        "How Stealthy This Rain." <u>Confr</u> (27/28) 84, p. 266.

2240. HEFFERNAN, Michael
        "Amid a Place of Stone." <u>MidwQ</u> (26:1) Aut 84, p. 73.
        "At the Tire Fire at the Landfill." <u>PoetryNW</u>
            (25:3) Aut 84, p. 36.
        "The Blessing of the Bones." <u>MemphisSR</u> (4:2) Spr
            84, p. 8.
        "The Garden Party." <u>MemphisSR</u> (4:2) Spr 84, p. 7.
        "Gifts." <u>NewL</u> (50:4) Sum 84, p. 55.
        "Jacob Limps Home over the River" (for Kathy).
            <u>MidwQ</u> (25:2) Wint 84, p. 166-167.
        "Liberty" (to Patrick Kavanagh). <u>GeoR</u> (38:4) Wint
            84, p. 720.
        "Pilgrimage." <u>MidwQ</u> (25:2) Wint 84, p. 164.
        "Presidents." <u>PoetryNW</u> (25:3) Aut 84, p. 35-36.
        "The Sea off Flanders." <u>MidwQ</u> (25:2) Wint 84, p.
            163.
        "To the Wreakers of Havoc." <u>MemphisSR</u> (4:2) Spr
            84, p. 7.
        "A Voyage to the Island." <u>MidwQ</u> (25:2) Wint 84,
            p. 165.

2241. HEFFERNAN, Thomas
        "The Sleeping Sonnets" (Selections: 53-55).
            <u>Ploughs</u> (10:1) 84, p. 80-81.

2242. HEFLIN, Jack
        "Respect the Birds." <u>AntR</u> (42:4) Aut 84, p. 452.

HEHIR, Diana O': <u>See</u> O'HEHIR, Diana

2243. HEIDE, Christopher
        "Coming Home to Pangnirtung." <u>PottPort</u> (6) 84, p.
            26-27.

2244. HEINE, Heinrich
        "Du Bist Wie Eine Blume." <u>NegC</u> (4:2) Spr 84, p. 74.
        "Jetzt Wohin?" <u>MassR</u> (25:4) Wint 84, p. 570, 572.
        "Sie Haben Heut' Abend Gesellschaft." <u>NegC</u> (4:2)
            Spr 84, p. 76.
        "This Evening They've a Party" (tr. by Stephen
            Town). <u>NegC</u> (4:2) Spr 84, p. 77.
        "Where?" (tr. by Stephen Town). <u>NegC</u> (4:2) Spr
            84, p. 79.
        "Whereto Now?" (tr. by Frederick C. Ellert).
            <u>MassR</u> (25:4) Wint 84, p. 571, 573.
        "Wo?" <u>NegC</u> (4:2) Spr 84, p. 78.
        "You Are Like a Flower" (tr. by Stephen Town).
            <u>NegC</u> (4:2) Spr 84, p. 75.

HEINE, Lala Koehn: <u>See</u> KOEHN-HEINE, Lala

2245. HEINEMAN, W. F.
        "Dark Seams of Water." <u>PikeF</u> (6) Aut 84, p. 3.

2246. HEINEMANN, W. F.
    "The Exile." Confr (27/28) 84, p. 43.

2247. HEINRICH, Peggy
    "Snorkeling." DekalbLAJ (17:1/2) 84, p. 130.

2248. HEISE, Hans-Jürgen
    "Paul Celan" (tr. by Carl Clifton Toliver).
    Sulfur (4:2, issue 11) 84, p. 94.

2249. HEJDUK, John
    "The Berlin Masque." Chelsea (42/43) 84, p. 427-434.

2250. HEJINIAN, Lyn
    "The Guard" (Selections: 5-6). Sulfur (3:3, issue
    9) 84, p. 130-135.

2251. HEKKANEN, Ernest
    "Dance of the Jolly Jugmen." Quarry (33:1) Wint
    84, p. 44.
    "The Myriad Footprints." Dandel (11:1) Spr-Sum
    84, p. 93-94.
    "The Stone Wafer." Dandel (11:1) Spr-Sum 84, p. 95.

2252. HELLER, Liane
    "The Dance." PoetryCR (6:1) Aut 84, p. 27.

2253. HELLER, Michael
    "A Night for Chinese Poets" (Newcastle, Wyoming).
    Pequod (16/17) 84, p. 127-128.

2254. HELLERSTEIN, Kathryn
    "Small Night-Music" (Selections: 1, 12, tr. of
    Jacob Glatshteyn, w. Benjamin Hrushovski).
    PartR (51:1) 84, p. 99-100.
    "Why Not" (tr. of M. L. Halpern, w. Benjamin
    Hrushovski). PartR (51:1) 84, p. 100-101.

2255. HELLWEG, Paul
    "Two Innocents." SanFPJ (6:2) 84, p. 80.
    "When Night Turns Day." SanFPJ (6:2) 84, p. 80.

2256. HELWIG, Maggie
    "Ekaterinburg, Kronstadt Shipyards." Grain (12:2)
    My 84, p. 8.
    "The Finland Station." Grain (12:2) My 84, p. 6.
    "The Name of the Magician." Waves (12:1) Aut 83,
    p. 66.
    "Notes for Les Ballets Russes." Grain (12:2) My
    84, p. 5-9.
    "Pisa-Crusader Dreams." CanLit (102) Aut 84, p.
    17-19.

2257. HEMAN, Bob
    "Guest." GreenfR (12:1/2) Sum-Aut 84, p. 124.
    "Passion." GreenfR (12:1/2) Sum-Aut 84, p. 124.
    "Source." GreenfR (12:1/2) Sum-Aut 84, p. 124.

2258. HEMINWAY, David
    "Allegory for Gisela " LitR (28:1) Aut 84, p. 63.

2259. HEMMINGSON, Michael A.
"Amazon River of the Mind." PoeticJ (4) 83, p. 16.
"Blades." PoeticJ (2) 83, p. 10.
"Breeze" (for Jennifer). PoeticJ (6) 84, p. 20.
"Grammer." PoeticJ (8) 84, p. 16-17.
"It Was a Day of Peace, a Night of Hell" (for
   Jennifer Crenshaw). Amelia (1:2) O 84, p. 57-58.
"A Nest." PoeticJ (1) 83, p. 21.
"One Hundred TVs." PoeticJ (1) 83, p. 11.
"Paths." Open24 (3) 84, p. 19.
"Poetry Lane." PoeticJ (4) 83, p. 16.
"Roof Eyes." Open24 (3) 84, p. 19.
"The Sculptor." PoeticJ (1) 83, p. 26.
"A Small Mirror." PoeticJ (5) 84, p. 39.
"The unfairness of all circumstances and events."
   PoeticJ (5) 84, p. 38.
"We Explore Our Present through the Past."
   PoeticJ (2) 83, p. 21.

2260. HENDERSON, Archibald
"The Hegira." NegC (4:2) Spr 84, p. 60.
"Table Turned." Swallow (3) 84, p. 21.

2261. HENDERSON, Bonnie Jo
"First Defense: I Didn't Give Adam the Apple."
   SanFPJ (6:3) 84, p. 10-11.

2262. HENDERSON, Brian
"Midnight Dawn" (for B.C.). PoetryCR (6:1) Aut
   84, p. 25.
"Vertigo." PoetryCR (6:1) Aut 84, p. 25.

2263. HENDRICKSON, Thomas M.
"Trenton Standard." Wind (14:51) 84, p. 20.

2264. HENKE, Mark
"Kassandra." SoDakR (22:4) Wint 84, p. 63.
"Zelda at Constantine." SoDakR (22:4) Wint 84, p.
   64.

2265. HENLEY, Don
"James Dean" (w. Jackson Browne, Glenn Frey, and J.
   D. Souther, 1974, Benchmark Music, ASCAP).
   NewOR (11:3/4) Aut-Wint 84, p. 95.

2266. HENLEY, Lloyd
"Shadows in the Cave." KanQ (16:1/2) Wint-Spr 84,
   p. 190-191.

2267. HENN, Mary Ann, Sister
"Beepbeepbeepbee   eep." SanFPJ (6:1) 84, p. 8.
"The Comet Is Coming -- 1986 (or Is That What It
   Is?)." SanFPJ (7:1) 84, p. 29.
"De Fence." YetASM (3) 84, p. 8.
"Euphoric Lies." SanFPJ (6:1) 84, p. 51.
"Flight 007." SanFPJ (6:1) 84, p. 50.
"Halley's Comet?" SanFPJ (7:1) 84, p. 32.
"Hands of Peace." SanFPJ (6:4) 84, p. 28.
"If you look at the sun and it's spotty." SanFPJ
   (7:1) 84, p. 32.

"It Comes Piecemeal." PoeticJ (8) 84, p. 17.
"Like a Nun." Wind (14:52) 84, p. 24-25.
"National symbol" (Haiku H665). SanFPJ (6:1) 84,
   p. 3.
"Ol' Buddy." PoeticJ (7) 84, p. 24.
"A Poet." Wind (14:52) 84, p. 24.
"Santa Hit." SanFPJ (6:4) 84, p. 27.
"Slogan for nuke squadron" (Haiku H728). SanFPJ
   (6:1) 84, p. 3.

2268. HENNING, Barbara
   "At Night." MichQR (23:2) Spr 84, p. 269.
   "The Difference." Vis (16) 84, p. 19.
   "Halloween." Vis (16) 84, p. 19.

2269. HENNING, Dianna
   "This Is How My Voice Will Rise." YellowS (12)
      Aut 84, p. 6.

2270. HENRY, Laurie
   "Downtown Newberry Destroyed by Tornado." AmerPoR
      (13:3) My-Je 84, p. 48.
   "No Tenure." PoetryNW (25:3) Aut 84, p. 26-27.

2271. HENRY, Marie
   "Cocoon." YellowS (12) Aut 84, p. 29.

2272. HENRY, Michael
   "Ward Round." Bogg (52) 84, p. 37.

2273. HENSON, Lance
   "Journal Entry 8/6/82" (for Annie West). Nimrod
      (27:2) Spr-Sum 84, p. 48.
   "Near the Wichita Mountains, January 18 1983."
      Nimrod (27:2) Spr-Sum 84, p. 48.

2274. HENTZ, Robert R.
   "The Apocalypse That Will Be." SanFPJ (6:2) 84,
      p. 49.
   "Elementary Aesthetics." Sam (37:3, 147th
      release) 83, p. 22.
   "Images Graven on a Television Screen and a Mind."
      SanFPJ (7:1) 84, p. 45-47.
   "Lest We Be Missiled." SanFPJ (6:2) 84, p. 50-51.
   "On the Curvature of Space." SanFPJ (7:1) 84, p. 48.
   "A Place Named Nicaragua." SanFPJ (6:2) 84, p. 45.
   "Silos, a Generation Gap." Sam (41:1, release
      161) 84, p. 9.
   "A Social Affair." SanFPJ (6:4) 84, p. 15.

2275. HERBERT, George
   "Easter-Wings." NewOR (11:3/4) Aut-Wint 84, p. 66.

2276. HERBERT, Zbigniew
   "Anabasis" (tr. by Bogdana and John Carpenter).
      ManhatR (3:2) Wint 84-85, p. 25.
   "Babylon" (tr. by Bogdana and John Carpenter).
      ManhatR (3:2) Wint 84-85, p. 31.
   "Cradle Song" (tr. by Bogdana and John Carpenter).
      ManhatR (3:2) Wint 84-85, p. 30.

"From the Top of the Stairs" (tr. by Bogdana
Carpenter and John Carpenter). MichQR (23:3)
Sum 84, p. 352-354.
"In Memoriam Nagy Laszlo" (tr. by Bogdana and John
Carpenter). ManhatR (3:2) Wint 84-85, p. 31-32.
"Lament" (To the memory of my mother, tr. by
Bogdana and John Carpenter). ManhatR (3:2)
Wint 84-85, p. 27.
"The Monster of Mr. Cogito" (tr. by Bogdana and
John Carpenter). ManhatR (3:2) Wint 84-85, p.
21-23.
"Mr. Cogito Looks at His Face in the Mirror" (tr.
by Bogdana and John Carpenter). ManhatR (3:2)
Wint 84-85, p. 19-20.
"Mr. Cogito--Notes from the House of the Dead" (tr.
by Bogdana and John Carpenter). ManhatR (3:2)
Wint 84-85, p. 34-37.
"Mr. Cogito on Virtue" (tr. by Bogdana and John
Carpenter). ManhatR (3:2) Wint 84-85, p. 24-25.
"Mr. Cogito Thinks about Blood" (tr. by Bogdana and
John Carpenter). ManhatR (3:2) Wint 84-85, p.
38-40.
"The Murderers of Kings" (tr. by Bogdana and John
Carpenter). ManhatR (3:2) Wint 84-85, p. 29.
"My inner voice" (tr. by Czeslaw Milosz and Peter
Dale Scott). ManhatR (3:2) Wint 84-85, p. 50-51.
"The Old Masters" (tr. by Bogdana and John
Carpenter). ManhatR (3:2) Wint 84-85, p. 26-27.
"Old Prometheus" (tr. by Bogdana and John
Carpenter). ManhatR (3:2) Wint 84-85, p. 20.
"On the Margin of the Trial" (tr. by Bogdana and
John Carpenter). ManhatR (3:2) Wint 84-85, p. 19.
"Photograph" (tr. by Bogdana and John Carpenter).
ManhatR (3:2) Wint 84-85, p. 28.
"Prayer of Mr. Cogito--Traveler" (tr. by Bogdana
and John Carpenter). ManhatR (3:2) Wint 84-85,
p. 32-34.
"Report from the Besieged City" (tr. by Bogdana and
John Carpenter). ManhatR (3:2) Wint 84-85, p.
42-43.
"Shameful Dreams" (tr. by Bogdana and John
Carpenter). ManhatR (3:2) Wint 84-85, p. 27-28.
"To Ryszard Krynicki--A Letter" (tr. by Bogdana and
John Carpenter). ManhatR (3:2) Wint 84-85, p.
40-41.
"We fall asleep on words" (tr. by Bogdana and John
Carpenter). ManhatR (3:2) Wint 84-85, p. 18.

2277. HERLIN, Louise
"Sleep" (tr. by Elton Glaser and Janice Fritsch).
WebR (9:1) Spr 84, p. 94-95.

2278. HERMAN, George Richard
"After Seeing Her Again." KanQ (16:1/2) Wint-Spr
84, p. 198.

2279. HERMAN, Peter
"The Day You Left." Waves (12:4) Spr 84, p. 44.
"Discovery of Language." Waves (12:4) Spr 84, p. 45.

2280. HERNANDEZ, David
"Ode to a Bowl of Yet-Ca-Main." TriQ (60) Spr-Sum 84, p. 174-175.

2281. HERNANDEZ MURIEL, Rodrigo
"Paisaje Erotico." Mairena (5:13) Spr 83, p. 99.
"Repercusion." Mairena (5:14) Aut 83, p. 94.

2282. HERNANDEZ SANCHEZ, Roberto
"Hombre a Diario." Mairena (5:13) Spr 83, p. 98.

HERNANDEZ TOVAR, Inèz: See TOVAR, Inèz Hernandez

2283. HERNTON, Calvin
"Black River Ode." GreenfR (11:1/2) Sum-Aut 83, p. 133-135.
"Ohio Klan." GreenfR (11:1/2) Sum-Aut 83, p. 133.
"Ohio Myself." GreenfR (11:1/2) Sum-Aut 83, p. 133.
"Rites." GreenfR (11:1/2) Sum-Aut 83, p. 132.

2284. HEROY, Susan
"Combing the Ashes." SouthernPR (24:2) Aut 84, p. 53-54.

2285. HERPORT, Susan Hall
"Genetic Weakness." PoetC (15:3) 84, p. 24.
"Sister Mary Whatshername." NeqC (4:4) Aut 84, p. 88.

2286. HERRERA, Juan Felipe
"Exiles." Metam (5:2/6:1) 84-85, p. 25.

HERRERA, Miguel Angel Muñoz: See MUÑOZ HERRERA, Miguel Angel

2287. HERRINGTON, Neva
"The Bakery Sonnet." SouthwR (69:3) Sum 84, p. 277.
"The Father Maker." Wind (14:50) 84, p. 26.

2288. HERRSTROM, David S.
"The Young Thief Makes Himself at Home." PikeF (6) Aut 84, p. 3.

2289. HERSHON, Robert
"Summer into Fall." PoetryNW (25:2) Sum 84, p. 34.

2290. HERVIANT, Claude
"Atlantide City" (excerpts, tr. by Louis A. Olivier). PikeF (6) Aut 84, p. 14.

2291. HERZBERG, Judith
"View." Vis (16) 84, p. 7.

2292. HERZING, Albert
"Vultures" (Excerpts, tr. of Joyce Mansour). Chelsea (42/43) 84, p. 276-277.

2293. HESFORD, Wendy
"The Carpenter Gathers the Light." Abraxas (31/32) 84, p. 51.

2294. HESKETH, Phoebe
       "Arrival." Stand (25:2) Spr 84, p. 52.

2295. HESS, Mary
       "El Hombre Illegal." SanFPJ (6:3) 84, p. 72.

2296. HESTER, M. L.
       "The Wives of Poets." Bogg (52) 84, p. 3.

2297. HETTICH, Michael
       "Your Mother Sings." NewL (50:4) Sum 84, p. 84-85.

2298. HEWITT, Geof
       "Missing Now 5 Days." NewL (50:2/3) Wint-Spr 84,
       p. 114.

2299. HEYD, Michael
       "Evening Cruise." PoeticJ (6) 84, p. 14.

2300. HEYEN, William
       "The Berries." AmerPoR (13:4) Jl-Ag 84, p. 9.
       "The Berries." Tendril (18, special issue) 84,
       p.92-93.
       "Memorial Day, Brockport, 1981." TriQ (59) Wint
       84, p. 91.
       "The New American Poetry." TriQ (59) Wint 84, p.
       88-89.
       "Over This Winter." TriQ (59) Wint 84, p. 90.

2301. HEYL, AnneLiese
       "Crayons Are Voracious." PikeF (6) Aut 84, p. 21.

2302. HEYMAN, Ann
       "The Biology Lab." DekalbLAJ (20th Anniversary
       Issue) 84, p. 94.
       "The Children" (Scholarship and Award Winners:
       First Place). DekalbLAJ (20th Anniversary
       Issue) 84, p. 16.
       "Dirge for the Piano Player" (Scholarship and Award
       Winners: First Place). DekalbLAJ (20th
       Anniversary Issue) 84, p. 15.
       "Dust." DekalbLAJ (20th Anniversary Issue) 84, p.
       94.
       "Razor." DekalbLAJ (20th Anniversary Issue) 84,
       p. 95.

2303. HEYNEN, Jim
       "Shortcomings." MemphisSR (5:1) Aut 84, p. 13.

2304. HEYWORTH, Blair
       "The Sheriff's Dilemma." BlackWR (11:1) Aut 84,
       p. 79-80.

2305. HIATT, Ben L.
       "16 Aug 82 Quivering Elbows." Abraxas (29/30) 84,
       p. 10-12.

2306. HICKEY, Gordon R.
       "The Great Owls." Abraxas (29/30) 84, p. 72-73.

2307. HICKMAN, Karrell
"Evening." Poem (52) N 84, p. 17.
"Return." Poem (52) N 84, p. 18-19.

2308. HICKS, Betty Brown
"Namesake." NeqC (4:1) Wint 84, p. 49-50.

2309. HICKS, John V.
"Corkboard." Quarry (33:1) Wint 84, p. 38-40.
"Gardener." Grain (12:3) Ag 84, p. 12.
"People before Sleep." Grain (12:3) Ag 84, p. 11.

2310. HIESTAND, Emily
"This Is Something Simple." Hudson (37:2) Sum 84,
p. 278-279.

2311. HIGGINBOTHAM, Keith
"Grammar Lesson." PoeticJ (4) 83, p. 13.
"The Rocket." PoeticJ (4) 83, p. 33.

2312. HILBERRY, Conrad
"For Katharine, 1952-1961" (September 1971). Peb
(23) 84, p. 16-17.

2313. HILDEBIDLE, John
"Freud in the Woods" (Putnam's Camp, New York,
1908). BelPoJ (35:2) Wint 84-85, p. 32-33.

2314. HILL, Beth Munroe
"Thomas and Nain." PottPort (6) 84, p. 21.

2315. HILL, Brian Merrikin
"Quays by the Rhone, at Lyons" (tr. of Pierre
Emmanuel). Argo (6:1) 84, p. 21.
"Simon of Cyrene" (tr. of Pierre Emmanuel). Argo
(6:1) 84, p. 21.

2316. HILL, Geoffrey
"A Pre-Raphaelite Notebook." Shen (35:2/3) 84, p.
174.

2317. HILL, Gerald
"As Slow Cattle Revolve." Waves (12:1) Aut 83, p.
68.
"Better Poems and Gardens." Quarry (33:3) Sum 84,
p. 56.
"The Day My Fingers Froze to the Earth." Grain
(12:1) F 84, p. 4.
"Emil's Dog Rises from His Hidden Self and Barks."
Grain (12:3) Ag 84, p. 54.
"The Horizon Sneaks across My Shoulders Like a
Mink." Waves (12:1) Aut 83, p. 68.
"A Kind of Sight." Grain (12:3) Ag 84, p. 52.
"Turning Twenty-One." Dandel (11:2) Aut-Wint 84-
85, p. 53.
"Water Leads to This." Grain (12:3) Ag 84, p. 53.

2318. HILL, Jack
"Response to 'Still in Saigon'" (Charlie Daniel's
Band). Wind (14:51) 84, p. 9.

2319. HILL, Kenneth
      "In the Hinterland." AntigR (58) Sum 84, p. 46.
      "Miscarried." AntigR (58) Sum 84, p. 45.

2320. HILL, Pati
      "Photocopied Garments." NewL (50:2/3) Wint-Spr
         84, p. 110-113.

2321. HILL, Terrence N.
      "Beware of the Meek." CrossC (6:1) 84, p. 10.
      "Mental Hospital Mornings." CrossC (6:1) 84, p. 10.

2322. HILLARD, Jeff
      "Highway 36, Eolia." MidAR (4:2) Aut 84, p. 9.

2323. HILLARD, Jeffrey
      "Appraisal of the New Year." SmPd (21:3) Aut 84,
         p. 23-24.

2324. HILLMAN, Brenda
      "Broken Dreams." AmerPoR (13:3) My-Je 84, p. 6-7.
      "Chess." Telescope (3:2) Spr 84, p. 5-6.
      "Cleave and Cleave." AmerPoR (13:3) My-Je 84, p. 5.
      "Fortress." AmerPoR (13:3) My-Je 84, p. 8-12.
      "Fragments." AmerPoR (13:3) My-Je 84, p. 3.
      "In the Provinces" (for J.M., Baltimore). AmerPoR
         (13:3) My-Je 84, p. 4-5.
      "A Life of Action." AmerPoR (13:3) My-Je 84, p. 3.
      "Rare Animals Display." Thrpny (16) Wint 84, p. 4.
      "The Shulamite Girl." AmerPoR (13:3) My-Je 84, p. 7.
      "Upon Hearing of Another Rescue" (for L.G.).
         AmerPoR (13:3) My-Je 84, p. 5.
      "Wooden Carousel." GrandS (3:2) Wint 84, p. 150.

2325. HILTON, David
      "1952." Spirit (7:1) 84, p. 142.
      "Crofter Tea, Skye." BelPoJ (34:4) Sum 84, p. 22.
      "Drinking Buddy." BelPoJ (34:4) Sum 84, p. 23.
      "Seeress in the Kozy Klub." Abraxas (29/30) 84,
         p. 48.

2326. HILTY, Peter
      "Prairie Valley School in Summer." CapeR (19:2)
         Sum 84, p. 18.

2327. HINE, Daryl
      "Aztec Tanka." Shen (35:1) 83-84, p. 30-31.
      "Letter to Shadow." Shen (35:2/3) 84, p. 175.
      "Palinode." CanLit (100) Spr 84, p. 147.

2328. HINES, Debra
      "Roulstone Once Removed." Iowa (14:3) Aut 84, p.
         60-61.

2329. HINRICHSEN, Dennis
      "The Anatomy of the Crab Is Repetitive and
         Rhythmical." GeoR (38:4) Wint 84, p. 762-764.

2330. HIONIS, Argyris
      "Metamorphoses" (Selections: XXI, XXIV, tr. by

Stavros Deligiorgis). <u>Iowa</u> (14:2) Spr-Sum 84,
p. 233-234.

2331. HIRATA, Hosea
"Because Your Body Gives Me Peace and Light."
<u>Quarry</u> (33:4) Aut 84, p. 41.
"Good Night." <u>Descant</u> (47, 15:4) Wint 84, p. 29-30.
"In Night Houses." <u>Descant</u> (47, 15:4) Wint 84, p.
26-28.
"On a Cold Night Missing a Hand." <u>Quarry</u> (33:4)
Aut 84, p. 39-40.
"A Walk." <u>Quarry</u> (33:4) Aut 84, p. 40.

HIROAKI, Sato: <u>See</u> SATO, Hiroaki

HIROMI, Ito: <u>See</u> ITO, Hiromi

2332. HIRSCH, David
"After Death" (tr. of Abraham Sutzkever, w. Roslyn
Hirsch). <u>GrahamHR</u> (7) Wint 84, p. 49-50.
"The Gray Crown" (tr. of Abraham Sutzkever, w.
Roslyn Hirsch). <u>GrahamHR</u> (7) Wint 84, p. 48.
"Stalks" (tr. of Abraham Sutzkever, w. Roslyn
Hirsch). <u>GrahamHR</u> (7) Wint 84, p. 51-52.

2333. HIRSCH, Edward
"Fever." <u>Poetry</u> (143:5) F 84, p. 271-272.
"Indian Summer." <u>Antaeus</u> (53) Aut 84, p. 234-235.
"Leningrad (1941-1943)." <u>MichQR</u> (23:3) Sum 84, p.
355-359.
"Poor Angels." <u>Poetry</u> (143:5) F 84, p. 273.
"Recovery." <u>Antaeus</u> (53) Aut 84, p. 233.

2334. HIRSCH, Roslyn
"After Death" (tr. of Abraham Sutzkever, w. David
Hirsch). <u>GrahamHR</u> (7) Wint 84, p. 49-50.
"The Gray Crown" (tr. of Abraham Sutzkever, w.
David Hirsch). <u>GrahamHR</u> (7) Wint 84, p. 48.
"Stalks" (tr. of Abraham Sutzkever, w. David
Hirsch). <u>GrahamHR</u> (7) Wint 84, p. 51-52.

2335. HIRSCHFIELD, Ted
"For a Dead Frog." <u>CapeR</u> (19:3) 20th Anniverary
Issue 84, p. 29.
"Poem for Annie on Her Birthday, 1974." <u>CapeR</u>
(19:3) 20th Anniverary Issue 84, p. 30-31.
"Sunday: A Hopewellian Village" (for Willie Smith).
<u>CapeR</u> (19:3) 20th Anniverary Issue 84, p. 32.
"What Animals Dream." <u>CapeR</u> (19:3) 20th
Anniverary Issue 84, p. 33.

2336. HIRSCHMAN, Jack
"Crane." <u>OroM</u> (2:3/4, issue 7/8) 84, p. 5.
"The Eagle Arcane." <u>OroM</u> (2:2) 84, p. 11-14.
"Head over Heels." <u>OroM</u> (2:2) 84, p. 23.
"Kallatumba" (Issue title. For Our Gentle Comrades.
Fremont, CA: Ruddy Duck Press). <u>OroM</u> (2:2) 84,
p. 1-24.
"Kallatumba." <u>OroM</u> (2:2) 84, p. 21.
"Marisolka." <u>OroM</u> (2:3/4, issue 7/8) 84, p. 24-25.

"Salt Point" (A Socialist Realist Poem). OroM
  (2:2) 84, p. 7-9.
"The Stalin Arcane." OroM (2:2) 84, p. 15-20.
"This Solitude." OroM (2:3/4, issue 7/8) 84, p. 25.
"Xhuxhimaxhuxh." OroM (2:3/4, issue 7/8) 84, p. 5.

2337. HIRSHFIELD, Jane
  "Coming, my eyes open." YellowS (10) Spr 84, p. 40.
  "In Moonlight." YellowS (12) Aut 84, p. 18.
  "Night quiets, cools." YellowS (10) Spr 84, p. 40.
  "The Speed with Which Blue Needles Move." OntR
    (20) Spr-Sum 84, p. 99.
  "Stars, still pond." YellowS (10) Spr 84, p. 40.
  "Woman in Red Coat." OntR (20) Spr-Sum 84, p. 98.

2338. HITCHCOCK, George
  "The Raid." Sparrow (46) 84, p. 15.
  "Ultima Thule Hotel." NewL (50:2/3) Wint-Spr 84,
    p. 38.

HITOMARO, Kakinomoto no: See KAKINOMOTO no HITOMARO

2339. HIX, Harvey
  "Funeral." TexasR (5:1/2) Spr-Sum 84, p. 86.
  "Garbage Bin." Poem (51) Mr [i.e. Jl] 84, p. 12.
  "Instructions to My Wife." TexasR (5:1/2) Spr-Sum
    84, p. 87.
  "Stone." Poem (51) Mr [i.e. Jl] 84, p. 13.

HO, Hon Leung: See LEUNG, Ho Hon

HO, Li: See LI, Ho

2340. HO, Xuan Huong
  "Landscape with Three Mountains" (tr. by John
    Balaban). Hudson (37:3) Aut 84, p. 430.

2341. HOAGLAND, Tony
  "Better." PoetryE (15) Aut 84, p. 61-62.

2342. HOAGWOOD, Terence
  "The Love Song of the Siamese Twin." HolCrit
    (21:4) O 84, p. 19.

2343. HODSON, Jennifer
  "Random Ideas." HangL (45) Spr 84, p. 61.
  "South of the Border." HangL (45) Spr 84, p. 62.

2344. HODSON, Stan
  "Movement in a Solid: A Composite Figure of the
    Poet This Century" (for M. H. Abrams, Pablo
    Neruda Prize for Poetry: Second Prize). Nimrod
    (28:1) Aut-Wint 84, p. 55-61.

2345. HODSON, Stanley
  "Translation Is a Kind of Trance." ConcPo (17:1)
    Spr 84, p. 12.

2346. HOEFER, David
  "Elegy: Life is speed led through ritual."

HiramPoR (36) Spr-Sum 84, p. 25.
"Photo Booth." HiramPoR (36) Spr-Sum 84, p. 24.

2347. HOEHN, Judy
"The 7:12." MemphisSR (5:1) Aut 84, p. 57.

2348. HOEY, Allen
"Felling Elms." Blueline (6:1) Sum-Aut 84, p. 37.
"Field Guide." SouthernHR (18:4) Aut 84, p. 324-325.

2349. HOFER, Mariann
"On a Farm outside Congress, Ohio" (for Dan).
Wind (14:51) 84, p. 21.
"Turn of the Century Postcard." Wind (14:51) 84,
p. 21.

2350. HOFF, Jennifer
"Short Term Life." SanFPJ (6:4) 84, p. 81.

2351. HOFFMAN, Chris
"The Shaman's Song." ThirdW (2) Spr 84, p. 12-13.

2352. HOFFMAN, Craig
"Raven at Grand Canyon." HiramPoR (37) Aut-Wint
84, p. 25.

2353. HOFFMAN, Daniel
"Instructions to a Medium to Be Transmitted to the
Shade of W. B. Yeats, the Latter Having
Responded in a Seance Held on 13 June 1965, Its
Hundredth Birthday." Shen (35:2/3) 84, p. 176-
177.
"Mark Twain, 1909." NewYorker (60:37) 29 O 84, p.
48.

2354. HOFFMAN, Helen
"Night Journey." OhioR (32) 84, p. 106.

2355. HOFFMAN, Jill
"Marigolds." NewYorker (60:22) 16 Jl 84, p. 87.

2356. HOFFMAN, N. M.
"Wolf Poem #7: At the Piano" (For Terri & Jay).
CapeR (19:2) Sum 84, p. 37.

2357. HOFMANNSTHAL, Hugo von
"An Experience" (tr. by Paul T. Hopper). Open24
(3) 84, p. 16.

2358. HOGGARD, James
"Out of Place, Far from Rain." OhioR (32) 84, p.
108.

2359. HOGUE, Cynthia
"Finding the Way Back." GreenfR (11:1/2) Sum-Aut
83, p. 120-121.

2360. HOHEISEL, Peter
"Winter Song." KanQ (16:1/2) Wint-Spr 84, p. 206-
207.

2361. HOLAMAN, Keith
"Little Song of the Maimed" (tr. of Benjamin
Pèret). Pequod (16/17) 84, p. 242.

2362. HOLAN, Vladimir
"Children at Christmas in 1945" (tr. by C. G.
Hanzlicek and Dana Habova). AmerPoR (13:2) Mr-
Ap 84, p. 48.
"The Vltava in 1946" (tr. by C. G. Hanzlicek and
Dana Habova). AmerPoR (13:2) Mr-Ap 84, p. 48.

2363. HOLCOMB, Gary
"The Crying of Sarah." WormR (24:1, issue 93) 84,
p. 6.
"Possessing Every Frozen Delicacy." WormR (24:1,
issue 93) 84, p. 5-6.

2364. HOLCOMBE, Emily G.
"A Dream Cometh." HiramPoR (37) Aut-Wint 84, p. 28.

2365. HOLDEN, Jonathan
"Father, Age 78." TarRP (24:1) Aut 84, p. 2-3.
"Geronimo" (After the earliest known photo of
Geronimo, taken by A. Frank Randall, in 1884,
when Geronimo was probably around 60). TarRP
(24:1) Aut 84, p. 5.
"Junk." Tendril (17) Wint 84, p. 90-91.
"Leverage." PoetL (79:2) Sum 84, p. 121.
"The Men in the Hoboken Bar." Tendril (17) Wint
84, p. 88-89.
"Mission." TarRP (24:1) Aut 84, p. 3-5.
"Night: Driving the Blizzard" (near Wayne,
Nebraska). IndR (7:3) Sum 84, p. 14-15.
"November." NewL (50:2/3) Wint-Spr 84, p. 105.
"Politics." Chelsea (42/43) 84, p. 370-371.
"Strolling Lovers." SouthwR (69:2) Spr 84, p. 129.
"Thanksgiving Day." TarRP (24:1) Aut 84, p. 1-2.
"Why We Bombed Haiphong." PoetL (79:2) Sum 84, p.
119-120.

2366. HOLDER, Barbara
"Elegy for Josephine." Wind (14:50) 84, p. 27.

2367. HOLINGER, Richard
"After Laughter" (On the death of Charles VIII at
the Chateau Amboise). WebR (9:2) Wint 85, p. 43.
"Its Coming." KanQ (16:1/2) Wint-Spr 84, p. 60-61.
"Moving toward the Dance." PaintedB (24) Aut 84,
p. 21.

2368. HOLLADAY, Hilary
"Gradually, the Snow." WestB (14) 84, p. 5.

HOLLAND, Kevin Crossley: See CROSSLEY-HOLLAND, Kevin

2369. HOLLAND, Larry
"Mutability." Wind (14:51) 84, p. 22.

2370. HOLLAND, William
"Legal Training." Gargoyle (24) 84, p. 45.

2371. HOLLANDER, John
"10/28/29 Loquitur." NewRep (191:3/4) 16-23 Jl
      84, p. 40.
"Anonymous Master, 'Standing Figure'." PoetryE
      (13/14) Spr-Sum 84, p. 18-19.
"The Court of Love: Special Sessions." Poetry
      (145:2) N 84, p. 97.
"Desires of Here and There." NewYorker (60:44) 17
      D 84, p. 48.
"Footnote to a Desperate Letter." NewYRB (31:16)
      25 O 84, p. 42.
"Glass Landscape." PoetryE (13/14) Spr-Sum 84, p.
      12.
"A Glimpse of Proserpina." NewYorker (60:17) 11
      Je 84, p. 38.
"In Fine Print." MichQR (23:4) Aut 84, p. 487.
"Inscribed on Shard of Household (?) Pottery."
      PoetryE (13/14) Spr-Sum 84, p. 13.
"Looking East in Winter." Poetry (145:2) N 84, p.
      95.
"O I." Poetry (145:2) N 84, p. 98.
"Ode to Landscape." PoetryE (13/14) Spr-Sum 84,
      p. 16-17.
"An Old Engraving." PoetryE (13/14) Spr-Sum 84,
      p. 15.
"On the Way to Summer." Shen (35:2/3) 84, p. 178-
      179.
"A Possible Fake." PoetryE (13/14) Spr-Sum 84, p.
      21.
"Skeleton Key." PoetryE (13/14) Spr-Sum 84, p. 20.
"A Statue of Something." PoetryE (13/14) Spr-Sum
      84, p. 14.
"Swan and Shadow." PoetryE (13/14) Spr-Sum 84, p.
      22.
"Thanks for a Bottle" (To Angus Fletcher).
      PoetryE (13/14) Spr-Sum 84, p. 10-11.
"Vintage Absence." Poetry (145:2) N 84, p. 96.
"When Song Will Not Do." NewRep (190:23) 11 Je
      84, p. 32.

2372. HOLLANDER, Martha
"The Soccer Game outside Munich." GrandS (3:2)
      Wint 84, p. 151.

2373. HOLLO, Anselm
"How It Works." Open24 (3) 84, p. 11.
"I.M. Charles Reznikoff." Open24 (3) 84, p. 9.
"Never a Dull Moment." Open24 (3) 84, p. 10.
"Never Send Out to Ask." Open24 (3) 84, p. 10.
"Personal Ad Valentine." Open24 (3) 84, p. 11.
"Richesse." Open24 (3) 84, p. 10.

2374. HOLLOWAY, Geoffrey
"The Elect." Argo (5:3) 84, p. 8-9.

2375. HOLLOWAY, Glenna
"The Best Thing My Father Did Was Lie." WestHR
      (38:1) Spr 84, p. 58-59.

2376. HOLLOWAY, John
"Hour Angle." <u>KenR</u> (NS 6:4) Aut 84, p. 83.
"A Poem of Light and Shade." <u>KenR</u> (NS 6:4) Aut
84, p. 84.

2377. HOLMAN, Amy
"Catching." <u>WoosterR</u> (1:2) N 84, p. 40.

2378. HOLMES, John Clellon
"Fayetteville Dawn" (1975). <u>NewL</u> (50:2/3) Wint-
Spr 84, p. 85.

2379. HOLMES, Olivia
"The Accident at Staplehurst." <u>Agni</u> (21) 84, p.
105-106.
"Dailiness" (for Tom). <u>Telescope</u> (3:1) Wint 84,
p. 95.
"The Equilibrium." <u>Telescope</u> (3:1) Wint 84, p. 94.
"A Short Spectacle." <u>Telescope</u> (3:1) Wint 84, p. 93.
"Vocabulary Exercise." <u>Telescope</u> (3:1) Wint 84,
p. 96.

2380. HOLOBORODKO, Vasyl
"Katerina" (fugue, tr. by Bohdan Boychuk). <u>Pequod</u>
(16/17) 84, p. 201-204.

2381. HOLSTEIN, Michael
"Garden Gossip." <u>LittleBR</u> (4:4) Sum 84, p. 62.
"Summer Poem." <u>LittleBR</u> (4:4) Sum 84, p. 63.

2382. HOLTOM, John
"Apple Pips." <u>Argo</u> (5:3) 84, p. 12.

2383. HOLTON, Milne
"Non-Metaphysical Sequence" (tr. of Veno Taufer, w.
the author). <u>Bound</u> (12:1) Aut 83, p. 213-218.

2384. HOLUB, Miroslav
"Collision" (tr. by David Young). <u>Field</u> (30) Spr
84, p. 29-31.

2385. HOM, Marlon K.
"America, I have come and landed" (in Chinese and
English, tr. of anonymous poem from <u>Songs of
Gold Mountain</u> I, 14a). <u>GreenfR</u> (11:1/2) Sum-
Aut 83, p. 157.
"American laws, more fierce than tigers" (in
Chinese and English, tr. of anonymous poem from
<u>Songs of Gold Mountain</u> I, 13b). <u>GreenfR</u>
(11:1/2) Sum-Aut 83, p. 160.
"Detention is called 'to await a review'" (in
Chinese and English, tr. of anonymous poem from
<u>Songs of Gold Mountain</u> I, 14a). <u>GreenfR</u>
(11:1/2) Sum-Aut 83, p. 155.
"Home in poverty" (in Chinese and English, tr. of
anonymous poem from <u>Songs of Gold Mountain</u> I,
14a). <u>GreenfR</u> (11:1/2) Sum-Aut 83, p. 149.
"I sojourn in America without proper documents" (in
Chinese and English, tr. of anonymous poem from
<u>Songs of Gold Mountain</u> I, 13b). <u>GreenfR</u>

(11:1/2) Sum-Aut 83, p. 152.
"In search of a petty gain" (in Chinese and
English, tr. of anonymous poem from Songs of
Gold Mountain I, 5a). GreenfR (11:1/2) Sum-
Aut 83, p. 150.
"The moment I heard we've entered port" (in Chinese
and English, tr. of anonymous poem from Songs
of Gold Mountain I, 13b). GreenfR (11:1/2)
Sum-Aut 83, p. 151.
"Poems on Immigration under the Chinese Exclusion
Act" (in Chinese and English, tr. of anonymous
poems from Songs of Gold Mountain anthologies,
San Francisco, 1911, 1915). GreenfR (11:1/2)
Sum-Aut 83, p. 149-160.
"So, liberty is the national principle" (in Chinese
and English, tr. of anonymous poem from Songs
of Gold Mountain I, 13b). GreenfR (11:1/2)
Sum-Aut 83, p. 159.
"Stay at home: many opportunities lost" (in Chinese
and English, tr. of anonymous poem from Songs
of Gold Mountain II, 11a). GreenfR (11:1/2)
Sum-Aut 83, p. 153.
"A weak country, a deprived voice" (in Chinese and
English, tr. of anonymous poem from Songs of
Gold Mountain I, 14a). GreenfR (11:1/2) Sum-
Aut 83, p. 158.
"The wooden barracks, all specially built" (in
Chinese and English, tr. of anonymous poem from
Songs of Gold Mountain I, 13b). GreenfR
(11:1/2) Sum-Aut 83, p. 154.
"The wooden cell: a steel barrel" (in Chinese and
English, tr. of anonymous poem from Songs of
Gold Mountain I, 14a). GreenfR (11:1/2) Sum-
Aut 83, p. 156.

2386. HOMER, Art
"Facing Up." PoetC (16:1) Aut 84, p. 52.
"Father in Knickers and Other Snapshots." CharR
(10:1) Spr 84, p. 42-43.
"Georgic on Insomnia." PoetC (16:1) Aut 84, p. 47.
"Postures in Snow." CharR (10:1) Spr 84, p. 45.
"Small Builders." PoetC (16:1) Aut 84, p. 50-51.
"Two Waterways." PoetC (16:1) Aut 84, p. 48-49.
"Visiting the Coast Alone." CharR (10:1) Spr 84,
p. 44.

2387. HONECKER, George J.
"Storybook Fossils" (Excerpts). Chelsea (42/43)
84, p. 367-369.

2388. HONGO, Garrett Kaoru
"On a Photograph of Civil Rights Demonstrators."
GreenfR (11:1/2) Sum-Aut 83, p. 162-163.

2389. HONIG, Edwin
"Last Poem." NegC (4:4) Aut 84, p. 65.
"Seeking Cover." NegC (4:4) Aut 84, p. 67.
"Translator's Tristesse." NegC (4:4) Aut 84, p. 69.
"Two Songs for Lot's Daughters" (1. "Deceived by
Age," 2. "Coming through Him"). NegC (4:4) Aut

HONIG 288

```
        84, p. 68-69.
    "Wapping 1912." NegC (4:4) Aut 84, p. 66.

2390. HOOBAN, Enid Iolanthe
    "The Missouri." AmerPoR (13:5) S-O 84, p. 41.
    "October." AmerPoR (13:5) S-O 84, p. 41.

2391. HOOBAN, Homer
    "Game Rules." AmerPoR (13:6) N-D 84, p. 43.
    "Love of Many Colors." AmerPoR (13:6) N-D 84, p. 43.

2392. HOOGESTRAAT, Jane
    "Broken Prairie." NoDaQ (52:2) Spr 84, p. 15.

2393. HOOVER, Paul
    "Some Polonius." Epoch (33:3) Sum-Aut 84, p. 281-
        283.

2394. HOPES, David
    "Parula Warbler." WindO (44) Sum-Aut 84, p. 24.

2395. HOPES, David B.
    "Always the Stars." StoneC (12:1/2) Aut-Wint 84,
        p. 24.
    "A Flower Called Peace-in-the-Valley." SouthernPR
        (24:1) Spr 84, p. 53-54.
    "I Give for Your Love." NegC (4:3) Sum 84, p. 105.
    "A Malediction" (after James Wright). WindO (44)
        Sum-Aut 84, p. 23.
    "Tell the River." StoneC (12:1/2) Aut-Wint 84, p.
        25.

2396. HOPES, David Brendan
    "The Cherub's Sword." KanQ (16:3) Sum 84, p. 34.
    "Clara Scifi Consults the Flowering Crab Concerning
        Her Lord Obedience" (Scifi was a debutante of
        Assisi who became a follower of St. Francis,
        later Saint Clare, founder of the Poor Clares).
        ThirdW (2) Spr 84, p. 50-52.
    "Julian" (A 14th century visionary, recluse and
        holy woman of Norwich). ThirdW (2) Spr 84, p.
        48-50.
    "Sassetta: The Meeting of St. Anthony and St.
        Paul." ThirdW (2) Spr 84, p. 47.

2397. HOPPER, Paul T.
    "An Experience" (tr. of Hugo von Hofmannsthal).
        Open24 (3) 84, p. 16.

2398. HORACE
    "Snow Drifts" (from Odes 1.9, tr. by Jim Powell).
        ParisR (26:94) Wint 84, p. 98-99.

HORIOKA, Takahashi: See TAKAHASHI, Horioka

2399. HORNER, Jan
    "Blue Beard." PraF (5:4) Sum 84, p. 69.
    "Novel Lovers." PraF (5:4) Sum 84, p. 71-72.
    "Walking on Air." PraF (5:4) Sum 84, p. 70.
```

2400. HORNEY, Philip
      "Bird Fish Birds." HangL (46) Aut 84, p. 76.
      "Cathedral, Ulm West-Germany." HangL (46) Aut 84,
         p. 75.

2401. HORNIG, Doug
      "César" (Mazatlan, Mexico--1958). Amelia (1:2)
         O 84, p. 70.

2402. HORNSEY, Richard
      "Prairie Winter." PoetryCR (6:1) Aut 84, p. 7.

2403. HOROVITZ, Frances
      "Irthing Valley." Argo (5:2) 84, p. 35.

2404. HOROWITZ, Mikhail
      "Imaginary Flora." YellowS (13) Wint 84, p. 23.

2405. HORSTING, Eric
      "At Woolworth's in Wyalusing." NewL (51:1) Aut
         84, p. 101.

2406. HORTON, Barbara
      "In December." SpoonRQ (9:4) Aut 84, p. 29.
      "Looking into the Night." StoneC (12:1/2) Aut-
         Wint 84, p. 40.

2407. HORTON, Louise
      "Thomas Gilcrease." Wind (14:51) 84, p. 23.

2408. HORVATH, Brooke
      "December Tulips." AntigR (56) Wint 84, p. 53.
      "October Frost." AntigR (56) Wint 84, p. 54.

2409. HORVATH, John
      "The Doctor's Son from Oroshaza." PoetC (15:3)
         84, p. 20.

2410. HOSKINS, Katherine
      "The red rose droops in a vase alone." GrandS
         (4:1) Aut 84, p. 187.
      "So now, invoke saints Carl and Sig." GrandS
         (4:1) Aut 84, p. 187.
      "Two Epigrams." GrandS (4:1) Aut 84, p. 187.

2411. HOUCHIN, Ron
      "Epimenides in Winter." ThirdW (2) Spr 84, p. 23.
      "Symbiosis." SouthwR (69:3) Sum 84, p. 332.

2412. HOUGHTON, Tim
      "Forest Animals." DenQ (19:1) Spr 84, p. 113.
      "Going to Sleep." DenQ (19:1) Spr 84, p. 112.
      "Indian Hill." TarRP (24:1) Aut 84, p. 20.
      "Legend of the Blue Spider." DenQ (19:1) Spr 84,
         p. 111.

2413. HOUSE, Tom
      "The Live Peepshow." Sam (37:3, 147th release)
         83, p. 54.
      "Mr. Positive." Sam (39:1, release 153) 84, p. 2.

"Sunday the Thoughts Come from Miles Around."
  Wind (14:52) 84, p. 26-27.
"West Durham Sunday." Wind (14:52) 84, p. 26.

2414. HOUSMAN, A. E.
  "Crossing alone the nighted ferry." Tendril (18,
  special issue) 84, p. 218.

HOUTEN, Lois van: See Van HOUTEN, Lois

HOVANESSIAN, Diana der: See Der HOVANESSIAN, Diana

2415. HOWARD, Ben
  "4 P.M." PraS (58:2) Sum 84, p. 90-91.
  "Cartographies." Poetry (144:4) Jl 84, p. 212.
  "Fado." Poetry (144:4) Jl 84, p. 213.
  "Figures." GeoR (38:1) Spr 84, p. 145.
  "Northern Interior" (for Wyatt Prunty in Virginia).
  MidwQ (26:1) Aut 84, p. 74-75.
  "Steady." PraS (58:2) Sum 84, p. 90.

2416. HOWARD, Eugene
  "Playing the Silence for All It's Worth."
  PaintedB (24) Aut 84, p. 40.

2417. HOWARD, Michelle
  "Another one died last week" (DeKalb County High
  Schools Literary Award Winners: First Place--
  Poetry). DekalbLAJ (17:1/2) 84, p. 152.

2418. HOWARD, Richard
  "Beyond Words." Shen (35:2/3) 84, p. 190-191.
  "Impersonations." GrandS (3:1) Aut 83, p. 16-23.
  "Narcissus Explains." GrandS (3:1) Aut 83, p. 13-15.
  "On Lately Looking into Chapman's 'Jane Austen: A
  Critical Bibliography'." GrandS (3:1) Aut 83,
  p. 24-25.

2419. HOWE, Fanny
  "Belfast." Ploughs (10:1) 84, p. 82-83.

2420. HOWE, Julia Ward
  "Battle Hymn of the Republic" (The first printing,
  The Atlantic Monthly (9:52) F 1862).
  LittleBR (4:4) Sum 84, p. 17.

2421. HOWE, Marie
  "Death, the Last Visit." Atlantic (253:6) Je 84,
  p. 76.

2422. HOWE, Susan
  "Bound Cupid sea washed." Sulfur (3:3, issue 9)
  84, p. 94.
  "Brute affirmation." Sulfur (3:3, issue 9) 84, p.
  88-89.
  "Corruptible first figure." Sulfur (3:3, issue 9)
  84, p. 89-90.
  "Double penetrable foreign sequel." Sulfur (3:3,
  issue 9) 84, p. 90-91.
  "Light inaccessible as darkness." Sulfur (3:3,

```
       issue 9) 84, p. 91-92.
       "Offering or gesture of offering." Sulfur (3:3,
       issue 9) 84, p. 92-93.

2423. HOWELL, Christopher
       "Albert Darby's Letter to John." Hudson (37:2)
       Sum 84, p. 280.
       "Elizabeth's Story." NowestR (22:3) 84, p. 13.

2424. HOWSARE, Katrine
       "Stories." Nat (238:1) 14 Ja 84, p. 26.

HOYOS, Ramón Ruiz de: See RUIZ De HOYOS, Ramón

2425. HRISTOZOV, Nikolai
       "In Front of the Cave" (adapted by William
       Meredith). AmerPoR (13:4) Jl-Ag 84, p. 6.

2426. HRUSHOVSKI, Benjamin
       "Fabius Lind's Days" (tr. of A. Leyeles, w. Barbara
       Benavie). PartR (51:1) 84, p. 101-102.
       "Letter to Sigmund Freud" (tr. of J. L. Teller, w.
       Barbara Benavie). PartR (51:1) 84, p. 102-103.
       "Small Night-Music" (Selections: 1, 12, tr. of
       Jacob Glatshteyn, w. Kathryn Hellerstein).
       PartR (51:1) 84, p. 99-100.
       "Why Not" (tr. of M. L. Halpern, w. Kathryn
       Hellerstein). PartR (51:1) 84, p. 100-101.

2427. HSU, Chao
       "The Locust Swarm." NewL (50:2/3) Wint-Spr 84, p.
       227.

2428. HUBBARD, Keith
       "Reading Depositions on Halloween Eve." PoetC
       (15:3) 84, p. 11.

2429. HUDDLE, David
       "Tour of Duty." Pig (12) 84, p. 40-41.

2430. HUDGINS, Andrew
       "Appeal to the Whirlwind." Iowa (14:3) Aut 84, p.
       51-52.
       "Consider." KenR (NS 6:1) Wint 84, p. 66.
       "Dangling." MassR (25:2) Sum 84, p. 302.
       "Homage to the Fox." Iowa (14:3) Aut 84, p. 48.
       "Judas, Flowering." Iowa (14:3) Aut 84, p. 50-51.
       "Late Spring in the Nuclear Age" (For Clare
       Rossini). NowestR (22:1/2) 84, p. 37.
       "The Liar's Psalm." Iowa (14:3) Aut 84, p. 48-52.
       "Madonna of the Pomegranate" (After Botticelli).
       Poetry (144:5) Ag 84, p. 271.
       "My Mother's Hands." Poetry (144:5) Ag 84, p. 272-
       273.
       "Night Moves." SouthwR (69:1) Wint 84, p. 32.
       "November Garden: An Elegy." Poetry (145:2) N 84,
       p. 63.
       "Repentance." Iowa (14:3) Aut 84, p. 49-50.
       "Returning Home to Babylon." NewEngR (7:1) Aut
       84, p. 114-116.
```

"Walking the Idiots." SouthernR (20:4) Aut 84, p.
    881--882.
"The Whale" (after Ponge). ChiR (34:3) Sum 84, p.
    42-43.
"Zelda Sayre in Montgomery" (1942). SouthernR
    (20:4) Aut 84, p. 882-884.

2431. HUDSON, Marc
    "An Icelandic Door" (In Memoriam Paul Skoog).
        KenR (NS 6:4) Aut 84, p. 36-41.
    "A Monk on Heimaey." MassR (25:1) Spr 84, p. 172.
    "Nondescript Landscape." MassR (25:3) Aut 84, p.
        444.

2432. HUDSPITH, Vicki
    "The Conservative." Tele (19) 83, p. 55.
    "Palm Beach." Tele (19) 83, p. 55.
    "This December." Tele (19) 83, p. 54.

2433. HUECKSTEDT, Robert A.
    "Alone I" (tr. of Nirālā). ConcPo (17:2)
        Aut 84, p. 107.
    "A Brahman's Son" (tr. of Nirālā). ConcPo
        (17:2) Aut 84, p. 106.
    "The King Saw to His Own Protection" (tr. of Nirā
        lā). ConcPo (17:2) Aut 84, p. 105.

2434. HUERTAS, Victor R.
    "Ana en Su Mecedora." Mairena (6:17) Aut 84, p. 89.

2435. HUETER, Diane
    "For Donn." DekalbLAJ (17:1/2) 84, p. 131.

2436. HUFF, Steven
    "At Penobscot Bay, Maine." MSS (3:2/3) Spr 84, p.
        38.
    "Before We Move into Aunt Harriet's House." MSS
        (3:2/3) Spr 84, p. 39.

2437. HUGGINS, Peter
    "The Day the Soldiers Came." Pig (12) 84, p. 79.

2438. HUGHES, Barbara
    "The Party" (for Ann Lewis). BelPoJ (35:1) Aut
        84, p. 18.
    "Pure Song" (for Dorothy Purves). BelPoJ (35:1)
        Aut 84, p. 18-19.

2439. HUGHES, Ed
    "Settlement." SnapD (7:2) Spr 84, p. 51.
    "Splash Light" (for Lea Baechler). SnapD (6:2)
        Spr 83, p. 37-39.

2440. HUGHES, Glenn
    "Day and Night of New Moon." PraS (58:3) Aut 84,
        p. 49.

2441. HUGHES, Henry John
    "Rain Lust." Poem (52) N 84, p. 20.

2442. HUGHES, Langston
"Imagine." Chelsea (42/43) 84, p. 67.

2443. HUGHES, Ted
"Big Poppy." NewRep (190:12) 26 Mr 84, p. 34.
"My Donkey." NewYorker (60:12) 7 My 84, p. 54.

2444. HUGO, Richard
"Cattails." Shen (35:2/3) 84, p. 192.

HUI-MING, Wang: See WANG, Hui-Ming

HUIDOBRO, Matías Montes: See MONTES HUIDOBRO, Matías

2445. HULL, Lynda
"Invisible Gestures." Telescope (3:3) Aut 84, p.
88-89.

2446. HULL, Lynda K.
"Autumn, Mist." NoAmR (269:2) Je 84, p. 11.

2447. HULSE, Michael
"Addressed to Shave." Argo (6:1) 84, p. 16-17.

2448. HULTSCH, Cindi
"The Ladybug." PikeF (6) Aut 84, p. 21.

2449. HUMES, Harry
"Bee Hive in Early December." WestB (14) 84, p. 62.
"The Christian Woman and Sasquatch." LittleM
(14:3) 84, p. 20.
"How the Festival of the Half Horses Ends."
PoetryNW (25:1) Spr 84, p. 29-30.
"Improvements on Empty Space." WestB (14) 84, p. 63.
"Survival Log." PoetryNW (25:1) Spr 84, p. 31-32.
"Walking the Anthracite." WestB (14) 84, p. 61.
"White Birch Father" (Honorable Mention). PoetL
(79:1) Spr 84, p. 15-18.

2450. HUMMA, John
"Why the Sons of Pharmacists Become Poets." CapeR
(19:2) Sum 84, p. 36.

2451. HUMMER, T. R.
"Any Time, What May Hit You." QW (19) Aut-Wint 84-
85, p. 72-73.
"The Beating." QW (19) Aut-Wint 84-85, p. 69.
"Because You Will Not Let Me Say I Will Love You
Forever." PoetC (15:2) Wint 84, p. 8.
"Cruelty." NewEngR (6:3) Spr 84, p. 469-470.
"The Future." NewYorker (60:2) 27 F 84, p. 126.
"The Second Story." GeoR (38:2) Sum 84, p. 323-326.
"The Cold" (a study in pushed time). QW (19) Aut-
Wint 84-85, p. 61-66.

2452. HUMPHREY, James
"Working Class Woman." StoneC (11:3/4) Spr-Sum
84, p. 15.

2453. HUNT, Leigh
       "On with the Story." <u>Amelia</u> (1:2) O 84, p. 56.
       "Red White and Blues for Langston Hughes."
          <u>Stepping</u> Wint 84, p. 21-22.
       "Sinking." <u>Stepping</u> (Anniversary Issue I) 84, p. 28.
       "The Story of a Very Funny Man." <u>Amelia</u> [1:1] Ap
          84, p. 33-35.

2454. HUNTER, Allyson
       "The Complete Takeover of America." <u>ThRiPo</u>
          (23/24) 84, p. 35.

2455. HUNTER, Deena
       "Arctic Circles." <u>Quarry</u> (33:1) Wint 84, p. 28-29.

2456. HUNTER, Donnell
       "Cowlick." <u>SnapD</u> (8:1) Aut 84, p. 11.

2457. HUNTSBERRY, Randy
       "Joe Dimaggio on the Right Field Fence." <u>SnapD</u>
          (7:1) Aut 83, p. 56-57.
       "A Sign" (for J. B.). <u>NewL</u> (51:1) Aut 84, p. 100.

HUONG, Ho Xuan: <u>See</u> HO, Xuan Huong

2458. HURDELSH, Mark D.
       "Child." <u>PoeticJ</u> (7) 84, p. 26.
       "Christmas Tree." <u>PoeticJ</u> (6) 84, p. 30.
       "A Creation." <u>PoeticJ</u> (5) 84, p. 6.

2459. HURLOW, Marcia
       "To Resolve a Dream." <u>Nimrod</u> (27:2) Spr-Sum 84,
          p. 22.
       "To Resolve a Dream" (for Greg). <u>WebR</u> (9:1) Spr
          84, p. 82.

2460. HURLOW, Marcia L.
       "Going Home." <u>Wind</u> (14:51) 84, p. 24-25.
       "Making a Dictionary." <u>Wind</u> (14:51) 84, p. 24.

2461. HURVITT, Mark
       "Imminent Onslaught." <u>BlueBldgs</u> (7) 84, p. 29.

2462. HUSS, Steven W.
       "Winter's Reds." <u>CapeR</u> (19:2) Sum 84, p. 50.

2463. HUSSEY, Charlotte
       "Birth." <u>StoneC</u> (11:3/4) Spr-Sum 84, p. 70.
       "The Straw Men on Duluth Street." <u>PoetryCR</u> (5:4)
          Sum 84, p. 19.

2464. HUSTED, Christina
       "Pumpkin Woman." <u>Vis</u> (14) 84, p. 37.

2465. HUSTON, Dorothy
       "Down." <u>MemphisSR</u> (4:2) Spr 84, p. 42.

2466. HUTCHINGS, Pat
       "After You Leave." <u>SpoonRQ</u> (9:4) Aut 84, p. 58.

"As If, after a Departure." <u>SpoonRQ</u> (9:4) Aut 84,
      p. 60.
"Dreams and Old Addresses." <u>SpoonRQ</u> (9:4) Aut 84,
      p. 59.
"Getting Back to Boise." <u>KanQ</u> (16:4) Aut 84, p. 152.
"Late October Cemetery Scene" (on rereading Joyce's
      "The Dead"). <u>Wind</u> (14:50) 84, p. 35.
"Pastorale: One Piano, Four Hands." <u>Northeast</u>
      (Series 3:17) Sum 84, p. 9.
"Sign Language." <u>Wind</u> (14:50) 84, p. 44.
"Spawning." <u>KanQ</u> (16:4) Aut 84, p. 148.
"Stroke" (for Lois). <u>SpoonRQ</u> (9:4) Aut 84, p. 57.
"Wakened by a Bird." <u>Abraxas</u> (31/32) 84, p. 31.

HUTCHINS, Pat: <u>See</u> HUTCHINGS, Pat

2467. HUTCHISON, Alexander
       "Goosegogs and Gorcocks." <u>MalR</u> (69) O 84, p. 35.
       "The Usual Story." <u>MalR</u> (69) O 84, p. 33.

2468. HUTCHISON, Joseph
       "Vander Meer's Revision." <u>TarRP</u> (24:1) Aut 84, p.
       13.

2469. HUTCHMAN, Laurence
       "Jacob in Edmonton." <u>PoetryCR</u> (5:4) Sum 84, p. 9.

2470. HUYETT, Pat
       "Come On In, the Water's Fine." <u>PoetC</u> (15:3) 84,
       p. 14.

2471. HYDE, Lewis
       "A Gentleman Living Alone" (tr. of Pablo Neruda,
       for Robert Bly). <u>Chelsea</u> (42/43) 84, p. 266-267.

2472. HYETT, Barbara Helfgott
       "Chambered Nautilus." <u>SouthernPR</u> (24:1) Spr 84,
       p. 51.
       "Elephant Hotel." <u>NewRep</u> (190:9) 5 Mr 84, p. 32.
       "The High Diving Horse." <u>NewRep</u> (189:25) 19 D 83,
       p. 34.
       "In the Woods near Munich" (April, 1945). <u>Ploughs</u>
       (10:4) 84, p. 176-177.

2473. HYMAN, Lateifa Ramona L.
       "Night Owls." <u>BlackALF</u> (18:1) Spr 84, p. 20.
       "Stephen." <u>BlackALF</u> (18:1) Spr 84, p. 19.

2474. IBARGOYEN, Saúl
       "Things" (tr. by John Oliver Simon). <u>Veloc</u> (3)
       Aut-Wint 83, p. 33.

2475. IBN KHAFAJA
       "The Ghost" (tr. by Jonathan Nevitt). <u>SenR</u> (14:1)
       84, p. 25-26.

2476. IBN ZUHR
       "Departure" (tr. by Jonathan Nevitt). <u>SenR</u> (14:1)
       84, p. 27.

2477. IDDINGS, Kathleen
"Suckering Tobacco." Vis (14) 84, p. 34.

2478. IGNATOW, David
"Aquarium" (To M.A., tr. of Oleh Olzhych, w. Bohdan
Boychuk). Pequod (16/17) 84, p. 188.
"Blessing Myself." Chelsea (42/43) 84, p. 43.
"Content." Chelsea (42/43) 84, p. 43.
"Different." PoetryE (15) Aut 84, p. 43-44.
"Dutch Painting" (tr. of Oleh Olzhych, w. Bohdan
Boychuk). Pequod (16/17) 84, p. 187.
"Five Poems on One Theme" (tr. of Bohdan Boychuk,
w. the author). Pequod (16/17) 84, p. 191-192.
"Here in bed behind a brick wall." Confr (27/28)
84, p. 155.
"I am lifted from my sadness." Confr (27/28) 84,
p. 156.
"I no longer want to feel with you." Confr
(27/28) 84, p. 155-156.
"I Turned My Back." Chelsea (42/43) 84, p. 107.
"No Theory." Chelsea (42/43) 84, p. 107.
"Proem." Bound (12:1) Aut 83, p. 61-67.
"Proud of Myself." PoetryE (15) Aut 84, p. 46.
"The Ride." PoetryE (15) Aut 84, p. 42.
"The Separate Dead." PoetryE (15) Aut 84, p. 45.
"Simultaneously." Chelsea (42/43) 84, p. 107.
"With the Door Open." Chelsea (42/43) 84, p. 43.
"Women" (tr. of Bohdan Boychuk, w. the author).
Confr (27/28) 84, p. 53.
"You are totally helpless in sleep." Confr
(27/28) 84, p. 156.
"You are unhappy with the way things." Confr
(27/28) 84, p. 156.
"You Who Gave Me Birth." Peb (23) 84, p. 95.

2479. IKEMOTO, Takashi
"Fish shop" (Haiku from the Japanese Masters, tr.
of Bashō, w. Lucien Stryk, calligraphy by
Lloyd J. Reynolds). NewL (50:2/3) Wint-Spr 84,
p. 140.
"Moor" (Haiku from the Japanese Masters, tr. of
Bashō, w. Lucien Stryk, calligraphy by Lloyd
J. Reynolds). NewL (50:2/3) Wint-Spr 84, p. 140.
"No need to cling" (Haiku from the Japanese
Masters, tr. of Joso, w. Lucien Stryk,
calligraphy by Lloyd J. Reynolds). NewL
(50:2/3) Wint-Spr 84, p. 140.
"Plum-viewing" (Haiku from the Japanese Masters,
tr. of Buson, w. Lucien Stryk, calligraphy by
Lloyd J. Reynolds). NewL (50:2/3) Wint-Spr 84,
p. 140.

2480. ILLYES, Gyula
"Mask" (tr. by Miklós Vajda). HolCrit (21:1) F
84, p. 9.
"The Sad Field-Hand" (tr. by William Jay Smith, w.
Miklós Vajda and Gyula Kodolányi). HolCrit
(21:1) F 84, p. 3.
"A Sentence for Tyranny" (Excerpt, tr. by Vernon
Watkins). HolCrit (21:1) F 84, p. 4.

"Tilting Sail" (tr. by William Jay Smith, w.
Miklós Vajda and Gyula Kodolányi). HolCrit
(21:1) F 84, p. 12.
"A Wreath" (tr. by William Jay Smith, w. Miklós
Vajda and Gyula Kodolányi). HolCrit (21:1) F
84, p. 10-11.

2481. IMAM, Hina Faisal
"Creation." Mund (14:2) 84, p. 67.
"Difference." Mund (14:2) 84, p. 68.
"She." Mund (14:2) 84, p. 67.

INES DE LA CRUZ, Juana, Sor: See CRUZ, Juana Inés de la, Sor

2482. INEZ, Colette
"Boats on the River, Party Lights." WestB (14)
84, p. 59.
"A Coverlet with Birds Beckoning Dreams." WestB
(14) 84, p. 58.
"In Ireland." Iowa (14:3) Aut 84, p. 5.
"Last Visit, Elizabeth." Ploughs (10:1) 84, p. 84.
"Notes from a Gutted House." VirQR (60:1) Wint
84, p. 67.
"The Parents." NeqC (4:2) Spr 84, p. 50.
"Prison Songs." AmerPoR (13:2) Mr-Ap 84, p. 6.

2483. INMAN, Will
"6 August 1981" (36 years later and how many days
before). Spirit (7:1) 84, p. 106-110.
"Giant Noctuid." Abraxas (29/30) 84, p. 34-35.

2484. IOANNOU, Susan
"Garden." Descant (47, 15:4) Wint 84, p. 94.
"Johnny." Descant (47, 15:4) Wint 84, p. 96-97.
"Song for a Separation." Descant (47, 15:4) Wint
84, p. 95.

2485. IRBY, James
"At the Sources" (tr. of Tomás Segovia). Iowa
(14:2) Spr-Sum 84, p. 147.
"Dawn of Tomorrow" (tr. of Tomás Segovia). Iowa
(14:2) Spr-Sum 84, p. 147-148.

2486. IRIE, Kevin
"Angelo." Waves (12:1) Aut 83, p. 41-43.
"Immigrants: The Second Generation." AntigR (56)
Wint 84, p. 73-74.
"Skinner's Rock." CapeR (19:2) Sum 84, p. 19.

2487. IRION, Mary Jean
"Chant." ChrC (101:37) 28 N 84, p. 1129.
"Fist." PraS (58:3) Aut 84, p. 88.
"Folding the Wash." ChrC (101:3) 25 Ja 84, p. 70.
"The Gift of Burial." PraS (58:3) Aut 84, p. 89.
"An October Weaving." ChrC (101:32) 24 O 84, p. 982.
"Seven Dromedaries at Whipsnade." SouthwR (69:2)
Spr 84, p. 210.

2488. IRVING, Leonard
"April Again." DekalbLAJ (17:1/2) 84, p. 132.

2489. IRWIN, Mark
      "Bucharest." OhioR (32) 84, p. 35.
      "The Creation of Man: The Sistine Chapel"
         (Prizewinning Poets--1984). Nat (238:18) 12 My
         84, p. 580.
      "To a Fallen Starling." MidAR (4:1) Spr 84, p. 139.
      "The Wisdom of the Body" (Selections: I, III-VII,
         IX). KenR (NS 6:2) Spr 84, p. 63-67.

2490. ISAAC, Melanie
      "Aftermath." Grain (12:4) N 84, p. 25.

2491. ISAACSON, Gail
      "First Kiss." WindO (44) Sum-Aut 84, p. 31.

2492. ISHIGAKI, Rin
      "Cliffs" (tr. by Harold P. Wright). Chelsea
         (42/43) 84, p. 262.
      "Living" (tr. by Harold P. Wright). Chelsea
         (42/43) 84, p. 263.

ISIS: See AREVALO, Marta de

2493. ISMAILI, Rashidah
      "Preparations 2." PoetryE (15) Aut 84, p. 29-30.

2494. ISOM, Joan
      "Running Away for a Day." Nimrod (27:2) Spr-Sum
         84, p. 11.

2495. ISRAEL, Inge
      "L'Adieu." PoetryCR (6:1) Aut 84, p. 8.
      "Courbure." PoetryCR (6:1) Aut 84, p. 8.
      "Univers Inflationniste." PoetryCR (6:1) Aut 84,
         p. 8.

2496. ISSENHUTH, Jean-Pierre
      "Averse." Os (18) 84, p. 16.
      "Nuit au Jardin." Os (18) 84, p. 17.

2497. ITO, Hiromi
      "February Cat" (in Japanese). YellowS (11) Sum
         84, p. 14.
      "February Cat" (tr. by Yuri Kageyama). YellowS
         (11) Sum 84, p. 14.
      "A Lot of Fun to Do" (in Japanese). YellowS (11)
         Sum 84, p. 22.
      "A Lot of Fun to Do" (tr. by Yuri Kageyama).
         YellowS (11) Sum 84, p. 22.
      "Probably a Toilet" (in Japanese). YellowS (11)
         Sum 84, p. 23.
      "Probably a Toilet" (tr. by Yuri Kageyama).
         YellowS (11) Sum 84, p. 23.

2498. ITZIN, Charles
      "The Brazilian Navy." NewL (50:4) Sum 84, p. 76.
      "Confessions." Nimrod (27:2) Spr-Sum 84, p. 49.
      "Eight O:Clock" (for Samuel Ray). NewL (51:2)
         Wint 84-85, p. 115.
      "Luz de Corral." NewL (50:2/3) Wint-Spr 84, p.

         260-261.
     "Os Alagados." <u>NewL</u> (50:4) Sum 84, p. 75.
     "Poet As a Mouth." <u>Nimrod</u> (27:2) Spr-Sum 84, p. 49.

2499. IVASK, Astrid
     "Tide" (tr. by Inara Cedrins). <u>Nimrod</u> (27:2) Spr-
         Sum 84, p. 55.

2500. IVEREM, Esther
     "Tsunami." <u>PaintedB</u> (22) Spr 84, p. 14.

2501. IVERSON, Roderick
     "The Edwardian Garden." <u>Veloc</u> (2) Spr 83, p. 54-57.
     "The Face." <u>Veloc</u> (3) Aut-Wint 83, p. 18.
     "Revelation and Demise" (Excerpt, tr. of Georg
         Trakl). <u>Field</u> (30) Spr 84, p. 70-71.
     "The Shape of Wind" (for Georg Trakl). <u>Veloc</u> (3)
         Aut-Wint 83, p. 17.

2502. JABES, Edmond
     "After the Deluge" (from <u>I Build My Dwelling</u>, tr.
         by Keith Waldrop). <u>DenQ</u> (19:1) Spr 84, p. 18.
     "Always This Image" (from <u>Of the Two Hands</u>, tr.
         by Keith Waldrop). <u>DenQ</u> (19:1) Spr 84, p. 31-32.
     "Groundless" (from <u>I Build My Dwelling</u>, tr. by
         Keith Waldrop). <u>DenQ</u> (19:1) Spr 84, p. 21-22.
     "Half Open, My Hand" (from <u>Of the Two Hands</u>, tr.
         by Keith Waldrop). <u>DenQ</u> (19:1) Spr 84, p. 30.
     "If There Were Anywhere But Desert" (Selected
         Poems, tr. by Keith Waldrop). <u>DenQ</u> (19:1) Spr
         84, p. 3-32.
     "Metamorphosis of the World" (from <u>I Build My
         Dwelling</u>, tr. by Keith Waldrop). <u>DenQ</u> (19:1)
         Spr 84, p. 18.
     "The Pact of Spring" (from <u>I Build My Dwelling</u>,
         tr. by Keith Waldrop). <u>DenQ</u> (19:1) Spr 84, p.
         23-24.
     "The Pilgrim" (from <u>I Build My Dwelling</u>, tr. by
         Keith Waldrop). <u>DenQ</u> (19:1) Spr 84, p. 19.
     "Screech-Owl with a Comet's Tail" (from <u>I Build My
         Dwelling</u>, tr. by Keith Waldrop). <u>DenQ</u> (19:1)
         Spr 84, p. 19.
     "Show" (from <u>I Build My Dwelling</u>, tr. by Keith
         Waldrop). <u>DenQ</u> (19:1) Spr 84, p. 15-17.
     "Slumber Inn" (from <u>I Build My Dwelling</u>, tr. by
         Keith Waldrop). <u>DenQ</u> (19:1) Spr 84, p. 5-12.
     "Sunland" (from <u>I Build My Dwelling</u>, tr. by Keith
         Waldrop). <u>DenQ</u> (19:1) Spr 84, p. 13-14.
     "Those from Whom" (from <u>Of the Two Hands</u>, tr. by
         Keith Waldrop). <u>DenQ</u> (19:1) Spr 84, p. 25-28.
     "Unmasked Hand" (from <u>Of the Two Hands</u>, tr. by
         Keith Waldrop). <u>DenQ</u> (19:1) Spr 84, p. 29.
     "Well Water" (from <u>I Build My Dwelling</u>, tr. by
         Keith Waldrop). <u>DenQ</u> (19:1) Spr 84, p. 20.

2503. JACKETTI, Maria T.
     "Inside my lover's mouth." <u>Mund</u> (14:2) 84, p. 48.
     "Meteor slices." <u>Mund</u> (14:2) 84, p. 49.
     "Optimism." <u>Mund</u> (14:2) 84, p. 49.
     "Soccer field." <u>Mund</u> (14:2) 84, p. 48.

"Speaking Three Languages." <u>Mund</u> (14:2) 84, p. 48.

2504. JACKOWSKA, Nicki
"Earth Rumour." <u>Stand</u> (25:2) Spr 84, p. 58.
"Winkling." <u>Stand</u> (25:1) Wint 83-84, p. 64.

2505. JACKSON, A. M.
"I'm Pissed." <u>EngJ</u> (73:3) Mr 84, p. 48.

2506. JACKSON, Angela
"Arachnia: Her Side of the Story." <u>13thM</u> (8:1/2)
    84, p. 64-65.
"The House of the Spider." <u>OP</u> (37) Spr-Sum 84, p. 4.
"In Her Solitude: The Inca Divining Spider." <u>OP</u>
    (37) Spr-Sum 84, p. 7.
"The Itsy Bitsy Spider Climbs and Analyzes." <u>OP</u>
    (37) Spr-Sum 84, p. 6.
"Rain." <u>YellowS</u> (13) Wint 84, p. 22.
"Rosaries" (For the Revolutionary Women of
    Nicaragua, for Melvin). <u>Stepping</u> (Anniversary
    Issue I) 84, p. 29.
"Spider Divine" (of the Cameroons). <u>OP</u> (37) Spr-
    Sum 84, p. 5.
"The Spider Speaks on the Need for Solidarity."
    <u>OP</u> (37) Spr-Sum 84, p. 8-9.
"The Spider's Mantra." <u>OP</u> (37) Spr-Sum 84, p. 3.
"Why I Must Make Language." <u>OP</u> (37) Spr-Sum 84,
    p. 10-11.
"Woman in Moonlight Washes Blues from Dreams".
    <u>YellowS</u> (11) Sum 84, p. 37.

2507. JACKSON, Fleda
"Mary Wollstonecraft Dies of Puerperal Fever."
    <u>NegC</u> (4:4) Aut 84, p. 26-29.

2508. JACKSON, Fleda Brown
"Apalachee Bay." <u>IndR</u> (7:2) Spr 84, p. 21.
"A Mother Watches Her Athletic Daughter." <u>CimR</u>
    (69) O 84, p. 22.
"Thousands Are Enjoying Their Sunday on the Beach."
    <u>StoneC</u> (11:3/4) Spr-Sum 84, p. 18.

2509. JACKSON, Gale P.
"New York Beirut Nagasaki" <u>BlackALF</u> (18:2) Sum
    84, p. 56.

2510. JACKSON, Haywood
"At the Theater--the Rush for Seats." <u>StoneC</u>
    (11:3/4) Spr-Sum 84, p. 43.
"Hugging and Kissing in Summer." <u>Swallow</u> (3) 84,
    p. 69.
"The Pink Blouse." <u>Swallow</u> (3) 84, p. 68.

2511. JACKSON, Richard
"All There Is." <u>Tendril</u> (17) Wint 84, p. 92.
"How Far the Light Travels." <u>AntR</u> (42:4) Aut 84,
    p. 456-457.
"How We See the Past." <u>TarRP</u> (23:2) Spr 84, p. 36-
    37.
"Morning Glory." <u>TarRP</u> (23:2) Spr 84, p. 37-38.

2512. JACKSON, Robert J. V.
     "The Queen Monarch." PoeticJ (7) 84, p. 2.

2513. JACKSON, Rodica S.
     "C." Mund (14:2) 84, p. 32.
     "Caltrop." Mund (14:2) 84, p. 32.

2514. JACKSON, William 'Haywood'
     "All the Unsavored Cherries." YellowS (10) Spr
     84, p. 8.

2515. JACOB, John
     "At the Red Fox." SpoonRQ (9:4) Aut 84, p. 19.
     "Suicide." SpoonRQ (9:4) Aut 84, p. 18.
     "The Union Man from Toluca, Illinois." SpoonRQ
     (9:4) Aut 84, p. 17.

2516. JACOBIK, Gray
     "In Music I Listen To." KanQ (16:1/2) Wint-Spr
     84, p. 75.
     "Telemann and Two Cats." KanQ (16:1/2) Wint-Spr
     84, p. 74.

2517. JACOBOWITZ, Judah
     "Black and White and Red." Poem (50) Mr 84, p. 2-3.
     "Nature Morte." Poem (50) Mr 84, p. 4.
     "Private Office Drama." CrabCR (2:1) Sum 84, p.
     10-11.
     "A Taste of Bonaparte." MassR (25:1) Spr 84, p.
     42-43.

2518. JACOBS, David
     "Mistress of the Flowers." Stand (25:2) Spr 84,
     p. 50.

2519. JACOBSEN, Josephine
     "Characters in Motion." NewL (50:2/3) Wint-Spr
     84, p. 216.
     "A Dream of Games." Poetry (145:2) N 84, p. 82-85.
     "Moon." TriQ (61) Aut 84, p. 120.
     "The Poem Itself." TriQ (61) Aut 84, p. 112.
     "The Spy." SouthernPR (24:1) Spr 84, p. 61-63.
     "The Steps." Comm (111:22) 14 D 84, p. 687.
     "Tiger" (Baltimore). TriQ (61) Aut 84, p. 118-119.

2520. JACOBSEN, Rolf
     "Briefing" (tr. by Roger Greenwald). Spirit (7:1)
     84, p. 141.
     "The Catacombs in San Callisto" (tr. by Roger
     Greenwald). Stand (25:1) Wint 83-84, p. 48.
     "Green Light" (tr. by Roger Greenwald). Spirit
     (7:1) 84, p. 95.
     "Thoughts upon Listening in on a Radio Telescope"
     (tr. by Roger Greenwald). Stand (25:1) Wint 83-
     84, p. 49.
     "Your Thoughts, Your Deeds" (tr. by Olav Grinde).
     Stand (25:4) Aut 84, p. 64.

2521. JACOX, Lynn C.
     "The Second Language" (for Mohammed Al-Abed).

MalR (67) F 84, p. 60-61.

2522. JAECH, Stephen
"Three Images." Wind (14:51) 84, p. 26.

2523. JAEGER, Lowell
"Blackbirds." CharR (10:1) Spr 84, p. 32-33.
"Coyote and the Stars." CharR (10:1) Spr 84, p.
    31-32.
"The Greasybears." CharR (10:1) Spr 84, p. 34-35.
"Native Land" (for Deb Allbery). CharR (10:1) Spr
    84, p. 27-31.

2524. JAEGER, Lowell L.
"The War at Home." WoosterR (1:1) Mr 84, p. 43-45.

2525. JAFFE, Dan
"The Day after the Election." NewL (50:2/3) Wint-
    Spr 84, p. 184.
"Survivor." NewL (51:2) Wint 84-85, p. 37.

2526. JAGASICH, Paul
"Are Your Poems Your Songs" (tr. of Jaroslav
    Seifert, w. Tom O'Grady). Spirit (8:1) 83-84,
    p. 37.
"The Artists' House" (tr. of Jaroslav Seifert, w.
    Tom O'Grady). Spirit (8:1) 83-84, p. 26-27.
"Before Those Few Light Kisses" (tr. of Jaroslav
    Seifert, w. Tom O'Grady). Spirit (8:1) 83-84,
    p. 49.
"Cannon Fire" (tr. of Jaroslav Seifert, w. Tom
    O'Grady). Spirit (8:1) 83-84, p. 23-24.
"The Casting of Bells" (tr. of Jaroslav Seifert, w.
    Tom O'Grady). Spirit (8:1) 83-84, p. 1-61.
"Crowned with Berries" (tr. of Jaroslav Seifert, w.
    Tom O'Grady). Spirit (8:1) 83-84, p. 21.
"Dance-Song" (tr. of Jaroslav Seifert, w. Tom
    O'Grady). Spirit (8:1) 83-84, p. 29-30.
"End of a Story" (tr. of Jaroslav Seifert, w. Tom
    O'Grady). Spirit (8:1) 83-84, p. 18-19.
"Heavenly Bonds" (tr. of Jaroslav Seifert, w. Tom
    O'Grady). Spirit (8:1) 83-84, p. 40-41.
"I don't Look at People's Souls" (tr. of Jaroslav
    Seifert, w. Tom O'Grady). Spirit (8:1) 83-84,
    p. 11.
"I Just Wanted to Tell You This" (tr. of Jaroslav
    Seifert, w. Tom O'Grady). Spirit (8:1) 83-84,
    p. 15.
"I Looked Only" (tr. of Jaroslav Seifert, w. Tom
    O'Grady). Spirit (8:1) 83-84, p. 46.
"I Remained on This Earth" (tr. of Jaroslav
    Seifert, w. Tom O'Grady). Spirit (8:1) 83-84,
    p. 14.
"If the Sand Could Sing" (tr. of Jaroslav Seifert,
    w. Tom O'Grady). Spirit (8:1) 83-84, p. 31.
"In Those Winters When" (tr. of Jaroslav Seifert,
    w. Tom O'Grady). Spirit (8:1) 83-84, p. 25.
"It Was Afternoon or Later" (tr. of Jaroslav
    Seifert, w. Tom O'Grady). Spirit (8:1) 83-84,
    p. 12.

"It's after All Saints Day" (tr. of Jaroslav
    Seifert, w. Tom O'Grady). Spirit (8:1) 83-84,
    p. 34.
"A Letter from Marienbad" (tr. of Jaroslav Seifert,
    w. Tom O'Grady). Spirit (8:1) 83-84, p. 55-61.
"Monument to a Kettle Drum" (tr. of Jaroslav
    Seifert, w. Tom O'Grady). Spirit (8:1) 83-84,
    p. 44-45.
"The Mount of Venus" (tr. of Jaroslav Seifert, w.
    Tom O'Grady). Spirit (8:1) 83-84, p. 50-51.
"My Star-Hung Window" (tr. of Jaroslav Seifert, w.
    Tom O'Grady). Spirit (8:1) 83-84, p. 38.
"Myrtle Wreath" (tr. of Jaroslav Seifert, w. Tom
    O'Grady). Spirit (8:1) 83-84, p. 35-36.
"Neither the Marble Tower" (tr. of Jaroslav
    Seifert, w. Tom O'Grady). Spirit (8:1) 83-84,
    p. 17.
"Not Too Long Ago" (tr. of Jaroslav Seifert, w. Tom
    O'Grady). Spirit (8:1) 83-84, p. 42-43.
"Orangeade" (tr. of Jaroslav Seifert, w. Tom
    O'Grady). Spirit (8:1) 83-84, p. 47-48.
"Poor Moon, She Is Helpless" (tr. of Jaroslav
    Seifert, w. Tom O'Grady). Spirit (8:1) 83-84,
    p. 13.
"Prologue" (tr. of Jaroslav Seifert, w. Tom
    O'Grady). Spirit (8:1) 83-84, p. 9-10.
"A Requiem for Dvorák" (tr. of Jaroslav Seifert,
    w. Tom O'Grady). Spirit (8:1) 83-84, p. 32-33.
"Ship in Flames" (tr. of Jaroslav Seifert, w. Tom
    O'Grady). Spirit (8:1) 83-84, p. 16.
"When Our Mulberry Trees" (tr. of Jaroslav Seifert,
    w. Tom O'Grady). Spirit (8:1) 83-84, p. 28.
"When We Are Denied" (tr. of Jaroslav Seifert, w.
    Tom O'Grady). Spirit (8:1) 83-84, p. 39.
"Where or Whenever I Had Heard" (tr. of Jaroslav
    Seifert, w. Tom O'Grady). Spirit (8:1) 83-84,
    p. 20.
"With the Roll of Our Blood" (tr. of Jaroslav
    Seifert, w. Tom O'Grady). Spirit (8:1) 83-84,
    p. 22.
"You Are Asking" (tr. of Jaroslav Seifert, w. Tom
    O'Grady). Spirit (8:1) 83-84, p. 52-54.

2527. JAGODZINSKE, Marcia
    "Fantasy." Sam (39:1, release 153) 84, back cover.
    "Man Standing at the Bar." Sam (39:1, release
        153) 84, p. 43.
    "A Middle Class Tradition." Sam (41:2, release
        162) 84 or 85, p. 13.
    "Reservoir." Sam (41:1, release 161) 84, p. 50.

2528. JAHN, Jerald D.
    "David Bohn at Oxford." SouthernHR (18:2) Spr 84,
        p. 106-107.

2529. JAMES, David
    "Asking the Moon." QW (18) Spr-Sum 84, p. 47.
    "Breaking." MidAR (4:2) Aut 84, p. 34.
    "Climbing Out." SouthernPR (24:2) Aut 84, p. 52.
    "A Song of Sleep." MidAR (4:2) Aut 84, p. 33.

"The Sparrow." KanQ (16:4) Aut 84, p. 14.

2530. JAMES, Joyce
"Catbirds." Ploughs (10:1) 84, p. 87-90.
"Dusk." Ploughs (10:4) 84, p. 195-196.
"The Wild Canaries on a Twenty-Mile Stretch of
Highway." Ploughs (10:1) 84, p. 85-86.

2531. JAMES, Norberto
"Apuntes para el Poema." Areíto (10:38) 84, p. 35.
"Pensar la Rosa." Areíto (10:38) 84, p. 35.

2532. JAMES, Sibyl
"Foreign Living." Telescope (3:3) Aut 84, p. 84.
"Forget your war talk" (Translitic in the manner of
the love sonnets of Louise Labé). Calyx
(8:3) Aut-Wint 84, p. 45.
"It don't mean a thing" (Translitic in the manner
of the love sonnets of Louise Labé). Calyx
(8:3) Aut-Wint 84, p. 46-47.

2533. JAMES-FRENCH, Dayv (See also FRENCH, Dayv James)
"At the Zoo: Albino Tiger." Quarry (33:3) Sum 84,
p. 36.
"Giant Panda." Quarry (33:3) Sum 84, p. 36.

2534. JAMID, Fayad
"Contémplala Es Muy Bella." Mairena (6:18) 84,
p. 171-172.

2535. JAMIESON, Patrick
"Brass Angel." AntigR (57) Spr 84, p. 44.

2536. JAMISON, Barbara
"The Mango Tree." OroM (2:3/4, issue 7/8) 84, p. 8.
"Nicaraguan Bus." OroM (2:3/4, issue 7/8) 84, p.
26-27.

2537. JAMISON, Stephen R.
"Rebecca and Omar and the Dance." AmerPoR (13:4)
Jl-Ag 84, p. 27.

2538. JAMMES, Francis
"The Farm Buildings Were Shiny Black" (tr. by
Antony Oldknow). WebR (9:2) Wint 85, p. 19-20.
"He Keeps Himself Busy" (For Marcel Schwob, tr. by
Antony Oldknow). WebR (9:2) Wint 85, p. 20-21.
"It's Going to Snow" (tr. by Dennis Tool, for Gary
Wilson). NewOR (11:3/4) Aut-Wint 84, p. 111.
"When Mist Made the Soil Glisten" (tr. by Antony
Oldknow). WebR (9:2) Wint 85, p. 22-23.

2539. JANIK, Phyllis
"The Coughing Architect of Taj Mahal." NewL
(51:2) Wint 84-85, p. 96-98.
"Mobile Still Life with Carnations and Baby's
Breath." NewL (51:1) Aut 84, p. 84-85.

2540. JANKIEWICZ, Henry
"A Problem in Topology." ThirdW (2) Spr 84, p. 4-6.

"A Voice from the Umbrella Stand." ThirdW (2) Spr
    84, p. 29-31.
"Waiting for Tea." ThirdW (2) Spr 84, p. 97-98.

2541. JANKOLA, Beth
    "Island Song." PoetryCR (5:4) Sum 84, p. 8.
    "The Snake Is Getting Bigger." WestCR (19:1) Je
        84, p. 46.
    "Thirteen Ways of Looking at a Crow." MalR (69) O
        84, p. 79-81.

2542. JANZEN, Jean
    "The Comfort of Rocks." ChrC (101:13) 18 Ap 84,
        p. 396.

2543. JAQUISH, Karen I.
    "Ode for Bessie." PoetL (79:1) Spr 84, p. 24-25.

2544. JARA, Gabriel
    "Caminante." Mairena (6:17) Aut 84, p. 82.

2545. JARMAN, Mark
    "Ideal Conditions." Hudson (37:1) Spr 84, p. 79-80.
    "If I Am Like Anything." AntR (42:3) Sum 84, p. 320.
    "Lost in a Dream." NewEngR (7:1) Aut 84, p. 102-103.
    "Poem for the Heartland." Thrpny (17) Spr 84, p. 20.
    "Poem in June." Hudson (37:1) Spr 84, p. 80-81.
    "The Seawall" (for Charles Wright). AntR (42:3)
        Sum 84, p. 321.
    "To the Reader." NewYorker (60:4) 12 Mr 84, p. 52.

2546. JARVIS, Kim
    "Chants, Moans, Screams." Stepping (Premier
        Issue) Sum 82, p. 28.
    "Fulton Street." Stepping (Premier Issue) Sum 82,
        p. 25-27.

2547. JASON, Philip K.
    "Livingroom." Telescope (3:2) Spr 84, p. 25-26.
    "Places." LitR (28:1) Aut 84, p. 52.

2548. JASPER, Pat
    "No Introduction Needed." CrossC (6:1) 84, p. 15.

2549. JASTRUN, Tomasz
    "Afghanistan" (tr. by Daniel Bourne). WebR (9:2)
        Wint 85, p. 16.
    "Hat" (tr. by Daniel Bourne). GreenfR (11:3/4)
        Wint-Spr 84, p. 131-132.
    "Interrogation and Map" (tr. by Daniel Bourne).
        GreenfR (11:3/4) Wint-Spr 84, p. 130.
    "Polish Dogs" (tr. by Daniel Bourne). WebR (9:2)
        Wint 85, p. 17.
    "Prose" (tr. by Daniel Bourne). GreenfR (11:3/4)
        Wint-Spr 84, p. 133.
    "Reunion" (tr. by Daniel Bourne). GreenfR
        (11:3/4) Wint-Spr 84, p. 132.
    "Rings" (tr. by Daniel Bourne). GreenfR (11:3/4)
        Wint-Spr 84, p. 131.
    "Tread" (tr. by Daniel Bourne). GreenfR (11:3/4)

Wint-Spr 84, p. 131.
"Visiting Day" (tr. by Daniel Bourne). GreenfR
(11:3/4) Wint-Spr 84, p. 132.
"Walk-ons" (tr. by Daniel Bourne). GreenfR
(11:3/4) Wint-Spr 84, p. 133.

2550. JEANNE, Ave
"A ll beautiful, once spacious skies." SanFPJ
(6:2) 84, p. 18.
"The Dead Never Know." SanFPJ (6:1) 84, p. 42.
"The empty cornfield." Amelia (1:2) O 84, p. 73.
"Gentle Thunderings." SanFPJ (7:1) 84, p. 9.
"Gnawing." SanFPJ (6:1) 84, p. 43.
"A Hug." PoeticJ (5) 84, p. 7.
"The Intelligence of a Missing Planet." SanFPJ
(7:1) 84, p. 12.
"The Last Harvest." SanFPJ (6:4) 84, p. 20.
"Letter to War Makers." SanFPJ (7:1) 84, p. 10.
"Muffled Voices." SanFPJ (6:2) 84, p. 64.
"A Nuclear Sunset." SanFPJ (6:4) 84, p. 17.
"The Null Set." SanFPJ (6:1) 84, p. 42.
"Ocelots." PoeticJ (5) 84, p. 7.
"Omen." SanFPJ (6:2) 84, p. 19.
"United We Fall." SanFPJ (6:2) 84, p. 63.
"Uprooted." SanFPJ (6:4) 84, p. 18.
"A Visit to Center City Philadelphia." SanFPJ
(7:1) 84, p. 11.
"Watching a Giant." PoeticJ (5) 84, p. 4.
"Where It All Began, It Ends." SanFPJ (6:2) 84,
p. 61.
"With Each Passing Breeze." SanFPJ (6:1) 84, p. 44.

2551. JEFFERS, Robinson
"Natural Music." Telescope (3:1) Wint 84, p. 131.

2552. JEFFREY, Mildred M.
"Law & Order." DekalbLAJ (17:1/2) 84, p. 133.

2553. JENCKES, Norma
"Quarry at Lime Rock." KanQ (16:1/2) Wint-Spr 84,
p. 155.

2554. JENDRYSCHIK, Manfred
"For William C. Williams" (tr. by F. H. König).
NoAmR (269:1) Mr 84, p. 55.
"Moment in Petzow" (tr. by F. H. König). NoAmR
(269:1) Mr 84, p. 53-54.
"The New Apartment" (tr. by F. H. König). NoAmR
(269:1) Mr 84, p. 55.

2555. JENKINS, Paul
"All Souls' Day." KenR (NS 6:2) Spr 84, p. 54.
"Dark Water." KenR (NS 6:2) Spr 84, p. 55.
"Exhalation." KenR (NS 6:2) Spr 84, p. 56.
"A House and a Vein of Water." KenR (NS 6:2) Spr
84, p. 53.
"Open Window." KenR (NS 6:2) Spr 84, p. 54-55.

2556. JENNINGS, Kate
"Coven." SouthernHR (18:1) Wint 84, p. 40.

"The Dark Side of the Moon." Hudson (37:3) Aut
    84, p. 428-429.
"Dime Store at Hallowe'en, Damascus, Virginia."
    LitR (28:1) Aut 84, p. 72.
"The Gifted Dreamer." Hudson (37:3) Aut 84, p.
    427-428.
"Kitchen Moon." LitR (28:1) Aut 84, p. 73.
"Malice." SouthernPR (24:2) Aut 84, p. 33.
"The Night Watch." Hudson (37:3) Aut 84, p. 426.
"Postcard." Hudson (37:3) Aut 84, p. 429-430.
"Pruning the Trees." Wind (14:50) 84, p. 28.
"Truffle Hunt." SouthernHR (18:2) Spr 84, p. 150.

2557. JENNINGS, Lane
    "Legend" (Hue Citadel -- Tet, 1968). ThirdW (2)
        Spr 84, p. 79.

2558. JENNINGS, Michael
    "A Man Squatting in the Shade." KanQ (16:1/2)
        Wint-Spr 84, p. 154.

2559. JENNINGS, Regina B.
    "To Langston." Stepping Wint 84, p. 16.

2560. JENNINGS, Richard J.
    "Birds." BallSUF (24:3) Sum 83, p. 82.
    "The Original Bozo." BallSUF (24:3) Sum 83, p. 52-
        53.

2561. JENSEN, Laura
    "The Clean One" (from Memory). IndR (7:3) Sum
        84, p. 67-68.
    "Sunburned Woman." AmerPoR (13:2) Mr-Ap 84, p. 12.
    "Triptych." PoetryNW (25:2) Sum 84, p. 22-23.

2562. JENSEN, Wollom, A.
    "Harvest." Wind (14:52) 84, p. 3.

2563. JEROME, Judson
    "Harvesting Together." Stepping (Anniversary
        Issue I) 84, p. 30-31.
    "The Sinew of Survival." Sparrow (46) 84, p. 30.

2564. JERSILD, Devon
    "Mother of the Birds." WebR (9:1) Spr 84, p. 73.
    "Sixth Sense." WebR (9:1) Spr 84, p. 72-73.
    "Waking in San Juan." WebR (9:1) Spr 84, p. 74.

2565. JESUS, Teresa de
    "Buscando con Ahinco." Mairena (6:17) Aut 84, p. 26.
    "Cosas que Suceden." Mairena (6:17) Aut 84, p. 25.
    "Deja Que Te Cante, Madre." Mairena (6:17) Aut
        84, p. 25-26.

2566. JEWELL, Terri L.
    "A Brother Returned." Wind (14:52) 84, p. 28.
    "Confiding in Open Waters." WoosterR (1:2) N 84,
        p. 56.
    "Ha'nt." WoosterR (1:2) N 84, p. 57.
    "Returning Anymore." Wind (14:52) 84, p. 28.

"Salvaging Blood, January 1983." BlackALF (18:1)
Spr 84, p. 35.
"Theurgy." BlackALF (18:1) Spr 84, p. 35.

2567. JEWINSKI, Ed
"The Earth As We Know It." ThRiPo (23/24) 84, p. 65.

2568. JILES, Paulette
"Night Flight to Attiwapiskat." Descant (44/45,
15:1/2) Spr-Sum 84, p. 13-15.
"Northern Reporter." Descant (44/45, 15:1/2) Spr-
Sum 84, p. 16.

2569. JIMENEZ, Vita Marie
"Have You Seen This Man?" HangL (46) Aut 84, p. 25.

2570. JIMENEZ GOMEZ, Florentino
"Abriste la ventana." Mairena (5:13) Spr 83, p.
74-75.

2571. JOEL, Gerd
"End of Autumn" (tr. of Leopoldo Chariarse, w.
Miriam Joel). Mund (14:2) 84, p. 9.
"Eternal Walls" (tr. of Leopoldo Chariarse, w.
Miriam Joel). Mund (14:2) 84, p. 11.

2572. JOEL, Miriam
"End of Autumn" (tr. of Leopoldo Chariarse, w.
Gerd Joel). Mund (14:2) 84, p. 9.
"Eternal Walls" (tr. of Leopoldo Chariarse, w.
Gerd Joel). Mund (14:2) 84, p. 11.

2573. JOGLAR CACHO, Manuel
"Desilusion." Mairena (5:13) Spr 83, p. 95.
"Oda a un Alfarero" (Selection: II). Mairena
(5:13) Spr 83, p. 95.

2574. JOHLER, Walt
"Horizon from the Ship." StoneC (12:1/2) Aut-Wint
84, p. 27.
"Moon Veil." Poem (52) N 84, p. 48.
"Steps in the Snow." Poem (52) N 84, p. 49.

2575. JOHN, Brian
"Scape." Argo (5:3) 84, p. 5.

2576. JOHNS, Leola
"To Commemorate and Celebrate Langston Hughes."
Stepping Wint 84, p. 23.

2577. JOHNSEN, Gretchen
"Dance." CreamCR (9:1/2) 84, p. 12.

2578. JOHNSON, Bill
"Traveling Camas Prairie." SnapD (6:2) Spr 83, p.
44.
"Wigwam Burner" (for M. K. Browning). SnapD (6:2)
Spr 83, p. 45.

2579. JOHNSON, David
"Une Espece Mourante: The Internationals."
SouthernHR (18:2) Spr 84, p. 148-149.

2580. JOHNSON, Denis
"Our Feature by the Waters." Telescope (3:3) Aut
84, p. 56.
"The Prayers of the Insane." Tendril (17) Wint
84, p. 95.
"The Skewbald Horse." NewYorker (59:49) 23 Ja 84,
p. 36-37.
"Someone They Aren't." Telescope (3:3) Aut 84, p.
57.
"Spaceman Tom and Commander Joe." Tendril (17)
Wint 84, p. 93.
"The Words of a Toast." Tendril (17) Wint 84, p. 94.

2581. JOHNSON, Doug
"Christmas Angel." RagMag (3:2) Aut 84, p. 7.
"Gray Forest, Late Autumn Light." RagMag (3:2)
Aut 84, p. 6.

2582. JOHNSON, Fred
"Mayakovsky Shot Himself (April 14, 1930)." MinnR
(N.S. 22) Spr 84, p. 5.

2583. JOHNSON, Gerald J.
"The Spider's Dance." PortR (30:1) 84, p. 136.

2584. JOHNSON, Greg
"The Burning House." SouthwR (69:4) Aut 84, p. 433.

2585. JOHNSON, Ida K.
"Ares Conquered." PoeticJ (6) 84, p. 35.

2586. JOHNSON, Jean Youell
"C. V. A. (Cerebral Vascular Accident)." PoeticJ
(7) 84, p. 16.
"I live in the night." PoeticJ (7) 84, p. 4.
"To Matisse." PoeticJ (7) 84, p. 5.
"White Quiet White." PoeticJ (8) 84, p. 8.

2587. JOHNSON, Jim
"When the Lynx Came Down from Canada." BelPoJ
(34:4) Sum 84, p. 32-33.

2588. JOHNSON, Joyce Sandeen
"In Memoriam." PoeticJ (2) 83, p. 20.

2589. JOHNSON, Kate Knapp
"James before Darkness." Tendril (17) Wint 84, p.
96.

2590. JOHNSON, Kathleen Jeffrie
"At Dusk." SouthernPR (24:1) Spr 84, p. 29.

2591. JOHNSON, Kent
"Circles of lichen." Northeast (Series 3:18) 84,
p. 10.
"Scuba divers breathing deeply." Northeast

          (Series 3:18) 84, p. 10.
          "Silent Screen." <u>Northeast</u> (Series 3:18) 84, p. 10.

2592. JOHNSON, Linda Wikene
          "At an Al Purdy Poetry Reading." <u>Waves</u> (12:2/3)
          Wint 84, p. 98.

2593. JOHNSON, Michael
          "A Hymn for the Eye" (tr. of Jorge Debravo). <u>Mund</u>
          (14:2) 84, p. 61.
          "Psalm to the Animal Earth of Your Abdomen" (tr. of
          Jorge Debravo). <u>Mund</u> (14:2) 84, p. 61, 63.

2594. JOHNSON, Michael L.
          "Death Is Naked" (tr. of Jorge Debravo).
          <u>BlueBldgs</u> (8) 84?, p. 24.
          "Fiesole" (For Kathleen). <u>KanQ</u> (16:3) Sum 84, p. 90.
          "A Lady Glimpsed at the End of Summer." <u>RagMag</u>
          (3:1) Spr 84, p. 7.
          "There Are Moments" (tr. of Jorge Debravo).
          <u>BlueBldgs</u> (8) 84?, p. 24.
          "To a Friend in the Hospital." <u>RagMag</u> (3:1) Spr
          84, p. 6.
          "To a Rose Dress: A Translation from Théophile
          Gautier." <u>KanQ</u> (16:3) Sum 84, p. 89.
          "Widows of Darkness" (tr. of Jorge Debravo).
          <u>BlueBldgs</u> (8) 84?, p. 24.

2595. JOHNSON, Nick
          "The Old Physics." <u>AmerPoR</u> (13:1) Ja-F 84, p. 6.

2596. JOHNSON, Robert K.
          "A Grey December Day." <u>WebR</u> (9:2) Wint 85, p. 39.
          "The Lecture." <u>WebR</u> (9:2) Wint 85, p. 39.
          "Some Day." <u>PoeticJ</u> (7) 84, p. 24.
          "A Summation." <u>PoeticJ</u> (8) 84, p. 29.

2597. JOHNSON, Ronald
          "Ark 47, Plow Spire" (for Ashland Kansas, Memorial
          Day, 1981). <u>Sulfur</u> (4:1, issue 10) 84, p. 124-
          131.

2598. JOHNSON, Sheila Golburgh
          "Chanterelles." <u>PoeticJ</u> (7) 84, p. 23.

2599. JOHNSON, Thomas
          "The Best Dance Hall in Iuka, Mississippi." <u>NewL</u>
          (50:2/3) Wint-Spr 84, p. 166.

2600. JOHNSON, Tom
          "The Chinese Wall." <u>Poetry</u> (145:1) O 84, p. 16-18.

2601. JOHNSON, W. R.
          "Mazes." <u>LitR</u> (27:2) Wint 84, p. 184-185.

2602. JOHNSTON, Fred
          "Territories" (for Mary Clancy). <u>Descant</u> (47,
          15:4) Wint 84, p. 187.

2603. JOHNSTON, George
"Elegy" (for George Whalley). Quarry (33:1) Wint
84, p. 22-23.

2604. JOHNSTON, Mark
"The Art of Erasure." Abraxas (29/30) 84, p. 65.
"Bones in the Woods." StoneC (12:1/2) Aut-Wint
84, p. 29.
"Night School." CarolQ (36:2) Wint 84, p. 90.

2605. JOLLY, Paulo de
"Luis XIV a la Infanta de España Marie Therese."
Mairena (5:14) Aut 83, p. 10.
"Luis XIV desde lo Alto de los Ventanales."
Mairena (5:14) Aut 83, p. 12.
"Luis XIV y la Alta Tonalidad de Alma." Mairena
(5:14) Aut 83, p. 11.
"Luis XIV y la Voluntad de Poder." Mairena (5:14)
Aut 83, p. 12.

JOLLY MONGE, Paulo: See JOLLY, Paulo de

2606. JONAID
"Ghazal: I am, O pious priest, one ungodly one"
(tr. by the author, w. Mary Jane White). Iowa
(14:2) Spr-Sum 84, p. 119.
"Poem: Here in the upper part of the village" (tr.
by the author). Iowa (14:2) Spr-Sum 84, p. 120.

2607. JONES, Andrew McCord
"Out to Lunch." StoneC (11:3/4) Spr-Sum 84, p. 13.

2608. JONES, D. G.
"Variations." CanLit (100) Spr 84, p. 157-163.

2609. JONES, Daryl
"The Horse." BlackWR (10:2) Spr 84, p. 35.

2610. JONES, Elba M.
"Revival." PoeticJ (4) 83, p. 27.

2611. JONES, Elizabeth
"6:37." Descant (47, 15:4) Wint 84, p. 151.
"Kansas." Descant (47, 15:4) Wint 84, p. 152.
"Wichita As Falls" (for Pat Metheny). Descant
(47, 15:4) Wint 84, p. 153.

JONES, Elizabeth Follin: See FOLLIN-JONES, Elizabeth

2612. JONES, Gayl
"Foxes." Callaloo (20, 7:1) Wint 84, p. 39-42.
"Mr. River's Love Story." Callaloo (20, 7:1) Wint
84, p. 43-45.

2613. JONES, Ina
"Going for a Ride." GreenfR (11:3/4) Wint-Spr 84,
p. 139-140.

2614. JONES, J. E. M.
"X Is a Constant in Time." Stepping Wint 83, p.

20-21.

2615. JONES, Joyce
"Pome to My Lover." BlackALF (18:1) Spr 84, p. 36.

2616. JONES, Patricia
"Bête Noire." Tele (19) 83, p. 28-29.

2617. JONES, Paul
"An Essay in Political Science." GeoR (38:3) Aut
84, p. 477.

2618. JONES, R. P.
"Los Desastres de la Guerra." Piq (12) 84, p. 71.

2619. JONES, Richard
"The Anchor." NewL (50:4) Sum 84, p. 96-97.
"Innocent Things." Pequod (16/17) 84, p. 103.
"Looking at My Father." NewL (50:4) Sum 84, p. 96.

2620. JONES, Robert C.
"The Sleeping Rocks Do Dream." NewL (50:4) Sum
84, p. 58-59.

2621. JONES, Robert L.
"The Stone House, Emma Cobb, Mr. Gin and Me" (to
David Grath, the Dwarf-King). ThRiPo (23/24)
84, p. 17-19.
"Tonight." ThRiPo (23/24) 84, p. 19.

2622. JONES, Rodney
"After Storms." Poetry (143:6) Mr 84, p. 326.
"Alma." PoetryNW (25:3) Aut 84, p. 6-7.
"Baby Angels." Atlantic (253:5) My 84, p. 84.
"Decadence." Swallow (3) 84, p. 106-109.
"A Distant Weather." PoetryNW (25:3) Aut 84, p. 8-9.
"The First Birth." NewEngR (7:2) Wint 84, p. 171-
172.
"For the Eating of Swine." Atlantic (253:1) Ja
84, p. 45.
"For Those Who Miss the Important Parts." Poetry
(143:6) Mr 84, p. 327-328.
"I Find Joy in the Cemetery Trees." NewEngR (7:2)
Wint 84, p. 172-173.
"Meditation on Birney Mountain." Poetry (143:6)
Mr 84, p. 328-330.
"Responsibilities." SouthernHR (18:4) Aut 84, p.
337.
"Some Futures." PoetryNW (25:3) Aut 84, p. 3-4.
"Unpainted Houses." PoetryNW (25:3) Aut 84, p. 5-6.

2623. JONES, Roger
"Crows: Night in New Hampshire Woods." Poem (52)
N 84, p. 37.
"Nothing in This Place" (--Millay, for my father).
Poem (52) N 84, p. 35.
"The Sound at the Edge of Sleep." Poem (52) N 84,
p. 36.

2624. JONES, Susan
        "East Tennessee Landscape" (as memory has it).
          AntR (42:1) Wint 84, p. 78-79.
        "The Transport." AntR (42:1) Wint 84, p. 80-81.

2625. JONSON, Ben
        "On My First Sonne." Peb (23) 84, p. 26.

2626. JOPP, Jessica
        "My Mother and I in a Field." GreenfR (12:1/2)
          Sum-Aut 84, p. 191.
        "My Mother, My Birthplace." GreenfR (12:1/2) Sum-
          Aut 84, p. 192.

2627. JORDAN, June
        "Who Would Be Free, Themselves Must Strike the
          Blow" (--Frederick Douglass). NowestR (22:1/2)
          84, p. 38.

2628. JORDAN, Milton
        "Better Things to Do." Wind (14:51) 84, p. 27.

2629. JORDAN, William R., Sr.
        "Piper Lad." Pig (12) 84, p. 1.
        "Soldier." Pig (12) 84, p. 82.

2630. JORIS, Pierre
        "German Landscape Revisited" (after Holderlin).
          Sulfur (3:3, issue 9) 84, p. 95.
        "The Second Cycle of Zeitgehöft" (tr. of Paul
          Celan). Sulfur (4:2, issue 11) 84, p. 17-26.

2631. JORON, Andrew
        "All Equations Are Lesion's Equal." Veloc (1) Sum
          82, p. 27-28.
        "Cascade" (w. Lee Ballentine). Veloc (1) Sum 82,
          p. 9-10.
        "Vehicular Man." Veloc (3) Aut-Wint 83, p. 15.

2632. JOSEPH, Lawrence
        "December 3rd, 1937." Stand (25:3) Sum 84, p. 54.

2633. JOSO
        "No need to cling" (Haiku from the Japanese
          Masters, tr. by Lucien Stryk and Takashi
          Ikemoto, calligraphy by Lloyd J. Reynolds).
          NewL (50:2/3) Wint-Spr 84, p. 140.

2634. JOYCE, Dianne
        "The Lull." CanLit (103) Wint 84, p. 62-63.
        "Strange Development." CanLit (103) Wint 84, p. 63.

2635. JOYCE, Jane Wilson
        "Bible Quilt, Circa 1900." PoetL (79:2) Sum 84,
          p. 72-73.
        "Changing the Ribbon." PoetC (16:1) Aut 84, p. 44.
        "Irish Chain." PoetL (79:2) Sum 84, p. 74-75.
        "A Retelling." PoetL (79:2) Sum 84, p. 75-77.
        "Sawtooth Bars, or Tree Everlasting." PoetL
          (79:2) Sum 84, p. 70-71.

"Threading My Way Back." <u>PoetL</u> (79:2) Sum 84, p.
    69-70.

2636. JOYCE, Jim
    "Against Graffiti." <u>KanQ</u> (16:1/2) Wint-Spr 84, p.
        127.
    "Dream-maker No. 2." <u>PraF</u> (5:4) Sum 84, p. 72.
    "Spring Fowl." <u>KanQ</u> (16:1/2) Wint-Spr 84, p. 126.

2637. JOYCE, Tom
    "Kite Flying." <u>Grain</u> (12:1) F 84, p. 16.

2638. JOYCE, William
    "The Mexico Poem." <u>SouthernPR</u> (24:2) Aut 84, p.
        41-42.

JUANA INES de la CRUZ, Sor: <u>See</u> CRUZ, Juana Inés de la, Sor

2639. JUDSON, John
    "Psalm for a Northern Field's Stream."
        <u>Abraxas</u> (29/30) 84, p. 40.
    "A Teacher's Story." <u>BelPoJ</u> (35:1) Aut 84, p. 36-39.

2640. JULANATO, Tereste
    "38 Special." <u>PoeticJ</u> (2) 83, p. 32.

2641. JUNGIC, Zoran
    "Beauty of the flower dust" (tr. by the author).
        <u>CapilR</u> (29) 83, p. 12.
    "Her marked eroded eye cover" (tr. by the author).
        <u>CapilR</u> (29) 83, p. 11.
    "This last tremble" (tr. by the author). <u>CapilR</u>
        (29) 83, p. 13.

2642. JUNIUS SECUNDUS
    "The Sohoiad: or, The Masque of Art" (A Satire in
        Heroic Couplets Drawn from Life, New York,
        MCMLXXXIV). <u>NewYRB</u> (31:5) 29 Mr 84, p. 17-19.

2643. JUNKINS, Donald
    "Kiting: A Reverie." <u>NewYorker</u> (60:10) 23 Ap 84,
        p. 48.
    "Swans Island, the Late 70's: Middle Age." <u>Confr</u>
        (27/28) 84, p. 175-176.
    "The Wounded Deer Leaps Highest." <u>Chelsea</u> (42/43)
        84, p. 96.

2644. JUSTICE, Donald
    "In Memory of My Friend the Bassoonist John Lenox."
        <u>AmerPoR</u> (13:1) Ja-F 84, p. 48.
    "In Memory of the Unknown Poet Robert Boardman
        Vaughn." <u>Antaeus</u> (52) Apr 84, p. 123.
    "The Map of Love." <u>NewEngR</u> (7:2) Wint 84, p. 222.
    "Men at Forty." <u>NewEngR</u> (7:2) Wint 84, p. 229.
    "October." <u>Nat</u> (238:20) 26 My 84, p. 648.
    "The Suicides." <u>NewEngR</u> (7:2) Wint 84, p. 224-226.

2645. KABOTIE, Michael
    "Rubber Bands." <u>GreenfR</u> (11:3/4) Wint-Spr 84, p. 41.
    "Snow Clan Visit" (For: Ella & Otis). <u>GreenfR</u>

(11:3/4) Wint-Spr 84, p. 42-43.
"Trilobite Flakes." <u>GreenfR</u> (11:3/4) Wint-Spr 84,
    p. 39-40.

2646. KACHINSKE, Timothy
    "Dark Christmas" (tr. of Benedek Kiss). <u>WebR</u>
        (9:1) Spr 84, p. 21.
    "Gypsy Wanderers" (tr. of Karoly Bari). <u>LitR</u>
        (27:3) Spr 84, p. 304-305.
    "In Memoriam Dylan Thomas" (tr. of Benedek Kiss).
        <u>WebR</u> (9:1) Spr 84, p. 20.
    "My Hands on the Head of My Son" (tr. of Benedek
        Kiss). <u>WebR</u> (9:1) Spr 84, p. 20.

2647. KAGEYAMA, Yuri
    "February Cat" (tr. of Hiromi Ito). <u>YellowS</u> (11)
        Sum 84, p. 14.
    "Lot of Fun to Do" (tr. of Hiromi Ito). <u>YellowS</u>
        (11) Sum 84, p. 22.
    "Probably a Toilet" (tr. of Hiromi Ito). <u>YellowS</u>
        (11) Sum 84, p. 23.
    "Selfish Martyrdom Series / Number One." <u>YellowS</u>
        (11) Sum 84, p. 15.

2648. KAHL, Marilyn
    "Ideas." <u>EngJ</u> (73:2) F 84, p. 96.

2649. KAISER-MARTIN, Billie
    "Detonation Simile." <u>SanFPJ</u> (7:1) 84, p. 39.
    "Killcount." <u>SanFPJ</u> (7:1) 84, p. 94.
    "The Poetry of While." <u>SanFPJ</u> (7:1) 84, p. 95.

2650. KAKASSY, Thomas
    "Timber." <u>BlackWR</u> (11:1) Aut 84, p. 90.

2651. KAKINOMOTO no HITOMARO
    "Mountain Wizard" (tr. by Graeme Wilson). <u>WestHR</u>
        (38:1) Spr 84, p. 60.

2652. KALAMARAS, George
    "The Longing." <u>GreenfR</u> (12:1/2) Sum-Aut 84, p.
        166-167.

2653. KALLET, Marilyn
    "Hunger." <u>GreenfR</u> (12:1/2) Sum-Aut 84, p. 184.
    "Yahrzeit, For My Father." <u>NewL</u> (50:4) Sum 84, p.
        49.

2654. KALLSEN, T. J.
    "The Temple of Dendur." <u>KanQ</u> (16:3) Sum 84, p. 22.

2655. KALMUS, Morris A.
    "Myopia." <u>SanFPJ</u> (6:4) 84, p. 12.
    "One Great Moment." <u>SanFPJ</u> (6:2) 84, p. 65.
    "The Overseer." <u>SanFPJ</u> (6:2) 84, p. 60.

2656. KALYNEC, Ihor
    "Castle" (tr. by Bohdan Boychuk). <u>Pequod</u> (16/17)
        84, p. 198.
    "In This Immense Aquarium" (tr. by Bohdan Boychuk).

Pequod (16/17) 84, p. 199.
"Our Whole Little Province" (tr. by Bohdan
Boychuk). Pequod (16/17) 84, p. 200.

2657. KAMBARA, Andrea
"2237 Giddings Street" (In Memoriam: Alice Lange,
1898-1982). SouthernR (20:2) Spr 84, p. 366-367.

2658. KAMBOURELI, Smaro
"In the Second Person" (Selections: Two poems).
PraF (5:2/3) Spr 84, p. 46-48.
"It's an act of love." PraF (5:2/3) Spr 84, p. 48.
"Yes, I'm a foreign country." PraF (5:2/3) Spr
84, p. 46-48.

2659. KAMENETZ, Rodger
"Incredible Luck." Abraxas (29/30) 84, p. 46-47.

2660. KAMINSKY, Marc
"Barrier" (from The Road from Hiroshima). NewL
(50:4) Sum 84, p. 80-81.
"Mourning" (from The Road from Hiroshima). NewL
(50:4) Sum 84, p. 81.

2661. KAMINSKY, Marsha
"Daisy." HangL (46) Aut 84, p. 26.

2662. KANE, Jean
"Lightning." PoetC (16:1) Aut 84, p. 20.
"Liners." PoetC (16:1) Aut 84, p. 22.
"Returning." PoetC (16:1) Aut 84, p. 21.

2663. KANE, Katherine
"The Arriviste." MissouriR (7:3) 84, p. 31-33.
"The Rabbi Said Never Go to Bed Angry." MissouriR
(7:3) 84, p. 34-36.

2664. KANGAS, J. R.
"Fistful of Daffodils." NewL (50:4) Sum 84, p. 84.

2665. KAPLINSKI, Jaan
"Eyes cast down, we must walk softly" (tr. by the
author and Sam Hamill). CharR (10:1) Spr 84,
p. 79.
"I Understood" (tr. by the author and Sam Hamill).
MidwQ (25:4) Sum 84, p. 413-414.
"Only to go along" (tr. by the author and Sam
Hamill). CharR (10:1) Spr 84, p. 78.
"Poetry Is Standing" (tr. by the author and Sam
Hamill). MidwQ (25:4) Sum 84, p. 412.
"Some roosters wake before dawn some islands grow
higher in a single day" (tr. by the author and
Sam Hamill). CharR (10:1) Spr 84, p. 77.
"Summer You Poor Summer" (tr. by the author and Sam
Hamill). MidwQ (25:4) Sum 84, p. 411.

2666. KAPPEL, A. J.
"Our World without Us." BelPoJ (34:3) Spr 84, p.
2-5.

2667. KAPPEL, Andrew J.
      "When I Roll." LitR (28:1) Aut 84, p. 53-55.

2668. KARR, Mary
      "Diogenes Invents a Game" (For John Engman).
      Poetry (145:2) N 84, p. 86.

2669. KARR, Muriel
      "Clerics Have Desired Me." YellowS (13) Wint 84,
      p. 17.

2670. KASPER, Vancy
      "Moody Violet" (For Jan, IV). Waves (13:1) Aut
      84, p. 78.
      "Resurrection." Waves (13:1) Aut 84, p. 78.

2671. KASSAK, Lajos
      "25" (tr. by Bruce Berlind). GrahamHR (7) Wint
      84, p. 54.

2672. KASTMILER, Peter
      "Phantasmagoria." ThirdW (2) Spr 84, p. 72.
      "Witness to the Temptation of Saint Anthony."
      ThirdW (2) Spr 84, p. 73.

2673. KATCHADOURIAN, Stina
      "The Day Cools" (tr. of Edith Södergran).
      YellowS (12) Aut 84, p. 36.
      "Love" (tr. of Edith Södergran). YellowS (12)
      Aut 84, p. 37.

2674. KATES, J.
      "Hail As If" (for Susan Gubernat). StoneC
      (12:1/2) Aut-Wint 84, p. 22.

2675. KATROVAS, Richard
      "The Disenfranchised." Telescope (3:1) Wint 84,
      p. 89--91.
      "Grieving for Hopkins." Iowa (14:3) Aut 84, p. 117.

2676. KATZ, Susan A.
      "Resemblances." NegC (4:2) Spr 84, p. 64.

2677. KATZENBERGER, Edward
      "Aliki at Lindos." TexasR (5:3/4) Aut-Wint 84, p.
      100.

2678. KAUFFMAN, Janet
      "Certain Cells." NewRep (190:22) 4 Je 84, p. 32.
      "Rally." Telescope (3:2) Spr 84, p. 148.
      "Round Lake." NewL (50:2/3) Wint-Spr 84, p. 240-241.
      "The Walk." IndR (7:3) Sum 84, p. 8.
      "Watching the Body." IndR (7:3) Sum 84, p. 7.
      "The Womb in the World." Telescope (3:2) Spr 84,
      p. 147-148.

2679. KAUFMAN, Debra
      "No Jazz in the Cornfields." SpoonRQ (9:2) Spr
      84, p. 44.

2680. KAUFMAN, Nancy
"The Birthday." <u>Shen</u> (35:1) 83-84, p. 51.

2681. KAUFMAN, Shirley
"After the Wars." <u>Ploughs</u> (10:1) 84, p. 94.
"The Dream of Completion." <u>CalQ</u> (23/24) Spr-Sum
     84, p. 44-45.
"Last Storm" (in memory of Yohevet Bat-Miriam, tr.
     of Abba Kovner). <u>Pequod</u> (16/17) 84, p. 119-123.
"Lazarus" (tr. of Avner Treinin). <u>Field</u> (31) Aut
     84, p. 86-88.
"Learning Distrust." <u>Ploughs</u> (10:1) 84, p. 93.
"Mother's Face Drowned in Her Palm" (tr. of Tuvia
     Ruebner, w. Grace Schulman). <u>Pequod</u> (16/17)
     84, p. 117.
"Potato Pie" (tr. of Abba Kovner). <u>Field</u> (30) Spr
     84, p. 18-20.
"Pots and Pans." <u>Ploughs</u> (10:1) 84, p. 95.
"Reasons." <u>Pequod</u> (16/17) 84, p. 115.
"The Way to Moriah." <u>Ploughs</u> (10:1) 84, p. 91-92.
"What Wrong Is." <u>Ploughs</u> (10:1) 84, p. 96.

2682. KAUL, A. J.
"Legends of Birds." <u>Wind</u> (14:51) 84, p. 28-29.

2683. KAVEN, Robert
"Dreaming of Speech." <u>WoosterR</u> (1:1) Mr 84, p. 98.
"The Study of Sleep." <u>WoosterR</u> (1:1) Mr 84, p. 97.

2684. KAZANECKI, Wiesław
"No Smoking" (tr. by Danuta Lopozyko and Peter
     Harris). <u>LitR</u> (28:1) Aut 84, p. 132.

2685. KEARNS, Josie
"Effects of Alcohol." <u>GreenfR</u> (12:1/2) Sum-Aut
     84, p. 163.
"River of No Return." <u>GreenfR</u> (12:1/2) Sum-Aut
     84, p. 162.

2686. KEARSEY, Greg
"Bridgett's." <u>PottPort</u> (6) 84, p. 16.
"The Settlement." <u>CanLit</u> (103) Wint 84, p. 49.

2687. KEATING, Diane
"No Birds or Flowers." <u>PoetryCR</u> (6:1) Aut 84, p. 14.

2688. KEATING-CLEMENTS, Judith
"The Grave Choice." <u>Tele</u> (19) 83, p. 86-89.

2689. KEEFER, Janice Kulyk
"Anniversary." <u>Grain</u> (12:3) Ag 84, p. 35.
"Field Flowers." <u>Grain</u> (12:1) F 84, p. 5.
"Love Words." <u>Grain</u> (12:1) F 84, p. 6-7.
"Nightsong." <u>Grain</u> (12:3) Ag 84, p. 37.
"Survey." <u>Grain</u> (12:3) Ag 84, p. 38.

2690. KEEGAN, James R.
"The Hog." <u>SouthernPR</u> (24:2) Aut 84, p. 46.
"Photograph of the Hunters and Their Kill."
     <u>SouthernPR</u> (24:2) Aut 84, p. 45-46.

2691. KEELEY, Edmund
"Among the Blind" (from <u>Eleven Poems</u>, tr. of
Yannis Ritsos). <u>Chelsea</u> (42/43) 84, p. 414.
"The Cheap Apartment Building" (from <u>Eleven
Poems</u>, tr. of Yannis Ritsos). <u>Chelsea</u> (42/43)
84, p. 413.
"Compulsory Assent" (from <u>Eleven Poems</u>, tr. of
Yannis Ritsos). <u>Chelsea</u> (42/43) 84, p. 416.
"The End of the Performance" (from <u>Eleven Poems</u>,
tr. of Yannis Ritsos). <u>Chelsea</u> (42/43) 84, p.
417.
"Identity Card" (from <u>Eleven Poems</u>, tr. of Yannis
Ritsos). <u>Chelsea</u> (42/43) 84, p. 414.
"Momentary Immobility" (from <u>Eleven Poems</u>, tr. of
Yannis Ritsos). <u>Chelsea</u> (42/43) 84, p. 416.
"Out of Place" (from <u>Eleven Poems</u>, tr. of Yannis
Ritsos). <u>Chelsea</u> (42/43) 84, p. 415.
"Sad Cunning" (from <u>Eleven Poems</u>, tr. of Yannis
Ritsos). <u>Chelsea</u> (42/43) 84, p. 415.

2692. KEENAN, Deborah
"Formal Presentations of Love." <u>Pequod</u> (16/17)
84, p. 74-75.

2693. KEENAN, Terrance
"After the Neutron." <u>Spirit</u> (7:1) 84, p. 184.

2694. KEENER, LuAnn
"Daphne." <u>SouthernHR</u> (18:4) Aut 84, p. 318.

2695. KEENEY, Bill
"To My Muse." <u>EngJ</u> (73:2) F 84, p. 80.

2696. KEHOE, Patrick
"The Blood Bank." <u>CreamCR</u> (9:1/2) 84, p. 62.
"Grey Girl, Wheat Girl." <u>CreamCR</u> (9:1/2) 84, p. 61.

2697. KEITHLEY, George
"In the Sky Are Two Bears." <u>MemphisSR</u> (5:1) Aut
84, p. 25.

2698. KELBER, Mim
"Questions for the Nuclear Age." <u>Sam</u> (41:1,
release 161) 84, p. 10.

2699. KELLER, David
"Boiling Up the Dead." <u>PoetryNW</u> (25:3) Aut 84, p.
10-11.
"Crossing the States." <u>PraS</u> (58:2) Sum 84, p. 41-42.
"The Doorstop in the Shape of a Calico Cat."
<u>Poetry</u> (144:2) My 84, p. 85-86.
"February Afternoon." <u>Telescope</u> (3:3) Aut 84, p. 51.
"Heat, Fireflies." <u>PoetryNW</u> (25:3) Aut 84, p. 9-10.
"How the Sioux Invented Cold." <u>Tendril</u> (17) Wint
84, p. 97.
"Longing." <u>Poetry</u> (144:2) My 84, p. 84-85.
"The Street with a Balloon Overhead." <u>BlackWR</u>
(11:1) Aut 84, p. 74-75.

2700. KELLER, Emily
       "Sculpture in the Gallery, 4 Horses: Butterfield."
       Confr (27/28) 84, p. 244.

2701. KELLMAN, Robbi
       "The Elevator--A Phobia." GreenfR (11:1/2) Sum-
       Aut 83, p. 128.

2702. KELLY, Brigit Pegeen
       "Baptizing an Illegitimate Child." PoetryNW
       (25:3) Aut 84, p. 37-38.
       "The Boy, the Bird, and the Window" (for Gordon
       Dudley). NowestR (22:3) 84, p. 7-8.
       "Dunfaire's Wood." PraS (58:3) Aut 84, p. 50.
       "Garden among Tombs." PoetryNW (25:3) Aut 84, p.
       38-39.
       "Harmony Stoneworks." NowestR (22:3) 84, p. 6.
       "In the Night." WestB (15) 84, p. 24.
       "Lines Spoken in Spite of Myself" (for Michael).
       NowestR (22:3) 84, p. 9-12.
       "Mr. Hummer's Cows." WestB (15) 84, p. 25.
       "The Reproach of Eva Alman Bech" (in 1922, after
       she had smothered her month old child). PraS
       (58:3) Aut 84, p. 51-52.
       "Skåne" (for Anders Bech, whose widowed mother
       deserted him and returned to Sweden after the
       death of her youngest child in 1922). GeoR
       (38:2) Sum 84, p. 378-379.
       "The Valiant." Poetry (144:6) S 84, p. 335.

2703. KELLY, Joseph
       "Saturday." KanQ (16:1/2) Wint-Spr 84, p. 37.

2704. KELLY, Michael
       "Catullus 8" (tr. of Catullus). Argo (5:3) 84, p.
       17.
       "Catullus 83" (tr. of Catullus). Argo (5:3) 84,
       p. 15.

2705. KELLY, Robert
       "The Book of Water" (Selection: Book Two--Water at
       Night). Epoch (34:1) 84-85, p. 68-81.
       "Epithalamion" (for Robert and Joan Levine).
       Chelsea (42/43) 84, p. 22-23.

2706. KELLY, Robert A.
       "Stealing Spring." CEACritic (46:1/2) Aut-Wint 83-
       84, p. 35.
       "Winter Wrestling." CEACritic (46:1/2) Aut-Wint
       83-84, p. 35.

2707. KELLY, Timothy
       "Chinese Finger Trap." Field (31) Aut 84, p. 76.
       "Red Radish." Field (31) Aut 84, p. 75.
       "Three Movements from Tai Chi Chuan." Field (31)
       Aut 84, p. 77-78.
       "Works in Olympia, Washington." Field (31) Aut
       84, p. 79.

2708. KEMMERER, Kathleen M.
    "Silent Rage, an Unemployment Poem." SanFPJ (6:3)
    84, p. 70-71.

2709. KEMP, P. J.
    "It Was a Different Age." Sam (41:2, release 162)
    84 or 85, p. 37.

2710. KEMP, Penny
    "Aerobics." Quarry (33:3) Sum 84, p. 62-63.
    "The Law of Sevens" (from Binding Twine).
    PoetryCR (5:4) Sum 84, p. 18.
    "Lies at Play." PoetryCR (6:2) Wint 84-85, p. 5.
    "Swimming Hole." Quarry (33:3) Sum 84, p. 63-64.

2711. KEMPHER, Ruth Moon
    "The Armadillo." WormR (24:2, issue 94) 84, p. 44.
    "Found Poem: In the Middle of American Lit. I."
    YetASM (3) 84, p. 2.
    "Go By." Bogg (52) 84, p. 14.
    "Hilda Halfheart's Notes to the Milkman: #42."
    DekalbLAJ (20th Anniversary Issue) 84, p. 95-96.
    "Patience, I Tell Myself, Is a Hard Virtue."
    Confr (27/28) 84, p. 234.

2712. KEMPTON, Karl
    "Accounting." Abraxas (31/32) 84, p. 39.

2713. KENDALL, John
    "Rough Draft." EngJ (73:4) Ap 84, p. 73.

2714. KENDALL, Robert
    "Autumn." Poem (52) N 84, p. 16.
    "Climber." CapeR (19:2) Sum 84, p. 33.
    "Matins for the Condemned." Tendril (17) Wint 84,
    p. 98.
    "The Rite of Spring." Poem (52) N 84, p. 14-15.

KENJI, Miyazawa: See MIYAZAWA, Kenji

2715. KENNEDY, Jo
    "The Quickening." CapeR (19:3) 20th Anniverary
    Issue 84, p. 34.

2716. KENNEDY, Mary
    "The End of the Journey." AmerS (53:4) Aut 84, p.
    513.

2717. KENNEDY, Terry
    "Manners." Confr (27/28) 84, p. 233.

2718. KENNEDY, X. J.
    "At World's End" (tr. of Robert Desnos). Chelsea
    (42/43) 84, p. 116.
    "Conformity" (after Baudelaire). TriQ (59) Wint
    84, p. 134.
    "The Medium Is the Message." Chelsea (42/43) 84,
    p. 204.
    "On a Given Book." TriQ (59) Wint 84, p. 134.
    "Poet Who Loves Obituaries." TriQ (59) Wint 84,

p. 135.
"Sappho to a Mummy Wrapped in Papyrus." TriQ (59)
Wint 84, p. 135.

2719. KENNER, Hugh
"Hugh Kenner's Nine Permutations of 'Alba' (w.
James Laughlin). ParisR (26:94) Wint 84, p.
202-203.
"Selection of Computer Permutations of Ezra Pound's
'In a Station of the Metro'" (w. James
Laughlin). ParisR (26:94) Wint 84, p. 196-198.

2720. KENNEY, Richard
"Driving Sleeping People." YaleR (73:4) Sum 84,
p. 523-524.
"The Invention of Zero" (Winner, NER/BLQ Narrative
Poetry Competition). NewEngR (7:1) Aut 84, p.
40-51.
"Rose." NewYorker (60:42) 3 D 84, p. 52.

2721. KENNY, Adele
"Reminders." Blueline (6:1) Sum-Aut 84, p. 44.
"Vision." Wind (14:52) 84, p. 31.

2722. KENNY, Maurice
"After the Reading" (Bernard/Laguna). PaintedB
(23) Sum 84, p. 31.
"Oroville High, California." Abraxas (29/30) 84,
p. 49.

2723. KENT, John
"Grub-Wood." MemphisSR (5:1) Aut 84, p. 56.

2724. KENT-STOLL, Marianne
"The Boy in Emergency." PraS (58:3) Aut 84, p. 70.

2725. KENYON, Jane
"The Appointment." NewRep (191:26) 24 D 84, p. 38.
"At the Town Dump." KenR (NS 6:2) Spr 84, p. 48.
"I hear the always-sad voice of the oriole" (tr. of
Anna Akhmatova, w. Vera Sandomirsky Dunham).
OhioR (33) 84, p. 30.
"Inpatient." Poetry (144:1) Ap 84, p. 34.
"The mysterious spring still lay under a spell"
(tr. of Anna Akhmatova, w. Vera Sandomirsky
Dunham). OhioR (33) 84, p. 30.
"Reading Late of the Death of Keats." SenR (14:1)
84, p. 62.
"Thinking of Madame Bovary." NewYorker (60:9) 16
Ap 84, p. 50.
"Travel: After a Death." NewRep (189:16) 17 O 83,
p. 32.
"Walking Alone in Late Winter." NewRep (189:10) 5
S 83, p. 37.
"Wash." NewYorker (60:13) 14 My 84, p. 46.
"Whirligigs." Poetry (144:1) Ap 84, p. 34.
"Who." KenR (NS 6:2) Spr 84, p. 49.
"Yes I loved them, those gatherings late at night"
(tr. of Anna Akhmatova, w. Vera Sandomirsky
Dunham). OhioR (33) 84, p. 31.

2726. KERR, Don
"Lefevre Gallery, Receptionist." Quarry (33:3)
Sum 84, p. 57.
"Ross Macdonald Love Story." Descant (47, 15:4)
Wint 84, p. 46-51.

2727. KERR, Nora
"Exchanges." RagMag (3:2) Aut 84, p. 15.
"First Step." RagMag (3:1) Spr 84, p. 12.
"Heavy." RagMag (3:1) Spr 84, p. 13.
"Lapsang Souchong." RagMag (3:1) Spr 84, p. 15.
"Prairie Winter." RagMag (3:1) Spr 84, p. 14.
"Rune." RagMag (3:2) Aut 84, p. 15.

2728. KERRIGAN, Anthony
"Noble Woman." SewanR (92:1) Ja-Mr 84, p. 61.

2729. KERRY, Paul May
"The Good Ones." NewEngR (6:3) Spr 84, p. 397.

2730. KESSELMAN, Sandra
"In the Nursing Room Lobby." SanFPJ (6:1) 84, p. 33.

2731. KESSLER, Clyde
"Rev. George Silsonne." Wind (14:51) 84, p. 29.

2732. KESSLER, Jascha
"Blade of Grass" (tr. of Ottó Orbán, w. Maria
Körösy). MichQR (23:4) Aut 84, p. 562.
"Broken Glass" (tr. of Zsuzsa Beney). GrahamHR
(7) Wint 84, p. 55-56.
"Concerned with Something Else While Turnovo's
Dying" (tr. of Luchezar Elenkov, w. Alexander
Shurbanov). GrahamHR (7) Wint 84, p. 59-60.
"Peace, Horror" (tr. of Miklos Radnoti). Confr
(27/28) 84, p. 58.
"Photograph" (tr. of Ottó Orbán, w. Maria
Körösy). MichQR (23:4) Aut 84, p. 561.
"Poet" (tr. of Luchezar Elenkov, w. Alexander
Shurbanov). GrahamHR (7) Wint 84, p. 58.
"Variations" (tr. of István Bella). GrahamHR
(7) Wint 84, p. 57.

2733. KESSLER, Miriam
"My Sister-in-law Is Ill." Paunch (57/58) Ja 84,
p. 87.

2734. KESSLER, T. J.
"Christopher asked me." SnapD (6:2) Spr 83, p. 21.

2735. KESTER, Marcia
"Northern Express" (For Marciano). PoeticJ (7)
84, p. 14.

KHAFAJA, Ibn: See IBN KHAFAJA

2736. KHAN, Balach
"I Have Long Owed You" (For G.) SenR (14:2) 84,
p. 52-53.
"It Is When the Young Die" (For Hoaran Marri).

<u>SenR</u> (14:2) 84, p. 48-49.
"Quetta." <u>SenR</u> (14:2) 84, p. 50-51.

KHANSA, al-: <u>See</u> AL-KHANSA

2737. KHERDIAN, David
       "Root River." <u>NewL</u> (50:2/3) Wint-Spr 84, p. 189.

2738. KHMELIUK, Vasyl
       "The Ladies' Pissoir" (tr. by Paul Pines). <u>Pequod</u>
       (16/17) 84, p. 182-183.
       "When Will My Auntie Come for Me" (tr. by Paul
       Pines). <u>Pequod</u> (16/17) 84, p. 184.

2739. KHRISTOV, Boris
       "The Window" (tr. by Vladimir Phillipov). <u>Iowa</u>
       (14:2) Spr-Sum 84, p. 224-225.

2740. KICH, Marty
       "In the Absence of Fire." <u>Wind</u> (14:50) 84, p. 30-31.
       "On Being Air-Lifted to the Burn Center." <u>Wind</u>
       (14:50) 84, p. 29-30.
       "Sunday Times" (for Michael Poskonski). <u>Wind</u>
       (14:50) 84, p. 29.

2741. KICKNOSWAY, Faye
       "Someone Is Always Dying." <u>HangL</u> (45) Spr 84, p.
       30-32.

2742. KIEFER, John
       "Fall." <u>CalQ</u> (25) Aut 84, p. 35.

2743. KIEFER, Rita Brady
       "The Students Are Asking." <u>SouthwR</u> (69:1) Wint
       84, p. 31.

2744. KILGRAS, Heidi
       "Sheik." <u>HangL</u> (45) Spr 84, p. 63.

2745. KILMER, Ann
       "Flannery O'Connor." <u>Comm</u> (111:8) 20 Ap 84, p. 239.

2746. KIM, Willyce
       "Makai/First Light." <u>Cond</u> (3:4, issue 10) 84, p. 67.

2747. KIMBALL, Karen
       "225. After midnight the heart steals" (tr. of Osip
       Mandelstam, w. Michael Cole). <u>CharR</u> (10:2) Aut
       84, p. 94.
       "395. I don't know the woman who searches" (tr. of
       Osip Mandelstam, w. Michael Cole). <u>CharR</u>
       (10:2) Aut 84, p. 94.

2748. KIMMET, Gene
       "Tacit Acquaintances." <u>Abraxas</u> (29/30) 84, p. 71.
       "Winter at Seventeen." <u>Ascent</u> (9:3) 84, p. 34.

2749. KING, Daniel J.
       "Divine Rights." <u>SanFPJ</u> (6:4) 84, p. 77.
       "Higher Sound." <u>SanFPJ</u> (6:4) 84, p. 60.

2750. KING, Lyn
"Description." <u>Descant</u> (47, 15:4) Wint 84, p. 148.
"Old Dice." <u>Descant</u> (47, 15:4) Wint 84, p. 146-147.
"The Perfect Now." <u>Waves</u> (12:2/3) Wint 84, p. 81.

2751. KING, Robert S.
"Discoveries of the Shovel." <u>CalQ</u> (25) Aut 84, p. 38.
"Dream of the Electric Eel." <u>SouthernPR</u> (24:1) Spr 84, p. 60.
"The Gravedigger Blows on the Bottle." <u>CalQ</u> (25) Aut 84, p. 39.

2752. KINKEAD, J. A.
"Ruby Slippers." <u>KanQ</u> (16:1/2) Wint-Spr 84, p. 192.

2753. KINNELL, Galway
"Freedom, New Hampshire" (For my brother, 1925-1957). <u>Peb</u> (23) 84, p. 66-70.
"The Fundamental Project of Technology." <u>AmerPoR</u> (13:4) Jl-Ag 84, p. 48.
"Goodbye." <u>AmerPoR</u> (13:4) Jl-Ag 84, p. 8.
"Goodbye." <u>Tendril</u> (18, special issue) 84, p. 89-90.
"Old Arrivals." <u>Chelsea</u> (42/43) 84, p. 76.
"River of Lead" (tr. of Yvan Goll). <u>Chelsea</u> (42/43) 84, p. 160.
"Under the Maud Moon." <u>Tendril</u> (18, special issue) 84, p. 32.

2754. KINSELLA, Thomas
"Office for the Dead." <u>Shen</u> (35:2/3) 84, p. 203.

2755. KINSEY, Ralph L.
"Manet's Sleeping Woman." <u>WoosterR</u> (1:1) Mr 84, p. 102-103.

2756. KINZIE, Mary
"Come Back." <u>SouthwR</u> (69:3) Sum 84, p. 248-249.
"The Crossing" (for D. H.). <u>SouthwR</u> (69:3) Sum 84, p. 247-248.
"David, 1979" (for Emilia Field Cresswell Marsh). <u>SouthwR</u> (69:3) Sum 84, p. 246.
"An Engraving of Blake." <u>CarolQ</u> (37:1) Aut 84, p. 10.
"First Storm." <u>AmerPoR</u> (13:1) Ja-F 84, p. 39.
"In the Parking Lot of the Faculty Club." <u>AmerPoR</u> (13:1) Ja-F 84, p. 39.
"The Pirate's Version." <u>CarolQ</u> (37:1) Aut 84, p. 9.
"Stundenbuch." <u>CarolQ</u> (36:3) Spr 84, p. 55.
"The Various Envies." <u>TriQ</u> (59) Wint 84, p. 133.

KIO, Kuroda: <u>See</u> KURODA, Kio

2757. KIRBY, David
"Baths." <u>SouthwR</u> (69:1) Wint 84, p. 87.
"The Dance of Husbands in Bathrobes." <u>CarolQ</u> (36:2) Wint 84, p. 87.

2758. KIRCHER, Pamela
"Window." <u>Tendril</u> (17) Wint 84, p. 99.

2759. KIRK, James
"Carib Nocturne." PoetL (79:3) Aut 84, p. 159.
"Dream Cow." PoetL (79:3) Aut 84, p. 158.
"Keeping the Fire at Night" (for Alan Richter).
Tendril (17) Wint 84, p. 100.

2760. KIRKENDALL, Susan
"Beside the Highway." Wind (14:50) 84, p. 32.
"Cemetery Picnic." WestB (14) 84, p. 87.
"Waiting." WestB (14) 84, p. 86.

2761. KIRKPATRICK, Kathryn
"Britomart Writes from Malecasta's Castle" (From
Book III, The Faerie Queene). SoCaR (17:1)
Aut 84, p. 110.
"The Traveler." SoCaR (17:1) Aut 84, p. 109.

2762. KIRSCH, Sarah
"In My Town" (tr. by E. Castendyk Briefs). Vis
(14) 84, p. 24.

2763. KIRSTEIN, Lincoln
"Siegfriedslage." Shen (35:2/3) 84, p. 25-29.

2764. KISS, Benedek
"Dark Christmas" (tr. by Timothy Kachinske). WebR
(9:1) Spr 84, p. 21.
"In Memoriam Dylan Thomas" (tr. by Timothy
Kachinske). WebR (9:1) Spr 84, p. 20.
"My Hands on the Head of My Son" (tr. by Timothy
Kachinske). WebR (9:1) Spr 84, p. 20.

2765. KITCHEN, Judith
"Perennials." GeoR (38:1) Spr 84, p. 78-79.
"Skin." Tendril (17) Wint 84, p. 101-102.

2766. KITTELL, Linda
"Cataloging the House." SnapD (7:1) Aut 83, p. 24-
25.
"Rhonda LaBombard." SnapD (7:1) Aut 83, p. 26.

2767. KITTELL, Ronald Edward
"Little Puffs." Abraxas (31/32) 84, p. 58.

2768. KIVI, Berta
"It's Good to Dream." WritersL (1) 84, p. 17.

KIVI, Tamara Shulz: See SHULZ-KIVI, Tamara

2769. KIYOOKA, Roy
"Wheels (a Journey in Process)." Descant (44/45,
15:1/2) Spr-Sum 84, p. 25-50.

2770. KIZER, Carolyn
"Exodus." Antaeus (52) Apr 84, p. 42-43.
"For Jan, in Bar Maria" (After Po Chü-I). Shen
(35:2/3) 84, p. 204.
"Lines to Accompany Flowers for Eve" (who took
heroin, then sleeping pills and who lies in a
New York hospital). Shen (35:2/3) 84, p. 204-205.

"On a Line from Sophocles." <u>Shen</u> (35:2/3) 84, p. 206.

2771. KLAINGUTI, Irma
"Aguoglias d'Utuon." <u>Os</u> (18) 84, p. 12.
"Chi So." <u>Os</u> (18) 84, p. 12.
"Late Leaves of Autumn" (tr. by John Allen and Elly Crol). <u>Os</u> (18) 84, p. 13.
"Who Knows" (tr. by John Allen and Elly Crol). <u>Os</u> (18) 84, p. 13.

2772. KLEBECK, William J.
"Bumps." <u>Dandel</u> (11:2) Aut-Wint 84-85, p. 73.
"Town Lights." <u>Dandel</u> (11:2) Aut-Wint 84-85, p. 71.
"Wash." <u>Dandel</u> (11:2) Aut-Wint 84-85, p. 72.

2773. KLEBER, Rodney
"The Case of the Mysterious Maiden." <u>NegC</u> (4:2) Spr 84, p. 17-19.

2774. KLEINSCHMIDT, Edward
"Avenues in Bloom." <u>MassR</u> (25:4) Wint 84, p. 513.
"Begonia." <u>Agni</u> (20) 84, p. 91.
"Catapult As a Form of Escape." <u>LittleM</u> (14:3) 84, p. 14-15.
"Celebrating Thinking." <u>MassR</u> (25:4) Wint 84, p. 514.
"Dog Walk." <u>LittleM</u> (14:3) 84, p. 13.
"Fly by Night." <u>Agni</u> (20) 84, p. 92-93.
"Gauguin: We Shall Not Go to Market Today." <u>CalQ</u> (23/24) Spr-Sum 84, p. 134.
"How You Continually Come As a Surprise." <u>LittleM</u> (14:3) 84, p. 12.
"In Late Afternoon As the Clock Sleeps." <u>LittleM</u> (14:3) 84, p. 9.
"Inside and Outside Rooms." <u>MSS</u> (3:2/3) Spr 84, p. 59.
"On the Occasion of Her Completed Portrait: Letter to Dora Maar, 1937." <u>LittleM</u> (14:3) 84, p. 11.
"Opening the Letters." <u>LittleM</u> (14:3) 84, p. 10.
"Passion on the Pullman." <u>ColEng</u> (46:1) Ja 84, p. 33.
"Random Panic in the U.S.A." <u>Poetry</u> (144:2) My 84, p. 101-103.
"Twelve Hours on the TV." <u>PoetryNW</u> (25:3) Aut 84, p. 27-28.

2775. KLEINZAHLER, August
"16. The creases in the schoolboy's pegged wool slacks" (from <u>Storm over Hackensack</u>). <u>Epoch</u> (33:2) Spr-Sum 84, p. 190.
"Abstruse Rap of the Wiseguy Scrapped." <u>Origin</u> (5:3) Spr 84, p. 78.
"Art & Youth." <u>CimR</u> (69) O 84, p. 34.
"English As a Second Language" (from <u>Storm over Hackensack</u>). <u>Epoch</u> (33:2) Spr-Sum 84, p. 191.
"Evening, Out of Town." <u>Origin</u> (5:3) Spr 84, p. 80.
"Gangster Jones' Analgesic and Anti-Gravitational Device." <u>Origin</u> (5:3) Spr 84, p. 76.
"Kid Clarinet." <u>Origin</u> (5:3) Spr 84, p. 77.

"November in West New York." Origin (5:3) Spr 84,
   p. 75.
"Shooting." Harp (269:1614) N 84, p. 22.
"Shooting" (from Storm over Hackensack). Epoch
   (33:2) Spr-Sum 84, p. 194-195.
"Show Business" (from Storm over Hackensack).
   Epoch (33:2) Spr-Sum 84, p. 189.
"Song." Origin (5:3) Spr 84, p. 79.
"Staying Home from Work." Origin (5:3) Spr 84, p.
   74.
"Staying Home from Work" (from Storm over
   Hackensack). Epoch (33:2) Spr-Sum 84, p. 196.
"Storm over Hackensack" (from Storm over
   Hackensack). Epoch (33:2) Spr-Sum 84, p. 188.
"Sunday Nocturne." Origin (5:3) Spr 84, p. 82.
"Sunday Nocturne" (from Storm over Hackensack).
   Epoch (33:2) Spr-Sum 84, p. 186.
"Trolley" (from Storm over Hackensack). Epoch
   (33:2) Spr-Sum 84, p. 192-193.
"Variations on Half of a Line by Mallarme" (from
   Storm over Hackensack). Epoch (33:2) Spr-Sum
   84, p. 187.
"Vikings of the Air." CimR (69) O 84, p. 60.
"Warm Night in February." CimR (69) O 84, p. 18.
"Where Souls Go." CimR (69) O 84, p. 46.
"Who Stole the Horses from the Indians?" Origin
   (5:3) Spr 84, p. 81.

2776. KLEPETAR, Steven
   "Buick." MidAR (4:1) Spr 84, p. 140.

2777. KLINE, Shaya
   "Prophesy" (for Judson). KanQ (16:1/2) Wint-Spr
   84, p. 180.

2778. KLINGSOR, Tristan
   "Dust" (tr. by Dorothy Aspinwall). WebR (9:2)
   Wint 85, p. 18.

2779. KLOEFKORN, William
   "The Burning." PaintedB (22) Spr 84, p. 7-8.
   "Edna." PaintedB (22) Spr 84, p. 9-10.
   "Feeling Good Because One of These Days It's Going
   to Be Spring." PaintedB (22) Spr 84, p. 5.
   "Greasing the Tracks." PoetC (16:1) Aut 84, p. 58-
   59.
   "Prove It." PaintedB (22) Spr 84, p. 6.
   "Solitude." PraS (58:2) Sum 84, p. 89.
   "Three Circles Out from My Hometown Unbroken."
   PoetC (16:1) Aut 84, p. 60-61.

2780. KLONGERBO, Ross
   "Wending Ball (Or: If Frost Had Only Played
   Tennis)." EngJ (73:4) Ap 84, p. 95.

2781. KNAFF, Deborah
   "From the Netherlands, Christmas." Sam (41:2,
   release 162) 84 or 85, back cover.
   "Tearing along the Dotted Line." Sam (37:3, 147th
   release) 83, p. 20.

2782. KNAPP, Trevor
      "Oak." KenR (NS 6:2) Spr 84, p. 68.

2783. KNAUTH, Stephen
      "Elegy for X." TarRP (23:2) Spr 84, p. 24.
      "For Now If Not for Long." SouthernPR (24:1) Spr
          84, p. 32.
      "Monsters." PraS (58:2) Sum 84, p. 93.
      "Philosophy." Abraxas (31/32) 84, p. 16.
      "The Runner." Abraxas (31/32) 84, p. 17.
      "The Way to the Mail." SmPd (21:1) Wint 84, p. 15.

2784. KNIGHT, Arthur (Arthur Winfield)
      "Bailing." SpoonRQ (9:3) Sum 84, p 46.
      "Between Friends." Vis (16) 84, p. 34.
      "The Breakdown." SpoonRQ (9:3) Sum 84, p 34.
      "The Buy." SpoonRQ (9:3) Sum 84, p 6.
      "The Cache." SpoonRQ (9:3) Sum 84, p 32.
      "Constellations." SpoonRQ (9:3) Sum 84, p 30.
      "Denial." SpoonRQ (9:3) Sum 84, p 52.
      "Destruction." SpoonRQ (9:3) Sum 84, p 28.
      "The Gentleman." Wind (14:50) 84, p. 33.
      "Great Place to Be." SpoonRQ (9:3) Sum 84, p 8-9.
      "Honeymoons." SpoonRQ (9:3) Sum 84, p 1-2.
      "John Wayne Is Dying." SpoonRQ (9:3) Sum 84, p 13.
      "Kevin." SpoonRQ (9:3) Sum 84, p 39.
      "Letter to Elmore in Marshall." Amelia (1:2) O
          84, p. 51-52.
      "Liars." Abraxas (29/30) 84, p. 54-55.
      "Marriage of Poets" (with Kit Knight. Foreword by
          James Drought). SpoonRQ (9:3) Sum 84, p 1-53.
      "Memorial Day." SpoonRQ (9:3) Sum 84, p 23.
      "On the Road." SpoonRQ (9:3) Sum 84, p 50.
      "On the Road." Wind (14:50) 84, p. 34-35.
      "Petting." SpoonRQ (9:3) Sum 84, p 44.
      "Petulance." CrossC (6:2) 84, p. 15.
      "Philosophy." SpoonRQ (9:3) Sum 84, p 4.
      "The Picnic" (For John Paul Minarik). Stepping
          (Anniversary Issue I) 84, p. 32-33.
      "The Picnic" (for John Paul Minarik). SpoonRQ
          (9:3) Sum 84, p 25.
      "Promise Me." SpoonRQ (9:3) Sum 84, p 37.
      "Scars." SpoonRQ (9:3) Sum 84, p 11.
      "Simple Things." SpoonRQ (9:3) Sum 84, p 48.
      "Sweet Potato" (for Dad). SpoonRQ (9:3) Sum 84, p
          15-18.
      "The Thief." SpoonRQ (9:3) Sum 84, p 42.
      "Woman of the Year." SpoonRQ (9:3) Sum 84, p 20-21.

2785. KNIGHT, Cranston
      "South African Miner." BlackALF (18:1) Spr 84, p.
          17.

2786. KNIGHT, Etheridge
      "Crown Hill Cemetery." NewL (50:2/3) Wint-Spr 84,
          p. 129.
      "Indianapolis War Memorial." NewL (50:2/3) Wint-
          Spr 84, p. 129.
      "Riverside Park." NewL (50:2/3) Wint-Spr 84, p. 129.
      "Three Songs" (I. Slim's Song, II. Song of the

Reverend Gatemouth Moore, III. Healing Song).
NewL (50:2/3) Wint-Spr 84, p. 127-128.

2787. KNIGHT, Kit
"Bananas Are for Dead People." SpoonRQ (9:3) Sum
84, p 45.
"Breakfast." SpoonRQ (9:3) Sum 84, p 43.
"Breast-feeding." SpoonRQ (9:3) Sum 84, p 7.
"Fat." SpoonRQ (9:3) Sum 84, p 5.
"His Grandson Is Uneasy." SpoonRQ (9:3) Sum 84, p
31.
"Horror Stories." SpoonRQ (9:3) Sum 84, p 38.
"Ink Stains." SpoonRQ (9:3) Sum 84, p 51.
"Is the Garbage on Fire Yet?" SpoonRQ (9:3) Sum
84, p 3.
"The Magic Day." SpoonRQ (9:3) Sum 84, p 10.
"Marriage of Poets" (with Arthur Knight. Foreword
by James Drought). SpoonRQ (9:3) Sum 84, p 1-53.
"Memorial Day Rose." SpoonRQ (9:3) Sum 84, p 24.
"Nice Thing to Do." SpoonRQ (9:3) Sum 84, p 35-36.
"The Queen Lives on Unemployment." SpoonRQ (9:3)
Sum 84, p 47.
"The Result." SpoonRQ (9:3) Sum 84, p 29.
"Russian Christmas." SpoonRQ (9:3) Sum 84, p 12.
"Specific Detail." SpoonRQ (9:3) Sum 84, p 26-27.
"Summer Roses." SpoonRQ (9:3) Sum 84, p 33.
"Symbols." SpoonRQ (9:3) Sum 84, p 22.
"That Clean Sun Smell." SpoonRQ (9:3) Sum 84, p 19.
"Too Old to Be Sexy." SpoonRQ (9:3) Sum 84, p 53.
"Two Women." SpoonRQ (9:3) Sum 84, p 40-41.
"Up with the Bourgeois." SpoonRQ (9:3) Sum 84, p 49.
"Valentine's Day Poem for Mark" SpoonRQ (9:3) Sum
84, p 14.

2788. KNOELLER, Christian
"The History Told." GreenfR (11:1/2) Sum-Aut 83,
p. 111.
"Inhabiting Halibut Point." GreenfR (11:1/2) Sum-
Aut 83, p. 110.
"Solstice." WestB (15) 84, p. 108-109.

2789. KNOEPFLE, John
"House wind sleep." NewL (50:2/3) Wint-Spr 84, p.
94.
"Some old plains drifter." NewL (50:2/3) Wint-Spr
84, p. 94.
"A table here." NewL (50:2/3) Wint-Spr 84, p. 94.

2790. KNOLL, Michael
"After Reading Wordsworth in Prison." MissR (36,
12:3) Spr 84, p. 81.
"The Dance." MissR (36, 12:3) Spr 84, p. 80.
"To a Deaf Mute." TriQ (61) Aut 84, p. 104.
"White Clouds, Wind." NegC (4:1) Wint 84, p. 34.
"Wintering at Santa Rita." TriQ (61) Aut 84, p. 103.

2791. KNOTT, Bill
"The Sculpture." Antaeus (53) Aut 84, p. 248.

2792. KNOX, Caroline
"To Newfoundland." Shen (35:4) 84, p. 54-58.
"Walden Remaindered." GeoR (38:1) Spr 84, p. 174.

2793. KNUPFER, Anne
"Song for T.S." (to Federico Peltzer, tr. of Cristina Piña). Iowa (14:2) Spr-Sum 84, p. 160-161.

2794. KOCH, Claude
"Pedigree" (For Joseph Meredith). FourQt (33:2) Wint 84, p. 3.

2795. KOCH, Kenneth
"The New Diana." GrandS (3:4) Sum 84, p. 68-89.
"Senegal." NewYRB (31:20) 20 D 84, p. 63.

2796. KOCH, Tom
"Playboy's Christmas Cards" (missives and missles for the jolly season). Playb (31:12) D 84, p. 180-181.
"To a Lottery Winner." Playb (31:12) D 84, p. 181.
"To a Trivial Pursuit Champ." Playb (31:12) D 84, p. 180.
"To Boy George." Playb (31:12) D 84, p. 181.
"To Jerry Mathers." Playb (31:12) D 84, p. 180.
"To John McEnroe." Playb (31:12) D 84, p. 181.

2797. KOCHER, Ellen
"9,600 Acres" (tr. of Gérard Bayo). Bound (12:1) Aut 83, p. 225.
"Au Sommet de la Nuit" (Selections, tr. of Gérard Bayo). Bound (12:1) Aut 83, p. 221-225.
"The Black Woods" (tr. of Gérard Bayo). Bound (12:1) Aut 83, p. 223.
"Law and Order" (tr. of Gérard Bayo). Bound (12:1) Aut 83, p. 223.
"Like a Clock" (tr. of Gérard Bayo). Bound (12:1) Aut 83, p. 221.
"Summer Evening" (tr. of Gérard Bayo). Bound (12:1) Aut 83, p. 221.

2798. KODOLANYI, Gyula
"The Sad Field-Hand" (tr. of Gyula Illyés, w. William Jay Smith and Miklós Vajda). HolCrit (21:1) F 84, p. 3.
"Tilting Sail" (tr. of Gyula Illyés, w. William Jay Smith and Miklós Vajda). HolCrit (21:1) F 84, p. 12.
"Wreath" (tr. of Gyula Illyés, w. William Jay Smith and Miklós Vajda). HolCrit (21:1) F 84, p. 10-11.

2799. KOEHN-HEINE, Lala
"Baba Jedza." PoetryCR (6:1) Aut 84, p. 12.
"Baba Jedza" (in Polish). PoetryCR (6:1) Aut 84, p. 12.
"The Coins of Hate." PoetryCR (6:2) Wint 84-85, p. 5.
"How Am I to Tell You What I Miss." PoetryCR

(6:1) Aut 84, p. 12.
"Jak Ci Mam Powiedziec Czego Mi Brak." <u>PoetryCR</u>
    (6:1) Aut 84, p. 12.
"Whatever You Wanted to Say You Said Long Ago."
    <u>PoetryCR</u> (6:1) Aut 84, p. 12.
"Wie Soll Ich Es Sagen Was Mir Fehlt." <u>PoetryCR</u>
    (6:1) Aut 84, p. 12.
"Wszystko Co Chciales Powiedziec Powiedziales Juz
    Dawno." <u>PoetryCR</u> (6:1) Aut 84, p. 12.

2800. KOERNER, Edgar
"Dry Day in the Waiting Room." <u>NewL</u> (51:1) Aut
    84, p. 48-49.

2801. KOERTGE, Ronald
"The Great Koertgini." <u>WormR</u> (24:1, issue 93) 84,
    p. 2.
"Not Only Naked Indian Girls and Booze But 10 Point
    Bucks That Line Up Just Begging To Be Shot and
    Bass in Shoals So Thick a Man Could Walk across
    the Water on Their Backs." <u>BelPoJ</u> (35:1) Aut 84,
    p. 4-5.
"On the Way Home from I.C.U." <u>BelPoJ</u> (35:1) Aut
    84, p. 6.
"Pathos Bill." <u>WormR</u> (24:1, issue 93) 84, p. 2.
"Secrets of Writing Revealed at Last" (for Billy
    Collins). <u>WormR</u> (24:1, issue 93) 84, p. 1.

2802. KOESTENBAUM, Phyllis
"Criminal Sonnet." <u>Thrpny</u> (17) Spr 84, p. 22.

2803. KOESTENBAUM, Wayne
"In Labor." <u>Agni</u> (21) 84, p. 104.
"In the Classroom." <u>Agni</u> (21) 84, p. 103.

KOFI, Awoonor: <u>See</u> AWOONOR, Kofi

2804. KOGAWA, Joy
"Grief Poem." <u>CanLit</u> (100) Spr 84, p. 171-172.
"In the Forest." <u>CanLit</u> (100) Spr 84, p. 171.

2805. KOLUMBAN, Nicholas
"Budapest." <u>NewL</u> (50:4) Sum 84, p. 95.
"Head Bowed" (tr. of Sandor Csoori). <u>CharR</u> (10:1)
    Spr 84, p. 76-77.
"Hermit Summer" (tr. of Sandor Csoori). <u>CharR</u>
    (10:1) Spr 84, p. 74-75.
"Midnight" (tr. of Sándor Csoóri). <u>NowestR</u>
    (22:3) 84, p. 91.
"Winter's Voice Softens" (tr. of Sándor
    Csoóri). <u>NowestR</u> (22:3) 84, p. 92.
"You Make a Poor Sky Dweller" (tr. of Sandor
    Csoori). <u>CharR</u> (10:1) Spr 84, p. 75-76.

2806. KOMUNYAKAA, Yusef
"1984." <u>Callaloo</u> (20, 7:1) Wint 84, p. 114-118.
"1984." <u>OP</u> (37) Spr-Sum 84, p. 48-51.
"After the Heart's Interrogation." <u>BlackALF</u>
    (18:1) Spr 84, p. 6.
"Articulation & Class." <u>NewOR</u> (11:1) Spr 84, p. 98.

"Crescent City Blues" (Excerpt). OP (37) Spr-Sum
    84, p. 52.
"From across Years." BlackALF (18:1) Spr 84, p. 6.
"Gift Horse." OP (37) Spr-Sum 84, p. 46-47.
"Insufficient Blue." OP (37) Spr-Sum 84, p. 45.
"Night Muse and Mortar Round." MSS (4:1/2) Aut
    84, p. 100.
"One More Loss to Count." MSS (4:1/2) Aut 84, p.
    101-102.
"Soliloquy: Man Talking to a Mirror." BlackALF
    (18:1) Spr 84, p. 6.
"Somewhere near Phu Bai." NewEngR (6:4) Sum 84,
    p. 608.
"Starlight Scope Myopia." NewEngR (6:4) Sum 84,
    p. 609-610.
"Unnatural State of the Unicorn." OP (37) Spr-Sum
    84, p. 44.
"Untitled Blues" (After a photo by Yevgeny
    Yevtushenko). Callaloo (20, 7:1) Wint 84, p.
    113-114.
"The Violinist Returns from War." BlackALF (18:1)
    Spr 84, p. 6.

2807. KONDOLEON, Harry
    "The Execution of You." HangL (45) Spr 84, p. 33-34.

2808. KONESKI, Blaze
    "Sick Doytchin" (tr. by Filip Korzenski). ConcPo
    (17:2) Aut 84, p. 164-165.

2809. KONIG, F. H.
    "For William C. Williams" (tr. of Manfred
    Jendryschik). NoAmR (269:1) Mr 84, p. 55.
    "Moment in Petzow" (tr. of Manfred Jendryschik).
    NoAmR (269:1) Mr 84, p. 53-54.
    "The New Apartment" (tr. of Manfred Jendryschik).
    NoAmR (269:1) Mr 84, p. 55.

2810. KOONCE, Thomas Henry, III
    "I Can Be Seen." CrossC (6:3) 84, p. 17.
    "Sunday Night in Prison." CrossC (6:3) 84, p. 17.

2811. KOONTZ, Tom
    "Awake unto Me." WindO (44) Sum-Aut 84, p. 21-22.
    "Backroads by Moonlight." SpoonRQ (9:2) Spr 84,
    p. 4.
    "Chicory Hermaphrodite." SpoonRQ (9:4) Aut 84, p.
    37.
    "Christmas Bombing, 1945." WindO (44) Sum-Aut 84,
    p. 21.
    "July beside the Supermarket." SpoonRQ (9:4) Aut
    84, p. 36.
    "Just Sitting Here." SpoonRQ (9:2) Spr 84, p. 4.
    "Sitting Empty." SpoonRQ (9:2) Spr 84, p. 4.

2812. KOOSER, Ted
    "Daddy Longlegs." NewL (50:4) Sum 84, p. 99.
    "Summer Night." Tendril (18, special issue) 84,
    p. 26.
    "Walking Alone to the Car." Iowa (14:3) Aut 84,

p. 7.

2813. KOPELKE, Kendra
"Winter." <u>GeoR</u> (38:4) Wint 84, p. 730.
"Woman Pouring Milk." <u>SenR</u> (14:1) 84, p. 21-22.

2814. KOPLAND, Rutger
"G" (tr. by Pleuke Boyce). <u>MalR</u> (68) Je 84, p. 31-
35.
"Our Gasworks" (tr. by James Brockway). <u>Stand</u>
(25:1) Wint 83-84, p. 55.
"Psalm" (tr. by James Brockway). <u>Stand</u> (25:1)
Wint 83-84, p. 55.

2815. KOPPERL, Helga
"Excavating Pots." <u>MinnR</u> (N.S. 22) Spr 84, p. 10-11.

2816. KORAY, Yunus
"Pendulum" (tr. by Talat Sait Halman). <u>NewRena</u>
(6:1, #18) Spr 84, p. 67.
"Sarkac." <u>NewRena</u> (6:1, #18) Spr 84, p. 66.

2817. KORIYAMA, Naoshi
"Air Raid" (tr. of Sachiko Yoshihara, w. Edward
Lueders). <u>Poetry</u> (143:6) Mr 84, p. 320.
"Guerrilla's Fantasy" (tr. of Kio Kuroda, w. Edward
Lueders). <u>Poetry</u> (143:6) Mr 84, p. 321-322.

2818. KOROSY, Maria
"Blade of Grass" (tr. of Ottó Orbán, w. Jascha
Kessler). <u>MichQR</u> (23:4) Aut 84, p. 562.
"Photograph" (tr. of Ottó Orbán, w. Jascha
Kessler). <u>MichQR</u> (23:4) Aut 84, p. 561.
"Wound and Knife" (tr. of György Somlyó, w.
William Jay Smith). <u>Iowa</u> (14:2) Spr-Sum 84, p.
202.

2819. KORP, Maureen
"Stepdaughter." <u>Quarry</u> (33:4) Aut 84, p. 18.

2820. KORSON, Michael
"Reading Chekhov." <u>NewRep</u> (191:27) 31 D 84, p. 38.

2821. KORZENSKI, Filip
"Sick Doytchin" (tr. of Blaze Koneski). <u>ConcPo</u>
(17:2) Aut 84, p. 164-165.

2822. KOSMICKI, Greg
"Carpentry." <u>CimR</u> (69) O 84, p. 4.
"Poem after a Bad Night." <u>CimR</u> (69) O 84, p. 44-45.
"The Solution." <u>NewL</u> (51:2) Wint 84-85, p. 113.
"Sunday Afternoon and Night." <u>Peb</u> (23) 84, p. 39-41.

2823. KOSTELANETZ, Richard
"Synthetic synopsis Syndrome Syntax." <u>PoetC</u>
(16:1) Aut 84, p. 10-13.

2824. KOTARY, Judith
"Heartland." <u>BelPoJ</u> (35:2) Wint 84-85, p. 2-3.
"Jellyfish." <u>BelPoJ</u> (35:2) Wint 84-85, p. 4.

2825. KOTSYBAR, James Philip
"Natural Selection." PoeticJ (5) 84, p. 12.

2826. KOTZIN, Miriam
"Portrait." MidAR (4:1) Spr 84, p. 115.

2827. KOVACIK, Karen
"Elsie Borden In & Out of the Shower." Paunch
(57/58) Ja 84, p. 92.

2828. KOVACS, Edna
"City." PortR (30:1) 84, p. 130-131.

2829. KOVACS, Steven
"Seventh Eclogue" (tr. of Miklós Radnóti).
LitR (27:3) Spr 84, p. 302-303.

2830. KOVLER, Allen
"Fruit Stands." NegC (4:3) Sum 84, p. 108-109.

2831. KOVNER, Abba
"Last Storm" (in memory of Yohevet Bat-Miriam, tr.
by Shirley Kaufman). Pequod (16/17) 84, p. 119-
123.
"Potato Pie" (tr. by Shirley Kaufman). Field (30)
Spr 84, p. 18-20.

2832. KOWIT, Steve
"Friendly Persuasion." Abraxas (31/32) 84, p. 22.

2833. KOZAK, Roberta
"Shot of the Garden at Dusk." BlackWR (11:1) Aut
84, p. 44-45.
"Their Inheritance." BlackWR (11:1) Aut 84, p. 42-
43.

2834. KOZER, José
"El Pájaro." Prismal (12/13) Aut 84, p. 63.
"Para Jomi García Ascot." Areíto (9:36) 84,
p. 101.
"El Recinto." Prismal (12/13) Aut 84, p. 64.
"Redencion." LindLM (3:1) Ja-Mr 84, p. 15.

2835. KOZLOWSKI, Bea
"Systems." YetASM (3) 84, p. 4.

2836. KRAFT, Frank
"Elegy from Trunk Bay" (St. John, the Virgin
Islands). CharR (10:1) Spr 84, p. 56-57.

2837. KRAFT, Kelley
"The Best Poem." RagMag (3:2) Aut 84, p. 18.

2838. KRAMER, Aaron
"At Night" (Two Poems). KenR (NS 6:1) Wint 84, p.
67-70.
"Birthday." AntigR (57) Spr 84, p. 75.
"The Cliche: a Ballad." Wind (14:50) 84, p. 37-38.
"Homecoming." KenR (NS 6:1) Wint 84, p. 67-69.
"Nocturne." KenR (NS 6:1) Wint 84, p. 70.

"Nocturne." <u>Vis</u> (16) 84, p. 24.
"Passing Lynbrook." <u>Wind</u> (14:50) 84, p. 36.
"Port Jefferson: A November Day." <u>Vis</u> (14) 84, p. 26.
"Raking." <u>AntigR</u> (57) Spr 84, p. 74.
"Southshore Line." <u>Wind</u> (14:50) 84, p. 37.

2839. KRAMER, Ernesto M.
"Cuestiones." <u>Mairena</u> (5:14) Aut 83, p. 86.

2840. KRAMER, Larry
"At Home." <u>QRL</u> (Poetry series 6, v. 25) 84, p. 36.
"The Bigmouth Bass." <u>QRL</u> (Poetry series 6, v. 25) 84, p. 44-45.
"Blackwater." <u>QRL</u> (Poetry series 6, v. 25) 84, p. 17.
"The Capitol of Washing Machines." <u>QRL</u> (Poetry series 6, v. 25) 84, p. 15.
"Child on the Staked Plain." <u>QRL</u> (Poetry series 6, v. 25) 84, p. 40-42.
"Clouds." <u>QRL</u> (Poetry series 6, v. 25) 84, p. 32.
"The Counterfeit." <u>QRL</u> (Poetry series 6, v. 25) 84, p. 12.
"The Covered Bridge." <u>QRL</u> (Poetry series 6, v. 25) 84, p. 31.
"The Dime Store Man." <u>QRL</u> (Poetry series 6, v. 25) 84, p. 35.
"Disappearance of the Future Chickens." <u>QRL</u> (Poetry series 6, v. 25) 84, p. 43.
"Dry Land." <u>QRL</u> (Poetry series 6, v. 25) 84, p. 39.
"House Wrecking." <u>QRL</u> (Poetry series 6, v. 25) 84, p. 23.
"Illinois Central." <u>QRL</u> (Poetry series 6, v. 25) 84, p. 37.
"Images of the San Francisco Disaster." <u>QRL</u> (Poetry series 6, v. 25) 84, p. 19.
"In the Sun." <u>QRL</u> (Poetry series 6, v. 25) 84, p. 24.
"Iowa." <u>QRL</u> (Poetry series 6, v. 25) 84, p. 8.
"John Carlson at Eighty." <u>QRL</u> (Poetry series 6, v. 25) 84, p. 13.
"The Junkman Dies." <u>QRL</u> (Poetry series 6, v. 25) 84, p. 18.
"Lost Wax." <u>QRL</u> (Poetry series 6, v. 25) 84, p. 16.
"The Man with the Most Beautiful Signature" (for my father, L.C. Kramer, 1911-1975). <u>QRL</u> (Poetry series 6, v. 25) 84, p. 48-57.
"Miserere." <u>QRL</u> (Poetry series 6, v. 25) 84, p. 26.
"Neighbors." <u>QRL</u> (Poetry series 6, v. 25) 84, p. 10.
"Overcoats." <u>QRL</u> (Poetry series 6, v. 25) 84, p. 25.
"Raw Milk." <u>QRL</u> (Poetry series 6, v. 25) 84, p. 20.
"The Rendering Works." <u>QRL</u> (Poetry series 6, v. 25) 84, p. 46.
"Requiem." <u>QRL</u> (Poetry series 6, v. 25) 84, p. 11.
"Scout Knives." <u>QRL</u> (Poetry series 6, v. 25) 84, p. 14.
"Silver Dollars." <u>QRL</u> (Poetry series 6, v. 25) 84, p. 9.
"The Story of My Father and the Great Cave-In." <u>QRL</u> (Poetry series 6, v. 25) 84, p. 38.

"String of Bronchos." QRL (Poetry series 6, v.
   25) 84, p. 21.
"Strong Winds below the Canyons" (Section title).
   QRL (Poetry series 6, v. 25) 84, p. 1-59.
"Strong Winds below the Canyons." QRL (Poetry
   series 6, v. 25) 84, p. 29-30.
"Trees and Vines." QRL (Poetry series 6, v. 25)
   84, p. 27.
"Victoria's Poem." QRL (Poetry series 6, v. 25)
   84, p. 28.
"Your Weight and Fortune." QRL (Poetry series 6,
   v. 25) 84, p. 34.

2841. KRAMER, Lotte
   "Friends." Stand (25:1) Wint 83-84, p. 56.
   "Tradition." Argo (5:2) 84, p. 4.

2842. KRAPF, Norbert
   "Bringing Bread." AmerS (53:2) Spr 84, p. 167-168.
   "Dandelion." Blueline (5:2) Wint-Spr 84, p. 44.
   "Wild Ginger." Blueline (5:2) Wint-Spr 84, p. 45.

2843. KRATT, Mary
   "Everything Already Has One." SouthernPR (24:2)
      Aut 84, p. 69.
   "Sweaters." KanQ (16:1/2) Wint-Spr 84, p. 182.
   "Yonder." SouthernHR (18:2) Spr 84, p. 164.

2844. KRAUSE, Mike R.
   "My Great Uncle Joe." PikeF (6) Aut 84, p. 20.

2845. KRAUSE, Richard
   "Isn't It Because." CalQ (25) Aut 84, p. 41.

2846. KRAUSS, Janet
   "Dispersion" (After Winslow Homer's The Dinner
      Horn). NegC (4:3) Sum 84, p. 87.
   "On Exhibit." ThirdW (2) Spr 84, p. 29.

2847. KREGAL, Ann
   "For Another Swimmer." Tele (19) 83, p. 70.
   "For Collin." Tele (19) 83, p. 69.
   "Miscellaneous Thoughts on Underemployment." Tele
      (19) 83, p. 71.

2848. KREITER-KURYLO, Carolyn
   "At the Lawn Party" (for Judy, undaunted by her
      blindness). PoetL (79:3) Aut 84, p. 145.
   "From a Café Window, Tangier." AntR (42:4) Aut
      84, p. 458.
   "Lately I Have Been Too Wrapped Up." PoetL (79:3)
      Aut 84, p. 146-147.
   "The Peasant Woman above Tarifa." PoetL (79:3)
      Aut 84, p. 144.

2849. KREKORIAN, Michael
   "With Great Delicacy" (in the story "Oh,
      Rauschenberg!"). KanQ (16:1/2) Wint-Spr 84, p.
      80-81.

2850. KRESH, David
"Carolina Moon 6/4." <u>KanQ</u> (16:1/2) Wint-Spr 84,
p. 93.

2851. KRESS, Leonard
"Bootleg Coal." <u>WestB</u> (15) 84, p. 21.
"The Frankford El." <u>PaintedB</u> (21) Wint 84, p. 15-16.
"Ruthenian Festival in Mahanoy City." <u>WestB</u> (15)
84, p. 23.
"To Spot the Centralia Mine Fire." <u>PaintedB</u> (23)
Sum 84, p. 6.
"To Spot the Centralia Mine Fire." <u>WestB</u> (15) 84,
p. 22.

2852. KRETZ, Thomas
"Blank Pages." <u>Sam</u> (37:3, 147th release) 83, p. 26.
"Dear Jane." <u>Waves</u> (12:4) Spr 84, p. 59.
"Experiment 14." <u>Quarry</u> (33:1) Wint 84, p. 53.
"From My Window." <u>ChrC</u> (101:4) 1-8 F 84, p. 101.
"Knoise." <u>Quarry</u> (33:1) Wint 84, p. 53.
"My Initials." <u>AntigR</u> (58) Sum 84, p. 15.
"Snowflake Fall." <u>KanQ</u> (16:1/2) Wint-Spr 84, p. 181.

2853. KRETZ, Tom
"Kudos." <u>SpoonRQ</u> (9:2) Spr 84, p. 37-38.

2854. KRIDLER, David
"Returning Home after a Few Days Away." <u>SenR</u>
(14:1) 84, p. 63.

2855. KRISTOFCO, John
"Father's Day 1983." <u>Poem</u> (50) Mr 84, p. 38.
"In the Art Museum." <u>Blueline</u> (6:1) Sum-Aut 84,
p. 40.
"Stoplight." <u>Poem</u> (50) Mr 84, p. 37.

2856. KROEKER, Ellen
"Lament for Mother." <u>KanQ</u> (16:1/2) Wint-Spr 84,
p. 189.

2857. KROETSCH, Robert
"Advice to My Friends." <u>CanLit</u> (100) Spr 84, p.
181-182.
"Advice to My Friends" (Selections). <u>Descant</u>
(44/45, 15:1/2) Spr-Sum 84, p. 7-9.
"Advice to My Friends" (Selections: 17. Having a
Word with Columbus: a Song for Ed Dyck. 18. Four
Questions for George Bowering. 19. Stairway: for
Giovanna Capone). <u>CrossC</u> (6:3) 84, p. 6.
"For Doug Jones: The Explanation" (from "Advice to
My Friends"). <u>Descant</u> (44/45, 15:1/2) Spr-Sum
84, p. 9.
"Late Fall Dirve: For Byrna Barclay" (from "Advice
to My Friends"). <u>Descant</u> (44/45, 15:1/2) Spr-
Sum 84, p. 7.
"November 9, 1983: For Robert Hilles" (from "Advice
to My Friends"). <u>Descant</u> (44/45, 15:1/2) Spr-
Sum 84, p. 8.

2858. KROGFUS, Miles
"Marion and Henry Adams on Tour." KanQ (16:3) Sum
84, p. 132-133.
"To a Friend in Therapy." KanQ (16:3) Sum 84, p. 63.

2859. KROLL, Ernest
"At the Grave of Willa Cather" (Jaffrey Center,
N.H.). KanQ (16:3) Sum 84, p. 79.
"Jack London." WebR (9:2) Wint 85, p. 90.
"Local View." WebR (9:2) Wint 85, p. 91.
"Nitty Gritty." TexasR (5:1/2) Spr-Sum 84, p. 34.
"Northeaster" (31 March 1980). LitR (27:2) Wint
84, p. 188-189.
"Swinburne." WebR (9:2) Wint 85, p. 91.

2860. KROLL, Judith
"Anniversary." Iowa (14:3) Aut 84, p. 116.
"Consolations." Tendril (17) Wint 84, p. 104.
"Hill Station." SouthernR (20:2) Spr 84, p. 344-345.
"Other Lives." SouthernR (20:2) Spr 84, p. 344.
"Soul Sharks." Tendril (17) Wint 84, p. 103.
"Sunday." SouthernR (20:2) Spr 84, p. 345-346.

2861. KRONEN, Steve
"Like a Chalice in a Piscina." KanQ (16:1/2) Wint-
Spr 84, p. 161.

2862. KRONENBERG, Mindy H.
"Water Course." PoeticJ (7) 84, p. 40.

2863. KRONENFELD, Judy
"What Shall I Wear?" HiramPoR (37) Aut-Wint 84,
p. 26-27.

2864. KROUSE, Lane
"From Apex to the Base." SanFPJ (6:1) 84, p. 14-15.

2865. KRUEGER, Robert
"Aprendizagem." Mester (13:2) Aut 84, p. 78.
"Nós Da Corda." Mester (13:2) Aut 84, p. 77.
"O Papagaio." Mester (13:2) Aut 84, p. 79.

2866. KRYNSKI, Magnus J.
"December 15, 1979: Dizzy with Success" (tr. of
Stanislaw Baranczak, w. Robert A. Maguire).
Confr (27/28) 84, p. 19.
"December 19, 1979: Clean Hands" (tr. of Stanislaw
Baranczak, w. Robert A. Maguire). Confr
(27/28) 84, p. 20.

2867. KRYSL, Marilyn
"September, You Remember the Ottoman Empire."
Iowa (14:3) Aut 84, p. 102.
"Sestina: People's Republic of China, the Foreign
Woman Laments the Revolution's Failure to
Accommodate Love." Iowa (14:3) Aut 84, p. 99-100.
"Thermodynamics." Iowa (14:3) Aut 84, p. 101.
"To the Tune 'Red Embroidered Shoes'." 13thM
(8:1/2) 84, p. 34-35.

2868. KRYSS, T. L.
    "Gauguin." <u>Abraxas</u> (29/30) 84, p. 13.
    "Hijacked." <u>Abraxas</u> (29/30) 84, p. 12.
    "Japanese Camera." <u>Abraxas</u> (29/30) 84, p. 14.

2869. KUBICEK, J. L.
    "Air and Variations on a Passage of Pierre de
    Ronsard." <u>ArizQ</u> (40:2) Sum 84, p. 188.

2870. KUDERKO, Lynne M.
    "Bedtime Story." <u>Ascent</u> (10:1) 84, p. 18.
    "Wintering Over." <u>Ascent</u> (10:1) 84, p. 19.

2871. KUFFEL, Frances
    "Bloodletting." <u>SouthernPR</u> (24:2) Aut 84, p. 60-61.
    "First Snow." <u>PraS</u> (58:1) Spr 84, p. 58-59.
    "Karamozov Applying for Land-Surveyor." <u>PraS</u>
    (58:1) Spr 84, p. 59-60.
    "The Runner." <u>Wind</u> (14:52) 84, p. 29.

2872. KULIK, William
    "Comrades" (tr. of Robert Desnos). <u>AmerPoR</u> (13:5)
    S-O 84, p. 48.

2873. KULYCKY, Michael
    "At a distance is better" ("Untitled"). <u>KanQ</u>
    (16:1/2) Wint-Spr 84, p. 226.

2874. KUMAR, Shiv K.
    "Hindu Boy Takes His Vow of Celibacy." <u>GreenfR</u>
    (11:3/4) Wint-Spr 84, p. 144-145.
    "Mother Teresa Feeds Her Lepers at Her Home for the
    Destitute, Calcutta." <u>GreenfR</u> (11:3/4) Wint-
    Spr 84, p. 143.

2875. KUMIN, Maxine
    "Atlantic City 1939." <u>Nat</u> (239:10) 6 O 84, p. 321.
    "The Chain." <u>MemphisSR</u> (5:1) Aut 84, p. 6-7.
    "How to Survive Nuclear War" (after reading Ibuse's
    <u>Black Rain</u>). <u>Ploughs</u> (10:4) 84, p. 171-173.
    "The Poet Visits Egypt and Israel." <u>SouthernPR</u>
    (24:2) Aut 84, p. 35-39.
    "Shopping in Ferney with Voltaire." <u>TriQ</u> (59)
    Wint 84, p. 124-126.

2876. KUMMINGS, Donald
    "Negative." <u>SpoonRQ</u> (9:2) Spr 84, p. 23.

2877. KUNITZ, Stanley
    "The Crystal Cage" (for Joseph Cornell). <u>PoetryE</u>
    (13/14) Spr-Sum 84, p. 231.
    "My Sisters." <u>Tendril</u> (18, special issue) 84, p.
    213.

2878. KUO, Alex
    "At Wolf Creek Pass, Colorado." <u>Bound</u> (12:1) Aut
    83, p. 179-180.
    "Coming Home" (for Zoe Filipkowski). <u>Bound</u> (12:1)
    Aut 83, p. 177-180.
    "Did You Not See." <u>LitR</u> (28:1) Aut 84, p. 70.

"El Salvador, Again." NewL (50:4) Sum 84, p. 76-77.
"The Immigrant." Bound (12:1) Aut 83, p. 180.
"Rose by Any Other Name." NowestR (22:3) 84, p.
   16-17.
"This Time I Think I'm Ready for January" (for
   Zoe). MalR (68) Je 84, p. 66.
"Winter Kill." Bound (12:1) Aut 83, p. 178-179.

2879. KURODA, Kio
"Guerrilla's Fantasy" (tr. by Naoshi Koriyama and
   Edward Lueders). Poetry (143:6) Mr 84, p. 321-
   322.

KURYLO, Carolyn Kreiter: See KREITER-KURYLO, Carolyn

2880. KUTCHINS, Laurie
"Night Driving, What the Prairie Says." SnapD
   (7:1) Aut 83, p. 41.
"Postcard from Inge, July." SnapD (7:1) Aut 83,
   p. 40.

2881. KUZMA, Greg
"America." MassR (25:2) Sum 84, p. 285.
"Beauty." KanQ (16:4) Aut 84, p. 79.
"The Brook." VirQR (60:1) Wint 84, p. 57.
"Cattails." NewL (50:2/3) Wint-Spr 84, p. 262.
"Coffee in the Morning." MidAR (4:1) Spr 84, p. 137.
"Dish." VirQR (60:1) Wint 84, p. 58.
"The Dove." TarRP (23:2) Spr 84, p. 21.
"For My Brother 1952-1977." TarRP (23:2) Spr 84,
   p. 22.
"History." VirQR (60:1) Wint 84, p. 57.
"How He Is Nearly Five Years Dead." Abraxas
   (29/30) 84, p. 70.
"In the Adirondacks." TarRP (23:2) Spr 84, p. 22.
"Kiss." KanQ (16:4) Aut 84, p. 78.
"The Lake." KanQ (16:4) Aut 84, p. 78.
"Poems for My Brother." Peb (23) 84, p. 71-79.
"Poems for the Dead" (Special issue, edited by Greg
   Kuzma. The Best Cellar Press). Peb (23) 84, p.
   1-95.
"The Retreat." VirQR (60:1) Wint 84, p. 58.
"The River." MidAR (4:1) Spr 84, p. 136.
"Twenty Dollar Bill." MinnR (N.S. 22) Spr 84, p. 29.
"Two." PoetryNW (25:1) Spr 84, p. 26.

2882. KWASNY, Melissa
"Grinding Cobalt and Vermilion." CutB (22) Spr-
   Sum 84, p. 48-49.

2883. KWIATKOWSKI, Diana
"Letter from the Islands" (The Caribbean, 1981).
   Amelia (1:2) O 84, p. 60.

2884. L. C. S.
"The whole idea of a woman as vice-prez." SanFPJ
   (6:4) 84, p. 76.

La . . .: See also names beginning with "La" without the
   following space, filed below in their alphabetic

positions, e.g., LaSALLE.

La CRUZ, Juana Inés de, Sor: See CRUZ, Juana Inés de la, Sor

La CUESTA, Francisco Ruiz de: See RUIZ de la CUESTA, Francisco

La FONTAINE, Jean de: See FONTAINE, Jean de la

La PUEBLA, Manuel de: See PUEBLA, Manuel de la

2885. La ROQUE, Catherine
"Civilization." SanFPJ (7:1) 84, p. 93.

2886. LaBARTHE, Penelope
"Ancient Child of Ancient Mothers." DekalbLAJ
(17:1/2) 84, p. 134.

2887. LACABA, Jose
"Force of Circumstance" (tr. by the author). Iowa
(14:2) Spr-Sum 84, p. 66-67.
"King's Orders" (tr. by the author). Iowa (14:2)
Spr-Sum 84, p. 68.
"The Sacred Passion of St. Joseph" (tr. by the
author). Iowa (14:2) Spr-Sum 84, p. 67-68.

2888. LACACI, Maria Elvira
"A la Poesia." Mairena (6:18) 84, p. 52-53.

2889. LACY, Ann
"Heartless." NeqC (4:4) Aut 84, p. 20-21.
"July 2 after Pit Cleanup." PoetL (79:1) Spr 84,
p. 22.
"Letter from 4th Avenue." Poem (50) Mr 84, p. 32.
"Monks and Nuns and Catholic Priests." NeqC (4:4)
Aut 84, p. 89.

2890. LADHA, Yasmin
"The Painting." Quarry (33:1) Wint 84, p. 49.

2891. LADISLAO, Maria L.
"Hizo suyas palabras." Mairena (5:14) Aut 83, p. 90.

2892. LaFORGE, Christopher Lyle
"Hope." SanFPJ (6:3) 84, p. 24.
"I Think." SanFPJ (6:3) 84, p. 23.
"When Down Is Up." SanFPJ (6:3) 84, p. 22.

2893. LaGATTUTA, Margo
"You." NeqC (4:2) Spr 84, p. 38.

2894. LAGOS, Janet
"The Animal Dentist." Tele (19) 83, p. 92.
"Counting (Backwards) Song." Tele (19) 83, p. 94.
"The Package." Tele (19) 83, p. 92.
"The Skunk and the Porcupine." Tele (19) 83, p. 93.
"Whales." Tele (19) 83, p. 93.

2895. LAIRD, R. Steven
"The Pull of Magnets." Grain (12:3) Ag 84, p. 44.

LAJOIE, Rhea Mouledoux: See MOULEDOUX-LAJOIE, Rhea

2896. LAKE, Paul
    "Boys Throwing Rocks at a Train." <u>KanQ</u> (16:1/2)
        Wint-Spr 84, p. 225.
    "Lost Driving in the Ozarks." <u>Thrpny</u> (18) Sum 84,
        p. 14.

2897. LAMKIN, Kurt
    "Touchdancers We." <u>PaintedB</u> (24) Aut 84, p. 22-24.

2898. LAMKIN, Kurt J.
    "West Gone." <u>Stepping</u> (Premier Issue) Sum 82, p.
        22-24.

2899. LAMPELL, Jacqueline
    "Open 24 Hours." <u>Open24</u> (3) 84, p. 2.

2900. LAMPPA, William R.
    "An American Rental Unit." <u>SanFPJ</u> (7:1) 84, p. 24.
    "An American Rental Unit." <u>SanFPJ</u> (7:1) 84, p. 88.
    "The Creationists." <u>SanFPJ</u> (7:1) 84, p. 36.

2901. LAMPRILL, Paul
    "Gary Glitter." <u>Bogg</u> (52) 84, p. 34.

2902. LAMPSON, David
    "The Cow Stands on One Leg" (Excerpts). <u>MalR</u> (68)
        Je 84, p. 53-62.

LAND, Thomas Orszag: <u>See</u> ORSZAG-LAND, Thomas

2903. LANDI, Patti
    "April Fool." <u>Tele</u> (19) 83, p. 49.
    "Nov. 26" (for Meeg Hamilton). <u>Tele</u> (19) 83, p. 48.
    "On Hearing the Siren" (for Jackie). <u>Tele</u> (19)
        83, p. 48.
    "She Finally Reaches the South" (Louisiana, a dream
        state). <u>Tele</u> (19) 83, p. 46-47.
    "Suicide II." <u>Open24</u> (3) 84, p. 31.
    "Touche." <u>Tele</u> (19) 83, p. 50.
    "William." <u>Tele</u> (19) 83, p. 47.

2904. LANDRON BOU, Iris M.
    "Buen Dia." <u>Mairena</u> (5:13) Spr 83, p. 64.
    "Contra-Tiempo." <u>Mairena</u> (6:16) Spr 84, p. 26.
    "Hora de Mar" (En homenaje al <u>Canto de la Locura</u>,
        de Francisco Matos Paoli). <u>Mairena</u> (6:16) Spr
        84, p. 23-25.
    "Silogismo." <u>Mairena</u> (6:16) Spr 84, p. 26.

2905. LANE, John
    "Building the Pheasant Cage." <u>VirQR</u> (60:3) Sum
        84, p. 425.
    "Grounds for Divorce." <u>SoCaR</u> (17:1) Aut 84, p. 27.
    "Road Gang." <u>VirQR</u> (60:3) Sum 84, p. 424-425.

2906. LANE, M. Travis
    "Corduroy." <u>CanLit</u> (100) Spr 84, p. 183.

2907. LANE, Pat
    "Blanc de Blanc." <u>WestCR</u> (18:4) Ap 84, p. 42.
    "The English." <u>WestCR</u> (18:4) Ap 84, p. 46.
    "Night Walked Right In." <u>WestCR</u> (18:4) Ap 84, p. 43.

"Poem for Sylvia." WestCR (18:4) Ap 84, p. 44.
"Story." WestCR (18:4) Ap 84, p. 45.
"Voices." WestCR (18:4) Ap 84, p. 41.

2908. LANE, Patrick
"Variations" (for Doug Jones). CanLit (100) Spr
84, p. 184-186.

2909. LANG, Stephen
"Coteries." Poem (50) Mr 84, p. 56.
"Gentleman in Silver." Poem (52) N 84, p. 23.
"Iconoclast--Ah, Forgive Me!" Poem (52) N 84, p. 24.
"In Sweethavens." Poem (52) N 84, p. 21.
"One of Those Jealous Types." Poem (52) N 84, p. 22.
"To Mr. McCormick." Poem (50) Mr 84, p. 57.

2910. LANG, Susanna
"In the Thickness" (tr. of Phillipe Denis). Iowa
(14:2) Spr-Sum 84, p. 177-179.

2911. LANGTON, Daniel J.
"After the Extraction." KanQ (16:4) Aut 84, p. 39.
"Ballade for My Wife." KanQ (16:3) Sum 84, p. 80.
"Dance Cycle." Spirit (7:1) 84, p. 175-177.
"Mark's Room." LitR (28:1) Aut 84, p. 121.
"Sage Advice." StoneC (11:3/4) Spr-Sum 84, p. 45.
"Turntables." CrabCR (1:3) Wint 84, p. 4.
"When You Get This." KanQ (16:4) Aut 84, p. 38.

2912. LANIER, Doris
"Accident." Wind (14:51) 84, p. 30.
"Writing." Wind (14:51) 84, p. 30-31.

2913. LANOUE, David
"Mississippi River." Wind (14:50) 84, p. 59.
"One Brown Hair." Wind (14:50) 84, p. 59.
"Two Poems Political" (1. Our President, 2. Moral
Majority). SanFPJ (6:2) 84, p. 96.

2914. LANZA, Robert M.
"To Her Persistent Master." EngJ (73:5) S 84, p. 99.

2915. LAPPIN, Linda
"Costa del Sol, at Night" (tr. of Vita Andersen, w.
Jannick Storm). Iowa (14:2) Spr-Sum 84, p. 183-
186.
"Funeral Song" (tr. of Patricio Esteve, w. the
author). Iowa (14:2) Spr-Sum 84, p. 159.

2916. LARDAS, Konstantinos
"The Comings and the Goings of Our Friend."
HolCrit (21:4) O 84, p. 16.
"Gordion." HolCrit (21:4) O 84, p. 9.

2917. LARIVEE, Adrien C.
"Love Letters." Waves (12:2/3) Wint 84, p. 91.

2918. LARSEN, Wendy
"My Father's Oldest Sister" (with Tran Thi Nga).
13thM (8:1/2) 84, p. 72.

"My Grandmother" (with Tran Thi Nga). 13thM
    (8:1/2) 84, p. 71.
"My Mother" (with Tran Thi Nga). 13thM (8:1/2)
    84, p. 70.
"Visiting My Auntie" (with Tran Thi Nga). 13thM
    (8:1/2) 84, p. 69.

2919. LARSON, Karl
    "Doe at 6 AM." Northeast (Series 3:17) Sum 84, p.
    16.

2920. LaSALLE, Peter
    "The Idea of Haiti." MassR (25:4) Wint 84, p. 617-
    618.

2921. LASDUN, James
    "On the Road to Chenonceaux." PoetryCR (5:3) Spr
    84, p. 12.
    "Picture of a Girl." PoetryCR (5:3) Spr 84, p. 12.

2922. LASH, Kenneth
    "Home." CalQ (23/24) Spr-Sum 84, p. 126-127.

2923. LASKIN, Pamela L.
    "Banana." SmPd (21:1) Wint 84, p. 17.

2924. LASOEN, Patricia
    "Still Life with Autumn Fruits" (tr. by Scott
    Rollins). Vis (16) 84, p. 24.

2925. LASSELL, Michael
    "Apostle's Creed: Après le Miroir le Déluge."
    Amelia (1:2) O 84, p. 40-41.
    "Cavafy" (for Jane Lagoudis Pinchin). Amelia
    (1:2) O 84, p. 42-43.
    "Dead Poets." Amelia (1:2) O 84, p. 42.
    "Desertions." Amelia (1:2) O 84, p. 41-42.
    "Keenings: After Rilke (Lamentations for Baritone
    and Chorus)" (for Eric Torgersen). HangL (46)
    Aut 84, p. 36-52.

2926. LATHAM, Cleveland
    "My Students in Military School." Spirit (7:1)
    84, p. 144-146.

2927. LAUBER, Peg Carlson
    "The Danger of Travel." Wind (14:50) 84, p. 40.
    "Near Lake Michigan." Wind (14:50) 84, p. 39.

2928. LAUGHLIN, J.
    "After I'm Gone." AntigR (57) Spr 84, p. 16.
    "Herodotus Reports." AntigR (57) Spr 84, p. 15.
    "Hi, Ben!" AntigR (57) Spr 84, p. 17.
    "You Came As a Thought." Poetry (144:3) Je 84, p.
    133.

2929. LAUGHLIN, James
    "Alba." ParisR (26:94) Wint 84, p. 199.
    "Hugh Kenner's Nine Permutations of 'Alba' (w. Hugh
    Kenner). ParisR (26:94) Wint 84, p. 202-203.

"The Non-World." <u>ParisR</u> (26:94) Wint 84, p. 163.
"Selection of Computer Permutations of Ezra Pound's
    'In a Station of the Metro'" (w. Hugh Kenner).
    <u>ParisR</u> (26:94) Wint 84, p. 196-198.

2930. LAUNIUS, Carl Judson
    "For Bobby Sands" (The Red Rose and the Fire).
        <u>SanFPJ</u> (6:3) 84, p. 20.
    "A song of Victor Jara." <u>SanFPJ</u> (6:2) 84, p. 26-27.

LAURA, Roland Legiardi: <u>See</u> LEGIARDI-LAURA, Roland

LAURENTIS, Louise Budde de: <u>See</u> deLAURENTIS, Louise Budde

2931. LAUTERMILCH, Steven
    "The Philosopher of the Beauty Mark." <u>HolCrit</u>
        (21:2, i.e. 21:3) Je 84, p. 13.

2932. LAVALLE, Tomás Guido
    "Regresando a Barcelona." <u>LindLM</u> (3:2/4) Ap-D 84,
        p. 4.

2933. LAVOINE, Frank
    "Outer Orbit." <u>PortR</u> (30:1) 84, p. 13-14.

2934. LAWLER, Patrick
    "Another Russian Novel: Fragment." <u>SouthernHR</u>
        (18:3) Sum 84, p. 256.
    "Burning Lady of Toronto." <u>SmPd</u> (21:1) Wint 84,
        p. 16.
    "Subsong." <u>StoneC</u> (12:1/2) Aut-Wint 84, p. 24.

2935. LAWLOR, William T.
    "The Crime" (tr. of Carlos Dobal). <u>NegC</u> (4:4) Aut
        84, p. 62.
    "I See My Country" (tr. of Tulio Galeas). <u>Vis</u>
        (15) 84, p. 23.

2936. LAWNER, Lynne
    "Lament of the Steam Shovel" (Part II, tr. of Pier
        Paolo Pasolini). <u>Chelsea</u> (42/43) 84, p. 103-105.

2937. LAWRENCE, D. H.
    "I wish I knew a woman." <u>Tendril</u> (18, special
        issue) 84, p. 81.
    "River Roses." <u>Tendril</u> (18, special issue) 84, p.
        81-82.
    "Song of a Man Who Has Come Through." <u>MassR</u>
        (25:2) Sum 84, p. 201.

2938. LAWRENCE, Nicholas
    "Sonnet: Behind his childhood is the running of
        water." <u>HarvardA</u> (118:2) Spr 84, p. 24.

2939. LAWRENCE, Robert
    "For Agnes in the Stromness Hotel." <u>GreenfR</u>
        (11:3/4) Wint-Spr 84, p. 99-100.
    "Watershed." <u>GreenfR</u> (11:3/4) Wint-Spr 84, p. 100-
        101.

2940. LAWRY, Mercedes
"Chinese Silk." PoetL (79:1) Spr 84, p. 31.
"The Choices Plain before Us." IndR (7:3) Sum 84,
p. 10-11.
"Hammer and Nails." WoosterR (1:1) Mr 84, p. 48.
"Parade." WoosterR (1:2) N 84, p. 66.
"Piano Lession" (for my father). SmPd (21:1) Wint
84, p. 20.
"The Scream." SmPd (21:1) Wint 84, p. 20.

2941. LAWS, Kyle
"Copper Skin." PoeticJ (8) 84, p. 15.
"The Horns." PoeticJ (4) 83, p. 10.
"Maize Rows Flowering Red." YellowS (10) Spr 84,
p. 24.
"Nighthawks." PoeticJ (8) 84, p. 14.
"Red Summer Moons." OroM (2:3/4, issue 7/8) 84,
p. 22.

2942. LAWSON, Christopher
"Possible Things to Do with the Robe after You Have
Quit the Klan." Wind (14:51) 84, p. 7.

2943. LAWSON, Helen
"Last Supper." YetASM (3) 84, p. 6.

2944. LAWTON, Susan
"Hysterical Fugue." Gargoyle (24) 84, p. 221-222.

2945. LAYTON, Elizabeth
"The Night the School Board Met." LittleBR (4:4)
Sum 84, p. 96-97.

2946. LAYTON, Irving
"The Cyst." AntigR (58) Sum 84, p. 116.
"Jude the Obscure." CanLit (100) Spr 84, p. 198.
"Juvenal Redidivus." AntigR (58) Sum 84, p. 115.
"New Year's Poem for Veneranda." CanLit (100) Spr
84, p. 198.

2947. LAYTON, Susan
"Poem" (To my unknown ancestor -- a lieutenant-
colonel in the civil war, tr. of Irina
Ratushinskaya). NewRep (190:11) 19 Mr 84, p. 34.

2948. LAZER, Hank
"Azaleas." WebR (9:1) Spr 84, p. 71.
"Deathwatch for My Father's Father." WebR (9:1)
Spr 84, p. 70.
"For Claes Oldenburg." LitR (28:1) Aut 84, p. 124-
125.

2949. LAZIN, Sharlene
"Force of Habit." WestCR (19:2) O 84, p. 30.
"Reconnaissance." WestCR (19:2) O 84, p. 30.
"Sunday Night, behind the Screen, or Waiting for
God." WestCR (19:2) O 84, p. 31.

Le . . . .: See also names beginning with "Le" without the
following space, filed below in their alphabetic

positions, e.g., LeFEVRE.

2950. Le MIEUX, Debbie
"Mushrooming on Olema Ridge." Ploughs (10:1) 84,
p. 106-107.
"Odalisque with Little Red Coffer" (after Matisse).
Ploughs (10:1) 84, p. 108-109.

2951. LEA, Sydney
"Facing the Revenant" (National Airport, 2 a.m.,
March). BlackWR (10:2) Spr 84, p. 55-56.
"The One Near Thought of the Stone in Autumn."
BlackWR (10:2) Spr 84, p. 57-59.
"Sereno." NewRep (190:18) 7 My 84, p. 39.
"Surviving Romance." BlackWR (10:2) Spr 84, p. 52-
54.

2952. LEASE, Joseph
"Overshadowed by Colors." ParisR (26:94) Wint 84,
p. 164.

2953. LEBOW, Jeanne
"The Boxer and the Queen of Hearts." MemphisSR
(4:2) Spr 84, p. 27.
"Headwaters." MemphisSR (4:2) Spr 84, p. 49.

2954. LECHLITNER, Ruth
"The Bridge." HolCrit (21:4) O 84, p. 20.

2955. LeCOUNT
"A sudden cloudburst." Northeast (Series 3:17)
Sum 84, p. 15.
"You ferns have me." Northeast (Series 3:17) Sum
84, p. 15.

2956. LEDBETTER, J. T.
"Dolly." SouthernPR (24:2) Aut 84, p. 47-48.

2957. LEDESMA, Luis Manuel
"Las Empleadas Públicas." Areíto (10:38) 84,
p. 35.

2958. LEDFORD, Loretta
"Program Strands (Based on Level of Interest)."
EngJ (73:3) Mr 84, p. 77.

2959. LEE, Alice
"Write a Villanelle." KanQ (16:1/2) Wint-Spr 84,
p. 178.

2960. LEE, David
"Building Pigpens." MidwQ (25:3) Spr 84, p. 333-337.
"The Chain Letter (An American Tragedy)." MidwQ
(25:3) Spr 84, p. 325-332.
"Day's Work" (for Chant & Ruth, with love). MidwQ
(25:3) Spr 84, p. 333-344.
"Digging Postholes." MidwQ (25:3) Spr 84, p. 338-
341.
"Shoveling Rolled Barley." MidwQ (25:3) Spr 84,
p. 342-344.

2961. LEE, Dean
       "200-Yard Inner Stampede." PikeF (6) Aut 84, p. 21.

2962. LEE, Dennis
       "Riff." CanLit (100) Spr 84, p. 199.
       "Riffs" (Excerpts). Epoch (33:3) Sum-Aut 84, p.
       310-318.

2963. LEE, George
       "Forsythia." Ploughs (10:1) 84, p. 97.
       "Pike Certificate." Ploughs (10:1) 84, p. 97.
       "Radiolaria: On a Drawing by Ernst Haeckel."
       Ploughs (10:1) 84, p. 98.

2964. LEE, John B.
       "The Clearing." AntigR (56) Wint 84, p. 24-25.
       "Come the Resolution." Quarry (33:3) Sum 84, p. 59.
       "In the Home for Old People." CrossC (6:2) 84, p.
       11.
       "Living on Easy Street." Waves (12:2/3) Wint 84,
       p. 79.
       "Photograph of a Soldier WWI." AntigR (56) Wint
       84, p. 23.
       "Thaw." Waves (12:2/3) Wint 84, p. 79.
       "This Was My Room." PoetryCR (6:2) Wint 84-85, p.
       20.

2965. LEE, Lance
       "Hawk in Mid-Dive." Poem (51) Mr [i.e. Jl] 84, p. 1.
       "Laugher." Poem (51) Mr [i.e. Jl] 84, p. 2.
       "Pick-Up Drop-Out Sobering-Up Poem in a Coffee
       House with Jazz in the Background." Poem (51)
       Mr [i.e. Jl] 84, p. 3.

2966. LEE, Li-Young
       "Dreaming of Hair." AmerPoR (13:1) Ja-F 84, p. 38.
       "The Gift." AmerPoR (13:1) Ja-F 84, p. 39.

2967. LEE, Myra
       "The Visitation." SanFPJ (6:2) 84, p. 69.

2968. LEEDY, David
       "Thinking of Sappho." Comm (111:9) 4 My 84, p. 280.

2969. LEET, Judith
       "Holding Court." Ploughs (10:4) 84, p. 178-179.

2970. LEFCOWITZ, Barbara
       "Condom Found off Crescent Harbor." Kayak (64) My
       84, p. 41.
       "My Poetry Retirement Dinner." Bogg (52) 84, p.
       21-22.

2971. LEFCOWITZ, Barbara F.
       "The Forgotten." WebR (9:2) Wint 85, p. 42.
       "The Remembered." WebR (9:2) Wint 85, p. 40-41.
       "Selected Correspondence of Sleeping Beauty."
       LitR (27:2) Wint 84, p. 214-216.

2972. LeFEVRE, Adam
     "December." <u>AmerPoR</u> (13:2) Mr-Ap 84, p. 36.
     "Humiliation." <u>AmerPoR</u> (13:2) Mr-Ap 84, p. 36.
     "So Long." <u>AmerPoR</u> (13:2) Mr-Ap 84, p. 36.

2973. LEGG, Thomas F.
     "Positive I.D." <u>BlueBuf</u> (2:2) Spr 84, p. 36.

2974. LEGIARDI-LAURA, Roland
     "Nervous Application" (w. Jeff Wright). <u>Tele</u> (19)
     83, p. 67-68.

2975. LEHMAN, David
     "Amnesia" (For Tom Disch). <u>Poetry</u> (144:4) Jl 84,
     p. 203-204.
     "Third and Icarus." <u>SouthwR</u> (69:3) Sum 84, p. 307-
     310.
     "Twenty Questions." <u>Shen</u> (35:1) 83-84, p. 94.

2976. LEHNER, Frank
     "Paper Hearts, Wooden Signs." <u>PoetryE</u> (15) Aut
     84, p. 12-13.

2977. LEIPER, Esther M.
     "Foreclosure." <u>Amelia</u> (1:2) O 84, p. 16.
     "Last Gift" (A Korean Sijo). <u>Amelia</u> (1:2) O 84,
     p. 68.
     "Passage of an Autumn Tramp." <u>Amelia</u> [1:1] Ap 84,
     p. 15-17.
     "Waumbek Woods in April" (Second Honorable Mention,
     13th Annual Kansas Poetry Contest). <u>LittleBR</u>
     (4:3) Spr 84, p. 66.

2978. LEITHAUSER, Brad
     "Flight from Osaka." <u>NewYorker</u> (60:22) 16 Jl 84,
     p. 36.
     "Hesitancy." <u>NewRep</u> (190:13) 2 Ap 84, p. 38.
     "In Minako Wada's House." <u>NewYorker</u> (60:22) 16 Jl
     84, p. 36.
     "Seaside Greetings" (Oki Islands, Japan Sea).
     <u>NewYorker</u> (60:22) 16 Jl 84, p. 36-37.
     "Three Poems from Japan." <u>NewYorker</u> (60:22) 16 Jl
     84, p. 36-37.
     "The Tigers of Nanzen-Ji" (Nanzen Temple, Kyoto).
     <u>Atlantic</u> (253:5) My 84, p. 75.

2979. LELAND, Blake
     "Lullabye of Birdland." <u>Epoch</u> (33:3) Sum-Aut 84,
     p. 229-238.

2980. LeMASTER, J. R.
     "I Thought of the Ships." <u>TexasR</u> (5:1/2) Spr-Sum
     84, p. 72.
     "Letter to the Late Robert Frost." <u>TexasR</u> (5:1/2)
     Spr-Sum 84, p. 70.
     "Lost at the Peking Zoo." <u>TexasR</u> (5:1/2) Spr-Sum
     84, p. 71.
     "Three Poems from China." <u>TexasR</u> (5:1/2) Spr-Sum
     84, p. 70-72.

2981. LEMBKE, Janet N.
"Hellfire to him who discovered hours!" (tr. of
Aquilius). Sparrow (46) 84, p. 9.

2982. LEMM, Richard
"Butterflies." PoetryCR (6:1) Aut 84, p. 24.
"Lady from South Africa." PottPort (6) 84, p. 10.
"Nineteen Eighty-Four." PottPort (6) 84, p. 5.
"The Side of the Blind" (for Lesley Choyce).
PottPort (6) 84, p. 22.
"Wet Blanket" (for Carolyn). PottPort (6) 84, p. 5.

2983. LeMON, Richard
"A man carries his wife through the street."
Ploughs (10:4) 84, p. 185.
"Moonglow soft as milk." Ploughs (10:4) 84, p. 186.

2984. LENHART, Michael
"66." PoeticJ (6) 84, p. 11.
"Bar." Sam (39:1, release 153) 84, p. 46.
"Child Science." PoeticJ (6) 84, p. 31.
"Fathers and Daughters." PoeticJ (4) 83, p. 28.
"Hangtown." Sam (41:1, release 161) 84, p. 38.
"Once More, into the Breach." PoeticJ (4) 83, p. 15.

2985. LENNEN, Elinor
"Non-Employment in Heaven" (from the October 16,
1929 issue). ChrC (101:20) 6-13 Je 84, p. 598.

2986. LENNICK, Donna
"Bedtime Stories." Descant (47, 15:4) Wint 84, p.
35.
"The Patient Wife." Waves (12:1) Aut 83, p. 62.
"The Sisters." Descant (47, 15:4) Wint 84, p. 33-34.
"Wash Day." Descant (47, 15:4) Wint 84, p. 36-37.

2987. LENSE, Edward
"The Back Ways." SmPd (21:2) Spr 84, p. 29.
"Drugstore Counter." Abraxas (29/30) 84, p. 55.

LEON, Abelardo Sánchez: See SANCHEZ LEON, Abelardo

2988. LEON, Cesar de
"Pedro Paramo." Mairena (6:18) 84, p. 216.

LEON, Daisy Mora de: See MORA de LEON, Daisy

LEON, José Castro de: See CASTRO de LEON, José

LEON, Kathie de: See De LEON, Kathie

2989. LEONHARD, Sigi
"Absence." RagMag (3:1) Spr 84, p. 20.
"Insignificant Encounter." RagMag (3:1) Spr 84,
p. 19.
"Record of Distances." RagMag (3:1) Spr 84, p. 18.
"Sonnet about Silence." RagMag (3:1) Spr 84, p. 21.

2990. LePONT, Henri
"Selaphobia" (for "Oppie"). Telescope (3:1) Wint

84, p. 33-34.

2991. LERGIER, Clara de
"Parece Igual." _Mairena_ (5:13) Spr 83, p. 100.

2992. LERMAN, Eleanor
"Taking Pictures" (for Allen Boretz). _NoAmR_
(269:1) Mr 84, p. 14.

2993. LERMONTOV, Mikhail
"The Cup of Life" (tr. by Anatoly Liberman).
NewYRB (31:9) 31 My 84, p. 30.

2994. LesCARBEAU, Mitchell
"Fauna in the Mirror" (Prizewinning Poets--1984).
Nat (238:18) 12 My 84, p. 581.
"The Reeds Speak to Psyche." _PoetL_ (79:2) Sum 84,
p. 90-91.

2995. LESLIE, Naton
"Fevered Hours." _WestB_ (15) 84, p. 78-79.
"Found House in Hemlock, Pennsylvania: 1963."
WestB (14) 84, p. 85.
"Where They Left Off Dancing." _CharR_ (10:2) Aut
84, p. 91.

2996. LESSER, Rika
"Away." _Nat_ (238:23) 16 Je 84, p. 741.

2997. LESTER-MASSMAN, Gordon
"The Body." _KanQ_ (16:4) Aut 84, p. 146-147.

2998. LESYTCH, Wadym
"Catharsis of War" (tr. by Elaine Epstein).
Pequod (16/17) 84, p. 189-190.

2999. LETKO, Ken
"Incarceration." _GreenfR_ (12:1/2) Sum-Aut 84, p.
181.

LEUDERS, Edward: _See_ LUEDERS, Edward

3000. LEUNG, Ho Hon
"After the 'Three Characters'" (for Stephen Bett).
AntigR (57) Spr 84, p. 121-125.
"Cubism & after the Long Silence of Dasein."
AntigR (59) Aut 84, p. 50.

3001. LEV, Donald
"The Republic." _GreenfR_ (11:1/2) Sum-Aut 83, p. 121.
"Routine Decision." _GreenfR_ (11:1/2) Sum-Aut 83,
p. 122.
"There Is Still Time." _GreenfR_ (11:1/2) Sum-Aut
83, p. 121.

3002. LEVANT, Howard
"Fishing at Sundown: A Meditation." _SewanR_ (92:4)
O-D 84, p. 536-537.

3003. LEVENTHAL, Ann Z.
"Snapshot." Pig (12) 84, p. 50.

3004. LEVER, Bernice
"Unable to Sway You, Father." CanLit (102) Aut
84, p. 6.

3005. LEVERING, Donald
"Country Junction." PoetC (16:1) Aut 84, p. 45.

3006. LEVERTOV, Denise
"The Gulf" (During the Detroit riots, 1967).
Chelsea (42/43) 84, p. 202-203.
"Losing Track." Tendril (18, special issue) 84,
p. 24-25.
"Of Necessity." Nimrod (27:2) Spr-Sum 84, p. 12.

LEVESQUE, Rosaire Dion: See DION-LEVESQUE, Rosaire

3007. LEVI, Toni Mergentime
"Comrade." Swallow (3) 84, p. 10.
"Transcending the Still Life." Wind (14:51) 84,
p. 32-33.

3008. LEVIN, Harriet
"Bukan" (tr. of Emha Ainunn Nadjib, w. the author).
Iowa (14:2) Spr-Sum 84, p. 65.

3009. LEVIN, John
"Audition." Open24 (3) 84, p. 20.
"Big Shoulders Does It Again." Open24 (3) 84, p. 20.

3010. LEVIN, Phillis
"Something about Windows." AntR (42:4) Aut 84, p.
450-451.

3011. LEVINE, Anita
"Cat Love." PoeticJ (1) 83, p. 22.
"The Gold Rush." PoeticJ (1) 83, p. 20.

3012. LEVINE, Ellen
"April 2." TarRP (23:2) Spr 84, p. 16.
"Herons." Tendril (17) Wint 84, p. 105.
"The Old Couple." CrabCR (2:1) Sum 84, p. 22.

3013. LEVINE, Miriam
"In the House of the Edge of the Railroad Flats."
Ploughs (10:1) 84, p. 99-100.

3014. LEVINE, Philip
"At Bessemer." MichQR (23:1) Wint 84, p. 68-69.
"Bare Facts." MichQR (23:1) Wint 84, p. 69-70.
"Late Light." NewYorker (60:27) 20 Ag 84, p. 36.
"Poem with No Ending." ParisR (26:92) Sum 84, p.
80-94.
"Ricky." Peb (23) 84, p. 58-61.
"Then." Ploughs (10:4) 84, p. 23-25.
"Winter Evening." MemphisSR (5:1) Aut 84, p. 14.
"Wisteria." NewYorker (60:16) 4 Je 84, p. 46.

3015. LEVIS, Larry
      "Decrescendo." <u>QW</u> (18) Spr-Sum 84, p. 64-65.
      "Joan of Arc: A Sonnet Sequence" (tr. of Agnes
         Gérgely, w. the author). <u>13thM</u> (8:1/2) 84,
         p. 102-109.
      "Letter." <u>Antaeus</u> (53) Aut 84, p. 103-110.
      "The Quilt." <u>QW</u> (18) Spr-Sum 84, p. 66-67.
      "Weldon Kees." <u>NewL</u> (50:2/3) Wint-Spr 84, p. 59.

3016. LEVITIN, Alexis
      "Biography" (tr. of Sophia de Mello Breyner).
         <u>WebR</u> (9:2) Wint 85, p. 9.
      "Blank Page" (tr. of Sophia de Mello Breyner).
         <u>WebR</u> (9:2) Wint 85, p. 10.
      "Crystallizations" (tr. of Eugenio de Andrade).
         <u>Mund</u> (14:2) 84, p. 41.
      "The Dead Soldier" (tr. of Sophia de Mello
         Breyner). <u>WebR</u> (9:2) Wint 85, p. 11.
      "Eurydice" (tr. of Sophia de Mello Breyner). <u>WebR</u>
         (9:2) Wint 85, p. 9.
      "His Beauty" (tr. of Sophia de Mello Breyner).
         <u>WebR</u> (9:2) Wint 85, p. 10.
      "Homage to Rimbaud" (tr. of Eugenio de Andrade).
         <u>GreenfR</u> (12:1/2) Sum-Aut 84, p. 87-88.
      "Inhabited Body" (tr. of Eugenio de Andrade).
         <u>Mund</u> (14:2) 84, p. 39.
      "Inhabited Heart" (tr. of Eugenio de Andrade).
         <u>Mund</u> (14:2) 84, p. 45.
      "The Minotaur" (tr. of Sophia de Mello Breyner).
         <u>WebR</u> (9:2) Wint 85, p. 9.
      "Names" (tr. of Eugenio de Andrade). <u>NewOR</u>
         (11:3/4) Aut-Wint 84, p. 118.
      "Of the Other Side" (tr. of Eugenio de Andrade).
         <u>GreenfR</u> (12:1/2) Sum-Aut 84, p. 88.
      "Of Transparency" (tr. of Sophia de Mello Breyner).
         <u>WebR</u> (9:2) Wint 85, p. 9.
      "Poetics" (tr. of Eugenio de Andrade). <u>GreenfR</u>
         (12:1/2) Sum-Aut 84, p. 84-85.
      "Silence" (tr. of Eugenio de Andrade). <u>Mund</u>
         (14:2) 84, p. 43.
      "Since Dawn" (tr. of Eugenio de Andrade). <u>Mund</u>
         (14:2) 84, p. 43, 45.
      "Solar Matter" (Selections: 45-46, 49, tr. of
         Eugenio de Andrade). <u>CutB</u> (22) Spr-Sum 84, p. 11.
      "Story of the South" (tr. of Eugenio de Andrade).
         <u>GreenfR</u> (12:1/2) Sum-Aut 84, p. 85-86.
      "While Asleep" (tr. of Eugenio de Andrade).
         <u>GreenfR</u> (12:1/2) Sum-Aut 84, p. 87.
      "Writing on the Wall" (tr. of Eugenio de Andrade).
         <u>GreenfR</u> (12:1/2) Sum-Aut 84, p. 86-87.

3017. LEVY, Howard
      "Grandfather." <u>MassR</u> (25:3) Aut 84, p. 366-367.
      "String Quintet in G Minor, K. 516." <u>GeoR</u> (38:3)
         Aut 84, p. 524.

3018. LEVY, Judy
      "Dedicatory Entry" (tr. of Anton Shammas). <u>Iowa</u>
         (14:2) Spr-Sum 84, p. 114.

3019. LEVY, Robert
      "Kappa." SenR (14:1) 84, p. 11-12.

3020. LEWIN, Rebecca
      "Where the Truth Was." Sam (41:1, release 161)
          84, back cover.

3021. LEWIS, Caryl
      "Paris." Bogg (52) 84, p. 46.

3022. LEWIS, Eugene Russell
      "Castigation" (On viewing the Viet Nam Veterans'
          Memorial, Washington, D.C.). SanFPJ (7:1) 84,
          p. 28.
      "Peaceful Planet." SanFPJ (7:1) 84, p. 35-36.

3023. LEWIS, J. Patrick
      "First Date." Wind (14:52) 84, p. 31.
      "The Gig at Powell's Mill." Wind (14:52) 84, p. 30.

3024. LEWIS, James
      "Call and Response." Os (19) 84, p. 6-8.

3025. LEWIS, Jeffrey
      "The Rebirth Blues." KanQ (16:4) Aut 84, p. 183-184.

3026. LEWIS, Joel
      "4.13.82." Tele (19) 83, p. 128.
      "Imp." Tele (19) 83, p. 127.
      "Interception." Tele (19) 83, p. 126.
      "Mood Music." Tele (19) 83, p. 127.

3027. LEWIS, Laurence
      "The Stone of Madness" (Untitled Prose Poems,
          Selections: 1-4, tr. of Fernando Arrabal).
          Chelsea (42/43) 84, p. 290-291.

3028. LEWIS, Lisa
      "Hatteras Lighthouse." TarRP (24:1) Aut 84, p. 31-
          32.
      "Leaving Sampson County in August." BlackWR
          (11:1) Aut 84, p. 46.
      "Raw Silk." TarRP (24:1) Aut 84, p. 32-33.
      "Sophistry on the Well-lit Desk." Iowa (14:3) Aut
          84, p. 53.
      "Watercolors." TarRP (24:1) Aut 84, p. 34.

3029. LEWIS, Melvyn J.
      "Father Crosses Over." PoeticJ (6) 84, p. 37.
      "Hearing." PoeticJ (4) 83, p. 36.
      "Seaside." PoeticJ (4) 83, p. 7.
      "Yesna." PoeticJ (4) 83, p. 9.

3030. LEWIS, Susan
      "By the River." Ascent (10:1) 84, p. 29.
      "Excavation." Ascent (10:1) 84, p. 29.

3031. LEWIS-DOC, Keith
      "The Other Side of Darkness." SanFPJ (6:1) 84, p.
          80.

"Reality." <u>SanFPJ</u> (6:1) 84, p. 77.
"Someone Crying." <u>SanFPJ</u> (6:1) 84, p. 77.

3032. LEYELES, A.
"Fabius Lind's Days" (tr. by Benjamin Hrushovski
and Barbara Benavie). <u>PartR</u> (51:1) 84, p. 101-
102.

3033. LI, Bai
"Tien-mu Mountain, Ascended in a Dream: a Farewell
Song" (tr. by Burton Raffel and Zuxin Ding).
<u>LitR</u> (27:3) Spr 84, p. 295-296.

3034. LI, Ho
"An Arrowhead from the Ancient Battlefield of
Ch'ang-P'ing" (tr. by Iain Bamforth). <u>KenR</u> (NS
6:2) Spr 84, p. 72-73.

LI, Pai: <u>See</u> PAI, Li

3035. LI, Po
"Alone" (tr. by Sam Hamill). <u>CrabCR</u> (1:3) Wint
84, p. 24.
"At Changmen Palace" (tr. by Sam Hamill). <u>CrabCR</u>
(2:1) Sum 84, p. 24.
"In the battlefield men grapple each other and
die." <u>NewL</u> (50:2/3) Wint-Spr 84, p. 226.

3036. LIAO, James S.
"Seeing an Old Love." <u>DekalbLAJ</u> (17:1/2) 84, p. 135.
"Winter Balance." <u>DekalbLAJ</u> (17:1/2) 84, p. 135.

3037. LIBBEY, Elizabeth
"1899: Girl and Her Father." <u>ThRiPo</u> (23/24) 84,
p. 57.
"Ablution." <u>OP</u> (37) Spr-Sum 84, p. 18-19.
"After the Fall." <u>ThRiPo</u> (23/24) 84, p. 58.
"The Calling." <u>OP</u> (37) Spr-Sum 84, p. 20.
"Engines." <u>ThRiPo</u> (23/24) 84, p. 56.
"Full Moon with Promise." <u>OP</u> (37) Spr-Sum 84, p. 17.
"Landscape for One Voice." <u>BlackWR</u> (10:2) Spr 84,
p. 24-25.
"Paraphernalia" (for Kelly Dobyns). <u>BlackWR</u>
(10:2) Spr 84, p. 22-23.

3038. LIBERMAN, Anatoly
"The Cup of Life" (tr. of Mikhail Lermontov).
<u>NewYRB</u> (31:9) 31 My 84, p. 30.

3039. LIBERTELLI, Bob
"The Muse in Museum." <u>Confr</u> (27/28) 84, p. 244.

3040. LIDDELL, Norrie
"Bears." <u>PoeticJ</u> (5) 84, p. 14.
"Burros." <u>PoeticJ</u> (8) 84, p. 28-29.
"The Man with the Gold Helmet" (painting by
Rembrandt). <u>PoeticJ</u> (3) 83, p. 11.
"Retrieval." <u>PoeticJ</u> (6) 84, p. 43.
"Swinging." <u>PoeticJ</u> (7) 84, p. 21.

3041. LIDDY, James
       "Letter to Eamonn Wall Esquire of Murphy Floods
       Hotel in the County of Wexford." CreamCR
       (9:1/2) 84, p. 68-69.

3042. LIEB, Patricia
       "Upon Boarding Flight #728." PikeF (6) Aut 84, p. 8.

3043. LIEBERMAN, L.
       "The Banana Dwarf." Nat (239:10) 6 O 84, p. 320.

3044. LIEBERMAN, Laurence
       "The Dominican Coachman." MichQR (23:2) Spr 84,
       p. 251-252.
       "Dominoes and Politics on the Morne" (Morne
       Fortuné, Castries, St. Lucia). Hudson (37:4)
       Wint 84-85, p. 578-582.
       "The Dungeon Amorist" (Fort Charlotte, Nassau,
       Bahamas). KenR (NS 6:4) Aut 84, p. 53-57.
       "Jamaica Flambeaux." TarRP (24:1) Aut 84, p. 38-40.
       "Queen of the Billiards." Hudson (37:4) Wint 84-
       85, p. 583-584.
       "The Telephone Piracies." CharR (10:2) Aut 84, p.
       65-70.
       "Woman's Tongue" (Barbados, Summer 1981). SewanR
       (92:3) Jl-S 84, p. 351-354.

3045. LIEBMAN, Maura
       "Closing the Door." Bogg (52) 84, p. 12.

3046. LIETZ, Robert
       "Autumn after a Lean Year." Epoch (33:2) Spr-Sum
       84, p. 128.
       "In a Late Hour." Epoch (33:2) Spr-Sum 84, p. 129.
       "The Island." CharR (10:1) Spr 84, p. 58-59.
       "Sledding in October." MemphisSR (4:2) Spr 84, p.
       24-25.
       "State of Shock." Tendril (17) Wint 84, p. 118-119.
       "Thanksgiving Week, 1982." CharR (10:1) Spr 84,
       p. 60-61.
       "Wyoming at the Midpoint." CharR (10:1) Spr 84,
       p. 59-60.

3047. LIFSHIN, Lyn
       "II-Damaged Madonna." WindO (44) Sum-Aut 84, p. 6.
       "1040 Madonna." Bogg (52) 84, p. 7, 13.
       "Adirondack Sunday " CrabCR (2:1) Sum 84, p. 3.
       "After the Fog." Amelia (1:2) O 84, p. 68.
       "After the Sixth Day." AntigR (57) Spr 84, p. 136.
       "Ballet Class." GreenfR (11:1/2) Sum-Aut 83, p. 62.
       "Barnstable Two Years Ago." NewL (50:4) Sum 84,
       p. 48.
       "Before the Stationery Store in the Mall Opens."
       NegC (4:2) Spr 84, p. 26.
       "Blarney Stone." SanFPJ (7:1) 84, p. 57.
       "Bobby Sands Is Dead." SanFPJ (7:1) 84, p. 60.
       "Branches Tangling." RagMag (3:1) Spr 84, p. 16.
       "The Cat in the Tall Grass off Balltown." GreenfR
       (11:1/2) Sum-Aut 83, p. 54.
       "Cherry Blossoms The." Abraxas (29/30) 84, p. 38.

"Damaged Madonna." <u>WindO</u> (44) Sum-Aut 84, p. 5.
"Damaged Madonna." <u>WormR</u> (24:4, issue 96) 84, p.
    152.
"Dandruff Madonna." <u>WormR</u> (24:4, issue 96) 84, p.
    153.
"Deep Radiation." <u>GreenfR</u> (11:1/2) Sum-Aut 83, p.
    66.
"The Dream after Friday." <u>OroM</u> (2:3/4, issue 7/8)
    84, p. 45.
"Elaine." <u>CalQ</u> (23/24) Spr-Sum 84, p. 46-47.
"Eyestrain Madonna." <u>WormR</u> (24:1, issue 93) 84,
    p. 12.
"Fat Madonna." <u>WormR</u> (24:1, issue 93) 84, p. 12.
"Fog Madonna." <u>WormR</u> (24:4, issue 96) 84, p. 153.
"For an Anthology of Masochistic Writing." <u>Open24</u>
    (3) 84, p. 17.
"Hangover Madonna." <u>WormR</u> (24:1, issue 93) 84, p.
    12.
"He Says You Know If You Don't Go to." <u>WormR</u>
    (24:4, issue 96) 84, p. 152.
"He Thinks He's a Teddy Bear Blue Blues." <u>WormR</u>
    (24:4, issue 96) 84, p. 151.
"Hot September Madonna." <u>WormR</u> (24:1, issue 93)
    84, p. 12.
"The Hotel Lifshin." <u>WormR</u> (24:4, issue 96) 84,
    p. 152.
"The Hotel Lifshin." <u>YetASM</u> (3) 84, p. 5.
"The Hotel Lifshin Is Raising Its Rates." <u>WormR</u>
    (24:1, issue 93) 84, p. 11.
"I Was Four, in Dotted." <u>HiramPoR</u> (37) Aut-Wint
    84, p. 29.
"In a Notebook from Paris." <u>AmerPoR</u> (13:4) Jl-Ag
    84, p. 28.
"In White Slopes, Snow." <u>HiramPoR</u> (36) Spr-Sum
    84, p. 26.
"It Was Like." <u>WormR</u> (24:1, issue 93) 84, p. 11.
"It Was Like Hearing." <u>WormR</u> (24:1, issue 93) 84,
    p. 11.
"Kent State 1970." <u>WormR</u> (24:4, issue 96) 84, p.
    151.
"Kent State May 1970." <u>SanFPJ</u> (6:1) 84, p. 94.
"Like the Butterfly on the Kitchen Ledge,
    Steepletop." <u>Abraxas</u> (31/32) 84, p. 54.
"Madonna Drawn to Difficult Men." <u>WormR</u> (24:4,
    issue 96) 84, p. 153.
"Madonna of the Imagined." <u>WindO</u> (44) Sum-Aut 84,
    p. 5.
"Madonna of the Love Lorn." <u>WormR</u> (24:4, issue
    96) 84, p. 152.
"Madonna of the Manuscripts." <u>WormR</u> (24:4, issue
    96) 84, p. 152.
"Madonna of the Married Man." <u>WindO</u> (44) Sum-Aut
    84, p. 7.
"Madonna of the Performance." <u>WormR</u> (24:4, issue
    96) 84, p. 152.
"Madonna Who Attracts Strangeness thru the Mail."
    <u>WormR</u> (24:4, issue 96) 84, p. 153.
"Madonna Who Fixes Neon Lights." <u>WormR</u> (24:4,
    issue 96) 84, p. 153.
"Madonna Who Thinks of Herself." <u>WormR</u> (24:4,

issue 96) 84, p. 153.
"Madonna with the Mother." WormR (24:4, issue 96)
    84, p. 152.
"May 4 1982." WindO (44) Sum-Aut 84, p. 6.
"Millay Hearing the News." GreenfR (11:1/2) Sum-
    Aut 83, p. 58-59.
"My Sister in Dripping Pines and Yes and Maples."
    AntiqR (57) Spr 84, p. 135.
"New Mexico Thru Blue Dust 32." GreenfR
    (11:1/2) Sum-Aut 83, p. 60.
"Night Slipping from Me." Bogg (52) 84, p. 4.
"On Mornings Like This." WormR (24:1, issue 93)
    84, p. 11.
"The Party." WindO (44) Sum-Aut 84, p. 7.
"Peter Kaplan." WormR (24:4, issue 96) 84, p. 151.
"Pied Piper of the Midwest." WormR (24:1, issue
    93) 84, p. 11.
"The Poem Machine." CalQ (23/24) Spr-Sum 84, p.
    47-48.
"Rensselaer." CrabCR (2:1) Sum 84, p. 3.
"She Said It Was Overnight." GreenfR (11:1/2) Sum-
    Aut 83, p. 70-71.
"Sometimes the Journal Has the Same." WormR
    (24:1, issue 93) 84, p. 12.
"Somewhere near Manning Blvd." WormR (24:1, issue
    93) 84, p. 12.
"Steeple Top The Forties." GreenfR (11:1/2) Sum-
    Aut 83, p. 56.
"Steepletop." GreenfR (11:1/2) Sum-Aut 83, p. 68.
"This Man Owns the Pickled Head of Legendary
    Mustachioed Bandit." CapeR (19:2) Sum 84, p.
    40-41.
"This Relationship Like Starting Ballet." WindO
    (44) Sum-Aut 84, p. 6.
"Those Cool Mornings." NegC (4:2) Spr 84, p. 24-25.
"Thru Blue Dust New Mexico 13." GreenfR
    (11:1/2) Sum-Aut 83, p. 64.
"When He Said His Wife Expected Him to Perform."
    WormR (24:1, issue 93) 84, p. 12.
"Writing All Night." GreenfR (11:1/2) Sum-Aut 83,
    p. 49-50.
"Writing Block Workshop and Single's Club."
    Open24 (3) 84, p. 17.
"Writing the Night Out of Me." WormR (24:4, issue
    96) 84, p. 151.
"You Take for Granted." MinnR (N.S. 23) Aut 84,
    p. 86-87.
"Zipper Magazine." Open24 (3) 84, p. 17.

3048. LIFSHITZ, Leatrice
    "Haiku: A Sequence." StoneC (11:3/4) Spr-Sum 84,
        p. 36.

3049. LIFSON, Martha
    "Dream / Embrace." Sulfur (3:3, issue 9) 84, p. 121.
    "From the Ironic Marriage Sequence: Dialogue."
        Sulfur (3:3, issue 9) 84, p. 123.
    "Her Love Changes It for Me." Sulfur (3:3, issue
        9) 84, p. 122.
    "Still Life" (by Willem Claesz Heda). Sulfur

(3:3, issue 9) 84, p. 120.

3050. LIGI
       "The Bottle." Abraxas (31/32) 84, p. 26.
       "I Read Once That." MinnR (N.S. 22) Spr 84, p. 30.
       "Problem Solving." Agni (21) 84, p. 97-98.

3051. LIGNELL, Kathleen
       "The Honeymoon." NewL (51:1) Aut 84, p. 24.
       "Red Trains." NewL (51:1) Aut 84, p. 24-25.

3052. LILBURN, Geoffrey R.
       "Australian Epiphany." ChrC (101:40) 19-26 D 84,
          p. 1198.

3053. LILBURNE, Geoffrey R.
       "Alan." Wind (14:52) 84, p. 32-33.
       "The Neighborhood: Five Years Later." Waves
          (12:1) Aut 83, p. 46-47.

3054. LILLARD, Charles
       "Certain Calligraphy near Vancouver Island."
          Descant (47, 15:4) Wint 84, p. 15.
       "Death by Water" (In Memoriam: Kelly). Descant
          (47, 15:4) Wint 84, p. 13-14.
       "Encounter, Waldron Island." Descant (47, 15:4)
          Wint 84, p. 16-17.
       "Petroglyph at Tidemark." Descant (47, 15:4) Wint
          84, p. 11-12.

3055. LILLYWHITE, Harvey
       "Below the Sound." GreenfR (12:1/2) Sum-Aut 84,
          p. 120-121.
       "Holding Hard" (for RJ and KD). GreenfR (12:1/2)
          Sum-Aut 84, p. 122.
       "Just Before I Died." PoetryE (15) Aut 84, p. 14.
       "Letter to a Friend." GreenfR (12:1/2) Sum-Aut
          84, p. 123.

3056. LIM, Shirley
       "Woman and Vase." Waves (12:2/3) Wint 84, p. 77.
       "The Worm." Waves (12:2/3) Wint 84, p. 76.

3057. LIMA, José Maria
       "Camaradas del sueño, os reconozco." Mairena
          (5:13) Spr 83, p. 100-101.

3058. LIMA, Robert
       "Cyclical Night" (tr. of Jorge Luis Borges).
          Chelsea (42/43) 84, p. 170-171.

3059. LIMON, Mercedes
       "Como Tantas Otras Veces." Mester (13:1) My 84,
          p. 52-53.
       "Visión del Mundo." Mester (13:1) My 84, p. 54.

3060. LINCOLN, C. Eric
       "Requiem for Malcolm X." Stepping Wint 83, p. 18-19.

3061. LINDEMAN, Jack
        "Sleepyhead." SouthwR (69:3) Sum 84, p. 334.

3062. LINDNER, Carl
        "The Arrow." StoneC (11:3/4) Spr-Sum 84, p. 37.
        "Fire at Night." SouthwR (69:1) Wint 84, p. 77.
        "Going Under." MidAR (4:1) Spr 84, p. 153.
        "Japanese Fishermen Slaughter 1000 Porpoises."
        MidAR (4:1) Spr 84, p. 154.

3063. LINDO, Hugo
        "El Invierno de la Raza." Mund (14:2) 84, p. 20-24.
        "Winter of the Race" (tr. by Elizabeth Gamble
        Miller). Mund (14:2) 84, p. 21-25.

3064. LINDSAY, Frannie
        "Goldfinch." CarolQ (36:2) Wint 84, p. 36.
        "Leaf for April." CarolQ (36:2) Wint 84, p. 34-35.

3065. LINEHAN, Don
        "Birds of Fire" (Selections: Nine Poems). Germ
        (8:2) Aut-Wint 84, p. 6-16.
        "Colour Transfusion." Germ (8:2) Aut-Wint 84, p. 8.
        "Kedge 1983 Evening." Germ (8:2) Aut-Wint 84, p. 16.
        "Mood of the Woods." Germ (8:2) Aut-Wint 84, p. 15.
        "Mornings." Germ (8:2) Aut-Wint 84, p. 14.
        "Poem: In the pool of sky." Germ (8:2) Aut-Wint
        84, p. 13.
        "Poem: The blond-haired children." Germ (8:2) Aut-
        Wint 84, p. 9.
        "Sea Ducks." Germ (8:2) Aut-Wint 84, p. 10.
        "September 10." Germ (8:2) Aut-Wint 84, p. 11.
        "Stillwater." Germ (8:2) Aut-Wint 84, p. 12.

3066. LINEHAN, Donal
        "Inistiogue 1983." AntigR (58) Sum 84, p. 16-17.

3067. LINEHAN, Moira
        "Sentence." BlueBldgs (7) 84, p. 14.

3068. LINSON, Eric
        "The Butcher Shop." PikeF (6) Aut 84, p. 21.

3069. LINTON, Deborah
        "Madame Bovary's Schizophrenia." IndR (7:2) Spr
        84, p. 17.

3070. LIPSCHUTZ, K.
        "America." SanFPJ (6:1) 84, p. 93.
        "Unofficial Advice to Nervous Nellies" (from the
        silver-tongued Choirmaster of the Lemmings Glee
        Club). SanFPJ (6:1) 84, p. 53.

3071. LIPSITZ, David
        "Nobody's Journal." PoeticJ (3) 83, p. 39.
        "Peace of Mind." PoeticJ (4) 83, p. 29.
        "Washington, D. C." PoeticJ (7) 84, p. 31.

3072. LIPSITZ, Lou
        "Big Dogs." Kayak (64) My 84, p. 18.

"Birth of the Bear Clan." <u>SouthernPR</u> (24:2) Aut
    84, p. 43-44.
"Health." <u>Kayak</u> (64) My 84, p. 17.
"Leaving the Psychiatrist's Office." <u>Antaeus</u> (52)
    Apr 84, p. 45-47.
"Metaphor." <u>NewL</u> (50:4) Sum 84, p. 24-25.
"On the Rivalry between Men and Women." <u>NewL</u>
    (50:4) Sum 84, p. 23.
"Song of the Divorced Father." <u>NewL</u> (50:4) Sum
    84, p. 27.
"Understanding." <u>NewL</u> (50:4) Sum 84, p. 24.
"When You Left." <u>NewL</u> (50:4) Sum 84, p. 26.

3073. LIPSKI, Donald
"As boring congressmen discussed energy." <u>PoetryE</u>
    (13/14) Spr-Sum 84, p. 169.
"A boy came down each fine green hill in jumps."
    <u>PoetryE</u> (13/14) Spr-Sum 84, p. 169.
"A budding country doctor." <u>PoetryE</u> (13/14) Spr-
    Sum 84, p. 169.

3074. LISH, Gordon
"The Lesson Which Is Sufficient Unto the Day
    Thereof." <u>WebR</u> (9:2) Wint 85, p. 5-8.

3075. LISOWSKI, Joseph
"Dark Root." <u>Swallow</u> (3) 84, p. 104.
"Stolen Moments." <u>Swallow</u> (3) 84, p. 103.

3076. LITKE, Suzanne
"It's Not Supposed to Happen Here." <u>YetASM</u> (3)
    84, p. 3.

3077. LITTLE, Carl
"Reminder" (Great Cranberry Island, Maine, for
    William Kienbusch, 1914-1980). <u>Hudson</u> (37:4)
    Wint 84-85, p. 569.

3078. LITTLE, Geraldine C.
"Abishag: Recollections in Old Age." <u>LitR</u> (27:2)
    Wint 84, p. 220-221.
"Atropos, Who Carried 'The Abhorred Shears'."
    <u>Shen</u> (35:1) 83-84, p. 85.
"The Breakfast Table, August 5, 1945." <u>NowestR</u>
    (22:1/2) 84, p. 39-40.
"Diptych: In the 'House of Special Purpose,'
    Ekaterinburg, May, 1918." <u>Shen</u> (35:1) 83-84,
    p. 83-85.
"For Jacqueline Du Pré, Cellist Extraordinaire,
    Stricken with Illness. She Will Not Play Again."
    <u>SenR</u> (14:1) 84, p. 61.
"Her Master's Voice." <u>StoneC</u> (12:1/2) Aut-Wint
    84, p. 33.
"Illuminated Page: Kellsian Fragment in the Pine
    Barrens of New Jersey." <u>LitR</u> (28:1) Aut 84, p.
    50-51.
"Journal Entries Written by Light through a
    Princeton Window: Robert Oppenheimer in Late
    Years, on a Visit." <u>NowestR</u> (22:1/2) 84, p. 41-
    42.

"Paris Attic: Marya Sklodovska, Madame Curie."
    SenR (14:1) 84, p. 59-60.
"Shizuka, 12th Century White Dress Dancer:
    Soliloquy." CalQ (23/24) Spr-Sum 84, p. 124-125.
"Snow." StoneC (12:1/2) Aut-Wint 84, p. 33.
"Voices, Greccio, Christmas Eve 1223." LitR
    (27:2) Wint 84, p. 217-219.

3079. LIVESAY, Dorothy
    "Care of the Hand." PoetryCR (5:4) Sum 84, p. 7.

3080. LLAMAZARES, Julio
    "Retrato de Bañista." Mairena (6:18) 84, p. 70.

3081. LLERENA, Edith
    "Siluetas." LindLM (3:1) Ja-Mr 84, p. 31.

LLOSA, Ricardo Pau: See PAU-LLOSA, Ricardo

3082. LLOYD, D. H.
    "Bible Bob Responds to a Jesus Honker." WormR
        (24:2, issue 94) 84, p. 52.
    "Like Father, Like Son." WormR (24:2, issue 94)
        84, p. 53.
    "Phases." WormR (24:2, issue 94) 84, p. 52.
    "Poetry Reading." WormR (24:2, issue 94) 84, p. 52.
    "Reaction to the Poetry Reading." WormR (24:2,
        issue 94) 84, p. 53.
    "Safety Meeting." WormR (24:2, issue 94) 84, p. 52.
    "Valley Poem." WormR (24:2, issue 94) 84, p. 53.

3083. LLOYD, David
    "Perception" (for Gabrielle). AntigR (59) Aut 84,
        p. 97.
    "Plum: For Jessica in Absentia." AntigR (59) Aut
        84, p. 96.

3084. LLOYD, Margaret
    "Fragments" (for my mother). LitR (28:1) Aut 84,
        p. 116-117.

3085. LOCKE, Duane
    "Dark Night in Sirimone." Northeast (Series 3:17)
        Sum 84, p. 19.
    "Eleonora of Toledo." Confr (27/28) 84, p. 242-243.
    "Life Imitates Art." LitR (28:1) Aut 84, p. 68-69.
    "Once More in Assisi." Os (18) 84, p. 5.

3086. LOCKLIN, Gerald
    "Another One that Got Away." WormR (24:1, issue
        93) 84, p. 23.
    "Bea and Orv, Orv and Bea." WormR (24:1, issue
        93) 84, p. 17.
    "Chinatown." WormR (24:1, issue 93) 84, p. 22.
    "The Christian Ministry to the Variously Colored
        Peoples." WormR (24:1, issue 93) 84, p. 21.
    "The Closest Distance Is Seldom Direct." Abraxas
        (31/32) 84, p. 21.
    "Closet Drama Is Not One In Which." WormR (24:1,
        issue 93) 84, p. 25.

"Cockatiel." <u>WormR</u> (24:1, issue 93) 84, p. 18.
"Constructive Criticism, or, Every Atrocity Must
    Have a Silver Lining." <u>Abraxas</u> (31/32) 84, p. 21.
"The Dolphin Market." <u>WormR</u> (24:1, issue 93) 84,
    p. 13-14.
"The Evening's Grading Was Not a Loss." <u>WormR</u>
    (24:1, issue 93) 84, p. 24.
"Father Damien." <u>WormR</u> (24:1, issue 93) 84, p. 23.
"The Fourth Volume of the Snopes Trilogy." <u>WormR</u>
    (24:2, issue 94) 84, p. 79.
"The Good Kid Gets Five Minutes at the Microphone."
    <u>WormR</u> (24:1, issue 93) 84, p. 26.
"Hand-in-Hand in the L.A. Arts Vanguard." <u>WormR</u>
    (24:1, issue 93) 84, p. 22.
"I Think It Was '72." <u>WormR</u> (24:1, issue 93) 84,
    p. 15.
"I'm Afraid She's Right." <u>Abraxas</u> (29/30) 84, p. 63.
"It Should Have Been a Great Week for a Yankee
    Fan." <u>WormR</u> (24:1, issue 93) 84, p. 20.
"It's Probably What Bukowski Likes about
    Beethoven." <u>WormR</u> (24:1, issue 93) 84, p. 19.
"Meeting the Press. <u>WormR</u> (24:1, issue 93) 84, p.
    27.
"My Daughter Is Studying Latin." <u>WormR</u> (24:1,
    issue 93) 84, p. 20.
"The Night Tom Snyder Said Something Intelligent."
    <u>WormR</u> (24:1, issue 93) 84, p. 21.
"No-Lose Proposition." <u>WormR</u> (24:1, issue 93) 84,
    p. 15.
"One Asks Oneself If One Is Losing One's Mind."
    <u>WormR</u> (24:1, issue 93) 84, p. 16.
"Overachievers, or, a Slow News Day." <u>WormR</u>
    (24:1, issue 93) 84, p. 17.
"Patterns." <u>WormR</u> (24:1, issue 93) 84, p. 16.
"Perfect Couple." <u>WormR</u> (24:1, issue 93) 84, p. 28.
"Poem: I thought I'd finally won an argument."
    <u>Bogg</u> (52) 84, p. 6.
"Reciprocal Solidarity." <u>WormR</u> (24:1, issue 93)
    84, p. 14.
"Respecting Our Betters." <u>WormR</u> (24:1, issue 93)
    84, p. 18.
"Reversing Fields." <u>WormR</u> (24:1, issue 93) 84, p.
    16.
"Shit." <u>WormR</u> (24:1, issue 93) 84, p. 25.
"So Few of Us Continue to Grow." <u>WormR</u> (24:1,
    issue 93) 84, p. 26.
"Social Security." <u>WormR</u> (24:1, issue 93) 84, p. 25.
"Spousal Support." <u>WormR</u> (24:2, issue 94) 84, p.
    78-79.
"Turkey Day Indeed." <u>WormR</u> (24:1, issue 93) 84,
    p. 27.
"Untrained Bear on a Vicious Cycle." <u>Bogg</u> (52)
    84, p. 14.
"Where Have the Great Sandbaggers Gone?" <u>WormR</u>
    (24:1, issue 93) 84, p. 24.
"Whip without Carrot." <u>WormR</u> (24:2, issue 94) 84,
    p. 79.
"Why Our Species Has Survived." <u>WormR</u> (24:2,
    issue 94) 84, p. 79.
"The Wild Bunch." <u>WormR</u> (24:1, issue 93) 84, p. 19.

"Will You Please Turn Off That Other Guy's Poem and
     Listen to Mine!" WormR (24:1, issue 93) 84,
     p. 18.
"Yeah, I'm the Guy in the Overcoat Ogling Minnie
     Mouse." Abraxas (29/30) 84, p. 62.

3087. LOCKLIN, Gerry
     "At Eleven My Son's Still Awake." OroM (2:3/4,
         issue 7/8) 84, p. 50.

3088. LOEB, Joan H.
     "Charlotte on the Coldest Day of the Year."
         DekalbLAJ (20th Anniversary Issue) 84, p. 96.

3089. LOGAN, John
     "Dawn and a Woman." Chelsea (42/43) 84, p. 264-265.
     "Day in the Sun" (for Stephen Logan). NewL
         (50:2/3) Wint-Spr 84, p. 108-109.
     "Gallery Walk" (Fifteen Italian Drawings 1780-
         1890). GreenfR (11:1/2) Sum-Aut 83, p. 1-5.
     "Manhattan Movements." MemphisSR (4:2) Spr 84, p.
         5-6.
     "Spirit of the Dead Watching." (After Gauguin).
         NewL (50:4) Sum 84, p. 62.
     "Staying Awake" (For Tom Lucas). Iowa (14:3) Aut
         84, p. 10.

3090. LOGAN, Lester
     "Water." PoeticJ (7) 84, p. 15.

3091. LOGAN, William
     "The Air of Cathedrals." Agni (21) 84, p. 17-18.
     "Anglian Music." Agni (21) 84, p. 15-16.
     "August in the Straits." ParisR (26:94) Wint 84,
         p. 169-170.
     "Babies." Agni (21) 84, p. 13-14.
     "Capability Brown in the Tropics." YaleR (74:1)
         Aut 84, p. 30.
     "Folly." SewanR (92:1) Ja-Mr 84, p. 62.
     "Green Island." SewanR (92:1) Ja-Mr 84, p. 63.
     "Horace." Nat (238:17) 5 My 84, p. 556.
     "The King of Black Pudding." Nat (239:10) 6 O 84,
         p. 322.
     "Moorhen." GrandS (4:1) Aut 84, p. 89-90.
     "The North Atlantic." NewYorker (60:32) 24 S 84,
         p. 52.
     "The Rivers of England." Agni (21) 84, p. 12.
     "The Shootist." Agni (20) 84, p. 5-8.

LOMAWYWESA: See KABOTIE, Michael

3092. LONDON, Jonathan
     "The Alligator Lady." WormR (24:2, issue 94) 84,
         p. 54.
     "The Carney Boy." WormR (24:2, issue 94) 84, p. 54.
     "The Carney King." WormR (24:2, issue 94) 84, p. 54.
     "Grey Fox." KanQ (16:1/2) Wint-Spr 84, p. 216-217.
     "The Ugliest Man in the World." WormR (24:2,
         issue 94) 84, p. 53.

3093. LONG, Charla
       "Kinship." PoeticJ (6) 84, p. 3.

3094. LONG, Charlotte Joyce
       "Ship for Curt." PoeticJ (3) 83, p. 19.

3095. LONG, Richard
       "Gifts." NegC (4:1) Wint 84, p. 37-38.
       "Matter of Poultry." SouthernPR (24:1) Spr 84, p.
       67-68.

3096. LONG, Robert
       "Cairo" (for Daniel Wolfe Levowitz). Tendril (17)
       Wint 84, p. 120.
       "Dreaming." Poetry (144:4) Jl 84, p. 209-210.
       "Hot Air." Poetry (144:4) Jl 84, p. 210.
       "Perfect Sunset." Poetry (144:4) Jl 84, p. 211.
       "What Happens." Kayak (64) My 84, p. 47.

3097. LONG, Robert Hill
       "Piece by Piece." Pig (12) 84, p. 50.
       "The Visitor." SenR (14:2) 84, p. 57.

3098. LONG, Virginia
       "The Winter of Our Divorce." Amelia (1:2) O 84,
       p. 77.

LONGCHAMPS, Joanne de: See De LONGCHAMPS, Joanne

LOO, Katie Wong: See SUI-YUN

3099. LOONEY, George
       "Artificial Lights" (for Leesa). TexasR (5:3/4)
       Aut-Wint 84, p. 101-103.
       "Birds." IndR (7:2) Spr 84, p. 43.
       "In the Shadow" (tr. of Dámaso Alonso, w. Robert
       Early and Mairi Meredith). MidAR (4:1) Spr 84,
       p. 83.
       "The Life of Man" (tr. of Dámaso Alonso, w.
       Robert Early and Mairi Meredith). MidAR (4:1)
       Spr 84, p. 85, 87.
       "Man" (tr. of Dámaso Alonso, w. Robert Early and
       Mairi Meredith). MidAR (4:1) Spr 84, p. 81.
       "A Man in the Company of Himself" (from Hijos de
       la Ira, tr. of Dámaso Alonso, w. Robert Early
       and Mairi Meredith. Translation Chapbook Series,
       Number One). MidAR (4:1) Spr 84, p. 79-102.
       "Misleading." TarRP (24:1) Aut 84, p. 14.
       "Monsters" (tr. of Dámaso Alonso, w. Robert Early
       and Mairi Meredith). MidAR (4:1) Spr 84, p.
       89, 91.
       "Myself" (tr. of Dámaso Alonso, w. Robert Early
       and Mairi Meredith). MidAR (4:1) Spr 84, p. 101.
       "Navigation without Numbers" (after a photograph by
       Wynn Bullock). MissR (37/38, 13:1/2) Aut 84,
       p. 88-91.
       "The Soul Is a Little Green Frog" (tr. of Dámaso
       Alonso, w. Robert Early and Mairi Meredith).
       MidAR (4:1) Spr 84, p. 97, 99.
       "To the Mite" (tr. of Dámaso Alonso, w. Robert

Early and Mairi Meredith). MidAR (4:1) Spr 84,
p. 93, 95.
"To the Victor." BlueBldgs (8) 84?, p. 33.

3100. LOOTS, Barbara
"The Whole Story" (for Sam and Agatha). Wind
(14:52) 84, p. 34.

3101. LOPES, Michael
"Metal Detectors." KanQ (16:1/2) Wint-Spr 84, p.
138.

LOPEZ, Antonio Dávila: See DAVILA LOPEZ, Antonio

LOPEZ, Hilda R. Mundo: See MUNDO LOPEZ, Hilda R.

3102. LOPEZ, Julio César
"Goteras en el Buzon." Mairena (5:14) Aut 83, p.
34-36.
"Goteras en el Buzon." Mairena (6:16) Spr 84, p.
43-46.
"La Mano." Mairena (6:17) Aut 84, p. 76.
"Mi Casa." Mairena (5:13) Spr 83, p. 63.

3103. LOPEZ, Nila
"Revirtiendo." Mairena (6:18) 84, p. 193.

3104. LOPEZ-ADORNO, Pedro
"Donde Vallejo Le Habla entre Sueños al Que
Escribe." Mairena (6:17) Aut 84, p. 69.

3105. LOPEZ FERNANDEZ, Alvaro
"Palabra mineral." Mairena (6:17) Aut 84, p. 92.

LOPEZ FLORES, Margarita: See FLORES, Margarita Lopez

3106. LOPEZ SURIA, Violeta
"Concha Meléndez, el olvido no existe." SinN
(14:2) Ja-Mr 84, p. 99-100.
"Rapto del Lapiz." Mairena (5:13) Spr 83, p. 70-71.
"Recordacion." SinN (14:2) Ja-Mr 84, p. 100-101.

3107. LOPOZYKO, Danuta
"Instinctive Self-Portrait" (tr. of Miron
Białoszdwski, w. Peter Harris). LitR (28:1)
Aut 84, p. 130.
"No Smoking" (tr. Wiesław Kazanecki, w. Peter
Harris). LitR (28:1) Aut 84, p. 132.
"The Pain" (tr. of Marek Wawrzykiewicz, w. Peter
Harris). LitR (28:1) Aut 84, p. 133.
"Young Faustus Visits the Institute of Oncology and
Does Research on Experience" (tr. of Jerzy
Gorzanski, w. Peter Harris). LitR (28:1) Aut
84, p. 131.

3108. LORCA, Federico García
"Llanto por Ignacio Sanchez Mejias." AmerPoR
(13:4) Jl-Ag 84, p. 32.
"Murió al Amanecer" (with music by Paul Bowles).
Chelsea (42/43) 84, p. 394-395.

3109. LORENZO, Rafael
    "Forensic Geography" (for James Sherry). Sulfur
    (3:3, issue 9) 84, p. 137-139.
    "Toy Store." Sulfur (3:3, issue 9) 84, p. 136-137.

3110. LOTT, Clarinda Harriss
    "Aunt Ritta." Open24 (3) 84, p. 37.
    "Couples." LitR (27:2) Wint 84, p. 225-226.
    "The Episcopal Squat." Vis (16) 84, p. 26.
    "The Innocent." Vis (16) 84, p. 25.
    "The Language of Rust." LitR (27:2) Wint 84, p. 224.
    "Soup." Open24 (3) 84, p. 37.
    "Stabat Mater." Open24 (3) 84, p. 38.

3111. LOTT, Rick
    "The Gift." PoetL (79:1) Spr 84, p. 30.
    "In the World." Pig (12) 84, p. 82.
    "Terminations." BlueBldgs (7) 84, p. 26.

3112. LOUTHAN, Robert
    "Something You Want." ParisR (26:94) Wint 84, p.
    176.

3113. LOUYS, Pierre
    "L'Abre." YellowS (12) Aut 84, p. 10.
    "Bilitis" (in French). YellowS (12) Aut 84, p. 11.
    "Bilitis" (tr. by Frederick Lowe). YellowS (12)
    Aut 84, p. 11.
    "Bucoliques en Pamphylie" (Selections in French
    with English tr. by Frederick Lowe). YellowS
    (12) Aut 84, p. 10-11.
    "Chanson." YellowS (12) Aut 84, p. 10.
    "Song" (tr. by Frederick Lowe). YellowS (12) Aut
    84, p. 11.
    "The Tree" (tr. by Frederick Lowe). YellowS (12)
    Aut 84, p. 10.

3114. LOVE, Sharri
    "At 47." PoeticJ (2) 83, p. 6.
    "Last State." PoeticJ (1) 83, p. 22.
    "Marshal Jim" (Jim Rea, 1876-1960). PoeticJ (2)
    83, p. 16.

3115. LOVITT, Swep
    "Somewhere in Tennessee." SmPd (21:2) Spr 84, p. 30.

3116. LOW, Jackson Mac
    "Giant Otters" Sulfur (4:1, issue 10) 84, p. 80.
    "The Pronouns--A Collection of 40 Dances--For the
    Dancers" (Selections: 1st Dance--Making Things
    New. 2nd Dance--Seeing Lines. 4th Dance--Being a
    Brother to Someone). Chelsea (42/43) 84, p. 142-
    143.
    "The Psychological Aspects of the Threat of Nuclear
    War." Sulfur (4:1, issue 10) 84, p. 80-81.

3117. LOWE, Frederick
    "Back by the Spring." BelPoJ (35:1) Aut 84, p. 2-3.
    "Bilitis" (tr. of Pierre Louÿs). YellowS (12)
    Aut 84, p. 11.

"Bucoliques en Pamphylie" (Selections in French with English tr. of Pierre Louÿs). YellowS (12) Aut 84, p. 10-11.
"Rhenane: Les Cloches" (from Alcools, tr. of Guillaume Apollinaire). YellowS (13) Wint 84, p. 41.
"Song" (tr. of Pierre Louÿs). YellowS (12) Aut 84, p. 11.
"The Tree" (tr. of Pierre Louÿs). YellowS (12) Aut 84, p. 10.
"Wet, Winter Dream in Machias, Maine." YellowS (12) Aut 84, p. 17.

3118. LOWE, Jonathan E.
"Apology." Wind (14:50) 84, p. 22.

3119. LOWELL, Robert
"Ford Madox Ford" (1873-1938). Shen (35:2/3) 84, p. 135.
"Our Afterlife" (For Peter Taylor). Shen (35:2/3) 84, p. 387-389.

3120. LOWENSTEIN, Robert
"Blank Epitaph." Poem (52) N 84, p. 40.
"Boys' Day." Sam (41:1, release 161) 84, p. 30.
"The Chess Master." Poem (52) N 84, p. 39.
"The Potter." Poem (50) Mr 84, p. 16.
"Scavengers." Wind (14:51) 84, p. 4.

3121. LOWEY, Mark
"Having Left." CrossC (6:1) 84, p. 14.

3122. LOWRY, Betty
"The Sea Witch." DekalbLAJ (17:1/2) 84, p. 136.

3123. LOWRY, Charlene
"Wolf Woman Dream." Calyx (8:2) Spr 84, p. 81.

3124. LOWRY, John
"Between the Acts." WormR (24:2, issue 94) 84, p. 44.
"Bulletins." Writ (16) Aut 84, p. 64-65.
"Cold Front." WormR (24:2, issue 94) 84, p. 43.
"Dry Run." WormR (24:2, issue 94) 84, p. 43.
"Laying On of Hands." WormR (24:2, issue 94) 84, p. 44.
"Motion Picture. WormR (24:2, issue 94) 84, p. 41.
"Situation Normal." WormR (24:2, issue 94) 84, p. 42.
"Stay Out of the Fun House." WormR (24:2, issue 94) 84, p. 42.
"Things Are Tough All Over." WormR (24:2, issue 94) 84, p. 42-43.

3125. LOWRY, Mary Ann
"Circulation." Wind (14:52) 84, p. 9.

3126. LU, Pei Wu
"Burning the Wasteland Grass" (tr. of Ai Qing, w. George Venn). NowestR (22:3) 84, p. 104.

"Fish Fossil" (tr. of Ai Qing, w. George Venn).
    NowestR (22:3) 84, p. 101.
"Hail" (tr. of Ai Qing, w. George Venn). NowestR
    (22:3) 84, p. 102.
"Persian Chrysanthemums" (tr. of Ai Qing, w. George
    Venn). NowestR (22:3) 84, p. 103.

3127. LUBETSKY, Elsen
    "Darling, We Are Growing Older." PoeticJ (8) 84,
        p. 31.
    "Drowning in Shallow Time." PoeticJ (3) 83, p. 38.
    "Goodbye to a Wide Narrow World." SanFPJ (6:2)
        84, p. 32.
    "In Your Blood." SanFPJ (6:2) 84, p. 29.
    "Music of a Sphere." PoeticJ (6) 84, p. 15.
    "Paradise Offed." SanFPJ (6:2) 84, p. 48.
    "Playing Cards with the Bees." PoeticJ (8) 84, p.
        24.
    "Rachel at Two Months." PoeticJ (7) 84, p. 27.
    "Step to the Tune of Extinction." SanFPJ (6:1)
        84, p. 69.
    "Thimbleful of Hope." SanFPJ (6:2) 84, p. 30.
    "War No More." SanFPJ (6:2) 84, p. 31.

3128. LUCAS, Barbara
    "Now That I'm Past Forty." HiramPoR (37) Aut-Wint
        84, p. 34.

3129. LUCINA, Mary, Sister
    "Bird." AntiqR (58) Sum 84, p. 13.
    "I Asked Hoping." AntiqR (58) Sum 84, p. 14.
    "Mining." Amelia (1:2) O 84, p. 12.

3130. LUDVIGSON, Susan
    "Love." SouthernPR (24:2) Aut 84, p. 28.
    "The Soul." SouthernPR (24:2) Aut 84, p. 29.
    "Trying to Come to Terms." VirQR (60:1) Wint 84,
        p. 60-61.

3131. LUDWIN, Peter
    "Hitting." Sam (41:1, release 161) 84, p. 28.
    "Hollis." Sam (41:1, release 161) 84, p. 17.
    "Still Life." Sam (41:2, release 162) 84 or 85,
        p. 25.

3132. LUEDERS, Edward
    "Air Raid" (tr. of Sachiko Yoshihara, w. Naoshi
        Koriyama). Poetry (143:6) Mr 84, p. 320.
    "Guerrilla's Fantasy" (tr. of Kio Kuroda, w. Naoshi
        Koriyama). Poetry (143:6) Mr 84, p. 321-322.

3133. LUHRMANN, Thomas
    "Limbo." Pequod (16/17) 84, p. 232.

3134. LUKAS, John
    "Six Paragraphs for Modern Living." CalQ (25) Aut
        84, p. 59-61.

3135. LUKAS, Susan Gimignani
    "Replacements." Sam (39:1, release 153) 84, p. 21.

3136. LUKE, Hugh
"Bequest." _Peb_ (23) 84, p. 45-46.

3137. LUMPKIN, Kenneth C.
"American Effigy." _SanFPJ_ (6:3) 84, p. 13-14.
"For Men Only." _SanFPJ_ (6:3) 84, p. 16.
"To Him, before the Flood." _SanFPJ_ (6:3) 84, p. 73.

3138. LUND, Mark
"Breakfast Station." _Quarry_ (33:1) Wint 84, p. 16.
"Mellon Tree." _Quarry_ (33:1) Wint 84, p. 15.
"Rags 'n' Tatters." _Quarry_ (33:1) Wint 84, p. 15-16.

3139. LUNDE, David
"Archaeology." _Veloc_ (4) Sum 84, p. 13.
"Night Songs." _NegC_ (4:3) Sum 84, p. 103.

3140. LUNDIN, Anne
"Freeing the Figure from Stone" (Michaelangelo).
EngJ (73:1) Ja 84, p. 80.

3141. LUNDIN, Judith
"Cereal." _Vis_ (14) 84, p. 39.

3142. LUNN, Jean
"Reading a Sequence of Love Poems." _StoneC_
(11:3/4) Spr-Sum 84, p. 42.

3143. LUPACK, Alan
"At a Performance of Tomaszewski's Knights of King
Arthur." _ThirdW_ (2) Spr 84, p. 78.

3144. LUSCHEI, Glenna
"Throwing Away My Shoes in Tokyo." _NegC_ (4:2) Spr
84, p. 32.

3145. LUSH, Richard M.
"After the Fact in San Francisco." _Writ_ (16) Aut
84, p. 45.
"From a Room That's Never Seen Sun." _Writ_ (16)
Aut 84, p. 43.
"In the Middle Kingdom." _Writ_ (16) Aut 84, p. 44.
"Through the Forest-green Fence." _Writ_ (16) Aut
84, p. 42.
"Under the Peak." _Writ_ (16) Aut 84, p. 40-41.

3146. LUSK, Daniel
"Country Life: Yellow." _PaintedB_ (23) Sum 84, p. 5.
"Joy." _Pequod_ (16/17) 84, p. 129-130.

3147. LUTHER, Susan M.
"Rain: Too Much to Say." _KanQ_ (16:4) Aut 84, p. 170.

3148. LUX, Thomas
"Snake Lake." _Atlantic_ (254:6) D 84, p. 116.

3149. LY, Dao Tai
"Pity for Prisoners." _NewL_ (50:2/3) Wint-Spr 84,
p. 233.

3150. LYLE, Steve
"Marginal Writer." EngJ (73:5) S 84, p. 26.

3151. LYLES, Peggy Willis
"Illusions." BlueBldgs (7) 84, p. 21.

3152. LYNCH, Jack
"1984." SanFPJ (7:1) 84, p. 49-51.

3153. LYNCH, Tamiko
"Communion." MidAR (4:2) Aut 84, p. 123.
"Sacrifice." MidAR (4:1) Spr 84, p. 157.

3154. LYNCH, Thomas
"Learning Gravity" (Excerpts, for Julie Tata
Young). Agni (20) 84, p. 46-48.
"Weekend in the Poconos." HiramPoR (36) Spr-Sum
84, p. 27.

3155. LYNCH, Thomas P.
"Marriage." QW (18) Spr-Sum 84, p. 48.
"Winterkill." QW (18) Spr-Sum 84, p. 49.

3156. LYNE, Sandford
"The Gold Pavilion." VirQR (60:1) Wint 84, p. 69.
"The Tadpole Pool." VirQR (60:1) Wint 84, p. 69-70.

LYNN, Elizabeth Cook: See COOK-LYNN, Elizabeth

3157. LYNSKEY, Edward C.
"The Bebop Ghosts." KanQ (16:1/2) Wint-Spr 84, p.
153.
"Death of a Madwoman." KanQ (16:1/2) Wint-Spr 84,
p. 154.
"True Form: Watery Grave." SmPd (21:3) Aut 84, p.
18.
"Wanted: Regular Love." Wind (14:50) 84, p. 63.

3158. LYON, Adriane R.
"Literary Affair." NegC (4:4) Aut 84, p. 84.

3159. LYON, George Ella
"Conjunction." WoosterR (1:1) Mr 84, p. 47.
"Fat Poem." ColEng (46:3) Mr 84, p. 255.
"Mrs. Bones." NegC (4:2) Spr 84, p. 42-45.
"Mrs. Bones." NegC (4:4) Aut 84, p. 74-76.
"Poem Is a Machine Made Out of Words" (William
Carlos Williams). WoosterR (1:1) Mr 84, p. 46.
"Poultry." PoetC (16:1) Aut 84, p. 41.
"Words, Leaves." PoetC (16:1) Aut 84, p. 40.

3160. LYON, Peggy
"Carp." Vis (14) 84, p. 6.

3161. LYONS, Richard
"Burning Stars" (Prizewinning Poets--1984). Nat
(238:18) 12 My 84, p. 580.
"DogDog." Chelsea (42/43) 84, p. 293.

3162. LYONS, Theresa
"When He Comes Home." PoetryE (15) Aut 84, p. 27.
"Winter Coming." PoetryE (15) Aut 84, p. 28.

3163. LYTLE, Leslie
"One on One." GeoR (38:2) Sum 84, p. 321-322.

MA'ARRI, al-: See Al-MA'ARRI

MAC . . .: See also names beginning with Mc . . .

MAC LOW, Jackson: See LOW, Jackson Mac

3164. MacAFEE, Norman
"Poet Assassinated" (after a photograph of Pasolini
at the site of his death). MinnR (N.S. 23) Aut
84, p. 112.

3165. MacBAIN, Walter D.
"House Party." Bogg (52) 84, p. 18-19.

3166. MacDIARMID, Hugh
"To Most of My Contemporaries." NewL (50:2/3)
Wint-Spr 84, p. 183.
"The Unicorn." NewL (50:2/3) Wint-Spr 84, p. 183.
"The Watergaw." SouthernR (20:2) Spr 84, p. 266.

3167. MacDONALD, Bernell
"After Raccoon Hunting." PottPort (6) 84, p. 5.
"Pyromania." PottPort (6) 84, p. 22.
"Still Life." PottPort (6) 84, p. 15.

3168. MacDONALD, Cynthia
"Francis Bacon, the Inventor of Spectacles Is the
Ringmaster." Shen (35:2/3) 84, p. 207-210.

3169. MacDOUGALL, Alan
"Lifeboat." PoeticJ (5) 84, p. 5.

3170. MacDUFFEE, Allison
"The News." Quarry (33:4) Aut 84, p. 58.

3171. MacEWEN, Gwendolyn
"Barker Fairley and the Blizzard." CanLit (100)
Spr 84, p. 206.

3172. MacFARLANE, Richard
"Quantum Quatrains." SanFPJ (6:1) 84, p. 13.
"The Relative Rubaiyat." SanFPJ (6:1) 84, p. 13.

MACHAN AAL, Katharyn: See AAL, Katharyn Machan

3173. MacINNES, Mairi
"Evening on the Estuary, Noon at Sea" (for
Estéban Vicente, painter, on his eightieth
birthday). LitR (28:1) Aut 84, p. 67.
"The Roman Road near Braich, Wales." LitR (28:1)
Aut 84, p. 66-67.

3174. MACKEY, Gerald
     "In Defense of Holden Caulfield: Censored for Being
     Obscene." EngJ (73:5) S 84, p. 58.

3175. MACKEY, Mary
     "Chamber Music". YellowS (11) Sum 84, p. 28.
     "Hibernating at High Elevations." YellowS (10)
     Spr 84, p. 10.
     "Hike." YellowS (10) Spr 84, p. 10.
     "Turning and Turning in My Arms. YellowS (11) Sum
     84, p. 28.

3176. MACKEY, Nathaniel
     "Bedouin Wind." Callaloo (20, 7:1) Wint 84, p. 79-
     80.
     "Maitresse Erzulie." Callaloo (20, 7:1) Wint 84,
     p. 81.

3177. MACKLIN, Cerene
     "Convalescent Home." HangL (45) Spr 84, p. 64.

3178. MACKLIN, Elizabeth
     "All Over." NewYorker (59:49) 23 Ja 84, p. 40.
     "A Woman at Ground Zero." MinnR (N.S. 23) Aut 84,
     p. 12-13.

3179. MACLAGAN, David
     "Pounding and Gism" (from Suppots et
     Supplications: Interjections, tr. of Antonin
     Artaud, w. A. James Arnold and Clayton
     Eshleman). Sulfur (3:3, issue 9) 84, p. 38-42.
     "Suppots et Supplications" (Selections, tr. of
     Antonin Artaud, w. A. James Arnold, David
     Rattray, and Clayton Eshleman). Sulfur (3:3,
     issue 9) 84, p. 15-59.

3180. MacLEOD, Alistair
     "On Hearing of the Death of Alden Nowlan, Early in
     the Morning, June 28, 1983." AntigR (57) Spr
     84, p. 12.

3181. MacLEOD, Kathryn
     "At Booth's Grave." MalR (69) O 84, p. 31-32.
     "Christening" (for the other Kathryn, the child who
     died in a well in Saskatchewan). Grain (12:3)
     Ag 84, p. 8.

MACLOW, Jackson: See LOW, Jackson Mac

3182. MacMILLAN, Sharon
     "Goodbye, Mabel Darlin'." Quarry (33:1) Wint 84,
     p. 17.
     "Shadows of Time." Quarry (33:1) Wint 84, p. 17-19.

3183. MACOMBER, Megan
     "Hart Crane." GreenfR (12:1/2) Sum-Aut 84, p. 193.

3184. MacPHERSON, Allen Roy
     "I Am the Rebel." AntigR (58) Sum 84, p. 90.
     "New Me Emerging." AntigR (58) Sum 84, p. 91.

3185. MACPHERSON, Jay
"Eve in Reflection." NoDaQ (52:3) Sum 84, p. 304.
"She." NoDaQ (52:3) Sum 84, p. 307.
"Some Ghosts and Some Ghouls." NoDaQ (52:3) Sum
84, p. 305.
"They Return." NoDaQ (52:3) Sum 84, p. 306.

3186. MacQUARRIE, Lachlan
"Peepshow: What the Mindreader Saw" (or, An Inquiry
into the Nature of Telepathy and Thought).
PottPort (6) 84, p. 32-33.

3187. MacQUEEN, Don
"Leaving" (for Nadea). PoeticJ (5) 84, p. 16.

3188. MacSWEEN, R. J.
"Because." AntigR (56) Wint 84, p. 51-52.
"Country Evening." AntigR (57) Spr 84, p. 30.
"Once in the Garden." AntigR (57) Spr 84, p. 31.
"Where Are They Gone." AntigR (57) Spr 84, p. 32.

3189. MADDOCK, Mary
"How do I differ from a woman with a flower" (tr.
of Bella Akhmadulina). AmerPoR (13:4) Jl-Ag
84, p. 12.
"Lunatics" (tr. of Bella Akhmadulina). AmerPoR
(13:4) Jl-Ag 84, p. 12.
"Muteness" (tr. of Bella Akhmadulina). AmerPoR
(13:4) Jl-Ag 84, p. 12.

3190. MADDOX, Everette
"Blue Moon of Kentucky" (for Bruce Cassidy). KanQ
(16:1/2) Wint-Spr 84, p. 174.

3191. MADIGAN, Mark
"Faith." CalQ (25) Aut 84, p. 66-67.

3192. MADOFF, Steven Henry
"The Funeral-Goers." Thrpny (19) Aut 84, p. 21.

3193. MADONICK, Michael David
"American Spring." NowestR (22:1/2) 84, p. 140-141.
"The Mind." Epoch (33:2) Spr-Sum 84, p. 150-151.

3194. MADZELAN, Pete
"American Dreaming." SanFPJ (6:3) 84, p. 53.
"Minimum Wage." SanFPJ (6:3) 84, p. 57.

MAGALY QUIÑONEZ, Marta: See QUIÑONEZ, Magaly

3195. MAGARRELL, Elaine
"Last Child." LitR (28:1) Aut 84, p. 108.
"Paperweight." Vis (16) 84, p. 31.
"Refusing the Eye." LitR (28:1) Aut 84, p. 109.

3196. MAGEE, Wes
"Littoral." BelPoJ (35:2) Wint 84-85, p. 16.

3197. MAGNUSSON, Sigurdur A.
"A Child Lost" (tr. by the author). Iowa (14:2)

Spr-Sum 84, p. 169.

3198. MAGOVERN, Susan
"Instructions on Becoming a Tree." MissR (36,
12:3) Spr 84, p. 70.

3199. MAGOWAN, Robin
"Icarus." Kayak (64) My 84, p. 32-33.

3200. MAGUIRE, Robert A.
"December 15, 1979: Dizzy with Success" (tr. of
Stanislaw Baranczak, w. Magnus J. Krynski).
Confr (27/28) 84, p. 19.
"December 19, 1979: Clean Hands" (tr. of Stanislaw
Baranczak, w. Magnus J. Krynski). Confr
(27/28) 84, p. 20.

MAGUT, Mohamed, al-: See Al-MAGUT, Mohamed

3201. MAHAPATRA, Jayanta
"Again the Rain Falls." Hudson (37:2) Sum 84, p.
274.
"Love Fragment" (for Panna). Hudson (37:2) Sum
84, p. 276.
"The Wind." Hudson (37:2) Sum 84, p. 275.

3202. MAHLER, Carol
"Firing Up the Furnace." NegC (4:4) Aut 84, p. 24.

3203. MAHON, Derek
"Ovid in Tomis." Stand (25:1) Wint 83-84, p. 79.

3204. MAHON, Jeanne
"Dingledy." HiramPoR (36) Spr-Sum 84, p. 28-29.

3205. MAHONY, Philip
"Blunt Trauma." Ploughs (10:1) 84, p. 110-112.

3206. MAIERS, Joan
"Power Outage." ThirdW (2) Spr 84, p. 45.

3207. MAILER, Norman
"At the Cathedral of St. Isaac in Leningrad."
PartR (51:4/52:1 Anniversary issue) 84-85, p.
535.

3208. MAINO, Jeannette
"Medea." KanQ (16:1/2) Wint-Spr 84, p. 36.
"Old Wine." KanQ (16:1/2) Wint-Spr 84, p. 37.
"Sing a Song of Hardware." KanQ (16:1/2) Wint-Spr
84, p. 36.

3209. MAISEL, Diane
"Hungry." Sam (39:1, release 153) 84, p. 30.
"The Three Temperaments of Circus Elephants." Sam
(41:1, release 161) 84, p. 29.

3210. MAJOR, Clarence
"Difficulty with Perspective." Callaloo (20, 7:1)
Wint 84, p. 36-38.

"Posing." Callaloo (20, 7:1) Wint 84, p. 32.
"Round Midnight." Callaloo (20, 7:1) Wint 84, p.
  33-35.
"Sexual Conduct." Chelsea (42/43) 84, p. 241.
"Study of a Geographical Trail." Callaloo (21,
  7:2) Spr-Sum 84, p. 72-76.

3211. MAKUCK, Peter
  "See Your Personal Banker." SouthwR (69:3) Sum
    84, p. 260.

3212. MALCOHN, Elissa
  "Every Action Has an Equal and Opposite Reaction."
    Veloc (4) Sum 84, p. 6-7.
  "Holograph Eye." Veloc (3) Aut-Wint 83, p. 9.
  "Running Moebius." Veloc (4) Sum 84, p. 9.
  "Thanksgiving Weekend: Two Rites of Passage"
    (Miami, 1981). Veloc (3) Aut-Wint 83, p. 10-14.

MALE, Belkis Cuza: See CUZA MALE, Belkis

3213. MALIN, Stephen
  "Closet Circus Lady: Epitaph for an Editor"
    (Margaret Hartley 1909-1983). SouthwR (69:1)
    Wint 84, p. 1.

3214. MALLARME, Stéphane
  "A Tomb for Anatole" (Selections: 8, 133, 160, tr.
    by Paul Auster). Pequod (16/17) 84, p. 227-228.

3215. MALLESS, Stan
  "Cape Breton, N.S." (July 1, 1983). AntigR (59)
    Aut 84, p. 7.

3216. MALLINSON, Anna
  "Technology." PoetryCR (6:2) Wint 84-85, p. 16.

3217. MALLORY, Norman
  "Halloween, 1949." AntigR (59) Aut 84, p. 52.

3218. MALLOY, Vivian
  "Reply to Yeats." PoetryE (15) Aut 84, p. 68.

3219. MALONE, Joe
  "Ishtar and the Shepherd-Man" (tr. of anonymous
    Babylonian poem). YellowS (13) Wint 84, p. 39-40.

3220. MALONEY, J. J.
  "The Empty Chair." NewL (50:2/3) Wint-Spr 84, p.
    58-59.

3221. MALONEY, Sally
  "Father." NegC (4:2) Spr 84, p. 52.
  "Mother." NegC (4:2) Spr 84, p. 53.

3222. MALPEZZI, Frances M.
  "Seminar." NegC (4:4) Aut 84, p. 40-41.

3223. MALTMAN, Kim
  "The Technology of the Persistence of Memory."

CanLit (100) Spr 84, p. 212.
"Whiskey." PoetryCR (5:4) Sum 84, p. 15.

3224. MALYON, Carol
"John Calvin and the Gerbils." MalR (67) F 84, p.
110-111.
"My Daughter Asks the Burning Question about God
and Immortality" (WQ Editors' Second Prize
Winner: Poetry). CrossC (6:1) 84, p. 8.

3225. MANCILLA, Yolanda
"Dream for Tía Cuca." Calyx (8:2) Spr 84, p. 11.
"En el Año de la Liberación, In the Year of the
Liberation." Calyx (8:2) Spr 84, p. 14-15.
"Niña." Calyx (8:2) Spr 84, p. 12-13.
"Río Piedras." Calyx (8:2) Spr 84, p. 16.

3226. MANDEL, Charlotte
"Under the Grating." GreenfR (11:1/2) Sum-Aut 83,
p. 170.

3227. MANDEL, Eli
"Wabamun Poems" (York Literary Review version).
PoetryCR (5:4) Sum 84, p. 10-11.

3228. MANDELKER, Barry
"The Death of Albert Einstein." Waves (12:4) Spr
84, p. 54-55.
"The Frog and Box." Grain (12:2) My 84, p. 15.

MANDELSHTAM, Osip: See MANDELSTAM, Osip

3229. MANDELSTAM, Osip
"#51. I have not died yet, nor am I yet alone" (tr.
by Marianne Andrea). Confr (27/28) 84, p. 54.
"84/ In a wild choir of girlish voices, tenderly"
(tr. by Stephen Tapscott). Epoch (33:3) Sum-
Aut 84, p. 261.
"85/ The Floor of the sleigh, packed with fatal
straw" (tr. by Stephen Tapscott). Epoch (33:3)
Sum-Aut 84, p. 262.
"90/ Failing to believe in the Afterlife, that
miracle" (tr. by Stephen Tapscott). Epoch
(33:3) Sum-Aut 84, p. 263.
"118/ We shall meet again in Petersburg" (tr. by
Stephen Tapscott). Epoch (33:3) Sum-Aut 84, p.
264.
"225. After midnight the heart steals" (tr. by
Michael Cole and Karen Kimball). CharR (10:2)
Aut 84, p. 94.
"395. I don't know the woman who searches" (tr. by
Michael Cole and Karen Kimball). CharR (10:2)
Aut 84, p. 94.
"Four Poems for Marina Tsvetaeva, ca 1916" (tr. by
Stephen Tapscott). Epoch (33:3) Sum-Aut 84, p.
260-264.
"The Horseshoe-Finder" (tr. by Amey Miller).
CarolQ (37:1) Aut 84, p. 35-37.
"I saw a lake, and it was standing sheer" (tr. by
R. H. Morrison). LitR (27:3) Spr 84, p. 313.

"In transparent Petropolis we'll die" (tr. by R. H.
    Morrison). LitR (27:3) Spr 84, p. 314.
"The Man Who Found a Horseshoe" (136, tr. by Robert
    Tracy). Ploughs (10:1) 84, p. 102-105.
"Still I have not yet died" (tr. by R. H.
    Morrison). LitR (27:3) Spr 84, p. 314.
"Succor me, O Lord, to live through this night"
    (tr. by R. H. Morrison). LitR (27:3) Spr 84,
    p. 314.
"Tristia" (tr. by Joseph Brodsky). Confr (27/28)
    84, p. 18.
"Upon the altar of the hazy ripples" (tr. by R. H.
    Morrison). LitR (27:3) Spr 84, p. 313.
"We will die in transparent Petropolis" (89, tr. by
    Robert Tracy). Ploughs (10:1) 84, p. 101.

3230. MANES, Christoph
    "Crows at Night." SnapD (6:2) Spr 83, p. 57.

3231. MANGAN, Kathy
    "A Still Life." GeoR (38:1) Spr 84, p. 92.

3232. MANHAE (Han Yong-Woon) (See also HAN, Yong-Woon)
    "Lover to Lover" (tr. by Bruce Taylor). StoneC
    (11:3/4) Spr-Sum 84, p. 26.
    "The Truth" (tr. by Bruce Taylor). StoneC
    (11:3/4) Spr-Sum 84, p. 27.

3233. MANICOM, David
    "After Our Children Had Gone to School." Descant
    (47, 15:4) Wint 84, p. 157.
    "Househusband, 5:30 P.M." Quarry (33:1) Wint 84,
    p. 50.
    "In the Circle." Quarry (33:1) Wint 84, p. 51.
    "Midnight, Doppler." Grain (12:3) Ag 84, p. 19.
    "Mot." Quarry (33:1) Wint 84, p. 50-51.
    "Paying the Rent, 1789-1861" (Bicentennial Contest
    Winners: Honourable Mention). Waves (12:4) Spr
    84, p. 90-91.
    "Signs of Evening." Descant (47, 15:4) Wint 84,
    p. 158.

3234. MANIS, Mike
    "A Woman Gone Mad" (for Inez Moore 1923-1983).
    PoetL (79:1) Spr 84, p. 26.

3235. MANNER, George
    "Among the Powers of Desire." Shen (35:1) 83-84,
    p. 96.
    "What Comes from the Willow at Pondside." Shen
    (35:1) 83-84, p. 97.

3236. MANNES, Marya
    "Satyr." NewL (50:2/3) Wint-Spr 84, p. 244.

3237. MANNING, Lynn
    "My Aunt." Vis (14) 84, p. 6.

3238. MANNING, Nichola
    "Ball/Square." WormR (24:1, issue 93) 84, p. 37.

"The Bus." WormR (24:1, issue 93) 84, p. 35.
"A Coward Dies a Thousand Deaths. WormR (24:1,
    issue 93) 84, p. 37-38.
"Feminist Women's Poetry Reading." Abraxas
    (29/30) 84, p. 27.
"The Girl Who'll Say Anything." WormR (24:4,
    issue 96) 84, p. 129-132.
"A Little Wooden House." WormR (24:1, issue 93)
    84, p. 37.
"Palm Trees." WormR (24:1, issue 93) 84, p. 35.
"Poetic Romance. WormR (24:1, issue 93) 84, p. 35.
"The Respected Poet." Abraxas (29/30) 84, p. 26.
"Three Cars." WormR (24:1, issue 93) 84, p. 36.
"Time Bomb." WormR (24:1, issue 93) 84, p. 36.
"Tomorrow's America." Abraxas (29/30) 84, p. 27.
"Turntabling." WormR (24:1, issue 93) 84, p. 36.

3239. MANSOUR, Joyce
    "Vultures" (Excerpts, tr. by Albert Herzing).
        Chelsea (42/43) 84, p. 276-277.

3240. MARAINI, Dacia
    "Blood of Woman" (tr. by Gerri Gunn). Waves
        (13:1) Aut 84, p. 63.
    "Go Ahead Devour Me Too" (tr. by Genni Gunn).
        Quarry (33:4) Aut 84, p. 50-51.
    "Sangue di Donne." Waves (13:1) Aut 84, p. 62.

3241. MARCELLO, Leo Luke
    "The Rocks in St. Brides Bay." SouthernR (20:1)
        Wint 84, p. 126-127.
    "Times Your Aunt Mary Needs You." Comm (111:17) 5
        O 84, p. 535.
    "Use the Common Present to Report What a Person or
        Thing Does Regularly" (Or Even the Mean Bluejay
        Looking into the Window Cannot Lift the Awning .
        . .). GreenfR (12:1/2) Sum-Aut 84, p. 194-195.
    "Using the Common Future to Report What Will Happen
        under Certain Conditions" (Or Is This One to
        Report What Will Occur Regardless of Human
        Intent?). GreenfR (12:1/2) Sum-Aut 84, p. 196.
    "William Faulkner, Sacred Cow." SouthernR (20:1)
        Wint 84, p. 124-125.

3242. MARCHAND, Millie
    "By the Miner's Grave." CapeR (19:3) 20th
        Anniverary Issue 84, p. 35.

3243. MARCHEWKA-BROWN, Nicole
    "Biographies." RagMag (3:2) Aut 84, p. 21.

3244. MARCUS, Leonard S.
    "The Letter." ManhatR (3:2) Wint 84-85, p. 63-64.

3245. MARCUS, Mordecai
    "Back Then." Amelia (1:2) O 84, p. 44.
    "Desert Days." Poem (51) Mr [i.e. Jl] 84, p. 56.
    "Handling Their Telephone Calls." GreenfR
        (12:1/2) Sum-Aut 84, p. 142.
    "Long Moments." Poem (51) Mr [i.e. Jl] 84, p. 55.

"On Being Asked Why People Rob Banks." GreenfR
(12:1/2) Sum-Aut 84, p. 141.
"Orange and Pear in Sunlight." SouthernPR (24:1)
Spr 84, p. 49-50.

3246. MARCUS, Ron
"April Fool's." Open24 (3) 84, p. 36.
"How to Cope with a Nuclear Attack." Open24 (3)
84, p. 36.

3247. MARCUS, Stanley
"Corporate Meeting." PraS (58:1) Spr 84, p. 77-78.
"Infant Crying." PraS (58:1) Spr 84, p. 75-76.

3248. MARGOLIS, Gary
"And Then Come Back." AntigR (59) Aut 84, p. 33.
"It's True." AntigR (59) Aut 84, p. 34.
"Waiting at the Office of Magritte." NoAmR
(269:2) Je 84, p. 28.
"When Your Shadow Gives Away Your Hand." ColEng
(46:5) S 84, p. 458.

3249. MARGOSHES, Dave
"Sartre Died for Our Sins." Waves (12:1) Aut 83,
p. 67.

3250. MARIANI, Paul
"A Bad Joke." TriQ (61) Aut 84, p. 89-90.
"The Ghost." NewL (50:4) Sum 84, p. 82-83.
"Light Streaming into the Head" (for Vince
DiMarco). TriQ (61) Aut 84, p. 91-93.
"Matadero, Riley & Company." Tendril (17) Wint
84, p. 121-123.
"On the Edge of the Atlantic." Swallow (3) 84, p.
17-18.
"Right and Left." NewEngR (7:1) Aut 84, p. 64.

MARICEVICH, Francisco Perez: See PEREZ MARICEVICH, Francisco

MARIS, Ron de: See De MARIS, Ron

3251. MARKERT, Lawrence
"Standing Mute." Open24 (3) 84, p. 39.

3252. MARKERT, Patricia
"Joan of Arc." AmerPoR (13:1) Ja-F 84, p. 15.
"Novena." AmerPoR (13:1) Ja-F 84, p. 15.

3253. MARKIN, Allan
"Home Movies: Starfish Odyssey." PoetryCR (5:3)
Spr 84, p. 18.
"On Static Cling and Other Things." PoetryCR
(5:4) Sum 84, p. 19.

3254. MARKS, Barry S.
"Long Distance." DekalbLAJ (20th Anniversary
Issue) 84, p. 97.

3255. MARLATT, Daphne
"Climbing the Canyon Even As" (from "Touch to My

Tongue"). <u>Descant</u> (44/45, 15:1/2) Spr-Sum 84,
p. 10.
"Down the Season's Avenue" (from "Touch to My
Tongue"). <u>Descant</u> (44/45, 15:1/2) Spr-Sum 84,
p. 12.
"Prairie" (from "Touch to My Tongue"). <u>Descant</u>
(44/45, 15:1/2) Spr-Sum 84, p. 11.
"Touch to My Tongue" (Selections). <u>Descant</u>
(44/45, 15:1/2) Spr-Sum 84, p. 10-12.
"Touch to My Tongue" (Selections: This Place Full
of Contradiction. Houseless. Where We Went).
<u>CanLit</u> (100) Spr 84, p. 223-224.

3256. MARLIS, Stefanie
"Building." <u>AmerPoR</u> (13:4) Jl-Ag 84, p. 19.
"Revolution." <u>PoetryE</u> (15) Aut 84, p. 49.
"Weapons." <u>Tendril</u> (17) Wint 84, p. 124.

3257. MARQUARDT, Barbara
"She Didn't Have to Kill It." <u>YetASM</u> (3) 84, p. 6.

3258. MARQUEZ, Enrique
"Fear of Words." <u>LindLM</u> (3:1) Ja-Mr 84, p. 15.

3259. MARQUEZ, Robert
"The New Muse" (tr. of Nicolas Guillen). <u>Vis</u> (15)
84, p. 16.
"The Rivers" (tr. of Nicolas Guillen). <u>Vis</u> (15)
84, p. 16.
"The Winds" (tr. of Nicolas Guillen). <u>Vis</u> (15)
84, p. 15.

3260. MARRA, Sue
"I Demand a Nuclear Freeze, But." <u>Bogg</u> (52) 84,
p. 19.
"I Think of an Old Friend." <u>PoeticJ</u> (6) 84, p. 4.
"Moving Day." <u>PoeticJ</u> (8) 84, p. 4.
"Old Friend." <u>PoeticJ</u> (5) 84, p. 37.

3261. MARRA, Susan
"The Egoless Poet." <u>PoeticJ</u> (4) 83, p. 23.
"Glass Fish." <u>PoeticJ</u> (2) 83, p. 7.
"Just a City Writer." <u>PoeticJ</u> (3) 83, p. 18.
"No Memories." <u>PoeticJ</u> (2) 83, p. 30.
"Trapped and Voiceless." <u>PoeticJ</u> (1) 83, p. 31.
"While You Dream." <u>PoeticJ</u> (2) 83, p. 2.

3262. MARRIOTT, Anne
"Anderson Lake at Twilight." <u>Waves</u> (12:1) Aut 83,
p. 44.
"The Black Rocks of Oregon." <u>PoetryCR</u> (6:2) Wint
84-85, p. 9.
"The Danish Sketches" (for Heather Spears.
Excerpts). <u>CanLit</u> (100) Spr 84, p. 225-227.
"Friend." <u>Waves</u> (12:1) Aut 83, p. 45.
"Port Renfrew." <u>NeqC</u> (4:1) Wint 84, p. 68-70.

3263. MARSH, David
"Respectability." <u>RagMag</u> (3:1) Spr 84, p. 29.

3264. MARSH, Donald
        "Respectability." RagMag (3:2) Aut 84, p. 1.

3265. MARSH, Kirk
        "The Graveyard." Wind (14:51) 84, p. 34.
        "Hard Sell." PoeticJ (1) 83, p. 15.

3266. MARSH, Tony
        "We'll Drink a Cup." KanQ (16:3) Sum 84, p. 100.
        "Who But the Moon?" CrabCR (1:3) Wint 84, p. 8.

3267. MARSHALL, J. M.
        "Through Purging Shades of Green Night." KanQ
        (16:1/2) Wint-Spr 84, p. 124-125.

3268. MARSHALL, John
        "Elmhurst Avenue." Dandel (11:1) Spr-Sum 84, p. 71.
        "The Fire Road" (Excerpt). PraF (5:4) Sum 84, p.
        81-83.
        "Winnipeg One." Dandel (11:1) Spr-Sum 84, p. 70.

3269. MARSHALL, Quitman
        "The Moustache Speaks." BlackWR (11:1) Aut 84, p.
        70-71.
        "Toads." BlueBldgs (7) 84, p. 9.

3270. MARSHALL, Tom
        "Dream Sequence: May 17, 1984" (for B.). Descant
        (47, 15:4) Wint 84, p. 134-145.
        "Dreamfields" (Selections: xxii, xxv, xxvi).
        CanLit (100) Spr 84, p. 228-229.
        "Lines for George Whalley." Descant (47, 15:4)
        Wint 84, p. 133.
        "Playing with Fire" (Selections: XVIII, XXVII).
        PoetryCR (6:2) Wint 84-85, p. 10.

MARTIN, Billie Kaiser: See KAISER-MARTIN, Billie

3271. MARTIN, Charles
        "Dido and Aeneas." Poetry (144:3) Je 84, p. 130-131.
        "Lines Freely Taken from Callimachus." Poetry
        (144:3) Je 84, p. 131-132.

3272. MARTIN, Charles Casey
        "Getting Fired." PoetryNW (25:4) Wint 84-85, p.
        18-19.
        "Miss September." PoetryNW (25:4) Wint 84-85, p.
        19-20.
        "Orange Blossom Special." PoetryNW (25:4) Wint 84-
        85, p. 15-17.

3273. MARTIN, Herbert Woodward
        "As the dawn edges." Paunch (57/58) Ja 84, p. 101.
        "Girl, Birds, Wind, Clouds." CentR (28:1) Wint
        84, p. 45.
        "The Revenant" (After the painting by Andrew
        Wyeth). Paunch (57/58) Ja 84, p. 78.

3274. MARTIN, Jennifer
        "The Reign." CarolQ (36:3) Spr 84, p. 31.

3275. MARTIN, Joe
"Cortes Passes Thirty Miles from the Hidden
  Metropolis of Palenque." GreenfR (11:3/4) Wint-
  Spr 84, p. 109-112.
"Visitation with the Past." AntigR (58) Sum 84,
  p. 18.

3276. MARTIN, Lynn
"Come June." PoetryNW (25:4) Wint 84-85, p. 45.
"Elegy for My Parents." PoetryNW (25:4) Wint 84-
  85, p. 45-46.
"The Talk of the Dying." PoetryNW (25:4) Wint 84-
  85, p. 44.

3277. MARTIN, Olivia
"Your Father Is Awake Shaking." NewL (50:2/3)
  Wint-Spr 84, p. 244.

3278. MARTIN, Paul
"Watching the News." Nimrod (28:1) Aut-Wint 84,
  p. 84.

3279. MARTIN, Richard
"By Zero." MidAR (4:2) Aut 84, p. 31.

3280. MARTINDALE, Sheila
"Different Strokes." Bogg (52) 84, p. 40-41.
"Parting gift." Bogg (52) 84, p. 38.

3281. MARTINEZ, Jan
"A Veces." Mairena (6:17) Aut 84, p. 41-42.
"El Bufon de Madera." Mairena (6:17) Aut 84, p. 40.
"Debe Ser." Mairena (6:17) Aut 84, p. 43.
"Ha Muerto la Rosa." Mairena (6:17) Aut 84, p. 40.
"Historia de un Angel." Mairena (6:17) Aut 84, p.
  42.
"Luciernagas." Mairena (6:17) Aut 84, p. 40.
"Moraleja." Mairena (6:17) Aut 84, p. 41.
"El Paraguas." Mairena (6:17) Aut 84, p. 41.
"Pequeño Homenaje a la Mariposa." Mairena
  (6:17) Aut 84, p. 44.
"Los Regalos." Mairena (6:17) Aut 84, p. 45.
"Stereo del Amor Imposible." Mairena (6:17) Aut
  84, p. 46.
"La Tarde." Mairena (6:17) Aut 84, p. 43.
"Tu Olor." Mairena (6:17) Aut 84, p. 46.
"El Viejo Quinque." Mairena (6:17) Aut 84, p. 46.

3282. MARTINEZ, Phyllis
"Metamorphosis." Calyx (8:3) Aut-Wint 84, p. 24.
"My Brother, Mon Semblable." Calyx (8:3) Aut-Wint
  84, p. 25.

3283. MARTINEZ RIVAS, Carlos
"Eunice Odio" (fragmento). Mairena (6:18) 84, p.
  157-158.

3284. MARTINS, Julio Monteiro
"The Position." Iowa (14:2) Spr-Sum 84, p. 155-157.

MARTIR, Doris Rios: See RIOS MARTIR, Doris

3285. MARTONE, Michael
"Plenty." WindO (44) Sum-Aut 84, p. 13.

MARTONE, Marjorie Hanft: See HANFT-MARTONE, Marjorie

3286. MARTOS, Marco
"Casti Connubi" (tr. by Lorraine Underwood). Vis
(15) 84, p. 29.

MARY LUCINA, Sister: See LUCINA, Mary, Sister

3287. MASARIK, Al
"Feeling Good." Piq (12) 84, p. 70.
"Overnight Pass." Piq (12) 84, p. 70.

3288. MASLEN, Cathy
"This moment exists only because I am bound to
him." Open24 (3) 84, p. 34-35.

3289. MASON, David
"The Buried Garden." Thrpny (18) Sum 84, p. 14.
"Plums" (for Linda Allardt). NegC (4:3) Sum 84,
p. 107.

3290. MASON, Deanna
"Death Hasn't Shoulders." SnapD (8:1) Aut 84, p.
40-43.
"How Does a Mother Grow." SnapD (8:1) Aut 84, p.
38-39.

MASSMAN, Gordon Lester: See LESTER-MASSMAN, Gordon

MASTER, J. R. le: See LeMASTER, J. R.

3291. MASTERS, Marcia Lee
"My Father's Return." NewL (50:4) Sum 84, p. 50-51.
"Running Away When I Was Young." SpoonRQ (9:4)
Aut 84, p. 34-35.
"Wind around the Moon." NewL (50:4) Sum 84, p. 51-
52.

3292. MASTERSON, Dan
"A Visit Home." SewanR (92:1) Ja-Mr 84, p. 64-65.
"Yardwork." SewanR (92:1) Ja-Mr 84, p. 65.

3293. MATHEWS, Aidan Carl
"Descartes at Daybreak." NewRep (190:16) 23 Ap
84, p. 36.

3294. MATHEWS, Harry
"Histoire." NewYRB (31:13) 16 Ag 84, p. 52.

3295. MATHIS, Cleopatra
"Body, Earth, Water." GrahamHR (7) Wint 84, p. 34-
35.
"Breath." GrahamHR (7) Wint 84, p. 31-33.
"The Creation of Adam" (After the etching by
William Blake). GrahamHR (7) Wint 84, p. 29.
"Night Storm." GrahamHR (7) Wint 84, p. 30.

3296. MATOS PAOLI, Francisco
"Biografia de un Poeta." _Mairena_ (6:18) 84, p. 23.
"La Expresion." _Mairena_ (6:17) Aut 84, p. 67.
"Pestaña del Llanto." _Mairena_ (5:13) Spr 83, p.
102.
"Soneto a Isabelita Freire." _Mairena_ (5:13) Spr
83, p. 101.

MATRE, C. van: _See_ Van MATRE, C. (Connie)

3297. MATTESON, Fredric
"Axe." _Sparrow_ (46) 84, p. 14.

3298. MATTHEWS, William
"Bad" (Excerpts). _AmerPoR_ (13:2) Mr-Ap 84, p. 13.
"Caddies' Day, the Country Club, a Small Town in
Ohio." _OhioR_ (32) 84, p. 6-7.
"Good" (Excerpts). _AmerPoR_ (13:2) Mr-Ap 84, p. 13.
"A Happy Childhood" (Excerpt). _OhioR_ (32) 84, p.
8-9.
"Listen." _Atlantic_ (253:1) Ja 84, p. 74.
"Loyal." _GeoR_ (38:4) Wint 84, p. 861.
"Right" (Excerpts). _AmerPoR_ (13:2) Mr-Ap 84, p. 14.
"Talk." _Chelsea_ (42/43) 84, p. 258.
"Whiplash." _Atlantic_ (253:3) Mr 84, p. 98.
"Wrong" (Excerpts). _AmerPoR_ (13:2) Mr-Ap 84, p. 14.

3299. MATTHIAS, John
"At a Screening of Gance's 'Napoleon': Arts
Theatre, Cambridge." _Salm_ (63/64) Spr-Sum 84,
p. 243-244.
"Edward." _Argo_ (5:2) 84, p. 19-20.
"Edward." _Salm_ (63/64) Spr-Sum 84, p. 240-241.
"F.M.F. from Olivet" (remembering Joseph Brewer).
Salm (63/64) Spr-Sum 84, p. 241-242.
"Horace Augustus Mandelstam Stalin." _Salm_ (63/64)
Spr-Sum 84, p. 238.
"My Youngest Daughter: Running toward an English
Village Church." _Salm_ (63/64) Spr-Sum 84, p. 245.
"Northern Summer." _Bound_ (12:1) Aut 83, p. 133-148.
"Northern Summer" (Selections: I. The Castle, II.
Pied-à-Terre, III. The Mine). _Argo_ (5:2) 84,
p. 13-18.
"Rhododendron." _Salm_ (63/64) Spr-Sum 84, p. 239.

3300. MATTISON, Alice
"The Committee." _MassR_ (25:3) Aut 84, p. 469-471.
"The Oyster Boats." _MassR_ (25:3) Aut 84, p. 471-472.
"Two Moons." _Shen_ (35:1) 83-84, p. 94-95.

3301. MATYAS, Cathy
"Nile." _PoetryCR_ (6:1) Aut 84, p. 16.

3302. MAURA, Sister
"Finding the Body." _Sparrow_ (46) 84, p. 24.

3303. MAUSOLF, Shelly Jo
"Death Comes Around" (1983-84 Literary Arts
Scholarship Winners: Third Place). _DekalbLAJ_
(17:1/2) 84, p. 106.

"Simon without Underwear" (1983-84 Literary Arts
   Scholarship Winners: Third Place). DekalbLAJ
   (17:1/2) 84, p. 106.
"Valentine's Day" (1983-84 Literary Arts
   Scholarship Winners: Third Place). DekalbLAJ
   (17:1/2) 84, p. 107.

3304. MAXHAM, Catherine
   "I Was Plump and Quiet and Ten." AntigR (59) Aut
   84, p. 95.

3305. MAXMIN, Jody
   "Archilochos Recollected in California." PraS
   (58:2) Sum 84, p. 94.

3306. MAXSON, Gloria (Gloria A.)
   "Carol after Christmas." ChrC (101::1) 4-11 Ja
   84, p. 15.
   "Extremist." ChrC (101:23) 18-25 Jl 84, p. 700.
   "Gerontologist." ChrC (101:21) 20-27 Je 84, p. 628.
   "On Robert Frost, Cremated." ChrC (101:10) 21-28
   Mr 84, p. 295.
   "Soldier." ChrC (101:14) 25 Ap 84, p. 424.

3307. MAXWELL, Richard
   "Ontology, In and About." CalQ (23/24) Spr-Sum
   84, p. 130-131.

3308. MAY, Connie
   "The Fear." Open24 (3) 84, p. 14.
   "Genetic Lace." Open24 (3) 84, p. 13.

3309. MAY, Frances
   "Port Holes." SpoonRQ (9:4) Aut 84, p. 52-53.

3310. MAYES, Frances
   "Into This View." MissR (36, 12:3) Spr 84, p. 74.
   "Red Digits Read 12:47." NewEngR (6:3) Spr 84, p.
   398-399.
   "Santa Fe, Winter Solstice." MissR (36, 12:3) Spr
   84, p. 75-76.
   "To Begin the Migraine." MissR (36, 12:3) Spr 84,
   p. 73.

3311. MAYFIELD, Suellen
   "After the War." VirQR (60:3) Sum 84, p. 426-427.

3312. MAYHALL, Jane
   "Butterfly" (music by Donald Ashwander). NegC
   (4:3) Sum 84, p. 100-102.
   "The Light-headed Petunias of Saratoga County."
   AmerPoR (13:4) Jl-Ag 84, p. 39.
   "The Unafraid." AmerPoR (13:4) Jl-Ag 84, p. 39.

3313. MAYNE, Seymour
   "At the Monastery of the Cross." CanLit (100) Spr
   84, p. 230.
   "Sacrifice." CanLit (100) Spr 84, p. 230.

3314. MAYO, E. L.
      "A Fair Warning." NewL (50:2/3) Wint-Spr 84, p. 164.
      "House." NewL (50:2/3) Wint-Spr 84, p. 165.
      "Serpent." NewL (50:2/3) Wint-Spr 84, p. 164.
      "The Shift." NewL (50:2/3) Wint-Spr 84, p. 165.

3315. MAYTE SANTIAGO, Beatriz
      "Cayeron." Mairena (5:13) Spr 83, p. 67.

3316. MAZUR, Gail
      "A Deck of Cards." Ploughs (10:4) 84, p. 67-68.
      "Fallen Angels." Ploughs (10:4) 84, p. 64-66.
      "In the Dark Our Story." Telescope (3:3) Aut 84,
         p. 42-43.
      "Reading Akhmatova." NewRep (190:15) 16 Ap 84, p.
         36.

3317. MAZUR, Rita Z.
      "And from the Summit" (Haiku, Fifth Honorable
         Mention, 13th Annual Kansas Poetry Contest).
         LittleBR (4:3) Spr 84, p. 70.

3318. MAZZARO, Jerome
      "Movements in Time." LitR (28:1) Aut 84, p. 42-43.

3319. MAZZOCCO, Robert
      "Cuba" (Primero de Mayo, the middle fifties).
         AmerPoR (13:5) S-O 84, p. 13.
      "Psalm" (the early seventies). AmerPoR (13:5) S-O
         84, p. 13.

3320. MBEMBE (Milton Smith)
      "African Art." NewL (50:2/3) Wint-Spr 84, p. 170.
      "African Art No. 2." NewL (50:2/3) Wint-Spr 84,
         p. 170.
      "Did They Help Me at the State Hospital for the
         Criminally Insane?" NewL (50:2/3) Wint-Spr 84,
         p. 170-171.
      "Survival Poem." NewL (50:2/3) Wint-Spr 84, p. 172.

Mc . . . : See also Names beginning with Mac . . .

3321. McADAM, Rhona
      "Anne, Doing Tai Chi in the Campground on Pender
         Island." MalR (68) Je 84, p. 65.
      "Life in Glass." Quarry (33:4) Aut 84, p. 4.

3322. McALEAVEY, David
      "Christmas Pageant." TarRP (24:1) Aut 84, p. 11.
      "Cowboy." GreenfR (11:1/2) Sum-Aut 83, p. 140.
      "Scrabble Jail." GreenfR (11:1/2) Sum-Aut 83, p.
         140-142.
      "Scrabble Jail" (corrected printing). GreenfR
         (11:3/4) Wint-Spr 84, p. 167-169.

3323. McALLASTER, Elva
      "Marienthal to Big Sur." KanQ (16:1/2) Wint-Spr
         84, p. 142.

3324. McANULLA, Charles
    "Distance." YetASM (3) 84, p. 5.
    "Guilt." PoeticJ (5) 84, p. 9.
    "Memo." PoeticJ (6) 84, p. 44.

3325. McBRIDE, Elizabeth
    "Deep Sea Fishing with My Father." BlueBldgs (7)
        84, p. 18.

3326. McBRIDE, Mekeel
    "After Grief." OntR (21) Aut-Wint 84, p. 70.
    "Castaway." Poetry (144:4) Jl 84, p. 197-198.
    "Here, for You." OntR (21) Aut-Wint 84, p. 69-70.
    "If I'd Been Born in Tennessee." OntR (21) Aut-
        Wint 84, p. 67-68.
    "Matins." Ploughs (10:4) 84, p. 124-125.
    "The Mechanics of Repair" (for Andy and Gail).
        Ploughs (10:4) 84, p. 126-127.
    "The Proper Offering." OntR (21) Aut-Wint 84, p.
        71-72.
    "Red Letters." OntR (21) Aut-Wint 84, p. 66.
    "A Short Autobiography of Inspiration" (for Anton
        Joseph, selections: 1-4, 8, 10, 11, 13).
        Nimrod (27:2) Spr-Sum 84, p. 50-53.

3327. McCABE, V.
    "History, or The Old House." DekalbLAJ (17:1/2)
        84, p. 137.

3328. McCABE, Victoria
    "The Body Private." LitR (28:1) Aut 84, p. 123.
    "Calendar." GreenfR (11:3/4) Wint-Spr 84, p. 117.
    "The First Articulation of Grief Is Spelled 'O'."
        TarRP (23:2) Spr 84, p. 23.
    "Friends, Teachers, Old Lovers, Fellow Writers,
        Kinsmen, Dogs, and Painters." NewL (51:1) Aut
        84, p. 26.
    "Locale." LitR (28:1) Aut 84, p. 122-123.
    "Modern Criticism." GreenfR (11:3/4) Wint-Spr 84,
        p. 118.
    "November Shadow." Abraxas (31/32) 84, p. 43.
    "On His Low Self-Esteem." NewL (50:2/3) Wint-Spr
        84, p. 217.
    "Prayer in a Late Hour." Abraxas (31/32) 84, p. 42.
    "Running Head American Heritage Dictionary." NewL
        (50:2/3) Wint-Spr 84, p. 217.
    "Salesman." GreenfR (11:3/4) Wint-Spr 84, p. 119.
    "The Valid Earth." SoDakR (22:1) Spr 84, p. 49.
    "The Woman Who Liked Her Thighs." HiramPoR (36)
        Spr-Sum 84, p. 30.

3329. McCAFFERY, Steve (See also FOUR HORSEMEN)
    "John Clare Adaptation" (based on Clare's "Written
        in Northhampton County Asylum"). CapilR (31)
        84, p. 37.
    "Oh Shut Up You Make Me Furious." CapilR (31) 84,
        p. 78-79.
    "Sizerz." CapilR (31) 84, p. 75.

3330. McCAFFREY, Phillip
       "Gourds." <u>Poetry</u> (145:2) N 84, p. 64.
       "Portraits." <u>CalQ</u> (23/24) Spr-Sum 84, p. 132-133.

3331. McCALLISTER, Ian
       "Sunday Painter." <u>Quarry</u> (33:3) Sum 84, p. 54.

3332. McCALLUM, Paddy
       "Orfeo." <u>Grain</u> (12:1) F 84, p. 23.

3333. McCANN, Janet
       "Shopping for the Gun." <u>PoeticJ</u> (1) 83, p. 9.

3334. McCANN, Richard
       "Afterwards." <u>PoetryNW</u> (25:2) Sum 84, p. 28.
       "Lace." <u>Shen</u> (35:1) 83-84, p. 22-23.
       "Slate Run, Pennsylvania, 1958." <u>PoetryNW</u> (25:2)
          Sum 84, p. 29.

3335. McCARRISTON, Linda
       "Grasshoppers." <u>MSS</u> (3:2/3) Spr 84, p. 111.
       "How Graciously the Animal." <u>MSS</u> (3:2/3) Spr 84,
          p. 110.
       "With the Horse in the Winter Pasture." <u>OhioR</u>
          (32) 84, p. 28.

3336. McCARTHY, Bill
       "God Said, 'Let There Be Light'" (Genesis 1:13).
          <u>SanFPJ</u> (6:3) 84, p. 31-32.
       "On the Nuclear Front." <u>SanFPJ</u> (6:3) 84, p. 35.

3337. McCARTHY, Gerald
       "Against the Rain" (for Sharif, Jimmy Z., Fitz and
          Sonny). <u>TriQ</u> (61) Aut 84, p. 105-106.
       "For a Friend in Prison." <u>TriQ</u> (61) Aut 84, p. 107.
       "The Hooded Legion." <u>TriQ</u> (59) Wint 84, p. 120.
       "Note in a Bottle." <u>NewL</u> (50:2/3) Wint-Spr 84, p.
          264.

3338. McCARTHY, Penny
       "First Match of the Season." <u>Argo</u> (6:1) 84, p. 18.

3339. McCARTHY, Tom
       "The Poet of the Mountains." <u>Iowa</u> (14:2) Spr-Sum
          84, p. 170.
       "Returning to De Valera's Cottage." <u>Iowa</u> (14:2)
          Spr-Sum 84, p. 171.

3340. McCARTIN, James T.
       "Collecting." <u>GreenfR</u> (12:1/2) Sum-Aut 84, p. 101.
       "My Mother." <u>NewL</u> (50:2/3) Wint-Spr 84, p. 190.
       "Thomas Eakins." <u>ArizQ</u> (40:2) Sum 84, p. 162.

3341. McCLATCHY, J. D.
       "The Approach." <u>Shen</u> (35:2/3) 84, p. 211.
       "The Lesson in Prepositions." <u>GrandS</u> (3:4) Sum
          84, p. 161-164.
       "The Luna Moth." <u>Poetry</u> (144:6) S 84, p. 311-313.
       "The Method." <u>GrandS</u> (3:4) Sum 84, p. 165.
       "Ovid's Farewell." <u>Poetry</u> (144:6) S 84, p. 314-318.

"Wells River." Nat (238:2) 21 Ja 84, p. 54.

3342. McCLEARY, Joy
"Lit. II--1st Hour." EngJ (73:5) S 84, p. 86.

3343. McCLOSKEY, Mark
"Adele Menken Stares at Her Ceiling." PoetryNW
(25:2) Sum 84, p. 20-21.
"The Poet Makes Believe He Is a Plumber."
PoetryNW (25:2) Sum 84, p. 21-22.
"The Way It Is with Sea-Elephants." Chelsea
(42/43) 84, p. 269.

3344. McCLURE, Michael
"Somebody's Dream" (After Celan). EvergR (98) 84,
p. 127.

3345. McCLURG, Kayla L.
"You Sure Don't Look Like a Poet." EngJ (73:2) F
84, p. 80.

3346. McCOLL, Michael
"I Mean Children." KanQ (16:1/2) Wint-Spr 84, p. 17.

3347. McCOMBS, Judith
"Mere eyer my error" (Contra-ceptual Art). Waves
(12:1) Aut 83, p. 26-27.

3348. McCORD, Howard
"At Pool." Gargoyle (24) 84, p. 233.
"Old Habits." Kayak (64) My 84, p. 54.

3349. McCORKLE, James
"Lying Awake Watching a Lighted Window." MinnR
(N.S. 22) Spr 84, p. 45-46.

3350. McCORMACK, Hope
"Waiting at the Sea-Well." ThirdW (2) Spr 84, p.
20-22.

3351. McCORMACK, Lee
"Momentary Gypsy Song" (for Garcia). StoneC
(11:3/4) Spr-Sum 84, p. 72-73.

3352. McCOWEN, David
"Edges." DekalbLAJ (17:1/2) 84, p. 138.

3353. McCOWN, Clint
"The Night before the Operation." SouthernPR
(24:1) Spr 84, p. 10.
"Splitting Up the Record Collection." SouthernPR
(24:1) Spr 84, p. 11.

3354. McCOY, Barbara
"Pale hands holding." Amelia (1:2) O 84, p. 11.

3355. McCOY, John
"Winter Night in Midwich." Amelia [1:1] Ap 84, p.
14.

3356. McCULLOUGH, Ken
"Elegy for Old Anna." NoDaQ (52:2) Spr 84, p. 16-29.
"Things To Do around Taos." NewL (50:2/3) Wint-
Spr 84, p. 213-215.

3357. McCURDY, Harold
"Newness." ChrC (101:10) 21-28 Mr 84, p. 304.

3358. McDERMOTT, Jeremiah
"The Night We Met." HangL (45) Spr 84, p. 35.

3359. McDONALD, Agnes
"Poetics of Sleep." SouthernPR (24:1) Spr 84, p.
59-60.

3360. McDONALD, Daniel
"My True Love." NegC (4:1) Wint 84, p. 51.

3361. McDONALD, Geordie, Percussionist
"The Complete Apocrypha." PoetryCR (5:3) Spr 84,
p. 18.
"The Completely Apocrypha." PoetryCR (6:1) Aut
84, p. 27.

3362. McDONALD, Walter
"Catching the Light at Lake Raven." Poetry
(144:6) S 84, p. 332.
"The Chimney Sweep." MidAR (4:2) Aut 84, p. 17-19.
"Cimarron." LitR (28:1) Aut 84, p. 57.
"The Constant Weather." HiramPoR (36) Spr-Sum 84,
p. 31.
"Cougar Hunt." WebR (9:1) Spr 84, p. 81.
"Fathers and Sons." Poetry (144:6) S 84, p. 332-333.
"Fifty." TarRP (24:1) Aut 84, p. 19.
"For Dawes, on Takeoff." Poetry (144:6) S 84, p.
333-334.
"Getting It Done." Vis (14) 84, p. 4.
"If the Accident Will." MidAR (4:2) Aut 84, p. 16.
"In the Tunnels." ColEng (46:2) F 84, p. 126-127.
"The Ladies of the Lake." SnapD (7:1) Aut 83, p.
12-13.
"Little Exercise." Vis (16) 84, p. 23.
"Living on a Little of Nothing." Swallow (3) 84,
p. 19-20.
"Loading the Steers." SenR (14:1) 84, p. 64.
"Mainly the Values Change." TarRP (24:1) Aut 84,
p. 19.
"Memento Mori." Poetry (144:6) S 84, p. 334.
"My Father Quits Another Job." MidAR (4:2) Aut
84, p. 14-15.
"Old Dog's Last Winter." Wind (14:51) 84, p. 59.
"Spending the Night near Matador." BelPoJ (35:2)
Wint 84-85, p. 5-6.
"Where the Trees Go." PoetryNW (25:4) Wint 84-85,
p. 43.
"Wringing." WebR (9:1) Spr 84, p. 80.

3363. McDONALD, Walter D.
"Hauling over Wolf Creek Pass in Winter." TriQ
(59) Wint 84, p. 121-122.

"Storm Warning." TriQ (59) Wint 84, p. 123.

3364. McDONOUGH, Robert E.
     "My Mother Changing My Father's Dressing." WestB
     (15) 84, p. 53.

3365. McDOUGALL, Linda
     "I Gorge Myself on Time." BlueBuf (2:2) Spr 84,
     p. 30.

3366. McDOWELL, Robert
     "The Librarian after Hours." PoetryNW (25:2) Sum
     84, p. 35-36.

3367. McELROY, Colleen J.
     "The Circus of the City." SouthernPR (24:2) Aut
     84, p. 61-62.
     "It Ain't the Blues That Blows an Ill Wind"
     (Valaida Snow: Cira 1930). BlackWR (11:1) Aut
     84, p. 40-41.
     "Shelley at Sequim Inlet." ManhatR (3:2) Wint 84-
     85, p. 72.
     "What I'd Least Like to Remember." ManhatR (3:2)
     Wint 84-85, p. 73.

3368. McFALL, Gardner
     "Describing the Middle Ages." Shen (35:1) 83-84,
     p. 33.
     "Needlepoint." Ploughs (10:4) 84, p. 58-59.
     "Peninsular Life." Ploughs (10:4) 84, p. 60-61.
     "The Pilot's Daughter." Agni (21) 84, p. 28-29.
     "Recife, the Venice of Brazil." Ploughs (10:4)
     84, p. 62-63.

3369. McFARLAND, Joanne
     "Lipstick." CapeR (19:3) 20th Anniverary Issue
     84, p. 36-37.

3370. McFARLAND, Ron
     "The Homecoming." SouthernPR (24:2) Aut 84, p. 48.
     "Meeting." MemphisSR (4:2) Spr 84, p. 23.
     "The Poet." SouthernHR (18:3) Sum 84, p. 232.

3371. McFEE, Michael
     "Asheville" (To Richard Hugo, after reading
     "Ashville"). PoetryNW (25:4) Wint 84-85, p. 24-
     26.
     "Bedtime Story." PoetryNW (25:4) Wint 84-85, p. 27.
     "From the Colonel's Journal." PoetryNW (25:4)
     Wint 84-85, p. 26.
     "Light Opera." GrahamHR (7) Wint 84, p. 18.
     "Mildew." GrahamHR (7) Wint 84, p. 19.

3372. McFERREN, Martha
     "The Author Receiveth Her First Lousy Review."
     NegC (4:3) Sum 84, p. 12.
     "Bridges." SouthernR (20:3) Sum 84, p. 594-596.
     "The Diamond Bessie Suite." Tendril (17) Wint 84,
     p. 127-129.
     "Going Public." SouthernR (20:4) Aut 84, p. 972.

"The Night Richard Nixon Quit." <u>Tendril</u> (17) Wint
    84, p. 125-126.
"Too Familiar." <u>Shen</u> (35:4) 84, p. 76.

3373. McGANN, Jerome
    "The Living Theater." <u>ChiR</u> (34:2) Spr 84, p. 62-64.

3374. McGARRY, Jean
    "Bath." <u>PoetC</u> (16:1) Aut 84, p. 28-29.
    "Black-Letter Vulgate." <u>AntR</u> (42:1) Wint 84, p.
        84-85.
    "Metallic Geraldine." <u>PoetC</u> (16:1) Aut 84, p. 27.
    "Royals." <u>PoetC</u> (16:1) Aut 84, p. 30-31.
    "Seven Last Words." <u>NewOR</u> (11:3/4) Aut-Wint 84,
        p. 79.
    "Whom They Loved." <u>PoetC</u> (16:1) Aut 84, p. 24-26.

3375. McGLYNN, Brian
    "Hemingway." <u>Wind</u> (14:50) 84, p. 14.
    "Rivermaster." <u>Wind</u> (14:50) 84, p. 10.

3376. McGONIGLE, Thomas
    "Moments before Entering the Corn Exchange" (A
        Prepared slide from St. Patrick's Day, Dublin,
        1974). <u>CreamCR</u> (9:1/2) 84, p. 71-78.

3377. McGOVERN, Martin
    "Christmas, Colorado." <u>Poetry</u> (145:3) D 84, p. 143.

3378. McGOWAN, Jim
    "Song of the Cooling Tower." <u>Bogg</u> (52) 84, p. 34.

3379. McGRATH, Kristina
    "The Life of the House." <u>13thM</u> (8:1/2) 84, p. 154-
        157.
    "The Tracks." <u>Confr</u> (27/28) 84, p. 265.

3380. McGUCKIAN, Medbh
    "The Rising Out." <u>Pequod</u> (16/17) 84, p. 44.

3381. McGUINK, Kevin
    "Tea Poem." <u>AntigR</u> (57) Spr 84, p. 112.

3382. McGUIRE, Jerry
    "Shut Up." <u>PaintedB</u> (21) Wint 84, p. 30-31.

3383. McGUIRE, Patrick
    "Changing the Name of the Game -- to Monopoly."
        <u>SanFPJ</u> (6:2) 84, p. 77-79.

3384. McHUGH, Heather
    "Animal Song." <u>Antaeus</u> (52) Apr 84, p. 82.
    "The Ghost." <u>NewRep</u> (191:22) 26 N 84, p. 34.
    "Physics." <u>AmerPoR</u> (13:2) Mr-Ap 84, p. 5.
    "The Trouble with 'In'." <u>AmerPoR</u> (13:2) Mr-Ap 84,
        p. 5.

3385. McINNIS, Nadine
    "For Every Mystery There Is an (Undiscovered)
        Equation." <u>AntigR</u> (59) Aut 84, p. 107-108.

"You Mother in Your Iron-coloured Hair." AntigR
(59) Aut 84, p. 109-110.

3386. McINTYRE, Mello
"Sanctus." AntigR (57) Spr 84, p. 42-43.

3387. McKAIN, David
"Portrait of an Aristocrat." Ploughs (10:1) 84,
p. 113.
"Witching." KanQ (16:1/2) Wint-Spr 84, p. 179.

3388. McKAY, Don
"The Drive." PoetryCR (5:4) Sum 84, p. 16.
"February Willows." PoetryCR (6:2) Wint 84-85, p. 5.
"The Fiddle in the Open Air." PoetryCR (5:4) Sum
84, p. 18.
"How to Imagine an Albatross" (assisted by the
report of a CIA observer near Christmas Island).
CanLit (103) Wint 84, p. 40-41.
"The Night Shift." CanLit (103) Wint 84, p. 49-50.
"Night Wind." Dandel (11:2) Aut-Wint 84-85, p. 51.
"You Who Never Arrived." Dandel (11:2) Aut-Wint
84-85, p. 52.

3389. McKAY, Jean
"Tonight My Body." Waves (12:1) Aut 83, p. 77.

3390. McKEE, Louis
"Emmaus." FourQt (33:3) Spr 84, p. 28.
"Her Dream." PoeticJ (3) 83, p. 15.
"What Is Missing." PaintedB (21) Wint 84, p. 8.

3391. McKEEVER, Carmelita, C.S.J.
"Icicles." ChrC (101:5) 15 F 84, p. 164.

3392. McKENZIE-PORTER, Patricia
"Scavengers." PottPort (6) 84, p. 6.

3393. McKERNAN, John
"A Dissertation on Jello." PoetC (15:2) Wint 84,
p. 12-13.

3394. McKERNAN, Llewellyn
"Faith." Agni (21) 84, p. 57.
"Oh." PoetC (15:2) Wint 84, p. 28.

3395. McKIM, Elizabeth
"My Ma." PaintedB (24) Aut 84, p. 30-31.
"Secrets." PaintedB (21) Wint 84, p. 26.
"Sometimes the Name Is Just a Small Shading, a
Shadow." PaintedB (21) Wint 84, p. 25.

3396. McKINLAY, Patricia
"Hook and Eye." PoetryNW (25:2) Sum 84, p. 43-44.

3397. McKINLEY, Maryann
"In Iowa City." NewL (51:2) Wint 84-85, p. 109.

3398. McKINLEY, Muriel
"Dark Night." Germ (8:2) Aut-Wint 84, p. 19.

"For C.D." <u>Germ</u> (8:2) Aut–Wint 84, p. 20.

3399. McKINNEY, Irene
"Visiting My Gravesite: Talbott Churchyard, West
Virginia." <u>Poetry</u> (143:5) F 84, p. 288.

3400. McKINNEY, Sandy
"The Front Room" (tr. of Rafael Guillén). <u>TriQ</u>
(59) Wint 84, p. 211-212.
"Mold" (tr. of Rafael Guillén). <u>TriQ</u> (59) Wint
84, p. 213-214.
"Task-Work" (tr. of Rafael Guillén). <u>TriQ</u> (59)
Wint 84, p. 209-210.

3401. McKINNON, Barry
"Cabin." <u>CapilR</u> (32) 84, p. 50.
"The Centre" (An Improvisation, for Marian).
<u>CapilR</u> (32) 84, p. 30-40.
"Clear north. First snow." <u>CapilR</u> (32) 84, p. 54-55.
"Composing." <u>CapilR</u> (32) 84, p. 57.
"A Few Thoughts." <u>CapilR</u> (32) 84, p. 44-45.
"I Really Really Think So" (for Sid Marty).
<u>CapilR</u> (32) 84, p. 52.
"I've wandered, not always lost." <u>CapilR</u> (32) 84,
p. 47.
"Journal" (after Pierre's paintings). <u>CapilR</u> (32)
84, p. 41-42.
"A Letter" (for Steve Stack). <u>CapilR</u> (32) 84, p. 53.
"Listen." <u>CapilR</u> (32) 84, p. 48.
"Ooga Booga" (for John Harris & Bill Little).
<u>CapilR</u> (32) 84, p. 43.
"Poetry Embarks Us on a Sea" (after George
Stanley). <u>CapilR</u> (32) 84, p. 54.
"Self Study" (for Peter Byl). <u>CapilR</u> (32) 84, p. 56.
"This Morning." <u>CapilR</u> (32) 84, p. 49.
"Thought to Joy." <u>CapilR</u> (32) 84, p. 53.
"Thoughts Driving." <u>CapilR</u> (32) 84, p. 51.
"Thoughts in Fall." <u>CapilR</u> (32) 84, p. 46-47.

3402. McKINNON, Patrick
"The Mailbox Poem." <u>RagMag</u> (3:2) Aut 84, p. 17.

3403. McKINNON, Patrick J.
"Casey Livingston Is an Epileptic." <u>YetASM</u> (3)
84, p. 5.
"The Kid Who Doesn't Sing." <u>RagMag</u> (3:1) Spr 84,
p. 10.

3404. McKINSEY, Martin
"Provincial Spring" (tr. of Yannis Ritsos).
<u>ParisR</u> (26:91) Spr 84, p. 122.
"Small Composition" (tr. of Yannis Ritsos).
<u>ParisR</u> (26:91) Spr 84, p. 123.
"Wavering Decisions" (tr. of Yannis Ritsos).
<u>ParisR</u> (26:91) Spr 84, p. 122.

3405. McLAUGHLIN, William
"Descent into the Decent." <u>WestB</u> (15) 84, p. 112-
113.
"Gigue." <u>WestB</u> (15) 84, p. 113-114.

"Learning to Boil Water." <u>BallSUF</u> (24:3) Sum 83,
    p. 53.
"Words for a Pro Quarterback in the Fall."
    <u>BallSUF</u> (24:3) Sum 83, p. 27.
"You May Go Home Now." <u>BallSUF</u> (24:3) Sum 83, p. 26.

3406. McLAURIN, Ken
    "Major Mode." <u>WindO</u> (44) Sum-Aut 84, p. 3.

3407. McLEAN, Anne
    "A Party." <u>Grain</u> (12:2) My 84, p. 10.

3408. McLEAN, Robert
    "Green Swamp." <u>Sam</u> (37:3, 147th release) 83, p. 50.

3409. McMAHON, Lynne
    "It's Like This Every Day." <u>AntR</u> (42:3) Sum 84,
    p. 319.

3410. McMAHON, Michael Beirne
    "Picnic at Taughannock." <u>SenR</u> (14:1) 84, p. 45-48.

3411. McMANUS, Fran, RSM
    "Masquerade." <u>EngJ</u> (73:7) N 84, p. 90.

3412. McMASTER, Susan
    "Lilacs." <u>Quarry</u> (33:4) Aut 84, p. 16-17.
    "Rheims Cathedral." <u>Quarry</u> (33:4) Aut 84, p. 16.

3413. McMILLAN, Hugh
    "Veterans." <u>Argo</u> (6:1) 84, p. 19.

3414. McMILLIN, Jan
    "Hamsin." <u>Grain</u> (12:3) Ag 84, p. 9.

3415. McMURRAY, Earl
    "Keeping Quiet." <u>Poetry</u> (145:2) N 84, p. 87.
    "A Man in a House." <u>Poetry</u> (145:2) N 84, p. 89.
    "A Perfect Stranger." <u>Poetry</u> (145:2) N 84, p. 88.

3416. McNAIR, Wesley
    "The Before People." <u>ThRiPo</u> (23/24) 84, p. 61.
    "Big Cars." <u>Poetry</u> (144:1) Ap 84, p. 10.
    "The Faith Healer." <u>Poetry</u> (144:3) Je 84, p. 157-
    158.
    "The Last Time Shorty Towers Fetched the Cows."
    <u>Atlantic</u> (253:4) Ap 84, p. 106.
    "The Minister's Death." <u>ThRiPo</u> (23/24) 84, p. 60-61.
    "Mute." <u>Poetry</u> (144:1) Ap 84, p. 9.
    "My Brother inside the Revolving Doors." <u>ThRiPo</u>
    (23/24) 84, p. 59.
    "The Portuguese Dictionary." <u>Poetry</u> (144:3) Je
    84, p. 158-160.
    "Remembering Aprons." <u>Poetry</u> (144:3) Je 84, p. 156.

3417. McNALL, Sally
    "Metaphors." <u>NewL</u> (50:2/3) Wint-Spr 84, p. 239.

3418. McNAMARA, Eugene
    "Breakfast Special at the Castle View." <u>PoetryCR</u>

(6:2) Wint 84-85, p. 7.

3419. McNEIL, Florence
"Mrs. Greene." CrossC (6:1) 84, p. 11.
"Rabbit Mary." CrossC (6:1) 84, p. 11.
"Renovation." PoetryCR (6:2) Wint 84-85, p. 9.

3420. McNULTY, Tim
"After Losing the Bid on a Season's Treeplanting to
an Out-of-Work Fisherman, We Take a Hike up
Barnes Creek and Reflect on the Nature of the
Times" (for Kevin & Finn). HangL (45) Spr 84, p.
36.
"Old Town." HangL (45) Spr 84, p. 37.

3421. McPHERSON, Sandra
"Alcatraz." NewRep (191:5) 30 Jl 84, p. 44.
"Approaching Robert Hayden." Obs (8:1) Spr 82, p.
206.
"Chicory at Night." YaleR (73:4) Sum 84, p. 568-572.
"Ledge." GrandS (3:3) Spr 84, p. 40-43.
"The Man on the Plane Proposes Sterilization of
Poor Women." YaleR (73:4) Sum 84, p. 568.
"On Being Told 'You Have Stars in Your Eyes' by a
Man Who Denied that 95.6% of Single-Parent
Households on Welfare in Our State Are Headed by
Women." GrandS (3:3) Spr 84, p. 37-38.
"Unspoken Request" (Assembly of God, 1980).
GrandS (3:3) Spr 84, p. 39.

3422. McQUEEN, Cilla
"Pink Neon Revolution." PoetryCR (6:1) Aut 84, p.
13.

3423. McQUILKIN, Rennie
"After Viewing the Daguerreotype 'Plaisir
d'Hiver'." KanQ (16:4) Aut 84, p. 59.
"Alive Alive in the Friendship Cemetery." CarolQ
(36:3) Spr 84, p. 7.
"At the Bar." Poetry (144:1) Ap 84, p. 18-19.
"The Burning Off." AntiqR (57) Spr 84, p. 85.
"A Country Death" (for Andrew Wyeth). Poem (50)
Mr 84, p. 40.
"The Dance." SmPd (21:1) Wint 84, p. 18.
"Doing Time at Gilead Regional." Poetry (144:1)
Ap 84, p. 16-17.
"In Wyeth." Poem (50) Mr 84, p. 39.
"Invitation" (for E.A.M.). LitR (27:2) Wint 84,
p. 187.
"Ladders to Glory, Woods Hole." Poetry (144:1) Ap
84, p. 17-18.
"Not Yet, Thank You" (for Jocie). AntiqR (57) Spr
84, p. 86.
"Song of Elpenor." SouthernR (20:2) Spr 84, p.
381-384.
"To Be Read Aloud in a Public Place." WindO (44)
Sum-Aut 84, p. 25.
"Twelve." Atlantic (253:1) Ja 84, p. 68.
"Van Gogh of Arles." WindO (44) Sum-Aut 84, p. 25-
26.

"We All Fall Down." <u>Atlantic</u> (253:5) My 84, p. 90.
"Your Things." <u>TarRP</u> (23:2) Spr 84, p. 25.

3424. McROBERTS, Robert
"Cove." <u>Northeast</u> (Series 3:18) 84, p. 12.
"Geography Lesson from a Friend." <u>Northeast</u>
(Series 3:18) 84, p. 32.
"Lizbeth Descending." <u>PoetryCR</u> (6:1) Aut 84, p. 14.

3425. McWHIRTER, George
"Wood Edge." <u>CanLit</u> (100) Spr 84, p. 204-205.

3426. MEADE, Gordon
"East Neuk Assizes." <u>Argo</u> (6:1) 84, p. 38.
"The River Tweed." <u>Argo</u> (5:3) 84, p. 9.

3427. MEADS, Kathy
"For the Sake of Alone." <u>StoneC</u> (11:3/4) Spr-Sum
84, p. 22.

3428. MEANS, David
"Bull Fighting in Boston." <u>WoosterR</u> (1:1) Mr 84,
p. 104-105.
"Winter 1967." <u>WoosterR</u> (1:2) N 84, p. 84.

3429. MEATS, Stephen
"A Child Falls Asleep." <u>MidwQ</u> (26:1) Aut 84, p. 80.
"False Spring." <u>MidwQ</u> (26:1) Aut 84, p. 76-77.
"Waiting in the Gritty Dark." <u>MidwQ</u> (26:1) Aut
84, p. 78-79.

3430. MECHCATIE, Oliver
"The evening turns and is gone." <u>Os</u> (18) 84, p. 9.
"Late afternoon when all the trees and fields."
<u>Os</u> (19) 84, p. 24-25.
"The night sky - open, clear, a black-blue." <u>Os</u>
(18) 84, p. 8.

3431. MECKEL, Christoph
"The Crow" (tr. by Carol Bedwell). <u>PoetL</u> (79:1)
Spr 84, p. 42-43.
"Jonas Speakes" (tr. by Carol Bedwell). <u>PoetL</u>
(79:1) Spr 84, p. 44.
"Rembrandt, Self-Portraits" (tr. by Carol Bedwell).
<u>PoetL</u> (79:1) Spr 84, p. 44.

MEDINA, Gladys Carmagnola de: <u>See</u> CARMAGNOLA de MEDINA,
Gladys

3432. MEDINA, Pablo
"October." <u>PoetL</u> (79:1) Spr 84, p. 37.

3433. MEDINA, Ramón Felipe
"Estacion 3." <u>Mairena</u> (5:13) Spr 83, p. 102-103.

3434. MEDNICK, Judy
"Staff Development Meeting." <u>EngJ</u> (73:6) O 84, p.
35.

3435. MEEHAN, Patrick
       "Jungle-rot." SanFPJ (6:1) 84, p. 65.
       "My Favorite Holiday." SanFPJ (6:1) 84, p. 84.

3436. MEEK, Jay
       "Child Molester." Chelsea (42/43) 84, p. 299.

3437. MEEKS, Dodie Messer
       "Plea." DekalbLAJ (17:1/2) 84, p. 139.

MEI, Yuan: See YUAN, Mei

3438. MEIER, Kay
       "My Parents at the Century of Progress, Chicago
        World's Fair, 1933." EngJ (73:4) Ap 84, p. 92.

3439. MEIJI, Emperor
       "Surely in this world men are brothers all." NewL
        (50:2/3) Wint-Spr 84, p. 230.

3440. MEINERS, R. K.
       "Cat Shadows." Stand (25:3) Sum 84, p. 4-5.
       "A Principle of Hearing." Stand (25:3) Sum 84, p. 5.

3441. MEISSNER, Bill
       "Dreams of Fish." SouthernPR (24:2) Aut 84, p. 11-
        12.
       "Drunk Man Walking the Trestle above the River."
        CarolQ (36:2) Wint 84, p. 89.
       "The Magician, Sawing His Woman in Half." IndR
        (7:2) Spr 84, p. 50.
       "The Passage." NowestR (22:1/2) 84, p. 43.
       "The Swimmer" (for Nathan, 7 months, seeing Lake
        Superior for the first time). MemphisSR (5:1)
        Aut 84, p. 20.
       "Swimming through the Darkness" (for Christine).
        MemphisSR (5:1) Aut 84, p. 19.
       "Twisters." ThRiPo (23/24) 84, p. 28.

3442. MEISSNER, William
       "November, 1963, the First Kill: After Dad Shot the
        Pheasant That Flew into Barbed Wire." MidAR
        (4:1) Spr 84, p. 27.
       "Opening the Season." MidAR (4:1) Spr 84, p. 25-26.
       "The Sons and Daughters Talk of the Drowned
        Fathers." MidAR (4:1) Spr 84, p. 28.

3443. MEISTER, Peter
       "Imagination." WoosterR (1:1) Mr 84, p. 99.

3444. MELHEM, D. H.
       "For Black Poets Who Think of Leadership."
        Stepping Wint 83, p. 14.
       "For Carl Harp." Stepping (Anniversary Issue I)
        84, p. 34-36.

3445. MELNYCZUK, Askold
       "The Sunday before Easter." Poetry (144:1) Ap 84,
        p. 35-38.

3446. MEMET, José Maria
"La Mision de un Hombre." <u>Mairena</u> (6:18) 84, p. 136.

3447. MENA SANTIAGO, William
"Todo Puede Matarme." <u>Mairena</u> (5:14) Aut 83, p. 89.

3448. MENDEZ SANTIAGO, Sabino
"Duermevela." <u>Mairena</u> (6:17) Aut 84, p. 92.

MENDOZA, Ester Feliciano: <u>See</u> FELICIANO MENDOZA, Ester

3449. MENEBROKER, Ann
"Bicycle." <u>WormR</u> (24:4, issue 96) 84, p. 140.
"Distance" (for K.R.). <u>WormR</u> (24:4, issue 96) 84,
     p. 139.
"Hot Air." <u>WormR</u> (24:4, issue 96) 84, p. 139.
"How It Is." <u>WormR</u> (24:4, issue 96) 84, p. 140.
"Phil W." <u>WormR</u> (24:4, issue 96) 84, p. 140.
"Poem fro Ben." <u>Open24</u> (3) 84, p. 45.
"Swagger." <u>WormR</u> (24:4, issue 96) 84, p. 140.
"What This Female Wears in the Mornings." <u>Bogg</u>
     (52) 84, p. 4.

3450. MENEFEE, Sarah
"Cop's Horse Seen." <u>OroM</u> (2:3/4, issue 7/8) 84,
     p. 24.
"You Sit on the Edge." <u>OroM</u> (2:3/4, issue 7/8)
     84, p. 23-24.

3451. MENFI, John
"Zarathustra." <u>SouthernPR</u> (24:1) Spr 84, p. 58.

3452. MENG, Hao-jan
"Spring Dreams" (tr. by Sam Hamill). <u>CrabCR</u> (2:1)
     Sum 84, p. 24.

3453. MENGDEN, Carol
"Lost/Found." <u>EngJ</u> (73:8) D 84, p. 45.

3454. MENZEL-DRATLER, Lynne
"Bhang Bhang." <u>SpoonRQ</u> (9:2) Spr 84, p. 29-30.
"Dustbunnies." <u>SpoonRQ</u> (9:2) Spr 84, p. 26-28.

3455. MERCHANT, N.
"To My Favorite Witch." <u>SanFPJ</u> (6:2) 84, p. 46-47.

3456. MERCHANT, Norris
"Campaign Season." <u>HiramPoR</u> (36) Spr-Sum 84, p. 32.

3457. MEREDITH, Joseph
"The Acid Test: Advice to My Son" (The Mary Elinore
     Smith Poetry Prize). <u>AmerS</u> (53:2) Spr 84, p.
     194-196.
"The Beach." <u>FourQt</u> (33:2) Wint 84, p. 4.
"The Beach" (revised version, 1974). <u>FourQt</u>
     (33:2) Wint 84, p. 4.
"The Conductor on the Media Local." <u>FourQt</u> (33:2)
     Wint 84, p. 8.
"For Andrew at Three Months." <u>FourQt</u> (33:2) Wint
     84, p. 6.

"The Handsome Young Poet and the Orange Eater."
    FourQt (33:2) Wint 84, p. 5.
"Hippel's Wilderness" (for E.H.). PaintedB (24)
    Aut 84, p. 6-7.
"The Little Boy-Girl." SouthwR (69:3) Sum 84, p.
    333.
"My Father's Chair" (revised version, 1974).
    FourQt (33:2) Wint 84, p. 5.
"The Operator" (for Anna McKenna Meredith at
    seventy-five). FourQt (33:2) Wint 84, p. 9.
"Our Walks" (for Claude Koch -- Spring, 1983).
    FourQt (33:2) Wint 84, p. 17.
"Pumpkin Time" (for Emily and Andrew). FourQt
    (33:2) Wint 84, p. 16.
"The Seduction of Gravity." FourQt (33:2) Wint
    84, p. 10-11.
"Splitting Day" (for JH). FourQt (33:2) Wint 84,
    p. 14-15.
"The Tumbler" (for Emily at four). FourQt (33:2)
    Wint 84, p. 11.
"The Voices" (for JMM). FourQt (33:2) Wint 84, p.
    12-13.
"When Mary Smiles." FourQt (33:2) Wint 84, p. 7.

3458. MEREDITH, Mairi
"In the Shadow" (tr. of Dámaso Alonso, w. Robert
    Early and George Looney). MidAR (4:1) Spr 84,
    p. 83.
"The Life of Man" (tr. of Dámaso Alonso, w.
    Robert Early and George Looney). MidAR (4:1)
    Spr 84, p. 85, 87.
"Man" (tr. of Dámaso Alonso, w. Robert Early and
    George Looney). MidAR (4:1) Spr 84, p. 81.
"A Man in the Company of Himself" (from Hijos de
    la Ira, tr. of Dámaso Alonso, w. Robert Early
    and George Looney. Translation Chapbook Series,
    Number One). MidAR (4:1) Spr 84, p. 79-102.
"Monsters" (tr. of Dámaso Alonso, w. Robert Early
    and George Looney). MidAR (4:1) Spr 84, p. 89,
    91.
"Myself" (tr. of Dámaso Alonso, w. Robert Early
    and George Looney). MidAR (4:1) Spr 84, p. 101.
"The Soul Is a Little Green Frog" (tr. of Dámaso
    Alonso, w. Robert Early and George Looney).
    MidAR (4:1) Spr 84, p. 97, 99.
"To the Mite" (tr. of Dámaso Alonso, w. Robert
    Early and George Looney). MidAR (4:1) Spr 84,
    p. 93, 95.

3459. MEREDITH, William
"The American Living-Room: A Tract." AmerPoR
    (13:4) Jl-Ag 84, p. 6.
"In Front of the Cave" (adapted from Nikolai
    Hristozov). AmerPoR (13:4) Jl-Ag 84, p. 6.
"An Old Photograph of Strangers." Shen (35:2/3)
    84, p. 212.

MERLO, Antonio Santiago: See SANTIAGO MERLO, Antonio

3460. MERRICLE, William
"Cathedral." Abraxas (29/30) 84, p. 22-25.
"Finery." Open24 (3) 84, p. 5.
"Fried Poem '84." Open24 (3) 84, p. 6.
"Rent." Open24 (3) 84, p. 4.
"The Seduction." Open24 (3) 84, p. 4.
"The Taste of Knowing When to Leave." Open24 (3) 84, p. 6.

MERRIKIN HILL, Brian: See HILL, Brian Merrikin

3461. MERRILL, James
"Bronze." GrandS (4:1) Aut 84, p. 16-26.
"Casual Wear." NewYRB (30:21/22) 19 Ja 84, p. 24.
"Country Music." Shen (35:2/3) 84, p. 213.
"A Day on the Connecticut River." NewYorker (60:34) 8 O 84, p. 44.
"Days of 1941 and '44" (for David Mixsell). YaleR (73:4) Sum 84, p. 518-520.
"The Help." Shen (35:2/3) 84, p. 215.
"Monday Morning." SouthernR (20:2) Spr 84, p. 333.
"Morning Glory" (for Howard Moss). Shen (35:1) 83-84, p. 5-9.
"Nike." Shen (35:2/3) 84, p. 214.
"Popular Demand." NewYRB (31:15) 11 O 84, p. 21.
"The Romance Language." Shen (35:2/3) 84, p. 213.
"Santo." Atlantic (254:3) S 84, p. 97.

3462. MERTON, Thomas
"The Woodcarver" (tr. of Chuang Tzu). Germ (8:1) Spr-Sum 84, p. 27-28.

3463. MERWIN, W. S.
"Age" (tr. of Jean Follain). Chelsea (42/43) 84, p. 230.
"Asia" (tr. of Jean Follain). Chelsea (42/43) 84, p. 231.
"Departure's Girlfriend." Chelsea (42/43) 84, p. 98-99.
"The Egg" (tr. of Jean Follain). Chelsea (42/43) 84, p. 231.
"Eyes of Summer." Tendril (18, special issue) 84, p. 31.
"The First Year." NewYorker (60:12) 7 My 84, p. 48.
"Full Moonlight in Spring." AmerPoR (13:4) Jl-Ag 84, p. 33.
"Late Spring." Antaeus (52) Apr 84, p. 128.
"Mementos." Iowa (14:3) Aut 84, p. 3.
"Native Trees." Iowa (14:3) Aut 84, p. 1.
"The Nest." Chelsea (42/43) 84, p. 256.
"Night above the Avenue." Iowa (14:3) Aut 84, p. 2.
"The Night of the Shirts." Tendril (18, special issue) 84, p. 37.
"The Night Surf." NewYorker (60:9) 16 Ap 84, p. 45.
"Signs" (tr. of Jean Follain). Tendril (18, special issue) 84, p. 208.
"Sky in September." Iowa (14:3) Aut 84, p. 4.
"The Sound of the Light." NewYorker (60:32) 24 S 84, p. 48.
"Summer '82." NewYorker (60:36) 22 O 84, p. 44.

"West Wall." <u>Antaeus</u> (52) Apr 84, p. 129.
"When You Go Away" (dedicated to his wife Dido).
    <u>Tendril</u> (18, special issue) 84, p. 207.

3464. MESA, Lauren
"Evening Walk." <u>Poetry</u> (144:5) Ag 84, p. 257.
"The Progress" (After Manet's "Bar at the Folies-
    Bergère"). <u>Poetry</u> (144:5) Ag 84, p. 255-256.

3465. MESHTET, Saheb
"Autumn of the Masks" (tr. of Mohamed al-Magut, w.
    Beth Tornes). <u>SenR</u> (14:1) 84, p. 41-42.
"Fear" (tr. of Mohamed al-Magut, w. Beth Tornes).
    <u>SenR</u> (14:1) 84, p. 39-40.
"In the Night" (tr. of Mohamed al-Magut, w. Beth
    Tornes). <u>SenR</u> (14:1) 84, p. 37-38.

3466. MESSER, Richard
"Invocation at the Sea of the Unborn." <u>SoDakR</u>
    (22:2) Sum 84, p. 21.
"This Is November." <u>SoDakR</u> (22:2) Sum 84, p. 20.

3467. MESSICK, Timothy B.
"On First Opening Shakespeare." <u>EngJ</u> (73:4) Ap
    84, p. 68.

3468. METRAS, Gary
"Bouquet." <u>PikeF</u> (6) Aut 84, p. 24.
"Curse." <u>PikeF</u> (6) Aut 84, p. 24.
"Seven Stones for Seven Poems." <u>PikeF</u> (6) Aut 84,
    p. 25-26.

3469. METZ, Roberta
"Ablutions." <u>GreenfR</u> (11:1/2) Sum-Aut 83, p. 127.

3470. METZGER, Deena
"Moon in Taurus." <u>NewL</u> (50:4) Sum 84, p. 57.

3471. MEUDT, Edna
"Perusing the Fashions." <u>Abraxas</u> (29/30) 84, p. 58.
"Wild Roses." <u>Abraxas</u> (29/30) 84, p. 59.

3472. MEYER, Bruce
"Beacon Street." <u>GreenfR</u> (11:3/4) Wint-Spr 84, p.
    103-105.
"I'll Huff and I'll Puff." <u>GreenfR</u> (11:3/4) Wint-
    Spr 84, p. 107.
"Letter to Haroldo Conti." <u>Descant</u> (47, 15:4)
    Wint 84, p. 113-115.
"The Lighthouse at Honfleur." <u>Shen</u> (35:1) 83-84,
    p. 12-13.
"Robbed!" <u>GreenfR</u> (11:3/4) Wint-Spr 84, p. 108.
"Shooting Pigeons." <u>GreenfR</u> (11:3/4) Wint-Spr 84,
    p. 106.
"Somewhere Short of Home." <u>GreenfR</u> (11:3/4) Wint-
    Spr 84, p. 102-103.
"Weyburn." <u>Descant</u> (47, 15:4) Wint 84, p. 112.

3473. MEYER, William
"Bill, Wyoming." <u>FourQt</u> (33:2) Wint 84, p. 24.

3474. MEYROVICH, Nick
"For the Fallen Especially Marguerite & Pepe."
CutB (22) Spr-Sum 84, p. 40-41.

3475. MICHAEL, Christine
"And As." _Vis_ (14) 84, p. 22.

3476. MICHAELS, Anne
"Letters from Martha." _Writ_ (16) Aut 84, p. 47.
"Rain Makes Its Own Night." _Writ_ (16) Aut 84, p. 46.
"To My Father." _Writ_ (16) Aut 84, p. 48-49.

3477. MICHAELS, Mary
"The Ice Land" (i.m. John Michaels 1944-75). _Argo_
(6:1) 84, p. 39.

MICHELE, Mary di: _See_ Di MICHELE, Mary

3478. MICHELINE, Jack
"Some Lines on Kerouac, Charles Mills, and Rambling
across the Pages of Time, Notes, Journals, and
the Road of the Real." _MoodySI_ (14) Spr 84, p.
21-22.

3479. MICHELUTTI, Dorina Carmen
"Balancing." _PoetryCR_ (5:3) Spr 84, p. 13.
"Centre Fold." _PoetryCR_ (5:3) Spr 84, p. 13.
"Double Bind." _PoetryCR_ (5:3) Spr 84, p. 13.
"Equilibrio." _PoetryCR_ (5:3) Spr 84, p. 13.
"Foto Modella." _PoetryCR_ (5:3) Spr 84, p. 13.
"Tra l'Incudine e il Martello." _PoetryCR_ (5:3)
Spr 84, p. 13.

3480. MICHIE, James
"Metaphors Mixed for Two." _GrandS_ (3:4) Sum 84,
p. 61.
"The Old Revolutionary." _GrandS_ (3:4) Sum 84, p.
58-59.
"Song." _GrandS_ (3:4) Sum 84, p. 60.

3481. MICKA, Mary Virginia
"This Sentence." _NewYorker_ (60:24) 30 Jl 84, p. 30.

3482. MIDDLETON, Christopher
"Bonnard." _Shen_ (35:2/3) 84, p. 216.
"Mandkind" (tr. of Georg Trakl). _Field_ (30) Spr
84, p. 68-69.

3483. MIDDLETON, David
"A Defendant Speaks." _SouthernR_ (20:3) Sum 84, p.
609.
"Elegy for a Father" (Francis L. Kerne, 1911-1979).
SouthernR (20:3) Sum 84, p. 608.

MIELES, Edgardo Nieves: _See_ NIEVES MIELES, Edgardo

MIEUX, Debbie le: _See_ Le MIEUX, Debbie

3484. MIGNON, Charles
"Alma Ata" (Excerpts, tr. of Piotr Sommer, w. the

author). <u>PraS</u> (58:1) Spr 84, p. 27-28.
"For My Mother" (tr. of Piotr Sommer, w. the
   author). <u>PraS</u> (58:1) Spr 84, p. 28-29.
"Home" (tr. of Piotr Sommer, w. the author). <u>PraS</u>
   (58:1) Spr 84, p. 29-30.
"I Know" (Tr. of Piotr Sommer, w. the author).
   <u>PraS</u> (58:1) Spr 84, p. 31.
"I'll put it down in tables" (from "Alma Ata", tr.
   of Piotr Sommer, w. the author). <u>PraS</u> (58:1)
   Spr 84, p. 28.
"I've brought many valuable things" (from "Alma
   Ata", tr. of Piotr Sommer, w. the author).
   <u>PraS</u> (58:1) Spr 84, p. 27.
"A Request" (tr. of Piotr Sommer, w. the author).
   <u>PraS</u> (58:1) Spr 84, p. 30.

3485. MIHALIC, Slavko
"Large Grieving Women" (tr. by Charles Simic).
   <u>LitR</u> (27:3) Spr 84, p. 301.
"The Morning Roar of the City" (tr. by Charles
   Simic). <u>LitR</u> (27:3) Spr 84, p. 300.
"Our Ancient Family Sign" (tr. by Charles Simic).
   <u>LitR</u> (27:3) Spr 84, p. 299.
"Pastoral" (tr. by Charles Simic). <u>LitR</u> (27:3)
   Spr 84, p. 299.
"Under the Microscope" (tr. by Charles Simic).
   <u>LitR</u> (27:3) Spr 84, p. 298.

3486. MILBURN, Michael
"At the Vision Center." <u>Ploughs</u> (10:1) 84, p. 117.
"Tiger." <u>Ploughs</u> (10:4) 84, p. 116-117.
"Visit." <u>AntR</u> (42:3) Sum 84, p. 330.

3487. MILES, Josephine
"Civilian." <u>Nat</u> (239:12) 20 O 84, p. 389.
"Doll." <u>Nat</u> (239:12) 20 O 84, p. 389.
"Mark." <u>Nat</u> (239:12) 20 O 84, p. 389.
"So Graven." <u>Nat</u> (239:12) 20 O 84, p. 389.
"Vigils." <u>Shen</u> (35:2/3) 84, p. 217.
"Witness." <u>Nat</u> (239:12) 20 O 84, p. 389.

3488. MILES, Ron
"Class of '62: Re-Union." <u>CanLit</u> (100) Spr 84, p.
   231.
"Living Together." <u>CanLit</u> (100) Spr 84, p. 232.

3489. MILEY, James D.
"Copyright 1980." <u>MinnR</u> (N.S. 23) Aut 84, p. 152.

3490. MILIZIANO, Erika
"Fall." <u>Abraxas</u> (31/32) 84, p. 30.
"New Roses." <u>Abraxas</u> (31/32) 84, p. 28.

3491. MILLER, A. McA.
"Boaz Pretends Again to Sleep" (Ruth 1-4). <u>NeqC</u>
   (4:3) Sum 84, p. 104-105.
"When the '48 Pontiac Rolled." <u>Blueline</u> (5:2)
   Wint-Spr 84, p. 8.

3492. MILLER, Alan
"Letter to Gregory." <u>BlackALF</u> (18:1) Spr 84, p. 7.
"Traveler." <u>BlackALF</u> (18:1) Spr 84, p. 7-8.

3493. MILLER, Amey
"The Horseshoe-Finder" (tr. of Osip Mandelstam).
<u>CarolQ</u> (37:1) Aut 84, p. 35-37.

3494. MILLER, Ann
"The Queen and Sir Philip Sidney Sit at Home on a
Sunday Night." <u>ColEng</u> (46:7) N 84, p. 667.

3495. MILLER, Brown
"Its Hour Come Round at Last." <u>Spirit</u> (7:1) 84,
p. 136.

3496. MILLER, Ceci
"The Spoon." <u>Iowa</u> (14:3) Aut 84, p. 64-65.

3497. MILLER, Christopher
"The Poem We Are In." <u>YellowS</u> (10) Spr 84, p. 19.

3498. MILLER, David
"Aura." <u>Origin</u> (5:4) Aut 84, p. 91-93.
"Focus." <u>Origin</u> (5:4) Aut 84, p. 88-90.
"The Image." <u>Origin</u> (5:4) Aut 84, p. 85-87.

3499. MILLER, David W.
"Beasts." <u>AntigR</u> (57) Spr 84, p. 34.
"Moon Rise." <u>AntigR</u> (57) Spr 84, p. 34.

3500. MILLER, Elizabeth Gamble
"Winter of the Race" (tr. of Hugo Lindo). <u>Mund</u>
(14:2) 84, p. 21-25.

3501. MILLER, Eric
"Bells" (for Michael). <u>CanLit</u> (102) Aut 84, p. 55.
"The Crow's Gate." <u>Quarry</u> (33:4) Aut 84, p. 43.
"A Dream." <u>Quarry</u> (33:4) Aut 84, p. 44.
"What the Nighthawk Said" (for Marien). <u>Quarry</u>
(33:4) Aut 84, p. 42.

3502. MILLER, Frances
"Of love speak simply." <u>StoneC</u> (12:1/2) Aut-Wint
84, p. 34.

3503. MILLER, Hugh
"Is Fall Effective?" (in memory of Alyn Brennen).
<u>AntigR</u> (58) Sum 84, p. 76.

3504. MILLER, James A.
"Don't, dear mankind, friends" (five poems: V).
<u>Paunch</u> (57/58) Ja 84, p. 106.
"Earth, Air, Water." <u>SmPd</u> (21:2) Spr 84, p. 18.
"Envoi Redux." <u>SmPd</u> (21:2) Spr 84, p. 25.
"We have become poets" (five poems: I). <u>Paunch</u>
(57/58) Ja 84, p. 102.
"We never could understand" (five poems: IV).
<u>Paunch</u> (57/58) Ja 84, p. 105.
"We'll keep dancing, friends" (five poems: III).

Paunch (57/58) Ja 84, p. 104.
"What's in it for us" (five poems: II). Paunch
   (57/58) Ja 84, p. 103.

3505. MILLER, Jeannette
      "La Muñeca." Areíto (10:38) 84, p. 34.
      "La Partida." Areíto (10:38) 84, p. 34.

3506. MILLER, Jeffrey
      "Cadillac Platitudes." Open24 (3) 84, p. 52.
      "Confessing My Time." Open24 (3) 84, p. 51.
      "The Inn of Loose Mercury." Open24 (3) 84, p. 53.
      "With a tasteful peck on the cheek." Open24 (3)
         84, p. 54.
      "Zen Ants." Open24 (3) 84, p. 53.

3507. MILLER, John N.
      "By the Sea" (tr. of Gabriele Wohmann). WebR
         (9:1) Spr 84, p. 97.
      "Pictures from an Institution." PraS (58:3) Aut
         84, p. 90-91.
      "Relatives" (tr. of Gabriele Wohmann). WebR (9:1)
         Spr 84, p. 96.

3508. MILLER, Julia M.
      "Sand Dollar." PoeticJ (5) 84, p. 28.

3509. MILLER, Leslie Adrienne
      "The Man in the Courtyard" (for Julie).
         SouthernPR (24:2) Aut 84, p. 65-66.

3510. MILLER, Leslie F.
      "Next--a Dictionary." Open24 (3) 84, p. 3.
      "Not My Neighborhood." Open24 (3) 84, p. 3.

3511. MILLER, Mary
      "The Final Ascent" (For Robert Hayden). Obs (8:1)
         Spr 82, p. 205.

3512. MILLER, Michael
      "Stations." SoDakR (22:1) Spr 84, p. 51.
      "White Owl." CentR (28:4/29:1) Aut 84-Wint 85, p.
         78.

3513. MILLER, Philip
      "Antiquing." CimR (66) Ja 84, p. 54-55.
      "Neighbors." Wind (14:52) 84, p. 35.
      "On the Run." Vis (16) 84, p. 36.
      "Serious Children." Confr (27/28) 84, p. 178.

3514. MILLER, Sandra Lake
      "St. Anne's--Moscow." AmerS (53:2) Spr 84, p. 238.

3515. MILLER, Stephen Paul
      "Assignment: Maureen Owen." Tele (19) 83, p. 75-77.

3516. MILLER, Vassar
      "Bout with Burning." Sparrow (46) 84, p. 6.
      "On a Weekend in September." Poetry (143:5) F 84,
         p. 274-275.

"The Sun Has No History." <u>NewL</u> (50:2/3) Wint-Spr
   84, p. 56.
"Tedium." <u>NewL</u> (50:2/3) Wint-Spr 84, p. 57.

3517. MILLER, Warren C.
    "De Profundis." <u>NegC</u> (4:4) Aut 84, p. 85.

3518. MILLETT, John
    "Miniature Battle Scene -- War Museum." <u>Sam</u>
      (38:3, release 151) 84, p. 2.
    "Tail Arse Charlie" (Edited, augmented and arranged
      by Grace Perry. Abridged from the 72-page
      original published as <u>Poetry Australia</u> #82,
      1980, by South Head Press, New South Wales). <u>Sam</u>
      (38:3, release 151) 84, p. 1-24.

3519. MILLION, Dian
    "Mu'gua." <u>Calyx</u> (8:2) Spr 84, p. 79.

3520. MILLIS, Christopher
    "Cassim." <u>KanQ</u> (16:4) Aut 84, p. 147.
    "Grandmother." <u>StoneC</u> (11:3/4) Spr-Sum 84, p. 61.
    "Separate Vacation." <u>StoneC</u> (11:3/4) Spr-Sum 84,
      p. 60.

3521. MILLS, Barriss
    "Cherries Are Overripe." <u>Sparrow</u> (46) 84, p. 32.

3522. MILLS, George
    "Island." <u>StoneC</u> (11:3/4) Spr-Sum 84, p. 68.
    "Stones." <u>StoneC</u> (11:3/4) Spr-Sum 84, p. 69.

3523. MILLS, Jim Ignatius
    "Ascension." <u>Kayak</u> (64) My 84, p. 63.
    "Final Poem on a Theme." <u>Kayak</u> (64) My 84, p. 64.
    "Fishermen." <u>SoDakR</u> (22:3) Aut 84, p. 23.
    "For Cesar Vallejo." <u>Kayak</u> (64) My 84, p. 62.
    "Old Man Dining." <u>SoDakR</u> (22:3) Aut 84, p. 22.
    "Swans." <u>SoDakR</u> (22:3) Aut 84, p. 24.

3524. MILLS, Paul
    "The Village Campaign." <u>Argo</u> (6:1) 84, p. 23.

3525. MILLS, Ralph J., Jr.
    "1/31." <u>Poem</u> (52) N 84, p. 2-3.
    "A Fall Song" (for R. S.). <u>Sparrow</u> (46) 84, p. 26.
    "The Lifting." <u>NewL</u> (50:2/3) Wint-Spr 84, p. 216-
      217.
    "You Were Saying." <u>Poem</u> (52) N 84, p. 1.

3526. MILLS, Robert
    "Celebrations." <u>SpoonRQ</u> (9:2) Spr 84, p. 49.
    "Diversey Harbor--Summer's End." <u>SpoonRQ</u> (9:2)
      Spr 84, p. 50.
    "Poetry Workshop." <u>SpoonRQ</u> (9:2) Spr 84, p. 48.

3527. MILLS, Sparling
    "Embroidery." <u>WestCR</u> (19:2) O 84, p. 24.
    "Emily Dickinson at Forty." <u>Quarry</u> (33:1) Wint
      84, p. 58.

"Eroica." AntigR (59) Aut 84, p. 119.
"Family Man." Descant (47, 15:4) Wint 84, p. 176.
"Found Poem." PoetryCR (6:2) Wint 84-85, p. 25.
"Good Friday." Quarry (33:1) Wint 84, p. 58-60.
"I See Her." Descant (47, 15:4) Wint 84, p. 177.
"Making Contact." AntigR (59) Aut 84, p. 119.
"Summer in Herring Cove." PoetryCR (6:2) Wint 84-
    85, p. 19.

3528. MILLS, William
      "The Meaning of Coyotes." SouthernR (20:4) Aut
          84, p. 869-870.
      "Rituals along the Arkansas." SouthernR (20:4)
          Aut 84, p. 870-872.
      "The White Tents of Arctic Summer." SouthernR
          (20:4) Aut 84, p. 872-873.

3529. MILNE, W. S.
      "Margaret." Stand (25:3) Sum 84, p. 4.

3530. MILOSZ, Czeslaw
      "City without a Name" (tr. by the author, Robert
          Hass and Robert Pinsky). Thrpny (16) Wint 84,
          p. 12-13.
      "Esse" (tr. by the author and Robert Pinsky).
          NewRep (189:20) 14 N 83, p. 32.
      "The Gates of the Arsenal" (tr. by Renata
          Gorczynski and Robert Hass). GrandS (3:2) Wint
          84, p. 94-96.
      "My inner voice" (tr. of Zbigniew Herbert, w. Peter
          Dale Scott). ManhatR (3:2) Wint 84-85, p. 50-51.
      "Slow River" (tr. by the author, Robert Hass and
          Robert Pinsky). NewRep (189:20) 14 N 83, p. 31.
      "Song of Porcelain" (tr. by the author and Robert
          Pinsky). NewRep (189:20) 14 N 83, p. 32.
      "Songs of Adrian Zielinsky" (tr. by the author and
          Robert Hass). NewRep (189:20) 14 N 83, p. 33.

3531. MINAR, Scott
      "The Factory As Sense of Place." WestB (15) 84,
          p. 71.
      "Luminare." GeoR (38:1) Spr 84, p. 73.
      "Music." FourQt (33:3) Spr 84, p. 25.

3532. MINARD, Murielle
      "Apostle." ChrC (101:21) 20-27 Je 84, p. 620.

3533. MINARD, Nancy
      "My Face Illustrates My Soul." PottPort (6) 84,
          p. 17.

3534. MINHINNICK, Robert
      "The Attic." Argo (5:3) 84, p. 38-39.

3535. MINOGUE, Frank
      "Fields." AntigR (56) Wint 84, p. 119.
      "Redemption Depot." AntigR (56) Wint 84, p. 119.

3536. MINTON, Helena
      "Burning the House" (Ossabaw Island, Georgia."

WestB (15) 84, p. 42-43.
"From the Same Cloth" (for the mill girls, Lowell,
   Massachusetts, circa, 1840). BelPoJ (34:3) Spr
   84, p. 34-35.
"Narcissus Speaks to Echo." Paunch (57/58) Ja 84,
   p. 81-82.

3537. MIR, Pedro
   "Hay un País en el Mundo" (fragmento). Areíto
   (10:38) 84, inside front cover.

3538. MIRABAL, Mili
   "Triptico." Mairena (5:13) Spr 83, p. 60-61.

3539. MIRSKIN, Jerry
   "Aurora." MSS (4:1/2) Aut 84, p. 16-17.
   "The Bronx." MSS (4:1/2) Aut 84, p. 23.
   "The Downstairs." MSS (4:1/2) Aut 84, p. 21.
   "Go Try." MSS (4:1/2) Aut 84, p. 19.
   "My Father." MSS (4:1/2) Aut 84, p. 14.
   "Outside the Supermarket, December." MSS (4:1/2)
      Aut 84, p. 15.
   "Small Animal." MSS (4:1/2) Aut 84, p. 18.

3540. MISCHNICK, Cynthia
   "Wildflowers." Northeast (Series 3:17) Sum 84, p. 8.

3541. MISHKIN, Julia
   "Desire Lies Down on the Quiet Lake of the Memory."
      BlackWR (11:1) Aut 84, p. 77.
   "Flight." YaleR (73:3) Spr 84, p. 432.
   "Ode to Waiting." Pequod (16/17) 84, p. 133-134.
   "Sestina on a Passage by Woolf." Thrpny (19) Aut
      84, p. 20.
   "Sleeper Alone near Water." BlackWR (11:1) Aut
      84, p. 76.

3542. MISHOE, Peggy
   "If I touch You." SanFPJ (6:1) 84, p. 49.
   "You Turned Loose." SanFPJ (6:2) 84, p. 93-94.

3543. MITCHAM, Judson
   "Epistles" (Excerpts). GeoR (38:3) Aut 84, p. 592-
      593.
   "Loss of Power." SouthernPR (24:1) Spr 84, p. 7.
   "Rocking Anna to Sleep." PoetryNW (25:3) Aut 84,
      p. 19-20.
   "To a Young Sleepwalker." GrahamHR (7) Wint 84,
      p. 20.

3544. MITCHELL, Roger
   "Aging Gracelessly." IndR (7:1) Wint 84, p. 60-61.
   "The History of the Wind" (for Lisel Mueller).
      IndR (7:1) Wint 84, p. 58-59.
   "The Life I Am Living." Ploughs (10:4) 84, p. 192-
      193.
   "Recognition." MidAR (4:2) Aut 84, p. 145.
   "School Dream." Ploughs (10:1) 84, p. 119-120.
   "The Story of the White Cup" (for Helen). Ploughs
      (10:1) 84, p. 118.

"Uneven Light." OhioR (33) 84, p. 32-33.
"Watching from the Bushes: A Last Farewell to the
    Sixties." ColEng (46:1) Ja 84, p. 32.
"Whatever It Is." IndR (7:1) Wint 84, p. 62.
"White." MidAR (4:2) Aut 84, p. 144.

3545. MITCHELL, Stan
"Pyramid Lake Poem to Women of Power" (poet's name
    omitted). YellowS (10) Spr 84, p. 28.

3546. MITSUI, James Masao
"Paris Windows: Some Linked Bantu" (after a
    photograph/silhouette by Fran Martiny).
    MemphisSR (4:2) Spr 84, p. 11.

3547. MITTON, M. Anne
"Grandfather." PottPort (6) 84, p. 33.
"Looking at the Album with Aunt Lena." PottPort
    (6) 84, p. 38.
"The Photography." PottPort (6) 84, p. 22.

3548. MIYAZAWA, Kenji
"Again, alone" (tr. by Hiroaki Sato). Tele (19)
    83, p. 34.
"Arms spread" (tr. by Hiroaki Sato). Tele (19)
    83, p. 36.
"As I move away from the Bunsen burner" (tr. by
    Hiroaki Sato). Tele (19) 83, p. 35.
"At daybreak" (tr. by Hiroaki Sato). Tele (19)
    83, p. 36.
"August 1919 Lamenting Dr. Ishimaru's Death" (tr.
    by Hiroaki Sato). Tele (19) 83, p. 36.
"Because sparklingly" (tr. by Hiroaki Sato). Tele
    (19) 83, p. 36.
"Because the flames" (tr. by Hiroaki Sato). Tele
    (19) 83, p. 34.
"Cobalt suffering stagnates" (tr. by Hiroaki Sato).
    Tele (19) 83, p. 35.
"Early Poems in Tanka Form" (Selections, tr. by
    Hiroaki Sato). Tele (19) 83, p. 34-36.
"Far-off mountains etched at back" (tr. by Hiroaki
    Sato). Tele (19) 83, p. 35.
"Frost-cloudy" (tr. by Hiroaki Sato). Tele (19)
    83, p. 35.
"In the autumn wind" (tr. by Hiroaki Sato). Tele
    (19) 83, p. 34.
"Kashiwa Field" (tr. by Hiroaki Sato). Tele (19)
    83, p. 36.
"My temple felt icy" (tr. by Hiroaki Sato). Tele
    (19) 83, p. 37.
"The night rain half-damaged" (tr. by Hiroaki
    Sato). Tele (19) 83, p. 34.
"Out of the navy blue" (tr. by Hiroaki Sato).
    Tele (19) 83, p. 35.
"Park" (tr. by Hiroaki Sato). Tele (19) 83, p. 36.
"Reflected on the wings" (tr. by Hiroaki Sato).
    Tele (19) 83, p. 35.
"Right below a nickel cloud" (tr. by Hiroaki Sato).
    Tele (19) 83, p. 36.
"The rock cliff" (tr. by Hiroaki Sato). Tele (19)

83, p. 35.
"Seven Forests" (tr. by Hiroaki Sato). Tele (19)
   83, p. 35.
"These pine trees on this street" (tr. by Hiroaki
   Sato). Tele (19) 83, p. 37.
"Through the night" (tr. by Hiroaki Sato). Tele
   (19) 83, p. 36.
"What do I eat things for?" (tr. by Hiroaki Sato).
   Tele (19) 83, p. 34.
"Winter Sketches" (Selections, tr. by Hiroaki
   Sato). Tele (19) 83, p. 37.

3549. MIZEJEWSKI, Linda
   "Anaerobics: Elaine Powers, Wheeling, West
      Virginia." ThRiPo (23/24) 84, p. 20.
   "Parents Sleeping." ThRiPo (23/24) 84, p. 21.

3550. MOBBERLEY, David W.
   "The Seeds of Descruction." SanFPJ (6:1) 84, p. 52.

3551. MODLIN, Edith
   "Obviously." PoeticJ (7) 84, p. 9.
   "Soots Him." PoeticJ (7) 84, p. 23.
   "Thumbs Up." PoeticJ (6) 84, p. 5.

3552. MOELLER, Jean
   "Of Many Colors." AntiqR (57) Spr 84, p. 54.
   "One." AntiqR (57) Spr 84, p. 54.

3553. MOELLER, Jean P.
   "The Suit." AntiqR (59) Aut 84, p. 118.

3554. MOFFEIT, Tony
   "Adobe Wall." Amelia (1:2) O 84, p. 80.
   "Adobe Wall Motel." PoeticJ (1) 83, p. 6.
   "After the Rain." PoeticJ (8) 84, p. 20.
   "Blues Outlaw." PoeticJ (6) 84, p. 10.
   "Buffalo Dance." OroM (2:3/4, issue 7/8) 84, p. 13.
   "High Village." PoeticJ (4) 83, p. 5.
   "Hung Out at My Dad's." OroM (2:3/4, issue 7/8)
      84, p. 21.
   "The Last Laugh." Amelia (1:2) O 84, p. 80.
   "Manolete." PoeticJ (7) 84, p. 12.
   "Marguerita." PoeticJ (3) 83, p. 32.
   "Micheline & Solomon" (Jack Micheline at the
      Kerouac conference 7/29/82). MoodySI (14) Spr
      84, p. 20.
   "Night Blowing a Solo." PoeticJ (5) 84, p. 8.
   "Phantom." PoeticJ (7) 84, p. 13.
   "Queen of Spades." PoeticJ (2) 83, p. 25.
   "A Silence of Fireflies Eating the Night."
      PoeticJ (5) 84, p. 8.
   "Those Who Speak Do Not Know, Those Who Know Do Not
      Speak." OroM (2:3/4, issue 7/8) 84, p. 12-13.

3555. MOFFITT, John
   "Formula." NegC (4:3) Sum 84, p. 13.

3556. MOHLER, Stephen C.
   "Call of the Hospitals" (tr. of Alvaro Mutis).

Vis (15) 84, p. 11-12.
"The Street" (tr. of Mario Riveros). Vis (15) 84,
    p. 10.

3557. MOIR, James M.
    "Lake of Ice." Waves (12:2/3) Wint 84, p. 86.
    "Two Ways of Life." Dandel (11:1) Spr-Sum 84, p. 30.

3558. MOLDAW, Carol
    "The Witch's Poems." CarolQ (37:1) Aut 84, p. 64-66.

MOLEN, Robert vander: See VanderMOLEN, Robert

3559. MOLLOHAN, Terrie
    "Beyond the Garden." Poem (51) Mr [i.e. Jl] 84,
        p. 41.
    "Review of a Stale Drama." Poem (51) Mr [i.e. Jl]
        84, p. 42.

3560. MOMADAY, N. Scott
    "The Bear." AmerPoR (13:4) Jl-Ag 84, p. 13.
    "The Delight Song of Tsoai-Talee." AmerPoR (13:4)
        Jl-Ag 84, p. 16.
    "Four Charms." GreenfR (11:3/4) Wint-Spr 84, p. 61.
    "The Great Fillmore Street Buffalo Drive."
        GreenfR (11:3/4) Wint-Spr 84, p. 62.
    "Plainview, 1." AmerPoR (13:4) Jl-Ag 84, p. 18.
    "Rings of Bone." GreenfR (11:3/4) Wint-Spr 84, p.
        63.

MON, Richard le: See LeMON, Richard

3561. MONAGHAN, Patricia
    "Burn Scars." YetASM (3) 84, p. 3.

3562. MONETTE, Paul
    "Bones and Jewels." Shen (35:2/3) 84, p. 218-225.

3563. MONFREDO, Louise
    "Country Cemetery." KanQ (16:4) Aut 84, p. 199.

MONGE, Paulo Jolly: See JOLLY, Paulo de

3564. MONOHAN, Carolyn
    "Sign." ChrC (101:11) 4 Ap 84, p. 338.

3565. MONTAG, Tom
    "I find the more." Sparrow (46) 84, p. 29.

3566. MONTAGUE, John
    "The Music Box." Pequod (16/17) 84, p. 34-35.

3567. MONTALE, Eugenio
    "Another Moon Effect" (tr. by William Arrowsmith).
        GrandS (3:1) Aut 83, p. 113.
    "Argyll Tour" (tr. by Charles Wright). Chelsea
        (42/43) 84, p. 121.
    "Arsenio" (tr. by John Paul Russo). DenQ (19:1)
        Spr 84, p. 109-110.
    "Beloved of the Gods" (tr. by Jonathan Galassi).

Thrpny (19) Aut 84, p. 12.
"The Black Trout" (tr. by Charles Wright).
Chelsea (42/43) 84, p. 120.
"Brooding" (tr. by Jonathan Galassi). ParisR
(26:92) Sum 84, p. 145.
"Chords: Feelings and Fantasies of an Adolescent
Girl" (tr. by Jonathan Galassi). Antaeus (53)
Aut 84, p. 84-88.
"Clizia in '34" (tr. by Jonathan Galassi). ParisR
(26:92) Sum 84, p. 146.
"Clizia Poems" (tr. by Jonathan Galassi). ParisR
(26:92) Sum 84, p. 145-151.
"Credo" (tr. by Jonathan Galassi). ParisR (26:92)
Sum 84, p. 151.
"Floating" (tr. by Jonathan Galassi). Antaeus
(53) Aut 84, p. 82-83.
"For an 'Homage to Rimbaud'" (tr. by Charles
Wright). Chelsea (42/43) 84, p. 122.
"Foursome" (tr. by Jonathan Galassi). ParisR
(26:92) Sum 84, p. 149.
"From the Train" (tr. by Charles Wright). Chelsea
(42/43) 84, p. 122.
"The Hiding Places II" (tr. by Jonathan Galassi).
PartR (51:3) 84, p. 382-383.
"I have such faith in you" (to C., tr. by Jonathan
Galassi). NewYRB (31:10) 14 Je 84, p. 4.
"In '38" (tr. by Jonathan Galassi). ParisR
(26:92) Sum 84, p. 148.
"Inside/Outside" (tr. by Jonathan Galassi).
ParisR (26:92) Sum 84, p. 147.
"Let's go down the road that slopes among tangles
of brambles" (tr. by Jonathan Galassi).
Antaeus (53) Aut 84, p. 89.
"Levantine Letter" (tr. by Jonathan Galassi).
Antaeus (53) Aut 84, p. 78-81.
"Low Tide" (tr. by William Arrowsmith). GrandS
(3:1) Aut 83, p. 114.
"On the Greve" (tr. by Charles Wright). Chelsea
(42/43) 84, p. 120.
"Predictions" (tr. by Jonathan Galassi). ParisR
(26:92) Sum 84, p. 146.
"Prose for A.M." (tr. by Jonathan Galassi). Stand
(25:3) Sum 84, p. 13.
"The Return" (Bocca di Magra, tr. by William
Arrowsmith). GrandS (3:1) Aut 83, p. 112.
"Since Life Is Fleeing" (tr. by Jonathan Galassi).
ParisR (26:92) Sum 84, p. 150.
"Toward Vienna" (tr. by William Arrowsmith).
GrandS (3:1) Aut 83, p. 113.
"Wind on the Halfmoon" (tr. by Charles Wright).
Chelsea (42/43) 84, p. 121.
"Winter Lingers On" (tr. by Jonathan Galassi).
Stand (25:3) Sum 84, p. 12.

3568. MONTAÑEZ CACERES, Fedora
"Mar Caribe en Puerto Rico" (Para ti, Julia).
Mairena (5:13) Spr 83, p. 67-69.

3569. MONTEIRO, George
"Notions about Linguistics" (tr. of Jorge de Sena).

ConcPo (17:2) Aut 84, p. 156.

3570. MONTES HUIDOBRO, Matías
"De Nada Vale." Mairena (6:17) Aut 84, p. 72.
"De Nada Vale." Mairena (6:18) 84, p. 174.
"Esta Obsesion del Verso." Mairena (5:13) Spr 83,
p. 59.

3571. MONTGOMERY, George
"Pizza Prose." MoodySI (14) Spr 84, p. 24.

3572. MONTGOMERY, John
"Merrimac vs. Monticello." MoodySI (14) Spr 84,
p. 7.

3573. MOODY, Margaret
"A Birth and a Death." Quarry (33:2) Spr 84, p.
79-80.
"Silly Cow." Quarry (33:2) Spr 84, p. 80-81.
"We Go Together." Quarry (33:2) Spr 84, p. 80.

3574. MOODY, Rodger
"What a Man Saw." Wind (14:52) 84, p. 44.

3575. MOODY, Shirley
"September Sentinel." SouthernPR (24:2) Aut 84,
p. 34.

3576. MOOERS, Vernon
"Hot Season." Sam (41:1, release 161) 84, p. 33.
"Just a Riot." Sam (41:2, release 162) 84 or 85,
p. 6.
"Military Men." SanFPJ (7:1) 84, p. 8.
"Sipping Drinks at the Central Hotel." SanFPJ
(6:4) 84, p. 94.
"Train to Kano." Waves (12:2/3) Wint 84, p. 99.

3577. MOORE, Barbara
"Braque Said." CutB (22) Spr-Sum 84, p. 6.
"Carnival." MassR (25:3) Aut 84, p. 382.
"Child Setting the Table for Breakfast." CutB
(22) Spr-Sum 84, p. 7.
"City." MassR (25:3) Aut 84, p. 381.
"Driving Home in Winter." NewOR (11:3/4) Aut-Wint
84, p. 94.
"Photograph Album." Poetry (144:3) Je 84, p. 165.
"To the Orphans." Poetry (144:3) Je 84, p. 164.

3578. MOORE, Berwyn J.
"A Cappella." SnapD (8:1) Aut 84, p. 54-55.
"My Son Writing Stories." SnapD (8:1) Aut 84, p.
52-53.
"Sister." TexasR (5:3/4) Aut-Wint 84, p. 17-18.

3579. MOORE, Dennis
"Reflecting." Wind (14:50) 84, p. 41.

3580. MOORE, Frank D.
"Seeing through Cataracts." PaintedB (22) Spr 84,
p. 11.

3581. MOORE, George B.
        "For the Dead Found in Argentina." YetASM (3) 84,
        p. 7.

3582. MOORE, Honor
        "Cleis." 13thM (8:1/2) 84, p. 66-67.
        "First Night." Cond (3:4, issue 10) 84, p. 83-84.

3583. MOORE, Janice Townley
        "Copperhead Wall." KanQ (16:4) Aut 84, p. 184.
        "The Way Back." NegC (4:4) Aut 84, p. 25.

3584. MOORE, Jonathan
        "For N." Abraxas (29/30) 84, p. 37.

3585. MOORE, Lenard D.
        "Heat." BlackALF (18:1) Spr 84, p. 28.
        "The noonday sunshine." BlackALF (18:1) Spr 84,
        p. 28.
        "The old country road" (Haiku, Second Prize, 13th
        Annual Kansas Poetry Contest). LittleBR (4:3)
        Spr 84, p. 69.
        "The old monk." ThirdW (2) Spr 84, p. inside back
        cover.
        "On the sunlit slope." ThirdW (2) Spr 84, p.
        inside back cover.
        "A Poem for Langston Hughes." Stepping Wint 84,
        p. 24.
        "Tanka Composed of Five Lines." BlueBldgs (8)
        84?, p. 37.

3586. MOORE, Marianne
        "Logic and 'The Magic Flute'" (First telecolorcast
        by RCA, January 15, 1956: impressions of a
        première). Shen (35:2/3) 84, p. 225-226.

3587. MOORE, Richard
        "Survivors." Ploughs (10:1) 84, p. 123.

3588. MOORE, Roger
        "After the Storm." Quarry (33:1) Wint 84, p. 27.
        "Danse Macabre." PottPort (6) 84, p. 39.
        "Heron." PottPort (6) 84, p. 33.
        "The Old Loyalist Burial Ground, Fredericton."
        AntigR (57) Spr 84, p. 117.
        "Repossession." PottPort (6) 84, p. 51.
        "This Carving May Be Gently Touched." AntigR (57)
        Spr 84, p. 118.
        "Winter Retreat." Waves (12:2/3) Wint 84, p. 97.

3589. MOORE, Rosalie
        "Chicago Airport." NewRena (6:1, #18) Spr 84, p.
        119.

3590. MOORE, Todd
        "Chewing Ice." RagMag (3:1) Spr 84, p. 28.
        "Grand Theft Auto." Open24 (3) 84, p. 50.
        "Last of." Open24 (3) 84, p. 50.
        "The Night." Abraxas (31/32) 84, p. 14.
        "Putting." PoeticJ (4) 83, p. 34.

"Shooting." <u>Bogg</u> (52) 84, p. 9.
"Sneaking Upstairs." <u>PoeticJ</u> (4) 83, p. 24.
"Touching the Dead." <u>RagMag</u> (3:1) Spr 84, p. 27.
"Trading Coats w/a kid." <u>RagMag</u> (3:1) Spr 84, p. 26.

3591. MOORHEAD, Andrea
"Amor." <u>Os</u> (18) 84, p. 27.
"Erie Plain." <u>Os</u> (19) 84, p. 14.
"A Halo in Darkness." <u>Os</u> (19) 84, p. 15.
"Morning Walk." <u>Os</u> (18) 84, p. 28.
"Offering." <u>Os</u> (18) 84, p. 26.
"Open Wings." <u>Os</u> (19) 84, p. 17.
"Song of a Dove." <u>Os</u> (18) 84, p. 29.

3592. MOOSE, Ruth
"Monday." <u>KanQ</u> (16:4) Aut 84, p. 134.
"Nodding Off." <u>Blueline</u> (5:2) Wint-Spr 84, p. 21.

3593. MOOTRY, Maria K.
"A Palace of Strangers: A Female Chicago Artist
Confronts Sally Mae Hunter, Bag Lady of the
Streets." <u>OP</u> (37) Spr-Sum 84, p. 24-27.

3594. MORA, Pat
"Bruja." <u>Calyx</u> (8:2) Spr 84, p. 26.
"Loss of Control." <u>Calyx</u> (8:2) Spr 84, p. 25.
"Village Therapy." <u>Calyx</u> (8:2) Spr 84, p. 25.

3595. MORA de LEON, Daisy
"Entremos aire, música." <u>Mairena</u> (5:13) Spr 83,
p. 103.

3596. MORAGA, Cherríe
"La Dulce Culpa." <u>Calyx</u> (8:2) Spr 84, p. 20-21.

3597. MORALES, Arqueles
"Decido Hablar a Mi Pais" (fragmentos: I, II,
VIII). <u>Mairena</u> (6:18) 84, p. 211.

MORALES, Emérito Santiago: <u>See</u> SANTIAGO MORALES, Emérito

3598. MORALES SANTOS, Francisco
"Cartas para Seguir con la Vida" (nacimiento del
sol). <u>Mairena</u> (6:18) 84, p. 214.

3599. MORAN, Lynda
"The Stars Are Screeching." <u>Pequod</u> (16/17) 84, p.
45.
"Vigil." <u>Pequod</u> (16/17) 84, p. 46.

3600. MORAN, Moore
"Dog Days in Puerto Vallarta." <u>NewL</u> (50:4) Sum
84, p. 42.
"The Face." <u>YaleR</u> (73:2) Wint 84, p. 303-304.
"Four." <u>Thrpny</u> (18) Sum 84, p. 22.

3601. MORAN, Ronald
"Life on the Rim." <u>NegC</u> (4:2) Spr 84, p. 36-37.

3602. MOREJON, Nancy
     "Desilusion para Ruben Dario." Mairena (6:18) 84,
        p. 177.

MORENO, César Fernandez: See FERNANDEZ MORENO, César

3603. MORGAN, David R.
     "Cracked Cathy" (July 27th, 1983). Bogg (52) 84,
        p. 56.

3604. MORGAN, Frederick
     "February 11, 1971." Peb (23) 84, p. 43.
     "July 30, 1968." Peb (23) 84, p. 42.
     "Song." SewanR (92:1) Ja-Mr 84, p. 66.

3605. MORGAN, John
     "Among the Beasts." PoetryNW (25:1) Spr 84, p. 34-
        35.
     "Cabin on the Yukon." NoAmR (269:1) Mr 84, p. 13.

3606. MORGAN, Richard Conrad
     "On the Way Down." Stand (25:3) Sum 84, p. 63.

3607. MORGAN, Robert
     "Chicago Delta." CarolQ (37:1) Aut 84, p. 26.
     "Christmas Play." Epoch (33:2) Spr-Sum 84, p. 126.
     "Coccidiosis." Epoch (33:2) Spr-Sum 84, p. 127.
     "Coccidiosis" (corrected printing). Epoch (33:3)
        Sum-Aut 84, p. 227.
     "Dead Dog on the Highway." VirQR (60:2) Spr 84,
        p. 235-236.
     "Family." CarolQ (37:1) Aut 84, p. 28.
     "Harrow." Poetry (144:1) Ap 84, p. 11.
     "Millstone." Epoch (33:2) Spr-Sum 84, p. 125.
     "Oranges." Poetry (145:3) D 84, p. 146.
     "Pumphouse." CarolQ (37:1) Aut 84, p. 27.
     "Rearview Mirror." Poetry (144:1) Ap 84, p. 12.
     "Sky Gift." VirQR (60:2) Spr 84, p. 234-235.
     "Sunday Toilet." Antaeus (53) Aut 84, p. 243.
     "Watershed." CarolQ (37:1) Aut 84, p. 25.

3608. MORGAN, S. K.
     "Conservation." PoeticJ (7) 84, p. 10.
     "He Kills Cats, You Know." WormR (24:4, issue 96)
        84, p. 144-145.
     "Hypertension." WormR (24:4, issue 96) 84, p. 142-
        143.
     "Jack." WormR (24:4, issue 96) 84, p. 148.
     "The John Belushi Memorial Poem." WormR (24:4,
        issue 96) 84, p. 142.
     "The Last Time." WormR (24:4, issue 96) 84, p. 146.
     "Maturity." WormR (24:4, issue 96) 84, p. 147-148.
     "The Milk of Human Kindness." WormR (24:4, issue
        96) 84, p. 145.
     "Music Plays." PoeticJ (8) 84, p. 21.
     "No Quarter." WormR (24:4, issue 96) 84, p. 141.
     "Nuclear Wino." SanFPJ (6:1) 84, p. 47.
     "The Season Is Upon Us." SanFPJ (6:1) 84, p. 46.
     "Something's Clicking." WormR (24:4, issue 96)
        84, p. 145-146.
     "This One's for My Old Man." WormR (24:4, issue

96) 84, p. 146-147.
"Three Guys Getting Older at Lunch" (for Ed M. &
    Bob J.). WormR (24:4, issue 96) 84, p. 144.
"The Time I Paid for It." WormR (24:4, issue 96)
    84, p. 143-144.
"White Angel" (for Marg Daly). WormR (24:4, issue
    96) 84, p. 147.

3609. MORGAN, William
    "Digby Church." OhioR (33) 84, p. 110.
    "King of Trash." OhioR (33) 84, p. 111.

3610. MORGENSTERN, Christian
    "Christ Forlorn" (tr. by Frederick C. Ellert).
        MassR (25:4) Wint 84, p. 569.
    "Der Einsame Christus." MassR (25:4) Wint 84, p.
        568.
    "Der Gaul." MassR (25:4) Wint 84, p. 566.
    "The Old Nag" (tr. by Frederick C. Ellert). MassR
        (25:4) Wint 84, p. 567.

3611. MORIN, Edward
    "Bullfinches' Mythology." Hudson (37:1) Spr 84,
        p. 85.
    "The Empty Nest Ghazal" (For Camille). Ploughs
        (10:1) 84, p. 121.
    "Hot Songs for Motown" (Selection: 5. "The Poem As
        a Deconstructed Car"). Ploughs (10:1) 84, p. 122.
    "One Swallow Flying" (Psalm #4 of "The Passion",
        from The Axion Esti, tr. of Odysseus Elytis,
        w. Lefteris Pavlides). Confr (27/28) 84, p. 57.
    "Petit Dejeuner." CharR (10:2) Aut 84, p. 76-77.

3612. MORISON, Ted
    "Homemade." SouthernHR (18:3) Sum 84, p. 234.

3613. MORITZ, A. F.
    "Crazy Girl." Waves (13:1) Aut 84, p. 64-65.
    "Indifference" (after Montale). Waves (13:1) Aut
        84, p. 66.
    "The Land of Colchis." Descant (47, 15:4) Wint
        84, p. 61-62.
    "Native Woman." Descant (47, 15:4) Wint 84, p. 63.
    "Song of a Married Man." Waves (13:1) Aut 84, p. 66.

3614. MORLEY, Hilda
    "Equinox." AmerPoR (13:5) S-O 84, p. 32.
    "That Walk." AmerPoR (13:5) S-O 84, p. 32.

3615. MORO, Diego
    "Arena." Mairena (5:14) Aut 83, p. 29.
    "Ayer." Mairena (5:14) Aut 83, p. 30.
    "Cancionero del Perro Muerto" (Selections).
        Mairena (5:14) Aut 83, p. 29-30.
    "Se Acabo el Mar." Mairena (5:14) Aut 83, p. 29.

3616. MORO, Liliam
    "Rompete el Pecho contra el Mundo." LindLM (3:1)
        Ja-Mr 84, p. 7.

MORREALE BARKER, Lucile Angela: <u>See</u> BARKER, Lucile Angela
    Morreale

3617. MORRILL, Donald
    "The Hair Wreath." <u>NewEngR</u> (7:2) Wint 84, p. 174.

3618. MORRIS, Herbert
    "Circus." <u>Poetry</u> (143:4) Ja 84, p. 217-227.
    "Daguerreotypie der Niagara Falls" (Aufgenommen von
      Babbitt 1852). <u>Shen</u> (35:2/3) 84, p. 227-232.
    "Delfina Flores and Her Niece Modesta." <u>Shen</u>
      (35:4) 84, p. 77-83.
    "Early Views of Rio, Passion, Night." <u>Poetry</u>
      (144:5) Ag 84, p. 276-280.
    "In the Dark" (Michael at New Hope, July 4).
      <u>ParisR</u> (26:93) Aut 84, p. 248-252.
    "Magic." <u>Salm</u> (65) Aut 84, p. 116-118.
    "The Park Hotel, Munich, 1907." <u>Shen</u> (35:1) 83-
      84, p. 39-51.
    "Tennessee." <u>Chelsea</u> (42/43) 84, p. 132-133.

3619. MORRIS, John N.
    "Flying Lessons." <u>GrandS</u> (3:2) Wint 84, p. 142-143.
    "The Gifts." <u>Shen</u> (35:2/3) 84, p. 232-233.
    "In the Restaurant Polar." <u>Shen</u> (35:2/3) 84, p. 233.
    "The Museum Shop Catalogue." <u>Poetry</u> (144:5) Ag
      84, p. 262-263.
    "Reading Myself Asleep." <u>Poetry</u> (144:5) Ag 84, p.
      260.
    "Reading the Writing." <u>Poetry</u> (144:5) Ag 84, p.
      261-262.
    "A Word from the Examiners." <u>Poetry</u> (144:5) Ag
      84, p. 260-261.

3620. MORRIS, Laurel
    "Fires Serenity." <u>WritersL</u> (2) 84, p. 7.

3621. MORRIS, Paul
    "In the Fields of Camphor" (tr. of Yvan Goll).
      <u>WebR</u> (9:1) Spr 84, p. 18.
    "The Lake of Salt" (tr. of Yvan Goll). <u>WebR</u> (9:1)
      Spr 84, p. 17.
    "Summer" (tr. of Georg Trakl). <u>BlueBldgs</u> (7) 84,
      p. 53.
    "To Claire" (Written December 1949 to January 1950
      in the hospital where he died. Tr. of Yvan
      Goll). <u>WebR</u> (9:1) Spr 84, p. 19.

3622. MORRIS, Peter
    "A Bunch of Vultures." <u>WormR</u> (24:4, issue 96) 84,
      p. 138.
    "Proud Poem." <u>WormR</u> (24:4, issue 96) 84, p. 138-139.

3623. MORRIS, Robert
    "Fragments from Texts for the Reliefs (1982)."
      <u>Sulfur</u> (4:1, issue 10) 84, p. 103-105.
    "Roller Disco: Cenotaph for a Public Figure."
      <u>Chelsea</u> (42/43) 84, p. 385.

3624. MORRISON, L. L.
    "The Ghosts of Jersey City." <u>Sparrow</u> (46) 84, p. 17.

3625. MORRISON, Lillian
    "In Terms of Physics." <u>Veloc</u> (4) Sum 84, p. 19.

3626. MORRISON, R. H.
"I saw a lake, and it was standing sheer" (tr. of
Osip Mandelstam). LitR (27:3) Spr 84, p. 313.
"In transparent Petropolis we'll die" (tr. of Osip
Mandelstam). LitR (27:3) Spr 84, p. 314.
"Still I have not yet died" (tr. of Osip
Mandelstam). LitR (27:3) Spr 84, p. 314.
"Succor me, O Lord, to live through this night"
(tr. of Osip Mandelstam). LitR (27:3) Spr 84,
p. 314.
"Upon the altar of the hazy ripples" (tr. of Osip
Mandelstam). LitR (27:3) Spr 84, p. 313.

3627. MORRISON, Thelma
"The Joker." Quarry (33:3) Sum 84, p. 38-39.
"Snake Streets." Quarry (33:3) Sum 84, p. 37-38.

3628. MORRISSETTE, Georges
"A L'Auberge du Violon." PraF (5:4) Sum 84, p. 56-
58.

3629. MORRISSETTE, M. P.
"End-of-the-Day Musings." YetASM (3) 84, p. 8.

3630. MORSE, Carl
"Humanities I." Shen (35:4) 84, p. 92-94.
"Humanities II." Shen (35:4) 84, p. 94-95.

3631. MORSE, Cheryl
"The D.H. Lawrence Tree." CapeR (19:2) Sum 84, p.
29.

3632. MORSE, Flo
"When It Was Over." Confr (27/28) 84, p. 196.

3633. MORSON, E. W.
"African Dream." WestCR (18:4) Ap 84, p. 29.
"Desert Ice." WestCR (18:4) Ap 84, p. 30.
"The Inheritance." WestCR (18:4) Ap 84, p. 29.
"Tundra." WestCR (18:4) Ap 84, p. 31.

3634. MORTON, Carl P.
"In Other Arms." NeqC (4:1) Wint 84, p. 105.
"Of Chimneys and the Heart." NeqC (4:4) Aut 84,
p. 80.
"Poetry." NeqC (4:1) Wint 84, p. 104.

3635. MORTON, Colin
"After all these years you." Grain (12:1) F 84,
p. 8.
"Bead of dew." Grain (12:1) F 84, p. 8.
"Forty-Five Years from Now." Grain (12:1) F 84,
p. 10.
"I want to make the night short for you." Grain
(12:1) F 84, p. 8.
"Li Po and Tu Fu at the Duck Lake Tavern." Grain
(12:1) F 84, p. 9.
"Quartier Libre" (English tr. of Jacques Prevert).
Quarry (33:1) Wint 84, p. 47.
"Spring Flood." Quarry (33:1) Wint 84, p. 48.

"Your face flowers in the light of the match."
   <u>Grain</u> (12:1) F 84, p. 8.

3636. MOSBY, George, Jr.
   "High Priestess." <u>HangL</u> (46) Aut 84, p. 54-55.
   "The Storm." <u>HangL</u> (46) Aut 84, p. 53.

3637. MOSER, John W.
   "Wind." <u>NewL</u> (50:2/3) Wint-Spr 84, p. 218.

3638. MOSES, Daniel David
   "Bee Muse." <u>Waves</u> (13:1) Aut 84, p. 72-73.
   "The End of the Night." <u>PoetryCR</u> (6:2) Wint 84-
      85, p. 6.
   "Grandmother in White." <u>Waves</u> (13:1) Aut 84, p. 74.

3639. MOSKIN, Ilene
   "Poem for Recuperation" (for my father). <u>Iowa</u>
      (14:3) Aut 84, p. 105-106.

3640. MOSS, Ed
   "Awakening from the Deep." <u>Pig</u> (12) 84, p. 36.

3641. MOSS, Greg
   "The Ducks." <u>AmerS</u> (53:2) Spr 84, p. 242.

3642. MOSS, Howard
   "Einstein's Bathrobe." <u>NewYorker</u> (60:6) 26 Mr 84,
      p. 46.
   "Heaven." <u>MemphisSR</u> (5:1) Aut 84, p. 4.
   "A Hill." <u>NewYorker</u> (60:10) 23 Ap 84, p. 44.
   "Miami Beach." <u>AmerPoR</u> (13:3) My-Je 84, p. 12.
   "The Miles Between." <u>GeoR</u> (38:4) Wint 84, p. 867.
   "The New York Notebooks." <u>AmerPoR</u> (13:3) My-Je
      84, p. 13.
   "Short Stories." <u>Shen</u> (35:2/3) 84, p. 234-236.
   "Weekend." <u>NewYorker</u> (60:1) 20 F 84, p. 54.

3643. MOSS, Stanley
   "In Front of a Poster of Garibaldi." <u>Nat</u> (238:19)
      19 My 84, p. 618.

3644. MOSS, Thylias
   "Acceptance of the Grave." <u>IndR</u> (7:1) Wint 84, p.
      66-67.
   "The Barren Midwife Speaks of Duty." <u>NoDaQ</u> (52:2)
      Spr 84, p. 98.
   "A Child's Been Dead a Week." <u>TexasR</u> (5:1/2) Spr-
      Sum 84, p. 138-139.
   "The Owl in Daytime." <u>IndR</u> (7:1) Wint 84, p. 63.
   "Secrets behind the Names." <u>IndR</u> (7:1) Wint 84,
      p. 68-69.
   "Taluca, Twenty Years Later." <u>TexasR</u> (5:1/2) Spr-
      Sum 84, p. 138.
   "The Undertaker's Daughter" (for M. Egolf). <u>IndR</u>
      (7:1) Wint 84, p. 64-65.

3645. MOTEN, Fred
   "Crisis of the Negro Intellectual." <u>HarvardA</u>
      (118:2) Spr 84, p. 22.

"The End of Poetry." HarvardA (118:2) Spr 84, p. 23.
"The End of Realism." HarvardA (118:2) Spr 84, p.
    23.

3646. MOTION, Andrew
"A Lyrical Ballad." ParisR (26:91) Spr 84, p. 88-90.

3647. MOUCHARD, Claude
"Black Animal Dependency" (tr. by Linda Orr).
    ParisR (26:92) Sum 84, p. 164-172.

3648. MOUL, Keith
"A Wisconsin Poplar." Wind (14:51) 84, p. 35-36.

3649. MOULEDOUX-LAJOIE, Rhea
"Domine Exaudi." PoetryCR (6:2) Wint 84-85, p. 27.
"Half Way Offering." AntigR (59) Aut 84, p. 132.
"Letter." AntigR (59) Aut 84, p. 133.
"Nature Reclaims." AntigR (59) Aut 84, p. 131.
"Suzanne/Secrets." AntigR (59) Aut 84, p. 133.

3650. MOULTON-BARRETT, Donalee
"In My Mother's House." Germ (8:1) Spr-Sum 84, p.
    18.
"The Lotus Mask." CrossC (6:4) 84, p. 8.
"Nationalism." Waves (12:1) Aut 83, p. 53.
"Nightwatch." PottPort (6) 84, p. 25.
"Toll Booths." Germ (8:1) Spr-Sum 84, p. 17.

3651. MOURE, Erin
"Be Sociable." CanLit (100) Spr 84, p. 234.
"Five Highways." Descant (47, 15:4) Wint 84, p. 22.
"Gary." PoetryCR (6:1) Aut 84, p. 25.
"Paradisical Vallejo." Descant (47, 15:4) Wint
    84, p. 23.
"Perfect Sight." PoetryCR (6:1) Aut 84, p. 25.
"Preparation for Dying, Performed for the Dying Man
    by His Wife of Forty Years." Quarry (33:3) Sum
    84, p. 66.
"Public Health." PoetryCR (6:1) Aut 84, p. 25.
"Shocks." CanLit (100) Spr 84, p. 234-235.
"Siksika." CanLit (100) Spr 84, p. 233.
"Speaking in Tongues." Descant (47, 15:4) Wint
    84, p. 21.
"The Words Mean What We Say, We Say" (reprinted
    from Quarry 32:4 where it appeared with an
    error in the last stanza). Quarry (33:3) Sum
    84, p. 67.

3652. MOVIUS, Geoffrey
"Angle of Incidence." LittleM (14:3) 84, p. 52.
"At Fenway." LittleM (14:3) 84, p. 51.
"Cadences of Desire." LittleM (14:3) 84, p. 51.

3653. MPINA, Edison
"Arlington." Iowa (14:2) Spr-Sum 84, p. 130.
"Naphiri." Iowa (14:2) Spr-Sum 84, p. 129.

3654. MUELLER, Lisel
"Bread and Apples." Tendril (17) Wint 84, p. 131.

"For the Strangers." PoetryNW (25:2) Sum 84, p. 3-4.
"Fulfilling the Promise." TriQ (60) Spr-Sum 84,
    p. 152-153.
"Identical Twins." TriQ (60) Spr-Sum 84, p. 150-151.
"Metaphor" (For Gregory Orr, who asked, How can one
    teach 'Spring and Fall: To a Young Child' in the
    Hawaiian Islands?). PoetryNW (25:2) Sum 84, p.
    4-5.
"Necessities." PoetryNW (25:2) Sum 84, p. 6-7.
"Reasons for Numbers." GeoR (38:1) Spr 84, p. 102-
    103.
"Rescues." Tendril (17) Wint 84, p. 130.
"Testimony." SenR (14:2) 84, p. 66.

3655. MULCAHY, Barbara Curry
"Desire." Quarry (33:4) Aut 84, p. 74.
"The Garden of the Man Whose Wife Has Left Him."
    Quarry (33:4) Aut 84, p. 74.
"I Am Folded In upon Myself." Waves (12:4) Spr
    84, p. 49.
"On a Dark Mountain." BlueBuf (2:2) Spr 84, p. 12.
"The Passage." Dandel (11:2) Aut-Wint 84-85, p.
    54-55.
"Season of the Winter Solstice." Quarry (33:3)
    Sum 84, p. 68-69.
"Three Beginnings." Quarry (33:3) Sum 84, p. 68.

3656. MULDOON, Paul
"Glanders." Pequod (16/17) 84, p. 47.

3657. MULDOON, Virginia
"Mr. Rose." PoeticJ (8) 84, p. 7.

3658. MULHALLEN, Karen
"Toward Punta Banda." Descant (44/45, 15:1/2) Spr-
    Sum 84, p. 198-201.

3659. MULL, Peter C.
"Grand Manan" (For John). WebR (9:1) Spr 84, p.
    56-57.

3660. MULLANY, Stephen W.
"The Flight of the Pelican." Vis (16) 84, p. 9.

3661. MULLEN, Charles
"The Ball Court" (Chichen Itza). ThirdW (2) Spr
    84, p. 37.

3662. MULLEN, Laura
"Black Satin Shoes." Thrpny (18) Sum 84, p. 22.
"Your Lovers Convene." Thrpny (16) Wint 84, p. 4.

3663. MULLER, Robert
"Lake George: A View." AmerPoR (13:4) Jl-Ag 84,
    p. 41.

3664. MULLIGAN, J. B.
"Caesar and Vercingetorix." Sam (38:4, release
    152) 84, p. 12.
"The Explosion." PoeticJ (3) 83, p. 36.

"The Flasher." <u>Sam</u> (38:4, release 152) 84, p. 3.
"The Neighbor." <u>Sam</u> (38:4, release 152) 84, p. 7.
"Office Workers." <u>Sam</u> (38:4, release 152) 84, p. 2.
"The Other." <u>PoeticJ</u> (3) 83, p. 38.
"The Shah of Iran." <u>Sam</u> (38:4, release 152) 84,
    p. 8.
"The Spot of Blood." <u>Sam</u> (38:4, release 152) 84,
    p. 4-5.
"Street Corner Incident." <u>Sam</u> (38:4, release 152)
    84, p. 6.
"A Suicide." <u>Wind</u> (14:50) 84, p. 42.
"This Way to the Egress" (Issue title). <u>Sam</u>
    (38:4, release 152) 84, p. 1-12.
"This Way to the Egress." <u>Sam</u> (38:4, release 152)
    84, back cover.
"The Unknown Soldier." <u>Sam</u> (38:4, release 152)
    84, p. 9-11.
"The Unspeakable." <u>Sam</u> (38:4, release 152) 84, p. 2.
"Voyeur." <u>Sam</u> (38:4, release 152) 84, p. 3.

3665. MULLINIX, Debra Kay
    "Post-Winter Ritual." <u>CapeR</u> (19:2) Sum 84, p. 3.

3666. MULRANE, Scott H.
    "The Confession of the Sage." <u>Bogg</u> (52) 84, p. 24.
    "Derailment." <u>Wind</u> (14:51) 84, p. 49.
    "January 6, 1980." <u>Abraxas</u> (29/30) 84, p. 18.
    "The Last Wild Man." <u>Abraxas</u> (29/30) 84, p. 19.

3667. MUMFORD, Erika
    "Black Fire." <u>Ploughs</u> (10:1) 84, p. 124-125.
    "Deeper into the Bog." <u>GreenfR</u> (11:3/4) Wint-Spr
    84, p. 148.
    "Pierre Loti Visits the Maharaja of Travancore."
    <u>Poetry</u> (143:5) F 84, p. 280-281.

3668. MUNDHENK, Michael
    "What Else Is There To Do." <u>Paunch</u> (57/58) Ja 84,
    p. 39-40.

3669. MUNDO LOPEZ, Hilda R.
    "Es como fabricar." <u>Mairena</u> (6:17) Aut 84, p. 87.

3670. MUÑOZ HERRERA, Miguel Angel
    "Atrasgos" (Selections). <u>Mairena</u> (5:14) Aut 83,
    p. 27-28.
    "Saltos del Dia." <u>Mairena</u> (5:14) Aut 83, p. 27.
    "Sueño." <u>Mairena</u> (5:14) Aut 83, p. 28.

3671. MUNRO, Jane
    "Creek Bed" (for Evelyn Southwell). <u>WestCR</u> (19:1)
    Je 84, p. 11-23.
    "Listing." <u>PoetryCR</u> (6:1) Aut 84, p. 23.
    "Satori." <u>PoetryCR</u> (6:2) Wint 84-85, p. 6.

3672. MURA, David
    "The Survivor" (for Kinzo Nishida and Hiroshima).
    <u>Spirit</u> (7:1) 84, p. 160-161.

3673. MURARI
      "In the morning her girlfriends press her" (tr. by
      Andrew Schelling). YellowS (13) Wint 84, p. 28.

3674. MURATORI, Fred
      "Corridors." CutB (22) Spr-Sum 84, p. 37.
      "Hiking in Winter" (for my father). LitR (27:2)
      Wint 84, p. 190.

3675. MURAWSKI, Elisabeth
      "And Now I Say to You." OhioR (32) 84, p. 25.
      "Davidsonville Farm." LitR (28:1) Aut 84, p. 113.
      "How We Learned about the War." LitR (28:1) Aut
      84, p. 112.
      "Midday Early June." SouthernPR (24:1) Spr 84, p.
      34.
      "Sculpture." OhioR (32) 84, p. 24.
      "Two Dreams of One Dead." SmPd (21:2) Spr 84, p. 26.

MURIEL, Rodrigo Hernandez: See HERNANDEZ MURIEL, Rodrigo

3676. MURILLO, Rosario
      "The Difficulties of a Poet Who Amidst Desks,
      Machines and Countless Other Things Scribbles
      Poems and Scribbles Them Again" (tr. by Barbara
      Paschke). Vis (15) 84, p. 25.
      "My Love Is Hard Right On" (For the compañeros of
      Gradas, tr. by Janet Brof). NewEngR (6:4) Sum
      84, p. 583-584.
      "Point Number 1 on the Agenda" (tr. by Marc
      Zimmerman and Ellen Banberger). MinnR (N.S.
      22) Spr 84, p. 69.
      "Requiem in Vita Pro Nobis" (tr. by Janet Brof).
      Vis (15) 84, p. 27.
      "Shadows at Dawn" (tr. by Barbara Paschke). Vis
      (15) 84, p. 26.

3677. MURPHY, Frank
      "Overheard in Quebec." HangL (45) Spr 84, p. 38.

3678. MURPHY, Kay
      "Eighties Meditation." SpoonRQ (9:2) Spr 84, p. 16.

3679. MURPHY, Kay A.
      "Christmas Card." Poetry (145:3) D 84, p. 145.
      "A Natural Thing." Tendril (17) Wint 84, p. 132.
      "Prophecy." SenR (14:1) 84, p. 10.
      "Telemachus' Sister" (for Mary Baron). SenR
      (14:1) 84, p. 9.

3680. MURPHY, P. D.
      "Human Sacrifice and the Hieratic State." SanFPJ
      (6:3) 84, p. 65.
      "A Real Emergency." SanFPJ (6:3) 84, p. 68.
      "Strike the Colors." SanFPJ (6:3) 84, p. 65.

3681. MURPHY, Ray
      "Genesis." TriQ (59) Wint 84, p. 119.
      "One Song." TriQ (59) Wint 84, p. 118.

3682. MURPHY, Rich
        "Alone in a Body Overgrown with a Man." <u>GreenfR</u>
        (12:1/2) Sum-Aut 84, p. 129-130.
        "Between Classes." <u>SanFPJ</u> (6:1) 84, p. 27.
        "Big Talk." <u>KanQ</u> (16:4) Aut 84, p. 79.
        "The Compromise of the Literal and Figurative."
        <u>SanFPJ</u> (6:1) 84, p. 89.
        "Pansy." <u>SanFPJ</u> (6:1) 84, p. 26.

3683. MURPHY, Richard
        "Family Seat." <u>GrandS</u> (3:2) Wint 84, p. 16.
        "Milford: East Wing." <u>GrandS</u> (3:2) Wint 84, p. 17.
        "Portico." <u>GrandS</u> (3:2) Wint 84, p. 15.
        "Roof-Tree." <u>GrandS</u> (3:2) Wint 84, p. 19.
        "Tony White's Cottage." <u>GrandS</u> (3:2) Wint 84, p. 20.
        "Wellington College." <u>GrandS</u> (3:2) Wint 84, p. 18.

3684. MURPHY, Sheila
        "Reading the Wedding Poem." <u>SpoonRQ</u> (9:4) Aut 84,
        p. 54.
        "Wild Rice Pantoum" (for Becky). <u>SpoonRQ</u> (9:4)
        Aut 84, p. 55.

3685. MURPHY, Sheila E.
        "Air-Conditioning Pantoum." <u>WindO</u> (44) Sum-Aut
        84, p. 9-10.
        "Derivation." <u>RagMag</u> (3:1) Spr 84, p. 1.
        "Haibun 16." <u>Amelia</u> (1:2) O 84, p. 76.

3686. MURPHY, Shelia E.
        "Fever." <u>Wind</u> (14:51) 84, p. 31.

3687. MURRAY, Donald M.
        "High School Reunion." <u>EngJ</u> (73:4) Ap 84, p. 85.
        "My Daughter Waits" (LEM 1957-1977). <u>Tendril</u> (17)
        Wint 84, p. 133.
        "Remembering to Call." <u>Tendril</u> (17) Wint 84, p. 134.

3688. MURRAY, G. E.
        "Shelby County, Indiana, February, 1977." <u>NewL</u>
        (50:2/3) Wint-Spr 84, p. 109.
        "Tyger on Michigan Avenue." <u>Gargoyle</u> (24) 84, p.
        235.

3689. MURRAY, Les A.
        "Flood Plains on the Coast Facing Asia." <u>LittleM</u>
        (14:3) 84, p. 5-8.
        "The Hypogeum." <u>NewYorker</u> (60:14) 21 My 84, p. 46.

3690. MURRAY, Marilyn
        "Imagine a Heart." <u>PoetryE</u> (15) Aut 84, back cover.
        "Imagine a Heart." <u>PoetryE</u> (15) Aut 84, p. 9.

3691. MURRAY, Philip
        "A Letter from the Lower East Side." <u>Sparrow</u> (46)
        84, p. 11.

3692. MUSGRAVE, John D.
        "Communion under Fire: Con Thien, Oct. '67." <u>Pig</u>
        (12) 84, p. 29.

3693. MUSGRAVE, Susan
       "Adrift." <u>CanLit</u> (100) Spr 84, p. 236.
       "Black Tulips." <u>NegC</u> (4:1) Wint 84, p. 77-78.
       "John Berryman, This Is for You." <u>CrossC</u> (6:3)
          84, p. 10.
       "Not a Love Poem." <u>PoetryCR</u> (6:2) Wint 84-85, p. 12.
       "Supposing You Have Nowhere to Go." <u>CrossC</u> (6:3)
          84, p. 10.

3694. MUSICK, Martin
       "The Battle." <u>PoeticJ</u> (8) 84, p. 5.
       "Fortress of Solitude." <u>PoeticJ</u> (8) 84, p. 5.

3695. MUSKE, Carol
       "August, Los Angeles, Lullaby." <u>Field</u> (31) Aut
          84, p. 56-58.
       "David." <u>Ploughs</u> (10:4) 84, p. 101-102.
       "A Fresco." <u>Ploughs</u> (10:4) 84, p. 99-100.
       "The Separator." <u>Poetry</u> (145:2) N 84, p. 66-68.
       "Sounding." <u>Poetry</u> (145:2) N 84, p. 68-69.
       "You Could." <u>Ploughs</u> (10:4) 84, p. 103-105.

3696. MUTIS, Alvaro
       "Call of the Hospitals" (tr. by Stephen C. Mohler).
          <u>Vis</u> (15) 84, p. 11-12.

3697. MYCUE, Edward
       "Creation Tears Apart." <u>YellowS</u> (13) Wint 84, p. 14.
       "Echoes of Arrival." <u>Veloc</u> (2) Spr 83, p. 4.
       "The Hanging Key." <u>Veloc</u> (2) Spr 83, p. 3.
       "Hot." <u>YetASM</u> (3) 84, p. 5.
       "Insane Floor." <u>Veloc</u> (3) Aut-Wint 83, p. 6.
       "Like a Wreath." <u>Open24</u> (3) 84, p. 29.
       "Richard Says Everyone Knows To." <u>AntigR</u> (57) Spr
          84, p. 58.
       "Skin." <u>Veloc</u> (3) Aut-Wint 83, p. 8.
       "Vision." <u>AntigR</u> (57) Spr 84, p. 57.
       "Wild / Sanctuary / Life." <u>SanFPJ</u> (6:4) 84, p. 86-
          87.

3698. MYERS, Jack
       "Coming to the Surface." <u>WoosterR</u> (1:1) Mr 84, p.
          39.
       "Leaves." <u>Tendril</u> (17) Wint 84, p. 137.
       "Natural Ice Cream." <u>Tendril</u> (17) Wint 84, p. 135.
       "Planting Stones." <u>Tendril</u> (17) Wint 84, p. 136.
       "Self-addressed Trains of Thought -- in Memory of
          My Memory." <u>WoosterR</u> (1:1) Mr 84, p. 40.
       "The Waiters." <u>OhioR</u> (32) 84, p. 38-39.
       "Waiting for the Part with the Bite out of Me to
          Snap." <u>NoAmR</u> (269:3) S 84, p. 70.

3699. MYERS, Joan Rohr
       "Something Worth Saving." <u>ChrC</u> (101:29) 3 O 84,
          p. 903.
       "When You Know." <u>PaintedB</u> (24) Aut 84, p. 20.

3700. MYERS, Marshall
       "Bob." <u>Wind</u> (14:51) 84, p. 17.

3701. MYERS, Neil
"Clara." PraS (58:2) Sum 84, p. 67.
"Day of Atonement." CharR (10:1) Spr 84, p. 62.
"Death Scenes." LitR (28:1) Aut 84, p. 38-41.
"Eliyahu." CharR (10:1) Spr 84, p. 61.
"Lot's Wife." CharR (10:1) Spr 84, p. 62.
"A Note for Jeremiah." CharR (10:1) Spr 84, p. 63.
"Poems on Hebrew Themes." CharR (10:1) Spr 84, p.
    61-63.
"Postcard, for Lee." CharR (10:1) Spr 84, p. 63.

3702. N. N.
"C H S.: . . . Allende Gossens." LindLM (3:2/4)
    Ap-D 84, p. 28.
"C H S.: . . . Pinochet Ugarte." LindLM (3:2/4)
    Ap-D 84, p. 28.

3703. NACKER-PAUL, Sali
"Avoir l'Apprenti dans le Soleil" (after Duchamp
    1914). SmPd (21:3) Aut 84, p. 33.
"Thief of Her Muse." SmPd (21:3) Aut 84, p. 34-35.

3704. NADJIB, Emha Ainunn
"Bukan" (tr. by the author and Harriet Levin).
    Iowa (14:2) Spr-Sum 84, p. 65.

3705. NAGY, Agnes Nemes
"Four Squares" (tr. by Bruce Berlind). Iowa
    (14:2) Spr-Sum 84, p. 196-197.
"The Ghost" (tr. by Bruce Berlind). Iowa (14:2)
    Spr-Sum 84, p. 200.
"Storm" (tr. by Bruce Berlind). Iowa (14:2) Spr-
    Sum 84, p. 199-200.
"Streetcar" (to the memory of Sidney Keyes, tr. by
    Bruce Berlind). Iowa (14:2) Spr-Sum 84, p. 197-
    199.
"To My Craft" (tr. by Bruce Berlind). Iowa (14:2)
    Spr-Sum 84, p. 201.

3706. NAJERA, Francisco
"Arráncame la piel para sentirme tuyo." Mairena
    (6:17) Aut 84, p. 69.
"En el Momento del Extasis." Mairena (5:14) Aut
    83, p. 76.

3707. NAJLIS, Michele
"Proverbs and Songs" (tr. by Marc Zimmerman and
    Ellen Banberger). MinnR (N.S. 22) Spr 84, p. 68.

3708. NAJLIS, Mitchelle
"Caos." Mairena (6:18) 84, p. 160.
"La Tarde." Mairena (6:18) 84, p. 160.

3709. NAKAGAMI, Tetsuo
"I'm Lying on the Bed at a Motel and" (tr. by the
    author and Marilyn Chin). Iowa (14:2) Spr-Sum
    84, p. 63.
"Wandering Was Always an Important Theme in My
    Lyric" (tr. by the author and Marilyn Chin).
    Iowa (14:2) Spr-Sum 84, p. 62.

3710. NAMEROFF, Rochelle
      "Letter Home." _Tendril_ (17) Wint 84, p. 138.
      "Narcissism." _Tendril_ (17) Wint 84, p. 139.
      "Saint Opossum." _AntR_ (42:4) Aut 84, p. 453.
      "Tiny Histories." _CharR_ (10:2) Aut 84, p. 91-92.

3711. NAMJOSHI, Suniti
      "Triptych." _CanLit_ (100) Spr 84, p. 237-238.

3712. NANCE, Kevin
      "Thermal" (Yellowstone, 1975). _PoetL_ (79:2) Sum
      84, p. 106-111.

3713. NANI, Christel
      "Bus Ride." _Amelia_ [1:1] Ap 84, p. 25.

NAOSHI, Koriyama: _See_ KORIYAMA, Naoshi

3714. NAPORA, Joe
      "Cronus." _MinnR_ (N.S. 22) Spr 84, p. 47-48.
      "Knots." _GreenfR_ (12:1/2) Sum-Aut 84, p. 40-41.
      "Titan." _MinnR_ (N.S. 22) Spr 84, p. 48-50.

NAPOUT, Lillian Stratta de: _See_ STRATTA de NAPOUT, Lillian

3715. NASDOR, Marc
      "Manhattan." _Open24_ (3) 84, p. 40.
      "No. 24" (for Elizabeth). _Tele_ (19) 83, p. 30.
      "Poem: He entered juggling." _Tele_ (19) 83, p. 31.
      "Someone Participates." _LittleM_ (14:3) 84, p. 34-35.
      "To Believe." _Tele_ (19) 83, p. 32.
      "Vermin." _Tele_ (19) 83, p. 31.
      "Where That Thing Is It Occur" (for Steve Carey).
      Open24 (3) 84, p. 40.

3716. NASH, C. L.
      "Beauty Will Be." _BlackALF_ (18:1) Spr 84, p. 34.
      "Cry for Me." _BlackALF_ (18:1) Spr 84, p. 35.

3717. NASH, Roger
      "After Her Stroke." _Quarry_ (33:3) Sum 84, p. 40-42.
      "An Invasion of Goats." _Waves_ (12:4) Spr 84, p. 57.
      "Poem of Probabilities." _CanLit_ (103) Wint 84, p.
      26.
      "Several Excuses for Having Stayed." _Quarry_
      (33:3) Sum 84, p. 40.

3718. NASIO, Brenda
      "Dear Papa." _NegC_ (4:4) Aut 84, p. 18-19.

3719. NASTER, Richard
      "Archaeology." _CapilR_ (29) 83, p. 74.
      "Crap-shoot. Nothing to Lose." _CapilR_ (29) 83, p.
      76-77.
      "Flatline. Between Visits." _CapilR_ (29) 83, p. 73.
      "For the Record." _CapilR_ (29) 83, p. 75.
      "Rousseau's Dream. The Begatting of the Beast."
      CapilR (29) 83, p. 72.

3720. NATHAN, Leonard
"The Emeritus." NewEngR (7:2) Wint 84, p. 153-157.
"The Fall." NewEngR (6:3) Spr 84, p. 471.
"Pledge." PoetL (79:1) Spr 84, p. 50.
"Surprise." NewEngR (6:3) Spr 84, p. 472-473.
"Them." PoetL (79:1) Spr 84, p. 51-52.
"The Third Wish." NewEngR (7:2) Wint 84, p. 158-161.

3721. NATHAN, Norman
"Alienated." Poem (51) Mr [i.e. Jl] 84, p. 18.
"All Is Mine, Says the Emperor's Chop." MalR (69)
    O 84, p. 56.
"Countdown." Poem (51) Mr [i.e. Jl] 84, p. 17.
"Escape." Quarry (33:3) Sum 84, p. 16.
"An Esp from Many at a Concert." Poem (51) Mr
    [i.e. Jl] 84, p. 19.
"Growing." MalR (69) O 84, p. 55.
"In the Distance in Every Direction." MalR (69) O
    84, p. 58.
"Magician." KanQ (16:1/2) Wint-Spr 84, p. 208.
"Odd Thoughts on Art." Poem (51) Mr [i.e. Jl] 84,
    p. 20.
"Through the Chasm." MalR (69) O 84, p. 54.
"Two Thousand-segmented Caterpillars." MalR (69)
    O 84, p. 57.

3722. NATHANIEL, Isabel
"Afternoon." PraS (58:2) Sum 84, p. 91.
"The Paintings." Confr (27/28) 84, p. 241.
"The Visit." PraS (58:2) Sum 84, p. 92.

3723. NATT, Gregory
"During a Time of Death." QW (19) Aut-Wint 84-85,
    p. 89.
"A Hole in the Earth" (after an Italian folk tale).
    QW (19) Aut-Wint 84-85, p. 90-91.

3724. NAVALES, Ana María
"XV. Gime la tarde de grises y geranios." Mairena
    (6:18) 84, p. 71.
"XVIII: Iluminado por el cansancio." Mairena
    (5:14) Aut 83, p. 81.
"XX: Invaden Mi Casa." Mairena (5:14) Aut 83, p. 81.

NAVARRO SALANGA, Alfredo: See SALANGA, Alfredo Navarro

3725. NEALE, Tom
"Mandelstam." Abraxas (29/30) 84, p. 33.
"Quick Brushstrokes." Abraxas (29/30) 84, p. 33.

3726. NEELON, Ann
"For African Flutes and Xylophone" (tr. of Leopold
    Sedar Senghor). CarolQ (37:1) Aut 84, p. 33.
"For Organ Flutes" (tr. of Leopold Sedar Senghor).
    CarolQ (37:1) Aut 84, p. 34.

3727. NELMS, Sheryl L.
"Fishing for Monsters." CrabCR (2:1) Sum 84, p. 27.
"Head under Glass." Amelia [1:1] Ap 84, p. 18.
"Head under Glass." KanQ (16:1/2) Wint-Spr 84, p.

224.
"October Comin Down." <u>PoeticJ</u> (4) 83, p. 4.

3728. NELSON, Bonnie J.
"One Moment, a Stranger." <u>KanQ</u> (16:4) Aut 84, p. 112.
"Toreador." <u>KanQ</u> (16:4) Aut 84, p. 112.

3729. NELSON, Howard
"Cows Walking Away from the Barn" (from <u>Creatures</u>). <u>AmerPoR</u> (13:2) Mr-Ap 84, p. 16.

3730. NELSON, Jo
"Aftermath." <u>SanFPJ</u> (6:3) 84, p. 61.
"Ailing Spirits." <u>SanFPJ</u> (6:1) 84, p. 68.
"Arming." <u>SanFPJ</u> (6:4) 84, p. 93.
"Ashes." <u>SanFPJ</u> (6:3) 84, p. 64.
"Enterprise." <u>SanFPJ</u> (6:1) 84, p. 81.
"Ostrich Talent." <u>SanFPJ</u> (6:4) 84, p. 31.
"Pass." <u>SanFPJ</u> (6:4) 84, p. 44.
"Rush." <u>SanFPJ</u> (6:4) 84, p. 31.
"Unleashed." <u>SanFPJ</u> (6:1) 84, p. 68.

3731. NELSON, John S.
"Anchor Man." <u>PoetL</u> (79:3) Aut 84, p. 149.

3732. NELSON, Liza
"Intersection." <u>BlackWR</u> (10:2) Spr 84, p. 94-95.
"Ode to a Dress." <u>Ploughs</u> (10:4) 84, p. 121-123.

3733. NELSON, Lonnie
"Brave Poets." <u>SanFPJ</u> (7:1) 84, p. 37-38.

3734. NELSON, Paul
"Benediction." <u>BlackWR</u> (11:1) Aut 84, p. 23.
"Children." <u>NoAmR</u> (269:1) Mr 84, p. 27.
"Days Off." <u>MassR</u> (25:2) Sum 84, p. 253-254.
"The Invention of Handball." <u>BlackWR</u> (11:1) Aut 84, p. 22.
"The Story." <u>Ploughs</u> (10:4) 84, p. 69-70.
"Tragedy." <u>Ploughs</u> (10:4) 84, p. 71-73.

3735. NELSON, Riki Kolbl
"Altweibersommer." <u>RagMag</u> (3:1) Spr 84, p. 35.
"Danae Brags." <u>RagMag</u> (3:1) Spr 84, p. 34.
"Each Year." <u>RagMag</u> (3:1) Spr 84, p. 36.
"Intaglio" (For my Mother). <u>RagMag</u> (3:1) Spr 84, p. 33.
"Old Names." <u>RagMag</u> (3:1) Spr 84, p. 31.
"Silk-Screen." <u>RagMag</u> (3:1) Spr 84, p. 32.

3736. NELSON, Rodney
"Revisiting Thrudvang Farm." <u>KanQ</u> (16:1/2) Wint-Spr 84, p. 172.

3737. NELSON, Shannon
"Charlotte McAllister at She-Nah-Nam" (Medicine Creek, Nisqually, Washington territory, 1846). <u>CrabCR</u> (1:3) Wint 84, p. 29.
"Memory That Broke a Thirty Year Depression" (for

my father). CrabCR (2:1) Sum 84, p. 23.

3738. NELSON, Stanley
"Northern Hare and Golden Eagle" (painting by J.J.
Audubon, Denver Museum). KanQ (16:3) Sum 84,
p. 44.
"Who Has Known." KanQ (16:3) Sum 84, p. 44.

3739. NELSON, W. Dale
"MacGregor." SouthwR (69:3) Sum 84, p. 258-259.

3740. NEMEROV, Howard
"The Distances They Keep." Shen (35:2/3) 84, p. 237.
"During a Solar Eclipse." Tendril (18, special
issue) 84, p. 264-265.
"Einstein & Freud & Jack" (to Allen Tate on his
75th Birthday). Telescope (3:1) Wint 84, p. 15-
16.
"Two Views of a Philosopher." Shen (35:2/3) 84,
p. 237.

3741. NEMSER, Paul
"Synthesis" (tr. of Ivan Drach, w. Mark Rudman).
Pequod (16/17) 84, p. 197.

3742. NEPO, Mark
"The Crazed Are Ever Fated." SouthernR (20:3) Sum
84, p. 606-607.
"The Moon Is Two Days into Scorpio." NewOR (11:2)
Sum 84, p. 44-45.
"Torch Song." KanQ (16:1/2) Wint-Spr 84, p. 78.

3743. NERUDA, Pablo
"A Gentleman Living Alone" (tr. by Lewis Hyde, for
Robert Bly). Chelsea (42/43) 84, p. 266-267.
"Oda a la Tristeza." CutB (22) Spr-Sum 84, p. 34.
"Ode to Gloom" (tr. by William Pitt Root). CutB
(22) Spr-Sum 84, p. 35.
"Ode to the Atom" (tr. by William Pitt Root).
Telescope (3:1) Wint 84, p. 97-101.
"Old Wall" (tr. by Sarah Arvio). AmerPoR (13:5) S-
O 84, p. 13.

3744. NESIN, Aziz
"Acili Gecenin Bitiminde." NewRena (6:1, #18) Spr
84, p. 28, 30.
"As the Night of Suffering Ends" (tr. by Talat Sait
Halman). NewRena (6:1, #18) Spr 84, p. 29, 31.

3745. NESTOR, Jack
"The Mill." Wind (14:52) 84, p. 36-37.
"She Speaks of Morning." Ascent (10:1) 84, p. 57-58.

3746. NEUGROSCHEL, Joachim
"Coagula your wound, too" (tr. of Paul Celan).
Chelsea (42/43) 84, p. 278.
"Narrow-Wood day under a retinerved sky-leaf" (tr.
of Paul Celan). Chelsea (42/43) 84, p. 278.
"Skull-thoughts, mute, on the arrow-path" (tr. of
Paul Celan). Chelsea (42/43) 84, p. 279.

3747. NEURON, Vesta
        "Circus, with Mirrors." PoeticJ (1) 83, p. 19.
        "Eavesdropper." PoeticJ (3) 83, p. 21.
        "For All Rationalists." PoeticJ (3) 83, p. 21.
        "For Misers of Yesterdays." PoeticJ (3) 83, p. 20.
        "Harvest." PoeticJ (6) 84, p. 23.
        "High Wire." PoeticJ (1) 83, p. 18.
        "July Afternoon." PoeticJ (3) 83, p. 20.
        "Messages Unsent." PoeticJ (5) 84, p. 23.
        "Night Ride." PoeticJ (4) 83, p. 23.
        "Suggestion for a Requiem." PoeticJ (2) 83, p. 22.
        "Trickster." PoeticJ (2) 83, p. 23.

3748. NEVILLE, Tam Lin
        "Grief Dance from a Distant Place." Spirit (7:1)
        84, p. 164.

3749. NEVITT, Jonathan
        "Departure" (tr. Ibn Zuhr). SenR (14:1) 84, p. 27.
        "The Ghost" (tr. of Ibn Khafāja). SenR (14:1)
        84, p. 25-26.

3750. NEW, Elisa
        "Amnon." CarolQ (37:1) Aut 84, p. 80.
        "Five Thirty." MSS (4:1/2) Aut 84, p. 62.
        "From the Eye of It." PraS (58:4) Wint 84, p. 28.
        "The Leap: A Jerusalem Suite" (Selection: 7. The
        Grove). SouthernR (20:2) Spr 84, p. 361-363.
        "The Leap: A Jerusalem Suite" (Selections: 1.
        Exile. 5. Ammunition Hill. 9. The Leap).
        CarolQ (37:1) Aut 84, p. 81-84.
        "Lore." PraS (58:4) Wint 84, p. 29.
        "Rebecca." CarolQ (37:1) Aut 84, p. 79.
        "Ventriloquism." PraS (58:4) Wint 84, p. 26-27.

3751. NEW, Joan
        "Lament." NeqC (4:4) Aut 84, p. 39.

3752. NEWCOMB, P. F.
        "Dust." CapeR (19:3) 20th Anniverary Issue 84, p.
        38.

3753. NEWCOMB, Richard
        "People Get the Faces." Poetry (143:5) F 84, p. 290.
        "Pressing and Mending." Poetry (143:5) F 84, p. 289.

3754. NEWCOMER, Katarzyna W.
        "Rings of the Earth to Venus." SanFPJ (6:1) 84,
        p. 10.

3755. NEWELL, Mike
        "The Quiet Monopoly All Poets Share." DekalbLAJ
        (20th Anniversary Issue) 84, p. 99.
        "The Unlived Life." DekalbLAJ (17:1/2) 84, p. 140-
        141.

3756. NEWMAN, C.
        "The Green Leaf Attached to the Stem" (tr. of
        Eugene Dubnov). NowestR (22:3) 84, p. 93.
        "Warming Your Hands" (tr. of Eugene Dubnov, w. the

author). <u>NowestR</u> (22:3) 84, p. 94-95.

3757. NEWMAN, Christopher
"These Squat Towns" (tr. of Eugene Dubnov, w. the
author). <u>PraS</u> (58:2) Sum 84, p. 64.

3758. NEWMAN, Janis
"First Snow." <u>MSS</u> (3:2/3) Spr 84, p. 60.

3759. NEWMAN, Michael
"Early Duty." <u>Bogg</u> (52) 84, p. 37.

3760. NEWMAN, P. B.
"New Hampshire Farm." <u>SouthernPR</u> (24:1) Spr 84,
p. 66.

3761. NEWMAN, Richard
"Yom Hashoam: The Ceremony and the Sermon." <u>Poem</u>
(51) Mr [i.e. Jl] 84, p. 40.

3762. NEWMAN, Wade
"Beating a Dead Horse." <u>NegC</u> (4:4) Aut 84, p. 48-49.
"Moses." <u>KenR</u> (NS 6:3) Sum 84, p. 53-55.
"Noah." <u>KenR</u> (NS 6:3) Sum 84, p. 55-56.

3763. NEWTON, Jerry
"And Someone Said." <u>BlackALF</u> (18:1) Spr 84, p. 20.
"Nonexistence." <u>BlackALF</u> (18:1) Spr 84, p. 20.
"Transition." <u>BlackALF</u> (18:1) Spr 84, p. 20.

3764. NGA, Tran Thi
"My Father's Oldest Sister" (with Wendy Larsen).
<u>13thM</u> (8:1/2) 84, p. 72.
"My Grandmother" (with Wendy Larsen). <u>13thM</u>
(8:1/2) 84, p. 71.
"My Mother" (with Wendy Larsen). <u>13thM</u> (8:1/2)
84, p. 70.
"Visiting My Auntie" (with Wendy Larsen). <u>13thM</u>
(8:1/2) 84, p. 69.

3765. NIATUM, Duane
"All We Need." <u>GreenfR</u> (11:3/4) Wint-Spr 84, p. 24.
"Apology." <u>GreenfR</u> (11:3/4) Wint-Spr 84, p. 7-8.
"Early Morning." <u>GreenfR</u> (11:3/4) Wint-Spr 84, p. 4.
"The Hard Task." <u>GreenfR</u> (11:3/4) Wint-Spr 84, p. 4.
"Klallam Song." <u>GreenfR</u> (11:3/4) Wint-Spr 84, p. 23.
"Meditation on Visiting Hurricane Ridge." <u>GreenfR</u>
(11:3/4) Wint-Spr 84, p. 6.
"Spider." <u>GreenfR</u> (11:3/4) Wint-Spr 84, p. 14.
"To the Woman Who Asked for a Name." <u>GreenfR</u>
(11:3/4) Wint-Spr 84, p. 5.
"Wolf." <u>GreenfR</u> (11:3/4) Wint-Spr 84, p. 23.

3766. NICASTRO, Kathleen
"The Tinker." <u>CarolQ</u> (36:3) Spr 84, p. 54.

3767. NICHOL, B. P. (<u>See also</u> FOUR HORSEMEN)
"Draft of an Epilogue to 'Inchoate World'" (from
<u>The Martyrology</u> Book VI Books). <u>CanLit</u> (100)
Spr 84, p. 239-241.

"Hour 23, 6:35 to 7:35" (in memory of Visvaldis
  Upenieks). CapilR (31) 84, p. 12-15.
"In the Plunkett Hotel" (from The Martyrology
  Book VI Books). MalR (69) O 84, p. 41-47.
"Interrupted Nap." CapilR (31) 84, p. 9-11.
"Two: Less Time." CapilR (31) 84, p. 38.

3768. NICOLLS, Alix
  "The Finish." PoeticJ (8) 84, p. 3.

3769. NIDITCH, B. Z.
  "Collected Poem." Os (19) 84, p. 26.
  "Ford Madox Ford." AntigR (57) Spr 84, p. 40.
  "Franz Kafka." AntigR (56) Wint 84, p. 19.
  "In My Exodus Season." AntigR (56) Wint 84, p. 18.
  "A Lasting Poem." GreenfR (12:1/2) Sum-Aut 84, p.
    197-198.
  "Marcel Proust." AntigR (57) Spr 84, p. 41.
  "Miklos Radnoti." Abraxas (31/32) 84, p. 32.
  "Miklos Radnoti." Confr (27/28) 84, p. 58.
  "Of an Age for Lawrence." Amelia (1:2) O 84, p. 66.
  "One Life." WebR (9:2) Wint 85, p. 96.
  "Pier Paolo Pasolini, 1922-1975." Veloc (2) Spr
    83, p. 28.
  "Playing Mozart." PoeticJ (5) 84, p. 39.
  "Simone Weil." AntigR (59) Aut 84, p. 49.
  "Snowstorm in Warsaw." AntigR (58) Sum 84, p. 120-
    121.
  "Someday Soon." WebR (9:2) Wint 85, p. 96.
  "Thoughts about Dostoyevsky." AntigR (57) Spr 84,
    p. 39.
  "Treblinka Liberation, 1945." Abraxas (29/30) 84,
    p. 57.
  "W. H. Auden (1907-1977) In Memoriam." AntigR
    (56) Wint 84, p. 20.
  "Warsaw, 1982." NegC (4:4) Aut 84, p. 73.
  "Warsaw Ghetto." NegC (4:4) Aut 84, p. 72.
  "Warsaw Market." GreenfR (12:1/2) Sum-Aut 84, p.
    197.
  "Warsaw May Day (1982)." MinnR (N.S. 22) Spr 84,
    p. 58.
  "Warsaw Spring (1982)." AntigR (58) Sum 84, p. 121.
  "Warsaw Waterfront." AntigR (58) Sum 84, p. 120.
  "The Year 194-." GreenfR (12:1/2) Sum-Aut 84, p.
    198.

3770. NIEDECKER, Lorine
  "South Dakota" (as lifted from a letter: 20 April
    1975). Origin (Series 5:1) Aut 83, p. 43.

3771. NIELSEN, Nancy L.
  "Dug In: The View from the Third Generation."
    PoetL (79:3) Aut 84, p. 150-151.
  "Nuclear Relocation Hearing, Bangor 3/22/84."
    BelPoJ (34:4) Sum 84, p. 7.
  "On Gaining a Name for Wisdom." BelPoJ (35:2)
    Wint 84-85, p. 21.
  "Sweet Sovereign Root." BelPoJ (34:4) Sum 84, p. 5.
  "That Fierce Energy." BelPoJ (34:4) Sum 84, p. 6.
  "Two Men Can't Run a Town This Small." BelPoJ

(35:2) Wint 84-85, p. 20.
"The Unattainable Coppery-Tailed Trogon." PoetL
(79:3) Aut 84, p. 151.

3772. NIELSON, Gretchen
"All over the world our closets are crowded with
saviors." Sam (37:3, 147th release) 83, p. 42.
"I'm exposing myself as a preacher as well as a
poet." Sam (37:3, 147th release) 83, p. 37.

3773. NIEMANN, Ernst
"There Is a Part of Us That's Incomplete." ConcPo
(17:1) Spr 84, p. 94-95.

NIETZCHE, Vicente Rodriguez: See RODRIGUEZ NIETZCHE, Vicente

NIEVES, Raúl Crespo: See CRESPO NIEVES, Raúl

3774. NIEVES MIELES, Edgardo
"Epitafio para un Poeta de Antologia Menor."
Mairena (5:14) Aut 83, p. 32-33.
"Quien le Pone el Cascabel a la Soledad"
(Selections). Mairena (5:14) Aut 83, p. 32-33.

3775. NIJMEIJER, Peter
"Euthanasia" (tr. of Hans Verhagen). Iowa (14:2)
Spr-Sum 84, p. 180-181.
"Summer Is Over" (tr. of Eddy van Vliet). Vis
(16) 84, p. 5.

3776. NIKOLOV, Spass
"Bulgaria" (tr. of Georgi Djagarov). ConcPo
(17:2) Aut 84, p. 100-101.

3777. NIMS, John Frederick
"Crutches and Canes." TriQ (59) Wint 84, p. 132.
"Old Age." TriQ (59) Wint 84, p. 132.
"Theology." TriQ (59) Wint 84, p. 132.

3778. NIMTZ, Steven
"How a Thing Is Made." VirQR (60:2) Spr 84, p. 237.
"Lotus Roots." Tendril (17) Wint 84, p. 147.
"Picture Book Language." VirQR (60:2) Spr 84, p.
236.

3779. NIRALA
"Alone I" (tr. by Robert A. Hueckstedt). ConcPo
(17:2) Aut 84, p. 107.
"A Brahman's Son" (tr. by Robert A. Hueckstedt).
ConcPo (17:2) Aut 84, p. 106.
"The King Saw to His Own Protection" (tr. by Robert
A. Hueckstedt). ConcPo (17:2) Aut 84, p. 105.

3780. NISETICH, Frank J.
"Epithalamium." NegC (4:4) Aut 84, p. 32-33.
"Semantic Shift." NegC (4:4) Aut 84, p. 31.

3781. NIXON, Colin
"New Year's Eve." NegC (4:1) Wint 84, p. 116.

3782. NIXON, John, Jr.
    "The General." Comm (111:7) 6 Ap 84, p. 220.
    "Heading for Titian." Comm (111:14) 10 Ag 84, p.
    443.

3783. NOBLE, Charles
    "Coins for a Gyroscope, or, I Turn South and the
    Moon Sails On" (Selection: IV Props). Dandel
    (11:2) Aut-Wint 84-85 p. 5-7.

3784. NOCERINO, Kathryn
    "Another Fine Day in the May Woods." Abraxas
    (29/30) 84, p. 66-67.

3785. NODA, Kesaya
    "Japan." GreenfR (12:1/2) Sum-Aut 84, p. 177.
    "Sansei." GreenfR (12:1/2) Sum-Aut 84, p. 178.

3786. NOEL, Bernard
    "Perhaps It Was Necessary." CrabCR (1:3) Wint 84,
    p. 28.
    "Spirit of the Mirror." CrabCR (1:3) Wint 84, p. 28.

3787. NOGUERAS, Luis Rogelio
    "Segunda Mano." Mairena (6:18) 84, p. 172.

3788. NOIN, Priest
    "Climbing to a Mountain Village" (tr. by Graeme
    Wilson). WestHR (38:2) Sum 84, p. 138.

3789. NOLAN, Pat
    "Aquarium (1917)" (Selections, tr. of Philippe
    Soupault). Tele (19) 83, p. 115-118.
    "Austin Creek." Tele (19) 83, p. 119-120.
    "Everybody's a Critic" (tr. of Philippe Soupault).
    Tele (19) 83, p. 116.
    "Extra Ordinary" (tr. of Philippe Soupault). Tele
    (19) 83, p. 117.
    "Flame" (tr. of Philippe Soupault). Tele (19) 83,
    p. 115.
    "Flash" (tr. of Philippe Soupault). Tele (19) 83,
    p. 118.
    "Flight" (tr. of Philippe Soupault). Tele (19)
    83, p. 115.
    "Poem: My words lead me to places unknown" (tr. of
    Philippe Soupault). Tele (19) 83, p. 116.
    "Seasonelle" (tr. of Philippe Soupault). Tele
    (19) 83, p. 117.

3790. NOLAND, John
    "Sea Lions at Cape Arago." KanQ (16:1/2) Wint-Spr
    84, p. 62.

3791. NOLD, John
    "Caught." Grain (12:3) Ag 84, p. 10.
    "Forehead." PoetryCR (6:2) Wint 84-85, p. 5.
    "North of Here." PoetryCR (5:4) Sum 84, p. 5.

3792. NOLL, Bink
    "The Dressing Room." NoAmR (269:3) S 84, p. 42.

"Paying for It." <u>MSS</u> (4:1/2) Aut 84, p. 145.

3793. NOLLA, Olga
"La Educacion Sentimental." <u>Mairena</u> (6:18) 84, p.
27-28.

NORD, Chard de: <u>See</u> DeNORD, Chard

3794. NORRIS, Gunilla
"Falling: Twenty-Five Years Later" (Special
Mention, Guy Owen Poetry Prize). <u>SouthernPR</u>
(24:2) Aut 84, p. 26-27.

3795. NORRIS, Kathleen
"Sleeping Beauty." <u>Nat</u> (238:16) 28 Ap 84, p. 525.
"Story Time." <u>PraS</u> (58:4) Wint 84, p. 47.
"The Wedding in the Courthouse." <u>PraS</u> (58:4) Wint
84, p. 45-46.

3796. NORRIS, Ken
"The Haunting." <u>Quarry</u> (33:3) Sum 84, p. 31.
"Heart Associations." <u>Waves</u> (12:1) Aut 83, p. 49.
"I don't know if I've got it in me" ("Untitled").
<u>Waves</u> (12:1) Aut 83, p. 49.
"I suppose I was never the man you were waiting
for." <u>PoetryCR</u> (6:2) Wint 84-85, p. 21.
"If" (For Daphne). <u>Quarry</u> (33:3) Sum 84, p. 31.
"One Morning." <u>Quarry</u> (33:3) Sum 84, p. 31.
"The Romantic Imagination" (from "The Better Part
of Heaven: Pacific Writings"). <u>Descant</u> (44/45,
15:1/2) Spr-Sum 84, p. 182-183.
"September Lament." <u>Quarry</u> (33:3) Sum 84, p. 32.
"So this is the life we come to be living."
<u>PoetryCR</u> (5:4) Sum 84, p. 8.
"Turning Thirty in Tonga" (from "The Better Part of
Heaven: Pacific Writings"). <u>Descant</u> (44/45,
15:1/2) Spr-Sum 84, p. 181.
"Worldly Angels." <u>AntigR</u> (57) Spr 84, p. 7.

3797. NORRIS, Leslie
"Hawk Music." <u>Atlantic</u> (254:4) O 84, p. 69.

3798. NORTHNAGEL, E. W.
"Flora and the Rocks." <u>SanFPJ</u> (6:3) 84, p. 85.
"Wanting." <u>SanFPJ</u> (6:3) 84, p. 88.

3799. NORTON, Edward
"A Sterile Heart." <u>Open24</u> (3) 84, p. 15.

3800. NORTON, John
"Air Transmigra." <u>Kayak</u> (64) My 84, p. 52-53.

3801. NORWOOD, Kyle
"Report to Walt Whitman." <u>KanQ</u> (16:3) Sum 84, p. 99.

3802. NOVAK, Michael Paul
"Archer's View." <u>NewL</u> (51:2) Wint 84-85, p. 46.

3803. NOVAK, Robert
"From the Editor of <u>The Windless Orchard</u>."

WindO (44) Sum-Aut 84, p. 34.

3804. NOWLAN, Alden A.
       "Three Choices." Sparrow (46) 84, p. 18.

3805. NOWLAN, Michael O.
       "Illusion." Germ (8:1) Spr-Sum 84, p. 21.
       "Saving It." Germ (8:1) Spr-Sum 84, p. 22.

NOYELLES, Bill de: See DeNOYELLES, Bill

3806. NOYES, Stanley
       "Reunion." GreenfR (12:1/2) Sum-Aut 84, p. 83.

3807. NOYES, Steve
       "Search for a Metaphor." Quarry (33:3) Sum 84, p.
          60-61.
       "When We Turn to Poets for Analysis They Say the
          Dancer Danced" (for Sue Smitten. Poet's surname
          corrected from "Hayden" in 13:1, p. 97). Waves
          (12:4) Spr 84, p. 58.

3808. NUGENT, Macushla
       "Staying Alive." HiramPoR (37) Aut-Wint 84, p. 30-
          31.
       "Universal." YetASM (3) 84, p. 2.

3809. NUNES, Shirley
       "Right Brain." EngJ (73:5) S 84, p. 84.

3810. NUNNELEE, Jane
       "The Bad Night." BlackWR (11:1) Aut 84, p. 91.
       "The Good Night." BlackWR (11:1) Aut 84, p. 91.

3811. NURKSE, D.
       "Closed Borders." Spirit (7:1) 84, p. 101.
       "Lamps and Fences." Spirit (7:1) 84, p. 100.
       "The Old Religion." NewL (50:4) Sum 84, p. 63.
       "The Other World." HangL (45) Spr 84, p. 39.
       "Shyness." CalQ (23/24) Spr-Sum 84, p. 127.
       "The Theft." NewL (50:4) Sum 84, p. 63.

3812. NURU, Njeri
       "All Afrikans Ain't Afrikan" (or, You Are What You
          Become). BlackALF (18:1) Spr 84, p. 15-16.
       "Atlanta Poem #1." BlackALF (18:1) Spr 84, p. 16.
       "Atlanta Poem #2." BlackALF (18:1) Spr 84, p. 16.
       "Bonding." BlackALF (18:1) Spr 84, p. 17.
       "Little Deaths Hurt Especially" (for Hodari and
          Mayimuna). BlackALF (18:1) Spr 84, p. 16.

3813. NUTBROWN, Graham
       "An Early Walk." Argo (5:2) 84, p. 31.

3814. NUTTING, Leslie
       "Brahe at Uraniborg." PoetryCR (5:4) Sum 84, p. 19.
       "The Clown in Winter." AntigR (59) Aut 84, p. 51.
       "Divorce." Waves (13:1) Aut 84, p. 67.
       "Etienne Brule." Quarry (33:3) Sum 84, p. 18-28.
       "My Wife Swimming." Waves (12:1) Aut 83, p. 63.

"Papa's Waltz" (after Theodore Roethke). <u>Grain</u>
(12:1) F 84, p. 17.
"Shunga." <u>Descant</u> (47, 15:4) Wint 84, p. 124.
"Toyoharu." <u>Descant</u> (47, 15:4) Wint 84, p. 125.

3815. NYE, Naomi Shihab
"Arabic Coffee." <u>PaintedB</u> (21) Wint 84, p. 19.
"The Brick" (For David & Barbara Clewell).
<u>PaintedB</u> (21) Wint 84, p. 17.
"February." <u>PaintedB</u> (21) Wint 84, p. 18.
"French Movies" (In memory of Patrick Dewaere).
<u>Telescope</u> (3:3) Aut 84, p. 82-83.
"New Year." <u>GeoR</u> (38:4) Wint 84, p. 855-856.
"No One Thinks of Tegucigalpa." <u>PraS</u> (58:3) Aut
84, p. 12-13.
"Office 337, Wheeler Hall, Berkeley." <u>PraS</u> (58:3)
Aut 84, p. 13-14.
"Telling the Story." <u>PraS</u> (58:3) Aut 84, p. 11-12.

3816. NYKIN, Ilya
"Ballad about a Wall" (tr. of Irina Ratushinskaya,
w. Pamela White Hadas). <u>GrandS</u> (3:3) Spr 84,
p. 83.
"Leningrad Triptych" (tr. of Irina Ratushinskaya,
w. Pamela White Hadas). <u>Agni</u> (21) 84, p. 37-38.
"My Lord" (tr. of Irina Ratushinskaya. w. Pamela
White Hadas). <u>Agni</u> (21) 84, p. 39.

3817. NYMARK, Mikki
"Eye on the Ball." <u>WebR</u> (9:2) Wint 85, p. 74.
"Signposts." <u>WebR</u> (9:2) Wint 85, p. 73.

3818. NYSTEDT, Bob
"Ferrets." <u>NeqC</u> (4:3) Sum 84, p. 69.
"Poets." <u>PoeticJ</u> (2) 83, p. 25.
"Words." <u>PoeticJ</u> (2) 83, p. 11.

3819. NYSTROM, Debra
"During Illness." <u>AntR</u> (42:1) Wint 84, p. 77.
"Leaving Dakota." <u>SenR</u> (14:2) 84, p. 32.
"Punishment." <u>Ploughs</u> (10:1) 84, p. 127.
"Waitress at a Window." <u>Ploughs</u> (10:1) 84, p. 126.

3820. OAKEY, Shaun
"Catalogue of Formative Experiences: Part 4 -- The
Males." <u>Grain</u> (12:3) Ag 84, p. 14-15.

3821. OAKS, Jeff
"Places I Have Seen Deer" (A Sequence: Excerpt).
<u>MSS</u> (3:2/3) Spr 84, p. 82.

3822. OANDASAN, William
"Ukom & No'm." <u>Spirit</u> (7:1) 84, p. 153-155.

3823. OATES, Joyce Carol
"Alone: A Threnody." <u>AntR</u> (42:1) Wint 84, p. 88.
"Dancer, Harshly Photographed." <u>Hudson</u> (37:3) Aut
84, p. 393-394.
"Foetal Song." <u>Chelsea</u> (42/43) 84, p. 186-187.
"I Saw a Woman." <u>Shen</u> (35:1) 83-84, p. 32-33.

"Love Letter, with Static Interference from
    Einstein's Brain." Iowa (14:3) Aut 84, p. 111-
    114.
"The Masquers." VirQR (60:3) Sum 84, p. 427-428.
"The Mountain Lion." SouthernR (20:3) Sum 84, p.
    600-602.
"New Jersey White-Tailed Deer." MichQR (23:2) Spr
    84, p. 253-255.
"Pain." SouthernR (20:3) Sum 84, p. 602-604.
"The Time Traveler." Hudson (37:3) Aut 84, p. 394-
    395.
"Two Masquers." VirQR (60:3) Sum 84, p. 428.
"The Vampire." SouthernR (20:3) Sum 84, p. 604.

3824. OBEJAS, Achy
    "Tiger Tiger." BelPoJ (35:1) Aut 84, p. 27-29.

3825. OBREGON, Roberto
    "Las Inscripciones" (fragmento). Mairena (6:18)
        84, p. 213.

3826. O'BRIEN, Geoffrey
    "Noh" (Selections: 2, 5). Tele (19) 83, p. 98-102.

3827. O'BRIEN, John
    "Americana." WebR (9:1) Spr 84, p. 86.
    "Upon Looking at Three Polaroid Pictures of Myself
        That Were Taken by My Foolish But Persistent
        Wife Who after Being Told Time and Time Again
        Not to Take My Photo Never-the-less Did . . ."
        WindO (44) Sum-Aut 84, p. 4.

3828. O'BRIEN, L. F.
    "The Third Circle (from Dante), or, The Student
        Smoking Area between Classes." EngJ (73:2) F
        84, p. 60.

3829. O'BRIEN, Michael
    "A Bird" (tr. of René Char). NewL (51:2) Wint
        84-85, p. 10.

3830. O'BRIEN, Peter
    "The Busy Old Fool." Quarry (33:3) Sum 84, p. 12.
    "Firmament." Quarry (33:3) Sum 84, p. 13.

3831. O'BRIEN, William P.
    "Moon Tide." WindO (44) Sum-Aut 84, p. 11.

3832. OBSSUTH, Karen E.
    "Tight Grip." PoeticJ (5) 84, p. 35.

3833. OCHART, Ivonne
    "Los Suspiros Luchan, I." Mairena (6:17) Aut 84,
        p. 70.

3834. OCHESTER, Ed
    "German War Primer (1937)" (Excerpts, tr. of
        Bertolt Brecht). MinnR (N.S. 23) Aut 84, p. 125.
    "The Latin American Solidarity Committee
        Fundraising Picnic." NewL (51:1) Aut 84, p. 91.

"Memorial Day, Elderton, Pennsylvania." WestHR
(38:4) Wint 84, p. 337-338.
"My Poorer Classmates from the Edge of the City"
(tr. of Bertolt Brecht). MinnR (N.S. 23) Aut
84, p. 126.
"Sunday Dinner." SouthernPR (24:1) Spr 84, p. 63.

3835. O'CONNOR, David
"These Quiet Hills" (County Sligo, Ireland).
PoeticJ (5) 84, p. 26.

3836. O'CONNOR, Mark
"Belle du Jour." Quarry (33:1) Wint 84, p. 68.
"Cliffs at Sounion." Quarry (33:1) Wint 84, p. 48.
"The First Hangings in Australia" (Abrolhos
Islands, 1629). Waves (12:2/3) Wint 84, p. 83.
"Greek Summer." Waves (12:2/3) Wint 84, p. 82.
"The Lake-Island at St. Naum." Quarry (33:1) Wint
84, p. 66-67.
"Medals for Motherhood" (Russia, 1980). Waves
(12:2/3) Wint 84, p. 82.

3837. O'CONNOR, Michael
"Night Dancing." Pig (12) 84, p. 80-81.
"Short Time." Pig (12) 84, p. 20.

3838. O'DRISCOLL, Dennis
"Journey." CreamCR (9:1/2) 84, p. 64.
"Passion." CreamCR (9:1/2) 84, p. 65.

3839. OESAU, Patricia
"Winter Lodge." SmPd (21:2) Spr 84, p. 17.

3840. O'FARRELL, Fran
"In This Time of Quick Identities." Sulfur (4:1,
issue 10) 84, p. 109.
"Ritual." Sulfur (4:1, issue 10) 84, p. 108.

3841. O'GARA, Gwynn
"The Etymology of You: Oh." YellowS (12) Aut 84,
p. 38.

3842. OGDEN, Hugh
"Late Winter." MidAR (4:1) Spr 84, p. 75-76.

3843. O'GRADY, Desmond
"Berlin Metro" (after Thomas Venclova).Agni (21)
84, p. 9-10.
"In Exile" (tr. of Shangi). Agni (21) 84, p. 11.

3844. O'GRADY, Tom
"Are Your Poems Your Songs" (tr. of Jaroslav
Seifert, w. Paul Jagasich). Spirit (8:1) 83-
84, p. 37.
"The Artists' House" (tr. of Jaroslav Seifert, w.
Paul Jagasich). Spirit (8:1) 83-84, p. 26-27.
"Before Those Few Light Kisses" (tr. of Jaroslav
Seifert, w. Paul Jagasich). Spirit (8:1) 83-
84, p. 49.
"Cannon Fire" (tr. of Jaroslav Seifert, w. Paul

Jagasich). <u>Spirit</u> (8:1) 83-84, p. 23-24.
"The Casting of Bells" (tr. of Jaroslav Seifert, w.
    Paul Jagasich). <u>Spirit</u> (8:1) 83-84, p. 1-61.
"Crowned with Berries" (tr. of Jaroslav Seifert, w.
    Paul Jagasich). <u>Spirit</u> (8:1) 83-84, p. 21.
"Dance-Song" (tr. of Jaroslav Seifert, w. Paul
    Jagasich). <u>Spirit</u> (8:1) 83-84, p. 29-30.
"End of a Story" (tr. of Jaroslav Seifert, w. Paul
    Jagasich). <u>Spirit</u> (8:1) 83-84, p. 18-19.
"Heavenly Bonds" (tr. of Jaroslav Seifert, w. Paul
    Jagasich). <u>Spirit</u> (8:1) 83-84, p. 40-41.
"I don't Look at People's Souls" (tr. of Jaroslav
    Seifert, w. Paul Jagasich). <u>Spirit</u> (8:1) 83-
    84, p. 11.
"I Just Wanted to Tell You This" (tr. of Jaroslav
    Seifert, w. Paul Jagasich). <u>Spirit</u> (8:1) 83-
    84, p. 15.
"I Looked Only" (tr. of Jaroslav Seifert, w. Paul
    Jagasich). <u>Spirit</u> (8:1) 83-84, p. 46.
"I Remained on This Earth" (tr. of Jaroslav
    Seifert, w. Paul Jagasich). <u>Spirit</u> (8:1) 83-
    84, p. 14.
"If the Sand Could Sing" (tr. of Jaroslav Seifert,
    w. Paul Jagasich). <u>Spirit</u> (8:1) 83-84, p. 31.
"In Those Winters When" (tr. of Jaroslav Seifert,
    w. Paul Jagasich). <u>Spirit</u> (8:1) 83-84, p. 25.
"It Was Afternoon or Later" (tr. of Jaroslav
    Seifert, w. Paul Jagasich). <u>Spirit</u> (8:1) 83-
    84, p. 12.
"It's after All Saints Day" (tr. of Jaroslav
    Seifert, w. Paul Jagasich). <u>Spirit</u> (8:1) 83-
    84, p. 34.
"A Letter from Marienbad" (tr. of Jaroslav Seifert,
    w. Paul Jagasich). <u>Spirit</u> (8:1) 83-84, p. 55-61.
"Monument to a Kettle Drum" (tr. of Jaroslav
    Seifert, w. Paul Jagasich). <u>Spirit</u> (8:1) 83-
    84, p. 44-45.
"The Mount of Venus" (tr. of Jaroslav Seifert, w.
    Paul Jagasich). <u>Spirit</u> (8:1) 83-84, p. 50-51.
"My Star-Hung Window" (tr. of Jaroslav Seifert, w.
    Paul Jagasich). <u>Spirit</u> (8:1) 83-84, p. 38.
"Myrtle Wreath" (tr. of Jaroslav Seifert, w. Paul
    Jagasich). <u>Spirit</u> (8:1) 83-84, p. 35-36.
"Neither the Marble Tower" (tr. of Jaroslav
    Seifert, w. Paul Jagasich). <u>Spirit</u> (8:1) 83-
    84, p. 17.
"Not Too Long Ago" (tr. of Jaroslav Seifert, w.
    Paul Jagasich). <u>Spirit</u> (8:1) 83-84, p. 42-43.
"Orangeade" (tr. of Jaroslav Seifert, w. Paul
    Jagasich). <u>Spirit</u> (8:1) 83-84, p. 47-48.
"Poor Moon, She Is Helpless" (tr. of Jaroslav
    Seifert, w. Paul Jagasich). <u>Spirit</u> (8:1) 83-
    84, p. 13.
"Prologue" (tr. of Jaroslav Seifert, w. Paul
    Jagasich). <u>Spirit</u> (8:1) 83-84, p. 9-10.
"A Requiem for Dvořák" (tr. of Jaroslav Seifert,
    w. Paul Jagasich). <u>Spirit</u> (8:1) 83-84, p. 32-33.
"Ship in Flames" (tr. of Jaroslav Seifert, w. Paul
    Jagasich). <u>Spirit</u> (8:1) 83-84, p. 16.
"When Our Mulberry Trees" (tr. of Jaroslav Seifert,

w. Paul Jagasich). <u>Spirit</u> (8:1) 83-84, p. 28.
"When We Are Denied" (tr. of Jaroslav Seifert, w.
    Paul Jagasich). <u>Spirit</u> (8:1) 83-84, p. 39.
"Where or Whenever I Had Heard" (tr. of Jaroslav
    Seifert, w. Paul Jagasich). <u>Spirit</u> (8:1) 83-
    84, p. 20.
"With the Roll of Our Blood" (tr. of Jaroslav
    Seifert, w. Paul Jagasich). <u>Spirit</u> (8:1) 83-
    84, p. 22.
"You Are Asking" (tr. of Jaroslav Seifert, w. Paul
    Jagasich). <u>Spirit</u> (8:1) 83-84, p. 52-54.

3845. O'HEHIR, Diana
"Apple." <u>Poetry</u> (144:3) Je 84, p. 134.
"My Father Owns This City." <u>Poetry</u> (144:3) Je 84,
    p. 135.

3846. OKAI
"Kwabenya." <u>Iowa</u> (14:2) Spr-Sum 84, p. 131.

3847. O'KEEFE, Richard
"As I Open a Window in Oregon, a Grasshopper Jumps
    on My Thumb" (for Bob Burt). <u>ThRiPo</u> (23/24)
    84, p. 33.

3848. O'KEEFE, Richard R.
"Alice Again." <u>TarRP</u> (23:2) Spr 84, p. 32.

3849. O'KEEFE, Virginia
"A Love Poem, of Sorts." <u>YetASM</u> (3) 84, p. 3.

3850. OKTENBERG, Adrian
"She Pleads Guilty." <u>NewL</u> (50:2/3) Wint-Spr 84,
    p. 243.

3851. OLDER, Julia
"Her/man Becomes Messenger." <u>NewL</u> (50:4) Sum 84,
    p. 60.
"Hermaphrodite in America" (Selections: Three
    Poems). <u>NewL</u> (50:4) Sum 84, p. 60-61.
"Pebbles." <u>NewL</u> (50:4) Sum 84, p. 61.
"Soup Run." <u>NewL</u> (50:4) Sum 84, p. 60.

3852. OLDKNOW, Antony
"The Farm Buildings Were Shiny Black" (tr. of
    Francis Jammes). <u>WebR</u> (9:2) Wint 85, p. 19-20.
"He Keeps Himself Busy" (For Marcel Schwob, tr. of
    Francis Jammes). <u>WebR</u> (9:2) Wint 85, p. 20-21.
"Impressionist." <u>CreamCR</u> (9:1/2) 84, p. 10-11.
"When Mist Made the Soil Glisten" (tr. of Francis
    Jammes). <u>WebR</u> (9:2) Wint 85, p. 22-23.
"Woman at the Window." <u>WebR</u> (9:2) Wint 85, p. 24.

3853. OLDS, Sharon
"After the Rapes in Our Building." <u>PoetryE</u>
    (13/14) Spr-Sum 84, p. 41.
"Bathing the New Born." <u>NewYorker</u> (60:35) 15 O
    84, p. 48.
"Bestiary." <u>PoetryE</u> (13/14) Spr-Sum 84, p. 40.
"Early Images of Heaven." <u>PoetryE</u> (13/14) Spr-Sum

84, p. 36.
"The Food-Thief" (Uganda, drought). PoetryE
(13/14) Spr-Sum 84, p. 35.
"The Gentlemen in the U-Boats." NewL (50:2/3)
Wint-Spr 84, p. 32.
"Greed and Aggression." Nat (238:5) 11 F 84, p. 172.
"I See My Girl." PoetryE (13/14) Spr-Sum 84, p. 34.
"The Indispensability of the Eyes." PoetryE
(13/14) Spr-Sum 84, p. 38.
"The Last Minute of My Father's Life and the First
Minute of His Death." PoetryE (13/14) Spr-Sum
84, p. 42-43.
"My Father in New York City." PoetryE (13/14) Spr-
Sum 84, p. 32-33.
"Race Riot, Tulsa, 1921." PoetryE (13/14) Spr-Sum
84, p. 39.
"When." PoetryE (13/14) Spr-Sum 84, p. 37.

3854. O'LEARY, Patrick
"FUNK (or Rip Van Radio Sleeps on Its Feet)" (After
Mojo 98 FM). LittleM (14:3) 84, p. 38.
"Necessary Night" (After Bergman's intro to the
screenplay of Wild Strawberries). LittleM
(14:3) 84, p. 37.
"Something Needed." LittleM (14:3) 84, p. 39-41.

3855. O'LEARY, Tomas
"Plan for the House." MidwQ (25:2) Wint 84, p. 168.

3856. OLES, Carole
"Between Talcy and Met." Ploughs (10:4) 84, p.
174-175.
"For the Drunk." TriQ (61) Aut 84, p. 98.
"To a Daughter at Fourteen Forsaking the Violin."
TriQ (61) Aut 84, p. 97.

3857. OLIPHANT, Dave
"Texas Indian Rock Art" (after a text by W. W.
Newcomb on work of Lula & Forrest Kirkland).
NewL (50:2/3) Wint-Spr 84, p. 55.

3858. OLIVA, Jorge
"Central Park 5:00 P.M.: Close Encounter of a
Second Kind (Physical Evidence)." LindLM
(3:2/4) Ap-D 84, p. 11.
"Postcard to Havana." LindLM (3:2/4) Ap-D 84, p. 11.

3859. OLIVER, Mary
"The Blackberry Fields." WestHR (38:3) Aut 84, p.
225-226.
"Bowing to the Empress." Atlantic (253:4) Ap 84,
p. 124.
"A Death." VirQR (60:1) Wint 84, p. 63-64.
"The Moths." Poetry (143:4) Ja 84, p. 215-216.
"Poem: The spirit likes to dress up like this."
KenR (NS 6:2) Spr 84, p. 50.
"The River." VirQR (60:1) Wint 84, p. 64-65.
"The Son." Poetry (143:4) Ja 84, p. 214-215.
"Stanley Kunitz." MemphisSR (5:1) Aut 84, p. 50.
"Trilliums." WestHR (38:1) Spr 84, p. 47-48.

"The Turtle." <u>WestHR</u> (38:4) Wint 84, p. 320-321.
"Two Kinds of Deliverance." <u>GeoR</u> (38:1) Spr 84,
    p. 62-63.
"A Visitor." <u>Atlantic</u> (254:1) Jl 84, p. 68.
"Voices." <u>WestHR</u> (38:4) Wint 84, p. 322-323.
"You are the dark song of the morning"
    ("Untitled"). <u>KenR</u> (NS 6:2) Spr 84, p. 51-52.

3860. OLIVER, Michael Brian
    "Pigs." <u>CanLit</u> (100) Spr 84, p. 244-245.

3861. OLIVER, Raymond
    "The Body Politic" (the late sixties). <u>TriQ</u> (59)
        Wint 84, p. 136.
    "Pay ce que vouldras." <u>TriQ</u> (59) Wint 84, p. 137.
    "Seventeenth-century Gravestone for a Child"
        (Chelmsford, Mass.). <u>TriQ</u> (59) Wint 84, p. 136.
    "To the Artist As a Young Child." <u>ChiR</u> (34:3) Sum
        84, p. 24.
    "What Is Our Life? A Play of Passion." <u>TriQ</u> (59)
        Wint 84, p. 137.

3862. OLIVEROS, Chuck
    "The Man Who Left Us Behind." <u>Veloc</u> (3) Aut-Wint
        83, p. 56.

3863. OLIVIER, Louis A.
    "Atlantide City" (excerpts, tr. of Claude
        Herviant). <u>PikeF</u> (6) Aut 84, p. 14.
    "Daily Bread" (from <u>Rêver à Haute Voix</u>, tr.
        of Gilbert Socard). <u>PikeF</u> (6) Aut 84, p. 14.
    "Descent under the Sea" (from <u>Le Temps</u>
        <u>Provisoire</u>, tr. of Raoul Bécousse). <u>PikeF</u>
        (6) Aut 84, p. 14.
    "Identifying Marks" (from <u>Ferrer le Sombre</u>, tr.
        of Vera Feyder, w. Lucia Cordell Getsi). <u>PikeF</u>
        (6) Aut 84, p. 14.

3864. OLLE, Carmen
    "El tiempo es un fantasma Masoch." <u>Mairena</u> (6:16)
        Spr 84, p. 72-73.

3865. OLOFSSON, Tommy
    "Every night I laugh at the moon" (tr. by Jean
        Pearson). <u>StoneC</u> (12:1/2) Aut-Wint 84, p. 42.
    "Varje kväll skrattar jag at manen." <u>StoneC</u>
        (12:1/2) Aut-Wint 84, p. 42.

3866. OLSEN, Don
    "Propaganda." <u>Northeast</u> (Series 3:17) Sum 84, p. 3.

3867. OLSEN, William
    "Over and under the Sun." <u>Telescope</u> (3:1) Wint
        84, p. 41-43.

3868. OLSON, Charles
    "Birth's Obituary." <u>Sulfur</u> (4:2, issue 11) 84, p.
        150.
    "The Collected Poems: 1940-1949" (Selections).
        <u>Sulfur</u> (4:2, issue 11) 84, p. 141-157.

"The Dragon-Fly." Sulfur (4:2, issue 11) 84, p.
   154-155.
"Dura." Sulfur (4:2, issue 11) 84, p. 157.
"Fable for Slumber." Sulfur (4:2, issue 11) 84,
   p. 144.
"A Fish Is the Flower of Water." Sulfur (4:2,
   issue 11) 84, p. 155.
"Her Dream, Half Remembered" (A translation from
   Havelock Ellis). Sulfur (4:2, issue 11) 84, p.
   151-152.
"The House." Sulfur (4:2, issue 11) 84, p. 145.
"Igor Stravinsky" (An Homage). Sulfur (4:2, issue
   11) 84, p. 156.
"Key West." Sulfur (4:2, issue 11) 84, p. 152-153.
"Marry the Marrow." Sulfur (4:2, issue 11) 84, p.
   142-143.
"Mindanao." Sulfur (4:2, issue 11) 84, p. 145-146.
"The Night." Sulfur (4:2, issue 11) 84, p. 147.
"Raphael." Sulfur (4:2, issue 11) 84, p. 146.
"She." Sulfur (4:2, issue 11) 84, p. 148.
"She, Thus." Sulfur (4:2, issue 11) 84, p. 148-149.
"A Translation" (from Havelock Ellis). Sulfur
   (4:2, issue 11) 84, p. 150-151.
"White Horse." Sulfur (4:2, issue 11) 84, p. 142.
"The Winter After." Sulfur (4:2, issue 11) 84, p.
   153-154.

3869. OLSON, Elder
"Anatole France: Advice on a Grandchild." NewL
   (50:4) Sum 84, p. 44.
"Auden." NewL (50:4) Sum 84, p. 44-45.
"Birthday Poem." TriQ (59) Wint 84, p. 127.
"City Streets." TriQ (59) Wint 84, p. 129.
"Epigram against an Epigrammatist." (Unfinished
   Because the Poet Could Not Think of a Rhyme).
   TriQ (59) Wint 84, p. 128.
"Fable." TriQ (59) Wint 84, p. 128.
"Finis." TriQ (59) Wint 84, p. 127.
"Mad Girl." TriQ (59) Wint 84, p. 129.
"Mermaid and Sailor." TriQ (59) Wint 84, p. 129.
"Merry Christmas!" NewL (50:2/3) Wint-Spr 84, p. 33.
"Returning a Knife to a 'friend'." TriQ (59) Wint
   84, p. 127.
"Revenant." TriQ (59) Wint 84, p. 128.
"Self-portrait." TriQ (59) Wint 84, p. 128.
"Undelivered Lecture on a Stabile." NewL (50:4)
   Sum 84, p. 45.

3870. OLSON, Lynda
"Sounds the Stream Remembers." GreenfR (11:1/2)
   Sum-Aut 83, p. 114.

3871. OLSON, Toby
"My Moon Girl." NewL (50:2/3) Wint-Spr 84, p. 92.

3872. OLZHYCH, Oleh
"Aquarium" (To M.A., tr. by Bohdan Boychuk and
   David Ignatow). Pequod (16/17) 84, p. 188.
"Dutch Painting" (tr. by Bohdan Boychuk and David
   Ignatow). Pequod (16/17) 84, p. 187.

3873. OMAR, K'ri
      "He Speaks." PoeticJ (1) 83, p. 8.

3874. ONDAATJE, Michael
      "Birch Bark" (for George Whalley). CanLit (100)
         Spr 84, p. 247.
      "Proust in the Waters" (for Scott and Krystyne).
         CanLit (100) Spr 84, p. 246-247.
      "Wordsworth in the Tropics." Descant (44/45,
         15:1/2) Spr-Sum 84, p. 175.

3875. O'NEILL, Brian
      "Burn Out." YaleR (73:2) Wint 84, p. 306-307.
      "How to Sit on a Porch." WoosterR (1:2) N 84, p. 58.

3876. O'NEILL, Patrick
      "Duality and Chief Charlie." SanFPJ (6:2) 84, p.
         86-87.
      "I Sit in the Balcony Eating Buttered Popcorn and
         Watch the Finale of a Most Sophisticated and
         Entertaining Fishing Production (Rated PG)."
         SanFPJ (6:2) 84, p. 42-43.

3877. OPENGART, Bea
      "Apogee." SmPd (21:1) Wint 84, p. 34.
      "Poem with Afternoon Light." Agni (21) 84, p. 83.

3878. OPPENHEIMER, J. R. (J. Robert)
      "Crossing." Telescope (3:1) Wint 84, p. 4.

3879. OPPENHEIMER, Joel
      "The Patriotess on the Centennial of William Carlos
         Williams' Birth." HiramPoR (36) Spr-Sum 84, p.
         33.

3880. OPYR, Linda
      "The Chase." EngJ (73:7) N 84, p. 75.
      "The Chase." PoeticJ (7) 84, p. 35.

3881. ORBAN, Ottó
      "A Blade of Grass" (tr. by Jascha Kessler and Maria
         Körösy). MichQR (23:4) Aut 84, p. 562.
      "Photograph" (tr. by Jascha Kessler and Maria
         Körösy). MichQR (23:4) Aut 84, p. 561.

3882. ORELLANA, Carlos
      "La Ciudad Va a Estallar, Flora." Mairena (6:18)
         84, p. 99.

3883. ORESICK, Peter
      "Anointing the Sick." ChrC (101:37) 28 N 84, p.
         1116.
      "Old Shevchenko." ChrC (101:31) 17 O 84, p. 957.

3884. ORFALEA, Gregory
      "In Memoriam: Colonel Azmi Saghiyeh, Defender of
         Tyre." GreenfR (12:1/2) Sum-Aut 84, p. 187-189.
      "The Little Finger of Carlos Montoya." GreenfR
         (12:1/2) Sum-Aut 84, p. 189-190.

3885. ORLEANS, Charles d'
"Rondeau LXII." NewOR (11:3/4) Aut-Wint 84, p. 20.

3886. ORLEN, Steve
"Paradise." Antaeus (53) Aut 84, p. 250.

3887. ORLICH, Rose
"Rosewood." Wind (14:51) 84, p. 37-38.

3888. ORR, Ed
"Aristocratic Lovers." Paunch (57/58) Ja 84, p. 84.
"Cow on Ferry-Boat: Dutch Field" (after Jan
Victors). SmPd (21:1) Wint 84, p. 35.
"Golden Style" (variation on a line by Verlaine).
Paunch (57/58) Ja 84, p. 83.
"Landscape As a Concavity of Vision" (after Miro).
YellowS (12) Aut 84, p. 28.
"The Mask." ThirdW (2) Spr 84, p. 44.
"Where the Unicorn Visits." RagMag (3:2) Aut 84,
p. 22.

3889. ORR, Greg
"Friday Lunch Break." Salm (65) Aut 84, p. 92.

3890. ORR, Gregory
"Equilibrium" (tr. of Evhen Pluzhnyk). Pequod
(16/17) 84, p. 180-181.

3891. ORR, Linda
"Black Animal Dependency" (tr. of Claude Mouchard).
ParisR (26:92) Sum 84, p. 164-172.
"Cafes." AntR (42:1) Wint 84, p. 83.

3892. ORSZAG-LAND, Thomas
"If Hatred Rules." Bogg (52) 84, p. 64.

ORTEGA, Adolfo Garcia: See GARCIA ORTEGA, Adolfo

3893. ORTEGA, Daniel
"In the Prison" (tr. by Marc Zimmerman and Ellen
Banberger). MinnR (N.S. 22) Spr 84, p. 70-72.

3894. ORTH, Kevin
"Walls That Look Back In." WestB (14) 84, p. 36.

ORTIZ, Ernesto Ruiz: See RUIZ ORTIZ, Ernesto

3895. ORTOLANI, Al
"The Last Hippie of Camp Fifty, Kansas" (First
Honorable Mention, 13th Annual Kansas Poetry
Contest). LittleBR (4:3) Spr 84, p. 65.

3896. OSBORN, Karen
"Ice Dance." YetASM (3) 84, p. 5.

OSBORNE, Elba Diaz de: See DIAZ de OSBORNE, Elba

3897. OSING, Gordon
"Dauphin Island." SouthernR (20:1) Wint 84, p.
131-133.

"European" (on the Reforma). GreenfR (12:1/2)
Sum-Aut 84, p. 135.
"Time Bombs" (Ciudad Mexico). GreenfR (12:1/2)
Sum-Aut 84, p. 134.

3898. OSLANDER, M. Marcuss
"News Story." Tele (19) 83, p. 104-105.
"There's No Way to Tell You." Tele (19) 83, p. 106.

3899. OSTASZEWSKI, Krzysztof
"I speak to you of flowers" (tr. by Wojtek
Stelmaszynski). Amelia (1:2) O 84, p. 55.
"Opus 63, a Tragedy" (tr. by Wojtek Stelmaszynski).
Amelia (1:2) O 84, p. 55.

3900. OSTASZEWSKI, Krzysztof M.
"I Am a Dark Cloud over the City" (tr. by the
author). PoeticJ (6) 84, p. 33.

3901. OSTRIKER, Alicia
"A Clearing by a Stream" (Roaring Fork, Aspen, June
1982). Poetry (144:6) S 84, p. 329-330.
"Death Is Only." NewEngR (7:1) Aut 84, p. 101.
"Digging to China." Nat (238:17) 5 My 84, p. 550.
"Single Woman Speaking." Poetry (144:6) S 84, p.
327-328.
"The Sky, Asleep, Dreams a Snowfall." Nat (239:1)
7-14 Jl 84, p. 28.
"Three Men Walking, Three Brown Silhouettes."
Iowa (14:3) Aut 84, p. 12-13.
"While Driving North." OntR (20) Spr-Sum 84, p.
37-40.

3902. OSTROFF, Anthony
"End of the War in Merida." NewL (50:2/3) Wint-
Spr 84, p. 169.

3903. OTERIÑO, Rafael Felipe
"Elegia: En la casa se respira el mismo aire de
entonces." Mairena (6:18) 84, p. 117.

3904. OTIS, Emily
"News." WestB (14) 84, p. 64.
"Tribute." WestB (14) 84, p. 65.

3905. OTT, Gil
"Reduced to the sun at noon." Origin (Series 5:2)
Wint 83, p. 88-89.

3906. OUTAVIT, R. U. (who has something to do with Jack Powers)
"Last of the Buffalo Heads." Sam (39:1, release
153) 84, p. 31.

3907. OUTRAM, Richard
"Dr. Dolittle." CanLit (100) Spr 84, p. 248-249.

3908. OVERALL, Suzanne
"Mind over Matter." SanFPJ (6:4) 84, p. 61.
"Why." PoeticJ (7) 84, p. 32.
"Without a Trace." PoeticJ (8) 84, p. 44.

3909. OVERTON, Ron
"Alcoholic Houses." OP (37) Spr-Sum 84, p. 42.
"And." OP (37) Spr-Sum 84, p. 40.
"Battle of the Network Stars." OP (37) Spr-Sum
    84, p. 38.
"Days of Baseball." OP (37) Spr-Sum 84, p. 41.
"The Magician." OP (37) Spr-Sum 84, p. 39.
"Midnight" (for Peter). OP (37) Spr-Sum 84, p. 43.
"The Rites." OP (37) Spr-Sum 84, p. 37.

3910. OVID
"The Tristia" (Selection: To His Wife, I, 6, tr. by
    David R. Slavitt). TexasR (5:1/2) Spr-Sum 84,
    p. 30-31.
"Tristia" (Selections: V-7, V-12, tr. by David R.
    Slavitt). MichQR (23:2) Spr 84, p. 221-225.

3911. OWEN, Sue
"Fortune Teller." SouthernR (20:2) Spr 84, p. 378-
    379.
"Hatred." VirQR (60:4) Aut 84, p. 614-615.
"Idle Hands." SouthernR (20:2) Spr 84, p. 380.
"Playing Dead." VirQR (60:4) Aut 84, p. 615-616.
"The Squirrels." SouthernR (20:2) Spr 84, p. 377-
    378.
"The White Rabbit." Poetry (145:3) D 84, p. 149-150.

3912. OWEN SOUND
"Every Day" (detail). CapilR (31) 84, p. 53.
"Für Dieter Schnebel (Tempus Est)." CapilR (31)
    84, p. 54.
"She Was a Visitor" (from a Robert Ashley work).
    CapilR (31) 84, p. 53.

3913. OWENS, Rochelle
"Long Before Homer Spoke" (from French Light).
    Nimrod (27:2) Spr-Sum 84, p. 60-62.

3914. OWENS, Tracy
"Going on a Lion Hunt." Writ (16) Aut 84, p. 66-67.

3915. OWER, John
"A Cross of Salt." AntigR (56) Wint 84, p. 100.
"Divorce." Confr (27/28) 84, p. 335.
"Me as a Raven and Crow." AntigR (56) Wint 84, p.
    100.
"Sonnet 3" (For M. C.). Poem (51) Mr [i.e. Jl]
    84, p. 50.

3916. OXENHORN, Harvey
"Fathers and Sons." Ploughs (10:1) 84, p. 128-129.

3917. OYAMA, Richard
"Dreams in Progress." GreenfR (11:1/2) Sum-Aut
    83, p. 165-166.
"Obon by the Hudson." GreenfR (11:1/2) Sum-Aut
    83, p. 167.

3918. OZAROW, Kent Jorgensen
"His Office." Confr (27/28) 84, p. 179.

3919. OZER, Kemal
       "Agit." <u>StoneC</u> (11:3/4) Spr-Sum 84, p. 38.
       "Elegy" (tr. by Dionis Coffin Riggs, William
          Fielder and Ozcan Yalim). <u>StoneC</u> (11:3/4) Spr-
          Sum 84, p. 39.

3920. OZICK, Cynthia
       "Bridled." <u>Chelsea</u> (42/43) 84, p. 130.
       "Red-Shift." <u>Chelsea</u> (42/43) 84, p. 131.

3921. PACERNICK, Gary
       "Mrs. Minster." <u>Wind</u> (14:52) 84, p. 38.

3922. PACEY, Michael
       "The Anthem of the Night." <u>PottPort</u> (6) 84, p. 52.
       "The Boston Suitcoat." <u>PottPort</u> (6) 84, p. 25.
       "The Old Neighbourhood." <u>PottPort</u> (6) 84, p. 33.

3923. PACK, Robert
       "Brother to Brother." <u>SewanR</u> (92:1) Ja-Mr 84, p.
          67-68.
       "Clayfeld's Dream." <u>WebR</u> (9:2) Wint 85, p. 25-27.
       "Clayfeld's Glove." <u>NewRep</u> (190:6) 13 F 84, p. 36.
       "Clayfeld's Microscope." <u>Poetry</u> (144:5) Ag 84, p.
          281-283.
       "Clayfeld's Vision of the Next Beginning." <u>GeoR</u>
          (38:4) Wint 84, p. 727-728.
       "The Homo Sapiens' Anniversary Song." <u>Antaeus</u>
          (52) Apr 84, p. 131-132.

3924. PACKIE, Susan
       "Beirut Massacre." <u>SanFPJ</u> (6:1) 84, p. 55.
       "Desert Indigestion." <u>Sam</u> (39:1, release 153) 84,
          p. 9.
       "Juxtaposition." <u>SanFPJ</u> (6:1) 84, p. 54.
       "Lab Specimens." <u>Sam</u> (37:3, 147th release) 83, p.
          49.

3925. PADGAONKAR, Mangesh
       "At a Quarter to Eight in the Morning" (tr. by
          Vinay Dharwadker). <u>MinnR</u> (N.S. 22) Spr 84, p. 60.
       "Salaam" (tr. by Vinay Dharwadker). <u>NewEngR</u> (6:4)
          Sum 84, p. 511-514.
       "You" (tr. by Vinay Dharwadker). <u>NewEngR</u> (6:4)
          Sum 84, p. 515-516.

3926. PADGETT, Ron
       "First Drift." <u>ParisR</u> (26:94) Wint 84, p. 167-168.

3927. PADHI, Bibhu
       "I Hear a Small Voice Speaking." <u>AntigR</u> (56) Wint
          84, p. 7-8.
       "Midnight." <u>SouthwR</u> (69:3) Sum 84, p. 311.
       "Siva." <u>AntigR</u> (56) Wint 84, p. 8.

3928. PADILLA, Heberto
       "Canto Sexto" (tr. of Hans Magnus Enzensberger).
          <u>LindLM</u> (3:1) Ja-Mr 84, p. 27.
       "Poetica." <u>Mairena</u> (6:18) 84, p. 172.

3929. PAETZNICK, Barbara
       "June Chill." Amelia [1:1] Ap 84, p. 19.

PAGAN, Angel A. Berríos: See BERRIOS PAGAN, Angel A.

3930. PAGE, P. K.
       "Concentration." MalR (67) F 84, p. 7.
       "Crow's Nest." MalR (67) F 84, p. 11-12.
       "Deaf-Mute in the Pear Tree." MalR (67) F 84, p.
           6-7.
       "Deep Sleep." MalR (67) F 84, p. 9.
       "Invisible Presences Fill the Air." MalR (67) F
           84, p. 5.
       "The Painting in Progress." CanLit (103) Wint 84,
           p. 50.
       "Remembering George Johnston Reading." MalR (67)
           F 84, p. 13.
       "To a Dead Friend." MalR (67) F 84, p. 8.
       "Visitants." MalR (67) F 84, p. 10.
       "What's in a Name?" MalR (67) F 84, inside back
           cover, p. 149.

3931. PAGE, William
       "Blister of Paint." TexasR (5:1/2) Spr-Sum 84, p.
           137.
       "The Carter House in Franklin, Tennessee."
           SouthernR (20:1) Wint 84, p. 136-137.
       "The Golden Apples." Wind (14:51) 84, p. 39.
       "Iron Creek, 1939." GreenfR (11:1/2) Sum-Aut 83,
           p. 102.
       "The Reappearance" (Jimmy Durante, 1893-1980).
           MidwQ (25:2) Wint 84, p. 169.

3932. PAGES, Irène
       "Automne." PoetryCR (5:3) Spr 84, p. 6.
       "Coucher de Soleil au Calendrier des Postes."
           PoetryCR (5:3) Spr 84, p. 6.
       "Les Pétrifiées." PoetryCR (5:3) Spr 84, p. 6.

3933. PAGIS, Dan
       "November '73" (tr. by W. Bargad). Pequod (16/17)
           84, p. 110.

3934. PAIEWONSKY CONDE, Edgar
       "Deya." Areíto (10:38) 84, p. 34.

3935. PAIN, Philip
       "Meditation 8." TriQ (61) Aut 84, p. 63.

3936. PAIR, Joyce
       "Free Will." DekalbLAJ (20th Anniversary Issue)
           84, p. 100-101.

3937. PALADINO, Thomas
       "The Director in the Jungle." Telescope (3:3) Aut
           84, p. 90-91.

3938. PALANDER, John
       "The Pickets." AntigR (56) Wint 84, p. 84.

3939. PALEY, Grace
      "Question." Chelsea (42/43) 84, p. 225.
      "When Drowning." Chelsea (42/43) 84, p. 224.

3940. PALEY, Roberta
      "Rain for Two Days." NewL (50:2/3) Wint-Spr 84,
        p. 218.

3941. PALMA, Marigloria
      "Aprietame en Tu Sombra." Mairena (5:14) Aut 83,
        p. 78.

3942. PALMER, Michael
      "First Figure" (for Ben Watkins). Sulfur (4:1,
        issue 10) 84, p. 121-122.
      "Music Rewritten" (after D.S.). Sulfur (4:1,
        issue 10) 84, p. 122-123.

3943. PANAGHIS, Afroditi
      "The Bard." Poem (51) Mr [i.e. Jl] 84, p. 64.
      "Threnody." Poem (51) Mr [i.e. Jl] 84, p. 65.

3944. PANEK, Denise Helene
      "Winter Garden." Calyx (8:2) Spr 84, p. 91.

3945. PANKEY, Eric
      "Chekhov on the Way to Singapore." KenR (NS 6:3)
        Sum 84, p. 46-47.
      "Encounters" (For My Father). KenR (NS 6:3) Sum
        84, p. 45-46.
      "Forfeiting Light." AntR (42:3) Sum 84, p. 324-325.
      "The Less It Seemed True." Telescope (3:3) Aut
        84, p. 111-112.
      "Photograph of My Parents: Ice Skating, 1954."
        SenR (14:1) 84, p. 65-66.
      "The Politic of Happiness." Telescope (3:2) Spr
        84, p. 10-11.
      "Returning in Winter" (after Czeslaw Milosz).
        Iowa (14:3) Aut 84, p. 11.
      "Winter Anniversary." LitR (28:1) Aut 84, p. 58.

3946. PANKOWSKI, Elsie
      "Barriers." Wind (14:51) 84, p. 40.
      "Cutting Posts on the Missouri." Wind (14:51) 84,
        p. 40-41.
      "Holding On" (To Geri). KanQ (16:1/2) Wint-Spr
        84, p. 195.

PAOLI, Francisco Matos: See MATOS PAOLI, Francisco

3947. PAPENHAUSEN, Carol
      "Separate, and Equal." SpoonRQ (9:2) Spr 84, p. 33.

3948. PAPPAS, Theresa
      "Olympia." PaintedB (24) Aut 84, p. 14.
      "Private Entrance." PaintedB (24) Aut 84, p. 13.

3949. PAPPAS, Tom
      "The Crazy Life." YellowS (12) Aut 84, p. 34.

3950. PARADIS, Philip
       "Dust Storm." MidAR (4:1) Spr 84, p. 128.

3951. PARE, Terence P.
       "Diminished Things." Poetry (144:4) Jl 84, p. 224-
       227.

3952. PARINI, Jay
       "Suburban Swamp." NewRep (190:14) 9 Ap 84, p. 34.

3953. PARISH, Barbara Shirk
       "In the Wake of the War." SmPd (21:1) Wint 84, p.
       23.
       "Outsider." SnapD (7:2) Spr 84, p. 13.
       "Spite Fence." SnapD (8:1) Aut 84, p. 17.
       "Taken from a Daughter's Journal." LittleBR (4:3)
       Spr 84, p. 13.

3954. PARKER, Doris
       "Buck Creek Road." Vis (16) 84, p. 17.

3955. PARKER, J. P.
       "El Padre of la Mesa." HiramPoR (37) Aut-Wint 84,
       p. 32-33.

3956. PARKER, Martha
       "Evensong." KanQ (16:4) Aut 84, p. 94.
       "Good Night." KanQ (16:4) Aut 84, p. 95.

3957. PARKEY, Donald E.
       "The Cellar." LittleBR (4:4) Sum 84, p. 74.

3958. PARKS, Gerald B.
       "Meditation of a Reader of Newspapers." WorldO
       (18:3) Spr 84, p. 43.

3959. PARKS, Ruth M.
       "In St. Paul's." PoeticJ (6) 84, p. 27.

3960. PARLATO, Stephen
       "Out Here in Northern California." Open24 (3) 84,
       p. 25-26.

3961. PARLATORE, Anselm
       "Bass from the Surf Reverie." Veloc (3) Aut-Wint
       83, p. 19-20.
       "Hunter at Mecox." Veloc (3) Aut-Wint 83, p. 24-26.
       "Winter Storm--Mecox." Veloc (3) Aut-Wint 83, p.
       22-23.

3962. PARRA, Nicanor
       "Chile." Mairena (6:18) 84, p. 133.
       "Vices of the Modern World" (tr. by Jorge Elliott).
       Chelsea (42/43) 84, p. 58-60.

3963. PARRAT, Anne
       "Grey." PoetryCR (6:2) Wint 84-85, p. 24.

3964. PARRATT, Anne
       "Black Tie." PortR (30:1) 84, p. 171-174.

3965. PARREÑO, E. José
"Racimo de Plátano en Nieve." Areíto (9:36)
84, p. 105.

3966. PARRIS, Peggy
"Newspaper" (cut-up poem). Kayak (64) My 84, p.
42-43.
"The Tease" (cut-up poem). Kayak (64) My 84, p. 44.

3967. PARRIS, Roger
"Colors and Smells" (Dedicated to Skip). Stepping
(Premier Issue) Sum 82, p. 29.

3968. PARRY, Marian
"Victorian Illustration." NegC (4:2) Spr 84, p.
20-21.

3969. PARSONS, Bruce
"Work, in Quotes." PottPort (6) 84, p. 4.

3970. PARSONS, Howard L.
"I, Hibakusha." NewWR (52:4) Jl-Ag 84, p. 23.

3971. PARTHASARATHY, R.
"Homecoming." Iowa (14:2) Spr-Sum 84, p. 81-83.

3972. PARTRIDGE, Dixie (Dixie L.)
"Aftermath." SnapD (8:1) Aut 84, p. 44.
"Change in a Landscape." SnapD (8:1) Aut 84, p. 45.
"Early Signs." SnapD (6:2) Spr 83, p. 40.
"Hypothermia." SnapD (6:2) Spr 83, p. 42-43.
"Sources." SnapD (6:2) Spr 83, p. 41.

3973. PASCHKE, Barbara
"Counter Voice" (tr. of Alfonsina Storni). Vis
(15) 84, p. 5.
"The Difficulties of a Poet Who Amidst Desks,
Machines and Countless Other Things Scribbles
Poems and Scribbles Them Again" (tr. of Rosario
Murillo). Vis (15) 84, p. 25.
"Shadows at Dawn" (tr. of Rosario Murillo). Vis
(15) 84, p. 26.
"To Dionysius, Companero" (tr. of Daisy Zamora).
Vis (15) 84, p. 24.
"Voice" (tr. of Alfonsina Storni). Vis (15) 84,
p. 4-5.
"The Wind Passes through Streets" (tr. of Otto Rene
Castillo). Vis (15) 84, p. 22.

3974. PASOLINI, Pier Paolo
"The Bells of Orvieto" (tr. by Paul Schmidt).
NewYRB (31:8) 10 My 84, p. 36.
"I Work All Day" (tr. by Lawrence R. Smith).
PoetryE (15) Aut 84, p. 79.
"Lament of the Steam Shovel" (Part II, tr. by Lynne
Lawner). Chelsea (42/43) 84, p. 103-105.
"Part of a Letter, to Young Codignola" (tr. by Paul
Schmidt). NewYRB (31:18) 22 N 84, p. 47.
"Supplication to My Mother" (tr. by Lawrence R.
Smith). PoetryE (15) Aut 84, p. 80.

3975. PASTAN, Linda
      "At My Desk" (To William Stafford). Poetry
         (145:1) O 84, p. 2-3.
      "The Death of a Parent." GeoR (38:3) Aut 84, p. 561.
      "Departures." TriQ (61) Aut 84, p. 77.
      "Donatello's Magdalene" (Wood sculpture, 15th
         Century). Poetry (144:5) Ag 84, p. 274.
      "Family Scene: Mid-Twentieth Century." Ploughs
         (10:4) 84, p. 108-109.
      "Folk Tale." Chelsea (42/43) 84, p. 280-281.
      "The Last Second Son Poem." NeqC (4:1) Wint 84,
         p. 101.
      "Notes for an Elegy: for John Gardner." Antaeus
         (52) Apr 84, p. 124-125.
      "Overture." Poetry (145:1) O 84, p. 1-2.
      "Routine Mammogram." TriQ (61) Aut 84, p. 75-76.
      "Shadows." TriQ (61) Aut 84, p. 78-79.
      "Suffocation" (for RJP). NewEnqR (7:1) Aut 84, p.
         90.
      "Waiting Room." Poetry (145:1) O 84, p. 3-4.
      "Why Not?" NewL (50:2/3) Wint-Spr 84, p. 188.

3976. PASTERNIK, Jean
      "Walk in Taos." Wind (14:52) 84, p. 39.

3977. PATCHEN, Kenneth
      "The Hands of the Air" (picture-poem)." PoetryE
         (13/14) Spr-Sum 84, p. 241.
      "The Impatient Explorer" (picture-poem)." PoetryE
         (13/14) Spr-Sum 84, p. 239.
      "With one tiny stick" (picture-poem)." PoetryE
         (13/14) Spr-Sum 84, p. 240.

3978. PATERSON, Andrea
      "Cinderella Story." WebR (9:1) Spr 84, p. 69.
      "Death by Drowning." WebR (9:1) Spr 84, p. 67-68.
      "The Senator's Ball." DekalbLAJ (17:1/2) 84, p. 141.

3979. PATTEN, Karl
      "Cardinal's Rocks, Marblehead." PaintedB (24) Aut
         84, p. 29.

3980. PATTERSON, Boydie C.
      "Rituals." Stepping (Anniversary Issue I) 84, p.
         37-38.

3981. PATTERSON, Cy
      "Bracing air." Bogg (52) 84, p. 52.

3982. PATTERSON, Raymond R.
      "The Poet and His People" (For Langston Hughes).
         Stepping Wint 84, p. 14-15.

3983. PATTERSON, Veronica
      "Perspective." IndR (7:3) Sum 84, p. 58.

3984. PATTON, Lee
      "Crossing the Missile Zone." Spirit (7:1) 84, p. 74.

3985. PATTON, Melinda
      "America the Beautiful." SanFPJ (6:4) 84, p. 6.
      "Atom Dead." SanFPJ (6:4) 84, p. 41.
      "Didn't Someone Once Say." SanFPJ (6:1) 84, p. 90.
      "No Man Can Take My Hand." SanFPJ (7:1) 84, p. 74.
      "Past Tense." SanFPJ (7:1) 84, p. 75.
      "Visions of El Salvador." SanFPJ (7:1) 84, p. 75.

3986. PAU-LLOSA, Ricardo
      "Foreign Language." Kayak (64) My 84, p. 25.
      "The Inventors." BelPoJ (35:1) Aut 84, p. 14.
      "The Poet." Confr (27/28) 84, p. 43.
      "The Sharing." BelPoJ (35:1) Aut 84, p. 13.
      "Swirling Lines." MissouriR (7:3) 84, p. 24-25.

3987. PAUL, David J.
      "Diver." Quarry (33:3) Sum 84, p. 10.
      "Pax." Quarry (33:3) Sum 84, p. 9-10.
      "There's Husbandry in Heaven." Quarry (33:3) Sum
          84, p. 9.

3988. PAUL, Jay S.
      "Old Mother of Mothers." BelPoJ (35:2) Wint 84-
          85, p. 25.
      "Upriver." StoneC (11:3/4) Spr-Sum 84, p. 12.

PAUL, Sali Nacker: See NACKER-PAUL, Sali

3989. PAULENICH, Craig
      "Defoliated." Pig (12) 84, p. 82.

3990. PAVESE, Cesare
      "Instinct" (tr. by Norman Thomas di Giovanni).
          Chelsea (42/43) 84, p. 123.

3991. PAVLIDES, Lefteris
      "One Swallow Flying" (Psalm #4 of "The Passion",
          from The Axion Esti, tr. of Odysseus Elytis,
          w. Edward Morin). Confr (27/28) 84, p. 57.

3992. PAWLOWSKI, Robert
      "Gulf Coast." MissR (37/38, 13:1/2) Aut 84, p. 78.
      "River." MissR (37/38, 13:1/2) Aut 84, p. 79.

3993. PAWLOWSKI, Robert S.
      "Margaret Reading." TexasR (5:3/4) Aut-Wint 84,
          p. 19.

3994. PAZ, Octavio
      "Objects and Apparitions" (for Joseph Cornell, tr.
          by Elizabeth Bishop). PoetryE (13/14) Spr-Sum
          84, p. 228-229.
      "Sun Stone" (Excerpts, tr. by Muriel Rukeyser).
          Chelsea (42/43) 84, p. 50-51.

3995. P'BITEK, Okot
      "Song of Lawino" (Excerpt). Iowa (14:2) Spr-Sum
          84, p. 132-134.

3996. PEACOCK, Molly
      "Among Tall Buildings." Pequod (16/17) 84, p. 26.
      "The Breach of Or." ParisR (26:93) Aut 84, p. 162.
      "Cloth God." ParisR (26:93) Aut 84, p. 163.
      "Desire." ParisR (26:93) Aut 84, p. 161.
      "Gesture." NewYorker (60:20) 2 Jl 84, p. 42.
      "Here." ParisR (26:93) Aut 84, p. 164.
      "Squirrel Disappears." GeoR (38:3) Aut 84, p. 631-
         632.
      "Violet Dusks." AntR (42:1) Wint 84, p. 82.

3997. PEARSON, Jean
      "Every night I laugh at the moon" (tr. of Tommy
         Olofsson). StoneC (12:1/2) Aut-Wint 84, p. 42.

3998. PEARSON, Julie
      "Consuelo." SanFPJ (6:1) 84, p. 88.

3999. PEASE, Deborah
      "Maintenance." Chelsea (42/43) 84, p. 420-421.

4000. PEATTIE, Noel
      "Tumbleweed Valley." GreenfR (12:1/2) Sum-Aut 84,
         p. 144-145.

4001. PECK, John
      "Begin's Autumn after the Late Massacre, 1982."
         TriQ (61) Aut 84, p. 86-87.
      "Boat near the Capo Miseno." NewRep (191:18) 29 O
         84, p. 34.
      "Buddy." TriQ (61) Aut 84, p. 83.
      "Hazelnut." TriQ (61) Aut 84, p. 88.
      "He, She, All of Them, Ay." TriQ (61) Aut 84, p.
         84-85.
      "Leaving the Central Station." Salm (65) Aut 84,
         p. 104-105.
      "Reading Late at Night in January." Salm (65) Aut
         84, p. 107.
      "Stanzas from the Bridge." TriQ (61) Aut 84, p.
         80-82.
      "Zürich, zum Storker." Salm (65) Aut 84, p. 105-
         106.

4002. PEDEN, Margaret Sayers
      "Modest Gift by Affection Made a Treat" (tr. of Sor
         Juana Inés de la Cruz). NewL (50:4) Sum 84,
         p. 64.
      "One day you buy something new" (Untitled, tr. of
         Luisa Valenzuela). Hudson (37:4) Wint 84-85,
         p. 570.
      "She Assures That She Will Hold a Secret in
         Confidence" (tr. of Sor Juana Inés de la
         Cruz). NewL (50:4) Sum 84, p. 64.
      "Urban Haiku" (tr. of Luisa Valenzuela). Hudson
         (37:4) Wint 84-85, p. 570.

4003. PEDITTO, Paul
      "Die the Death of a Rag Doll." HangL (46) Aut 84,
         p. 56-57.

4004. PEDROZO, Armanda
       "Copula." Mairena (6:18) 84, p. 191.

4005. PEELER, Tim
       "As the Train Approaches." PoeticJ (7) 84, p. 15.
       "Blue's Baby." PoeticJ (8) 84, p. 19.
       "The Conservative Prostitute." Sam (39:1, release
         153) 84, p. 48.
       "Ferris Wheel Ride." PoeticJ (7) 84, p. 11.
       "Going to California." PoeticJ (2) 83, p. 11.
       "Technically Pioneer." Amelia (1:2) O 84, p. 24.

4006. PELLETIER, Gus
       "For Archibald MacLeish (1892-1982): A
         Retrospective." Wind (14:52) 84, p. 40.
       "For Roger Duchamp, USMC." PoeticJ (4) 83, p. 18-19.

4007. PELLISIER, Hank
       "Nightmare." SanFPJ (6:2) 84, p. 36.

PEÑA, Alfredo Cardona: See CARDONA PEÑA, Alfredo

4008. PEÑA, Horacio
       "Recuerdos de Nefertili, Princesa Egipcia."
         Mairena (6:18) 84, p. 156-157.

4009. PENHA, James W.
       "A-Changing." SanFPJ (6:1) 84, p. 21.

4010. PENNANT, Edmund
       "Beginning." Comm (111:7) 6 Ap 84, p. 220.
       "The Mummies of Guanajuato." NegC (4:1) Wint 84,
         p. 26-27.
       "The Saint." Comm (111:7) 6 Ap 84, p. 220.

4011. PEPPER, Patric
       "Three Views of a Biker." Wind (14:50) 84, p. 31.

4012. PERCHIK, Simon
       "As a shadow brings down the dark." HolCrit
         (21:2) Ap 84, p. 18.
       "My arm asleep, numb." CreamCR (9:1/2) 84, p. 90.
       "My wall again and under its paper." Os (18) 84,
         p. 19.
       "Nothing Will Collide." MidAR (4:1) Spr 84, p.
         141-142.
       "Poem: This penny has the name my father gave."
         Bogg (52) 84, p. 7.
       "Sharp As Coral." SouthwR (69:3) Sum 84, p. 261.
       "What Nag." CalQ (25) Aut 84, p. 36.

4013. PERDOMO, Miguel Aníbal
       "El Prisionero." Areíto (10:38) 84, p. 33.

4014. PEREIRA, Sam
       "1983" (for Norman Dubie). Telescope (3:3) Aut
         84, p. 92-93.
       "Cat Galaxies." Telescope (3:1) Wint 84, p. 92.
       "Something about Sailing." Poetry (144:2) My 84,
         p. 104-105.

4015. PEREIRA VARELA, Marisol
"Mensis." Mairena (6:17) Aut 84, p. 87.

4016. PERET, Benjamin
"Little Song of the Maimed" (tr. by Keith Holaman).
Pequod (16/17) 84, p. 242.

4017. PEREZ, Hildebrando
"Mutatis Mutandis." Mairena (6:18) 84, p. 93.

4018. PEREZ CASTELLON, Ninoska
"Absoluta Negadora de Realidades." LindLM (3:2/4)
Ap-D 84, p. 23.
"You and Your Eternal Quest." LindLM (3:2/4) Ap-D
84, p. 23.

4019. PEREZ FIRMAT, Gustavo
"Dias de los Padres en Chapel Hill." LindLM
(3:2/4) Ap-D 84, p. 21.
"Romance de Coral Gables." LindLM (3:2/4) Ap-D
84, p. 21.

4020. PEREZ MARICEVICH, Francisco
"Noche Arriba." Mairena (6:18) 84, p. 190.

4021. PERI ROSSI, Cristina (See also ROSSI, Christina Peri)
"Aquellos que alguna vez la amaron." Cond (3:4,
issue 10) 84, p. 48.
"Penétrame occidental y perversa." Cond (3:4,
issue 10) 84, p. 49.
"Penétrame profunda y larvariamente." Cond
(3:4, issue 10) 84, p. 50.
"Penetrate me deep and sinuously". (tr. by Patrice
Titterington). Cond (3:4, issue 10) 84, p. 50.
"Penetrate me occidental and perverse" (tr. by
Patrice Titterington). Cond (3:4, issue 10)
84, p. 49.
"Those who once loved her" (tr. by Patrice
Titterington). Cond (3:4, issue 10) 84, p. 48.

4022. PERKINS, David
"1946 Nickel." NewL (50:2/3) Wint-Spr 84, p. 86.
"Doing Time." NewL (50:2/3) Wint-Spr 84, p. 86-87.

4023. PERKINS, James A.
"Not Considering Gravity." SmPd (21:3) Aut 84, p.
17.
"Saranac Time Bomb." CapeR (19:2) Sum 84, p. 44.

4024. PERKINS, James Ashbrook
"First Frost/Fall 1975." CapeR (19:3) 20th
Anniverary Issue 84, p. 39.

4025. PERLBERG, Mark
"Night Too Hot to Sleep." Peb (23) 84, p. 38.

4026. PERLMAN, Mira-Lani
"About Which Was More Important." Telescope (3:1)
Wint 84, p. 116-118.
"Love Song." Telescope (3:1) Wint 84, p. 114-115.

4027. PERMANENT COMMISSION ON HUMAN RIGHTS
      "Forms and Levels of Human Rights Violations in
      Nicaragua." MinnR (N.S. 22) Spr 84, p. 78.

4028. PERRICONE, Christopher, Jr.
      "The Cellar." KanQ (16:4) Aut 84, p. 200.

4029. PERRINE, Laurence
      "Janus." Poetry (144:3) Je 84, p. 133.
      "Limerick: The sex-life her husband dreamed of."
      Poetry (144:3) Je 84, p. 133.

4030. PERROW, Mike
      "Listen, He Chop on Down." HolCrit (21:1) F 84,
      p. 19.

4031. PERRY, Georgette
      "Specter." Veloc (4) Sum 84, p. 53.

4032. PERRY, Jeanne
      "South James County." Tendril (17) Wint 84, p.
      148-149.

4033. PERRY, Maggie
      "Lake Michigan Summers." Northeast (Series 3:17)
      Sum 84, p. 23.
      "Skaters." SpoonRQ (9:4) Aut 84, p. 15.
      "Stone & Light." SpoonRQ (9:4) Aut 84, p. 16.

4034. PERRY, Robert
      "In Memory of Earl Organ." PraS (58:1) Spr 84, p.
      50-52.

4035. PESEROFF, Joyce
      "Exercise." NewRep (190:21) 28 My 84, p. 39.
      "The Glad Cafe." NewL (51:2) Wint 84-85, p. 114.
      "The Long March." Ploughs (10:4) 84, p. 128-129.
      "Study." NewRep (189:12/13) 19-26 S 83, p. 36.
      "Uncle Ben." Shen (35:1) 83-84, p. 57.

4036. PETERS, Patricia Claire
      "For Joanna." Hudson (37:1) Spr 84, p. 75-78.
      "Nighttime" (from "For Joanna"). Hudson (37:1)
      Spr 84, p. 75-76.
      "Skating" (from "For Joanna"). Hudson (37:1) Spr
      84, p. 77-78.
      "Walking" (from "For Joanna"). Hudson (37:1) Spr
      84, p. 76-77.

4037. PETERS, Robert
      "Blood Countess" (Excerpts). Bogg (52) 84, p. 5-6.
      "The Blood Countess" (Excerpts). Sulfur (4:1,
      issue 10) 84, p. 68-74.
      "Iconoclast." Sam (41:1, release 161) 84, p. 31.

4038. PETERSON, Geoffrey
      "Fishing off Okinawa." ThirdW (2) Spr 84, p. 16-17.

4039. PETERSON, Jim
      "Clean Undecorated Hall." GeoR (38:3) Aut 84, p.

575-576.
"The Inheritance." <u>GeoR</u> (38:3) Aut 84, p. 576-577.

4040. PETERSON, Marsha
"In the Grays." <u>Blueline</u> (6:1) Sum-Aut 84, p. 20-21.

4041. PETERSON, Robert
"Geography." <u>NowestR</u> (22:3) 84, p. 14-15.

4042. PETESCH, Donald A.
"David Frost Show, May 4, 1977." <u>Pig</u> (12) 84, p. 82.
"The Generals on the Evening News." <u>SouthernPR</u>
(24:1) Spr 84, p. 44.
"Maps." <u>PoetryNW</u> (25:2) Sum 84, p. 32.

4043. PETO, Sylvia
"Ghosts." <u>Tendril</u> (17) Wint 84, p. 150.
"The Kid Who Loved Water Too Much." <u>Tendril</u> (17)
Wint 84, p. 151-152.

4044. PETRAKOS, Chris
"Love, Sleep, Travelling." <u>PoetryE</u> (15) Aut 84,
p. 11.
"One Snowy Night." <u>PoetryE</u> (15) Aut 84, p. 10.
"Spirits." <u>OhioR</u> (32) 84, p. 107.

4045. PETREMAN, David A.
"Borrowing Dusk." <u>StoneC</u> (11:3/4) Spr-Sum 84, p. 36.

4046. PETRIE, Paul
"After the Long Winter." <u>ChrC</u> (101:10) 21-28 Mr
84, p. 304.
"The Break Up." <u>NewL</u> (51:1) Aut 84, p. 52.
"The Lost Child." <u>Comm</u> (111:5) 9 Mr 84, p. 150.
"The Lost Child." <u>NegC</u> (4:4) Aut 84, p. 22-23.
"The Margin." <u>SouthernR</u> (20:1) Wint 84, p. 143.
"Once Again, Spring." <u>ChrC</u> (101:12) 11 Ap 84, p.
364.
"The Onset of Senility." <u>Poetry</u> (144:3) Je 84, p.
150-151.
"The Superannuated Couple." <u>Poetry</u> (144:3) Je 84,
p. 149-150.
"Unseasonable New Years." <u>MSS</u> (4:1/2) Aut 84, p.
147.

4047. PETROSKY, Anthony
"Streetlight: The Wedding Photograph." <u>OhioR</u> (33)
84, p. 137.

4048. PETTEE, Dan
"The Epigrammatist." <u>NegC</u> (4:3) Sum 84, p. 119.

4049. PEVEAR, Richard
"The Clouds" (tr. of Yves Bonnefoy). <u>ParisR</u>
(26:92) Sum 84, p. 132-144.

4050. PFEFFERLE, Susan
"Reflections on a Harvest." <u>Quarry</u> (33:4) Aut 84,
p. 21.

4051. PFINGSTON, Roger
"Bones." NewL (50:2/3) Wint-Spr 84, p. 31.
"Milk." ColEng (46:7) N 84, p. 665-666.
"November Night." PoetL (79:3) Aut 84, p. 175.

4052. PHIFER, Marjorie Maddox
"Somewhere in Yugoslavia." TarRP (23:2) Spr 84,
p. 15.

4053. PHILIP, Dawad
"Cries." Stepping (Premier Issue) Sum 82, p. 30-32.

4054. PHILIP, Marlene
"Black Fruit" (for Bruce). Dandel (11:1) Spr-Sum
84, p. 36-37.
"Habit of Angels." Dandel (11:1) Spr-Sum 84, p.
38-39.
"Salmon Courage." Dandel (11:1) Spr-Sum 84, p. 34-
35.

4055. PHILLIPOV, Vladimir
"The Window" (tr. of Boris Khristov). Iowa (14:2)
Spr-Sum 84, p. 224-225.

4056. PHILLIPPY, Patricia
"Queen Street." LitR (28:1) Aut 84, p. 118-119.
"The Strand." AntR (42:4) Aut 84, p. 455.

4057. PHILLIPS, Ben
"Apple Juice." WestCR (19:2) O 84, p. 22.
"Ice Dream Fishing on College Street." WestCR
(19:2) O 84, p. 20.
"Old Poets." WestCR (19:2) O 84, p. 21.

4058. PHILLIPS, David
"English Bay" (a draft). CapilR (32) 84, p. 84-88.
"For Diane Turning 36." CapilR (32) 84, p. 76.
"For the Birds" (season this with changes).
CapilR (32) 84, p. 80-81.
"The Last Strip Show." CapilR (32) 84, p. 82.
"The Muse." CapilR (32) 84, p. 68-75.
"The Outside." CapilR (32) 84, p. 79.
"Timing." CapilR (32) 84, p. 83.
"View from Barry McKinnon's Deck, Sechelt."
CapilR (32) 84, p. 77.
"Your Guess Is As Good As Mine." CapilR (32) 84,
p. 78.

4059. PHILLIPS, Frances
"Leading Up to Monday." HangL (45) Spr 84, p. 40-41.
"The Woman next Door." HangL (45) Spr 84, p. 42-45.

4060. PHILLIPS, James
"Orpheus" (tr. of Johannes Poethen). Sulfur (4:2,
issue 11) 84, p. 100-102.

4061. PHILLIPS, Louis
"The Bear of Sleep Growls All Night." Nimrod
(27:2) Spr-Sum 84, p. 63.
"I Ought Not to Be Writing Stories But Falling in

467 PIERCY

Love" (Chekhov). Nimrod (27:2) Spr-Sum 84, p. 63.

4062. PHILLIPS, Robert
"Adam Speaks." GrahamHR (7) Wint 84, p. 40.
"Chicory." Nat (239:10) 6 O 84, p. 322.
"Collaborations." OntR (20) Spr-Sum 84, p. 54-60.
"Here & There." Shen (35:1) 83-84, p. 92.
"In August." Shen (35:1) 83-84, p. 92-93.
"Three Artists" (I. Le Papillon: Emma-Marie Livry,
1842-1863. II. Chambered Nautilus: Robert T. S.
Lowell, 1917-1977. III. A Local Artist: Henry M.
Progar, 1927-1982). OntR (20) Spr-Sum 84, p. 61-
64.
"Wear" (for Philip Booth). Chelsea (42/43) 84, p.
438.

4063. PHILLIS, Yannis
"Nocturnal Song in Salvador." StoneC (11:3/4) Spr-
Sum 84, p. 42.

4064. PHOENIX, David D.
"Animus." SmPd (21:1) Wint 84, p. 23.
"Leaving Eden at Dawn." SmPd (21:1) Wint 84, p. 22.

4065. PICASSO, Pablo
"Journal Entry: Christmas 1939" (tr. by Roger
Shatuck). PoetryE (13/14) Spr-Sum 84, p. 81.
"Untitled Poem (The Caseta Text)" (tr. by Angel
Florès). PoetryE (13/14) Spr-Sum 84, p. 115-
117.

4066. PIERCE, Edith Lovejoy
"For Our Sake" (from the March 16, 1955 issue).
ChrC (101:22) 4-11 Jl 84, p. 674.
"Returning to Jerusalem" (Luke 2:45-47). ChrC
(101::1) 4-11 Ja 84, p. 7.

4067. PIERCE, Joy Rogers
"Vow to Pattern." Poem (50) Mr 84, p. 55.

4068. PIERCE, Karen
"History II: Paternal Heritage." PoeticJ (7) 84,
p. 39.
"Tomales Bay - December '83." PoeticJ (6) 84, p. 40.

4069. PIERCE, Neal
"July." Wind (14:52) 84, p. 39.
"Small Talk." PoeticJ (7) 84, p. 37.

4070. PIERCY, Marge
"How We Make Nice." NegC (4:2) Spr 84, p. 13.
"The Night the Moon Got Drunk." SouthernHR (18:3)
Sum 84, p. 216.
"The Place Where Everything Changed." NegC (4:2)
Spr 84, p. 14-15.
"Return of the Prodigal Darling." NegC (4:2) Spr
84, p. 11-12.
"The Sun and the Moon in the Morning Sky of
Charlotte" (for Julian Mason). SouthernPR
(24:2) Aut 84, p. 67-68.

"Tashlich." NegC (4:2) Spr 84, p. 9-10.
"This Prowling Zoo." Chelsea (42/43) 84, p. 144.
"The Track of the Master Builder." Spirit (7:1)
   84, p. 102.
"Your Cats Are Your Children." Stepping
   (Anniversary Issue I) 84, p. 40-41.

PIERO, W. S. di: See Di PIERO, W. S.

4071. PIETKIEWICZ, Karen
   "To My Father." Waves (12:4) Spr 84, p. 50.

4072. PIETRI, Pedro
   "Tata." Mairena (6:18) 84, p. 30.

4073. PIGNO, Antonia Quintana
   "La Recien Casada." KanQ (16:3) Sum 84, p. 90.

4074. PIGOTT, Yvonne
   "After a Long Countdown." AntigR (57) Spr 84, p. 87.

4075. PIJEWSKI, John
   "Happy." Tendril (17) Wint 84, p. 154.
   "On My Back." Tendril (17) Wint 84, p. 153.

4076. PIKE, Charles
   "Interlude." ConcPo (17:1) Spr 84, p. 26-28.

4077. PILCHER, Barry Edgar
   "Poem: The bird looks up at me." Bogg (52) 84, p.
   51.
   "Power cut." Bogg (52) 84, p. 37.

4078. PILINSZKY, Janos
   "Apocrypha" (tr. by Stephen Polgar). AmerPoR
   (13:6) N-D 84, p. 22.
   "Fish in a Net." AmerPoR (13:6) N-D 84, p. 20.

4079. PIMENTEL, Jorge
   "Balada para un Caballo" (fragmento). Mairena
   (6:18) 84, p. 94.

4080. PIÑA, Cristina
   "Song for T.S." (to Federico Peltzer, tr. by Anne
   Knupfer). Iowa (14:2) Spr-Sum 84, p. 160-161.

4081. PIÑERA, Virgilio
   "Uno de los Duques de Alba" (A Lezama). LindLM
   (3:2/4) Ap-D 84, p. 7.

4082. PINES, Paul
   "The Ladies' Pissoir" (tr. of Vasyl Khmeliuk).
   Pequod (16/17) 84, p. 182-183.
   "When Will My Auntie Come for Me" (tr. of Vasyl
   Khmeliuk). Pequod (16/17) 84, p. 184.

4083. PINSKER, Sanford
   "At the Pool." CEACritic (45:3/4) Mr-My 83, p. 27.
   "Poem, Nearly Anonymous." GeoR (38:1) Spr 84, p. 91.
   "Waiting for My IBM PCII." CEACritic (45:3/4) Mr-

My 83, p. 27.

4084. PINSKY, Robert
"The Changes" (from History of My Heart).
AmerPoR (13:1) Ja-F 84, p. 7.
"City without a Name" (tr. of Czeslaw Milosz, w.
the author and Robert Hass). Thrpny (16) Wint
84, p. 12-13.
"Daughter." Shen (35:2/3) 84, p. 261-263.
"Esse" (tr. of Czeslaw Milosz, w. the author).
NewRep (189:20) 14 N 83, p. 32.
"The Questions" (from History of My Heart).
AmerPoR (13:1) Ja-F 84, p. 7.
"Slow River" (tr. of Czeslaw Milosz, w. the author
and Robert Hass). NewRep (189:20) 14 N 83, p. 31.
"Song of Porcelain" (tr. of Czeslaw Milosz, w. the
author). NewRep (189:20) 14 N 83, p. 32.
"Song of Reasons." Antaeus (52) Apr 84, p. 35-36.
"Sonnet: Afternoon sun on her back." Thrpny (17)
Spr 84, p. 14.
"Waiting" HolCrit (21:5) D 84, p. 7-8.

4085. PIRKLE, Thomas
"Brambles, Rocks, Low-lying Trees." SouthernPR
(24:1) Spr 84, p. 52.

4086. PITA, Juana Rosa
"Oficio." Mairena (6:18) 84, p. 175.

4087. PITKIN, Anne
"Robin." Ploughs (10:1) 84, p. 130-132.

4088. PITKIN, Jo
"Grace." QW (19) Aut-Wint 84-85, p. 94.

4089. PITNER, Erin Clayton
"To a Child on Her Sixth Birthday" (For Erin
Abbott). CapeR (19:3) 20th Anniverary Issue
84, p. 40.

4090. PITZEN, Jim
"Harassing Fire." Pig (12) 84, p. 17.
"It's So Soon Over." Pig (12) 84, p. 36.

4091. PIZARNIK, Alejandra
"The Awakening" (tr. by Jim Fitzgerald and Frank
Graziano). CharR (10:1) Spr 84, p. 72-73.
"Poema: Tú eliges el lugar de la herida."
Mairena (6:18) 84, p. 113.
"Roads from the Mirror" (tr. by Jim Fitzgerald and
Frank Graziano). CharR (10:1) Spr 84, p. 69-71.
"Los Trabajos y las Noches." Mairena (6:18) 84,
p. 113.

4092. PLANTOS, Ted
"After the Fire." PoetryCR (5:3) Spr 84, p. 20.
"Edible Heart." PoetryCR (5:3) Spr 84, p. 20.
"Famished Light." PoetryCR (5:3) Spr 84, p. 20.
"Ontario Rains" (Bicentennial Contest Winners,
Poetry: Tie for Second). Waves (12:4) Spr 84,

p. 86.

4093. PLANZ, Allen
"Game." Chelsea (42/43) 84, p. 128-129.

4094. PLATH, James
"After the Swim-Meet, at MacDonalds." Northeast
(Series 3:18) 84, p. 9.

4095. PLATH, Sylvia
"The Beggars." Chelsea (42/43) 84, p. 54.
"The Eye-mote." Chelsea (42/43) 84, p. 55.

4096. PLAZA, Ramon
"Calle de Tierra." Mairena (6:18) 84, p. 117.

4097. PLOTKIN, Frederick
"Antique." CapeR (19:3) 20th Anniverary Issue 84,
p. 41.

4098. PLUMLY, Stanley
"After Whistler." Field (30) Spr 84, p. 95-96.

4099. PLUZHNYK, Evhen
"Equilibrium" (tr. by Gregory Orr). Pequod
(16/17) 84, p. 180-181.

PO, Li: See LI, Po

4100. POBO, Kenneth
"Iowa." Wind (14:50) 84, p. 18.
"Oklahoma." Wind (14:50) 84, p. 12.
"The Roomful of Brains." Veloc (4) Sum 84, p. 37.
"Sometimes at Night" (The Phillips Poetry Award--
Fall/Winter-1983/84). StoneC (11:3/4) Spr-Sum
84, p. 77.

4101. POELLOT, Ray (Raymond)
"American Central." SanFPJ (6:4) 84, p. 69.
"Barrel: Oily and Slick." SanFPJ (7:1) 84, p. 19.
"Guitarless." SanFPJ (7:1) 84, p. 17-18.
"Poverty's Space." SanFPJ (7:1) 84, p. 60.

4102. POETHEN, Johannes
"Orpheus" (tr. by James Phillips). Sulfur (4:2,
issue 11) 84, p. 100-102.

4103. POINTEK, H. L.
"Clockstroke" (tr. by E. Castendyk Briefs). Vis
(14) 84, p. 16.
"Consolation" (tr. by E. Castendyk Briefs). Vis
(14) 84, p. 16.
"Names" (tr. by E. Castendyk Briefs). Vis (14)
84, p. 16.

4104. POLAK, Maralyn Lois
"You Wouldn't Know." PaintedB (22) Spr 84, p. 24-25.

4105. POLAVARAPU, Malu
"For Grandmother." Writ (16) Aut 84, p. 34-35.

"The Other Woman." <u>Waves</u> (12:2/3) Wint 84, p. 57.
"White Walls." <u>Writ</u> (16) Aut 84, p. 36.

4106. POLGAR, Stephen
"Apocrypha" (tr. of Janos Pilinszky). <u>AmerPoR</u>
(13:6) N-D 84, p. 22.

4107. POLITO, Robert
"What the Dead Know." <u>NewYorker</u> (59:48) 16 Ja 84,
p. 44.

4108. POLLACK, Frederick
"The Abandoned Man" (Selections: 1, 3). <u>Hudson</u>
(37:3) Aut 84, p. 443-450.

4109. POLLAK, Felix
"Countdown" (tr. of Hans Magnus Enzensberger, w.
Reinhold Grimm). <u>NowestR</u> (22:1/2) 84, p. 71.
"A Course in Poetics" (tr. of Hans Magnus
Enzensberger, w. Reinhold Grimm). <u>TriQ</u> (61)
Aut 84, p. 100.
"Delete Whatever Inapplicable" (tr. of Hans Magnus
Enzensberger, w. Reinhold Grimm). <u>AmerPoR</u>
(13:5) S-O 84, p. 7.
"The Doctrine of Categories" (tr. of Hans Magnus
Enzensberger, w. Reinhold Grimm). <u>NowestR</u>
(22:1/2) 84, p. 65.
"Doomsday" (tr. of Hans Magnus Enzensberger, w.
Reinhold Grimm). <u>NowestR</u> (22:1/2) 84, p. 67.
"The Dresses" (tr. of Hans Magnus Enzensberger, w.
Reinhold Grimm). <u>AmerPoR</u> (13:5) S-O 84, p. 6.
"The Empty House" (tr. of Hans Magnus Enzensberger,
w. Reinhold Grimm). <u>NowestR</u> (22:1/2) 84, p. 69.
"For the Primer of Senior High" (tr. of Hans Magnus
Enzensberger, w. Reinhold Grimm). <u>AmerPoR</u>
(13:5) S-O 84, p. 7.
"Historical Process" (tr. of Hans Magnus
Enzensberger, w. Reinhold Grimm). <u>AmerPoR</u>
(13:5) S-O 84, p. 7.
"Hotel Room, Mexico City." <u>Abraxas</u> (31/32) 84, p.
53.
"The Junta Issues Guidelines on Torture." <u>NewL</u>
(51:1) Aut 84, p. 66-67.
"My Country, 'Tis of Thee." <u>NewL</u> (51:1) Aut 84,
p. 66.
"Obsession" (tr. of Hans Magnus Enzensberger, w.
Reinhold Grimm). <u>TriQ</u> (61) Aut 84, p. 102.
"Peace Conference" (tr. of Hans Magnus
Enzensberger, w. Reinhold Grimm). <u>NowestR</u>
(22:1/2) 84, p. 63.
"Rain Times Four." <u>Northeast</u> (Series 3:18) 84, p. 7.
"Regardless of" (tr. of Hans Magnus Enzensberger,
w. Reinhold Grimm). <u>AmerPoR</u> (13:5) S-O 84, p. 6.
"Residual Light" (tr. of Hans Magnus Enzensberger,
w. Reinhold Grimm). <u>TriQ</u> (61) Aut 84, p. 101.
"Shit" (tr. of Hans Magnus Enzensberger, w.
Reinhold Grimm). <u>AmerPoR</u> (13:5) S-O 84, p. 6.
"Vision." <u>Northeast</u> (Series 3:18) 84, p. 6.
"Visitation." <u>Abraxas</u> (31/32) 84, p. 52.
"Widow." <u>NewL</u> (50:2/3) Wint-Spr 84, p. 134-135.

"You'll Never Be Asked." <u>Abraxas</u> (31/32) 84, p. 53.

4110. POLLEY, M.
"Broken Down in Mud Guard Montana, 3 AM." <u>SnapD</u>
(6:2) Spr 83, p. 52.
"Hot on the Heels of Love" (found poem). <u>SnapD</u>
(6:2) Spr 83, p. 53.

4111. POLLITT, Katha
"Chinese Finches." <u>Shen</u> (35:2/3) 84, p. 264.

4112. POLSON, Don
"The Swamp." <u>PoetryCR</u> (5:4) Sum 84, p. 12.

4113. PONGE, Francis
"The Butterfly" (from <u>Le Parti Pris des choses</u>,
tr. by Lane Dunlop). <u>Chelsea</u> (42/43) 84, p. 191.
"The Mollusc" (from <u>Le Parti Pris des choses</u>, tr.
by Lane Dunlop). <u>Chelsea</u> (42/43) 84, p. 191.

4114. PONGER, Edward
"Self-Portrait" (for my father, Herman Ponger, 1910-
1982). <u>Confr</u> (27/28) 84, p. 243.

4115. PONSOT, Marie
"Take Time, Take Place." <u>13thM</u> (8:1/2) 84, p. 7-12.

PONT, Henri Le: <u>See</u> LePONT, Henri

4116. POPE, Dan
"Lost City." <u>AntigR</u> (58) Sum 84, p. 92.

4117. PORRAS, José A.
"Diaria Agonia." <u>Mairena</u> (6:17) Aut 84, p. 71.

4118. PORRITT, R.
"First Frost." <u>Nimrod</u> (27:2) Spr-Sum 84, p. 65.
"I Saw You Walking with Two Children Whose Hair Was
the New Color of Another Woman." <u>Nimrod</u> (27:2)
Spr-Sum 84, p. 64.

4119. PORTER, Anne
"Thérèse." <u>Comm</u> (111:14) 10 Ag 84, p. 443.

4120. PORTER, Bern
"My Life* on the Islands" (*The author has lived
among the Yapese, the Ulithians, the Guamanians
and the off-shore Laplanders). <u>CreamCR</u> (9:1/2)
84, p. 29.

4121. PORTER, Helen
"Sound Poets." <u>PottPort</u> (6) 84, p. 15.

PORTER, Patricia McKenzie: <u>See</u> McKENZIE-PORTER, Patricia

4122. POSNER, David
"A Man about to Dream" (for John Logan). <u>Chelsea</u>
(42/43) 84, p. 296-297.

4123. POST, Jonathan V.
      "The Neurophysiologist." _Veloc_ (2) Spr 83, p. 27.

4124. POTASH, L.
      "Commie, Cracker, Redneck, Radical." _SanFPJ_ (6:3)
         84, p. 84.
      "Minutes, an Arms Control Disarmament Agency
         Meeting." _SanFPJ_ (6:2) 84, p. 58-59.
      "People Got to Eat." _SanFPJ_ (6:2) 84, p. 76.
      "Return Engagement." _SanFPJ_ (6:3) 84, p. 82-83.

4125. POTTER, Carol
      "On Water." _NewL_ (51:2) Wint 84-85, p. 108-109.
      "The Trouble with Chickens." _NewL_ (51:2) Wint 84-
         85, p. 108.

4126. POTTER, Jacklyn
      "Waking Up during an Imaginary Snowstorm When Acid
         Rain Is Falling." _Stepping_ (Anniversary Issue
         I) 84, p. 42.

4127. POTTS, Richard
      "Ode to Jefferson." _SouthwR_ (69:3) Sum 84, p. 234.

4128. POULIN, A., Jr.
      "Husbands and Lovers" (For David Plante). _NewEngR_
         (7:2) Wint 84, p. 213-215.
      "Love" (tr. of Anne Hébert). _NewEngR_ (6:4) Sum
         84, p. 561.

4129. POUND, Ezra
      "The Coming of War: Actaeon." _SouthernR_ (20:2)
         Spr 84, p. 280-281.
      "Notes for an Unpublished Canto" (1935). _Shen_
         (35:2/3) 84, p. 275-276.
      "A Selection of Computer Permutations of Ezra
         Pound's 'In a Station of the Metro'" (by James
         Laughlin and Hugh Kenner). _ParisR_ (26:94) Wint
         84, p. 196-198.

4130. POUND, Omar S.
      "The Dying Expatriate." _AntigR_ (56) Wint 84, p. 12.
      "Images from Bhartrihari" (Sanscrit anthologist,
         ca. 650 a.d.). _AntigR_ (56) Wint 84, p. 13.
      "Moon-Catch in Snowlight." _AntigR_ (56) Wint 84,
         p. 11.
      "Saint Erkenwald." _AntigR_ (57) Spr 84, p. 99-111.
      "Saint Erkenwald." _Origin_ (Series 5:2) Wint 83,
         p. 45-54.
      "Siege" (Lucknow: 1857). _MissouriR_ (7:3) 84, p.
         18-22.
      "Siege" (Lucknow: 1857). _Origin_ (Series 5:1) Aut
         83, p. 73-77.

4131. POUPARD, B. A.
      "Darkness returns." _PoeticJ_ (3) 83, p. 44.

4132. POWELL, Craig
      "Prelude." _Quarry_ (33:1) Wint 84, p. 80-81.

4133. POWELL, Jim
        "Cleopatra" (Horace, Odes I.37). ChiR (34:2) Spr
            84, p. 9-10.
        "Heat." ParisR (26:94) Wint 84, p. 92-93.
        "Heights" (A Letter, for Paul Lake). ChiR (34:2)
            Spr 84, p. 4-8.
        "A Letter." ParisR (26:94) Wint 84, p. 94-97.
        "Snow Drifts" (from Odes 1.9, tr. of Horace).
            ParisR (26:94) Wint 84, p. 98-99.

4134. POWELL, Joseph
        "Canetops." PoeticJ (3) 83, p. 4.
        "Red Tides." CrabCR (2:1) Sum 84, p. 4-5.

4135. POWELL, Katherine Anne
        "Jonah" (tr. of Günter Eich). Field (30) Spr
            84, p. 47.
        "Keys" (tr. of Günter Eich). Field (30) Spr 84,
            p. 48.

4136. POWER, Marjorie
        "Floor Poem Number Three." CapeR (19:2) Sum 84,
            p. 6.
        "On Her Spindle." StoneC (12:1/2) Aut-Wint 84, p. 26.

4137. POWERS, Arthur
        "Angry Women." KanQ (16:1/2) Wint-Spr 84, p. 163.

4138. POWERS, Jack (See also OUTAVIT, R. U.)
        "A Dandelion Baby." Sam (38:2, release 150) 84,
            p. 10.
        "Drifting." Sam (38:2, release 150) 84, p. 1-12.
        "Fountainhead." Sam (37:3, 147th release) 83, p. 41.
        "Her Diaphragm." Sam (38:2, release 150) 84, p. 9.
        "Hobo, from Boston, West." Sam (38:2, release
            150) 84, p. 3.
        "In the Time of Caesar Augustus." Sam (38:2,
            release 150) 84, p. 12.
        "A Lament." Sam (38:2, release 150) 84, p. 2.
        "Our Father." Sam (38:2, release 150) 84, p. 11.
        "Perhaps, at a time like this." Sam (38:2,
            release 150) 84, p. 6-7.
        "Playing Ted Williams" (for Gene Stephens). Sam
            (38:2, release 150) 84, p. 4-5.
        "Talking to Herself Again." Sam (38:2, release
            150) 84, p. 8.

4139. POWERS, P. J.
        "Earth Fragrance" (tr. of Halldis M. Vesaas, w.
            Ronald Wakefield, George Schoolfield, and the
            author). LitR (27:3) Spr 84, p. 305.

4140. POWERS, Richard S.
        "Cook's Tour." PoetL (79:3) Aut 84, p. 141.

4141. POWERS, William
        "Perhaps Imagined." KanQ (16:1/2) Wint-Spr 84, p.
            159.

POY, Phillip de: See DePOY, Phillip

4142. POYNER, Ken
"The Belief in Progress." HiramPoR (36) Spr-Sum 84,
p. 36.
"The Challenge." HiramPoR (36) Spr-Sum 84, p. 34-35.
"The Chauvinist." PoetL (79:3) Aut 84, p. 154-155.
"The Covenant." PoetL (79:3) Aut 84, p. 153-154.
"Currituck, N.C." IndR (7:2) Spr 84, p. 44-45.
"Father and Son." CapeR (19:2) Sum 84, p. 20.
"The Happiness." WestB (14) 84, p. 56-57.
"The Interface." WestB (15) 84, p. 99.
"The Last Afternoon." Iowa (14:3) Aut 84, p. 67.
"Living in the Tropics." KanQ (16:1/2) Wint-Spr
84, p. 97.
"McClellan Shoots His Dogs." Iowa (14:3) Aut 84,
p. 66.
"The Milking Cow." Wind (14:51) 84, p. 42.
"Place." WestB (15) 84, p. 98-99.
"Self-Taught." WestB (14) 84, p. 55-56.
"The State." Iowa (14:3) Aut 84, p. 68-69.

4143. POYNTER, Jean
"Rodeo Man." PoeticJ (8) 84, p. 2.
"Trout Man." PoeticJ (7) 84, p. 8.

4144. PRADO, Adélia
"The Alphabet in the Park" (tr. by Ellen Watson).
AmerPoR (13:1) Ja-F 84, p. 24.
"The Black Umbrella" (tr. by Ellen Watson). Field
(30) Spr 84, p. 52.
"Blossoms" (tr. by Ellen Watson). AmerPoR (13:1)
Ja-F 84, p. 25.
"Day" (tr. by Ellen Watson). AmerPoR (13:1) Ja-F
84, p. 25.
"Dysrhythmia" (tr. by Ellen Watson). AmerPoR
(13:1) Ja-F 84, p. 24.
"In the Middle of the Night" (tr. by Ellen Watson).
AmerPoR (13:1) Ja-F 84, p. 25.
"Legend with the Word Map" (tr. by Ellen Watson).
AmerPoR (13:1) Ja-F 84, p. 25.
"Lesson" (tr. by Ellen Watson). AmerPoR (13:1) Ja-
F 84, p. 26.
"Lineage" (tr. by Ellen Watson). Field (30) Spr
84, p. 53.
"Not Even One Line in December" (tr. by Ellen
Watson). AmerPoR (13:1) Ja-F 84, p. 24.
"Pieces for a Stained-Glass Window" (tr. by Ellen
Watson). AmerPoR (13:1) Ja-F 84, p. 25.
"Some Other Names for Poetry" (tr. by Ellen
Watson). AmerPoR (13:1) Ja-F 84, p. 26.
"Subject-ive" (tr. by Ellen Watson). AmerPoR
(13:1) Ja-F 84, p. 26.
"Tyrants" (tr. by Ellen Watson). AmerPoR (13:1)
Ja-F 84, p. 26.
"With Poetic License" (tr. by Ellen Watson).
AmerPoR (13:1) Ja-F 84, p. 24.
"Young Girl in Bed" (tr. by Ellen Watson). Field
(30) Spr 84, p. 54-55.

4145. PRANGE, Marnie
"Key West, 1953" (for my mother). PoetryNW (25:1)
Spr 84, p. 17-18.

"No One Was Out: A Letter." <u>PoetryNW</u> (25:1) Spr
        84, p. 19-20.

4146. PRATT, C. W.
        "The Drunken Boat" (tr. of Arthur Rimbaud). <u>LitR</u>
            (27:3) Spr 84, p. 306-308.
        "The Sober Boat" (for Patrick Jones). <u>LitR</u> (27:3)
            Spr 84, p. 309.
        "The Supermarket" (after Andrew Marvell, "The
            Garden"). p. 180.
        "The Telephone." <u>LitR</u> (27:2) Wint 84, p. 181.

4147. PRATT, Charles
        "Father and Son." <u>KanQ</u> (16:1/2) Wint-Spr 84, p. 123.

4148. PREIL, Gabriel
        "Opening to the Light" (tr. by Robert Friend).
            <u>Pequod</u> (16/17) 84, p. 118.

4149. PRESTON, D. S.
        "Settings." <u>HolCrit</u> (21:2, i.e. 21:3) Je 84, p. 18.

4150. PRESTON, Hank
        "I Send My Words Like Falcons." <u>PoeticJ</u> (5) 84,
            p. 18.
        "Maybe -- Just Maybe." <u>SanFPJ</u> (6:1) 84, p. 30.
        "Priorities." <u>SanFPJ</u> (6:1) 84, p. 31.
        "Song for the Cottonwood Tree." <u>PoeticJ</u> (6) 84,
            p. 39.
        "Songs Heard in the Market-Place." <u>SanFPJ</u> (6:1)
            84, p. 92.
        "To a Creature Out of Place." <u>PoeticJ</u> (8) 84, p. 33.
        "Unwelcome Fact #7." <u>SanFPJ</u> (6:1) 84, p. 30.
        "War, Peace, and Then What?" <u>SanFPJ</u> (6:1) 84, p. 91.

4151. PRESTON, Scott
        "River as a Picasso, 1903." <u>SnapD</u> (7:2) Spr 84,
            p. 12.

4152. PREVERT, Jacques
        "Breakfast" (tr. by Edward Fettman). <u>GreenfR</u>
            (11:1/2) Sum-Aut 83, p. 90.
        "The Dunce" (tr. by Chael Graham). <u>Spirit</u> (7:1)
            84, p. 105.
        "The Dunce" (tr. by Edward Fettman). <u>GreenfR</u>
            (11:1/2) Sum-Aut 83, p. 90-91.
        "Home Life" (tr. by Edward Fettman). <u>GreenfR</u>
            (11:1/2) Sum-Aut 83, p. 91.
        "Quartier Libre." <u>Quarry</u> (33:1) Wint 84, p. 47.
        "Quartier Libre" (English tr. by Colin Morton).
            <u>Quarry</u> (33:1) Wint 84, p. 47.

4153. PRICE, Alice L.
        "The Anthropologists at Bandelier." <u>GreenfR</u>
            (11:3/4) Wint-Spr 84, p. 135.
        "Massacre at Marais des Cygnes." <u>LittleBR</u> (4:4)
            Sum 84, p. 38.

4154. PRICE, Caroline
        "Child and Gypsies." <u>Argo</u> (6:1) 84, p. 3.

4155. PRICE, Gale
      "Kiera's Mother." <u>SanFPJ</u> (6:4) 84, p. 83.
      "Policy on Central America (Among Other Places)."
          <u>SanFPJ</u> (6:4) 84, p. 82.
      "Resignation." <u>SanFPJ</u> (6:4) 84, p. 84.

4156. PRICE, Reynolds
      "A Heaven for Elizabeth Rodwell, My Mother."
          <u>Poetry</u> (144:3) Je 84, p. 144-148.
      "House Snake." <u>TriQ</u> (61) Aut 84, p. 15-26.
      "Porta Nigra" (after Stefan George). <u>OntR</u> (20)
          Spr-Sum 84, p. 89.
      "Rincon: The Strangers." <u>NewYorker</u> (60:45) 24 D
          84, p. 34.

4157. PRICE, V. B.
      "Duranes Lateral." <u>SoDakR</u> (22:1) Spr 84, p. 42-43.

4158. PRICE-GRESTY, David Ian
      "The Inlet." <u>Vis</u> (16) 84, p. 8.
      "West Wales Winter Night." <u>Amelia</u> [1:1] Ap 84, p.
          5-6.

4159. PRIDA, Dolores
      "January Blues." <u>Areíto</u> (9:36) 84, p. 103.

4160. PRIEST, Robert
      "Bubbles and Pins." <u>Descant</u> (47, 15:4) Wint 84,
          p. 102.
      "Darth Orange." <u>Descant</u> (47, 15:4) Wint 84, p.
          106-107.
      "Elastic People." <u>Descant</u> (47, 15:4) Wint 84, p.
          110.
      "Instructions for Prayer." <u>CrossC</u> (6:1) 84, p. 10.
      "Meatball Maniacs." <u>Descant</u> (47, 15:4) Wint 84,
          p. 109.
      "Once upon a Pea." <u>Descant</u> (47, 15:4) Wint 84, p.
          111.
      "Private Laughter." <u>Descant</u> (47, 15:4) Wint 84,
          p. 104.
      "Prophecy." <u>PoetryCR</u> (5:4) Sum 84, p. 15.
      "Puzzle Kids." <u>Descant</u> (47, 15:4) Wint 84, p. 108.
      "The Secret Invasion of Bananas." <u>Descant</u> (47,
          15:4) Wint 84, p. 105.
      "Treatment of a New Faith." <u>CrossC</u> (6:1) 84, p. 10.
      "A Very Strange Creature." <u>Descant</u> (47, 15:4)
          Wint 84, p. 103.

4161. PRILL, David
      "The Floating Man." <u>Veloc</u> (3) Aut-Wint 83, p. 47.

4162. PRINS, Johanna H.
      "Eros has my uprooted wits" (Sappho 47)" (tr. of
          Sappho). <u>AmerPoR</u> (13:2) Mr-Ap 84, p. 37.
      "Eros makes me feel weak in the knees" (Sappho
          130)" (tr. of Sappho). <u>AmerPoR</u> (13:2) Mr-Ap
          84, p. 37.
      "Like a hyacinth in the mountains" (Sappho 105c)"
          (tr. of Sappho). <u>AmerPoR</u> (13:2) Mr-Ap 84, p. 37.
      "Some say an army of men on horse" (Sappho 16)"

(tr. of Sappho). <u>AmerPoR</u> (13:2) Mr-Ap 84, p. 37.

4163. PRIOR, Tim
"Meditation in a Time of Death." <u>AntiqR</u> (59) Aut
84, p. 99.
"Nerves." <u>AntiqR</u> (59) Aut 84, p. 98.
"Prayer to the Voice of His Lover." <u>AntiqR</u> (59)
Aut 84, p. 98.

4164. PROCSAL, Gloria H.
"Commuter." <u>PoeticJ</u> (2) 83, p. 26.
"Girl in a Yellow Hat" (1885). <u>PoeticJ</u> (1) 83, p.
14.
"Intensive Care Unit." <u>PoeticJ</u> (3) 83, p. 31.
"Night-Eyes of the Mountain." <u>PoeticJ</u> (2) 83, p. 4.

4165. PROCTOR, Clint
"Final Defensive Fire." <u>Vis</u> (14) 84, p. 18.

4166. PROCTOR, Margaret
"Paper." <u>Bogg</u> (52) 84, p. 41.

4167. PROKES, Gary M.
"Conversations over Gin." <u>BlueBldgs</u> (8) 84?, p. 9-
11.

4168. PROPER, Stan
"The Greatest Army." <u>SanFPJ</u> (6:4) 84, p. 45.
"Spring Morning." <u>SanFPJ</u> (6:4) 84, p. 48.

4169. PROPERTIUS
"III.8 Our candlelit brawl last night was lovely"
(tr. by Michael West). <u>NewEngR</u> (6:3) Spr 84,
p. 452-453.

4170. PROPP, Karen
"Girls on a Bridge." <u>CarolQ</u> (36:3) Spr 84, p. 32.
"In Brooklyn." <u>Agni</u> (20) 84, p. 97-98.
"The Men in Paris." <u>Agni</u> (20) 84, p. 95-96.
"Poem: When our blood had sung." <u>Agni</u> (20) 84, p.
94.

4171. PROSPERE, Susan
"The Company We Keep." <u>NewYorker</u> (60:43) 10 D 84,
p. 58.
"Stargazing" (Prizewinning Poets--1984). <u>Nat</u>
(238:18) 12 My 84, p. 581.
"Sub Rosa." <u>Antaeus</u> (52) Apr 84, p. 33-34.

4172. PROTHRO, Nancy
"Morning Glory." <u>CimR</u> (68) Jl 84, p. 63.

4173. PROVENCHER, Richard
"A Winter Scene." <u>WritersL</u> (2) 84, p. 12.

4174. PROVONCHEE, Catherine A.
"After the Stillbirth." <u>YetASM</u> (3) 84, p. 2.

4175. PROVOST, Sara
"The Angel in Front of the Fountain." <u>HolCrit</u>

(21:1) F 84, p. 20.

4176. PROVOST, Sarah
"The Lonely Man Plans a Picnic." Poetry (145:1) O
84, p. 12-13.
"Mercurochrome." Poetry (145:1) O 84, p. 10-11.
"Pastoral." Poetry (145:1) O 84, p. 11-12.

4177. PRUNTY, Wyatt
"Baseball" (For Howard Nemerov). SouthernR (20:4)
Aut 84, p. 886.
"Black Water." NewYorker (60:29) 3 S 84, p. 80.
"Geography." SouthernR (20:4) Aut 84, p. 887-889.
"The Vireo." NewEngR (6:3) Spr 84, p. 451.

4178. PUEBLA, Manuel de la
"Carta a los Jovenes Poetas Puertorriqueños."
Mairena (6:17) Aut 84, p. 53-60.
"Itinerario." Mairena (5:13) Spr 83, p. 73.
"Mujer con Llave." Mairena (5:14) Aut 83, p. 77.

4179. PUFF, Mary A. M.
"The Only Way to Leave." Paunch (57/58) Ja 84, p.
88.

4180. PULLEN, Emma E.
"Avenue of the Americas." SanFPJ (6:4) 84, p. 92.
"Black Aggression." SanFPJ (6:3) 84, p. 83.
"February 15, 1978, or the Night Ali Lost."
SanFPJ (6:4) 84, p. 40.
"The Griot" (For John Oliver Killens). SanFPJ
(6:4) 84, p. 40.
"Harlem Sunday Stroll." SanFPJ (6:4) 84, p. 10.
"Next Week's Paycheck Blues." SanFPJ (6:4) 84, p.
11.
"Next Week's Paycheck Blues." SanFPJ (6:4) 84, p.
88.
"Rock Gone Reggae." Stepping (Anniversary Issue
I) 84, p. 44.
"Unc Allen." SanFPJ (6:4) 84, p. 37.

4181. PULTZ, Constance
"Breaking Away." TarRP (23:2) Spr 84, p. 13.
"For a Child Born Deaf." NegC (4:2) Spr 84, p. 63.
"Frog." StoneC (11:3/4) Spr-Sum 84, p. 29.

4182. PURCELL, Sally
"Twice I Have Crossed Acheron." SenR (14:1) 84,
p. 57.

4183. PURDY, Al
"Bestiary." CanLit (100) Spr 84, p. 250-251.
"Friends." PoetryCR (6:2) Wint 84-85, p. 21.
"In the Beginning Was the Word." Waves (13:1) Aut
84, p. 54-55.
"Man Without a Country." Waves (13:1) Aut 84, p.
56-57.
"Time Past / Time Now." Waves (13:1) Aut 84, p. 58.
"Vancouver." CanLit (102) Aut 84, p. 54-55.

4184. PURENS, Ilmars
"Clues to a Riddle of the Place" (for Edvins
Strautmanis). BlueBldgs (8) 84?, p. 1.

4185. PYBUS, Rodney
"Paternities (1942-74)" (from Annals). Stand
(25:4) Aut 84, p. 53.

QING, Ai: See AI, Qing

4186. QUAGLIANO, Tony
"Papeete Poem." NewL (51:1) Aut 84, p. 88-89.

4187. QUANDT, J.
"The Scenic Route." PoetryCR (6:1) Aut 84, p. 27.

4188. QUANDT, James
"In the White City." AntigR (58) Sum 84, p. 7.
"The Scarecrow." Waves (12:4) Spr 84, p. 48-49.
"A Vacation by the Sea." AntigR (58) Sum 84, p. 8.

4189. QUATRONE, Rich
"Maintenance." EngJ (73:8) D 84, p. 68.
"School I." EngJ (73:5) S 84, p. 64.
"School II." EngJ (73:5) S 84, p. 64.

4190. QUEEN, Don J.
"California's Most Perfect Organic Pear." NegC
(4:2) Spr 84, p. 22.
"Enduring Friend and Lover, Do Not Die Before I
Exit into Eternity" (for Ms. Longbird). NegC
(4:2) Spr 84, p. 23.

4191. QUEMADA, David V.
"To Frank." NewL (50:2/3) Wint-Spr 84, p. 239.

4192. QUENEAU, Raymond
"Ah the Lovely Holidays" (tr. by Elton Glaser).
CharR (10:2) Aut 84, p. 93.
"Prophecy for Yesterday" (tr. by Elton Glaser).
CharR (10:2) Aut 84, p. 93-94.

4193. QUERENGESSER, Neil
"Arithmetic." Dandel (11:2) Aut-Wint 84-85, p. 75.
"Flight 107 Arriving from Montreal and Points
East." Dandel (11:2) Aut-Wint 84-85, p. 74.

4194. QUINN, Bernetta, Sister
"Night in Norfolk." NewL (50:4) Sum 84, p. 47.
"Poet on a Terrace" (for R.P.W.) KanQ (16:3) Sum
84, p. 28.
"Theatre of Dionysius, Athens." NewL (50:4) Sum
84, p. 47.

4195. QUINN, John
"The Camas Meadow War" (for J. R.). Hudson (37:2)
Sum 84, p. 239-243.

4196. QUINN, John Robert
"Hedgerows." SpoonRQ (9:4) Aut 84, p. 46.

"The Orchard." <u>ChrC</u> (101:15) 2 My 84, p. 454.

4197. QUINN, Nancy
"When They Say She's Detached." <u>SoDakR</u> (22:4)
Wint 84, p. 72.
"Winter in New York, 1976." <u>SoDakR</u> (22:4) Wint
84, p. 73.

4198. QUIÑONES, Fernando
"Industrial Venus" (tr. by Reginald Gibbons).
<u>TriQ</u> (59) Wint 84, p. 217-218.

4199. QUIÑONES, Magaly
"Clave del Juego." <u>Mairena</u> (6:16) Spr 84, p. 16.
"Cuando Desampare Mi Paloma." <u>Mairena</u> (6:16) Spr
84, p. 18.
"Edades." <u>Mairena</u> (6:16) Spr 84, p. 18.
"Lo Imposible." <u>Mairena</u> (5:14) Aut 83, p. 13.
"Insomnio." <u>Mairena</u> (5:14) Aut 83, p. 13.
"Lo Que el Poeta Aprende." <u>Mairena</u> (5:14) Aut 83,
p. 15-16.
"Memoria del Mar." <u>Mairena</u> (6:16) Spr 84, p. 16-17.
"Un Miedo Extraño." <u>Mairena</u> (5:13) Spr 83, p.
103-104.
"La Palabra." <u>Mairena</u> (5:14) Aut 83, p. 13.
"Para Nombrar las Cosas" (Selections). <u>Mairena</u>
(5:14) Aut 83, p. 13-16.
"Un Sastre." <u>Mairena</u> (5:14) Aut 83, p. 14.
"Tu Sufrimiento." <u>Mairena</u> (6:16) Spr 84, p. 17.

QUIÑONEZ, Marta Magaly: <u>See</u> QUIÑONEZ, Magaly

QUINTANA PIGNO, Antonia: <u>See</u> PIGNO, Antonia Quintana

4200. R. C. (<u>See</u> <u>also</u> CLOKE, Richard)
"1.9 trillion $ for proposed military build up."
<u>SanFPJ</u> (6:2) 84, p. 56.
"$1,800,000,000,000." <u>SanFPJ</u> (6:1) 84, p. 37.
"About 25 million years ago." <u>SanFPJ</u> (6:3) 84, p.
87.
"All this massive escalation." <u>SanFPJ</u> (6:3) 84,
p. 37.
"The Big H." <u>SanFPJ</u> (6:1) 84, p. 72.
"Big turnaround in the economy." <u>SanFPJ</u> (6:2) 84,
p. 64.
"The bland smiler." <u>SanFPJ</u> (6:4) 84, p. 87.
"Can't stop the nuclear arms race now." <u>SanFPJ</u>
(6:3) 84, p. 63.
"CIA psych warfare manual." <u>SanFPJ</u> (7:1) 84, p. 22.
"The deficit's a time bomb." <u>SanFPJ</u> (7:1) 84, p. 57.
"Establishment poet sits in his cubicle." <u>SanFPJ</u>
(6:4) 84, p. 12.
"Every second somewhere." <u>SanFPJ</u> (6:1) 84, p. 12.
"Export of Revolution." <u>SanFPJ</u> (6:2) 84, p. 76.
"FBI and CIA paramilitary." <u>SanFPJ</u> (6:3) 84, p. 14.
"Freedom in US." <u>SanFPJ</u> (6:2) 84, p. 32.
"God is in favor of." <u>SanFPJ</u> (6:1) 84, p. 47.
"Hey what's going on?" <u>SanFPJ</u> (6:2) 84, p. 87.
"A hot dog is not a hot dog anymore." <u>SanFPJ</u>

(6:1) 84, p. 18.
"How best can one." SanFPJ (6:3) 84, p. 75.
"Human error." SanFPJ (6:1) 84, p. 17.
"I tell you now that." SanFPJ (6:1) 84, p. 37.
"If 16 inch artillery." SanFPJ (6:3) 84, p. 46.
"If it be murder." SanFPJ (6:2) 84, p. 25.
"If we're nuked by the Soviets." SanFPJ (6:1) 84,
    p. 63.
"If you've got 2 mil." SanFPJ (6:4) 84, p. 37.
"I'm in favor of." SanFPJ (6:2) 84, p. 18.
"Inflation's down." SanFPJ (6:1) 84, p. 23.
"Inter. Monetary Fund." SanFPJ (6:3) 84, p. 40.
"An international incident." SanFPJ (6:1) 84, p. 39.
"Jody Powell and Brzezinski." SanFPJ (6:1) 84, p.
    69.
"The KAL airliner." SanFPJ (6:1) 84, p. 19.
"Limited nuclear war." SanFPJ (6:4) 84, p. 7.
"London news item." SanFPJ (6:2) 84, p. 88.
"Messages sent." SanFPJ (6:3) 84, p. 84.
"A moderate." SanFPJ (7:1) 84, p. 18.
"News accounts echo." SanFPJ (6:1) 84, p. 50.
"Nothing can go faster." SanFPJ (7:1) 84, p. 79.
"Now I've had it." SanFPJ (6:1) 84, p. 8.
"Nuclear bombs." SanFPJ (6:2) 84, p. 53.
"The nuclear game." SanFPJ (6:3) 84, p. 59.
"Nuclear war causes cloud covers." SanFPJ (6:2)
    84, p. 95.
"Nuclear war causes earthquakes." SanFPJ (6:2)
    84, p. 95.
"Nuclear war destroys ozone." SanFPJ (6:2) 84, p.
    95.
"Nuclear war has very few advocates." SanFPJ
    (6:2) 84, p. 51.
"Nuclear war is a mess." SanFPJ (6:2) 84, p. 95.
"Nuclear war is like a two way gun." SanFPJ (6:3)
    84, p. 11.
"Nuclear war kills all plants." SanFPJ (6:2) 84,
    p. 95.
"Nuclear war sprays radiation all over." SanFPJ
    (6:2) 84, p. 95.
"Nuclear warfare." SanFPJ (6:2) 84, p. 39.
"Odd how we make distinctions." SanFPJ (6:2) 84,
    p. 30.
"One Trident sub launched." SanFPJ (7:1) 84, p. 9.
"One Trident submarine." SanFPJ (7:1) 84, p. 44.
"Panel of scientists." SanFPJ (6:1) 84, p. 28.
"The question arises." SanFPJ (6:2) 84, p. 43.
"Right to life." SanFPJ (6:2) 84, p. 85.
"Sending signals and messages with troops."
    SanFPJ (6:2) 84, p. 95.
"Set of three rings." SanFPJ (6:1) 84, p. 60.
"Some day there will be." SanFPJ (6:3) 84, p. 52.
"Soviet offers to reduce missiles." SanFPJ (6:1)
    84, p. 11.
"Soviets will increase defense outlays 2%."
    SanFPJ (6:3) 84, p. 32.
"Suppose an H-bomb." SanFPJ (6:2) 84, p. 94.
"Talk about the Dark Ages." SanFPJ (6:2) 84, p. 27.
"Thousands of marines." SanFPJ (6:2) 84, p. 65.
"Too expensive to get sick any more." SanFPJ

(6:1) 84, p. 9.
"A trillion and a half dollars federal debt."
SanFPJ (6:3) 84, p. 67.
"Turn the atomic clock." SanFPJ (6:2) 84, p. 11.
"The ultimate irony." SanFPJ (6:2) 84, p. 21.
"U.N. stats." SanFPJ (6:3) 84, p. 57.
"U.S. government official." SanFPJ (6:2) 84, p. 28.
"Unemployment drops." SanFPJ (6:1) 84, p. 56.
"US says Soviets." SanFPJ (6:2) 84, p. 71.
"US senator says." SanFPJ (6:2) 84, p. 84.
"US takes a holier than thou stance on everything."
SanFPJ (6:2) 84, p. 91.
"US visa questionnaires." SanFPJ (6:2) 84, p. 79.
"Use of 10% of arsenals." SanFPJ (6:3) 84, p. 56.
"We abound in dichotomies." SanFPJ (6:2) 84, p. 85.
"What goes on?" SanFPJ (6:4) 84, p. 73.
"What if a nuclear war does happen." SanFPJ (6:2)
84, p. 85.
"What of the rights." SanFPJ (6:2) 84, p. 23.
"When hunting a bear." SanFPJ (6:2) 84, p. 55.
"Whenever there's an international incident."
SanFPJ (6:2) 84, p. 75.
"Why don't those opposed." SanFPJ (6:2) 84, p. 19.
"World horrified over 260." SanFPJ (6:1) 84, p. 46.
"The world stumbles." SanFPJ (6:1) 84, p. 43.
"You see there are terrorists." SanFPJ (6:1) 84,
p. 7.

4201. R. J. S.
"Ground Zero." Sam (41:1, release 161) 84, p. 4.
"Of All the Things." Sam (41:2, release 162) 84
or 85, p. 16.

4202. RABINOWITZ, Sima
"Poems" (tr. of Christina Peri Rossi). Vis (15)
84, p. 30.
"The Unwanted Angel" (tr. of Jose Watanabe). Vis
(15) 84, p. 28.

4203. RABORG, Frederick A., Jr.
"Above Mirage." LittleBR (4:4) Sum 84, p. 95.
"Fresh-Cut Timber." LittleBR (4:3) Spr 84, p. 14.
"Fridays, When I Was Young." PoeticJ (8) 84, p. 10.
"New Wave Look." SanFPJ (6:1) 84, p. 32.
"Night Walking." CapeR (19:2) Sum 84, p. 17.
"On Knocking Down a Friend behind Town Hall."
PoeticJ (8) 84, p. 36.

4204. RACHEL, Naomi
"Cul-de-Sac." ThirdW (2) Spr 84, p. 39-40.

4205. RADDYSH, Garry
"The Child." Grain (12:2) My 84, p. 45.
"Stunned by Rhetoric, the Answer Folded Neatly in
the Words." Grain (12:2) My 84, p. 46.

4206. RADHUBER, Stanley
"The Swans on Lac Leman." LitR (28:1) Aut 84, p. 46.

4207. RADIN, Doris
     "Anne and the Saloon." <u>Confr</u> (27/28) 84, p. 322.
     "The Collector." <u>BlueBldgs</u> (7) 84, p. 23.
     "Every Day." <u>KanQ</u> (16:4) Aut 84, p. 95.
     "Hiding" (Prose sections from The Kabuki Theatre by
         Earle Ernst, Hiding by Dorothy Aldis).
         <u>BlueBldgs</u> (7) 84, p. 16.
     "Presence in Tarastcha." <u>CarolQ</u> (37:1) Aut 84, p.
         29-30.

4208. RADNER, Rebecca
     "Dream the Geese Come." <u>CalQ</u> (23/24) Spr-Sum 84,
         p. 129.

4209. RADNOTI, Miklós
     "Peace, Horror" (tr. by Jascha Kessler). <u>Confr</u>
         (27/28) 84, p. 58.
     "Seventh Eclogue" (tr. by Steven Kovács). <u>LitR</u>
         (27:3) Spr 84, p. 302-303.

4210. RADU, Kenneth
     "Aschenputtel's Sisters." <u>PoetryCR</u> (5:4) Sum 84,
         p. 11.
     "Criticism." <u>Quarry</u> (33:3) Sum 84, p. 51-52.
     "Daffodils in Snow." <u>Quarry</u> (33:3) Sum 84, p. 51.
     "Icarus." <u>CrossC</u> (6:1) 84, p. 15.
     "Pornography." <u>PoetryCR</u> (5:4) Sum 84, p. 11.

4211. RAEBURN, Nancy
     "Incident at the Zoo in October." <u>BelPoJ</u> (34:4)
         Sum 84, p. 20-21.

4212. RAFFA, Joseph
     "The Last Nayaug." <u>HiramPoR</u> (37) Aut-Wint 84, p. 35.

4213. RAFFEL, Burton
     "In Spring: Looking into the Distance, on the Wall"
         (tr. of Du Fu, w. Zuxin Ding). <u>LitR</u> (27:3) Spr
         84, p. 296.
     "Moonlit Night" (tr. of Du Fu, w. Zuxin Ding).
         <u>LitR</u> (27:3) Spr 84, p. 297.
     "Spring Rain" (tr. of Du Fu, w. Zuxin Ding). <u>LitR</u>
         (27:3) Spr 84, p. 297.
     "Tien-mu Mountain, Ascended in a Dream: a Farewell
         Song" (tr. of Li Bai, w. Zuxin Ding). <u>LitR</u>
         (27:3) Spr 84, p. 295-296.

4214. RAGAN, James
     "The River in the Tree." <u>IndR</u> (7:3) Sum 84, p. 61.

4215. RAINE, Craig
     "Again." <u>GrandS</u> (3:3) Spr 84, p. 54-57.
     "The Gift." <u>AntR</u> (42:2) Spr 84, p. 214-215.
     "A Hungry Fighter." <u>SewanR</u> (92:1) Ja-Mr 84, p. 69-
         71.
     "In Modern Dress." <u>AntR</u> (42:2) Spr 84, p. 206-208.
     "Inca." <u>AntR</u> (42:2) Spr 84, p. 209-210.
     "Plain Song." <u>AntR</u> (42:2) Spr 84, p. 211.
     "Purge." <u>AntR</u> (42:2) Spr 84, p. 212-213.
     "Rich." <u>GrandS</u> (3:3) Spr 84, p. 58-59.

"The Widower." <u>AntR</u> (42:2) Spr 84, p. 216-218.
"Wulf and Eadwacer." <u>GrandS</u> (3:3) Spr 84, p. 60.

4216. RAISOR, Philip
"Metamorphosis." <u>KanQ</u> (16:1/2) Wint-Spr 84, p. 64.

4217. RAIZISS, Sonia
"In Your Sleep" (Selections: I-III, V, tr. of
Vittorio Sereni). <u>Chelsea</u> (42/43) 84, p. 147.

4218. RAKOSI, Carl
"Americana" (Selections: XXVII, XXXI). <u>Chelsea</u>
(42/43) 84, p. 288-289.

4219. RAMIREZ CORDOVA, Antonio
"Si la Violeta Cayese de Tus Manos." <u>Mairena</u>
(6:16) Spr 84, p. 5-7.

4220. RAMIREZ de ARELLANO, Diana
"Hay un Poema Solo." <u>Mairena</u> (6:17) Aut 84, p. 75-
76.

4221. RAMIREZ de ARELLANO, Olga
"Poema 11." <u>Mairena</u> (5:13) Spr 83, p. 76-77.

4222. RAMIREZ GUISCAFRE, Marilyn R.
"Palabras." <u>Mairena</u> (5:13) Spr 83, p. 75.

4223. RAMIREZ ROSADO, Wanda
"Carta de Adios a Mi Amor" (Primer premio del
Certamen organizado por la Escuela Cupeyville
entre estudiantes de la Enseñanza Secundaria
de San Juan). <u>Mairena</u> (5:14) Aut 83, p. 91-93.

4224. RAMKE, Bin
"The Consolation of Touch." <u>GeoR</u> (38:4) Wint 84,
p. 761.
"What We Learned to Do to Each Other." <u>OhioR</u> (33)
84, p. 141.

4225. RAMOS-GASCON, Antonio
"Cuesta Trabajo Ser de Alli." <u>Mairena</u> (5:14) Aut
83, p. 87.

4226. RAMSEY, Jarold
"Hand-Shadows" (for a daughter, eighteen).
<u>PoetryNW</u> (25:2) Sum 84, p. 46-47.

4227. RAMSEY, Paul
"Subterfuges for Listening to Time." <u>SouthernR</u>
(20:1) Wint 84, p. 149-150.

4228. RANDALL, Dudley
"Langston Blues." <u>Stepping</u> Wint 84, p. 12.

4229. RANDALL, Julia
"Video Games." <u>KenR</u> (NS 6:2) Spr 84, p. 74-75.

4230. RANDALL, Margaret
"Girl with a Parasol" (tr. of Daisy Zamora).

<u>Calyx</u> (8:3) Aut-Wint 84, p. 11.
"March 6, 1982" (Managua, Nicaragua). <u>Spirit</u>
     (7:1) 84, p. 73.
"The News Vendor" (tr. of Daisy Zamora). <u>Calyx</u>
     (8:3) Aut-Wint 84, p. 12.
"Technical Problem" (Havana--halfway to Managua--
     Havana August 5, 1983). <u>NewL</u> (50:4) Sum 84, p.
     78.
"The Waitress" (tr. of Daisy Zamora). <u>Calyx</u> (8:3)
     Aut-Wint 84, p. 10.

4231. RANDLETT, Mary McAlister
     "Back in Sardis, Mississippi." <u>WebR</u> (9:2) Wint
          85, p. 88-89.

4232. RANKIN, Paula
     "A Poem for Spring." <u>ThRiPo</u> (23/24) 84, p. 66-68.

4233. RANKIN, Rush
     "Body Language." <u>PoetryNW</u> (25:1) Spr 84, p. 24-25.
     "Dante, Missing Beatrice." <u>NewL</u> (51:1) Aut 84, p.
          46.
     "Ersatz Dying." <u>ThRiPo</u> (23/24) 84, p. 16.
     "Single LIfe." <u>PoetryNW</u> (25:1) Spr 84, p. 23-24.

4234. RANSBERRY, Jayne
     "Bloody Shame, 1980." <u>CalQ</u> (23/24) Spr-Sum 84, p.
          128.

4235. RANSOM, Bill
     "Food Chain." <u>Tendril</u> (17) Wint 84, p. 156.
     "Petén, 1983." <u>Tendril</u> (17) Wint 84, p. 155.

4236. RANTALA, Kathryn
     "Interstellar Reports: The Microbe Invasion,
          Earth." <u>Veloc</u> (2) Spr 83, p. 9-10.
     "Weightlessness." <u>Veloc</u> (2) Spr 83, p. 8.

4237. RATNER, Rochelle
     "Acquaintances." <u>GreenfR</u> (11:1/2) Sum-Aut 83, p.
          109.
     "First Steps." <u>GrahamHR</u> (7) Wint 84, p. 38-39.
     "From a Letter." <u>GreenfR</u> (11:1/2) Sum-Aut 83, p.
          108.

4238. RATTAN, Cleatus
     "Free of the Flesh." <u>TexasR</u> (5:1/2) Spr-Sum 84,
          p. 58.

4239. RATTI, John
     "Knowing and Not Knowing" (my father). <u>HangL</u> (45)
          Spr 84, p. 51-53.
     "Samson's Riddle." <u>HangL</u> (45) Spr 84, p. 46-48.
     "Tibet" (for Robert Gilday, 1925-1980). <u>HangL</u>
          (45) Spr 84, p. 49-50.

4240. RATTRAY, David
     "Mothers to the Stable" (from <u>Suppots et
          Supplications</u>: Fragmentations, tr. of Antonin
          Artaud). <u>Sulfur</u> (3:3, issue 9) 84, p. 17-19.

"Suppots et Supplications" (Selections, tr. of
Antonin Artaud, w. A. James Arnold, Clayton
Eshleman, and David Maclagan). Sulfur (3:3,
issue 9) 84, p. 15-59.

4241. RATUSHINSKAYA, Irina
"Ballad about a Wall" (tr. by Pamela White Hadas
and Ilya Nykin). GrandS (3:3) Spr 84, p. 83.
"Leningrad Triptych" (tr. by Pamela White Hadas and
Ilya Nykin). Agni (21) 84, p. 37-38.
"My Lord" (tr. by Ilya Nykin and Pamela White
Hadas). Agni (21) 84, p. 39.
"Poem" (To my unknown ancestor -- a lieutenant-
colonel in the civil war, tr. by Susan Layton).
NewRep (190:11) 19 Mr 84, p. 34.

4242. RATZLAFF, Keith
"Harley Ridge." Telescope (3:1) Wint 84, p. 54.
"In the Garden." Telescope (3:1) Wint 84, p. 55.
"The Invention." MidAR (4:1) Spr 84, p. 41.
"My Daughter After an Illness." MidAR (4:1) Spr
84, p. 43.
"Negotiations." Telescope (3:1) Wint 84, p. 104-105.
"Out Here." ColEng (46:5) S 84, p. 459.
"Outside Hutchinson, Kansas." Telescope (3:1)
Wint 84, p. 53.

4243. RAVICZ, Tanyo
"The Doll." HarvardA (117:4/118:1) D 84, p. 28.
"Enabled now to cry watercolors." HarvardA
(118:2) Spr 84, p. 36.

4244. RAVIKOVITCH, Dahlia
"Pride" (tr. by Chana Bloch). Pequod (16/17) 84,
p. 113.

4245. RAWLINS, Susan
"Body Language." GrandS (3:2) Wint 84, p. 146-147.
"Didier Pironi's Departure Creates an Opening at
L'Equipe Ligier-Gitanes." GrandS (3:2) Wint
84, p. 144-145.
"Exeunt Severally." Shen (35:1) 83-84, p. 29.

4246. RAWSON, Eric
"Ghosts Again." MidAR (4:2) Aut 84, p. 125.
"Written in a Small Circle of Wind." MidAR (4:2)
Aut 84, p. 126.

4247. RAY, David
"Anniversary Poem" (for J.). Amelia (1:2) O 84,
p. 19.
"The Assassin." GreenfR (12:1/2) Sum-Aut 84, p.
174-175.
"At a Fortress in India" (for the Mulders: Bill,
Helen, and Alice). NewL (51:2) Wint 84-85, p.
91-95.
"The Battered House." GreenfR (12:1/2) Sum-Aut
84, p. 175-176.
"The Buffalo Waiting Room." Chelsea (42/43) 84,
p. 126.

"Cobalt" (for Sam). PoetryE (15) Aut 84, p. 67.
"Edison Winter Home, Fort Myers." Kayak (64) My
    84, p. 56.
"For Harry S. Truman in Hell." Spirit (7:1) 84,
    p. 58-59.
"For Wang Hui-Ming." Amelia (1:2) O 84, p. 17.
"Hitch-Hiker." Amelia (1:2) O 84, p. 18.
"Mr. Tittle's Cabin." CharR (10:2) Aut 84, p. 81.
"An Old Woodcut." Spirit (7:1) 84, p. 182.
"On a Photograph by Art Sinsabaugh." CreamCR
    (9:1/2) 84, p. 34.
"Visit to a Tenement, Ludlow Street (Jacob Riis)."
    CharR (10:2) Aut 84, p. 82.
"The Woodpecker." MemphisSR (4:2) Spr 84, p. 22-23.

4248. RAY, Judy
    "Sleeping in the Larder in World War II." Amelia
        (1:2) O 84, p. 32-33.

4249. RAY, Nandita
    "Montage." MalR (68) Je 84, p. 21-22.
    "The Traveller." MalR (68) Je 84, p. 23-25.
    "Uncle Vanya." MalR (68) Je 84, p. 20.

4250. RAYMOND, Kathy
    "Jelly Road." PoeticJ (4) 83, p. 39.

4251. RAYMOND, Mark J.
    "Fate of a Child Locked in the Pantry Closet."
        HangL (45) Spr 84, p. 65.
    "Snapshot." HangL (45) Spr 84, p. 66.

4252. RAYNER, Mindi
    "Qualitative Judgment." Stepping (Anniversary
        Issue I) 84, p. 45.

4253. RAYSHICH, Steve
    "Intrusions." Sam (41:2, release 162) 84 or 85,
        p. 29.
    "Street Poem." Sam (39:1, release 153) 84, p. 51.

4254. RAZ, Jonathan
    "For an Imaginary One." Veloc (1) Sum 82, p. 16.

4255. REA, Susan
    "Poem for My Father." SouthernPR (24:2) Aut 84,
        p. 56-57.
    "Testimony for a Divorce." CrabCR (1:3) Wint 84,
        p. 22-23.

4256. REA, Susan Irene
    "Girl, Drowning." FourQt (33:4) Sum 84, p. 16.

4257. REA, Tom
    "Over Vitebsk, Chagall, 1914." CutB (22) Spr-
        Sum 84, p. 43.

4258. READER, Willie
    "Squaw." Sparrow (46) 84, p. 22.

4259. REARDON, Patrick
"Weight." StoneC (11:3/4) Spr-Sum 84, p. 25.

4260. RECTOR, Liam
"The Eventual Music" (for David St. John). Shen
(35:2/3) 84, p. 303.
"Showing." GeoR (38:3) Aut 84, p. 635.
"The Sorrow of Architecture." AmerPoR (13:1) Ja-F
84, p. 4-5.
"Three Portraits of Boy." AmerPoR (13:1) Ja-F 84,
p. 3-4.

4261. REDGROVE, Peter
"Childhood Thoughts." Sulfur (3:3, issue 9) 84,
p. 73-74.
"Fly Buddha." Sulfur (3:3, issue 9) 84, p. 67-68.
"The Funeral" (For N.). Sulfur (3:3, issue 9) 84,
p. 68-70.
"The Impossibility, the No-Body." Sulfur (3:3,
issue 9) 84, p. 72-73.
"Nan's Last Seance." Sulfur (3:3, issue 9) 84, p.
74-75.
"The Party in the Woods." GreenfR (11:3/4) Wint-
Spr 84, p. 87-89.
"The Quiet Woman." GreenfR (11:3/4) Wint-Spr 84,
p. 89-90.
"Some Music." Sulfur (3:3, issue 9) 84, p. 70-71.

4262. REDWINE, Nancy
"I lay on the beach remembering Lot's wife."
YellowS (12) Aut 84, p. 19.

4263. REECE, Spencer
"The Retarded." WindO (44) Sum-Aut 84, p. 38.

4264. REED, Alison T.
"Amadeus" (From One to the Other, in Love with the
Same Man). Poem (52) N 84, p. 25.
"Keats in Kentucky." Poem (52) N 84, p. 29.
"Reports Home on the Inter-University Forum for
Educators in Community Psychiatry with Responses
from the Left Wife." Poem (52) N 84, p. 30-34.
"The Shape-Changers at Larne." Vis (16) 84, p. 16-
17.
"To the Innocent." Poem (52) N 84, p. 26-28.

4265. REED, Crystal
"These Days." MSS (3:2/3) Spr 84, p. 9-10.

4266. REED, Ishmael
"Datsun's Death." Nimrod (27:2) Spr-Sum 84, p. 66-
67.
"On the Fourth of July in Sitka, 1982." CreamCR
(9:1/2) 84, p. 30-31.

4267. REED, Jeremy
"The Fishshack Couple." PoetryCR (5:3) Spr 84, p.
12.
"Night Fishing" (for Robin Robertson). Waves
(12:1) Aut 83, p. 54-55.

"September Cycle." <u>PoetryCR</u> (5:3) Spr 84, p. 12.

4268. REED, Jim
"In Memory Of." <u>AntigR</u> (56) Wint 84, p. 111.
"Loss." <u>AntigR</u> (56) Wint 84, p. 111.

4269. REED, John R.
"Crusoe's Cats." <u>OntR</u> (21) Aut-Wint 84, p. 90-91.
"Elegy for Chris." <u>OntR</u> (21) Aut-Wint 84, p. 84-85.
"The Fifth Cavalry." <u>WoosterR</u> (1:1) Mr 84, p. 42-43.
"Fourth of July at Grandmother's House" (Aurora,
    Minnesota, 1945). <u>OntR</u> (21) Aut-Wint 84, p. 83.
"Loneliness." <u>OntR</u> (21) Aut-Wint 84, p. 89.
"Oscar." <u>FourQt</u> (33:4) Sum 84, p. 15.
"Space Telescope." <u>Poem</u> (50) Mr 84, p. 5.
"Sunbathers at Catanzaro Lido." <u>OntR</u> (21) Aut-
    Wint 84, p. 87.
"Three Snapshots from Georgia." <u>NegC</u> (4:3) Sum
    84, p. 15.
"To the Andes Survivors." <u>OntR</u> (21) Aut-Wint 84,
    p. 88-89.
"Troubled Waters." <u>OntR</u> (21) Aut-Wint 84, p. 86-87.
"Uncle Emil." <u>OntR</u> (21) Aut-Wint 84, p. 82.

4270. REES, Elizabeth
"Public Transportation." <u>Abraxas</u> (31/32) 84, p. 46.

4271. REES, Ennis
"The Watch Mender." <u>SouthernR</u> (20:4) Aut 84, p. 885.

4272. REEVE, F. D.
"Carving the Circle." <u>SewanR</u> (92:1) Ja-Mr 84, p.
    1-3.
"Running in Central Park." <u>NewL</u> (51:1) Aut 84, p.
    68-69.
"The South Windows at Chartres." <u>NewL</u> (51:1) Aut
    84, p. 68.

4273. REEVES, Troy Dale
"Baptism I." <u>ChrC</u> (101:27) 12-19 S 84, p. 834.

4274. REICHOW, V. L.
"Breaking." <u>IndR</u> (7:1) Wint 84, p. 32.
"The Deer." <u>IndR</u> (7:1) Wint 84, p. 35.
"Sudden Changes." <u>IndR</u> (7:1) Wint 84, p. 33.
"Summer." <u>IndR</u> (7:1) Wint 84, p. 34.

4275. REID, Colin Way
"The Sleeping Gypsy" (On the painting of that name
    by Henri Rousseau, at the Museum of Modern Art
    in New York). <u>SewanR</u> (92:4) O-D 84, p. 599.
"Temenos" (A sacred precinct. After sculptures
    from the East Frieze of the Parthenon, in the
    British Museum, London). <u>SewanR</u> (92:4) O-D 84,
    p. 600.

4276. REID, Monty
"For the Paleo Expedition." <u>PoetryCR</u> (5:3) Spr
    84, p. 9.

4277. REID, P . C.
       "In the Dead of Night." WebR (9:1) Spr 84, p. 51.
       "Stolen Hours." WebR (9:1) Spr 84, p. 50-51.
       "Thoughts from Genji." WebR (9:1) Spr 84, p. 49-50.

4278. REIMER, Dolores
       "Old Man Riverbottom." NoDaQ (52:3) Sum 84, p. 235.

4279. REINER, Cary York
       "Jazz Woman with Reed Instrument." ThirdW (2) Spr
       84, p. 91-94.

4280. REINFRANK, Arno
       "Lament for Paul Celan" (On the death of my friend
       in Paris, tr. by Suzanne Shipley Toliver).
       Sulfur (4:2, issue 11) 84, p. 95.

4281. REINSCH, Margo
       "Incoming Tide." HiramPoR (36) Spr-Sum 84, p. 37.

4282. REISS, James
       "Woodland Sketches." Nat (238:16) 28 Ap 84, p. 523.

4283. REISS, Pat
       "The Encounter." WritersL (1) 84, p. 17.

4284. REITER, David
       "After-Thoughts." WestCR (19:2) O 84, p. 25.
       "She spins on a point" ("Untitled"). WestCR
       (19:2) O 84, p. 25.

4285. REITER, Thomas
       "The Fare." PoetryNW (25:1) Spr 84, p. 38-39.
       "Mulberry-Picking on Waste Ground." PoetryNW
       (25:1) Spr 84, p. 37-38.
       "Pitch and Kerosene." CimR (69) O 84, p. 58-59.
       "Sodbusters." CimR (69) O 84, p. 61-62.

4286. RENDALL, Barbara
       "Postcards." PoetryCR (5:4) Sum 84, p. 9.
       "Sentieri." PoetryCR (5:4) Sum 84, p. 9.
       "Shakespeare's Women." PoetryCR (6:2) Wint 84-85,
       p. 6.
       "Watching for a Child." PoetryCR (5:4) Sum 84, p. 9.

4287. RENO, Janet
       "Dancing Sand." WebR (9:2) Wint 85, p. 94-95.

4288. REPETTO, Vittoria
       "A.E. has jet-black hair." Tele (19) 83, p. 82.
       "A.E. takes a ride in an elevator." Tele (19) 83,
       p. 83.
       "At Newton's Birthday party." Tele (19) 83, p. 84.
       "The diet of cafes." Tele (19) 83, p. 84.
       "E = mc^2." Tele (19) 83, p. 82.
       "The Einstein Poems." Tele (19) 83, p. 82-85.
       "Flip a coin." Tele (19) 83, p. 85.
       "Quote." Tele (19) 83, p. 85.
       "Young A.E. in catholic school." Tele (19) 83, p.
       83.

4289. REPP, John
      "On Assateague Island." <u>Telescope</u> (3:2) Spr 84,
         p. 24.

4290. RESS, Lisa
      "Late Spring Trip." <u>PraS</u> (58:3) Aut 84, p. 94.
      "One of Everything, Two of Us" (for H-J. W.).
         <u>PraS</u> (58:3) Aut 84, p. 93.
      "Spaghetti Sauce, Good Red." <u>PraS</u> (58:3) Aut 84,
         p. 92.
      "War Movie over Iowa." <u>MSS</u> (3:2/3) Spr 84, p. 112.

RETAMAR, Roberto Fernandez: <u>See</u> FERNANDEZ RETAMAR, Roberto

4291. REVARD, Carter
      "January." <u>GreenfR</u> (11:3/4) Wint-Spr 84, p. 45.
      "The Only Other Poncas in Los Angeles." <u>GreenfR</u>
         (11:3/4) Wint-Spr 84, p. 44-45.

4292. REVELL, Donald
      "Charleston." <u>NewEngR</u> (7:1) Aut 84, p. 58-60.
      "A Setting" (in memory of John Cheever). <u>AntR</u>
         (42:3) Sum 84, p. 334.

4293. REVERDY, Pierre
      "Galleries." <u>AmerPoR</u> (13:4) Jl-Ag 84, p. 34.

4294. REXROTH, Kenneth
      "Andree Rexroth." <u>Peb</u> (23) 84, p. 1-4.
      "Kings River Canyon." <u>Peb</u> (23) 84, p. 2-4.
      "Mt. Tamalpais." <u>Peb</u> (23) 84, p. 1-2.

4295. REYES, Kathleen M.
      "Punishments." <u>Calyx</u> (8:2) Spr 84, p. 18.
      "The Volunteer Protectionist." <u>Calyx</u> (8:2) Spr
         84, p. 17.

4296. REYES DAVILA, Marcos
      "El Llamado" (Envio a Marcos Ariel, hijo).
         <u>Mairena</u> (5:14) Aut 83, p. 80-81.

4297. RHENISCH, Harold
      "A Skeleton of Breath." <u>AntigR</u> (59) Aut 84, p. 8-12.
      "The View across the Valley." <u>Grain</u> (12:3) Ag 84,
         p. 20-22.

4298. RHINEHART, Rosalyn G.
      "Glory's Song." <u>BlackALF</u> (18:1) Spr 84, p. 18.
      "Jazz Man." <u>BlackALF</u> (18:1) Spr 84, p. 17.
      "Roots." <u>BlackALF</u> (18:1) Spr 84, p. 17.

4299. RHODES, Barbara
      "Burning Bright." <u>Wind</u> (14:52) 84, p. 42-43.
      "Marguerite in New Orleans." <u>Wind</u> (14:52) 84, p.
         41-42.

4300. RHYMER, Parke
      "Nagging Suspicion." <u>DekalbLAJ</u> (17:1/2) 84, p. 142.

493   RIEL

4301. RIBOVICH, John
      "Come Morning." <u>Poem</u> (51) Mr [i.e. Jl] 84, p. 59.
      "Front Range." <u>Poem</u> (51) Mr [i.e. Jl] 84, p. 60.

4302. RICARDO, Cassiano
      "The Horse in the Garden" (tr. by Eloah T.
        Giacomelli). <u>AntigR</u> (59) Aut 84, p. 120.

4303. RICE, Pamela
      "Album, Altered Figures." <u>CarolQ</u> (36:3) Spr 84,
        p. 66.

4304. RICE, Paul
      "For a One-Legged Man with a Crutch, Cutting Grass
        with a Push Mower, a Dollar Bill Hanging from
        His Back Trouser Pocket, 1956." <u>NegC</u> (4:2) Spr
        84, p. 30-31.

4305. RICH, Adrienne
      "North American Time" (Extract). <u>NowestR</u> (22:3)
        84, p. i.

4306. RICHARDSON, Iris
      "Parting." <u>PoeticJ</u> (2) 83, p. 35.

4307. RICHESON, William
      "Shoes." <u>Vis</u> (14) 84, p. 28.

4308. RICHMOND, Steve
      "Gagaku." <u>OroM</u> (2:3/4, issue 7/8) 84, p. 35-36.
      "Riches." <u>Bogg</u> (52) 84, p. 15.

4309. RICHTER, Harvena
      "Black Eggs." <u>NewL</u> (50:4) Sum 84, p. 46.
      "The Self in Variation" (more scenes from
        meditation). <u>SoDakR</u> (22:1) Spr 84, p. 45-48.

4310. RICKEL, Boyer
      "Exposure." <u>YaleR</u> (73:2) Wint 84, p. 259.
      "My Dear Flaubert." <u>YaleR</u> (73:2) Wint 84, p. 259-
        260.

4311. RIDEN, Bradley D.
      "Fourth Step." <u>PikeF</u> (6) Aut 84, p. 3.
      "A Song for Dorothy." <u>PikeF</u> (6) Aut 84, p. 3.

4312. RIDLAND, John
      "Aria for Lady Alice, Tarzan's Mother." <u>Hudson</u>
        (37:4) Wint 84-85, p. 551-553.
      "Aria for Tarzan's Father." <u>Hudson</u> (37:4) Wint 84-
        85, p. 549-551.
      "Laudate." <u>Peb</u> (23) 84, p. 28-29.
      "Swimming for Jeni." <u>Poetry</u> (143:5) F 84, p. 276-
        277.
      "The Thalidomide Kids on Televison (1978)."
        <u>Chelsea</u> (42/43) 84, p. 237.
      "Who's Angry." <u>Peb</u> (23) 84, p. 30-31.

4313. RIEL, Steven
      "Manna." <u>AntigR</u> (58) Sum 84, p. 62.

4314. RIGGS, Dionis Coffin
      "Elegy" (tr. of Kemal Ozer, w. William Fielder and
         Ozcan Yalim). StoneC (11:3/4) Spr-Sum 84, p. 39.
      "Hegira" (tr. of Orhan Veli, w. William Fielder and
         Ozcan Yalim). StoneC (11:3/4) Spr-Sum 84, p. 41.
      "Salem." StoneC (11:3/4) Spr-Sum 84, p. 65.

4315. RIGSBEE, David
      "Crickets." GeoR (38:2) Sum 84, p. 345.

4316. RILEY, Joanne M.
      "Darning with Light." CalQ (25) Aut 84, p. 64-65.

4317. RILEY, Judas Mary-Ellen
      "Julius Caesar Speaks of His Seizures." MSS
         (4:1/2) Aut 84, p. 270-271.

4318. RILEY, Michael D.
      "Assignation." KanQ (16:4) Aut 84, p. 121.
      "Commuting." YetASM (3) 84, p. 4.
      "Of a Sparrow, Doris and John." KanQ (16:4) Aut
         84, p. 122.
      "Panther." PoeticJ (4) 83, p. 32.

4319. RILEY, Sam
      "New Salem, Illinois 1837." SpoonRQ (9:2) Spr 84,
         p. 41.
      "Sparrow." SpoonRQ (9:2) Spr 84, p. 40.

4320. RILKE, Rainer Maria
      "Autumn's End" (tr. by Robert Bly). NewL (51:2)
         Wint 84-85, p. 35.
      "The Bowl of Roses" (tr. by Edward Snow). Thrpny
         (18) Sum 84, p. 27.
      "Serious Moment" (tr. by Robert Bly). NewL (51:2)
         Wint 84-85, p. 36.
      "Sonnets to Orpheus" (Selections: I.4, I.11, I.13,
         I.14, I.17, I.20, II.5, II.20, II.25, tr. by
         Barbara Feyerabend). SenR (14:1) 84, p. 67-75.

4321. RILLING, David
      "Blank Sheet of Paper Poems, Part II: Land-Mark
         Poem." SmPd (21:3) Aut 84, p. 35.
      "Blank Sheet of Paper Poems, Part III: Worm Hole
         Poem." SmPd (21:3) Aut 84, p. 36.

4322. RILLING, Helen E.
      "Saga of the Sangamo." Amelia [1:1] Ap 84, p. 26-27.

4323. RIMBAUD, Arthur
      "The Drunken Boat" (tr. by C. W. Pratt). LitR
         (27:3) Spr 84, p. 306-308.

RIN, Ishigaki: See ISHIGAKI, Rin

4324. RINALDI, Nicholas
      "Shagging Flies in Flushing Meadow Park." GreenfR
         (11:1/2) Sum-Aut 83, p. 104.
      "Violin" (Eve of Saint Agnes Contest Winners I).
         NegC (4:1) Wint 84, p. 10-17.

4325. RINDO, Ronald J.
      "David." SmPd (21:2) Spr 84, p. 27.

4326. RIOS, Alberto
      "Street, Cloud." BlackWR (11:1) Aut 84, p. 24.

4327. RIOS de TORRES, Rosario Esther
      "Hay una palabra que nos hiere en lejanía."
      Mairena (5:13) Spr 83, p. 105.
      "Soy tu propia soledad de hombre." Mairena (5:13)
      Spr 83, p. 104.

4328. RIOS MARTIR, Doris
      "Quiero vivir." Mairena (5:13) Spr 83, p. 105-106.

4329. RIOS RUIZ-TAGLE, Mariela I.
      "Madre Espina de Campos Absolutos." Mairena
      (6:16) Spr 84, p. 8-10.

4330. RIPLEY, Lonnie
      "First Grader." DekalbLAJ (20th Anniversary
      Issue) 84, p. 101.

4331. RIPOLL, Carlos
      "Boniato Jail: Account of a Massacre" (tr. of
      Armando Valladares). Confr (27/28) 84, p. 32-35.
      "Lend Me Your Legs for an Instant" (tr. of Armando
      Valladares). Confr (27/28) 84, p. 36.

4332. RISTOVIC, Alexander
      "About Death and Other Things" (tr. by Charles
      Simic). Iowa (14:3) Aut 84, p. 16.
      "Flirting with a Pig" (tr. by Charles Simic).
      Iowa (14:3) Aut 84, p. 15.
      "Gingerbread Heart" (tr. by Charles Simic). Iowa
      (14:3) Aut 84, p. 14.

4333. RITCHIE, Diane
      "Progress." SanFPJ (6:4) 84, p. 14-15.

4334. RITCHIE, Elisavietta
      "My Editor Asks Me to Consider Substituting 'Seed'
      for 'Sperm'" (for Karen Alenier). StoneC
      (11:3/4) Spr-Sum 84, p. 35.
      "To Ride the White Camel" (Nefta, Tunisia, October
      1983). PoetL (79:2) Sum 84, p. 96-97.

4335. RITSOS, Yǎnnis
      "Among the Blind" (from Eleven Poems, tr. by
      Edmund Keeley). Chelsea (42/43) 84, p. 414.
      "The Cheap Apartment Building" (from Eleven
      Poems, tr. by Edmund Keeley). Chelsea (42/43)
      84, p. 413.
      "Compulsory Assent" (from Eleven Poems, tr. by
      Edmund Keeley). Chelsea (42/43) 84, p. 416.
      "The Conjunction 'Or'" (tr. by Kimon Friar).
      AmerPoR (13:6) N-D 84, p. 25.
      "Counterfeit" (tr. by Kimon Friar). AmerPoR
      (13:6) N-D 84, p. 26.
      "Countryside" (tr. by Kimon Friar). AmerPoR

(13:6) N-D 84, p. 24.
"Deterioration" (tr. by Kimon Friar). AmerPoR
(13:6) N-D 84, p. 26.
"Encounter" (tr. by Kimon Friar). AmerPoR (13:6)
N-D 84, p. 23.
"The End of the Performance" (from Eleven Poems,
tr. by Edmund Keeley). Chelsea (42/43) 84, p.
417.
"The Final Obel" (tr. by Kimon Friar). AmerPoR
(13:6) N-D 84, p. 25.
"Forged Passport" (tr. by Kimon Friar). AmerPoR
(13:6) N-D 84, p. 26.
"The Great Hypocrite" (tr. by Kimon Friar).
AmerPoR (13:6) N-D 84, p. 27.
"Helen's House" (tr. by Kimon Friar). AmerPoR
(13:6) N-D 84, p. 27.
"Identity Card" (from Eleven Poems, tr. by Edmund
Keeley). Chelsea (42/43) 84, p. 414.
"Known Consequences" (tr. by Kimon Friar).
AmerPoR (13:6) N-D 84, p. 27.
"The Meaning of Simplicity" (tr. by Kimon Friar).
AmerPoR (13:6) N-D 84, p. 23.
"The Models" (tr. by Kimon Friar). AmerPoR (13:6)
N-D 84, p. 25.
"Momentary Immobility" (from Eleven Poems, tr. by
Edmund Keeley). Chelsea (42/43) 84, p. 416.
"The Mountain's Daughter" (tr. by Kimon Friar).
AmerPoR (13:6) N-D 84, p. 26.
"Nocturnal Episode" (tr. by Kimon Friar). AmerPoR
(13:6) N-D 84, p. 26.
"Nocturne" (tr. by Kimon Friar). AmerPoR (13:6) N-
D 84, p. 24.
"The Other Precision" (tr. by Kimon Friar).
AmerPoR (13:6) N-D 84, p. 24.
"Out of Place" (from Eleven Poems, tr. by Edmund
Keeley). Chelsea (42/43) 84, p. 415.
"Partial Resignation" (tr. by Kimon Friar).
AmerPoR (13:6) N-D 84, p. 26.
"Provincial Spring" (tr. by Martin McKinsey).
ParisR (26:91) Spr 84, p. 122.
"The Relation of the Unrelated" (tr. by Kimon
Friar). AmerPoR (13:6) N-D 84, p. 24.
"Reverential Comparison" (tr. by Kimon Friar).
AmerPoR (13:6) N-D 84, p. 24.
"Romiosini" (Selection: II, tr. by N. C.
Germanakos). Chelsea (42/43) 84, p. 249-251.
"Sad Cunning" (from Eleven Poems, tr. by Edmund
Keeley). Chelsea (42/43) 84, p. 415.
"Silence" (tr. by Kimon Friar). AmerPoR (13:6) N-
D 84, p. 24.
"Small Composition" (tr. by Martin McKinsey).
ParisR (26:91) Spr 84, p. 123.
"Strange Times" (tr. by Kimon Friar). AmerPoR
(13:6) N-D 84, p. 25.
"Stripped Naked" (tr. by Kimon Friar). AmerPoR
(13:6) N-D 84, p. 27.
"Summer at Dhiminio" (tr. by Kimon Friar).
AmerPoR (13:6) N-D 84, p. 24.
"Summer Noon at Karlóvasi" (tr. by Kimon Friar).
AmerPoR (13:6) N-D 84, p. 24.

"Summer Sorrow" (tr. by Kimon Friar). AmerPoR
(13:6) N-D 84, p. 27.
"The Unacceptable Man" (tr. by Kimon Friar).
AmerPoR (13:6) N-D 84, p. 25.
"The Uncompromising" (tr. by Kimon Friar).
AmerPoR (13:6) N-D 84, p. 25.
"Wavering Decisions" (tr. by Martin McKinsey).
ParisR (26:91) Spr 84, p. 122.
"Wells and People" (tr. by Kimon Friar). AmerPoR
(13:6) N-D 84, p. 26.

4336. RITTY, Joan
"The Afterwards." PoeticJ (1) 83, p. 28.
"Drought in a Boy." PoeticJ (7) 84, p. 18.
"Homily." PoeticJ (4) 83, p. 8.
"Illusion." PoeticJ (3) 83, p. 13.
"Night Tree." PoeticJ (4) 83, p. 22.
"Porch Swing: The Jumping-Off Place." NegC (4:2)
Spr 84, p. 51.
"A Sense of Family." PoeticJ (8) 84, p. 34-35.
"Stanza." PoeticJ (3) 83, p. 5.
"Whole Courage." PoeticJ (6) 84, p. 29.

4337. RIUS GALINDO, José María
"Desde mí hasta mí." Mairena (6:18) 84, p. 73.
"Y cuando ya no me quede la palabra." Mairena
(6:17) Aut 84, p. 81.

4338. RIVARD, David
"Double Indemnity." Telescope (3:3) Aut 84, p.
104-105.
"Leaving the Gateway Cinema." PoetryE (15) Aut
84, p. 40-41.

4339. RIVARD, Ken
"Precise Moment." Waves (12:4) Spr 84, p. 60.

RIVAS, Carlos Martinez: See MARTINEZ RIVAS, Carlos

4340. RIVERA, Aureo
"Vivir el Presente." Mairena (5:13) Spr 83, p. 106.

RIVERA, Carmelo Colón: See COLON RIVERA, Carmelo

RIVERA, Cecilia Colón: See COLON RIVERA, Cecilia

4341. RIVERA, Etnairis
"El Pulso de una Estrella Aguardando" (Selections).
Mairena (5:14) Aut 83, p. 20-22.

RIVERA, Guillermo Rodriguez: See RODRIGUEZ RIVERA, Guillermo

RIVERA, Rafael Barreto: See BARRETO RIVERA, Rafael

4342. RIVERA RODRIGUEZ, Luis A.
"Oye Poeta!" Mairena (6:17) Aut 84, p. 78-79.

4343. RIVERO, Eliana
"Going West." Calyx (8:2) Spr 84, p. 23.
"Huachuca" (The Mountain Poems). Calyx (8:2) Spr

84, p. 22-23.
"Tan Lejos del Azúcar." <u>Areíto</u> (9:36) 84, p.
106.

4344. RIVEROS, Mario
"The Street" (tr. by Stephen C. Mohler). <u>Vis</u> (15)
84, p. 10.

4345. RIVERS, J. W.
"Enemy Forces Set a Trap for Francis Marion on His
Own Plantation." <u>SoCaR</u> (17:1) Aut 84, p. 42.
"Late at Night in the Kitchen." <u>OhioR</u> (33) 84, p.
138-139.
"Modesty Silsbee Finds Her Father's Bible in a
Trunk." <u>SpoonRQ</u> (9:4) Aut 84, p. 43.

4346. RIVERS, Jim
"Diary Entries of Jochebed Sloan, Wife of Lt. Simon
Sloan, Just before a Massacre" (Fort Dearborn,
Illinois, 13 August 1812). <u>SpoonRQ</u> (9:2) Spr
84, p. 56.
"From Phoebe Campbell to Her Sister" (Fort Wayne,
Indiana, August 15, 1812). <u>SpoonRQ</u> (9:2) Spr
84, p. 57.

4347. RIVERS, Kinloch
"Misfortune." <u>PoeticJ</u> (8) 84, p. 11.
"Twigs." <u>NeqC</u> (4:4) Aut 84, p. 44.

4348. ROA BASTOS, Augusto
"Del Regreso." <u>Mairena</u> (6:18) 84, p. 187.

4349. ROACH, Irene
"'Widow' in printing." <u>YetASM</u> (3) 84, p. 2.

4350. ROBBINS, Martin
"Blind Student Reading." <u>StoneC</u> (12:1/2) Aut-Wint
84, p. 37.
"Demolition Derby." <u>WebR</u> (9:1) Spr 84, p. 40.
"Exercise for a New Season." <u>CapeR</u> (19:3) 20th
Anniverary Issue 84, p. 42.
"Guidebook/Mountain Streams." <u>WebR</u> (9:1) Spr 84,
p. 39.
"In Willow Fly Time." <u>GreenfR</u> (11:1/2) Sum-Aut
83, p. 106.
"Motorcycle Death." <u>WebR</u> (9:1) Spr 84, p. 41.
"Notes/Maker of Death Masks." <u>Mund</u> (14:2) 84, p. 13.
"On a Dime, Struck in Denver." <u>GreenfR</u> (12:1/2)
Sum-Aut 84, p. 113.
"Passacaglia." <u>Mund</u> (14:2) 84, p. 14.
"Winter in the Newspaper Room." <u>GreenfR</u> (12:1/2)
Sum-Aut 84, p. 113.

4351. ROBBINS, Richard
"5608 Springhill Place." <u>StoneC</u> (12:1/2) Aut-Wint
84, p. 31.
"After the Miracle." <u>NoAmR</u> (269:3) S 84, p. 12.
"Earthquake Weather." <u>CharR</u> (10:1) Spr 84, p. 39.
"A Glider Takes Off from the Cliff." <u>CharR</u> (10:1)
Spr 84, p. 41-42.

"In Eastern Montana." ThirdW (2) Spr 84, p. 58-59.
"Living near the Refuge." PoetryNW (25:1) Spr 84,
   p. 5.
"March Day on a North County Marsh." CharR (10:1)
   Spr 84, p. 38.
"The Symbolists." CharR (10:1) Spr 84, p. 40-41.
"Vegetarianism." PoeticJ (3) 83, p. 40.
"Whaleships in Winter Quarters at Herschel Island."
   CharR (10:1) Spr 84, p. 40.

4352. ROBBINS, Tim
"Harvest." HangL (46) Aut 84, p. 58.
"Mi-Lo (the Laughing Buddha)." HangL (45) Spr 84,
   p. 54.
"Scarface." HangL (45) Spr 84, p. 55-56.

4353. ROBERSON, Katherine
"Fashionable Causes." SanFPJ (6:4) 84, p. 34.
"Speaking Out." SanFPJ (6:4) 84, p. 35.

4354. ROBERTS, Elizabeth Madox
"At Morning." SouthernR (20:4) Aut 84, p. 807.

4355. ROBERTS, Kim
"Yellow." Tendril (17) Wint 84, p. 157.

4356. ROBERTS, Len
"And I'd Fear Some Terrible Accident Like His War."
   WestB (15) 84, p. 104.
"During My Yearly Visit I Eat a Ham Sandwich and
   Discuss My Brother's Madness with My Mother."
   WestB (15) 84, p. 106.
"Hearing the Girl Story While Shoveling Snow."
   OhioR (32) 84, p. 126.
"It Will Wait." PaintedB (22) Spr 84, p. 19.
"Talking to My Brother about the Day he Was Raped
   by a Man Twenty Years Earlier." WestB (15) 84,
   p. 106.
"When the Jukebox Plays Sousa." WestB (15) 84, p.
   105.

4357. ROBERTS, Mark
"Renfield." Bogg (52) 84, p. 53.

4358. ROBERTSON, Kirk
"Adjusting to the Desert" (for Michael Hogan).
   OroM (2:3/4, issue 7/8) 84, p. 33-35.
"Carpinteria." Abraxas (29/30) 84, p. 21.

4359. ROBERTSON, Robin
"Bale-Fire." Descant (47, 15:4) Wint 84, p. 190.
"Child Lost." PoetryCR (5:4) Sum 84, p. 14.
"Embankment." Descant (47, 15:4) Wint 84, p. 188-
   189.
"Pibroch." PoetryCR (5:4) Sum 84, p. 14.

4360. ROBERTSON, Wm. B.
"Coffee Room Gun." Quarry (33:4) Aut 84, p. 56-57.
"Mothers' Wishes." Quarry (33:4) Aut 84, p. 56.
"Neighbours." Descant (47, 15:4) Wint 84, p. 52-53.

"The Pursuit of Happiness." <u>Descant</u> (47, 15:4)
Wint 84, p. 54-55.

4361. ROBERTSON, William P.
"Lady Bug's Aphids." <u>PoeticJ</u> (2) 83, p. 40.

4362. ROBIN, Ralph
"Camera Angle." <u>SouthernHR</u> (18:2) Spr 84, p. 108.

4363. ROBINS, Corinne
"In the Nest." <u>Confr</u> (27/28) 84, p. 337.

4364. ROBINSON, Bain
"Trains/Departure Time." <u>CutB</u> (22) Spr-Sum 84, p.
50-51.

4365. ROBINSON, Bruce
"Crossing into Wisconsin." <u>StoneC</u> (12:1/2) Aut-
Wint 84, p. 32.
"West Virginia" (from <u>Calendar</u>: August).
<u>GreenfR</u> (11:1/2) Sum-Aut 83, p. 136.

4366. ROBINSON, Colin
"The Enchanted Wood." <u>Argo</u> (5:2) 84, p. 31.

4367. ROBINSON, Edward Arlington
"Eros Turannos." <u>NewRep</u> (189:9) 29 Ag 83, p. 26.

4368. ROBINSON, James Miller
"Beans and Tortilla." <u>Poem</u> (52) N 84, p. 8-9.
"The Beggar on the Ground." <u>Poem</u> (52) N 84, p. 10.
"Birthday." <u>Poem</u> (52) N 84, p. 11.
"Daughter of a Servant." <u>SpoonRQ</u> (9:4) Aut 84, p.
33.
"Green Night at the Texas Cowgirl." <u>WormR</u> (24:4,
issue 96) 84, p. 135.
"Morning in Saltillo." <u>Poem</u> (52) N 84, p. 7.
"Report." <u>WormR</u> (24:4, issue 96) 84, p. 135-136.

4369. ROBINSON, Kim Stanley
"Sense and Science: Davis, March 1979." <u>Veloc</u> (4)
Sum 84, p. 61-62.

4370. ROBINSON, Peter
"Letters and Dreams: The War Poems of Marian
Elmsley, 1939-1945" (Selections: III. "History,"
VI. "The Stone Animals," VII. "Letters").
<u>Quarry</u> (33:3) Sum 84, p. 29-30.
"On Hokusai's 'The Great Wave'." <u>PoetryCR</u> (5:3)
Spr 84, p. 14.

4371. ROBISON, Margaret Richter
"They Say in the Mountain Village." <u>BlueBldgs</u> (7)
84, p. 15.

4372. ROBSON, Ruthann
"An Apple a Day." <u>ThirdW</u> (2) Spr 84, p. 70-71.
"Each Winter." <u>Calyx</u> (8:3) Aut-Wint 84, p. 21.
"Fibers." <u>CrabCR</u> (1:3) Wint 84, p. 16.
"Simmer Over Medium Heat." <u>NegC</u> (4:2) Spr 84, p. 48.

4373. ROCA, Juan Manuel
"The Horse in Flames" (tr. by Lorraine Underwood).
Vis (15) 84, p. 12.

4374. ROCHE, Judith
"The Change." ThirdW (2) Spr 84, p. 11.

4375. RODEFER, Stephen
"Imitation W." Sulfur (4:1, issue 10) 84, p. 82-83.

4376. RODIER, Katharine
"Atlantic City." Poetry (145:2) N 84, p. 81.
"Belongings." SouthernPR (24:1) Spr 84, p. 12-13.

4377. RODNEY, Janet
"Lost in Thought" (Summer 1983). Sulfur (3:3,
issue 9) 84, p. 82-87.

RODRIGUEZ, Luis A. Rivera: See RIVERA RODRIGUEZ, Luis A.

4378. RODRIGUEZ, Magda Graniela
"Poema al Viento." Mairena (6:17) Aut 84, p. 94.

4379. RODRIGUEZ, Maria
"If I Could Mumble Like Marlon Brando." Telescope
(3:3) Aut 84, p. 58-59.

4380. RODRIGUEZ, Norman
"El Rodeo." Mairena (6:18) 84, p. 174.

RODRIGUEZ, Rafael A. Acevedo: See ACEVEDO RODRIGUEZ, Rafael
A.

4381. RODRIGUEZ NIETZSCHE, Vicente
"Disfrazada de azul." SinN (14:2) Ja-Mr 84, p. 101.
"Un Poema de Rosas Necesario." Mairena (6:18) 84,
p. 24.

4382. RODRIGUEZ RIVERA, Guillermo
"Dar con la Palabra." Mairena (6:18) 84, p. 178.
"Historia de Cuba" (fragmento). Mairena (6:17)
Aut 84, p. 84.

4383. ROESSLER, Marjorie
"The Mirrored Face." Quarry (33:1) Wint 84, p. 52.
"A Taste of Sun." Quarry (33:1) Wint 84, p. 52.

4384. ROETHKE, Theodore
"My Papa's Waltz." Hudson (37:1) Spr 84, p. 60.

4385. ROGAL, Stanley Wm.
"Familiar." PoetryCR (5:4) Sum 84, p. 15.

ROGELIO NOGUERAS, Luis: See NOGUERAS, Luis Rogelio

4386. ROGERS, Anne
"Letter to My Father Concerning a Chair." WestB
(14) 84, p. 66.

4387. ROGERS, C. D.
"Blue Turtles." EngJ (73:4) Ap 84, p. 45.

"The boy with pimples." <u>SanFPJ</u> (6:1) 84, p. 48.
"Genesis." <u>SanFPJ</u> (6:1) 84, p. 48.

4388. ROGERS, Del Marie
"Our Voices Cross in the Sky." <u>SouthernPR</u> (24:1)
Spr 84, p. 32.

4389. ROGERS, John
"Housewarming" (for Christine). <u>TarRP</u> (23:2) Spr
84, p. 11-12.

4390. ROGERS, Pattiann
"The Art of Imitation." <u>MissouriR</u> (7:3) 84, p. 29.
"Being Remembered." <u>PraS</u> (58:3) Aut 84, p. 37.
"Canis, A Knowledge of." <u>Nimrod</u> (27:2) Spr-Sum
84, p. 7.
"Creating Something Out of Nothing." <u>KenR</u> (NS
6:2) Spr 84, p. 60-61.
"The Creation of the Inaudible." <u>GeoR</u> (38:2) Sum
84, p. 264.
"A Dedication." <u>Nimrod</u> (27:2) Spr-Sum 84, p. 10.
"The Documentation of Absence." <u>Nimrod</u> (27:2) Spr-
Sum 84, p. 8.
"Duality." <u>PraS</u> (58:3) Aut 84, p. 38.
"The Elegance of the Dichotomous Experience."
<u>Poetry</u> (144:6) S 84, p. 341.
"Entomological Research." <u>Iowa</u> (14:3) Aut 84, p.
120.
"An Experiment of Faith" (A Group of Poems). <u>PraS</u>
(58:3) Aut 84, p. 31-40.
"An Experiment of Faith." <u>PraS</u> (58:3) Aut 84, p. 39.
"Filling-in Spaces." <u>PraS</u> (58:3) Aut 84, p. 40.
"The Importance of the Whale in the Field of Iris."
<u>PoetryNW</u> (25:2) Sum 84, p. 8-9.
"Investigative Logic in a Study of Love." <u>Poetry</u>
(144:6) S 84, p. 340.
"The Limitations of Death." <u>Poetry</u> (144:6) S 84,
p. 339.
"The Objects of Immortality." <u>Amelia</u> [1:1] Ap 84,
p. 3-4.
"On Watching My Child Swim to the 12 Foot Bottom."
<u>CapeR</u> (19:3) 20th Anniverary Issue 84, p. 43.
"Rhythmic Brushwork." <u>KenR</u> (NS 6:2) Spr 84, p. 61-
62.
"A Seasonal Tradition." <u>ChiR</u> (34:3) Sum 84, p. 49-
50.
"Sight and Sound." <u>AmerPoR</u> (13:4) Jl-Ag 84, p. 5.
"The Structure of Sustenance." <u>Iowa</u> (14:3) Aut
84, p. 118-119.
"The Study of the Splinter Expert." <u>SouthernR</u>
(20:4) Aut 84, p. 879-880.
"Traveling by Circles." <u>Nimrod</u> (27:2) Spr-Sum 84,
p. 9.
"The Well-Wisher from Half-Way around the World."
<u>PraS</u> (58:3) Aut 84, p. 35-36.
"White Prayer." <u>PoetryNW</u> (25:2) Sum 84, p. 9-10.
"The Witness of Death." <u>PraS</u> (58:3) Aut 84, p. 33-
34.

4391. ROGERS, Ron
"White Shaman Nocturne." GreenfR (11:3/4) Wint-
Spr 84, p. 65.

ROGOFF, Jay Grover: See GROVER-ROGOFF, Jay

4392. ROHDE, Karl
"Key to the Universe." PoeticJ (5) 84, p. 3.

4393. ROJAS, Gonzalo
"Rey." Mairena (6:18) 84, p. 133.

4394. ROLDAN BLAS, Israel
"Encontraste el amor?" Mairena (5:13) Spr 83, p.
106.

4395. ROLLINS, Scott
"Still Life with Autumn Fruits" (tr. of Patricia
Lasoen). Vis (16) 84, p. 24.

4396. ROMAINE, E.
"The Eye of Heaven." GeoR (38:3) Aut 84, p. 620.

4397. ROMELL, Karen
"Pigeons." MalR (68) Je 84, p. 81-82.
"Sleep." MalR (68) Je 84, p. 80-81.

4398. ROMERO, Aide
"Lentamente." Mairena (6:18) 84, p. 97.

4399. ROMERO, Elvio
"Vacio." Mairena (6:18) 84, p. 187.

4400. ROMERO, Julia
"El Beso." Mairena (5:14) Aut 83, p. 75.

4401. ROMERO, Julia E.
"Este Corazon." Mairena (6:17) Aut 84, p. 80.

4402. RONAY, György
"Conflagration" (tr. by Iván de Beky). Descant
(47, 15:4) Wint 84, p. 201.
"He Who Has Arrived" (tr. by Iván de Beky).
Descant (47, 15:4) Wint 84, p. 200.
"On the Skeleton of a Primary Reptile" (tr. by
Iván de Beky). Descant (47, 15:4) Wint 84,
p. 199.
"Report" (tr. by Iván de Beky). Descant (47,
15:4) Wint 84, p. 198.

4403. RONER, C. J.
"And So Was Our Soul." SanFPJ (6:3) 84, p. 48.
"Another Pesticide Birthing." SanFPJ (6:3) 84, p.
78.
"A Defense Team for the Sea." SanFPJ (6:3) 84, p.
77.
"Gods of Tumor Cell Madness." SanFPJ (6:3) 84, p.
79.
"Happily May I Walk." SanFPJ (6:3) 84, p. 80.
"On to Saturn." SanFPJ (6:3) 84, p. 18-19.
"So Keep a Geiger Counter around the House."

SanFPJ (6:4) 84, p. 50-51.

4404. RONNOW, Robert
"Ken Is Practicing a Song." PoetryE (15) Aut 84,
p. 22-23.
"The Listener." PoetryE (15) Aut 84, p. 21.

4405. ROOT, Judith
"Matinee." NoAmR (269:2) Je 84, p. 39.
"Picking Berries." MinnR (N.S. 22) Spr 84, p. 9.

4406. ROOT, William Pitt
"The Day the Sun Rises Twice." Spirit (7:1) 84,
p. 103.
"For the Better Maker." Poetry (144:5) Ag 84, p.
284-286.
"For the Furbearers." CreamCR (9:1/2) 84, p. 26-28.
"Ode to Gloom" (tr. of Pablo Neruda). CutB (22)
Spr-Sum 84, p. 35.
"Ode to the Atom" (tr. of Pablo Neruda).
Telescope (3:1) Wint 84, p. 97-101.
"Peripheral Vision." Nat (239:6) 8 S 84, p. 180.
"Remembering the Sea Elephant." Poetry (144:5) Ag
84, p. 286-288.
"Sea-Grape Tree and the Miraculous" (Guy Owen
Poetry Prize Recipient, Siv Cedering, Judge).
SouthernPR (24:2) Aut 84, p. 5-11.

ROQUE, Catherine la: See La ROQUE, Catherine

4407. RORIPAUGH, Robert
"Coyotes." Wind (14:50) 84, p. 43-44.
"Northern Light." Wind (14:50) 84, p. 43.

ROSADO, Wanda Ramírez: See RAMIREZ ROSADO, Wanda

4408. ROSADO AQUINO, Mario
"Poema de la Realidad." Mairena (6:17) Aut 84, p.
96.

4409. ROSBERG, Rose
"New York Initiation." PoetryCR (6:2) Wint 84-85,
p. 24.

4410. ROSE, Harriet
"Poem for the Maker." PoetryCR (6:2) Wint 84-85,
p. 24.

4411. ROSE, Jennifer
"Britons Leaving France" (Boulogne-sur-Mer). Agni
(21) 84, p. 109-110.

ROSE, Lynne Cheney: See CHENEY-ROSE, Lynne

4412. ROSE, Wendy
"Between Earth and Elsewhere: Song of the Last
Survivor." Veloc (1) Sum 82, p. 31.
"The Building of the Trophy." GreenfR (12:1/2)
Sum-Aut 84, p. 71-74.
"Coalinga." GreenfR (12:1/2) Sum-Aut 84, p. 75.

"Comment on Ethnopoetics and Literacy." GreenfR
    (12:1/2) Sum-Aut. 84, p. 68-69.
"Earth Place" (For Mary Simmons). Calyx (8:2) Spr
    84, p. 66.
"Every Planet We Ever Took." Veloc (1) Sum 82, p.
    32.
"Georgeline." GreenfR (12:1/2) Sum-Aut 84, p. 63-64.
"Halfbreed Cry." GreenfR (12:1/2) Sum-Aut 84, p. 65.
"Indian Man in His Prison (Halfbreed Chronicle)."
    GreenfR (12:1/2) Sum-Aut 84, p. 70-71.
"Mission Bells." GreenfR (12:1/2) Sum-Aut 84, p. 50.
"Story Keeper." GreenfR (12:1/2) Sum-Aut 84, p.
    66-68.
"Ta Tiopa Maza Win/Iron Door Woman." Calyx (8:2)
    Spr 84, p. 67-69.
"Truganinny." GreenfR (12:1/2) Sum-Aut 84, p. 58-59.

4413. ROSE, Wilga
       "Cross Country." Bogg (52) 84, p. 64.
       "Shoreline." Bogg (52) 84, p. 45.

4414. ROSEBURY, Pauline P.
       "Alienation." SanFPJ (6:4) 84, p. 16.
       "Dreamer." SanFPJ (6:4) 84, p. 13.
       "Oppression." SanFPJ (6:1) 84, p. 62-63.

4415. ROSELIEP, Raymond
       "Artist." ChrC (101:10) 21-28 Mr 84, p. 304.
       "I whispered of death" (haiku). PoetryCR (5:3)
           Spr 84, p. 9.
       "My Father's Gait." HolCrit (21:5) D 84, p. 18.
       "Sunset gilds the wings." Sparrow (46) 84, p. 18.

4416. ROSEN, Aaron
       "Giorgio di Chirico" (from The Taps for Space).
           AmerPoR (13:4) Jl-Ag 84, p. 38.

4417. ROSEN, Kenneth
       "The Fall (Bababadalgharag., etc.)." Agni (21)
           84, p. 49-51.
       "The String Quartet of the Birds." Agni (21) 84,
           p. 52-53.

4418. ROSEN, Michael J.
       "At Brunch We Entertain the Notion of the Perfect
           Place to Live." MichQR (23:1) Wint 84, p. 67.
       "Blind Minotaur Guided by a Little Girl in the
           Night" (Picasso). Nat (238:4) 4 F 84, p. 134.
       "A Colder Spring" (In memory of E.B.). SenR
           (14:2) 84, p. 58-59.
       "A Guide to the Old World." Shen (35:4) 84, p. 34-
           35.
       "The Map of Emotions." Shen (35:4) 84, p. 33-34.
       "Next." Nat (238:23) 16 Je 84, p. 746.
       "Reading on the Roof." NewOR (11:3/4) Aut-Wint
           84, p. 133.
       "Refrigerium" (a song of respite to quench the
           burning souls in hell). ParisR (26:94) Wint
           84, p. 161.
       "Strand." Nat (238:21) 2 Je 84, p. 682.

4419. ROSENBERG, Chuck
"Landfall." <u>Salm</u> (65) Aut 84, p. 76.

4420. ROSENBERG, Joel
"On Being Photographed" (for Bill Aron). <u>Ploughs</u>
(10:4) 84, p. 189.

4421. ROSENBERG, L. M.
"Alone with the Shoe Manufacturer in His Memorial
Park." <u>Blueline</u> (6:1) Sum-Aut 84, p. 48.
"The Bells of Saint Simon." <u>ParisR</u> (26:94) Wint
84, p. 165.
"Blue Mountain Lake" (for my sister). <u>Blueline</u>
(6:1) Sum-Aut 84, p. 24-25.
"A Suburban Childhood." <u>ParisR</u> (26:94) Wint 84,
p. 166.

4422. ROSENBERG, Liz
"It Is Snowing on the House of the Dead." <u>Bound</u>
(12:1) Aut 83, p. 116.
"The Speed of Death." <u>Bound</u> (12:1) Aut 83, p. 115.

4423. ROSENBERGER, F. C.
"Ars Poetica." <u>ArizQ</u> (40:1) Spr 84, p. 34.
"Litmus." <u>ArizQ</u> (40:3) Aut 84, p. 268.

4424. ROSENMAN, John B.
"Beside the Riverrun." <u>CentR</u> (28:3) Sum 84, p. 223.
"Loss." <u>CentR</u> (28:3) Sum 84, p. 223-224.

4425. ROSENSTOCK, Carl
"From the Bureau of Personnel." <u>GreenfR</u> (12:1/2)
Sum-Aut 84, p. 119.
"I Depend on You for Accurate" (for Ginny
MacKenzie). <u>GreenfR</u> (12:1/2) Sum-Aut 84, p. 118.

4426. ROSENTHAL, Amy G.
"Counting." <u>SouthernPR</u> (24:1) Spr 84, p. 48.

4427. ROSENTHAL, Bob
"Bob--Get New Finance Accordian--Allen." <u>Tele</u>
(19) 83, p. 60.
"F M L N." <u>Tele</u> (19) 83, p. 61.
"Little Night." <u>Tele</u> (19) 83, p. 62.
"Pith." <u>Tele</u> (19) 83, p. 62.
"Song Sung." <u>Tele</u> (19) 83, p. 61.

4428. ROSENZWEIG, Gerry
"Love of the Dark." <u>PoeticJ</u> (6) 84, p. 16.
"Quince." <u>PoeticJ</u> (6) 84, p. 21.
"Weather." <u>PoeticJ</u> (3) 83, p. 2.

4429. ROSS, Mary Waller
"From Another Rosebush to a Nightingale." <u>Poem</u>
(50) Mr 84, p. 30.
"Miss Rosemary, for Remembrance" (b. 1890, d.
1962). <u>Poem</u> (50) Mr 84, p. 29.
"Pity the Penguin." <u>Poem</u> (50) Mr 84, p. 31.

4430. ROSS-GOTTA, Loretta
"Holy Ground." ChrC (101:19) 30 My 84, p. 572.

4431. ROSSI, Christina Peri (See also PERI ROSSI, Cristina)
"Poems" (tr. by Sima Rabinowitz). Vis (15) 84, p.
30.

4432. ROSSKOPF, Allen
"Teacher." EngJ (73:3) Mr 84, p. 62.

4433. ROTELLA, Alexis
"Ch'in Kuan." Northeast (Series 3:17) Sum 84, p. 21.
"In the mirror" (haiku). PoetryCR (5:3) Spr 84,
p. 9.
"Purple." Sam (41:2, release 162) 84 or 85, p. 14.
"X." NewL (51:1) Aut 84, p. 49.

4434. ROTELLA, Guy
"Swimmers." WestB (15) 84, p. 110-111.

4435. ROTHENBERG, Jerome
"Blood River Shaman Chant" (Nenets). Sulfur (4:1,
issue 10) 84, p. 75-76.
"A Song in Praise of the Chiefs" (Aztec, tr. from
A. M. Garibay K.'s Spanish version). Chelsea
(42/43) 84, p. 246-247.
"Song of an Initiate" (Huichol, Mexico, tr. from A.
M. Garibay K.'s Spanish version). Chelsea
(42/43) 84, p. 245.

4436. ROTHFORK, John
"Texas Jukebox." TexasR (5:3/4) Aut-Wint 84, p.
82-83.

4437. ROUGHTON, Becke
"Your Last War." SouthernPR (24:1) Spr 84, p. 13.

4438. ROUNTREE, Thomas
"Gulfcoast Dis/connections." NegC (4:2) Spr 84,
p. 126-127.

4439. ROUTE, Deborah
"The Tattered Beanie." YetASM (3) 84, p. 4.

4440. ROWDON, Larry
"Dirge." Waves (12:2/3) Wint 84, p. 102.

4441. ROYSTER, Philip M.
"Black Mythology." BlackALF (18:1) Spr 84, p. 33.
"The Black Scholar." BlackALF (18:1) Spr 84, p. 33.
"Sarah's Blues." BlackALF (18:1) Spr 84, p. 34.
"Song of the People." BlackALF (18:1) Spr 84, p. 33.
"You can look at a nude woman" (for Virgo).
BlackALF (18:1) Spr 84, p. 33.

4442. RUARK, Gibbons
"Proof." Ploughs (10:1) 84, p. 134.
"A Small Rain." Ploughs (10:1) 84, p. 133.
"To Janey, Address Unknown." Ploughs (10:1) 84,
p. 136.

"What's Water But the Generated Soul?" Ploughs
(10:1) 84, p. 135.
"With the Bust of Maecenas at Coole." NewRep
(191:6) 6 Ag 84, p. 36.

4443. RUBENS, Philip M.
"The Picture Book." StoneC (12:1/2) Aut-Wint 84,
p. 17.

4444. RUBIN, Anele
"Hurt." Abraxas (29/30) 84, p. 69.

4445. RUBIN, Larry
"Escape." SouthwR (69:1) Wint 84, p. 15.
"Lines to a Lawyer-Piranha." DekalbLAJ (20th
Anniversary Issue) 84, p. 104.
"Lines to an Old Friend, Newly Widowed, Whose
Husband Played Chopin." Comm (111:1) 13 Ja 84,
p. 18.
"The Loner Gets to the Theatre Early." Shen
(35:1) 83-84, p. 21.
"March Treachery." SouthernPR (24:1) Spr 84, p. 33.
"A Note on Sublimation through Poetry." DekalbLAJ
(20th Anniversary Issue) 84, p. 105.
"The Phone Rings at 3 A.M." LitR (28:1) Aut 84,
p. 127.
"Poem for Halloween." NegC (4:4) Aut 84, p. 9.
"The Sightseeing Bus Goes Up the Mountian"
(Seattle). DekalbLAJ (20th Anniversary Issue)
84, p. 104.

4446. RUBIN, Mark
"Catherine Prudhomme." MidAR (4:1) Spr 84, p. 114.
"Crossing the Sound." PoetL (79:1) Spr 84, p. 49.
"A Slight Bird Shifting One Foot to Another."
PoetL (79:1) Spr 84, p. 48.
"Sunday Afternoon." VirQR (60:1) Wint 84, p. 61.
"Three Women." SouthernPR (24:1) Spr 84, p. 21-23.

4447. RUDMAN, Mark
"After a Death." Origin (5:4) Aut 84, p. 46.
"August Is Not a Month." PartR (51:3) 84, p. 385-
388.
"Before." Pequod (16/17) 84, p. 219-220.
"Bitter Night" (tr. of Bohdan Antonych). Pequod
(16/17) 84, p. 186.
"Cipher." PartR (51:3) 84, p. 384-385.
"Enigma after the Dreadful Thunderclap." Origin
(5:4) Aut 84, p. 49-50.
"The Evening" (tr. of Bohdan Boychuk, w. the
author). Confr (27/28) 84, p. 53.
"Making Belief." Origin (5:4) Aut 84, p. 47-48.
"Orphanos." Pequod (16/17) 84, p. 221-225.
"Perspective." Origin (5:4) Aut 84, p. 45.
"Pictures at an Exhibition" (after Manet).
Telescope (3:3) Aut 84, p. 98-101.
"Running Out." Ploughs (10:4) 84, p. 180-181.
"Song on the Indestructability of Matter" (tr. of
Bohdan Antonych). Pequod (16/17) 84, p. 185.
"Synthesis" (tr. of Ivan Drach, w. Paul Nemser).

Pequod (16/17) 84, p. 197.

4448. RUEBNER, Tuvia
"Mother's Face Drowned in Her Palm" (tr. by Grace
Schulman and Shirley Kaufman). Pequod (16/17)
84, p. 117.

4449. RUEFLE, Mary
"How History Begins." OhioR (32) 84, p. 37.
"This Untouched Thing." OhioR (32) 84, p. 36.

4450. RUESCHER, Scott
"Dog Gone Ode." Agni (20) 84, p. 42.
"The Driver Kept on Going." Agni (21) 84, p. 92-93.
"For Starts." Agni (20) 84, p. 45.
"Mouse Chase." Agni (20) 84, p. 43-44.
"Taking the Cue." Agni (20) 84, p. 41.
"Unintentional Lullaby." Agni (21) 84, p. 90-91.

4451. RUFF, John
"The Story of St. Christopher." PoetryNW (25:3)
Aut 84, p. 33-34.

4452. RUFFIN, Paul
"Boy in a Polythelene Bag." PortR (30:1) 84, p. 45.
"Building a Fire in Deep Winter." SoDakR (22:2)
Sum 84, p. 49-52.
"Frozen Over." MidAR (4:1) Spr 84, p. 46.
"Grass-Fire." CalQ (25) Aut 84, p. 40.
"His Grandmother Speaks on Canning." QW (19) Aut-
Wint 84-85, p. 92.
"In Dejection His Grandmother Receives a Promise."
QW (19) Aut-Wint 84-85, p. 93.

4453. RUFFUS, Stephen
"Incident Regarding Cell Block 'A'." QW (18) Spr-
Sum 84, p. 95.

4454. RUGO, Mariève
"Rain." WestB (14) 84, p. 93.

4455. RUIZ, J. A.
"Death in the Streets." Vis (15) 84, p. 29.

RUIZ, José O. Colón: See COLON RUIZ, José O.

4456. RUIZ, Víctor
"El tiempo es el deleite de tu mano sobre la
mía." Mairena (6:17) Aut 84, p. 90.

4457. RUIZ de HOYOS, Ramón
"A una Lajeña." Mairena (5:13) Spr 83, p. 107.

4458. RUIZ de la CUESTA, Francisco
"Mensajeros de la Alborada." Mairena (6:17) Aut
84, p. 77.

4459. RUIZ de TORRES, Juan
"Capitular." Mairena (5:13) Spr 83, p. 62.
"Castilla." Mairena (6:18) 84, p. 72.

4460. RUIZ ORTIZ, Ernesto
        "Como Si Tuviese Derecho a Exigir el Angel
        Dormido." _Mairena_ (5:13) Spr 83, p. 107-108.

RUIZ-TAGLE, Mariela I. Rios: _See_ RIOS RUIZ-TAGLE, Mariela I.

4461. RUKEYSER, Muriel
        "For My Son." _Chelsea_ (42/43) 84, p. 223.
        "Sun Stone" (Excerpts, tr. of Octavio Paz).
        Chelsea (42/43) 84, p. 50-51.

4462. RUMENS, Carol
        "His Story." _Argo_ (5:3) 84, p. 26.
        "How to Live Here." _Argo_ (5:3) 84, p. 27.

4463. RUNCIMAN, Lex
        "Fairmoor." _ColEng_ (46:6) O 84, p. 570.
        "Family Albums." _CharR_ (10:1) Spr 84, p. 46.
        "Furniture." _ColEng_ (46:6) O 84, p. 571.
        "Nostalgia." _CharR_ (10:1) Spr 84, p. 47.
        "Touring Arizona." _CharR_ (10:1) Spr 84, p. 48.

4464. RUSH, Jerry
        "A Five Minute Morning." _MalR_ (68) Je 84, p. 86.
        "Plastic Curtains." _MalR_ (68) Je 84, p. 87.

4465. RUSH, Jerry M.
        "The Everyday Absence of Event." _Grain_ (12:4) N
        84, p. 42-46.
        "Letters We Might Have Written: Our Shadow Selves."
        Grain (12:4) N 84, p. 41.
        "The Walls of His Walking." _Grain_ (12:4) N 84, p.
        40.

4466. RUSS, Lawrence
        "How We Are Fooled." _GreenfR_ (11:1/2) Sum-Aut 83,
        p. 129-130.

4467. RUSS, Lee
        "Good Morning." _NegC_ (4:3) Sum 84, p. 114-115.

4468. RUSSAKOFF, Molly
        "Lament of the Conductor." _ParisR_ (26:91) Spr 84,
        p. 91.

4469. RUSSELL, CarolAnn
        "Things We Talk About at Home." _OhioR_ (32) 84, p.
        10.

4470. RUSSELL, Frank
        "Another Little World." _MemphisSR_ (4:2) Spr 84,
        p. 21.
        "Asking Too Much." _Poem_ (50) Mr 84, p. 22.
        "Back Home." _GreenfR_ (12:1/2) Sum-Aut 84, p. 127.
        "Dear Exquisite Fingers in My Gut." _GreenfR_
        (12:1/2) Sum-Aut 84, p. 125.
        "Drunken Wood." _GreenfR_ (12:1/2) Sum-Aut 84, p. 126.
        "O Children of Wichita!" _NewL_ (50:4) Sum 84, p. 29.
        "Quitting the Script." _MemphisSR_ (5:1) Aut 84, p.
        24.

"Salt of the Void." GreenfR (12:1/2) Sum-Aut 84,
   p. 127-128.
"Simply Cicadas." GreenfR (12:1/2) Sum-Aut 84, p.
   128.
"Simply Cicadas." Poem (50) Mr 84, p. 21.
"What Uncle Wants." MemphisSR (4:2) Spr 84, p. 48.

4471. RUSSELL, Hilary
      "Chub Newman's Bodywork." StoneC (11:3/4) Spr-Sum
         84, p. 34.

4472. RUSSELL, John A.
      "Walking through This Green Valley." Pig (12) 84,
         p. 79.

4473. RUSSELL, R. F. Gillian (Harding)
      "The Existentialist." Grain (12:4) N 84, p. 37-39.

4474. RUSSELL, Timothy
      "The Fifty Things Wrong with This Picture." WestB
         (14) 84, p. 8.
      "In Esse." WestB (15) 84, p. 41.
      "In Posse." WestB (15) 84, p. 39.
      "In Rem." WestB (15) 84, p. 40.
      "Inertia." WestB (14) 84, p. 9.
      "Stars and Stripes." WestB (14) 84, p. 10.

4475. RUSSELL, Tony
      "Bru Mike." PoetryCR (6:1) Aut 84, p. 14.

4476. RUSSO, John Paul
      "Arsenio" (tr. of Eugenio Montale). DenQ (19:1)
         Spr 84, p. 109-110.

4477. RUTER, Allan J.
      "1964: The Hardy Boys." EngJ (73:3) Mr 84, p. 107.

4478. RUTSALA, Vern
      "Darkening World." YaleR (73:2) Wint 84, p. 304-305.
      "Going to England." Stand (25:2) Spr 84, p. 53.
      "Lela and Others" (For Kirsten). Poetry (143:4)
         Ja 84, p. 201-203.
      "Sunday Drives." PoetryE (15) Aut 84, p. 51-52.
      "Uncle." Poetry (143:4) Ja 84, p. 203-204.
      "The Windowsill over the Sink." Atlantic (254:2)
         Ag 84, p. 88.

4479. RYAN, Dennis
      "Hokkaido, Road to the North Sea." Poem (51) Mr
         [i.e. Jl] 84, p. 10-11.
      "A One-Armed Man." Poem (51) Mr [i.e. Jl] 84, p.
         8-9.

4480. RYAN, Kay
      "Black Purse/White Gloves." Poem (51) Mr [i.e.
         Jl] 84, p. 47.
      "The Brain." Poem (51) Mr [i.e. Jl] 84, p. 48.
      "Bridge." StoneC (12:1/2) Aut-Wint 84, p. 30.
      "The Egyptians." Poetry (144:2) My 84, p. 88.
      "Marianne Moore Announces Lunch." Poetry (144:2)

My 84, p. 87.
"Morning Sun" (oil, 1952, Edward Hopper). MidAR
    (4:2) Aut 84, p. 117.
"Necessary Music." SmPd (21:2) Spr 84, p. 31.
"To Speak of Need." NewOR (11:2) Sum 84, p. 85.
"Why Insects Will Outlast Us." Poem (51) Mr [i.e.
    Jl] 84, p. 49.

4481. RYAN, Margaret
    "Blue Luna Coombs." Amelia (1:2) O 84, p. 69-70.

4482. RYAN, Michael
    "Consider a Move." Tendril (18, special issue)
        84, p. 210-211.
    "Larkinesque." Poetry (143:5) F 84, p. 266-267.
    "Presences." NewEngR (7:2) Wint 84, p. 232.
    "Tanglewood" (For H). Poetry (143:5) F 84, p. 267-
        268.
    "This Is Why." NewRep (191:2) 9 Jl 84, p. 34.
    "Winter Drought" (P. K., 1957-1977). Poetry
        (143:5) F 84, p. 269-270.

4483. RYDER, Lyn C.
    "Wild Dog." SnapD (7:1) Aut 83, p. 23.

4484. RYERSON, Alice
    "Calling-People." BelPoJ (35:2) Wint 84-85, p. 24.
    "The Double Solitude." SpoonRQ (9:4) Aut 84, p. 31.

4485. RYOMEI
    "He died from the fire of his own troops" (senryu).
        NewL (50:2/3) Wint-Spr 84, p. 230.

4486. RZEZAK, E. Ruth
    "Reencuentro." Mairena (6:17) Aut 84, p. 90.

4487. RZEZAK, Ruth
    "Conexion." Mairena (5:14) Aut 83, p. 88.

S., L. C.: See L. C. S.

S., R. J.: See R. J. S.

4488. SABA, Umberto
    "L'Arboscello." NeqC (4:4) Aut 84, p. 59.
    "Autobiographia, 3." Chelsea (42/43) 84, p. 110.
    "The Sapling" (tr. by Will Wells). NeqC (4:4) Aut
        84, p. 58.

4489. SACERIO GARI, Enrique
    "Se despierta un reflejo niuyorquino." Areíto
        (9:36) 84, p. 106.

SACHIKO, Yoshihara: See YOSHIHARA, Sachiko

4490. SACKS, Gustavo Rafael
    "El Cafe." Mairena (5:13) Spr 83, p. 66.

4491. SACKS, Peter
    "Giraffe." Nat (238:25) 30 Je 84, p. 809.

"Transvaal: Under Frost." PartR (51:3) 84, p. 389-
390.

4492. SADOFF, Ira
"After Being Depressed by a Bad Book of Philosophy,
I Sit beside a Total Stranger at a Horror
Movie." PoetryNW (25:3) Aut 84, p. 30-31.
"Honduras." NewEngR (6:4) Sum 84, p. 532.
"I'm Tired of the Old Oedipal Dramas." PoetryNW
(25:3) Aut 84, p. 31-32.
"Les Malheurs des Immortels" (Selections: Between
the Two Poles of Politeness. The Modesty Well in
View. Tr. of Paul Eluard). Chelsea (42/43) 84,
p. 292.
"Memorial Days" (for Yvette and Robert Sadoff).
Shen (35:4) 84, p. 62-63.
"Nazis." NewEngR (6:4) Sum 84, p. 530-531.
"Notre Dame (1909)" (after Francis Jammes).
NewEngR (6:4) Sum 84, p. 533.
"The Threat of Another New England Winter and a
Faltering Economy Drives Me Deep into the
Woods." Agni (20) 84, p. 37-38.
"The Wooden Desk." Shen (35:4) 84, p. 63-64.
"Zinfandel." Antaeus (52) Apr 84, p. 74-75.

SAEED, Abu: See ABU SAEED

4493. SAFIR, Natale
"The Dance." SmPd (21:2) Spr 84, p. 31.

4494. SAGAN, Miriam
"Buddha Hall with Fog and Bride." StoneC (11:3/4)
Spr-Sum 84, p. 11.
"A Different Eden." AmerPoR (13:3) My-Je 84, p. 44.

4495. SAGEL, Jim
"Homeland" (tr. by the author). OroM (2:3/4,
issue 7/8) 84, p. 31.
"Patria." OroM (2:3/4, issue 7/8) 84, p. 30.
"Treaty." OroM (2:3/4, issue 7/8) 84, p. 14-15.

SAGUIER, Ruben Bareiro: See BAREIRO SAGUIER, Ruben

4496. SAID, Amina
"En d'autres temps l'île." PoetryCR (6:2) Wint
84-85, p. 8.
"Jeux de mirages." PoetryCR (6:2) Wint 84-85, p. 8.

SAINT: See also ST. (filed as spelled)

4497. SAKAKI, Nanao
"An Abandoned Farmhouse." GreenfR (11:1/2) Sum-
Aut 83, p. 185.

4498. SALAMON, Joanna
"Ballad for a Solonaut" (to the memory of Przemek
Golba, tr. by Marianna Abrahamowicz). Iowa
(14:2) Spr-Sum 84, p. 195.

4499. SALANGA, Alfredo Navarro
      "Barber." <u>Dandel</u> (11:1) Spr-Sum 84, p. 55-56.
      "Death Is No Rectangle." <u>Dandel</u> (11:1) Spr-Sum
          84, p. 59-60.
      "Letter to an Old Friend." <u>Dandel</u> (11:1) Spr-Sum
          84, p. 57-58.

4500. SALAS, Horacio
      "Los Relojes." <u>Mairena</u> (6:18) 84, p. 115.

4501. SALASIN, R.
      "Japanese Garden." <u>Abraxas</u> (29/30) 84, p. 9.
      "Only one day you notice." <u>MinnR</u> (N.S. 23) Aut
          84, p. 37.
      "Poem on a Line by Po Chu-Yi." <u>HangL</u> (45) Spr 84,
          p. 57.
      "Poem on the Eve of War." <u>HangL</u> (45) Spr 84, p.
          58-59.
      "Two Poems on Esther Williams." <u>Abraxas</u> (29/30)
          84, p. 8-9.

4502. SALASIN, Robert
      "My mother is a Democrat." <u>Tele</u> (19) 83, p. 79.
      "Oh! An orchid." <u>Tele</u> (19) 83, p. 78.
      "Poem on Two Lines from Rimbaud." <u>Tele</u> (19) 83,
          p. 78.
      "This is the great illumination." <u>Tele</u> (19) 83,
          p. 79.

4503. SALAZAR, Deborah
      "Sisters set the table." <u>SouthernHR</u> (18:1) Wint
          84, p. 63.
      "Two Sonnets" (For Carrie). <u>SouthernHR</u> (18:1)
          Wint 84, p. 63.
      "You quit speaking in our parents' Spanish."
          <u>SouthernHR</u> (18:1) Wint 84, p. 63.

4504. SALERNO, Salvatore
      "A Potter Has His Say." <u>SoCaR</u> (16:2) Spr 84, p.
          14-15.

4505. SALES, Miguel
      "Calculation of Probabilities" (To Julio Morejon,
          tr. by Maria Cignarella and Robert M.
          Glickstein). <u>Confr</u> (27/28) 84, p. 37.
      "Profile of Winter" (tr. by Maria Cignarella and
          Robert M. Glickstein). <u>Confr</u> (27/28) 84, p. 38.

4506. SALINAS, Judy
      "All's Fair: In Response to Locklin's 'The Women
          Have Won'." <u>WormR</u> (24:4, issue 96) 84, p. 132-
          133.

4507. SALINAS, Luis Omar
      "Among the Flowers." <u>SenR</u> (14:1) 84, p. 43.
      "Until Daybreak." <u>SenR</u> (14:1) 84, p. 44.

4508. SALINAS, Mercedes
      "Drum Beat." <u>PikeF</u> (6) Aut 84, p. 20.
      "Smile." <u>PikeF</u> (6) Aut 84, p. 20.

4509. SALINAS, Pedro
"The Truth of Two" (tr. by Harry Thomas). AmerPoR
(13:2) Mr-Ap 84, p. 6.

4510. SALINERO, Amelia
"Poemas del Horizonte." Mairena (6:17) Aut 84, p.
51-52.

4511. SALISBURY, Ralph
"Cherokee Ghost Story: My Father's." NeqC (4:1)
Wint 84, p. 102.
"Out of This World." NowestR (22:1/2) 84, p. 142.
"The War One Wins." NewL (51:1) Aut 84, p. 95.

SALLE, Peter la: See LaSALLE, Peter

4512. SALLIS, James
"Albert." Bogg (52) 84, p. 12.
"Corrida " SmPd (21:1) Wint 84, p. 12.
"A Little Imagination." Confr (27/28) 84, p. 198.
"Revisions." SoDakR (22:3) Aut 84, p. 25.
"The Science of Poetry." CharR (10:1) Spr 84, p. 51.
"Temptation of Silence." SoDakR (22:3) Aut 84, p.
26-27.

4513. SALTER, Mary Jo
"Among the Ningyo." NewRep (190:8) 27 F 84, p. 36.
"Expectancy" (Japan Baptist Hospital, Kyoto).
NewYorker (60:28) 27 Ag 84, p. 40.
"Luminary." Nat (239:10) 6 O 84, p. 322.
"Mary Cazzato, 1921." YaleR (74:1) Aut 84, p. 25-27.
"On Reading a Writer's Letters." GrandS (3:4) Sum
84, p. 103.
"Shisendō" (The Hall of the Hermit-Poets).
GrandS (3:4) Sum 84, p. 104-107.

4514. SALTMAN, Benjamin
"The Russian Movie." Hudson (37:2) Sum 84, p. 281.

4515. SAMPSON, Dennis
"Bite Down on the Azalea." SoDakR (22:3) Aut 84,
p. 68-69.

4516. SAMS, Jeffrey
"On Speaking with a Dark Woman." Open24 (3) 84,
p. 30.

4517. SAMSON, Sue
"After Picking Dogwood." PoeticJ (6) 84, p. 17.
"Before Dawn." PoeticJ (5) 84, p. 17.
"Black on White." PoeticJ (6) 84, p. 32.
"Night Driving." PoeticJ (3) 83, p. 10.

SAN MARTIN VIEYRA, Mario Antonio: See VIEYRA, Antonio

4518. SANAZARO, Leonard
"Laundry Day." CentR (28:4/29:1) Aut 84-Wint 85,
p. 78-79.
"Then." KanQ (16:4) Aut 84, p. 162.

4519. SANCHEZ, Carmen
       "En la Sombra." Mairena (6:17) Aut 84, p. 91.

SANCHEZ, Francisco Feliciano: See FELICIANO SANCHEZ,
       Francisco

SANCHEZ, Jesús Francisco Feliciano: See FELICIANO SANCHEZ,
       Jesús Francisco

SANCHEZ, Roberto Hernandez: See HERNANDEZ SANCHEZ, Roberto

4520. SANCHEZ, Sonia
       "For Unborn Malcolms." Stepping Wint 83, p. 17.
       "Malcolm." Stepping Wint 83, p. 16.

4521. SANCHEZ LEON, Abelardo
       "Paginas Sueltas" (fragmento). Mairena (6:18) 84,
       p. 97.

4522. SANDEEN, Ernest
       "Interrogation." Poetry (143:4) Ja 84, p. 193-194.
       "Seventy-Fourth Birthday." Poetry (143:4) Ja 84,
       p. 195.
       "Translating the Latin." Poetry (143:4) Ja 84, p.
       195-196.

4523. SANDERS, Mark
       "After Snow, Work." Northeast (Series 3:18) 84,
       p. 13.
       "Winter Fields." KanQ (16:1/2) Wint-Spr 84, p. 196.

4524. SANDRY, Ellen S.
       "Image of Age." SanFPJ (6:3) 84, p. 17.
       "A Question of Survival." SanFPJ (6:1) 84, p. 61.

4525. SANDY, Stephen
       "Command Performance" (for Robert Lowell). MichQR
       (23:1) Wint 84, p. 95-96.
       "Expecting Fathers." Salm (63/64) Spr-Sum 84, p.
       250.
       "Figure on a Wooded Path." Poetry (144:4) Jl 84,
       p. 222-223.
       "Forbidden City." Salm (63/64) Spr-Sum 84, p. 246.
       "Letter from Stoney Creek." Salm (63/64) Spr-Sum
       84, p. 249.
       "Man in the Open Air." Poetry (144:4) Jl 84, p. 222.
       "Mrs. Gale." Salm (63/64) Spr-Sum 84, p. 247-248.
       "A Sketch: New Haven." Salm (63/64) Spr-Sum 84,
       p. 248.

4526. SANER, Reg
       "Curve." TarRP (24:1) Aut 84, p. 15.
       "Depot." WestB (15) 84, p. 76.
       "Guidelines." Poetry (145:3) D 84, p. 159-160.
       "In This Snapshot of Nuptial Clouds." TarRP
       (24:1) Aut 84, p. 16.
       "Stroke." GeoR (38:1) Spr 84, p. 163.
       "Vespers." GeoR (38:1) Spr 84, p. 172-173.
       "Where the Desert Knows One or Two Word." OhioR
       (32) 84, p. 44.

"Where the Sky's Always Strongest." OhioR (32)
    84, p. 45.
"The Wisdom of the Ages." WestB (15) 84, p. 77.

4527. SANFIELD, Steve
    "Inventory." GreenfR (11:1/2) Sum-Aut 83, p. 183.
    "Preparing for Winter." GreenfR (11:1/2) Sum-Aut
        83, p. 184.
    "The Quality of Life." GreenfR (11:1/2) Sum-Aut
        83, p. 183-184.
    "Summer Report." GreenfR (11:1/2) Sum-Aut 83, p.
        184.

4528. SANFORD, Christy Sheffield
    "The Honeymoon(s). YellowS (10) Spr 84, p. 25.

4529. SANGE, Sally Harris
    "Epithalamium." KenR (NS 6:1) Wint 84, p. 71-73.

4530. SANGER, Richard
    "A Body Is Man's Best Friend" (tr. of Jaime Gil de
        Biedma). TriQ (59) Wint 84, p. 203.
    "Le Prince d'Aquitaine a la Tour Abolie" (tr. of
        Jaime Gil de Biedma). TriQ (59) Wint 84, p. 204.

4531. SANGUINETI, Edoardo
    "Hell's Purgatory" (Selections: 14-17, tr. by
        Baxter Hathaway). Chelsea (42/43) 84, p. 153-155.

SANJURJO, José María Gomez: See GOMEZ SANJURJO, José María

4532. SANSIRENE, Teresa
    "Esos Dias de Lluvia." LindLM (3:2/4) Ap-D 84, p.
        14.
    "Paraiso del Infierno." LindLM (3:2/4) Ap-D 84,
        p. 14.

4533. SANTANA, Lázaro
    "Family Chronicle" (tr. by Reginald Gibbons).
        TriQ (59) Wint 84, p. 215.
    "P.S." (tr. by Reginald Gibbons). TriQ (59) Wint
        84, p. 216.

4534. SANTI, Enrico Mario
    "Cinco Ejercicios Barrocos." LindLM (3:1) Ja-Mr
        84, p. 11.

SANTIAGO, Beatriz Mayté: See MAYTE SANTIAGO, Beatriz

SANTIAGO, José Manuel Torres: See TORRES SANTIAGO, José
    Manuel

SANTIAGO, Sabino Méndez: See MÉNDEZ SANTIAGO, Sabino

SANTIAGO, William Mena: See MENA SANTIAGO, William

4535. SANTIAGO BERMUDEZ, Ariel
    "Pasaporte de Ida." Mairena (6:17) Aut 84, p. 91.

4536. SANTIAGO MERLO, Antonio
    "Las Alas de la Inconciencia en la Decepcion."
    Mairena (6:17) Aut 84, p. 88.

4537. SANTIAGO MORALES, Emérito
    "Retorno." Mairena (5:13) Spr 83, p. 108-109.

SANTISTEBAN, Ricardo Silva: See SILVA SANTISTEBAN, Ricardo

SANTOS, Francisco Morales: See MORALES SANTOS, Francisco

4538. SANTOS, Sherod
    "Death." NewYorker (60:21) 9 Jl 84, p. 40.
    "Driving out of the Keys." Antaeus (52) Apr 84,
        p. 40-41.
    "Goodbye." QW (18) Spr-Sum 84, p. 45.
    "Photograph of My Father" (Public Gardens, Berlin,
        1948). ParisR (26:94) Wint 84, p. 177.

4539. SANTOS SILVA, Loreina
    "La noche, un zarpazo gigante." Mairena (5:13)
        Spr 83, p. 109.
    "Porque el mar como la hembra." Mairena (5:13)
        Spr 83, p. 109-110.

4540. SAPIA, Yvonne
    "Dirty Pictures." CalQ (25) Aut 84, p. 68.
    "The Possibility of Heaven" (for Joan, Eve of Saint
        Agnes Contest Winners III). NegC (4:1) Wint
        84, p. 22.

4541. SAPINKOPF, Lisa
    "Assassination of Simonetta Vespucci" (tr. of
        Sophia de Mello Breyner Andresen). NewOR
        (11:2) Sum 84, p. 73.
    "Give me the sun of the blue waters, of the
        spheres" (tr. of Sophia de Mello Breyner
        Andresen). Mund (14:2) 84, p. 93.
    "I sent the boat out after the wind" (tr. of Sophia
        de Mello Breyner Andresen). Mund (14:2) 84, p.
        95.
    "Luminous the abolished days" (tr. of Sophia de
        Mello Breyner Andresen). Mund (14:2) 84, p. 93.
    "On the beaches, which are the white faces of dead
        fleets" (tr. of Sophia de Mello Breyner
        Andresen). Mund (14:2) 84, p. 93.
    "Only then did I leave my darkness" (tr. of Sophia
        de Mello Breyner Andresen). Mund (14:2) 84, p.
        95.
    "Our fingers opened closed hands" (tr. of Sophia de
        Mello Breyner Andresen). Mund (14:2) 84, p. 95.
    "Poem of geometry and silence" (tr. of Sophia de
        Mello Breyner Andresen). Mund (14:2) 84, p. 93.
    "The Summer of Night" (Excerpted from Words in
        Stone, tr. of Yves Bonnefoy). MissR (37/38,
        13:1/2) Aut 84, p. 83-87.
    "Women by the Seashore" (Excerpted from Coral,
        tr. of Sophia de Mello Breyner Andresen).
        MissR (37/38, 13:1/2) Aut 84, p. 76.

4542. SAPPHO
"Eros has my uprooted wits" (Sappho 47) (tr. by
Johanna H. Prins). AmerPoR (13:2) Mr-Ap 84, p.
37.
"Eros makes me feel weak in the knees" (Sappho 130)
(tr. by Johanna H. Prins). AmerPoR (13:2) Mr-
Ap 84, p. 37.
"Like a hyacinth in the mountains" (Sappho 105c)
(tr. by Johanna H. Prins). AmerPoR (13:2) Mr-
Ap 84, p. 37.
"Some say an army of men on horse" (Sappho 16) (tr.
by Johanna H. Prins). AmerPoR (13:2) Mr-Ap 84,
p. 37.

4543. SARABIA, Gil
"A Change of Season." SanFPJ (6:1) 84, p. 41.
"The Second Apple." SanFPJ (6:1) 84, p. 41.

4544. SARAH, Robyn
"Anyone Skating on That Middle Ground." MalR (67)
F 84, p. 54-55.

4545. SARGENT, Elizabeth
"Throughout 10, 000 worlds" (from the Sanskrit).
LittleBR (4:4) Sum 84, p. 52.

4546. SARIKAHYA, Teoman
"The Girl Grows Smaller" (tr. by Talat Sait
Halman). NewRena (6:1, #18) Spr 84, p. 71.
"Kuculur Kiz." NewRena (6:1, #18) Spr 84, p. 70.

4547. SASANOV, Catherine
"4 Brazilian Lives - No Food." Kayak (64) My 84,
p. 13-15.
"Competition." WebR (9:1) Spr 84, p. 36.
"Nijinsky's Last Word Being 'Edison'." WebR (9:1)
Spr 84, p. 35.

4548. SATO, Hiroaki
"Again, alone" (tr. of Kenji Miyazawa). Tele (19)
83, p. 34.
"Arms spread" (tr. of Kenji Miyazawa). Tele (19)
83, p. 36.
"As I move away from the Bunsen burner" (tr. of
Kenji Miyazawa). Tele (19) 83, p. 35.
"At daybreak" (tr. of Kenji Miyazawa). Tele (19)
83, p. 36.
"August 1919 Lamenting Dr. Ishimaru's Death" (tr.
of Kenji Miyazawa). Tele (19) 83, p. 36.
"Because sparklingly" (tr. of Kenji Miyazawa).
Tele (19) 83, p. 36.
"Because the flames" (tr. of Kenji Miyazawa).
Tele (19) 83, p. 34.
"Cobalt suffering stagnates" (tr. of Kenji
Miyazawa). Tele (19) 83, p. 35.
"Early Poems in Tanka Form" (Selections, tr. of
Kenji Miyazawa). Tele (19) 83, p. 34-36.
"Far-off mountains etched at back" (tr. of Kenji
Miyazawa). Tele (19) 83, p. 35.
"Frost-cloudy" (tr. of Kenji Miyazawa). Tele (19)

83, p. 35.
"In the autumn wind" (tr. of Kenji Miyazawa).
    Tele (19) 83, p. 34.
"Kashiwa Field" (tr. of Kenji Miyazawa). Tele
    (19) 83, p. 36.
"My temple felt icy" (tr. of Kenji Miyazawa).
    Tele (19) 83, p. 37.
"The night rain half-damaged" (tr. of Kenji
    Miyazawa). Tele (19) 83, p. 34.
"Out of the navy blue" (tr. of Kenji Miyazawa).
    Tele (19) 83, p. 35.
"Park" (tr. of Kenji Miyazawa). Tele (19) 83, p. 36.
"Reflected on the wings" (tr. of Kenji Miyazawa).
    Tele (19) 83, p. 35.
"Right below a nickel cloud" (tr. of Kenji
    Miyazawa). Tele (19) 83, p. 36.
"The rock cliff" (tr. of Kenji Miyazawa). Tele
    (19) 83, p. 35.
"Seven Forests" (tr. of Kenji Miyazawa). Tele
    (19) 83, p. 35.
"These pine trees on this street" (tr. of Kenji
    Miyazawa). Tele (19) 83, p. 37.
"Through the night" (tr. of Kenji Miyazawa). Tele
    (19) 83, p. 36.
"What do I eat things for?" (tr. of Kenji
    Miyazawa). Tele (19) 83, p. 34.
"Winter Sketches" (Selections, tr. of Kenji
    Miyazawa). Tele (19) 83, p. 37.

4549. SATTERFIELD, Ben
    "Spelling." Swallow (3) 84, p. 97.

4550. SATTERFIELD, Ellen
    "Disillusionment" (DeKalb County High Schools
    Literary Award Winners: Third Place--Poetry).
    DekalbLAJ (17:1/2) 84, p. 153.

4551. SAULTER, Bea
    "Hub-Bub in the Kitchen." PoeticJ (7) 84, p. 21.

4552. SAUNDERS, Josephine
    "One Thing Following Another." NewYorker (60:14)
    21 My 84, p. 40.

4553. SAUNDERS, Linda
    "Shrunken Head." Stand (25:1) Wint 83-84, p. 65.

4554. SAVAGE, Gail
    "In April--In Iowa." SpoonRQ (9:2) Spr 84, p. 34.

4555. SAVAGE, Tom
    "Bookkeeper's Son." Tele (19) 83, p. 39.
    "The Crush of Age." Tele (19) 83, p. 39.
    "Funeral March for a Parrot." LittleM (14:3) 84,
        p. 53.
    "Halloween Poem." Tele (19) 83, p. 40.
    "The Mortar Remarks." Tele (19) 83, p. 38.
    "Out Takes." LittleM (14:3) 84, p. 53.
    "Preparatory Rite for a Celebration" (For John
        Richard and Gene Stilp). Abraxas (31/32) 84,

p. 62.
"Wiping the Pavement Off Yr Shoulder." <u>Tele</u> (19)
83, p. 40.
"With Barrault in Venezuela." <u>Tele</u> (19) 83, p. 38.

4556. SAVARD, Jeannine
"Shadow As an Article of Faith." <u>Telescope</u> (3:2)
Spr 84, p. 17.
"Who Dance and Sing" (for my daughter). <u>AntR</u>
(42:3) Sum 84, p. 322.

4557. SAVOIE, Terry
"Farm Auction: Muscatine County, Iowa." <u>BlueBldgs</u>
(7) 84, p. 28.
"Nineteen." <u>Ploughs</u> (10:1) 84, p. 137-138.
"Requited Love." <u>BlueBldgs</u> (7) 84, p. 18.

4558. SAVORY, Elaine
"To a Man after My Own Heart" (for B.). <u>NegC</u>
(4:3) Sum 84, p. 110-111.

4559. SAVRE, Joyce
"I Believe This Is the Home of Georgia O'Keeffe."
<u>MinnR</u> (N.S. 23) Aut 84, p. 88-90.

4560. SAVREN, Shelley
"Packing." <u>PoeticJ</u> (5) 84, p. 3.

4561. SCALAPINO, Leslie
"That They Were at the Beach--Aeolotropic Series."
<u>Epoch</u> (33:2) Spr-Sum 84, p. 197-207.

4562. SCAMMELL, Michael
"Open-Air Concert" (tr. of Veno Taufer). <u>Vis</u> (14)
84, p. 15.

4563. SCANLON, Larry
"Double Shift As an Act of Landscape." <u>MinnR</u>
(N.S. 22) Spr 84, p. 25-26.

4564. SCANLON, Leone
"Allhallows." <u>NegC</u> (4:4) Aut 84, p. 10.

4565. SCANNELL, Edward James
"Astronomy." <u>WebR</u> (9:2) Wint 85, p. 93.

4566. SCARBORO, Ann Armstrong
"Golden Relection of the Sea" (tr. of Jocelyn
Valverde). <u>ConcPo</u> (17:2) Aut 84, p. 136.
"Soweto" (for James Mange, condemned to death, tr.
of Jocelyn Valverde). <u>ConcPo</u> (17:2) Aut 84, p.
135.

4567. SCARBROUGH, George
"Address." <u>SpiritSH</u> (50) Aut-Wint 84, p. 69.
"Aftermath." <u>SpiritSH</u> (50) Aut-Wint 84, p. 19-20.
"Dedication to the Book." <u>SpiritSH</u> (50) Aut-Wint
84, p. 3-6.
"The God Hunter." <u>SpiritSH</u> (50) Aut-Wint 84, p.
55-57.

"Hansel in Old Age." SpiritSH (50) Aut-Wint 84,
    p. 57-59.
"Impasse." SpiritSH (50) Aut-Wint 84, p. 12-18.
"Job, a Verse Play." SpiritSH (50) Aut-Wint 84,
    p. 6-11.
"John James Audubon: A Reverie" (for David Rogers).
    SpiritSH (50) Aut-Wint 84, p. 49-54.
"Leathers." SpiritSH (50) Aut-Wint 84, p. 68.
"Madness Maddened." SpiritSH (50) Aut-Wint 84, p.
    27-42.
"Matins." SpiritSH (50) Aut-Wint 84, p. 70.
"Metamorphosis." SpiritSH (50) Aut-Wint 84, p. 20-
    21.
"Moving Day." SpiritSH (50) Aut-Wint 84, p. 43-45.
"Order." SpiritSH (50) Aut-Wint 84, p. 23-24.
"Still Life." SpiritSH (50) Aut-Wint 84, p. 21-22.
"Sunday School Picnic." SpiritSH (50) Aut-Wint
    84, p. 66-67.
"Tenantry." SpiritSH (50) Aut-Wint 84, p. 24-25.
"To a Woman Seeking a Position" (After the
    Chinese). SpiritSH (50) Aut-Wint 84, p. 18.
"Troll Poem." SpiritSH (50) Aut-Wint 84, p. 45-49.
"Variations on a Blue Theme" (For Wallace Stevens).
    SpiritSH (50) Aut-Wint 84, p. 60-65.
"Victory Song." SpiritSH (50) Aut-Wint 84, p. 26.

4568. SCATES, Maxine
    "A Boat." AmerPoR (13:4) Jl-Ag 84, p. 45.
    "The Orchard." AmerPoR (13:4) Jl-Ag 84, p. 45.

4569. SCHAEFFER, Susan Fromberg
    "Alphabet." Chelsea (42/43) 84, p. 253-255.
    "Loss." KanQ (16:3) Sum 84, p. 50-51.
    "A Walk in the Woods." NewL (50:4) Sum 84, p. 18-19.

4570. SCHAFER, R. Murray
    "Smoke (a Novel)" (detail). CapilR (31) 84, p. 49.

4571. SCHANEN, Peggy
    "Ben W." Northeast (Series 3:18) 84, p. 27.
    "Bill J." Northeast (Series 3:18) 84, p. 25.
    "Crossroads." Northeast (Series 3:18) 84, p. 21-31.
    "Danny R." Northeast (Series 3:18) 84, p. 29.
    "John D." Northeast (Series 3:18) 84, p. 28.
    "Katie J." Northeast (Series 3:18) 84, p. 24.
    "Lou B." Northeast (Series 3:18) 84, p. 26.
    "The Room." Northeast (Series 3:18) 84, p. 30.
    "The Street." Northeast (Series 3:18) 84, p. 23.

4572. SCHARTNER, Adelaide
    "A Softer Touch." WritersL (1) 84, p. 23.

4573. SCHECHTER, Robert
    "Almost Singing." PoetryE (15) Aut 84, p. 59-60.

4574. SCHECHTER, Ruth Lisa
    "Who's Afraid of Maurice Schwartz?" GreenfR
        (11:3/4) Wint-Spr 84, p. 141-142.

4575. SCHECHTER, Toby
"I Keep House." <u>LittleM</u> (14:3) 84, p. 16.
"Separation." <u>LittleM</u> (14:3) 84, p. 16.

4576. SCHEELE, Roy
"Advent." <u>ChrC</u> (101:38) 5 D 84, p. 1142.
"At the Drought's Height." <u>SouthernHR</u> (18:4) Aut
84, p. 325.
"Corot's Clouds." <u>PraS</u> (58:2) Sum 84, p. 80-81.
"The Gap in the Cedar" (In memory of my father).
<u>Peb</u> (23) 84, p. 55.
"Househunting." <u>PraS</u> (58:2) Sum 84, p. 82-84.
"Lightning Bugs." <u>GreenfR</u> (12:1/2) Sum-Aut 84, p.
153.
"Uncle Lou." <u>PraS</u> (58:2) Sum 84, p. 85.
"Upriver" (The Missouri). <u>PraS</u> (58:2) Sum 84, p. 81.

4577. SCHEER, Linda
"Aligi Sassu, Painter" (tr. of Rafael Alberti).
<u>QRL</u> (Poetry series 6, v. 25) 84, p. 66.
"Arthrocious (I)" (Sonnet IV, tr. of Rafael
Alberti). <u>QRL</u> (Poetry series 6, v. 25) 84, p. 56.
"Arthrocious (II)" (Sonnet V, tr. of Rafael
Alberti). <u>QRL</u> (Poetry series 6, v. 25) 84, p.
56-57.
"Autumn in Rome" (tr. of Rafael Alberti). <u>QRL</u>
(Poetry series 6, v. 25) 84, p. 33.
"Boredom" (Scenic poem, tr. of Rafael Alberti).
<u>QRL</u> (Poetry series 6, v. 25) 84, p. 36-37.
"Bruno Caruso, Etcher" (tr. of Rafael Alberti).
<u>QRL</u> (Poetry series 6, v. 25) 84, p. 65-66.
"Campo de'Fiori" (Sonnet IV, tr. of Rafael
Alberti). <u>QRL</u> (Poetry series 6, v. 25) 84, p. 13.
"Carlo Quattrucci Paints the Botanic Gardens" (tr.
of Rafael Alberti). <u>QRL</u> (Poetry series 6, v.
25) 84, p. 68-69.
"Corrado Cagli, Painter" (tr. of Rafael Alberti).
<u>QRL</u> (Poetry series 6, v. 25) 84, p. 71-72.
"Finally" (Sonnet VIII, tr. of Rafael Alberti).
<u>QRL</u> (Poetry series 6, v. 25) 84, p. 16.
"Free Verses, Scenes and Songs" (tr. of Rafael
Alberti). <u>QRL</u> (Poetry series 6, v. 25) 84, p. 18.
"Giuseppe Mazzullo, Sculptor" (tr. of Rafael
Alberti). <u>QRL</u> (Poetry series 6, v. 25) 84, p. 70.
"Guido Strazza, Painter" (In Search of Atlantis,
tr. of Rafael Alberti). <u>QRL</u> (Poetry series 6,
v. 25) 84, p. 67.
"I Enter Your Churches, Lord" (Sonnet III, tr. of
Rafael Alberti). <u>QRL</u> (Poetry series 6, v. 25)
84, p. 55.
"Is It a Crime?" (tr. of Rafael Alberti). <u>QRL</u>
(Poetry series 6, v. 25) 84, p. 32.
"It Would Be So Lovely" (tr. of Rafael Alberti).
<u>QRL</u> (Poetry series 6, v. 25) 84, p. 46.
"Love" (tr. of Rafael Alberti). <u>QRL</u> (Poetry
series 6, v. 25) 84, p. 25.
"Il Mascherone" (tr. of Rafael Alberti). <u>QRL</u>
(Poetry series 6, v. 25) 84, p. 19.
"Nocturne: Rome is empty, suddenly" (tr. of Rafael
Alberti). <u>QRL</u> (Poetry series 6, v. 25) 84, p. 44.

"Nocturne: The other night I saw" (tr. of Rafael
    Alberti). QRL (Poetry series 6, v. 25) 84, p. 24.
"Now Only" (Sonnet I, tr. of Rafael Alberti). QRL
    (Poetry series 6, v. 25) 84, p. 54.
"Pasquinade" (Sonnet IX, tr. of Rafael Alberti).
    QRL (Poetry series 6, v. 25) 84, p. 16-17.
"Poems with Names" (Written in Rome, tr. of Rafael
    Alberti). QRL (Poetry series 6, v. 25) 84, p.
    64-75.
"The Poet Begs in the Streets" (tr. of Rafael
    Alberti). QRL (Poetry series 6, v. 25) 84, p.
    62-63.
"Poetic Life" (Sonnet V, tr. of Rafael Alberti).
    QRL (Poetry series 6, v. 25) 84, p. 14.
"Prediction" (tr. of Rafael Alberti). QRL (Poetry
    series 6, v. 25) 84, p. 39.
"La Puttana Andaluza" (Scenic poem, tr. of Rafael
    Alberti). QRL (Poetry series 6, v. 25) 84, p.
    21-22.
"Roman Religious Art" (Question and plea of J.B.,
    Sonnet VI, tr. of Rafael Alberti). QRL (Poetry
    series 6, v. 25) 84, p. 14-15.
"Rome: Danger to Pedestrians" (tr. of Rafael
    Alberti, w. Brian Swann). QRL (Poetry series
    6, v. 25) 84, p. 1-75.
"Silent Dialogue with a Neighbor" (Scenic poem, tr.
    of Rafael Alberti). QRL (Poetry series 6, v.
    25) 84, p. 26-27.
"The Son" (Scenic poem, tr. of Rafael Alberti).
    QRL (Poetry series 6, v. 25) 84, p. 31-32.
"St. Peter's Basilica" (to José Miguel Velloso,
    tr. of Rafael Alberti). QRL (Poetry series 6,
    v. 25) 84, p. 29.
"Still on the subject of piss" (tr. of Rafael
    Alberti). QRL (Poetry series 6, v. 25) 84, p.
    28-29.
"Strophe for a Monument to the Heroes of the
    Resistance" (for Federico Brook, sculptor, tr.
    of Rafael Alberti). QRL (Poetry series 6, v.
    25) 84, p. 49.
"Take Pity, Lord!" (tr. of Rafael Alberti). QRL
    (Poetry series 6, v. 25) 84, p. 34.
"Ten Sonnets" (To Giuseppe Gioachino Belli, homage
    from a Spanish poet in Rome, tr. of Rafael
    Alberti, w. Brian Swann). QRL (Poetry series
    6, v. 25) 84, p. 11-17.
"The Two Friends" (Scenic poem, tr. of Rafael
    Alberti). QRL (Poetry series 6, v. 25) 84, p.
    42-43.
"Ugo Attardi, Painter" (Spain today, tr. of Rafael
    Alberti). QRL (Poetry series 6, v. 25) 84, p.
    64-65.
"Umberto Mastroianni, Sculptor" (tr. of Rafael
    Alberti). QRL (Poetry series 6, v. 25) 84, p.
    73-75.
"What to Do?" (Sonnet X, tr. of Rafael Alberti).
    QRL (Poetry series 6, v. 25) 84, p. 17.
"When I Leave Rome" (for Ignazio Delogu, tr. of
    Rafael Alberti). QRL (Poetry series 6, v. 25)
    84, p. 53.

"When Rome Is" (tr. of Rafael Alberti). QRL
    (Poetry series 6, v. 25) 84, p. 41.
"While I Sleep" (tr. of Rafael Alberti). QRL
    (Poetry series 6, v. 25) 84, p. 37.
"You Haven't Come to Rome to Dream" (tr. of Rafael
    Alberti). QRL (Poetry series 6, v. 25) 84, p. 52.

4578. SCHEERER, Constance
    "Country Woman." NewL (51:1) Aut 84, p. 42.
    "Crows." NewL (51:1) Aut 84, p. 41.
    "In the Museum." NewL (51:1) Aut 84, p. 40.
    "Salesman." NewL (51:1) Aut 84, p. 39.
    "Saying Grace." NewL (51:1) Aut 84, p. 40-41.

4579. SCHEIER, Libby
    "Assassin." Waves (13:1) Aut 84, p. 13.

4580. SCHELHAAS, David
    "Covert Reader." EngJ (73:6) O 84, p. 93.

4581. SCHELLING, Andrew
    "In the morning her girlfriends press her" (tr. of
        Murāri). YellowS (13) Wint 84, p. 28.
    "O neighbor, please keep an eye on my house" (tr.
        of Vidyā). YellowS (13) Wint 84, p. 29.
    "On makeshift bedding in the cucumber garden" (tr.
        of Vidyā). YellowS (13) Wint 84, p. 28.
    "A south wind stirs" (tr. of anonymous Sanskrit
        poem). YellowS (13) Wint 84, p. 28.
    "Tell me, Murala River" (tr. of Vidyā).
        YellowS (13) Wint 84, p. 29.
    "You mount repeatedly this playful woman's firm-set
        breasts" (tr. of Vācaspati). YellowS (13)
        Wint 84, p. 29.

SCHENDEL, Michel van: See Van SCHENDEL, Michel

4582. SCHEVILL, James
    "The Indian Mayor in Guatemala." Ploughs (10:1)
        84, p. 141.
    "Pirandello." MichQR (23:1) Wint 84, p. 31-32.
    "The Sound Magician" (After listening to a talk by
        Darrell De Vore). Ploughs (10:1) 84, p. 139-140.
    "Stunned Silence." Ploughs (10:1) 84, p. 142.

4583. SCHIFF, Jeff
    "At Random." Quarry (33:3) Sum 84, p. 33.
    "Summer Comes for the Maker." MalR (67) F 84, p.
        109.
    "Who's Keeping Score?" Quarry (33:3) Sum 84, p.
        33-34.
    "Work." MalR (67) F 84, p. 108.

4584. SCHILTZ, M.
    "The Cop" (for Mark). DekalbLAJ (20th Anniversary
        Issue) 84, p. 105-106.
    "One Way." DekalbLAJ (20th Anniversary Issue) 84,
        p. 106.

4585. SCHLEY, Jim
        "Recollect" (for Doc). BlueBldgs (8) 84?, p. 4.
        "Three Fires." BlueBldgs (8) 84?, p. 2-3.
        "Whistler." BlueBldgs (8) 84?, p. 5.

4586. SCHLOSS, David
        "Do Human Babies Need Stimulation, Air, Light,
          Nourishment, Love, etc.?" Shen (35:1) 83-84,
          p. 20-21.
        "A Face Transfigured by Love." OhioR (33) 84, p. 88.

4587. SCHLOSSER, Robert
        "Bangkok 1970." PoeticJ (4) 83, p. 29.
        "Bangkok 1979." PoeticJ (4) 83, p. 3.
        "From an Autumn Night on Skagit Flats." Sam
          (39:1, release 153) 84, p. 40.
        "Give Pause to Planetary Tilting." Sam (41:1,
          release 161) 84, p. 25.
        "Memorial Day 1984." Sam (41:2, release 162) 84
          or 85, p. 28.
        "Red Monkey." PoeticJ (2) 83, p. 34.
        "Sea of Cortez Impressions." PoeticJ (2) 83, p. 19.

4588. SCHMIDT, Jan
        "Changing Rhythms: After a Child Is Born." KanQ
          (16:4) Aut 84, p. 80.

4589. SCHMIDT, Jan Zlotnik
        "The Fall of Woman." Wind (14:51) 84, p. 43.
        "Journey with My Son." Poem (50) Mr 84, p. 12.
        "The Taste of the Sixties." Poem (50) Mr 84, p.
          10-11.

4590. SCHMIDT, Paul
        "The Bells of Orvieto" (tr. of Pier Paolo
          Pasolini). NewYRB (31:8) 10 My 84, p. 36.
        "Part of a Letter, to Young Codignola" (tr. of Pier
          Paolo Pasolini). NewYRB (31:18) 22 N 84, p. 47.

4591. SCHMIDT, Paulette
        "Horizon" (for Tristan Tzara, tr. of Philippe
          Soupault). MissouriR (7:3) 84, p. 16.
        "Let Old Fools Have the Floor" (tr. of Philippe
          Soupault). MissouriR (7:3) 84, p. 17.

4592. SCHMIDT, Steven
        "Killing Deer." Blueline (6:1) Sum-Aut 84, p. 36.

4593. SCHMITT, Cannon
        "Driving to Georgia." DekalbLAJ (20th Anniversary
          Issue) 84, p. 107-108.

4594. SCHMITZ, Dennis
        "The Apparatus." TriQ (60) Spr-Sum 84, p. 398.
        "Brand Loyalty." NowestR (22:1/2) 84, p. 44-45.
        "Eden." Field (31) Aut 84, p. 80-81.
        "Hunting." Field (31) Aut 84, p. 82-83.
        "Ladder." Field (30) Spr 84, p. 39-40.
        "State & Van Buren." TriQ (60) Spr-Sum 84, p. 397.
        "Thirteen." Field (30) Spr 84, p. 41.

4595. SCHNACKENBERG, Gjertrud
"Complaint." NewYorker (60:40) 19 N 84, p. 48.
"The Heavenly Feast" (Simone Weil, 1909-43).
NewYorker (60:31) 17 S 84, p. 48.
"Imaginary Prisons" (A version of Sleeping Beauty
in memory of C.W.R.). ParisR (26:94) Wint 84,
p. 66-78.
"The Painter to His Wife" (Based on the Self-
Portrait of Ivan Generalić, The School of
Naïve Painters, Hlebine, Yugoslavia).
NewYorker (60:36) 22 O 84, p. 50.

4596. SCHNEIDER, R. T.
"Wind Chill." KanQ (16:1/2) Wint-Spr 84, p. 180.

4597. SCHOEBERLEIN, Marion
"Needles." Confr (27/28) 84, p. 162.

4598. SCHOEMPERLEN, Diane
"What You Don't Know Won't Hurt You." PoetryCR
(5:4) Sum 84, p. 11.

4599. SCHOENBERGER, Nancy
"Audubon's Shrews." Antaeus (52) Apr 84, p. 83.
"October Poem: Baynard's Irises." SouthernR
(20:3) Sum 84, p. 597-598.
"Quiet and Getting Quieter." Ploughs (10:1) 84,
p. 143.
"Shiraz." SouthernR (20:3) Sum 84, p. 598-599.

4600. SCHOERKE, Meg
"Flight of Cranes on a Mountainous Landscape."
AmerS (53:2) Spr 84, p.182.

4601. SCHOFIELD, Paul
"Cloudy summer day." Amelia (1:2) O 84, p. 38.

4602. SCHOOLFIELD, George
"Earth Fragrance" (tr. of Halldis M. Vesaas, w.
Ronald Wakefield, P. J. Powers, and the author).
LitR (27:3) Spr 84, p. 305.

4603. SCHORR, David
"Magnesium Chloride." PortR (30:1) 84, p. 17-18.

4604. SCHOTT, Lynn Rigney
"Spring Training." NewYorker (60:6) 26 Mr 84, p. 54.

4605. SCHREIBER, Ron
"August 31 et Seq." Wind (14:50) 84, p. 45-47.
"The Landslide on Guilt Mountain." Tendril (17)
Wint 84, p. 158.
"New York City Weekend." Abraxas (29/30) 84, p. 64.

4606. SCHREIBMAN, Susan
"I Feel Like." Wind (14:52) 84, p. 44.
"It Was Like." PoetL (79:2) Sum 84, p. 95.
"The Next One." PoetL (79:2) Sum 84, p. 94.

4607. SCHROCK, Glenda
"Emil in the Private Nursing Home." Thrpny (17)
Spr 84, p. 6.

4608. SCHROEDER, Bethany
"Blackberry Winter." Poetry (145:2) N 84, p. 70-71.
"Spooner's Cove" (At Montana d'Oro). Poetry
(145:2) N 84, p. 71-72.

4609. SCHROEDER, Gary
"In Defense of a Barter System." KanQ (16:4) Aut
84, p. 96.

4610. SCHROEDER, Sandra
"Chain Reaction." PoetryNW (25:2) Sum 84, p. 47.
"The Poet's Version of Molloy's 'Dress for
Success'." CrabCR (2:1) Sum 84, p. 8-9.

4611. SCHULER, Robert
"Action Painting: Apple Orchard." SpoonRQ (9:1)
Wint 84, p. 45.
"After an Icestorm." SpoonRQ (9:1) Wint 84, p. 35.
"Alameda de las Pulgas." SpoonRQ (9:1) Wint 84,
p. 70.
"Around the World." SpoonRQ (9:1) Wint 84, p. 9.
"At Bisla his castle." SpoonRQ (9:1) Wint 84, p. 37.
"Berkeley: Summer, 1965." SpoonRQ (9:1) Wint 84,
p. 71.
"Blizzard." SpoonRQ (9:1) Wint 84, p. 39.
"Breakwater: the headlands above Mendocino" (for
James Ensor). SpoonRQ (9:1) Wint 84, p. 7-8.
"Carolyn." SpoonRQ (9:1) Wint 84, p. 22.
"Cranky Spanky's San Francisco Ritual." SpoonRQ
(9:1) Wint 84, p. 69.
"Danae" (painting, 1907-1908, by Gustav Klimt).
SpoonRQ (9:1) Wint 84, p. 30.
"Dream." SpoonRQ (9:1) Wint 84, p. 4.
"Dream." TarRP (24:1) Aut 84, p. 53.
"Early California Morning." SpoonRQ (9:1) Wint
84, p. 68.
"Easter Landscape." SpoonRQ (9:1) Wint 84, p. 19.
"Fall Poem for M." SpoonRQ (9:1) Wint 84, p. 25.
"Gathering Moon Salt." SpoonRQ (9:1) Wint 84, p. 23.
"Haying Day: August." SpoonRQ (9:1) Wint 84, p. 54.
"Heatwave: January, 1981." SpoonRQ (9:1) Wint 84,
p. 42.
"A History of Daisies." SpoonRQ (9:1) Wint 84, p.
50.
"A History of Tourism." SpoonRQ (9:1) Wint 84, p.
66.
"I want to write." SpoonRQ (9:1) Wint 84, p. 72.
"In James Ensor's 'Musique Russe'." SpoonRQ (9:1)
Wint 84, p. 6.
"In James Ensor's 'Musique Russe'." TarRP (24:1)
Aut 84, p. 53.
"In This Revery I Lose a Thousand Kalpas."
SpoonRQ (9:1) Wint 84, p. 29.
"Irises: Last Love Poem for M." SpoonRQ (9:1)
Wint 84, p. 26.
"Joan." SpoonRQ (9:1) Wint 84, p. 21.

"July Midnight, Midwest." SpoonRQ (9:1) Wint 84,
    p. 64.
"June Dawn." SpoonRQ (9:1) Wint 84, p. 46.
"June for Julie." SpoonRQ (9:1) Wint 84, p. 47.
"The Lake" (dream while listening to David Friesen,
    acoustic bass, & John Stowell, mandolin).
    SpoonRQ (9:1) Wint 84, p. 13.
"Legends of Gypsy Bands Lost in the Plains."
    SpoonRQ (9:1) Wint 84, p. 15.
"Little Song." SpoonRQ (9:1) Wint 84, p. 56.
"Martha." SpoonRQ (9:1) Wint 84, p. 24.
"Martha remember." SpoonRQ (9:1) Wint 84, p. 44.
"Music for Monet" (dedicated to Carol). SpoonRQ
    (9:1) Wint 84, p. 1-72.
"Nevada." SpoonRQ (9:1) Wint 84, p. 67.
"Night Music: 'Shaker Loops' by John Adams."
    SpoonRQ (9:1) Wint 84, p. 14.
"Night rain." SpoonRQ (9:1) Wint 84, p. 53.
"Nightsong, July." SpoonRQ (9:1) Wint 84, p. 49.
"North, Late March" (for Hayden Carruth). SpoonRQ
    (9:1) Wint 84, p. 43.
"Northern Wisconsin, January, 1983." SpoonRQ
    (9:1) Wint 84, p. 36.
"Old Amana." SpoonRQ (9:1) Wint 84, p. 65.
"Out of the circling." SpoonRQ (9:1) Wint 84, p. 48.
"Pam." SpoonRQ (9:1) Wint 84, p. 28.
"Poem / Dance for Nass El Riwan." SpoonRQ (9:1)
    Wint 84, p. 10.
"Poem for Cream." SpoonRQ (9:1) Wint 84, p. 11.
"Poplar tips whip rain across sun." SpoonRQ (9:1)
    Wint 84, p. 55.
"Progress Report: July, 1982." SpoonRQ (9:1) Wint
    84, p. 51.
"Record Wisconsin Snowfall." SpoonRQ (9:1) Wint
    84, p. 40.
"Records of Gypsy Bands Lost in the Plains: No. 2."
    SpoonRQ (9:1) Wint 84, p. 27.
"Rotary Perception" (improvisation, in memory of
    Charles Mingus). SpoonRQ (9:1) Wint 84, p. 12.
"Savanna." SpoonRQ (9:1) Wint 84, p. 63.
"Self-portrait No. 11: Still-life -- Postcard from
    Tretyakov Gallery, Moscow / Wisconsin, late
    March." SpoonRQ (9:1) Wint 84, p. 5.
"Skiing midnight." SpoonRQ (9:1) Wint 84, p. 34.
"Space-Time." SpoonRQ (9:1) Wint 84, p. 3.
"Splitting Wood." Northeast (Series 3:18) 84, p. 16.
"Sunday: Prelude to the Trail Scroll." SpoonRQ
    (9:1) Wint 84, p. 33.
"Susan." SpoonRQ (9:1) Wint 84, p. 20.
"This morning." SpoonRQ (9:1) Wint 84, p. 52.
"Twenty below." SpoonRQ (9:1) Wint 84, p. 41.
"Vermeer's 'Head of a Girl with Turban,' 1664."
    Northeast (Series 3:18) 84, p. 14.
"Vermeer's World." Northeast (Series 3:18) 84, p.
    15.
"Weather Report: Ishtar's Suite." SpoonRQ (9:1)
    Wint 84, p. 57-60.
"Winter Poetics" (for William Witherup).
    Northeast (Series 3:18) 84, p. 17.
"Winter Solstice." SpoonRQ (9:1) Wint 84, p. 38.

4612. SCHULER, Ruth Wildes
"Farewell to the Florida Panther." PoeticJ (1)
83, p. 32.
"The Gray of Black and White." PoeticJ (6) 84, p.
34.
"Hart Crane" (Jumped from the cruise ship, Orizaba,
April 27, 1932). PoeticJ (2) 83, p. 27.
"Interlude." PoeticJ (8) 84, p. 18.
"Love Goddess." PoeticJ (4) 83, p. 35.
"The Poet's Place." PoeticJ (5) 84, p. 24.
"Requiem to a Poet and Playwright" (For A.E.).
PoeticJ (3) 83, p. 30.

4613. SCHULMAN, Grace
"The Ceiba" (tr. of Pablo Antonio Cuadra). Nat
(238:3) 28 Ja 84, p. 101.
"Dawn over the East River." OntR (20) Spr-Sum 84,
p. 91.
"Echocardiogram." GrandS (3:3) Spr 84, p. 128-129.
"The Gate" (tr. of T. Carmi). Pequod (16/17) 84,
p. 111.
"His Shutters Close" (tr. of T. Carmi). Pequod
(16/17) 84, p. 112.
"Let There Be Translators." Shen (35:2/3) 84, p.
323.
"Mother's Face Drowned in Her Palm" (tr. of Tuvia
Ruebner, w. Shirley Kaufman). Pequod (16/17)
84, p. 117.
"The Swans." OntR (20) Spr-Sum 84, p. 90.

4614. SCHULTE, Rainer
"Behind the Shutters" (of Wolfgang Bächler).
Mund (14:2) 84, p. 59.
"The Dead" (tr. of Wolfgang Bächler). Mund
(14:2) 84, p. 57, 59.
"My Boundaries" (tr. of Wolfgang Bächler). Mund
(14:2) 84, p. 57.
"On the Train" (tr. of Wolfgang Bächler). Mund
(14:2) 84, p. 59.
"Roads" (tr. of Wolfgang Bächler). Mund (14:2)
84, p. 57.

4615. SCHULTZ, Philip
"Deep within the Ravine." AmerPoR (13:3) My-Je
84, p. 34-36.
"A Letter Found on a January Night in Front of the
Public Theater." Pequod (16/17) 84, p. 149-150.
"The Quality." Nat (239:10) 6 O 84, p. 321.

4616. SCHULTZ, Robert
"When the Magnitude of the Possible Dawned."
Hudson (37:3) Aut 84, p. 371-375.

4617. SCHULZ, Hart
"The First Time Wesly Sees the Ocean" (Wesly is
four). SnapD (7:2) Spr 84, p. 52.

4618. SCHULZE, Axel
"Landscape" (tr. by Frederic Will). Iowa (14:2)
Spr-Sum 84, p. 193.

4619. SCHUMACHER, Rose
"Nadine Makes a Quilt." FourQt (33:4) Sum 84, p. 3.

4620. SCHUT, Laurie
"Six Quadrants" (to David Hockney's swimming pool
paintings). BlueBuf (2:2) Spr 84, p. 11.
"Still Life in Black and White." Dandel (11:1)
Spr-Sum 84, p. 53.
"Two Ways." BlueBuf (2:2) Spr 84, p. 12.

4621. SCHUYLER, James
"This Notebook." YaleR (74:1) Aut 84, p. 31.

4622. SCHWAGER, Elaine
"Body of Water." Writ (16) Aut 84, p. 25.
"Moving." Writ (16) Aut 84, p. 27.
"Progression." Writ (16) Aut 84, p. 26.

4623. SCHWARTZ, Hillel
"Burning Down the House." Descant (47, 15:4) Wint
84, p. 181-182.
"Fantasiestücke 1: The Woman of My Dreams Makes a
Pass at Me in the Generic Section of a
Supermarket." PoetL (79:3) Aut 84, p. 157.
"The Frozen Zoo." Descant (47, 15:4) Wint 84, p.
183-184.
"Galatea's Newsstand." Spirit (7:1) 84, p. 90-91.
"Grandma at Grand Canyon, 1938." PoetryNW (25:4)
Wint 84-85, p. 46-47.
"Romance." Descant (47, 15:4) Wint 84, p. 185-186.
"Stock." BelPoJ (35:2) Wint 84-85, p. 22-23.
"Taking of Lives." PoetryNW (25:1) Spr 84, p. 3-4.
"Upon the Death of an Uncle, I Inherit a Raccoon
Coat." CalQ (25) Aut 84, p. 30-31.
"Whether Regret and Compassion Are of the Same
Species." PoetL (79:3) Aut 84, p. 156.

4624. SCHWARTZ, Jeffrey
"Gingko Trees on Beeler." HangL (46) Aut 84, p. 59.
"The Story of the Horse." ThRiPo (23/24) 84, p. 43.
"What We Work For" (for Jim Daniels). MinnR (N.S.
22) Spr 84, p. 27.

4625. SCHWARTZ, Lloyd
"Love." Poetry (144:3) Je 84, p. 125-127.

4626. SCHWERNER, Armand
"Tablet XXIV." Origin (Series 5:1) Aut 83, p. 57-60.

4627. SCHWITZGEBE, Eric
"The Prophet." PortR (30:1) 84, p. 40-41.

4628. SCIBERRAS, Lillian
"To a Chilean Woman" (tr. by Oliver Friggieri).
Vis (15) 84, p. 38-39.

4629. SCOTT, Anne
"The Chemist." PottPort (6) 84, p. 17.
"Falling." Waves (12:1) Aut 83, p. 50.
"The Field." Waves (12:1) Aut 83, p. 51.

"Therese." <u>PottPort</u> (6) 84, p. 14.

4630. SCOTT, Herbert
"The Derelict." <u>Chelsea</u> (42/43) 84, p. 227.
"The Rapist Speaks to Himself." <u>Chelsea</u> (42/43)
84, p. 226.

4631. SCOTT, Jo
"2084 AD." <u>SanFPJ</u> (6:4) 84, p. 58.
"Custody." <u>SanFPJ</u> (7:1) 84, p. 76.
"Liberty." <u>SanFPJ</u> (7:1) 84, p. 61.
"Not Applicable." <u>SanFPJ</u> (6:1) 84, p. 11.
"A Poem for All the Military Widows." <u>SanFPJ</u>
(6:4) 84, p. 24.
"Runaway." <u>SanFPJ</u> (6:4) 84, p. 57.

4632. SCOTT, L. E.
"A dying Race." <u>Stepping</u> (Anniversary Issue I)
84, p. 46.

4633. SCOTT, Nathaniel
"The Last Summer." <u>PortR</u> (30:1) 84, p. 159-160.

4634. SCOTT, Peter Dale
"My inner voice" (tr. of Zbigniew Herbert, w.
Czeslaw Milosz). <u>ManhatR</u> (3:2) Wint 84-85, p.
50-51.

4635. SCOTT, Virginia
"Epifania." <u>PraS</u> (58:4) Wint 84, p. 62-64.
"Wild Roses Offer No Embrace." <u>AntigR</u> (58) Sum
84, p. 114.

4636. SCRIBNER, Douglas
"Pieces of a Memory." <u>Vis</u> (14) 84, p. 31.
"The Prophets on the Edge." <u>Sam</u> (41:1, release
161) 84, p. 47.

4637. SCULLY, James
"Lumpen! If." <u>MinnR</u> (N.S. 23) Aut 84, p. 59-60.
"Unskilled Labor." <u>MinnR</u> (N.S. 23) Aut 84, p. 61-62.

4638. SEABURG, Alan
"Virginia Woolf." <u>CapeR</u> (19:3) 20th Anniverary
Issue 84, p. 44.

4639. SEARLES, George J.
"Cool Breeze, Constant." <u>GreenfR</u> (11:1/2) Sum-Aut
83, p. 107-108.

4640. SEARS, Vickie
"Grandmother." <u>Calyx</u> (8:2) Spr 84, p. 76-77.
"Oldways Keeper." <u>Calyx</u> (8:2) Spr 84, p. 78.

4641. SEATON, J. P.
"Alone" (tr. of Yuan Mei). <u>NeqC</u> (4:3) Sum 84, p. 40.
"A Guest Arrives" (tr. of Yuan Mei). <u>NeqC</u> (4:3)
Sum 84, p. 42.
"Idleness" (tr. of Yuan Mei). <u>LitR</u> (28:1) Aut 84,
p. 137.

"Ill" (tr. of Yuan Mei). NeqC (4:3) Sum 84, p. 38.
"In Idleness I" (tr. of Yuan Mei). LitR (28:1)
Aut 84, p. 136.
"In Idleness II" (tr. of Yuan Mei). LitR (28:1)
Aut 84, p. 137.
"Jeering at Myself" (tr. of Yuan Mei). NeqC (4:3)
Sum 84, p. 37.
"March" (tr. of Yuan Mei). NeqC (4:3) Sum 84,
back cover.
"Mornings arise" (tr. of Yuan Mei). NeqC (4:3)
Sum 84, p. 46.
"Opening the Window" (tr. of Yuan Mei). NeqC
(4:3) Sum 84, p. 46.
"Returned from Yang-chou up the Hill to View the
Snow" (tr. of Yuan Mei). LitR (28:1) Aut 84,
p. 136.
"River village sands white bright moon" (tr. of
Yuan Mei). NeqC (4:3) Sum 84, p. 44.

4642. SEDGWICK, Eve Kosofsky
"Sestina Lente." MassR (25:4) Wint 84, p. 576-578.

4643. SEETCH, Beth
"After You Left." ThRiPo (23/24) 84, p. 54.
"Unchained Melody." ThRiPo (23/24) 84, p. 55.

4644. SEGALL, Pearl B.
"I Remember." PoeticJ (6) 84, p. 5.
"Mad-Lib." SanFPJ (6:3) 84, p. 95.
"The Polls Show." SanFPJ (6:3) 84, p. 94.
"Pure Polyester People." SanFPJ (6:3) 84, p. 86-87.
"Re: Union." PoeticJ (4) 83, p. 38.
"Rebel." SanFPJ (6:3) 84, p. 96.
"Rick Says." SanFPJ (6:3) 84, p. 93.
"Youngstown: Ghosts of Steel, an Elegy." SanFPJ
(6:3) 84, p. 66-67.

4645. SEGARRA, Samuel
"Poesimusica." Mairena (5:13) Spr 83, p. 72-73.

4646. SEGOVIA, Tomás
"At the Sources" (tr. by James Irby). Iowa (14:2)
Spr-Sum 84, p. 147.
"Canciones sin Su Música" (tr. by Nathaniel
Tarn). Iowa (14:2) Spr-Sum 84, p. 149.
"Dawn of Tomorrow" (tr. by James Irby). Iowa
(14:2) Spr-Sum 84, p. 147-148.
"Interludio Idilico: Coda" (tr. by Nathaniel Tarn).
Iowa (14:2) Spr-Sum 84, p. 148.

4647. SEID, Christopher
"Bird Dreams." Nimrod (27:2) Spr-Sum 84, p. 69.
"Black Moth." Nimrod (27:2) Spr-Sum 84, p. 68.
"Lines of the Young Dwarf." Nimrod (27:2) Spr-Sum
84, p. 68.

4648. SEIDEL, Frederick
"Elms." ParisR (26:93) Aut 84, p. 213.

4649. SEIDMAN, Hugh
"Model." Origin (Series 5:1) Aut 83, p. 44.
"To Hikmet." Origin (Series 5:1) Aut 83, p. 40-41.

4650. SEIFERLE, Rebecca
"As If It Never Belonged Here." Poem (50) Mr 84,
     p. 60.
"As Sweet As Water." Poem (50) Mr 84, p. 61.
"A Finer Justice." Poem (50) Mr 84, p. 58.
"An Herbal Conceit." PoeticJ (5) 84, p. 27.
"A Salt Landscape." LitR (28:1) Aut 84, p. 127.
"The Tongues of Angels." Poem (50) Mr 84, p. 59.

4651. SEIFERT, Edward
"Jeremiah." ChrC (101:25) 15-22 Ag 84, p. 772.

4652. SEIFERT, Jaroslav
"Abacus" (tr. by Lyn Coffin). ConcPo (17:2) Aut
     84, p. 188.
"Are Your Poems Your Songs" (tr. by Paul Jagasich
     and Tom O'Grady). Spirit (8:1) 83-84, p. 37.
"The Artists' House" (tr. by Paul Jagasich and Tom
     O'Grady). Spirit (8:1) 83-84, p. 26-27.
"Before Those Few Light Kisses" (tr. by Paul
     Jagasich and Tom O'Grady). Spirit (8:1) 83-84,
     p. 49.
"Cannon Fire" (tr. by Paul Jagasich and Tom
     O'Grady). Spirit (8:1) 83-84, p. 23-24.
"The Casting of Bells" (tr. by Paul Jagasich and
     Tom O'Grady). Spirit (8:1) 83-84, p. 1-61.
"Crowned with Berries" (tr. by Paul Jagasich and
     Tom O'Grady). Spirit (8:1) 83-84, p. 21.
"Dance-Song" (tr. by Paul Jagasich and Tom
     O'Grady). Spirit (8:1) 83-84, p. 29-30.
"End of a Story" (tr. by Paul Jagasich and Tom
     O'Grady). Spirit (8:1) 83-84, p. 18-19.
"Heavenly Bonds" (tr. by Paul Jagasich and Tom
     O'Grady). Spirit (8:1) 83-84, p. 40-41.
"I don't Look at People's Souls" (tr. by Paul
     Jagasich and Tom O'Grady). Spirit (8:1) 83-84,
     p. 11.
"I Just Wanted to Tell You This" (tr. by Paul
     Jagasich and Tom O'Grady). Spirit (8:1) 83-84,
     p. 15.
"I Looked Only" (tr. by Paul Jagasich and Tom
     O'Grady). Spirit (8:1) 83-84, p. 46.
"I Remained on This Earth" (tr. by Paul Jagasich
     and Tom O'Grady). Spirit (8:1) 83-84, p. 14.
"If the Sand Could Sing" (tr. by Paul Jagasich and
     Tom O'Grady). Spirit (8:1) 83-84, p. 31.
"In Those Winters When" (tr. by Paul Jagasich and
     Tom O'Grady). Spirit (8:1) 83-84, p. 25.
"It Was Afternoon or Later" (tr. by Paul Jagasich
     and Tom O'Grady). Spirit (8:1) 83-84, p. 12.
"It's after All Saints Day" (tr. by Paul Jagasich
     and Tom O'Grady). Spirit (8:1) 83-84, p. 34.
"A Letter from Marienbad" (tr. by Paul Jagasich and
     Tom O'Grady). Spirit (8:1) 83-84, p. 55-61.
"Monument to a Kettle Drum" (tr. by Paul Jagasich
     and Tom O'Grady). Spirit (8:1) 83-84, p. 44-45.

"The Mount of Venus" (tr. by Paul Jagasich and Tom
    O'Grady). Spirit (8:1) 83-84, p. 50-51.
"My Star-Hung Window" (tr. by Paul Jagasich and Tom
    O'Grady). Spirit (8:1) 83-84, p. 38.
"Myrtle Wreath" (tr. by Paul Jagasich and Tom
    O'Grady). Spirit (8:1) 83-84, p. 35-36.
"Neither the Marble Tower" (tr. by Paul Jagasich
    and Tom O'Grady). Spirit (8:1) 83-84, p. 17.
"Not Too Long Ago" (tr. by Paul Jagasich and Tom
    O'Grady). Spirit (8:1) 83-84, p. 42-43.
"Orangeade" (tr. by Paul Jagasich and Tom O'Grady).
    Spirit (8:1) 83-84, p. 47-48.
"Paradise Lost" (tr. by Lyn Coffin). ConcPo
    (17:2) Aut 84, p. 186-188.
"A Poem at the End" (tr. by Lyn Coffin). ConcPo
    (17:2) Aut 84, p. 185.
"Poor Moon, She Is Helpless" (tr. by Paul Jagasich
    and Tom O'Grady). Spirit (8:1) 83-84, p. 13.
"Prologue" (tr. by Paul Jagasich and Tom O'Grady).
    Spirit (8:1) 83-84, p. 9-10.
"A Requiem for Dvorák" (tr. by Paul Jagasich and
    Tom O'Grady). Spirit (8:1) 83-84, p. 32-33.
"Ship in Flames" (tr. by Paul Jagasich and Tom
    O'Grady). Spirit (8:1) 83-84, p. 16.
"When Our Mulberry Trees" (tr. by Paul Jagasich and
    Tom O'Grady). Spirit (8:1) 83-84, p. 28.
"When We Are Denied" (tr. by Paul Jagasich and Tom
    O'Grady). Spirit (8:1) 83-84, p. 39.
"Where or Whenever I Had Heard" (tr. by Paul
    Jagasich and Tom O'Grady). Spirit (8:1) 83-84,
    p. 20.
"With the Roll of Our Blood" (tr. by Paul Jagasich
    and Tom O'Grady). Spirit (8:1) 83-84, p. 22.
"You Are Asking" (tr. by Paul Jagasich and Tom
    O'Grady). Spirit (8:1) 83-84, p. 52-54.

4653. SELAWSKY, John T.
    "The Tomatoes." LittleBR (4:4) Sum 84, p. 57.

4654. SELE, Baraka
    "Gerald Cheatom, 1970." BlackALF (18:1) Spr 84,
        p. 8.
    "Listen." BlackALF (18:1) Spr 84, p. 8.
    "Spirit People." BlackALF (18:1) Spr 84, p. 9.
    "Uprising: A Day in the History of Revolutionary
        Warfare." BlackALF (18:1) Spr 84, p. 8.

4655. SELENDER, Mike
    "Transit." NegC (4:4) Aut 84, p. 77-78.

4656. SELF, Lynda
    "Catfish." SouthernR (20:1) Wint 84, p. 147-148.

4657. SELINGER, Eric
    "Large Religious Poem." HarvardA (117:4/118:1) D
        84, p. 27.
    "Large Sentimental Poem." HarvardA (117:4/118:1)
        D 84, p. 12-13.
    "Once, Well Yes." HarvardA (118:2) Spr 84, p. 33-35.

4658. SELLERS, Bettie
    "Charlie Walks the Night." Poem (50) Mr 84, p. 42.
    "Leah's Prayer in August." Poem (50) Mr 84, p. 41.

4659. SELLIN, Eric
    "In the Roman Cemetery at Tipasa." CapeR (19:3)
    20th Anniverary Issue 84, p. 45.

4660. SELVAGGIO, Marc
    "The Street of Lilies." GeoR (38:1) Spr 84, p. 128.

4661. SEMENOVICH, Joseph
    "Drunkard's Lament." Paunch (57/58) Ja 84, p. 79.
    "Even if you're a half-assed poet." Amelia (1:2)
    O 84, p. 81.
    "Penelope says." RagMag (3:1) Spr 84, p. 17.
    "A Proletariat's Dream." Paunch (57/58) Ja 84, p.
    80.
    "Vincent, one of the other poets at my job."
    Abraxas (29/30) 84, p. 60.
    "Way in the back of my head." Abraxas (31/32) 84,
    p. 59.

4662. SEMONES, Charles
    "In the Funeral Home: A Reminiscence" (for Jeff).
    Wind (14:50) 84, p. 48.
    "The People of Inverness" (for Wade Hall). Wind
    (14:50) 84, p. 48-49.

4663. SENA, Jorge de
    "Noções de Linguiistica." ConcPo (17:2) Aut
    84, p. 155.
    "Notions about Linguistics" (tr. by George
    Monteiro). ConcPo (17:2) Aut 84, p. 156.

4664. SENGHOR, Léopold Sédar
    "To New York" (for jazz orchestra: trumpet solo,
    tr. by Serge Gavronsky). Chelsea (42/43) 84,
    p. 242-244.
    "For African Flutes and Xylophone" (tr. by Ann
    Neelon). CarolQ (37:1) Aut 84, p. 33.
    "For Organ Flutes" (tr. by Ann Neelon). CarolQ
    (37:1) Aut 84, p. 34.

4665. SEÑORET, Raquel
    "Cantos al Sortilegio de la Imagination" (Cantos
    VII-VIII: fragmentos). Mairena (5:14) Aut 83,
    p. 31.

4666. SERCHUK, Peter
    "A Christmas Card from Wyandotte, Michigan." NewL
    (50:4) Sum 84, p. 28-29.
    "In the Attic Where She Sleeps." MidAR (4:2) Aut
    84, p. 12-13.
    "The Long Nights of Waiting." MidAR (4:2) Aut 84,
    p. 11.
    "The Woman in the Dream." SouthwR (69:3) Sum 84,
    p. 303.

4667. SERENI, Vittorio
      "In Your Sleep" (Selections: I-III, V, tr. by Sonia
      Raiziss). Chelsea (42/43) 84, p. 147.

4668. SERGEANT, Howard
      "Lines for a Young Lady's Autograph Album."
      AntigR (58) Sum 84, p. 117.

4669. SERRANO, Pio E.
      "Memoria Elegiaca Mientras Escucho a Glenn Miller."
      LindLM (3:1) Ja-Mr 84, p. 5.

4670. SESSIONS, W. A.
      "After a Fight on July 31." SouthernR (20:4) Aut
      84, p. 894-895.
      "How Myths Are Made." SouthernR (20:4) Aut 84, p.
      895-897.
      "Taking a Chance." SouthernR (20:4) Aut 84, p.
      897-899.

4671. SETH, Vikram
      "The Golden Gate: A Novel in Verse" (Selection:
      Chapter 2). Shen (35:4) 84, p. 3-32.

4672. SEVIN, Jeff
      "Division." YellowS (10) Spr 84, p. 18.

4673. SEXTON, Tom
      "Denali." TexasR (5:1/2) Spr-Sum 84, p. 46.
      "Minus 60." TexasR (5:1/2) Spr-Sum 84, p. 44.
      "Poolshark." TexasR (5:1/2) Spr-Sum 84, p. 45.

4674. SEYFRIED, Robin
      "Truth and Beauty." AmerS (53:3) Sum 84, p. 379.

4675. SEYLER, Deborah
      "Lust for Life." DekalbLAJ (17:1/2) 84, p. 143.
      "Shugah." RagMag (3:2) Aut 84, p. 45.

4676. SHAFFER, Craig
      "Responsibility." SouthernPR (24:2) Aut 84, p. 54-
      55.

4677. SHAFTON, Anthony
      "Balthazar's Lullaby." WebR (9:2) Wint 85, p. 53.
      "Thanksgiving at the Porcelain Room." WebR (9:2)
      Wint 85, p. 54-56.
      "That Mood." Tendril (17) Wint 84, p. 159.

SHAHID ALI, Agha: See ALI, Agha Shahid

4678. SHAKESPEARE, Sheila
      "After the Death of a Son." AntigR (56) Wint 84,
      p. 72.

4679. SHAKESPEARE, William
      "That time of year thou mayst in me behold" (Sonnet
      #42). Ploughs (10:1) 84, p. 198-199.

4680. SHALLY, Judith
"Two Gardeners' Graves" (For Berthe and Harry
Margoshes). LitR (28:1) Aut 84, p. 126.

4681. SHAMMAS, Anton
"Dedicatory Entry" (tr. by Judy Levy). Iowa
(14:2) Spr-Sum 84, p. 114.
"Goodboy" (tr. by the author). Iowa (14:2) Spr-
Sum 84, p. 114-117.

4682. SHAMOSH, Amnon
"Anna Frank and I" (three versions, tr. by Ada
Aharoni). Descant (47, 15:4) Wint 84, p. 202-204.

4683. SHANAHAN, Deirdre
"Learning." Argo (5:2) 84, p. 30.

4684. SHANGI
"In Exile" (tr. by Desmond O'Grady). Agni (21)
84, p. 11.

4685. SHANNON, Jeanne
"Sirocco." Wind (14:51) 84, p. 44-45.

4686. SHAPIRO, Alan
"Homage." AmerS (53:3) Sum 84, p. 380.

4687. SHAPIRO, Daniel
"On Leave." BlackWR (10:2) Spr 84, p. 71.

4688. SHAPIRO, Daniel E.
"The Woman on the Wing." PoetryNW (25:1) Spr 84,
p. 28-29.

4689. SHAPIRO, David
"House (Blown Apart)". ParisR (26:93) Aut 84, p.
212.

4690. SHAPIRO, Gregg
"California." SnapD (7:1) Aut 83, p. 55.

4691. SHAPIRO, Harvey
"American Words." Chelsea (42/43) 84, p. 204.
"Getting through the Day." Atlantic (253:1) Ja
84, p. 62.
"Memorial Day." Pequod (16/17) 84, p. 126.
"Movie." Pequod (16/17) 84, p. 125.
"Things Unseen." Atlantic (253:1) Ja 84, p. 62.

4692. SHAPIRO, Karl
"The Sawdust Logs." NewYorker (59:52) 13 F 84, p.
52.

SHARAT CHANDRA, G. S.: See CHANDRA, G. S. Sharat

4693. SHARE, Don
"5th Month Lotus." PaintedB (24) Aut 84, p. 5.

4694. SHATTUCK, Roger
"Incompatible Components." PartR (51:4/52:1

Anniversary issue) 84-85, p. 599-600.
"Journal Entry: Christmas 1939" (tr. of Pablo
    Picasso). PoetryE (13/14) Spr-Sum 84, p. 82.
"Trespass." Shen (35:1) 83-84, p. 100-101.

4695. SHAW, H. E.
    "Fate defined by the fast emptiness of winter."
        Tele (19) 83, p. 132.
    "Red. Fresh cream would not be image enough."
        Tele (19) 83, p. 131.
    "She will certainly scream." Tele (19) 83, p. 131-
        132.

4696. SHAW, Jeanne Osborne
    "Gnat in Amber." DekalbLAJ (20th Anniversary
        Issue) 84, p. 108.

4697. SHAW, Phillip
    "Now I Know." Stepping Wint 84, p. 27-30.

4698. SHAWGO, Lucy
    "Sparrows." AmerS (53:3) Sum 84, p. 328.

4699. SHEA, Shawn Christopher
    "The House." DekalbLAJ (17:1/2) 84, p. 144-145.

4700. SHEARD, Norma Voorhees
    "December" (for Jill remembering our mothers).
        CapeR (19:2) Sum 84, p. 49.
    "Flight." CapeR (19:2) Sum 84, p. 48.

4701. SHEARER, Ellen
    "Listening." Quarry (33:4) Aut 84, p. 20.

4702. SHECK, Laurie
    "Childlessness: Frida Kahlo to Her Doctor." SenR
        (14:2) 84, p. 54-56.
    "Distance." PoetryNW (25:3) Aut 84, p. 44-45.
    "The Madwoman in the Attic." PoetryNW (25:3) Aut
        84, p. 45-46.
    "Picture for Sale above a Cash Register."
        PoetryNW (25:3) Aut 84, p. 43-44.
    "The Red Cow at Lascaux." PoetryNW (25:3) Aut 84,
        p. 47.
    "The Soul Revisiting the Body" (The Papyrus of Ani,
        1400 B.C.). Poetry (144:6) S 84, p. 337-338.

4703. SHECTMAN, Robin
    "For a Lost Watch." AmerS (53:3) Sum 84, p. 312.

4704. SHEEHAN, Paul R.
    "Aftermath." SanFPJ (6:1) 84, p. 87.
    "Categorically." SanFPJ (6:1) 84, p. 86.
    "Meaninglessness" (A Scrap of Truth). SanFPJ
        (6:1) 84, p. 45.
    "Soldiers of Oblivion." SanFPJ (6:1) 84, p. 45.
    "The Unconscionable Truth." SanFPJ (6:1) 84, p. 87.

4705. SHEEHAN, T.
    "Backyard Hieroglyphics." Poem (51) Mr [i.e. Jl]

84, p. 14-15.
"Bearing Investigation." <u>Poem</u> (51) Mr [i.e. Jl]
84, p. 16.

4706. SHEEHAN, Thomas
"Streetlight." <u>StoneC</u> (12:1/2) Aut-Wint 84, p. 36-
37.

4707. SHEEHAN, Timothy
"At Camino." <u>Telescope</u> (3:1) Wint 84, p. 160.
"Here." <u>Telescope</u> (3:1) Wint 84, p. 160.

4708. SHEEHAN, Tom
"Cold Night Thoughts beside an Empty Cave." <u>CutB</u>
(22) Spr-Sum 84, p. 12.
"Empty." <u>CapeR</u> (19:2) Sum 84, p. 23.
"Silence, Night Pear Falling, Earth Movement."
<u>CapeR</u> (19:2) Sum 84, p. 24-25.

4709. SHEFTEL, Harry B.
"Tales of Elixir." <u>NeqC</u> (4:3) Sum 84, p. 88.

SHEKERJIAN, Regina de Cormier: <u>See</u> DeCORMIER-SHEKERJIAN,
Regina

4710. SHELLEY, Anne
"Journal Entry (March 10, 1636, Boston)" (from
<u>Letters</u> <u>and</u> <u>Journals</u> <u>of</u> <u>Mary</u> <u>Dyer</u> <u>1614?-1660</u>).
<u>Nimrod</u> (27:2) Spr-Sum 84, p. 72.
"Miss Parret." <u>Nimrod</u> (27:2) Spr-Sum 84, p. 70.
"Prayer (1656, Boston Prison)" (from <u>Letters</u> <u>and</u>
<u>Journals</u> <u>of</u> <u>Mary</u> <u>Dyer</u> <u>1614?-1660</u>). <u>Nimrod</u>
(27:2) Spr-Sum 84, p. 72.
"She Takes the Stand" (from <u>Letters</u> <u>and</u> <u>Journals</u>
<u>of</u> <u>Mary</u> <u>Dyer</u> <u>1614?-1660</u>). <u>Nimrod</u> (27:2) Spr-
Sum 84, p. 72.

4711. SHELNUTT, Eve
"Inductor." <u>OhioR</u> (33) 84, p. 134.

4712. SHELOR, R. S.
"Cat at Midnight." <u>WebR</u> (9:2) Wint 85, p. 97.
"From the Kitchen Table." <u>WebR</u> (9:1) Spr 84, p. 84.
"There Is a Woman." <u>WebR</u> (9:1) Spr 84, p. 85.

4713. SHELTON, Mark
"Parimutuel." <u>ThRiPo</u> (23/24) 84, p. 34.

4714. SHELTON, Richard
"The Rain the Stones the Darkness." <u>Peb</u> (23) 84,
p. 80-82.

4715. SHEPARD, Neil
"Late Spring at the Farm." <u>Blueline</u> (6:1) Sum-Aut
84, p. 12-13.

4716. SHEPHERD, J. Barrie
"Bomb Fragment." <u>ChrC</u> (101:23) 18-25 Jl 84, p. 704.
"Inquiry." <u>ChrC</u> (101:12) 11 Ap 84, p. 358.
"November One." <u>ChrC</u> (101:33) 31 O 84, p. 1005.

"Pinnacle." <u>ChrC</u> (101:9) 14 Mr 84, p. 276.

4717. SHEPHERD, Jamie
"Six-thirty A.M." <u>SnapD</u> (8:1) Aut 84, p. 50.

4718. SHEPHERD, Judith
"Weeds in the Garden." <u>SoCaR</u> (17:1) Aut 84, p. 43.

4719. SHEPPARD, Patricia
"The Woods, Late April." <u>Iowa</u> (14:3) Aut 84, p. 115.

4720. SHERBURNE, James C.
"Quicksilver." <u>Vis</u> (16) 84, p. 35.

4721. SHERER, Joan M.
"Second Tuesday in November." <u>SanFPJ</u> (6:1) 84, p. 78-80.
"To Nurture the Bird of Prey." <u>SanFPJ</u> (6:1) 84, p. 76.

4722. SHERIDAN, David
"Adultery in a Freightyard Flat -- 1943." <u>Wind</u> (14:51) 84, p. 27.

4723. SHERIDAN, Michael
"Poem for My Wife." <u>NewL</u> (50:2/3) Wint-Spr 84, p. 188-189.

4724. SHERMAN, Alana
"Letter for Mark, Abroad." <u>PoeticJ</u> (4) 83, p. 24.
"Peas in a Bowl." <u>WindO</u> (44) Sum-Aut 84, p. 26.
"Snake in My Garden." <u>PoeticJ</u> (7) 84, p. 7.

4725. SHERMAN, G. W.
"The Death of the General." <u>Sam</u> (41:1, release 161) 84, p. 26.

4726. SHERMAN, Joseph
"Parking Lot" (or Shnippishok Transposed). <u>PottPort</u> (6) 84, p. 24.

4727. SHERMAN, Kenneth
"Diane Arbus: Ground Glass." <u>PoetryCR</u> (5:4) Sum 84, p. 16.
"In Hiroshima." <u>AntigR</u> (57) Spr 84, p. 132-133.

4728. SHIELDS, Michael
"Super Hanc Petram." <u>Os</u> (19) 84, p. 27.

4729. SHIELDS, Tom
"Dandelion Wars." <u>PoeticJ</u> (3) 83, p. 14.
"Robin Hood." <u>PoeticJ</u> (3) 83, p. 7.

4730. SHIKATANI, Gerry
"As Is." <u>Waves</u> (13:1) Aut 84, p. 53.
"Gas Station, Vocables." <u>Waves</u> (13:1) Aut 84, p. 51.
"In the Air" (for Sam Johnson). <u>PoetryCR</u> (6:1) Aut 84, p. 7.
"On an Afternoon." <u>Waves</u> (13:1) Aut 84, p. 52.
"Parked Cars." <u>Waves</u> (13:1) Aut 84, p. 53.

"Sound Piece for Three Voices." <u>CapilR</u> (31) 84,
    p. 66.
"Spanish Dharma." <u>PoetryCR</u> (5:4) Sum 84, p. 11.
"Speech." <u>Waves</u> (13:1) Aut 84, p. 52.

4731. SHILLIDAY, Gregg
    "Poincon." <u>Grain</u> (12:2) My 84, p. 27.

4732. SHIMOSE, Pedro
    "Ciego y Baston." <u>LindLM</u> (3:1) Ja-Mr 84, p. 17.

4733. SHIN, Tae-ch'ul
    "For the Desert Island" (tr. by the author and
        Marilyn Chin). <u>Iowa</u> (14:2) Spr-Sum 84, p. 64.

4734. SHINEO, Shoda
    "These big bones" (tanka). <u>NewL</u> (50:2/3) Wint-Spr
        84, p. 231.

4735. SHIPLEY, Vivian
    "Auction Day: August, 1979" (for Larry 2Cambron).
        <u>GreenfR</u> (11:3/4) Wint-Spr 84, p. 134.
    "White Chickens." <u>GreenfR</u> (11:3/4) Wint-Spr 84,
        p. 134-135.

4736. SHIRES, Linda M.
    "Some Woman. What Woman?" <u>WebR</u> (9:2) Wint 85, p.
        46-48.

4737. SHIRLEY, Aleda
    "The Book of the Ocean to Cynthia." <u>Shen</u> (35:1)
        83-84, p. 56-57.
    "Dreams of You Come in Pairs." <u>MissR</u> (36, 12:3)
        Spr 84, p. 88.
    "Moving around Time." <u>TarRP</u> (23:2) Spr 84, p. 8.
    "One Summer Night." <u>MissR</u> (36, 12:3) Spr 84, p. 89.
    "Reasons for Flight." <u>PoetryNW</u> (25:3) Aut 84, p.
        34-35.
    "Still Life." <u>TarRP</u> (23:2) Spr 84, p. 9.

4738. SHIVELY, Bill
    "Where Does the Red Lip Go?" <u>Wind</u> (14:51) 84, p. 55.

4739. SHIVELY, Joellen
    "Ft. Peck Indian Reservation: 1963-1983." <u>Calyx</u>
        (8:2) Spr 84, p. 85.

4740. SHIVELY, Sharon
    "Hey Bud!" <u>Tele</u> (19) 83, p. 123.
    "Nine-Thirty P.M." <u>Tele</u> (19) 83, p. 125.
    "Pencil Sharpener." <u>Tele</u> (19) 83, p. 124.

SHODA, Shineo: <u>See</u> SHINEO, Shoda

4741. SHOLL, Betsy
    "The Goose-Girl." <u>Field</u> (31) Aut 84, p. 65-67.
    "Milkweed." <u>Field</u> (31) Aut 84, p. 63-64.
    "Plowshares." <u>WestB</u> (14) 84, p. 94-95.

4742. SHOMER, Enid
"A Bestiary" (Eve of Saint Agnes Contest Winners
    II). NeqC (4:1) Wint 84, p. 18-21.
"Customs." HiramPoR (37) Aut-Wint 84, p. 37.
"Making Out." NeqC (4:3) Sum 84, p. 14.
"The Mother Dream." HiramPoR (37) Aut-Wint 84, p.
    36.
"Sun and Moon in Mrs. Sussman's Tap Dancing Class."
    HiramPoR (37) Aut-Wint 84, p. 38-39.
"Thinking of Alexander" (for Richard Eberhart).
    NeqC (4:2) Spr 84, p. 70-71.
"The Tomato Packing Plant Line." DekalbLAJ
    (17:1/2) 84, p. 145.

SHOPTAW, John Willet: See WILLET-SHOPTAW, John

4743. SHORB, Michael
"The Dolphin." WebR (9:1) Spr 84, p. 32.
"Galloping Horse Unearthed at Leitai, China."
    ThirdW (2) Spr 84, p. 95-96.

4744. SHORE, Jane
"Dresses." NewRep (191:1) 2 Jl 84, p. 36-37.
"Pharaoh." NewRep (191:23) 3 D 84, p. 32.

4745. SHORT, Dinah
"Crazy Old Woman inside an Old House." PortR
    (30:1) 84, p. 163.

4746. SHREVE, Virginia
"Madwoman Throwing Mangoes." SouthernPR (24:2)
    Aut 84, p. 63-64.

4747. SHU, Ting
"Boat." ConcPo (17:2) Aut 84, p. 39.

4748. SHULZ-KIVI, Tamara
"Name-Dropping Stars." Ploughs (10:1) 84, p. 144-
    145.

4749. SHUMAKER, Peggy
"Cutting the Storm." GreenfR (12:1/2) Sum-Aut 84,
    p. 199.
"Ira and Amy Pratt." Nimrod (28:1) Aut-Wint 84,
    p. 75-78.

SHUNTARO, Tanigawa: See TANIGAWA, Shuntaro

4750. SHURBANOV, Alexander
"Concerned with Something Else While Turnovo's
    Dying" (tr. of Luchezar Elenkov, w. Jascha
    Kessler). GrahamHR (7) Wint 84, p. 59-60.
"Poet" (tr. of Luchezar Elenkov, w. Jascha
    Kessler). GrahamHR (7) Wint 84, p. 58.

4751. SHUTTLE, Penelope
"7 Dream Stairs." ManhatR (3:2) Wint 84-85, p. 64-
    65.
"Biographical Note." ManhatR (3:2) Wint 84-85, p.
    67-68.

"Giving Birth." <u>ManhatR</u> (3:2) Wint 84-85, p. 66-67.

4752. SHUTTLEWORTH, Paul
"Bullpen Catcher" (Issue title. For Luke). <u>Sam</u>
(40:3, release 159) 84, p. 1-16.
"Bullpen Catcher." <u>Sam</u> (40:3, release 159) 84, p.
8-15.
"Encirclement." <u>Sam</u> (40:3, release 159) 84, p. 16.
"A House with Carved and Painted Shutters." <u>SnapD</u>
(8:1) Aut 84, p. 58.
"How to Throw a Knuckleball." <u>Sam</u> (40:3, release
159) 84, p. 6-7.
"June's Innings." <u>Sam</u> (40:3, release 159) 84, p. 5.
"A Poem to Tell You Why I Named My Son Luke Appling
after the White Sox Hall of Fame Shortstop."
<u>Sam</u> (40:3, release 159) 84, p. 2-4.

4753. SICOLI, Dan
"Dennis." <u>PoeticJ</u> (5) 84, p. 34-35.

4754. SIDERIS, Hilary
"The Passenger." <u>PoetryNW</u> (25:2) Sum 84, p. 30.

4755. SIDNEY, Joan Seliger
"That Woman We Still Hope to Find" (on a line from
Reg Saner's "Essay on Earth"). <u>YellowS</u> (12)
Aut 84, p. 21.

4756. SIDNEY, Philip
"Astrophil and Stella" (Excerpt). <u>SouthernHR</u>
(18:1) Wint 84, p. 10.

4757. SIEBERT, Charles
"Crossing Central Park in Late Winter." <u>NewYorker</u>
(59:48) 16 Ja 84, p. 40.

4758. SIEGEL, Robert
"Connection." <u>SewanR</u> (92:4) O-D 84, p. 538-539.
"Mowing." <u>SewanR</u> (92:4) O-D 84, p. 539-540.

4759. SIEGEL, Suzie
"Exposure." <u>SouthernR</u> (20:2) Spr 84, p. 385.

4760. SIGURDARDOTTIR, Steinunn
"A Consolation" (tr. by the author and Sebastian
Barry). <u>NewOR</u> (11:2) Sum 84, p. 22.

4761. SILBERT, Layle
"Prayer." <u>WestB</u> (14) 84, p. 97-98.

4762. SILES, Jaime
"El Corazon del Agua." <u>Mairena</u> (6:18) 84, p. 67.

4763. SILESKY, Barry
"Something about Driving" (for I.S.). <u>Abraxas</u>
(29/30) 84, p. 36.

4764. SILKIN, Jon
"Climbing to Jerusalem" (for Moshe and Ziona Dor).
<u>GrahamHR</u> (7) Wint 84, p. 23.

"Innocence Barbs the Lake." GrahamHR (7) Wint 84,
     p. 21.
"Naming Souls" (tr. of Uri Zvi Greenberg, w. Ezra
     Spicehandler). Stand (25:4) Aut 84, p. 65.
"A Socket of Plain Water." GrahamHR (7) Wint 84,
     p. 21.
"The Sun's Body, Resting." GrahamHR (7) Wint 84,
     p. 22.
"Three Poems about Fear and Grief." GrahamHR (7)
     Wint 84, p. 21-22.

4765. SILVA, Fernando Antonio
     "Demonstration" (tr. by Marc Zimmerman and Ellen
     Banberger). MinnR (N.S. 22) Spr 84, p. 71-72.

SILVA, Loreina Santos: See SANTOS SILVA, Loreina

4766. SILVA SANTISTEBAN, Ricardo
     "Poiesis." Mairena (6:18) 84, p. 93.

4767. SILVER, Howard
     "Preparations." Shen (35:1) 83-84, p. 90.
     "Struggling toward the Literal." Shen (35:1) 83-
     84, p. 91.

4768. SILVER, Mara
     "Comfort." HangL (45) Spr 84, p. 68.
     "Geology Music." HangL (45) Spr 84, p. 67.

4769. SILVERMAN, Maxine
     "Death by Imagination." GreenfR (11:3/4) Wint-Spr
     84, p. 137-138.
     "Death by Imagination." GreenfR (12:1/2) Sum-Aut
     84, p. 169-170.
     "Fantasia on My Mother's Death." GreenfR (11:3/4)
     Wint-Spr 84, p. 138-139.
     "Fantasia on My Mother's Death." GreenfR (12:1/2)
     Sum-Aut 84, p. 168-169.
     "Somewhere on the Delta." Pig (12) 84, p. 71.

4770. SILVERMAN, Stuart
     "The Shop." CapeR (19:3) 20th Anniverary Issue
     84, p. 46.

4771. SIMIC, Charles
     "About Death and Other Things" (tr. of Alexander
     Ristovic). Iowa (14:3) Aut 84, p. 16.
     "Bed." Chelsea (42/43) 84, p. 182-183.
     "Birthday Star Atlas." MissouriR (7:3) 84, p. 78-79.
     "Cold Blue Tinge." Hudson (37:2) Sum 84, p. 336.
     "Ever So Tragic." MissouriR (7:3) 84, p. 76.
     "Flirting with a Pig" (tr. of Alexander Ristovic).
     Iowa (14:3) Aut 84, p. 15.
     "For the Sake of Amelia." BlackWR (10:2) Spr 84,
     p. 69.
     "The Fork." Chelsea (42/43) 84, p. 182.
     "Gingerbread Heart" (tr. of Alexander Ristovic).
     Iowa (14:3) Aut 84, p. 14.
     "History." KenR (NS 6:2) Spr 84, p. 58-59.
     "Instead of Counting Sheep." KenR (NS 6:2) Spr

84, p. 57-58.
"The Kid." <u>Field</u> (30) Spr 84, p. 60.
"Large Grieving Women" (tr. of Slavko Mihalić).
    <u>LitR</u> (27:3) Spr 84, p. 301.
"The Morning Roar of the City" (tr. of Slavko
    Mihalić). <u>LitR</u> (27:3) Spr 84, p. 300.
"Muttering Perhaps, or Humming." <u>MissouriR</u> (7:3)
    84, p. 77.
"My Weariness of Epic Proportions." <u>Salm</u> (65) Aut
    84, p. 65.
"Notice." <u>KenR</u> (NS 6:2) Spr 84, p. 59.
"On Thursday." <u>Field</u> (30) Spr 84, p. 59.
"Our Ancient Family Sign" (tr. of Slavko
    Mihalić). <u>LitR</u> (27:3) Spr 84, p. 299.
"Outside a Dirtroad Trailer." <u>Field</u> (30) Spr 84,
    p. 61.
"Painters of Angels and Seraphim." <u>MissouriR</u>
    (7:3) 84, p. 75.
"Pastoral" (tr. of Slavko Mihalić). <u>LitR</u> (27:3)
    Spr 84, p. 299.
"Promises of Leniency and Forgiveness." <u>Field</u>
    (30) Spr 84, p. 63.
"The Road Home." <u>BlackWR</u> (10:2) Spr 84, p. 66-68.
"Under the Microscope" (tr. of Slavko Mihalić).
    <u>LitR</u> (27:3) Spr 84, p. 298.
"Wherein Obscurely." <u>Field</u> (30) Spr 84, p. 62.
"With Souls as White as Butterflies." <u>BlackWR</u>
    (10:2) Spr 84, p. 70.

4772. SIMISON, Greg
    "Grendel, Closing." <u>AntigR</u> (58) Sum 84, p. 78.
    "Making Waves." <u>MalR</u> (67) F 84, p. 113.

4773. SIMMERMAN, Jim
    "Ars Poetica." <u>PoetC</u> (15:2) Wint 84, p. 4-5.
    "Division of Property." <u>NewEngR</u> (6:4) Sum 84, p.
        612.
    "Hide'n'go Seek." <u>NewEngR</u> (6:4) Sum 84, p. 611.
    "The Housewife Laments Her Purchase of Floating
        Eggs." <u>GeoR</u> (38:1) Spr 84, p. 175-176.
    "With Shadows." <u>NewEngR</u> (6:4) Sum 84, p. 613-614.

4774. SIMMONS, James
    "The Farther Shore." <u>Pequod</u> (16/17) 84, p. 33.

4775. SIMMONS, Judith D.
    "Don't Blame Him" (for Thelonius Monk). <u>Stepping</u>
        (Premier Issue) Sum 82, p. 33.

4776. SIMMONS, Thomas
    "First Sunday of Advent, 1967." <u>NewRep</u> (189:6) 8
        Ag 83, p. 36.

4777. SIMMONS, Tony
    "You divided our things." <u>Abraxas</u> (29/30) 84, p. 62.

SIMMS, Michael Garcia: <u>See</u> GARCIA-SIMMS, Michael

4778. SIMON, John Oliver
    "Even in the Morning." <u>Veloc</u> (3) Aut-Wint 83, p. 32.

"Headlands, 2365." Veloc (1) Sum 82, p. 33-34.
"The House of Corn." Abraxas (31/32) 84, p. 55.
"Losing Power under the Bed." Abraxas (31/32) 84,
    p. 55.
"Nimitz Freeway." Veloc (1) Sum 82, p. 35-38.
"Things" (tr. of Saûl Ibargoyen). Veloc (3) Aut-
    Wint 83, p. 33.
"Vaqueros of Eden." Veloc (3) Aut-Wint 83, p. 31.

4779. SIMON, Leslie
    "The Economy of Use." OroM (2:3/4, issue 7/8) 84,
        p. 10-11.
    "I Am a Poem." OroM (2:3/4, issue 7/8) 84, p. 11.
    "A Jew: To Such a World in Such a Time" (Israeli
        Invasion of Lebanon, 1982). OroM (2:3/4, issue
        7/8) 84, p. 37-38.

4780. SIMON, Maurya
    "Return to Dresden, 1945" (For the Idelovici
        family, killed in the firebombing of Dresden).
        Poetry (143:6) Mr 84, p. 315-316.
    "Venice, 1959." CalQ (23/24) Spr-Sum 84, p. 135.
    "The Wedding." CutB (22) Spr-Sum 84, p. 46-47.

4781. SIMONS, Louise
    "The Motel." MinnR (N.S. 22) Spr 84, p. 6-8.

4782. SIMPSON, Betty Jane
    "The Pioneer Man" (Fourth Honorable Mention, 13th
        Annual Kansas Poetry Contest). LittleBR (4:3)
        Spr 84, p. 68.

4783. SIMPSON, Grace
    "Palm Sunday." ChrC (101:12) 11 Ap 84, p. 367.

4784. SIMPSON, Louis
    "26th Precinct Station." GeoR (38:3) Aut 84, p. 523.
    "In Otto's Basement." Pequod (16/17) 84, p. 2.
    "Red-Avoiding Pictures." Pequod (16/17) 84, p. 1.
    "The Unwritten Poem." Field (30) Spr 84, p. 79.
    "The Unwritten Poem." KenR (NS 6:3) Sum 84, p. 123.
    "The Unwritten Poem." OhioR (33) 84, p. 133.
    "The Wall Test." Chelsea (42/43) 84, p. 201.

4785. SIMPSON, Matt
    "Heading Out." Stand (25:3) Sum 84, p. 66.

4786. SIMPSON, Nancy
    "Touching Ground." Nimrod (28:1) Aut-Wint 84, p. 83.
    "Two A.M." Nimrod (28:1) Aut-Wint 84, p. 82.

4787. SINCLAIR, Roy
    "Oyster Bank." Waves (12:1) Aut 83, p. 56.

SINH, Truong: See TRUONG, Sinh

4788. SINIKKA
    "Bones." Dandel (11:1) Spr-Sum 84, p. 96.
    "Roof of Sod." WestCR (19:1) Je 84, p. 48.
    "Workshop." WestCR (19:1) Je 84, p. 47.

4789. SION ap BRYDYDD
"Cloves and cedar smoke in the air" (29 englynion:
II, tr. by Michael Donaghy). <u>SenR</u> (14:2) 84,
p. 40.
"Dull the journey. Feeble and muttering the old
men" (29 englynion: XXVIII, tr. by Michael
Donaghy). <u>SenR</u> (14:2) 84, p. 41.
"Dull the journey. Long the road reeled in toward
the lantern" (29 englynion: XXVII, tr. by
Michael Donaghy). <u>SenR</u> (14:2) 84, p. 41.
"The moment you touch the whorl of my ear" (29
englynion: IV, tr. by Michael Donaghy). <u>SenR</u>
(14:2) 84, p. 41.
"Morfydd, daughter of Gwyn" (29 englynion: I, tr.
by Michael Donaghy). <u>SenR</u> (14:2) 84, p. 40.
"Say this rhyme, reader, aloud to yourself" (29
englynion: XXIX, tr. by Michael Donaghy). <u>SenR</u>
(14:2) 84, p. 41.
"Smooth the skin on a bowl of milk" (29 englynion:
III, tr. by Michael Donaghy). <u>SenR</u> (14:2) 84,
p. 40.

4790. SIOTIS, Dino
"Immigrant" (in Greek). <u>Os</u> (19) 84, p. 20.
"Immigrant" (tr. by John Chioles). <u>Os</u> (19) 84, p.
21.
"The Spring" (in Greek). <u>Os</u> (19) 84, p. 18.
"The Spring" (tr. by John Chioles). <u>Os</u> (19) 84,
p. 19.

4791. SIPORIN, Ona
"Questions / Answers." <u>SnapD</u> (7:1) Aut 83, p. 14-15.

4792. SIROWITZ, Hal
"Glue." <u>Waves</u> (12:2/3) Wint 84, p. 78.
"Memorized Women." <u>Waves</u> (12:2/3) Wint 84, p. 78.
"My Favorite Weeping Willow." <u>KanQ</u> (16:1/2) Wint-
Spr 84, p. 181.
"Serenade." <u>NewL</u> (50:4) Sum 84, p. 94.
"Skimping." <u>PortR</u> (30:1) 84, p. 67.

4793. SIRR, Peter
"Winter Light" (after reading a poem by
Mandelstam). <u>Pequod</u> (16/17) 84, p. 55.

4794. SITTERLY, Cassandra
"Red Lipstick." <u>Abraxas</u> (31/32) 84, p. 49.

4795. SKEEN, Anita
"Bulb." <u>Nimrod</u> (28:1) Aut-Wint 84, p. 67.
"Coffee." <u>Nimrod</u> (28:1) Aut-Wint 84, p. 67.
"Fixing the Moon." <u>PraS</u> (58:2) Sum 84, p. 98-99.
"Furnishings: a Collection of Prose Poems"
(Selections). <u>Nimrod</u> (28:1) Aut-Wint 84, p. 65-
68.
"How to Find Poems." <u>EngJ</u> (73:3) Mr 84, p. 42.
"Laundry." <u>Nimrod</u> (28:1) Aut-Wint 84, p. 65.
"Lesson." <u>PraS</u> (58:2) Sum 84, p. 97.
"Oven." <u>Nimrod</u> (28:1) Aut-Wint 84, p. 66.
"Pool." <u>Nimrod</u> (28:1) Aut-Wint 84, p. 66.

"Shower." <u>Nimrod</u> (28:1) Aut-Wint 84, p. 66.
"Suitcase." <u>Nimrod</u> (28:1) Aut-Wint 84, p. 68.
"Toilet." <u>Nimrod</u> (28:1) Aut-Wint 84, p. 67.
"Wallpaper." <u>Nimrod</u> (28:1) Aut-Wint 84, p. 65.
"Window." <u>Nimrod</u> (28:1) Aut-Wint 84, p. 65.

4796. SKEETER, Sharyn Jeanne
"General Alexandre Dumas de la Pailléterie."
<u>GreenfR</u> (11:3/4) Wint-Spr 84, p. 154-155.
"Liberté ou Mort: 'Volunteer Chasseurs' at
Savannah, 1779." <u>GreenfR</u> (11:3/4) Wint-Spr 84,
p. 153-154.
"The Love of Anne Fidèle and Kébinda, 1777."
<u>GreenfR</u> (11:3/4) Wint-Spr 84, p. 152-153.

4797. SKELTON, Robin
"Bushed." <u>Quarry</u> (33:1) Wint 84, p. C96.
"Note on the Economy." <u>CanLit</u> (100) Spr 84, p. 286.

4798. SKILLMAN, Judith
"Afternoon of the Child Genius." <u>PoetryNW</u> (25:3)
Aut 84, p. 20-21.
"For Tom." <u>SmPd</u> (21:1) Wint 84, p. 21.
"The Heart, A Study." <u>SenR</u> (14:1) 84, p. 51.
"The Left Hand of the Artist." <u>PoetC</u> (16:1) Aut
84, p. 32-33.
"The Sunflowers." <u>CreamCR</u> (9:1/2) 84, p. 36.
"Working Woman" (for Leona). <u>PoetryNW</u> (25:3) Aut
84, p. 21-22.

4799. SKINKER, Bertha Rives
"To Mr. T.S. Eliot, on reading 'Old Possum's Book
of Practical Cats'." <u>KenR</u> (NS 6:3) Sum 84, p.
28-29.

4800. SKIPPER, Louis
"Fico Trover." <u>PoetryNW</u> (25:4) Wint 84-85, p. 28-29.

4801. SKLAR, Morty
"Going to Camp / Leaving Camp & Getting Divorced"
(for Shelley, who went to camp once too).
<u>Abraxas</u> (31/32) 84, p. 64-65.
"Poem to the Sun." <u>Spirit</u> (7:1) 84, p. 138.

4802. SKLOOT, Floyd
"Rules of the Game." <u>Spirit</u> (7:1) 84, p. 147-148.

4803. SKRANDE, Evita
"Treasure Hunt to Find the Handkerchief." <u>Iowa</u>
(14:3) Aut 84, p. 62-63.

4804. SLACHMAN, Virginia
"Lance Delivers His Valedictory." <u>QW</u> (18) Spr-Sum
84, p. 68.

4805. SLACK, Ellen
"The Funeral of My Cousin Phil Maddux: Tinicum,
Bucks County, in the Spring." <u>PaintedB</u> (24)
Aut 84, p. 25.
"Holding Cousin/Bond of Kinship." <u>PaintedB</u> (24)

Aut 84, p. 26.
"Just Country." <u>PaintedB</u> (24) Aut 84, p. 28.

4806. SLATE, Ron
"Comfort Levels." <u>PoetryNW</u> (25:3) Aut 84, p. 24.
"Determination." <u>PoetryNW</u> (25:3) Aut 84, p. 23-24.
"Munch Post Card in My Office." <u>PoetryNW</u> (25:3)
Aut 84, p. 22-23.
"A Prepared Statement." <u>PoetryNW</u> (25:3) Aut 84,
p. 25-26.

4807. SLATER, Robert
"Morning Raga." <u>NewL</u> (50:2/3) Wint-Spr 84, p. 167.
"Presence." <u>NewL</u> (50:4) Sum 84, p. 94.

4808. SLAUGHTER, Caryl
"Housecalls." <u>Tele</u> (19) 83, p. 97.
"Mandala." <u>Tele</u> (19) 83, p. 96.
"Visian." <u>Tele</u> (19) 83, p. 96.

4809. SLAUGHTER, William
"Holes." <u>Kayak</u> (64) My 84, p. 60.
"An Odd Song." <u>Kayak</u> (64) My 84, p. 61.
"What I Hear from My Window in Alexandria, Egypt"
(an early morning poem). <u>NewL</u> (51:1) Aut 84,
p. 23.

4810. SLAVITT, David R.
"The Tristia" (Selection: To His Wife, I, 6, tr. of
Ovid). <u>TexasR</u> (5:1/2) Spr-Sum 84, p. 30-31.
"Tristia" (Selections: V-7, V-12, tr. of Ovid).
<u>MichQR</u> (23:2) Spr 84, p. 221-225.

4811. SLEIGH, Tom
"Elk at Black Fork Canyon." <u>Ploughs</u> (10:4) 84, p.
169-170.
"Hope" (For Aunt Hope). <u>Ploughs</u> (10:4) 84, p. 165-
166.
"Last Wish" (For my grandmother). <u>Ploughs</u> (10:4)
84, p. 167-168.

4812. SLESINGER, Warren
"Heartache, Heartbeat, Heartbreak." <u>ThRiPo</u>
(23/24) 84, p. 48.
"Letter." <u>ThRiPo</u> (23/24) 84, p. 46.
"Telephone." <u>ThRiPo</u> (23/24) 84, p. 47.

4813. SLOAN, De Villo
"Painting Concept." <u>Os</u> (18) 84, p. 6.

4814. SMALL, Deborah
"1905." <u>MinnR</u> (N.S. 23) Aut 84, p. 6-10.

4815. SMALL, Virginia
"The Hamburger Stand People Next Door." <u>NewL</u>
(51:1) Aut 84, p. 90.

4816. SMARIO, Tom
"A Barefoot Journey." <u>PoeticJ</u> (3) 83, p. 9.
"A Bouquet for Michelle." <u>PoeticJ</u> (4) 83, p. 25.

"The Dazzle of Dawn." <u>PoeticJ</u> (4) 83, p. 14.
"Legacy." <u>PoeticJ</u> (3) 83, p. 28-29.
"The Rescue." <u>PoeticJ</u> (4) 83, p. 19.
"The World's Greatest Poet." <u>PoeticJ</u> (8) 84, p. 30.

4817. SMART, Carolyn
      "Driving Home" (for Kenneth). <u>PoetryCR</u> (6:1) Aut
      84, p. 15.

4818. SMART, Marjory
      "3rd Quarter." <u>Waves</u> (12:1) Aut 83, p. 73.

4819. SMELAND, Cathe
      "Age of Woman." <u>AntigR</u> (59) Aut 84, p. 78.
      "Just Thinking." <u>AntigR</u> (59) Aut 84, p. 78.
      "Per Te." <u>AntigR</u> (59) Aut 84, p. 77.

4820. SMETZER, Michael
      "The New Arrival." <u>HangL</u> (46) Aut 84, p. 60.
      "Working the Tar House." <u>NewL</u> (51:2) Wint 84-85,
      p. 39-41.

4821. SMITH, Allen
      "Coexistence." <u>CrossC</u> (6:1) 84, p. 15.

4822. SMITH, Arthur
      "Extra Innings." <u>NewYorker</u> (60:17) 11 Je 84, p.
      42-43.
      "My Father's Garden." <u>ThRiPo</u> (23/24) 84, p. 45.
      "Pictures from the Floating World." <u>NewEngR</u> (7:1)
      Aut 84, p. 7-8.
      "Pike's Head." <u>ThRiPo</u> (23/24) 84, p. 44-45.
      "Those Goats." <u>NewYorker</u> (60:11) 30 Ap 84, p. 93.
      "Twelve Pole" (for my mother). <u>NewEngR</u> (7:1) Aut
      84, p. 6-7.

4823. SMITH, Bruce
      "Snow on the Ocean." <u>Poetry</u> (145:2) N 84, p. 73.

4824. SMITH, Charlie
      "The Sweetness of a Peach." <u>Field</u> (31) Aut 84, p.
      73-74.
      "The Unseen Piers upon Which the World Rides."
      <u>Field</u> (31) Aut 84, p. 72.

SMITH, D. L. Crockett: <u>See</u> CROCKETT-SMITH, D. L.

4825. SMITH, Dave
      "An Antipastoral Memory of One Summer." <u>NewYorker</u>
      (60:5) 19 Mr 84, p. 52.
      "Chopping Wood." <u>NewYorker</u> (60:7) 2 Ap 84, p. 44.
      "The Family." <u>Antaeus</u> (53) Aut 84, p. 236-238.
      "The Isle of Wight." <u>Shen</u> (35:1) 83-84, p. 67-73.
      "A Nest of Mice." <u>Nat</u> (238:22) 9 Je 84, p. 713.
      "Stroke." <u>NewYorker</u> (60:13) 14 My 84, p. 50.

4826. SMITH, David (1906-1965, sculptor)
      "The Question--What Are Your Influences." <u>PoetryE</u>
      (13/14) Spr-Sum 84, p. 207-209.
      "The Question--What Is Your Hope." <u>PoetryE</u>

(13/14) Spr-Sum 84, p. 204-205.

4827. SMITH, Dean Wesley
"Dating While Waiting for a Divorce." SnapD (7:2)
Spr 84, p. 50.

4828. SMITH, Douglas
"A Canadian Tourist Flies to St. Paul on
Thanksgiving Weekend in Search of Great
Bargains." NoDaQ (52:3) Sum 84, p. 179-180.
"Flowers of Fire: Canada Turns 116." NoDaQ (52:3)
Sum 84, p. 178-179.
"Lives" (from the Soap Opera Synopsis column in the
Winnipeg Free Press, 1983). Kayak (64) My 84,
p. 59.
"What the Moon Cannot Bear." PoetryE (15) Aut 84,
p. 26.

4829. SMITH, Hugh T.
"48 Hour Pass." Wind (14:51) 84, p. 46.

4830. SMITH, James Steel
"Desert Highway." Epoch (33:3) Sum-Aut 84, p. 257.
"Linkings." Epoch (33:3) Sum-Aut 84, p. 258.
"Mission Box." Epoch (33:3) Sum-Aut 84, p. 259.

SMITH, James Sutherland: See SUTHERLAND-SMITH, James

4831. SMITH, Jayne R.
"Dungeons and Dragons" (To Brion). EngJ (73:5) S
84, p. 84.

4832. SMITH, Jennifer E.
"So Many Mountains." Stepping Wint 84, p. 20.

4833. SMITH, Jim
"And When the Kid Drowned on My Mother It Became an
Angel." Grain (12:2) My 84, p. 41.
"Baby Film Review" (for Megan). Grain (12:2) My
84, p. 40.
"Found Text -- Incident 2." Waves (13:1) Aut 84,
p. 34.
"Mayakovsky: The Phillistine Reefs" (4b).
PoetryCR (5:4) Sum 84, p. 16.

4834. SMITH, Jordan
"Days of 1974." Poetry (143:5) F 84, p. 293-294.
"Two Pen and Ink Studies for Despair" (from Six
Poems after the drawings and paintings by
Edvard Munch). Chelsea (42/43) 84, p. 418-419.

4835. SMITH, Ken
"They Call It the Window of Vulnerability."
Stand (25:4) Aut 84, p. 6.

4836. SMITH, Kristin
"Great Grandpa." PikeF (6) Aut 84, p. 21.

4837. SMITH, Lawrence R.
"Advice from a Depressed Area" (tr. of Giovanni

Giudici). <u>PoetryE</u> (15) Aut 84, p. 75.
"April 1961" (tr. of Franco Fortini). <u>PoetryE</u>
    (15) Aut 84, p. 74.
"Childish Canzonetta" (tr. of Alfredo Giuliani).
    <u>PoetryE</u> (15) Aut 84, p. 77.
"Convalescence" (tr. of Alfredo Giuliani).
    <u>PoetryE</u> (15) Aut 84, p. 78.
"I Work All Day" (tr. of Pier Paolo Pasolini).
    <u>PoetryE</u> (15) Aut 84, p. 79.
"One September Evening" (tr. of Franco Fortini).
    <u>PoetryE</u> (15) Aut 84, p. 73.
"Supplication to My Mother" (tr. of Pier Paolo
    Pasolini). <u>PoetryE</u> (15) Aut 84, p. 80.
"A Woman" (tr. of Giovanni Giudici). <u>PoetryE</u> (15)
    Aut 84, p. 76.

4838. SMITH, Le Roy, Jr.
    "The Whole." <u>Comm</u> (111:2) 27 Ja 84, p. 46.

4839. SMITH, LeRoy
    "The Rejected Image." <u>Comm</u> (111:7) 6 Ap 84, p. 220.

4840. SMITH, Leonora Anderson
    "Missing Legacy." <u>CentR</u> (28:3) Sum 84, p. 225-227.

4841. SMITH, Loueva
    "Locust." <u>TexasR</u> (5:3/4) Aut-Wint 84, p. 26-27.
    "The Operation." <u>TexasR</u> (5:3/4) Aut-Wint 84, p. 28.

4842. SMITH, Macklin
    "Birding the Battle of Attu." <u>Ploughs</u> (10:1) 84,
        p. 146-147.
    "What a Clever Design." <u>Ploughs</u> (10:1) 84, p. 148.

4843. SMITH, Melinda B.
    "I've Heard the Laughter." <u>Poem</u> (50) Mr 84, p. 24.
    "Terra." <u>Poem</u> (50) Mr 84, p. 23.

4844. SMITH, Michael
    "Male and Female Poets" (tr. of Lucía Fox).
        <u>ConcPo</u> (17:2) Aut 84, p. 181.

SMITH, Milton: <u>See</u> MBEMBE (Milton Smith)

4845. SMITH, Patty
    "The memory of drugged and pain-filled hours."
        <u>TriQ</u> (61) Aut 84, p. 68.

4846. SMITH, R. T.
    "After Quarreling." <u>MemphisSR</u> (5:1) Aut 84, p. 48.
    "Apple-Light" (for Jo). <u>CimR</u> (68) Jl 84, p. 10.
    "Bats." <u>MemphisSR</u> (5:1) Aut 84, p. 49.
    "The Climbers." <u>TexasR</u> (5:3/4) Aut-Wint 84, p. 20-
        21.
    "Los Hurdes: A Film." <u>CrabCR</u> (2:1) Sum 84, p. 21.
    "Painting Osceola: An Epistle from George Catlin to
        His Wife." <u>CimR</u> (68) Jl 84, p. 23-26.

4847. SMITH, Ron
    "Seasonal." <u>CapilR</u> (30) 84, p. 46-53.

4848. SMITH, Russell C.
      "April's Autobiography." LittleM (14:3) 84, p. 30.
      "In the Jaws of the Beast." LittleM (14:3) 84, p.
      29.

4849. SMITH, Stephen
      "Michael." SouthernPR (24:2) Aut 84, p. 49-50.

4850. SMITH, Stephen E.
      "Eulogy for a Friend Killed near Da Nang." KanQ
      (16:1/2) Wint-Spr 84, p. 207.

4851. SMITH, Steven
      "Probable Jazz" (a conducted piece for two voices).
      CapilR (31) 84, p. 52.

4852. SMITH, Sue M.
      "Both of Me." PottPort (6) 84, p. 5.

SMITH, Sybil Woods: See WOODS-SMITH, Sybil

4853. SMITH, Thomas R.
      "Ezekiel." BlueBldgs (7) 84, p. 35.
      "The Gift." YellowS (11) Sum 84, p. 12.
      "Keeping the Star." ThirdW (2) Spr 84, p. 33.

4854. SMITH, Tom
      "Buying Condoms." BelPoJ (34:4) Sum 84, p. 18-19.
      "The Last Child." BelPoJ (34:4) Sum 84, p. 15-18.

4855. SMITH, Virginia E.
      "Upbeat News Item -- L. A. Times." PoeticJ (1)
      83, p. 4.

4856. SMITH, William Jay
      "The Sad Field-Hand" (tr. of Gyula Illyés, w.
      Miklós Vajda and Gyula Kodolányi). HolCrit
      (21:1) F 84, p. 3.
      "Tilting Sail" (tr. of Gyula Illyés, w. Miklós
      Vajda and Gyula Kodolányi). HolCrit (21:1) F
      84, p. 12.
      "We Say This Prayer" (tr. of Jozsef Tornai). Iowa
      (14:2) Spr-Sum 84, p. 209.
      "Wound and Knife" (tr. of György Somlyó, w.
      Maria Korosy). Iowa (14:2) Spr-Sum 84, p. 202.
      "A Wreath" (tr. of Gyula Illyés, w. Miklós
      Vajda and Gyula Kodolányi). HolCrit (21:1) F
      84, p. 10-11.

4857. SMITH-BOWERS, Cathy
      "The Fat Lady Travels." GeoR (38:1) Spr 84, p. 74.
      "A Sequence of Women." SouthernPR (24:1) Spr 84,
      p. 15-17.
      "Turning the Myth Around." SouthernHR (18:1) Wint
      84, p. 64.

4858. SMYTH, Gerard
      "Loneliness." CreamCR (9:1/2) 84, p. 70.

4859. SMYTH, Paul
       "The Lie." CapeR (19:3) 20th Anniverary Issue 84,
       p. 47.

4860. SNEYD, Steve
       "Call of Duty." Bogg (52) 84, p. 46.
       "Coming to Set You Free." Sam (41:1, release 161)
       84, p. 42.
       "You Owe It to the Profession." Veloc (4) Sum 84,
       p. 26.

4861. SNODGRASS, Ann
       "Porterfield: Morning in an Orchard." AntR (42:4)
       Aut 84, p. 460.

4862. SNODGRASS, W. D.
       "Reichsmarschall Hermann Goering" (22 April 1945).
       Salm (65) Aut 84, p. 113-114.
       "Who Wants to Cure a Migraine" (tr. of Gabriel
       Bataille). NeqC (4:1) Wint 84, p. 53-55.

4863. SNOW, Carol
       "Positions of the Body." Antaeus (53) Aut 84, p.
       95-102.

4864. SNOW, Edward
       "The Bowl of Roses" (tr. of Rainer Maria Rilke).
       Thrpny (18) Sum 84, p. 27.

4865. SNOW, Karen
       "Secretary." BelPoJ (35:1) Aut 84, p. 8-12.

4866. SNYDAL, Laurence
       "Homefield." CapeR (19:2) Sum 84, p. 11.
       "Preserving." CapeR (19:2) Sum 84, p. 10.

4867. SNYDER, Gary
       "August on Sourdough, a Visit from Dick Brewer."
       Tendril (18, special issue) 84, p. 159-160.
       "Strategic Air Command" (VIII, 82, Koip Peak,
       Sierra Nevada). Spirit (7:1) 84, p. 19.
       "True Night." TexasR (5:3/4) Aut-Wint 84, p. 140-
       142.

4868. SOBIN, A. G.
       "The Artist's Intention." NewL (50:2/3) Wint-Spr
       84, p. 215.

4869. SOBIN, Anthony
       "Rio de Janeiro." KanQ (16:1/2) Wint-Spr 84, p. 8.

4870. SOBIN, Gustaf
       "Flowering Almonds: Outside and In." Pequod
       (16/17) 84, p. 79-80.
       "Madrigal." Pequod (16/17) 84, p. 77-78.

4871. SOBOTKA, Henry
       "Dirge." SanFPJ (6:4) 84, p. 25.
       "Disembowelment." SanFPJ (6:4) 84, p. 74-75.

4872. SOCARD, Gilbert
"Daily Bread" (from Rêver à Haute Voix, tr.
by Louis A. Olivier). PikeF (6) Aut 84, p. 14.

4873. SOCOLOW, Elizabeth Anne
"Beautiful Is Hard." Ploughs (10:4) 84, p. 130-131.
"Of Cloves, Cleats, Bad Luck, Old Friends."
Ploughs (10:4) 84, p. 132-133.

4874. SODERGRAN, Edith
"Dagen Svalnar." YellowS (12) Aut 84, p. 36.
"The Day Cools" (tr. by Stina Katchadourian).
YellowS (12) Aut 84, p. 36.
"Kårlek." YellowS (12) Aut 84, p. 37.
"Love" (tr. by Stina Katchadourian). YellowS (12)
Aut 84, p. 37.

4875. SODERLING, Janice
"Change of Earth" (Three poems from the section
"Bellevue Hospital, New York, tr. of Heidi von
Born). MalR (67) F 84, p. 104-105.
"Have You Seen the Wild Dogs in Benidorm." MalR
(67) F 84, p. 106-107.

4876. SOKOLSKY, Helen H.
"It Is Not So Simple." Confr (27/28) 84, p. 293.
"The Navigators." Confr (27/28) 84, p. 294.

4877. SOLARI, Rose
"Juggling." PoetL (79:3) Aut 84, p. 148.

4878. SOLDOFSKY, Alan
"Hitchhiking." CalQ (25) Aut 84, p. 32.

4879. SOLHEIM, James
"Atoms." PoetryNW (25:4) Wint 84-85, p. 13.
"Midnight on the Maryville High Football Field."
PoetryNW (25:4) Wint 84-85, p. 14.
"Poem around My Father." MalR (67) F 84, p. 63-64.
"Riding to the Hospital." CimR (66) Ja 84, p. 56.
"Trespassing in Job's, the Abandoned Hospital."
CimR (69) O 84, p. 42-43.
"A Young Couple Coming Home." MalR (67) F 84, p.
62-63.

4880. SOLIS, Pedro Xavier
"In My Country" (tr. by Marc Zimmerman and Ellen
Banberger). MinnR (N.S. 22) Spr 84, p. 67.

4881. SOLLY, Richard
"For My Student, Sister Rose." PoeticJ (6) 84, p.
24.

4882. SOLOMON, Carl
"La Condition Humaine." MoodySI (14) Spr 84, p. 23.
"Coptic." MoodySI (14) Spr 84, p. 23.

4883. SOLOMON, Sherry
"The Lifesaver" (for Gail). BelPoJ (35:2) Wint 84-
85, p. 17.

4884. SOLONCHE, J. R.
    "Arrowhead." SmPd (21:3) Aut 84, p. 28.
    "Fault Finding." SmPd (21:3) Aut 84, p. 24.
    "First Snow." SmPd (21:3) Aut 84, p. 25.
    "The Poet at Home." LitR (28:1) Aut 84, p. 120-121.
    "Suggested Photographs" (For J. & her new camera).
        SmPd (21:3) Aut 84, p. 26-27.
    "A Walk around the Lake." Poem (51) Mr [i.e. Jl]
        84, p. 54.

4885. SOLT, John
    "The Street" (tr. of Sachiko Yoshihara). Iowa
        (14:2) Spr-Sum 84, p. 60.
    "Woman" (tr. of Sachiko Yoshihara). Iowa (14:2)
        Spr-Sum 84, p. 60-61.

4886. SOLWAY, David
    "The Oracle." CanLit (100) Spr 84, p. 298.

4887. SOMAN, Jeanne B.
    "Symbiotic Detachment." SanFPJ (6:1) 84, p. 16.

4888. SOMERVILLE, Jane
    "In the Cruel Month." StoneC (12:1/2) Aut-Wint
        84, p. 14.
    "The Summer Storm." NegC (4:3) Sum 84, p. 89.
    "Talking to My Mother on the Telephone." Wind
        (14:50) 84, p. 50.

4889. SOMLYO, György
    "Fable of First Person" (tr. by Donald Davie).
        Iowa (14:2) Spr-Sum 84, p. 202-203.
    "Wound and Knife" (tr. by Maria Korosy and William
        Jay Smith). Iowa (14:2) Spr-Sum 84, p. 202.

4890. SOMMER, Jason
    "The Ballad of Fighting with My Father." Ploughs
        (10:1) 84, p. 157-158.

4891. SOMMER, Piotr
    "Alma Ata" (Excerpts, tr. by the author and Charles
        Mignon). PraS (58:1) Spr 84, p. 27-28.
    "For My Mother" (tr. by the author and Charles
        Mignon). PraS (58:1) Spr 84, p. 28-29.
    "Home" (tr. by the author and Charles Mignon).
        PraS (58:1) Spr 84, p. 29-30.
    "I Know" (Tr. by the author and Charles Mignon).
        PraS (58:1) Spr 84, p. 31.
    "I'll put it down in tables" (from "Alma Ata", tr.
        by the author and Charles Mignon). PraS (58:1)
        Spr 84, p. 28.
    "I've brought many valuable things" (from "Alma
        Ata", tr. by the author and Charles Mignon).
        PraS (58:1) Spr 84, p. 27.
    "A Request" (tr. by the author and Charles Mignon).
        PraS (58:1) Spr 84, p. 30.

4892. SOMOZA, Joseph
    "The Chinese Print." GreenfR (11:3/4) Wint-Spr
        84, p. 151.

"Seaside." <u>Sam</u> (37:3, 147th release) 83, p. 51.

4893. SONDE, Susan
"Pater Noster for the Days Leading Up to the New
Year." <u>NewL</u> (51:2) Wint 84-85, p. 44-45.

4894. SONIAT, Katherine
"Cages." <u>MSS</u> (3:2/3) Spr 84, p. 40.
"Domestication." <u>SouthernR</u> (20:2) Spr 84, p. 339.
"Free-Spirited Rabbit Looking for Home." <u>MalR</u>
(68) Je 84, p. 63.
"Fresh Hardware." <u>SouthernR</u> (20:2) Spr 84, p. 338-
339.
"Horizon." <u>PoetryCR</u> (5:4) Sum 84, p. 19.
"Night Tracking." <u>MalR</u> (68) Je 84, p. 64.
"North." <u>SouthernR</u> (20:2) Spr 84, p. 340.
"Notes of Departure." <u>Poetry</u> (144:1) Ap 84, p. 4-6.
"Primary Motif." <u>Poetry</u> (144:1) Ap 84, p. 4.
"Summer Resurrection." <u>SouthernR</u> (20:2) Spr 84,
p. 337.

4895. SORENSEN, Sally Jo
"ABC Products." <u>PoetL</u> (79:2) Sum 84, p. 100.
"Before the Revolution." <u>PoetL</u> (79:2) Sum 84, p.
101.
"Grandmother's Tale." <u>WestB</u> (15) 84, p. 79.
"Industrial Accident." <u>PoetL</u> (79:2) Sum 84, p. 101.

4896. SORENSON, Preben Major
"Thanatos" (tr. by Anne Born). <u>Stand</u> (25:3) Sum
84, p. 55.
"This Picture" (tr. by Anne Born). <u>Stand</u> (25:3)
Sum 84, p. 55.

4897. SORESCU, Marin
"Poisons" (tr. by Michael Hamburger). <u>NowestR</u>
(22:3) 84, p. 124.

4898. SORESTAD, Glen
"Bennett Halkett." <u>PoetryCR</u> (5:3) Spr 84, p. 5.
"Goldfish and Bumblebees" (for Joe). <u>CanLit</u> (100)
Spr 84, p. 299.
"The Road from Nelson to Vernon." <u>CrossC</u> (6:3)
84, p. 14.
"Shelling Peas." <u>PoetryCR</u> (6:1) Aut 84, p. 15.

4899. SORKIN, Adam
"At Night on the Shore" (tr. of Anghel Dumbraveanu,
w. Irina Grigorescu). <u>Mund</u> (14:2) 84, p. 31.
"Heralds" (tr. of Anghel Dumbraveanu, w. Irina
Grigorescu). <u>Mund</u> (14:2) 84, p. 27.
"Horses of Time" (tr. of Anghel Dumbraveanu, w.
Irina Grigorescu). <u>Mund</u> (14:2) 84, p. 27.
"The Masks" (tr. of Anghel Dumbraveanu, w. Irina
Grigorescu). <u>Mund</u> (14:2) 84, p. 29.

4900. SORKIN, Adam J.
"Hidden Portrait" (tr. of Anghel Dumbraveanu, w.
Irina Grigorescu). <u>ConcPo</u> (17:2) Aut 84, p. 70.
"Interior" (tr. of Anghel Dumbraveanu, w. Irina

Grigorescu). <u>ConcPo</u> (17:2) Aut 84, p. 70.

4901. SOSA, Roberto
"The Elect of Violence" (tr. by Zoe Anglesey).
<u>OroM</u> (2:3/4, issue 7/8) 84, p. 7.
"Los Elegidos de la Violencia." <u>OroM</u> (2:3/4,
issue 7/8) 84, p. 6.

4902. SOSAYA, Elizabeth
"Fall." <u>AntigR</u> (57) Spr 84, p. 116.

4903. SOTO, Gary
"Ambition" (For Two Friends). <u>Poetry</u> (144:4) Jl
84, p. 192-193.
"Between Words." <u>Poetry</u> (143:4) Ja 84, p. 191-192.
"Desire." <u>Poetry</u> (144:4) Jl 84, p. 188-189.
"Finding a Lucky Number" (To a Nephew). <u>Poetry</u>
(144:4) Jl 84, p. 187-188.
"The Jungle Cafe." <u>Poetry</u> (144:4) Jl 84, p. 193-194.
"Looking Around, Believing." <u>Poetry</u> (143:4) Ja
84, p. 189.
"Morning on This Street." <u>Poetry</u> (144:4) Jl 84,
p. 190-191.
"The Plum's Heart." <u>Poetry</u> (144:4) Jl 84, p. 189-
190.
"Seeing Things." <u>Thrpny</u> (18) Sum 84, p. 6.
"When We Wake." <u>Poetry</u> (143:4) Ja 84, p. 190-191.

4904. SOTO, Nilda
"Cuándo amaneceras mota de luna." <u>Mairena</u>
(6:17) Aut 84, p. 98.

SOTO, Salvador Arana: <u>See</u> ARANA SOTO, Salvador

4905. SOUPAULT, Philippe
"Aquarium (1917)" (Selections, tr. by Pat Nolan).
<u>Tele</u> (19) 83, p. 115-118.
"Everybody's a Critic" (tr. by Pat Nolan). <u>Tele</u>
(19) 83, p. 116.
"Extra Ordinary" (tr. by Pat Nolan). <u>Tele</u> (19)
83, p. 117.
"Flame" (tr. by Pat Nolan). <u>Tele</u> (19) 83, p. 115.
"Flash" (tr. by Pat Nolan). <u>Tele</u> (19) 83, p. 118.
"Flight" (tr. by Pat Nolan). <u>Tele</u> (19) 83, p. 115.
"Horizon" (for Tristan Tzara, tr. by Paulette
Schmidt). <u>MissouriR</u> (7:3) 84, p. 16.
"Let Old Fools Have the Floor" (tr. by Paulette
Schmidt). <u>MissouriR</u> (7:3) 84, p. 17.
"Poem: My words lead me to places unknown" (tr. by
Pat Nolan). <u>Tele</u> (19) 83, p. 116.
"Seasonelle" (tr. by Pat Nolan). <u>Tele</u> (19) 83, p.
117.

4906. SOUSTER, Raymond
"Blue Heron near the Old Mill Bridge." <u>PoetryCR</u>
(6:1) Aut 84, p. 18.
"The Nine O'Clock School Bell Ringing." <u>PoetryCR</u>
(6:1) Aut 84, p. 18.
"Outburst." <u>PoetryCR</u> (6:2) Wint 84-85, p. 10.
"Queen Anne's Lace." <u>Quarry</u> (33:1) Wint 84, p. C100.

"Saturday Afternoon at Kensington Market" (for Bill
Brooks). <u>CanLit</u> (100) Spr 84, p. 300.

4907. SOUTHER, J. D.
"James Dean" (w. Jackson Browne, Glenn Frey, and
Don Henley, 1974, Benchmark Music, ASCAP).
<u>NewOR</u> (11:3/4) Aut-Wint 84, p. 95.

4908. SOUTHWICK, Marcia
"Blood." <u>AntR</u> (42:1) Wint 84, p. 90-91.
"Child, Invisible Fire." <u>Field</u> (30) Spr 84, p. 42-
43.

4909. SPACKS, Barry
"Body My Familiar." <u>Stand</u> (25:4) Aut 84, p. 42.
"Courting the Moon." <u>AmerPoR</u> (13:3) My-Je 84, p. 38.
"Ease." <u>AmerPoR</u> (13:3) My-Je 84, p. 37.
"Gesture of Air." <u>AmerPoR</u> (13:3) My-Je 84, p. 38.
"Introduction to Poetry." <u>VirQR</u> (60:1) Wint 84,
p. 62.
"Little Things." <u>AmerPoR</u> (13:3) My-Je 84, p. 37.
"The Model." <u>IndR</u> (7:3) Sum 84, p. 59.

4910. SPANG, Bruce
"August 6." <u>NowestR</u> (22:1/2) 84, p. 46.

4911. SPANGLE, Douglas
"Question" (A Fragment from the long poem Steel
Bridge). <u>ThirdW</u> (2) Spr 84, p. 60-61.
"Steel Bridge" (Selections). <u>ThirdW</u> (2) Spr 84,
p. 60-68.
"Three Sparks for Muster Mark" (From the long poem
Steel Bridge). <u>ThirdW</u> (2) Spr 84, p. 62-68.

4912. SPARSHOTT, Francis
"Chewing the Fat." <u>PoetryCR</u> (5:3) Spr 84, p. 7.
"Listen Eugenia." <u>PoetryCR</u> (6:2) Wint 84-85, p. 26.
"On the Brocken." <u>PoetryCR</u> (6:1) Aut 84, p. 18.
"Santayana." <u>CanLit</u> (100) Spr 84, p. 301.
"State Visit." <u>PoetryCR</u> (6:2) Wint 84-85, p. 19.

4913. SPEAKES, Richard
"Decorations." <u>Tendril</u> (17) Wint 84, p. 162.
"Geisha." <u>Tendril</u> (17) Wint 84, p. 160.
"Last Chance Cafe." <u>QW</u> (18) Spr-Sum 84, p. 100.
"Things That Go Bump in the Night." <u>Tendril</u> (17)
Wint 84, p. 161.

4914. SPEAR, Roberta
"Cinque Terre: The Land of Five Noises" (For
Shula). <u>Poetry</u> (144:4) Jl 84, p. 200.
"Ice." <u>Poetry</u> (144:4) Jl 84, p. 199.

4915. SPEARS, Heather
"Købmagergade (1)." <u>Waves</u> (13:1) Aut 84, p. 61.
"Købmagergade (2)." <u>Waves</u> (13:1) Aut 84, p. 61.
"Procedure." <u>Waves</u> (13:1) Aut 84, p. 60.
"Viking Excavations, Runegaard." <u>PoetryCR</u> (6:2)
Wint 84-85, p. 16.

4916. SPEARS, Monroe
"Academic Nightmare" (Vier Ernste Gesänge, I).
SouthernR (20:4) Aut 84, p. 865-866.
"Security" (Vier Ernste Gesänge, III).
SouthernR (20:4) Aut 84, p. 867.
"The Shepherds' Complaint: Academic Variations on a
Theme from Auden." SouthernR (20:4) Aut 84, p.
861-865.
"The Third Ashram" (Vier Ernste Gesänge, II).
SouthernR (20:4) Aut 84, p. 866.
"To the Reader" (Vier Ernste Gesänge, IV).
SouthernR (20:4) Aut 84, p. 867-868.
"Vier Ernste Gesänge." SouthernR (20:4) Aut 84,
p. 865-868.

4917. SPEER, Laurel
"Bathing with Gide on the Beach." LittleM (14:3)
84, p. 17.
"The Cat Sits Inside." CapeR (19:3) 20th
Anniverary Issue 84, p. 48.
"Famous Ames Charm." NegC (4:4) Aut 84, p. 15.
"Putting on a Girdle for the Wallace Sterling Tea"
(1958). MidAR (4:1) Spr 84, p. 138.

4918. SPENCE, Michael
"The Darkening." SoDakR (22:3) Aut 84, p. 66.
"Dusk and After." SoDakR (22:3) Aut 84, p. 65.
"Stripping." GreenfR (12:1/2) Sum-Aut 84, p. 132.

4919. SPENCER, Jane
"The Dark." Mund (14:2) 84, p. 51.
"Meanings." Mund (14:2) 84, p. 50.
"My Black Wool Coat." Mund (14:2) 84, p. 50.
"Summer in New York." Mund (14:2) 84, p. 51.

4920. SPENDER, Stephen
"After Stefan George -- Mein Kind Kam Heim." Shen
(35:2/3) 84, p. 324.
"Auden Aetat XX, LX." Shen (35:2/3) 84, p. 30.
"A Chorus of Oedipus." PartR (51:4/52:1
Anniversary issue) 84-85, p. 609.
"Chorus of Oedipus at Colonos." PartR (51:4/52:1
Anniversary issue) 84-85, p. 610.
"From My Diary." PartR (51:4/52:1 Anniversary
issue) 84-85, p. 608.
"A Girl Who Has Drowned Herself Speaks." PartR
(51:4/52:1 Anniversary issue) 84-85, p. 608.

4921. SPERO, Nancy
"Codex Artaud" (Excerpts). Sulfur (3:3, issue 9)
84, p. 60-66.

4922. SPICEHANDLER, Ezra
"Naming Souls" (tr. of Uri Zvi Greenberg, w. Jon
Silkin). Stand (25:4) Aut 84, p. 65.

4923. SPICER, David
"The Man Who Wore the Beautiful Hats." AmerPoR
(13:3) My-Je 84, p. 46.

4924. SPICHER, Julia M.
"Handling Tools." WestB (15) 84, p. 80.

4925. SPIEGEL, Robert
"Mourning Doves" (for Maggie). Wind (14:52) 84,
p. 45-46.
"One Night Locked Forever." YellowS (11) Sum 84,
p. 11.

4926. SPIGLE, Naomi
"The Driving Lesson." WindO (44) Sum-Aut 84, p.
17-18.

4927. SPINGARN, Lawrence P.
"Cleaning Out the Desk." Salm (65) Aut 84, p. 120-
121.
"Horn and Hardart" (New York: 1935). Salm (65)
Aut 84, p. 119-120.
"Rudy." Salm (65) Aut 84, p. 119.

4928. SPINKS, Randall
"The Mind Is Like an Hourglass." TexasR (5:3/4)
Aut-Wint 84, p. 104-105.

4929. SPIRES, Elizabeth
"Angel" (Amiens Cathedral). Poetry (145:3) D 84,
p. 153.
"April: First Movement." Ploughs (10:1) 84, p.
160-161.
"Café Luna." SouthwR (69:3) Sum 84, p. 304-306.
"The Falling." Ploughs (10:1) 84, p. 159-160.
"Mascara." NewYorker (60:40) 19 N 84, p. 58.
"Sky above Clouds." QW (18) Spr-Sum 84, p. 44.
"Storyville Portrait" (New Orleans red light
district, 1912: a photograph by E. J. Bellocq).
PartR (51:3) 84, p. 388-389.
"Waving Goodbye." NewYorker (60:3) 5 Mr 84, p. 52.

4930. SPIVACK, Kathleen
"The Doctor." MichQR (23:3) Sum 84, p. 400-401.
"The Flower Bed." GreenfR (11:3/4) Wint-Spr 84,
p. 120-121.
"Hold On Hold back." NoDaQ (52:2) Spr 84, p. 30.
"Horses Dreaming." NoDaQ (52:2) Spr 84, p. 31.
"Letter from a Friend." StoneC (11:3/4) Spr-Sum
84, p. 16-17.
"Living Secretly." PoetL (79:2) Sum 84, p. 86.
"The Path into Night." Atlantic (254:5) N 84, p. 60.
"Present Participle." MinnR (N.S. 23) Aut 84, p.
151.
"She Dreams." PoetL (79:2) Sum 84, p. 88-89.
"Someone Is Leaving." StoneC (11:3/4) Spr-Sum 84,
p. 17.
"Storm Warnings." NoDaQ (52:2) Spr 84, p. 32.
"The Suitability Quiz." GreenfR (11:3/4) Wint-Spr
84, p. 120.
"Three Generations." PoetL (79:2) Sum 84, p. 87.
"The Traveller." NoDaQ (52:2) Spr 84, p. 33.
"West Virginia Handicrafts." Ploughs (10:1) 84,
p. 149-151.

4931. SPIVACK, Susan Fantl
"Cat, Snake, and Frog." Blueline (5:2) Wint-Spr
84, p. 43.
"The Metal Cage: A Fable." 13thM (8:1/2) 84, p.
176-177.
"My Skin Is Not Yours." YellowS (12) Aut 84, p. 8.
"Sarah in Her Daughter's House with Fancy Faucets
Remembers the Shul." GreenfR (12:1/2) Sum-Aut
84, p. 136.
"Signalling." YellowS (10) Spr 84, p. 7.
"Visit to the Province." Tele (19) 83, p. 95.

4932. SPIVEY, Ted R.
"Two Poets at Eighty." DekalbLAJ (20th
Anniversary Issue) 84, p. 109.

4933. SPLAKE, T. Kilgore
"Biorhythm." PoeticJ (1) 83, p. 23.
"Broken Rainbow." PoeticJ (1) 83, p. 30.

4934. SPOTTSWOOD, H. M.
"Driving after Snow." PoeticJ (7) 84, p. 9.
"Morning Air." Wind (14:50) 84, p. 51-52.
"Pete and Luther" (Down but not out). PoeticJ (3)
83, p. 16-17.
"Urban Narrative." Wind (14:50) 84, p. 52.

4935. SPUTE, Penny M.
"Forgotten." PoeticJ (7) 84, p. 17.

SRI SURYAKANT TRIPATHI: See NIRALA

4936. ST. ANDREWS, Bonnie
"The Sisyphus Shuffle." DekalbLAJ (17:1/2) 84, p.
142.

4937. ST. CLAIR, Philip
"Coyote Cantina." TexasR (5:1/2) Spr-Sum 84, p. 60.

4938. ST. CYR, Napoleon
"Scratch Me." SmPd (21:2) Spr 84, p. 11.

4939. ST. JOHN, David
"Chapter Forever." GrandS (3:3) Spr 84, p. 106.
"Crossroads." Field (30) Spr 84, p. 37.
"The Day of the Sentry." Antaeus (52) Apr 84, p.
79-80.
"Desire." NewYorker (60:26) 13 Ag 84, p. 36.
"The Flute." YaleR (74:1) Aut 84, p. 56-57.
"Gin." Tendril (18, special issue) 84, p. 61-62.
"Leap of Faith." NewYorker (60:41) 26 N 84, p. 52.
"Many Rivers." YaleR (74:1) Aut 84, p. 56.
"Night." Antaeus (52) Apr 84, p. 81.
"No Heaven." Poetry (145:3) D 84, p. 154-156.
"Occasions for Monuments." NewRep (190:10) 12 Mr
84, p. 34.
"The Reef." NewYorker (60:39) 12 N 84, p. 48.

4940. ST. MARTIN, Hardie
"Hospital" (tr. of José Adán Castelar). Nat

(238:3) 28 Ja 84, p. 100.
"Small Hours of the Night" (tr. of Roque Dalton).
<u>Nat</u> (238:3) 28 Ja 84, p. 100.

4941. STAFFORD, Kim R.
"Aunt Charlotte Said." <u>Field</u> (30) Spr 84, p. 58.
"Back Home in the Shopping Center." <u>VirQR</u> (60:4)
Aut 84, p. 626.
"Indian Languages." <u>VirQR</u> (60:4) Aut 84, p. "627-
628.
"Medieval Prayerbook." <u>Field</u> (30) Spr 84, p. 56-57.
"Shockley." <u>PoetryNW</u> (25:2) Sum 84, p. 24-25.

4942. STAFFORD, William
"1940." <u>SouthernHR</u> (18:3) Sum 84, p. 233.
"Across Kansas." <u>AmerPoR</u> (13:4) Jl-Ag 84, p. 30.
"Burning a Book." <u>Field</u> (31) Aut 84, p. 51.
"Friend Who Never Came." <u>NewL</u> (50:2/3) Wint-Spr
84, p. 29.
"Geography Lesson." <u>TexasR</u> (5:1/2) Spr-Sum 84, p.
59.
"High School." <u>CarolQ</u> (36:3) Spr 84, p. 17.
"Incident." <u>Spirit</u> (7:1) 84, p. 60.
"Losing a Friend." <u>Chelsea</u> (42/43) 84, p. 259.
"Maybe Alone on My Bike." <u>Poetry</u> (144:4) Jl 84,
p. 232.
"Maybe This Way." <u>PoetC</u> (15:2) Wint 84, p. 33.
"A Note Slid under the Door." <u>NowestR</u> (22:1/2)
84, p. 143.
"Ode to Garlic." <u>PoetC</u> (15:2) Wint 84, p. 32.
"Our Time." <u>WoosterR</u> (1:1) Mr 84, p. 9.
"Saint Matthew and All." <u>CarolQ</u> (36:3) Spr 84, p.
16.
"Saying It." <u>CarolQ</u> (36:3) Spr 84, p. 18.
"A Song of Widows and Orphans." <u>NewL</u> (50:2/3)
Wint-Spr 84, p. 29.
"The Spirit of '75." <u>NewL</u> (50:2/3) Wint-Spr 84,
p. 30-31.
"Tides." <u>GeoR</u> (38:4) Wint 84, p. 854.
"Wearing Ear Protectors." <u>GeoR</u> (38:4) Wint 84, p.
853-854.

4943. STANDING, Sue
"How to Be Angry." <u>Ploughs</u> (10:1) 84, p. 152.

4944. STANFORD, Ann
"After Winslow Homer" (3 poems). <u>Nimrod</u> (28:1)
Aut-Wint 84, p. 62-64.
"Homeward Bound" (After Winslow Homer: Wood-
engraving, Harper's Weekly, December 21, 1867).
<u>Nimrod</u> (28:1) Aut-Wint 84, p. 63.
"Saved" (After Winslow Homer: Etching, 1889).
<u>Nimrod</u> (28:1) Aut-Wint 84, p. 64.
"The Wreck" (After Winslow Homer: Oil painting,
1896). <u>Nimrod</u> (28:1) Aut-Wint 84, p. 62.

4945. STANFORD, Janet Holmes
"Aviary." <u>Antaeus</u> (52) Apr 84, p. 84.
"Charleston." <u>Agni</u> (21) 84, p. 88-89.

4946. STANHOPE, Rosamund
"Moving House." <u>WebR</u> (9:2) Wint 85, p. 82.
"This World Is Paper." <u>WebR</u> (9:2) Wint 85, p. 81.

4947. STANTON, Maura
"Attendant Lord." <u>Ploughs</u> (10:4) 84, p. 28-29.
"The Cuckoo Clock." <u>Ploughs</u> (10:4) 84, p. 26-27.
"Heaven." <u>Ploughs</u> (10:4) 84, p. 30-32.
"Sorrow and Rapture." <u>Telescope</u> (3:3) Aut 84, p.
49-50.

4948. STAP, Don
"It Is Winter." <u>PoetryE</u> (15) Aut 84, p. 25.
"The Neighbors." <u>PoetryE</u> (15) Aut 84, p. 24.

4949. STAPLETON, Patty
"Honey Light." <u>CapeR</u> (19:2) Sum 84, p. 7.

4950. STAPLETON, Wilson
"Cedes." <u>Bogg</u> (52) 84, p. 34.

4951. STARBUCK, George
"Telemetry before Impact." <u>GrandS</u> (3:4) Sum 84,
p. 23-28.

4952. STARCK, Clemens
"Man Studying a Map." <u>MalR</u> (68) Je 84, p. 67.

4953. STARK, Jennifer
"Confessions of a Pool-Side Romantic." <u>EngJ</u>
(73:3) Mr 84, p. 99.

4954. STAVELY, Margaret
"Of Change and Swift Glimpses" (Second Prize, 13th
Annual Kansas Poetry Contest). <u>LittleBR</u> (4:3)
Spr 84, p. 63.

4955. STAW, Jane
"Poem after Several Images in Calvino." <u>Agni</u> (21)
84, p. 107-108.

4956. STEAD, C. K.
"The Craft of Poetry." <u>MalR</u> (68) Je 84, p. 37.
"The Poetry Room" (Four Poems). <u>MalR</u> (68) Je 84,
p. 36-37.
"Professor Moon at the Lectern." <u>MalR</u> (68) Je 84,
p. 36.
"Steady." <u>MalR</u> (68) Je 84, p. 36.

4957. STEELE, Paul Curry
"Juniperus Virginiana." <u>AmerPoR</u> (13:6) N-D 84, p.
30.
"Special Detachment." <u>AmerPoR</u> (13:1) Ja-F 84, p. 20.
"Window Tree in Winter." <u>AmerPoR</u> (13:2) Mr-Ap 84,
p. 10.

4958. STEELE, Timothy
"Guessing Game." <u>TriQ</u> (59) Wint 84, p. 133.
"Life Portrait" (thinking of Dora Spenlow and David
Copperfield). <u>Thrpny</u> (19) Aut 84, p. 17.

"The Skull at the Crossroads." TriQ (59) Wint 84,
    p. 133.
"Social Reform." TriQ (59) Wint 84, p. 134.
"The Wartburg, 1521-22" (where Luther hides for ten
    months after the Diet of Worms). Thrpny (18)
    Sum 84, p. 12.

4959. STEFANILE, Felix
    "For the Hurdy-Gurdy" (tr. of Sergio Corazzini).
        Sparrow (46) 84, p. 23.

4960. STEFANILE, Selma
    "As if the cardinal." Sparrow (46) 84, p. 18.

4961. STEFFENS, Bradley
    "The Surf Horse." PoeticJ (7) 84, p. 25.

4962. STEFFEY, Duane
    "The Butt of Jokes." HiramPoR (37) Aut-Wint 84,
        p. 42.
    "Cinderella." Poem (52) N 84, p. 55.
    "Construction from the Forest." Poem (52) N 84,
        p. 57.
    "Liquid." Poem (52) N 84, p. 56.

4963. STEIN, Donna Baier
    "Between Seasons." KanQ (16:1/2) Wint-Spr 84, p.
        217.
    "Sometimes You Sense the Difference." KanQ
        (16:1/2) Wint-Spr 84, p. 218.

4964. STEIN, Hannah
    "The Country of Hope." PoetryNW (25:2) Sum 84, p.
        14.
    "Improvisation." PoetryNW (25:2) Sum 84, p. 15.

4965. STEIN, Jill
    "Loyalties." PoetryNW (25:1) Spr 84, p. 12-13.
    "Scenes from the Life of a Friend." PoetryNW
        (25:1) Spr 84, p. 10-11.
    "The Tipping Moment." PoetryNW (25:1) Spr 84, p.
        11-12.

4966. STEIN, Karen
    "February." YetASM (3) 84, p. 6.

4967. STEIN, Kevin
    "Beggarweed." KanQ (16:4) Aut 84, p. 120.
    "Blue Willow China." Telescope (3:2) Spr 84, p. 13.
    "Cousins." SnapD (7:1) Aut 83, p. 61.
    "Hold Still." SouthernPR (24:1) Spr 84, p. 24.
    "In a Certain Angular Light." SouthernPR (24:1)
        Spr 84, p. 25.
    "Those Trees above Us." Telescope (3:2) Spr 84,
        p. 12.

4968. STEINARR, Steinn
    "Time and Water" (Selections, tr. by Alan Boucher).
        Vis (16) 84, p. 6.
    "Water That Runs" (tr. by Alan Boucher). Vis (16)

84, p. 6.
"Wave That Breaks" (tr. by Alan Boucher). Vis
(16) 84, p. 6.

4969. STEINBERGH, Judith
"Nights under the Trumpet Vine." Calyx (8:3) Aut-
Wint 84, p. 36.
"These Days." Calyx (8:3) Aut-Wint 84, p. 35.

4970. STEINGRABER, Sandra
"Inscription in a Birthday Card." MichQR (23:1)
Wint 84, p. 97-98.

4971. STEINMAN, Lisa
"The Often Regrettable Ease with Which Things,
through Death or Dissolution, Enter the Category
of Stuff." Tendril (17) Wint 84, p. 163.

4972. STELIGA, Heather S. J.
"Ana's Dance." Writ (16) Aut 84, p. 38.
"Like a Cadence It Is Saturday." Writ (16) Aut
84, p. 39.
"The Miniature Boathouse: 1." Writ (16) Aut 84,
p. 37.

4973. STELLINO, Beatriz Marcela
"Insomnio." Mairena (5:13) Spr 83, p. 65.

4974. STELMACH, Marjorie
"At the Kirkwood Clock Shop." WebR (9:1) Spr 84,
p. 42-45.
"Elizabeth Bishop's Poems." WebR (9:1) Spr 84, p.
47-48.
"Flies." WebR (9:1) Spr 84, p. 46.
"This Clean Clutter." CapeR (19:3) 20th
Anniverary Issue 84, p. 49.

4975. STELMASZYNSKI, Wojtek
"I speak to you of flowers" (tr. of Krzysztof
Ostaszewski). Amelia (1:2) O 84, p. 55.
"Opus 63, a Tragedy" (tr. of Krzysztof
Ostaszewski). Amelia (1:2) O 84, p. 55.

4976. STEPHEN, Ian
"Broken Oar." WorldO (18:4) Sum 84, p. 38.
"Traveller in a Gallery." WorldO (18:4) Sum 84,
p. 38.
"Workshop." Waves (12:1) Aut 83, p. 57.

4977. STEPHENS, Jack
"Thanatophobia." AntR (42:3) Sum 84, p. 328.

4978. STEPHENS, Jan. M.
"Hot Footing It to Your House." PoetryCR (5:4)
Sum 84, p. 14.

4979. STEPHENS, Rosemary
"Feet." CapeR (19:3) 20th Anniversary Issue 84, p.
50.

4980. STEPHENSON, Sallie
        "Interview, 1982." Pig (12) 84, p. 78.

4981. STEPHENSON, Shelby
        "Duck and Percy Bolling." CrabCR (1:3) Wint 84,
          p. 3.
        "I Feel the Grief of Growing Up." Hudson (37:4)
          Wint 84-85, p. 567.
        "Sleeping in the Old House in Winter." CrabCR
          (1:3) Wint 84, p. 3.
        "When I Prop My Feet." PoetryNW (25:2) Sum 84, p.
          42-43.

4982. STERLING, Phillip
        "Smelt." NegC (4:4) Aut 84, p. 16-17.

4983. STERN, Gerald
        "82/83." AmerPoR (13:2) Mr-Ap 84, p. 22.
        "Adler." AmerPoR (13:2) Mr-Ap 84, p. 24.
        "The Dancing." OhioR (33) 84, p. 29.
        "The Dogs." AmerPoR (13:2) Mr-Ap 84, p. 20.
        "The Expulsion." AmerPoR (13:2) Mr-Ap 84, p. 19-20.
        "Fritz." Antaeus (53) Aut 84, p. 241-242.
        "Ground Hog Lock." Antaeus (53) Aut 84, p. 239-240.
        "Huzza!" GeoR (38:2) Sum 84, p. 347.
        "John's Mysteries." AmerPoR (13:2) Mr-Ap 84, p. 21.
        "July 2, 1983." AmerPoR (13:2) Mr-Ap 84, p. 20.
        "Kissing Stieglitz Goodbye." NewYorker (60:5) 19
          Mr 84, p. 46.
        "My Swallows." GeoR (38:2) Sum 84, p. 346-347.
        "The Nettle Tree." AmerPoR (13:2) Mr-Ap 84, p. 20.
        "The New Moses." AmerPoR (13:2) Mr-Ap 84, p. 22.
        "Of Blessed Name." Poetry (144:5) Ag 84, p. 289-290.
        "One Bird to Love Forever." Poetry (144:5) Ag 84,
          p. 290-292.
        "Red Bird" (For Greg and Marnie). BlackWR (10:2)
          Spr 84, p. 60-61.
        "Soap." AmerPoR (13:2) Mr-Ap 84, p. 23.
        "Three Skies." AmerPoR (13:2) Mr-Ap 84, p. 25.

4984. STERN, Robert
        "Even the Moon." AntigR (59) Aut 84, p. 134-135.
        "There Is No Face in the Sun." AntigR (59) Aut
          84, p. 135.

4985. STERNLIEB, Barry
        "Nixon at Yaddo." MinnR (N.S. 23) Aut 84, p. 58.
        "Origami." PraS (58:2) Sum 84, p. 96.
        "Shi Huang Ti" (d. 210 B.C.). PraS (58:2) Sum 84,
          p. 95.

4986. STETLER, Charles
        "Faint Praise." Wind (14:50) 84, p. 53.
        "Slice of Life." Wind (14:50) 84, p. 53.

4987. STEURY, Tim
        "Again and Again." SouthernPR (24:2) Aut 84, p.
          22-23.

4988. STEVENS, Alex
"Another Life's Land." <u>PraS</u> (58:1) Spr 84, p. 55-56.
"The Letter." <u>PraS</u> (58:1) Spr 84, p. 57.
"Lost Embassy." <u>Shen</u> (35:1) 83-84, p. 53-54.

4989. STEVENS, Allen
"Heraclitus in the Fen." <u>Stand</u> (25:1) Wint 83-84,
p. 47.

4990. STEVENS, C. J.
"Parsnips." <u>LitR</u> (28:1) Aut 84, p. 119.

4991. STEVENS, Elisabeth
"Conversation." <u>PortR</u> (30:1) 84, p. 61.
"The Fowler." <u>PortR</u> (30:1) 84, p. 90-91.
"Intimation." <u>PortR</u> (30:1) 84, p. 69.
"The Wives of Old, Important Men." <u>Wind</u> (14:51)
84, p. 41.

4992. STEVENS, Kevin
"Visiting a Civil War Museum in West Virginia."
<u>WebR</u> (9:2) Wint 85, p. 78.

4993. STEVENS, Peter
"March Weather." <u>CanLit</u> (103) Wint 84, p. 24-26.
"Yorkshire Spring." <u>CanLit</u> (103) Wint 84, p. 23-24.

4994. STEVENS, Ralph S., III
"On Looking at Kandinsky's 'Composition'." <u>CrabCR</u>
(2:1) Sum 84, p. 28.

4995. STEVENS, Wallace
"The House Was Quiet and the World Was Calm."
<u>Tendril</u> (18, special issue) 84, p. 215.
"How Now, O, Brightener." <u>Shen</u> (35:2/3) 84, p. 360.
"Note on Moonlight." <u>Shen</u> (35:2/3) 84, p. 361.
"The Sun This March." <u>YaleR</u> (73:2) Wint 84, p. 291.

4996. STEVENSON, Anne
"Where the Animals Go." <u>Stand</u> (25:1) Wint 83-84,
p. 28.

4997. STEVENSON, Diane
"Riding the River." <u>GreenfR</u> (12:1/2) Sum-Aut 84,
p. 171.

4998. STEVENSON, Richard
"(7) Avocado." <u>Grain</u> (12:4) N 84, p. 36.
"Amadeus Macaw." <u>AntigR</u> (58) Sum 84, p. 57-58.
"Another Hansel and Gretel Story." <u>Grain</u> (12:2)
My 84, p. 53-59.
"Auguries and Hijinks." <u>Quarry</u> (33:1) Wint 84, p.
25.
"Building Flaws." <u>CrossC</u> (6:3) 84, p. 15.
"Cassette Letter to My Son." <u>PoetryCR</u> (6:2) Wint
84-85, p. 22.
"Colquitz Creek Improvement Project" (3
selections). <u>Quarry</u> (33:1) Wint 84, p. 24-26.
"From the Mouths of Angels." <u>AntigR</u> (58) Sum 84,
p. 59.

"Houseplant Series" (Selections: 1. "Teddy Bear
   Plant," 2. "Jade Plant," 3. "Prayer Plant," 4.
   "Spider Plant," 5. "Aloe Vera"). MalR (67) F
   84, p. 85-89.
"Job Security" (for Tom Wayman). Quarry (33:1)
   Wint 84, p. 24.
"Outer Rings." Quarry (33:1) Wint 84, p. 26.
"Quick's Bottom." AntigR (58) Sum 84, p. 58.
"Quick's Bottom." NoDaQ (52:3) Sum 84, p. 213.
"Riot, Gwonge Ward." PoetryCR (6:2) Wint 84-85,
   p. 22.
"The Tallest Totem" (with apologies to Margaret
   Hurdon Keifer). NoDaQ (52:3) Sum 84, p. 212.
"Wreck Beach." NoDaQ (52:3) Sum 84, p. 214.

4999. STEWARD, D. E.
   "8 de Mayo." Abraxas (29/30) 84, p. 16-17.
   "Unity." Abraxas (29/30) 84, p. 15.
   "Voids." GreenfR (11:1/2) Sum-Aut 83, p. 137.

5000. STEWARD, Dave
   "BOGG." Bogg (52) 84, p. 32.

5001. STEWART, Frank
   "Searching for Ice." Agni (20) 84, p. 39-40.

5002. STEWART, Jack
   "For My Stillborn Brothers." Poem (50) Mr 84, p. 51.
   "The Purple Tree." Poem (50) Mr 84, p. 52.
   "Samson." CalQ (25) Aut 84, p. 55.

5003. STEWART, James B.
   "Tichakunda." Stepping (Anniversary Issue I) 84,
   p. 48.

5004. STEWART, Jean
   "My Dead Father." HangL (46) Aut 84, p. 61.

5005. STEWART, Pamela
   "Benediction" (for Sheila). AmerPoR (13:5) S-O
   84, p. 37.
   "A Formal Problem." PaintedB (23) Sum 84, p. 17.
   "Sea Longing" (for E.J.C.). AmerPoR (13:5) S-O
   84, p. 37.

5006. STEWART, R. S.
   "Young Man in a Shoe." StoneC (11:3/4) Spr-Sum
   84, p. 20-21.

5007. STEWART, Robert
   "Evacuation Plan." Spirit (7:1) 84, p. 86-87.
   "Furnace Dream." CharR (10:1) Spr 84, p. 52.
   "Kegel's." CharR (10:1) Spr 84, p. 53.
   "Litany of Tools." CharR (10:1) Spr 84, p. 54-55.

5008. STEWART, Robert J.
   "Ballet under the Stars." NewL (50:2/3) Wint-Spr
   84, p. 186.

5009. STEWART, Susan
        "Budapest, March 1928: The Genius of Friendship"
          (For Edward Hirsch). Poetry (144:3) Je 84, p.
          153-155.
        "Man Dancing with a Baby." Poetry (144:3) Je 84,
          p. 152.

5010. STEWART, Wayne W.
        "Lines for a Monk." Poem (51) Mr [i.e. Jl] 84, p.
          21.

5011. STICKNEY, John
        "A Sacramental Affair." Abraxas (31/32) 84, p. 45.
        "Sacrifices in the Age of Shortages." Sam (39:1,
          release 153) 84, p. 25.
        "We Greet the Plague." Abraxas (31/32) 84, p. 44.

5012. STIEBER, Christopher
        "Paul Newman and First Holy Communion: Sunday
          Dinner at Home." WindO (44) Sum-Aut 84, p. 12,
          51.

5013. STILL, James
        "Madly to Learn." NewL (51:2) Wint 84-85, p. 38-39.
        "What Have Your Heard Lately?" NewL (51:2) Wint
          84-85, p. 38.

5014. STILLMAN, Terri D.
        "Nature's Passion." PoeticJ (8) 84, p. 40.

5015. STILLWELL, Marie
        "Fantasy." WebR (9:2) Wint 85, p. 99.
        "Night Storm." WebR (9:2) Wint 85, p. 95.
        "Ondine." WebR (9:2) Wint 85, p. 98.

5016. STILLWELL, Mary Kathryn
        "The Letter." SoDakR (22:4) Wint 84, p. 91.
        "Yesterday Buying a Dracaena." EngJ (73:8) D 84,
          p. 35.

5017. STOCK, Bud
        "Burnished by Moonlight." Poem (50) Mr 84, p. 33.
        "Drifting." Poem (50) Mr 84, p. 34.
        "Tincture of Rust." PoeticJ (5) 84, p. 36.

5018. STOCK, Norman
        "My Uncle's Pajamas." NewEngR (6:4) Sum 84, p.
          585-586.

5019. STOCKDALE, John C.
        "The Important Things of Life." PottPort (6) 84,
          p. 10.
        "Respectability's Anachronistic." PottPort (6)
          84, p. 15.

5020. STOKES, Martin
        "First Flight." Argo (5:3) 84, p. 28-37.

5021. STOKESBURY, Leon
        "Adventures in Bronze." NewEngR (6:3) Spr 84, p.

438-439.
"Day Begins at Governor's Square Mall." <u>SouthernR</u>
    (20:1) Wint 84, p. 134-135.
"Luncheon of the Boating Party." <u>QW</u> (18) Spr-Sum
    84, p. 42-43.
"Often in Different Landscapes." <u>PoetC</u> (15:2)
    Wint 84, p. 25.
"Wakulla Springs." <u>Swallow</u> (3) 84, p. 37.

STOLL, Marianne Kent: <u>See</u> KENT-STOLL, Marianne

5022. STONE, Arlene
    "California Rainman." <u>YellowS</u> (10) Spr 84, p. 12.
    "The Shirt: (Svengali in Istanbul)." <u>YellowS</u> (12)
        Aut 84, p. 32-33.

5023. STONE, Carole
    "The Muse" (For Sister Bernetta Quinn, O.S.F.).
        <u>NewL</u> (50:4) Sum 84, p. 54-55.
    "Over the Pulaski Skyway." <u>CalQ</u> (23/24) Spr-Sum
        84, p. 137.
    "Receiving a Letter from My Son." <u>NewL</u> (50:4) Sum
        84, p. 53.
    "Western Motel, 1957." <u>NewL</u> (50:4) Sum 84, p. 54.

5024. STONE, Ken
    "So Long: A Landscape." <u>Amelia</u> (1:2) O 84, p. 73.
    "Today, Fiesta Music." <u>PoeticJ</u> (4) 83, p. 40.

5025. STONE, Ruth
    "Curtains." <u>Field</u> (30) Spr 84, p. 38.
    "Some Things You'll Need to Know Before You Join
        the Union." <u>CalQ</u> (25) Aut 84, p. 27-29.

5026. STORACE, Patricia
    "August: Blues." <u>Agni</u> (21) 84, p. 65.
    "Death: A Betrothal." <u>Agni</u> (21) 84, p. 71-72.
    "Exile's Matins." <u>Agni</u> (21) 84, p. 73.
    "Illegitimacy." <u>NewYRB</u> (31:7) 26 Ap 84, p. 21.
    "Intaglio." <u>Agni</u> (21) 84, p. 69-70.
    "Pamina's Marriage Speech." <u>Agni</u> (21) 84, p. 60-61.
    "Perdita." <u>Agni</u> (21) 84, p. 62.
    "Simple Sums." <u>Agni</u> (21) 84, p. 68.
    "Spring Afternoon." <u>Agni</u> (21) 84, p. 63-64.
    "Varieties of Religious Experience." <u>Agni</u> (21)
        84, p. 74.
    "Vocation." <u>Agni</u> (21) 84, p. 59.
    "A Weekend at the Last Resort." <u>Agni</u> (21) 84, p.
        66-67.

5027. STOREY, Sandra
    "Patrol" (For Milton). <u>Pig</u> (12) 84, p. 17.

5028. STORM, Jannick
    "Costa del Sol, at Night" (tr. of Vita Andersen, w.
        Linda Lappin). <u>Iowa</u> (14:2) Spr-Sum 84, p. 183-
        186.

5029. STORNI, Alfonsina
    "Counter Voice" (tr. by Barbara Paschke). <u>Vis</u>

573   STRAUS

(15) 84, p. 5.
"Voice" (tr. by Barbara Paschke). <u>Vis</u> (15) 84, p. 4-5.

5030. STOTLER, Michael
"Perry the Pinhead." <u>SanFPJ</u> (6:2) 84, p. 81.

5031. STOUT, Robert Joe
"Anniversary." <u>DekalbLAJ</u> (17:1/2) 84, p. 147.
"Clearing Up the Garden." <u>Sam</u> (37:3, 147th release) 83, p. 23.
"East Liberty, Mississippi." <u>StoneC</u> (12:1/2) Aut-Wint 84, p. 21.
"Lover." <u>Sam</u> (39:1, release 153) 84, p. 36.
"Premonition: Fixing New Year's Dinner." <u>DekalbLAJ</u> (17:1/2) 84, p. 146.
"Separation." <u>KanQ</u> (16:4) Aut 84, p. 59.
"Teenaged Maid, Calle San Luis de Potosi." <u>NegC</u> (4:3) Sum 84, p. 115.
"When Will I Quit Playing Softball?" <u>Poem</u> (50) Mr 84, p. 28.

5032. STOWELL, Phyllis
"You Come with Your Dreams." <u>SouthwR</u> (69:2) Spr 84, p. 147.

5033. STRAHAN, B. R. (Bradley R.)
"Latin Lullaby." <u>Vis</u> (15) 84, p. inside front cover.
"Love in the Vacation." <u>Vis</u> (14) 84, p. 36.
"The Nose." <u>CrabCR</u> (1:3) Wint 84, p. 14.

5034. STRAND, Mark
"Keeping Things Whole." <u>HolCrit</u> (21:4) O 84, p. 3.
"The Kite" (for Bill and Sandy Bailey). <u>PoetryE</u> (13/14) Spr-Sum 84, p. 53-54.
"The Marriage." <u>HolCrit</u> (21:4) O 84, p. 4.
"Night Piece" (after Dickens, for Bill and Sandy Bailey). <u>PoetryE</u> (13/14) Spr-Sum 84, p. 61-62.
"Only If the Landscape Is Correct." <u>PoetryE</u> (13/14) Spr-Sum 84, p. 52.
"The Poem." <u>Atlantic</u> (254:3) S 84, p. 77.
"The Room." <u>PoetryE</u> (13/14) Spr-Sum 84, p. 55-58.
"She" (for Bill and Sandy Bailey). <u>PoetryE</u> (13/14) Spr-Sum 84, p. 59-60.

5035. STRATTA de NAPOUT, Lillian
"Poema 15: Puedo ponerle." <u>Mairena</u> (6:18) 84, p. 194.

5036. STRATTON, R. E.
"Simplification." <u>SoDakR</u> (22:3) Aut 84, p. 67.

5037. STRAUS, Austin
"4/7/83." <u>StoneC</u> (12:1/2) Aut-Wint 84, p. 38.
"All-Purpose Apology Poem." <u>NewL</u> (51:2) Wint 84-85, p. 111-113.
"Austin's Book of Lists (Partial Contents)." <u>NewL</u> (51:2) Wint 84-85, p. 110-111.
"Certainties / Sonnet to Wanda." <u>StoneC</u> (12:1/2) Aut-Wint 84, p. 38.

"The Inventor Worm" (Found poem: from Encyclopedia
    Britannica, "Inventions and Discoveries," by E.
    E. Free). NegC (4:3) Sum 84, p. 99.
"Islands." SanFPJ (6:2) 84, p. 68.

5038. STRECKER, James
    "The Dhow." WritersL (2) 84, p. 12.
    "Queen Street Odyssey." PoetryCR (6:1) Aut 84, p. 3.

5039. STRECKFUS, Charles F.
    "After It's Over." SanFPJ (6:4) 84, p. 52.
    "A G.I. in El Salvador." SanFPJ (6:4) 84, p. 49.

5040. STREIF, Jan
    "At last, the mocking bird stops." Sparrow (46)
        84, p. 18.

5041. STRICKLAND, Stephanie
    "Consort." Ploughs (10:1) 84, p. 153.
    "First Couple." Agni (20) 84, p. 36.
    "Living on Air." Ploughs (10:1) 84, p. 154-156.
    "The Old Woman Said." WestB (14) 84, p. 12-13.
    "Seeing Red." WestB (14) 84, p. 11.

5042. STROBERG, Paul
    "Algebra." WormR (24:2, issue 94) 84, p. 69.
    "AWOL." WormR (24:2, issue 94) 84, p. 70.
    "Finance Company." WormR (24:2, issue 94) 84, p. 68.
    "Going Back to School." WormR (24:2, issue 94)
        84, p. 71.
    "Life of Crime." WormR (24:2, issue 94) 84, p. 69.
    "Out." WormR (24:2, issue 94) 84, p. 70.
    "Thunder and Lightning." WormR (24:2, issue 94)
        84, p. 67.
    "Trash." WormR (24:2, issue 94) 84, p. 70-71.
    "Two Out of Three." WormR (24:2, issue 94) 84, p.
        71-72.
    "What I Like about the Railroad." WormR (24:2,
        issue 94) 84, p. 68.

5043. STROHM, Paul Martin
    "On the Wharf." Wind (14:50) 84, p. 55.

5044. STRUNK, Orlo
    "A Backyard." ChrC (101:8) 7 Mr 84, p. 238.

5045. STRUTHERS, Ann
    "Anna Margaret Smith's Brooch." NewL (51:1) Aut
        84, p. 98.
    "Esterville Meteorite." NewL (51:1) Aut 84, p. 99.
    "Stoneboat." NewL (51:1) Aut 84, p. 98.

5046. STRUTHERS, Betsy
    "Vigil" (for Redvers Donavon Day). Waves (13:1)
        Aut 84, p. 75.

5047. STRYK, Dan
    "Affirmations of Faith in the Concrete World."
        CharR (10:2) Aut 84, p. 85.
    "Bag-Ladies" (St. James's Park). Confr (27/28)

84, p. 291.
"Bats." TriQ (60) Spr-Sum 84, p. 172-173.
"Bird Island, Grey Light." BelPoJ (34:3) Spr 84,
      p. 32-33.
"Crocus Garden." KanQ (16:1/2) Wint-Spr 84, p. 94.
"The Female Cardinal." WestHR (38:3) Aut 84, p.
      243-244.
"Metamorphosis and Fusion." Confr (27/28) 84, p.
      292.
"Pet Shop." HolCrit (21:2) Ap 84, p. 15.
"Pumpkins." SouthernHR (18:4) Aut 84, p. 336-337.
"The Sad and Noble Poems of the Ancient Chinese
      Concubines." PoetryNW (25:3) Aut 84, p. 12.
"Whales." HolCrit (21:2) Ap 84, p. 14.
"Winter Bound." KanQ (16:1/2) Wint-Spr 84, p. 94-95.

5048. STRYK, Lucien
      "Farmer." NewL (50:2/3) Wint-Spr 84, p. 90.
      "Fish shop" (Haiku from the Japanese Masters, tr.
      of Bashō, w. Takashi Ikemoto, calligraphy by
      Lloyd J. Reynolds). NewL (50:2/3) Wint-Spr 84,
      p. 140.
      "Moor" (Haiku from the Japanese Masters, tr. of
      Bashō, w. Takashi Ikemoto, calligraphy by
      Lloyd J. Reynolds). NewL (50:2/3) Wint-Spr 84,
      p. 140.
      "No need to cling" (Haiku from the Japanese
      Masters, tr. of Joso, w. Takashi Ikemoto,
      calligraphy by Lloyd J. Reynolds). NewL
      (50:2/3) Wint-Spr 84, p. 140.
      "Plum-viewing" (Haiku from the Japanese Masters,
      tr. of Buson, w. Takashi Ikemoto, calligraphy by
      Lloyd J. Reynolds). NewL (50:2/3) Wint-Spr 84,
      p. 140.
      "Where We Are." NowestR (22:1/2) 84, p. 144.
      "Willows" (for Taigan Takayama, Zen master).
      AmerPoR (13:5) S-O 84, p. 35.

5049. STUART, Dabney
      "Anniversary II." MassR (25:2) Sum 84, p. 197-198.
      "Ex-Wife." NoAmR (269:4) D 84, p. 29.
      "Hidden Meanings." MassR (25:2) Sum 84, p. 199.
      "Traces of a Bicameral Mind." NoAmR (269:3) S 84,
      p. 47.
      "Variable Service." Shen (35:2/3) 84, p. 362.

5050. STUART, Francis
      "Borges." AntigR (57) Spr 84, p. 56.
      "In Time of War." AntigR (57) Spr 84, p. 56.
      "Remembering Yeats." AntigR (57) Spr 84, p. 55.

5051. STUART, Jesse
      "I hate to leave springtime among the hills."
      Poetry (144:4) Jl 84, inside back cover.

STUBBS, John Heath: See HEATH-STUBBS, John

5052. STUCK, Anne F.
      "Study in Proportions." Waves (12:2/3) Wint 84,
      p. 100-101.

5053. STUDEBAKER, William
"Sandpoint." TarRP (24:1) Aut 84, p. 22.

5054. STUDING, Richard
"Early April." Confr (27/28) 84, p. 263.

5055. STULL, Dalene Workman
"Symbols at Parting." KanQ (16:4) Aut 84, p. 220.
"Undercurrent." KanQ (16:4) Aut 84, p. 219.

5056. STULL, Richard
"Position." Shen (35:1) 83-84, p. 55.

5057. STURM, John Edward
"Victim(s) in the Park." SpoonRQ (9:4) Aut 84, p.
48-49.

5058. SUARDIAZ, Luis
"Una Muchacha Muy Extraña." Mairena (6:18) 84,
p. 173.

5059. SUAREZ, Elena
"Sad Music" (tr. by the author). Vis (15) 84, p. 30.

5060. SUAREZ, Michael
"Esperanza, August 1983." Sam (37:3, 147th
release) 83, p. 33.
"Report from El Salvador." Sam (37:3, 147th
release) 83, p. 32.

5061. SUAREZ ARAUZ, Nicomedes
"Iguanas" (tr. of Alfredo Cardona Peña). Nat
(238:3) 28 Ja 84, p. 100.

5062. SUAREZ FERNANDEZ, Jenri
"No sé por qué resido en el silencio."
Mairena (6:17) Aut 84, p. 95.

5063. SUDERMAN, Elmer F.
"Thinking of Lois." Wind (14:52) 84, p. 47.

5064. SUGAI, Susan
"Shelves in a Visqueen Tent" (for Barry Spell).
GreenfR (11:1/2) Sum-Aut 83, p. 164.

5065. SUI-YUN
"I Capitulo." Mairena (5:13) Spr 83, p. 58.
"El cielo parece asfixiarse." Mairena (6:16) Spr
84, p. 83.
"Mis pies rugen esta tarde, al igual que me alma."
Mairena (6:16) Spr 84, p. 84.
"Las noches rudimentarias han vuelto a poblar mis
alas de hierro." Mairena (5:14) Aut 83, p. 84.
"Quizás tengas que desvirgar me alma junto a mi
carne." Mairena (6:16) Spr 84, p. 83-84.
"Redonda y húmeda." Mairena (6:16) Spr 84, p. 84.

5066. SUK, Julie
"Chartres." TarRP (23:2) Spr 84, p. 18.
"The Eye of a Feather." TarRP (23:2) Spr 84, p. 19.

5067. SUKNASKI, Andrew
      "Floating Entry" (from "Divining for West" of
      Celestial Mechanics / life fragment in
      progress). CanLit (100) Spr 84, p. 305-306.
      "Tony's Crabapple Tree" (1982 In Regina). CanLit
      (100) Spr 84, p. 302-305.
      "Vurma to Kaplitska / Flight from Margins of Lvov"
      (fragments from Divining for West / part II of
      Celestial Mechanics / life fragment in
      progress). PraF (5:2/3) Spr 84, p. 9-26.
      "Wordsketch on Indian Summer" (w. Kristjana
      Gunnars). PraF (5:2/3) Spr 84, p. 30-31.

5068. SULLIVAN, Chuck
      "The Juggler on the Radio: For Gary at 40" (Special
      Mention, Guy Owen Poetry Prize). SouthernPR
      (24:2) Aut 84, p. 30-31.

5069. SULLIVAN, Francis
      "Enigma #11." LittleM (14:3) 84, p. 21.
      "Enigma #12." LittleM (14:3) 84, p. 22.
      "Enigma #13." LittleM (14:3) 84, p. 23.
      "Enigma #18." LittleM (14:3) 84, p. 24.

5070. SULLIVAN, Luke Longstreet
      "White Marble." RagMag (3:1) Spr 84, p. 38.

5071. SUMMERHAYES, Don
      "Bravura." Quarry (33:3) Sum 84, p. 8.
      "Lost in the Cypress Hills above Eastend, Sask."
      Grain (12:4) N 84, p. 26-27.

5072. SUMMERS, Hollis
      "Everybody Has a Surprise in Store for Him or
      Herself, Even at Easter." LitR (28:1) Aut 84,
      p. 115.
      "The Traveler." WestB (14) 84, p. 67.

SUNG, Tsao: See TSAO, Sung

5073. SUPERVIELLE, Jules
      "A Dead Woman's Eyes" (tr. by Geoffrey Gardner).
      NewL (50:2/3) Wint-Spr 84, p. 91.
      "Family of This World" (tr. by George Bogin).
      PoetryE (15) Aut 84, p. 85-86.
      "Finale" (tr. by George Bogin). PoetryE (15) Aut
      84, p. 82.
      "Night" (tr. by George Bogin). PoetryE (15) Aut
      84, p. 84.
      "The Sun Speaks Softly" (tr. by George Bogin).
      PoetryE (15) Aut 84, p. 83.

5074. SUPRANER, Robyn
      "Asylum." BlueBldgs (8) 84?, p. 25.
      "At Yalta." Ploughs (10:1) 84, p. 162.
      "Cradle Song." BlueBldgs (8) 84?, p. 26.
      "Details from a Garden." BlueBldgs (8) 84?, p. 26.
      "Oops!" Ploughs (10:1) 84, p. 163.
      "Red Cat." BlueBldgs (8) 84?, p. 25.

5075. SUREYA, Cemal
        "Iste Tam Bu Saatlerde." NewRena (6:1, #18) Spr
          84, p. 24, 26.
        "Just at These Hours" (tr. by Talat Sait Halman).
          NewRena (6:1, #18) Spr 84, p. 25, 27.

SURIA, Violeta López: See LOPEZ SURIA, Violeta

SURYAKANT TRIPATHI, Sri: See NIRALA

5076. SUSSKIND, Harriet
        "Family Matters." PraS (58:1) Spr 84, p. 73-74.
        "The House Dress." PraS (58:1) Spr 84, p. 72-73.
        "The Morning after the Storm." MSS (3:2/3) Spr
          84, p. 81.
        "When You Are Travelling." PraS (58:1) Spr 84, p.
          71.

5077. SUSSMAN, Leona Mahler
        "Not a Saturday Night Shooting." Abraxas (31/32)
          84, p. 47.

5078. SUTHERLAND, E. L.
        "Blood Strangers." AntigR (57) Spr 84, p. 76.

5079. SUTHERLAND-SMITH, James
        "The Autopsy." WestB (14) 84, p. 90-91.
        "An Execution in Riyadh." StoneC (11:3/4) Spr-Sum
          84, p. 14.
        "An Execution in Riyadh" (The Phillips Poetry Award
          -- Spring/Summer--1984). StoneC (12:1/2) Aut-
          Wint 84, p. 44.
        "Killing a Sheep." LitR (28:1) Aut 84, p. 60-61.
        "Oboe." NeqC (4:4) Aut 84, p. 46.

5080. SUTHERLIN, Susan
        "Coming Home, Then Leaving." ThRiPo (23/24) 84,
          p. 25.
        "Dream, the Fourteenth of July ." ThRiPo (23/24)
          84, p. 26.
        "In the Beginning Merlin Says Seven." ThRiPo
          (23/24) 84, p. 27.

5081. SUTTER, Barton
        "The Snowman." MinnR (N.S. 23) Aut 84, p. 149-150.

5082. SUTZKEVER, Abraham
        "After Death" (tr. by David and Roslyn Hirsch).
          GrahamHR (7) Wint 84, p. 49-50.
        "The Gray Crown" (tr. by David and Roslyn Hirsch).
          GrahamHR (7) Wint 84, p. 48.
        "Stalks" (tr. by David and Roslyn Hirsch).
          GrahamHR (7) Wint 84, p. 51-52.

5083. SUVIN, D. Ronald
        "Hiroshige's Iris Garden at Horikiri." Amelia
          (1:2) O 84, p. 8.
        "The Sunflower of Sense" (For BM: Death be not
          proud). Veloc (2) Spr 83, p. 53.

5084. SVEHLA, John
"A Dusty Sunday." Wind (14:51) 84, p. 53.
"Red Sun." Wind (14:51) 84, p. 60.

5085. SVEVO, Italo
"Fables." Origin (Series 5:2) Wint 83, p. 94-96.

5086. SVOBODA, Robert J.
"A Rogue's Thesaurus" (D-H). SmPd (21:1) Wint 84,
p. 25-31.
"A Rogue's Thesaurus" (I-M). SmPd (21:2) Spr 84,
p. 12-16.

5087. SVOBODA, Terese
"Fleur-de-Lis." VirQR (60:4) Aut 84, p. 619-620.
"Keep House." VirQR (60:4) Aut 84, p. 621.

5088. SWAIM, Alice MacKenzie
"Come, Drink a Toast to Eccentricity!" Amelia
[1:1] Ap 84, p. 24.
"Late Leaves for Burning." Amelia (1:2) O 84, p. 59.

5089. SWAN, Diane
"Watching the Game." TarRP (23:2) Spr 84, p. 10.

5090. SWANBERG, Christine
"The Boat People." SpoonRQ (9:2) Spr 84, p. 45-46.
"Nightshift." SpoonRQ (9:4) Aut 84, p. 30.
"Please Pass This Note." EngJ (73:2) F 84, p. 44.

5091. SWANBERG, Ingrid
"Regret." Northeast (Series 3:18) 84, p. 11.

5092. SWANDER, Mary
"At the Country Farm." Pequod (16/17) 84, p. 13-15.
"Braiding Rugs." Nat (238:11) 24 Mr 84, p. 358.

5093. SWANGER, David
"Confession." NewL (51:1) Aut 84, p. 70-71.
"Elissa Plays the Piano." PoetryNW (25:1) Spr 84,
p. 42-43.
"The Hand Becomes." NewL (50:4) Sum 84, p. 21.
"The Heart's Education." PoetryNW (25:1) Spr 84,
p. 43-44.
"Knob Pines." PoetryNW (25:1) Spr 84, p. 44.
"Lost Dogs." NewL (51:1) Aut 84, p. 71.
"What the Wing Says." GeoR (38:3) Aut 84, p. 463.

5094. SWANN, Brian
"Application to the Doors." MalR (67) F 84, p. 92.
"The Birds" (for Roberta). Ploughs (10:1) 84, p.
164.
"The Bridge of Breasts" (Remembered from Rome, tr.
of Rafael Alberti). QRL (Poetry series 6, v.
25) 84, p. 48.
"Catbird." MassR (25:1) Spr 84, p. 59-60.
"Cats, Cats, and Cats" (Sonnet II, tr. of Rafael
Alberti). QRL (Poetry series 6, v. 25) 84, p.
54-55.
"Charcoal and the Child." MalR (67) F 84, p. 91.

"Comet" (tr. of Rafael Alberti). QRL (Poetry
  series 6, v. 25) 84, p. 34.
"Danger" (tr. of Rafael Alberti). QRL (Poetry
  series 6, v. 25) 84, p. 44.
"The Day When the Night Rain Stopped the Birds from
  Dying." BlueBldgs (7) 84, p. 40.
"Earning a Living." MassR (25:1) Spr 84, p. 57-58.
"Even the Monks Deal in Contraband" (tr. of Rafael
  Alberti). QRL (Poetry series 6, v. 25) 84, p. 43.
"Forging the Keys." MalR (67) F 84, p. 90.
"In Rome You Hear" (Sonnet X, tr. of Rafael
  Alberti). QRL (Poetry series 6, v. 25) 84, p.
  60-61.
"Increasing." BlueBldgs (8) 84?, p. 12.
"Infernal Congratulations" (tr. of Rafael Alberti).
  QRL (Poetry series 6, v. 25) 84, p. 30.
"Instead of worshippers" (tr. of Rafael Alberti).
  QRL (Poetry series 6, v. 25) 84, p. 50.
"Intermediate Nocturne 2: Today dark things pass
  by" (Sonnet VII, tr. of Rafael Alberti). QRL
  (Poetry series 6, v. 25) 84, p. 58-59.
"Invitation in August" (To Vittorio Bodini, tr. of
  Rafael Alberti). QRL (Poetry series 6, v. 25)
  84, p. 25.
"A Jump in the Lake." SouthwR (69:1) Wint 84, p. 61.
"Koan of the White Birch." BlueBldgs (7) 84, p. 40.
"Lizard" (tr. of Rafael Alberti). QRL (Poetry
  series 6, v. 25) 84, p. 39.
"Monserrato, 20" (tr. of Rafael Alberti). QRL
  (Poetry series 6, v. 25) 84, p. 9-10.
"Nocturne 1: For a long time I hear your whiskers
  rain" (Sonnet VI, tr. of Rafael Alberti). QRL
  (Poetry series 6, v. 25) 84, p. 58.
"Nocturne 2: I speak to you today from Rome"
  (Sonnet VIII, tr. of Rafael Alberti). QRL
  (Poetry series 6, v. 25) 84, p. 59.
"Nocturne: Nights of pain" (tr. of Rafael Alberti).
  QRL (Poetry series 6, v. 25) 84, p. 30.
"Nocturne: Suddenly, there's no one in Rome" (tr.
  of Rafael Alberti). QRL (Poetry series 6, v.
  25) 84, p. 35.
"Nocturne: Take hold of the key to Rome" (tr. of
  Rafael Alberti). QRL (Poetry series 6, v. 25)
  84, p. 47.
"A nymph on the patio of my house" (tr. of Rafael
  Alberti). QRL (Poetry series 6, v. 25) 84, p. 23.
"Open and Closed." BlueBldgs (7) 84, p. 41.
"Open and Closed." BlueBldgs (8) 84?, p. 12.
"Roman gatomaquia" (tr. of Rafael Alberti). QRL
  (Poetry series 6, v. 25) 84, p. 40.
"Rome: Danger to Pedestrians" (Section title, tr.
  of Rafael Alberti, w. Linda Scheer). QRL
  (Poetry series 6, v. 25) 84, p. 1-75.
"Rome, Danger to Pedestrians" (Sonnet II, tr. of
  Rafael Alberti). QRL (Poetry series 6, v. 25)
  84, p. 12.
"The Seine's chestnut trees" (tr. of Rafael
  Alberti). QRL (Poetry series 6, v. 25) 84, p. 38.
"Self Reliance." MalR (67) F 84, p. 93.
"Sets of Threes" (tr. of Rafael Alberti). QRL

(Poetry series 6, v. 25) 84, p. 20.
"Shadows." MemphisSR (4:2) Spr 84, p. 16.
"Si Proibisce di Buttare Immondezze" (Sonnet VII,
   tr. of Rafael Alberti). QRL (Poetry series 6,
   v. 25) 84, p. 15.
"The Skull on Its Occiput." BlueBldgs (8) 84?, p.
   13.
"The Stars." BlueBldgs (7) 84, p. 38.
"Ten Sonnets" (To Giuseppe Gioachino Belli, homage
   from a Spanish poet in Rome, tr. of Rafael
   Alberti, w. Linda Scheer). QRL (Poetry series
   6, v. 25) 84, p. 11-17.
"Three Poems of a Childhood." MalR (67) F 84, p.
   90-92.
"Three Roman Nocturnes with Don Ramón del Valle-
   Inclán" (tr. of Rafael Alberti). QRL (Poetry
   series 6, v. 25) 84, p. 58-59.
"Time's Answer" (Sonnet IX, To Bertolt Brecht, tr.
   of Rafael Alberti). QRL (Poetry series 6, v.
   25) 84, p. 60.
"To Marco, Dog of Santa Maria in Trastevere" (tr.
   of Rafael Alberti). QRL (Poetry series 6, v.
   25) 84, p. 51.
"Two Songs of the Earth" (for Kathleen Spivack).
   Ploughs (10:1) 84, p. 165-167.
"Urinating Prohibited" (Sonnet III, tr. of Rafael
   Alberti). QRL (Poetry series 6, v. 25) 84, p.
   12-13.
"Vietnam" (Sonnet XI, tr. of Rafael Alberti). QRL
   (Poetry series 6, v. 25) 84, p. 61.
"Water of innumerable fountains" (tr. of Rafael
   Alberti). QRL (Poetry series 6, v. 25) 84, p. 45.
"What I've Given Up for You" (Sonnet I, tr. of
   Rafael Alberti). QRL (Poetry series 6, v. 25)
   84, p. 11.

5095. SWANN, Gethsemane Ely
   "Professional Help." WestCR (19:1) Je 84, p. 31.

5096. SWANN, Roberta Metz
   "Bounty." Stepping (Anniversary Issue I) 84, p. 49.
   "Grey Fox." Ploughs (10:1) 84, p. 114.
   "Like Garlic." Ploughs (10:1) 84, p. 115-116.

5097. SWANNELL, Anne
   "Poetry Reading on Broadway." PoetryCR (6:1) Aut
      84, p. 27.

5098. SWANSON, Danielle
   "Garden Politics." Vis (15) 84, p. 31.

5099. SWANSON, R. A.
   "Eight Blackfeet." GreenfR (11:3/4) Wint-Spr 84,
      p. 35.
   "Three Months Later." GreenfR (11:3/4) Wint-Spr
      84, p. 36.

5100. SWANSON, Robert
   "Illinois in Winter." KanQ (16:1/2) Wint-Spr 84,
      p. 111.

"Our Lives, the Other Lives." <u>Comm</u> (111:22) 14 D
    84, p. 687.
"Sappy Days Are Here Again." <u>Shen</u> (35:1) 83-84,
    p. 98.
"There Is That." <u>MassR</u> (25:2) Sum 84, p. 300.
"Weight." <u>MassR</u> (25:2) Sum 84, p. 301.

5101. SWANSON, Susan Marie
    "How the Island Got This Way." <u>RagMag</u> (3:1) Spr
        84, p. 41.
    "Lillian Gish's Mother Sitting for Her Portrait."
        <u>Northeast</u> (Series 3:17) Sum 84, p. 5.
    "Old School." <u>RagMag</u> (3:1) Spr 84, p. 40.

5102. SWARD, Robert
    "Basketball's the American Game Bacause It's
        Hysterical." <u>Waves</u> (12:4) Spr 84, p. 64-65.
    "Continuous Topless Strippers." <u>NewL</u> (50:4) Sum
        84, p. 98-99.
    "Kiss, Bite & Moo Softly." <u>Waves</u> (12:4) Spr 84,
        p. 61.
    "Mr. Amnesia." <u>Waves</u> (12:4) Spr 84, p. 62-63.
    "Toronto Island Suite" (Excerpt). <u>GreenfR</u>
        (11:3/4) Wint-Spr 84, p. 96.

5103. SWARTZ, Gerald
    "A Troll Manifeto." <u>Abraxas</u> (29/30) 84, p. 32-33.

5104. SWEENEY, Jackie Piperno
    "Pregnant Poetry." <u>NegC</u> (4:2) Spr 84, p. 54-55.

5105. SWEENEY, Kevin
    "Sensitivity." <u>SpoonRQ</u> (9:2) Spr 84, p. 59-60.
    "Solidarity." <u>SanFPJ</u> (7:1) 84, p. 92.

5106. SWEENEY, Matthew
    "Airports Aren't Deserted." <u>Argo</u> (5:3) 84, p. 4.
    "Blondbeard." <u>Stand</u> (25:3) Sum 84, p. 77.
    "That Place." <u>Argo</u> (5:3) 84, p. 3-4.

5107. SWENSON, Karen
    "The Idaho Egg Woman." <u>GreenfR</u> (11:1/2) Sum-Aut
        83, p. 112.
    "Playing Jacks in Bhaktapur." <u>CalQ</u> (23/24) Spr-
        Sum 84, p. 43.
    "A Problem in Esthetics." <u>AmerPoR</u> (13:1) Ja-F 84,
        p. 6.
    "The State of Wyoming." <u>GreenfR</u> (11:1/2) Sum-Aut
        83, p. 113.

5108. SWENSON, May
    "A Bird's Life." <u>Chelsea</u> (42/43) 84, p. 108-109.
    "The Elect." <u>Nat</u> (239:10) 6 O 84, p. 321.
    "Goodbye, Goldeneye." <u>Nat</u> (238:6) 18 F 84, p. 204.
    "Night Visits with the Family." <u>Shen</u> (35:2/3) 84,
        p. 362-364.
    "Pale Sun." <u>Nat</u> (238:20) 26 My 84, p. 646.
    "The People Wall." <u>Chelsea</u> (42/43) 84, p. 166-167.
    "Summerfall." <u>NewYorker</u> (60:31) 17 S 84, p. 54.

5109. SWICKARD, David
"Bringing in the Barbarians." PoetL (79:1) Spr
84, p. 46-47.
"Dedicatory Epistle." PoetL (79:1) Spr 84, p. 45.
"October." StoneC (11:3/4) Spr-Sum 84, p. 30-31.

5110. SWIFT, Joan
"Testimony." PoetryNW (25:2) Sum 84, p. 10-13.

5111. SWIFT, Jonathan
"An Elegy on Dicky and Dolly." Hudson (37:4) Wint
84-85, p. 613.

5112. SWISS, Thomas
"Journal." Ploughs (10:4) 84, p. 112-113.

5113. SWIST, Wally
"Amputee's Litany - Miami, 1959." Tele (19) 83,
p. 13.

5114. SYLVESTER, Janet
"Interval." Tendril (17) Wint 84, p. 165.
"Solo." Tendril (17) Wint 84, p. 164.

5115. SYLVESTER, Sherry
"My Grandmother Smiling." Calyx (8:2) Spr 84, p.
70-72.

5116. SYMONS, Betsy
"Hunger." Vis (14) 84, p. 22.

5117. SZE, Arthur
"The Ansel Adams Card." GreenfR (11:1/2) Sum-Aut
83, p. 186.
"Dazzled." NewL (50:2/3) Wint-Spr 84, p. 1860187.
"The House." GreenfR (11:1/2) Sum-Aut 83, p. 188.
"New Wave." GreenfR (11:1/2) Sum-Aut 83, p. 187.

5118. SZEMAN, Sherri
"The Horses." CapeR (19:2) Sum 84, p. 32.
"Penelope to Ulysses" (on their first night
together after his return). CentR (28:2) Spr
84, p. 106-108.

5119. SZLYK, Marianne
"Montreal 1978." AntigR (56) Wint 84, p. 83.

5120. SZUMIGALSKI, Anne
"Clarrie." CanLit (100) Spr 84, p. 307-308.
"Sandblind at the Crossing." CanLit (100) Spr 84,
p. 308-309.

TAGLE, Mariela I. Ríos Ruiz: See RIOS RUIZ-TAGLE, Mariela I.

5121. TAGLIABUE, John
"Answering the Call-or-Religious Joy." PraS
(58:1) Spr 84, p. 32.
"Archilochos." NewL (50:2/3) Wint-Spr 84, p. 62.
"Arion on the Dolphin's Back." GreenfR (12:1/2)
Sum-Aut 84, p. 152.

"Clouds Are Superior to Theologies." BlueBldgs
    (7) 84, p. 44.
"Crowded Shanghai Market Including and Surrounded
    by Many Vegetables and Trucks and Bicycles."
    MassR (25:4) Wint 84, p. 536.
"Debussy and Proust." NewL (50:2/3) Wint-Spr 84,
    p. 62.
"Frequently Enough Some One Is Sent Dreaming or
    Flying." GreenfR (12:1/2) Sum-Aut 84, p. 150.
"A Grain Field at the Edge of a Forest" (Palm
    Sunday at a Ruysdael Exhibit, notes/poems).
    BlueBldgs (7) 84, p. 52.
"Nature's Nuptial." BlueBldgs (7) 84, p. 44.
"Princess Nausikaa to Odysseus: 'You Have No Choice
    But to Endure'." GreenfR (12:1/2) Sum-Aut 84,
    p. 150-151.
"Scattering Dynasties along the Way." MassR
    (25:4) Wint 84, p. 537.
"Smooth and Gleaming." GreenfR (12:1/2) Sum-Aut
    84, p. 151.
"There's a Porpoise to This Singing." GreenfR
    (12:1/2) Sum-Aut 84, p. 151.
"The Underground Pressure." Chelsea (42/43) 84,
    p. 372.

5122. TAHANA
"I Am of a Sovereign Nation." SanFPJ (7:1) 84, p.
    16.
"Reservations." SanFPJ (7:1) 84, p. 13.
"Wicasasni." SanFPJ (7:1) 84, p. 14-15.

TAI, Ly Dao: See LY, Dao Tai

TAI-CH'UL, Shin: See SHIN, Tai-Ch'ul

5123. TAIT, George Edward
"The Choice Blues." Stepping (Premier Issue) Sum
    82, p. 35.
"A Dull Brilliance." Stepping (Premier Issue) Sum
    82, p. 34.

5124. TAKAHASHI, Horioka
"In Hiroshima Salvias are in bloom" (tr. of
    anonymous Hiroshima A-bomb victim). NewL
    (50:2/3) Wint-Spr 84, p. 231.
"The spot where the bomb fell" (tr. of anonymous
    Hiroshima A-bomb victim). NewL (50:2/3) Wint-
    Spr 84, p. 231.
"Undressing to the waist" (tr. of anonymous
    Hiroshima A-bomb victim). NewL (50:2/3) Wint-
    Spr 84, p. 231.

TAKASHI, Ikemoto: See IKEMOTO, Takashi

5125. TALBOT, Kathrine
"The Mistress." Argo (5:2) 84, p. 32-34.

5126. TALENS, Jenaro
"Intermezzo." Mairena (6:18) 84, p. 70.

5127. TALL, Deborah
"Daybreak." Ploughs (10:1) 84, p. 168.
"The Miraculous Mandarin." Ploughs (10:1) 84, p.
169-171.

5128. TALLOSI, Jim
"An Autumn Field." PraF (5:2/3) Spr 84, p. 96-97.
"Bergamot." PraF (5:2/3) Spr 84, p. 95.
"Planets." PraF (5:2/3) Spr 84, p. 94.

5129. TAMMINGA, Frederick W.
"Kanaka Creek Stones (To Be Specific) or Love
Language (To Be Abstract)." AntigR (59) Aut
84, p. 124.
"Moonlit Dream in the Faraway Nude." AntigR (59)
Aut 84, p. 125.
"Saint Francis or Anyone." AntigR (59) Aut 84, p.
126.

5130. TANDORI, Dezso
"And There Isn't" (tr. by Bruce Berlind).
GrahamHR (7) Wint 84, p. 53.

5131. TANER, Renato O.
"Dear Lover" (from The Widower's Tango). PoetryCR
(5:4) Sum 84, p. 19.
"I tripped over a winter boot" (from The Widower's
Tango). PoetryCR (5:4) Sum 84, p. 19.

5132. TANIKAWA, Shuntaro
"Billy the Kid" (tr. by Harold P. Wright).
Chelsea (42/43) 84, p. 257.

5133. TANNER, Anita
"Cellar Hole." SnapD (8:1) Aut 84, p. 9.
"Of Time and Purpose." SnapD (8:1) Aut 84, p. 10.
"Stacking against Winter." SnapD (8:1) Aut 84, p. 8.

5134. TANTICLAIUX, Leticia
"The Signature of Things" (tr. of Rafael Vargas).
Iowa (14:2) Spr-Sum 84, p. 150.

5135. TAPSCOTT, Stephen
"84/ In a wild choir of girlish voices, tenderly"
(tr. of Osip Mandelstam). Epoch (33:3) Sum-Aut
84, p. 261.
"85/ The Floor of the sleigh, packed with fatal
straw" (tr. of Osip Mandelstam). Epoch (33:3)
Sum-Aut 84, p. 262.
"90/ Failing to believe in the Afterlife, that
miracle" (tr. of Osip Mandelstam). Epoch
(33:3) Sum-Aut 84, p. 263.
"118/ We shall meet again in Petersburg" (tr. of
Osip Mandelstam). Epoch (33:3) Sum-Aut 84, p.
264.
"Appaloosa." Ploughs (10:4) 84, p. 39-41.
"Chronic." Ploughs (10:4) 84, p. 35.
"Four Poems for Marina Tsvetaeva, ca 1916" (tr. of
Osip Mandelstam). Epoch (33:3) Sum-Aut 84, p.
260-264.

"Hank." Ploughs (10:4) 84, p. 33-34.
"Landscape with Mares and Foals." Ploughs (10:4)
     84, p. 36-38.
"Nocturne." Agni (20) 84, p. 66-67.
"You." Agni (20) 84, p. 64-65.

5136. TARASOVIC, Marcia M.
"The Girl with the Roan Mare." SoDakR (22:2) Sum
     84, p. 25.
"Saturday Poem." Wind (14:51) 84, p. 2.

5137. TARN, Nathaniel
"Canciones sin Su Música" (tr. of Tomás
     Segovia). Iowa (14:2) Spr-Sum 84, p. 149.
"Interludio Idílico: Coda" (tr. of Tomás
     Segovia). Iowa (14:2) Spr-Sum 84, p. 148.

5138. TARNAWSKY, Yuriy
"Every Wound Has a Name" (tr. by the author).
     Pequod (16/17) 84, p. 193.
"Questionnaire XVIII" (tr. by the author). Pequod
     (16/17) 84, p. 194-196.

5139. TATE, James
"Cleaning the Streets." MissR (36, 12:3) Spr 84,
     p. 69.
"The Life of Poetry" (Riven Doggeries 31). WestHR
     (38:4) Wint 84, p. 372-373.
"The Wheelchair Butterfly." Chelsea (42/43) 84,
     p. 228-229.
"The Wild Cheese." Tendril (17) Wint 84, p. 6.

5140. TAUB, Michael
"Don Quijote" (tr. of Lucian Blaga, w. William
     Harmon). ConcPo (17:2) Aut 84, p. 64.
"Eve" (tr. of Lucian Blaga, w. William Harmon).
     ConcPo (17:2) Aut 84, p. 65.

5141. TAUFER, Veno
"Non-Metaphysical Sequence" (tr. by the author and
     Milne Holton). Bound (12:1) Aut 83, p. 213-218.
"Open-Air Concert" (tr. by Michael Scammell). Vis
     (14) 84, p. 15.

5142. TAYLOR, Brigham
"Weekend at Branchport." SenR (14:2) 84, p. 34.

5143. TAYLOR, Bruce
"The Compilations of Rumi" (Excerpts). StoneC
     (12:1/2) Aut-Wint 84, p. 43.
"The Distance" (tr. of Han Yong-Woon). LitR
     (27:3) Spr 84, p. 310.
"Foolish Women." Abraxas (29/30) 84, p. 48.
"Lover to Lover" (tr. of Manhae, i.e. Han Yong-
     Woon). StoneC (11:3/4) Spr-Sum 84, p. 26.
"My Sorrow" (tr. of Han Yong-Woon). LitR (27:3)
     Spr 84, p. 312.
"My Way" (tr. of Han Yong-Woon). LitR (27:3) Spr
     84, p. 311.
"The Truth" (tr. of Manhae, i.e. Han Yong-Woon).

StoneC (11:3/4) Spr-Sum 84, p. 27.
"Waiting" (tr. of Han Yong-Woon). LitR (27:3) Spr
     84, p. 311.

5144. TAYLOR, Christopher
     "Ch'ien -- The Creative." Quarry (33:1) Wint 84,
          p. 71.
     "Elegy." Descant (47, 15:4) Wint 84, p. 98.
     "Geostrophe." Quarry (33:1) Wint 84, p. 69.
     "Morning Raga." Quarry (33:1) Wint 84, p. 70.
     "A Short Meditation on Death." Descant (47, 15:4)
          Wint 84, p. 99.
     "They Want to Tell You about God." Descant (47,
          15:4) Wint 84, p. 100-101.
     "The Very Late T'ang." Quarry (33:1) Wint 84, p. 71.

5145. TAYLOR, Eleanor Ross
     "In the Echoes, Wintering." Shen (35:1) 83-84, p.
          14.
     "Motherhood, 1880." MichQR (23:4) Aut 84, p. 598.
     "Rachel Plummer's Dream Winter 1836." Shen
          (35:2/3) 84, p. 364-367.
     "To the Rest Home." MichQR (23:4) Aut 84, p. 599-
          600.

5146. TAYLOR, Henry
     "Taking to the Woods." Poetry (145:1) O 84, p. 33-
          35.

5147. TAYLOR, Joan
     "How Tall She Is." Dandel (11:1) Spr-Sum 84, p. 72.

5148. TAYLOR, John
     "The Attic." WestB (14) 84, p. 15.
     "Comfort in Fear." WestB (14) 84, p. 17.
     "My Love Waiting Here for You." Bogg (52) 84, p. 58.
     "The Wings of the Storm." WestB (14) 84, p. 15.

5149. TAYLOR, Laurie
     "Grandmother." CapeR (19:3) 20th Anniverary Issue
          84, p. 51.
     "The Old Man's Tapestry." SouthwR (69:3) Sum 84,
          p. 331.

5150. TAYLOR, Linda
     "Fun Blood." PoetryNW (25:2) Sum 84, p. 44-45.

5151. TAYLOR, Marilyn J.
     "Nostalgia." RagMag (3:2) Aut 84, p. 34.
     "On Top of the Abandoned Shoe Factory." RagMag
          (3:2) Aut 84, p. 34.
     "Three Years Later." RagMag (3:2) Aut 84, p. 34.

5152. TAYLOR, Mervyn
     "The Outing." Stepping (Premier Issue) Sum 82, p.
          37.
     "Refugees." Stepping (Premier Issue) Sum 82, p. 36.

5153. TAYLOR, Peter
     "The Hand of Emmagene." Shen (35:2/3) 84, p. 368-

386.

5154. TEASDALE, Sara
"Afterwards." Poetry (144:3) Je 84, p. 129.
"Conflict." Poetry (144:3) Je 84, p. 128.
"In Florence." Poetry (144:5) Ag 84, p. 275.
"Nights without Sleep." Poetry (144:3) Je 84, p.
128.
"To a Loose Woman." Poetry (144:3) Je 84, p. 129.

5155. TEILLIER, Jorge
"Alegria." WoosterR (1:2) N 84, p. 53.
"Happiness" (tr. by Mary Crow). WoosterR (1:2) N
84, p. 52.
"The Last Island" (tr. by Mary Crow). WoosterR
(1:2) N 84, p. 54.
"La Ultima Isla." WoosterR (1:2) N 84, p. 55.
"El Viento y el Miedo Golpean." Mairena (6:18)
84, p. 134.

5156. TEKST
"Broken Tantra." CapilR (31) 84, p. 68.

5157. TELLER, J. L.
"Letter to Sigmund Freud" (tr. by Benjamin
Hrushovski and Barbara Benavie). PartR (51:1)
84, p. 102-103.

5158. TELLEZ, Dora Maria
"We Live in a Rush" (tr. by Marc Zimmerman and
Ellen Banberger). MinnR (N.S. 22) Spr 84, p.
72-73.

5159. TEM, Steve Rasnic
"After the Collapse." Veloc (2) Spr 83, p. 13-14.

Ten HARMSEN von der BEEK, F.: See BEEK, F. Ten Harmsen V. D.

5160. TENPAS, Kathleen
"1925." Blueline (5:2) Wint-Spr 84, p. 35.

5161. TERASHIMA, Robert
"The Caterpillar." GreenfR (12:1/2) Sum-Aut 84,
p. 172.
"Finches." HangL (46) Aut 84, p. 62.
"The Meaning of Meaning." GreenfR (12:1/2) Sum-
Aut 84, p. 173.

5162. TERPSTRA, John
"The Loo." Quarry (33:1) Wint 84, p. 43-44.

5163. TERRANOVA, Elaine
"The Rocking Chair." SouthernPR (24:2) Aut 84, p.
58.

5164. TERRIS, Virginia
"Anxieties." Confr (27/28) 84, p. 334.

5165. TERRIS, Virginia R.
"Ripping Seams." GreenfR (11:1/2) Sum-Aut 83, p.

107.
"Traveling." <u>GreenfR</u> (11:1/2) Sum-Aut 83, p. 106.

5166. TETI, Zona
"Susanna Not Thinking of the Elders." <u>Shen</u> (35:1)
83-84, p. 38.

TETSUO, Nakagami: <u>See</u> NAKAGAMI, Tetsuo

5167. THALMAN, Mark
"The Companion." <u>SnapD</u> (6:2) Spr 83, p. 23.
"Siletz." <u>SnapD</u> (6:2) Spr 83, p. 22.

5168. THAM, Hilary
"Letter from Malaysia." <u>PoetL</u> (79:3) Aut 84, p. 152.

5169. THANIEL, George
"The Lady Who Plays the Piano." <u>AntigR</u> (56) Wint
84, p. 118.
"The Old Album." <u>AntigR</u> (56) Wint 84, p. 117.

5170. THENIOR, Ralf
"Feierabend." <u>PortR</u> (30:1) 84, p. 155.
"Friday Night" (tr. by Marilyn Waniek). <u>PortR</u>
(30:1) 84, p. 154.

5171. THENON, Susana
"Distances" (Selections: 4, 5, 15, 35, tr. by
Renata Treitel). <u>Mund</u> (14:2) 84, p. 33-37.
"Distancias" (Selections: 4, 5, 15, 35). <u>Mund</u>
(14:2) 84, p. 34, 36.

5172. THESEN, Sharon
"Poem in Memory of an Earlier Poem." <u>CanLit</u> (100)
Spr 84, p. 310-311.
"Turgenev's Huntsmen." <u>CanLit</u> (100) Spr 84, p. 310.

5173. THICH, Nhat Hanh (<u>See also</u> HANH, Thich Nhat)
"Promise me this day." <u>NewL</u> (50:2/3) Wint-Spr 84,
p. 236.

5174. THIEL, Robert
"El Coquí: Little Frog at Night." <u>AntigR</u> (56)
Wint 84, p. 35.
"Matilija Adolescence." <u>YellowS</u> (12) Aut 84, p. 16.
"Your Tranquil Smile." <u>AntigR</u> (56) Wint 84, p. 36.

5175. THILLET, Yves
"Vivaldi." <u>FourQt</u> (33:3) Spr 84, p. 2-3.

5176. THOMAS, Caroline
"Tea Is Very Sane." <u>SanFPJ</u> (6:2) 84, p. 12.

5177. THOMAS, Colette
"Winter Solstice." <u>GrandS</u> (4:1) Aut 84, p. 142-144.

5178. THOMAS, D. M.
"Friday Evening." <u>NewL</u> (50:2/3) Wint-Spr 84, p. 61.

5179. THOMAS, David J.
"Stopping by Splices on a Typical Evening." EngJ
(73:1) Ja 84, p. 86.

5180. THOMAS, Debra
"The Carpenter's Woman." YetASM (3) 84, p. 8.
"Your Story." PoetL (79:3) Aut 84, p. 142.

5181. THOMAS, Diana
"Eclipse." Stand (25:1) Wint 83-84, p. 46.

5182. THOMAS, Elizabeth
"Atlantic City." MissR (36, 12:3) Spr 84, p. 85.
"Love Again." MissR (36, 12:3) Spr 84, p. 86.

5183. THOMAS, George
"Skating Thin Ice." Sam (39:1, release 153) 84,
p. 11.

5184. THOMAS, Harry
"Gorbunov and Gorchakov" (tr. of Joseph Brodsky).
ParisR (26:93) Aut 84, p. 102-145.
"The Truth of Two" (tr. of Pedro Salinas).
AmerPoR (13:2) Mr-Ap 84, p. 6.

5185. THOMAS, Jim
"Afternoon Painter." KanQ (16:1/2) Wint-Spr 84,
p. 152.
"Great Jays." CapeR (19:2) Sum 84, p. 47.
"On Vocations." CapeR (19:3) 20th Anniverary
Issue 84, p. 52.

5186. THOMAS, Lorenzo
"The Invasion of Cuba, 17 April 1961." Sparrow
(46) 84, p. 12.

5187. THOMAS, Lynne
"America." SanFPJ (6:1) 84, p. 31.

5188. THOMAS, Michael
"Forties Movies, American." Bogg (52) 84, p. 38.

5189. THOMAS, Stephen
"Crow Song." MalR (68) Je 84, p. 38-40.

5190. THOMPSON, Brent
"Leatherjackets." MalR (69) O 84, p. 29-30.

5191. THOMPSON, Gary
"Gothic." NewL (50:4) Sum 84, p. 88-89.

5192. THOMPSON, J.
"En Route." HiramPoR (36) Spr-Sum 84, p. 38.

5193. THOMPSON, Jeanie
"Allegro Assaii." Telescope (3:1) Wint 84, p. 38.
"Obeying My Hands" (for Kay Dorsch). Telescope
(3:2) Spr 84, p. 23.

5194. THOMPSON, Joanna
       "Mnemosyne." AmerPoR (13:3) My-Je 84, p. 47.

5195. THOMPSON, John
       "Ending on Paumanok." NewYRB (31:1) 2 F 84, p. 18.
       "The Skins of a Dream." Germ (8:1) Spr-Sum 84, p.
           29.

5196. THOMPSON, Nance E.
       "I Quit." Sam (39:1, release 153) 84, p. 13.

5197. THOMPSON, Perry
       "An Attack of the Heart" (Scholarship and Award
           Winners: First Place). DekalbLAJ (20th
           Anniversary Issue) 84, p. 18.
       "City Angels Jet My Breath Away" (Scholarship and
           Award Winners: First Place). DekalbLAJ (20th
           Anniversary Issue) 84, p. 17.
       "Grow Fresh Spring Water at Home in Your Spare
           Time" (1983-84 Literary Arts Scholarship
           Winners: First Place). DekalbLAJ (17:1/2) 84,
           p. 91.
       "The Runner's Ghost Hovers about the Runner" (1983-
           84 Literary Arts Scholarship Winners: First
           Place). DekalbLAJ (17:1/2) 84, p. 91.
       "There Are People My Teachers Have Eaten" (1983-84
           Literary Arts Scholarship Winners: First Place).
           DekalbLAJ (17:1/2) 84, p. 92.

5198. THOMPSON, Phil
       "November Nuance." PottPort (6) 84, p. 10.
       "Too Much Pride." PottPort (6) 84, p. 24.

5199. THOMPSON, Susan Scott
       "Poem for My Mother." CalQ (25) Aut 84, p. 70.

5200. THOMSON, Gary
       "Getting to Work." SnapD (7:1) Aut 83, p. 65.

5201. THOMSON, Nancy Jean
       "Erosion." BlueBuf (2:2) Spr 84, p. 25.

5202. THORNBRUGH, David
       "Lizards." WebR (9:1) Spr 84, p. 78.
       "Physics." WebR (9:1) Spr 84, p. 79.
       "Travelogue." WebR (9:1) Spr 84, p. 79.

5203. THORNE, Evelyn
       "The Silent Turning." Wind (14:50) 84, p. 54-55.
       "Voyage." Wind (14:50) 84, p. 54.

5204. THORNTON, Russell
       "Siesta Shower." AntigR (57) Spr 84, p. 83.
       "The Water." AntigR (57) Spr 84, p. 84.

5205. THORSEN, Victoria Wysznski
       "Once giant-birch me was green and naive"
           ("Untitled"). WorldO (18:3) Spr 84, p. 32.

5206. TICE, David
"The Secret of Tropical Heights." <u>DekalbLAJ</u>
(17:1/2) 84, p. 148.

5207. TIERNEY, Terry
"The Lives of a Cell." <u>SoDakR</u> (22:3) Aut 84, p. 64.
"The Rattlesnake Exchanges Its Skin." <u>CalQ</u> (25)
Aut 84, p. 58.
"What to Do in the Case of a Gas Attack." <u>SoDakR</u>
(22:3) Aut 84, p. 63.

5208. TIHANYI, Eva
"Autobiography." <u>CanLit</u> (100) Spr 84, p. 318.
"Breakthrough." <u>CanLit</u> (100) Spr 84, p. 319-320.
"Death by History." <u>AntigR</u> (56) Wint 84, p. 82.
"Kitchen Scene." <u>AntigR</u> (56) Wint 84, p. 81.
"Solar Fugue." <u>CanLit</u> (100) Spr 84, p. 318-319.

5209. TILLEY, Barrie
"Sleek Drive." <u>Bogg</u> (52) 84, p. 51-52.

5210. TILLINGHAST, David
"The Autumn Deer." <u>SoCaR</u> (16:2) Spr 84, p. 125.

5211. TILLINGHAST, Richard
"Easter Week: Vermont" (For Robert Fitzgerald).
<u>Antaeus</u> (52) Apr 84, p. 126-127.

TING, Chu-Hsin: <u>See</u> DING, Zuxin

TING, Shu: <u>See</u> SHU, Ting

5212. TIO, Elsa
"A Arnaldo Torres Rosado y Carlos Soto Arrivi."
<u>Mairena</u> (6:16) Spr 84, p. 21.
"A Jorge Luis Borges." <u>Mairena</u> (6:16) Spr 84, p. 20.
"Cisterna, honda, oculta." <u>Mairena</u> (6:16) Spr 84,
p. 22.
"Desde el día gigante de tu ausencia." <u>Mairena</u>
(6:16) Spr 84, p. 19.
"Envio." <u>Mairena</u> (6:16) Spr 84, p. 22.
"Saudade." <u>Mairena</u> (6:16) Spr 84, p. 19.
"Voz de caracol." <u>Mairena</u> (6:16) Spr 84, p. 20.

5213. TIPTON, David
"The Salt Flats" (tr. of Antonio Cisneros). <u>Stand</u>
(25:3) Sum 84, p. 66-67.

5214. TISDALE, Charles
"Nicodemus." <u>ChrC</u> (101:11) 4 Ap 84, p. 328.

5215. TISERA, Mary
"Aphrodisiac." <u>WestB</u> (15) 84, p. 44-46.
"Aunt Wilhelmina at the Family Reunion." <u>WestB</u>
(14) 84, p. 28.
"Before and After." <u>Abraxas</u> (31/32) 84, p. 34-35.
"Obeying the Rock Candy Horse." <u>WestB</u> (14) 84, p.
29.
"On Ash Wednesday." <u>Poetry</u> (143:5) F 84, p. 287.

5216. TITTERINGTON, Patrice
"Penetrate me deep and sinuously". (tr. of Cristina
Peri Rossi). Cond (3:4, issue 10) 84, p. 50.
"Penetrate me occidental and perverse" (tr. of
Cristina Peri Rossi). Cond (3:4, issue 10) 84,
p. 49.
"Those who once loved her" (tr. of Cristina Peri
Rossi). Cond (3:4, issue 10) 84, p. 48.

5217. TOBIAS, Arthur
"Climbing Shi-Tou Shan Lion-Head Mountain."
GreenfR (11:1/2) Sum-Aut 83, p. 147.
"Inland Waterways." GreenfR (11:1/2) Sum-Aut 83,
p. 147.
"Walking with Han Shan Summertime." GreenfR
(11:1/2) Sum-Aut 83, p. 147.

5218. TODD, Theodora
"The Beaver Pond: Cause and Effect." BelPoJ
(34:4) Sum 84, p. 24-25.
"Epithalamium for a July Wedding." BelPoJ (34:4)
Sum 84, p. 25-26.

5219. TOHE, Laura
"Easter Sunday." Calyx (8:2) Spr 84, p. 84.
"No Parole Today." Calyx (8:2) Spr 84, p. 88.

5220. TOLIVER, Carl Clifton
"In Memoriam Paul Celan" (tr. of Rose Ausländer).
Sulfur (4:2, issue 11) 84, p. 91.
"Paul Celan" (tr. of Annemarie Zornack). Sulfur
(4:2, issue 11) 84, p. 96.
"Paul Celan" (tr. of Hans-Jürgen Heise). Sulfur
(4:2, issue 11) 84, p. 94.

5221. TOLIVER, Suzanne Shipley
"Jewish Cemetery in Prague" (tr. of Erich Arendt).
Sulfur (4:2, issue 11) 84, p. 89-90.
"Lament for Paul Celan" (On the death of my friend
in Paris, tr. of Arno Reinfrank). Sulfur (4:2,
issue 11) 84, p. 95.
"Oradea" (In memory of Paul Celan, tr. of Heinz
Czechowski). Sulfur (4:2, issue 11) 84, p. 92-93.

5222. TOLKIEN, J. R. R.
"Among the people of earth one has poetry in him"
(for W. H. A.). Shen (35:2/3) 84, p. 32.
"For W. H. A." Shen (35:2/3) 84, p. 31-32.
"Woruldbüendra sum bid wödbora" (For W. H. A.).
Shen (35:2/3) 84, p. 31.

5223. TOLL, Chris
"SASE Enclosed." Open24 (3) 84, p. 2.

5224. TOLL, Joshua
"How to Be a Safe Knight." Open24 (3) 84, p. 12.

5225. TOLLIVER, Jeri
"Two for the Price of One." PoeticJ (7) 84, p. 33.

5226. TOME, Jesús
"Suplica Final." Mairena (6:18) 84, p. 73.
"Tres Impromptus." Mairena (5:13) Spr 83, p. 64-65.

5227. TOMFOHRDE, Mitchell G.
"Impression." ArizQ (40:3) Aut 84, p. 218.

5228. TOMPKINS, Leslie C.
"Pronoun Substitutes." Northeast (Series 3:18) 84, p. 5.

5229. TOMPKINS, R. D. Wayne
"Walking Down Country Roads." PoetryCR (6:2) Wint 84-85, p. 27.

5230. TOOL, Dennis
"It's Going to Snow" (tr. of Francis Jammes, for Gary Wilson). NewOR (11:3/4) Aut-Wint 84, p. 111.

5231. TOPP, Patricia
"Poem for Baby Kate." PoeticJ (6) 84, p. 28.

5232. TORNAI, Jozsef
"We Say This Prayer" (tr. by William Jay Smith). Iowa (14:2) Spr-Sum 84, p. 209.
"Without Voice, without Hope" (tr. by the author and Daniel Weissbort). Iowa (14:2) Spr-Sum 84, p. 208.

5233. TORNES, Beth
"Autumn of the Masks" (tr. of Mohamed al-Magut, w. Saheb Meshtet). SenR (14:1) 84, p. 41-42.
"Fear" (tr. of Mohamed al-Magut, w. Saheb Meshtet). SenR (14:1) 84, p. 39-40.
"In the Night" (tr. of Mohamed al-Magut, w. Saheb Meshtet). SenR (14:1) 84, p. 37-38.

5234. TORNLUND, Niklas
"Homeward in the Night" (tr. by John Tritica). GreenfR (12:1/2) Sum-Aut 84, p. 34.
"The Old Land" (tr. by John Tritica). GreenfR (12:1/2) Sum-Aut 84, p. 29-34.
"Train-Rattle" (tr. by John Tritica). CreamCR (9:1/2) 84, p. 86-88.
"The Tree" (tr. by John Tritica). GreenfR (12:1/2) Sum-Aut 84, p. 34-35.

5235. TORRENS, James
"The American Way." BilingR (10:1) Ja-Ap 83, p. 68.
"Shine On, la Rubia." BilingR (10:1) Ja-Ap 83, p. 68.

5236. TORRES, Alba Azucena
"Communique Number 1,000 for My Love" (tr. by Marc Zimmerman and Ellen Banberger). MinnR (N.S. 22) Spr 84, p. 79.

5237. TORRES, César G.
"Borinqueñita." Mairena (5:13) Spr 83, p. 110.

TORRES, Juan Ruiz de: See RUIZ de TORRES, Juan

5238. TORRES SANTIAGO, José Manuel
"Desahuciados." Mairena (6:18) 84, p. 25.

5239. TORRESON, Rodney
"Matthew Schnell (1951-1981)." SpoonRQ (9:2) Spr
84, p. 36.

TOSTERIN, Lola Lemire: See TOSTEVIN, Lola Lemire

5240. TOSTESON, Heather
"Advent." SmPd (21:3) Aut 84, p. 10.
"The Grove." SmPd (21:3) Aut 84, p. 16.
"January, 1978." SmPd (21:3) Aut 84, p. 12.
"The Logic of the Heart." SmPd (21:3) Aut 84, p.
13-15.
"Objective Correlatives." SmPd (21:3) Aut 84, p. 11.
"They Know." SmPd (21:3) Aut 84, p. 16.
"Wind." SmPd (21:3) Aut 84, p. 8-9.

5241. TOSTEVIN, Lola Lemire
"Not a Poem." CanLit (100) Spr 84, p. 321-322.
"To the Heart's Discontent." CapilR (28) 83, p.
82-87.

5242. TOTH, Eva
"The Creation of the World" (tr. by Marianna
Abrahamowicz). Iowa (14:2) Spr-Sum 84, p. 210-
211.

5243. TOTH, Linda Beth
"The Country Boy." Wind (14:51) 84, p. 47.

TOV, Sharona Ben: See BEN-TOV, Sharona

5244. TOVAR, Inéz Hernandez
"Momentos." Calyx (8:2) Spr 84, p. 10.
"Yollotl." Calyx (8:2) Spr 84, p. 9.

5245. TOWN, Stephen
"This Evening They've a Party" (tr. of Heinrich
Heine). NegC (4:2) Spr 84, p. 77.
"Where?" (tr. of Heinrich Heine). NegC (4:2) Spr
84, p. 79.
"You Are Like a Flower" (tr. of Heinrich Heine).
NegC (4:2) Spr 84, p. 75.

5246. TOWNER, Daniel
"Books by Nobody." Agni (21) 84, p. 40.
"The Fountain." NewL (50:4) Sum 84, p. 79.
"The Outer Banks, North Carolina." OhioR (33) 84,
p. 107-108.
"Ragged Figure." GeoR (38:1) Spr 84, p. 124.
"What Steamboat Rock Was Like." OhioR (33) 84, p.
109.

5247. TOY, Judith Baldwin
"Given Life Like Ra" (taken from the hieroglyphic
spell on the outmost coffin of Tut). PoetL
(79:2) Sum 84, p. 92.

"Stolen Reflections during Siege of Flu" (Sermon to
      Myself on Daughters). PoetL (79:2) Sum 84, p. 93.

5248. TRACY, Robert
      "The Man Who Found a Horseshoe" (136, tr. of Osip
         Mandelstam). Ploughs (10:1) 84, p. 102-105.
      "We will die in transparent Petropolis" (89, tr. of
         Osip Mandelstam). Ploughs (10:1) 84, p. 101.

5249. TRAIL, Nell
      "Percept" (Third Honorable Mention, 13th Annual
         Kansas Poetry Contest). LittleBR (4:3) Spr 84,
         p. 67.

5250. TRAKL, Georg
      "Mandkind" (tr. by Christopher Middleton). Field
         (30) Spr 84, p. 68-69.
      "Metamorphosis" (tr. by Stuart Friebert). Field
         (30) Spr 84, p. 66.
      "On the Death of an Old Woman." Field (30) Spr
         84, p. 65.
      "The Rats" (tr. by James Wright). Field (30) Spr
         84, p. 67.
      "The Rats" (tr. by R. Grenier). Field (30) Spr
         84, p. 66.
      "Revelation and Demise" (Excerpt, tr. by Roderick
         Iverson). Field (30) Spr 84, p. 70-71.
      "Sleep." MidAR (4:2) Aut 84, p. 108.
      "Sommer." BlueBldgs (7) 84, p. 53.
      "Summer" (tr. by Paul Morris). BlueBldgs (7) 84,
         p. 53.
      "To My Sister." GeoR (38:1) Spr 84, p. 192.

5251. TRAMMELL, Robert
      "The Biggest Attraction." SouthwR (69:3) Sum 84,
         p. 302.

5252. TRANBARGER, Ossie E.
      "Serenity" (A Klōang). Amelia (1:2) O 84, p. 44.
      "Sunday Man." Amelia [1:1] Ap 84, p. 32.

5253. TRANSTROMER, Tomas
      "After a Death" (tr. by Robert Bly). Tendril (18,
         special issue) 84, p. 291.
      "Face to Face." Tendril (18, special issue) 84,
         p. 206.

5254. TREBY, Ivor
      "The Scampering." Argo (5:3) 84, p. 11-12.

5255. TREGEBOV, Rhea
      "Alive." Grain (12:4) N 84, p. 4-6.
      "At the Roman Ruins Vaison, France." Dandel
         (11:1) Spr-Sum 84, p. 40-41.
      "Basya Reva." PraS (58:4) Wint 84, p. 48-49.
      "Bowls of Fruit & Rabbits." Grain (12:3) Ag 84,
         p. 45.
      "Bring It with You." Grain (12:4) N 84, p. 4.
      "I Could Put." Grain (12:4) N 84, p. 6.
      "It Doesn't Stop." Grain (12:4) N 84, p. 6.

"Looking Out." PoetryCR (5:4) Sum 84, p. 18.
"Not a Penny." Grain (12:4) N 84, p. 4.
"Not Happy." Grain (12:4) N 84, p. 5.
"On the Phone." PraS (58:4) Wint 84, p. 48.
"Too Much World." Grain (12:4) N 84, p. 5.
"Under the Regime." Grain (12:3) Ag 84, p. 46.

5256. TREININ, Avner
      "Lazarus" (tr. by Shirley Kaufman). Field (31)
      Aut 84, p. 86-88.

5257. TREITEL, Margot
      "Family Plot." BlueBldgs (7) 84, p. 12.
      "Guidebook." PoetC (16:1) Aut 84, p. 54.
      "In the Kibbutz Kitchen." Nimrod (27:2) Spr-Sum
      84, p. 73-74.
      "Kitchen Utensils." RagMag (3:1) Spr 84, p. 39.
      "Living in Town." PoetC (16:1) Aut 84, p. 55.
      "Naming Day." CentR (28:4/29:1) Aut 84-Wint 85,
      p. 76.
      "Passing Through Cotonou." GreenfR (11:1/2) Sum-
      Aut 83, p. 98.
      "The White Man's Burden." GreenfR (11:1/2) Sum-
      Aut 83, p. 97.
      "Your Life in the Suburbs." Open24 (3) 84, p. 18.

5258. TREITEL, Renata
      "Distances" (Selections: 4, 5, 15, 35, tr. of
      Susana Thènon). Mund (14:2) 84, p. 33-37.
      "Hens." Calyx (8:2) Spr 84, p. 24.
      "To Grandmother." Wind (14:50) 84, p. 56.
      "World's End." Wind (14:50) 84, p. 56-57.

5259. TREMBLAY, Bill
      "1957." GreenfR (12:1/2) Sum-Aut 84, p. 143.
      "Rock from the Foothills." MinnR (N.S. 22) Spr
      84, p. 51.

5260. TREMBLAY, Gail
      "Urban Indians, Pioneer Square, Seattle." Calyx
      (8:2) Spr 84, p. 89.

5261. TRESHAN, Sheryl
      "Dear Carolyn." Tele (19) 83, p. 81.
      "Journal Entry 1/10/82." Tele (19) 83, p. 80.

5262. TRESSIN, Deanna
      "Ugly Eva." EngJ (73:5) S 84, p. 51.

5263. TRETHEWEY, Eric
      "'52 Pickup." Wind (14:52) 84, p. 48.
      "Ars Poetica." AntigR (58) Sum 84, p. 11.
      "August Tableau, Burnt Coat Head." Waves (12:1)
      Aut 83, p. 48.
      "A Dream." SouthernR (20:2) Spr 84, p. 370.
      "Hawks." PottPort (6) 84, p. 9.
      "It's Easy." SouthernR (20:2) Spr 84, p. 369.
      "Rescue." YaleR (73:2) Wint 84, p. 302-303.
      "Roadgang." PottPort (6) 84, p. 49.
      "Seven Questions Overlooking the Gulf." AntigR

(58) Sum 84, p. 12.

5264. TRIANA, José
"Juegos del Tiempo." LindLM (3:1) Ja-Mr 84, p. 5.
"Mi Padre." LindLM (3:1) Ja-Mr 84, p. 5.
"Voto de Penitencia." LindLM (3:1) Ja-Mr 84, p. 5.

5265. TRIMBLE, Mary
"Grief." TriQ (60) Spr-Sum 84, p. 399.

TRIPATHI, Sri Suryakant: See NIRALA

5266. TRISTE, Juan Aníbal
"Pajaro Negro." Mairena (6:17) Aut 84, p. 96.

5267. TRITEL, Barbara
"A Visit from Mother." KanQ (16:4) Aut 84, p. 60.

5268. TRITICA, John
"The Electric Body." GreenfR (12:1/2) Sum-Aut 84,
p. 37-38.
"Homeward in the Night" (tr. of Niklas Törnlund).
GreenfR (12:1/2) Sum-Aut 84, p. 34.
"The Old Land" (tr. of Niklas Törnlund).
GreenfR (12:1/2) Sum-Aut 84, p. 29-34.
"Shaking Trees of Alphabet" (For Joe Napora).
GreenfR (12:1/2) Sum-Aut 84, p. 39.
"Train-Rattle" (tr. of Niklas Törnlund).
CreamCR (9:1/2) 84, p. 86-88.
"The Tree" (tr. of Niklas Törnlund). GreenfR
(12:1/2) Sum-Aut 84, p. 34-35.

5269. TRIVELPIECE, Laurel
"The Snow Leopards." PoetryNW (25:3) Aut 84, p. 13.

5270. TROENDLE, Yves
"Aubade to Hidden Lovers: Ode to Hans Arp." Kayak
(64) My 84, p. 45.
"Epitaph: I'm standing in her dream." Kayak (64)
My 84, p. 46.
"Shadow." PoetryCR (5:4) Sum 84, p. 19.
"Song: to Recognition." PoetryCR (5:3) Spr 84, p.
18.

5271. TROWBRIDGE, William
"Albert Speer Lies Deep in Spandau." TarRP (23:2)
Spr 84, p. 28.
"In 1949." PoetC (16:1) Aut 84, p. 62-63.
"In the Castle." TarRP (23:2) Spr 84, p. 29.
"Kindergarten." TarRP (23:2) Spr 84, p. 30.
"Kong Breaks a Leg at the William Morris Agency."
PoetC (15:2) Wint 84, p. 39.
"Kong Settles Down." PoetC (15:2) Wint 84, p. 41.
"Kong Tries for a Mature Audience." PoetC (15:2)
Wint 84, p. 40.
"Layover in Dubuque." Wind (14:51) 84, p. 48.
"The Madness of Kong." PoetC (15:2) Wint 84, p. 38.
"Meditation on Our New Ceiling Fan." BelPoJ
(35:1) Aut 84, p. 1.
"The Professor's Mail." TarRP (23:2) Spr 84, p. 31.

"Self Help." PoetC (16:1) Aut 84, p. 67-69.
"Uncle Bud's Nature Remedy Poem." Wind (14:51)
    84, p. 48-49.
"The Waste Land." PoetC (16:1) Aut 84, p. 64-66.

5272. TROYANOVICH, Steve
    "Blooz" (for Eric V. Burdon). Quarry (33:1) Wint
        84, p. 57.
    "The Conspiracy of Morning" (for Alain Grandbois).
        Quarry (33:1) Wint 84, p. 54.
    "Harlequin Autumn." Quarry (33:1) Wint 84, p. 55.
    "The Last Gizzlestine." Quarry (33:1) Wint 84, p.
        56.
    "May 22, 1979." Quarry (33:1) Wint 84, p. 55-56.
    "Prehistoric Nights." Quarry (33:1) Wint 84, p. 54.
    "Returning Home." Quarry (33:1) Wint 84, p. 54-57.

TROYER, Gene van: See Van TROYER, Gene

5273. TRU, Vu
    "I am neither a communist nor a nationalist."
        NewL (50:2/3) Wint-Spr 84, p. 234.

5274. TRUDELL, Dennis
    "The Brown of Longing" (Two Photographs from
        Central America, Susan Meiselas, photographer).
        PraS (58:4) Wint 84, p. 53-54.
    "Central America" (photograph by Susan Meiselas).
        IndR (7:2) Spr 84, p. 24-25.
    "The Disappeared" (Desaparecidos). MinnR (N.S.
        23) Aut 84, p. 40.
    "If It Dies" (from a photograph by Susan Meiselas).
        TriQ (59) Wint 84, p. 116-117.
    "Isthmus." TriQ (59) Wint 84, p. 114-115.
    "Medic" (for Rich). MinnR (N.S. 23) Aut 84, p. 38-
        39.
    "The Rain that Falls" (Two Photographs from Central
        America, Susan Meiselas, photographer). PraS
        (58:4) Wint 84, p. 52-53.
    "A Small Black Album." NewEngR (7:2) Wint 84, p.
        233-234.
    "Somoza's Nicaragua" (from a photograph by Susan
        Meiselas). NewEngR (7:2) Wint 84, p. 235-236.
    "The Window." GeoR (38:2) Sum 84, p. 290.

5275. TRUDELL, Janet
    "Costumes." PoeticJ (5) 84, p. 44.
    "Not Yet." PoeticJ (7) 84, p. 10.

5276. TRUDELL, Janet L.
    "Confinement." PoeticJ (5) 84, p. 10.
    "Sunrise in Prison." PoeticJ (6) 84, p. 25.
    "That Look." PoeticJ (5) 84, p. 10.
    "Yesterdays." PoeticJ (6) 84, p. 6.

5277. TRUESDALE, C. W.
    "Doña Baby." Paunch (57/58) Ja 84, p. 124-130.
    "The Old Conductor" (for Tanja Jovanovic Kasnar).
        Abraxas (31/32) 84, p. 18.

5278. TRUHLAR, Richard
       "Glaucoma Sonata." CapilR (31) 84, p. 26.
       "Three Native Texts for Richard Heulsenbeck."
         CapilR (31) 84, p. 22.
       "Turner Visits Blacking House." CapilR (31) 84,
         p. 24-25.

5279. TRUMPENER, Katie
       "The Desert Song." MalR (68) Je 84, p. 83-84.
       "From the First Winter of a Big White Dog Whose
         Name Means Snowflake." MalR (68) Je 84, p. 85.

5280. TRUNCELLITO, Barbara
       "In Allegiance." Wind (14:51) 84, p. 50-51.
       "My Body." SnapD (8:1) Aut 84, p. 46-47.

5281. TRUONG, Sinh
       "Devastated." NewL (50:2/3) Wint-Spr 84, p. 235.

5282. TRUSSLER, Michael
       "It Appears That." Waves (12:1) Aut 83, p. 59.

5283. TSAO, Sung
       "Written in the Year Chi-Hai." NewL (50:2/3) Wint-
         Spr 84, p. 226.

5284. TSCHACBASOV, Nahum
       "The Moon Is My Uncle" (Excerpts). Chelsea
         (42/43) 84, p. 270-273.

5285. TSIMICALIS, Stavros
       "Fishing for Moon Pieces." Descant (47, 15:4)
         Wint 84, p. 84.
       "The Incipient Voice." Descant (47, 15:4) Wint
         84, p. 82-83.
       "Waiting for Layton." Descant (47, 15:4) Wint 84,
         p. 80-81.

5286. TSVETAEVA, Marina
       "On Love" (from a diary, tr. by Liza Tucker).
         Pequod (16/17) 84, p. 3-12.

TU, Fu: See DU, Fu

5287. TUCKER, Jim
       "Key West/Dover." Vis (16) 84, p. 14.

5288. TUCKER, Liza
       "On Love" (from a diary, tr. of Marina Tsvetaeva).
         Pequod (16/17) 84, p. 3-12.

5289. TUCKER, Memye Curtis
       "Airport Phone Booth." SouthernHR (18:3) Sum 84,
         p. 202.
       "Chipped Tooth." SouthernPR (24:2) Aut 84, p. 59.
       "The Last Day of Fulvius Agrippa." ConcPo (17:1)
         Spr 84, p. 93.

5290. TULLOSS, Rod
       "Finding the Masculine Principle in Babyshit."

Gargoyle (24) 84, p. 151-152.

5291. TURCO, Lewis
"The Day the Shed Came Apart." YaleR (73:2) Wint
84, p. 307-308.
"Memory." Nat (238:15) 21 Ap 84, p. 490.
"Night Song." MassR (25:2) Sum 84, p. 251-252.
"Recollections XI." Hudson (37:1) Spr 84, p. 86-87.
"Seventeen Haiku" ((After Bashō). CreamCR
(9:1/2) 84, p. 4-5.
"Terminal." MSS (4:1/2) Aut 84, p. 103-104.

5292. TURGEON, Gregoire
"Renoir, Two Girls at the Piano." NegC (4:3) Sum
84, p. 118.

5293. TURLOCK, Maggie
"Deadly Weapons." KanQ (16:1/2) Wint-Spr 84, p. 197.

5294. TURNBULL, Gael
"The Sun Inflates the Sky." Sparrow (46) 84, p. 27.

5295. TURNER, Alberta
"Matter." LittleM (14:3) 84, p. 28.
"Stuff." WoosterR (1:1) Mr 84, p. 64.
"Stumping Wise." Poetry (144:2) My 84, p. 99-100.

5296. TURNER, Frederick
"Against the Sad Poets." Shen (35:1) 83-84, p. 60.
"The Cave at Zhoukoudian." YaleR (74:1) Aut 84,
p. 58-63.
"Freeze Tag." Shen (35:1) 83-84, p. 60-61.
"On Goya's 'Saturn'." Poetry (143:6) Mr 84, p.
337-341.

5297. TURNER, Myron
"God Is My Co-Pilot." NoDaQ (52:3) Sum 84, p. 6-7.
"The Mark." NoDaQ (52:3) Sum 84, p. 3-5.

5298. TUSCHEN, John
"The Wild West" (For Barbara Stanwick -- Every
Outlaw's Mother). Abraxas (31/32) 84, p. 36.

5299. TWICHELL, Chase
"The Colorless Center of Everything." BlackWR
(10:2) Spr 84, p. 26-27.
"Evening, Herron's Farm." OhioR (33) 84, p. 112.
"Rhymes for Old Age." Thrpny (19) Aut 84, p. 19.

5300. TWISS, Dorothy
"Letters to My Sister in Her Distance." CimR (67)
Ap 84, p. 33-36.

5301. TYLER, Robert L.
"Gentle Brother." Wind (14:51) 84, p. 52.

5302. TZARA, Tristan
"To make a dadist poem." SewanR (92:3) Jl-S 84,
p. 390-391.

TZU, Chuang: See CHUANG, Tzu

5303. UCHMANOWICZ, Pauline
        "Queen of the Pickpockets." MassR (25:2) Sum 84,
            p. 223-224.
        "Tin Can Trout." YetASM (3) 84, p. 5.

5304. UDRY, Susan
        "Scrap Paper." CarolQ (37:1) Aut 84, p. 7-8.

5305. UGURLU, Nurer
        "Guilt" (tr. by Talat Sait Halman). NewRena (6:1,
            #18) Spr 84, p. 69.
        "Suc." NewRena (6:1, #18) Spr 84, p. 68.

5306. ULLRICH, David
        "Reverie." Poem (50) Mr 84, p. 50.

5307. ULMER, James
        "Building the Fence." NewYorker (60:38) 5 N 84,
            p. 46.
        "Gathering." VirQR (60:3) Sum 84, p. 431-432.

5308. UMAVIJANI, Montri
        "A Thai Divine Comedy" (Selections). Iowa (14:2)
            Spr-Sum 84, p. 70-71.

5309. UMPIERRE, Luz María
        "Carta a los Hispanos." Mairena (5:13) Spr 83, p.
            110-111.
        "Carta a los Hispanos" (a mis alumnos). BilingR
            (10:1) Ja-Ap 83, p. 67.
        "Una Defensa" (A Aida). BilingR (10:1) Ja-Ap 83,
            p. 66-67.
        "Oración ante una Imagen Derrumbada" (hágase
            con mucha devoción--mil eyaculaciones).
            BilingR (10:1) Ja-Ap 83, p. 66.

5310. UMPIERRE, Luzma
        "In Response." Cond (3:4, issue 10) 84, p. 46-47.

5311. UNDERWOOD, Lorraine
        "Casti Connubi" (tr. of Marco Martos). Vis (15)
            84, p. 29.
        "The Horse in Flames" (tr. of Juan Manuel Roca).
            Vis (15) 84, p. 12.

5312. UNDERWOOD, Robert
        "Joe Easy." WormR (24:2, issue 94) 84, p. 67.
        "Random Man." WormR (24:2, issue 94) 84, p. 67.

5313. UNGARETTI, Giuseppe
        "Il Tempo E Muto." NegC (4:4) Aut 84, p. 61.
        "Time Is Mute" (tr. by Will Wells). NegC (4:4)
            Aut 84, p. 60.

5314. UNGER, Barbara
        "After the Consciousness-Raising Group." NegC
            (4:4) Aut 84, p. 38.

"At the Singles Social." Abraxas (31/32) 84, p. 48.
"Ragtime Solo." BelPoJ (35:2) Wint 84-85, p. 15.

5315. UNTERECKER, John
"Cameras." Ploughs (10:1) 84, p. 172-173.
"The River Is Stained with Blue Sky, But That Does
Not Deny Stars." VirQR (60:1) Wint 84, p. 59.

5316. UPDIKE, John
"Aerie." NewYorker (60:41) 26 N 84, p. 46.
"The Code." OntR (20) Spr-Sum 84, p. 34.
"Cunts" (Upon Receiving the Swingers Life Club
Membership Solicitation). Playb (31:1) Ja 84,
p. 162.
"The Furniture." NewYorker (60:33) 1 O 84, p. 36.
"Gradations of Black" (Third Floor, Whitney
Museum). NewYorker (60:26) 13 Ag 84, p. 30.
"Ode to Evaporation." NewYorker (60:46) 31 D 84,
p. 30.
"Ode to Fragmentation." ParisR (26:94) Wint 84,
p. 178-179.
"Ode to Growth." MichQR (23:4) Aut 84, p. 485-486.
"Ode to Healing." MichQR (23:4) Aut 84, p. 483-484.
"Pain." NewRep (189:26) 26 D 83, p. 34.

5317. UPTON, Lee
"The Art Student at the Reformatory." PoetL
(79:2) Sum 84, p. 104-105.
"Fortune Cookies." KanQ (16:1/2) Wint-Spr 84, p.
162.
"Happiness." NoAmR (269:2) Je 84, p. 20.
"Introductions." KanQ (16:1/2) Wint-Spr 84, p. 162.
"Migration." SouthernPR (24:1) Spr 84, p. 70-71.
"Mud Dog." PoetL (79:2) Sum 84, p. 103.

5318. URDANG, Constance
"The Game of Troy." OntR (20) Spr-Sum 84, p. 43.
"Journeys." Shen (35:1) 83-84, p. 80.
"Meeting Again." OntR (20) Spr-Sum 84, p. 41.
"The Old Woman." Chelsea (42/43) 84, p. 127.
"The Other One." OntR (20) Spr-Sum 84, p. 42.
"Paris." Ploughs (10:4) 84, p. 110.
"The River." Poetry (144:4) Jl 84, p. 214.
"Robert's Knee." Shen (35:1) 83-84, p. 81-82.
"Son." Ploughs (10:4) 84, p. 111.
"Travelling without a Camera." Shen (35:1) 83-84,
p. 81.

5319. URIBE ARCE, Armando
"Una Emocion Baldia." Mairena (6:18) 84, p. 138.

5320. URQUHART, Jane
"Birds." PoetryCR (5:4) Sum 84, p. 17.
"Hall of Mirrors." PoetryCR (5:4) Sum 84, p. 17.
"Horses." PoetryCR (5:4) Sum 84, p. 17.

URTECHO, José Coronel: See CORONEL URTECHO, José

5321. USCHUK, Pamela
"After Reading Louise Bogan's Journals." Poetry

(145:3) D 84, p. 134-135.
"Black Ice." Poetry (145:3) D 84, p. 135-138.
"The Eye Saints Dream." Vis (16) 84, p. 10-11.
"Going Second Class." PoetC (16:1) Aut 84, p. 42.
"Meditations beside Kootenai Creek" (For William).
    Poetry (144:2) My 84, p. 74-77.
"Of Simple Intent" (for William). Telescope (3:1)
    Wint 84, p. 102-103.
"Through the Dark, a Brilliance." Tendril (17)
    Wint 84, p. 166.

5322. UU, David
"Corn Plasters & My Heart." CapilR (31) 84, p. 81.
"For D.A. Levy." CapilR (31) 84, p. 80.
"Salmon River Soliloquy II." CapilR (31) 84, p. 80.

5323. VACASPATI
"You mount repeatedly this playful woman's firm-set
    breasts" (tr. by Andrew Schelling). YellowS
    (13) Wint 84, p. 29.

5324. VACLAVICEK, Susan
"Orpheum." PoetryE (15) Aut 84, p. 50.

5325. VAJDA, Miklós
"Mask" (tr. of Gyula Illyès). HolCrit (21:1) F
    84, p. 9.
"The Sad Field-Hand" (tr. of Gyula Illyès, w.
    William Jay Smith and Gyula Kodolányi).
    HolCrit (21:1) F 84, p. 3.
"Tilting Sail" (tr. of Gyula Illyès, w. William
    Jay Smith and Gyula Kodolányi). HolCrit
    (21:1) F 84, p. 12.
"A Wreath" (tr. of Gyula Illyès, w. William Jay
    Smith and Gyula Kodolányi). HolCrit (21:1) F
    84, p. 10-11.

5326. VALAORITIS, Nanos
"Melancholia." Veloc (1) Sum 82, p. 20.
"My Style." Veloc (1) Sum 82, p. 17-18.
"Progressive Distortion of 16th Century Oil
    Painting with Castle Soldier Shepherd and
    Woman." Veloc (1) Sum 82, p. 19.

5327. VALDERRAMA, Pilar
"Quiero Vivir Contigo." Mairena (6:18) 84, p. 54.

5328. VALENTE, Lynn Manning
"Mars." Vis (16) 84, p. 4.
"Nurse." Northeast (Series 3:17) Sum 84, p. 20.

5329. VALENTINE, Jean
"Visit." NewYorker (60:28) 27 Ag 84, p. 63.

5330. VALENZUELA, Luisa
"One day you buy something new" (Untitled, tr. by
    Margaret Sayers Peden). Hudson (37:4) Wint 84-
    85, p. 570.
"Urban Haiku" (tr. by Margaret Sayers Peden).
    Hudson (37:4) Wint 84-85, p. 570.

5331. VALERY, Paul
"La Jeune Parque" (lines 34-101, tr. by Suzette
Haden Elgin). <u>Veloc</u> (2) Spr 83, p. 35-38.

5332. VALIQUETTE, Lynne
"Leave of Absence: A Ballad." <u>Northeast</u> (Series
3:17) Sum 84, p. 22.

5333. VALIS, Noel M.
"The Lamb of Marks and Spencer's." <u>NeqC</u> (4:4) Aut
84, p. 81.

VALKENBERG, Rick van: <u>See</u> Van VALKENBERG, Rick

5334. VALLADARES, Armando
"Boniato Jail: Account of a Massacre" (tr. by
Carlos Ripoll). <u>Confr</u> (27/28) 84, p. 32-35.
"Lend Me Your Legs for an Instant" (tr. by Carlos
Ripoll). <u>Confr</u> (27/28) 84, p. 36.

5335. VALLADARES, Carmen
"Cansancio." <u>Mairena</u> (5:13) Spr 83, p. 111.
"Cansancio." <u>Mairena</u> (6:18) 84, p. 176.

5336. VALLEJO, César
"Trilce" (Excerpts, tr. by James Wright). <u>Chelsea</u>
(42/43) 84, p. 52-53.

5337. VALLEJOS, Roque
"Poema 12: Todos velávamos a Dios." <u>Mairena</u>
(6:18) 84, p. 192.

5338. VALVERDE, Jocelyn
"Golden Relection of the Sea" (tr. by Ann Armstrong
Scarboro). <u>ConcPo</u> (17:2) Aut 84, p. 136.
"Le Reflet d'Or de la Mer." <u>ConcPo</u> (17:2) Aut 84,
p. 136.
"Soweto" (for James Mange, condemned to death, tr.
by Ann Armstrong Scarboro). <u>ConcPo</u> (17:2) Aut
84, p. 135.

Van . . .: <u>See also</u> names beginning with "Van" without the
following space, filed below in their alphabetic
positions.

5339. Van BEEK, Edith
"Collections." <u>Waves</u> (13:1) Aut 84, p. 33.

5340. Van BRUNT, Lloyd
"Dirge for the Pileated Woodpecker." <u>SouthernPR</u>
(24:1) Spr 84, p. 68-69.
"Pretty Things." <u>NewL</u> (50:4) Sum 84, p. 89.
"Sunday Morning--1982." <u>SoDakR</u> (22:4) Wint 84, p.
6-7.

5341. Van DUYN, Mona
"A Christmas Card, after the Assassination."
<u>Chelsea</u> (42/43) 84, p. 201.

5342. Van HOUTEN, Lois
"Coming to Terms with Geese." StoneC (12:1/2) Aut-
Wint 84, p. 15.

5343. Van MATRE, C. (Connie)
"Acid Rain." SanFPJ (6:1) 84, p. 85.
"The Deal." SanFPJ (7:1) 84, p. 64.
"Five Four Three." SanFPJ (6:1) 84, p. 85.
"Naked Words of Truth." SanFPJ (6:4) 84, p. 19.
"A Nuclear Bomb Explodes." SanFPJ (6:2) 84, p. 51.
"Peace." SanFPJ (6:4) 84, p. 76.
"Taking Count." SanFPJ (6:2) 84, p. 52.
"The Yellow Cat" (from "A Poets Dream"). SanFPJ
(7:1) 84, p. 62.
"To Help the Needy." SanFPJ (7:1) 84, p. 63.
"The Who and What of the Eightys." SanFPJ (6:1)
84, p. 56.

5344. Van SCHENDEL, Michel
"Lacis." CanLit (100) Spr 84, p. 333-334.
"Poeme: Etrangement l'extrême." CanLit (100)
Spr 84, p. 333.
"Répartition." CanLit (100) Spr 84, p. 334.
"Suite pour un Silence." CanLit (100) Spr 84, p.
334-335.

5345. Van TROYER, Gene
"Falling Astronauts." Veloc (3) Aut-Wint 83, p. 57.
"The Whole Message." Veloc (2) Spr 83, p. 17-23.

5346. Van VALKENBERG, Rick
"Why New Beat." MoodySI (14) Spr 84, p. 26.

Van VLIET, Eddy: See VLIET, Eddy van

5347. Van WALLEGHEN, Michael
"Blue Tango." SouthernR (20:2) Spr 84, p. 357-359.
"The Bottom Line." Ploughs (10:1) 84, p. 174-175.
"Roberta and Wilbur." SouthernR (20:2) Spr 84, p.
359-360.

5348. Van WINCKEL, Nance
"The Bomber's Misgiving." Ascent (9:2) 84, p. 56.
"Change of Heart." PoetryNW (25:2) Sum 84, p. 25-26.
"Deserting the Town." PoetryNW (25:4) Wint 84-85,
p. 32-33.
"Force of Habit." Ascent (10:1) 84, p. 1-5.
"The Inarticulate Organ." Ascent (9:3) 84, p. 23.
"Learning to Dive." PoetryNW (25:4) Wint 84-85,
p. 31-32.
"Nightfall on the Boardwalk." PoetryNW (25:2) Sum
84, p. 26.
"Repossession." Ascent (9:2) 84, p. 55.

5349. Van WYCK, Marcia
"Introducing Man to His Cave." Veloc (4) Sum 84,
p. 35-36.
"Needle's Eye." Veloc (4) Sum 84, p. 33-34.

5350. VANCE, Scott
"Cluttered." WindO (44) Sum-Aut 84, p. 8.

5351. VanderMOLEN, Robert
"Of Pines." Epoch (34:1) 84-85, p. 5-9.
"Snow." NewL (51:2) Wint 84-85, p. 116-117.
"Sunset." NewL (51:2) Wint 84-85, p. 117.

VARELA, Marisol Pereira: See PEREIRA VARELA, Marisol

5352. VARGA, Jon
"Night Tide." PoeticJ (2) 83, p. 38.

5353. VARGAS, Rafael
"The Signature of Things" (tr. by Leticia
Tanticlaiux). Iowa (14:2) Spr-Sum 84, p. 150.

5354. VARMA, Shrikant
"The Half-Hour Argument" (tr. by Aparna Dharwadker
and Vinay Dharwadker). NewEngR (7:2) Wint 84,
p. 265-268.

5355. VARNADO, S. L.
"An Evening at the Cinema." NegC (4:1) Wint 84,
p. 117-122.

5356. VARON, Jodi
"Carp." CutB (22) Spr-Sum 84, p. 44-45.

5357. VAZAKAS, Byron
"The Marble Distances." NewL (50:2/3) Wint-Spr
84, p. 107.

5358. VEACH, Cindy
"Walks." PraS (58:4) Wint 84, p. 49-51.

5359. VEENENDAAL, Cornelia
"Coal Days." HangL (46) Aut 84, p. 63.

5360. VEGA, Cajina
"Ballad of Monimbo" (tr. by Marc Zimmerman and
Ellen Banberger). MinnR (N.S. 22) Spr 84, p.
77, 81.

5361. VEGA, José Luis
"Go-Go Girl." Mairena (6:18) 84, p. 28.

5362. VEIGA, Marisella L.
"As Gentle As a Lamb." Ploughs (10:1) 84, p. 177.
"Sitting." Ploughs (10:1) 84, p. 176.

5363. VELASCO, Isabel
"Como Explicarte." Mairena (6:17) Aut 84, p. 20.
"Es Bueno." Mairena (6:17) Aut 84, p. 20.
"Nuevas Vidas." Mairena (6:18) 84, p. 140.
"Si Dijera Lo Que Siento." Mairena (6:17) Aut 84,
p. 19.

5364. VELI, Orhan
"Hegira" (tr. by Dionis Coffin Riggs, William

Fielder and Ozcan Yalim). <u>StoneC</u> (11:3/4) Spr-
Sum 84, p. 41.
"Hicret." <u>StoneC</u> (11:3/4) Spr-Sum 84, p. 40.

5365. VENN, George
"Burning the Wasteland Grass" (tr. of Ai Qing, w.
Lu Pei Wu). <u>NowestR</u> (22:3) 84, p. 104.
"Fish Fossil" (tr. of Ai Qing, w. Lu Pei Wu).
<u>NowestR</u> (22:3) 84, p. 101.
"Hail" (tr. of Ai Qing, w. Lu Pei Wu). <u>NowestR</u>
(22:3) 84, p. 102.
"Persian Chrysanthemums" (tr. of Ai Qing, w. Lu Pei
Wu). <u>NowestR</u> (22:3) 84, p. 103.

VENTI, T. (Tom) di: <u>See</u> DiVENTI, T. (Tom)

5366. VEQUIST, Betty
"My Hex." <u>LittleBR</u> (4:4) Sum 84, p. 47.

5367. VERAS, Paulo
"Beauty and the Beast" (tr. by Clara Angelica).
<u>Tele</u> (19) 83, p. 20.
"Family Album" (tr. by Clara Angelica). <u>Tele</u> (19)
83, p. 21.
"Of What Is Not Human" (tr. by Clara Angelica).
<u>Tele</u> (19) 83, p. 18-19.
"With Marginal Fury" (tr. by Clara Angelica).
<u>Tele</u> (19) 83, p. 20.

5368. VERHAGEN, Hans
"Euthanasia" (tr. by Peter Nijmeijer). <u>Iowa</u>
(14:2) Spr-Sum 84, p. 180-181.

5369. VERHULST, Pat
"Guard." <u>CrabCR</u> (1:3) Wint 84, p. 23.

5370. VERLAINE, Paul
"Le Bon Disciple." <u>AntigR</u> (57) Spr 84, p. 24.
"Poor Gaspard" (tr. by Dr. Don D. Wilson). <u>Amelia</u>
(1:2) O 84, p. 75.
"The True Disciple" (tr. by Bernhard Frank).
<u>AntigR</u> (57) Spr 84, p. 25.
"Tu Crois au Marc de Café." <u>AntigR</u> (57) Spr 84,
p. 26.
"You Believe in Tea-Leaves" (tr. by Bernhard
Frank). <u>AntigR</u> (57) Spr 84, p. 27.

5371. VERNON, William
"Ash Like Sand Like the People." <u>Sam</u> (40:2,
release 158) 84, p. 6.
"Ask a Marine." <u>Sam</u> (40:2, release 158) 84, p. 20.
"Bare Feet on Coral." <u>Sam</u> (40:2, release 158) 84,
p. 16.
"Brass Pickers." <u>Sam</u> (40:2, release 158) 84, p. 10.
"Carnival: Inside the Tent." <u>Sam</u> (40:2, release
158) 84, p. 17.
"Carnival: On the Edge of Town." <u>Sam</u> (40:2,
release 158) 84, p. 19.
"Cleaning the Bones." <u>Sam</u> (40:2, release 158) 84,
p. 1-20.

"Climb to the Summit." Sam (40:2, release 158) 84, p. 8.
"Cold Weather Training." Sam (40:2, release 158) 84, p. 5.
"Depot." Sam (40:2, release 158) 84, p. 3.
"Habv." Sam (40:2, release 158) 84, p. 11.
"Hiding from the Wind." Sam (40:2, release 158) 84, p. 9.
"On Leave at Subic Bay." Sam (40:2, release 158) 84, p. 15.
"The Secret of the Rosary." Sam (40:2, release 158) 84, p. 2.
"Taking Care of the Bones." Sam (40:2, release 158) 84, p. 13.

5372. VERNON, William J.
"Cyclotron." PoeticJ (1) 83, p. 7.
"Gorge-Out." SouthernHR (18:4) Aut 84, p. 317.
"Mining the Wind." PoeticJ (3) 83, p. 3.
"Pouch of Magic." PoeticJ (7) 84, p. 28.
"Razing a Barn." WoosterR (1:2) N 84, p. 67.
"Swimming a Witch." BelPoJ (34:3) Spr 84, p. 35-36.
"They Go to School to Learn." PoeticJ (7) 84, p. 29.

5373. VERVAECKE, Kris
"Killing Chickens." KanQ (16:1/2) Wint-Spr 84, p. 196-197.

5374. VESAAS, Halldis M.
"Earth Fragrance" (tr. by Ronald Wakefield, George Schoolfield, P. J. Powers, and the author). LitR (27:3) Spr 84, p. 305.

5375. VEUHOFF, Heinz
"1st 'A' Print for New Printer, New York, May 2, 1981." KanQ (16:3) Sum 84, p. 43.

5376. VICKERS, Edward Davin
"Grandmother's Recipe." DekalbLAJ (20th Anniversary Issue) 84, p. 110.

5377. VICUÑA, Cecilia
"Historias de Astros." Mairena (6:17) Aut 84, p. 21-22.
"Luxumei." Mairena (6:17) Aut 84, p. 21.

5378. VIDYA
"O neighbor, please keep an eye on my house" (in Sanskrit). YellowS (13) Wint 84, p. 29.
"O neighbor, please keep an eye on my house" (tr. by Andrew Schelling). YellowS (13) Wint 84, p. 29.
"On makeshift bedding in the cucumber garden" (tr. by Andrew Schelling). YellowS (13) Wint 84, p. 28.
"Tell me, Murala River" (in Sanskrit). YellowS (13) Wint 84, p. 29.
"Tell me, Murala River" (tr. by Andrew Schelling). YellowS (13) Wint 84, p. 29.

5379. VIERECK, Peter
        "Archer in the Marrow: The Applewood Cycles"
        (Selections: "Motifs: Archer in the Marrow,"
        "Duel on Land's End," "Epilogue: Prologue to New
        Spiral"). Agni (20) 84, p. 113-117.

5380. VIEYRA, Antonio
        "Ansia" (Selections: III-VI). Mairena (5:14) Aut
        83, p. 18-19.
        "Balardas." Mairena (6:17) Aut 84, p. 74.
        "Espantapajaros" (Selections: III, VI). Mairena
        (5:14) Aut 83, p. 19.
        "Otredad" (Selections). Mairena (5:14) Aut 83, p.
        17.
        "Prolongo mi palabra." Mairena (6:18) 84, p. 138.
        "Soy el que sufre y se rebela." Mairena (6:18)
        84, p. 138.

VIEYRA, Mario Antonio San Martin: See VIEYRA, Antonio

5381. VIGNOLA, Ralph A.
        "Outlaws." SanFPJ (6:2) 84, p. 75.
        "Partial Suicide." SanFPJ (6:2) 84, p. 73.
        "Venom." SanFPJ (6:2) 84, p. 74.

5382. VILARIÑO, Idea
        "Noche de Sabado." BlackWR (10:2) Spr 84, p. 38.
        "Saturday Night" (tr. by Patsy Boyer and Mary
        Crow). BlackWR (10:2) Spr 84, p. 39.

5383. VILLA, Emilio
        "Brunt H" (Excerpts). Chelsea (42/43) 84, p. 335-
        339.

5384. VILLANI, Jim
        "Sweeping Up after the Mob." Wind (14:50) 84, p. 58.

5385. VILLANUEVA, Salvador
        "Poema de las Mutaciones y los Rompimientos."
        Mairena (6:18) 84, p. 29.

5386. VILLAR, Luis
        "Errante en la Noche." Mairena (5:14) Aut 83, p. 85.

5387. VILLARRUBIA, Jan
        "Ta'a Ta Moo" ("Land of the Lizard People," based
        on a Tahitian myth). ThirdW (2) Spr 84, p. 8-9.

5388. VILLEGAS, Juan
        "In Honor of Truth and the Prophet Malcolm X."
        Stepping Wint 83, p. 22-23.
        "A Tribute to our nearly decimated Brethren: The
        Song of Rising Cloud." Stepping (Premier
        Issue) Sum 82, p. 38-40.

VILLEGAS, Nestor Diaz de: See DIAZ de VILLEGAS, Nestor

5389. VILLENA, Luis Antonio de
        "Di Pagani." Mairena (6:18) 84, p. 69.

5390. VILLIAS, Josette Liliane
"African Drought." SanFPJ (7:1) 84, p. 52.
"Black Star Sapphire." SanFPJ (7:1) 84, p. 51.
"Feast of Poor Souls." SanFPJ (7:1) 84, p. 68.
"Hail Woman!" SanFPJ (7:1) 84, p. 68.
"Mz Frankenstein." SanFPJ (7:1) 84, p. 65.

5391. VINCIGUERRA, Theresa
"For Ungaretti." CalQ (23/24) Spr-Sum 84, p. 136.

5392. VINZ, Mark
"Against the Wall." MidwQ (25:4) Sum 84, p. 415.
"First Rites and Last." SouthernPR (24:2) Aut 84,
    p. 70-73.
"House for Rent." SpoonRQ (9:4) Aut 84, p. 4.
"Kansas, August, Keeping the Faith." SpoonRQ
    (9:4) Aut 84, p. 2.
"Lost and Found." SpoonRQ (9:4) Aut 84, p. 3.
"The Silver Dollar Bar" (for the Poets at Southwest
    State University." SpoonRQ (9:4) Aut 84, p. 1.

VITO, E. B. de: See De VITO, E. B.

5393. VIZCAYA, Sergio
"1978" (w. Condega Poetry Workshop, tr. by Marc
    Zimmerman and Ellen Banberger). MinnR (N.S.
    22) Spr 84, p. 70.

5394. VLASAK, Keith
"Together." Wind (14:52) 84, p. 38.

5395. VLIET, Eddy van
"Summer Is Over" (tr. by Peter Nijmeijer). Vis
    (16) 84, p. 5.

VOE, Bill de: See DeVOE, Bill

5396. VOIGT, Ellen Bryant
"Bright Leaf." AmerPoR (13:6) N-D 84, p. 48.
"The Drowned Man." SenR (14:2) 84, p. 75-76.
"Landscape, Dense with Trees." NewYorker (60:27)
    20 Ag 84, p. 40.
"Memorial Day." NewYorker (60:15) 28 My 84, p. 44.
"The Storm." Atlantic (254:2) Ag 84, p. 50.
"Sweet Everlasting." AmerPoR (13:6) N-D 84, p. 46.

5397. VOLDSETH, Beverly
"Five Violets." PoeticJ (2) 83, p. 29.
"Hay Creek Sunday Morning." PoeticJ (2) 83, p. 12-
    13.

5398. VOLEK, Bronislava
"It Is Raining" (tr. by Willis Barnstone and the
    author). Nimrod (27:2) Spr-Sum 84, p. 75.
"Supper" (tr. by Willis Barnstone and the author).
    Nimrod (27:2) Spr-Sum 84, p. 75.

5399. VOLLMER, Judith
"Music Lessons." YetASM (3) 84, p. 4.
"Nursing the Sunburn." HangL (45) Spr 84, p. 60.

"Troy Hill Voices." <u>TarRP</u> (23:2) Spr 84, p. 33-34.

5400. VOLMER, Janet
"Outline." <u>Wind</u> (14:51) 84, p. 53.

5401. VOLPENDESTA, David
"Mourning Flavor" (tr. of Otto Rene Castillo).
<u>Vis</u> (15) 84, p. 20-21.
"Other People's Blood" (tr. of Gioconda Belli).
<u>Vis</u> (15) 84, p. 27.

Von BORN, Heidi: <u>See</u> BORN, Heidi von

5402. Von CUTTER, Lionel
"Appetite." <u>Bogg</u> (52) 84, p. 34.

Von der BEEK, F. Ten Harmsen: <u>See</u> BEEK, F. Ten Harmsen V. D.

Von HOFMANNSTHAL, Hugo: <u>See</u> HOFMANNSTHAL, Hugo von

5403. VORONCA, Ilarie
"It is perhaps the snow that sets you on fire"
("Untitled", tr. by Dorothy Aspinwall). <u>WebR</u>
(9:2) Wint 85, p. 18.

5404. VOSS, Lori
"Making Coffee." <u>CapeR</u> (19:2) Sum 84, p. 42.
"Marriage." <u>CapeR</u> (19:2) Sum 84, p. 43.

5405. VOSSEKUIL, Cheryl
"Beneath the Surface." <u>CentR</u> (28:2) Spr 84, p.
109-111.

VRIES, Carrow de: <u>See</u> De VRIES, Carrow

VRIES, Daniel de: <u>See</u> De VRIES, Daniel

VRIES, N. de: <u>See</u> De VRIES, N.

VU, Tru: <u>See</u> TRU, Vu

5406. WADDEN, Paul
"Littoral" (for L.R.). <u>WebR</u> (9:1) Spr 84, p. 33.
"Mirror." <u>Northeast</u> (Series 3:18) 84, p. 8.

5407. WADDINGTON, Miriam
"The Gift." <u>CanLit</u> (100) Spr 84, p. 337-338.
"The New Seasons: Light and Dark." <u>CanLit</u> (100)
Spr 84, p. 336-337.

5408. WADE, Cory
"Coming In." <u>SoDakR</u> (22:1) Spr 84, p. 41.
"Orpheus." <u>SouthernR</u> (20:2) Spr 84, p. 386.

5409. WADE, John Stevens
"Fart." <u>Northeast</u> (Series 3:17) Sum 84, p. 7.
"I Was Laughing." <u>Paunch</u> (57/58) Ja 84, p. 86.

5410. WADE, Seth
"For an Album." <u>CapeR</u> (19:3) 20th Anniversary
Issue 84, p. 53.

5411. WADE, Sidney
"Local Habitation." <u>GrandS</u> (4:1) Aut 84, p. 102.
"Snowy Owl." <u>GrandS</u> (4:1) Aut 84, p. 100-101.
"White Birds." <u>NewYorker</u> (60:38) 5 N 84, p. 159.

5412. WADLEY, Kenya
"Simple Thank You." <u>Stepping</u> Wint 84, p. 26.

5413. WAGES, Nancy Susan
"Summer." <u>DekalbLAJ</u> (17:1/2) 84, p. 148-149.

5414. WAGNER, Anneliese
"Thank You." <u>WestB</u> (14) 84, p. 14.

5415. WAGNER, Charles
"The Overcoming Church." <u>KanQ</u> (16:4) Aut 84, p. 40.

5416. WAGNER, Kathleen
"Sampler" (Rebecca Steele, Age 10, November 26,
1839). <u>BlueBldgs</u> (7) 84, p. 25.

5417. WAGONER, David
"The Caterpillar." <u>Nat</u> (238:8) 3 Mr 84, p. 262.
"My Father's Football Game." <u>TriQ</u> (60) Spr-Sum
84, p. 400-401.
"Round Dance." <u>Chelsea</u> (42/43) 84, p. 424-425.
"Their Bodies" (To the students of anatomy at
Indiana University). <u>ColEng</u> (46:5) S 84, p.
456-457.
"There." <u>AntR</u> (42:4) Aut 84, p. 449.
"To the Last Man." <u>Antaeus</u> (53) Aut 84, p. 249.
"The Track Scale Weigher." <u>TriQ</u> (60) Spr-Sum 84,
p. 402-403.

5418. WAHLE, F. Keith
"Always the Blood." <u>WestB</u> (15) 84, p. 114.
"The Father." <u>MidAR</u> (4:2) Aut 84, p. 127-128.
"The Hundred-Word Story." <u>WormR</u> (24:4, issue 96)
84, p. 161.
"One Night Stand." <u>YellowS</u> (11) Sum 84, p. 33.

5419. WAIN, John
"Twofold." <u>Hudson</u> (37:2) Sum 84, p. 189-198.

5420. WAKEFIELD, Ronald
"Earth Fragrance" (tr. of Halldis M. Vesaas, w.
George Schoolfield, P. J. Powers, and the
author). <u>LitR</u> (27:3) Spr 84, p. 305.

5421. WAKOSKI, Diane
"Amaryllis Belladonna" (for Joyce Benvenuto who
said she did not see how I could say that Darwin
represented "freedom from savagery" when I
depicted him torturing (sic) an insect). <u>PraS</u>
(58:4) Wint 84, p. 79-80.
"Gourds." <u>PraS</u> (58:4) Wint 84, p. 77.

"Head Life." <u>PraS</u> (58:4) Wint 84, p. 78.
"The Orange." <u>Agni</u> (20) 84, p. 72-73.
"Screw, a Technical Love Poem." <u>Chelsea</u> (42/43)
    84, p. 164-165.
"The Story of Richard Maxfield." <u>Peb</u> (23) 84, p.
    32-35.
"Winning & Losing." <u>PraS</u> (58:4) Wint 84, p. 75-76.

5422. WAKOWSKI, Diane
"The Tightrope Walker." <u>Sparrow</u> (46) 84, p. 13.

5423. WALCOTT, Derek
"Cul de Sac Valley." <u>NewRep</u> (191:19) 5 N 84, p.
    32-33.
"Elsewhere" (for Stephen Spender). <u>NewYRB</u> (31:13)
    16 Ag 84, p. 16.
"Eulogy to W. H. Auden." <u>NewRep</u> (189:21) 21 N 83,
    p. 38-39.
"God Rest Ye Merry Gentlemen, Part II." <u>NewYRB</u>
    (31:20) 20 D 84, p. 34.
"Midsummer" (Excerpts). <u>NewRep</u> (190:3) 23 Ja 84,
    p. 31-33.
"Midsummer" (Selections: VI, XIV, VII). <u>GreenfR</u>
    (12:1/2) Sum-Aut 84, p. 26-27.
"Semper Eadem" (June 1973). <u>NewL</u> (50:2/3) Wint-
    Spr 84, p. 60-61.

5424. WALDMAN, Anne
"Canzone" (for Ted Berrigan, 1934-1983). <u>ParisR</u>
    (26:93) Aut 84, p. 209-211.

5425. WALDOR, Peter
"Mortgage Business." <u>Ploughs</u> (10:4) 84, p. 140-141.

5426. WALDROP, Keith
"After the Deluge" (from <u>I</u> <u>Build</u> <u>My</u> <u>Dwelling</u>, tr.
    of Edmond Jabès). <u>DenQ</u> (19:1) Spr 84, p. 18.
"Always This Image" (from <u>Of</u> <u>the</u> <u>Two</u> <u>Hands</u>, tr.
    of Edmond Jabès). <u>DenQ</u> (19:1) Spr 84, p. 31-32.
"Groundless" (from <u>I</u> <u>Build</u> <u>My</u> <u>Dwelling</u>, tr. of
    Edmond Jabès). <u>DenQ</u> (19:1) Spr 84, p. 21-22.
"Half Open, My Hand" (from <u>Of</u> <u>the</u> <u>Two</u> <u>Hands</u>, tr.
    of Edmond Jabès). <u>DenQ</u> (19:1) Spr 84, p. 30.
"If There Were Anywhere But Desert" (Selected
    Poems, tr. of Edmond Jabès). <u>DenQ</u> (19:1) Spr
    84, p. 3-32.
"Metamorphosis of the World" (from <u>I</u> <u>Build</u> <u>My</u>
    <u>Dwelling</u>, tr. of Edmond Jabès). <u>DenQ</u> (19:1)
    Spr 84, p. 18.
"The Pact of Spring" (from <u>I</u> <u>Build</u> <u>My</u> <u>Dwelling</u>,
    tr. of Edmond Jabès). <u>DenQ</u> (19:1) Spr 84, p.
    23-24.
"The Pilgrim" (from <u>I</u> <u>Build</u> <u>My</u> <u>Dwelling</u>, tr. of
    Edmond Jabès). <u>DenQ</u> (19:1) Spr 84, p. 19.
"Screech-Owl with a Comet's Tail" (from <u>I</u> <u>Build</u> <u>My</u>
    <u>Dwelling</u>, tr. of Edmond Jabès). <u>DenQ</u> (19:1)
    Spr 84, p. 19.
"Show" (from <u>I</u> <u>Build</u> <u>My</u> <u>Dwelling</u>, tr. of Edmond
    Jabès). <u>DenQ</u> (19:1) Spr 84, p. 15-17.
"Slumber Inn" (from <u>I</u> <u>Build</u> <u>My</u> <u>Dwelling</u>, tr. of

Edmond Jabès). <u>DenQ</u> (19:1) Spr 84, p. 5-12.
"Sunland" (from <u>I</u> <u>Build</u> <u>My</u> <u>Dwelling</u>, tr. of
Edmond Jabès). <u>DenQ</u> (19:1) Spr 84, p. 13-14.
"Those from Whom" (from <u>Of</u> <u>the</u> <u>Two</u> <u>Hands</u>, tr. of
Edmond Jabès). <u>DenQ</u> (19:1) Spr 84, p. 25-28.
"Unmasked Hand" (from <u>Of</u> <u>the</u> <u>Two</u> <u>Hands</u>, tr. of
Edmond Jabès). <u>DenQ</u> (19:1) Spr 84, p. 29.
"Well Water" (from <u>I</u> <u>Build</u> <u>My</u> <u>Dwelling</u>, tr. of
Edmond Jabès). <u>DenQ</u> (19:1) Spr 84, p. 20.

5427. WALDROP, Rosmarie
"Of Salem." <u>GrandS</u> (3:1) Aut 83, p. 151.
"Of the American Character according to Santayana."
<u>GrandS</u> (3:1) Aut 83, p. 152.
"Shorter American Memories" (Of Salem. Of the
American Character according to Santayana).
<u>GrandS</u> (3:1) Aut 83, p. 151-152.

5428. WALKER, Dee
"Good Woman." <u>KanQ</u> (16:4) Aut 84, p. 77.

5429. WALKER, Don T.
"The Eighth Limerick." <u>LittleBR</u> (4:4) Sum 84, p. 87.

5430. WALKER, Eric
"Images on the Beach" (tr. of Elsa Cross, w. Abby
Wolf). <u>Iowa</u> (14:2) Spr-Sum 84, p. 145-146.

5431. WALKER, Ida Crane
"Chansonettes and Violettes" (Third Prize, 13th
Annual Kansas Poetry Contest). <u>LittleBR</u> (4:3)
Spr 84, p. 64.

5432. WALKER, Lynne
"Big Red Chronology." <u>PaintedB</u> (22) Spr 84, p. 23.
"I Wanta Go Back, Grown Up." <u>PaintedB</u> (22) Spr
84, p. 21.
"Schizogony." <u>PaintedB</u> (22) Spr 84, p. 22.
"What You Want? Baby, I Got It!" <u>WormR</u> (24:4,
issue 96) 84, p. 153-156.

5433. WALKER, Robert
"Silver." <u>WebR</u> (9:2) Wint 85, p. 79-80.

5434. WALKER, Sue
"Letter from a Confederate Soldier" (Camp Close,
Ohio, Jan. 10, 1865, Music by Donald Ashwander).
<u>NegC</u> (4:2) Spr 84, p. 81-83.

5435. WALL, Eamonn
"Museo Leon Trotsky." <u>Abraxas</u> (29/30) 84, p. 42-43.

5436. WALLACE, Anthony
"The Bell System." <u>SmPd</u> (21:1) Wint 84, p. 33.

5437. WALLACE, Bronwen
"How It Will Happen." <u>Descant</u> (47, 15:4) Wint 84,
p. 139-142.
"My Son Is Learning to Invent." <u>CrossC</u> (6:4) 84,
p. 5.

"Place of Origin." <u>Descant</u> (47, 15:4) Wint 84, p.
    136-138.
"To Get to You." <u>Descant</u> (47, 15:4) Wint 84, p.
    143-145.

5438. WALLACE, Linda
    "Priorities at 13." <u>SnapD</u> (6:2) Spr 83, p. 24-25.

5439. WALLACE, Naomi
    "Hours." <u>NegC</u> (4:2) Spr 84, p. 49.

5440. WALLACE, Robert
    "Hurricane." <u>SouthernPR</u> (24:2) Aut 84, p. 18-21.
    "Kick the Can." <u>OhioR</u> (32) 84, p. 124.
    "We." <u>OhioR</u> (32) 84, p. 125.

5441. WALLACE, Ronald
    "The Art of Love." <u>Poem</u> (50) Mr 84, p. 44.
    "An Impossible Sonnet" (for Angela, who told me the
        six words in English for which there is no
        rhyme). <u>KanQ</u> (16:3) Sum 84, p. 51.
    "Merida: The Market." <u>QW</u> (18) Spr-Sum 84, p. 63.
    "Poem Written Mostly by Fourth Graders." <u>PoetryNW</u>
        (25:1) Spr 84, p. 46-47.
    "Potatoes." <u>Poem</u> (50) Mr 84, p. 43.
    "The Secret of Levitation." <u>WoosterR</u> (1:1) Mr 84,
        p. 89-90.
    "Short History of the Tongue." <u>WoosterR</u> (1:1) Mr
        84, p. 90-91.
    "Sinbad the Sailor." <u>AmerPoR</u> (13:4) Jl-Ag 84, p. 44.
    "Trash-Picking for Emily, Age 6." <u>PoetC</u> (15:2)
        Wint 84, p. 22.
    "Yucatan: In the Mayan Village." <u>NegC</u> (4:2) Spr
        84, p. 29.

5442. WALLACE, T. S.
    "Garrulous in Gaza" (Samson survives to old age).
        <u>Swallow</u> (3) 84, p. 11-12.
    "Imperatives." <u>PoetL</u> (79:3) Aut 84, p. 143.
    "The Language of Blood." <u>MidAR</u> (4:1) Spr 84, p. 24.
    "Manifest Destiny." <u>YetASM</u> (3) 84, p. 6.
    "We Are Not What We Think." <u>StoneC</u> (12:1/2) Aut-
        Wint 84, p. 41.
    "You Who Are Martyrs." <u>StoneC</u> (11:3/4) Spr-Sum
        84, p. 15.

5443. WALLACE-CLARK, Ruth
    "Leaving My Son at Twin Oaks Commune." <u>Wind</u>
        (14:52) 84, p. 33.
    "New Tupelo: Night of Sad Guitars." <u>Wind</u> (14:52)
        84, p. 37.

WALLEGHEN, Michael van: <u>See</u> Van WALLEGHEN, Michael

5444. WALLER, Gary
    "Skaneateles Lake, January." <u>Blueline</u> (5:2) Wint-
        Spr 84, p. 7.

5445. WALLS, Doyle Wesley
    "This Common Flight." <u>PoetC</u> (16:1) Aut 84, p. 56-57.

"The Woman He Married." NegC (4:2) Spr 84, p. 40-41.

5446. WALSH, Chad
"They Are Coming Between Us, Robert Hayden." Obs
(8:1) Spr 82, p. 195-196.

5447. WALSH, Marty
"Land of Milk and Honey." StoneC (12:1/2) Aut-
Wint 84, p. 16.

5448. WALTER, R. R.
"Time Was: Christmas." BallSUF (24:3) Sum 83, p.
71-73.

5449. WALTERS, LaWanda
"Grandmother's Blue Willow Dishes." SouthernPR
(24:2) Aut 84, p. 73-74.

5450. WALTHALL, Hugh
"Spell in the Pokey." Shen (35:1) 83-84, p. 89.

5451. WALTON, Angela
"Icarian Letter." SoCaR (17:1) Aut 84, p. 48.
"Life Says the Clown." SoCaR (17:1) Aut 84, p. 47.
"Vici, Vidi, Veni" (Irish blues for Calley).
SoCaR (17:1) Aut 84, p. 49.

5452. WALTON, Gary
"A.D.C. 4th." SanFPJ (6:3) 84, p. 34.
"Cosmology on a Budget." SanFPJ (6:3) 84, p. 33.
"Political Masque" (on reading Robert Bly).
SanFPJ (6:3) 84, p. 36.

5453. WANG, Hui-Ming
"Possess nothing." NewL (50:2/3) Wint-Spr 84, p.
238.
"The Song of the Draftee." LittleBR (4:4) Sum 84,
p. 49.
"The Song of the Draftee" (Chinese calligraphy).
LittleBR (4:4) Sum 84, p. 48.

5454. WANG, Jesse
"My Hometown's Base Creatures" (tr. of Wu Cheng, w.
Marilyn Chin). Iowa (14:2) Spr-Sum 84, p. 57-58.

5455. WANG, V. S. M.
"La Mer (After Debussy)." HarvardA (117:4/118:1)
D 84, p. 14-15.

5456. WANIEK, Marilyn
"Friday Night" (tr. of Ralf Thenior). PortR
(30:1) 84, p. 154.

5457. WARD, Diane
"The Fourth of July Is Geography." Sulfur (3:3,
issue 9) 84, p. 76-81.

5458. WARD, Jennie
"Brother Blood." PoetL (79:3) Aut 84, p. 133-134.

5459. WARD, Jerry
"Black Boy." <u>BlackALF</u> (18:1) Spr 84, p. 19.
"Danger in the Human Zone." <u>BlackALF</u> (18:1) Spr
84, p. 19.
"For Rachel." <u>BlackALF</u> (18:1) Spr 84, p. 18.
"Lawd Today." <u>BlackALF</u> (18:1) Spr 84, p. 18.
"Meditation 83/US." <u>BlackALF</u> (18:1) Spr 84, p. 18.
"The Outsider Inside." <u>BlackALF</u> (18:1) Spr 84, p.
18.
"Two for Certain Leaders." <u>BlackALF</u> (18:1) Spr
84, p. 19.

5460. WARD, Jerry W., Jr.
"Langston / Blues Griot." <u>Stepping</u> Wint 84, p. 13.

5461. WARD, Joanne
"Fresh Cut of Grass." <u>Confr</u> (27/28) 84, p. 264.

5462. WARDEN, Marine Robert
"Requiem for KAL 007." <u>Abraxas</u> (29/30) 84, p. 17.
"September." <u>NegC</u> (4:4) Aut 84, p. 47.

5463. WARLAND, Betsy
"No words" (XVII). <u>Waves</u> (12:4) Spr 84, p. 42.
"This Map Is Not the Territory." <u>Waves</u> (12:4) Spr
84, p. 42.
"Untying the Tongue" (Exceprts). <u>Waves</u> (12:4) Spr
84, p. 38-43.
"When she began she used words like moon, egg"
(VIII). <u>Waves</u> (12:4) Spr 84, p. 42.

5464. WARNE, Candice
"The Dead." <u>Spirit</u> (7:1) 84, p. 172-173.

5465. WARREN, Barbara L.
"Poet in Residence." <u>EngJ</u> (73:5) S 84, p. 37.

5466. WARREN, Chris
"The Peever Graveyard." <u>Quarry</u> (33:4) Aut 84, p.
52-54.
"Photograph of Franz Kafka at 13." <u>Quarry</u> (33:4)
Aut 84, p. 52.

5467. WARREN, Michael
"On the Surface: In the Mirror." <u>Waves</u> (12:4) Spr
84, p. 55.

5468. WARREN, Norma
"Dichotomy." <u>RagMag</u> (3:2) Aut 84, p. 43.
"Late Afternoon on Slim Creek Lake." <u>RagMag</u> (3:2)
Aut 84, p. 42.

5469. WARREN, Robert Penn
"Arizona Midnight." <u>NewEngR</u> (6:3) Spr 84, p. 417.
"Far West Once." <u>NewYorker</u> (60:8) 9 Ap 84, p. 44-45.
"First Moment of Autumn Recognized." <u>YaleR</u> (73:3)
Spr 84, p. 429.
"Hope." <u>YaleR</u> (73:3) Spr 84, p. 430.
"Instant on Crowded Street." <u>NewEngR</u> (6:3) Spr
84, p. 415.

"Last Meeting." AmerPoR (13:4) Jl-Ag 84, p. 22.
"Literal Dream" (Twenty years after reading
   "Tess...," and without ever having seen the
   movie). NewYorker (59:46) 2 Ja 84, p. 28.
"Myth of Mountain Sunrise." NewEngR (6:3) Spr 84,
   p. 418.
"Old Love." SewanR (92:3) Jl-S 84, p. 348-350.
"Upwardness." PartR (51:4/52:1 Anniversary issue)
   84-85, p. 611.
"Whistle of the Three A.M. Express." AmerPoR
   (13:4) Jl-Ag 84, p. 22.
"Winter Wheat: Oklahoma." NewEngR (6:3) Spr 84,
   p. 416.

5470. WARREN, Rosanna
      "Boy in Kayak." SouthernHR (18:4) Aut 84, p. 324.
      "Funerary Portraits." SenR (14:1) 84, p. 13-14.
      "History As Decoration." PartR (51:4/52:1
         Anniversary issue) 84-85, p. 612.
      "In a Tuscan Landscape." SenR (14:1) 84, p. 17-18.
      "Invitation au Voyage: Baltimore." Agni (21) 84,
         p. 75-76.
      "Lily." ThRiPo (23/24) 84, p. 81-82.
      "Orchard" (in memoriam W.K.). Agni (21) 84, p. 77-
         78.
      "Painting a Madonna." GeoR (38:2) Sum 84, p. 400-
         401.
      "'Sea Gate and Goldenrod': Cranberry Island Elegy"
         (for W.K.). SenR (14:1) 84, p. 15-16.

5471. WARSH, Sylvia Maultash
      "Relic." Waves (12:1) Aut 83, p. 65.

5472. WASHBURN, Katharine
      "Blue of the Lodes in your mouth" (tr. of Paul
         Celan). Sulfur (4:2, issue 11) 84, p. 16.
      "Gone into the night, complicit" (tr. of Paul
         Celan). Sulfur (4:2, issue 11) 84, p. 16.
      "Once, when death was mobbed" (tr. of Paul Celan).
         Sulfur (4:2, issue 11) 84, p. 16.

5473. WASKOWSKY, Nicolaus
      "Eftsoon" (for M.K.G., July 1980). BlueBldgs (7)
         84, p. 10.
      "The Healing" (Asylum Lake, Kalamazoo: July, 1975.
         Calvin College: July, 1981). BlueBldgs (8)
         84?, p. 6.
      "Those Left at Sunrise" (After Czeslaw Milosz, 1975
         Winter, 1978-1979). BlueBldgs (7) 84, p. 10.

5474. WATANABE, José
      "Acerca de la Libertad." Mairena (6:18) 84, p. 96.
      "The Unwanted Angel" (tr. by Sima Rabinowitz).
         Vis (15) 84, p. 28.

5475. WATERHOUSE, Elizabeth
      "Kaleidoscope." NewRep (190:7) 20 F 84, p. 34.

5476. WATERMAN, Cary
      "Graduation." WoosterR (1:1) Mr 84, p. 66.

"In the Year of the Anti-Nuclear Demonstrations,
   1982." WoosterR (1:1) Mr 84, p. 67.
"New Physics." RagMag (3:2) Aut 84, p. 3.
"Poem before Sleeping." RagMag (3:2) Aut 84, p. 4.
"September Comes." RagMag (3:2) Aut 84, p. 2.

5477. WATERS, Mary Ann
   "Airplane Conversation with an Engineer Who
      Designed Ammunition." Poetry (143:6) Mr 84, p.
      324-325.
   "Although It Was Late in the Season." Poetry
      (145:1) O 84, p. 6-7.
   "As Your Car Approaches." Telescope (3:2) Spr 84,
      p. 9.
   "Diver." Poetry (145:1) O 84, p. 7.
   "Seeking the Elements." Poetry (143:6) Mr 84, p.
      323-324.
   "Something for Nothing." Telescope (3:2) Spr 84,
      p. 7-8.
   "Taxi." Poetry (145:1) O 84, p. 5-6.

5478. WATERS, Michael
   "Leaves & Ashes." Tendril (18, special issue) 84,
      p. 60.
   "Lunch Hour" (for Jody Swilky). OhioR (32) 84, p.
      104-105.
   "Mythology." Ploughs (10:1) 84, p. 178-179.
   "Negative Space." ThRiPo (23/24) 84, p. 52-53.
   "Pollen." Poetry (144:4) Jl 84, p. 219.
   "Romance." ThRiPo (23/24) 84, p. 51.
   "Who Started the River Flowing." GreenfR (11:1/2)
      Sum-Aut 83, p. 103.

5479. WATERS, Susan C.
   "The red cat." CapeR (19:2) Sum 84, p. 1.
   "Still Life with Spiderwort Flower." CapeR (19:2)
      Sum 84, p. 2.

5480. WATHALL, Agnes
   "The Magic Glass." PoeticJ (6) 84, p. 26.

5481. WATKINS, Vernon
   "Sentence for Tyranny" (Excerpt, tr. of Gyula
      Illyés). HolCrit (21:1) F 84, p. 4.

5482. WATSON, Craig
   "Dissolve." Origin (5:4) Aut 84, p. 67.
   "Emotion." Origin (5:4) Aut 84, p. 67-71.
   "Fate." Origin (5:4) Aut 84, p. 69.
   "Friction." Origin (5:4) Aut 84, p. 68.
   "Relief." Origin (5:4) Aut 84, p. 70.
   "Surrender." Origin (5:4) Aut 84, p. 71.

5483. WATSON, Ellen
   "The Alphabet in the Park" (tr. of Adélia Prado).
      AmerPoR (13:1) Ja-F 84, p. 24.
   "The Black Umbrella" (tr. of Adélia Prado).
      Field (30) Spr 84, p. 52.
   "Blossoms" (tr. of Adélia Prado). AmerPoR
      (13:1) Ja-F 84, p. 25.

"Day" (tr. of Adélia Prado). AmerPoR (13:1) Ja-
    F 84, p. 25.
"Dysrhythmia" (tr. of Adélia Prado). AmerPoR
    (13:1) Ja-F 84, p. 24.
"In the Middle of the Night" (tr. of Adélia
    Prado). AmerPoR (13:1) Ja-F 84, p. 25.
"Legend with the Word Map" (tr. of Adélia Prado).
    AmerPoR (13:1) Ja-F 84, p. 25.
"Lesson" (tr. of Adélia Prado). AmerPoR (13:1)
    Ja-F 84, p. 26.
"Lineage" (tr. of Adélia Prado). Field (30) Spr
    84, p. 53.
"Not Even One Line in December" (tr. of Adélia
    Prado). AmerPoR (13:1) Ja-F 84, p. 24.
"Pieces for a Stained-Glass Window" (tr. of
    Adélia Prado). AmerPoR (13:1) Ja-F 84, p. 25.
"Some Other Names for Poetry" (tr. of Adélia
    Prado). AmerPoR (13:1) Ja-F 84, p. 26.
"Subject-ive" (tr. of Adélia Prado). AmerPoR
    (13:1) Ja-F 84, p. 26.
"Tyrants" (tr. of Adélia Prado). AmerPoR (13:1)
    Ja-F 84, p. 26.
"With Poetic License" (tr. of Adélia Prado).
    AmerPoR (13:1) Ja-F 84, p. 24.
"Young Girl in Bed" (tr. of Adélia Prado).
    Field (30) Spr 84, p. 54-55.

5484. WATSON, Harold
    "The Cafflick Effick." PaintedB (21) Wint 84, p. 32.

5485. WATSON, Morris Taylor
    "The Ceremony." Wind (14:52) 84, p. 49.

5486. WATSON, Wilfred
    "Diana Rigg." CanLit (100) Spr 84, p. 346-347.
    "Sonnet Times Three" (for Jack Shadbolt,
        Archipenko, BJ). CanLit (100) Spr 84, p. 347-348.

5487. WATTEN, Barrett
    "Progress" (Excerpt). Sulfur (4:1, issue 10) 84,
        p. 39-45.

5488. WATTS, Stephen
    "The Conversation with Dante" (Excerpts). Ploughs
        (10:1) 84, p. 180-185.

5489. WAWRZYKIEWICZ, Marek
    "The Pain" (tr. by Danuta Lopozyko and Peter
        Harris). LitR (28:1) Aut 84, p. 133.

5490. WAYMAN, Tom
    "Country Feuds." Hudson (37:1) Spr 84, p. 51-52.
    "The Drawer." MinnR (N.S. 23) Aut 84, p. 114-115.
    "La Lluvia de tu Muerte." Peb (23) 84, p. 13-14.
    "Mike." Hudson (37:1) Spr 84, p. 49-50.
    "Motion Pictures." Hudson (37:1) Spr 84, p. 52-53.
    "Wood." CanLit (100) Spr 84, p. 349-350.

5491. WAYNE, J. O.
    "The Eavesdropper." Ploughs (10:1) 84, p. 186.

"Lapsing." <u>Ploughs</u> (10:1) 84, p. 187.

5492. WAYNE, Jane O.
     "Autumnal Equinox." <u>Poetry</u> (144:6) S 84, p. 322-323.
     "The Family Album." <u>Poetry</u> (144:6) S 84, p. 322.

5493. WAYNE-WRIGHT, Roger
     "Dixieland Blue." <u>LitR</u> (28:1) Aut 84, p. 56.
     "Mummy Face." <u>LitR</u> (28:1) Aut 84, p. 56.
     "Wheat Burning." <u>LitR</u> (28:1) Aut 84, p. 57.

5494. WEATHERS, Winston
     "An Alexandrian Ghost." <u>SouthernR</u> (20:1) Wint 84,
        p. 129-130.
     "At the Crematorium, on the Edge of History."
        <u>SouthernR</u> (20:1) Wint 84, p. 128.
     "Epitaph for the Children Drowned in the River."
        <u>Poetry</u> (143:4) Ja 84, p. 212.

5495. WEAVER, Kathleen
     "Lake in Bucharest" (tr. of Samuel Feijöo).
        <u>MinnR</u> (N.S. 22) Spr 84, p. 57.

5496. WEAVER, Margaret
     "Onion." <u>Vis</u> (14) 84, p. 38.

5497. WEAVER, Michael S.
     "The Aftermath." <u>HangL</u> (46) Aut 84, p. 68-70.
     "Atlantic City." <u>Callaloo</u> (20, 7:1) Wint 84, p. 77.
     "Currents." <u>HangL</u> (46) Aut 84, p. 64-67.
     "Photograph of Negro Mania." <u>Gargoyle</u> (24) 84, p.
        55-56.
     "Poem for Uncles." <u>Callaloo</u> (20, 7:1) Wint 84, p.
        78.
     "Water Song." <u>Callaloo</u> (20, 7:1) Wint 84, p. 74-76.

5498. WEAVER, Richard
     "Father's Day." <u>NoAmR</u> (269:1) Mr 84, p. 19.

5499. WEBB, Martha
     "Dance Piece/Kalaupapa." <u>VirQR</u> (60:1) Wint 84, p.
        70-71.
     "History." <u>VirQR</u> (60:1) Wint 84, p. 71-72.

5500. WEBB, Michael A.
     "Six Years Past." <u>Vis</u> (14) 84, p. 32.

5501. WEBB, Paddy
     "Bryony." <u>Dandel</u> (11:1) Spr-Sum 84, p. 63-64.
     "Evening." <u>AntigR</u> (59) Aut 84, p. 14.
     "Skate." <u>AntigR</u> (59) Aut 84, p. 13.

5502. WEBB, Phyllis
     "Following" (for Daphne Marlatt). <u>CanLit</u> (100)
        Spr 84, p. 351-352.
     "Performance." <u>CanLit</u> (100) Spr 84, p. 352-353.

5503. WEBSTER, Diane
     "Fire Escape." <u>PoeticJ</u> (4) 83, p. 24.

5504. WEBSTER, Tom
"Ninety-Nine White Flapping." CalQ (25) Aut 84,
p. 33.
"Why August." CalQ (25) Aut 84, p. 34-35.

5505. WEDGE, Philip
"The Sandpits." KanQ (16:1/2) Wint-Spr 84, p. 164.

5506. WEE, Karen Herseth
"Eleven Ways of Looking at a Loon" (Minnesota
Views). RagMag (3:1) Spr 84, p. 25.
"Of all the world's afternoons." RagMag (3:1) Spr
84, p. 22.
"Small Town Commencement." RagMag (3:2) Aut 84,
p. 32.
"Unicorn Quest." RagMag (3:2) Aut 84, p. 30.

5507. WEEDON, Syd
"Buildings Fall." Sam (41:2, release 162) 84 or
85, p. 2.
"Captions/Portraits" (I-III). RagMag (3:2) Aut
84, p. 41.
"Captions/Thoughtscapes, Variation 1." RagMag
(3:2) Aut 84, p. 40.
"The curve of your hip." Sam (37:3, 147th
release) 83, p. 55.

5508. WEEKLEY, Richard J.
"The Dance of the Yuccas." WindO (44) Sum-Aut 84,
p. 33.
"Rediscovering the Stick." WindO (44) Sum-Aut 84,
p. 32.
"The White Electric Light." CapeR (19:2) Sum 84,
p. 46.

5509. WEEKS, Ramona
"Dream of Snowbirds." CalQ (23/24) Spr-Sum 84, p.
122.
"Virginia Woolf." SouthernHR (18:1) Wint 84, p.
38-39.
"Zucchini Crop." CalQ (23/24) Spr-Sum 84, p. 122.

5510. WEIDMAN, Phil
"1962 Sum." WormR (24:4, issue 96) 84, p. 149.
"Archer." WormR (24:1, issue 93) 84, p. 8.
"Bodega Tides." WormR (24:1, issue 93) 84, p. 7.
"Buck." WormR (24:4, issue 96) 84, p. 149.
"Burnout." WormR (24:1, issue 93) 84, p. 7.
"George F." WormR (24:4, issue 96) 84, p. 150.
"Growing Pain." WormR (24:1, issue 93) 84, p. 8.
"Hi Ho Game." WormR (24:4, issue 96) 84, p. 150.
"Homemade Wine." WormR (24:4, issue 96) 84, p. 149.
"Hungryman." WormR (24:4, issue 96) 84, p. 150.
"Levis for Men." WormR (24:4, issue 96) 84, p. 150.
"Light Junkie." WormR (24:1, issue 93) 84, p. 8.
"Lost." WormR (24:1, issue 93) 84, p. 7.
"Match." WormR (24:1, issue 93) 84, p. 7.
"Nat Shinner & the Night Hawks." WormR (24:1,
issue 93) 84, p. 8.
"Patch." WormR (24:4, issue 96) 84, p. 149.

"Pathfinder." <u>WormR</u> (24:1, issue 93) 84, p. 7.
"Rancho Palos Verdes." <u>WormR</u> (24:4, issue 96) 84,
    p. 150.
"Reprieve." <u>WormR</u> (24:4, issue 96) 84, p. 149.
"Rocker." <u>WormR</u> (24:1, issue 93) 84, p. 7.
"Scramble." <u>WormR</u> (24:1, issue 93) 84, p. 8.
"Sharp Shooter." <u>WormR</u> (24:4, issue 96) 84, p. 149.
"Thursday before Christmas." <u>WormR</u> (24:4, issue
    96) 84, p. 150.
"Vacationing at Donner." <u>PoeticJ</u> (5) 84, p. 40.
"White Painting." <u>WormR</u> (24:4, issue 96) 84, p. 149.
"Xmas Tree in July." <u>WormR</u> (24:1, issue 93) 84,
    p. 8.

5511. WEIGL, Bruce
    "Amnesia" (for Lee Childress). <u>TriQ</u> (59) Wint 84,
        p. 108.
    "The Artificial Waterfall and Woods Scene Clock."
        <u>Tendril</u> (17) Wint 84, p. 168.
    "Debris." <u>Tendril</u> (17) Wint 84, p. 169.
    "Elegy for A." <u>TriQ</u> (59) Wint 84, p. 101-102.
    "Noise." <u>TriQ</u> (59) Wint 84, p. 106.
    "Paper Moon." <u>TriQ</u> (59) Wint 84, p. 103.
    "Regret for the Mourning Doves Who Failed to Mate."
        <u>TriQ</u> (59) Wint 84, p. 107.
    "Snowy Egret." <u>TriQ</u> (59) Wint 84, p. 104-105.
    "Song for the Lost Private." <u>Tendril</u> (17) Wint
        84, p. 167.
    "Weeds among the Garlic." <u>Tendril</u> (17) Wint 84,
        p. 170.

5512. WEIL, James L.
    "The Oboe Player." <u>Sparrow</u> (46) 84, p. 25.

5513. WEILER, Sarah
    "His conceit is everywhere, it follows him."
        <u>HangL</u> (45) Spr 84, p. 69.
    "I am sleeping in the freezer frozen." <u>HangL</u> (46)
        Aut 84, p. 77.

5514. WEINER, Rebecca
    "Your Winter's Tale." <u>Pequod</u> (16/17) 84, p. 100.

5515. WEINGARTEN, Roger
    "Life Drawing in El Dorado." <u>Tendril</u> (17) Wint
        84, p. 171-172.
    "Two Sons Drowning." <u>Tendril</u> (17) Wint 84, p. 173.
    "Welcome to the Encyclopedia of Thieves." <u>AntR</u>
        (42:4) Aut 84, p. 462-463.

5516. WEINMAN, Paul
    "Adam Gets Eden." <u>StoneC</u> (12:1/2) Aut-Wint 84, p.
        30.
    "Carp Lay." <u>Sam</u> (39:1, release 153) 84, p. 33.
    "High in the Tree." <u>Wind</u> (14:50) 84, p. 59.
    "Split Tongues Licking." <u>DekalbLAJ</u> (20th
        Anniversary Issue) 84, p. 111.
    "Staring at Feet." <u>Wind</u> (14:50) 84, p. 59.
    "There's No Luncheon Tomorrow." <u>CrabCR</u> (2:1) Sum
        84, p. 11.

5517. WEINTRAUB, Rachel
       "Undulation." <u>PoetC</u> (15:3) 84, p. 4.

5518. WEISERT, Hilde
       "Night Again." <u>Writ</u> (16) Aut 84, p. 50.
       "The Scheme of Things." <u>Writ</u> (16) Aut 84, p. 51.

5519. WEISS, David
       "Big Bang." <u>Ploughs</u> (10:1) 84, p. 189.
       "Canoeing on the Loxahatchee." <u>VirQR</u> (60:1) Wint
          84, p. 68-69.
       "Elle, Ella, Sie." <u>Pequod</u> (16/17) 84, p. 231.
       "The Fountains." <u>Telescope</u> (3:1) Wint 84, p. 39-40.
       "Heat Wave." <u>PraS</u> (58:4) Wint 84, p. 31-32.
       "Olive." <u>Ploughs</u> (10:1) 84, p. 188.
       "This Sweet Thing." <u>VirQR</u> (60:1) Wint 84, p. 68.
       "The White Road." <u>PraS</u> (58:4) Wint 84, p. 30.

5520. WEISS, Dora
       "Seems Strange." <u>SanFPJ</u> (6:1) 84, p. 29.

5521. WEISS, Sanford
       "Black Walnuts." <u>Kayak</u> (64) My 84, p. 48.
       "Confinement." <u>Kayak</u> (64) My 84, p. 49.
       "Disappearances." <u>Kayak</u> (64) My 84, p. 49.

5522. WEISS, Sigmund
       "The 1940's and Today" (From notes of 9/28/82 reve.
          9/4/83). <u>SanFPJ</u> (6:1) 84, p. 25.
       "The Last Hello." <u>SanFPJ</u> (6:4) 84, p. 65.
       "Madame de Porchilian." <u>SanFPJ</u> (6:4) 84, p. 66-68.

5523. WEISS, Theodore
       "As If a Rain." <u>AmerPoR</u> (13:5) S-O 84, p. 35.
       "Camel in the Snow." <u>YaleR</u> (73:4) Sum 84, p. 572-
          573.
       "Collaboration." <u>AmerPoR</u> (13:5) S-O 84, p. 33.
       "The Hostage." <u>AmerPoR</u> (13:5) S-O 84, p. 33.
       "In Passing" (Section title). <u>OntR</u> (21) Aut-Wint
          84, p. 45-54.
       "In Passing." <u>OntR</u> (21) Aut-Wint 84, p. 48-49.
       "In Praise of What Passes." <u>OntR</u> (21) Aut-Wint
          84, p. 51-52.
       "The Jupon." <u>Nat</u> (239:10) 6 O 84, p. 322.
       "Living It Up." <u>OntR</u> (21) Aut-Wint 84, p. 52.
       "Living Room" (for Hannah Arendt and Heinrich
          Blücher). <u>SouthwR</u> (69:2) Spr 84, p. 104-118.
       "Looking Back." <u>AmerPoR</u> (13:5) S-O 84, p. 33.
       "Pair of Shoes." <u>AmerPoR</u> (13:5) S-O 84, p. 34.
       "Piecemeal." <u>YaleR</u> (73:4) Sum 84, p. 574-575.
       "The Readings." <u>NewL</u> (51:1) Aut 84, p. 50-51.
       "Slow Fuse." <u>AmerPoR</u> (13:5) S-O 84, p. 34.
       "Sound." <u>AmerPoR</u> (13:5) S-O 84, p. 35.
       "Studying French." <u>Chelsea</u> (42/43) 84, p. 138-139.
       "Under the Appearance of." <u>AmerPoR</u> (13:5) S-O 84,
          p. 34.
       "Variations on a Favorite Theme." <u>OntR</u> (21) Aut-
          Wint 84, p. 46-48.
       "Walk in the Park." <u>OntR</u> (21) Aut-Wint 84, p. 53-54.
       "Word for Word." <u>OntR</u> (21) Aut-Wint 84, p. 50.

5524. WEISSBORT, Daniel
"Without Voice, without Hope" (tr. of Jozsef
Tornai, w. the author). Iowa (14:2) Spr-Sum
84, p. 208.

5525. WEITZMAN, Sarah Brown
"My Muse." Abraxas (29/30) 84, p. 45.

5526. WELCH, Anne
"Tattletale Tit." CarolQ (37:1) Aut 84, p. 39.

5527. WELCH, Don
"Snipe Hunter." SpoonRQ (9:2) Spr 84, p. 35.

5528. WELCH, Jennifer
"Its a Tennessee Williams Scenario." Amelia (1:2)
O 84, p. 64.
"Unappreciatively beside Real Dahlias." PoeticJ
(7) 84, p. 19.

5529. WELCH, Liliane
"The Bath." Descant (47, 15:4) Wint 84, p. 165.
"The Disperazione's Roof." Grain (12:2) My 84, p.
21.
"Dwelling." AntigR (56) Wint 84, p. 33.
"Hands." Descant (47, 15:4) Wint 84, p. 167.
"Her Cats." CanLit (101) Sum 84, p. 14.
"Knots." AntigR (56) Wint 84, p. 34.
"Lady of the Path." Descant (47, 15:4) Wint 84,
p. 166.
"Landscape 1982." PoetryCR (5:4) Sum 84, p. 9.
"Nova Scotia." PottPort (6) 84, p. 6.
"One Collar a Day." StoneC (11:3/4) Spr-Sum 84,
p. 33.
"One Collar Each Day." Descant (47, 15:4) Wint
84, p. 169.
"Planting Trees." Descant (47, 15:4) Wint 84, p.
168.
"Printing." Descant (47, 15:4) Wint 84, p. 170.
"The Rug." StoneC (11:3/4) Spr-Sum 84, p. 32.
"Sugar Harvest." PottPort (6) 84, p. 9.
"Vallon Manstorna" (for Ghigno Timillero). Grain
(12:4) N 84, p. 40.
"The Vase." StoneC (11:3/4) Spr-Sum 84, p. 32.

5530. WELLS, J. D.
"Elegy for Yoshitada." Argo (5:3) 84, p. 24-25.

5531. WELLS, Valerie
"How I Was Grown." BlueBldgs (7) 84, p. 33.
"This Was My Bird" (Phrase found written in a
child's hand on an envelope containing five
pigeon feathers, inside on 1910 sewing machine).
BlueBldgs (7) 84, p. 34.

5532. WELLS, Will
"The Sapling" (tr. of Umberto Saba). NegC (4:4)
Aut 84, p. 58.
"Time Is Mute" (tr. of Giuseppe Ungaretti). NegC
(4:4) Aut 84, p. 60.

WEN-CHUN, Cho, Lady: See CHO, Wen-Chun, Lady

5533. WENDELL, Julia
"Possibilities." AntR (42:3) Sum 84, p. 331.

5534. WENDT, Ingrid
"Mussels." CalQ (23/24) Spr-Sum 84, p. 120-121.
"Sestina" (For Rich). Poetry (144:3) Je 84, p.
139-140.
"Singing the Mozart Requiem" (for the Eugene
Concert Choir). Calyx (8:3) Aut-Wint 84, p. 39-44.

5535. WERDINGER, Roberta
"Never the Cup." YellowS (12) Aut 84, p. 7.

5536. WERUP, Jacques
"The Time in Malmö on the Earth" (Excerpts, tr.
by Roger Greenwald). PoetryE (15) Aut 84, p.
88-93.

5537. WESLOWSKI, Dieter
"The Dead in Winter." PortR (30:1) 84, p. 153.
"The Even Number of Life." MassR (25:2) Sum 84,
p. 181.
"From Beneath a Willow Tree, I Watch My Children at
Sunset." PortR (30:1) 84, p. 11.
"Nothing's Safe from Kurt" (for Kurt Schwitters).
WestB (14) 84, p. 84.
"The Promise." Abraxas (31/32) 84, p. 45.
"The Snow Phoenix." BlueBldgs (8) 84?, p. 35.
"Song of the Living Alone Heart." BlueBldgs (8)
84?, p. 35.

5538. WEST, Bob
"Edges." BelPoJ (34:4) Sum 84, p. 27.

5539. WEST, Charles
"Thirteen Ways of Looking at a Black Hole" (A
Variation on a Theme by Wallace Stevens).
Veloc (4) Sum 84, p. 27-28.

5540. WEST, Charles Ross
"Summer wind" (Haiku, Third Honorable Mention, 13th
Annual Kansas Poetry Contest). LittleBR (4:3)
Spr 84, p. 70.
"Sunset" (Haiku, First Prize, 13th Annual Kansas
Poetry Contest). LittleBR (4:3) Spr 84, p. 69.

5541. WEST, Kathleene
"Wind Chill." PraS (58:3) Aut 84, p. 95-96.

5542. WEST, Kevin
"Antique." PoetC (15:3) 84, p. 27.

5543. WEST, Michael
"III.8 Our candlelit brawl last night was lovely"
(tr. of Propertius). NewEngR (6:3) Spr 84, p.
452-453.
"Combing Her Hair God Daydreams the World Reflected
in Her Vanity." HiramPoR (37) Aut-Wint 84, p.
40-41.

"Shaking Hands with Myself." BelPoJ (34:4) Sum
    84, p. 12-14.

5544. WEST, Michael David
    "Apprenticeship." YetASM (3) 84, p. 2.

5545. WEST, Thomas A., Jr.
    "Questions." PoeticJ (4) 83, p. 37.
    "White Flies in Her Eyes." PoetL (79:1) Spr 84,
        p. 39.

5546. WESTERFIELD, Nancy G.
    "Amnesty." Comm (111:9) 4 My 84, p. 275.
    "Finding Time." Grain (12:3) Ag 84, p. 27.
    "For Glad Tidings." Wind (14:50) 84, p. 60-61.
    "Foregone Conclusion." NegC (4:2) Spr 84, p. 116-
        117.
    "The Hour of Immortality." Comm (111:14) 10 Ag
        84, p. 437.
    "The Meteorite." ChrC (101:6) 22 F 84, p. 196.
    "Le Mot: Sitting for the Calligrapher." Wind
        (14:50) 84, p. 60.
    "Nebraska." FourQt (33:3) Spr 84, p. 5.
    "Nude Descending an Up Staircase." NegC (4:2) Spr
        84, p. 120.

5547. WESTWOOD, Norma
    "Losing Parts." PaintedB (24) Aut 84, p. 11.

5548. WETTEROTH, Bruce
    "Toast to Sobriety." Abraxas (31/32) 84, p. 33.

5549. WEXELBLATT, Robert
    "The Hermit." FourQt (33:3) Spr 84, p. 13-14.

5550. WEXLER, Philip
    "Churning Golden." PoetL (79:1) Spr 84, p. 23.

5551. WHALEN, Tom
    "Aubade." NewOR (11:2) Sum 84, p. 16.
    "The Cataclysmic Variables." Veloc (3) Aut-Wint
        83, p. 37-38.
    "The Epidemic." Telescope (3:1) Wint 84, p. 83-85.
    "I don't remember the hour" ("untitled"). Veloc
        (3) Aut-Wint 83, p. 36.
    "Lustspielabend." Veloc (3) Aut-Wint 83, p. 34.

5552. WHEALDON, Everett
    "Mystical Mary & Reasonable Robert." Sam (37:3,
        147th release) 83, p. 38.

5553. WHEATCROFT, John
    "At a Certain Table in a Bar." GrahamHR (7) Wint
        84, p. 73-74.
    "Beyond the Oubliette." GrahamHR (7) Wint 84, p.
        44-45.
    "Runagate." GrahamHR (7) Wint 84, p. 42-43.
    "Village Church, Yorkshire." GrahamHR (7) Wint
        84, p. 46-47.

5554. WHEATLEY, Lili
"You Asked Me to Write a Poem about Love."
PoetryCR (5:3) Spr 84, p. 18.

5555. WHEATLEY, Patience
"Picking Raspberries with Gerda." Quarry (33:4)
Aut 84, p. 5.

5556. WHEELER, Alice H.
"Getting a Word in Edgewise." WestB (15) 84, p. 100.

5557. WHEELER, E. D.
"At the Cottage of Sidney Lanier" (For Addie B.
Early). DekalbLAJ (20th Anniversary Issue) 84,
p. 112.

5558. WHEELER, Emily
"Back Country Possibilities." Ploughs (10:1) 84,
p. 190.
"This Is How I Remember You." Ploughs (10:1) 84,
p. 191.

5559. WHIPP, Les
"April 11, 1984, Driving Westward" (for Sandy, d.
April 17, 1984). PraS (58:3) Aut 84, p. 67-68.

5560. WHISLER, Robert F.
"Reflections in a Mirror" (a trilogy for W.S.).
KanQ (16:3) Sum 84, p. 62-63.

5561. WHITE, Brenda Black
"The Well." TexasR (5:3/4) Aut-Wint 84, p. 106-107.

5562. WHITE, Carolyn
"On the Curbing of Passion." KanQ (16:1/2) Wint-
Spr 84, p. 63.

5563. WHITE, Gail
"Ballade of a Latter-Day Faust." CEACritic
(45:3/4) Mr-My 83, p. 32-33.
"Comparison." CEACritic (45:3/4) Mr-My 83, p. 33.
"For John Donne and Many Others." PikeF (6) Aut
84, p. 36.
"Jeremiah in Egypt." Amelia (1:2) O 84, p. 72.
"Miss Emily Dickinson Goes to the Office."
CEACritic (45:3/4) Mr-My 83, p. 32.
"Prospero in Milan." CEACritic (45:3/4) Mr-My 83,
p. 33.
"Silo." PraS (58:3) Aut 84, p. 65.
"Slow Leafing." PraS (58:3) Aut 84, p. 66.

5564. WHITE, J. P.
"The Arctic Balloonists Talk to the Ones They Left
Behind." Poetry (145:3) D 84, p. 157-158.
"Descending into the Moscow Metro." IndR (7:3)
Sum 84, p. 16.
"The Dream of Swans in Moscow." OntR (21) Aut-
Wint 84, p. 23-24.
"The Pomegranate Tree Speaks from the Dictator's
Garden." NoAmR (269:1) Mr 84, p. 7.

"You Will Write the Book." <u>Tendril</u> (17) Wint 84,
     p. 174.

5565. WHITE, J. Richard
      "Black Barbara." <u>BlueBldgs</u> (7) 84, p. 18.

5566. WHITE, Joan
      "Eclipse." <u>ThirdW</u> (2) Spr 84, p. 46.

5567. WHITE, Kathy M.
      "Jack in the Pulpit." <u>Veloc</u> (2) Spr 83, p. 40.

5568. WHITE, Mary Jane
      "Ghazal: I am, O pious priest, one ungodly one"
         (tr. of Jonaid, w. the author). <u>Iowa</u> (14:2)
         Spr-Sum 84, p. 119.

5569. WHITE, Mimi
      "8mm." <u>Tendril</u> (17) Wint 84, p. 176.
      "Battered Wives." <u>Tendril</u> (17) Wint 84, p. 178.
      "Night Song." <u>BlueBldgs</u> (7) 84, p. 50.
      "The Plague." <u>Tendril</u> (17) Wint 84, p. 177.
      "September." <u>Tendril</u> (17) Wint 84, p. 175.

5570. WHITE, Robert
      "Archipelagoes" (tr. of Bartolo Cattafi). <u>Chelsea</u>
         (42/43) 84, p. 152.
      "Measurements" (tr. of Bartolo Cattafi). <u>Chelsea</u>
         (42/43) 84, p. 152.

5571. WHITE, William M.
      "Last Summer." <u>Wind</u> (14:51) 84, p. 36.

5572. WHITE, William W.
      "Dividing." <u>NegC</u> (4:3) Sum 84, p. 11.

5573. WHITEHEAD, James
      "Below Is What He Said That Troubles Me."
         <u>SouthernR</u> (20:3) Sum 84, p. 605.

5574. WHITELAW, Scott
      "Rose." <u>Germ</u> (8:1) Spr-Sum 84, p. 24.

5575. WHITEN, Clifton
      "Curve of Drift." <u>PoetryCR</u> (6:1) Aut 84, p. 14.
      "Departure of a Friend." <u>Waves</u> (12:1) Aut 83, p. 64.
      "Poetry Canada Review 1979-1984 -- Retrospective
         and Glance Ahead." <u>PoetryCR</u> (6:1) Aut 84, p. 3.
      "Simple Affair." <u>WestCR</u> (19:2) O 84, p. 27.
      "Sloppy over Patsy." <u>WestCR</u> (19:2) O 84, p. 26.

5576. WHITING, Nathan
      "Turn Signal to the Dome." <u>HiramPoR</u> (36) Spr-Sum
         84, p. 39.

5577. WHITLOW, Carolyn Beard
      "Poem for the Children." <u>Stepping</u> (Anniversary
         Issue I) 84, p. 50.

5578. WHITMAN, Cedric
"Winter in Tomi or Dido's Complaint." KenR (NS
6:3) Sum 84, p. 20-24.

5579. WHITMAN, Marie Monroe
"Lament in Monroe County" (in memory of E. Dyer --
a timid, silent man, frightened of wind, killed
in a case of mistaken identity). Wind (14:50)
84, p. 62-63.
"Toward New Orleans" (for Cheryl and John). Wind
(14:50) 84, p. 62.

5580. WHITMAN, Walt
"Pictures." Antaeus (52) Apr 84, p. 184-196.
"Reconciliation." Origin (Series 5:1) Aut 83, p. 72.
"Song of Myself" (Selection: Section 5). Tendril
(18, special issue) 84, p. 82-83.

5581. WHITSON, Lori
"Eyes of a Gemini" (for Marie). PoeticJ (6) 84,
p. 19.
"Rosebud" (for Nonnie). PoeticJ (6) 84, p. 40.

5582. WHITT, Laurie Ann
"How It Happens." Waves (12:2/3) Wint 84, p. 90.

5583. WHITT, Laurie Anne
"Man with a Beating Heart" (from Max Ernst's
sculpture, "Young Man with Beating Heart").
Quarry (33:4) Aut 84, p. 47-48.
"Uneasy Pieces." Quarry (33:4) Aut 84, p. 45-47.

5584. WHITTEMORE, Reed
"Summer Concert." Shen (35:2/3) 84, p. 451.

5585. WHYTE, Jon
"The Conquest of Killimanjaro" (IV--No Leopards).
BlueBuf (2:2) Spr 84, p. 19-20.
"The Descent of Killimanjaro." BlueBuf (2:2) Spr
84, p. 20.
"The Last Ascent of Killimanjaro" (I, II--Horombo,
III--Kibo Hut). BlueBuf (2:2) Spr 84, p. 17-19.

5586. WICKER, Nina A.
"Letting Go." Wind (14:52) 84, p. 35.

5587. WICKERS, Brian
"Poem: A poor metaphor." Grain (12:4) N 84, p. 35.
"Rain." Grain (12:4) N 84, p. 34.

5588. WICKERT, Max
"Having sunk back in the places where they rose."
Shen (35:1) 83-84, p. 53.
"Parsifal." SewanR (92:4) O-D 84, p. 541-542.
"They got it all together and the dance." Shen
(35:1) 83-84, p. 52.
"They tried to move as if they liked it but."
Shen (35:1) 83-84, p. 52-53.
"The Unholy Weeks" (Selections: Three Sonnets).
Shen (35:1) 83-84, p. 52-53.

5589. WICKLESS, Harrison
        "Rejection Slip." Poetry (144:2) My 84, p. 106.

5590. WICKSTROM, Lois
        "Slice of Life." Veloc (4) Sum 84, p. 29.

5591. WIDMER, Kingsley
        "Curse on Crows" (Three Sample Cancer Poems: I).
          Paunch (57/58) Ja 84, p. 145.
        "Malediction Forbidding Mourning" (Three Sample
          Cancer Poems: II). Paunch (57/58) Ja 84, p. 145.
        "Ode to My Cancer" (Three Sample Cancer Poems:
          III). Paunch (57/58) Ja 84, p. 146.
        "Three Sample Cancer Poems." Paunch (57/58) Ja
          84, p. 145-146.

5592. WIEGMAN, Robyn
        "August in New York City." KanQ (16:1/2) Wint-Spr
          84, p. 127.
        "Betrothal." SoDakR (22:1) Spr 84, p. 50.
        "Bread and Fire." 13thM (8:1/2) 84, p. 174-175.
        "Familiar Row of Houses." PraS (58:3) Aut 84, p. 69.
        "Route 4." IndR (7:2) Spr 84, p. 48.
        "Somewhere." IndR (7:2) Spr 84, p. 49.
        "Vacation." MidAR (4:2) Aut 84, p. 118.
        "Walking with My Father." CalQ (25) Aut 84, p. 69.
        "What We Knew." PraS (58:3) Aut 84, p. 68.

5593. WIEGNER, Kathleen
        "The Fading Art of Stealing Home." HangL (46) Aut
          84, p. 71.

5594. WIENER, Leo
        "How Come." PoeticJ (2) 83, p. 5.

5595. WIER, Dara
        "Daytrip to Paradox." BlackWR (10:2) Spr 84, p.
          64-65.
        "Dreamland." BlackWR (10:2) Spr 84, p. 62-63.
        "Faith." CimR (66) Ja 84, p. 22.
        "Here." CimR (66) Ja 84, p. 16.
        "Sleeping in Cars." CimR (66) Ja 84, p. 42.

5596. WIESELTHIER, Vicki
        "Jane Sauer's Basket." WebR (9:1) Spr 84, p. 31.

5597. WIESELTIER, Leon
        "Hope." NewRep (189:5) 1 Ag 83, p. 34.

5598. WIEZELL, Elsa
        "Esto." Mairena (6:18) 84, p. 194.

5599. WIGGIN, Neurine
        "The Drifter." PikeF (6) Aut 84, p. 18.
        "Heart Attack." KanQ (16:4) Aut 84, p. 135.

5600. WILBORN, William
        "Conch." CalQ (25) Aut 84, p. 62-63.
        "From the Chorus." YaleR (73:2) Wint 84, p. 261.
        "On Welfare." TriQ (59) Wint 84, p. 137.

5601. WILBUR, Richard
    "For Dudley." Peb (23) 84, p. 36-37.
    "The Undead." Telescope (3:3) Aut 84, p. 154-155.
    "The Writer." Tendril (18, special issue) 84, p.
        282-283.

5602. WILD, Peter
    "Beaver." SouthernPR (24:1) Spr 84, p. 71.
    "Farm Dogs." Swallow (3) 84, p. 86-87.
    "Greenland." KanQ (16:1/2) Wint-Spr 84, p. 35.
    "In Spain." IndR (7:2) Spr 84, p. 18-19.
    "Lies between Fires." PraS (58:1) Spr 84, p. 69-70.
    "Love." CutB (22) Spr-Sum 84, p. 8.
    "Ornithologists." KanQ (16:1/2) Wint-Spr 84, p. 34.
    "The Peaceable Kingdom." PraS (58:1) Spr 84, p.
        66-67.
    "Salvation." PraS (58:1) Spr 84, p. 68-69.
    "Shark." Sparrow (46) 84, p. 13.
    "The Shroud of Turin." BlackWR (10:2) Spr 84, p.
        72-73.
    "Successful Gardening." TarRP (24:1) Aut 84, p. 12.
    "Vegetarian Merchants." ChiR (34:3) Sum 84, p. 45.

5603. WILDE, Heather
    "Introduction." NewL (50:2/3) Wint-Spr 84, p. 93.

5604. WILDER, Amos N.
    "Prayer" (from the July 24, 1935 issue). ChrC
        (101:22) 4-11 Jl 84, p. 665.

5605. WILDER, Rex
    "The Source of Every Flame is Blue." Wind (14:51)
        84, p. 54-55.

5606. WILJER, Robert
    "Carnival Glass." KanQ (16:1/2) Wint-Spr 84, p. 173.

5607. WILK, David
    "Coyote in a Fever Sings." GreenfR (12:1/2) Sum-
        Aut 84, p. 146.
    "Coyote Tells All in a Fit of Anger." GreenfR
        (12:1/2) Sum-Aut 84, p. 147.
    "Old Coyote's Travel Journal of Sleep." GreenfR
        (12:1/2) Sum-Aut 84, p. 148-149.

5608. WILL, Frederic
    "Dürer at Work." AmerPoR (13:5) S-O 84, p. 36-37.
    "Landscape" (tr. of Axel Schulze). Iowa (14:2)
        Spr-Sum 84, p. 193.

5609. WILL, Fredrio
    "Neruda's Urine." BlueBldgs (7) 84, p. 19.

5610. WILLARD, Nancy
    "Life at Sea: The Naming of Fish." Field (30) Spr
        84, p. 46.
    "Science Fiction." Field (30) Spr 84, p. 44.
    "Walking Poem." IndR (7:2) Spr 84, p. 6-7.
    "Wreath to the Fish." Field (30) Spr 84, p. 45.

5611. WILLET-SHOPTAW, John
"Now What?" HarvardA (118:2) Spr 84, p. 21.

5612. WILLEY, Edward
"Back Then." SoCaR (16:2) Spr 84, p. 34.

5613. WILLIAMS, Cathy
"Spring Winds." PoeticJ (5) 84, p. 20.

5614. WILLIAMS, Christie
"My Grandmother's Dream." Nimrod (27:2) Spr-Sum
84, p. 77.

5615. WILLIAMS, John A.
"The Caretaker." Stepping (Anniversary Issue I)
84, p. 51-52.
"More Journeys without Title" (From Safari West).
Callaloo (21, 7:2) Spr-Sum 84, p. 83-85.

5616. WILLIAMS, Jonathan
"Bunk Johnson's Grave at New Iberia" (Elegy from
Poeticules Criticasters Kitschdiggers &
Justfolks). Chelsea (42/43) 84, p. 100.
"The Gastronaut (1886-1959)" (Elegy from
Poeticules Criticasters Kitschdiggers &
Justfolks). Chelsea (42/43) 84, p. 101.

5617. WILLIAMS, Karen
"Conquering Fear." CentR (28:1) Wint 84, p. 46-47.

5618. WILLIAMS, Leianne
"Now I Become Myself." Quarry (33:1) Wint 84, p. 5.

5619. WILLIAMS, Miller
"The man at the station where I go buy gas." TriQ
(59) Wint 84, p. 131.

5620. WILLIAMS, Norman
"The Dream of South." NewYorker (60:11) 30 Ap 84,
p. 52.
"The Tremors at Balvano" (6 December 1980). GeoR
(38:2) Sum 84, p. 380.

5621. WILLIAMS, Umar A. K. I.
"Undistinguished Marathon." Stepping (Anniversary
Issue I) 84, p. 54-55.

5622. WILLIAMS, William Carlos
"Between Walls." Salm (65) Aut 84, p. 69.
"Fine Work with Pitch and Copper." PoetryE
(13/14) Spr-Sum 84, p. 244.
"June 9." Shen (35:2/3) 84, p. 472.
"Love Song." SouthernR (20:2) Spr 84, p. 282.
"Negro Woman." Origin (5:3) Spr 84, p. 68.
"The Sea-Elephant." Tendril (18, special issue)
84, p. 267-268.
"The Semblables." Tendril (18, special issue) 84,
p. 155-156.
"Sort of a Song." Tendril (18, special issue) 84,
p. 144-145.

"Still Life." <u>Shen</u> (35:2/3) 84, p. 473.
"The Yachts." <u>Tendril</u> (18, special issue) 84, p. 152-153.
"Young Sycamore." <u>Tendril</u> (18, special issue) 84, p. 148.

5623. WILLOUGHBY, Ron
"Summer Beach." <u>NegC</u> (4:3) Sum 84, p. 90.

5624. WILLSON, Robert
"Putsch--1923." <u>NewL</u> (50:2/3) Wint-Spr 84, p. 63.

5625. WILMARTH, Christopher
"Blue" (from Sigh). <u>PoetryE</u> (13/14) Spr-Sum 84, p. 175.
"Breath" (Selections). <u>PoetryE</u> (13/14) Spr-Sum 84, p. 174-176.
"Doors" (from Saint). <u>PoetryE</u> (13/14) Spr-Sum 84, p. 175.
"Edges" (from Toast). <u>PoetryE</u> (13/14) Spr-Sum 84, p. 175.
"Pages" (from "My old books closed"). <u>PoetryE</u> (13/14) Spr-Sum 84, p. 174.
"Was" (from "When Winter on forgotten woods moves somber"). <u>PoetryE</u> (13/14) Spr-Sum 84, p. 174.
"Wine and Stones" (from "The whole soul summed up"). <u>PoetryE</u> (13/14) Spr-Sum 84, p. 176.
"You" (from "Insert myself within your story"). <u>PoetryE</u> (13/14) Spr-Sum 84, p. 174-175.

5626. WILMER, Clive
"At the Grave of Ezra Pound" (S. Michele, Venice). <u>Thrpny</u> (16) Wint 84, p. 16.

5627. WILNER, Eleanor
"The Daughters of Midas." <u>ChiR</u> (34:3) Sum 84, p. 46-47.
"High Noon at Los Alamos." <u>NowestR</u> (22:1/2) 84, p. 47-48.
"The Last Man" (for Vivian). <u>Calyx</u> (8:3) Aut-Wint 84, p. 18-19.
"Reading the Bible Backwards." <u>ThirdW</u> (2) Spr 84, p. 88-90.
"Time Out of Mind." <u>ThirdW</u> (2) Spr 84, p. 80-83.
"What Do Myths Have to Do with the Price of Fish?" (for Arthur). <u>ThirdW</u> (2) Spr 84, p. 83-87.

5628. WILOCH, Thomas
"The Butterfly Woman." <u>Bogg</u> (52) 84, p. 9.

5629. WILSON, Andrew L.
"Grass" (Mekong Delta, 1965). <u>TarRP</u> (24:1) Aut 84, p. 10.

5630. WILSON, Ann
"I Couldn't and I Wouldn't." <u>BlackWR</u> (11:1) Aut 84, p. 80-81.

5631. WILSON, Barbara
"Reflexive Act." <u>PoetryCR</u> (6:1) Aut 84, p. 16.

"Virginia to Anne." NegC (4:1) Wint 84, p. 86-97.

5632. WILSON, Don D.
      "Poor Gaspard" (tr. of Paul Verlaine). Amelia
      (1:2) O 84, p. 75.

5633. WILSON, Edmund
      "To Wystan Auden on His Birthday" (w. Louise Bogan:
      Alternate lines by E. W. and L. B. -- first line
      by E. W. Composed in 1956). Shen (35:2/3) 84,
      p. 24.

5634. WILSON, Edward
      "The Cunning to Get Near Enough." MidwQ (25:2)
      Wint 84, p. 170.
      "Fighter Pilot." MidwQ (25:2) Wint 84, p. 171.
      "Sestina." MidwQ (25:2) Wint 84, p. 172-173.

5635. WILSON, Graeme
      "Climbing to a Mountain Village" (tr. of Priest
      Noin, 998-1050). WestHR (38:2) Sum 84, p. 138.
      "The Lad Who Last Night Slept Here" (tr. of Yi
      Chong-Bo, 1693-1766). WestHR (38:2) Sum 84, p.
      132.
      "Mountain Wizard" (tr. of Kakinomoto no Hitomaro,
      681-729). WestHR (38:1) Spr 84, p. 60.

5636. WILSON, John
      "Ink Wash I." KanQ (16:1/2) Wint-Spr 84, p. 163.
      "Southern California Snow" (Ojai, Summer 1984).
      Poetry (145:3) D 84, p. 144.

5637. WILSON, Keith
      "Cow Dogs." Kayak (64) My 84, p. 65.
      "Portrait of a Father." Kayak (64) My 84, p. 67.
      "Spring" (for Rudy Anaya). Kayak (64) My 84, p. 66.

5638. WILSON, Miles
      "Getting There." SewanR (92:2) Ap-Je 84, p. 204-205.
      "Husband in the Garden." SewanR (92:2) Ap-Je 84,
      p. 202-203.

5639. WILSON, Paul
      "Buffalofish." Grain (12:4) N 84, p. 28.

5640. WILSON, R. T.
      "Settling." CharR (10:2) Aut 84, p. 90.
      "Snowbound." CharR (10:2) Aut 84, p. 89.

5641. WILSON, Robert D.
      "Exile without Honor." SanFPJ (7:1) 84, p. 56.
      "Guernica." SanFPJ (7:1) 84, p. 53-55.

5642. WILSON, Robley, Jr.
      "The Mornings I Oversleep." Poetry (144:4) Jl 84,
      p. 228.
      "Shadows." GeoR (38:1) Spr 84, p. 64-65.
      "The Summer Place." Poetry (144:4) Jl 84, p. 228-
      230.

5643. WILSON, Saunie Kaye
      "Summer Daze, Summer Haze." Calyx (8:2) Spr 84,
         p. 86-87.

5644. WILSON, William J.
      "Done For." Poem (51) Mr [i.e. Jl] 84, p. 44.
      "Eve." Poem (51) Mr [i.e. Jl] 84, p. 46.
      "Joy of Rotting." Poem (51) Mr [i.e. Jl] 84, p. 45.
      "Lost Things." Poem (51) Mr [i.e. Jl] 84, p. 43.

5645. WINANS, A. D.
      "And God Looked Down and Saw His Children Playing
         at Amchitka." Spirit (7:1) 84, p. 167-170.
      "For Marilyn Monroe." OroM (2:3/4, issue 7/8) 84,
         p. 17-19.
      "Reflections." PoeticJ (1) 83, p. 29.

WINCKEL, Nance van: See Van WINCKEL, Nance

5646. WINDER, Louise Somers
      "Some bird--unseen" (Haiku, Second Honorable
         Mention, 13th Annual Kansas Poetry Contest).
         LittleBR (4:3) Spr 84, p. 70.
      "Yard Sale" (Haiku, Fourth Honorable Mention, 13th
         Annual Kansas Poetry Contest). LittleBR (4:3)
         Spr 84, p. 70.

5647. WINDSOR, Paul D.
      "They Await." AntigR (58) Sum 84, p. 132.

5648. WINFIELD, William
      "Alba." Poem (50) Mr 84, p. 46.
      "Birthday." BlueBldgs (8) 84?, p. 17.
      "Boy and Car." DekalbLAJ (17:1/2) 84, p. 150.
      "Descent." BlueBldgs (8) 84?, p. 20.
      "Descent." DekalbLAJ (17:1/2) 84, p. 149.
      "Desert Music." Poem (50) Mr 84, p. 49.
      "Dusk." Poem (50) Mr 84, p. 45.
      "House on the Hill." BlueBldgs (8) 84?, p. 19.
      "In a Vision." PoetL (79:1) Spr 84, p. 36.
      "Lunar Days." BlueBldgs (8) 84?, p. 21.
      "Moon in the Mirror." BlueBldgs (8) 84?, p. 19.
      "Negative Exposure." BlueBldgs (8) 84?, p. 21.
      "On White Winter Mornings." Poem (50) Mr 84, p. 48.
      "The Poet." NegC (4:2) Spr 84, p. 57.
      "The Road." Poem (50) Mr 84, p. 47.
      "Roses in November." BlueBldgs (8) 84?, p. 18.
      "Shadow of No Object." BlueBldgs (8) 84?, p. 18.
      "Sphere." BlueBldgs (8) 84?, p. 17.
      "The Unseen." WestB (14) 84, p. 60.
      "White World." BlueBldgs (8) 84?, p. 20.
      "Zone." BlueBldgs (8) 84?, p. 18.

5649. WINK, Johnny
      "She Wept for Hamlet." KanQ (16:3) Sum 84, p. 124.

5650. WINN, Howard
      "Insomnia." BlueBldgs (7) 84, p. 30.
      "Presence." KanQ (16:1/2) Wint-Spr 84, p. 73.

5651. WINNER, Robert
      "Into My Dream." <u>Confr</u> (27/28) 84, p. 176.

5652. WINWOOD, David
      "Unforgettable Summers" (tr. by the author). <u>Iowa</u>
      (14:2) Spr-Sum 84, p. 182.

5653. WISEMAN, Christopher
      "Kensington Gardens, May 1982." <u>CanLit</u> (100) Spr
      84, p. 361.

5654. WITT, Harold
      "Barbie." <u>NewL</u> (50:2/3) Wint-Spr 84, p. 259.
      "For Whom the Bell Tolls." <u>Amelia</u> (1:2) O 84, p. 61.
      "George Morton, Manager, Citrus Empire Hotel."
          <u>Bogg</u> (52) 84, p. 25.
      "Hershey, the Cop." <u>WindO</u> (44) Sum-Aut 84, p. 37.
      "Hope." <u>TexasR</u> (5:3/4) Aut-Wint 84, p. 22.
      "Jeffers." <u>WestB</u> (15) 84, p. 46.
      "Josephine Mandala, Sing-Tel." <u>Wind</u> (14:51) 84,
          p. 57.
      "Marcus Welby." <u>Sparrow</u> (46) 84, p. 31.
      "Melvin." <u>Wind</u> (14:51) 84, p. 56.
      "Mrs. Asquith among the Daffodils." <u>Poem</u> (52) N
          84, p. 50.
      "Mrs. Asquith Rejoices That There Are Still Willing
          and Able Workers in the World." <u>Poem</u> (52) N
          84, p. 51.
      "One." <u>KanQ</u> (16:1/2) Wint-Spr 84, p. 74.
      "Self-Reliance." <u>GreenfR</u> (12:1/2) Sum-Aut 84, p.
          159.
      "Wolfeian." <u>TexasR</u> (5:3/4) Aut-Wint 84, p. 23.
      "Zoom." <u>ConcPo</u> (17:1) Spr 84, p. 78.

5655. WITTE, John
      "Home." <u>NewYorker</u> (60:19) 25 Je 84, p. 34.
      "Rubbing" (for J.A.). <u>OhioR</u> (32) 84, p. 40.

5656. WITTLINGER, Ellen
      "The Diver." <u>Pequod</u> (16/17) 84, p. 229-230.

5657. WOESSNER, Warren
      "Looking at Power." <u>Spirit</u> (7:1) 84, p. 174.
      "Maggie May" (Rod Stewart, 1971). <u>Abraxas</u> (31/32)
          84, p. 63.
      "Moving." <u>Abraxas</u> (29/30) 84, p. 20.
      "Open Poetry Reading." <u>Abraxas</u> (29/30) 84, p. 20.
      "What'd I Say" (Ray Charles, 1965). <u>SpoonRQ</u> (9:4)
          Aut 84, p. 40.

5658. WOHLFELD, Valerie
      "Artificial Devices." <u>Tendril</u> (17) Wint 84, p.
          179-181.
      "The Bird Woman and I." <u>BlueBldgs</u> (8) 84?, p. 30.

5659. WOHMANN, Gabriele
      "By the Sea" (tr. by John N. Miller). <u>WebR</u> (9:1)
          Spr 84, p. 97.
      "Relatives" (tr. by John N. Miller). <u>WebR</u> (9:1)
          Spr 84, p. 96.

5660. WOJAHN, David
        "Census." VirQR (60:3) Sum 84, p. 435-436.
        "Les Enfants de Paradis." Agni (20) 84, p. 99-100.
        "Glassworks at Saratoga" (In memory of James L.
          White). Poetry (145:1) O 84, p. 25-26.
        "North by Northwest." BlackWR (11:1) Aut 84, p.
          18-19.
        "Past the Dark Arroyo." VirQR (60:3) Sum 84, p.
          436-437.
        "Satin Doll." AntR (42:3) Sum 84, p. 332-333.
        "Steam." NoAmR (269:3) S 84, p. 61.
        "The Third Language." SewanR (92:4) O-D 84, p.
          543-544.
        "This Moment." Poetry (145:1) O 84, p. 26-27.
        "The Widow" (The Portuguese Cemetery, Cape Cod).
          SewanR (92:4) O-D 84, p. 544-545.
        "The World of Donald Evans." BlackWR (11:1) Aut
          84, p. 20-21.

5661. WOLANSKYJ, Lidia Alexandra
        "Seasonal Sketch: Eastern Townships." PoetryCR
          (6:2) Wint 84-85, p. 27.
        "The Telephone Affair." AntigR (59) Aut 84, p. 63.

5662. WOLF, Abby
        "Images on the Beach" (tr. of Elsa Cross, w. Eric
          Walker). Iowa (14:2) Spr-Sum 84, p. 145-146.

5663. WOLF, Jami
        "Drawing Class." TarRP (24:1) Aut 84, p. 24.
        "Measuring Time." PoetryNW (25:2) Sum 84, p. 27.
        "Our Separate Ways." TarRP (24:1) Aut 84, p. 23.

5664. WOLF, Joan
        "The Alternative Newspaper Astrologer." RagMag
          (3:1) Spr 84, p. 42-45.
        "What Promise." PikeF (6) Aut 84, p. 3.

5665. WOLF, Leonard
        "How to Begin" (From a recipe by Ari the Learned in
          his twelfth-century Book of Icelanders).
          Atlantic (254:3) S 84, p. 75.

5666. WOLFE, Cary
        "Mahogany." CarolQ (36:3) Spr 84, p. 67.
        "Words at the Door." CarolQ (36:3) Spr 84, p. 68.

5667. WOLFE, Ellen
        "Findings." BelPoJ (34:4) Sum 84, p. 3-4.

5668. WOLFE, Tence
        "Coal Town Caves." SanFPJ (7:1) 84, p. 34.
        "Coal Town Christmas." SanFPJ (6:4) 84, p. 93.

5669. WOLFF, Daniel
        "Heading home late, in the black on black." Shen
          (35:1) 83-84, p. 63.
        "It seems that we are beautiful." Shen (35:1) 83-
          84, p. 62.
        "Lost Child." Thrpny (16) Wint 84, p. 14.

"Mugumbo's Bar." Stepping (Anniversary Issue I)
    84, p. 56-58.
"Sonnet: The hands are in forward, so the head goes
    idle." Thrpny (17) Spr 84, p. 14.
"Soon, they'll be sending the President packing."
    Shen (35:1) 83-84, p. 62-63.
"Work Sonnets." Shen (35:1) 83-84, p. 62-63.

5670. WONG, Nellie
    "Elegy for the Crisco Kid" (For Michael Hammond who
        died from a cardiac arrest, Gainesville, Florida
        February 14, 1981). PoeticJ (5) 84, p. 30-31.
    "The Moving Trees." GreenfR (11:1/2) Sum-Aut 83,
        p. 169.
    "Remembering Chinese Opera" (for Joseph Bruchac).
        GreenfR (11:1/2) Sum-Aut 83, p. 168-169.
    "Traveling Light." GreenfR (11:1/2) Sum-Aut 83,
        p. 168.

WONG LOO, Katie: See SUI-YUN

5671. WOOD, Kathy
    "Land Scape." AntigR (56) Wint 84, p. 70.
    "Tornado Watch at the Towers." AntigR (56) Wint
        84, p. 71.

5672. WOOD, Mary Gill
    "Denver/NCTE 1983." EngJ (73:6) O 84, p. 52.

5673. WOOD, Susan
    "1669 Oxford Street." Tendril (17) Wint 84, p. 189.
    "Birthright" (For Kenneth Millar 1915-1983 (Ross
        Macdonald)). Tendril (17) Wint 84, p. 203-205.
    "Bodies Terrestrial." Tendril (17) Wint 84, p. 186.
    "Carnation, Lily, Lily, Rose." Tendril (17) Wint
        84, p. 208.
    "Counting the Losses." Tendril (17) Wint 84, p. 194.
    "Education." Tendril (17) Wint 84, p. 187.
    "First Summer." Tendril (17) Wint 84, p. 195.
    "For Joseph Cornell." Tendril (17) Wint 84, p.
        190-191.
    "Hills above Half Moon Bay." Tendril (17) Wint
        84, p. 188.
    "Hope." Tendril (17) Wint 84, p. 197.
    "Monday." Tendril (17) Wint 84, p. 196.
    "Pinetum." Tendril (17) Wint 84, p. 206-207.
    "Pirate's Beach." Tendril (17) Wint 84, p. 192-193.
    "Presence." Tendril (17) Wint 84, p. 202.
    "Provincetown." Tendril (17) Wint 84, p. 200-201.
    "Too Good to Be True." Tendril (17) Wint 84, p.
        198-199.

5674. WOODRUFF, William
    "Carl Sandburg in Burbank." PoeticJ (8) 84, p. 25.

5675. WOODS, Christopher
    "The Bee Keeper" (for Edward Albee). Nimrod
        (27:2) Spr-Sum 84, p. 78.
    "Divers." Poem (51) Mr [i.e. Jl] 84, p. 22-23.
    "Gulliver." NegC (4:2) Spr 84, p. 67.

"Rapids." <u>Wind</u> (14:51) 84, p. 33.

5676. WOODS, Dan
       "Ceremonial Visit in the Irish Manner." <u>AntiqR</u>
       (58) Sum 84, p. 107.
       "To My Absent Father." <u>AntiqR</u> (58) Sum 84, p. 105-
       106.

5677. WOODS, Elizabeth
       "Again." <u>PoetryCR</u> (5:3) Spr 84, p. 3.
       "Contemplating Snail Ponds." <u>PoetryCR</u> (5:3) Spr
       84, p. 3.

5678. WOODS, John
       "How It Might Come to Us." <u>Ploughs</u> (10:4) 84, p.
       50-51.
       "Under the Lidless Eye." <u>Ploughs</u> (10:4) 84, p. 46-
       47.
       "Why Mothers Fear the Lost Guitar." <u>Ploughs</u>
       (10:4) 84, p. 44-45.
       "The Woman Who Was Forgotten." <u>Ploughs</u> (10:4) 84,
       p. 48-49.

5679. WOODS, Phil
       "Pike Creek." <u>NewL</u> (51:2) Wint 84-85, p. 118.

5680. WOODS-SMITH, Sybil
       "Angeline Ruby, 1920." <u>NewEngR</u> (6:3) Spr 84, p. 434.
       "Darwin Free." <u>NewEngR</u> (6:3) Spr 84, p. 433.
       "John Wesley Johnson." <u>NewEngR</u> (6:3) Spr 84, p. 435.

5681. WOODY, Elizabeth
       "Speaking Hands." <u>Calyx</u> (8:2) Spr 84, p. 82-82a.

5682. WOOLSON, Peter
       "Insectarium." <u>KanQ</u> (16:1/2) Wint-Spr 84, p. 126.
       "Thinly Disguised." <u>KanQ</u> (16:1/2) Wint-Spr 84, p.
       125.

5683. WORDSWORTH, William
       "A slumber did my spirit seal." <u>Tendril</u> (18,
       special issue) 84, p. 165-166.

5684. WORLEY, James
       "Einstein As Second Violinist." <u>ChrC</u> (101:34) 7 N
       84, p. 1029.
       "One More Time." <u>ChrC</u> (101:35) 14 N 84, p. 1055.

5685. WORLEY, Jeff
       "Alvin Cornelius Tells the Crowd at the Dew Drop
       Inn How It Was." <u>GreenfR</u> (12:1/2) Sum-Aut 84,
       p. 164-165.
       "Confession to the Townsmen." <u>Confr</u> (27/28) 84,
       p. 27.
       "Digger's Complaint." <u>IndR</u> (7:2) Spr 84, p. 52-53.
       "Geek Show." <u>Tendril</u> (17) Wint 84, p. 182.
       "Knife Creek Uprising." <u>SoDakR</u> (22:2) Sum 84, p.
       46-47.
       "Midwest Poem" (for Dave Etter). <u>LitR</u> (28:1) Aut
       84, p. 59.

5686. WORLEY, LaVon
    "Entering the Camps." CharR (10:1) Spr 84, p. 55.
    "Moving West" (for Becky Klusmeyer). CharR (10:1)
        Spr 84, p. 56.

5687. WORMSER, Baron
    "1969." ParisR (26:93) Aut 84, p. 165-166.
    "The American Intelligentsia." SouthernR (20:1)
        Wint 84, p. 144-145.
    "Annuals" (For Janet). Poetry (144:3) Je 84, p. 163.
    "An Art of Remoteness." Agni (21) 84, p. 22-23.
    "By-Products." Tendril (17) Wint 84, p. 183.
    "The Delegates." VirQR (60:3) Sum 84, p. 433.
    "Elegy for a Detective." ParisR (26:93) Aut 84,
        p. 168.
    "The Fall of the Human Empire." PoetryE (15) Aut
        84, p. 5.
    "Families." VirQR (60:3) Sum 84, p. 432-433.
    "Fishing." PoetryE (15) Aut 84, p. 8.
    "For My Brother Who Died Before I Was Born."
        Poetry (144:3) Je 84, p. 161.
    "For My Friend Greg, Twice-Decorated in Vietnam,
        Who Answers the Phone, 'Alive and Well'."
        Tendril (17) Wint 84, p. 184.
    "I Try to Explain to My Children a Newspaper
        Article." Harp (269:1610) Jl 84, p. 22.
    "I Try to Explain to My Children a Newspaper
        Article Which Says That According to a Computer
        a Nuclear War Is Likely to Occur in the Next
        Twenty Years." Poetry (143:6) Mr 84, p. 342-343.
    "In Baseball" (For Tom Hart). Poetry (144:3) Je
        84, p. 162.
    "Letter from the Countryside." PoetryE (15) Aut
        84, p. 6-7.
    "My Old Man." Agni (21) 84, p. 24.
    "Postcard Bearing a Portrait of Chief Joseph."
        ParisR (26:93) Aut 84, p. 166-167.
    "Satirist." NewRep (189:15) 10 O 83, p. 30.

5688. WORTH, Dorothy W.
    "From Hades." DekalbLAJ (20th Anniversary Issue)
        84, p. 113.
    "Salamander in Winter." DekalbLAJ (20th
        Anniversary Issue) 84, p. 114.

5689. WORTHY, Andre
    "Untitled: A noon sun shines brightly overhead."
        PoeticJ (6) 84, p. 18.

5690. WRAY, Bettye K.
    "Depression in Recession." NegC (4:2) Spr 84, p. 72.

5691. WRAY, Elizabeth
    "The Limits of the Town." NewL (50:2/3) Wint-Spr
        84, p. 37.

5692. WREGGITT, Andrew
    "Bridge to Greenville, Nass Valley." CrossC (6:3)
        84, p. 11.
    "Fairview Floats." Dandel (11:1) Spr-Sum 84, p. 66.

"Fishing." <u>CrossC</u> (6:3) 84, p. 11.
"Fishing, Kloiya Creek." <u>Dandel</u> (11:1) Spr-Sum
    84, p. 67.
"The Green Diamond." <u>Dandel</u> (11:1) Spr-Sum 84, p.
    68-69.

5693. WRIGHT, A. J.
    "The Burning Chair." <u>NeqC</u> (4:2) Spr 84, p. 61.
    "Down in Flotsam County." <u>Amelia</u> (1:2) O 84, p. 78.

5694. WRIGHT, Arthur
    "In My Own Lifetime." <u>Stepping</u> (Premier Issue)
    Sum 82, p. 41.

5695. WRIGHT, C. D.
    "The Complete Birth of the Cool." <u>Field</u> (31) Aut
        84, p. 47.
    "Elements of the Night." <u>TriQ</u> (59) Wint 84, p. 111.
    "Little Sisters." <u>BlackWR</u> (11:1) Aut 84, p. 72-73.
    "Nothing to Declare." <u>Field</u> (31) Aut 84, p. 49-50.
    "The Spirit Hunter." <u>Field</u> (31) Aut 84, p. 48.
    "Spread Rhythm." <u>Field</u> (31) Aut 84, p. 46.
    "Treatment" (for the children of Atlanta). <u>TriQ</u>
        (59) Wint 84, p. 112-113.
    "Wages of Love." <u>TriQ</u> (59) Wint 84, p. 109-110.

5696. WRIGHT, Carolyne
    "Fire Season" (Temecula, California). <u>MemphisSR</u>
        (4:2) Spr 84, p. 10.
    "Hard Beauty." <u>MemphisSR</u> (4:2) Spr 84, p. 9.
    "Note from the Stop-Gap Motor Inn." <u>NewL</u> (51:1)
        Aut 84, p. 64-65.
    "Woman Blooming for the Wind Machine." <u>VirQR</u>
        (60:1) Wint 84, p. 65-66.

5697. WRIGHT, Charles
    "Argyll Tour" (tr. of Eugenio Montale). <u>Chelsea</u>
        (42/43) 84, p. 121.
    "Arkansas Traveller." <u>NewYorker</u> (60:2) 27 F 84,
        p. 46-47.
    "Autumn Garden" (Florence, tr. of Dino Campana).
        <u>MissouriR</u> (7:3) 84, p. 45.
    "Autumn Garden" (Florence, tr. of Dino Campana).
        <u>Thrpny</u> (19) Aut 84, p. 11.
    "The Black Trout" (tr. of Eugenio Montale).
        <u>Chelsea</u> (42/43) 84, p. 120.
    "For an 'Homage to Rimbaud'" (tr. of Eugenio
        Montale). <u>Chelsea</u> (42/43) 84, p. 122.
    "From the Train" (tr. of Eugenio Montale).
        <u>Chelsea</u> (42/43) 84, p. 122.
    "Genoa Woman" (from "Donna Genovese," tr. of Dino
        Campana). <u>Thrpny</u> (17) Spr 84, p. 20.
    "Homage to Paul Cézanne." <u>PoetryE</u> (13/14) Spr-
        Sum 84, p. 66-73.
    "I have nothing to say about the way the sky tilts"
        (the first poem from "Three Poems for the New
        Year). <u>QW</u> (19) Aut-Wint 84-85, p. 184.
    "In the Mountains" (From the Falterona to Corniolo -
        - deserted valleys, tr. of Dino Campana).
        <u>MissouriR</u> (7:3) 84, p. 46.

"Italian Days." NewYorker (59:51) 6 F 84, p. 50-51.
"Journal of English Days." Field (30) Spr 84, p.
    5-15.
"Looking at Pictures." PoetryE (13/14) Spr-Sum
    84, p. 74-75.
"March Journal." Field (31) Aut 84, p. 89-91.
"Night Journal." Field (31) Aut 84, p. 92-94.
"On the Greve" (tr. of Eugenio Montale). Chelsea
    (42/43) 84, p. 120.
"Orphic Songs" (tr. of Dino Campana). MissouriR
    (7:3) 84, p. 43-47.
"Portrait of Mary" (After Montale). Shen (35:2/3)
    84, p. 474.
"Song of Darkness" (tr. of Dino Campana).
    MissouriR (7:3) 84, p. 47.
"To Giacomo Leopardi in the Sky." GeoR (38:2) Sum
    84, p. 408-409.
"Toscanita" (For Bino Binazzi, tr. of Dino
    Campana). Thrpny (19) Aut 84, p. 11.
"Voyage to Montevideo" (tr. of Dino Campana).
    MissouriR (7:3) 84, p. 43-44.
"Wind on the Halfmoon" (tr. of Eugenio Montale).
    Chelsea (42/43) 84, p. 121.

5698. WRIGHT, Eric
"Amsterdam." Descant (47, 15:4) Wint 84, p. 89.
"Corfu." Descant (47, 15:4) Wint 84, p. 90.
"Love Is What You Make It." Descant (47, 15:4)
    Wint 84, p. 93.
"Psychoanalysis." Descant (47, 15:4) Wint 84, p. 91.
"This Living Hand." Descant (47, 15:4) Wint 84,
    p. 92.

5699. WRIGHT, Franz
"Alcohol." Field (31) Aut 84, p. 70-71.
"Day Comes." VirQR (60:3) Sum 84, p. 434-435.
"Guests." Field (31) Aut 84, p. 69.
"Ill Lit." Field (31) Aut 84, p. 68.

5700. WRIGHT, Fred W., Jr.
"Harry the Vendor." PoeticJ (2) 83, p. 18.

5701. WRIGHT, Harold P.
"Billy the Kid" (tr. of Shuntaro Tanikawa).
    Chelsea (42/43) 84, p. 257.
"Cliffs" (tr. of Rin Ishigaki). Chelsea (42/43)
    84, p. 262.
"Living" (tr. of Rin Ishigaki). Chelsea (42/43)
    84, p. 263.

5702. WRIGHT, James
"Blessing." Germ (8:2) Aut-Wint 84, p. 35-36.
"Confession to J. Edgar Hoover." Chelsea (42/43)
    84, p. 68.
"Devotions." Peb (23) 84, p. 5-6.
"Eisenhower's Visit to Franco, 1959." Tendril
    (18, special issue) 84, p. 47-48.
"The Jewel." Germ (8:2) Aut-Wint 84, p. 35.
"The Jewel." Tendril (18, special issue) 84, p. 38.
"Late November in a Field." MidAR (4:2) Aut 84,

p. 110.
"The Life." Tendril (18, special issue) 84, p. 75-
76.
"Lightning Bugs Asleep in the Afternoon." Germ
(8:2) Aut-Wint 84, p. 40-41.
"Lying in a Hammock at William Duffy's Farm at Pine
Island, Minnesota." OhioR (33) 84, p. 22.
"Lying in a Hammock at William Duffy's Farm in Pine
Island, Minnesota." Agni (21) 84, p. 122.
"Outside Fargo, North Dakota." AmerPoR (13:4) Jl-
Ag 84, p. 30-31.
"Outside Fargo, North Dakota." Tendril (18,
special issue) 84, p. 214.
"The Rats" (tr. of Georg Trakl). Field (30) Spr
84, p. 67.
"To a Blossoming Pear Tree." Germ (8:2) Aut-Wint
84, p. 39.
"To a Shy Girl." OhioR (33) 84, p. 17.
"To the Saguaro Cactus Tree in the Desert Rain."
Tendril (18, special issue) 84, p. 286-287.
"Trilce" (Excerpts, tr. of César Vallejo).
Chelsea (42/43) 84, p. 52-53.
"The Vestal in the Forum." Tendril (18, special
issue) 84, p. 224-225.
"Written during Illness." OhioR (33) 84, p. 20.

5703. WRIGHT, Jay
"Twenty-Two Tremblings of the Postulant"
(Improvisations Surrounding the Body:
Selections). Obs (8:1) Spr 82, p. 197-202.

5704. WRIGHT, Jeff
"Flicker." Abraxas (29/30) 84, p. 39.
"God Is a Road" (for Diane Burns). Tele (19) 83,
p. 66.
"Good Fucking Bye." Tele (19) 83, p. 65.
"Nervous Application" (w. Roland Legiardi-Laura).
Tele (19) 83, p. 67-68.
"Play Along." Abraxas (31/32) 84, p. 66-67.
"Yankee Dogs." Tele (19) 83, p. 63-64.

5705. WRIGHT, Jonathan
"After the Image." Germ (8:1) Spr-Sum 84, p. 35.
"The Dream of the Book of Passion and Sorrow."
Germ (8:1) Spr-Sum 84, p. 36.

5706. WRIGHT, Richard
"I am nobody" (Haiku, calligraphy by Lloyd
Reynolds). NewL (50:2/3) Wint-Spr 84, p. 6.
"In the fallking snow" (Haiku, calligraphy by Lloyd
Reynolds). NewL (50:2/3) Wint-Spr 84, p. 6.
"Make up your mind snail" (Haiku, calligraphy by
Lloyd Reynolds). NewL (50:2/3) Wint-Spr 84, p. 6.
"Standing in the field" (Haiku, calligraphy by
Lloyd Reynolds). NewL (50:2/3) Wint-Spr 84, p. 6.
"With a twitching nose" (Haiku, calligraphy by
Lloyd Reynolds). NewL (50:2/3) Wint-Spr 84, p. 6.

5707. WRIGHT, Roger W.
"Southern Romance." DekalbLAJ (20th Anniversary

Issue) 84, p. 115.

WRIGHT, Roger Wayne: See WAYNE-WRIGHT, Roger

5708. WRIGHT, Terry
"Last Dance before Curfew." SanFPJ (6:2) 84, p. 20.

5709. WRIGLEY, Robert
"Aubade for Mothers" (Selection: "The Ritual of
Expulsion and Yearning"). PartR (51:3) 84, p.
391-392.
"Collection" (for my son). NewEngR (6:3) Spr 84,
p. 436-437.
"Ice Storm." MidAR (4:2) Aut 84, p. 10.
"Lover of Fire." CimR (68) Jl 84, p. 51-52.
"Spring Tillage." SnapD (7:1) Aut 83, p. 63.

5710. WRONSKY, Gail
"The Female Centaur" (for Natalie Barney). Calyx
(8:3) Aut-Wint 84, p. 48.

5711. WU, Cheng
"The Morning Reading" (tr. by Marilyn Chin and
Eunice Chen). Iowa (14:2) Spr-Sum 84, p. 58-59.
"My Hometown's Base Creatures" (tr. by Marilyn Chin
and Jesse Wang). Iowa (14:2) Spr-Sum 84, p. 57-
58.

WU, Lu Pei: See LU, Pei Wu

5712. WYATT, David
"Nap." NowestR (22:1/2) 84, p. 49.
"The White-Throat Calling in the Poplars before
Dawn" (--WCW). NowestR (22:1/2) 84, p. 50-51.

WYCK, Marcia van: See Van WYCK, Marcia

5713. WYNAND, Derk
"The Other Version." CanLit (100) Spr 84, p. 373.
"Outward from the Pool's Dry Edge." CanLit (100)
Spr 84, p. 372-373.
"Twin." CanLit (100) Spr 84, p. 372.

5714. WYTTENBERG, Victoria
"The Children's Clothing." PoetryNW (25:4) Wint
84-85, p. 6.
"Grieving on the Suicide of the Groom" (to my
sister). PoetryNW (25:4) Wint 84-85, p. 3-4.
"Listening to Birds." PoetryNW (25:1) Spr 84, p.
41-42.
"The Sea Lion." PoetryNW (25:1) Spr 84, p. 40-41.
"Visiting the Dollhouse." PoetryNW (25:4) Wint 84-
85, p. 5.
"The Woman Who Lives over the Funeral Home."
PoetryNW (25:4) Wint 84-85, p. 4-5.

5715. YALIM, Ozcan
"Elegy" (tr. of Kemal Ozer, w. Dionis Coffin Riggs
and William Fielder). StoneC (11:3/4) Spr-Sum
84, p. 39.

"Hegira" (tr. of Orhan Veli, w. Dionis Coffin Riggs
and William Fielder). StoneC (11:3/4) Spr-Sum
84, p. 41.

5716. YAMAMOTO, Judith
"Youngest Brother." PartR (51:3) 84, p. 390-391.

5717. YAMAMOTO, Traise
"Learning to Talk." NewRep (190:3) 23 Ja 84, p. 38.

5718. YAMRUS, John
"Today's Numbers." Bogg (52) 84, p. 20.

5719. YARROW, Bill
"The Reclamation of Virginity." Poem (52) N 84,
p. 62-63.
"Taking Off the Knives." Poem (52) N 84, p. 64.

5720. YASAR, Izzet
"Bleeding" (tr. by Talat Sait Halman). NewRena
(6:1, #18) Spr 84, p. 111, 113.
"Kanama." NewRena (6:1, #18) Spr 84, p. 110, 112.

5721. YATES, J. Michael
"The Queen Charlotte Islands Meditations"
(Excerpts). NewOR (11:1) Spr 84, p. 112-113.
"The Queen Charlotte Islands Meditations"
(Selections: 48, 57). PoetryCR (5:4) Sum 84,
p. 6.
"The Queen Charlotte Islands Meditations"
(Selections: 63, 76-79). GreenfR (11:3/4) Wint-
Spr 84, p. 92-95.
"The Queen Charlotte Islands Meditations"
(Selections: 81, 91). Grain (12:2) My 84, p.
38-39.

5722. YAU, John
"Cenotaph." Sulfur (4:1, issue 10) 84, p. 132-133.
"Halfway to China." Sulfur (4:1, issue 10) 84, p.
133-135.

5723. YEATS, William Butler
"Three Things." Hudson (37:1) Spr 84, p. 68.

5724. YENSER, Pamela
"Dear Heart." MassR (25:3) Aut 84, p. 401.
"Finding Her Brother Lost." MassR (25:3) Aut 84,
p. 398-399.
"The Running Dream." MassR (25:3) Aut 84, p. 400.

5725. YEO, Robert
"A Dragon for the Family." Iowa (14:2) Spr-Sum
84, p. 69.

5726. YI, Chong-Bo
"The Lad Who Last Night Slept Here" (tr. by Graeme
Wilson). WestHR (38:2) Sum 84, p. 132.

YONG-WOON, Han: See MANHAE

5727. YORK, Judy
"O Canada." Waves (12:1) Aut 83, p. 52.

5728. YOSELOFF, T. R.
"Paris (Left Bank Blues)." LitR (28:1) Aut 84, p.
61.

5729. YOSHIHARA, Sachiko
"Air Raid" (tr. by Naoshi Koriyama and Edward
Lueders). Poetry (143:6) Mr 84, p. 320.
"The Street" (tr. by John Solt). Iowa (14:2) Spr-
Sum 84, p. 60.
"Woman" (tr. by John Solt). Iowa (14:2) Spr-Sum
84, p. 60-61.

5730. YOTS, Michael
"Michaelangelo off the Record on His Inspiration
for the Sistine Chapel Ceiling" (for Stanton
Millet). Wind (14:51) 84, p. 58-59.

5731. YOUNG, Bernard
"He Is Here." Bogg (52) 84, p. 43.

5732. YOUNG, David
"Collision" (tr. of Miroslav Holub). Field (30)
Spr 84, p. 29-31.

5733. YOUNG, Dean
"Last Night's Bread." Telescope (3:2) Spr 84, p. 15.
"Our Life in California." Telescope (3:2) Spr 84,
p. 16.
"Vulnerability." Kayak (64) My 84, p. 55.
"Zebras." BlueBldgs (7) 84, p. 36.

5734. YOUNG, Ellen Roberts
"Incompletes." ChrC (101:16) 9 My 84, p. 484.

5735. YOUNG, Irene S.
"Going Home." SanFPJ (7:1) 84, p. 41-42.

5736. YOUNG, Jill
"At El Patio the Workers Fraternize." WormR
(24:4, issue 96) 84, p. 125-129.
"My Neighbor's Dog." Abraxas (31/32) 84, p. 27.

5737. YOUNG, Kathryn
"Father." WindO (44) Sum-Aut 84, p. 8.

5738. YOUNG, Louis C., Jr.
"A Libationary Chant-Prayer for Malcolm and His
Sacred Autobiography." Stepping Wint 83, p. 15.

5739. YOUNG, Mary Bownsberger
"On the Death of David." ChrC (101:9) 14 Mr 84,
p. 269.

5740. YOUNG, Patricia
"Ape-Woman." Grain (12:1) F 84, p. 18-19.

5741. YOUNG, Ree
       "Main Street." SouthernHR (18:4) Aut 84, p. 318.

5742. YOUNG BEAR, Ray A.
       "A Drive to Lone Ranger." NowestR (22:1/2) 84, p.
          122-125.
       "Eagle Crossing, July 1975." GreenfR (11:3/4)
          Wint-Spr 84, p. 28-29.
       "The First Dimension of Skunk." AmerPoR (13:6) N-
          D 84, p. 36.
       "From the Spotted Night." AmerPoR (13:6) N-D 84,
          p. 36.
       "The King Cobra As Political Assassin" (May 30,
          1981). TriQ (59) Wint 84, p. 97-99.
       "March Eight/1979." GreenfR (11:3/4) Wint-Spr 84,
          p. 27-28.
       "Nothing Could Take Away the Bear-King's Image."
          Sulfur (4:1, issue 10) 84, p. 115-120.
       "Wadasa Nakamoon, Vietnam Memorial." TriQ (59)
          Wint 84, p. 100.

5743. YRARRAZAVAL, Renato
       "He tratado de enmendar palabras." Mairena (6:18)
          84, p. 139.

5744. YUAN, Mei
       "Alone" (tr. by J. P. Seaton). NegC (4:3) Sum 84,
          p. 40.
       "A Guest Arrives" (tr. by J. P. Seaton). NegC
          (4:3) Sum 84, p. 42.
       "Idleness" (tr. by J. P. Seaton). LitR (28:1) Aut
          84, p. 137.
       "Ill" (tr. by J. P. Seaton). NegC (4:3) Sum 84,
          p. 38.
       "In Idleness I" (tr. by J. P. Seaton). LitR
          (28:1) Aut 84, p. 136.
       "In Idleness II" (tr. by J. P. Seaton). LitR
          (28:1) Aut 84, p. 137.
       "Jeering at Myself" (tr. by J. P. Seaton). NegC
          (4:3) Sum 84, p. 37.
       "March" (tr. by J. P. Seaton). NegC (4:3) Sum 84,
          back cover.
       "Mornings arise" (tr. by J. P. Seaton). NegC
          (4:3) Sum 84, p. 46.
       "Opening the Window" (tr. by J. P. Seaton). NegC
          (4:3) Sum 84, p. 46.
       "Returned from Yang-chou up the Hill to View the
          Snow" (tr. by J. P. Seaton). LitR (28:1) Aut
          84, p. 136.
       "River village sands white bright moon" (tr. by J.
          P. Seaton). NegC (4:3) Sum 84, p. 44.

5745. YUP, Paula
       "Possessions." YetASM (3) 84, p. 7.

5746. YURGEL, Danae
       "Escape: A Grande Ronde Fantasy." PoeticJ (1) 83,
          p. 3.
       "Sage Harvest." PoeticJ (1) 83, p. 6.

YURI   650

YURI, Kageyama: See KAGEYAMA, Yuri

5747. YURKIEVICH, Saûl
      "The Door" (tr. by Cola Franzen). Mund (14:2) 84,
          p. 87, 89.
      "Para Que Leerlo." Mund (14:2) 84, p. 86.
      "La Puerta." Mund (14:2) 84, p. 86, 88.
      "Ronda." Mund (14:2) 84, p. 88, 90.
      "Rounds" (tr. by Cola Franzen). Mund (14:2) 84,
          p. 89, 91.
      "Why Bother to Read It" (tr. by Cola Franzen).
          Mund (14:2) 84, p. 87.

5748. YURMAN, Rich
      "Two Grandmothers Are Better Than One." YetASM
          (3) 84, p. 2.

5749. ZABLE, Jeffrey A. Z.
      "The End." Wind (14:51) 84, p. 60.
      "The End." WormR (24:2, issue 94) 84, p. 74.
      "The End of a Relationship." WormR (24:2, issue
          94) 84, p. 74.
      "Guilty." WormR (24:2, issue 94) 84, p. 75.
      "The Race." Wind (14:51) 84, p. 60.
      "The Unfortunate Request" (for Russell Edson).
          WormR (24:2, issue 94) 84, p. 75-76.

5750. ZABRANSKY, Richard
      "The Owl." Ascent (9:3) 84, p. 40-41.

5751. ZACHARIN, Noah
      "The Gardener." Quarry (33:3) Sum 84, p. 71.
      "The Highway Toll Collector." MalR (68) Je 84, p.
          96-97.
      "The Men Who Break Fingers." MalR (68) Je 84, p.
          95-96.
      "Moth." PoetryCR (5:4) Sum 84, p. 16.
      "Ships in the Forest." MalR (68) Je 84, p. 94-95.
      "When I Am Wind." Quarry (33:3) Sum 84, p. 70.

5752. ZAGAJEWSKI, Adam
      "Going to Lvov" (tr. by Renata Gorczynski).
          NewRep (190:5) 6 F 84, p. 40.

ZAHURUL HAQUE, Abu Saeed: See ABU SAEED

5753. ZALAMEA, Luis
      "Las Cartas de Amor de Mi Abuela" (tr. of Hart
          Crane). LindLM (3:2/4) Ap-D 84, p. 25.

5754. ZAMORA, Daisy
      "Commander Two" (tr. by Marc Zimmerman and Ellen
          Banberger). MinnR (N.S. 22) Spr 84, p. 73.
      "Girl with a Parasol" (tr. by Margaret Randall).
          Calyx (8:3) Aut-Wint 84, p. 11.
      "The News Vendor" (tr. by Margaret Randall).
          Calyx (8:3) Aut-Wint 84, p. 12.
      "The Rigoberto Lopez Perez Unit" (tr. by Marc
          Zimmerman and Ellen Banberger). MinnR (N.S.
          22) Spr 84, p. 73-74.

"A Time Will Come" (tr. by Marc Zimmerman and Ellen
    Banberger). MinnR (N.S. 22) Spr 84, p. 80.
"To Dionysius, Companero" (tr. by Barbara Paschke).
    Vis (15) 84, p. 24.
"The Waitress" (tr. by Margaret Randall). Calyx
    (8:3) Aut-Wint 84, p. 10.

5755. ZANDER, William
    "Mammals." PoetryNW (25:4) Wint 84-85, p. 29-30.

5756. ZAPATA, Miguel Angel
    "Nunca Fui un Muchacho de Puerto" (a los criollos
        peruanos). LindLM (3:2/4) Ap-D 84, p. 19.
    "Si Tan Solo Pudiera." LindLM (3:2/4) Ap-D 84, p.
        19.

5757. ZAPOCAS, Andrés
    "Kirkpatrick." Metam (5:2/6:1) 84-85, p. 27.
    "Nuclear." Metam (5:2/6:1) 84-85, p. 26.

5758. ZARANKA, William
    "Blessing's Anatomy." PraS (58:1) Spr 84, p. 54-55.
    "Blessing's Candid." DenQ (19:1) Spr 84, p. 82.
    "Blessing's Chariots." DenQ (19:1) Spr 84, p. 72.
    "Blessing's Flashback." DenQ (19:1) Spr 84, p. 84.
    "Blessing's Goats and Monkeys." DenQ (19:1) Spr
        84, p. 73-74.
    "Blessing's Grand Tour Fantasia." DenQ (19:1) Spr
        84, p. 78-80.
    "Blessing's Inspiration." DenQ (19:1) Spr 84, p. 81.
    "Blessing's Zone." PraS (58:1) Spr 84, p. 53-54.
    "His Argument with His Machine." DenQ (19:1) Spr
        84, p. 76.
    "His Recovery." DenQ (19:1) Spr 84, p. 83.
    "Like Having a Trick Knee." DenQ (19:1) Spr 84,
        p. 77-78.
    "Misogyny." DenQ (19:1) Spr 84, p. 75.
    "The Technological Eye." DenQ (19:1) Spr 84, p.
        71-84.
    "Toad Song." Sparrow (46) 84, p. 20.

5759. ZARIN, Cynthia
    "The Near and Dear." NewYorker (59:52) 13 F 84,
        p. 46.
    "Now." NewYorker (60:11) 30 Ap 84, p. 46.

5760. ZARZYSKI, Paul
    "The Noonhour Westbound." CharR (10:2) Aut 84, p.
        80-81.
    "Silos." NowestR (22:1/2) 84, p. 145.
    "Speckled Trout." CharR (10:2) Aut 84, p. 79-80.
    "Zarzyski Goes Daffy with Zupan on the Last Day of
        Quacker Season." CharR (10:2) Aut 84, p. 78-79.

5761. ZAWADIWSKY, Christina
    "Burning Statues." LittleM (14:3) 84, p. 18-19.

5762. ZAWADIWSKY, Christine
    "All Smoke Will Rise." Abraxas (31/32) 84, p. 50.

5763. ZEIDNER, Lisa
"Dementia Colander." <u>MissR</u> (37/38, 13:1/2) Aut
84, p. 56-75.
"God's Jukebox." <u>Telescope</u> (3:2) Spr 84, p. 152.
"Safety in Numbers." <u>Poetry</u> (144:2) My 84, p. 80-83.
"What Really Happens When the Plane Goes Down."
<u>Poetry</u> (144:2) My 84, p. 80.

5764. ZEIGER, David
"Homage to Twyla Tharp and Company." <u>WindO</u> (44)
Sum-Aut 84, p. 34-35.
"Waiting." <u>Vis</u> (14) 84, p. 19.

5765. ZEIGER, L. L.
"Woods/Words." <u>NewL</u> (51:1) Aut 84, p. 16-17.

5766. ZEISER, Linda
"Passion's Nest" (Excerpt). <u>Amelia</u> (1:2) O 84, p.
74.

5767. ZEISS, Todd Rolf
"Man to Man" (For my son, jilted by his sweetheart,
Grace). <u>CapeR</u> (19:2) Sum 84, p. 15.
"Other Poets, Other Lines." <u>CapeR</u> (19:2) Sum 84,
p. 14.
"A Portrait of My Father in Myself." <u>CapeR</u> (19:2)
Sum 84, p. 12.
"We See Only Hawks" (after poems by Wordsworth and
Hopkins). <u>CapeR</u> (19:2) Sum 84, p. 13.

5768. ZENIK, Robert L. J.
"Man." <u>WritersL</u> (1) 84, p. 23.

5769. ZEPEDA, Rafael
"After Hours." <u>WormR</u> (24:1, issue 93) 84, p. 29.
"The Competitive Spirit." <u>WormR</u> (24:1, issue 93)
84, p. 31.
"The Origin of the Species." <u>WormR</u> (24:1, issue
93) 84, p. 30.
"A Source of Inspiration." <u>WormR</u> (24:1, issue 93)
84, p. 29-30.

5770. ZIEROTH, Dale
"1956: Mrs. Wrungren, Storekeeper." <u>MalR</u> (67) F
84, p. 57-58.
"1956: The Old Lutheran Pastor." <u>MalR</u> (67) F 84,
p. 58-59.
"1956: The School Teacher Falls in Love." <u>MalR</u>
(67) F 84, p. 56-57.
"De-Horning." <u>CrossC</u> (6:3) 84, p. 13.
"The Party Line." <u>CanLit</u> (100) Spr 84, p. 374-375.
"Returning to a Town." <u>CrossC</u> (6:3) 84, p. 12.
"We Must Face This." <u>CrossC</u> (6:3) 84, p. 12.
"Winter." <u>CrossC</u> (6:3) 84, p. 13.

5771. ZIMMER, Paul
"Blues for Old Dogs." <u>BlackWR</u> (10:2) Spr 84, p. 18.
"Driving North from Savannah on My Birthday."
<u>Poetry</u> (144:4) Jl 84, p. 234.
"The Great Bird of Love over the Kingdom."

BlackWR (10:2) Spr 84, p. 17.
"The News of the Day." Swallow (3) 84, p. 56.
"Zimmer Speaks of the King's Roads." Swallow (3)
   84, p. 55.

5772. ZIMMERMAN, Marc
    "1978" (tr. of Sergio Vizcaya and Condega Poetry
       Workshop, w. Ellen Banberger). MinnR (N.S. 22)
       Spr 84, p. 70.
    "Ballad of Monimbo" (tr. of Cajina Vega, w. Ellen
       Banberger). MinnR (N.S. 22) Spr 84, p. 77, 81.
    "Commander Two" (tr. of Daisy Zamora, w. Ellen
       Banberger). MinnR (N.S. 22) Spr 84, p. 73.
    "Communique Number 1,000 for My Love" (tr. of Alba
       Azucena Torres, w. Ellen Banberger). MinnR
       (N.S. 22) Spr 84, p. 79.
    "Demonstration" (tr. of Fernando Antonio Silva, w.
       Ellen Banberger). MinnR (N.S. 22) Spr 84, p.
       71-72.
    "The Gourd" (tr. of Pablo Antonio Cuadra, w. Ellen
       Banberger). MinnR (N.S. 22) Spr 84, p. 67.
    "In la Bartolina" (tr. of Ivan Guevara, w. Ellen
       Banberger). MinnR (N.S. 22) Spr 84, p. 69.
    "In My Country" (tr. of Pedro Xavier Solis, w.
       Ellen Banberger). MinnR (N.S. 22) Spr 84, p. 67.
    "In the Prison" (tr. of Daniel Ortega, w. Ellen
       Banberger). MinnR (N.S. 22) Spr 84, p. 70-72.
    "In This Country" (tr. of Ernesto Castillo, w.
       Ellen Banberger). MinnR (N.S. 22) Spr 84, p.
       79-80.
    "Let's Go, Comrades" (tr. of Francisco de Asis
       Fernández, w. Ellen Banberger). MinnR (N.S.
       22) Spr 84, p. 81.
    "Letter" (tr. of Alejandro Bravo, w. Ellen
       Banberger). MinnR (N.S. 22) Spr 84, p. 80.
    "Manifesto" (tr. of Alejandro Bravo, w. Ellen
       Banberger). MinnR (N.S. 22) Spr 84, p. 74-76.
    "Monimbo" (tr. of Alejandro Bravo, w. Ellen
       Banberger). MinnR (N.S. 22) Spr 84, p. 68.
    "Point Number 1 on the Agenda" (tr. of Rosario
       Murillo, w. Ellen Banberger). MinnR (N.S. 22)
       Spr 84, p. 69.
    "Proverbs and Songs" (tr. of Michele Najlis, w.
       Ellen Banberger). MinnR (N.S. 22) Spr 84, p. 68.
    "The Rigoberto Lopez Perez Unit" (tr. of Daisy
       Zamora, w. Ellen Banberger). MinnR (N.S. 22)
       Spr 84, p. 73-74.
    "There Are Discourses Like These" (tr. of Ivan
       Guevara, w. Ellen Banberger). MinnR (N.S. 22)
       Spr 84, p. 74-77.
    "A Time Will Come" (tr. of Daisy Zamora, w. Ellen
       Banberger). MinnR (N.S. 22) Spr 84, p. 80.
    "We Live in a Rush" (tr. of Dora Maria Tellez, w.
       Ellen Banberger). MinnR (N.S. 22) Spr 84, p.
       72-73.

5773. ZIMMERMAN, Robert N.
    "Canoe in the Morning." PoeticJ (7) 84, p. 6.

5774. ZIMMERMAN, Toni
"If Life Could Only Be As Simple." CapeR (19:3)
20th Anniverary Issue 84, p. 54.

5775. ZIMROTH, Evan
"The Drama Critic Warns of Clichès." Poetry
(144:1) Ap 84, p. 7-8.

5776. ZLOTKOWSKI, Edward
"Lauds." AntigR (57) Spr 84, p. 126.

5777. ZOLLER, Ann
"Fighting Fair." WebR (9:1) Spr 84, p. 61.

5778. ZOLLER, Ann L.
"Genesis of Man" (Myth of the Haida Tribe of
Vancouver). ThirdW (2) Spr 84, p. 7.

5779. ZOLLER, James A.
"Untitled Domestic Poem." Blueline (5:2) Wint-Spr
84, p. 20.

5780. ZOLYNAS, Al
"Under Ideal Conditions." Veloc (4) Sum 84, p. 5.

5781. ZONAILO, Carolyn
"The Heart Can Be a Mountain" (for Gerry Gerein).
PoetryCR (5:4) Sum 84, p. 7.

5782. ZONTELLI, Patricia
"First Snow Storm." BelPoJ (34:4) Sum 84, p. 1.

5783. ZORNACK, Annemarie
"Paul Celan" (tr. by Carl Clifton Toliver).
Sulfur (4:2, issue 11) 84, p. 96.

5784. ZUCKERMAN, Anne
"Olympia on the Couch." StoneC (11:3/4) Spr-Sum
84, p. 75.

5785. ZUCKERMAN, Ryki
"Lying Low." Paunch (57/58) Ja 84, p. 85.

ZUHR, Ibn: See IBN ZUHR

5786. ZUKOFSKY, Louis
"Stay where the casement suns unapproachably high."
Origin (Series 5:1) Aut 83, p. 46.

5787. ZUKOR-COHN, Mareé
"Dream of an Old Man." Paunch (57/58) Ja 84, p. 94.

5788. ZURITA, Raul
"Pastoral de Chile (IV)." Mairena (6:18) 84, p. 137.

ZUXIN, Ding: See DING, Zuxin

5789. ZWEIG, Paul
"Black Poet" (tr. of Antonin Artaud). Chelsea
(42/43) 84, p. 117.

"The Classroom." _AmerPoR_ (13:6) N-D 84, p. 9.
"Early Waking." _AmerPoR_ (13:6) N-D 84, p. 9.
"Jacob and the Angel." _Antaeus_ (52) Apr 84, p. 48.

5790. ZYDEK, Fredrick
    "This Too Was Vapor" (for Gary Numan). _SouthwR_
        (69:3) Sum 84, p. 265.
    "Touching the Distance." _Grain_ (12:1) F 84, p. 22.

TITLE INDEX

Titles are arranged alphanumerically, with numerals filed in numerical order before letters. Each title is followed by one or more author entry numbers, which refer to the numbered entries in the first part of the volume.

1899: Girl and Her Father:
3037.
1905: 4814.
1923, Albert Einstein Invents
Birds: 1283.
1925: 5160.
1929: 178.
1940: 4942.
The 1940's and Today: 5522.
1943: 1003.
1946 Nickel: 4022.
1952: 2325.
1956: Mrs. Wrungren,
Storekeeper: 5770.
1956: The Old Lutheran Pastor:
5770.
1956: The School Teacher Falls
in Love: 5770.
1957: 5259.
1962 Sum: 5510.
1964: The Hardy Boys: 4477.
1969: 5687.
1974: 2081.
1978: 262, 1034, 5393, 5772.
1983: 4014.
1983, San Antonio: 2206.
1984: 178, 2806, 2806, 3152.
2084 AD: 4631.
2237 Giddings Street: 2657.
3464 Hutchison: 3 for Easter:
637.
3.885 Hectares: 341.
5608 Springhill Place: 4351.
9,600 Acres: 341, 2797.
10,000 Volts, Seven Black
Widows, All Adults and My
Wife's New Red Pants: 291.
$1,800,000,000,000: 4200.
A Arnaldo Torres Rosado y
Carlos Soto Arrivi: 5212.
A Cappella: 3578.
A-Changing: 4009.
A.D.C. 4th: 5452.
A.E. has jet-black hair: 4288.
A.E. takes a ride in an
elevator: 4288.
A Jorge Luis Borges: 5212.
A Juan Carlos: 1315.
A la Poesia: 2888.
A la Sombra de Leon Felipe:
1123.
A L'Auberge du Violon: 3628.
A 11 beautiful, once spacious
skies: 2550.
A.M: 1550.
A Mère Meera: 1744.
A Mi Hermano el Obrero: 423.
A Pizca: 94.
A. R. Ammons amid the Fungi:
18.
A una Lajeña: 4457.
A Veces: 3281.
A Veces No Quisiera Ser Poeta:
1024.
A Vermeer de Delft: 930.
Abacus: 991, 4652.

An Abandoned Farmhouse: 4497.
The Abandoned Man: 4108.
Abandonment: 564.
Abattoir: 1366.
Abbatoir: 967.
ABC Products: 4895.
Abishag: Recollections in Old
Age: 3078.
Ablution: 3037.
Ablutions: 3469.
About 25 million years ago:
4200.
About Death: 227.
About Death and Other Things:
4332, 4771.
About Which Was More
Important: 4026.
Above Mirage: 4203.
L'Abre: 3113.
Abriste la ventana: 2570.
Abschied von der Eifel: 590.
Absence: 806, 2989.
Absent Star: 1442.
Absoluta Negadora de
Realidades: 4018.
Abstruse Rap of the Wiseguy
Scrapped: 2775.
The Absurd, Off Broadway: 628.
Academic Nightmare: 4916.
Acapulco: 1341.
Acceptance of the Grave: 3644.
Accepting Death: 1707.
Accident: 2912.
The Accident at Staplehurst:
2379.
Accomplishment: 1794.
Accounting: 2712.
The Accusation: 742.
Acerca de la Libertad: 5474.
Acid Rain: 5343.
The Acid Test: Advice to My
Son: 3457.
Acili Gecenin Bitiminde: 3744.
Acontece: 867.
Acquaintances: 4237.
Acre of Love: 1174.
Across Kansas: 4942.
Across the River: 1466.
Action: 1741.
Action Painting: Apple
Orchard: 4611.
Adam Gets Eden: 5516.
Adam Gives Thanks: 286.
Adam Laments: 286.
Adam Speaks: 4062.
Adam's Stroke of Genius: 286.
Adan, Adan: 1178.
Address: 4567.
Addressed to Shave: 2447.
Adele Menken Stares at Her
Ceiling: 3343.
L'Adieu: 2495.
Adirondack Sunday: 3047.
Adivinanza al Final: 1313.
Adjusting to the Desert: 4358.
Adler: 4983.

has poetry in him: 5222.
Among the Powers of Desire: 3235.
Amor: 3591.
Amos: 923.
Amputee's Litany - Miami, 1959: 5113.
Amsterdam: 5698.
Ana en Su Mecedora: 2434.
Anabasis: 827, 830, 2276.
Anaerobics: Elaine Powers, Wheeling, West Virginia: 3549.
Anagrammagic: 1993.
Ana's Dance: 4972.
Anatole France: Advice on a Grandchild: 3869.
Anatomy Lesson: 89.
Anatomy of a Spider Monkey: 2161.
The Anatomy of the Crab Is Repetitive and Rhythmical: 2329.
Ancestor: 1543.
The Anchor: 1550, 2619.
Anchor Man: 3731.
Ancient Child of Ancient Mothers: 2886.
The Ancient of Days: 1853.
And: 3909.
And All the Lambs Go Down to Their Final Resting Place: 323.
And As: 3475.
And can see the many hidden ways merit drains out: 203.
And from the Summit: 3317.
And God Looked Down and Saw His Children Playing at Amchitka: 5645.
And I'd Fear Some Terrible Accident Like His War: 4356.
And if I read pomes: 1550.
And in a Moment: 894.
And must I see him, the father of lies: 3, 912.
And Now I Say to You: 3675.
And So Was Our Soul: 4403.
And Someone Said: 3763.
And Then Come Back: 3248.
And Then We Got the Green: 711.
And There Are, Also, Other Awakenings: 1158.
And There Isn't: 408, 5130.
And What Did the Soldier's Wife Receive?: 603, 1493.
And When the Kid Drowned on My Mother It Became an Angel: 4833.
And You Too, Merry Andropov: 1329.
Anderson Lake at Twilight: 3262.
Andree Rexroth: 4294.

Andromeda: 2036.
Anecdota del Abuelito: 2062.
Anemophobia: 1483.
Anette: 185.
The Angel: 303.
Angel: 4929.
The Angel in Front of the Fountain: 4175.
Angel Peak: A 2nd Road Song: 595.
Los Angeles: 2219.
Angeline Ruby, 1920: 5680.
Angelo: 2486.
Angels: 755.
Angels of Ascent: 1344.
The Angelus: 1522.
Angle of Incidence: 3652.
Anglian Music: 3091.
Angry Women: 4137.
The Animal Dentist: 2894.
Animal Song: 3384.
Animation: 1073.
Animus: 4064.
Ankunft: 260.
Anna Frank and I: 42, 4682.
Anna Margaret Smith's Brooch: 5045.
Anne and the Saloon: 4207.
Anne, Doing Tai Chi in the Campground on Pender Island: 3321.
Annie Sadler: 5.
Anniversaries: 549.
The Anniversary: 559.
Anniversary: 2689, 2860, 5031.
Anniversary II: 5049.
Anniversary of Dismay: 1069.
The Anniversary of Silence: 244.
Anniversary Poem: 1186, 4247.
An Annual of the Dark Physics: 1413.
Annuals: 5687.
Annulus: 1869.
The Annunciation: 815.
Annunciation: 2192.
Anny Tarpley: 1898.
Anointing the Sick: 3883.
Anonymous Master, 'Standing Figure': 2371.
Anonymous Poems on Immigration under the Chinese Exclusion Act: 152.
Anorexia: 1911.
The Anorexic: 1588.
Another Fine Day in the May Woods: 3784.
Another Hansel and Gretel Story: 4998.
Another Life's Land: 4988.
Another Link: 2195.
Another Little World: 4470.
Another Moon Effect: 193, 3567.
Another Old Photograph: 1438.
Another one died last week:

Are You Aware of Gender When
    You Write?: 2081.
Are Your Poems Your Songs:
    2526, 3844, 4652.
Areíto por Carlos Muñiz:
    848.
Arena: 3615.
Ares Conquered: 2585.
Argument: 539.
An Argument in Support of
    Letters: 1923.
Argumentum e Silentio: 781,
    883.
Argus, Dreaming: 1467.
Argyll Tour: 3567, 5697.
Aria for Lady Alice, Tarzan's
    Mother: 4312.
Aria for Tarzan's Father:
    4312.
Arion on the Dolphin's Back:
    5121.
Aristocratic Lovers: 3888.
Arithmetic: 4193.
Arizona Midnight: 5469.
Ark 47, Plow Spire: 2597.
Arkansas Traveller: 5697.
Arlington: 3653.
Arm and Arm: 148.
Arm Wrestling with My Father:
    1407.
The Armadillo: 459, 2711.
Armageddon: 1330.
The Armchair Philosopher:
    1133.
Arming: 3730.
Arms spread: 3548, 4548.
Around the World: 4611.
Arqueologia Divina: 1606.
Arráncame la piel para
    sentirme tuyo: 3706.
Arrival: 260, 2294.
The Arrival of the Future:
    1569.
The Arriviste: 2663.
The Arrow: 3062.
Arrowhead: 4884.
An Arrowhead from the Ancient
    Battlefield of Ch'ang-
    P'ing: 261, 3034.
Ars Poetica: 4423, 4773, 5263.
Arsenio: 3567, 4476.
Arson: 1646.
Art & Youth: 2775.
The Art of Dying: 204, 1514.
The Art of Erasure: 2604.
The Art of Imitation: 4390.
The Art of Love: 5441.
An Art of Remoteness: 5687.
The Art Student at the
    Reformatory: 5317.
Arte Poetica: 1056, 1842.
Artesana de Sueños: 99.
Arthrocious (I): 57, 4577.
Arthrocious (II): 57, 4577.
Articulation & Class: 2806.
Artificial Devices: 5658.

Artificial Lights: 3099.
The Artificial Waterfall and
    Woods Scene Clock: 5511.
The Artist: 632.
Artist: 4415.
The Artist As Historian: 103.
Artists: 124.
The Artists' House: 2526,
    3844, 4652.
The Artist's Intention: 4868.
Arts & Sciences: 1929.
As a Fragment, Fourteen Years:
    1544.
As a shadow brings down the
    dark: 4012.
As boring congressmen
    discussed energy: 3073.
As Gentle As a Lamb: 5362.
As I move away from the Bunsen
    burner: 3548, 4548.
As I Open a Window in Oregon,
    a Grasshopper Jumps on My
    Thumb: 3847.
As I Walk I Turn over Leaves:
    426.
As If a Rain: 5523.
As If, after a Departure:
    2466.
As If It Never Belonged Here:
    4650.
As if the cardinal: 4960.
As Is: 4730.
As Myself, Dulled: 1001.
As Slow Cattle Revolve: 2317.
As Sweet As Water: 4650.
As the Apparition Walked: 721.
As the dawn edges: 3273.
As the Night of Suffering
    Ends: 2105, 3744.
As the Train Approaches: 4005.
As Your Car Approaches: 5477.
Ascension: 3523.
Ascension Day: 346.
Aschenputtel's Sisters: 4210.
Ash: 30, 1127.
Ash Like Sand Like the People:
    5371.
Ash Wednesday Again: 1671.
Ashes: 3730.
Asheville: 3371.
The Ashtray: 846.
Asia: 1697, 3463.
Asiatic Day-Flower: 1651.
Ask a Marine: 5371.
Ask me no questions I'll still
    tell you lies: 2157.
Asking the Moon: 2529.
Asking Too Much: 4470.
Assassin: 2067.
The Assassin: 4247.
Assassin: 4579.
Assassinated on the Street:
    421, 468, 735, 1196.
Assassination of Simonetta
    Vespucci: 142, 4541.
Assholes: 420.

Assignation: 4318.
Assignment: Maureen Owen:
  3515.
Assimilation: 1200.
Assumer l'ogive de ma main:
  979.
Assumptions: 1474.
Astoria Boulevard: 1898.
Astronomy: 4565.
Astrophil and Stella: 4756.
Asylum: 5074.
At 3 A.M: 1688.
At 5th & Howard: 497.
At 47: 3114.
At a Certain Table in a Bar:
  5553.
At a distance is better: 2873.
At a Fortress in India: 4247.
At a Performance of
  Tomaszewski's Knights of
  King Arthur: 3143.
At a Quarter to Eight in the
  Morning: 1308, 3925.
At a Screening of Gance's
  'Napoleon': Arts Theatre,
  Cambridge: 3299.
At an Al Purdy Poetry Reading:
  2592.
At Bessemer: 3014.
At Billings' Bridge Graveyard:
  449.
At Bisla his castle: 4611.
At Booth's Grave: 3181.
At Brunch We Entertain the
  Notion of the Perfect Place
  to Live: 4418.
At Camino: 4707.
At Changmen Palace: 2119,
  3035.
At Damariscotta Mills: 2108.
At daybreak: 3548, 4548.
At Dusk: 2590.
At Easter: 346.
At El Patio the Workers
  Fraternize: 5736.
At Eleven My Son's Still
  Awake: 3087.
At Fenway: 3652.
At Home: 2840.
At last, the mocking bird
  stops: 5040.
At Montale's Grave: 1790.
At Morning: 4354.
At My Desk: 3975.
At Newton's Birthday party:
  4288.
At Night: 2268, 2838.
At Night on the Shore: 1428,
  2026, 4899.
At North Farm: 203, 203.
At Penobscot Bay, Maine: 2436.
At Peredelkino with Pasternak,
  1936: 140.
At Pool: 3348.
At Random: 4583.
At that from which the tide

pool fills: 1550.
At the Bar: 3423.
At the Cathedral of St. Isaac
  in Leningrad: 3207.
At the Cottage of Sidney
  Lanier: 5557.
At the Country Farm: 5092.
At the Country Wedding: 188.
At the Crematorium, on the
  Edge of History: 5494.
At the Drought's Height: 4576.
At the End: 265, 1293.
At the End of the Hunt: 1249.
At the Fishhouses: 459.
At the Grave of Ezra Pound:
  5626.
At the Grave of Willa Cather:
  2859.
At the Iron Works: 483.
At the Kirkwood Clock Shop:
  4974.
At the Koin-o-Kleen: 1654.
At the Lawn Party: 2848.
At the Monastery of the Cross:
  3313.
At the Old Dancing School:
  112.
At the Piano: 752.
At the Place of the Skull:
  1249.
At the Pool: 4083.
At the Red Fox: 2515.
At the Roman Ruins Vaison,
  France: 5255.
At the Singles Social: 5314.
At the Sound: 1550.
At the Sources: 2485, 4646.
At the Theater--the Rush for
  Seats: 2510.
At the Tire Fire at the
  Landfill: 2240.
At the Town Dump: 2725.
At the University of
  Melancholy: 1821.
At the Vision Center: 3486.
At the Winter Solstice: 1037.
At the Zoo: 2072.
At the Zoo: Albino Tiger:
  2533.
At This Instant All Over
  America: 1758.
At Wolf Creek Pass, Colorado:
  2878.
At Woolworth's in Wyalusing:
  2405.
At World's End: 1298, 2718.
At Yalta: 5074.
At Your Father's Funeral:
  1330.
Atlanta Poem #1: 3812.
Atlanta Poem #2: 3812.
An Atlantiad: 1603.
Atlantic City 1939: 2875.
Atlantic City: 4376, 5182,
  5497.
Atlantide City: 2290, 3863.

Atlas of Oregon: 1276.
The Atom Bomb Will Cure My
   Impotence: 2230.
Atom Dead: 3985.
Atomic Sunset: 1881.
Atoms: 4879.
Atrasgos: 3670.
Atropos, Who Carried 'The
   Abhorred Shears': 3078.
An Attaché Case: 1569.
An Attack of the Heart: 5197.
The Attack of the Zombie
   Poets: 751.
Attendant Lord: 4947.
Attending a Young Man Resting
   beside a Stream: Twilight
   Image of a Japanese Scroll:
   789.
The Attic: 3534, 5148.
Attics of Useful Artifacts:
   488.
Au Sommet de la Nuit: 341,
   2797.
Aubade: 1061, 2010, 5551.
Aubade for Mothers: 5709.
Aubade to Hidden Lovers: Ode
   to Hans Arp: 5270.
Auction Day: August, 1979:
   4735.
Auden: 3869.
Auden Aetat XX, LX: 4920.
Audition: 3009.
Audubon's Shrews: 4599.
Auguries and Hijinks: 4998.
August 2, 1981: 1182.
August 6: 4910.
August 31 et Seq: 4605.
August 1919 Lamenting Dr.
   Ishimaru's Death: 3548,
   4548.
August 1953: 872.
August and a Pond: 1475.
August: Blues: 5026.
August in New York City: 5592.
August in the Straits: 3091.
August Is Not a Month: 4447.
August, Los Angeles, Lullaby:
   3695.
August on Sourdough, a Visit
   from Dick Brewer: 4867.
August Tableau, Burnt Coat
   Head: 5263.
Auld Acquaintance: 1323.
Aunt Charlotte Said: 4941.
Aunt Jenny Quotes: 1912.
Aunt Ritta: 3110.
Aunt Wilhelmina at the Family
   Reunion: 5215.
Aura: 3498.
The Aurignacian Summation:
   1541.
Aurora: 3539.
Ausência: 806.
Austin Creek: 3789.
Austin's Book of Lists
   (Partial Contents): 5037.

Australian Epiphany: 3052.
The Author Receiveth Her First
   Lousy Review: 3372.
Autobiographia, 3: 4488.
Autobiography: 5208.
Autobiography Concluding in
   Seance: 83.
Automne: 3932.
The Autopsy: 5079.
Autumn: 606, 896, 2714.
Autumn 1980: 2081.
Autumn after a Lean Year:
   3046.
The Autumn Deer: 5210.
An Autumn Field: 5128.
Autumn Garden: 785, 5697.
Autumn in Rome: 57, 4577.
Autumn Lament: 1647.
Autumn Leaves: 702.
Autumn Maneuver: 127, 233.
Autumn, Mist: 2446.
Autumn of the Masks: 55, 3465,
   5233.
Autumn Villanelle: 1509.
Autumnal: 2108.
Autumnal Equinox: 5492.
Autumn's End: 504, 4320.
Avenue of the Americas: 4180.
Avenues in Bloom: 2774.
Averse: 2496.
The Aviary: 1751.
Aviary: 4945.
Aviation: 1779.
Avilov Writes to Chekhov:
   1274.
Avocado: 1521.
Avoir l'Apprenti dans le
   Soleil: 3703.
Awake: 1373.
Awake unto Me: 2811.
Awakening: 282.
The Awakening: 1679, 1999,
   4091.
Awakening from the Deep: 3640.
Away: 2996.
Away from the Game: 231.
Away with Boards: 2234.
Awesome: 2120.
AWOL: 5042.
The Axe: 1063.
Axe: 3297.
Ayer: 3615.
Azaleas: 2948.
Aztec Tanka: 2327.
Azubah Nye: 1909.
B Is for Beast: 1645.
Baba Jedza: 2799, 2799.
Babies: 1779, 3091.
Babilonia está cerca: 1316.
Babushka: 932.
Baby Angels: 2622.
Baby Film Review: 4833.
Babylon: 827, 830, 2276.
Babysitter: 2171.
Bachelor Party: 381.
Bachelor's Wives: 2010.

Baybrook: 817.
Be Sociable: 3651.
Be Specific, Young Man: 1594.
Bea and Orv, Orv and Bea:
3086.
The Beach: 2019, 3457, 3457.
Beachcomber: 1136.
Beached Whale: 1550.
The Beached Whale: Wellfleet,
Massachusetts, 1840: 725.
Beachplums: 1797.
Beacon Street: 3472.
Bead of dew: 3635.
Beans and Tortilla: 4368.
The Bear: 3560.
The Bear of Sleep Growls All
Night: 4061.
Bear Spell: 1715.
Bearing Investigation: 4705.
Bears: 3040.
Beasts: 3499.
The Beating: 2451.
Beating a Dead Horse: 3762.
A Beautiful Day: 230.
Beautiful Is Hard: 4873.
Beauty: 2881.
Beauty and the Beast: 149,
5367.
Beauty of the flower dust:
2641.
Beauty Will Be: 3716.
Beaver: 5602.
The Beaver Pond: Cause and
Effect: 5218.
The Bebop Ghosts: 3157.
Because: 3188.
Because sparklingly: 3548,
4548.
Because the flames: 3548,
4548.
Because You Will Not Let Me
Say I Will Love You
Forever: 2451.
Because Your Body Gives Me
Peace and Light: 2331.
Becoming: 289, 806.
Bed: 4771.
Bed of Stones: 2040.
Bedouin Wind: 3176.
Bedtime Stories: 2986.
Bedtime Story: 2870, 3371.
Bee Hive in Early December:
2449.
The Bee Keeper: 5675.
Bee Muse: 3638.
Beepbeepbeepbee   eep: 2267.
Bees and Their Problems: 782.
Beetle: 1981.
Beetle Picking: 357.
Before: 4447.
Before and After: 5215.
Before Dawn: 4517.
Before Divorce: 1351.
Before Names of Things: 605.
Before Nightfall: 741.
The Before People: 3416.

Before the Beginning: 179.
Before the Revolution: 4895.
Before the Stationery Store in
the Mall Opens: 3047.
Before Those Few Light Kisses:
2526, 3844, 4652.
Before We Move into Aunt
Harriet's House: 2436.
The Beggar on the Ground:
4368.
The Beggars: 4095.
Beggarweed: 4967.
The Beginning: 1157.
Beginning: 4010.
The Beginning of the
Beginning: 631.
Beginnings: 34, 1731.
Begin's Autumn after the Late
Massacre, 1982: 4001.
Begonia: 2774.
Behavior Modification: 1488.
Behind Mount Temple: 1715.
Behind the Shutters: 232,
4614.
Behind the Stone: 1745.
Being Remembered: 4390.
Being Young: 485.
Beings of the Womb: 1915.
Beirut Massacre: 3924.
Belfast: 2419.
The Belief in Progress: 4142.
Belinda Fuller: 1955.
The Bell Is Struck: 2145.
The Bell System: 5436.
Belladonna: 1641, 1826.
Belle du Jour: 3836.
Bells: 1281, 3501.
The Bells of Orvieto: 3974,
4590.
The Bells of Saint Simon:
4421.
Belly Stove: 1057.
Belongings: 4376.
Beloved of the Gods: 1790,
3567.
Below Is What He Said That
Troubles Me: 5573.
Below Keats' Room, Early
Morning: 2108.
Below the Sound: 3055.
Ben Uyandim Bir Ask Demekti Bu
Dunyada: 405.
Ben W: 4571.
Beneath the Surface: 5405.
Beneath the Veneer: 853.
Benediction: 114, 1664, 3734,
5005.
Bennett Halkett: 4898.
Benzedrine Music: 2230.
Bequest: 3136.
Bergamot: 5128.
Berkeley: Summer, 1965: 4611.
Berkeley Where Anything Can
Happen: 178.
The Berlin Masque: 2249.
Berlin Metro: 3843.

The Berries: 2300, 2300.
Beside the Highway: 2760.
Beside the Riverrun: 4424.
El Beso: 4400.
The Best Dance Hall in Iuka,
    Mississippi: 2599.
The Best Days: 1442.
The Best Poem: 2837.
The Best Thing My Father Did
    Was Lie: 2375.
The Best Watermelon Since the
    First World War: 933.
Bestiary: 3853, 4183.
A Bestiary: 4742.
The Bestowal: 2215.
The Bet: Horse in Motion:
    1665.
Bete Noire: 2117.
Bête Noire: 2616.
The Bethlehem Birth: 1330.
Betrayal: 880.
Betrothal: 5592.
Better: 2341.
Better Poems and Gardens:
    2317.
Better Things to Do: 2628.
Between Classes: 3682.
Between Earth and Elsewhere:
    Song of the Last Survivor:
    4412.
Between Friends: 2784.
Between Nehalem and Manzanita –
    – Oregon Coast, 1983: 298.
Between Seasons: 642, 4963.
Between Talcy and Met: 3856.
Between the Acts: 3124.
Between the Lover and the
    Beloved How Many Distances
    and Legends Spell the
    Circle to Be Unbroken: 178.
Between the Rivers: 845.
Between Walls: 5622.
Between Words: 4903.
Beware of the Meek: 2321.
Beyond the Garden: 3559.
Beyond the Oubliette: 5553.
Beyond Words: 2418.
Bhang Bhang: 3454.
Bible Bob Responds to a Jesus
    Honker: 3082.
Bible Quilt, Circa 1900: 2635.
Bible Sonnet I: 609.
Bicycle: 3449.
Biddulph's Grove: 2069.
Big Bang: 5519.
Big Cars: 3416.
Big Dogs: 3072.
Big Eyes: 383.
The Big H: 4200.
The Big Money: 731.
Big Poppy: 2443.
Big Red Chronology: 5432.
Big Shoulders Does It Again:
    3009.
Big Talk: 3682.
Big Top: 1926.

Big turnaround in the economy:
    4200.
Bigfoot: 1738.
The Biggest Attraction: 5251.
The Bigmouth Bass: 2840.
Bilitis: 3113, 3113, 3117.
Bill: 208.
Bill J: 4571.
Bill of Divorcement: 1932.
Bill, Wyoming: 3473.
Billy in the Street: His Wife
    Considers Her Plight: 682.
Billy the Kid: 5132, 5701.
Biochips: 1743.
Biografia de un Poeta: 3296.
Biographical Note: 4751.
Biographies: 3243.
Biography: 422, 620, 3016.
A Biography: 1163.
The Biology Lab: 2302.
Biorhythm: 4933.
Birch Bark: 3874.
Birches: 1773.
Bird: 3129.
A Bird: 907, 3829.
Bird Dreams: 4647.
Bird Fish Birds: 2400.
Bird Island, Grey Light: 5047.
Bird Songs: 2068.
The Bird Woman and I: 5658.
Birding in Mt. Auburn
    Cemetery: 1543.
Birding the Battle of Attu:
    4842.
Birds: 2560, 3099, 5320.
The Birds: 5094.
Birds at Night: 651.
The Bird's Day: 1550.
The Birds in Paradise: 602.
Birds in the Garden: 714.
The Birds Know: 692.
A Bird's Life: 5108.
Birds of Fire: 3065.
Birds That Come from Trees:
    952.
Birth: 2463.
A Birth and a Death: 3573.
Birth of the Baptist: 1306.
Birth of the Bear Clan: 3072.
The Birth of Time: 92.
The Birthday: 2680.
Birthday: 2838, 4368, 5648.
Birthday Gift: 1434.
Birthday Poem: 3869.
Birthday Star Atlas: 4771.
Birthday: The Water Pump:
    1241.
Birthmarks: 1655.
Birthright: 5673.
Birth's Obituary: 3868.
Bite Down on the Azalea: 4515.
Bitter Night: 158, 4447.
Black Aggression: 4180.
Black and White and Red: 2517.
Black Animal Dependency: 3647,
    3891.

Blue Willow China: 4967.
Blueberry Juice: 1672.
Blueprint of St. Francis:
  2067.
Blue's Baby: 4005.
Blues for December 21st: 1869.
Blues for Old Dogs: 5771.
Blues Outlaw: 3554.
The Bluesman: 783.
Bluffing Your Way through an
  Exam: 1543.
Blunt Trauma: 3205.
Blurred Impression: 112.
A Boat: 4568.
Boat: 4747.
Boat near the Capo Miseno:
  4001.
The Boat People: 5090.
Boat Ride: 1794, 1794.
Boating Incident: 251.
Boats on the River, Party
  Lights: 2482.
Boaz Pretends Again to Sleep:
  3491.
Bob: 3700.
Bob--Get New Finance Accordian-
  -Allen: 4427.
Bob Hosey Is Dead: 1242.
Bobby Sands Is Dead: 3047.
Bodega Tides: 5510.
Bodies Terrestrial: 5673.
The Body: 2997.
The Body Casts Aside Its Vest
  and Sings: 1558.
Body, Earth, Water: 3295.
Body Is Man's Best Friend:
  1877.
A Body Is Man's Best Friend:
  4530.
Body Language: 2168, 4233,
  4245.
Body My Familiar: 4909.
Body of Water: 4622.
The Body Poetic: 1680.
The Body Politic: 3861.
The Body Private: 3328.
Body Surfing: 39, 1696.
The Body Theory: 1929.
BOGG: 5000.
Boiling Up the Dead: 2699.
Le Bois Noir: 341.
Boliche: 16.
Bologna, November 1978: 517.
Bomb Fragment: 4716.
The Bomb under Big Boy's Butt:
  958.
Bombed: 1129.
The Bomber's Misgiving: 5348.
Le Bon Disciple: 5370.
Bonding: 3812.
Bones: 2219, 4051, 4788.
Bones and Jewels: 3562.
Bones in the Woods: 2604.
Boniato Jail: Account of a
  Massacre: 4331, 5334.
Bonnard: 3482.

Bonsai Growers: 975.
Book about Rembrandt: 1929.
Book Fair/The Topic: 1929.
The Book of Days: 2007.
Book of Mercy: 998.
A Book of Spells: 728.
Book of the Jungle: 2087.
The Book of the Ocean to
  Cynthia: 4737.
The Book of Water: 2705.
Bookcase: 1122.
Bookkeeper's Son: 4555.
Books by Nobody: 5246.
Boom Town: 712.
Boomerang: 978.
Boor: 711.
Bootleg Coal: 2851.
Borders: 1543.
Boredom: 57, 4577.
Borges: 5050.
Borinqueñita: 5237.
Borrowing Dusk: 4045.
Böses Spiel: 590.
Boston 1.12.70: 816.
The Boston Suitcoat: 3922.
Both of Me: 4852.
The Bottle: 3050.
Bottleships: 1860.
The Bottom Line: 5347.
Bound Cupid sea washed: 2422.
Bounty: 5096.
Bouquet: 3468.
A Bouquet for Michelle: 4816.
Bout with Burning: 3516.
Bow Down: 2066.
Bowhead: 1568.
Bowing to the Empress: 3859.
The Bowl of Roses: 4320, 4864.
Bowl with Splatter-Painted
  Hand: 971.
Bowls of Fruit & Rabbits:
  5255.
Box Love: 1904.
The Boxer and the Queen of
  Hearts: 2953.
Boy: 1299.
A Boy Adds Black Vultures to
  His Life-List: 1071.
Boy and Car: 5648.
A boy came down each fine
  green hill in jumps: 3073.
Boy in a Polythelene Bag:
  4452.
The Boy in Emergency: 2724.
Boy in Kayak: 5470.
The Boy in the Mirror: 1346.
The Boy, the Bird, and the
  Window: 2702.
The boy with pimples: 4387.
Boys: 272.
Boys' Day: 3120.
Boys Throwing Rocks at a
  Train: 2896.
Bracing air: 3981.
Brahe at Uraniborg: 3814.
A Brahman's Son: 2433, 3779.

Braiding Rugs: 5092.
The Brain: 4480.
Brambles, Rocks, Low-lying
Trees: 4085.
The Branch: 683.
Branches Tangling: 3047.
Brand Loyalty: 4594.
Brandeburgo 1526: 266.
Braque Said: 3577.
Brass Angel: 2535.
Brass Pickers: 5371.
Brave Poets: 3733.
Bravura: 5071.
The Brazilian Navy: 2498.
The Breach of Or: 3996.
Bread and Apples: 3654.
Bread and Fire: 5592.
Break-in on Old Bill: 208.
The Break Up: 4046.
The Breakdown: 2784.
Breakfast: 1628, 2787, 4152.
Breakfast Piece: 1543.
Breakfast Special at the
Castle View: 3418.
Breakfast Station: 3138.
The Breakfast Table, August 5,
1945: 3078.
Breaking: 2529, 4274.
Breaking Away: 4181.
Breaking the Rock Down: 148.
Breakthrough: 5208.
Breakwater: the headlands
above Mendocino: 4611.
Breast-feeding: 2787.
Breath: 1562, 1999, 3295,
5625.
Breeze: 2259.
Breve Carta de Amor y
Despedida: 363.
The Brick: 3815.
The Brickmen: 1053.
The Bride Wore Grey: 1341.
Bridge: 682, 4480.
The Bridge: 2954.
The Bridge of Breasts: 57,
5094.
Bridge to Greenville, Nass
Valley: 5692.
Bridges: 3372.
Bridgett's: 2686.
Bridled: 3920.
Brief Encounter: 1253.
A Brief Exercise in
Megalomania: 787.
Briefing: 2006, 2520.
Bright-Eyed Shining Star:
1427.
Bright Leaf: 5396.
Bring It with You: 5255.
Bring them all back to life:
203.
Bringing Bread: 2842.
Bringing in the Barbarians:
5109.
Britomart Writes from
Malecasta's Castle: 2761.

Britons Leaving France: 4411.
Broken Down in Mud Guard
Montana, 3 AM: 4110.
Broken Dreams: 2324.
A Broken Glass: 384.
Broken Glass: 2732.
Broken Mirror: 34.
Broken Oar: 4976.
The Broken Pianola(for Heitor
Villa-Lobos): 2072.
Broken Prairie: 2392.
Broken Rainbow: 4933.
A Broken Shutter in the Wind:
2131.
Broken Tantra: 5156.
The Bronx: 3539.
Bronze: 3461.
Brooding: 1790, 3567.
The Brook: 2881.
The Brook That Flowed from the
Mountain: 245.
Brooklyn, 2 A.M: 1562.
Brother Blood: 5458.
Brother Plans to Move, 1983:
1348.
A Brother Returned: 2566.
Brother to Brother: 3923.
The Brown of Longing: 5274.
Bru Mike: 4475.
Bruges: 1016.
Bruja: 3594.
Brujería: 1164.
Bruno Caruso, Etcher: 57,
4577.
Brunt H: 5383.
Brute affirmation: 2422.
Bryony: 5501.
Bubbles and Pins: 4160.
Bucharest: 2489.
Buck: 5510.
Buck Creek Road: 3954.
Bucoliques en Pamphylie: 3113,
3117.
Budapest: 2805.
Budapest, March 1928: The
Genius of Friendship: 5009.
Buddha Hall with Fog and
Bride: 4494.
Buddha in the Limelight: 106.
A budding country doctor:
3073.
Buddy: 4001.
Buen Dia: 2904.
Buffalo Dance: 3554.
The Buffalo Waiting Room:
4247.
Buffalofish: 5639.
El Bufon de Madera: 3281.
Buick: 2776.
Building: 1177, 3256.
Building a Fire in Deep
Winter: 4452.
Building Flaws: 4998.
The Building of the Trophy:
4412.
Building Pigpens: 2960.

Calm Jazz Sea: 299.
Caltrop: 2513.
Calvin Coolidge Asleep: 310.
Camaradas del sueño, os
   reconozco: 3057.
The Camas Meadow War: 4195.
Cambodia: 1613.
Camel in the Snow: 5523.
The Camellia Grill: 1246.
Camels Led by an Angel: 92.
Camera Angle: 4362.
Cameras: 5315.
Caminante: 2544.
Caminante Adjunto: 984.
Campaign Season: 3456.
El Campesino: 1026.
Campo de'Fiori: 57, 4577.
A Canadian Tourist Flies to
   St. Paul on Thanksgiving
   Weekend in Search of Great
   Bargains: 4828.
Canción de Placer: 1469.
Cancion de Siempre: 1082.
Cancionero del Perro Muerto:
   3615.
Canciones sin Su Música:
   4646, 5137.
Candy Cane in July: 146.
Canetops: 4134.
Canicula di Anna: What Do We
   Have Here?: 840.
Canis, A Knowledge of: 4390.
The Cannon: 1902.
Cannon Fire: 2526, 3844, 4652.
Canoe in the Morning: 5773.
Canoeing on the Loxahatchee:
   5519.
Cansancio: 5335, 5335.
Can't stop the nuclear arms
   race now: 4200.
Canto: 1888.
Canto a Cesar Vallejo: 99, 99.
Canto al Nuevo Tiempo: 374.
Canto Popular: 95.
Canto Sexto: 1529, 3928.
Cantos al Sortilegio de la
   Imaginacion: 4665.
Canzone: 5424.
Caos: 3708.
Capability Brown in the
   Tropics: 3091.
Cape Breton, N.S: 3215.
A Cape of Wild Flies: 235.
Cape of Wild Flies: 1541.
The Capitol of Washing
   Machines: 2840.
Capitular: 4459.
The Captain Learns Doubt: 975.
Captain Norman Knight: 922.
Captions/Portraits: 5507.
Captions/Thoughtscapes,
   Variation 1: 5507.
Car Pool: 1249.
Car Radio: 1499.
Cara o Cruz? Aguila o Sol?:
   1608.

Card Island or Cod Island?:
   1808.
Cardiac Arrest: 939.
Cardinal and Lilies: 449.
Cardinal's Rocks, Marblehead:
   3979.
Cardiophobia: 1483.
Care of the Hand: 3079.
The Caretaker: 5615.
The Caretaker's Daughter:
   1543.
Carib Nocturne: 2759.
Carillon for Cambridge Women:
   378.
Caring: 1176.
Carl Sandburg in Burbank:
   5674.
Carlitos Gardel: 316.
Carlo Quattrucci Paints the
   Botanic Gardens: 57, 4577.
Carnation, Lily, Lily, Rose:
   5673.
The Carney Boy: 3092.
The Carney King: 3092.
Carnies: 78.
Carnival: 3577.
Carnival Glass: 5606.
Carnival: Inside the Tent:
   5371.
Carnival: On the Edge of Town:
   5371.
Carol after Christmas: 3306.
Carolina Moon 6/4: 2850.
Carolyn: 4611.
Carp: 3160, 5356.
Carp Lay: 5516.
The Carpenter Gathers the
   Light: 2293.
The Carpenter's Woman: 5180.
Carpentry: 2822.
Carpinteria: 4358.
Carpool: 669.
Carrying Pain: 1954.
The Cars: 668.
Carta a los Hispanos: 5309,
   5309.
Carta a los Jovenes Poetas
   Puertorriqueños: 4178.
Carta de Adios a Mi Amor:
   4223.
Las Cartas de Amor de Mi
   Abuela: 1115, 5753.
Cartas para Seguir con la
   Vida: 3598.
The Carter House in Franklin,
   Tennessee: 3931.
The Cartographers: 85.
Cartographer's Nightmare:
   1512.
Cartographies: 2415.
Cartography: 2184.
Cartography of the Subtle
   Heart: 1102.
Carving the Circle: 4272.
Una Casa Nueva: 174.
Cascade: 258, 2631.

Definitive Things: 383.
Deflections: 1480.
Defoliated: 3989.
Deja Que Te Cante, Madre:
   2565.
Deja Vu: 96.
Déjà Vu: 1924.
Del Regreso: 4348.
Delaying: 1589.
The Delegates: 5687.
Delete Whatever Inapplicable:
   1529, 2031, 4109.
Deletions: 23.
Delfina Flores and Her Niece
   Modesta: 3618.
The Delight Song of Tsoai-
   Talee: 3560.
Deliverance: 1943.
Delivery: 1929.
Delivery Boy: 989.
The Delta at Sunset: 872.
Dementia Colander: 5763.
Demise of the Thunderstorms on
   the Eighth: 2053.
Democracy Freedom: 978.
The Democrats: 753.
Demolition Derby: 4350.
Demonstration: 262, 4765,
   5772.
Denali: 4673.
Denial: 2784.
Dennis: 4753.
Denver/NCTE 1983: 5672.
Departing from 28th Street:
   2095.
The Department: 2039.
Departure: 402, 2476, 3749.
Departure of a Friend: 5575.
Departures: 3975.
Departure's Girlfriend: 3463.
The Deposition: 1657.
Depot: 4526, 5371.
Depression: 1299.
Depression in Recession: 5690.
Derailment: 3666.
The Derelict: 4630.
Derivation: 3685.
Des cris soyeux: 979.
Desahuciados: 5238.
Los Desastres de la Guerra:
   2618.
Descartes at Daybreak: 3293.
Descending into the Moscow
   Metro: 5564.
The Descent: 432.
Descent: 1175, 5648, 5648.
Descent into the Decent: 3405.
The Descent of Killimanjaro:
   5585.
Descent under the Sea: 349,
   3863.
Describing the Middle Ages:
   3368.
Description: 2750.
Descriptions of the Falling
   Snow: 752, 752.

Desde a Aurora: 136.
Desde el día gigante de tu
   ausencia: 5212.
Desde mí hasta mí: 4337.
Desert Days: 3245.
Desert Highway: 4830.
Desert Ice: 3633.
Desert Indigestion: 3924.
Desert Music: 5648.
The Desert Song: 5279.
Desert Water: 2214.
Deserting the Town: 5348.
Desertions: 2925.
Desilusion: 2573.
Desilusion para Ruben Dario:
   3602.
Desire: 1461, 3655, 3996,
   4903, 4939.
Desire Lies Down on the Quiet
   Lake of the Memory: 3541.
Desires of Here and There:
   2371.
The Desk: 559, 2037.
Despair: 516, 1196.
Destruction: 2784.
The Detachable Man: 1651.
Details: 338.
Details from a Garden: 5074.
Detasseling Corn: 1411.
Detention is called 'to await
   a review': 152, 2385.
Deterioration: 1756, 4335.
Determination: 4806.
Detonation Simile: 2649.
Deus: 806.
Deuterium Sonnet for a
   Cassette-Recorder: 751.
Devastated: 5281.
Devotions: 5702.
Deya: 3934.
The Dhow: 5038.
Di Pagani: 5389.
El Dia de la Ira: 1313.
Dialoge: 1818.
Dialysis: 2073.
The Diamond Bessie Suite:
   3372.
The Diamond Persona: 1413.
Diana Rigg: 5486.
Diane Arbus: Ground Glass:
   4727.
Diaphragm: 2123.
Diaria Agonia: 4117.
The Diary: 932.
Diary, 14th Entry: 648.
Diary Entries of Jochebed
   Sloan, Wife of Lt. Simon
   Sloan, Just before a
   Massacre: 4346.
Dias de los Padres en Chapel
   Hill: 4019.
Dicen que estuvieron contigo y
   te ayudaban a ir: 930.
Dichotomy: 5468.
Diciendo lo Indecible: 354.
Dickinson: 1020.

Dusk and After: 4918.
Dusk: Mallards on the Charles River: 503.
Dust: 204, 2302, 2778, 3752.
Dust Bowl #2: 671.
Dust Storm: 3950.
Dustbunnies: 3454.
A Dusty Sunday: 5084.
Dutch Painting: 578, 2478, 3872.
Dwelling: 5529.
Dying: 560.
The Dying Expatriate: 4130.
A dying Race: 4632.
Dysrhythmia: 4144, 5483.
E. A. Robinson: 155.
E.C.T: 469.
E = mc^2: 4288.
E só então sai das minhas trevas: 142.
Each Bird Walking: 1794.
Each Morning, and Each Morning Again: 483.
Each Thing in Time Finds: 1990.
Each Winter: 4372.
Each Year: 3735.
The Eager Interpreter: 1870.
The Eagle Arcane: 2336.
Eagle Crossing, July 1975: 5742.
The Eagle Flies: 196.
Earhart Flies through the Monsoon: 377.
Earlee Wintr Song in th Forest: 462.
Early: 1929.
Early April: 5054.
Early Arrival: 1141.
Early California Morning: 4611.
Early Duty: 3759.
Early Images of Heaven: 3853.
The Early Moon: 135.
Early Morning: 1916, 3765.
Early Poems in Tanka Form: 3548, 4548.
Early Signs: 3972.
Early Traders in Southern China: 128.
Early Views of Rio, Passion, Night: 3618.
Early Waking: 5789.
An Early Walk: 3813.
Earning a Living: 5094.
Earth, Air, Water: 3504.
The Earth As We Know It: 2567.
Earth-Body, Light-Body: 1102.
Earth Fragrance: 4139, 4602, 5374, 5420.
Earth Place: 4412.
Earth Rumour: 2504.
Earth Song LIX: 558.
The Earth Was Tepid and the Moon Was Dark: 503.
Earthquake Weather: 4351.

Ease: 4909.
East Liberty, Mississippi: 5031.
East Neuk Assizes: 3426.
East Tennessee Landscape: 2624.
Easter 1964: 2217.
Easter 1983: 240.
The Easter House: 2232.
Easter Landscape: 4611.
Easter Sunday: 5219.
Easter Traffic Jam, San Salvador: 1092.
Easter Week: 1322.
Easter Week: Vermont: 5211.
Easter-Wings: 2275.
Eastern Standard Time: 1892.
An Easy Death: 699.
Easy Desktop Human Rights Policy for Bureaucrats of the U.S. State Dept: 1716.
Eating: 1870.
Eating the Fruit: 502.
Eating Your Lasagna: 1064.
Eavesdropper: 3747.
The Eavesdropper: 5491.
Ebb Tide: 768.
Echo: 50, 140.
Echocardiogram: 4613.
Echoes of Arrival: 3697.
Echoes of Great Cavities: 1149, 1255.
The Eclectic Chair: 1558.
Eclipse: 5181, 5566.
Economic Alchemy: 1915.
Economics: 242, 2219.
The Economy of Use: 4779.
Edades: 4199.
Eden: 4594.
The Edge of My Speech: 932.
Edges: 3352, 5538, 5625.
Edible Heart: 4092.
Edipo y la Esfinge: 2062.
Edison Winter Home, Fort Myers: 4247.
Edna: 2779.
Eduardo Mondlane: 2216.
La Educacion Sentimental: 3793.
Education: 523, 5673.
Edvard Munch: 434.
Edward: 3299.
The Edwardian Garden: 2501.
Eerie: 721.
Effects of Alcohol: 2685.
Eftsoon: 5473.
The Egg: 1697, 3463.
Eggs: 30.
The Egoless Poet: 3261.
Egon Schiele's Self Portraits: 2035.
Egyptian Chorus: 1361.
The Egyptians: 4480.
Eight Blackfeet: 5099.
Eight O:Clock: 2498.
The Eighth Limerick: 5429.

Erie: 1341.
Erie Plain: 3591.
Eroica: 3527.
Eros has my uprooted wits
    (Sappho 47): 4162, 4542.
Eros makes me feel weak in the
    knees (Sappho 130): 4162,
    4542.
Eros Turannos: 4367.
Erosion: 5201.
Errante en la Noche: 5386.
Ersatz Dying: 4233.
Es Bueno: 5363.
Es como fabricar: 3669.
Escape: 702, 3721, 4445.
Escape: A Grande Ronde
    Fantasy: 5746.
O Escorpião ea Valsinha:
    806.
Escort: 1956.
Esos Dias de Lluvia: 4532.
An Esp from Many at a Concert:
    3721.
Espantapajaros: 5380.
Une Espece Mourante: The
    Internationals: 2579.
Esperanza, August 1983: 5060.
An Essay in Political Science:
    2617.
Essay on Elements: 1380.
Essay on the Personal: 1434.
Esse: 3530, 4084.
The Essentials of Poetry:
    1527.
Esta Obsesion del Verso: 3570.
Establishment poet sits in his
    cubicle: 4200.
Estacion 3: 3433.
Estación de Buses: 1532.
Este Corazon: 4401.
Este Tiempo Que Me Lleva:
    1357.
Esteli: 65, 173, 1405.
Esterville Meteorite: 5045.
Esto: 5598.
Estrangement in Athens: 1155.
Estudios Innecesarios: 1010.
Et s'illuminèrent les grands
    pas bleus: 979.
Etait-ce une neige de fleurs:
    1708.
The Eternal Husband: 721.
Eternal Walls: 910, 2571,
    2572.
Eternidad con el Recuerdo:
    224.
Eternity Blues: 839.
Ethel Rosenberg: A Sestina:
    1201.
The Ethics of Altruism in
    Altoona: 839.
Ethnic Diagnosis: 858.
Etienne Brule: 3814.
The Etymology of You: Oh:
    3841.
Eulogy for a Friend Killed

near Da Nang: 4850.
Eulogy to W. H. Auden: 5423.
Eunice Odio: 3283.
Euphoric Lies: 2267.
Eurocentric: 591.
Europe: 1657.
European: 3897.
European Lions: A Dozen Views:
    124.
Eurydice: 620, 3016.
Euthanasia: 3775, 5368.
Evacuation Plan: 5007.
Evangelist & Peregrine: 1562.
Eve: 178, 474, 2157, 5140,
    5644.
Eve in Reflection: 3185.
Evelyn: 851.
Even God must tire: 1005.
Even if we don't know: 978.
Even if you're a half-assed
    poet: 4661.
Even in the Morning: 4778.
Even Love Dresses for the
    Weather: 457.
The Even Number of Life: 5537.
Even That Routine: 1375.
Even the Monks Deal in
    Contraband: 57, 5094.
Even the Moon: 4984.
Evening: 939, 2307, 5501.
The Evening: 578, 4447.
An Evening at the Cinema:
    5355.
Evening Cruise: 2299.
Evening, Herron's Farm: 5299.
Evening in the Adirondacks:
    1806.
Evening on the Estuary, Noon
    at Sea: 3173.
Evening Out: 103.
Evening, Out of Town: 2775.
The evening turns and is gone:
    3430.
Evening Walk: 3464.
The Evening's Grading Was Not
    a Loss: 3086.
Evenly Spaced Out around the
    Court, the Cheerleaders Are
    Jumping High, Kicking Their
    Legs in the Air: 2204.
Evensong: 3956.
Event: 1227.
The Eventual Music: 4260.
Ever So Tragic: 4771.
Everett Morgan's Horses: 1174.
Every Action Has an Equal and
    Opposite Reaction: 3212.
Every Day: 1088, 3912, 4207.
Every Day Is the 4th of July:
    1651.
Every night I laugh at the
    moon: 3865, 3997.
Every Planet We Ever Took:
    4412.
Every second somewhere: 4200.
Every Wound Has a Name: 5138.

Flyer: 1016.
Flying Lessons: 3619.
Flying Mountain: 1180.
Focus: 3498.
Foetal Song: 3823.
The Fog Horns at Port
 Townsend: 504.
Fog Madonna: 3047.
Folding the Wash: 2487.
Folk Tale: 3975.
Following: 1774, 5502.
Folly: 3091.
Food Chain: 4235.
Food for Thought: 2177.
The Food-Thief: 3853.
Foolish Women: 5143.
Foot Soldier: 739.
Football Weather: 837.
Footnote to a Desperate
 Letter: 2371.
Footsteps: 983.
For a Child Born Deaf: 4181.
For a Dead Frog: 2335.
For a Friend in Prison: 3337.
For a Lost Watch: 4703.
For a One-Legged Man with a
 Crutch, Cutting Grass with
 a Push Mower, a Dollar Bill
 Hanging from His Back
 Trouser Pocket, 1956: 4304.
For African Flutes and
 Xylophone: 3726, 4664.
For Agnes in the Stromness
 Hotel: 2939.
For All Rationalists: 3747.
For an Album: 5410.
For an Anthology of
 Masochistic Writing: 3047.
For an 'Homage to Rimbaud':
 3567, 5697.
For an Imaginary One: 4254.
For Andrew at Three Months:
 3457.
For Another Swimmer: 2847.
For Any Memorial Day: 319.
For Archibald MacLeish (1892-
 1982): A Retrospective:
 4006.
For Ariadne: 505.
For Billie Holiday: Finally,
 Lady, You Were Done from
 Us: 1353.
For Black Poets Who Think of
 Leadership: 3444.
For Bobby Sands: 2930.
For Brandon: 1988.
For C.D.: 3398.
For Carl Harp: 3444.
For Celeste: Fifteen and
 Doubting: 2046.
For Cesar Vallejo: 3523.
For Claes Oldenburg: 2948.
For Collin: 2847.
For D.A. Levy: 5322.
For Dawes, on Takeoff: 3362.
For Dennis Brutus: 809.

For Diablo Canyon: 1113.
For Diane Turning 36: 4058.
For Donn: 2435.
For Doug Jones: The
 Explanation: 2857.
For Dudley: 5601.
For Earle Birney: 2124.
For Every Mystery There Is an
 (Undiscovered) Equation:
 3385.
For George Archibald: 993.
For Georgia O'Keefe and Silk:
 1446.
For Ginya: 332.
For Giselbertus the Stone-
 Carver: 2221.
For Glad Tidings: 5546.
For Grandmother: 4105.
For Gwendolyn MacEwen: 2124.
For Harold Town: 2124.
For Harry S. Truman in Hell:
 4247.
For Jacqueline Du Pré,
 Cellist Extraordinaire,
 Stricken with Illness. She
 Will Not Play Again: 3078.
For Jan, in Bar Maria: 2770.
For Jim Dine: 1122.
For Joanna: 4036.
For John Donne and Many
 Others: 5563.
For Joseph Cornell: 5673.
For Karl Kline (1935-1971):
 1759.
For Katharine, 1952-1961:
 2312.
For Kay: 1003.
For Marilyn Monroe: 5645.
For Men Only: 3137.
For Misers of Yesterdays:
 3747.
For Muhammad Ali: 944.
For My Brother 1952-1977:
 2881.
For My Brother Who Died Before
 I Was Born: 5687.
For My Daughter, Ruma: 13, 13,
 2200.
For My First Love, Roses and
 Streams: 332.
For My Friend Greg, Twice-
 Decorated in Vietnam, Who
 Answers the Phone, 'Alive
 and Well': 5687.
For My Mother: 3484, 4891.
For My Son: 2147, 4461.
For My Stillborn Brothers:
 5002.
For My Student, Sister Rose:
 4881.
For My Unwanted Shadow: 293.
For N: 3584.
For Now If Not for Long: 2783.
For One on Whom Murder Was
 Attempted: 390.
For Organ Flutes: 3726, 4664.

For Our Better Graces: 1798.
For Our Sake: 4066.
For Paul Blackburn: 1491.
For Peg: A Remnant of Song
    Still Distantly Sounding:
    839.
For Rachel: 5459.
For Randall Jarrell, 1914-
    1965: 1413.
For Richard: 1217.
For Roger Duchamp, USMC: 4006.
For Rosie B_____: 661.
For Sir John Davies: 1089.
For Starts: 4450.
For the Better Maker: 4406.
For the Birds: 4058.
For the Dead: 1180.
For the Dead Found in
    Argentina: 3581.
For the Desert Island: 924,
    4733.
For the Drunk: 3856.
For the Eating of Swine: 2622.
For the Eye in the Keyhole:
    421, 468, 735, 1196.
For the Fallen Especially
    Marguerite & Pepe: 3474.
For the Frost Belt: Three
    Prayers and One Curse: 952.
For the Furbearers: 4406.
For the Girl Most Likely to
    Exceed: 1333.
For the Hurdy-Gurdy: 1068,
    4959.
For the Lately Dead: 1521.
For the Older Writers: 2098.
For the Paleo Expedition:
    4276.
For the Primer of Senior High:
    1529, 2031, 4109.
For the Record: 3719.
For the Sake of Alone: 3427.
For the Sake of Amelia: 4771.
For the Scrapbook of Mrs.
    Charles Black: 857.
For the Strangers: 3654.
For the Women Cotton-Pickers
    of Chinandega: 1934.
For Those I've Saved Names
    For: 1200.
For Those Who Miss the
    Important Parts: 2622.
For Tom: 4798.
For Unborn Malcolms: 4520.
For Ungaretti: 5391.
For W. H. A: 5222.
For W. H. Applewhite: 162.
For Wang Hui-Ming: 4247.
For Whom the Bell Tolls: 5654.
For William C. Williams: 2554,
    2809.
For Young Kerem: 1978.
Forbidden City: 4525.
Force of Circumstance: 2887.
Force of Habit: 2949, 5348.
Les Forces de l'Ordre: 341.

Ford Madox Ford: 3119, 3769.
Forecast 1978: 1074, 1633.
Forecast of Snow in Minnesota:
    2.
Foreclosure: 2977.
Foregone Conclusion: 5546.
Forehead: 3791.
Foreign Language: 3986.
Foreign Living: 2532.
Forensic Geography: 3109.
Forest Animals: 2412.
Forfeiting Light: 3945.
Forged Passport: 1756, 4335.
Forget your war talk: 2532.
Forgetting: 287, 1293.
Forging the Keys: 5094.
The Forgotten: 2971.
Forgotten: 4935.
The Fork: 4771.
Form and Variation: 570.
Formal Presentations of Love:
    2692.
A Formal Problem: 5005.
Forms and Levels of Human
    Rights Violations in
    Nicaragua: 4027.
Formula: 3555.
Forsythia: 2963.
Fort Lauderdale Beach Surf
    Etiquette: 968.
Fort Ord, California, 1953:
    814.
Fort Rock: 129.
Forties Movies, American:
    5188.
Fortress: 2324.
Fortress of Solitude: 3694.
Fortune Cookie Future: 1054.
Fortune Cookies: 5317.
The Fortune Teller: 550.
Fortune Teller: 3911.
Fortune-Telling: 209.
The Forty-Acre Lot: 1467.
Forty-Five Years from Now:
    3635.
Fossils: 541, 820.
Foto Modella: 3479.
Found House in Hemlock,
    Pennsylvania: 1963: 2995.
Found Poem: 3527.
Found Poem: In the Middle of
    American Lit. I: 2711.
Found Text -- Incident 2:
    4833.
The Fountain: 1230, 5246.
Fountainhead: 4138.
The Fountains: 5519.
Four: 3600.
Four Charms: 3560.
Four hours on a bus across
    Saskatchewan: 591.
Four Poems for Marina
    Tsvetaeva, ca 1916: 3229,
    5135.
Four Poems from India: 1385.
Four Poems from Maine: 954.

441.
From the Ironic Marriage
    Sequence: Dialogue: 3049.
From the Kitchen Table: 4712.
From the Mouths of Angels:
    4998.
From the Mouths of Lizards:
    557.
From the Netherlands,
    Christmas: 2781.
From the Same Cloth: 3536.
From the Second Canto: 944,
    1213.
From the Spotted Night: 5742.
From the Top of the Stairs:
    827, 830, 2276.
From the Train: 3567, 5697.
From Underneath: 1434.
From Your Window: 2018.
Front Range: 4301.
The Front Room: 2060, 3400.
Frontier: 138, 807.
The Frontier: 1406.
Frontiers: 1361.
Frost: 1903.
Frost Breath: 1587.
Frost-cloudy: 3548, 4548.
Frosties: 1069.
Frozen Over: 4452.
The Frozen Zoo: 4623.
Fruit Stands: 2830.
Ft. Peck Indian Reservation:
    1963-1983: 4739.
The FTL Addict Fixes: 557.
Fugue: 256, 1323.
Der Fuhrer: 774.
Fulfilling the Promise: 3654.
Full Circle: 1926.
Full Moon: 260.
Full Moon with Promise: 3037.
Full Moonlight in Spring:
    3463.
Fulton Street: 2546.
Fun Blood: 5150.
The Fundamental Project of
    Technology: 2753.
The Funeral: 1413.
Funeral: 2339.
The Funeral: 4261.
The Funeral-Goers: 3192.
Funeral March for a Parrot:
    4555.
The Funeral of My Cousin Phil
    Maddux: Tinicum, Bucks
    County, in the Spring:
    4805.
Funeral Song: 1546, 2915.
Funerary Portraits: 5470.
FUNK (or Rip Van Radio Sleeps
    on Its Feet): 3854.
Funnels: 1234.
The Funnies: 1438.
Für Dieter Schnebel (Tempus
    Est): 3912.
Die Furie des Verschwindens:
    1529, 1984.

Furnace Dream: 5007.
Furnishings: a Collection of
    Prose Poems: 4795.
Furniture: 4463.
The Furniture: 5316.
The Future: 2451.
Future Talk: 737.
G: 576, 2814.
A G.I. in El Salvador: 5039.
Gaeilge: 811.
Gagaku: 4308.
Galatea's Newsstand: 4623.
Galleries: 4293.
Gallery of the Sarcophagi:
    Heraklion Museum: 1276.
Gallery Walk: 3089.
Galloping Horse Unearthed at
    Leitai, China: 4743.
Galway Kinnel: 152.
Game: 4093.
The Game of Troy: 5318.
The Game Protector: 1713.
Game Rules: 2391.
Games in the Back Hills: 712.
Gangster Jones' Analgesic and
    Anti-Gravitational Device:
    2775.
The Gap in the Cedar: 4576.
Garbage Bin: 2339.
The Garden: 549.
Garden: 2484.
Garden among Tombs: 2702.
The Garden at Twickenham:
    2107.
The Garden Cafeteria: 1677.
The Garden Girls: 1452.
Garden Gossip: 2381.
The Garden of Acclimatization:
    2009.
The Garden of the Man Whose
    Wife Has Left Him: 3655.
The Garden Party: 2240.
Garden Politics: 5098.
Garden Spider: 828.
Gardener: 2309.
The Gardener: 2087, 5751.
Gardenias: 1386.
Gardening: 1929.
The Garrison: 213.
Garrulous in Gaza: 5442.
Gary: 3651.
Gary Glitter: 2901.
Gas Station: 81.
Gas Station, Vocables: 4730.
Gaspé: 831.
The Gastronaut (1886-1959):
    5616.
The Gate: 821, 4613.
The Gates of the Arsenal:
    1961, 2202, 3530.
The Gathering: 110.
Gathering: 5307.
Gathering Moon Salt: 4611.
Gauguin: 2868.
Gauguin: We Shall Not Go to
    Market Today: 2774.

Gradually, the Snow: 2368.
Graduate Student: 31.
Graduation: 5476.
Graffiti from the Gare Saint-
  Manquè: 2081.
The Grafting of Hybrids: 367.
A Grain Field at the Edge of a
  Forest: 5121.
Grain of Hope Rime at the End
  of the World: 21.
Grains and Tears: 221.
The Gramma Poems: Wheelchair:
  234.
Grammar Lesson: 2311.
Grammer: 2259.
Grammy: 1426.
Grand Manan: 3659.
Grand Prix Prayer Wheels:
  1641.
Grand Theft Auto: 3590.
Grandfather: 3017, 3547.
Grandfather Was a Soldier:
  570.
Grandma at Grand Canyon, 1938:
  4623.
Grandmother: 3520, 4640, 5149.
Grandmother in White: 3638.
Grandmother in White,
  Courting: 2101.
Grandmother's Blue Willow
  Dishes: 5449.
Grandmother's Recipe: 5376.
Grandmother's Tale: 4895.
Grandpa's Hands: 618.
Grandson's Elegy of the
  Cherokee: 2053.
Grange: 1356.
Granting the Wolf: 960.
Grasmere: 954.
Grass: 5629.
Grass-Fire: 4452.
Grasshoppers: 3335.
The Grave Choice: 2688.
The Gravedigger Blows on the
  Bottle: 2751.
Graves: 1366.
Graves and Vines: 162.
Graveyard: 1138.
The Graveyard: 3265.
The Graveyard at Rochester,
  Iowa: 1704.
The Gray Crown: 2332, 2334,
  5082.
Gray Forest, Late Autumn
  Light: 2581.
The Gray of Black and White:
  4612.
Gray Squirrel: 1732.
Greasing the Tracks: 2779.
The Greasybears: 2523.
The Great Bear over Grand
  Junction, Colorado: 1657.
The Great Bird of Love over
  the Kingdom: 5771.
The Great Chain of Being:
  1455.

The Great Falls: 1264.
The Great Fillmore Street
  Buffalo Drive: 3560.
Great Grand Story: 1251.
Great Grandpa: 4836.
Great-Grandparents Wedding
  Portrait: 1836.
The Great Hypocrite: 1756,
  4335.
Great Jays: 5185.
The Great Koertgini: 2801.
The Great Owls: 2306.
Great Place to Be: 2784.
Great South Bay: 1411.
The Greatest Army: 4168.
Greed and Aggression: 3853.
The Greek Anthology: 1341.
Greek Summer: 3836.
Green Darkness: 1031.
The Green Diamond: 5692.
The Green House: 1020.
Green Island: 3091.
The Green Leaf Attached to the
  Stem: 1414, 3756.
Green Light: 2006, 2520.
Green Night at the Texas
  Cowgirl: 4368.
Green Stew: 227.
Green Swamp: 3408.
Green Violence: 1311.
Green Volvos: 1378.
The Greenhouse Blues: 79.
Greening: 1136.
Greenland: 5602.
Greenwood Hill in Winter:
  1848: 449.
Greetings, Friends: 150.
Greetings from Tranquility
  Lake: 604.
The Grenada Invasion 1983:
  658.
Grendel, Closing: 4772.
Gretel: 1092.
Grey: 3963.
A Grey December Day: 2596.
Grey Fox: 3092, 5096.
Grey Girl, Wheat Girl: 2696.
Grey Green Mist: 146.
Greyhound/Science Fiction:
  2209.
Greylag: 2067.
Grief: 550, 5265.
Grief Dance from a Distant
  Place: 3748.
Grief Poem: 2804.
Grieving for Hopkins: 2675.
Grieving on the Suicide of the
  Groom: 5714.
Grinding Cobalt and Vermilion:
  2882.
The Griot: 4180.
Ground & Figure: 1929.
Ground Hog Lock: 4983.
Ground Zero: 4201.
Groundless: 2502, 5426.
Grounds for Divorce: 2905.

The Grove: 5240.
Grove Street Cemetery, New
  Haven: 1462.
Grow Fresh Spring Water at
  Home in Your Spare Time:
  5197.
Growing: 3721.
Growing Pain: 5510.
Growing Up and Anxious: 386.
Growing Up in Kankakee: 539.
Growing Up Maine: 712.
Growing Up with Guns: 1407.
Grub-Wood: 2723.
Guanzhou: 1754.
The Guard: 2250.
Guard: 5369.
The Guardian: 2039.
Guarding the Door: 510.
Guatemalan Exodus: Los
  Naturales: 1934.
Guatemalan Morning: 27.
Guernica: 178, 5641.
Guerrilla's Fantasy: 2817,
  2879, 3132.
Guessing Game: 4958.
Guest: 711, 2257.
A Guest Arrives: 4641, 5744.
Guests: 5699.
A Guide to the Old World:
  4418.
Guidebook: 5257.
Guidebook/Mountain Streams:
  4350.
Guidelines: 4526.
Guido Strazza, Painter: 57,
  4577.
Guilt: 2105, 3324, 5305.
Guilty: 5749.
Guitarless: 4101.
The Gulf: 3006.
Gulf Coast: 3992.
Gulfcoast Dis/connections:
  4438.
Gulliver: 5675.
Gulls Inland: 1327.
Gusano de la Conciencia: 946.
Gut Shot: 314.
The Guttural Muse: 2232.
Gypsy Wanderers: 288, 2646.
Ha Muerto la Rosa: 3281.
Habit of Angels: 4054.
The Habit of Surfaces: 2097.
Habit, Those Yards: 2009.
Habv: 5371.
Had Death Not Had Me in Tears:
  221.
Hades: 178.
Hagios Panaghiotes: The Church
  in Tolon: 1276.
Haibun 16: 3685.
Haiku: A Sequence: 3048.
Haikuku: 913.
Hail: 44, 3126, 5365.
Hail As If: 2674.
Hail on Stone Mountain: 209.
Hail to the Cockroach!: 1365.

Hail Woman!: 5390.
Hair: 1569.
The Hair Wreath: 3617.
Haiti: 1124.
Hakka Woman: 757.
The Half-Hour Argument: 1307,
  1308, 5354.
Half Open, My Hand: 2502,
  5426.
Half Way Offering: 3649.
Halfbreed Cry: 4412.
Halfway to China: 5722.
Hall of Mirrors: 5320.
Halley's Comet?: 2267.
Halloween: 2268.
Halloween, 1949: 3217.
Halloween Poem: 4555.
A Halo in Darkness: 3591.
Halves: 1434.
Ham, the Father of Canaan:
  2181.
Hamburg: 1016.
The Hamburger Stand People
  Next Door: 4815.
Hammer and Nails: 2940.
Hamsin: 3414.
The Hand: 1559.
The Hand Becomes: 5093.
Hand-in-Hand in the L.A. Arts
  Vanguard: 3086.
The Hand of Emmagene: 5153.
Hand-Shadows: 4226.
Handful of Dust: 1538.
Handling Their Telephone
  Calls: 3245.
Handling Tools: 4924.
Hands: 189, 756, 5529.
Hands of Peace: 2267.
The Hands of the Air: 3977.
The Handsome Young Poet and
  the Orange Eater: 3457.
The Hanging Key: 3697.
Hangover Madonna: 3047.
Hangtown: 2984.
Hank: 5135.
Hansel in Old Age: 4567.
Ha'nt: 2566.
Happily May I Walk: 4403.
Happiness: 1138.
The Happiness: 4142.
Happiness: 5155, 5317.
Happy: 4075.
A Happy Childhood: 3298.
Harassing Fire: 4090.
Hard Beauty: 5696.
Hard Sell: 3265.
The Hard Spirit: 526.
The Hard Task: 3765.
Hardy Street: 1437.
Harlem Sunday Stroll: 4180.
Harlequin Autumn: 5272.
Harley Ridge: 4242.
Harmony Stoneworks: 2702.
Harp Seals: 1092.
A Harrison Fisher Poem: 145.
Harrow: 3607.

Harry the Vendor: 5700.
Hart Crane: 3183, 4612.
The Harvest: 1236.
Harvest: 2562, 3747, 4352.
Harvesting Together: 2563.
The Harvestman: 1550.
Hat: 565, 2549.
Hatred: 3911.
Hatteras Lighthouse: 3028.
Hauling over Wolf Creek Pass
    in Winter: 3363.
The Haunting: 196, 3796.
Haunting Eyes: 1943.
Haunts: 244.
Have You Seen the Wild Dogs in
    Benidorm: 4875.
Have You Seen This Man?: 2569.
Have You Watered the Elephant
    Today?: 736.
Having Left: 3121.
Having sunk back in the places
    where they rose: 5588.
Hawk in Mid-Dive: 2965.
Hawk Music: 3797.
Hawks: 5263.
Hay Creek Sunday Morning:
    5397.
Hay Frente al Tiempo: 1085.
Hay Lake, Minnesota: 286.
Hay un Cuerpo Que Anda: 1409.
Hay un País en el Mundo:
    3537.
Hay un Poema Solo: 4220.
Hay una palabra que nos hiere
    en lejanía: 4327.
Haying Day: August: 4611.
Hazelnut: 4001.
He: 118, 1997.
He Can Go Home, I Guess We
    Pulled the Wrong Nigga This
    Time: 1540.
He died from the fire of his
    own troops: 4485.
He Is Here: 5731.
He Keeps Himself Busy: 2538,
    3852.
He Kills Cats, You Know: 3608.
He Said To: 369.
He Says You Know If You Don't
    Go to: 3047.
He, She, All of Them, Ay:
    4001.
He Speaks: 3873.
He Thinks He's a Teddy Bear
    Blue Blues: 3047.
He tratado de enmendar
    palabras: 5743.
He was smoking a joint: 1550.
He Who Has Arrived: 1255,
    4402.
He who tries to bring down a
    cloud: 191.
Head Bowed: 1149, 2805.
Head Examined: 1191.
Head Life: 5421.
Head over Heels: 2336.

Head under Glass: 3727, 3727.
Headgear from the American
    Collection: 1685.
Heading for an Epilogue: 231.
Heading for Titian: 3782.
Heading home late, in the
    black on black: 5669.
Heading Out: 4785.
Headlands, 2365: 4778.
Headwaters: 2953.
Healer of the Light-Body:
    1102.
The Healing: 5473.
Health: 3072.
Hear the Sky: 1792.
Hearing: 3029.
Hearing Fourth of July Drums:
    504.
Hearing the Girl Story While
    Shoveling Snow: 4356.
The Heart, A Study: 4798.
Heart Act to Follow: 1680.
Heart Associations: 3796.
Heart Attack: 5599.
The Heart Can Be a Mountain:
    5781.
Heart Test with an Echo
    Chamber: 211.
Heart Transplant: 653.
Heartache, Heartbeat,
    Heartbreak: 4812.
Heartland: 2824.
Heartless: 2889.
The Heart's Education: 5093.
Heat: 2077, 3585, 4133.
Heat, Fireflies: 2699.
Heat Rising: 660.
Heat Wave: 935, 5519.
Heatwave: January, 1981: 4611.
Heaven: 3642, 4947.
A Heaven for Elizabeth
    Rodwell, My Mother: 4156.
Heavenly Bonds: 2526, 3844,
    4652.
The Heavenly Feast: 4595.
Heavy: 2727.
The Heavy Freight: 127, 233.
Hector's Return: 1286.
Hedgerows: 4196.
Hedging: 571.
Hegira: 1639.
The Hegira: 2260.
Hegira: 4314, 5364, 5715.
Height: 1646.
Heights: 4133.
Helen: 264.
Helen's House: 1756, 4335.
Hellfire to him who discovered
    hours!: 163, 2981.
Hell's Purgatory: 2205, 4531.
The Help: 3461.
Help Heaven: 1122.
Hemingway: 1184, 3375.
Hemlocks: 1003.
The Hemophiliac: 1407.
Hens: 5258.

Her Cats: 5529.
Her Diaphragm: 4138.
Her Dream: 3390.
Her Dream, Half Remembered:
    1497, 3868.
Her Final Portrait: 1501.
Her Friends: 740.
Her House: 1874.
Her Husband Was a Boxer: 2171.
Her Love Changes It for Me:
    3049.
Her/man Becomes Messenger:
    3851.
Her marked eroded eye cover:
    2641.
Her Master's Voice: 3078.
Her Rage: 1020.
Heraclitus in the Fen: 4989.
Heralds: 1428, 2026, 4899.
The Herb Garden: 1127.
An Herbal Conceit: 4650.
Here: 3996, 4707, 5595.
Here & There: 4062.
Here Cums the Bride All Dresst
    in Fire: 2230.
Here, for You: 3326.
Here I am: 711.
Here in bed behind a brick
    wall: 2478.
Here, in the Desolate City:
    1467.
Here Was Buried Thomas
    Jefferson: 1987.
Here, We Are the Hawk: 2225.
Hereditary Divinity: 1330.
La Herida de Tu Voz: 1658.
Hermaphrodite: 2067.
Hermaphrodite in America:
    3851.
The Hermit: 504, 5549.
Hermit Summer: 1149, 2805.
Herodotus Reports: 2928.
Heron: 1974, 3588.
Herons: 3012.
Hershey, the Cop: 5654.
Herta: 568.
Herzog II: 1723.
Hesitancy: 2978.
Hey Bud!: 4740.
Hey what's going on?: 4200.
Hi, Ben!: 2928.
Hi Ho Game: 5510.
Hibernating at High
    Elevations: 3175.
Hicksville: 1463.
Hicret: 5364.
Hidden Farm Road: 1736.
Hidden Meanings: 5049.
Hidden Portrait: 1428, 2026,
    4900.
Hide'n'go Seek: 4773.
Hiding: 4207.
Hiding from the Wind: 5371.
The Hiding Places II: 1790,
    3567.
Higdon Cove: 295.

The High Diving Horse: 2472.
High in the Tree: 5516.
High Noon at Los Alamos: 5627.
High Priestess: 3636.
The High Road to Harar: 809.
High School: 4942.
High School Reunion: 3687.
High Village: 3554.
High Wire: 3747.
Higher Sound: 2749.
Highway 36, Eolia: 2322.
The Highway Toll Collector:
    5751.
Hijacked: 2868.
Hike: 3175.
Hiking in Winter: 3674.
Hilda Halfheart's Notes to the
    Milkman: #42: 2711.
A Hill: 3642.
The Hill Land: 1929.
Hill Station: 2860.
Hills above Half Moon Bay:
    5673.
Un Himno Para el Ojo: 1269.
Hindu Boy Takes His Vow of
    Celibacy: 2874.
Hinter den Fensterläden:
    232.
Hippel's Wilderness: 3457.
Hiroshige's Iris Garden at
    Horikiri: 5083.
His and Her Binoculars: 1536.
His Argument with His Machine:
    5758.
His Beauty: 620, 3016.
His conceit is everywhere, it
    follows him: 5513.
His Grandmother Speaks on
    Canning: 4452.
His Grandson Is Uneasy: 2787.
His Hair, His Eyes: 2065.
His Name John Thompson: 723.
His Neck: 76.
His Office: 3918.
His Recovery: 5758.
His Shutters Close: 821, 4613.
His Story: 4462.
His Three Women: 1892.
His watch adlibbed: 1031.
Histoire: 3294.
Historia de Amor: 1469.
Historia de Cuba: 4382.
Historia de un Angel: 3281.
Historia Trivial: 283.
Historias de Astros: 5377.
Historical Process: 1529,
    2031, 4109.
History: 148, 2881, 4771,
    5499.
A History: 922.
History As Decoration: 5470.
History II: Paternal Heritage:
    4068.
History Is for Strangers: 690.
A History of Daisies: 4611.
The History of Stone: 952.

How to Winter Out: 1348.
How W. H. Auden Spends the
    Night in a Friend's House:
    1243.
How We Are Fooled: 4466.
How We Learned about the War:
    3675.
How We Make Nice: 4070.
How We See the Past: 2511.
How We Survived the Cretaceous
    Age Together: 844.
How You Continually Come As a
    Surprise: 2774.
Howard Nemerov: 744.
Hoy las nubes me trajeron: 57.
Hua-Lien: 914.
Huachuca: 4343.
Hub-Bub in the Kitchen: 4551.
A Hug: 2550.
Hugging and Kissing in Summer:
    2510.
Hugh Kenner's Nine
    Permutations of 'Alba':
    2719, 2929.
Hum, quietly: 1644.
Human error: 4200.
Human life is nothing more
    than the sum of its
    appetites: 686.
Human Sacrifice and the
    Hieratic State: 3680.
Humana Trascendencia: 424.
Humanities I: 3630.
Humanities II: 3630.
Humiliation: 2972.
The Hummingbird Feeder: 2179.
Hummingbirds: 1413.
Hundred Names: 152.
The Hundred-Word Story: 5418.
Hung Out at My Dad's: 3554.
Hunger: 2653, 5116.
Hungry: 3209.
A Hungry Fighter: 4215.
Hungryman: 5510.
Hunt: 1929.
Hunter at Mecox: 3961.
Hunters and Wives: 1004.
Hunting: 198, 924, 4594.
Los Hurdes: A Film: 4846.
Hurricane: 5440.
Hurt: 4444.
Husband in the Garden: 5638.
Husbands: 1900.
Husbands and Lovers: 4128.
Huzza!: 4983.
Hyacinth: 1375.
Hyaena: 2067.
Hydrangea Blue: 2229.
Hyla Brook: 1773, 1773.
Hymn: And many voices
    marshalled in one hymn:
    350.
Hymn for the Eye: 1269.
A Hymn for the Eye: 2593.
Hymn to Allison on Her Natal
    Day: 1104.

Hymn to the Buffalo: 1226.
Hypertension: 3608.
The Hypogeum: 3689.
Hypothermia: 3972.
Hysterical Fugue: 2944.
I Am a Dark Cloud over the
    City: 3900.
I Am a Poem: 4779.
I am always beginning: 88.
I Am Discontented: 1848.
I Am Folded In upon Myself:
    3655.
I am lifted from my sadness:
    2478.
I Am Mirror: 65, 172, 1405.
I am neither a communist nor a
    nationalist: 5273.
I am nobody: 5706.
I Am of a Sovereign Nation:
    5122.
I am sleeping in the freezer
    frozen: 5513.
I Am the Light of the World:
    1396.
I Am the Rebel: 3184.
I Am the Silent Warrior: 2022.
I Am the Washerwoman: 2132.
I Am This Wooden Humming: 395.
I Asked Hoping: 3129.
I Believe This Is the Home of
    Georgia O'Keeffe: 4559.
I Bild Myself a Littl House:
    2230.
I Can Be Seen: 2810.
I Capitulo: 5065.
I Could Put: 5255.
I Couldn't and I Wouldn't:
    5630.
I Demand a Nuclear Freeze,
    But: 3260.
I Depend on You for Accurate:
    4425.
I don't know if I've got it in
    me: 3796.
I don't Look at People's
    Souls: 2526, 3844, 4652.
I don't remember the hour:
    5551.
I dream the school will not
    hold us: 544.
I Enter Your Churches, Lord:
    57, 4577.
I Feel Like: 4606.
I Feel the Grief of Growing
    Up: 4981.
I Find Joy in the Cemetery
    Trees: 2622.
I find the more: 3565.
I Get Jealous of an Old Home
    Movie: 1348.
I Give for Your Love: 2395.
I Gorge Myself on Time: 3365.
I hate to leave springtime
    among the hills: 5051.
I have always had two skulls:
    515, 555.

I Welcome the Dark: 2115.
I whispered of death: 4415.
I wish I knew a woman: 2937.
I Woke, This Meant a Love in
    the World: 405, 2105.
I Work All Day: 3974, 4837.
I work Underground: 254.
I wrote two letters, both to
    you, last night: 1245.
Icarian Letter: 5451.
Icarus: 3199, 4210.
Ice: 559, 4914.
Ice Cream: 1983.
Ice Dance: 3896.
Ice Dream Fishing on College
    Street: 4057.
Ice-God: 1004.
The Ice Land: 3477.
Ice Storm: 5709.
Ice Storm in the Sun Belt:
    1543.
An Icelandic Door: 2431.
The Iceman: 1312.
Icicles: 3391.
Iconoclast--Ah, Forgive Me!:
    2909.
Iconoclast: 4037.
The Idaho Egg Woman: 5107.
The Idea of Haiti: 2920.
Ideal Conditions: 2545.
Ideas: 2648.
Identical Twins: 3654.
Identification: 47, 1444.
Identifying Marks: 1629, 1861,
    3863.
Identifying the Body: 1527.
Identifying w/ Slime-Dazzle:
    1001.
Identity Card: 2691, 4335.
Idle Hands: 3911.
Idleness: 4641, 5744.
Idolatry: 347.
If: 1126, 3796.
If 16 inch artillery: 4200.
If God wants to give you
    wings: 1448.
If Hatred Rules: 3892.
If I Am Like Anything: 2545.
If I Could Mumble Like Marlon
    Brando: 4379.
If I touch You: 3542.
If I trace silence: 1528.
If I'd Been Born in Tennessee:
    3326.
If it be murder: 4200.
If It Dies: 5274.
If Life Could Only Be As
    Simple: 5774.
If the Accident Will: 3362.
If the Sand Could Sing: 2526,
    3844, 4652.
If There Were Anywhere But
    Desert: 2502, 5426.
If Those Memories Have Left
    Me, How: 1126.
If We Could Just Be Certain:

2230.
If We Had Foreseen All This:
    666.
If we're nuked by the Soviets:
    4200.
If you ever worry: 978.
If You Have O Soul: 54, 2191.
If you look at the sun and
    it's spotty: 2267.
If you've got 2 mil: 4200.
Ignominy: 1498.
Ignorance: 1547.
Ignorance Is Unbounded: 68.
Igor Stravinsky: 3868.
Iguana: 2067.
Iguanas: 805, 5061.
Il aurait fallu t'aimer: 979.
Il neige sur le toit: 1425.
The Iliad: 1654.
Ill: 4641, 5744.
Ill at Fifteen: 739.
I'll Huff and I'll Puff: 3472.
Ill Lit: 5699.
I'll Not Cop Out on
    Rhododendrons This Ti:
    1126.
I'll Not Cop Out on
    Rhododendrons This Time:
    1126.
I'll put it down in tables:
    3484, 4891.
Illegal Immigrants Entering
    the City: 872.
Illegitimacy: 5026.
Illinois at Christmas: 2064.
Illinois Central: 2840.
Illinois in Winter: 5100.
Illuminated Page: Kellsian
    Fragment in the Pine
    Barrens of New Jersey:
    3078.
Illusion: 3805, 4336.
The Illusion Still Unbroken:
    1227.
Illusions: 3151.
I'm Afraid She's Right: 3086.
I'm exposing myself as a
    preacher as well as a poet:
    3772.
I'm in favor of: 4200.
I'm Lying on the Bed at a
    Motel and: 924, 3709.
I'm Not Into Nothingness:
    1853.
I'm Pissed: 2505.
I'm sick and tired: 1260.
I'm Tired of the Old Oedipal
    Dramas: 4492.
I'm waiting for you: 1423.
Im Zug: 232.
The Image: 3498.
Image of Age: 4524.
Imagery without Purpose: 391.
Images: 1901.
Images II: 817.
Images from Bhartrihari: 4130.

In Labor: 2803.
In Late Afternoon As the Clock
  Sleeps: 2774.
In Memoriam: 2588.
In Memoriam: Colonel Azmi
  Saghiyeh, Defender of Tyre:
  3884.
In Memoriam Dylan Thomas:
  2646, 2764.
In Memoriam Nagy Laszlo: 827,
  830, 2276.
In Memoriam Paul Celan: 214,
  5220.
In Memory Of: 4268.
In Memory of Earl Organ: 4034.
In Memory of EW, 1st World
  Soldier, Socialist: 1689.
In Memory of My Friend the
  Bassoonist John Lenox:
  2644.
In Memory of the Unknown Poet
  Robert Boardman Vaughn:
  2644.
In Michigan: 1981.
In Minako Wada's House: 2978.
In Modern Dress: 4215.
In Mokelumne Wilderness: 1550.
In Moonlight: 2337.
In Music I Listen To: 2516.
In My Ascendancy: 1543.
In My Brother's Garden: 225.
In My Country: 262.
In my country: 1208, 1208.
In My Country: 4880, 5772.
In My Darker Moments: 768.
In My Day We Used to Call it
  Pussy-Whipped: 711.
In My Dream You Are: 1954.
In My Exodus Season: 3769.
In My Father's Study: 1217.
In My Mother's Dresser Drawer:
  2089.
In My Mother's House: 3650.
In My Own Lifetime: 5694.
In My Town: 623, 2762.
In My Twenty-fifth Year: 327.
In New Guinea: 515, 555.
In Night Houses: 2331.
In October: 617.
In Other Arms: 3634.
In Otto's Basement: 4784.
In Our Last World: 660.
In Passing: 5523, 5523.
In Pieces: 1550.
In Posse: 4474.
In Praise of Caveman: 2230.
In Praise of Caveman: The Atom
  Bomb Poems: 2230.
In Praise of What Passes:
  5523.
In Rainy September: 504.
In Rem: 4474.
In Response: 5310.
In Rome You Hear: 57, 5094.
In search of a petty gain:
  152, 2385.

In Spain: 5602.
In Spring: Looking into the
  Distance, on the Wall:
  1331, 1412, 4213.
In St. Paul's: 3959.
In Sweethavens: 2909.
In Terms of Physics: 3625.
In the Absence of Fire: 2740.
In the Adirondacks: 2881.
In the Air: 4730.
In the Art Museum: 2855.
In the Attic Where She Sleeps:
  4666.
In the autumn wind: 3548,
  4548.
In the battlefield men grapple
  each other and die: 3035.
In the Beginning: 2024.
In the Beginning Merlin Says
  Seven: 5080.
In the Beginning Was the Word:
  4183.
In the Blessed Seconds: 1199.
In the Castle: 5271.
In the Circle: 3233.
In the City: 1903.
In the Clare Glens: 1435.
In the Classroom: 2803.
In the Country: 60.
In the Cruel Month: 4888.
In the Dark: 3618.
In the Dark Our Story: 3316.
In the Dead of Night: 4277.
In the desert: 1116.
In the Desert Botanical
  Garden: 568.
In the Distance in Every
  Direction: 3721.
In the Echoes, Wintering:
  5145.
In the fallking snow: 5706.
In the Fields of Camphor:
  1945, 3621.
In the Fifth Week: 583.
In the Forest: 1954, 2804.
In the Funeral Home: A
  Reminiscence: 4662.
In the Garden: 4242.
In the Grays: 4040.
In the Greenhouse: 1339.
In the Hinterland: 2319.
In the Home for Old People:
  2964.
In the House: 2112.
In the House of the Edge of
  the Railroad Flats: 3013.
In the Jaws of the Beast:
  4848.
In the Kibbutz Kitchen: 5257.
In the Kitchen: 1518.
In the Lake: 2043.
In the Middle Kingdom: 3145.
In the Middle of the Night:
  4144, 5483.
In the Midnight Hours: 279.
In the mirror: 4433.

It's Probably What Bukowski
  Likes about Beethoven:
  3086.
It's Really Easy: 1426.
It's So Soon Over: 4090.
It's Summer at My Sister's
  House: Mahone Bay 1982:
  892.
It's True: 3248.
It's Your Hands I'm Afraid Of:
  287.
The Itsy Bitsy Spider Climbs
  and Analyzes: 2506.
I've Been Up All Night: 2147.
I've brought many valuable
  things: 3484, 4891.
I've Ex-: 1126.
I've Heard the Laughter: 4843.
I've Never Been to War: 1611.
I've wandered, not always
  lost: 3401.
Ives: 1456.
Jabben: 715.
Jack: 3608.
Jack in the Pulpit: 5567.
Jack London: 2859.
Jack-O-Lantern: 1370.
Jack, the Following Summer:
  1143.
Jacob and the Angel: 5789.
Jacob in Edmonton: 2469.
Jacob Limps Home over the
  River: 2240.
J'ai toujours eu deux
  crânes: 555.
J'aime tant ma maison: 979.
Jak Ci Mam Powiedziec Czego Mi
  Brak: 2799.
Jamaica Flambeaux: 3044.
James before Darkness: 2589.
James Dean: 676, 1755, 2265,
  4907.
Jane Goodall's Chimps Revert
  to Cannibalism: 1757.
Jane Sauer's Basket: 5596.
Jane Todd Crawford, Kentucky,
  1830: 1092.
January: 510, 1451, 1869,
  4291.
January 1, 1973: 944.
January 6, 1980: 3666.
January, 1978: 5240.
January Blues: 4159.
Janus: 4029.
Japan: 3785.
Japanese Camera: 2868.
Japanese Fishermen Slaughter
  1000 Porpoises: 3062.
Japanese Garden: 4501.
The Jay: 731.
Jazz Man: 4298.
Jazz Woman with Reed
  Instrument: 4279.
Je fuyais le réel: 555.
Jeering at Myself: 4641, 5744.
Jeffers: 5654.

Jelly Road: 4250.
Jellyfish: 2824.
Jennifer and the Maple Keys:
  2181.
Jeremiah: 4651.
Jeremiah in Egypt: 5563.
Jerry: 1524.
Jetzt Wohin?: 2244.
La Jeune Parque: 1486, 5331.
Jeux de mirages: 4496.
Jew Learning German: 1615.
A Jew: To Such a World in Such
  a Time: 4779.
The Jewel: 5702, 5702.
Jewish Cemetery in Prague:
  176, 5221.
The Jilted Poet: 330.
Jimmy Fendel's Elegy for the
  Laundromat Owner: 1759.
Joan: 4611.
Joan of Arc: 3252.
Joan of Arc: A Sonnet
  Sequence: 1852, 3015.
Job, a Verse Play: 4567.
Job Security: 4998.
Jocelyn's House: Wellfleet:
  1926.
Jody Powell and Brzezinski:
  4200.
Joe Dimaggio on the Right
  Field Fence: 2457.
Joe Easy: 5312.
Joe Prichard: 476.
Johanna Barns: 472.
John: 72.
The John Belushi Memorial
  Poem: 3608.
John Berryman, This Is for
  You: 3693.
John Burroughs Thanks Henry
  Ford for a New Car, 1914:
  1071.
John Calvin and the Gerbils:
  3224.
John Carlson at Eighty: 2840.
John Clare Adaptation: 3329.
John D: 4571.
John / Henry: 1780.
John James Audubon: A Reverie:
  4567.
John Keats: He Dreams of Being
  Warm: 954.
John Wayne Is Dying: 2784.
John Wesley Johnson: 5680.
Johnathan Moon: 1387.
Johnny: 2484.
Johnny Cash: 145.
John's Mysteries: 4983.
The Joker: 3627.
Jonah: 1476, 4135.
Jonas Speakes: 351, 3431.
Joplin's Joplin: 1377.
Joseph: 275.
Josephine Mandala, Sing-Tel:
  5654.
Joshua: 1768.

Lake Michigan Summers: 4033.
Lake of Ice: 3557.
The Lake of Salt: 1945, 3621.
The Lamb: 182.
The Lamb of Marks and
Spencer's: 5333.
Lament: 225, 827, 830, 929,
2119, 2276, 3751.
A Lament: 4138.
Lament for Mother: 2856.
Lament for Paul Celan: 4280,
5221.
Lament in Monroe County: 5579.
Lament of the Conductor: 4468.
Lament of the Steam Shovel:
2936, 3974.
Lamps and Fences: 3811.
Lance Delivers His
Valedictory: 4804.
Land Grab in Bolivian Boom
Town: 1585.
The Land of Colchis: 3613.
Land of Milk and Honey: 5447.
The Land of Nod: 1995.
Land Scape: 5671.
The Land Where Rooflines
Parallel the Ground: 88.
Landfall: 4419.
The Landlocked Bride: 1374.
Land's End: 1550.
Landscape: 506, 4618, 5608.
Landscape 1982: 5529.
Landscape As a Concavity of
Vision: 3888.
Landscape, Dense with Trees:
5396.
Landscape for One Voice: 3037.
Landscape with Mares and
Foals: 5135.
Landscape with the Fall of
Icarus: 189.
Landscape with Three
Mountains: 248, 2340.
The Landslide on Guilt
Mountain: 4605.
Langston Blues: 4228.
Langston / Blues Griot: 5460.
Langston Hughes Attends the
Festival: 25.
Langston Hughes Is Merry
Glory: 649.
Language: 869.
The Language of Blood: 5442.
The Language of Rust: 3110.
Language: Post-Feminist: 1309.
Laps: 1968.
Lapsang Souchong: 2727.
Lapsing: 5491.
Large Families: 310.
Large Grieving Women: 3485,
4771.
Large Religious Poem: 4657.
Large Sentimental Poem: 4657.
The Lark Ascending: 46.
Larkinesque: 4482.
The Last Afternoon: 4142.

The Last Ascent of
Killimanjaro: 5585.
Last Chance: Atlantic City
3:45 AM: 556.
Last Chance Cafe: 4913.
Last Child: 3195.
The Last Child: 4854.
Last Dance before Curfew:
5708.
The Last Day of Fulvius
Agrippa: 5289.
The Last Day to Write Poems:
1646.
The Last Days of Heaven: 1009.
The Last Dream: 746.
Last Evening: 2180.
Last Gift: 2977.
The Last Gizzlestine: 5272.
The Last Harvest: 2550.
The Last Hello: 5522.
The Last Hippie of Camp Fifty,
Kansas: 3895.
Last Honeymoon: 1853.
Last Infirmity: 1250.
The Last Island: 1138, 5155.
The Last Laugh: 3554.
Last Letter: 319.
The Last Man: 5627.
The Last Man in the Quabbin:
1797.
Last Meeting: 5469.
The Last Minute of My Father's
Life and the First Minute
of His Death: 3853.
Last Names: 310.
The Last Nayaug: 4212.
The Last Night at Home: 1954.
Last Night's Bread: 5733.
Last Night's Sleep: 1077.
Last of: 3590.
Last of the Buffalo Heads:
3906.
Last of the Coffee: 608.
The Last of the Herrigs: 1570.
The Last Poem: 2100.
Last Poem: 2389.
Last Rites: 1093, 1520.
The Last Scene: 598.
The Last Second Son Poem:
3975.
The Last Sermon: 1918.
Last State: 3114.
Last Storm: 2681, 2831.
The Last Strip Show: 4058.
The Last Summer: 4633.
Last Summer: 5571.
Last Supper: 2943.
The Last Time: 2198, 3608.
The Last Time Shorty Towers
Fetched the Cows: 3416.
Last Visit, Elizabeth: 2482.
The Last Wild Man: 3666.
Last Wish: 4811.
Last Words: 2095.
The Last Year: 526.
A Lasting Poem: 3769.

Luminous the abolished days:
142, 4541.
Lumpen! If: 4637.
The Luna Moth: 3341.
Lunar Days: 5648.
Lunatics: 49, 3189.
Lunch: 259.
Lunch at Helen
Frankenthaler's: 2054.
Lunch-Break on the Edge of
Town: 2018.
Lunch Hour: 5478.
Lunch Time: 291.
Luncheon of the Boating Party:
5021.
The Lush Earth: 747.
Lust: 1547.
Lust for Life: 4675.
Lustspielabend: 5551.
Luxumei: 5377.
Luz de Corral: 2498.
Lying Awake Watching a Lighted
Window: 3349.
Lying in a Hammock at William
Duffy's Farm at Pine
Island, Minnesota: 5702.
Lying in a Hammock at William
Duffy's Farm in Pine
Island, Minnesota: 5702.
Lying Low: 5785.
Lyre: 907.
A Lyrical Ballad: 3646.
Lyrical Sonnet: 1261.
Lytton's Corners: 2216.
M.P.H.: 693.
MacGregor: 3739.
The Machine Age: 146.
Mad Girl: 3869.
Mad-Lib: 4644.
Mad Magdalens and North
American Holy Men: 1637.
Mad Poem: 991.
Madame Bovary's Schizophrenia:
3069.
Madame de Porchilian: 5522.
Made-in-the-U.S.A: 688.
Madly to Learn: 5013.
Madness Maddened: 4567.
The Madness of Kong: 5271.
Madonna: 1902.
Madonna Drawn to Difficult
Men: 3047.
Madonna of the Imagined: 3047.
Madonna of the Love Lorn:
3047.
Madonna of the Manuscripts:
3047.
Madonna of the Married Man:
3047.
Madonna of the Performance:
3047.
Madonna of the Pomegranate:
2430.
Madonna Who Attracts
Strangeness thru the Mail:
3047.

Madonna Who Fixes Neon Lights:
3047.
Madonna Who Thinks of Herself:
3047.
Madonna with the Mother: 3047.
Madre Espina de Campos
Absolutos: 4329.
Madrigal: 4870.
Madrona: 664.
The Madwoman in the Attic:
4702.
Madwoman Throwing Mangoes:
4746.
Mae West: 1635.
Magalópole: 806.
Magdalene: 264.
Maggie May: 5657.
Magic: 3618.
The Magic Day: 2787.
The Magic Glass: 5480.
Magic Mongers: 722.
The Magic Words: 209.
The Magician: 1954.
Magician: 3721.
The Magician: 3909.
The Magician, Sawing His Woman
in Half: 3441.
Magnesium Chloride: 4603.
Magnificat: 2207.
Mahogany: 5666.
The Mail: 1217.
Mail: 1547.
Mail Stop: 452.
The Mailbox Poem: 3402.
The Main Enemy Is at Home:
753.
The Main Man: 1117.
Main Street: 5741.
Mainly the Values Change:
3362.
Maintenance: 3999, 4189.
Maitines: 1358.
Maitresse Erzulie: 3176.
Maize Rows Flowering Red:
2941.
Major Mode: 3406.
Makai/First Light: 2746.
Make Me an Angel: 682.
Make up your mind snail: 5706.
Making a Dictionary: 2460.
Making a Garden: 981.
Making Beds: 1799.
Making Belief: 4447.
Making Coffee: 5404.
Making Contact: 3527.
Making It Turkey: 2123.
Making Out: 4742.
Making the Strange Familiar:
125.
Making Waves: 4772.
Malcolm: 4520.
Malcolm X: 649.
Male and Female Poets: 1728,
4844.
A Malediction: 2395.
Malediction Forbidding

Marion and Henry Adams on
    Tour: 2858.
Marion, in Winter: 1372.
Marisolka: 2336.
Mark: 3487.
The Mark: 5297.
Mark Twain, 1909: 2353.
Marked with D: 2183.
Market-Day: 1954.
Mark's Room: 2911.
Marooned: 739.
Marriage: 3155, 5404.
The Marriage: 888, 5034.
Marriage of Poets: 2784, 2787.
Marry the Marrow: 3868.
Mars: 5328.
Marshal Jim: 3114.
Martha: 4611.
Martha remember: 4611.
Martial Arts: 1275.
Mary: 257.
Mary and Martha: 1286.
Mary Cazzato, 1921: 4513.
Mary Wollstonecraft Dies of
    Puerperal Fever: 2507.
März in Basel: 590.
Más allá de la
    delgadísima voz que no
    cesa: 363.
Mascara: 4929.
Il Mascherone: 57, 4577.
Mask: 2480, 5325.
The Mask: 3888.
Masking to Meet Ourselves:
    2144.
The Masks: 1428, 2026, 4899.
Masquerade: 3411.
The Masquers: 3823.
Massacre at Marais des Cygnes:
    4153.
Massacres: 1341.
Massage: 32.
Mastile: 1428.
Matadero, Riley & Company:
    3250.
The Matala Cafe: 1121.
Match: 5510.
Matchbox: 1929.
Math: 2224.
Matilija Adolescence: 5174.
Matinee: 4405.
The Mating Reflex: 2095.
Matins: 3326, 4567.
Matins for the Condemned:
    2714.
Matisse: 116.
The Matrix: 19.
Matter: 5295.
Matter of Poultry: 3095.
A Matter of Trust: 111.
Matthew Schnell (1951-1981):
    5239.
Matthiola: 1645.
Maturity: 3608.
Mau Than: 248.
May: 771, 882.

May 4 1982: 3047.
May 22, 1979: 5272.
Mayakovsky Is Dead: 1903.
Mayakovsky Shot Himself (April
    14, 1930): 2582.
Mayakovsky: The Phillistine
    Reefs: 4833.
Mayaro Sea Sculpture: 1145.
Maybe Alone on My Bike: 4942.
Maybe Dats Your Pwoblem Too:
    2095.
Maybe It's the Rinse Cycle:
    291.
Maybe -- Just Maybe: 4150.
Maybe This Way: 4942.
Maze: 2023.
Mazes: 2601.
McClellan Shoots His Dogs:
    4142.
Me as a Raven and Crow: 3915.
Me, Contemplating
    'Astrological Facts and
    Cosmological Theories' in
    Kung's Does God Exist One
    Morning in June: 335.
Me n Arleen Usd to Drive Evree
    Wher: 462.
Me queda la mar media en el
    triunfo del agua: 143.
Me veréis un cometa
    enloquecido: 57.
Mea Culpa: 1926.
Meal: 610.
The Meaning of Coyotes: 3528.
The Meaning of Meaning: 5161.
The Meaning of Simplicity:
    1756, 4335.
Meaninglessness: 4704.
Meanings: 4919.
Measurements: 873, 5570.
Measuring Time: 5663.
Meat Dreams: 543.
Meatball Maniacs: 4160.
The Mechanics of Repair: 3326.
Medals: 985.
Medals for Motherhood: 3836.
Medea: 3208.
Medic: 5274.
Medicine: 846.
Medieval Prayerbook: 4941.
Meditation: 1653, 1736.
Meditation 8: 3935.
Meditation 83/US: 5459.
A Meditation after Battle:
    319.
Meditation at Lagunitas: 2202.
Meditation at the Edge of Lake
    Superior: 357.
Meditation in a Time of Death:
    4163.
Meditation in Late August
    Drought: 1910.
Meditation of a Reader of
    Newspapers: 3958.
Meditation on Birney Mountain:
    2622.

The Meteorite: 5546.
The Method: 3341.
Methuselah (Dart-Man): 1498.
Metro Dodo Foucault: 1065.
The Mexico Divorce Hotel:
   1048.
The Mexico Poem: 2638.
Mi Casa: 3102.
Mi-Lo (the Laughing Buddha):
   4352.
Mi Mas Preciado Lector: 1804.
Mi Padre: 5264.
Miami Beach: 3642.
Michael: 4849.
Michaelangelo off the Record
   on His Inspiration for the
   Sistine Chapel Ceiling:
   5730.
Micheline: 145.
Micheline & Solomon: 3554.
Midas Dream: 1963.
Midday Early June: 3675.
Middle Age: 896.
A Middle Class Tradition:
   2527.
Midnight: 1149, 2805, 3909,
   3927.
Midnight Dawn: 2262.
Midnight, Doppler: 3233.
Midnight in Anchorage: 1636.
Midnight in the City: 829.
Midnight Marching Band: 320.
Midnight on the Maryville High
   Football Field: 4879.
Midsummer: 5423, 5423.
Midwest Poem: 5685.
Un Miedo Extraño: 4199.
Migrants: 471.
Migrating Hawks: 66.
Migration: 1562, 5317.
The Migration of Butterflies:
   1770.
Migrations: 1543.
Mike: 5490.
Miklos Radnoti: 3769, 3769.
Mildew: 3371.
Miles Away: 1209.
The Miles Between: 3642.
Milford: East Wing: 3683.
Military Men: 3576.
Military Presence, Cobh 1899:
   974.
Milk: 4051.
The Milk of Human Kindness:
   3608.
Milk, Seed, Sun: 131.
The Milking Cow: 4142.
Milkweed: 4741.
The Mill: 3745.
Millay Hearing the News:
   3047.
Millers: 1738.
Millstone: 3607.
The Mind: 3193.
The Mind Is Like an Hourglass:
   4928.

Mind over Matter: 3908.
Mindanao: 3868.
Mine Disaster: 1249.
Los Mineros: 1382.
Miniature Battle Scene -- War
   Museum: 3518.
The Miniature Boathouse: 1:
   4972.
Minimum Wage: 3194.
Mining: 3129.
Mining the Wind: 5372.
The Minister's Death: 3416.
Minotaur: 234.
The Minotaur: 620, 3016.
Minus 60: 4673.
Minutes, an Arms Control
   Disarmament Agency Meeting:
   4124.
The Miracle Worker: 872.
The Miraculous Mandarin: 5127.
Mirage Verbal: Writings
   through Marcel Duchamp,
   Notes: 767, 1417.
Mirame hacia Adentro: 274.
Mirror: 5406.
Mirror Up to Nature: 485.
The Mirrored Face: 4383.
The Mirroring of Man through
   Beasts: 460, 1749.
The Mirror's Place: 168, 2165.
Mis pies rugen esta tarde, al
   igual que me alma: 5065.
Misanthrope: 364.
Miscarried: 2319.
Miscellaneous Thoughts on
   Underemployment: 2847.
Miscount: 353.
Miserere: 2840.
Misericordia General: 103.
Misery in the World: 2104.
Misfortune: 4347.
La Mision de un Hombre: 3446.
Misleading: 3099.
Misogyny: 5758.
Miss Denby: 1569.
Miss Emily Dickinson Goes to
   the Office: 5563.
Miss Johnson Dances for the
   First Time: 1451.
Miss Juergensen: 1904.
Miss Kelly: 1795.
Miss Parret: 4710.
Miss Rosemary, for
   Remembrance: 4429.
Miss September: 3272.
Missiles and Picnics: 1937.
Missing: 709.
Missing Legacy: 4840.
Missing Now 5 Days: 2298.
Missing Person: 1721.
Mission: 2365.
Mission Bells: 4412.
Mission Box: 4830.
Mississippi River: 2913.
The Missouri: 2390.
Missouri at Flood-Time: 1835.

Missouri Litany: 511.
Missouri Voices: 1748.
The Mistress: 5125.
Mistress of the Flowers: 2518.
Mitologia Familiar: 444.
Los Mitos del Hombre: 1318.
Mnemosyne: 5194.
Mobile Still Life with
    Carnations and Baby's
    Breath: 2539.
Modalities: 1543.
Model: 4649.
The Model: 4909.
The Models: 1756, 4335.
A moderate: 4200.
Modern Criticism: 3328.
Modern Day: 415.
Modern Day Companions #2: 415.
Modern Day Companions #3: 415.
Modern Day Diversions #1: 415.
Modern Day Diversions #7: 415.
Modern Day Entertainment #1:
    415.
Modern Day Flukes #37: 415.
Modern Day Professions #2:
    415.
Modern Day Professions #3:
    415.
Modern Day Professions #9:
    415.
Modern Day Professions #13:
    415.
Modern Days 21: 415.
Modern Flukes: 415.
A Modern Girl: 109, 990.
A Modest Gift by Affection
    Made a Treat: 1146.
Modest Gift by Affection Made
    a Treat: 4002.
Modesty Silsbee Finds Her
    Father's Bible in a Trunk:
    4345.
Mojave: 507.
Mold: 2060, 3400.
The Mollusc: 1431, 4113.
The moment I heard we've
    entered port: 152, 2385.
Moment in Petzow: 2554, 2809.
The moment you touch the whorl
    of my ear: 1360, 4789.
Momentary Gypsy Song: 3351.
Momentary Immobility: 2691,
    4335.
Momentos: 5244.
Moments before Entering the
    Corn Exchange: 3376.
Mon ami le plus cher: 555.
Mon dernier mot: 979.
Monday: 526, 3592, 5673.
Monday Morning: 1120, 3461.
Monet's Last Self-Portrait:
    2043.
Monimbo: 262, 600, 5772.
A Monk on Heimaey: 2431.
Monkhood: 428.
Monks and Nuns and Catholic

Priests: 2889.
Monochromes: 932.
Monologue: 1368.
Monologue to His Own
    Reflection: 1439.
Monologue with Its Wife: 504,
    1482.
The Monroe Doctrine Applied
    Domestically: 973.
Monserrato, 20: 57, 5094.
The Monster in the Park: 832.
The Monster of Mr. Cogito:
    827, 830, 2276.
Monsters: 94, 114, 1454, 2783,
    3099, 3458.
Monstruos: 94.
Montage: 4249.
Montana Rusa: 530.
Months Later, Your Image:
    1506.
Montmartre: 325.
Montreal 1978: 5119.
Monument to a Kettle Drum:
    2526, 3844, 4652.
Monuments on the Mall: 468.
Mood Music: 3026.
Mood of the Woods: 3065.
Moody Violet: 2670.
Moon: 2519.
Moon-Catch in Snowlight: 4130.
Moon-Fever: 1727.
Moon in Taurus: 3470.
Moon in the Mirror: 5648.
The Moon Is My Uncle: 5284.
The Moon Is Two Days into
    Scorpio: 3742.
Moon over Vermont: 347.
Moon Rise: 3499.
Moon Sharks: 1311.
Moon Tide: 3831.
Moon Veil: 2574.
Moonglow soft as milk: 2983.
Moonlight Nuptials: 909.
Moonlit Dream in the Faraway
    Nude: 5129.
Moonlit Night: 1331, 1412,
    4213.
Moor: 329, 2479, 5048.
Moorhen: 3091.
Moraleja: 3281.
Morbid Fascinations: 1103.
More about That Summer: 50,
    140.
More Beautiful Than Beauty
    Itself: 1645.
More Blessed to Receive: 208.
More Journeys without Title:
    5615.
More Music: 1286.
More Songs from Holcomb
    County: 700.
Morfydd, daughter of Gwyn:
    1360, 4789.
Morganitas: 719.
Morning: 1550.
The Morning after the Storm:

5076.
Morning Air: 4934.
Morning Coffee: 1945: 1295.
Morning Conversation: 1332.
Morning Excuse for Not Mowing: 2005.
Morning Fragments: 850.
The Morning Glory: 504.
Morning Glory: 2511, 3461, 4172.
Morning in Saltillo: 4368.
Morning on the Orient Express: 2078.
Morning on This Street: 4903.
Morning Raga: 4807, 5144.
The Morning Reading: 917, 924, 5711.
The Morning Roar of the City: 3485, 4771.
Morning Song: 477, 1272.
A Morning Spent Waiting for Rain: 2182.
The Morning Star: 263, 807.
Morning Sun: 4480.
Morning Walk: 3591.
Mornings: 3065.
Mornings arise: 4641, 5744.
The Mornings I Oversleep: 5642.
Mortal, imagine here beneath the face: 3, 912.
The Mortar Remarks: 4555.
Mortgage Business: 5425.
Moses: 3762.
Mosquito Fleet: 1797.
Mosquitoes: 244.
The Most Beautiful Bird in the World: 2230.
Most worldmen murder for gold: 1385.
Mostly It Is the Future Which Haunts This House: 549.
Mot: 3233.
Le Mot: Sitting for the Calligrapher: 5546.
The Motel: 4781.
Motel 6: 1302.
Moth: 5751.
Mother: 1540, 3221.
The Mother Dream: 4742.
Mother Dying: 1433.
Mother Merrill: 1530.
Mother Myself: 1352.
Mother Nature: 413.
Mother of the Birds: 2564.
Mother Ruin: 2010.
Mother Taught Her Daughers to Fish: 497.
Mother Teresa Feeds Her Lepers at Her Home for the Destitute, Calcutta: 2874.
Mother Was Gentle: 327.
A Mother Watches Her Athletic Daughter: 2508.
Motherhood, 1880: 5145.
Mother's Face Drowned in Her

Palm: 2681, 4448, 4613.
Mother's Glowing Embers: 180.
The Mothers of the Plaza de Mayo: 1416.
Mothers to the Stable: 195, 4240.
Mothers' Wishes: 4360.
The Moths: 3859.
Motion Picture: 3124.
Motion Pictures: 5490.
Motorcycle Death: 4350.
The Mount of Venus: 2526, 3844, 4652.
Mountain Jack Blues: 217.
The Mountain Lion: 3823.
Mountain Wizard: 2651, 5635.
Mountains: 714.
The Mountain's Daughter: 1756, 4335.
The Mountains of Evening: 503.
Mourning: 2045, 2660.
Mourning Doves: 4925.
Mourning Flavor: 864, 5401.
The Mourning of Lot's Wife: 2181.
Mouse: 1509.
Mouse Chase: 4450.
The Moustache Speaks: 3269.
The Move West: 587.
Movement: 846.
Movement in a Solid: A Composite Figure of the Poet This Century: 2344.
Movements in Time: 3318.
Movie: 4691.
Moving: 4622, 5657.
Moving around Time: 4737.
Moving Day: 3260, 4567.
Moving House: 4946.
Moving into Memory: 1250.
Moving On: 2110.
Moving toward the Dance: 2367.
The Moving Trees: 5670.
Moving West: 5686.
The Mower in Therapy: 961.
Mowing: 4758.
Mr. Amnesia: 5102.
Mr. Burdoff's Visit to Germany: 1243.
Mr. Celentano Remembers the Night Johnny Paris Sang 'Heartbreak Hotel': 1241.
Mr. Cogito Looks at His Face in the Mirror: 827, 830, 2276.
Mr. Cogito--Notes from the House of the Dead: 827, 830, 2276.
Mr. Cogito on Virtue: 827, 830, 2276.
Mr. Cogito Thinks about Blood: 827, 830, 2276.
Mr. Hummer's Cows: 2702.
Mr. Positive: 2413.
Mr Potato Kills Time: 629.
Mr. Rhizor's Geese: 207.

lay under a spell: 50,
1429, 2725.
Mystery: 2067.
Mystic Meditations: 152.
Mystical Aspirations: 536,
1699, 1921.
Mystical Mary & Reasonable
Robert: 5552.
Myth of Mountain Sunrise:
5469.
Mythology: 5478.
Myths: 1274.
Mz Frankenstein: 5390.
Nadine Makes a Quilt: 4619.
Nagging Suspicion: 4300.
Nahuatl Icnocuicatl Song: 152.
Naked to the Sun: 1017.
The Naked Truth: 1125.
Naked Words of Truth: 5343.
A Name: 950.
Name-Dropping Stars: 4748.
The Name of the Magician:
2256.
Names: 136, 623, 839, 1209,
3016, 4103.
Namesake: 2308.
Naming Day: 5257.
Naming Flowers: 449.
Naming Souls: 2004, 4764,
4922.
Naming the Dead: 1164.
Nana del Limonero: 1605.
Nan's Last Seance: 4261.
The Nap: 936.
Nap: 5712.
Napalm, Minh, and the Holy
Ghost: 1726.
Naphiri: 3653.
Narcissism: 3710.
Narcissism on Rye: 648.
Narcissus Explains: 2418.
Narcissus Speaks to Echo:
3536.
Narrow-Wood day under a
retinerved sky-leaf: 883,
3746.
Nas praias que são o rosto
branco das amadas mortas:
142.
Nat Shinner & the Night Hawks:
5510.
Nat Turner: 1080.
Natale Embrasure: 1216.
Natalie: 30.
National symbol: 2267.
Nationalism: 3650.
Native Land: 2523.
Native Tongue: 2068.
Native Trees: 3463.
Native Woman: 3613.
Nativity: 1575.
The Nativity of Thought: 557.
The Natural and Social
Sciences: 1360.
Natural Beauty: 1311.
Natural Ice Cream: 3698.

Natural Music: 2551.
Natural Selection: 943, 2825.
Natural Theology in the
Garden: 1445.
A Natural Thing: 3679.
Nature Morte: 2517.
Nature Reclaims: 3649.
Nature's Nuptial: 5121.
Nature's Passion: 5014.
Naval Photograph: 25 October
1942: What the Hand May be
Saying: 559.
Navigation without Numbers:
3099.
The Navigators: 4876.
Nazis: 4492.
The Near and Dear: 5759.
Near Lake Michigan: 2927.
Near Peggy's Cove: 1586.
Near the Wichita Mountains,
January 18 1983: 2273.
Nearing: 721.
Nebraska: 5546.
Nebraska, U.S.A: 539.
Necessary Music: 4480.
Necessary Night: 3854.
Necessities: 3654.
Necessity Is the Mother of the
'Bullet': 1997.
Need: 2.
Needlepoint: 3368.
Needles: 4597.
Needle's Eye: 5349.
Negative: 2876.
Negative Capability: 1853.
Negative Exposure: 5648.
Negative Space: 5478.
Negotiated Settlements and
Immediate Withdrawals:
1401.
Negotiations: 1792, 4242.
Negro sin Nada en su Casa:
762.
Negro Woman: 5622.
The Neighbor: 3664.
The Neighborhood: Five Years
Later: 3053.
Neighbors: 2840, 3513.
The Neighbors: 4948.
Neighbours: 4360.
Neither Man Nor Mouse: 1227.
Neither the Marble Tower:
2526, 3844, 4652.
Nelly Myers: 110.
Neologisms: 1929.
Neoplatonism Comes to an End
in the French Quarter:
1158.
Neruda's Urine: 5609.
Nerves: 4163.
Nervous Application: 2974,
5704.
A Nest: 2259.
The Nest: 3463.
A Nest of Mice: 4825.
Nestucca River Poem: 1119.

Netsuke: 851.
The Nettle Tree: 4983.
Neuchatlitz: 780.
The Neurophysiologist: 4123.
Nevada: 4611.
Nevada, in Season: 1543.
Never a Dull Moment: 2373.
Never Done: 1952.
Never Seek to Tell They Love:
    479.
Never Send Out to Ask: 2373.
Never the Cup: 5535.
Never Too Late: 2234.
New Alliance: 45, 905.
The New American Poetry: 2300.
The New Apartment: 2554, 2809.
The New Arrival: 4820.
New Colt: 509.
The New Diana: 2795.
New England Autumn: 1413.
A New Equilibrium: 1145.
The New Fish Store: 1671.
New Hampshire Farm: 3760.
New Hartford: 839.
New Jersey Turnpike Night:
    748.
New Jersey White-Tailed Deer:
    3823.
The New Love Poem: 1186.
New Me Emerging: 3184.
New Mexico Thru Blue Dust
    32: 3047.
The New Moon: 778.
New Moon: 1560.
The New Moses: 4983.
The New Muse: 2059, 3259.
New Orleans, 1983: 2007.
New Physics: 5476.
New Roses: 3490.
New Sacrament: 1915.
New Salem, Illinois 1837:
    4319.
The New Seasons: Light and
    Dark: 5407.
New Stars: 1910.
New Territory: 1759.
New Tribes: 1286.
New Tupelo: Night of Sad
    Guitars: 5443.
New Wave: 5117.
New Wave Look: 4203.
New Year: 3815.
New Year's Eve: 3781.
New Year's Poem for Veneranda:
    2946.
New York Beirut Nagasaki:
    2509.
New York City Weekend: 4605.
New York Initiation: 4409.
The New York Notebooks: 3642.
The Newcomer: 1089.
Newness: 3357.
The News: 3170.
News: 3904.
News accounts echo: 4200.
News Blackout: 1952.

News Brief: 1748.
News Item: 1543.
News of the Day: 417.
The News of the Day: 5771.
News of the Occluded Cyclone:
    1779.
News of the Tropics: 1938.
News Story: 3898.
The News Vendor: 4230, 5754.
Newscast: 166.
Newsclips 2. (Dec/6-7): 470.
Newspaper: 3966.
Next: 4418.
Next--a Dictionary: 3510.
Next: Arlington Station: 1948.
The Next Instar: 1543.
Next Mistake: 1180.
The Next One: 4606.
Next to Nothing: 1075.
Next Week's Paycheck Blues:
    4180, 4180.
Nicaragua: 438.
Nicaragua Woman: 531.
Nicaraguan Bus: 2536.
Nice, Dec. 1983: 1730.
Nice Thing to Do: 2787.
Nice to End: 2123.
The Niche: 1455.
Nicodemus: 5214.
Night: 30, 515, 4939, 5073.
The Night: 3590, 3868.
Night above the Avenue: 3463.
Night Again: 5518.
Night before Moving: 309.
The Night before the
    Operation: 3353.
Night Blowing a Solo: 3554.
Night Dancing: 3837.
Night Driving: 4517.
Night: Driving the Blizzard:
    2365.
Night Driving, What the
    Prairie Says: 2880.
The Night Energy Moves in
    Waves: 1981.
Night-Eyes of the Mountain:
    4164.
Night Fantasies: 104.
Night Fishing: 1771, 4267.
Night Flight to Attiwapiskat:
    2568.
Night Flights: 739.
Night Flying: 776.
A Night for Chinese Poets:
    2253.
Night Gold: 1779.
Night in Norfolk: 4194.
Night Journal: 1191, 5697.
Night Journey: 2354.
Night Meetings: 1211.
Night Moves: 2430.
Night Muse and Mortar Round:
    2806.
Night Music: 'Shaker Loops' by
    John Adams: 4611.
The Night of the Shirts: 3463.

Night on the Nile: 18.
Night Owls: 2473.
Night Piece: 5034.
Night Piece with Cats (1): 2083.
Night Piece with Cats (2): 2083.
Night Portrait of Rome: 127, 233.
Night quiets, cools: 2337.
Night rain: 4611.
The night rain half-damaged: 3548, 4548.
The Night Richard Nixon Quit: 3372.
Night Ride: 3747.
Night Rider: 76.
Night Sail off Raber: 358.
The Night-Scented Stock Opens in Bartok's Music for Strings, Percussion and Celesta: 1645.
Night School: 30, 880, 2604.
Night Shift: 2015.
The Night Shift: 3388.
The night sky - open, clear, a black-blue: 3430.
Night Slipping from Me: 3047.
Night Song: 5291, 5569.
Night Songs: 3139.
Night Storm: 3295, 5015.
The Night Surf: 3463.
The Night the Moon Got Drunk: 4070.
The Night the School Board Met: 2945.
Night Thoughts for My Brother: 1248.
Night Tide: 5352.
The Night Tom Snyder Said Something Intelligent: 3086.
Night Too Hot to Sleep: 4025.
Night Tracking: 4894.
Night Traveling: 1412, 2119.
Night Tree: 4336.
Night Visits with the Family: 5108.
Night Walked Right In: 2907.
Night Walking: 4203.
Night Walks: 1366.
The Night-Wanderers: 2184.
Night Watch: 1352.
The Night Watch: 2556.
Night Ways: 1797.
The Night We Met: 3358.
Night Wind: 3388.
Night Winds: 504.
Night Work: 1646.
The Night Your Dress Lifted: 1449.
Nightfall: 962.
Nightfall on the Boardwalk: 5348.
Nighthawks: 2941.
Nightingale: 303.

Nightly Vigil: 2048.
Nightmare: 4007.
Nights under the Trumpet Vine: 4969.
Nights without Sleep: 5154.
Nightshift: 5090.
Nightsky: 1205.
Nightsong: 2689.
Nightsong, July: 4611.
Nighttime: 4036.
Nightwatch: 3650.
Nihil Obstat: 2119.
Nijinsky's Last Word Being 'Edison': 4547.
Nike: 3461.
Nile: 3301.
Nimitz Freeway: 4778.
Niña: 3225.
The Nine O'Clock School Bell Ringing: 4906.
Nine-Thirty P.M: 4740.
Nineteen: 4557.
Nineteen Eighty-Four: 2982.
Ninety-Nine White Flapping: 5504.
Nitty Gritty: 2859.
Nixon at Yaddo: 4985.
No. 24: 3715.
No Birds or Flowers: 2687.
No Body Counts on Holidays: 1520.
No digas más: 1232.
No hand holds me either: 781, 883.
No Hanukah Bush: 2096.
No Heaven: 4939.
No Introduction Needed: 2548.
No Jazz in the Cornfields: 2679.
No Lack of Space: 664.
No Lo Contendere: 738.
No-Lose Proposition: 3086.
No Man Can Take My Hand: 3985.
No Matter: 1141.
No Memories: 3261.
No Middle Leg to Stand On: 1203.
No Names, No Pack Drill: 403.
No need to cling: 2479, 2633, 5048.
No One Calls Me Any More: 291, 291.
No One Thinks of Tegucigalpa: 3815.
No One Wants to be Horatio: 134.
No One Was Out: A Letter: 4145.
No Paradise Is Lost: 614.
No Parole Today: 5219.
No Quarter: 3608.
No sé por qué resido en el silencio: 5062.
No Smoking: 2174, 2684, 3107.
No Tenure: 2270.
No Theory: 2478.

On Claudine Goux: 801.
On Cognition: 1543.
On Discovering Canada's First
  Observatory: 1373.
On Exhibit: 2846.
On First Opening Shakespeare:
  3467.
On Gaining a Name for Wisdom:
  3771.
On Golden Land: 1947.
On Goya's 'Saturn': 5296.
On Hearing of the Death of
  Alden Nowlan, Early in the
  Morning, June 28, 1983:
  3180.
On Hearing the Siren: 2903.
On Her Spindle: 4136.
On His Low Self-Esteem: 3328.
On His Own Prowess: 156, 1630.
On Hokusai's 'The Great Wave':
  4370.
On I-74: 186.
On Knocking Down a Friend
  behind Town Hall: 4203.
On Lately Looking into
  Chapman's 'Jane Austen: A
  Critical Bibliography':
  2418.
On Leave: 4687.
On Leave at Subic Bay: 5371.
On Looking at Kandinsky's
  'Composition': 4994.
On Looking into Chinggaltai's
  Grammar of the Mongol
  Language: 1645.
On Love: 5286, 5288.
On makeshift bedding in the
  cucumber garden: 4581,
  5378.
On Mornings Like This: 3047.
On My Back: 4075.
On My First Sonne: 2625.
On My Mother's Birthday: 2188.
On Picking Blueberries with My
  Grandmother for the Last
  Time: 1747.
On Putting the Grandchild to
  Bed: 1704.
On Reading a Writer's Letters:
  4513.
On Robert Frost, Cremated:
  3306.
On Saul Bellow's Thesis, That
  We Think Our Era's Awful
  Because We'll Die in It:
  1122.
On Soap Operas: 1502.
On Speaking with a Dark Woman:
  4516.
On Static Cling and Other
  Things: 3253.
On Straightening Utrillo:
  2170.
On Sunset Boulevard: 1645.
On the back of a letter in
  French: 2081.

On the Beach: 1145.
On the beaches, which are the
  white faces of dead fleets:
  142, 4541.
On the Brocken: 4912.
On the Curbing of Passion:
  5562.
On the Curvature of Space:
  2274.
On the Death of an Old Woman:
  5250.
On the Death of David: 5739.
On the Death of Her Brother:
  53, 1630.
On the Death of One of Our
  Fathers: 770.
On the Death of the Evansville
  University Basketball Team
  in a Plane Crash, December
  13, 1977: 2113.
On the Diamond behind Garfield
  Elementary, Melvin White
  Proves There Is But One
  Boog Powell: 394.
On the Disappearance of the
  Mummy Bound for the World's
  Fiar: 1067.
On the Dole in 1984: 1534.
On the Edge of the Atlantic:
  3250.
On the Ever-Blooming Road:
  1519.
On the Failure of All
  Political Poems: 394.
On the Fourth of July in
  Sitka, 1982: 4266.
On the Greve: 3567, 5697.
On the Heights with You: 1600.
On the Line: 1363.
On the Margin of the Trial:
  827, 830, 2276.
On the Nuclear Front: 3336.
On the Occasion of Her
  Completed Portrait: Letter
  to Dora Maar, 1937: 2774.
On the Phone: 5255.
On the Rivalry between Men and
  Women: 3072.
On the Road: 1249, 2784, 2784.
On the Road to Chenonceaux:
  2921.
On the Run: 3513.
On the Skeleton of a Primary
  Reptile: 1255, 4402.
On the Soul: 1286.
On the Stone of a Bully
  Muscle: 1435.
On the sunlit slope: 3585.
On the Surface: In the Mirror:
  5467.
On the Train: 232, 4614.
On the Veranda We Drink Gin-
  and-Tonic: 60.
On the Verandah: 1645.
On the Way Down: 3606.
On the Way Home from I.C.U:

Perth's Last Total Eclipse of
the Sun Happened over 400
Years Ago: 1991.
Perusing the Fashions: 3471.
Pestaña del Llanto: 3296.
Pet Shop: 5047.
Petals: 397.
Pete and Luther: 4934.
Petén, 1983: 4235.
Peter Kaplan: 3047.
Petit Dejeuner: 3611.
Les Pétrifiées: 3932.
Petroglyph at Tidemark: 3054.
Petting: 2784.
Petty Dreads: 6 Poems in Five
Lines: 1033.
Petulance: 2784.
Phantasmagoria: 2672.
Phantom: 3554.
Pharaoh: 4744.
Phases: 3082.
Phil W: 3449.
The Philistine Woman: 1801.
The Philosopher of the Beauty
Mark: 2931.
Philosopher's Stone: 2196.
Philosophy: 2783, 2784.
Phone Book Isolation: 255.
The Phone Rings at 3 A.M:
4445.
Photo: 1716.
Photo Booth: 2346.
Photo Circa 1969: 1443.
Photocopied Garments: 2320.
Photograph: 827, 830, 1191,
2276, 2732, 2818, 3881.
The Photograph: 1521.
Photograph Album: 3577.
The Photograph I Keep of Them:
1141.
Photograph of a Soldier WWI:
2964.
Photograph of Franz Kafka at
13: 5466.
A Photograph of Her Breath, an
Echo of Her Hair: 178.
Photograph of My Father: 4538.
Photograph of My Parents: Ice
Skating, 1954: 3945.
Photograph of Negro Mania:
5497.
Photograph of the Hunters and
Their Kill: 2690.
The Photographer Discovers
America: 60.
Photographic Memory: 219.
Photographs: 1979: 2079.
The Photography: 3547.
Physics: 92, 3384, 5202.
Piano Lession: 2940.
Pibroch: 4359.
Picasso Used to Gaze at the
Sun: 226.
Picasso's Eyes: 1282.
Pick-Up Drop-Out Sobering-Up
Poem in a Coffee House with

Jazz in the Background:
2965.
The Pickets: 3938.
Picking Berries: 4405.
Picking Raspberries with
Gerda: 5555.
The Picnic: 2784, 2784.
Picnic at Taughannock: 3410.
Pictorial: Upper Volta: 1677.
The Picture Book: 4443.
Picture Book Language: 3778.
Picture for Sale above a Cash
Register: 4702.
Picture of a Girl: 2921.
Picture Window: 312.
Pictures: 5580.
Pictures at an Exhibition:
4447.
Pictures from an Institution:
3507.
Pictures from the Floating
World: 4822.
Piece by Piece: 3097.
Piece of a Thing: 2016.
Piece of Shadow Work: 1645.
Piecemeal: 5523.
Pieces for a Stained-Glass
Window: 4144, 5483.
Pieces of a Memory: 4636.
Piecework: 416.
Pied Piper of the Midwest:
3047.
Pier, P. M: 425.
Pier Paolo: 363.
Pier Paolo Pasolini, 1922-
1975: 3769.
Pierre Loti Visits the
Maharaja of Travancore:
3667.
Pietà: 346.
Pigeons: 4397.
Piggyback Ride: 313.
Pigs: 703, 3860.
Pike Certificate: 2963.
Pike County: 1547.
Pike Creek: 5679.
Pike's Head: 4822.
The Pilgrim: 2502, 5426.
Pilgrimage: 2240.
Pilgrim's Progress: 977.
The Pillow: 504.
The Pilot's Daughter: 3368.
The Pimple: 1704.
The Pine Cone: 2047.
Pinetum: 5673.
The Pink Blouse: 2510.
Pink Flamingoes: 1018.
Pink Neon Revolution: 3422.
Pinnacle: 4716.
Pinnacle Farm: 1403.
The Pioneer Man: 4782.
Pioneer Ranching: 1169.
Pipe Smoking: 1547.
Piper Lad: 2629.
The Piper of Farragut: 811.
Pirandello: 4582.

Report from El Salvador: 5060.
Report from the Besieged City:
    827, 830, 2276.
Report from the State Capitol:
    768.
Report to Walt Whitman: 3801.
Reports Home on the Inter-
    University Forum for
    Educators in Community
    Psychiatry with Responses
    from the Left Wife: 4264.
Repossession: 3588, 5348.
Representative Women: 1041.
Reprieve: 5510.
The Reproach of Eva Alman
    Bech: 2702.
The Republic: 3001.
A Request: 3484, 4891.
Requiem: 2840.
A Requiem for a Lover of
    Bigger Thomas: 1167.
A Requiem for Dvorák: 2526,
    3844, 4652.
Requiem for KAL 007: 5462.
Requiem for Malcolm X: 3060.
Requiem in Vita Pro Nobis:
    645, 3676.
Requiem to a Poet and
    Playwright: 4612.
Requiescat: 1733.
Requited Love: 4557.
Reruns, For All My Sons: 1407.
The Rescue: 4816.
Rescue: 5263.
Rescues: 3654.
Resemblances: 2676.
Reservations: 5122.
Reservoir: 2527.
Residual Light: 1529, 2031,
    4109.
Resignation: 4155.
Respect the Birds: 2242.
Respectability: 3263, 3264.
Respectability's
    Anachronistic: 5019.
The Respected Poet: 3238.
Respecting Our Betters: 3086.
Response to 'Still in Saigon':
    2318.
Responsibilities: 2622.
Responsibility: 4676.
Responso: 280.
The Result: 2787.
The Resurrection: 872.
Resurrection: 2670.
The Retarded: 4263.
A Retelling: 2635.
Retorno: 4537.
Retrato de Bañista: 3080.
The Retreat: 2000, 2881.
Retrieval: 3040.
Retrospective: 420.
Return: 1977, 2170, 2307.
The Return: 193, 1395, 1434,
    1869, 3567.
Return Engagement: 4124.

The Return of Frankenstein:
    1635.
Return of the Prodigal
    Darling: 4070.
The Return of the Repressed:
    1603.
Return to Dresden, 1945: 4780.
Return to the Lake: 1083.
Returned from Yang-chou up the
    Hill to View the Snow:
    4641, 5744.
Returning: 2662.
Returning a Knife to a
    'friend': 3869.
Returning Anymore: 2566.
Returning Home: 5272.
Returning Home after a Few
    Days Away: 2854.
Returning Home from the Field:
    798.
Returning Home to Babylon:
    2430.
Returning in Winter: 3945.
Returning to a Town: 5770.
Returning to De Valera's
    Cottage: 3339.
Returning to Jerusalem: 4066.
Reunion: 565, 2549, 3806.
Rev. George Silsonne: 2731.
Revaluations: 1954.
Revelation and Demise: 2501,
    5250.
Revelations: 995.
The Revenant: 1250, 3273.
Revenant: 3869.
Reverential Comparison: 1756,
    4335.
Reverie: 5306.
Reversing Fields: 3086.
Review of a Stale Drama: 3559.
Revirtiendo: 3103.
Revision: 1073.
Revisions: 1928, 4512.
Revisiting Thrudvang Farm:
    3736.
Revival: 428, 2610.
Revolution: 1113, 3256.
Revolution in Albania: 635.
Rey: 4393.
Rhapsody on Old Clothes: 2083.
Rheims Cathedral: 3412.
Rhenane: Les Cloches: 159,
    3117.
Rhododendron: 3299.
Rhonda LaBombard: 2766.
Rhymes for Old Age: 5299.
Rhythmic Brushwork: 4390.
Rich: 4215.
Richard Hunt's Jacob's Ladder:
    1706.
Richard Says Everyone Knows
    To: 3697.
Riches: 4308.
Richesse: 2373.
Rick Says: 4644.
Ricky: 3014.

Le Scorpion et le Menuet: 289,
  806.
Scotch and Water: 707.
Scout: 188.
Scout Knives: 2840.
Scrabble Babble: 311.
Scrabble Jail: 3322, 3322.
Scramble: 5510.
Scrap Paper: 5304.
Scrapbook (Trio): 1662.
Scratch Danial's: 964.
Scratch Daniel's: 964.
Scratch Me: 4938.
A Scream: 11.
The Scream: 2940.
Screech-Owl with a Comet's
  Tail: 2502, 5426.
Screw, a Technical Love Poem:
  5421.
Scripts: 1395.
Scroll of Sky Unrolled: 1758.
Scuba divers breathing deeply:
  2591.
The Sculptor: 2259.
The Sculpture: 2791.
Sculpture: 3675.
Sculpture in the Gallery, 4
  Horses: Butterfield: 2700.
Scumbling: 1779.
Se Acabo el Mar: 3615.
Se despierta un reflejo
  niuyorquino: 4489.
Sea Ducks: 3065.
The Sea-Elephant: 5622.
'Sea Gate and Goldenrod':
  Cranberry Island Elegy:
  5470.
Sea-Grape Tree and the
  Miraculous: 4406.
The Sea Lion: 5714.
Sea Lions at Cape Arago: 3790.
Sea Longing: 5005.
The sea. My sea: 57, 419.
Sea of Cortez Impressions:
  4587.
The Sea off Flanders: 2240.
Sea Urchin Harakiri: 235,
  1541.
The Sea Witch: 3122.
Seafarers: 484.
Seagull: 1388.
Seagulls: 145.
Seal Rock: 2067.
Search: 1194.
Search for a Metaphor: 3807.
Search Party: 2018.
Searching Breezes through Me:
  227.
Searching for Ice: 5001.
Seascapes: 911.
Seaside: 793, 3029, 4892.
Seaside Greetings: 2978.
The Season for Dancing: 1038.
The Season Is Upon Us: 3608.
The Season of Devastation:
  876, 877, 1545.

The Season of the Plains: 75.
Season of the Winter Solstice:
  3655.
Season Ticket: 1941.
Seasonal: 4847.
Seasonal Sketch: Eastern
  Townships: 5661.
A Seasonal Tradition: 4390.
Seasonelle: 3789, 4905.
The Seasons: A Primer: 1477.
Seasons: A Round: 1604.
The Seawall: 2545.
The Second Apple: 4543.
The Second Coming: 189.
The Second Cycle of
  Zeitgehöft: 883, 2630.
The Second Decade of
  Illustrations or Captions
  for Chinese Artifacts:
  1247.
Second Fantasia on the Eve of
  Saint Agnes: 443.
The Second Language: 2521.
Second Level: 1929.
Second Movement: Adagio: 2009.
Second Nature: 1969.
The Second Nuclear Attack, or
  the Completion: 331.
Second Skin: 1488.
The Second Story: 2451.
Second Tuesday in November:
  4721.
Second Winter: 948.
Secret Clearance Sale: 1197.
The Secret Invasion of
  Bananas: 4160.
The Secret Life of Mr. Yves
  Tanguy: 1219.
The Secret of Levitation:
  5441.
The Secret of the Rosary:
  5371.
The Secret of Tropical
  Heights: 5206.
Secretary: 4865.
Secrets: 504, 1768, 1901,
  3395.
Secrets behind the Names:
  3644.
Secrets of the Fur Trade:
  Everywoman's Encyclopedia,
  1895: 2201.
Secrets of Writing Revealed at
  Last: 2801.
Security: 4916.
Sedako's cranes are flying:
  687.
The Seduction: 3460.
The Seduction of Gravity:
  3457.
See the Specialist: 223.
See Your Personal Banker:
  3211.
Seeattuuuuuuuuuuuuuulllll:
  462.
Seedbed: 855.

Silos, a Generation Gap: 2274.
Siluetas: 3081.
Silver: 906, 5433.
The Silver Dollar Bar: 5392.
Silver Dollars: 2840.
Silver Lake: 1866.
Silver Pennies: 1827.
Simmer Over Medium Heat: 4372.
Simon de Cyrène: 1514.
Simon of Cyrene: 1514, 2315.
Simon without Underwear: 3303.
Simone Weil: 3769.
Simple Affair: 5575.
Simple Sums: 5026.
Simple Thank You: 5412.
Simple Things: 2784.
Simplification: 5036.
Simply Cicadas: 4470, 4470.
Simultaneously: 2478.
Sin Volver: 1164.
Sinbad the Sailor: 5441.
Since Dawn: 136, 3016.
Since Life Is Fleeing: 1790,
   3567.
The Sinew of Survival: 2563.
Sing a Song of Hardware: 3208.
The Singer: 952.
Singing: 1437.
The Singing Cabbie: 798.
Singing in the Rain: A Success
   Story: 784.
Singing the Mozart Requiem:
   5534.
Single LIfe: 4233.
Single Woman Speaking: 3901.
Sinking: 2453.
Sipping Drinks at the Central
   Hotel: 3576.
Siren: 855.
Sirocco: 4685.
Sister: 507, 1386, 1946, 3578.
Sister Mary Appassionata
   Blesses the Kindergarten
   Class: 952.
Sister Mary Appassionata
   Explains to the Classics
   Class Why So Many of the
   Greatest Lovers, Heroes and
   Saints Were Shepherds: 952.
Sister Mary Appassionata
   Lectures the Anatomy Class:
   Doctrines of the Nose: 952.
Sister Mary Appassionata
   Lectures the Biorhythm
   Class: Doctrines of Time:
   952, 952.
Sister Mary Appassionata
   Lectures the Eighth Grade
   Boys and Girls on the
   Nature of Symmetry: 952.
Sister Mary Appassionata
   Lectures the Eighth Grade
   Boys and Girls: To Punish
   the Cities: 952.
Sister Mary Appassionata
   Lectures the Eighth Grade

Boys: You're Born with Two
   Heads, Don't Let the Little
   One Rule the Big One: 952.
Sister Mary Appassionata
   Lectures the Journalism
   Class: Doctrines of Belief:
   952, 952.
Sister Mary Appassionata
   Lectures the Natural
   History Class: Love and
   Curse, the Wind, the Words:
   952.
Sister Mary Appassionata
   Lectures the Parents of the
   Eighth Grade Boys and
   Girls: 952, 952.
Sister Mary Appassionata
   Lectures the Pre-Med Class:
   Doctrines of Sweat: 952.
Sister Mary Appassionata
   Lectures the Science Class:
   Doctrines of the Elements:
   952, 952.
Sister Mary Appassionata
   Lectures the Social
   Behavior Class: Friends,
   Those Who Love: 952.
Sister Mary Appassionata
   Lectures the Theology
   Class: 952.
Sister Mary Appassionata
   Lectures the Urban Studies
   Class: Gunfire, Bedroom,
   Passion's Trash: 952.
Sister Mary Appassionata
   Lectures the Zoology Class:
   Doctrines of the Beast:
   952.
Sister Mary Appassionata to
   the Eighth Grade Boys and
   Girls: Doctrines of
   Divination: 952.
Sister Mary Appassionata to
   the Introductory Astronomy
   Class: Heartbeat and Mass,
   Every Last Breath: 952.
Sister Mary Appassionata to
   the Optometry Class:
   Doctrines of the Eye: 952.
Sister Mary Appassionata to
   the Pre-Med Class: Thinking
   Ourselves to Death: 952.
Sister Mary Whatshername:
   2285.
A Sister on the Tracks: 2092.
The Sisters: 1380, 2986.
Sisters set the table: 4503.
The Sisyphus Shuffle: 4936.
Sit. Anx. Reg. Fert: 1862.
The Sitter: 84.
Sitting: 5362.
Sitting Empty: 2811.
Sitting Up with the Dead: 571.
Situation Normal: 3124.
Siva: 3927.
Six Days of Thunderstorms:

Snow As a Way of Light: 2043.
Snow-Bed: 883.
Snow Clan Visit: 2645.
Snow Drifts: 2398, 4133.
Snow in Carolina: 84.
Snow in the Heartland: 1396.
The Snow Leopards: 5269.
Snow on the Ocean: 4823.
The Snow Phoenix: 5537.
Snow Up: 1912.
Snowbound: 5640.
Snowed In: 953, 1190.
Snowflake Fall: 2852.
The Snowman: 5081.
The Snows: 515.
Snowstorm in Warsaw: 3769.
Snowy Egret: 5511.
Snowy Morning: 44, 924.
Snowy Owl: 5411.
So Few of Us Continue to Grow:
  3086.
So Graven: 3487.
So Keep a Geiger Counter
  around the House: 4403.
So, liberty is the national
  principle: 152, 2385.
So Little Time: 1087.
So Long: 2972.
So Long: A Landscape: 5024.
So Long to the Eifel: 590,
  1757.
So many divers torments thrive
  in us: 3, 912.
So Many Mountains: 4832.
So Many Selves: 1820.
So now, invoke saints Carl and
  Sig: 2410.
So the World Changes: 221.
So this is the life we come to
  be living: 3796.
Soap: 4983.
Soap Opera in Five Easy
  Pieces: 865.
The Sober Boat: 4146.
Soccer field: 2503.
The Soccer Game outside
  Munich: 2372.
A Social Affair: 2274.
Social Reform: 4958.
Social Security: 130, 3086.
Social Unrealism: 1641.
A Socket of Plain Water: 4764.
Sodbusters: 4285.
Soft Rain: 2070.
Softening to Heaven: 1641.
A Softer Touch: 4572.
The Sohoiad: or, The Masque of
  Art: 2642.
Un Soir de Carnaval: 1544.
Soir d'Eté: 341.
Solar Creed: 56, 1705.
Solar Fugue: 5208.
Solar Matter: 136, 136, 3016.
Sold: 2107.
Soldier: 2629, 3306.
Soldier's Dream: 1389.

Soldiers of Oblivion: 4704.
Soldiers of Orange: 857.
Soledad es una vieja casona:
  859.
Solidarity: 5105.
Soliloquy: Man Talking to a
  Mirror: 2806.
Solitaire: 227.
Solitude: 2779.
Solo: 5114.
Solo Concert: 1587.
Solstice: 2788.
The Solution: 2822.
Some: 1980.
Some bird--unseen: 5646.
Some Day: 2596.
Some day there will be: 4200.
Some Examples of 'Computer
  Poems': 913.
Some Futures: 2622.
Some Ghosts and Some Ghouls:
  3185.
Some Laws Are: 2147.
Some Lines on Kerouac, Charles
  Mills, and Rambling across
  the Pages of Time, Notes,
  Journals, and the Road of
  the Real: 3478.
Some Modern Good Turns: 1319.
Some Music: 4261.
Some of My Readers: 711.
Some old plains drifter: 2789.
Some Other Names for Poetry:
  4144, 5483.
Some Poems: 1577.
Some Polonius: 2393.
Some Responses to Aegis:
  1528.
Some roosters wake before dawn
  some islands grow higher in
  a single day: 2119, 2665.
Some say an army of men on
  horse (Sappho 16): 4162,
  4542.
Some Soap: 1928.
Some Things: 697.
Some Things You Can't Forget:
  1481.
Some Things You'll Need to
  Know Before You Join the
  Union: 5025.
Some Thoughts on Dying: 54,
  1630.
Some Times: 670.
Some twenty years of marital
  agreement: 1166.
Some Vegetables: 1929.
Some Woman. What Woman?:
  4736.
Some Writing from a Journal
  (1959, NY): 1889.
Somebody: 579.
Somebody's Dream: 3344.
Someday Soon: 3769.
Someone Crying: 3031.
Someone Is Always Dying: 2741.

Louis: 2033.
To a Greased Pole Climber:
1523.
To a Kid Who Believes in
Astrology: 1423.
To a Loose Woman: 5154.
To a Lottery Winner: 2796.
To a Man after My Own Heart:
4558.
To a Rapist: 2008.
To a Rose Dress: A Translation
from Théophile Gautier:
1831, 2594.
To a Shy Girl: 5702.
To a Trivial Pursuit Champ:
2796.
To a Woman Seeking a Position:
4567.
To a Young Selectric Dying:
2045.
To a Young Sleepwalker: 3543.
To a Young Woman Dying at
Weir: 1413.
To Alberta: 1110.
To Alexander Blok: 50, 140.
To All the Gods at Once: A
Prayer for Mercy: 1935.
To an Adolescent Weeping
Willow: 369.
To an Overly Literary Lady:
383.
To Be: 369.
To Be Human: 515.
To be involved in every phase
of directing: 203.
To Be Read Aloud in a Public
Place: 3423.
To Begin the Migraine: 3310.
To Believe: 3715.
To Boy George: 2796.
To Christopher: 619.
To Claire: 1945, 3621.
To Commemorate and Celebrate
Langston Hughes: 2576.
To Dionysius, Companero: 3973,
5754.
To Frank: 4191.
To Frank O'Hara: 640.
To Galway: 368.
To Get to You: 5437.
To Giacomo Leopardi in the
Sky: 5697.
To Grandmother: 5258.
To Have Known a Prophet Isn't
Everything: 567.
To Help the Needy: 5343.
To Her Persistent Master:
2914.
To Hikmet: 4649.
To Him, before the Flood:
3137.
To Issei, the First
Generation: 1517.
To Janey, Address Unknown:
4442.
To Jerry Mathers: 2796.

To John McEnroe: 2796.
To Johnny Who Could Not See:
1121.
To Kill a Deer: 1770.
To Langston: 2559.
To Life: 1337.
To make a dadist poem: 5302.
To Make It Like Ray!: 2123.
To Mama Lizzie: 82.
To Marco, Dog of Santa Maria
in Trastevere: 57, 5094.
To Market, to Market:
Hawthorne's Shopping List:
1450.
To Market, To Market:
Shakespeare's Shopping
List: 1450.
To Matisse: 2586.
To Most of My Contemporaries:
3166.
To Mr. McCormick: 2909.
To Mr. T.S. Eliot, on reading
'Old Possum's Book of
Practical Cats': 4799.
To My 8th Grade Class: 2168.
To My Absent Father: 5676.
To My Brother, Who Wasn't
Wearing a Helmet: 1424.
To My Craft: 408, 3705.
To My Father: 3476, 4071.
To My Favorite Witch: 3455.
To My Grandmother: 45, 905.
To My Green Lady, with Regret:
1543.
To My Muse: 2695.
To My Sister: 1884, 5250.
To My Wife in Time of War:
677.
To New York: 1833, 4664.
To Newfoundland: 2792.
To Nurture the Bird of Prey:
4721.
To Our Lady of the Battle:
1427.
To Patricia at Massanutten
Mountain, Virginia:
Watching for Stars: 2033.
To People Who Pick Food: 858.
To Poetry: 1635.
To Praise the Music: 647.
To Relocate: 2230.
To Resolve a Dream: 2459,
2459.
To Ride the White Camel: 4334.
To Rise, So Suddenly: 358.
To Ronnie, Like Your Father:
416.
To Russia--Who Are You: 80.
To Ryszard Krynicki--A Letter:
827, 830, 2276.
To Speak of Need: 4480.
To Speak Or: 1753.
To Split a Round of Oak: 208.
To Spot the Centralia Mine
Fire: 2851, 2851.
To Stop Thinking With: 1587.

To That Dark Handsome Youth Named Death: 1865, 1865, 1978.
To the Andes Survivors: 4269.
To the Artist As a Young Child: 3861.
To the Colonised Body: 1935.
To the Dead: 439.
To the Government of Nova Scotia: 964.
To the Heart's Discontent: 5241.
To the Innocent: 4264.
To the King from the Candle: 991.
To the Lady Who Refused to Purchase My Book of War Poems: 319.
To the Last Man: 5417.
To the Mite: 94, 1454, 3099, 3458.
To the Orphans: 3577.
To the Planetoids and You: 206.
To the Poet Jimenez, Man of Andalucia: 996.
To the Reader: 2545, 4916.
To the Rest Home: 5145.
To the Saguaro Cactus Tree in the Desert Rain: 5702.
To the Sun: 127, 233.
To the Tune 'Red Embroidered Shoes': 2867.
To the Tyrant: 975.
To the Victor: 3099.
To the Woman Who Asked for a Name: 3765.
To the Wreakers of Havoc: 2240.
To Whom It May Concern: 732.
To William Blake: 1156.
To Wystan Auden on His Birthday: 512, 5633.
Toad Song: 5758.
Toads: 3269.
Toast: 16.
The Toast: 1303.
Toast to Sobriety: 5548.
Tobacco Barn: 117.
Tocar un cascabel de porcelana en el aire: 363.
Today, Fiesta Music: 5024.
Today the clouds brought to me: 57, 419.
Today, the Only Certainty Is Winter: 2192.
Today, the Rain Walks: 251.
Today's Numbers: 5718.
Todo Concluido: 868.
Todo Continuara en su Puesto: 600.
Todo Puede Matarme: 3447.
Together: 5394.
Tohopekaliga: 854.
Toilet: 4795.
The Token: 92.

Token Drunk: 711.
Toll Booths: 3650.
Tom McAfee: 1695.
Tomales Bay - December '83: 4068.
The Tomato Packing Plant Line: 4742.
Tomato Vines: 1664.
The Tomatoes: 4653.
A Tomb for Anatole: 215, 3214.
The Tombkeeper, St. Louis Cemetery #1: 1246.
Tomorrow in the Desert: 765.
Tomorrow the World: 774.
Tomorrow's America: 3238.
Tom's Tavern Revisited: a Tale of Ambition: 396.
Tongue: 2219.
The Tongues of Angels: 4650.
Tonight: 2621.
Tonight I Feel Mortal: 1048.
Tonight My Body: 3389.
Tonight, Old Bones: 899.
Tony White's Cottage: 3683.
Tony's Crabapple Tree: 5067.
Too expensive to get sick any more: 4200.
Too Familiar: 3372.
Too Good to Be True: 5673.
Too Much Pride: 5198.
Too Much World: 5255.
Too Old to Be Sexy: 2787.
Tooling the Vesper: 1435, 1435.
The Tools: 432.
The Tooth Fairy: 1048.
Torch Song: 3742.
Toreador: 3728.
The Tornado: 383, 886.
The Tornado Chaser: 1003.
The Tornado Month: 1757.
Tornado Watch at the Towers: 5671.
Tornado Weather: 8.
Toronto Island Suite: 5102.
Toronto-London One Way Gray Coach Lines: 894.
Toscanita: 785, 5697.
Die Toten: 232.
Touch to My Tongue: 3255, 3255.
Touchdancers We: 2897.
Touche: 2903.
Touching Ground: 4786.
Touching the Dead: 3590.
Touching the Distance: 5790.
Tour of Duty: 2429.
Tourette's Syndrome: 679.
Touring Arizona: 4463.
Tourist: 178.
The Tourist: 1761.
Tournant: 289, 806.
Tout le bleu du monde: 979.
Toward New Orleans: 5579.
Toward Penelope: 1362.
Toward Punta Banda: 3658.

Watching Us Sleep: 725.
Watching You Swim: 412.
Water: 3090.
The Water: 5204.
Water Course: 2862.
Water Leads to This: 2317.
Water Moving through Concrete:
    2064.
Water Music: 838.
Water Music and the Seven Gram
    Soul: 93.
Water of innumerable
    fountains: 57, 5094.
Water Song: 5497.
Water That Runs: 563, 4968.
Watercolors: 3028.
The Watergaw: 3166.
Watering the Garden: 480.
Watering the Lawn: 300.
Waters Have Held Us: 612.
Watershed: 2939, 3607.
Waumbek Woods in April: 2977.
The Wave: 1031.
Wave That Breaks: 563, 4968.
Wavering Decisions: 3404,
    4335.
The Wavering Line: 711.
Waves: 1419.
The Waves at Matsushima: 390.
Waving Goodbye: 4929.
Wawenock: 1040.
The Way Back: 3583.
Way back in my hand-wrestling
    days: 2157.
The Way He Turns: 504.
The Way Home from School: 739.
Way in the back of my head:
    4661.
The Way It Is with Sea-
    Elephants: 3343.
The Way to Moriah: 2681.
The Way to the Mail: 2783.
The Ways: 1929.
We: 5440.
We abound in dichotomies:
    4200.
We All Fall Down: 3423.
We Are Not What We Think:
    5442.
We don't have castes in the
    good old U S of A: 978.
We Explore Our Present through
    the Past: 2259.
We fall asleep on words: 827,
    830, 2276.
We Go Together: 3573.
We Greet the Plague: 5011.
We Grew Up Playing Bomb
    Shelter: 2101.
We have become poets: 3504.
We Have Looked Everywhere:
    2029.
We Have Risen and the
    Cloisters Are Empty: 127,
    233.
We Interrupt This Broadcast:

417.
We Live in a Rush: 262, 5158,
    5772.
We Must Face This: 5770.
We never could understand:
    3504.
We Say This Prayer: 4856,
    5232.
We See Only Hawks: 5767.
We Walk: 1055.
We Want to Bless Yu All th
    Stars undr Holee Hevns
    Wing: 462.
We will die in transparent
    Petropolis: 3229, 5248.
A weak country, a deprived
    voice: 152, 2385.
Wealth Affords an Opulent
    Grief: 1645.
Weapons: 3256.
Wear: 4062.
Wearing Ear Protectors: 4942.
Wearing the White Night Gown:
    1100.
Weather: 4428.
Weather Breeder: 1797.
Weather Report: Ishtar's
    Suite: 4611.
Weathering: 1638.
Weaverbird's Vacuum Behavior
    in the Laboratory: 1567.
Webern's Mountain: 906.
Wedding: 2007.
The Wedding: 4780.
The Wedding in the Courthouse:
    3795.
The Wedding of That Year:
    1543.
Wednesday, 8 February: 817.
Weed: 89.
Weed Farm: 368.
The Weed Pullers: 1241.
Weeds: 1869.
Weeds among the Garlic: 5511.
Weeds in the Garden: 4718.
A Week on the Drawhorse: 107.
Weekend: 3642.
Weekend at Branchport: 5142.
A Weekend at the Last Resort:
    5026.
Weekend in the Poconos: 3154.
Wege: 232.
Weight: 4259, 5100.
The Weight of the Day: 1138.
Weightlessness: 4236.
Welcome to the Encyclopedia of
    Thieves: 5515.
The Welder: 1174.
Weldon Kees: 3015.
The Well: 5561.
The Well-cropped attracts
    danger: 1550.
We'll Drink a Cup: 3266.
We'll keep dancing, friends:
    3504.
Well Water: 2502, 5426.

The Well-Wisher from Half-Way
  around the World: 4390.
Wellington College: 3683.
Wells and People: 1756, 4335.
Wells River: 3341.
Welsh Encounters: 382.
Wending Ball (Or: If Frost Had
  Only Played Tennis): 2780.
We're all dancing: 978.
Das Wernher von Braun Lied:
  91.
West Durham Sunday: 2413.
West Gone: 2898.
West Virginia: 4365.
West Virginia Handicrafts:
  4930.
West Wales Winter Night: 4158.
West Wall: 3463.
Western Motel, 1957: 5023.
Western Wind: 152, 152.
Wet Are the Boards: 203.
Wet Blanket: 2982.
Wet, Winter Dream in Machias,
  Maine: 3117.
Weyburn: 3472.
WH: 1168.
The Whale: 2430.
Whales: 2894, 5047.
Whaleships in Winter Quarters
  at Herschel Island: 4351.
What: 256.
What?: 370.
What a Clever Design: 4842.
What a Man Saw: 3574.
What a Time!: 503.
What Animals Dream: 2335.
What Calls You Home: 1573.
What Comes from the Willow at
  Pondside: 3235.
What do I eat things for?:
  3548, 4548.
What Do Myths Have to Do with
  the Price of Fish?: 5627.
What Else Is There To Do:
  3668.
What goes on?: 4200.
What Happens: 3096.
What Have Your Heard Lately?:
  5013.
What Holds Them Apart: 1798.
What Hunter? II: 1792.
What I Did in the War: 1772.
What I Hear from My Window in
  Alexandria, Egypt: 4809.
What I Know: 2171.
What I Like about the
  Railroad: 5042.
What I'd Least Like to
  Remember: 3367.
What if a nuclear war does
  happen: 4200.
What Is a Poet: 2147.
What is it you want?: 1528.
What Is Known: 1001.
What Is Mine: 1380.
What Is Missing: 3390.

What Is Most Needed: 1815.
What Is Our Life? A Play of
  Passion: 3861.
What Is Written in Clouds:
  1645, 1645.
What Is Written in Dust: 1645.
What Is Written in Fields:
  1645, 1645.
What Is Written in Furniture:
  1645, 1645.
What Is Written in Gardens:
  1645.
What Is Written in Glass:
  1645.
What Is Written in Leaves:
  1645.
What Is Written in Mist: 1645.
What Is Written in Moonlight:
  1645.
What Is Written in Pine
  Branches: 1645.
What Is Written in Porcelain:
  1645.
What Is Written in Rain: 1645.
What Is Written in Rooms:
  1645, 1645.
What Is Written in Sand: 1645.
What Is Written in Stars:
  1645.
What Is Written in Stone:
  1645.
What Is Written in the Sky:
  1645.
What Is Written in the Wind:
  1645, 1645.
What Is Written on the
  Ceiling: 1645.
What Is Written on the Floor:
  1645.
What Is Written on the Shore:
  1645.
What Is Written on the Window:
  1645.
What I've Given Up for You:
  57, 5094.
What Matters: 2234.
What Nag: 4012.
What of the rights: 4200.
What Promise: 5664.
What Really Happens When the
  Plane Goes Down: 5763.
What Salina Sees: 1435.
What Shall I Wear?: 2863.
What Springs to Life: 2209.
What Steamboat Rock Was Like:
  5246.
What the Dead Know: 4107.
What the Heart Can Bear: 1869.
What the Moon Cannot Bear:
  4828.
What the Nighthawk Said: 3501.
What the Right Hand Gives, the
  Left Takes Away: 764.
What the Wing Says: 5093.
What the Woman Who Said She
  Was Not Crazy Told Me: 357.